Problems in Contract Law

ASPEN PUBLISHERS

Problems in Contract Law
Cases and Materials

Sixth Edition

Charles L. Knapp
Joseph W. Cotchett Distinguished Professor of Law
University of California, Hastings College of the Law
Max E. Greenberg Professor Emeritus of Contract Law
New York University School of Law

Nathan M. Crystal
Class of 1969 Professor of Contract Law and Professional Responsibility
University of South Carolina

Harry G. Prince
Professor of Law
University of California, Hastings College of the Law

Wolters Kluwer
Law & Business

AUSTIN   BOSTON   CHICAGO   NEW YORK   THE NETHERLANDS

Aspen Publishers
Attn: Permissions Department
76 Ninth Avenue, 7th Floor
New York, NY 10011-5201

To contact Customer Care, e-mail customer.care@aspenpublishers.com,
call 1-800-234-1660, fax 1-800-901-9057, or mail correspondence to:

Aspen Publishers
Attn: Order Department
PO Box 990
Frederick, MD 21705

Printed in the United States of America.

1 2 3 4 5 6 7 8 9 0

ISBN 978-0-7355-6255-4

Library of Congress Cataloging-in-Publication Data

Knapp, Charles L.
    Problems in contract law: cases and materials / Charles L. Knapp, Nathan M.
Crystal, Harry G. Prince. — 6th ed.
        p. cm.
    Includes index.
    ISBN 978-0-7355-6255-4
    1. Contracts — United States — Cases. I. Crystal, Nathan M. II. Prince, Harry G.,
1953 — III. Title.
KF801.A7K5 2007

                                                                            2007016341

About Wolters Kluwer Law & Business

Wolters Kluwer Law & Business is a leading provider of research information and workflow solutions in key specialty areas. The strengths of the individual brands of Aspen Publishers, CCH, Kluwer Law International and Loislaw are aligned within Wolters Kluwer Law & Business to provide comprehensive, in-depth solutions and expert-authored content for the legal, professional and education markets.

CCH was founded in 1913 and has served more than four generations of business professionals and their clients. The CCH products in the Wolters Kluwer Law & Business group are highly regarded electronic and print resources for legal, securities, antitrust and trade regulation, government contracting, banking, pension, payroll, employment and labor, and health-care reimbursement and compliance professionals.

Aspen Publishers is a leading information provider for attorneys, business professionals and law students. Written by preeminent authorities, Aspen products offer analytical and practical information in a range of specialty practice areas from securities law and intellectual property to mergers and acquisitions and pension/benefits. Aspen's trusted legal education resources provide professors and students with high-quality, up-to-date and effective resources for successful instruction and study in all areas of the law.

Kluwer Law International supplies the global business community with comprehensive English-language international legal information. Legal practitioners, corporate counsel and business executives around the world rely on the Kluwer Law International journals, loose-leafs, books and electronic products for authoritative information in many areas of international legal practice.

Loislaw is a premier provider of digitized legal content to small law firm practitioners of various specializations. Loislaw provides attorneys with the ability to quickly and efficiently find the necessary legal information they need, when and where they need it, by facilitating access to primary law as well as state-specific law, records, forms and treatises.

Wolters Kluwer Law & Business, a unit of Wolters Kluwer, is headquartered in New York and Riverwoods, Illinois. Wolters Kluwer is a leading multinational publisher and information services company.

To Lex.

C.L.K.

To Chuck and H. G. — great coauthors and wonderful people.

N.M.C.

To Sue, Andrew, James, and Callie — with love.

H.G.P.

Summary of Contents

Contents

4 | The Statute of Frauds

5 | The Meaning of the Agreement: Principles of Interpretation and the Parol Evidence Rule

6 | Supplementing the Agreement: Implied Terms, the Obligation of Good Faith, and Warranties   437

7 | Avoiding Enforcement: Incapacity, Bargaining Misconduct, Unconscionability, and Public Policy   517

8 ‖ **Justification for Nonperformance: Mistake, Changed Circumstances, and Contractual Modifications** — **663**

9 | Rights and Duties of Third Parties   741

10 | Consequences of Nonperformance: Express Conditions, Material Breach, and Anticipatory Repudiation   783

Preface

When the first edition of these materials was being prepared, more than thirty years ago, many American social and legal institutions had recently been called into serious question by those — students and others — who had heard in the spirit of "the Sixties" a call to action. In those circumstances, it seemed necessary to stress the extent to which the rules of contract law could still be important to lawyers and their clients in the modern world and to suggest that the study of law in law school could provide a solid foundation for a lawyering career. The title *Problems in Contract Law* was chosen to reflect two related notions: that the rules of contract law could be usefully studied through analysis of multi-issue, integrative problems, and that those rules, once mastered, could be creatively used by attorneys to solve the problems of their clients.

Over the intervening decades, American society has seen vast political, social, and technological change — much of it unimaginable back in 1976. Contract law is commonly considered one of the more stable areas of law, but it, too, is visibly in a state of flux. As technological and political changes gradually merge the American marketplace into a global one, judges and lawyers will have to keep pace. All of these factors make a realistic survey of contract law today a substantially more complex and challenging undertaking than it was (or seemed to be) a quarter century ago.

To give the student some sense of the complexity of our legal world, this new edition attempts, like its predecessors, to sound several themes. The first of these, of course, is to give an overview of contract doctrine — the rules and principles, both common law and statutory, that make up what we think of as "contract law." For those instructors who rely substantially on the case method for this purpose, we continue to present a varied collection of judicial opinions for study and analysis. As in previous editions, introductory text summarizes basic concepts, enabling the cases to focus on more challenging applications of doctrine; the Notes and Questions after each case help the student to analyze that case and to place it in context with other parts of the material. Complementing case study with the problem method, we present throughout the book a series of lengthy, multi-issue Problems, to help the student understand and apply the principles reflected in the text and cases studied. And through text, Notes, and occasional Comments we point out some of the places where contract law overlaps with or is affected by other areas of law, such as Tort, Agency, Professional Responsibility, and forms of Alternate Dispute Resolution.

With contract law, as with all areas of law, however, knowledge of doctrine is not the end of study, but only the beginning. Starting with the introduction in Chapter 1 and continuing throughout the book, we urge the student to view the material from a variety of other perspectives. The first of these is *historical*. Text, cases, and Comments describe the development of our common law of contract in the English courts of Law and Equity, and trace the historical progression of American contract law from Holmes and Williston through Corbin and Llewellyn to the present day. With this added historical perspective, students may better see contract law for what it really is — not simply a collection of discrete rules, but a complex and constantly evolving system.

The second perspective these materials stress is the *theoretical* one. From the outset, the student encounters the various strands of modern academic thought about contract law. The materials present extended quotations from scholars representing all modern schools of analysis (some notion of their number and variety can be gained from the Acknowledgments, which follow this Preface), and text, Notes, and Comments provide citations to dozens of other scholarly works, for the guidance of instructors or students who wish to pursue these questions further. (For easy reference we have again included in the back of the book a table of scholarly authorities cited, along with the usual tables of cases and statutes.)

Besides the historical and theoretical aspects, these materials focus on the *lawyering* perspective — reminding the student constantly that the rules of law we encounter have an impact on real people in real disputes, and that creative lawyering in the contract area requires not merely knowledge of the rules of law but the ability to analyze and predict the effects of various courses of conduct that a client might undertake, in the light of those rules. Many of the Notes following the cases invite the student to consider two practice-related questions: How could an attorney have either prevented this dispute from arising or helped her client to obtain a better outcome than was achieved in the actual case? How will this decision affect attorneys in the future, in their roles as counselors, negotiators, and advocates? The Problems, which often cast the student in the role of an attorney at the predispute stage, also raise questions of both law and lawyering, but without the benefit of already reached judicial outcomes. The Problems can serve a number of functions for the student, such as integrating various strands of doctrine and providing a useful preparation for law school examinations. Probably their most important purpose, however, is to suggest that in real life there is likely to be not just one answer to a client's problem but a whole range of possible answers, some of which are clearly wrong, but many of which are at least plausibly right, in varying degrees. Living with ambivalence and uncertainty is not always pleasant, but the ability to do so is surely a more necessary lawyering skill than mastering the niceties of citation form.

The book comprises 12 chapters, which fall generally into the following parts:

Introduction	Chapter 1
Formation	Chapters 2-4
Interpretation and implication	Chapters 5-6

Defenses or grounds for nonenforcement	Chapters 7-8
Third parties	Chapter 9
Breach and remedies	Chapters 10-12

Material on the UCC is integrated throughout wherever it is relevant to our understanding of the general law of contract. A separate supplement, *Rules of Contract Law,* reprints important provisions and comments from Articles 1, 2, and 9 of the UCC and the Restatement (Second) of Contracts, along with the Articles of the Convention on International Sales of Goods (CISG) and the Principles of International Commercial Contracts. It also presents material on contract drafting, and a selection of sample law school examination questions (some with suggested answers).

For the three of us, collaboration on these materials continues to be not only an educational experience but a great pleasure as well. We hope that those who use this volume will likewise find enjoyment as well as information in its pages. As our last word to students and teachers about to embark on this journey with us, we sound once again our traditional closing note:

No study of law is adequate if it loses sight of the fact that law operates first and last *for, upon,* and *through* individual human beings. This, of course, is what rescues law from the status of a science, and makes its study so frustrating — and so fascinating.

It was true in 1976, and it still is.

Charles L. Knapp
Nathan M. Crystal
Harry G. Prince

April 2007

Acknowledgments

Professors Knapp and Prince would like to thank the University of California Hastings College of the Law for its generous research support, and the following Hastings students for valuable research assistance: Yoori Choi, Mary McDonald, Thom Neale, and Linh Judiee Tran. Professor Crystal would like to thank the University of South Carolina School of Law for its generous support of his research, and Stephania Bondurant for her extraordinary research assistance. We are grateful to our many colleagues who have used previous editions of this work and have been generous with their comments and suggestions for improvement.

We would also like to thank the following authors and copyright holders for permission to reprint portions of their work:

Ross A. Albert, Comment, Restitutionary Recovery for Rescuers of Human Life, 74 Cal. L. Rev. 85, 124-125 (1986). Copyright © 1986. Reprinted with permission of the California Law Review.

Richard M. Alderman, Pre-Dispute Mandatory Arbitration in Consumer Contracts: A Call for Reform, 38 Hous. L. Rev. 1238-1242 (2001). Reprinted with permission.

P.S. Atiyah, Contracts, Promises and the Law of Obligations, 94 L.Q. Rev. 193, 211-212 (1978). Copyright © 1978. Reprinted with permission of Stevens & Sons, Ltd. and the author.

Douglas G. Baird & Robert Weisberg, Rules, Standards, and the Battle of the Forms: A Reassessment of §2-207, 68 Va. L. Rev. 1217, 1233-1235 (1982). Copyright © 1982. Reprinted with permission of the Virginia Law Review Association and Fred B. Rothman & Co.

Lisa Bernstein, Merchant Law in a Merchant Court: Rethinking the Code's Search for Immanent Business Norms, 144 U. Pa. L. Rev. 1765, 1770-1771 (1996). Copyright © 1996. Reprinted with permission of the University of Pennsylvania Law Review.

Robert L. Birmingham, Breach of Contract, Damage Measures and Economic Efficiency, 24 Rutgers L. Rev. 273, 288-289, 291 (1970). Copyright © 1970. Reprinted with permission of the Rutgers Law Review.

James T. Brennan, Injunction Against Professional Athletes' Breaching Their Contracts, 34 Brooklyn L. Rev. 61, 70 (1967). Copyright © 1967 Brooklyn Law School, Brooklyn Law Review. Reprinted with permission.

Arthur L. Corbin, Corbin on Contracts, Vol. 1, §29, at 82-85; Vol. 3, §539, at 81. Reprinted from Corbin on Contracts (1971) with permission of West Publishing Co.

William Dodge, Teaching the CISG in Contracts, 50 J. Leg. Ed. 75, 82-83 (2002). Copyright © 2002 by the Journal of Legal Education. Reprinted by permission.

Melvin A. Eisenberg, The Bargain Principle and Its Limits, 95 Harv. L. Rev. 741, 788-789, 794-797 (1982). Copyright © 1982 by the Harvard Law Review Association. Reprinted with permission.

Melvin A. Eisenberg, Donative Promises, 47 U. Chi. L. Rev. 1, 4-6, 29 (1979). Copyright © 1979. Reprinted with permission of the author.

Daniel A. Farber & John H. Matheson, Beyond Promissory Estoppel: Contract Law and the "Invisible Handshake," 52 U. Chi. L. Rev. 903, 945 (1985). Copyright © 1985. Reprinted with permission of the University of Chicago Law Review.

E. Allan Farnsworth, Contracts §12.9, at 791-795 (3rd ed. 1999). Copyright © 1999 by E. Allan Farnsworth. Published by Aspen Law & Business. Reprinted with permission.

E. Allan Farnsworth, Legal Remedies for Breach of Contract, 70 Colum. L. Rev. 1145, 1149-1156 (1970). Copyright © 1970 by the Directors of the Columbia Law Review Association, Inc. All rights reserved. Reprinted by permission.

E. Allan Farnsworth, Your Loss or My Gain? The Dilemma of the Disgorgement Principle in Breach of Contract, 94 Yale L.J. 1339, 1382 (1985). Copyright © 1985. Reprinted with permission of the Yale Law Journal, Fred B. Rothman & Co., and the author.

Marc A. Franklin, When Worlds Collide: Liability Theories and Disclaimers in Defective Product Cases, 18 Stan. L. Rev. 974, 984 (1966). Copyright © 1966 by the Board of Trustees of the Leland Stanford Junior University. Reprinted with permission.

Charles Fried, Contract as Promise 16-17, 37 (1981). Copyright © 1981 by the President and Fellows of Harvard College. Reprinted with permission of the Harvard University Press.

Daniel Friedmann, The Efficient Breach Fallacy, 18 J. Legal Stud. 1, 6-7 (1989). Copyright © 1989 by the University of Chicago. All rights reserved. Reprinted with permission.

Daniel Friedmann, Restitution of Benefits Obtained Through the Appropriation of Property or the Commission of a Wrong, 80 Colum. L. Rev. 504, 551, 553-554 (1980). Copyright © 1980 by the Directors of the Columbia Law Review Association, Inc. All rights reserved. Reprinted by permission.

Roger C. Henderson, The Doctrine of Reasonable Expectations in Insurance Law After Two Decades, 51 Ohio St. L.J. 823, 846-847, 853 (1990). Copyright © 1990 by the Ohio State University. Reprinted with permission.

Robert A. Hillman, Keeping the Deal Together After Material Breach — Common Law Mitigation Rules, the UCC, and the Restatement (Second) of Contracts, 47 U. Colo. L. Rev. 553, 591-592 (1976). Copyright © 1976. Reprinted with permission of the University of Colorado Law Review and the author.

Morton J. Horwitz, The Historical Foundations of Modern Contract Law, 87 Harv. L. Rev. 917, 923, 927, 944-945 (1974). Copyright © 1974 by the Harvard Law Review Association. Reprinted with permission.

W. Page Keeton et al., Prosser and Keeton on the Law of Torts §106, at 739 (5th ed. 1984). Reprinted from Prosser & Keeton on Torts (5th ed. 1984) with permission of the West Publishing Co.

Charles L. Knapp, Enforcing the Contract to Bargain, 44 N.Y.U. L. Rev. 673, 682-684 (1969). Copyright © 1969. Reprinted with permission of New York University Law Review and the author.

Charles L. Knapp, Rescuing Reliance: The Perils of Promissory Estoppel, 49 Hastings L.J. 1191, 1322-1323, 1325, 1334 (1998). Copyright © 1999 by the University of California, Hastings College of the Law. Reprinted with permission.

Candace S. Kovacic, A Proposal to Simplify Quantum Meruit Litigation, 35 Am. U.L. Rev. 547, 550-551 (1986). Copyright © 1986. Reprinted with permission of the author.

Arthur Allen Leff, Unconscionability and the Code — The Emperor's New Clause, 115 U. Pa. L. Rev. 485, 554 (1967). Copyright © 1967. Reprinted with permission of the University of Pennsylvania Law Review and Fred B. Rothman & Co.

Peter Linzer, The Decline of Assent: At-Will Employment as a Case Study of the Breakdown of Private Law Theory, 20 Ga. L. Rev. 323, 423 (1986). Copyright © 1986. Reprinted with permission of the University of Georgia Law Review and the author.

Leon Lipson, The *Allegheny College* Case, 23 Yale L. Rep. No. 2, at 11 (1977). Copyright © 1977. Reprinted with permission of Yale Law School.

Ian R. Macneil, Efficient Breach of Contract: Circles in the Sky, 68 Va. L. Rev. 947, 968-969 (1982). Copyright © 1982. Reprinted with permission of the Virginia Law Review Association and Fred B. Rothman & Co.

Judith L. Maute, *Peevyhouse v. Garland Coal & Mining Co.* Revisited: The Ballad of Willie and Lucille, 89 Nw. U. L. Rev. 1341, 1358-1363 (1995). Copyright © 1995. Reprinted by special permission of Northwestern University School of Law, Law Review.

William A. Mayhew, Reasonable Expectations: Seeking a Principled Application, 13 Pepp. L. Rev. 267, 288-289 (1986). Copyright © 1986. Reprinted with permission of the Pepperdine Law Review.

Ralph James Mooney, The New Conceptualism in Contract Law, 74 Or. L. Rev. 1131, 1170-1171 (1995). Copyright © 1995 by the University of Oregon. Reprinted by permission.

John E. Murray, Jr., Contracts §54, at 112-113 (2d ed. 1974). Copyright © 1974. Reprinted with permission of the Michie Company.

National Conference of Commissioners on Uniform State Laws, Model Residential Landlord and Tenant Act, 7B U.L.A. §2.104 (Supp. 1998). Reprinted from Uniform Laws Annotated (Supp. 1998) with permission of the West Publishing Co. and the National Conference of Commissioners on Uniform State Laws.

Edwin Patterson, The Interpretation and Construction of Contracts, 64 Colum. L. Rev. 833, 853-854 (1964). Copyright © 1964 by the Directors of the Columbia Law Review Association, Inc. All rights reserved. Reprinted by permission.

Lee A. Pizzimenti, Prohibiting Lawyers from Assisting in Unconscionable Transactions: Using an Overt Tool, 72 Marq. L. Rev. 151, 174 (1989). Copyright © 1988. Reprinted with permission of the Marquette Law Review.

Richard A. Posner, Economic Analysis of Law 131-133, 151-152 (5th ed. 1998). Copyright © 1998. Reprinted with permission of Richard A. Posner.

Richard A. Posner, Gratuitous Promises in Economics and Law, 6 J. Legal Stud. 411, 418-419 (1977). Copyright © 1977 by the University of Chicago. All rights reserved. Reprinted with permission.

Harry G. Prince, Contract Interpretation in California: Plain Meaning, Parol Evidence and Use of the "Just Result" Principle, 31 Loy. L.A. L. Rev. 557, 584-585 (1998). Copyright © 1998. Reprinted with permission.

Todd D. Rakoff, Contracts of Adhesion: An Essay in Reconstruction, 96 Harv. L. Rev. 1173, 1176-1177 (1983). Copyright © 1983 by the Harvard Law Review Association. Reprinted with permission.

Robert S. Summers, "Good Faith" in General Contract Law and the Sales Provisions of the Uniform Commercial Code, 54 Va. L. Rev. 195, 202-203 (1968). Copyright © 1968. Reprinted with permission of the Virginia Law Review Association and Fred B. Rothman & Co.

Kellye Y. Testy, An Unlikely Resurrection, 90 Nw. U. L. Rev. 219, 226 (1995). Copyright © 1995. Reprinted by special permission of Northwestern University School of Law, Law Review.

Roberto Mangabeira Unger, The Critical Legal Studies Movement, 96 Harv. L. Rev. 561, 629 (1983). Copyright © 1983 by the Harvard Law Review Association. Reprinted with permission.

Craig S. Warkol, Note, Resolving the Paradox Between Legal Theory and Legal Fact: The Judicial Rejection of the Theory of Efficient Breach, 20 Cardozo L. Rev. 321, 343 (1998). Copyright © 1998 by Yeshiva University. All rights reserved. Reprinted with permission of the Cardozo Law Review.

Geoffrey R. Watson, In the Tribunal of Conscience: Mills v. Wyman Reconsidered, 71 Tul. L. Rev. 1749, 1751 (1997). Copyright © 1997. Reprinted with the permission of the Tulane Law Review Association. All rights reserved.

James J. White & Robert S. Summers, Uniform Commercial Code §8-4, at 312 (4th ed. 1995). Reprinted with permission of the West Publishing Co.

Eyal Zamir, The Inverted Hierarchy of Contract Interpretation and Supplementation, 97 Colum. L. Rev. 1710, 1771-1773 (1997). Copyright © 1997 by the Directors of the Columbia Law Review Association, Inc. All rights reserved. Reprinted by permission.

Provisions, comments, and illustrations from the Restatement of Contracts (copyright © 1932), the Restatement (Second) of Contracts (copyright © 1981), the Restatement of Restitution (copyright © 1937), and the Restatement (Second) of Torts (copyright © 1965) are reprinted with permission of the American Law Institute. Portions of the comments to the

Uniform Commercial Code, by the American Law Institute and the National Conference of Commissioners on Uniform State Laws (copyright © 1991), are reprinted with permission of the Permanent Editorial Board for the Uniform Commercial Code.

Unless otherwise indicated, references to Corbin on Contracts are to the revised edition, copyright dates from 1962 through 1971; references to Williston on Contracts are to the third edition (W. Jaeger ed.), copyright dates from 1957 through 1979. Footnotes from cases and other quoted material have been omitted without indication; where footnotes have been included, their original numbering has been retained.

1 | An Introduction to the Study of Contract Law

   Legal education, at least as inflicted upon first-year students in American law schools, used to be a sink-or-swim process. For many years students learned legal analysis by reading cases and responding in class to questions and hypotheticals posed by their professors; casebooks rarely provided explanatory textual material; instructors took great pride in refusing to answer questions in class (except with questions of their own) and frowned on the use of "hornbooks" as study aids outside of class. The whole enterprise was not unlike teaching beginning drivers how to handle an automobile by setting them down unceremoniously in the middle of a freeway at rush hour. Perhaps of even greater consequence, in terms of the quality of education provided, was the widely held view that teaching the student the skills of legal analysis — "thinking like a lawyer," as it was usually described — was essentially the only task of legal education. Law schools virtually ignored other lawyering skills such as counseling, advocacy, or negotiation, and they paid little attention to philosophical, historical, or sociological studies of law.

   In recent years, legal educators have come to realize that the traditional goals and methods of legal education had to be modified and expanded. Like other modern casebooks, these materials will attempt to present to the student a broader view of contract law than might have been visible with the traditional approach. Through problems, textual material, and supplementary readings we hope to stimulate you to think about both the theoretical and the practical side of contract law. We hope also to convey our shared sense that contract law — like all other bodies of law, particularly those that make up what we call "common law" — is not merely a static set of rules. It is rather at any given moment a vast and complex composite of what was, what is now, and what is in the process of becoming. Law students of today will, when they enter practice, deal with lawyers and judges who recall vividly the last century's Seventies and Eighties, and themselves will someday be the lawyers of this century's Twenties and Thirties. We hope therefore to set before you at least some glimpses of the history of our law of contract, a reasonably accurate picture of its present state, and some sense of what a contract law of the future might look like.

A. CONTRACT LAW IN THE FIRST-YEAR LAW CURRICULUM

Certainly it is possible to talk for hours about something without ever defining it. Many terms in everyday use—"justice," "love," "medium-rare"—are notoriously elusive in meaning. Nevertheless, at the risk of spelling out what to many students may already be obvious, we would like at the outset to present some working definitions of terminology we will be using throughout these materials.

Contract, as we will use that term, ordinarily connotes an *agreement* between two or more persons—not merely a shared belief, but a common understanding as to something that is to be done in the future by one or both of them. Sometimes, the term *contract* is used also to refer to a *document*—the set of papers in which such an agreement is set forth. For lawyers, *contract* usually is used to refer to an agreement that has *legal effect;* that is, it creates obligations for which some sort of legal enforcement will be available if performance is not forthcoming as promised. Thus, it will sometimes be necessary to distinguish among three elements in a transaction, each of which may be called a "contract": (1) the agreement-in-fact between the parties, (2) the agreement-as-written (which may or may not correspond accurately to the agreement-in-fact), and (3) the set of rights and duties created by (1) and (2). Without trying at this point to state a short but comprehensive definition of *law* (if that were possible), it is perhaps sufficient to suggest that we will be surveying the ways in which such agreements are made and enforced in our legal system—the role of lawyers and judges in creating contracts, in deciding disputes that may arise with respect to their performance, and in fashioning appropriate remedies for their breach.

Contract law is but one of several subjects that make up the traditional first-year law curriculum. Besides the course in contracts, most law schools have first-year courses in torts, criminal law, and property (as well as courses in procedure—civil procedure and perhaps criminal procedure as well). How does contract law fit into this pattern?

In the Anglo-American legal system, a great number of things—both tangible and intangible—are susceptible of "ownership." A diamond ring, the Empire State Building, "Spider-Man," computer software—all may be the "property" of one person or group of persons, which means that the state will protect the right of the "owner" to use, enjoy, and even consume that thing, to the exclusion of all other persons. The first-year property course traditionally focuses on the detailed rules that in Anglo-American law govern the ownership of "real property" (land and the buildings on it), as well as some types of "personal" property, such as "goods" (tangible moveable property). Later you will have the opportunity to explore bodies of law relating to ownership of other, less tangible kinds of property such as copyrights, patents, shares of corporate stock, and negotiable instruments.

Any society that recognizes property rights must also address the question of how it should respond when someone violates those rights. And property rights are not the only kind of individual rights that may need legal protection. Even societies that do not permit private ownership of wealth to the degree that ours does are likely to recognize the personal rights of individuals to be free from certain kinds of conduct such as the infliction of physical injury or other interferences with their individual freedom or dignity. The courses in criminal law and torts deal with different aspects of this question: Criminal law focuses on those violations of personal and property rights that society deems serious enough to be deterred by the threat of punishment for their commission (robbery, rape, and murder are obvious examples); tort law considers what remedy should be made available to the individuals so injured. Because of the nature of the conduct regulated, criminal law and tort law overlap to a great degree, but they are not congruent. Many acts are criminal but not tortious, because they are offenses not against individuals but against the state — treason, for example, or tax evasion; others, such as slander, may be tortious but not criminal.

Where does contract law fit into this picture? We have noted already that our society recognizes and protects a variety of types of property and personal rights. Ownership of property ordinarily includes the right to use and consume the thing owned, but in many cases it will be more to the advantage of the owner to transfer, or "convey," the right of ownership to some other person in exchange for something else of value (money, perhaps, or the ownership of some other property). A piano is more valuable to one who can play it than to one who cannot, and two lots of adjoining real property may be worth much more when combined into one parcel than when held separately. Similarly, the ownership of factory machinery may be much more valuable when it is combined with a right to the work of skilled technicians and laborers, a dependable source of supply of raw materials, and licenses to use patented processes in the manufacturing of goods. Agreements for exchange are the means by which such resources are assembled and put to productive use. Some such agreements call for the immediate and simultaneous exchange of money for goods or services (your purchase of a morning newspaper, for instance, or of a hamburger or a haircut). Where exchanges of any significant size are concerned, however, it is much more common for both the planning and the performance to be spread over a considerable period of time. The law of contracts is our society's legal mechanism for protecting the expectations that arise from the making of agreements for the future exchange of various types of performance, such as the conveyance of property (tangible and intangible), the performance of services, and the payment of money. (Such agreements are often referred to as "executory contracts.")

Before proceeding to examine contract law in more detail, we should point out here that our description of the relationship between the various "substantive" bodies of law that you will be encountering this year is necessarily an oversimplified one. Legal problems do not always fit neatly into the pigeonholes that legal theorists have created; frequently they raise issues involving more than one body of law. For instance, you will learn in this course that some types of conduct that we call "fraud" can constitute both a breach of contract and a tort. Lease agreements between landlord and tenant have historically been governed by rules of property law, but recently courts have tended to analyze their legal effect more in the manner traditionally applied to contracts. The web of the law may not be quite as seamless as the old saying would have it, but students and teachers alike must beware of falling into the trap of believing that our various legal categories are ironclad and unchanging; they are not.

PROBLEM 1-1

(A) Think about your activities during the last week before your first day of class in law school. What types of contracts did you enter into?

(B) Consider the following hypothetical transactions, each of which obviously has numerous real counterparts. In which ones is a "contract" (using that term in one or more of the senses suggested above) involved?

1. Amalgamated Rubber Products, Inc., agrees to buy 35 percent (700,000 shares) of the outstanding common stock of Fargo Petroleum Corp. for $85 million.

2. Marian Gerber buys a used car from Tiptop Motors, Inc. She pays $2500 down and agrees to pay $300 per month for 24 months. Tiptop assigns its rights under that document to Sunshine Finance Corp. As required by the laws of her state, Gerber obtains a policy of auto liability insurance from Fidelity Underwriters Co.

3. Oscar Bennett is hired as a driver for Interstate Motorfreight, Inc. The Teamsters Union acts as the bargaining representative of all employees of Interstate, and Bennett becomes a dues-paying member of the Union.

4. On his way to work in the morning, Frederico Montoya leaves an overcoat at the neighborhood dry cleaning shop. The proprietor gives him a ticket with a serial number on it and says "Friday."

5. Ruth Harmon boards a bus to ride to a neighboring city. On the way the bus is struck by another car; Ruth and several other passengers are slightly injured.

6. Sondra Michaels accepts Jay Krieger's proposal of marriage, and he gives her a lovely sapphire engagement ring. Sondra's parents send out invitations to 400 people, inviting them to the wedding on May 28. About 150 of those people are also invited to a reception, "r.s.v.p." Nearly 130 of the latter do respond, indicating their intention to attend the reception. All the invited guests who attend the wedding send (or bring) presents to Sondra and Jay.

7. Before leaving for work in the morning, Mr. Kovaks promises his wife that he will take the entire family out to dinner that evening. Mr. Kovaks takes the family to a local fast, food restaurant for dinner. Numerous hamburgers, French fries, and milkshakes are consumed; the bill is $77.85, which Mr. Kovaks pays with a credit card.

8. Jack Clawson, a wealthy resident of Tuscon, dies unexpectedly, leaving a will providing that his considerable estate is to go

three-quarters to his daughter Maria and one-quarter to his son John. John is thinking of challenging the will because his father had told him that he was going to leave everything to his children equally.

9. Marc and Edna, law students, have a regular game of Texas Hold 'Em poker with several of their fellow students. Edna is the big winner at this week's game, to the tune of $15.

10. A candidate for President promises not to raise taxes. The candidate wins the election with more than 60 million votes.

B. THE SOURCES OF CONTRACT LAW

Having presented our general definition of contract law, we next face the question: Where is this law to be found? From what sources — what "authority" — do courts derive the rules of law they apply to decide contract disputes? The types of authority we will consider fall generally into two categories: primary and secondary. Primary authority, commonly viewed by lawyers and judges as "the law" itself, consists of prior judicial decisions (which collectively make up what we call the "common law") and statutes, ordinances, and the like (expressions of the will of a duly constituted legislative body on a subject within its proper sphere of action). Secondary authority might be very loosely defined as anything else that could appropriately influence a court; the examples we will consider, however, consist mainly of the two principal types of persuasive authority that have had marked influence on the common law of contract: commentary by legal scholars and the American Law Institute's Restatements of the Law.

1. Judicial Opinions

Historically, contract law developed in the Anglo-American system as judge-made law, rules distilled from a composite of court decisions in prior cases. Thus, one of your principal tasks in using these materials will be to learn how to read, understand, and apply judicial decisions. You will find at first that they seem to be written in a foreign language; like any technical jargon, legal language is full of strange words (like *assumpsit* and *quantum meruit*) as well as words that are familiar but appear to be used with an unfamiliar or specialized meaning (like *consideration* and *offer*). We will try to help you by signaling in the text with quotation marks or italics when a familiar word has a special meaning in the legal lexicon. You may find at first that a law dictionary is not only useful but indispensable to comprehending what is going on. Soon enough, however, you will find that you can not only read but fluently speak the legal language that the courts are using. (For a time you may also drive your family and friends to distraction with it, but this too will pass.)

Our judicial system of decisionmaking is commonly said to be one of "stare decisis" — adherence to past decisions, or "precedents." A precedent is a prior decision with facts sufficiently similar to the case "sub judice" — under adjudication — that the court feels obliged to follow it and to render a similar decision. A regime of law based primarily on precedent is commonly justified on two grounds. First, it offers a high degree of predictability of decision, enabling those who so desire to order their affairs in accordance with ascertainable rules of law. Second, it puts a rein on what might otherwise be the natural proclivity of judges to decide cases on the basis of prejudice, personal emotion, or other factors that we might regard as improper grounds for decision. Such a system also will obviously have the characteristic — which may sometimes be a virtue, sometimes a defect — of being static and conservative, generally oriented toward preservation of the status quo.

There will be times, however, when a common law judge concludes that blind adherence to precedent would produce an unjust result in the case presented for decision. There are a number of ways such a result may be avoided. To begin with, a precedent is considered to be "binding" on a court only if it was decided by that same court or by an appellate court of higher rank in the same jurisdiction. Other precedents — from lower courts or from other jurisdictions — are said to be merely "persuasive." If a precedent of the latter type is in fact *un*persuasive, the judge is free to disregard it. If the precedent is not merely persuasive, but binding, it cannot simply be ignored. It may, however, be avoided: If the facts of the present case do not include a fact that appears to have been necessary ("material") to the earlier decision, the court may "distinguish" the precedent and render a different decision. If the earlier precedent is indeed binding, but is difficult or impossible to distinguish, there is one other way to avoid its effect: If the court of decision is the one that created the precedent (or is a higher court), it can simply "overrule" the earlier decision. (This does not retroactively change the outcome for the parties to that earlier case, but it does change the rule for the case under decision and subsequent similar cases.) Over-ruling is considered a relatively drastic action and is usually reserved for instances in which the court feels that the rule established by the earlier precedent is simply wrong, that is, unjust in its general application because either it was ill conceived at the outset or it has been outmoded by later developments.

Some cases cannot be decided on the basis of precedent alone, either because no precedent exists (a somewhat unlikely occurrence in our litigious society) or because the applicability of precedent to the case at hand is unclear. In these cases courts turn to "policy" to resolve the case. Policy may be regarded generally as any societal goal that will be furthered by a particular decision. This may be economic, political, social, or moral, and it may have to do with the particular parties themselves or with the good of society as a whole (or some definable segment of it). Often a court will discern a public policy in statutes or court decisions, even when those do not apply directly to the case at hand; at other times the court will apparently be following the judge's own sense of what is just or moral. As we shall see, some legal commentators believe that "all law is policy" and should be frankly viewed as such; others feel that policy is too ill-defined or too ungovernable a factor to furnish any guide at all to decisionmaking. Some have a particular policy that they would have the courts seek to promote — economic efficiency, for example. As you review the court decisions in these materials, keep your eyes open for both overt and covert judicial applications of policy as a basis for decision.

2. Statutory Law

In 1677 the English Parliament enacted what is commonly referred to as the "statute of frauds." Subsequently adopted in virtually every American state, this statute requires certain types of contracts to be evidenced by a signed writing to be enforceable in court. With this notable exception, until the twentieth century contract law has been largely judge-made. As we shall see, even the statute of frauds has itself become so overlaid by court decisions that it has more of the quality of common law than of a modern statute.

The common law character of contract law changed significantly in the twentieth century, although it is still accurate to characterize contract law as predominantly judge-made rather than statutory. Probably the most important inroad on the historical character of contract law was the development of the Uniform Commercial Code, begun in the 1940s. In the 1960s, a wave of consumer protection statutes at both the federal and state levels modified traditional contract principles. Other statutory influences on contract law will be mentioned throughout these materials. It should also be noted that in a few states, most importantly California, significant principles of the common law have been "codified," enacted into statutory form.

Although its name suggests otherwise, the Uniform Commercial Code (UCC, or the Code) does not govern all commercial transactions. It does not apply, for example, to transactions in real estate or to personal service contracts. Nevertheless, it has become the major statute with general importance to all phases of contract law. The Code had its origins in the late nineteenth century, when rapid industrialization and the growth of a national commercial economy first highlighted the expense, inconvenience, and uncertainty occasioned by differences between the states in matters of commercial law. Led by New York, a number of states created a National Conference of Commissioners on Uniform State Laws (NCCUSL) to address these problems. Although it did not have the power to make law, the NCCUSL drafted and recommended to the state legislatures a series of "uniform acts," dealing with various commercial matters, such as negotiable instruments and bills of lading. The Uniform Sales Act, which was widely adopted, was composed largely of provisions applicable by their nature only to sales of goods (e.g., passage of title and means of delivery); like the other uniform acts, it assumed the existence of an underlying body of common law governing contract formation in general.

By 1940, it appeared that an updating was in order for a number of the uniform acts, including the Uniform Sales Act. As that project proceeded, however, it grew into something rather different. Joining with the American Law Institute (a prestigious and influential organization of lawyers, judges, and law teachers), the NCCUSL produced a general revision and consolidation of all the existing uniform commercial laws, the Uniform Commercial Code. Professor Karl Llewellyn was the architect of the UCC and the principal drafter of Article 2, its Sales article. Reflecting his influence, the Code represented a determined effort to bring the law applicable to commercial transactions more in line with business practice, so as to effectuate the legitimate expectations of those engaged in business dealings. Although its acceptance by the states was at first slow in coming, all or part of the UCC has been adopted and is now in force in every American state.

The UCC, like contract law in general, has not been static. In 1987, a new Article 2A was adopted, dealing with leases of goods (a topic that had previously been covered, if at all, only "analogically" by Article 2, Sales). Various articles of the UCC have been comprehensively revised since the Code's widespread adoption in the 1960s, some, such as Article 9, more than once. In 2001, a revised version of Article 1 was promulgated by ALI/ NCCUSL, but it has been adopted by less than half the states. In recent years, however, two other attempts to bring the UCC further abreast of current technical and business developments have run into difficulty. Attempts to create a new Article 2B to deal with computer software foundered on the shoals of deep differences among the various affected interests; instead of a new ALI-sponsored addition to the UCC, that effort has now produced a proposed Uniform Computer Information Transactions Act ("UCITA"). This statute has been adopted in two states but has run into heavy opposition from consumer advocates as well as business interests outside the software industry, and its ultimate success is still in doubt.

A major effort to rewrite Article 2 has run into similar difficulties. Originally planned as a comprehensive revision of Article 2 as a whole, it also ran into heavy opposition from some business interests who feared that some provisions of the proposed Article 2 would be too favorable to consumers. That story is told by one of the Reporters of the proposed revised article, Richard E. Speidel, in Revising Article 2, A View from the Trenches, 52 Hastings L.J. 607 (2002). (Professor Speidel's article is part of a symposium discussion of the Uniform Laws revision process, with contributions by prominent academics, attorneys, and others involved in or concerned with the revision process. See 52 Hastings L.J. 603 et seq.) The result of this process has been only a partial revision of Article 2, itself the subject of intense debate. Revised Article 2 has not yet been adopted by any state.

When a court decides a case governed by a statute, its reasoning differs from that used when common law principles are applied. Any court, even the highest court of the jurisdiction, is bound to follow the provisions of a valid statute that apply to the dispute before it. This duty stems from a fundamental political tenet of our society: The legislature has ultimate lawmaking power so long as it acts within the bounds of its constitutional authority. Thus, the legislature may if it wishes modify or eliminate any of the rules of common law. Sometimes, of course, the language of a statute may be subject to differing interpretations; in such cases, courts ordinarily seek to ascertain the legislature's purpose in enacting it, in order to adopt a construction that will best effectuate that purpose. Sometimes there is "legislative history" — legislative debates, committee reports, and the like — which sheds light on that purpose. It should be noted, however, that a few judges and scholars believe that courts should not resort to legislative history, but should only examine the text of a statute in deciding what it means. These critics of the use of legislative history argue that such sources are often self-serving and in any event only the language of the statute, not its history, has been enacted into law. See Antonin Scalia, A Matter of Interpretation: Federal Courts and the Law (1997). Nonetheless, the vast majority of judges continue to resort to legislative history when interpreting statutes. As we shall see, the UCC has its own peculiar form of legislative history, the "Official Comments" of the drafters. (These are not literally legislative history; they are the product not of the state legislatures themselves but of the authors of the "Official" UCC, on which the various state statutes are based.)

When drafting Article 2 of the UCC, Professor Llewellyn and his colleagues departed from the pattern of the prior Uniform Sales Act. Instead of merely assuming a body of applicable contract law as a background, they included in the Code a number of provisions that altered the rules of the common law of contract as applied to sales of goods. These provisions express principles that could also be applied to contracts other than sales of goods. (It should be noted that despite its placement in what is entitled "The Uniform Commercial Code," Article 2 applies to all sales of goods, not just to transactions in which one or both of the parties are "merchants"; sales by merchants to consumers and even transactions in which neither party is a merchant are within its scope.) Once Article 2 was generally adopted, courts began to apply some of its provisions "by analogy" in contract cases to which Article 2 does not directly apply. This tendency has in turn had its influence on another form of authority, one which, although persuasive rather than binding, has had an immeasurably strong impact on contract law: The Restatement of Contracts.

3. The Restatements

As we have seen, the National Conference of Commissioners on Uniform State Laws and its various model acts represented one response to the growing uncertainty and lack of uniformity in commercial law. In the early twentieth century, another institutional effort emerged to address these problems. In 1923, the American Law Institute (ALI) was formed. The major project undertaken by this organization was the preparation and promulgation of what purported to be accurate and authoritative summaries of the rules of common law in various fields, including contracts, torts, and property. The first such "Restatement" to be issued—and perhaps the most successful in terms of acceptance and use by the bench and bar—was the Restatement of Contracts, officially adopted by the ALI in 1932. (It had been gradually emerging in draft form over the several years preceding.) The Restatement resembled a statute in form, consisting of "black-letter" statements of the "general rule" (or, where the cases appeared to conflict, the "better rule"). In addition, most sections were supported with at least some commentary and illustrations. None of the ALI Restatements have the force of law, as does a statute or an individual court decision. Although they constitute only secondary authority, the Restatements have in fact proved to be remarkably persuasive; not infrequently, a court will justify its decision by simply citing and quoting (perhaps with approving discussion) the Restatement's rule on a given point.

Recognizing that contract law had undergone substantial development since 1932, the ALI in 1962 began to prepare a revised version of its Restatement. Finally adopted in full in 1979, the Restatement (Second) of Contracts reflects some shifts in philosophy from the original Restatement. (Throughout these materials, references to "the Restatement" or "Restatement (Second)" will mean the Restatements of Contracts; other ALI Restatements, such as Agency, Property, or Torts, will be specifically identified.) The first Restatement tended to emphasize generalization and predictability, at the expense of diversity and flexibility; the second attempts, with more extended supporting commentary and editorial notes, to acknowledge some of the complexity the first Restatement preferred to ignore and to suggest a freer rein for judicial discretion. As we shall see, the Restatement (Second) also reflects to a great degree the influence of the Uniform Commercial Code. This has solidified the incorporation of many of Article 2's innovative features into general contract law, making it less necessary for courts in non-goods cases to invoke the UCC as "analogical" authority.

4. Legal Commentary

Although they are no more than secondary authority, the Restatements of Contracts have clearly had a powerful effect in shaping judicial views of what the common law of contract ought to be. Perhaps no other secondary authority has had quite that impact on the law, but over the years a variety of published articles, books, and multivolume treatises has been devoted to analyzing, evaluating, and synthesizing the immense body of contract cases that has accumulated in the reported decisions of American courts. Authors of these works have sought to clarify the law, to propose solutions for unresolved issues, and in some cases to argue strenuously and often effectively for legal change. In the aggregate, such commentary has been extremely influential in shaping the course of the common law of contract.

Perhaps the most weighty (certainly in pounds and probably in influence as well) of these commentaries are the two multivolume treatises by Professors Samuel Williston and Arthur Corbin. Williston was the Reporter for the original Restatement of Contracts, and his ideas were reflected in its organization and content; the Williston treatise (first published in 1920 and periodically revised thereafter) was thus naturally regarded with particular respect by judges who viewed the Restatement itself as authoritative. Professor Corbin's treatise was not published until 1950, capping a long and distinguished scholarly career. Although he and Williston were friends and associates, and Corbin himself took part in the writing of the Restatement, the two differed in fundamental philosophy. Williston tended to regard the law as a set of abstract rules that courts could by deduction use to decide individual cases; Corbin regarded his task as a legal scholar to be to discover what the courts were actually doing and to attempt to weave those findings into what he called "working rules" of law. The Corbin Treatise is currently being revised and updated by scholars under the leadership of Professor Joseph M. Perillo.

Besides the works of these two giants of contract law, many shorter commentaries have appeared over the years. Among those currently in print, perhaps the most influential is the one-volume treatise by Professor E. Allan Farnsworth, who served as Reporter for the Restatement (Second) of Contracts. For issues arising under the UCC, lawyers and courts frequently turn to James J. White & Robert S. Summers, Uniform Commercial Code (5th ed. 2000).

5. International Commercial Law

Most transactions in which American lawyers are involved take place entirely within the United States, but international commercial transactions are of growing importance to our economy. Today, exports and imports of goods are a significant percentage of gross domestic product. Moreover, it is likely that international business will continue to grow in importance as various legal and technological barriers to cross-border dealings diminish. Students entering the practice of law in the twenty-first century must be familiar with the sources of law for international transactions.

Historically, tariffs have probably been the most significant barrier to international trade. Countries erect tariffs on imported goods for a variety of reasons, including to protect domestic industries and to raise revenue. As part of the international reconstruction that took place after World War II, most countries became parties to a treaty known as the General Agreement on Tariffs and Trade, or "GATT." Two of the central purposes of GATT were reduction of tariff and nontariff barriers to trade and clarification of member countries' rules regarding trade (the term "transparency" is used to refer to this goal). The United States has been a member of GATT since its inception, although Congress did not give its formal approval of United States participation until ratification of the 1994 amendments to GATT, which created a central body for administering GATT, the World Trade Organization (WTO). In the 50 years since its formation, GATT has been quite successful in reducing trade barriers.

Lack of uniformity of the rules governing international commercial transactions has been another major barrier to international trade. Attempts to overcome this problem go back at least to the 1930s. In 1980 under the sponsorship of the United Nations Commission on International Trade Law (UNCITRAL), a number of countries adopted a treaty, the United Nations Convention on the International Sale of Goods ("CISG"). The Convention formally became effective January 1, 1988. The CISG is analogous to the UCC. Like the UCC it applies to the sale of goods. Also, like the UCC it has the force of law, because it is a treaty. On the other hand, there are important differences between the CISG and the UCC. For example, the CISG does not apply to consumer transactions, while the UCC does. See CISG Article 2(a). The CISG generally applies when the parties to a contract have places of business in countries that have adopted the Convention. Thus, the CISG would apply to a sale of a machine from an American manufacturer to a French company, since both countries are parties to the CISG. The full text of the CISG is reprinted in the Rules Supplement; we will also refer to various articles of the CISG throughout these materials to compare its provisions with domestic law.

The CISG does not purport to cover all issues of international contract law. To fill in the gaps left by the CISG, a private organization, the International Institute for the Unification of Private Law (UNIDROIT), has sponsored the preparation of Principles of International Commercial Contracts. Published in 1994 and revised in 2004, the Principles are analogous to the Restatements, providing scholarly opinion as to what the law is (or should be), but without the force of law that the CISG has. The Principles are also reprinted in the Supplement.

C. THE PERSPECTIVE OF CONTRACT THEORY

Throughout our study of contract law, we will of course be centrally concerned with learning to understand and apply the body of rules that courts and lawyers commonly regard as making up the present-day law of contract, both common law and statutory. At the same time, students and teachers should be aware that, particularly in recent years, many commentators and analysts have tried to go beyond mere identification and classification of such rules of law to examine the fundamental nature of contract law itself: what it consists of; how it has evolved; what goals and policies it serves; and where it fits into the broader picture of law as viewed through the lens of legal or moral philosophy, economics, political or social science, historiography, or any of the various other branches of inquiry into human life and thought.

From time to time in the course of these materials, we will attempt to paraphrase the conclusions of those writers or will present excerpts from their writings. Such descriptions and quotations will of necessity fail to do justice to the arguments and analyses presented in those works; the best evidence is always the original writings themselves. Any attempt at "thumbnail sketching" must be open to the charge that it omits significant matters and inaccurately summarizes or generalizes about the matters that it does include. Nevertheless, the following discussion is our attempt briefly to introduce you to some of the points of view you will see reflected in the commentaries that are cited at the end of this chapter and in the chapters that follow.

During the Willistonian period, contract law was viewed as a set of universal rules distilled from decided cases; it did not appear necessary either to explain or to justify its existence. Because cases were to be decided by the virtually mechanical application of rules to reach a doctrinally "correct" result, judges had no need to use — indeed, were in effect forbidden to use — moral or political values in reaching their decisions. This "formalist" approach to law is initially identified with Christopher Columbus Langdell, Dean of Harvard Law School, father of the case method and author of the first legal casebook, on contracts. Professor Williston is usually regarded as the heir to the Langdellian tradition; his ideas, as we have seen, in turn permeated the original Restatement of Contracts.

In the early years of the twentieth century, legal scholars began to produce works that rejected the tenets of formalism. Dean Roscoe Pound of the Harvard Law School argued for a "sociological jurisprudence," in which rules of law would be evaluated on the basis of the social interests that they served. In the 1920s and 1930s a group of scholars working in diverse fields of law called for a "realistic" jurisprudence. The "Legal Realists," as they came to be called, had a view of the legal system different from that of Langdell and Williston. They saw court decisions not as products of the application of neutral principles to given sets of facts, but rather as the end results of a decisionmaking process in which both the finding of facts and the application of rules were affected by the personalities, points of view, interests, and goals of the decisionmakers. Since all lawmaking was in effect policymaking, they argued, the formation of legal rules should be the result of a conscious application of all relevant knowledge of human affairs—including that furnished by other disciplines such as economics, political science, psychology, and anthropology—rather than a process (real or pretended) of "discovering" neutral principles from which abstract rules could be deduced.

Not surprisingly, the Realists were particularly critical of the "black-letter" law approach of the Restatements. One of the most influential of the Realists was Karl Llewellyn, who later became the principal drafter of the UCC. In his numerous books and articles, Llewellyn propounded the notion that judges should reach their decisions only after having immersed themselves in the factual details of the disputes before them. From this process, he believed, would come the "situation sense" that would lead to the right result. Llewellyn's influence on the UCC can be seen in its emphasis on general standards (such as "good faith" and "unconscionability") rather than on mechanical rules and in the Code's reliance on such broad sources of "law" as trade custom and business practice.

Because they focused almost exclusively on the impossibility of achieving true objectivity in legal decisionmaking, the Realists were criticized by many—including even Dean Pound—for failing to address the social purposes and goals of the legal process. This criticism may not have been well founded, however, because at least some of the Realists appear to have had a social program of their own; they believed that by the application of "scientific" knowledge, the decisionmaking process could be tamed and (along with other social institutions) made to serve the ideal of a perfectible, "liberal" state. Events during and after World War II dealt a sharp blow to the liberal belief in the progressive improvement of human institutions, however, and the Vietnam War and the social ferment we know as "the Sixties" probably also contributed to this process. As a result, legal scholarship in general and contract scholarship in particular have appeared over the last several decades to be engaged in a process of deconstruction and reconstruction, attempting both to show the inherent failings of the old system and to find some new basis on which to give theoretical legitimacy to a body of legal principles applicable to contract disputes.

One school of thought that gained many adherents during this period applies methods of economic analysis to legal issues. Central to this economic approach to law is the notion of "efficiency." (While writers differ over the appropriate definition of "efficiency," generally efficiency is thought to be increased when the cost of transactions in society is reduced, and resources are allocated to their most highly valued uses.) Scholars identified with the economic-analysis school of legal thought ordinarily make two claims about the relationship between law and economics: (1) the "positive" or empirical argument that legal rules (particularly those of the common law) tend in general to reach "efficient" outcomes and (2) the "normative" claim that "inefficient" rules of law should be modified in the direction of greater efficiency.

Economic theorists differ among themselves on a number of issues in contract law. The predominant wing, the "Chicago school," led by former University of Chicago Professor (now Judge) Richard Posner, has reached conclusions that are generally regarded as conservative, politically as well as economically. Thus, Chicago school theorists have argued that courts should not refuse to enforce agreements merely because they are unfair or "unconscionable"; enforcement should be withheld only when an agreement is the product of such defined bargaining misconduct as "fraud" or "duress." Other economic scholars have challenged the Chicago school's noninterventionist conclusions, arguing for statutes that require disclosure of information to consumers, regulate the language of contracts, and impose increased warranty obligations on manufacturers. Interestingly, now that he is on the bench, Judge Posner has tempered his rigorous application of economic principles and has instead argued for a pragmatic approach to judicial decisionmaking. See Richard A. Posner, The Problems of Jurisprudence (1990).

Other scholars, without necessarily rejecting the possibility that useful insights can be gained from economic analysis, argue that the focus on efficiency is much too narrow. Professor Ian Macneil claims that most significant modern contracts arise in settings in which the parties have long-term commercial or personal relationships. Relying on this insight, Macneil and other scholars have argued that contract law should embody principles designed to preserve such relationships. Thus, relational scholars place emphasis on concepts such as good faith and fair dealing. Other scholars have turned to moral philosophy to construct principles of contract law. Professors Melvin Eisenberg, Charles Fried, and Randy Barnett — just to name three who have proceeded independently, and from diverse perspectives — have argued for principles of contract law based primarily on the concepts of fairness, morality, and consent.

Beginning in the 1970s, a loosely connected group of scholars engaged in work in a variety of fields of law that came to be known as "Critical Legal Studies" (CLS). Acknowledging a debt to the Legal Realists of an earlier day, the CLS scholars go even further with the process of deconstruction, to argue that it is impossible to discover or develop any rational system of decision-making within our legal system as it now exists. They maintain that attempts to justify the existing legal process are essentially a form of political ideology, mere rhetoric having as its consequence the preservation of existing distributions of power and wealth in society. Although (as they themselves readily concede) the critical side of the CLS movement is much more fully developed than is its program for social change, there are nevertheless indications that, at least for some of its members, the ultimate goal is a utopian society based on altruistic and communitarian values.

More recently, other scholars have expanded upon the insights of Critical Legal Studies. Arguing from perspectives of race and gender, these theorists have maintained that the law has often served the interests of white males at the expense of women and members of minority groups. This new group of critical scholars contends that both the substance and teaching of law should become more sensitive to the values and goals of these groups. By contrast, Professors Robert Scott, Lisa Bernstein, and Omri Ben-Shahar have recently argued for a return to formalism in contract law. Professor John Murray, on the other hand, finds that most theoretical scholarship creates "products that are useless to courts and practitioners." At the same time he finds "no redeeming virtue" in a revival of formalism because that approach would ignore the context in which disputes and transactional matters arise. Murray argues instead for a return to the practical reasoning used by Corbin and Llewellyn.

D. THE LAWYERING PERSPECTIVE

As teachers, students, and scholars, it is necessary and appropriate for us to consider the theoretical bases that may explain, justify, or even help to create our law of contract. However, we assume that most readers of these materials will have the goal of becoming practicing attorneys. If you are indeed an aspiring lawyer, you should from the very beginning of your law studies be addressing the material not only from the perspective of a student or scholar, but also from the standpoint of what the law as you encounter it may mean to you as a practicing attorney, to your clients, and to the judges before whom you may appear.

We suggested at the outset that law schools traditionally did not aspire to teach very much about "lawyering," other than the modes of legal analysis that are an essential part of the lawyer's skills. In recent years, courses involving "simulation" of lawyering experience or even the actual representation of real clients in various "clinical" settings have done much to remedy this omission. Particularly in the first year of legal education, however, the primary vehicle for learning continues to be the study of appellate court decisions. These, while undeniably forming the major source of our common law rules, also have a serious drawback as training for lawyers: They usually convey little sense of what the attorneys either did or should have done before the litigation to avoid the dispute or to minimize its impact on their clients. Winning a lawsuit may be very satisfying for an attorney and for her client, but it is never a victory when an attorney wins a lawsuit that she could and *should* have enabled her client to avoid. We will try with questions and problems to remind you throughout these materials that although the lawyer's task may sometimes end with a lawsuit, it typically does not begin there. Particularly where commercial contracting is concerned, lawyers are frequently consulted by their clients before disputes arise, at a time when contracts are being negotiated and drafted.

As a practicing attorney, you can be sure that you will be called on to play all of the following roles:

Counselor. Your first task will invariably be to assist your client in identifying the nature and scope of his legal problem(s), ascertaining the client's legal position as objectively as you can. If your client is already a party to a dispute, this may involve predicting how a court is likely to respond to the case if presented; if the client is merely looking toward entering into a commercial transaction, this may mean exploring the legal consequences of the different forms that transaction might take. In any case, it will mean identifying the options available, making sure the client understands the legal and practical consequences of each, helping the client to choose between those alternatives, and then helping him to implement that choice. The product of your analysis may be orally conveyed or it may take the form of an opinion letter or a memorandum of law.

Negotiator. You might be called on to represent your client in discussions looking toward an agreement with some other party. These might be attempts to reach an agreement on some sort of contractual arrangement or they might be discussions aimed at settling a dispute that has already arisen. Negotiation requires first understanding the client's needs and aspirations, then working out with the client the parameters for agreement; only then can you be ready to meet with the opposing party in an attempt to reach an agreement within those parameters. In negotiations, the lawyer's skill of legal analysis will of course be called on: Whether the subject is the settlement of a lawsuit or the creation of a contractual relationship, it will be important for the lawyer to have and to be able to convey an accurate assessment of the legal position of the parties (either as it already exists or as it might be affected by a proposed agreement). But rational legal analysis is only one aspect of negotiation. The skills of a bargainer include the ability to employ a variety of negotiating techniques, many of which are designed not merely to appeal to rational intellect but to capitalize on the other side's emotions, conscience, greed, or fear, or even its incompetence. The skills of a negotiator may to some extent be inborn, but skills training programs in law school address the possibility that they can also be taught.

Drafter. Perhaps your client has already reached an agreement; perhaps your skill as a negotiator has produced an agreement on your client's behalf. In either case, it will ordinarily appear necessary for a variety of legal and practical reasons to reduce that agreement to a writing that the parties can adopt as the final and complete expression of their bargain. Here is perhaps the greatest call on the lawyer's skill with words — the ability to organize a complicated package into a coherent, accessible structure; the ability to write with economy, clarity, and precision; sometimes, the ability to say as little as possible on a point where this is preferable in the circumstances. For some types of agreement a "form book" may supply a useful pattern, but even then the attorney must fully understand the ways in which the form needs to be modified to serve her client's own particular needs.

Advocate. Traditionally in the English system, certain attorneys serve as "barristers" and argue cases in court; others are known as "solicitors" and have an office practice. (Even in the English system, time and practice have blurred these distinctions. For a number of years solicitors have tried cases in the lower courts. In recognition of these changes, Parliament passed the Courts and Legal Services Act of 1990, which ended the barristers' monopoly on rights of audience in the high courts.) Except in the largest of firms, law practice in the United States is usually not so specialized, and the chances are that you will from time to time find yourself in court. In approaching the case, you must of course engage in rigorous and completely objective analysis, in order to know what legal arguments there may be and the relative strengths and weaknesses of each. As an advocate, however, you will be required to present the most persuasive arguments you can on behalf of your client. While bound to represent your client's interests zealously, you of course may not engage in illegal or fraudulent conduct on behalf of a client. Your advocacy may take the form of oral argument or of written briefs and trial memoranda addressed to the court; you will also have to prepare formal written pleadings in the action.

We have stressed the role of the lawyer as counselor, negotiator, and drafter as well as advocate in the hope of making you aware from the outset of a very simple but important truth: Contract law in action is not just a body of rules. It is a complicated process by which attorneys and their clients make, perform (or sometimes breach), and enforce exchange agreements. While contract litigation is an important component of practice for many attorneys, you should never forget that the vast majority of disputes that the rules of contract law *could* solve are *never submitted to a court for decision.* On any given day, the number of individual contracts entered into in even one of the United States must number in the millions. Of that huge total, a tiny fraction—but still a large number, in absolute terms—will eventually give rise to a dispute between the parties. Of these relatively few disputes, the overwhelming majority will be resolved without even coming to the threshold of a court, much less to judgment or a decision on appeal. The number of written opinions on which the common law is based, incredibly large though it may be, is to the commercial life of our country as is a sand castle, not just to the beach on which it sits, but to the globe of which that beach is a part.

This observation should not be taken to mean that case law is therefore irrelevant to commercial practice. Once a dispute has arisen, a lawyer's estimate of how that dispute would be resolved in court will be one of the most important factors she weighs in advising her client on what terms that dispute should be settled. It will not, however, be the only factor. Knowledge of the rules of law is an important, indeed indispensable, tool for the lawyer, but it may be no more important than a number of other ones, such as knowledge of business practices, human understanding, and simple common sense.

SELECTED BIBLIOGRAPHY

Judicial Decisionmaking

Benjamin N. Cardozo, The Nature of the Judicial Process (1921)
Ronald M. Dworkin, Taking Rights Seriously (1977)
Edward H. Levi, An Introduction to Legal Reasoning (1949)
Karl N. Llewellyn, The Common Law Tradition (1960)
Richard A. Posner, The Problems of Jurisprudence (1990)

Uniform State Laws, the Restatements, and the Uniform Commercial Code

Peter A. Alces & David Frisch, On the UCC Revision Process: A Reply to Dean Scott, 37 Wm. & Mary L. Rev. 1217 (1996)

Robert Braucher, The Legislative History of the Uniform Commercial Code, 2 Am. Bus. L.J. 137 (1964)

Nathan M. Crystal, Codification and the Rise of the Restatement Movement, 54 Wash. L. Rev. 239 (1979)

John Honnold, The Life of the Law, 100-180 (1964)

Gregory E. Maggs, Ipse Dixit: The Restatement (Second) of Contracts and the Modern Development of Contract Law, 66 Geo. Wash. L. Rev. 508 (1998)

Alan Schwartz & Robert E. Scott, The Political Economy of Private Legislatures, 143 U. Pa. L. Rev. 595 (1995)

International and Comparative Contract Law

Michael J. Bonell, An International Restatement of Contract Law: The UNIDROIT Principles of International Commercial Contracts (3d ed. 2005)

Conference on Commercial Law Theory and the Convention on the International Sale of Goods (CISG), 25 Int'l Rev. L. & Econ. 311 (2005)

Larry A. DiMatteo et al., The Interpretive Turn in International Sales Law: An Analysis of Fifteen Years of CISG Jurisprudence, 24 Nw. J. Int'l L. & Bus. 299 (2004)

The Enforceability of Promises in European Contract Law (James Gordley ed. 2001)

Formalism and Neoformalism

P.S. Atiyah & Robert S. Summers, Form and Substance in Anglo-American Law (2002)

Omri Ben-Shahar, The Tentative Case Against Flexibility in Commercial Law, 66 U. Chi. L. Rev. 781 (1999)

Lisa Bernstein, Merchant Law in a Merchant Court: Rethinking the Code's Search for Immanent Business Norms, 144 U. Pa. L. Rev. 1765 (1996)

Jay M. Feinman, Un-Making Law: The Conservative Campaign to Roll Back the Common Law (2004)

Grant Gilmore, The Death of Contract (1974)

Duncan Kennedy, Form and Substance in Private Law Adjudication, 89 Harv. L. Rev. 1685 (1976)

Ralph James Mooney, The New Conceptualism in Contract Law, 74 Or. L. Rev. 1131 (1995)

Mark L. Movsesian, Rediscovering Williston, 62 Wash. & Lee L. Rev. 207 (2005)

John E. Murray, Jr., Contract Theories and the Rise of Neoformalism, 71 Fordham L. Rev. 869 (2002)

Robert E. Scott, The Case for Formalism in Relational Contract, 94 Nw. U. L. Rev. 847 (2000)

Legal Realism

George C. Christie, Jurisprudence: Text and Readings On the Philosophy of Law (2d ed. 1995)

American Legal Realism (William W. Fisher III et al. eds. 1993)

Michael Steven Green, Legal Realism as Theory of Law, 46 Wm. & Mary L. Rev. 1915 (2005)

Brian Leiter, Rethinking Legal Realism: Toward a Naturalized Jurisprudence, 76 Tex. L. Rev. 267 (1997)

John Henry Schlegel, American Legal Realism and Empirical Social Science (1995)

William L. Twining, Karl Llewellyn and the Realist Movement (rev. ed. 1985)

Economic Analysis of Law

Readings in the Economics of Contract Law (Victor P. Goldberg ed. 1989)

A. Mitchell Polinsky, An Introduction to Law and Economics (3d ed. 2003)

Eric A. Posner, Economic Analysis of Contract Law After Three Decades: Success or Failure?, 112 Yale L.J. 829 (2003)

Richard A. Posner, Economic Analysis of Law (7th ed. 2007)

Relational Contract Law

Randy E. Barnett, Conflicting Visions: A Critique of Ian Macneil's Relational Theory of Contract, 78 Va. L. Rev. 1175 (1992)

Ian R. Macneil, The New Social Contract (1980)

Relational Contract Theory: Unanswered Questions—A Symposium in Honor of Ian R. Macneil, 94 Nw. U. L. Rev. 735 (2000)

Alan Schwartz & Robert E. Scott, Contract Theory and the Limits of Contract Law, 113 Yale L.J. 541 (2003)

Richard E. Speidel, Article 2 and Relational Sales Contracts, 26 Loy. L.A. L. Rev. 789 (1993)

Symposium, Law, Private Governance and Continuing Relationships, 1985 Wis. L. Rev. 461 (1985)

Other Contract Scholars

Randy E. Barnett, A Consent Theory of Contract, 86 Colum. L. Rev. 269 (1986)

Melvin A. Eisenberg, The Bargain Principle and Its Limits, 95 Harv. L. Rev. 741 (1982)

Charles Fried, Contract as Promise (1981)

Lawrence M. Friedman & Stewart Macaulay, Law and the Behavioral Sciences (2d ed. 1977)

Charles L. Knapp, Opting Out or Copping Out? An Argument for Strict Scrutiny of Individual Contracts, 40 Loy. L.A. L. Rev. 95 (2006)

Peter Linzer, Rough Justice: A Theory of Restitution and Reliance, Contracts and Torts, 2001 Wis. L. Rev. 695

Daniel Markovits, Contract and Collaboration, 113 Yale L.J. 1417 (2004)

W. David Slawson, Binding Promises (1996)

Critical Legal Studies and Other Critical Scholars

Anthony R. Chase, Race, Culture, and Contract: From the Cottonfield to the Courtroom, 28 Conn. L. Rev. 1 (1995)

Critical Race Theory: The Key Writings That Formed the Movement (Kimberle Crenshaw et al. eds. 1995)

Jay M. Feinman, Critical Approaches to Contract Law, 30 UCLA L. Rev. 829 (1983)

Mary Joe Frug, Postmodern Legal Feminism (1992)

Symposium on Critical Legal Studies, 36 Stan. L. Rev. 1 (1984)

Symposium: Critical Race Perspectives for the New Millennium, 31 New Eng. L. Rev. 705 (1997)

Patricia A. Tidwell & Peter Linzer, The Flesh-Colored Band Aid—Contracts, Feminism, Dialogue, and Norms, 28 Hous. L. Rev. 791 (1991)

Mark Tushnet, Critical Legal Studies: A Political History, 100 Yale L.J. 1515 (1991)

Neil G. Williams, Offer, Acceptance, and Improper Considerations: A Common-Law Model for the Prohibition of Racial Discrimination in the Contracting Process, 62 Geo. Wash. L. Rev. 183 (1994)

Contract Theory in General

Perspectives on Contract Law (Randy E. Barnett ed. 3d ed. 2005)

The Theory of Contract Law: New Essays (Peter Benson ed. 2001)

Foundations of Contract Law (Richard Craswell & Alan Schwartz eds. 1994)

Jay M. Feinman, The Significance of Contract Theory, 58 U. Cin. L. Rev. 1283 (1990)

Robert A. Hillman, The Richness of Contract Law (1997)

Duncan Kennedy, From the Will Theory to the Principle of Private Autonomy: Lon Fuller's "Consideration and Form," 100 Colum. L. Rev. 94 (2000)

A Contracts Anthology (Peter Linzer ed. 2d ed. 1995)

Symposium, Proceedings and Papers of the Conference on Contract Law: From Theory to Practice, 1988 Ann. Surv. Am. L. 1

Lawyering Skills

Robert M. Bastress & Joseph D. Harbaugh, Interviewing, Counseling and Negotiating: Skills for Effective Representation (1990)

Gary Bellow & Bea Moulton, The Lawyering Process (1978)

David A. Binder, Paul Bergman & Susan C. Price, Lawyers as Counselors: A Client-Centered Approach (2004)

Scott J. Burnham, Drafting and Analyzing Contracts (3d ed. 2003)

Charles B. Craver, Effective Legal Negotiation and Settlement (5th ed. 2005)

Thomas C. Haggard, Contract Law From a Drafting Perspective: An Introduction to Contract Drafting for Law Students (2003)

Thomas A. Mauet, Trial Techniques (6th ed. 2002)

2 | The Basis of Contractual Obligation: Mutual Assent and Consideration

We begin our study of contract law by examining the traditional or "classical" requirements for formation of a contract. In this and other chapters we will often compare "classical" with "modern" contract law. A few words of explanation about these terms may be helpful. During the latter part of the nineteenth and early twentieth centuries, judges and scholars (particularly Justice Oliver Wendell Holmes Jr., Professor Christopher Columbus Langdell, and Professor Samuel Williston) developed a particular approach to contract law, which was eventually embodied in the first Restatement of Contracts, issued in 1932. We use the terms classical or traditional contract law to refer to the principles and rules that emerged during this period. You will gain a feel for classical contract law as you proceed through these materials, but in reading cases you should be on the lookout for two important aspects of classical law that you can contrast with more modern decisions.

First, classical contract law showed a preference for clear rules (sometimes referred to as "legal formalism") over general standards (such as "reasonableness"). Second, traditional contract law was relatively indifferent to issues of morality or social policy presented by contract cases (other than the policy that contracts should be kept, *pacta sunt servanda*). Scholars have pointed out that these aspects of classical contract law reflected deeper notions of laissez faire economics and limited governmental interference in private transactions.

Over the middle part of the last century, influenced by scholars such as Professors Arthur Corbin and Karl Llewellyn, and reflecting the influence of the Uniform Commercial Code as well as case law, a more "modern" contract law emerged—more attentive to the needs of the commercial marketplace, characterized less by rules than by standards, and frequently more responsive to issues of social justice and economic power than the classical system. Doctrines such as *good faith* and *unconscionability* exemplify this modern approach. Toward the end of the twentieth century, however, renewed emphasis on the workings of a free market economy and the scholarly analyses of the "law and economics" movement produced to some degree a swing back toward a more "conceptual" or "formalist" view of contract law, less concerned with imbalances of power and more concerned with enforcing the agreement-as-made, or at least as-adhered-to.

While the above descriptions of historical trends may be accurate enough to be useful, do not think that the courts in any period necessarily speak with one voice. The tension between the classical (or perhaps "conceptualist") and modern approaches persists, and it can be seen in the varying attitudes of courts toward such formalities as the statute of frauds and the parol evidence rule, as well as the availability of equitable defenses of various kinds. As your study progresses, you may find that you temperamentally align yourself more with one tendency than the other, but try to remain open to the arguments on both sides — the effective attorney may prefer one side of a case to the other, but she will fully understand both the strengths and weaknesses of the arguments for both sides. (So, it should be added, will the effective law student.)

A. MUTUAL ASSENT

The Restatement (Second) in §17 states that formation of a contract requires "a bargain in which there is a manifestation of mutual assent to the exchange and a consideration." Section A of this chapter examines the traditional bargaining process resulting in mutual assent, section B explores the doctrine of consideration, and section C probes a number of important issues that have confronted courts in applying the fundamental concept of mutual assent.

Several points about the Restatement's requirements for formation of a contract are worth noting. First, the Restatement refers to the concept of a bargain, in which the parties manifest mutual assent. Under the traditional model of contract formation, applicable to many commercial transactions, parties engage in the give-and-take of bargaining through a process of offer and acceptance, ultimately either reaching a deal (a "manifestation of mutual assent") or breaking off negotiations. It is important to recognize, however, that a contract can be formed even when the parties do not engage in bargaining. Noncommercial transactions involving family members, friends, or charitable entities may, but will not necessarily, result in contracts even though the parties may not have engaged in a formal negotiation. We will consider a number of these noncommercial transactions in this chapter. Even within the commercial realm, contracts can arise despite the absence of bargaining between the parties. Consider, for example, the many contracts that you have entered into over the Internet, in which you check a box stating that "I agree" to various terms that you have scrolled through, probably without reading and certainly without bargaining. We will see later in this chapter that substantial controversy exists over how the law should treat such "contracts." One of the principal reasons for this controversy is that these contracts typically involve inequality of bargaining power between the parties. The important point to recognize at this stage of your studies is that a bargain resulting in mutual assent is the traditional and probably most important way in which a contract can be formed, but it is not the only way.

Second, when parties are in a bargaining relationship, it is also possible that one party can incur legal obligations to another person even though they have not entered into a contract. The doctrines of *restitution* and *promissory estoppel*, which we will examine in Chapter 3, involve liability between parties even though no contract has been formed or even contemplated. We will consider the policy reasons why contract law has come to recognize these additional bases of obligation.

Third, even if a contract has been formed, that is far from the end of the analysis. As we will see in subsequent chapters, a party who has entered into a contract may be relieved of that obligation if the other party has engaged in some form of bargaining misconduct, such as fraud, duress, or undue influence (to name just three), or if circumstances that existed at the time of the contract have changed sufficiently to justify nonperformance.

1. Intention to be Bound: The Objective Theory of Contract

In applying the concept of mutual assent, some courts state that the formation of a contract requires a "meeting of the minds" between the parties. A subtle but important distinction exists, however, between the ideas of "mutual assent" and "meeting of the minds." Suppose S and B sign a written document in which B agrees to buy a condominium in a new development. B later claims that he did not understand that he was signing a contract and that he did not intend to buy the condo. B might claim that he thought that the document he signed simply "reserved" the condo for him but did not obligate him to buy the property. The case goes to a trial before a jury. Suppose the jury believes that B is telling the truth and that he honestly did not understand that he was obligated to buy the property. If contract law requires a "meeting of the minds" for contract formation, then the jury should find for B. This view of contract formation has been described as "subjective" in that the actual intention of a party, rather than that party's conduct, determines the party's legal obligations. On the other hand, if contract law requires a manifestation of mutual assent, then (absent some fraud or other misconduct by S) the jury should find for S because both S and B manifested their assent by signing the document of sale. This approach has been described as "objective," in that it looks at the conduct of the parties from the perspective of a reasonable person rather than their actual, subjective intentions. Which approach should contract law use? Consider the following case.

Ray v. William G. Eurice & Bros., Inc.
Maryland Court of Appeals
201 Md. 115, 93 A.2d 272 (1952)

HAMMOND, Judge.

In an action in the Circuit Court for Baltimore County by the owners of an unimproved lot against a construction company for a complete breach of a written contract to build a house, the court, sitting without a jury, found for the defendant and the plaintiffs appealed.

Calvin T. Ray and Katherine S. J. Ray, his wife, own a lot on Dance Mill Road in Baltimore County. Late in 1950, they decided to build a home on it, and entered into negotiations with several builders, including William G. Eurice & Bros., Inc., the appellee, which had been recommended by friends. They submitted stock plans and asked for an estimate — not a bid — to see whether the contemplated house was within their financial resources. John M. Eurice, its President, acted for the Eurice Corporation. He indicated at the first meeting that the cost of the house would be about $16,000. Mr. Ray then employed an architect who redrew the plans and wrote a rough draft of specifications. Mr. Ray had copies of each mechanically reproduced, and in January, 1951, arranged a meeting with Mr. Eurice to go over them so that a final bid, as opposed to an estimate, could be arrived at. In the Ray living room, Mr. Ray and Mr. John Eurice went over the redrawn plans dated January 9, 1951, and the specifications prepared by the architect, consisting of seven pages and headed "Memorandum Specifications, Residence for Mr. and Mrs. C. T. Ray, Dance Mill Road, Baltimore County, Maryland, 9 January, 1951," and discussed each item. Mr. Eurice vetoed some items and suggested change in others. For example, foundation walls were specified to be of concrete block. Mr. Eurice wanted to pour concrete walls, as was his custom. Framing lumber was to be fir. Mr. Eurice wanted this to be fir or pine. In some instances, Mr. Eurice, wanting more latitude, asked that the phrase "or equivalent" be added after a specified product or brand make. All the changes agreed on were noted by Mr. Ray in green ink on the January 9th specifications, and Mr. Eurice was given a set of plans and a set of the specifications so that he could make a formal bid in writing. On February 14, the Eurice Corporation submitted unsigned, its typewritten three-page proposed contract to build a house for $16,300 "according to the following specifications." Most of the three pages consisted of specifications which did not agree in many, although often relatively unimportant, respects with those in the January 9th seven-page specifications. Mr. Ray advised Mr. Eurice that he would have his own lawyer draw the contract. This was done. In the contract, as prepared and as finally signed, the builder agrees to construct a house for $16,300 "strictly in accordance with the Plans hereto attached and designated residence for Mr. and Mrs. C. T. Ray, Dance Mill Road, Baltimore County, Maryland, Sheets 1 through 7 dated 9 January 1951 . . . and to supply and use only those materials and building supplies shown on the Specifications hereto attached and designated Memorandum Specifications — Residence for Mr. C. T. Ray, Dance Mill Road, Baltimore County, Maryland, Sheets 1 through 5 dated 14 February 1951 it being understood and agreed that any deviation from the said Plans shall be made only with the prior assent of the Owner. Deviations from the Specifications shall be made only in the event any of the items shown thereon is unavailable at the time its use is required, and then only after reasonable effort and diligence on the part of the Builder to obtain the specific item has failed and the owner has given his prior approval to the use of a substitute item."

The Memorandum Specifications referred to in the contract, consisting of five pages and dated February 14, 1951, had been prepared by Mr. and Mrs. Ray, the night of the day the Eurice Corporation delivered its three-page proposal, and after Mr. Ray had said that his own lawyer would draw the contract. On the 14th of February the January 9 seven pages, as they had emerged from the green ink deletions and additions made at the meeting in January, were retyped and from the stencil so cut at the Ray apartment, Mr. Ray had many copies mechanically reproduced at the Martin Plant where he is an aeronautical engineer. The rewritten specifications were identified as they are designated in the contract, namely as "... Sheets 1 through 5, dated 14 February 1951."

On February 22, at the office of the Eurice Corporation, on the Old Philadelphia Road, the contract was signed. Present, at the time, were Mr. Ray — Mrs. Ray was absent and had signed the contract earlier because she could not get a babysitter — Mr. John Eurice and Mr. Henry Eurice, who is Secretary of the Eurice Corporation. Mr. Ray relates the details of the meeting, as follows:

> I had copies, plans and specifications before me, as well as two copies of the contract. We sat down, Mr. John Eurice and I sat down and went over all of the items in the specifications. I volunteered to show him I had in fact changed the specifications to reflect their building idiosyncrasies, such as wanting to build the house with a poured cellar. We also went over the contract document item by item. Following that, we each signed the contract and Mr. Henry Eurice, being the other party there at the time, witnessed our signature. He was in the room during the entire discussion or review of the contract.

After the contract had been signed, Mr. Ray says he asked that the Eurice brothers help him fill out the F.H.A. form of specifications (required to obtain the mortgage he needed) since he was not familiar with the intricacies of that form. This they did, with Mr. Henry Eurice giving most of the aid. They used the memorandum specifications of February 14 where they corresponded with the F.H.A. form and in other instances, as where the memorandum specifications were not adequate, Mr. Henry Eurice gave the necessary information. After the F.H.A. specifications were completed, the meeting broke up and a copy of the signed contract and copies of the Plans and Specifications were retained by the Eurice Corporation.

Mr. Ray then obtained a loan from the Loyola Savings & Loan Association. To do this it was necessary that he furnish it with his copy of the contract as well as copies of the Plans, the specifications of February 14 and the F.H.A. specifications. Neither the plans nor specifications which were left with the Building Association were signed by the Eurice Corporation, nor, through a misunderstanding, had they been signed by either Mr. or Mrs. Ray. When they applied for the loan, Mr. and Mrs. Ray did sign the reverse side of each page of the drawings and of the contract specifications. Thereafter, in response to a call from the Building Association, Mr. John Eurice went to its office and signed the reverse side of each page of the contract, each page of the specifications of the five-page specifications of February 14, referred to in the contract, and each page of the plans dated January 9, and referred to in the contract, although he says that he did not look at any of these prior to signing them.

Settlement of the mortgage loan was made on April 19 and thereafter, Mr. Ray phoned Mr. John Eurice repeatedly in order to set a starting date for the construction work. He finally came to the Ray home on April 22 and indicated that he would start construction sometime about the middle of May. Other details of the work were discussed and Mr. Ray was given the names of a plumber and a supply company so that he could pick out and buy direct various products which would be incorporated in the house. Mr. Eurice, at that time, brought up the question of a dry well which had not been noted in the specifications, and which was required by the Baltimore County Building Code, and Mr. Ray agreed that he would make allowance for this, as he felt it was an honest mistake.

On May 8, Mr. Ray received urgent messages from the Eurice Corporation that his presence was desired for a conference. As he walked into the office, Mr. Henry Eurice picked up the drawings, specifications and the contract, and threw them across the desk at him, and onto the floor, with the announcement that he had never seen them, and that if he had to build according to those specifications he did not propose to go ahead. Attempts were made at the meeting to iron out the differences which apparently caused Mr. Henry Eurice to state that he would not live up to the contract. A second meeting was held at the Ray apartment several days later, and these efforts were continued by Mr. John Eurice, and that was the last contact that the Ray family had with any officer or agent of the Eurice Corporation. Realization that to build according to contract specifications would cost more than their usual "easy going, hatchet and saw manner" as Judge Gontrum described it, undoubtedly played a part in the refusal of the Eurice brothers to build the Ray house, although they testified that the excess cost would be only about $1,000. More decisive, in all probability, was Mr. Ray's precision and his insistence on absolute accuracy in the smallest details which certainly made the Eurices unhappy, and to them was the shadow cast by harassing and expensive events to come. For example, at the meeting where the specifications were thrown across the desk, Mr. Ray agreed that certain millwork and trim which the Eurices had on hand was the equal of the specified Morgan millwork. Mr. Henry Eurice testified as to this:

> He said that he thought ours were better. I said "if we put that in your house how will we determine it was right or not?" He said he would bring a camera and take a picture of the moldings in our shed and when they were constructed in the house take another picture, and see if it would correspond. I said, "Man we can't build you a house under those conditions. It is not reasonable." It created a heated argument for a while.

After written notice by Mr. Ray's lawyer to the lawyer for Eurice Corporation, that Mr. and Mrs. Ray considered that the contract had been breached and unless recognized within the week they would hold the Eurice Corporation "for any additional amount necessary to construct the house over and above the price called for in the agreement which has been breached by your client" had been ignored, suit was filed.

Mr. John Eurice agrees, in his testimony, that the Memorandum Sheets 1 to 7, dated January 9, had been gone over by him with Mr. and Mrs. Ray, but only as he says, to pick up "pointers." He also agrees that he had been told that the contract was to be drawn by Mr. Ray's lawyer, but says that he agreed only "so long as it is drawn up to our three page contract." He says that no specifications were attached to the contract which was signed, at the time it was signed, and Mr. and Mrs. Ray cannot say definitely that the specifications were physically attached, although both say that they were unquestionably in existence and Mr. Ray is unequivocal and positive in his statement that they were present, stapled together, and discussed at the time of signing the contract. Mr. John Eurice says that the first time he saw the specifications was when his brother Henry "chucked them out," and in response to a question as to where they came from, said: "They were laying on the desk on the opened mail." This, he says, was some two weeks after the signing of the contract. No effort has been made by the appellee to show how the specifications arrived in the office at this time, with the opened mail. No envelope, with what could be a significant postmark, was introduced. No stenographer or clerk was brought into court to say that the specifications had been received in the mail, or to say that they had been delivered by messenger, or by Mr. Ray. Mr. John Eurice does not deny that he signed the plans and specifications, as well as the back of the contract at the office of the Loyola Building and Loan Association, but dismisses this as a practice necessary in all cases where financing is to be obtained, which has no relation to or significance in connection with the actual agreement between builder and owner.

Mr. Henry Eurice says that, although he was present at the time the contract was signed, and signed as a witness, that no specifications were attached to either copy of the signed contract, and that he did not see Specifications 1 to 5 until "right smart later, maybe a month." When he did first see them "they were laying on the desk on the opened mail."

Mr. John Eurice says in his testimony that the contract which was signed February 22 was not the proposal the Eurice Corporation had made. He sets forth that he read the contract of February 22 before he signed it, and he admits that he read paragraph B, whereby the builder agreed to construct the building strictly in accordance with the plans and specifications identified by description and date. He says he thought that the specifications, although they referred to pages 1 through 5, were those in his proposal which covered only three pages. Mr. Henry Eurice says that he read the contract of February 22, and that he read the paragraph with respect to the plans and specifications, but that he, too, thought it referred to the three-page proposal. Both agree that the plans were present at the time of the signing of the contract.

On the basis of the testimony which has been cited at some length, Judge Gontrum found the following:

> The plaintiff, Mr. Ray, is an aeronautical engineer, a highly technical, precise gentleman, who has a truly remarkable memory for figures and dates and a meticulous regard for detail. Apparently, his profession and his training have schooled him to approach all problems in an exceedingly technical and probably very efficient manner. He testified with an exceptional fluency and plausibility. His mastery of language and recollection of dates and figures are phenomenal.
>
> The defendants in the case are what might be termed old fashioned country or community builders. Their work is technical but it doesn't call for the specialized ability that Mr. Ray's work demands. They conduct their business in a more easy going, hatchet and saw manner, and have apparently been successful in a small way in their field of home construction.
>
> The contract in question was entered into, in my judgment, in a hasty and rather careless fashion.

Judge Gontrum then cites the testimony of the Eurice Brothers that they had not seen Specifications 1 through 5 when they signed, and then says:

> . . . There is real doubt in my mind about the matter. Why the defendants signed the agreement without checking up on the specifications, I do not know, but they clearly were under the impression that the specifications referred to in the agreement were the specifications they had submitted some time prior and which they had permitted to be redrafted by the attorney for Mr. Ray. They both stated with absolute emphasis, and I do not question their veracity, that they were under the impression that the specifications in the agreement were the same which they had prepared.

He concludes by saying that he feels that Mr. and Mrs. Ray were under one impression, and that the Messrs. Eurice were under another impression, saying:

> . . . In my opinion there was an honest mistake; that there was no real meeting of the minds and that the plaintiffs and defendants had different sets of specifications in mind when this agreement was signed. The minds of the parties, so different in their approach, to use a mechanical phrase, did not mesh.

It is unnecessary to decide, as we see it, whether there was or was not a mistake on the part of the Eurice Corporation. It does strain credulity to hear that the Messrs. Eurice, builders all their adult lives and, on their own successful builders for fifteen years of some twenty houses a year, would sign a simple contract to build a house, after they had read it, without knowing exactly what obligations they were assuming as to specifications requirements. The contract clearly referred to the specifications by designation, by number of pages and by date. It permits, in terms, no deviations from the specified makes or brands to be incorporated in the house, without the express permission of the owner. This would have been unimportant if the Eurice three-page specifications had been intended, since generality and not particularity was the emphasis there. Again, the contract could scarcely have intended to incorporate by reference the specifications in the three-page proposal because they were not set forth in a separate writing, but were an integral part of a proposed contract, which itself was undated, and which was of *three* pages, while the specifications designated in the contract were dated and were stated to be in the contract, *five* pages. Further, it is undisputed that the five pages of February 14th were the seven pages of January 9, corrected to reflect the deletions and changes made and agreed to by Mr. Ray and Mr. John Eurice. The crowning challenge to credulity in finding mistake is the fact that admittedly the contract, the plans and the specifications were all signed at one sitting by the President of the Eurice Corporation at the Loyola Building Association, after they had been signed by Mr. and Mrs. Ray.

If we assume the view as to mistake held by Judge Gontrum, in effect the mistake in the written agreement which prevented its execution by the Eurice Corporation from making it a contract was an unilateral one. It consisted, in the opinion of the Court, in the Eurice Corporation thinking it was assenting to its own specifications, while in form it was assenting to the Ray specifications. If there was such a mistake, the legal result the Court found to follow, we think does not follow.

The law is clear, absent fraud, duress or mutual mistake, that one having the capacity to understand a written document who reads and signs it, or, without reading it or having it read to him, signs it, is bound by his signature in law, at least. . . .

Neither fraud nor duress are in the case. If there was mistake it was unilateral. The Rays intended their specifications to be a part of the contract, and the contract so stated, so the misconception, if it existed, was in the minds of the Messrs. Eurice.

Williston, Contracts (Rev. Ed.), Sec. 1577, says as to unilateral mistake:

> But if a man acts negligently, and in such a way as to justify others in supposing that the terms of the writing are assented to by him and the writing is accepted on that supposition, he will be bound both at law and in equity. Accordingly, even if an illiterate executes a deed under a mistake as to its contents, he is bound if he did not require it to be read to him or its object explained.

In Maryland there may be exceptions in proceedings for specific performance, but otherwise the rule is in accord. . . . See also the Restatement, Contracts, Section 70, where it is said:

> One who makes a written offer which is accepted, or who manifests acceptance of the terms of a writing which he should reasonably understand to be an offer or proposed contract, is bound by the contract, though ignorant of the terms of the writing or of its proper interpretation.

It does not lie in the mouth of the appellee, then, to say that it intended to be bound to build only according to its specifications. First, its claimed intent is immaterial, where it has agreed in writing to a clearly expressed and unambiguous intent to the contrary. Next, it may not vary that clearly expressed written intent by parol. And, finally, it may not put its own interpretation on the meaning of the written agreement it has executed. The Restatement, Contracts, Section 20, states the first proposition:

> A manifestation of mutual assent by the parties to an informal contract is essential to its formation and the acts by which such assent is manifested, must be done with the intent to do those acts, but neither mental assent to the promises in the contract nor real or apparent intent that the promises shall be legally binding, is essential.

Williston (work cited), Sec. 21, states the rule as follows: "The only intent of the parties to a contract which is essential, is an intent to say the words and do the acts which constitute their manifestation of assent." Judge Learned Hand expressed it in this wise: "A contract has, strictly speaking, nothing to do with the personal, or individual, intent of the parties. A contract is an obligation attached by the mere force of law to certain acts of the parties, usually words, which ordinarily accompany and represent a known intent. If, however, it were proved by twenty bishops that either party, when he used the words, intended something else than the usual meaning which the law imposes upon them, he would still be held, unless there were some mutual mistake, or something else of the sort." Hotchkiss v. National City Bank, D.C., 200 F. 287, 293.

. . . The test in such case is objective and not subjective. Restatement, Contracts, Sec. 230. . . . Williston (work cited), Sec. 94, page 294, says: "It follows that the test of a true interpretation of an offer or acceptance is not what the party making it thought it meant or intended it to mean, but what a reasonable person in the position of the parties would have thought it meant.". . .

We conclude that the appellee wrongfully breached its contract to build the plaintiffs a house for $16,300. The measure of damage in such a case presents no difficulty. Keystone Engineering Corp. v. Sutter, Md., 78 A.2d 191, 195. Here Judge Marbury said for the Court: "When a contractor on a building contract fails to perform, one of the remedies of the owner is to complete the contract, and charge the cost against the wrongdoer. Williston on Contracts, Rev. Ed. Vol. 5, §1363, p.3825, Restatement Contracts, ch. 12, §346, Subsec. (1)(a)(i), p.573 and Comment 1, p.576." See also, Carrig v. Gilbert-Varker Corp., 314 Mass. 351, 50 N.E.2d 59, 62, 147 A.L.R. 927. There the court said: "The owner was entitled to be put in the same position that he would have been in if the contractor had performed its contract. . . . We think the proper measure of damages was the cost in excess of the contract price that would be incurred by the owner in having the houses built. . . ." That figure is ascertainable with sufficient definiteness in the instant case. . . .

Judgment reversed with costs and judgment entered for appellants against appellee in the sum of $5,993.40.

Notes and Questions

1. *Credibility of the parties.* Does it appear to you that Judge Hammond, the author of the Maryland Court of Appeals' opinion in *Ray,* believed the Eurice brothers' testimony? Do you? Under the view of the case taken by the court, is the question of their veracity material to the outcome of the case? Should it be?

2. *Nature of the parties.* Although classical contract law typically assumes the interaction of hypothetical individuals (see the ubiquitous *A, B,* and sometimes *C* of the illustrations to both Restatements), in modern life it is of course more typical for at least one of the contracting parties to be a business enterprise, conducting its affairs through the medium of a corporation. This was true in the *Ray* case, where the defendant was a corporation, although it seems to have been essentially the creature of the two Eurice brothers, John and Henry. We will see repeatedly in these materials the problems that can arise when more than one invidual acts on behalf of a party to contractual negotiations. (Problems can also develop where there are two allied individuals, although in the Rays' case, Mrs. Ray appears to have played a less active role than her husband, at least in the final meetings.) Do you think John and Henry Eurice were equally involved in and aware of the negotiations with Calvin and Katherine Ray? If not, what effect might that fact have had on the progress of those negotiations?

3. *The objective theory of contractual intent.* At one point the law may have looked for a true, or "subjective" intention on the part of the promisor. (See, however, Professor Joseph Perillo's historical study, The Origins of the Objective Theory of Contract Formation and Interpretation, 69 Fordham L. Rev. 427 (2000), suggesting that such was not necessarily the case even in earlier periods of the common law.) In any event, at least since Oliver Wendell Holmes's lectures and writings in the 1880s began to have their effect, both the rhetoric and the actions of courts and writers have stressed an "objective theory" of contract obligation, by which one is ordinarily bound or not bound, not by her "secret intent" to that effect, but by the reasonable interpretation of her words and actions. Indeed, the objective approach to contract formation and interpretation was seen as one of the central tenets of classical contract law.

In his famous 1881 set of lectures, Holmes stated, "The law has nothing to do with the actual state of the parties' minds. In contract, as elsewhere, it must go by externals, and judge parties by their conduct." Oliver Wendell Holmes, The Common Law 242 (Mark DeWolfe Howe ed. 1963). Later Holmes offered a pragmatic justification for the objective approach:

> In the case of contracts, . . . it is obvious that they express the wishes not of one person but of two, and those two adversaries. If it turns out that one meant one thing and the other another, speaking generally, the only choice possible . . . is either to hold both parties to the judge's interpretation of the words in the sense which I have explained, or to allow the contract to be avoided because there has been no meeting of minds. The latter course not only would greatly enhance the difficulty of enforcing contracts against losing parties, but would run against a plain principle of justice. For each party to a contract has notice that the other will understand his words according to the usage of the normal speaker of English under the circumstances, and therefore cannot complain if his words are taken in that sense.

Oliver Wendell Holmes, The Theory of Legal Interpretation, 12 Harv. L. Rev. 417, 419 (1899). Judge Hand's "twenty bishops" observation has become the classic statement of the strict objectivist position, which as the court indicates was espoused also by Williston. The Restatement (Second) rejects the subjective approach in §21. As we shall see, this does not mean that the promisor's intention to be bound (real or apparent) may not be significant in some situations; for the most part, however, the law looks merely for a sufficient expression of commitment to perform.

What social policies are served by the objective theory of contracts, as advocated by Holmes, Williston, and Hand? Are those policies reflected in the *Ray* decision? Does it appear to you that any important social goals would be served by using a subjective test, enforcing only those contracts that appear to reflect a true "meeting of the minds?"

4. *Disparity in bargaining power.* One of the central features of classical contract law was that it ignored any imbalances in bargaining power — in economic resources, knowledge, and a host of other factors — that may exist between the parties. In *Ray*, the Eurice brothers appear to have been knowledgeable in the construction business and the Rays were not (although Calvin Ray seems to have made up in compulsive attention to detail what he might have lacked in expertise), so it is perhaps not surprising if the court

holds the Eurices to a high standard of self-protection in the bargaining process. But the principle applied in *Ray* is not limited in its application to knowledgeable or powerful contractors. In Skrbina v. Fleming Cos., 53 Cal. Rptr. 2d 481, 485 (Ct. App. 1996), plaintiff employee claimed wrongful termination on a variety of grounds, including violation of both state and federal antidiscrimination statutes; the defendant employer countered by asserting a release signed by plaintiff, which by its terms barred "any claims . . . regarding my employment, benefits and separation from" defendant, "including any and all claims under state or federal employment laws and regulations." Plaintiff, who had been employed as a journeyman mechanic, testified that he had understood that his signing was merely a necessary prerequisite to his receiving severance benefits. Affirming the lower court's grant of summary judgment for defendant, the appellate court observed:

> As to whether he signed the release knowingly and voluntarily, plaintiff asserts first that he never intended to abandon his discrimination and harassment claims and that neither the company nor the union told him that signing the release might affect those claims; he was told only that he must sign in order to collect his severance benefits. Absent fraud, deception, misrepresentation, duress, or undue influence, however, these assertions do not raise a triable issue as to the knowing and voluntary character of his act. By his own admission, he read the release, then signed it "willingly" to obtain the benefits provided in return for his signature. He has offered no evidence that defendants told him the release did not encompass employment discrimination claims or that he asked anyone's advice as to whether it did. If he signed the release on the mere unspoken belief that the release did not encompass such claims, despite express language in the release to the contrary, he may not now rely on his unspoken intention not to waive these claims in order to escape the effect of the release.

Id. at 489.

5. *Presence of a promise.* The Restatement defines a promise as "a manifestation of intention to act or refrain from acting in a specified way, so made as to justify a promisee in understanding that a commitment has been made." Restatement (Second) §2. The comments point out that mere expressions of present intention (as opposed to a manifestation of actual intention), predictions, or opinions do not constitute promises. Are these distinctions clear in theory? In practice? They can be seen in the case law; see, e.g., Peters v. Bower, 63 So. 2d 629 (Fla. 1953) (developer's sworn declaration that it intended to grade and pave all streets held to be merely a statement of intention, and not a promise); Basch v. George Washington University, 370 A.2d 1364 (D.C. Ct. App. 1977) (university's statement in bulletin that "every effort will be made to keep tuition increases within . . . limits" of previous increases not a promise, merely an "expectancy of a continued course of conduct").

6. *Is the promisor serious?* Occasionally, the maker of a promise will claim that it was not made with serious intent — it was only a joke, and the other party either knew that, or at least reasonably should have. In Lucy v. Zehmer, 84 S.E.2d 516 (Va. 1954), a land-purchase contract was enforced by the buyer over the seller's contention that he had only been joking and had believed that the buyer was, too. The court in that case found that, despite the setting (a conversation over drinks in a bar), the past dealings between the parties

made it reasonable for the buyer to believe that the seller was serious, and the seller should reasonably have known that. See also Keith A. Rowley, You Asked for It, You Got It . . . Toy Yoda: Practical Jokes, Prizes, and Contract Law, 3 Nev. L.J. 526 (2003).

In Leonard v. Pepsico, Inc., 88 F. Supp. 2d 116 (S.D.N.Y. 1999), *aff'd*, 210 F.3d 88 (2d Cir. 2000), the defendant conducted an advertising campaign based on the redeemability of "Pepsi points" found on specially marked packages of its products for various items of merchandise (T-shirts, jackets, cameras, etc.) shown in a "Pepsi Stuff" catalog. Plaintiff Leonard asserted the right to buy a Harrier jet plane for 15 Pepsi points and $700,000. The plane was not listed in the catalog, but was shown in the defendant's TV commercial as being available for 7 million Pepsi points. The Pepsi points, as described in defendant's catalog, were also available for purchase at ten cents apiece; apparently, plaintiff had actually raised $700,000 "through acquaintances" which he asserted to be the equivalent of 7 million points, entitling him to purchase the plane. (He included the 15 points because the plaintiff's catalog indicated that each offer had to be accompanied by a minimum of 15 actual points; the rest could be the cash equivalent.) In the court's opinion the plane was described as being worth some $23 million, a fact of which the plaintiff was apparently aware when he set out to raise the money. The United States District Court held for the defendant, finding that although other items identified in the commercial actually were available for given amounts of Pepsi points (the T-shirt, the camera, etc.), no reasonable viewer could have understood that the jet plane shown in the ad was seriously offered as a premium for purchase of the defendant's soft drinks. In an opinion which is itself obviously intended to be funny, the court gives a long description of the commercial in terms designed to make it clear that no one could have taken it seriously. The court does not, however, mention that there were three versions of the "Harrier jet" commercial shown on television. The first was the one on which the plaintiff based his asserted "acceptance"; the second increased the number of Pepsi points for the plane from 7 million to 700 million (the equivalent of $70 million, much more than the value of the plane); the third added an explicit disclaimer of contractual intent. Are these added facts relevant to the issue of whether the plaintiff could reasonably have believed the original offer to be seriously intended?

2. Offer and Acceptance in Bilateral Contracts

In the first chapter of these materials, we suggested that the notion of "contract" typically involves an element of futurity: commitment to some course of action to be undertaken in the future. Although important types of transactions clearly are exceptions, it also seems likely that most contracts of commercial importance will involve commitments on *both* sides: an exchange of promises. Such agreements have traditionally been referred to in the contract lexicon as "bilateral contracts." Since they involve an exchange of reciprocal commitments, bilateral contracts were seen by the classical theorists as typically being the product of a negotiating process usually known as "offer and acceptance."

This process was envisioned as ordinarily involving something like the following: First, the parties engage in a period of preliminary negotiation, exchanging communications of a more or less detailed nature about the type of exchange of performances to which each would be willing to agree. Next, one party (the "offeror") makes an "offer" — a direct, complete proposal that a contract be entered into, providing for an exchange of defined performances. This has the effect of creating in the party to which that offer is addressed a "power of acceptance." If that other party (the "offeree") manifests her "acceptance" of the offer in a legally effective way, then at that moment a contract comes into being. If the initial offer is not acceptable, however, the offeree may respond by making a "counter-offer" of her own, which may in turn be accepted by the original offeror (thus giving rise to a contract different from the one he originally proposed). Of course, a contract may never come into being at all; the offeree may simply reject the offer without making one of her own in return. Or, the offeree may delay too long in accepting, so that the power of acceptance created by the offer has been terminated either by a time limit (explicit or implicit) contained in the offer itself or by the offeror's withdrawal ("revocation") of his offer.

Such is the process of agreement-making on which the rules of classical contract law are premised. As succeeding chapters will suggest, one might well have some reservations about the extent to which this model of the bargaining process conforms to the way people actually behave; the number of types of exchange-agreements that fall within our definition of contract is staggeringly large, and in many instances the process of contract formation is radically different from the one described above. Postponing such questions for the time being, however, let us proceed to consider some characteristic applications of the rules of classical contract law to disputes between persons who have engaged in the process of attempting to reach mutual agreement to a bargained-for exchange of promises.

Lonergan v. Scolnick
California District Court of Appeal
129 Cal. App. 2d 179, 276 P.2d 8 (1954)

BARNARD, Presiding Justice.

This is an action for specific performance or for damages in the event specific performance was impossible.

The complaint alleged that on April 15, 1952, the parties entered into a contract whereby the defendant agreed to sell, and plaintiff agreed to buy a 40-acre tract of land for $2,500; that this was a fair, just and reasonable value of the property; that on April 28, 1952, the defendant repudiated the contract and refused to deliver a deed; that on April 28, 1952, the property was worth $6,081; and that plaintiff has been damaged in the amount of $3,581. The answer denied that any contract had been entered into, or that anything was due to the plaintiff.

By stipulation, the issue of whether or not a contract was entered into between the parties was first tried, reserving the other issues for a further trial if that became necessary. The issue as to the existence of a contract was submitted upon an agreed statement, including certain letters between the parties, without the introduction of other evidence.

The stipulated facts are as follows: During March, 1952, the defendant placed an ad in a Los Angeles paper reading, so far as material here, "Joshua Tree vic. 40 acres, . . . need cash, will sacrifice." In response to an inquiry resulting from this ad the defendant, who lived in New York, wrote a letter to the plaintiff dated March 26, briefly describing the property, giving directions as to how to get there, stating that his rock-bottom price was $2,500 cash, and further stating that "This is a form letter." On April 7, the plaintiff wrote a letter to the defendant saying that he was not sure he had found the property, asking for its legal description, asking whether the land was all level or whether it included certain jutting rock hills, and suggesting a certain bank as escrow agent "should I desire to purchase the land." On April 8, the defendant wrote to the plaintiff saying "From your description you have found the property"; that this bank "is O.K. for escrow agent"; that the land was fairly level; giving the legal description; and then saying, "If you are really interested, you will have to decide fast, as I expect to have a buyer in the next week or so." On April 12, the defendant sold the property to a third party for $2,500. The plaintiff received defendant's letter of April 8 on April 14. On April 15 he wrote to the defendant thanking him for his letter "confirming that I was on the right land," stating that he would immediately proceed to have the escrow opened and would deposit $2,500 therein "in conformity with your offer," and asking the defendant to forward a deed with his instructions to the escrow agent. On April 17, 1952, the plaintiff started an escrow and placed in the hands of the escrow agent $100, agreeing to furnish an additional $2,400 at an unspecified time, with the provision that if the escrow was not closed by May 15, 1952, it should be completed as soon thereafter as possible unless a written demand for a return of the money or instruments was made by either party after that date. It was further stipulated that the plaintiff was ready and willing at all times to deposit the $2,400.

The matter was submitted on June 11, 1953. On July 10, 1953, the judge filed a memorandum opinion stating that it was his opinion that the letter of April 8, 1952, when considered with the previous correspondence, constituted an offer of sale which offer was, however, qualified and conditioned upon prompt acceptance by the plaintiff; that in spite of the condition thus imposed, the plaintiff delayed more than a week before notifying the defendant of his acceptance; and that since the plaintiff was aware of the necessity of promptly communicating his acceptance to the defendant his delay was not the prompt action required by the terms of the offer. Findings of fact were filed on October 2, 1953, finding that each and all of the statements in the agreed statement are true, and that all allegations to the contrary in the complaint are untrue. As conclusions of law, it was found that the plaintiff and defendant did not enter into a contract as alleged in the complaint or otherwise, and that the defendant is entitled to judgment against the plaintiff. Judgment was entered accordingly, from which the plaintiff has appealed.

The appellant contends that the judgment is contrary to the evidence and to the law since the facts, as found, do not support the conclusions of law upon which the judgment is based. It is argued that there is no conflict in the evidence, and this court is not bound by the trial court's construction of the written instruments involved; that the evidence conclusively shows that an offer was made to the plaintiff by the defendant, which offer was accepted by the mailing of plaintiff's letter of April 15; that upon receipt of defendant's letter of April 8 the plaintiff had a reasonable time within which to accept the offer that had been made; that by his letter of April 15 and his starting of an escrow the plaintiff accepted said offer; and that the agreed statement of facts establishes that a valid contract was entered into between the parties. In his briefs the appellant assumes that an offer was made by the defendant, and confined his argument to contending that the evidence shows that he accepted that offer within a reasonable time.

There can be no contract unless the minds of the parties have met and mutually agreed upon some specific thing. This is usually evidenced by one party making an offer which is accepted by the other party. Section 25 of the Restatement of the Law on Contracts reads:

> If from a promise, or manifestation of intention, or from the circumstances existing at the time, the person to whom the promise or manifestation is addressed knows or has reason to know that the person making it does not intend it as an expression of his fixed purpose until he has given a further expression of assent, he has not made an offer.

The language used in Niles v. Hancock, 140 Cal. 157, 73 P. 840, 842, "It is also clear from the correspondence that it was the intention of the defendant that the negotiations between him and the plaintiff were to be purely preliminary," is applicable here. The correspondence here indicates an intention on the part of the defendant to find out whether the plaintiff was interested, rather than an intention to make a definite offer to the plaintiff. The language used by the defendant in his letters of March 26 and April 8 rather clearly discloses that they were not intended as an expression of fixed purpose to make a definite offer, and was sufficient to advise the plaintiff that some further expression of assent on the part of the defendant was necessary.

The advertisement in the paper was a mere request for an offer. The letter of March 26 contains no definite offer, and clearly states that it is a form letter. It merely gives further particulars, in clarification of the advertisement, and tells the plaintiff how to locate the property if he was interested in looking into the matter. The letter of April 8 added nothing in the way of a definite offer. It merely answered some questions asked by the plaintiff, and stated that if the plaintiff was really interested he would have to act fast. The statement that he expected to have a buyer in the next week or so indicated that the defendant intended to sell to the first-comer, and was reserving the right to do so. From this statement, alone, the plaintiff knew or should have known that he was not being given time in which to accept an offer that was being made, but that some further assent on the part of the defendant was required. Under the language used the plaintiff was not being given a right to act within a reasonable time after receiving the letter; he was plainly told that the defendant intended to sell to another, if possible, and warned that he would have to act fast if he was interested in buying the land. . . .

The judgment is affirmed.

GRIFFIN and MUSSELL, JJ., concur.

Notes and Questions

1. *Was there an offer?* To the appellate court that decided *Lonergan*, the principal issue in that case was whether an offer had been made. Many contract cases have turned on the question whether a given communication did amount in legal contemplation to an offer, or whether it was merely a "preliminary negotiation" or an "invitation for an offer." The words used by the parties will be relevant, but not necessarily decisive; even a communication that uses the word *offer* may not be held an offer in the legal sense. E.g., Moulton v. Kershaw, 18 N.W. 172 (Wis. 1884) ("we are authorized to offer Michigan fine salt, in full car-load lots of 80 to 95 bbls. . . . at 85c. per bbl. . . ." held to be only an invitation for offers); as to factors that may influence a court one way or the other on this issue, see generally E. Allan Farnsworth, Contracts §3.10 (4th ed. 2004). The court in *Lonergan* quotes §25 of the first Restatement, describing the offer as an expression of the offeror's "fixed purpose," requiring no "further expression of assent" on her part; the Restatement (Second) §26 is essentially similar. See also Restatement (Second) §24. Applying these Restatement rules, what factors are relevant to resolution of this issue? Would you agree that the defendant's letter of April 8 did not rise to the level of an offer?

2. *Time of acceptance: The "mailbox rule."* From the parties' point of view, it may make no difference at all whether the case is decided on one ground or another: You either win or you lose. (This is not always the case, of course; sometimes *how much* the victorious plaintiff wins will depend on the legal basis for that victory, as we shall see later in the chapters dealing with remedies.) It may matter to the judges and attorneys in future cases, however. In *Lonergan*, the trial court held that plaintiff could not recover, not because defendant never made an offer, but because plaintiff did not make a timely acceptance. Does the appellate court's basis for decision appear to you a better one? If the defendant's letter of April 8 had amounted to an offer, then it would appear necessary to decide how long the plaintiff's power of acceptance would last, and whether he effectively accepted before it terminated. The plaintiff responded by mailing a letter of attempted acceptance on April 15; if on that date an offer was open for acceptance, could plaintiff's act of mailing that letter have completed their contract?

Anglo-American common law has traditionally held that although both an offer and a revocation (by the offeror) must be *communicated* to be effective, an acceptance will in some circumstances be treated as effective as soon as dispatched (mailed, telegraphed, etc.) by the offeree. E.g., Morton's of Chicago/Great Neck LLC v. Crab House, Inc., 746 N.Y.S.2d 317 (App. Div. 2002) (oral acceptance of written lease renewal agreement effective; even if not, acceptor mailed written acceptance before offeror faxed its notice of revocation); compare Gibbs v. American Sav. & Loan Assn., 266 Cal. Rptr. 517 (Ct. App. 1990) (offer not accepted merely by plaintiff giving it to mail clerk in her office; acceptance would occur only when deposited in U.S. mail, by which time revocation had been received). See generally Restatement (Second) §§63 (basic rule, exception for option contracts), 65 (medium of acceptance must be reasonable in circumstances), 66 (only applies where acceptance properly stamped, addressed, etc.), 68 (when revocation, rejection or acceptance are deemed to be communicated).

This rule — commonly known as the "deposited acceptance," or "mailbox" rule — was originally justified in terms of the offeror's designation of the post as an "agent" for communication of acceptance; later cases discarded this rationale as essentially fictional, and focused instead on the practical need of the offeree to have a firm basis for action in reliance on the effectiveness of her acceptance once it had been dispatched. The rule is discussed, and its various applications are considered, in Ian R. Macneil, Time of Acceptance: Too Many Problems for a Single Rule, 112 U. Pa. L. Rev. 947 (1964). As its nickname suggests, the mailbox rule is particularly likely to be applied where the offeree is replying by mail to an offer made through the mail (as of course was the case in *Lonergan*), but it may also apply where the offer was made by other means, so long as a reply by post is reasonable in the circumstances. E.g., Cantu v. Central Education Agency, 884 S.W.2d 565 (1994) (teacher's attempt to withdraw letter of resignation, hand-delivered earlier to school district, was too late; school district had already mailed letter accepting resignation, and its reply by post was reasonable in circumstances). The mailbox rule will not apply, however, if the offeror has stated (expressly or by implication) that he must *receive* the acceptance for it to be effective — an idea often expressed in the catchphrase, "The offeror is master of the offer."

3. *The deposited acceptance rule under the CISG.* We mentioned in Chapter 1 that the United States is party to an important treaty dealing with international sales contracts, the Convention on Contracts for the International Sale of Goods (CISG). Because international transactions are of growing importance for lawyers, throughout these materials we will compare the provisions of the CISG to US contract law. In Article 16(1), the CISG generally adopts the mailbox rule, by providing that an otherwise revocable offer cannot be revoked once an acceptance has been dispatched. CISG Article 18(2) modifies the common law mailbox rule, however, by placing the risk of non-arrival of the acceptance on the offeree rather than the offeror. Thus, to be effective in ultimately concluding the bargain, the acceptance must actually reach the offeror in a timely fashion. See William S. Dodge, Teaching the CISG in Contracts, 50 J. Leg. Ed. 72, 81 (2000) ("CISG's rule . . . places the risk of a lost communication on the party who is in the best position to prevent that loss by choosing a more reliable means of communication").

Izadi v. Machado (Gus) Ford, Inc.
Florida District Court of Appeal
550 So.2d 1135 (1989)

Before SCHWARTZ, C.J., and HUBBART and JORGENSON, JJ.
SCHWARTZ, Chief Judge.

This is an appeal from the dismissal with prejudice of a three count complaint for damages arising out of the following advertisement placed by the appellee in the February 21, 1988 edition of the Miami Herald: [see figure on p. 39]

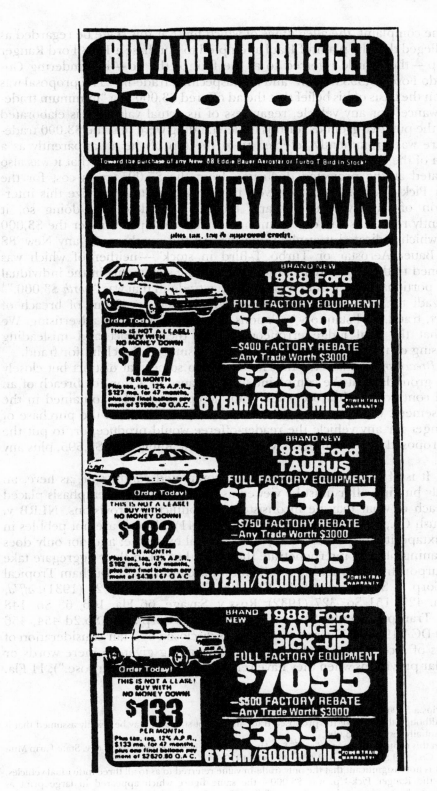

The complaint, the allegations of which must at this stage be regarded as true, alleged that the plaintiff Izadi attempted to purchase a 1988 Ford Ranger Pick-Up — the vehicle referred to at the foot of the ad — by tendering Gus Machado Ford $3,595 in cash[1] and an unspecified trade-in.[2] The proposal was made on the basis of his belief that the ad offered $3,000 as a "minimum trade-in allowance" for any vehicle, regardless of its actual value. As is elaborated below, the putative grounds for this understanding were that the $3,000 trade-in figure was prominently referred to at the top of the ad apparently as a portion of the consideration needed to "buy a[3] new Ford" and that it was also designated as the projected deduction from the $7,095 gross cost for the Ranger Pick-Up. Machado, however, in fact refused to recognize this interpretation of its advertisement and turned Izadi down. In doing so, it apparently relied instead on the infinitesimally small print under the $3,000 figure which indicated it applied only toward the purchase of "any New '88 Eddie Bauer Aerostar or Turbo T-Bird in stock" — neither of which was mentioned in the remainder of the ad — and the statements in the individual vehicle portions that the offer was based on a trade-in that was "*worth* $3,000."[4] [e.s.] Izadi then brought the present action based on claims of breach of contract, fraud, and statutory violations involving misleading advertising. We hold that the trial judge erroneously held the contract and misleading advertising counts insufficient, but correctly dismissed the claim for fraud.

1. *Breach of Contract.* We first hold, on two somewhat distinct but closely related grounds, that the complaint states a cause of action for breach of an alleged contract which arose when Izadi accepted an offer contained in the advertisement, which was essentially to allow $3,000 toward the purchase of the Ranger for any vehicle the reader-offeree would produce, or, to put the same proposed deal in different words, to sell the Ranger for $3,595, plus any vehicle.

(a) It is of course well settled that a completed contract or, as here, an allegedly binding offer must be viewed as a whole, with due emphasis placed upon each of what may be inconsistent or conflicting provisions. NLRB v. Federbush Co., 121 F.2d 954, 957 (2d Cir. 1941) ("Words are not pebbles in alien juxtaposition; they have only a communal existence; and not only does the meaning of each interpenetrate the other, but all in their aggregate take their purport from the setting in which they are used. . . ."); Durham Tropical Land Corp. v. Sun Garden Sales Co., 106 Fla. 429, 138 So. 21 (1931), *aff'd*, 106 Fla. 429, 151 So. 327 (1932); Ross v. Savage, 66 Fla. 106, 63 So. 148 (1913); Transport Rental Systems, Inc. v. Hertz Corp., 129 So.2d 454, 456 (Fla. 3d DCA 1961) ("The real intention, as disclosed by a fair consideration of all parts of a contract, should control the meaning given to mere words or particular provisions when they have reference to the main purpose."); 11 Fla.

---

1. Plus a $500 factory rebate allowance.

2. Although the value of the proposed trade-in was not stated, it may be readily assumed that it was substantially less than $3,000.

3. In this context, "a" means "any." See United States Fidelity & Guaranty Co. v. State Farm Mut. Auto. Ins. Co., 369 So.2d 410, 412 (Fla. 3d DCA 1979).

4. It is not insignificant that the only trade-in value referred to as to all three individual vehicles, including the Ranger Pick-Up, was $3,000 — the same figure which appeared in large print as representing a "minimum trade-in allowance" for "a new Ford."

Jur. 2d Contracts §121 (1979). In this case, that process might well involve disregarding both the superfine print and apparent qualification as to the value of the trade-in, as contradictory to the far more prominent thrust of the advertisement to the effect that $3,000 will be allowed for any trade-in on any Ford. Transport Rental Systems, Inc. v. Hertz Corp., 129 So.2d at 456 ("If a contract contains clauses which are apparently repugnant to each other, they must be given such an interpretation as will reconcile them."); 11 Fla. Jur. 2d Contracts §118; see supra Notes 1-3, and accompanying text. We therefore believe that the complaint appropriately alleges that, objectively considered, the advertisement indeed contained just the unqualified $3,000 offer which was accepted by the plaintiff.[6] On the face of the pleadings, the case thus is like many previous ones in which it has been held, contrary to what is perhaps the usual rule, see 1 Williston on Contracts §27 (W. Jaeger 3d ed. 1957); 1 Corbin on Contracts §25 (1963), that an enforceable contract arises from an offer contained in an advertisement. R.E. Crummer & Co. v. Nuveen, 147 F.2d 3 (7th Cir. 1945); Lefkowitz v. Great Minneapolis Surplus Store, 251 Minn. 188, 86 N.W.2d 689 (1957); . . . see Steinberg v. Chicago Medical School, 69 Ill.2d 320, 13 Ill.Dec. 699, 371 N.E.2d 634 (1977); 1 Williston on Contracts §27, at 65 (1957). See generally Annot., Advertisement Addressed to Public Relating to Sale or Purchase of Goods at the Specified Price As an Offer the Acceptance of Which Will Consummate a Contract, 43 A.L.R. 3d 1102 (1972).

Of course, if an offer were indeed conveyed by an objective reading of the ad, it does not matter that the car dealer may subjectively have not intended for its chosen language to constitute a binding offer. As Williston states:

> [T]he test of the true interpretation of an offer or acceptance is not what the party making it thought it meant or intended it to mean, but what a reasonable person in the position of the parties would have thought it meant.

1 Williston on Contracts §94, at 339-340; see also *Crummer*, 147 F.2d at 3; *Lefkowitz*, 251 Minn. at 191, 86 N.W.2d at 691. . . .[7] That rule seems directly to apply to this situation.

(b) As a somewhat different, and perhaps more significant basis for upholding the breach of contract claim, we point to the surely permissible conclusion from the carefully chosen language and arrangement of the

---

6. It goes almost without saying that the plaintiff's ability eventually to recover on the theories suggested in this opinion depends on the showing that he was, in fact, led or misled into a genuine — even if unjustified — belief that such an offer had indeed been made. If he were merely attempting to take a knowing advantage of imprecise language in the advertisement and did not, in fact, rely upon it, he may not recover. See Vance v. Indian Hammock Hunt & Riding Club, Ltd., 403 So.2d 1367 (Fla. 4th DCA 1981); Restatement (Second) of Contracts §167 comment a (1981) ("A misrepresentation is not a cause of a party's making a contract unless he relied on the misrepresentation in manifesting his assent.").

7. To borrow from Oliver Wendell Holmes:

> I do not suppose that you could prove, for purposes of construction as distinguished from avoidance, an oral declaration of even an agreement that words in a dispositive instrument making sense as they stand should have a different meaning from the common one; for instance that the parties to a contract orally agreed that when they wrote five hundred feet it should mean one hundred inches, or that Bunker Hill Monument should signify Old South Church.

O.W. Holmes, The Theory of Legal Interpretation, 12 Harv. L. Rev. 417, 420 (1898-99).

advertisement itself that Machado — although it did not intend to adhere to the $3,000 trade-in representation — affirmatively, but wrongly sought to make the public believe that it would be honored; that, in other words, the offer was to be used as the "bait" to be followed by a "switch" to another deal when the acceptance of that offer was refused.[8] Indeed, it is difficult to offer any other explanation for the blanket representation of a $3,000 trade-in for *any* vehicle — which is then hedged in sub-microscopic print to apply only to two models which were not otherwise referred to in the ad — or the obvious non-coincidence that the only example of the trade-in for the three vehicles which was set out in the ad was the very same $3,000. This situation invokes the applicability of a line of persuasive authority that a binding offer may be implied from the very fact that deliberately misleading advertising intentionally leads the reader to the conclusion that one exists. See Corbin on Contracts §64, at 139 (Supp. 1989) (where "bait and switch" advertising suspected, public policy "ought to justify a court in holding deceptive advertising to be an offer despite the seller's . . . intent not to make any such offer"). See generally Annot., Advertisement Addressed to Public Relating to Sale or Purchase of Goods at the Specified Price as an Offer the Acceptance of Which Will Consummate a Contract, 43 A.L.R. 3d 1102 §2[b], at 1107. . . . In Johnson v. Capital City Ford Co., 85 So.2d 75 (La. App. 1955), the court dealt with a case very like this one, in which the issue was whether a newspaper advertisement stating that any purchaser who bought a 1954 automobile before a certain date could exchange it for a newer model without an extra charge constituted a binding offer. The dealership argued that, despite the plain wording of the advertisement, it had no intention of making an offer, but merely sought to lure customers to the sales lot; it claimed also that, because of the small print at the bottom of the contract, any promises by the purchaser to exchange the vehicle for a later model were not binding. The court rejected these contentions on the holding that a contract had been formed even though the dealership "had an erroneous belief as to what the advertisement, as written, meant, or what it would legally convey." *Johnson*, 85 So.2d at 80. As the court said:

> There is entirely too much disregard of law and truth in the business, social, and political world of to-day. . . . It is time to hold men to their primary engagements to tell the truth and observe the law of common honesty and fair dealing.

Johnson, 85 So.2d at 82. We entirely agree. . . .

. . .

3. *Statutory Violation.* It follows from what we have said concerning the allegedly misleading "'nature of the advertisement in making an offer which the advertiser did not intend to keep, that the complaint properly alleged claims for violations of the Florida Deceptive and Unfair Trade Practices Act,

---

8. "'Bait and switch' describes an offer which is made not in order to sell the advertised product at the advertised price, but rather to draw the customer to the store to sell him another similar product which is more profitable to the advertiser." Tashof v. Federal Trade Commission, 437 F.2d 707, 709 n.3 (D.C. Cir. 1970).

sections 501.201-501.213, Florida Statutes (1987),[9] and the statutory prohibition against misleading advertising, section 817.41, Florida Statutes (1987).[10] . . .

Affirmed in part, reversed in part and remanded.

Notes and Questions

1. *Reading the ad in* **Izadi.** The court in *Izadi* interprets the advertisement as possibly conveying to a reasonable reader the impression that the defendant was offering to sell any car on its lot for the listed price minus a $3,000 allowance for any trade-in vehicle, and it quotes Williston and Holmes for the proposition that a communication should be interpreted as a reasonable person would interpret it, regardless of the secret intention of the person making it. This is of course consistent with the "objective theory" which we encountered earlier. Would you have so understood the ad in *Izadi*? If the court is right on this point, would it follow that the defendant should be held to have made such an offer to the plaintiff, even if the plaintiff himself did not in fact understand it that way? We will return in Chapter 5 to a discussion of various approaches to contract interpretation.

2. *Advertisements as offers.* Although it concedes that the "usual rule" may be otherwise, the court in *Izadi* holds that the defendant's ad could constitute an "offer" that the plaintiff could accept. As the court suggests, the traditional rule has been that advertisements in newspapers, magazines, etc., are not offers but merely invitations for offers. See comment *b* to Restatement (Second) §26: "Advertisements of goods by display, sign, handbill, newspaper, radio or television are not ordinarily intended or understood as offers to sell. . . . [T]o make an offer by an advertisement . . . there must ordinarily be some language of commitment or some invitation to take action without further communication"; see also Litton Microwave Cooking Products v. Leviton Mfg. Co., 15 F.3d 790 (8th Cir. 1994) (price quotations and catalogs usually do not amount to offers). What justifies this approach to advertising messages? There are holdings to the contrary; the leading case is Lefkowitz v. Great Minneapolis Surplus Store, cited by the court in *Izadi,* where the defendant advertised one or two items of each kind — fur coats, etc. — at extremely low prices, with the additional language "first come, first served." The ad in *Lefkowitz* appeared to be an example of "bait and switch" advertising, a category in which the Florida court appears willing to place the ad in *Izadi.* In Donovan v. RRL Corp., 27 P.3d 702 (Cal. 2001), discussed in the notes following the *Wil-Fred's* case in Chapter 8, the court held that defendant auto dealer had indeed made an offer by its newspaper advertisement, but declined to enforce a contract, on the ground of unilateral mistake.

9. 501.204 Unlawful acts and practices. — (1) Unfair methods of competition and unfair or deceptive acts or practices in the conduct of any trade or commerce are hereby declared unlawful.

10. 817.41 Misleading advertising prohibited. — (1) It shall be unlawful for any person to make or disseminate or cause to be made or disseminated before the general public of the state, or any portion thereof, any misleading advertisement. Such making or dissemination of misleading advertising shall constitute and is hereby declared to be fraudulent and unlawful, designed and intended for obtaining money or property under false pretenses.

3. *Scholarly Commentary*. In a 1994 article, Professor Melvin Eisenberg asserted that the traditional rule does not conform to the reasonable expectations of most readers, who would assume that an advertiser does indeed commit itself to sell on a first-come-first-served basis until its supply of the advertised goods is exhausted. Eisenberg also claims that a majority of modern cases have followed *Lefkowitz* in imposing liability on the advertiser. Melvin A. Eisenberg, Expression Rules in Contract Law and Problems of Offer and Acceptance, 82 Cal. L. Rev. 1127, 1166-1172 (1994). Jay Feinman and Stephen Brill go even further than Eisenberg:

> Courts and scholars uniformly recite the contract law rule familiar to all first-year students: An advertisement is not an offer. The courts and scholars are wrong. An advertisement is an offer. This article explains why the purported rule is not the law, why the actual rule is that an advertisement is an offer, and what this issue tells us about contract law in particular and legal doctrine in general.

Jay M. Feinman & Stephen R. Brill, Is an Advertisement an Offer? Why It Is, and Why It Matters, 58 Hastings L.J. 61 (2006).

Normile v. Miller
Supreme Court of North Carolina
313 N.C. 98, 326 S.E.2d 11 (1985)

FRYE, Justice.

Defendant Hazel Miller owned real estate located in Charlotte, North Carolina. On 4 August 1980, the property was listed for sale with a local realtor, Gladys Hawkins. On that same day, Richard Byer, a real estate broker with the realty firm Gallery of Homes, showed the property to the prospective purchasers, Plaintiffs Normile and Kurniawan. Afterwards, Byer helped plaintiffs prepare a written offer to purchase the property. A Gallery of Homes form, entitled "DEPOSIT RECEIPT AND CONTRACT FOR PURCHASE AND SALE OF REAL ESTATE," containing blanks for the insertion of terms pertinent to the purchasers' offer, was completed in quadruplicate and signed by Normile and Kurniawan. One specific standard provision in Paragraph 9 included a blank that was filled in with the time and date to read as follows: "OFFER & CLOSING DATE: Time is of the essence, therefore this offer must be accepted on or before *5:00 P.M. Aug. 5th 1980*. A signed copy shall be promptly returned to the purchaser."

Byer took the offer to purchase form to Gladys Hawkins, who presented it to defendant. Later that evening, Gladys Hawkins returned the executed form to Byer. It had been signed under seal by defendant, with several changes in the terms having been made thereon and initialed by defendant. The primary changes made by defendant were an increase in the earnest money deposit ($100 to $500); an increase in the down payment due at closing ($875 to $1,000); a decrease in the unpaid principal of the existing mortgage amount ($18,525 to $18,000); a decrease in the term of the loan from seller (25 years to 20 years); and a purchaser qualification contingency added in the outer margin of the form.

That same evening, Byer presented defendant's counteroffer to Plaintiff Normile. Byer testified in his deposition that Normile did not have $500 for the earnest money deposit, one of the requirements of defendant's counteroffer. Also, Byer stated that Normile did not "want to go 25 [sic] years because he wanted lower payments." Byer was under the impression at this point that Normile thought he had first option on the property and that "nobody else could put an offer in on it and buy it while he had this counteroffer, so he was going to wait awhile before he decided what to do with it." Normile, however, neither accepted or rejected the counteroffer at this point, according to Byer. When this meeting closed, Byer left the pink copy of the offer to purchase form containing defendant's counteroffer with Normile. Byer stated that he thought that Normile had rejected the counteroffer at this point.

At approximately 12:30 A.M. on 5 August, Byer went to the home of Plaintiff Segal, who signed an offer to purchase with terms very similar to those contained in defendant's counteroffer to Plaintiffs Normile and Kurniawan. This offer was accepted, without change, by defendant. Later that same day, at approximately 2:00 P.M., Byer informed Plaintiff Normile that defendant had revoked her counteroffer by commenting to Normile, "[Y]ou snooze, you lose; the property has been sold." Prior to 5:00 P.M. on that same day, Normile and Kurniawan initialed the offer to purchase form containing defendant's counteroffer and delivered the form to the Gallery of Homes' office, along with the earnest money deposit of $500.

Separate actions were filed by plaintiff-appellants and appellee seeking specific performance. Plaintiff Segal's motion for consolidation of the trials was granted. Defendant, in her answer, recognized the validity of the contract between her and Plaintiff Segal. However, because of the action for specific performance commenced by Plaintiffs Normile and Kurniawan, defendant contended that she was unable to legally convey title to Plaintiff Segal. Both plaintiffs filed a motion for summary judgment. Plaintiff Segal's motion for summary judgment was granted by the trial court, and defendant was ordered to specifically perform the contract to convey the property to Segal. Plaintiffs Normile and Kurniawan appealed to the Court of Appeals from the trial court's denial of their motion for summary judgment. That court unanimously affirmed the trial court's actions. Discretionary review was allowed by this Court on petition of Plaintiffs Normile and Kurniawan.

I

. . . [We] begin with a brief description of how a typical sale of real estate is consummated. The broker, whose primary duty is to secure a ready, willing, and able buyer for the seller's property, generally initiates a potential sale by procuring the prospective purchaser's signature on an offer to purchase instrument. J. Webster, North Carolina Real Estate for Brokers and Salesmen, §8.03 (1974). "An 'offer to purchase' is simply an offer by a purchaser to buy property, . . ." J. Webster, supra, §8.03. This instrument contains the prospective purchaser's "offer" of the terms he wishes to propose to the seller. Id.

Usually, this offer to purchase is a printed form with blanks that are filled in and completed by the broker. Among the various clauses contained in such an instrument, it is not uncommon for the form to contain "a clause stipulating that the seller must accept the offer and approve the sale within a certain specified period of time, . . . The inclusion of a date within which the seller must accept simply indicates that the offer will automatically expire at the termination of the named period if the seller does not accept before then." Id. §8.10. Such a clause is contained in Paragraph 9 of the offer to purchase form in the case *sub judice*.

In the instant case, the offerors, plaintiffs-appellants, submitted their offer to purchase defendant's property. This offer contained a Paragraph 9, requiring that "this offer must be accepted on or before 5:00 P.M. Aug. 5th 1980." Thus the offeree's, defendant-seller's, power of acceptance was controlled by the duration of time for acceptance of the offer. Restatement (Second) of Contracts §35 (1981). "The offeror is the creator of the power, and before it leaves his hands, he may fashion it to his will . . . if he names a specific period for its existence, the offeree can accept only during this period." Corbin, Offer and Acceptance, and Some of the Resulting Legal Relations, 26 Yale L.J. 169, at 183 (1917); see Restatement, supra, §41; S. Williston, A Treatise on the Law of Contracts §53 (1957).

This offer to purchase remains only an offer until the seller accepts it on the terms contained in the original offer by the prospective purchaser. J. Webster, supra, §8.10. If the seller does accept the terms in the purchaser's offer, he denotes this by signing the offer to purchase at the bottom, thus forming a valid, binding, and irrevocable purchase contract between the seller and purchaser. However, if the seller purports to accept but changes or modifies the terms of the offer, he makes what is generally referred to as a qualified or conditional acceptance. Richardson v. Greensboro Warehouse & Storage Co., 223 N.C. 344, 26 S.E.2d 897 (1943); Wilson v. W. M. Storey Lumber Co., 180 N.C. 271, 104 S.E. 531 (1920); 17 Am. Jur. 2d Contracts §62 (1964). "The effect of such an acceptance so conditioned is to make a new counter-proposal upon which the parties have not yet agreed, but which is open for acceptance or rejection." (Citations omitted.) *Richardson*, 223 N.C. at 347, 26 S.E.2d at 899. Such a reply from the seller is actually a counteroffer and a rejection of the buyer's offer. J. Webster, supra, §8.10.

These basic principles of contract law are recognized not only in real estate transactions but in bargaining situations generally. It is axiomatic that a valid contract between two parties can only exist when the parties "assent to the same thing in the same sense, and their minds meet as to all terms." Goeckel v. Stokely, 236 N.C. 604, 607, 73 S.E.2d 618, 620 (1952). This assent, or meeting of the minds, requires an offer and acceptance in the exact terms and that the acceptance must be communicated to the offeror. . . . "If the terms of the offer are changed or any new ones added by the acceptance, there is no meeting of the minds and, consequently, no contract." G. Thompson, supra, §4452. This counter-offer amounts to a rejection of the original offer. S. Williston, supra, §51. "The reason is that the counter-offer is interpreted as being in effect the statement by the offeree not only that he will enter into the transaction on the terms stated in his counteroffer, but also by implication that he will not assent to the terms of the original offer." Id. §36.

The question then becomes, did defendant-seller accept plaintiff-appellants' offer prior to the expiration of the time limit contained within the offer? We conclude that she did not. The offeree, defendant-seller, changed the original offer in several material respects, most notably in the terms regarding payment of the purchase price. S. Williston, supra, §77 (any alteration in the method of payment creates a conditional acceptance). This qualified acceptance was in reality a rejection of the plaintiff-appellants original offer because it was coupled with certain modifications or changes that were not contained in the original offer. G. Thompson, supra, §4452. Additionally, defendant-seller's conditional acceptance amounted to a counter-offer to plaintiff-appellants. "A counter-offer is an offer made by an offeree to his offeror relating to the same matter as the original offer and proposing a substituted bargain differing from that proposed by the original offer." Restatement, supra, §39. Between plaintiff-appellants and defendant-seller there was no meeting of the minds, since the parties failed to assent to the same thing in the same sense.

In substance, defendant's conditional acceptance modifying the original offer did not manifest any intent to accept the terms of the original offer, including the time-for-acceptance provision, unless and until the original offeror accepted the terms included in defendant's counteroffer. The offeree, by failing to unconditionally assent to the terms of the original offer and instead qualifying his acceptance with terms of his own, in effect says to the original offeror, "I will accept your offer, provided you [agree to my proposed terms]." Rucker v. Sanders, 182 N.C. 607, 609, 109 S.E. 857, 858 (1921). Thus, the time-for-acceptance provision contained in plaintiff-appellants' original offer did not become part of the terms of the counter-offer. And, of course, if they had accepted the counteroffer from defendant, a binding purchase contract, which would have included the terms of the original offer and counteroffer, would have then resulted. J. Webster, supra, §8.03. . . .

It is generally recognized that "[a]n 'option' is a contract by which the owner agrees to give another the exclusive right to buy property at a fixed price within a specified time." 8A G. Thompson, Commentaries on the Modern Law of Real Property, §4443 (1963); Sandlin v. Weaver, 240 N.C. 703, 83 S.E.2d 806 (1954). In effect, an owner of property agrees to hold his offer open for a specified period of time. G. Thompson, supra, §4443. This option contract must also be supported by valuable consideration. Id. Disregarding the issue of consideration, it is more significant that defendant's counteroffer did not contain any promise or agreement that her counteroffer would remain open for a specified period of time.

Several of the cases cited by plaintiff-appellants are useful in illustrating how a seller expressly agrees to hold his offer open. For instance, in Ward v. Albertson, 165 N.C. 218, 81 S.E. 168 (1914), this Court stated, "An option, in the proper sense, is a contract by which the owner of property agrees with another that he shall have the right to purchase the same at a fixed price within a certain time." Id at 222-23, 81 S.E. at 169. In that case, defendant-seller had agreed in writing as follows: ". . . I agree that if [prospective purchaser] pays me nine hundred and ninety five dollars prior to January 1, 1913, to convey to him all the timber and trees. . . ." Id. at 219, 81 S.E. at 168. . . . And finally, in Kidd v. Early, 289 N.C. 343, 222 S.E.2d 392 (1976), defendant-sellers agreed in writing: ". . . we C.F. Early and Bessie D. Early, hereby irrevocably agree to convey to [prospective purchasers] upon demand by him within 30 days from the date hereof, . . . a certain tract or parcel of land. . . ." Id. at 346, 222 S.E.2d at 396.

In each of these . . . cases, this Court recognized that the sellers had given the prospective purchasers a contractual option to purchase the seller's property. In the present case we find no comparable language within defendant-seller's counteroffer manifesting any similar agreement. There is no language indicating that defendant-seller in any way agreed to sell or convey her real property to plaintiff-appellants at their request within a specified period of time. There is, however, language contained within the prospective purchasers' offer to purchase that does state, "DESCRIPTION: I/we Michael M. Normile and Wawie Kurniawan hereby *agree to purchase* from the sellers, . . ." and "*this* offer must be accepted on or before 5:00 P.M. Aug. 5th 1980." (Emphasis added.) Nowhere is there companion language to the effect that Defendant Miller "hereby agrees to sell or convey to the purchasers" if they accept by a certain date.

Therefore, regardless of whether or not the seal imported the necessary consideration, we conclude that defendant-seller made no promise or agreement to hold her offer open. Thus, a necessary ingredient to the creation of an option contract, i.e., a promise to hold an offer open for a specified time, is not present. Accordingly, we hold that defendant's counteroffer was not transformed into an irrevocable offer for the time limit contained in the original offer because the defendant's conditional acceptance did not include the time-for-acceptance provision as part of its terms and because defendant did not make any promise to hold her counteroffer open for any stated time.

II

The foregoing preliminary analysis of both the Court of Appeals' opinion and plaintiff-appellants' argument in their brief prefaces what we consider to be decisive of the ultimate issue to be resolved. Basic contract principles effectively and logically answer the primary issue in this appeal. That is, if a seller rejects a prospective purchaser's offer to purchase but makes a counteroffer that is not accepted by the prospective purchaser, does the prospective purchaser have the power to accept after he receives notice that the counteroffer has been revoked? The answer is no. The net effect of defendant-seller's counteroffer and rejection is twofold. First, plaintiff-appellants' original offer was rejected and ceased to exist. S. Williston, supra, §51. Secondly, the counteroffer by the offeree requires the original offeror, plaintiff-appellants, to either accept or reject. Benya v. Stevens & Thompson Paper Co., Inc., 143 Vt. 521, 468 A.2d 929 (1983).

Accordingly, the next question is did plaintiff-appellants, the original offerors, accept or reject defendant-seller's counteroffer? Plaintiff-appellants in their brief seem to answer this question when they state, "At the time Byer presented the counteroffer to Normile, Normile neither accepted nor rejected it. . . ." Therefore, plaintiff-appellants did not manifest any intent to agree to or accept the terms contained in defendant's counteroffer. Normile instead advised Byer that he, though mistakenly, had an option on the property and that it was off the market for the duration of the time limitation contained in his original offer. As was stated by Justice Bobbitt in Howell v. Smith, 258 N.C. 150, 128 S.E.2d 144 (1962): "'The question whether a contract has been made must be determined from a consideration of the expressed intention of the parties — that is from a consideration of their words and acts.'" Id. at 153, 128 S.E.2d at 146. Although Normile's mistaken belief that he had an option is unfortunate, he still failed to express to Byer his agreement to or rejection of the counteroffer made by defendant-seller. . . .

Plaintiff-appellants in the instant case . . . did not accept, either expressly or by conduct, defendant's counteroffer. In addition to disagreeing with the change in payment terms, Normile stated to Byer that "he was going to wait awhile before he decided what to do with [the counteroffer]." Neither did plaintiffs explicitly reject defendant's counteroffer. Instead, plaintiff-appellants in this case chose to operate under the impression, though mistaken, that they had an option to purchase and that the property was "off the market." Absent either an acceptance or rejection, there was no meeting of the minds or mutual assent between the parties, a fortiori, there was no contract. Horton v. Humble Oil & Refining Co., 255 N.C. 675, 122 S.E.2d 716 (1961); Goeckel, 236 N.C. 604, 73 S.E.2d 618 (1952).

It is evident from the record that after plaintiff-appellants failed to accept defendant's counteroffer, there was a second purchaser, Plaintiff-appellee Segal, who submitted an offer to defendant that was accepted. This offer and acceptance between the latter parties, together with consideration in the form of an earnest money deposit from plaintiff-appellee, ripened into a valid and binding purchase contract.

By entering into the contract with Plaintiff-appellee Segal, defendant manifested her intention to revoke her previous counteroffer to plaintiff-appellants. "It is a fundamental tenet of the common law that an offer is generally freely revocable and can be countermanded by the offeror at any time before it has been accepted by the offeree." E. Farnsworth, Contracts, §3.17 (1982); Restatement, supra, §42. The revocation of an offer terminates it, and the offeree has no power to revive the offer by any subsequent attempts to accept. G. Thompson, supra, §4452.

Generally, notice of the offeror's revocation must be communicated to the offeree to effectively terminate the offeree's power to accept the offer. It is enough that the offeree receives reliable information, even indirectly, "that the offeror had taken definite action inconsistent with an intention to make the contract." E. Farnsworth, supra, §3.17 (the author cites Dickinson v. Dodds, 2 Ch. Div. 463 (1876), a notorious English case, to support this proposition); Restatement, supra, §43.

In this case, plaintiff-appellants received notice of the offeror's revocation of the counteroffer in the afternoon of August 5, when Byer saw Normile and told him, "[Y]ou snooze, you lose; the property has been sold." Later that afternoon, plaintiff-appellants initialed the counteroffer and delivered it to the Gallery of Homes, along with their earnest money deposit of $500. These subsequent attempts by plaintiff-appellants to accept defendant's revoked counteroffer were fruitless, however, since their power of acceptance had been effectively terminated by the offeror's revocation. Restatement, supra, §36. Since defendant's counteroffer could not be revived, the practical effect of plaintiff-appellants' initialing defendant's counteroffer and leaving it at the broker's office before 5:00 P.M. on August 5 was to resubmit a new offer. This offer was not accepted by defendant since she had already contracted to sell her property by entering into a valid, binding, and irrevocable purchase contract with Plaintiff-appellee Segal.

For the reasons stated herein, the decision of the Court of Appeals is modified and affirmed.

Notes and Questions

1. *Classical Principles of offer and acceptance.* The court in *Normile* cites and applies many classical rules of offer and acceptance embodied in the first Restatement of Contracts and carried forward in the Restatement (Second), including the following: The power of acceptance created by an offer will be terminated by the offeree's rejection (as well as by other events, such as revocation by the offeror, or his death or incapacity). Restatement (Second) of Contracts §36. An acceptance must be unequivocal and unqualified in order for a contract to be formed. Restatement (Second) §§57 and 58. (Note that silence by the offeree rarely amounts to acceptance, but in some limited circumstances an offeree's silence may result in the formation of a contract. See Restatement (Second) §69; James J. White, Autistic Contracts, 45 Wayne L. Rev. 1693 (2000).) A "qualified acceptance" constitutes a counter-offer, Restatement (Second) §59, and as such will have the same effect as a rejection, insofar as the original power of acceptance is concerned. Restatement (Second) of Contracts §39. See Melvin A. Eisenberg, The Revocation of Offers, 2004 Wis. L. Rev. 271 (discussing classical and modern principles of offer and acceptance and arguing that contract law has partially but not completely broken away from doctrinal restrictions of classical contract law). See also Charles L. Knapp, An Offer You Can't Revoke, 2004 Wis. L. Rev. 309 (criticizing Eisenberg for failing to take into account many of the principles of modern contract law). For an argument that the rules of offer and acceptance have developed to promote efficient reliance see Richard Craswell, Offer, Acceptance, and Efficient Reliance, 48 Stan. L. Rev. 481 (1996).

2. *Policy analysis of classical rules.* What policy justifies the rule that the offeree's power of acceptance is terminated by his rejection of the offer? Does that policy apply with equal force to the case where the offeree makes a counter-offer? Professor Melvin Eisenberg has argued that the counter-offer-equals-rejection rule of Restatement (Second) §39(2) is not congruent with the normal understanding of most bargainers, and ought to be either abandoned entirely, or "dropped to the form of a maxim." Melvin A. Eisenberg, Expression Rules in Contract Law and Problems of Offer and Acceptance, 82 Cal. L. Rev. 1127, 1158-1161 (1994). Note, however, that the rule of termination-by-counter-offer is not stated as an inflexible one: Restatement (Second) §39(2) indicates that effect should be given to the expressed intention of either offeror or offeree to the contrary.

3. *Option contracts.* Plaintiff Normile testified that when he received the defendant's counter-offer he believed he had "first option" on the property, that Miller had bound herself to sell to no one else until Normile had accepted or rejected that counter-offer. The court indicates, however, that the defendant had made no promise to keep her offer open, and that Normile

thus could not have had such an option. Even if Miller's counter-offer had been accompanied by an express promise on her part to keep that offer open for a stated period of time, Normile and Kurniawan would still not have had an enforceable option contract because they did not provide "consideration" for Miller's promise to hold the offer open. We will examine both the doctrine of consideration and option contracts in more detail in part B of this chapter. For now it is sufficient for you to know that under the modern theory of consideration a promise is generally enforceable only if the promisee has given either a promise or a performance in exchange for the promise that that promisee seeks to enforce. Normille and Kurniawan did not give anything to Miller to hold the offer open.

4. *Possibility of multiple acceptances.* In the course of its opinion in *Normile,* the North Carolina Supreme Court indicates that because the parties "failed to assent to the same thing in the same sense" there was "no meeting of the minds," and hence no contract. Suppose the plaintiffs had signed and returned Miller's counter-offer before they learned from Byer that Miller had in the meantime contracted to sell the property to Segal. Would a binding contract between Miller and plaintiffs have been formed? And, if so, what about the contract between Miller and Segal?

3. Offer and Acceptance in Unilateral Contracts

Perhaps no aspect of the classical contract law system was more vividly impressed on the minds of generations of law students than the distinction between bilateral and unilateral contracts. As we have seen, a bilateral contract is formed when the parties exchange promises of performance to take place in the future: Each party is both a promisor and a promisee; the offeree's communicated acceptance also constitutes in effect her promise to perform. However, if the offeror should offer to exchange his promise of a future performance only in return for the offeree's actual rendering of performance, rather than her mere promise of future performance, then the transaction would give rise to a unilateral contract. In that case, only one party (the offeror) would be a promisor, and the offeree's rendering of performance would also constitute her acceptance of the offer.

This view of the unilateral contract affords maximum protection to the offeror, who would not be bound unless and until he had received the performance he sought. For the offeree, however, it carries certain risks. If the offeror should revoke his offer at a time when the offeree had commenced but not yet completed the requested performance, classical theory denied the offeree any remedy on the contract because the offer was revoked before the proposed contract ever came into being. In 1916, Professor Maurice Wormser stated the classical view of this situation:

> Suppose *A* says to *B,* "I will give you $100 if you walk across the Brooklyn Bridge," and *B* walks — is there a contract? It is clear that *A* is not asking *B* for *B's promise* to walk across the Brooklyn Bridge. What *A* wants from *B* is the *act* of walking across the bridge. When *B* has walked across the bridge there is a contract, and *A* is

then bound to pay to B $100. At that moment there arises a unilateral contract. A has bartered away his volition for B's act of walking across the Brooklyn Bridge.

When an act is thus wanted in return for a promise, a unilateral contract is created when the act is done. It is clear that only one party is bound. B is not bound to walk across the Brooklyn Bridge, but A is bound to pay B $100 if B does so. Thus, in unilateral contracts, on one side we find merely an act, on the other side a promise. . . .

It is plain that in the Brooklyn Bridge case . . . , what A wants from B is the act of walking across the Brooklyn Bridge. A does not ask for B's promise to walk across the bridge and B has never given it. B has never bound himself to walk across the bridge. A, however, has bound himself to pay $100 to B, if B does so. Let us suppose that B starts to walk across the Brooklyn Bridge and has gone about one-half of the way across. At that moment A overtakes B and says to him, "I withdraw my offer." Has B then any rights against A? Again, let us suppose that after A has said, "I withdraw my offer," B continues to walk across the Brooklyn Bridge and completes the act of crossing. Under these circumstances, has B any rights against A?

. . . What A wanted from B, what A asked for, was the act of walking across the bridge. Until that was done, B had not given to A what A had requested. The acceptance by B of A's offer could be nothing but the act on B's part of crossing the bridge. It is elementary that an offeror may withdraw his offer until it has been accepted. It follows logically that A is perfectly within his rights in withdrawing his offer before B has accepted it by walking across the bridge — the act contemplated by the offeror and the offeree as the acceptance of the offer. A did not want B to walk half-way across or three-quarters of the way across the bridge. What A wanted from B, and what A asked for from B, was a certain and entire act. B understood this. It was for that act that A was willing to barter his volition with regard to $100. B understood this also. Until this act is done, therefore, A is not bound, since no contract arises until the completion of the act called for. Then, and not before, would a unilateral contract arise. Then, and not before, would A be bound.

The objection is made, however, that it is very "hard" upon B that he should have walked half-way across the Brooklyn Bridge and should get no compensation. This suggestion, invariably advanced, might be dismissed with the remark that "hard" cases should not make bad law. But going a step further, by way of reply, the pertinent inquiry at once suggests itself, "Was B bound to walk across the Brooklyn Bridge?" The answer to this is obvious. By hypothesis, B was not bound to walk across the Brooklyn Bridge. . . . If B is not bound to continue to cross the bridge, if B is will-free, why should not A also be will-free? Suppose that after B has crossed half the bridge he gets tired and tells A that he refuses to continue crossing. B, concededly, would be perfectly within his rights in so speaking and acting. A would have no cause of action against B for damages. If B has a *locus poenitentiae*, so has A. They each have, and should have, the opportunity to reconsider and withdraw. Not until B has crossed the bridge, thereby doing the act called for, and accepting the offer, is a contract born. At that moment, and not one instant before, A is bound, and there is a unilateral contract. . . . So long as there is freedom of contract and parties see fit to integrate their understanding in the form of a unilateral contract, the courts should not interfere with their evident understanding and intention simply because of alleged fanciful hardship.

I. Maurice Wormser, The True Conception of Unilateral Contracts, 26 Yale L.J. 136, 136-138 (1916). Professor Wormser's argument, with its pointed if somewhat redundant disdain for "alleged fanciful hardship," may suggest why it has been sometimes said that "taught law is tough law." (And it may have some bearing on the fact that the fictional Professor Kingsfield of *The Paper Chase* was a contracts teacher.) The next case, Petterson v. Pattberg, illustrates the problem faced by an offeree in attempting to accept an offer for a unilateral contract when the offeror changes his mind and attempts to withdraw his offer.

Petterson v. Pattberg
New York Court of Appeals
248 N.Y. 86, 161 N.E. 428 (1928)

KELLOGG, J. The evidence given upon the trial sanctions the following statement of facts: John Petterson, of whose last will and testament the plaintiff is the executrix, was the owner of a parcel of real estate in Brooklyn, known as 5301 Sixth Avenue. The defendant was the owner of a bond executed by Petterson, which was secured by a third mortgage upon the parcel. On April 4th, 1924, there remained unpaid upon the principal the sum of $5,450. This amount was payable in installments of $250 on April 25th, 1924, and upon a like monthly date every three months thereafter. Thus the bond and mortgage had more than five years to run before the entire sum became due. Under date of the 4th of April, 1924, the defendant wrote Petterson as follows: "I hereby agree to accept cash for the mortgage which I hold against premises 5301 6th Ave., Brooklyn, N.Y. It is understood and agreed as a consideration I will allow you $780 providing said mortgage is paid on or before May 31, 1924, and the regular quarterly payment due April 25, 1924, is paid when due." On April 25, 1924, Petterson paid the defendant the installment of principal due on that date. Subsequently, on a day in the latter part of May, 1924, Petterson presented himself at the defendant's home, and knocked at the door. The defendant demanded the name of his caller. Petterson replied: "It is Mr. Petterson. I have come to pay off the mortgage." The defendant answered that he had sold the mortgage. Petterson stated that he would like to talk with the defendant, so the defendant partly opened the door. Thereupon Petterson exhibited the cash and said he was ready to pay off the mortgage according to the agreement. The defendant refused to take the money. Prior to this conversation Petterson had made a contract to sell the land to a third person free and clear of the mortgage to the defendant. Meanwhile, also, the defendant had sold the bond and mortgage to a third party. It, therefore, became necessary for Petterson to pay to such person the full amount of the bond and mortgage. It is claimed that he thereby sustained a loss of $780, the sum which the defendant agreed to allow upon the bond and mortgage if payment in full of principal, less that sum, was made on or before May 31st, 1924. The plaintiff has had a recovery for the sum thus claimed, with interest.

Clearly the defendant's letter proposed to Petterson the making of a unilateral contract, the gift of a promise in exchange for the performance of an act. The thing conditionally promised by the defendant was the reduction of the mortgage debt. The act requested to be done, in consideration of the offered promise, was payment in full of the reduced principal of the debt prior to the due date thereof. "If an act is requested, that very act and no other must be given." (Williston on Contracts, sec. 73.) "In case of offers for a consideration, the performance of the consideration is always deemed a condition." (Langdell's Summary of the Law of Contracts, sec. 4.) It is elementary that any offer to enter into a unilateral contract may be withdrawn before the act requested to be done has been performed. (Williston on Contracts, sec. 60; Langdell's Summary, sec. 4; Offord v. Davies, 12 C.B. [N.S.] 748.) A bidder at a sheriff's sale may revoke his bid at any time before the property is struck down to him. (Fisher v. Seltzer, 23 Penn. St. 308.) The offer of a reward in consideration of an act to be performed is revocable before the very act requested has been done. (Shuey v. United States, 92 U.S. 73; Biggers v. Owen, 79 Ga. 658; Fitch v. Snedaker, 38 N.Y. 248.) So, also, an offer to pay a broker commissions, upon a sale of land for the offeror, is revocable at any time before the land is sold, although prior to revocation the broker performs services in an effort to effectuate a sale. (Stensgaard v. Smith, 43 Minn. 11; Smith v. Cauthen, 98 Miss. 746.) An interesting question arises when, as here, the offeree approaches the offeror with the intention of proffering performance and, before actual tender is made, the offer is withdrawn. Of such a case Williston says: "The offeror may see the approach of the offeree and know that an acceptance is contemplated. If the offeror can say 'I revoke' before the offeree accepts, however brief the interval of time between the two acts, there is no escape from the conclusion that the offer is terminated." (Williston on Contracts, sec. 60-b.) In this instance Petterson, standing at the door of the defendant's house, stated to the defendant that he had come to pay off the mortgage. Before a tender of the necessary moneys had been made the defendant informed Petterson that he had sold the mortgage. That was a definite notice to Petterson that the defendant could not perform his offered promise and that a tender to the defendant, who was no longer the creditor, would be ineffective to satisfy the debt. "An offer to sell property may be withdrawn before acceptance without any formal notice to the person to whom the offer is made. It is sufficient if that person has actual knowledge that the person who made the offer has done some act inconsistent with the continuance of the offer, such as selling the property to a third person." (Dickinson v. Dodds, 2 Ch. Div. 463, headnote.) To the same effect is Coleman v. Applegarth (68 Md. 21). Thus, it clearly appears that the defendant's offer was withdrawn before its acceptance had been tendered. It is unnecessary to determine, therefore, what the legal situation might have been had tender been made before withdrawal. It is the individual view of the writer that the same result would follow. This would be so, for the act requested to be performed was the completed act of payment, a thing incapable of performance unless assented to by the person to be paid. (Williston on Contracts, sec. 60-b.) Clearly an offering party has the right to name the precise act performance of which would convert his offer into a binding promise. Whatever the act may be until it is performed the offer must be revocable. However, the supposed case is not before us for decision. We think that in this particular instance the offer of the defendant was withdrawn before it became a binding promise, and, therefore, that no contract was ever made for the breach of which the plaintiff may claim damages.

The judgment of the Appellate Division and that of the Trial Term should be reversed and the complaint dismissed, with costs in all courts.

LEHMAN, J. (dissenting). The defendant's letter to Petterson constituted a promise on his part to accept payment at a discount of the mortgage he held, provided the mortgage is paid on or before May 31st, 1924. Doubtless by the terms of the promise itself, the defendant made payment of the mortgage by the plaintiff, before the stipulated time, a condition precedent to performance by the defendant of his promise to accept payment at a discount. If the condition precedent has not been performed, it is because the defendant made performance impossible by refusing to accept payment, when the plaintiff came with an offer of immediate performance. "It is a principle of fundamental justice that if a promisor is himself the cause of the failure of performance either of an obligation due him or of a condition upon which his own liability depends, he cannot take advantage of the failure." (Williston on Contracts, sec. 677.) The question in this case is not whether payment of the mortgage is a condition precedent to the performance of a promise made by the defendant, but, rather, whether at the time the defendant refused the offer of payment, he had assumed any binding obligation, even though subject to condition.

The promise made by the defendant lacked consideration at the time it was made. Nevertheless the promise was not made as a gift or mere gratuity to the plaintiff. It was made for the purpose of obtaining from the defendant something which the plaintiff desired. It constituted an offer which was to become binding whenever the plaintiff should give, in return for the defendant's promise, exactly the consideration which the defendant requested.

Here the defendant requested no counter promise from the plaintiff. The consideration requested by the defendant for his promise to accept payment was, I agree, some act to be performed by the plaintiff. Until the act requested was performed, the defendant might undoubtedly revoke his offer. Our problem is to determine from the words of the letter read in the light of surrounding circumstances what act the defendant requested as consideration for his promise.

The defendant undoubtedly made his offer as an inducement to the plaintiff to "pay" the mortgage before it was due. Therefore, it is said, that "the act requested to be performed was the completed act of payment, a thing incapable of performance unless assented to by the person to be paid." In unmistakable terms the defendant agreed to accept payment, yet we are told that the defendant intended, and the plaintiff should have understood, that the act requested by the defendant, as consideration for his promise to accept payment, included performance by the defendant himself of the very promise for which the act was to be consideration. The defendant's promise was to become binding only when fully performed; and part of the consideration to be furnished by the plaintiff for the defendant's promise was to be the performance of that promise by the defendant. So construed, the defendant's promise or offer, though intended to induce action by the plaintiff, is but a snare and delusion. The plaintiff could not reasonably suppose that the defendant was asking him to procure the performance by the defendant of the very act which the defendant promised to do, yet we are told that even after the plaintiff had done all else which the defendant requested, the defendant's promise was still not binding because the defendant chose not to perform.

I cannot believe that a result so extraordinary could have been intended when the defendant wrote the letter. "The thought behind the phrase proclaims itself misread when the outcome of the reading is injustice or absurdity." (See opinion of Cardozo, Ch. J., in Surace v. Danna, 248 N.Y. 18.) If the defendant intended to induce payment by the plaintiff and yet reserve the right to refuse payment when offered he should have used a phrase better calculated to express his meaning than the words: "I agree to accept." A promise to accept payment, by its very terms, must necessarily become binding, if at all, not later than when a present offer to pay is made.

I recognize that in this case only an offer of payment, and not a formal tender of payment, was made before the defendant withdrew his offer to accept payment. Even the plaintiff's part in the act of payment was then not technically complete. Even so, under a fair construction of the words of the letter I think the plaintiff had done the act which the defendant requested as consideration for his promise. The plaintiff offered to pay with present intention and ability to make that payment. A formal tender is seldom made in business transactions, except to lay the foundation for subsequent assertion in a court of justice of rights which spring from refusal of the tender. If the defendant acted in good faith in making his offer to accept payment, he could not well have intended to draw a distinction in the act requested of the plaintiff in return, between an offer which unless refused would ripen into completed payment, and a formal tender. Certainly the defendant could not have expected or intended that the plaintiff would make a formal tender of payment without first stating that he had come to make payment. We should not read into the language of the defendant's offer a meaning which would prevent enforcement of the defendant's promise after it had been accepted by the plaintiff in the very way which the defendant must have intended it should be accepted, if he acted in good faith.

The judgment should be affirmed.

CARDOZO, Ch. J., POUND, CRANE and O'BRIEN, JJ., concur with KELLOGG, J.; LEHMAN, J., dissents in opinion, in which ANDREWS, J., concurs.

Judgments reversed, etc.

Notes and Questions

1. *Analyzing* **Petterson**. After Petterson stated that he had come to pay off the mortgage, Pattberg told Petterson that he had sold the mortgage. Why did that statement amount to a revocation? Suppose Pattberg had not in fact sold the mortgage. In response to Petterson's statement that he was appearing to pay the mortgage, suppose Pattberg had said that he had changed his mind and was no longer willing to accept a discount of $780. If Petterson had then exhibited the cash, would a contract have been formed?

2. *Reactions to* **Petterson**. The *Petterson* decision got mixed reviews from the law review commentators of its day. See, e.g., Samuel Blinkoff, Note, 14 Cornell L.Q. 81, 82, 84 (1928) ("court gives the strict orthodox answer" but "it seems that the demands of good faith in business dealings would require a

more liberal decision in cases of this kind"); Note, 27 Mich. L. Rev. 465, 466 (1929) ("reached a result in accord with the weight of authority" but "results in great unfairness to the offeree"); Jack C. Peppin, Comment, 17 Cal. L. Rev. 153, 155, 157 (1929) ("strict logic and principle stand in the way of allowing a recovery on mere tender without the acceptance thereof" but "the injustice of applying these strict rules to particular situations is often so shocking that many courts have in effect held that the offer becomes irrevocable after the offeree has taken substantial steps in reliance on the offer"). The California note went on to describe several types of cases in which some protection against revocation had frequently been afforded; the list includes offers of rewards made to the general public, offers of commission to a real estate broker, and offers calling for a long series of acts involving substantial time, trouble, or expense on the part of the offeree. 17 Cal. L. Rev. at 157-158 n.13.

As we have seen, one of the principal characteristics of the offer for a unilateral contract, in the eyes of the contract classicists, was that it remained revocable until the offeree's full performance of the act(s) called for in the offer; when rendered, that performance furnished the acceptance of the offer. As we will see, performance also constituted the consideration necessary to bind the offeror to the promise it expressed.

The drafters of the Restatements have attempted to ameliorate the harsh results sometimes reached under the classical analysis. Section 32 of the second Restatement now declares that in cases of doubt courts should conclude that the offeror intended to allow the offeree to accept *either* by making a return promise or by rendering the performance requested by the offeror. Unfortunately, this rule only provides partial protection to the offeree against revocation of the offer. Section 32 does not apply when it was clear that the offeror sought an act and only an act in exchange for the promise of performance. The rule would also not apply if the offeree simply began performance without making a return promise. Presumably in that situation the offeror would remain free to revoke until the offeree's completion of performance.

Responding to the same concerns about good faith and fair dealing reflected in Justice Lehman's dissenting opinion and in contemporary scholarly criticisms of the case, the drafters of the first and second Restatements created another rule that provided much broader protection to the offeree under a unilateral contract. Restatement (Second) §45 now provides that when an offeree tenders or begins the requested performance under a unilateral contract, the offeror becomes bound and cannot revoke his offer so long as the offeree completes performance in accordance with the terms of the offer. (The Restatement uses the concept of an "option" contract to reach this result. As we will see, the situation covered by §45 is not truly an option contract because the offeror under a unilateral contract has not made an express promise to hold the offer open for a stated period of time. The Restaters used the concept of an option contract in an effort to make the significant change in the law reflected in §45 appear less revolutionary. Use of an old concept in a creative way to show legal continuity is a technique that some judges will employ and that advocates who are seeking to change the law can use effectively.)

Like §90, its more celebrated sibling (dealing with "promissory estoppel"), a concept we will discuss in the next chapter, §45 of the first Restatement appears to have reflected the view of Professor Arthur Corbin rather than that of Professor Samuel Williston. Compare 1 Williston on Contracts §60 (1920) with Arthur L. Corbin, Offer and Acceptance, and Some of the Resulting Legal Relations, 26 Yale L.J. 169, 191-196 (1917). In that respect Restatement §45 may have been part of what Professor Gilmore has referred to as the "Corbinization" of the first Restatement. Grant Gilmore, The Death of Contract 165 (1974).

Even Professor Wormser — the prototypical proponent of a hard-shelled approach to unilateral contract offers — ultimately acquiesced in the rule of §45. See I. Maurice Wormser, Book Review, 3 J. Legal Ed. 145, 146 (1950). Would the application of either §32 or §45 of the Second Restatement have changed the result of the *Petterson* case?

Cook v. Coldwell Banker/Frank Laiben Realty Co.
Missouri Court of Appeals
967 S.W.2d 654 (1998)

KATHIANNE KNAUP CRANE, Presiding Judge.

Defendant real estate brokerage firm appeals from a judgment entered on a jury verdict awarding defendant's former salesperson $24,748.89 as damages for breach of a bonus agreement. Defendant claims that the salesperson failed to make a submissible case in that she did not accept the bonus offer before it was revoked. Defendant also asserts trial court errors relating to instructions, evidence, and closing argument. We affirm.

Plaintiff, Mary Ellen Cook, a licensed real estate agent, worked as a real estate salesperson or agent pursuant to a verbal agreement for defendant Coldwell Banker/Frank Laiben Realty Co. and its predecessors. Plaintiff listed and sold real estate for defendant as an independent contractor. Frank Laiben was a co-owner of defendant.

At a sales meeting in March, 1991, defendant, through Laiben, orally announced a bonus program in order to remain competitive with other local brokerage firms and to retain its agents. The bonus program provided that an agent earning $15,000.00 in commissions would receive a $500.00 bonus payable immediately, an agent earning $15,000.00 to $25,000.00 in commissions would receive a twenty-two percent bonus, and an agent earning above $25,000.00 in commissions would receive a thirty percent bonus. Bonuses over the first $500.00 were to be paid at the end of the year. The first year of the program would be January 1, 1991 to December 31, 1991 and it would continue on an annual basis after that. Laiben kept track of the agents' earnings in a separate bonus account.

At the end of April, 1991, plaintiff surpassed $15,000.00 in earnings, entitling her to a $500.00 bonus which defendant paid to her in September, 1991. By September, 1991 plaintiff surpassed $32,400.00 in commissions.

At another sales meeting in September, 1991, Laiben indicated that bonuses would be paid at a banquet to be held in March of the following year instead of at the end of the year. Plaintiff asked if that meant that an agent had to be "here" in March in order to collect the bonus. Laiben indicated that was what it meant. Plaintiff testified that, at the time of the change in the bonus agreement, she had no intention of leaving defendant, but stayed with defendant until the end of 1991 in reliance on the promise of a bonus.

During 1991 plaintiff was contacted about joining Remax, another real estate brokerage firm. Although she was not initially interested, in January, 1992 she accepted a position with Remax and advised Laiben of her departure. Laiben informed her that she would not be receiving her bonus. At the end of 1991, plaintiff had total earnings of $75,638.47, which made her eligible for a combined bonus of $17,391.54. After placing her license with Remax, plaintiff finished closing four or five contracts that she had been working on prior to leaving defendant. In March, 1992 plaintiff sent a demand letter to defendant, seeking payment for the bonus she believed she had earned. Defendant did not pay plaintiff.

On December 17, 1992 plaintiff filed an action against defendant for breach of a bonus contract, seeking damages in the amount of $18,404.31. She amended this petition to include prejudgment interest. At trial Laiben denied that at the March meeting he had stated the bonuses would be paid at the end of the year and testified that at that meeting he had told the agents the bonuses would not be paid until the following March. The jury returned a verdict in favor of plaintiff and awarded her damages in the amount of $24,748.89. The court entered judgment in this amount.

In its first point defendant contends that the trial court erred in overruling its motions for directed verdict because plaintiff failed to make a submissible case of breach of the bonus agreement. In particular, defendant argues that plaintiff did not adduce sufficient evidence to establish a reasonable inference that 1) she tendered consideration to support defendant's offer of a bonus, or that 2) she accepted defendant's offer to give a bonus. *Issue #1*

A directed verdict is a drastic action and should only be granted where reasonable and honest persons could not differ on a correct disposition of the case. Seidel v. Gordon A. Gundaker Real Estate Co., 904 S.W.2d 357, 361 (Mo. App. 1995). In determining whether a plaintiff has made a submissible case in a contract action, we view the evidence in a light most favorable to plaintiff, presume plaintiff's evidence is true, and give plaintiff the benefit of all reasonable and favorable inferences to be drawn from the evidence. Gateway Exteriors Inc. v. Suntide Homes Inc., 882 S.W.2d 275, 279 (Mo. App. 1994).

Plaintiff adduced evidence of a unilateral contract offered in March, 1991 to pay a bonus under certain conditions at the end of the year. She also adduced evidence that in September, 1991 defendant attempted to revoke that offer and make the bonus contingent upon the agent's remaining until March of the following year.

A unilateral contract is a contract in which performance is based on the wish, will, or pleasure of one of the parties. Klamen v. Genuine Parts Co., 848 S.W.2d 38, 40 (Mo. App. 1993). A promisor does not receive a promise as consideration for his or her promise in a unilateral contract. Id. A unilateral contract lacks consideration for want of mutuality, but when the promisee performs, consideration is supplied, and the contract is enforceable to the extent performed. Leeson v. Etchison, 650 S.W.2d 681, 684 (Mo. App. 1983). An offer to make a unilateral contract is accepted when the requested performance is rendered. Nilsson v. Cherokee Candy & Tobacco Co., 639

S.W.2d 226, 228 (Mo. App. 1982). A promise to pay a bonus in return for an at-will employee's continued employment is an offer for a unilateral contract which becomes enforceable when accepted by the employee's performance. Id. at 228.

In the absence of any contract to the contrary, plaintiff could terminate her relationship with defendant at any time and was not obligated to earn a certain level of commissions. There was sufficient evidence that the bonus offer induced plaintiff to remain with defendant through the end of 1991 and to earn a high level of commissions for the court to submit the issue of acceptance by performance to the jury.

Defendant next argues that it was free to revoke the first offer with the second offer because, as of the time the second offer was made, plaintiff had not yet accepted the first offer. Defendant maintains that, because plaintiff did not stay until March, 1992, she did not accept the second offer and thus, did not earn the bonus.

Generally, an offeror may withdraw an offer at any time prior to acceptance unless the offer is supported by consideration. Coffman Industries, Inc. v. Gorman-Taber Co., 521 S.W.2d 763, 772 (Mo. App. 1975). However, an offeror may not revoke an offer where the offeree has made substantial performance. Id. (citing 1 Williston on Contracts, Third Edition Section 60A (1957)). *Coffman* set out the general rule of law as follows:

> Where one party makes a promissory offer in such form that it can be accepted by the rendition of the performance that is requested in exchange, without any express return promise or notice of acceptance in words, the offeror is bound by a contract just as soon as the offeree has rendered a substantial part of that requested performance.

1 Corbin on Contracts Section 49 (1952), quoted in *Coffman*, 521 S.W.2d at 772. The court stated the rationale for the rule as follows:

> The main offer includes a subsidiary promise, necessarily implied, that if part of the requested performance is given, the offeror will not revoke his offer, and that if tender is made it will be accepted. **Part performance** or tender may thus furnish consideration for the subsidiary promises. Moreover, merely acting in justifiable reliance on an offer may in some cases serve as sufficient reason for making a promise binding. (Emphasis supplied.)

Restatement [First] of Contracts Section 45 cmt. b (1932), quoted in *Coffman*, 521 S.W.2d at 772. Thus, in the context of an offer for unilateral contract, the offer may not be revoked where the offeree has accepted the offer by substantial performance. Id. at 771-72.

In this case there was evidence that, before the offer was modified in September, 1991, plaintiff had remained with defendant and had earned over $32,400.00 in commissions, making her eligible for the offered bonus. This constitutes sufficient evidence of substantial performance.

Plaintiff adduced evidence that defendant offered to pay a bonus at the end of 1991 if she would continue to work for it, that she stayed through 1991 with an intent to accept the offer, that she sold and listed enough property to qualify for all three bonus levels, that defendant knew of plaintiff's performance, that defendant paid $500.00 of the bonus but did not pay the remainder, and that she was damaged. This evidence was sufficient to make a submissible case for breach of a unilateral contract. Point one is denied.

. . .

MARY RHODES RUSSELL and JAMES R. DOWD, JJ., concur.

Notes and Questions

1. *Continuing evolution of unilateral contract theory.* We have already noted that §§31 and 45 of the first Restatement were aimed at minimizing the importance of the unilateral contract concept. Writing in 1938, Professor Karl Llewellyn sharply criticized the common law emphasis on the dichotomy between bilateral and unilateral contracts. He declared that "true" unilateral contracts—where the offeror seeks only performance and *not* a promise—were in fact so few in proportion to the ordinary run of commercial contracts that they should be viewed not as one-half of the contracting universe (as the classical categories would appear to suggest) but rather as aberrations—just a sideshow to the center ring of the contract circus. There were, Llewellyn conceded, a few types of true unilateral contracts; these would include offers of commissions to real estate brokers and the like, offers of rewards, etc. What these offers had in common, however, was not merely that acceptance could be made by performing, but the speculative nature of the offeree's performance: Where it is not at all certain that the offeree will be able to perform, *even if she wants to,* an offeror is unlikely to be interested in a mere promissory acceptance. What he wants is the specified performance; for that, and that alone, he is willing to pay the promised price. Professor Llewellyn's thesis is set forth throughout his article, On Our Case-Law of Contract: Offer and Acceptance (Pts. 1 & 2), 48 Yale L.J. 1, 779 (1938-1939), and is quoted and summarized in an article by Professor Mark Pettit, Jr., Modern Unilateral Contracts, 63 B.U. L. Rev. 551, 552-556 (1983). Influenced greatly by Professor Llewellyn's argument, the drafters of the Second Restatement abandoned the terminology he had attacked. Henceforth, they suggested, the terms *unilateral contract* and *bilateral contract* should generally be avoided, as "productive of confusion." See the Reporter's Note to Restatement (Second) §1, Comment *f.* Glimpses of the old unilateral contract can still be caught here and there in the revised Restatement, however. E.g., §32 (successor to former §31), Comment *b:* "Language or circumstances sometimes make it clear that the offeree is not to bind himself in advance of performance. . . . In such cases, the offer does not invite a promissory acceptance. . . ."

2. *Application to* **Cook.** Would the transaction in *Cook* fall within Professor Llewellyn's category of the "true" unilateral contract? Note that the court, referring to both Professors Williston and Corbin, indicates that in order to prevent revocation of the defendant's offer, plaintiff Cook had to have rendered "substantial" performance. Does §45 impose this requirement? Should it? (The phrase "substantial performance" has another application in determining remedies for breach of contract, which we will encounter later, in Chapter 10.)

3. *Modern use of unilateral contract analysis.* In his 1983 article, cited in Note 1, Professor Mark Pettit suggested that the obituary for the unilateral contract delivered in Restatement (Second) may have been a trifle premature. Despite the strictures of Professor Llewellyn and others, Pettit noted, judges persist in

using the unilateral contract analysis as a basis for decision. E.g., Abbott v. Schnader Harrison Segal & Lewis LLP, 2001 WL 819796 (Pa. Com. Pl.) (law firm's pension plan could not be unilaterally amended after partners had fulfilled service requirements; court cites and discusses Restatement (Second) §45 in justifying its decision). Having gone full circle from the classical days of Wormser and his Bridge, courts are now using unilateral contract analysis not to avoid liability but to *enforce* it, by imposing liability on an offeror in cases where no promissory acceptance was invited or required. These "new-style" unilateral contracts (Professor Pettit's phrase) do not involve performance by the offeree that is inherently speculative; they are simply cases in which the offeree is not necessarily committed to full performance. See Mark Pettit, Jr., Modern Unilateral Contracts, 3 B.U. L. Rev. 551, 577-583 (1983) (discussing employee benefit cases).

Comment: Remedies for Breach of Contract

As the reader is probably by now aware, the editors of these materials have chosen to postpone full discussion of remedies for breach of contract until later in the book, after the formation process and the principal defenses to contract enforcement have been surveyed. This is not uncommon among contracts casebooks, but some authors take other approaches; notable examples include John P. Dawson, William B. Harvey & Stanley D. Henderson, Contracts (8th ed. 2003) (remedies first), and Lon L. Fuller & Melvin A. Eisenberg, Basic Contract Law (8th ed. 2006) (remedies after consideration, but before formation). We continue to adhere to our basic plan of organization not merely because it has a certain chronological logic, but because we believe that the student's appreciation of the issues raised in a survey of remedial principles can be enhanced by prior exposure to the process by which agreements are made (by the parties) and obligations are defined (by the courts). On the other hand, we recognize that the most elementary Legal Realism requires some awareness even at this early stage of what is — and what is *not* — ordinarily entailed in the judicial enforcement of binding contractual obligations.

The conventional approach to contract enforcement is to award relief that will protect the plaintiff's "expectation interest" — the net value that the plaintiff expected to realize from due performance of the contract at issue. Other "interests," which contract remedies may attempt to protect, are the "restitution" and "reliance" interests — the extent to which the defendant has been enriched by, or the plaintiff injured by, plaintiff's actions in reliance on the defendant's commitment to perform. (These three remedial interests will be more fully defined and examined in Chapters 11 and 12.)

The simplest form of relief to protect the plaintiff's expectation interest would be an award of "specific performance" — ordering the defendant to cooperate with the plaintiff in exchanging performances as originally agreed to. As we shall see, however, such "specific" relief is often unavailable to the plaintiff in a contract action. Sometimes the defendant is simply unable to perform what she promised. (Recall our discussion of the possibility that the defendant in *Normile* might have found herself bound by two valid contracts to two separate buyers. Both contracts might have been enforceable, but only one buyer could have obtained specific performance; the other would have had to be content with a damage award.) Beyond that, specific relief in Anglo-American law is the exception, not the rule. For a variety of reasons—historical, theoretical, and practical—English and American courts have traditionally used as their primary vehicle for contract enforcement the award of money damages, computed if possible so as to give the plaintiff the economic equivalent of her net expectation under the contract.

In some situations, the court's award of money damages may have an effect much like specific performance, because payment of money was the defendant's performance obligation under the contract. This was the situation in Cook v. Coldwell Banker, where the defendant breached its promise to pay Cook her bonus. Where the defendant's obligation is something other than the payment of money, however, the court will ordinarily have to compute a money equivalent of the plaintiff's lost expectation. Thus, if a contractor breaches a contract with the owner to construct a residence, the owner will generally be entitled to recover the difference between the price for which the breaching contractor had agreed to perform the work and the price that the owner was required to pay another contractor to perform the same work. Ray v. William G. Eurice Bros., Inc., which presented the objective theory of contract earlier in this chapter, illustrates this aspect of expectation damages.

In Chapters 11 and 12, we will address directly some of the theoretical and practical problems involved in formulating remedies for breach of contract. In the meantime, as we move through a variety of cases illustrating issues of formation, validation, and excuse, keep an eye out for remedies issues as well. In the *Lonergan* case, for instance, the plaintiff lost because the court resolved the issues of offer and acceptance in favor of defendant Skolnick. Suppose instead that Lonergan had prevailed on those issues, so that Skolnick was indeed liable to Lonergan for wrongful breach of a contract to sell him Skolnick's California property. From the information available in the court's opinion in that case, what remedy might the court have awarded Lonergan?

4. Other Methods of Reaching Mutual Assent

The next case, Harlow & Jones, Inc. v. Advance Steel Co., provides your first extensive exposure to Article 2 of the Uniform Commercial Code (UCC). Before reading the case, an introduction to the UCC is useful. See also the text material in Chapter 1 and the Editors' Note to the UCC in the rules supplement.

One of the first issues you must consider in analyzing a contracts problem is whether Article 2 of the UCC or general common law principles govern the transaction. Article 2 of the UCC deals with transactions in "goods." UCC §2-102. (As discussed in Chapter 1, the ALI and the NCCUSL have adopted a revised version of Article 2, but as of late 2006, the revision had not been adopted by any state and its prospects are unclear. Accordingly, these materials cite both the prior version of Article 2, which remains governing law with some variations in all states, and Revised Article 2 when the revised version makes significant changes.)

Goods are generally defined as any tangible, moveable property, such as a car or a computer. Compare UCC §2-105(1), with Revised §2-103(1)(k). Article 2 does not cover contracts for the sale of real estate, contracts to provide services, or contracts to lease goods. (Article 2A, which has many provisions similar to Article 2, governs contracts for the lease of goods.) Article 2 does not cover contracts involving patents, trademarks, or other intellectual property.

Article 2 does apply, however, to both consumer and commercial sales of goods. Thus, if a consumer buys an automobile from a dealer (a consumer-merchant contract), Article 2 applies. If a person buys bric-a-brac from the owner at a yard sale (a consumer-consumer contract), Article 2 applies. If a hospital buys an MRI from the maker of the equipment (a merchant-merchant contract), Article 2 applies. Students often make the mistake of stating that Article 2 does not apply unless the parties to the contract are merchants. Certain provisions of the Article 2 apply only to merchants, but absent specific language in a particular section, Article 2 applies to all three types of contracts described above.

Even if Article 2 applies, this does not mean that common law principles are irrelevant. The drafters of Article 2 wrote against a common law background. To the extent that Article 2 specifically deals with a problem, then Article 2 controls. But if Article 2 does not cover an issue, then courts and lawyers must turn to common law principles to resolve the issue, even if the contract is one that is subject to Article 2. UCC §1-103(b) expresses this important principle regarding the relationship between Article 2 and the common law. To take one example, Article 2 often uses the term "offer," but it does not define the word. Thus, you must turn to common law principles (recall the *Lonergan* case) to determine if an offer has been made.

Sometimes a transaction may involve both the sale of goods and the provision of services. For example, when you take your car to be serviced, the dealer will typically sell you certain goods, for example oil to lubricate the car or replacement parts. In addition, the dealer charges you for the labor to repair the vehicle. Does the UCC apply to such a transaction? You can probably easily think of several possible approaches to this issue. We will return to this subject in connection with the *Princess Cruises* case later in this chapter.

Regardless of whether Article 2 applies, other statutory law may also govern the contract. For example, if a consumer buys an automobile from a dealer, Article 2 applies to the sale, but various consumer protection statutes may also apply. Similarly, a contract for the sale of real estate would not be subject to Article 2; general common law principles would control the contractual aspects of the transactions. However, a host of federal and state statutes also regulate the transaction.

Harlow & Jones, Inc. v. Advance Steel Co.
United States District Court
424 F.Supp. 770 (E.D. Mich. 1976)

MEMORANDUM OPINION

FEIKENS, District Judge.
This is an action in contract, brought by the seller, Harlow and Jones, Inc. (hereinafter "Harlow"), against the buyer, Advance Steel Co. (hereinafter

"Advance"), to recover damages and costs for an alleged breach of an agreement to purchase 1000 tons of imported European steel. Defendant denies liability, claiming that the shipment of steel was late and was therefore properly rejected under the contract. The parties agree that their respective rights and liabilities in this action are governed by the Uniform Commercial Code. The pertinent facts, as established by the testimony and exhibits presented at trial, are summarized:

In late June, 1974, Robert Stewart, president of Advance, had several telephone conversations with a William VanAs, an independent steel broker who is authorized to solicit orders on a commission basis from customers in the Great Lakes area on behalf of Harlow. During these conversations, VanAs informed Stewart of the availability of some 5000 metric tons of cold-rolled steel which Harlow could import from a West German mill for shipment during September–October, 1974. On July 2, 1974, Stewart advised VanAs that he was interested in purchasing 1000 tons of this shipment. The terms of the transaction were recorded by VanAs on his worksheet of July 2, 1974, and later that same day were relayed by VanAs to Carl Greve, president of Harlow.

On July 9, 1974, Greve mailed to Stewart a sales form, S–2373, confirming a sale of 1000 metric tons of cold-rolled steel, with shipment from a European port during September–October, 1974. That same day, Greve placed an order with Centro Stahlhandel GMBH for the 1000 tons and included a copy of its sales form to Advance. Stewart received Harlow's confirmation form but never signed or returned the enclosed copy as requested. On July 19, 1974, Stewart prepared a worksheet for the transaction in question, and on the basis of this worksheet prepared and mailed Advance's purchase order, B–04276, containing the same quantities, specifications (with minor revisions), and shipping dates as Harlow's confirmation form. Advance's purchase order was received by Harlow on July 25, 1974, but was never signed or returned.

The steel was shipped from Europe on three separate vessels. Approximately 214 tons were shipped on the M.S. Federal Lakes in September, 1974, and arrived in Detroit in October, 1974. Another 195 metric tons were shipped on the M.S. Ermis in October, 1974, and arrived in Detroit in early November, 1974. These two shipments were accepted and paid for by Advance. The balance of the steel was shipped from Antwerp on November 14, 1974, and arrived in Detroit on November 27, 1974. In a letter to Harlow dated October 29, 1974, Advance rejected this third shipment because of "late delivery." In a letter dated November 7, 1974, Harlow rejected Advance's cancellation and denied that a delay had yet developed which would justify Advance's action.

Further exchanges of correspondence ensued, with each party reaffirming its position that the other had breached its responsibilities under the contract. After arrival, the steel was warehoused in Detroit for a time and eventually sold at a loss by Harlow to other buyers, including Advance.

Harlow has taken the position throughout these proceedings that its sales confirmation form S–2373 of July 9, 1974 was an offer which defendant accepted by mailing back Advance purchase order form B–04276 on July 19, 1974.

. . .

Under this construction of the evidence, the terms of Harlow's S–2373 form would control. Specifically, there are a host of fine print terms on the back of this document which state that all delivery dates are approximate, contingent upon timely delivery by Harlow suppliers, and qualified by disclaimers of liability for "force majeure," acts of God, labor strikes, etc.[2]

Though no delivery date in fact appears on Harlow's S–2373, the form does specify a shipment date of "September–October, 1974." Harlow produced testimony from VanAs, Greve, and two disinterested local steel importers who all agreed that, according to an accepted steel importing trade usage, shipment in September–October means delivery in October–November. Since delivery here of the final shipment occurred before the end of November, Harlow contends that its shipping obligations were met and that Advance improperly and prematurely rejected this shipment on October 29. Harlow also sought to establish that the delay in shipment past the end of October was caused by bad weather, a Canadian pilot strike, and an accident in the Welland Canal — all contingencies which Harlow claims were unanticipated and beyond its control.

Advance takes the position that Harlow's sales form S–2373 was an offer which Advance rejected shortly after its receipt through a series of oral communications with VanAs. Stewart testified that he telephoned VanAs some time between July 9 and July 22 and informed him that he could not accept the boilerplate disclaimers regarding delivery on the back of Harlow's sales form and that VanAs had told him to just circle the objectionable terms and return the form. Stewart also testified to a second conversation with VanAs during this period in Stewart's office during which Stewart circled certain terms on the back of Harlow's S–2373 form and wrote on the front "delivery no later than October 31"; VanAs was reported to have said, "fine, no problem."

Advance contends that it had good reason to be concerned about the shipping dates. According to the testimony of Stewart and others, the market for steel was high and unstable during the summer and fall of 1974, and in any purchase of imported European steel, time was therefore of the essence.

2. 5. Delivery

(a) All delivery dates are approximate and not guaranteed.

(b) Time of delivery is indicated on the basis of a corresponding promise of delivery by our suppliers. We shall not be responsible in case of delays or failure to deliver on the part of our suppliers, unavailability of shipping space, changes of sailing schedules and/or diversion of steamer while in transit.

(c) If force majeure, acts of God, labor disturbances, or other causes beyond our control should result in delays or nondelivery on our part, or on the part of our suppliers, or of the manufacturers, we shall not be liable, and the buyer agrees to accept delivery within a reasonable time after the aforementioned circumstances cease to exist and correspondingly extend time of delivery. Any extra expenses incurred because of any delays or failure of buyer in accepting delivery shall be for buyer's account.

(d) "Force majeure" shall include fire, strikes, breakdown of machinery or accidents of any kind, any delay in, interference with or inability to obtain transportation, inability to obtain suitable insurance or any license or permit now or hereafter required; Municipal, State, Federal or any government action, regulation or prohibition effecting the production, transportation, sale or delivery of, any of the goods affected by this contract; the present or, any subsequent war conditions or any development thereof or any new outbreak of war; loss, destruction, or detention of ship, embargo; failure for any reason whatsoever of subcontractors, carriers, manufacturers or Seller's vendors to perform any contract relating to the goods hereby sold; or any and all causes beyond Seller's control.

S-2373
Harlow
would control

B-04276 - Advance
would control

A. Mutual Assent | 67

Having rejected the shipping terms contained in Harlow's sales form S–2373 for this reason, Advance argues that its purchase order B–04276, sent on July 22, 1974, was a counter-offer which Harlow accepted by making two partial shipments in October. Under this analysis, the terms of Advance's purchase order B–04276 would control. B–04276 contains a shipment date of "Sept–Oct 74," and further specifies that a failure to ship within this time allows Advance to cancel the order without notice.[3] Since these terms of shipment were bargained for and crucial, in Advance's view, and since the balance of the steel was not in fact shipped until November 14, Advance argues that its rejection of this last shipment was fully justified under the contract.

Each party has sought to establish that the terms of this agreement are governed by the provisions of its own contract form. This is certainly understandable, since both S–2373 and B–04276 provide ample disclaimers of liability for late shipment and delivery. But in taking these respective positions, both Harlow and Advance have misread the evidence. The court finds that an oral contract for the purchase of steel was formed before either party began sending or receiving written contract forms.

The court finds that an agreement to purchase the 1000 tons of European steel was made through the several telephone conversations between Stewart and VanAs during the week of July 2, 1974. Greve testified that much of the steel importing business is conducted by phone and that oral contracts are often made in this way and then later confirmed in writing. This method of contract formation is also recognized by the Uniform Commercial Code, §2-204(1):

> A contract for sale of goods may be made in any manner sufficient to show agreement, including conduct by both parties which recognizes the existence of such a contract.

The conduct of the parties here indicates a common understanding that the sale had been arranged as of July 9, 1974. Harlow apparently assumed such an understanding, since on July 9, 1974, it mailed an order to its German supplier for the 1000 tons and included the size and grade specifications which Advance had given to VanAs. Harlow's S–2373 form sent that same day could hardly be an offer to Advance then, especially since Harlow styled it as a sales confirmation form and never followed up on Advance's failure to sign and return it as requested.

Advance's conduct also corroborates the existence of an oral contract as of July 9. Advance has always taken the position that VanAs had at least apparent authority to negotiate contracts on behalf of Harlow, and this was apparently Stewart's understanding at the time of his telephone conversations with VanAs in early July, 1974. Stewart having indicated to VanAs during these conversations not only Advance's interest in purchasing 1000 tons of steel but also the various size and grade specifications and shipping dates which Advance wanted, it becomes difficult to accept his testimony that Advance had made no firm commitment to purchase at this point.

---

3. This order not valid unless acknowledged and accepted immediately. If the material is not shipped on or before the time specified herein, the purchaser has the privilege of cancelling without notice.

Advance's conduct upon receiving Harlow's confirmation form does not undercut the court's conclusion that an oral contract had already been negotiated at this point. Even if believed, Stewart's testimony indicates only an objection to S–2373's boilerplate terms regarding delivery and does not show any disagreement with Harlow's assertion in the cover letter to this form that a contract for the purchase of steel had already been agreed upon. It is worth noting that VanAs flatly denies the assertion that Stewart ever informed him that delivery was to be made by October 31, and VanAs denies that he ever agreed to any such modification of Harlow's sales confirmation. Stewart did not remember ever having mailed to Harlow the copy of S–2373 with Advance's written notation for delivery by October 31. Moreover, the purchase order form B–04276 which Advance did eventually send to Harlow on or about July 22, 1974 was admittedly prepared in reference to Harlow's sales form, yet contains no indication that delivery was to be made by this date.

Even though it is difficult to identify the exact point at which a binding contract was formed, that does not prevent the court from finding that an agreement was in fact made during the series of telephone conversations conducted by the parties between July 2 and July 9, 1974. U.C.C. §2-204 speaks directly to this point:

(2) An agreement sufficient to constitute a contract for sale may be found even though the moment of its making is undetermined.

The fact that shipping and delivery terms were not completely ironed out during oral negotiations is likewise unimportant. U.C.C. §2-204(3) provides:

(3) Even though one or more terms are left open, a contract for sale does not fail for indefiniteness if the parties have intended to make a contract and there is a reasonably certain basis for giving an appropriate remedy.

Having found that a contract to purchase the steel in question was made initially on an oral basis, the written forms sent by both parties must be construed as confirmatory memoranda. In order to determine the specifics of a contract formed in this manner, U.C.C. §2-207(3) provides for an integration of the parties' confirmations on the following basis:

(3) Conduct by both parties which recognizes the existence of a contract is sufficient to establish a contract for sale although the writings of the parties do not otherwise establish a contract. In such case the terms of the particular contract consist of those terms on which the writings of the parties agree, together with any supplementary terms incorporated under any other provisions of this Act.

There is in this case a substantial agreement between the confirmation forms of the parties. The forms contain the same price terms, weight and grade specifications (with one minor exception), and the same shipment date of September–October, 1974.

[The court went on to conclude that defendant Advance had breached the contract by rejecting the last shipment. Even though Harlow was required to ship the steel by the end of October, under UCC §2-504 Advance was entitled to reject this shipment only if there was a "material delay." Harlow introduced evidence that in the international steel trade, steel shipped by the end of October should arrive by the end of November. In this case, although the steel was shipped late, it did arrive in Detroit on November 29, so there was no material delay. — EDS.]

Notes and Questions

1. *Application of the UCC.* As discussed in the text preceding *Harlow & Jones*, the UCC applies to transactions in goods but not to services. Thus, Article 2 governed the contract between Harlow & Jones and Advance Steel for the sale of steel. The separate contract between Harlow & Jones and its sales agent, VanAs, however, was probably not subject to Article 2. While the goal of the contract was the sale of goods, the subject matter was a brokerage service rendered by VanAs.

2. *Contract formation under the UCC.* We have seen that under common law principles a contract requires a bargain in which there is a manifestation of mutual assent. We have also seen that the process of offer and acceptance is the typical way in which parties manifest mutual assent, at least in commercial contracts. Under the principles of offer and acceptance that we previously discussed, was a contract formed on the facts of the *Harlow & Jones* case? What principles of contract formation did you learn from the case? How do these principles compare to the common law principles we examined earlier?

3. *Oral contracts and the statute of frauds.* In *Harlow & Jones* the court found that a contract was formed under UCC §2-204(1) by "several telephone conversations between Stewart and VanAs during the week of July 2, 1974." Under the UCC a contract for the sale of goods of $500 or more must comply with the writing requirement of the UCC statute of frauds, UCC §2-201. Revised Article 2 raises the amount to $5,000. Chapter 4 examines the requirements of the UCC statute of frauds in more detail. It is sufficient for you to know at this point that the UCC does not necessarily require a formal signed contract in order to satisfy the statute of frauds, so even though there was no such document in the case, the requirements of the statute may still have been met.

4. *Battle of the forms, UCC §2-207.* In *Harlow & Jones* the parties exchanged conflicting documents, but neither party signed or agreed to the terms of the other party's document. The court did not have to resolve issues regarding conflicts between the documents because it found that the parties had agreed by their conduct to form a contract. We will address in more detail the problem of the battle of the forms later in this chapter.

Comment: Introduction to the CISG

We have previously referred several times to the Convention on Contracts for the International Sale of Goods (CISG), an international treaty to which the United States is a party. It is useful to think of the CISG as the international equivalent to Article 2 of the UCC. If a contract has international aspects, one of the first issues you must analyze is whether the CISG applies. For further discussion of the CISG see the Editors' Note to the CISG in the rules supplement.

Scope. The scope provisions of the CISG, however, are quite different from those of Article 2. First, the CISG generally applies to contracts for the sale of goods when the contracting parties have places of business in different countries that are signatories to the CISG. See Article 1(a). For a list of signatory countries see the Editors' Note to the CISG in the supplement. Most of the United States's major trading partners, with the exception of Japan and the UK, are parties to the CISG. Thus, if a Chinese garment manufacturer sells goods to a New York department store, the contract would be subject to the CISG. Keep in mind, however, that many foreign companies establish U.S. subsidiaries. A contract between a U.S. subsidiary of a Chinese company and a U.S. company would not be subject to the CISG. Second, unlike Article 2 of the UCC, which applies to sales of goods to consumers, the CISG excludes consumer transactions. See Article 2(a). Third, parties to an international contract that is otherwise subject to the CISG may by contract agree that the CISG does not apply and that some other source of law governs. See Article 6. Under the UCC the parties may, subject to some limitations, vary the provisions by agreement, but the parties do not have the power to exclude the application of the UCC entirely. UCC §1-302.

Contract formation under the CISG. When the *Harlow & Jones* case was decided in 1976 the CISG had not yet come into existence. If the CISG had been in effect, it would not have governed the contract between Harlow & Jones and Advance Steel because both were U.S. companies. Article 2 of the UCC controlled that transaction. Harlow & Jones brought the steel that it sold to Advance from a German company, Centro Stahlhandel GMBH (GMBH is the German abbreviation for their equivalent of a corporation, like our "Inc."). That transaction today would be subject to the CISG unless the parties agreed by contract to exclude the CISG pursuant to Article 6.

A problem on offer and acceptance under the CISG. Consider the following hypothetical based on the facts of *Harlow & Jones:* Suppose that the dispute that arose in the case between Advance Steel and Harlow & Jones had instead arisen between Advance Steel and Centro, the German steel manufacturer. In other words, assume the same facts except that Advance Steel dealt directly with Centro rather than with Harlow & Jones. Suppose also the dispute was taken to commercial arbitration rather than a court. (For a variety of legal and practical reasons, commercial arbitration is a common method of dispute resolution for international sales transactions.) The lawyer for Advance Steel makes the following argument to the arbitrators: "The CISG requires an offer and an acceptance in order for a contract to be formed. See Articles 14-24. In particular, Article 23 provides that a contract is concluded when an acceptance becomes effective. Advance Steel never accepted Centro's offer to sell steel. Instead, it made a counteroffer under Article 19. Centro never accepted Advance Steel's counteroffer. Therefore, no contract was formed between the parties and Advance Steel was not required to accept the last shipment of the steel." If you were the lawyer for Centro, how would you respond to this argument? In formulating your response, review Articles 7-13 of the CISG, as well as the provisions of Articles 14-24.

B. CONSIDERATION

Suppose the parties have mutually assented to form a contract, either through a process of offer and acceptance or some less formal method of assent. In the case of a bilateral contract, both of the parties will have made promises, while in a unilateral contract only one of the parties will be a promisor. Is the making of a promise when part of a process of mutual assent sufficient to result in the formation of a contract? Whatever may be the moral obligations that arise from the making of a promise, in the Anglo-American legal system the making of a promise is insufficient by itself to result in the formation of a contract. An additional requirement is necessary — the presence of "consideration."

This feature of Anglo-American law has not been without its vigorous critics. E.g., Wright, Ought the Doctrine of Consideration to Be Abolished from the Common Law?, 49 Harv. L. Rev. 1225 (1936); James D. Gordon III, A Dialogue about the Doctrine of Consideration, 75 Cornell L. Rev. 987 (1990); Andrew Kull, Reconsidering Gratuitous Promises, 21 J. Leg. Studies 39 (1992); see also Charles L. Knapp, The Promise of The Future — and Vice Versa: Some Reflections on the Metamorphosis of Contract Law, 82 Mich. L. Rev. 932 (1984) (reviewing E. Allan Farnsworth, Contracts (1st ed. 1982)). On the other hand, it has also had its defenders. E.g., Edwin W. Patterson, An Apology for Consideration, 58 Colum. L. Rev. 929 (1958). A particularly thoughtful and balanced evaluation of the consideration doctrine and all its various corollaries can be found in a pair of articles by Professor Mark B. Wessman, Should We Fire the Gatekeeper? An Examination of the Doctrine of Consideration, 48 U. Miami L. Rev. 45 (1993), and Retraining the Gatekeeper: Further Reflections on the Doctrine of Consideration, 29 Loyola L.A. L. Rev. 713 (1996).

International contract law recognizes that a contract can be formed simply by agreement without the additional requirement of consideration. The UNIDROIT Principles of International Commercial Contracts (2004) state: "A contract may be concluded either by the acceptance of an offer or by conduct of the parties that is sufficient to show agreement." Article 2.1.1. In international transactions covered by the CISG consideration is not required. See CISG Art. 23 (contract formed when acceptance of offer becomes effective) and Art. 11 (contract not subject to any requirements as to form).

The revised Restatement for the most part adheres to the doctrine of consideration in its traditional form; the drafters of the Uniform Commercial Code, while limiting its effect in some commercially important instances (e.g., §2-209(1), dealing with contract modification) did not attempt to repeal generally the law of consideration as it affects the sale of goods under Article 2 of the Code.

Despite the tendency of classically trained lawyers to regard consideration as the most obvious *sine qua non* of contractual obligation, however, the presence of consideration is not today — if indeed it ever was — the *only* basis on which liability for breach of a promise may rest. In the next chapter we will explore a variety of other circumstances that may cause such promissory liability to arise even in the absence of any "consideration," in the conventional legal sense of that term. Despite the possibility of alternatives to consideration as a basis for enforcement, however, the historical primacy of consideration doctrine in the classical contract system makes it of fundamental importance to our understanding of contractual obligation.

1. Defining Consideration

Hamer v. Sidway
New York Court of Appeals
124 N.Y. 538, 27 N.E. 256 (1891)

Appeal from order of the General Term of the Supreme Court in the fourth judicial department, made July 1, 1890, which reversed a judgment in favor of plaintiff entered upon a decision of the court on trial at Special Term and granted a new trial.

This action was brought upon an alleged contract.

The plaintiff presented a claim to the executor of William E. Story, Sr., for $5,000 and interest from the 6th day of February, 1875. She acquired it through several mesne assignments from William E. Story, 2d. The claim being rejected by the executor, this action was brought. It appears that William E. Story, Sr., was the uncle of William E. Story, 2d; that at the celebration of the golden wedding of Samuel Story and wife, father and mother of William E. Story, Sr., on the 20th day of March, 1869, in the presence of the family and invited guests he promised his nephew that if he would refrain from drinking, using tobacco, swearing and playing cards or billiards for money until he became twenty-one years of age he would pay him a sum of $5,000. The nephew assented thereto and fully performed the conditions inducing the promise. When the nephew arrived at the age of twenty-one years and on the 31st day of January, 1875, he wrote to his uncle informing him that he had performed his part of the agreement and had thereby become entitled to the sum of $5,000. The uncle received the letter and a few days later and on the sixth of February, he wrote and mailed to his nephew the following letter:

Buffalo, Feb. 6, 1875

W. E. Story, Jr.:

Dear Nephew—Your letter of the 31st ult. came to hand all right, saying that you had lived up to the promise made to me several years ago. I have no doubt but you have, for which you shall have five thousand dollars as I promised you. I had the money in the bank the day you was 21 years old that I intend for you, and you shall have the money certain. Now, Willie I do not intend to interfere with this money in any way till I think you are capable of taking care of it and the sooner that time comes the better it will please me. I would hate very much to have you start out in some adventure that you thought all right and lose this money in one year. . . . Willie, you are 21 and you have many a thing to learn yet. This money you have earned much easier than I did besides acquiring good habits at the same time and you are quite welcome to the money; hope you will make good use of it. I was ten long years getting this together after I was your age. Now, hoping this will be satisfactory, I stop. One thing more. Twenty-one years ago I bought you 15 sheep. These sheep were put out to double every four years. I kept track of them the first eight years; I have not heard much about them since. Your father and grandfather promised me that they would look after them till you were of age. Have they done so? I hope they have. By this time you have between five and six hundred sheep, worth a nice little income this spring. Willie, I have said much more than I expected to; hope you can make out what I have written. To-day is the seventeenth day that I have not been out of my room, and have had the doctor as many days. Am a little better to-day; think I will get out next week. You need not mention to father, as he always worries about small matters.

Truly Yours,
W. E. Story.

P.S.—You can consider this money on interest.

The nephew received the letter and thereafter consented that the money should remain with his uncle in accordance with the terms and conditions of the letters. The uncle died on the 29th day of January, 1887, without having paid over to his nephew any portion of the said $5,000 and interest.

PARKER, J. The question which provoked the most discussion by counsel on this appeal, and which lies at the foundation of plaintiff's asserted right of recovery, is whether by virtue of a contract defendant's testator William E. Story became indebted to his nephew William E. Story, 2d, on his twenty-first birthday in the sum of five thousand dollars. The trial court found as a fact that "on the 20th day of March, 1869, . . . William E. Story agreed to and with William E. Story, 2d, that if he would refrain from drinking liquor, using tobacco, swearing, and playing cards or billiards for money until he should become 21 years of age then he, the said William E. Story, would at that time pay him, the said William E. Story, 2d, the sum of $5,000 for such refraining, to which the said William E. Story, 2d, agreed," and that he "in all things fully performed his part of said agreement."

The defendant contends that the contract was without consideration to support it, and, therefore, invalid. He asserts that the promisee by refraining from the use of liquor and tobacco was not harmed but benefited; that that which he did was best for him to do independently of his uncle's promise, and insists that it follows that unless the promisor was benefited, the contract was without consideration. A contention, which if well founded, would seem to leave open for controversy in many cases whether that which the promisee did or omitted to do was, in fact, of such benefit to him as to leave no consideration to support the enforcement of the promisor's agreement. Such a rule could not be tolerated, and is without foundation in the law. The Exchequer Chamber, in 1875, defined consideration as follows: "A valuable consideration in the sense of the law may consist either in some right, interest, profit or benefit accruing to the one party, or some forbearance, detriment, loss or responsibility given, suffered or undertaken by the other." Courts "will not ask whether the thing which forms the consideration does in fact benefit the promisee or a third party, or is of any substantial value to anyone. It is enough that something is promised, done, forborne or suffered by the party to whom the promise is made as consideration for the promise made to him." (Anson's Prin. of Con. 63.)

"In general a waiver of any legal right at the request of another party is a sufficient consideration for a promise." (Parsons on Contracts, 444.)

"Any damage, or suspension, or forbearance of a right will be sufficient to sustain a promise." (Kent, vol. 2, 465, 12th ed.)

Pollock, in his work on contracts, page 166, after citing the definition given by the Exchequer Chamber already quoted, says: "The second branch of this judicial description is really the most important one. Consideration means not so much that one party is profiting as that the other abandons some legal right in the present or limits his legal freedom of action in the future as an inducement for the promise of the first."

Now, applying this rule to the facts before us, the promisee used tobacco, occasionally drank liquor, and he had a legal right to do so. That right he abandoned for a period of years upon the strength of the promise of the testator that for such forbearance he would give him $5,000. We need not speculate on the effort which may have been required to give up the use of those stimulants. It is sufficient that he restricted his lawful freedom of action within certain prescribed limits upon the faith of his uncle's agreement, and now having fully performed the conditions imposed, it is of no moment whether such performance actually proved a benefit to the promisor, and the court will not inquire into it, but were it a proper subject of inquiry, we see nothing in this record that would permit a determination that the uncle was not benefited in a legal sense. Few cases have been found which may be said to be precisely in point, but such as have been support the position we have taken.

In Shadwell v. Shadwell (9 C.B. [N.S.] 159), an uncle wrote to his nephew as follows:

My Dear Lancey —

I am so glad to hear of your intended marriage with Ellen Nicholl, and as I promised to assist you at starting, I am happy to tell you that I will pay you 150 pounds yearly during my life and until your annual income derived from your profession of a chancery barrister shall amount to 600 guineas, of which your own admission will be the only evidence that I shall require.

Your affectionate uncle,
Charles Shadwell.

It was held that the promise was binding and made upon good consideration.

In Lakota v. Newton, an unreported case in the Superior Court of Worcester, Mass., the complaint averred defendant's promise that "if you (meaning plaintiff) will leave off drinking for a year I will give you $100," plaintiff's assent thereto, performance of the condition by him, and demanded judgment therefor. Defendant demurred on the ground, among others, that the plaintiff's declaration did not allege a valid and sufficient consideration for the agreement of the defendant. The demurrer was over-ruled.

In Talbott v. Stemmons (a Kentucky case not yet reported), the step-grandmother of the plaintiff made with him the following agreement: "I do promise and bind myself to give my grandson, Albert R. Talbott, $500 at my death, if he will never take another chew of tobacco or smoke another cigar during my life from this date up to my death, and if he breaks his pledge he is to refund double the amount to his mother." The executor of Mrs. Stemmons demurred to the complaint on the ground that the agreement was not based on a sufficient consideration. The demurrer was sustained and an appeal taken therefrom to the Court of Appeals, where the decision of the court below was reversed. In the opinion of the court it is said that "the right to use and enjoy the use of tobacco was a right that belonged to the plaintiff and not forbidden by law. The abandonment of its use may have saved him money or contributed to his health, nevertheless, the surrender of that right caused the promise, and having the right to contract with reference to the subject-matter, the abandonment of the use was a sufficient consideration to uphold the promise." Abstinence from the use of intoxicating liquors was held to furnish a good consideration for a promissory note in Lindell v. Rokes (60 Mo. 249). . . .

[The defendant also argued that even if the uncle's promise had originally given rise to an enforceable obligation, the plaintiff's action to enforce that promise was barred by the statute of limitations — too much time had passed since the cause of action arose. The court held, however, that the uncle's letter amounted to a "declaration of trust," making the uncle himself a "trustee" of the promised sum on behalf of his nephew as "beneficiary." The case thus was viewed not as the mere attempt to enforce an executory promise, but as an action to compel the delivery of a sum of money held in trust; the uncle's original promise was viewed as having in a legal sense already been performed. — EDS.]

The order appealed from should be reversed and the judgment of the Special Term affirmed, with costs payable out of the estate.

All concur.

Order reversed and judgment of Special Term affirmed.

Notes and Questions

1. *Hypothetical variations of **Hamer**.* (a) Recall our discussion of Lucy v. Zehmer, in the notes following the Ray v. William G. Eurice & Bros., Inc. case. Suppose that when young Mr. Story turned 21 and wrote his uncle, the uncle had responded (truthfully) that his "promise" of $5000 had not been seriously intended, that it had been made only as a boast to impress the guests at the golden wedding celebration. Should the outcome of the case have been different?

(b) Suppose a modern-day *Hamer* case, in which the uncle, concerned about the effects of drug abuse, promises his fifteen-year-old nephew $5000 if he refrains from using such drugs as marijuana, heroin, or cocaine at least until the age of 21. Suppose the nephew initially promises to refrain, and keeps that promise until age 21, but by that time the uncle has died, and his estate resists payment. Should the promise be enforced? What would be the legal arguments for and against enforcement? What would the policy arguments be? If consulted by the uncle at the outset, could you suggest ways in which the eventual enforcement of such a promise might be made more likely?

2. *Historical background.* As we shall see, the test for consideration employed by the court in *Hamer* is not the only one a court might use; the Restatement uses a somewhat different approach, which we will encounter below. The "benefit/detriment" test used in *Hamer* has deep roots in Anglo-American contract law, however, as the following Comment attests.

Comment: History of the Consideration Doctrine

The origins of the modern consideration doctrine can be traced back at least to thirteenth-century English law. At that time the English courts did not yet recognize our modern concept of breach of contract. They did, however, enforce legal rights that were similar to those arising under contracts today. In particular, the English courts allowed two causes of action of a contractual nature: covenant and debt. Each of these had its own particular limitations.

The action of covenant was available only to enforce a promise made in writing and under seal. The "seal" at this stage was exceedingly formal: Typically, wax was melted onto the document and, before it cooled, was impressed with a signet ring or other device. The sealed document was often referred to as a "deed," or "specialty." Such documents were seldom employed in informal, day-to-day business affairs, so the action of covenant had limited utility for enforcing promises made in such transactions.

The action of debt had more practical importance, because it was available to enforce both formal promises (through the action of debt "sur obligation") and informal ones (debt "sur contract"). The debt action had a different limitation, however: It was unavailable unless the plaintiff claimed that he was owed a definite or certain sum of money. This limitation did not prevent the action of debt from being used to enforce informal promises, such as loans, purchases of goods, and agreements to pay for services rendered, so long as the plaintiff could claim a definite sum and could establish that the defendant had received a quid pro quo for the asserted debt.

Both covenant and debt were effective remedies for the cases in which they were available, but neither provided a useful remedy for the improper performance of an informal promise. For instance, suppose a nobleman took a piece of heirloom silver to a silversmith for repair, and the smith did the work improperly, damaging it further. The customer could not seek a remedy in the action of covenant, because the parties would not have used a sealed instrument for such a routine transaction. The action of debt would not lie, because the damage caused by the defective performance was not a definite sum.

In addition, the action of debt suffered from two further limitations. First, it was not available if the debtor had died in the meantime. More importantly, the court rules of the time permitted the defendant in a debt action to have the benefit of "wager of law." Under this procedure, the defendant could appear in court with "oath-helpers" (usually 11 in number), each of whom would swear that the defendant was not indebted to the plaintiff. If the defendant successfully performed this ceremony, he won his case. Obviously, the less scrupulous the debtor (and his friends), the greater the likelihood that the debt would go uncollected.

Because of these shortcomings, the actions of covenant and debt were gradually replaced during the fifteenth and sixteenth centuries by a new action, called "assumpsit." Assumpsit eventually became the general remedy for breach of promise. Like most changes in the common law system, this one came incrementally. In the fourteenth century, the English courts had recognized the action for damages resulting from a wrongful act (what today we would call a "tort"). This action, known as "trespass," originally applied to public wrongs, such as breach of the peace. Later, in the form of "trespass on the case," it was extended to apply to private wrongs as well. Thus, an action in trespass on the case would lie for the nonperformance of an obligation voluntarily undertaken (such as the silversmith's promise of repair). The action in such cases came to be known as assumpsit, because the pleading alleged that the defendant had "assumed" — that is, voluntarily undertaken — the obligation of performance.

By the year 1400 it was well established that assumpsit could be used to recover damages for improper performance of a voluntary obligation. The English courts, however, distinguished between "misfeasance" (improper performance) and "nonfeasance" (failure to render any performance at all). Assumpsit was only available to remedy the former. For nonfeasance, plaintiff was remitted to an action of covenant, where he could recover only if he could produce a specialty. Throughout the fifteenth century, a number of exceptions to this rule accumulated, permitting assumpsit to be used for various types of mere nonfeasance. By the first quarter of the sixteenth century, the rule disappeared entirely, and the plaintiff was generally permitted to recover for either misfeasance or nonfeasance without producing a sealed document. Assumpsit had completely superseded covenant.

The use of assumpsit instead of an action for debt had obvious attraction for the unpaid creditor, because of the procedural advantage enjoyed by the defendant in a debt action. Defendants' attorneys therefore objected strenuously when plaintiffs attempted to bring an assumpsit in any case where an action of debt would be available. This heated dispute was ultimately resolved by the Exchequer Chamber in Slade's Case, 76 Eng. Rep. 1074 (1602), which held that plaintiff might elect between assumpsit and debt in any case where both would lie. The natural consequence was that assumpsit effectively replaced debt as well.

Once assumpsit had taken over the field of contractual obligation, the English courts faced another question: What should be its scope? Both covenant and debt were limited by specific requirements — the production of a sealed instrument and the obligation to pay a sum certain, incurred in exchange for a quid pro quo. Assumpsit did not have these limitations, but it did develop limitations of its own. These came to be expressed in the doctrine of consideration, which — like the action of assumpsit itself — developed incrementally. As assumpsit evolved, it became customary to plead the factors that the defendant considered in making his promise. Over time the process of pleading such "considerations" grew into a formal requirement. Case decisions gradually outlined the kinds of consideration for which an action in assumpsit would lie. The concepts of detriment to the promisee and benefit to the promisor, which were used quite early, came to represent the paradigms of consideration. The historical link is not clear, but at least it can be said that the "detriment" suffered by the promisee has a resemblance to the harm suffered by the plaintiff in the early trespass action, while the "benefit" to the promisor is akin to the quid pro quo received by the defendant in a debt action. Even today, courts will use these concepts to describe the factors in a case that justify the finding of sufficient consideration to support liability for breach of a promise. Accounts of the development of the consideration doctrine can be found in the writings of many legal historians. One in-depth exploration is contained in Alfred W. B. Simpson, A History of the Common Law of Contract (1987).

Pennsy Supply, Inc. v. American Ash Recycling Corp. of Pennsylvania
Pennsylvania Superior Court
895 A.2d 595 (2006)

Before: Joyce, Orie Melvin and Tamila, JJ.
Opinion by Orie Melvin, J.:

1. Appellant, Pennsy Supply, Inc. ("Pennsy"), appeals from the grant of preliminary objections in the nature of a demurrer in favor of Appellee, American Ash Recycling Corp. of Pennsylvania ("American Ash"). We reverse and remand for further proceedings.

2. The trial court summarized the allegations of the complaint as follows:

The instant case arises out of a construction project for Northern York High School (Project) owned by Northern York County School District (District) in York County, Pennsylvania. The District entered into a construction contract for the Project with a general contractor, Lobar, Inc. (Lobar). Lobar, in turn, subcontracted the paving of driveways and a parking lot to [Pennsy].

The contract between Lobar and the District included Project Specifications for paving work which required Lobar, through its subcontractor Pennsy, to use certain base aggregates. The Project Specifications permitted substitution of the aggregates with an alternate material known as Treated Ash Aggregate (TAA) or AggRite.

The Project Specifications included a "notice to bidders" of the availability of AggRite at no cost from [American Ash], a supplier of AggRite. The Project Specifications also included a letter to the Project architect from American Ash confirming the availability of a certain amount of free AggRite on a first come, first served basis.

Pennsy contacted American Ash and informed American Ash that it would require approximately 11,000 tons of AggRite for the Project. Pennsy subsequently picked up the AggRite from American Ash and used it for the paving work, in accordance with the Project Specifications.

Pennsy completed the paving work in December 2001. The pavement ultimately developed extensive cracking in February 2002. The District notified . . . Lobar[] as to the defects and Lobar in turn directed Pennsy to remedy the defective work. Pennsy performed the remedial work during summer 2003 at no cost to the District.

The scope and cost of the remedial work included the removal and appropriate disposal of the AggRite, which is classified as a hazardous waste material by the Pennsylvania Department of Environmental Protection. Pennsy requested American

Ash to arrange for the removal and disposal of the AggRite; however, American Ash did not do so. Pennsy provided notice to American Ash of its intention to recover costs.

Trial Court Opinion, 5/27/05, at 1-3 (footnote omitted). Pennsy also alleged that the remedial work cost it $251,940.20 to perform and that it expended an additional $133,777.48 to dispose of the AggRite it removed. Compl. ¶¶ 26, 29.

3. On November 18, 2004, Pennsy filed a five-count complaint against American Ash alleging breach of contract (Count I); breach of implied warranty of merchantability (Count II); breach of express warranty of merchantability (Count III); breach of warranty of fitness for a particular purpose (Count IV); and promissory estoppel (Count V). American Ash filed demurrers to all five counts. Pennsy responded and also sought leave to amend should any demurrer be sustained. The trial court sustained the demurrers by order and opinion dated May 25, 2005, and dismissed the complaint. This appeal followed.

4. Pennsy raises three questions for our review:

. . .

(2) Whether Pennsy's relief of [American Ash's] legal obligation to dispose of a material classified as hazardous waste, such that [American Ash] avoided the costs of disposal thereof at a hazardous waste site, is sufficient consideration to ground contract and warranty claims.

. . .

Appellant's Brief at 3.

5. "Preliminary objections in the nature of a demurrer test the legal sufficiency of the complaint." Hospodar v. Schick, 885 A.2d 986, 988 (Pa. Super. 2005).

When reviewing the dismissal of a complaint based upon preliminary objections in the nature of a demurrer, we treat as true all well-pleaded material, factual averments and all inferences fairly deducible therefrom. Where the preliminary objections will result in the dismissal of the action, the objections may be sustained only in cases that are clear and free from doubt. To be clear and free from doubt that dismissal is appropriate, it must appear with certainty that the law would not permit recovery by the plaintiff upon the facts averred. Any doubt should be resolved by a refusal to sustain the objections. Moreover, we review the trial court's decision for an abuse of discretion or an error of law.

Id. In applying this standard to the instant appeal, we deem it easiest to order our discussion by count.

6. Count I raises a breach of contract claim. "A cause of action for breach of contract must be established by pleading (1) the existence of a contract, including its essential terms, (2) a breach of a duty imposed by the contract and (3) resultant damages." Corestates Bank, N.A. v. Cutillo, 723 A.2d 1053, 1058 (Pa. Super. 1999). While not every term of a contract must be stated in complete detail, every element must be specifically pleaded. Id. at 1058. Clarity is particularly important where an oral contract is alleged. Snaith v. Snaith, 422 A.2d 1379, 1382 (Pa. Super. 1980).

7. Instantly, the trial court determined that "any alleged agreement between the parties is unenforceable for lack of consideration." Trial Court

Opinion, 5/27/05, at 5. The trial court also stated "the facts as pleaded do not support an inference that disposal costs were part of any bargaining process *or* that American Ash offered the AggRite with an intent to avoid disposal costs." Id. at 7 (emphasis added). Thus, we understand the trial court to have dismissed Count I for two reasons related to the necessary element of consideration: one, the allegations of the Complaint established that Pennsy had received a conditional gift from American Ash, see Id. 6, 8, and, two, there were no allegations in the Complaint to show that American Ash's avoidance of disposal costs was part of any bargaining process between the parties. See Id. at 7.

8. It is axiomatic that consideration is "an essential element of an enforceable contract." Stelmack v. Glen Alden Coal Co., 339 Pa. 410, 414-415, 14 A.2d 127, 128 (1940). See also Weavertown Transport Leasing, Inc v. Moran, 834 A.2d 1169, 1172 (Pa. Super. 2003) (stating, "[a] contract is formed when the parties to it (1) reach a mutual understanding, (2) exchange consideration, and (3) delineate the terms of their bargain with sufficient clarity"). Consideration consists of a benefit to the promisor or a detriment to the promisee." *Weavertown*, 834 A.2d at 1172 (citing *Stelmack*). "Consideration must actually be bargained for as the exchange for the promise." *Stelmack*, 339 Pa. at 414, 14 A.2d at 129.

> It is not enough, however, that the promisee has suffered a legal detriment at the request of the promisor. The detriment incurred must be the "quid pro quo", or the "price" of the promise, and the inducement for which it was made. . . . If the promisor merely intends to make a gift to the promisee upon the performance of a condition, the promise is gratuitous and the satisfaction of the condition is not consideration for a contract. The distinction between such a conditional gift and a contract is well illustrated in Williston on Contracts, Rev. Ed., Vol. 1, Section 112, where it is said: "If a benevolent man says to a tramp, 'If you go around the corner to the clothing shop there, you may purchase an overcoat on my credit,' no reasonable person would understand that the short walk was requested as the consideration for the promise, but that in the event of the tramp going to the shop the promisor would make him a gift."

Weavertown, 834 A.2d at 1172 (quoting *Stelmack*, 339 Pa. at 414, 14 A.2d at 128-29). Whether a contract is supported by consideration presents a question of law. Davis & Warde, Inc. v. Tripodi, 616 A.2d 1384 (Pa. Super. 1992).

9. The classic formula for the difficult concept of consideration was stated by Justice Oliver Wendell Holmes, Jr., as "the promise must induce the detriment and the detriment must induce the promise." John Edward Murray, Jr., Murray on Contracts §60 (3d. ed. 1990), at 227 (citing Wisconsin & Michigan Ry. v. Powers, 191 U.S. 379 (1903)). As explained by Professor Murray:

> If the promisor made the promise for the purpose of inducing the detriment, the detriment induced the promise. *If, however, the promisor made the promise with no particular interest in the detriment that the promisee had to suffer to take advantage of the promised gift or other benefit, the detriment was incidental or conditional to the promisee's receipt of the benefit.* Even though the promisee suffered a detriment induced by the

promise, the purpose of the promisor was not to have the promisee suffer the detriment because she did not seek that detriment in exchange for her promise.

Id. §60.C, at 230 (emphasis added). This concept is also well summarized in American Jurisprudence:

> As to the distinction between consideration and a condition, it is often difficult to determine whether words of condition in a promise indicate a request for consideration or state a mere condition in a gratuitous promise. An aid, though not a conclusive test, in determining which construction of the promise is more reasonable is an inquiry into *whether the occurrence of the condition would benefit the promisor. If so, it is a fair inference that the occurrence was requested as consideration.* On the other hand, if the occurrence of the condition is no benefit to the promisor but is merely to enable the promisee to receive a gift, the occurrence of the event on which the promise is conditional, though brought about by the promisee in reliance on the promise, is not properly construed as consideration.

17A Am. Jur. 2d §104 (2004 & 2005 Supp.) (emphasis added). See also Restatement (Second) of Contracts §71 comment c (noting "the distinction between bargain and gift may be a fine one, depending on the motives manifested by the parties"); Carlisle v. T & R Excavating, Inc., 704 N.E.2d 39 (Ohio App. 1997) (discussing the difference between consideration and a conditional gift and finding no consideration where promisor who promised to do excavating work for preschool being built by ex-wife would receive no benefit from wife's reimbursement of his material costs).

10. Upon review, we disagree with the trial court that the allegations of the Complaint show only that American Ash made a conditional gift of the AggRite to Pennsy. In paragraphs 8 and 9 of the Complaint, Pennsy alleged:

> American Ash actively promotes the use of AggRite as a building material to be used in base course of paved structures, and provides the material free of charge, in an effort to have others dispose of the material and thereby avoid incurring the disposal costs itself . . . American Ash provided the AggRite to Pennsy for use on the Project, which saved American Ash thousands of dollars in disposal costs it otherwise would have incurred.

Compl. ¶¶ 8, 9. Accepting these allegations as true and using the Holmesian formula for consideration, it is a fair interpretation of the Complaint that American Ash's promise to supply AggRite free of charge induced Pennsy to assume the detriment of collecting and taking title to the material, and critically, that it was this very detriment, whether assumed by Pennsy or some other successful bidder to the paving subcontract, which induced American Ash to make the promise to provide free AggRite for the project. Paragraphs 8-9 of the Complaint simply belie the notion that American Ash offered AggRite as a conditional gift to the successful bidder on the paving subcontract for which American Ash desired and expected nothing in return.

11. We turn now to whether consideration is lacking because Pennsy did not allege that American Ash's avoidance of disposal costs was part of any bargaining process between the parties. The Complaint does not allege that the parties discussed or even that Pennsy understood at the time it requested

or accepted the AggRite that Pennsy's use of the AggRite would allow American Ash to avoid disposal costs.[5] However, we do not believe such is necessary. The bargain theory of consideration does not actually require that the parties bargain over the terms of the agreement. . . . According to Holmes, an influential advocate of the bargain theory, what is required [for consideration to exist] is that the promise and the consideration be in "the relation of reciprocal conventional inducement, each for the other." Allen Farnsworth, Farnsworth on Contracts §2.6 (1990) (citing O. Holmes, The Common Law 293-94 (1881)); see also Restatement (Second) of Contracts §71 (defining "bargained for" in terms of the Holmesian formula). Here, as explained above, the Complaint alleges facts which, if proven, would show the promise induced the detriment and the detriment induced the promise. This would be consideration. Accordingly, we reverse the dismissal of Count I.

[The court went on to hold that the trial court also erred in dismissing the counts for breach of warranty under the UCC and for promissory estoppel.]

22. For all of the foregoing reasons, we reverse the trial court's order granting the demurrers and dismissing the Complaint and remand for further proceedings. Jurisdiction relinquished.

Notes and Questions

1. *Disposal costs.* It may seem odd that Pennsy Supply sought to recover the costs it incurred to dispose of the AggRite when it claimed that the consideration for its contract with American Ash was that it relieved American Ash of disposal costs. However, Pennsy planned on using the AggRite in paving work, which did not involve any disposal expenses. The only reason Pennsy incurred these costs was that the AggRite was defective, requiring its removal and disposal. Put another way: Pennsy agreed to take the AggRite "off American Ash's hands," but it did not agree to dispose of the AggRite and pay the resulting disposal costs.

2. *Pennsy's claims for breach of warranty under Article 2.* Pennsy's complaint alleged causes of action for breach of various warranties under Article 2 of the UCC. We will examine these warranties in Chapter 6. Most courts have limited Article 2 warranties to contracts for the sale of goods. (Article 2A, dealing with leasing transactions, imposes somewhat similar warranties.) If the court had accepted American Ash's contention that it made only a conditional gift to Pennsy, then Pennsy would have been unable to recover on these theories, although it might still have had a claim for promissory estoppel, which, as we will see in the next chapter, does not depend on the existence of a contract between the parties.

5. Pennsy's complaint, by placing the allegation in ¶ 8 that American Ash promotes AggRite and provides it free of charge, before the allegations in ¶¶ 9-10 related to formation of the oral contract, is arguably structured to suggest Pennsy did contemplate American Ash's avoidance of disposal costs. We note also that during oral argument on the preliminary objections, Pennsy's counsel represented "it was understood by everybody that this [i.e., avoidance of disposal costs] was what American Ash was getting in return for [providing the AggRite for free]." Transcript of Proceedings, Feb. 1, 2005, at 14-15.

3. *Consideration or condition to a gift.* The trial court had held that Pennsy's disposal costs did not constitute consideration because these costs were a mere condition to American Ash's gift of AggRite to Pennsy. The appellate court rejects this conclusion. (Notice that the court states that the presence of consideration is a question of law for the court to decide; courts in other jurisdictions might treat this matter differently, leaving it up to the jury to decide whether a contract is present based on the court's instructions about the requirements for contract formation.) The distinction between conduct that constitutes consideration and conduct that is a condition to a gift is not a clear one because the very same conduct may be consideration or a condition to a gift depending on how the parties treat the conduct. (Williston's reference to a "tramp" sounds a little archaic today, and perhaps ambiguous as well. As Williston used it, synonyms would be "hobo" or "vagrant"; today we might simply say "homeless person".) What test does the court use to distinguish between consideration and a condition to a gift? Can you think of other factors that should be relevant in determining whether conduct constitutes consideration rather than a condition to a gift?

4. *Relationship of the benefit/detriment test and bargain theory of consideration.* Citing prior case law, the court holds that consideration requires a benefit to the promisor or a detriment to the promise that is bargained for. See also Cobaugh v. Klick-Lewis, Inc., 561 A.2d 1248, 1250 (Pa. Super. Ct. 1989) (golfer who shot hole-in-one entitled to car offered by defendant as prize; court applies both bargained-for-exchange and benefit/detriment tests for consideration). In other words, benefit or detriment are insufficient to constitute consideration. Notice, however, that according to the court in *Pennsy Supply* the requirement that consideration be bargained for does not require actual bargaining between the parties. The court uses the Holmesian test of "reciprocal conventional inducement, each for the other." Under this test American Ash affirmatively sought companies to take AggRite so that American Ash could avoid the disposal costs of this material. Correspondingly, Pennsy's assumption of this disposal obligation induced American Ash to deliver AggRite to it. Thus, each party's promise and resulting performance induced the corresponding promise and performance by the other party.

You will probably read other cases in which the test for consideration is stated differently than the test used by the court in *Pennsy Supply*. Some courts may simply refer to benefit to the promisor or detriment to the promisee without mentioning the bargain theory. Such a statement probably occurs when the court is giving a general statement of the requirements for a contract, but the facts of the case do not raise an issue regarding whether the benefit or the detriment was bargained for.

At the other extreme you will find courts that simply refer to the bargain theory of consideration without mentioning benefit or detriment. For example, in Baehr v. Penn-O-Tex Oil Corp., 104 N.W.2d 661 (1960), the court stated:

Consideration requires that a contractual promise be the product of a bargain. However, in this usage, "bargain" does not mean an exchange of things of equivalent, or any, value. It means a negotiation resulting in the voluntary assumption of an obligation by one party upon condition of an act or forbearance by the other. Consideration thus insures that the promise enforced as a contract is not accidental, casual, or gratuitous, but has been uttered intentionally as the result of some deliberation, manifested by reciprocal bargaining or negotiation. In this view, the requirement of consideration is no mere technicality, historical anachronism, or arbitrary formality. It is an attempt to be as reasonable as we can in deciding which promises constitute contracts. Id. at 665.

Notice that the court in *Baehr*, unlike the court in *Pennsy Supply*, does not mention benefit or detriment. The Restatement (Second) in §71 adopts the bargain theory of consideration and in §79 it rejects any additional requirement of benefit or detriment. The court in *Baehr*, also unlike the court in *Pennsy Supply*, seems to require actual negotiation between the parties. On this issue, the Restatement appears to agree with *Pennsy Supply* that actual negotiation is not required. Restatement §71(2) states that a "performance or return promise is bargained for if it is sought by the promisor in exchange for his promise and is given by the promise in exchange for that promise." Comment *b* to §71 adopts the Holmesian test of a "reciprocal relation of motive or inducement." Which view on the issue of negotiation do you think is better as a matter of policy? Consider the functions performed by legal formalities discussed in note 7 below.

5. *Practical effect of different tests for consideration.* For the student attempting to grapple with the niceties of consideration theory, developed over centuries of obscure and often inconsistent case law and commentary, a spoonful of Legal Realism may at this point help the doctrinal medicine go down. In the vast majority of real-world cases, it will be unnecessary to worry unduly about whether a benefit/detriment or a bargained-for-exchange test for consideration is employed, because the ordinary commercial contract will pass both tests with flying colors. Take for example a contract to sell a parcel of real estate for cash, where the parties exchange promises that at some future date they will exchange performances—cash from the purchaser in return for a conveyance of land from the vendor. Will the parties at that point be bound by their promises? The law's traditional answer is yes. Even if both parties do no more than exchange promises of future performance, the law regards the making of a (non-"illusory") promise as sufficient legal "detriment" to bind the promisee to perform a return promise of his own, under the benefit/detriment test for consideration. (Of course, the purchaser at the time of signing such an agreement is likely to pay the vendor a sum of money, either as a "down payment" or as "earnest money," but that payment, while it furnishes additional consideration for the vendor's promise to sell, is not necessary to bind the vendor to her bargain.) On the other hand, if the Holmes "bargain" test is applied, the answer is the same: This land-purchase transaction would obviously be viewed as a bargained-for exchange and thus would be supported by consideration. See Restatement (Second) §§71, 77.

In light of the above analysis, the choice between the "benefit/detriment" and "bargained-for exchange" tests for consideration will ordinarily have little effect on the outcome of the question: Is this promise enforceable? As Professor Farnsworth has pointed out, the principal effect of Holmes's doctrinal shift to the "bargain" test seems to be at the margin: Promises made in a family setting, or otherwise "on the periphery of the marketplace," might under the bargain theory be more likely to go unenforced, as non-exchange transactions. By the same token, reliance on a promise, no matter how truly "detrimental," would unless bargained for as the price of that promise fail the consideration test. Such reliance would thus go uncompensated, unless some other theory of liability should apply. E. Allan Farnsworth, Contracts 48 (4th ed. 2004). In the next chapter we will explore the concept of "promissory estoppel," which may protect detrimental reliance that was not bargained for.

6. *The **Newman & Snells Bank** case.* Even if most cases would be decided the same under either test for consideration, there are situations where the choice could make a difference. In Newman & Snell's Bank v. Hunter, 220 N.W. 665 (Mich. 1928), a widow was sued by the bank to enforce her promise to pay her late husband's debt to the plaintiff bank; in exchange for that promise, the bank had surrendered to her his promissory note evidencing the debt. As the deceased husband had died insolvent, the bank had no way of collecting the debt from his estate, and the defendant would not have been personally liable on the debt unless she voluntarily obligated herself to pay it. The court denied enforcement, on the ground that because the note was worthless, its surrender could be no detriment to the bank and its receipt no benefit to the defendant. If the transaction were viewed purely from the "bargain" standpoint, however, it could be argued that the widow got what she bargained for—her husband's promissory note. Here again, however, legal realism requires us to recognize that under either test, judgment for the bank could have been rationalized by a court so inclined. (Even if the note could not in fact have been enforced, physically surrendering it to the widow was something the bank was certainly free *not* to do.) On the other hand, whatever the niceties of doctrine, the possibility that the plaintiff knowingly took advantage of the defendant's grief and ignorance of the law seems strong enough to suggest that denial of recovery was appropriate, whether that result be justified on grounds of lack of consideration, or on some other basis, such as wrongful nondisclosure or undue influence, defenses that we will examine later in these materials.

7. *The functions of legal formality.* Although our legal system is less concerned in general with matters of "form" than was the old English common law, there are even today some formalities that do have a particular legal effect when properly employed. The execution of a will is one example; another is the marriage ceremony. In the early days of English law, the seal was employed as a means of creating a binding contractual obligation. Today, however, the seal has little or no force in most jurisdictions, and promises are not generally enforceable merely because "formally" expressed, with or without the presence of a seal. For a recent survey of the present-day law regarding the use of seals, see Eric Mills Holmes, Stature and Status of a Promise under Seal as a Legal Formality, 29 Willamette L. Rev. 617 (1993). Although clearly out of fashion today, the seal in its heyday did offer a clearly defined method by which persons seeking to create a legally enforceable promise could do so with confidence in its effectiveness. Building on the notion that formality as a legal device does have its uses, Professor Lon Fuller offered in 1941 the following analysis of the functions that a legal formality may serve:

The Functions Performed by Legal Formalities

The Evidentiary Function. — The most obvious function of a legal formality is, to use Austin's words, that of providing "evidence of the existence and purport of the contract, in case of controversy." The need for evidentiary security may be satisfied in a variety of ways: by requiring a writing, or attestation, or the certification of a notary. It may even be satisfied, to some extent, by such a device as the Roman *stipulatio*, which compelled an oral spelling out of the promise in a manner sufficiently ceremonious to impress its terms on participants and possible bystanders.

The Cautionary Function. — A formality may also perform a cautionary or deterrent function by acting as a check against inconsiderate action. The seal in its original form fulfilled this purpose remarkably well. The affixing and impressing of a wax wafer — symbol in the popular mind of legalism and weightiness — was an excellent device for inducing the circumspective frame of mind appropriate in one pledging his future. To a less extent any requirement of a writing, of course, serves the same purpose, as do requirements of attestation, notarization, etc.

The Channeling Function. — Though most discussions of the purposes served by formalities go no further than the analysis just presented, this analysis stops short of recognizing one of the most important functions of form. That a legal formality may perform a function not yet described can be shown by the seal. The seal not only insures a satisfactory memorial of the promise and induces deliberation in the making of it. It serves also to mark or signalize the enforceable promise; it furnishes a simple and external test of enforceability. This function of form Ihering described as "the facilitation of judicial diagnosis," and he employed the analogy of coinage in explaining it. . . .

Interrelations of the Three Functions. — Though I have stated the three functions of legal form separately, it is obvious that there is an intimate connection between them. Generally speaking, whatever tends to accomplish one of these purposes will also tend to accomplish the other two. He who is compelled to do something which will furnish a satisfactory memorial of his intention will be induced to deliberate. Conversely, devices which induce deliberation will usually have an evidentiary value. Devices which insure evidence or prevent inconsiderateness will normally advance the desideratum of channeling, in two different ways. In the first place, he who is compelled to formulate his intention carefully will tend to fit it into legal and business categories. In this way the party is induced to canalize his own intention. In the second place, wherever the requirement of a formality is backed by the sanction of the invalidity of the informal transaction (and this is the means by which requirements of form are normally made effective), a degree of channeling results automatically. Whatever may be its legislative motive, the formality in such a case tends to effect a categorization of transactions into legal and non-legal.

Just as channeling may result unintentionally from formalities directed toward other ends, so these other ends tend to be satisfied by any device which accomplishes a channeling of expression. There is an evidentiary value in the clarity and definiteness of contour which such a device accomplishes. Anything which effects a neat division between the legal and the non-legal, or between different kinds of legal transactions, will tend also to make apparent to the party the consequences of his action and will suggest deliberation where deliberation is needed.

Lon L. Fuller, Consideration and Form, 41 Colum. L. Rev. 799, 800-803 (1941). Professor Fuller's article goes on to argue that although the seal for various reasons has "decayed," the doctrine of consideration can and often does serve one or all of the above functions that the seal used to serve. More recent writers have been skeptical of Fuller's "functions of form" thesis. E.g., Andrew Kull, Reconsidering Gratuitous Promises, 21 J. Legal Studies 39, 51-55 (1992) (seal may have served such functions well, but consideration doctrine does so so poorly that the absence of consideration should not be a conclusive argument against enforcement of a promise). Does the requirement of consideration serve the evidentiary, cautionary, and channeling functions?

Professor Duncan Kennedy has recently provided a critique of Professor Fuller's classic article, placing it in the development of contract between the nineteenth-century ascendancy of the "will theory" and the twentieth-century rise of legal realism and sociological jurisprudence. Kennedy also describes the evolution of contract scholarship in the post–World War II era from moderate-left-liberal vs. moderate-right-conservative (up to circa 1970), to a more vigorously left vs. a more vigorously right (economically and politically) division in the latter years of the century. Duncan Kennedy, From the Will Theory to the Principle of Private Autonomy: Lon Fuller's "Consideration and Form," 100 Colum. L. Rev. 94 (2000).

2. Applying the Consideration Doctrine

Dougherty v. Salt
New York Court of Appeals
227 N.Y. 200, 125 N.E. 94 (1919)

CARDOZO, J. The plaintiff, a boy of eight years, received from his aunt, the defendant's testatrix, a promissory note for $3,000 payable at her death or before. Use was made of a printed form, which contains the words "value received." How the note came to be given, was explained by the boy's guardian, who was a witness for his ward. The aunt was visiting her nephew. "When she saw Charley coming in, she said 'Isn't he a nice boy?' I answered her, yes, that he is getting along very nice, and getting along nice in school, and I showed where he had progressed in school, having good reports, and so forth, and she told me that she was going to take care of that child, that she loved him very much. I said, 'I know you do, Tillie, but your taking care of the child will be done probably like your brother and sister done, take it out in talk.' She said: 'I don't intend to take it out in talk, I would like to take care of him now.' I said, 'Well, that is up to you.' She said, 'Why can't I make out a note to him?' I said, 'You can, if you wish to.' She said, 'Would that be right?' And I said, 'I do not know, but I guess it would; I do not know why it would not.' And she said, 'Well, will you make out a note for me?' I said, 'Yes, if you wish me to,' and she said, 'Well, I wish you would.'" A blank was then produced, filled out, and signed. The aunt handed the note to her nephew with these words, "You have always done for me, and I have signed this note for you. Now, do not lose it. Some day it will be valuable."

The trial judge submitted to the jury the question whether there was any consideration for the promised payment. Afterwards, he set aside the verdict in favor of the plaintiff, and dismissed the complaint. The Appellate Division, by a divided court, reversed the judgment of dismissal, and reinstated the verdict on the ground that the note was sufficient evidence of consideration.

We reach a different conclusion. The inference of consideration to be drawn from the form of the note has been so overcome and rebutted as to leave no question for a jury. This is not a case where witnesses summoned by the defendant and friendly to the defendant's cause, supply the testimony in disproof of value (Strickland v. Henry, 175 N.Y. 372). This is a case where the testimony in disproof of value comes from the plaintiff's own witness, speaking at the plaintiff's instance. The transaction thus revealed admits of one interpretation, and one only. The note was the voluntary and unenforcible promise of an executory gift (Harris v. Clark, 3 N.Y. 93; Holmes v. Roper, 141 N.Y. 64, 66). This child of eight was not a creditor, nor dealt with as one. The aunt was not paying a debt. She was conferring a bounty (Fink v. Cox, 18 Johns. 145). The promise was neither offered nor accepted with any other purpose. "Nothing is consideration that is not regarded as such by both parties" (Philpot v. Gruninger, 14 Wall. 570, 577; Fire Ins. Assn. v. Wickham, 141 U.S. 564, 579; Wisconsin & M. Ry. Co. v. Powers, 191 U.S. 379, 386; DeCicco v. Schweizer, 221 N.Y. 431, 438). A note so given is not made for "value received," however its maker may have labeled it. The formula of the printed blank becomes, in the light of the conceded facts, a mere erroneous conclusion, which cannot overcome the inconsistent conclusion of the law (Blanshan v. Russell, 32 App. Div. 103; *affd., on opinion below*, 161 N.Y. 629; Kramer v. Kramer, 181 N.Y. 477; Bruyn v. Russell, 52 Hun. 17). The plaintiff, through his own witness, has explained the genesis of the promise, and consideration has been disproved (Neg. Instr. Law, sec. 54; Consol. Laws, chap. 43). . . .

Judgment accordingly.

Notes and Questions

1. **Dougherty** *compared with* **Hamer.** In *Dougherty*, as in *Hamer*, an older person makes a promise to a younger relative, enforcement of which is later resisted, after the promisor has died. The promise in *Dougherty* was made in a more formal manner than the one in *Hamer*, but the latter was enforced while the former was not. Why? The promissory note that went unenforced in *Dougherty* is not quoted in the opinion, but presumably it was a written, signed promise by the aunt to pay her nephew the stated sum at the designated time. There is no indication that the promise was stated to be conditional on anything other than the aunt's death (that being the event defining the time when payment would be due). Suppose, however, that the note had begun, "In consideration of my nephew Charley having been a good boy until the age of 21 or until my death (whichever shall first occur), I hereby promise. . . ." Should the promise in the note have been in that case an obligation enforceable against the aunt's estate, just as the uncle's promise was enforceable in *Hamer*?

In *Dougherty*, as in *Hamer*, suit was brought not against the individual promisor, but against the representative of the deceased promisor's estate. (The defendant in *Hamer* is referred to as the "executor" and the aunt in *Dougherty* as the "testatrix," in both cases indicating that the decedent left a valid will. Where the decedent has died "intestate"—without a will—the representative of the estate is often referred to as the "administrator." Today the term "personal representative" is used in many jurisdictions to refer to all such representatives.) In *Hamer*, the case was further complicated by the fact that the plaintiff was not the promisee himself, but an "assignee"—someone to whom Story had transferred ("assigned") his right to payment. (The general topic of assignment is addressed in Chapter 9.) That might have influenced defendant Sidway's unwillingness to pay. In *Dougherty*, however, the plaintiff was Charley himself. There seems to have been no real dispute about the genuineness of the aunt's promise; nor does it appear that the aunt had changed her mind about Charley's merits before she died. Why didn't defendant Salt simply pay the note when it was presented?

2. *Should donative promises be enforced?* The court in *Dougherty* indicates that the promise was not supported by any consideration because it was no more than the promise of an "executory gift" (i.e., a gift to be performed in the future). There was no value received by the aunt for her promise, and the mere recital of value would not suffice, where it was plain that none had in fact been given. Such "donative" promises are frequently made, sometimes by one family member to another and occasionally between persons bound to each other not by blood relationship but by other ties of affection. Such promises also often go unenforced, sometimes because the promisor changes his mind or the promisee declines to press the point; and sometimes, as in *Dougherty*, because the promisor dies before her intent has been carried out. Should the law enforce the purely donative promise, without insisting that it be supported by consideration? Professor Melvin Eisenberg has made a survey of this area, concluding that generally enforcement of the purely donative promise seems unnecessary where the promise has not been substantially relied on by the promisee. (The possibility of enforcement in the event of reliance is addressed in the next section of this chapter.) He goes on to suggest some reasons why enforcement of purely donative promises is ordinarily not appropriate:

> These substantive considerations are reinforced by the administrative problems that would be raised by attempts to enforce informal unrelied-upon donative promises. Initially, this type of promise raises serious problems of proof. Since such a promise is, by hypothesis, both informal and gratuitous, it would be too easy (or so it may be thought) for a plaintiff falsely to convince a jury that a promise was made, despite the lack of either objective proof or corroborating circumstances. Moreover, in a context that involves neither formality nor explicit reciprocity, it may often be difficult to distinguish a promise from a statement of present intent. Indeed, the speaker himself may hardly understand "just what he means or (which is perhaps even more important) what he is understood to mean."
>
> Furthermore, if one is to come under a legal obligation simply by virtue of having exercised his will, it might at least be required that the will has probably been exercised in a deliberate manner. But since actors involved in a donative transaction are often emotionally involved, and since the donative promisor tends to look mainly to the interests of the promisee, an informal donative promise is more likely to be uncalculated than deliberative. Indeed, such promises may raise a problem akin to capacity, because they are frequently made in highly emotional states brought on by surges of gratitude, impulses of display, or other intense but transient feelings. (One reason that donative promises often fail to arouse a secure expectation is that the promisee realizes the promisor may back off when a sober self returns.) In theory, the law could deal with this problem by examining for deliberation on an individual basis. In practice, however, an inquiry into so subjective an element seems unlikely to produce reliable results.
>
> Finally, the obligation created by a donative promise may be excused by acts of the promisee amounting to *ingratitude*, or by personal circumstances of the promisor that render keeping the promise *improvident*. If Uncle promises to give Nephew $20,000 in two years, and Nephew later wrecks Uncle's living room in an angry rage,

no one, not even Nephew, is likely to expect Uncle to remain obliged. The same result may follow if Uncle suffers a serious financial setback, and is barely able to take care of the needs of his immediate family; or if Uncle's wealth remains constant, but his personal obligations significantly increase in an unexpected manner, as through marriage, the birth of children, or illness; or perhaps even if Uncle's wealth and personal obligations both remain constant, but, due to miscalculation, execution of the gift would jeopardize his ability to maintain his immediate family in a proper manner. The potential availability of these excuses further explains the insecurity of a donative promisee's expectation. More to the point, what constitutes ingratitude and improvidence is very difficult to determine, particularly in the context of the intimate relationships that often give rise to donative promises, and this difficulty would add substantially to the problem of administration. Thus, despite occasional protests that the law should put its weight behind all promises that are seriously made, there seems to be widespread agreement that informal unrelied-upon donative promises should not be legally enforced.

Melvin A. Eisenberg, Donative Promises, 47 U. Chi. L. Rev. 1, 4-6 (1979). In a later article Professor Eisenberg suggested two additional substantive reasons why unrelied-on affective, donative promises should not be enforceable:

(1) The world of gift would be impoverished if simple donative promises that are based on affective considerations, such as love or friendship, were folded into the hard-headed world of contract. (2) Where a donative promise is based on affective considerations, in the absence of reliance a donative promisee is morally obliged to release a repenting promisor.

Melvin A. Eisenberg, The World of Contract and the World of Gift, 85 Cal. L. Rev. 821 (1997). Are Eisenberg's arguments persuasive? Do they apply to *Dougherty*?

For a skeptical response to many of Professor Eisenberg's arguments, see Andrew Kull, Reconsidering Gratuitous Promises, 21 J. Legal Studies 39, 63 (1992)("person who makes a serious gratuitous promise of a magnitude that will later justify litigation is particularly unlikely to do so except as a matter of conscious choice"); see also Jane B. Baron, Gifts, Bargains, and Form, 64 Ind. L.J. 155 (1988/89) (questioning the way in which contract and other areas of law tend to undervalue gratuitous transfers by insisting on distinguishing them from bargains and then according them disfavoring treatment).

3. *Counseling Aunt Tillie.* Charley's guardian was apparently the aunt's only source of legal advice in *Dougherty*, and he was obviously not a reliable one. If Charley's aunt had consulted an attorney, could she have accomplished her purpose? The Comment that follows explores some of the possibilities that a lawyer would consider.

Comment: The Lawyer's Role in Counseling for Legal Effect

Suppose a present-day Aunt Tillie should come to you as her attorney, seeking advice as to how best to effectuate her wish to confer a future benefit on her nephew Charley. We have already suggested that the lawyer's role as counselor involves understanding the objectives that the client wishes to achieve; identifying the alternative options for achieving those objectives; evaluating the legal effects of each and any possible pitfalls involved; making sure the client understands the legal and practical consequences of each of those alternatives; helping the client to choose among them; and, finally, helping her to implement that choice. Given the aunt's objective of somehow presently effecting a gift that will benefit her nephew Charley at some future time, what legal devices could you suggest to accomplish for her the result she seeks?

Promissory Note. The device actually employed in the *Dougherty* case — a promissory note with a recital of consideration — would probably have no more success with a modern judge than it did with Judge Cardozo in 1919. Comment *b* to Restatement (Second) §71 states: "Moreover, a mere pretense of bargain does not suffice, as where there is a false recital of consideration or where the purported consideration is merely nominal." Suppose that instead of just reciting "value received," the aunt were to receive from her nephew a small amount of money (a dollar or so) in exchange for her promise? Would that — in light of the minimal nature of the law's requirement of "legal detriment" — supply sufficient consideration for enforcement of her promise? The first Restatement (§75) appeared to sanction such "nominal consideration" as a device for making a promise enforceable, but Restatement (Second) §71 unequivocally rejects in comment *b* and the following illustration:

5. *A* desires to make a binding promise to give $1000 to his son *B*. Being advised that a gratuitous promise is not binding, *A* offers to buy from *B* for $1000 a book worth less than $1. *B* accepts the offer knowing that the purchase of the book is a mere pretense. There is no consideration for *A*'s promise to pay *B* $1000.

Assuming therefore that a mere written promise that recites consideration will probably not create an obligation enforceable against the promisor's estate, what other devices might you advise your client to employ?

Promise Under Seal. We have seen earlier that the common law enforced promises under seal, in the action of covenant, without requiring any showing of consideration. Could your client confer an enforceable right on her nephew by signing and delivering to him a *sealed* promissory note? Such a document will have varying effect today depending on the jurisdiction involved. The past several centuries have witnessed a steady decline in the efficacy of this legal form: As the volume of commercial transactions increased, the original formality of the seal was relaxed, so that it might be no more than a preprinted notation on a contract form (see Restatement (Second) §96(3)); as the seal thus came to be less and less "special," legislatures responded by depriving it of its special legal effect. Today, nearly every state has passed legislation affecting the legal significance of the seal. Some have simply abolished the device altogether; others have reduced its effect to a mere presumption of consideration. (Statutes dealing with the seal are collected and discussed in the Introductory Note to Topic 3, §§95-109 of the Restatement (Second); for a more recent report, see Eric Mills Holmes, Stature and Status of a Promise under Seal as a Legal Formality, 29 Willamette L. Rev. 617 (1993).) See also Knott v. Racicot, 812 N.E.2d 1207 (Mass. 2004) (discussing the history and declining importance of the seal; abolishing the common law rule that option contracts under seal import consideration). The Uniform

Commercial Code abolished the significance of the seal in sales of goods (UCC §2-203). Restatement (Second) §95 states a rule for enforcement of instruments under "seal." However, as a "restatement" of the common law, the rule of §95 can have effect only where the common law relating to seals has not been displaced by statutes abolishing or weakening the seal's legal effect. Despite a few recent statutory attempts to create a comparable device, there is today no generally available equivalent of the old English seal for use in creating binding gratuitous obligations.

Executed Gift. The surest way to guarantee that the intended beneficiary of the aunt's generosity ends up with the money would, obviously, be for her to simply give him (or his guardian, on his behalf) the money now, in cash. While a promise to make a gift in the future is not an enforceable obligation under contract law, property law provides that once a gift has been "executed" — delivered by the donor with the intent to make a gift, and accepted by the donee — it is irrevocable and may not be recovered by the donor. Ray A. Brown, The Law of Personal Property 77-78 (3d ed. 1975). (There is an exception for gifts made "in contemplation of death" — causa mortis — which are revocable if the donor recovers his health. Id. at 131.) What justifies the law's refusal on the one hand to carry out the unexecuted promise of a gift, while on the other refusing to undo an equally gratuitous transaction merely because it has been executed? The notion of making a present gift of the money is an alternative that your client should consider, but she may not wish to do so, as she may not have the money to spare at this time. (She may also — consciously or subconsciously — wish to use the prospect of receiving the money in the future as a means of keeping her nephew's attention and affection in the meantime.)

Testamentary Gift. In light of your client's expressed wish that her nephew receive the money at her death, it would seem logical to suggest that a "testamentary gift" be employed: She could make a will, a "last testament" of her desires as to the disposition of her property after death. If her will is made with such formality as the law requires (typical requirements include a signed writing and the presence of witnesses who also sign, attesting the genuineness of the document), its provisions would after her death be carried out (executed) by her personal representative, the executor of her estate. Assuming that sufficient assets remained after payment of any debts of the estate, the bequest to the nephew would be paid along with any other bequests. In this case, the absence of consideration for the gift would be legally irrelevant. The testamentary-gift option has the disadvantage of requiring somewhat more effort than the promissory note used in *Dougherty*, since the will must be formally signed and witnessed. On the other hand, it should achieve its purpose (assuming the aunt is presently of sufficient mental capacity as required by law). What are its drawbacks? Only two readily appear: This bequest, along with any others, will not be payable until the debts of the estate have been satisfied; should the estate have insufficient assets, an enforceable promissory note (along with any other enforceable debt of the estate) would take priority over a mere testamentary gift. Also, unlike an apparently unconditional promissory note, a testamentary gift is "ambulatory" — it may be freely revoked by a later will. (Of course your client may not regard this latter feature as a drawback, although her nephew might.)

Gift in Trust. One other legal device merits mention here. You may recall that in *Hamer* the court seized on the fact that the uncle had assertedly set aside the money owed his nephew, in order to find that a "trust" had been created (thereby avoiding what would have otherwise been the bar of the statute of limitations, and allowing enforcement of the obligation). If your client presently has the funds to make the gift to her nephew, but does not wish to give him (or his guardian) present control over those funds, she could create a trust on his behalf. (She could appoint another person to serve as "trustee," or she could do so herself.) As a trust "beneficiary," he would eventually enjoy the benefits of the gift, while being relieved of both the responsibility and the power that immediate control over the funds would represent. For a variety of legal and practical reasons, such "inter vivos" trusts have become a frequently employed vehicle for the gratuitous transfer of wealth between family members. Courses in Trusts and Estate Planning will give you a chance to explore them in depth later in your legal studies.

Batsakis v. Demotsis
Texas Court of Civil Appeals
226 S.W.2d 673 (1949)

McGILL, Justice.

This is an appeal from a judgment of the 57th judicial District Court of Bexar County. Appellant was plaintiff and appellee was defendant in the trial court. The parties will be so designated.

Plaintiff sued defendant to recover $2,000 with interest at the rate of 8% per annum from April 2, 1942, alleged to be due on the following instrument, being a translation from the original, which is written in the Greek language:

Peiraeus
April 2, 1942

Mr. George Batsakis
Konstantinou Diadohou #7
Peiraeus

Mr. Batsakis:

I state by my present (letter) that I received today from you the amount of two thousand dollars ($2,000.00) of United States of America money, which I borrowed from you for the support of my family during these difficult days and because it is impossible for me to transfer dollars of my own from America.

The above amount I accept with the expressed promise that I will return to you again in American dollars either at the end of the present war or even before in the event that you might be able to find a way to collect them (dollars) from my representative in America to whom I shall write and give him an order relative to this.

You understand until the final execution (payment) to the above amount an eight per cent interest will be added and paid together with the principal.

I thank you and I remain yours with respects.

The recipient,

(Signed) *Eugenia The. Demotsis.*

Trial to the court without the intervention of a jury resulted in a judgment in favor of plaintiff for $750.00 principal, and interest at the rate of 8% per annum from April 2, 1942 to the date of judgment, totaling $1163.83, with interest thereon at the rate of 8% per annum until paid. Plaintiff has perfected his appeal.

The court sustained certain special exceptions of plaintiff to defendant's first amended original answer on which the case was tried, and struck therefrom paragraphs II, III and V. Defendant excepted to such action of the court, but has not cross-assigned error here. The answer, stripped of such paragraphs, consisted of a general denial contained in paragraph I thereof, and of paragraph IV, which is as follows:

> IV. That under the circumstances alleged in Paragraph II of this answer, the consideration upon which said written instrument sued upon by plaintiff herein is founded, is wanting and has failed to the extent of $1975.00, and defendant pleads specially under the verification hereinafter made the want and failure of consideration stated, and now tenders, as defendant has here-tofore tendered to plaintiff, $25.00 as the value of the loan of money received by defendant from plaintiff, together with interest thereon.
>
> Further, in connection with this plea of want and failure of consideration defendant alleges that she at no time received from plaintiff himself or from anyone for plaintiff any money or thing of value other than, as hereinbefore alleged, the original loan of 500,000 drachmae. That at the time of the loan by plaintiff to defendant of said 500,000 drachmae the value of 500,000 drachmae in the Kingdom of Greece in dollars of money of the United States of America, was $25.00, and also at said time the value of 500,000 drachmae of Greek money in the United States of America in dollars was $25.00 of money of the United States of America. The plea of want and failure of consideration is verified by defendant as follows.

The allegations in paragraph II which were stricken, referred to in paragraph IV, were that the instrument sued on was signed and delivered in the Kingdom of Greece on or about April 2, 1942, at which time both plaintiff and defendant were residents of and residing in the Kingdom of Greece, and

> [Defendant] avers that on or about April 2, 1942 she owned money and property and had credit in the United States of America, but was then and there in the Kingdom of Greece in straitened financial circumstances due to the conditions produced by World War II and could not make use of her money and property and credit existing in the United States of America. That in the circumstances the plaintiff agreed to and did lend to defendant the sum of 500,000 drachmae, which at that time, on or about April 2, 1942, had the value of $25.00 in money of the United States of America. That the said plaintiff, knowing defendant's financial distress and desire to return to the United States of America, exacted of her the written instrument plaintiff sues upon, which was a promise by her to pay to him the sum of $2,000.00 of United States of America money.

Plaintiff specially excepted to paragraph IV because the allegations thereof were insufficient to allege either want of consideration or failure of consideration, in that it affirmatively appears therefrom that defendant received what was agreed to be delivered to her, and that plaintiff breached no agreement. The court overruled this exception, and such action is assigned as error. Error is also assigned because of the court's failure to enter judgment for the whole unpaid balance of the principal of the instrument with interest as therein provided.

Defendant testified that she did receive 500,000 drachmas from plaintiff. It is not clear whether she received all the 500,000 drachmas or only a portion of them before she signed the instrument in question. Her testimony clearly shows that the understanding of the parties was that plaintiff would give her the 500,000 drachmas if she would sign the instrument. She testified:

Q. . . . who suggested the figure of $2,000.00?
A. That was how he asked me from the beginning. He said he will give me five hundred thousand drachmas provided I signed that I would pay him $2,000.00 American money.

The transaction amounted to a sale by plaintiff of the 500,000 drachmas in consideration of the execution of the instrument sued on, by defendant. It is not contended that the drachmas had no value. Indeed, the judgment indicates that the trial court placed a value of $750.00 on them or on the other consideration which plaintiff gave defendant for the instrument if he believed plaintiff's testimony. Therefore the plea of want of consideration was unavailing. A plea of want of consideration amounts to a contention that the instrument never became a valid obligation in the first place. National Bank of Commerce v. Williams, 125 Tex. 619, 84 S.W.2d 691.

Mere inadequacy of consideration will not void a contract. 10 Tex. Jur., Contracts, Sec. 89, p.150; Chastain v. Texas Christian Missionary Society, Tex. Civ. App., 78 S.W.2d 728, loc. cit. 731(3), Wr. Ref.

Nor was the plea of failure of consideration availing. Defendant got exactly what she contracted for according to her own testimony. The court should have rendered judgment in favor of plaintiff against defendant for the principal sum of $2,000.00 evidenced by the instrument sued on, with interest as therein provided. . . . As so reformed, the judgment is affirmed.

Reformed and affirmed.

Notes and Questions

1. *Adequacy of consideration.* Closely allied to the view of consideration as reflecting the exchange element of a transaction is the rule that, in ascertaining the presence of consideration, the courts will not "weigh" the consideration, or insist on a "fair" or "even" exchange. In his treatise, Williston put it thus: "It is an 'elementary principle that the law will not enter into an inquiry as to the adequacy of the consideration.' This rule is almost as old as the law of consideration itself." Williston on Contracts §115; see also Restatement (Second) §79 (no requirement of "equivalence in the values exchanged"). Comment *e* to §79 points out, however, that "gross inadequacy of consideration may be relevant" to the application of other issues, such as fraud, mistake, lack of capacity, duress or undue influence. Although the first Restatement had no such explicit caveat, it is possible that courts nevertheless frequently "policed" bargains of this sort by finding a complete lack of

consideration where in fact bargained-for consideration was present but was "grossly inadequate." Recall Newman & Snell's State Bank v. Hunter, discussed in Note 6 following the *Pennsy Supply* case, above, in which a widow's promise to pay her late husband's debts was not enforced. Present-day courts faced with a grossly unfair bargain coupled with other factors tending toward excuse are probably more likely to rely on other doctrines, as suggested by Comment *e* to Restatement (Second) §79, rather than on a lack of consideration. Cf. Howard v. Diolosa, 574 A.2d 995 (N.J. Super. Ct. 1990), *cert. denied*, 585 A.2d 409 (N.J. 1990) (sellers permitted to avoid sale of their home for grossly unfair price to purchaser who promised to lease it back to them on vague terms pursuant to lease that was never executed; no finding of fraud, mistake or undue influence, but transaction was unconscionable, and the product of disproportionate bargaining power).

2. *Exploring the **Batsakis** case.* The trial court judge who decided the *Batsakis* case apparently concluded that the 500,000 drachmas that the defendant received from the plaintiff were then worth $750 in American money. Would the appellate court's disposition of the case have been any different if the trial court had accepted defendant's contention that the Greek money she received was worth only 25 American dollars? If you as trial judge had heard and believed the defendant's story, would you have had any reluctance to enforce her promise to the plaintiff? Are there any legal theories other than lack of consideration that might have been invoked in her behalf? Consider the following facts:

In the spring of 1941, German, Italian, and Bulgarian forces invaded and occupied Greece, taking control of food and medical supplies. The Allies imposed a naval blockade that restricted supplies to Greece throughout the winter of 1941-1942, and the Germans systematically looted the country; the result was a devastating famine that killed many thousands of Greeks during that period, possibly as many as 40,000 in the Athens-Piraeus area alone. Rampant inflation during the same period drove the price of bread from 70 drachmas to 2,350. See generally Mark Mazower, Inside Hitler's Greece 23-41, 65-67 (1993). Against this backdrop, how should one evaluate the *Batsakis* case? Are these circumstances relevant, and if so, how?

3. *Change in the law's concern for fairness.* Some analysts, particularly those associated with the Critical Legal Studies movement, have seen in the ascendancy of the bargain theory of consideration a movement on the law's part away from an earlier willingness to police the "fairness" of bargains, and toward a view of contract particularly adaptable to commercial speculation in commodities and securities, where the parties determine the contract price of the commodity in question based on their appraisal of the market. The following excerpt is from a 1974 article by Professor Morton Horwitz, perhaps the leading proponent of this thesis.

The most important aspect of the eighteenth century conception of exchange is an equitable limitation on contractual obligation. Under the modern will theory, the extent of contractual obligation depends upon the convergence of individual desires. The equitable theory, by contrast, limited and sometimes denied contractual obligation by reference to the fairness of the underlying exchange....

What we have seen of eighteenth century doctrines suggests that contract law was essentially antagonistic to the interests of commercial classes. The law did not assure a businessman the express value of his bargain, but at most its specific performance. Courts and juries did not honor business agreements on their face, but scrutinized them for the substantive equality of the exchange.

For our purposes, the most important consequence of this hostility was that contract law was insulated from the purposes of commercial transactions. Business-men settled disputes informally among themselves when they could, referred them to a more formal process of arbitration when they could not, and relied on merchant juries to ameliorate common law rules. And, finally, they endeavored to find legal forms of agreement with which to conduct business transactions free from the equalizing tendencies of courts and juries. . . .

Morton J. Horwitz, The Historical Foundations of Modern Contract Law, 87 Harv. L. Rev. 917, 923, 927 (1974). (This article was later incorporated into Morton J. Horwitz, The Transformation of American Law, 1780-1860 (1977).) Other writers have differed sharply with Horwitz and his colleagues over the extent to which classical contract law did indeed represent a change from past law in this respect. See, e.g., Alfred W. B. Simpson, The Horwitz Thesis and the History of Contracts, 46 U. Chi. L. Rev. 533 (1979). Whether the classical view of consideration did indeed mark a sharp break with the past or merely a change in emphasis, it does appear to be particularly consistent with a society in which the law fully supports a "free market" economy, permitting commercial entities (individuals or corporations) to make whatever agreements of exchange they wish at whatever relative values they can agree to.

4. *The question of "illusory" promises.* One form of bargain-imbalance that may result in nonenforcement of a promise can be found in the Restatement's qualification of the bargained-for-exchange principle by the rule of Restate-ment (Second) §77, comment *a*, that a promise, even if bargained for, will not serve as consideration for a promise in return if it is "illusory" — if it makes performance entirely optional with the promisor. In Marshall Durbin Food Corp. v. Baker, 909 So.2d 1267 (Miss. 2005), the court explained the concept of the illusory promise as follows:

By the phrase "illusory promise" is meant words in promissory form that promise nothing; they do not purport to put any limitation on the freedom of the alleged promisor, but leave his future action subject to his own future will, just as it would have been had he said no words at all . . . A prediction of future willingness is not an expression of present willingness and is not a promise. To see a promise in it is to be under an illusion. We reach the same result if B's reply to A is, "I promise to do as you ask if I please to do so when the time arrives." In form this is a conditional promise, but the condition is the pleasure or future will of the promisor himself. The words used do not purport to effect any limitation upon the promisor's future freedom of choice. They do not lead the promisee to have an expectation of performance because of a present expression of will. He may hope that a future willingness will exist; but he has no more reasonable basis for such a hope than if B had merely made a prediction or had said nothing at all. As a promise, B's words are mere illusion. Such an illusory promise is neither enforceable against the one making it, nor is it operative as a consideration for a return promise.

Id. at 1275 (quoting 1 Corbin, *Contracts*, §145 (1 vol. ed.1952)).

Probably the most common application of the illusory promise doctrine is when the agreement is "at will," i.e., the promisor reserves the right to terminate the agreement with the promisee at any time without any period of notice to the promisee. (Suppose the promisor must give notice a relatively short period of time before terminating the agreement, for example seven days. Is the promise illusory?) As the Corbin quote states, an illusory promise is not enforceable against the one making it because by definition that person has not made any commitment. In addition, an illusory promise cannot serve as consideration for a return promise made by the other party, thus rendering that promise unenforceable, unless supported by some other consideration. See, e.g., E.I. Du Pont de Nemours & Co. v. Claiborne-Reno Co., 64 F.2d 224 (8th Cir.), *cert. denied,* 290 U.S. 646 (1933) (manufacturer's promise to continue distributorship operation not supported by consideration when distributor was free to terminate arrangement at any time).

Two qualifications to the illusory promise doctrine are worth noting. First, the concept does not apply to the promisee under a unilateral contract because the promisee does not make any promises. If a promisor offers to enter into a unilateral contract, the promisor does not seek a return promise. Under a unilateral contract the promisee's performance constitutes both acceptance of the promisor's promise and consideration for that promise. Thus, in *Marshall Durbin Food Corp.,* above, the company argued that its promise to pay Baker certain retirement benefits was unenforceable because Baker's employment was at will; the company had the right to discharge him and he remained free to leave his employment at any time. The court agreed that Baker had made no promise or commitment to the company, but it still found that the company's promise was enforceable because the company sought Baker's continued employment and he continued to work for the company as requested. The court said: "In the instant case, the Company focuses only on the alleged return promise of Mr. Baker and ignores the fact that other consideration, such as Mr. Baker's actual performance, is equally sufficient consideration." Id. at 1276. (The *Marshall Durbin Food Corp.* case is another example of Professor Pettit's thesis that modern courts frequently use the unilateral contract concept to enforce promises where there is no return promise, rather than to deny enforcement as was the situation in Peterson v. Pattberg. Recall note 3 following Cook v. Coldwell Banker, above.)

Second, even when the principal aspects of a contract do not impose obligations on either or both of the parties, a court may find consideration present in the "secondary" commitments that the parties make. See, e.g. Larson v. Green Tree Financial Corp., 983 P.2d 357 (Mont. 1999) (even though arrangement between plaintiff mobile home dealer and defendant financing company did not require defendant to purchase contracts from plaintiff nor plaintiff to offer to sell them to defendant, agreement nevertheless did impose some obligations on each party sufficient to constitute consideration; plaintiff was obligated to conform to HUD regulations it otherwise would not necessarily have been bound by, and plaintiff in return was permitted to hold itself out as a dealer approved by defendant for customer financing).

The illusory promise doctrine at one time impeded enforcement of such useful commercial arrangements as requirement and output contracts, now generally regarded as being enforceable despite the indefiniteness of commitment involved. See UCC §2-306, discussed further in Chapter 6.

5. *"Mutuality of obligation."* Courts have sometimes also subjected contracts to a "mutuality of obligation" test, usually articulated as "both parties must be bound or neither is bound." As a broad generality, that is clearly an overstatement: We have already seen that unilateral contracts lack mutuality. A promisee under a unilateral contract is free to perform or not, while the promisor becomes bound once the promisee tenders a beginning of performance. As we shall see, many a promise is enforceable by a party who is not herself bound to performance in return. (E.g., the "promissory estoppel" case, where the relying promisee may be protected even in the absence of any commitment on her part.) The Restatement (Second) strongly asserts the absence of any "mutuality of obligation" test for contract enforcement; if the consideration requirement is met, it declares, that is enough. Restatement (Second) §79(c). Nevertheless, some courts continue to apply a "mutuality of obligation" test for enforceability. E.g., Pick Kwik Food Stores, Inc. v. Tenser, 407 So. 2d 216 (Fla. Dist. Ct. App. 1981) (gasoline company could not enforce agreement for operation of pump on food store's premises where company had right to remove pump at any time); Gull Laboratories, Inc. v. Diagnostic Technology, Inc., 695 F. Supp. 1151 (D. Utah. 1988) (distributorship agreement unenforceable against manufacturer for lack of consideration or mutuality; agreement did not bind distributor to order any goods).

Plowman v. Indian Refining Co.
United States District Court
20 F. Supp. 1 (E.D. Ill. 1937)

LINDLEY, District Judge.

Thirteen persons and the administrators of five deceased persons brought this suit, alleging that defendant, in 1930, made separate contracts to pay each of the individual plaintiffs and each of the deceased persons whose administrators sued, monthly sums equal to one-half of the wages formerly earned by such parties as employees of the defendant for life. Each of the claimants had been employed for some years at a fixed rate of wages, usually upon an hourly basis but payable monthly or semimonthly.

The theory of plaintiffs is that on July 28, 1930 (with two exceptions), the vice-president and general manager of the refinery plant called the employees, who had rendered long years of service separately into his office and made with each a contract, to pay him, for the rest of his natural life, a sum equal to one-half of the wages he was then being paid. The consideration for the contracts, it is said, arose out of the relationship then existing, the desire to provide for the future welfare of these comparatively aged employees and the provision in the alleged contracts that the employees would call at the office for their several checks each pay-day.

Most of the employees were participants in group insurance, the premiums for which had been paid approximately one-half by the employee and one-half by the company, and, according to plaintiffs, their parts of the premiums were to be deducted from their payments as formerly. This procedure was followed.

The employees were retained on the pay roll, but, according to their testimony, they were not to render any further services, their only obligation being to call at the office for their remittances. Most of them testified that it was agreed that the payments were to continue throughout the remainder of their lives. But two testified that nothing was said as to the time during which the payments were to continue. As to still others the record is silent as to direct testimony in this respect.

The payments were made regularly until June 1, 1931, when they were cut off and each of the employees previously receiving the same was advised by defendant's personnel officer that the arrangement was terminated.

Defendant does not controvert many of these facts, but insists that the whole arrangement was included in a letter sent to each of the employees as follows:

> Confirming our conversation of today, it is necessary with conditions as they are throughout the petroleum industry, to effect substantial economies throughout the plant operation. This necessitates the reducing of the working force to a minimum necessary to maintain operation. In view of your many years of faithful service, the management is desirous of shielding you as far as possible from the effect of reduced plant operation and has, therefore, placed you upon a retirement list which has just been established for this purpose.
>
> Effective August 1, 1930, you will be carried on our payroll at a rate of $_____$ per month. You will be relieved of all duties except that of reporting to Mr. T. E. Sullivan at the main office for the purpose of picking up your semi-monthly checks. Your group insurance will be maintained on the same basis as at present, unless you desire to have it cancelled. (Signed by the vice-president.)

It contends and offered evidence that nothing was said to any employee about continuing the payments for his natural life; that the payments were gratuitous, continuing at the pleasure and will of defendant; that the original arrangement was not authorized, approved, or ratified by the board of directors, the executive committee thereof, or any officer endowed with corporate authority to bind the company; that there was no consideration for the promise to make the payments; and that it was beyond the power of any of the persons alleged to have contracted to create by agreement or by estoppel any liability of the company to pay wages to employees during the remainders of their lives, if they did not render actual services. Defendant admits the payments as charged and the termination of the arrangement on June 1, 1931.

The employees assert that there was ample authority in the vice-president and general manager to make a binding contract of the kind alleged to have existed; that, irrespective of the existence or nonexistence of such authority, the conduct of the company in making payment was ratification of the original agreement and that defendant is now estopped to deny validity of the same.

Plaintiff Kogan, an employee aged 72, testified that for some years prior to July 28, 1930, he had been employed as a drill pressman and in general repair work in the machine shops; that on July 28, 1930, he talked to Mr. Anglin, the vice-president and general manager, in the latter's private office; that Anglin said then that the oil industry was in a deplorable condition; that the management found it necessary to cut down expenses, and therefore, to lay off certain employees; that the witness was to be relieved of his duties, but that he would receive one-half of his salary and would be retained upon the pay roll; that this was being done because of the witness' many years of services; that the company did not desire to discharge him without further compensation; that he would be excused from all labor and required only to report to the main office to get his checks; that the company would carry his insurance in accord with previous practice; and that he would have all the privileges of hospitalization and in other respects of regular employees. The witness said he expressed his preference to work, but was told that that was impossible. He says that he was told that the arrangement was permanent, that is, for as long as he lived; that he would receive a letter confirming this conversation, which he should keep; that his labor would end on July 31, 1930; that he received the letter within a day or two; that thereafter he reported regularly at the office and obtained the checks until May 29, 1931, when he was told by the personnel department that the check then received would be the last one. This action, he said he was then told, was taken because of the necessity for further retrenchment. He testified that he sought no other employment; that nothing was said to him about working or not working for other parties, and that when he received the letter he kept it without comment or objection.

Other claimants testified substantially the same. . . .

In behalf of defendant, the assistant secretary testified that there were no minutes showing any corporate action with regard to the arrangement and that there was nothing in the records of the corporation, in bylaws, resolution or minutes authorizing, directing, or ratifying the payments or giving anybody authority to make the same. Anglin, vice-president and general manager in charge of manufacturing at the Lawrenceville Refinery where these men were employed, testified that he said to Kogan that, due to depressed conditions the company found it necessary to reduce expenses and lay off certain men; that it had no pension plan; that in an effort to be perfectly fair the company would keep him on the pay roll but relieve him of all duties except to pick up his check; that he said that the arrangement was voluntary with the company, and terminable at its pleasure, and that he hoped it would last during Kogan's lifetime, but that there might be a change in the policy of the company. His testimony as to the other employees was the same. He denied promising any of them that the payments would persist so long as they lived. He sent the letters as he promised confirming the arrangement. He testified that the letters were in compliance with what he had said; that no complaint or demand for any additional provisions was thereafter made; that he himself was employed orally; that he had no written contract; that he had no authority from the directors to make the arrangement; that he hired and fired men in Lawrenceville upon recommendation of the foreman; that a change in the management occurred when the Indian Refining Company was purchased by the Texas Company between October, 1930, and January, 1931; and that after the latter date he was not general manager at Lawrenceville. . . .

The present vice-president and general manager testified that he came into office January, 1931; and that no complaint was received by him by any plaintiff until suit was started.

Thus it is undisputed that a separate arrangement was made by the local office with each of the claimants, most of them on July 28, 1930, to continue them upon the pay roll, deliver to them semimonthly a check, upon their calling for same, for one-half of the former wages; that this was done until June 1, 1931. It is also undisputed that the letters sent out said nothing about how long the payments should continue but were wholly silent in that respect. It is also undisputed that insurance payments were deducted from the checks that were delivered; that the employees were retained on the pay roll; that they did no active work after August 1, 1931 [sic; 1930?]; that they received their checks as mentioned; that the payments terminated on June 1, 1931; that most of them called at the office for their checks and received same; and that in at least two instances the checks were mailed. The controverted question of fact arises upon the testimony of most of the plaintiffs that each of them was told that the payments would continue until their death. This is denied.

Let us assume, without so deciding, for the purpose of disposition of this case, that each of the employees was told that the payments would continue for his lifetime. Then the questions remaining are legal in character. The arrangement was made by no corporate officer having authority to make such a contract. Under the bylaws, corporation transactions as recorded in the minutes, there was no authorization or ratification of any such contract. It is urged, however, that by continuing to pay the checks the corporation ratified the previously unauthorized action. The facts render such conclusion dubious. I am unable to see how knowledge of the mere fact that men's names were on the pay roll and checks paid to them could create any estoppel to deny authority, in the absence of proof of knowledge upon the part of the duly authorized officers of the company that the men were not working but were receiving in effect pensions or that they had been promised payments for life. Consequently, there was no ratification express or implied and no estoppel.

Presented also is the further question of whether, admitting the facts as alleged by plaintiffs, there was any consideration for a contract to pay a pension for life. However strongly a man may be bound in conscience to fulfill his engagements, the law does not recognize their sanctity or supply any means to compel their performance, except when founded upon a sufficient consideration. Volume 6, American & English Encyclopedia of Law, p.673 (2d Ed.)

The long and faithful services of the employees are relied upon as consideration; but past or executed consideration is a self-contradictory term. Consideration is something given in exchange for a promise or in a reliance upon the promise. Something which has been delivered before the promise is executed, and, therefore, made without reference to it, cannot properly be legal consideration. Williston on Contracts, vol. 1, §142; 13 Corpus Juris, 359; Shields v. Clifton Hill Land Co., 94 Tenn. 123, 28 S.W. 668, 26 L.R.A. 523, 45 Am. St. Rep. 700; Restatement of the Law of Contracts, vol. 1, p.88.

It is further contended that there was a moral consideration for the alleged contracts. The doctrine of validity of moral consideration has received approval in some courts, but quite generally it is condemned because it is contrary in character to actual consideration. . . . Thus in Hart v. Strong, 183 Ill. 349, 55 N.E. 629, 631, the court said: "The agreement to receive less than the amount due on the note was made upon the purely moral consideration that John W. Hart, believing himself about to die, thought he ought not to have exacted so large a consideration for the reconveyance. But such an obligation does not form a valid consideration unless the moral duty were once a legal one. 'But the morality of the promise, however certain or however urgent the duty, does not, of itself, suffice for a consideration.' 1 Pars. Cont. 434."

Upon the same ground, appreciation of past services or pleasure afforded the employer thereby is not a sufficient consideration. . . . So Williston says (Contracts, vol. 1, p.230): ". . . if there be no legal consideration, no motive, such as love and respect, or affection for another or a desire to do justice, or fear of trouble, or a desire to equalize the shares in an estate, or to provide for a child, or regret for having advised an unfortunate investment, will support a promise."

Plaintiffs have proved that they were ready, willing, and able to travel to and report semimonthly to the main office. But this does not furnish a legal consideration. The act was simply a condition imposed upon them in obtaining gratuitous pensions and not a consideration. The employees went to the office to obtain their checks. Such acts were benefits to them and not detriments. They were detriments to defendant and not benefits. This is not consideration. Williston on Contracts, vol. 1, pp.231-235, and cases cited; Restatement of Contracts, par. 75, Illus. 2.

In the absence of valid agreement to make payments for the rest of their natural lives, clearly the arrangement was one revocable at the pleasure of defendant. If defendant agreed to make the payments for life, then, fatal to plaintiffs' cases is the lack of consideration. We have merely a gratuitous arrangement without consideration, and therefore, void as a contract.

In this enlightened day, I am sure, no one controverts the wisdom, justice, and desirability of a policy, whether promoted and fostered by industry voluntarily or by state or federal government, looking to the promotion and assurance of financial protection of deserving employees in their old age. We have come to realize that the industry wherein the diligent worker labors for many years should bear the cost of his living in some degree of comfort through his declining years until the end of his life. To impose this expense upon the industry, to the creation of whose product he has contributed, is not unfair or unreasonable, for, eventually, obviously, under wise budgeting and cost accounting systems, this element of cost is passed on to the consumer of the product. The public bears the burden — as, indeed, it does eventually of all governmental expenditures and corporate costs, either in taxes or price of products purchased. Surely no one would have the temerity to urge that such a policy is not more fair and reasonable, more humane and beneficent, than the poorhouse system of our earlier days. The recognition of the soundness of this proposition is justified by the resulting contribution to the advance of standards of living, hygienic and sanitary environment, and, in some degree at least, of culture and civilization.

But, in the absence of statute creating it, such a policy does not enter into the relationship of employer or employee, except when so provided by contract of the parties. The court is endowed with no power of legislation; nor may it read into contracts provisions upon which the parties' minds have not met.

Viewing the testimony most favorably for the plaintiffs, despite the desirability of the practice of liberality between employer and employee, the court must decide a purely legal question — whether under plaintiffs' theory there were valid contracts. The obvious answer is in the negative. Consequently, there will be a decree in favor of defendant dismissing plaintiffs' bill for want of equity. The foregoing includes my findings of fact and conclusions of law.

Notes and Questions

1. *Consideration or condition?* The court holds that the plaintiffs' travel to the defendant's office, to pick up their checks, did not constitute consideration; it was "simply a condition imposed upon them in obtaining gratuitous pensions." Do you agree? Recall the analysis in *Pennsy Supply*, above.

2. *Hypothetical variations of **Plowman**.* The judge also dismisses (quoting Williston) the possibility that "love and respect, . . . affection for another or a desire to do justice" could amount to consideration; "legal consideration," he says, is necessary. It is frequently stated, however, that where bargained-for consideration is present, the fact that the promisor may have had some other motive or inducement for making the promise will not of itself defeat the agreement. See Restatement (Second) §81, and Comment *b*. Assuming that the principal motive for the defendant's promise may have been the welfare of its senior employees, should the promise have been enforceable if any of the following had also been part of the case?

(a) Each promisee was required to pick up his check in person at the office of the defendant, at a time when the employees of the defendant would be picking up their regular paychecks.

(b) Each pensioned employee was required, before receiving any payments, to submit a signed resignation, waiving all right to future employment with the defendant and any claim to wages or payments other than the promised "pension."

(c) Each promisee was required, before receiving payments, to sign an agreement that he would, on request, assist in training new employees of the defendant. (Would it matter whether the employees had ever been called on to do so?)

3. *"Past consideration."* The court also rejects the possibility that the "long and faithful service" of the plaintiffs could constitute consideration, using two related arguments. Services already performed could be, at best, only "past consideration," which is a "self-contradictory" term: Something already done cannot constitute consideration for a later promise. Nor can any "moral obligation" arising out of past faithful service constitute consideration, unless the "moral" duty was also a "legal" one. If this is indeed the law, *should* it be? Professor Charles Fried has argued that the making of a promise is an act that of itself creates a moral obligation that the law should respect and enforce.

> The obligation to keep a promise is grounded not in arguments of utility but in respect for individual autonomy and in trust. Autonomy and trust are grounds for the institution of promising as well, but the argument for *individual* obligation is not the

same. Individual obligation is only a step away, but that step must be taken. An individual is morally bound to keep his promises because he has intentionally invoked a convention whose function it is to give grounds — moral grounds — for another to expect the promised performance. To renege is to abuse a confidence he was free to invite or not, and which he intentionally did invite. To abuse that confidence now is like (but only *like*) lying: the abuse of a shared social institution that is intended to invoke the bonds of trust. . . .

The utilitarian counting the advantages affirms the general importance of enforcing *contracts*. The moralist of duty, however, sees *promising* as a device that free, moral individuals have fashioned on the premise of mutual trust, and which gathers its moral force from that premise. The moralist of duty thus posits a general obligation to keep promises, of which the obligation of contract will be only a special case — that special case in which certain promises have attained legal as well as moral force. But since a contract is first of all a promise, the contract must be kept because a promise must be kept.

To summarize: There exists a convention that defines the practice of promising and its entailments. This convention provides a way that a person may create expectations in others. By virtue of the basic Kantian principles of trust and respect, it is wrong to invoke that convention in order to make a promise, and then to break it.

Charles Fried, Contract as Promise 16-17 (1981). Do you agree with Fried's position? Even if you would stop short of enforcing the moral obligation implicit in *every* promise, would you as judge in *Plowman* have felt impelled to enforce the moral obligation of the Indian Refining Co.? We return later in this chapter to the question of "past consideration" and "moral obligation" as possible bases for promissory liability.

4. *The issue of authority.* Would plaintiffs' legal position have been improved if the defendant's board of directors had adopted by formal resolution a plan to pay the disputed pensions to the plaintiffs, specifically providing that such payments should continue for the lives of the discharged employees? Although his opinion is perhaps slightly unclear on the point, Judge Lindley appears to find that the promises, if made, were made by agents lacking in authority to bind the defendant, and were not made binding on the defendant by later events. The issue of whether a person or organization is legally responsible for the acts of an employee is one of the issues addressed by agency law. This body of law has, like contract law, been the subject of two ALI Restatements; agency law can be, and often is, the subject of a separate law school course. Agency issues frequently arise in contract cases, however, and not every law school today offers a separate agency course. The following Comment is therefore designed to provide an introduction to some basic agency concepts.

Comment: The Power of Agents to Bind Their Principals

Agency is a consensual relationship in which one person, the agent, agrees to act on behalf of, and subject to the control of, another person, the principal. Restatement (Third) of Agency §1.01. ("Person" in this context means a "legal" person, which can include corporations as well as individuals; corporations, being artificial persons, can act only through agents.) The agency relationship is often described as "fiduciary," because it involves a relationship of trust and confidence in which one person is bound to act in the interests of another. Id. §8.01. The principal's right to control the agent is the essence of the relationship. As indicated, the agency relationship is a consensual one; it is usually created by contract between the principal and its agent, although agency may also be gratuitous.

If an agent has "actual authority" to enter into a contract on behalf of the principal, then the principal is bound by the agent's actions in the same way as if the principal had engaged in those actions himself. As a matter of law, the principal becomes a party to the contract by virtue of the agent's actions, while the agent is not a party. Id. §6.01. The Restatement of Agency provides that an agent can have actual authority in several ways. First, an agent has actual authority to take actions "designated . . . in the principal's manifestations." Id. §2.02(1). Many courts and the former Restatement use the term "express authority" to refer to this form of authorization. Id. §2.01, comment b. Thus, if the Board of Directors of Indian Refining Co. had passed a resolution directing its vice president to send the letters in question to the plaintiffs, those letters would in law have been sent by the company itself and the promises therein would have been its promises, because the officer would have had actual authority to act on its behalf. (Note that this conclusion would not by itself have resolved the question whether the company, by making the promises in those letters, had incurred contractual liability.)

Second, an agent has actual authority to take actions "implied in the principal's manifestations." Id. §2.02(1). For example, suppose the board of directors had directed the vice president to develop a plan to reduce the company's work force to a level sufficient to maintain the company's operations despite the economic conditions then prevailing (a national depression) with appropriate provision for payment of partial salary to any long-term employees who were laid off as part of this plan. In this case the board would not have expressly authorized the sending of these particular letters, but authority to do so might fairly have been implied from the vice president's general mandate.

Third, an agent has actual authority to perform "acts necessary or incidental to achieving the principal's objectives." Id. §2.02(1). Thus, if the board had passed a resolution authorizing the vice president to enter into contracts with long-term employees on the terms discussed in the case, the vice president would have had actual authority to sign the contracts and other documents necessary or incidental to carrying out the resolution and would also have had actual authority to instruct the payroll department to make the necessary changes to effectuate the board's resolution. Id. §2.02, comment d.

Suppose, on the other hand, that the board had passed a resolution authorizing the vice president to develop a plan to reduce the company's work force to a level sufficient to maintain the company's operations despite the economic conditions then prevailing. However, suppose that in this situation the board did not specify that the vice president had authority to pay reduced salaries to workers who were laid off without any corresponding obligation by these workers to the company. In this example the vice president might well lack actual authority to enter into the contracts involved in the case because the arrangement would probably amount to a gift by the corporation to its long-term employees. Generally, the authorization of an agent to make a gift of the principal's property must be quite specific. Id. §2.02, comment *h*.

Even in the absence of any actual authority, however, a principal may be legally bound by the actions of its agent if the principal has done or said something that leads the other party reasonably to believe that the agent does indeed have actual authority to do the act in question. Suppose that Indian Refining's Board of Directors had ordered that a letter be sent to all employees, advising them that "Vice President Anglin will shortly be communicating with you about the way in which our company will respond to the drastic change in economic conditions, in order to assure its survival and the continued well-being of its employees." Even if the board had made it plain to the vice president that his actual authority merely extended to the reshuffling of work shifts and the discharge of some employees, such a letter might be held to have created in the minds of the employees a reasonable belief that he also had the authority to promise pension payments. In that case he would have had "apparent authority" to make the promises in the letters. Id. §2.03. See also §3.03, comment *e* (discussing the apparent authority of organizational executives and corporate officers).

Finally, even where an agent has no authority at all—either actual or apparent—to enter into a particular contract on behalf of the principal, a principal that later learns of its agent's action and approves of it will be liable on that contract by virtue of such "ratification." Id. §4.01. This sort of after-the-fact approval was at issue in *Plowman*. The plaintiffs argued that the board of directors had ratified the vice president's promises to them by continuing to make salary payments after the plaintiffs stopped work. The judge rejected that argument on the ground that effective ratification requires knowledge of all material facts; the board, he declared, could not have known merely from payroll records that the employees were no longer working or were receiving lifetime pensions. See Id. §4.06.

The court also referred to the notion of "estoppel," a concept that crops up in a variety of legal contexts. (In the next chapter we will see another application of the estoppel concept in a contractual context.) Under agency law a principal may be estopped to deny that its agent's actions were unauthorized, where the principal by words or actions caused the other to rely to his detriment on the agent's authority to act. Id. §2.05. This notion is obviously very similar to that of apparent authority. Apparent authority, however, is based on the principal's manifestations, while an estoppel could result from other acts or even inaction by the principal that place the agent in position to lead the third party to believe that the agent has authority to act for the principal. Id. §2.05, comment *d*. For example, suppose the vice president had on his own without board approval adopted the plan described in the case. Suppose further that the board became aware of the vice president's actions, but failed to take action to prevent him from going forward with his plan. In this case the corporation would probably be estopped to deny that the vice president acted with authority. Id. §2.05(2).

C. ISSUES IN APPLYING THE CONCEPT OF MUTUAL ASSENT

In the first sections of this chapter we explored two requirements for formation of a contract: mutual assent and consideration. While consideration remains an element of contract formation, in most modern commercial contracts consideration is rarely a problem. Typically parties exchange mutual promises, and each party's promise serves as consideration for the promise made by the other party. However, issues involving mutual assent arise frequently. This section considers a number of these issues.

1. Limiting the Offeror's Power to Revoke: The Effect of Pre-Acceptance Reliance

Earlier in this chapter we saw that the traditional method of mutual assent was through the process of offer and acceptance. We also encountered the fundamental Anglo-American common law rule that an offer is revocable unless and until it is accepted by the offeree, even if the offer itself expressly states that it cannot and will not be revoked. (Even the "mailbox" rule does not so much curtail the offeror's power of revocation as it does expand the notion of what constitutes "acceptance.") This principle of free revocability, however logical it may have seemed as part of the structure of classical contract law, is certainly no manifestation of a necessary "natural law" of contract. For example, Article 16 of the Convention on Contracts for the International Sale of Goods (see the text in Chapter 1 and the Rules Supplement) provides as follows:

> (1) Until a contract is concluded an offer may be revoked if the revocation reaches the offeree before he has dispatched an acceptance.
> (2) However, an offer cannot be revoked:
>   (a) If it indicates, whether by stating a fixed time for acceptance or otherwise, that it is irrevocable; or
>   (b) If it was reasonable for the offeree to rely on the offer as being irrevocable and the offeree has acted in reliance on the offer.

Of course, even classical contract law recognized the possibility that an offer could be made irrevocable by contract. Suppose that a landowner offers to sell his land for a stated price to a prospective purchaser, who wants some time to consider the deal—perhaps to investigate its feasibility or desirability or to make related arrangements. If the offeree/vendee gives the offeror some consideration (a sum of money, perhaps) to hold the offer open for a stated period of time, under the classical system the offer will be irrevocable during that period, as an "option contract."

The option contact actually has at least two promises by the offeror. In our example, the landowner makes a promise (offer) to sell the land for a stated price. In addition, the landowner promises to hold the offer open (i.e., not exercise the common law right to revoke) in exchange for some consideration, typically payment of money, although the consideration could instead be some performance by the offeree, such as conducting engineering studies of the land, if that performance was bargained for. If the offeree (option holder) decides to exercise the option, then the offeree accepts the offeror's first promise to sell the land. The option holder could, if she so desires, allow the option to lapse and not exercise the right to purchase the land. In that case the consideration paid for the option is retained by the offeror, unless the parties have agreed otherwise.

Option contracts serve a useful purpose in commercial relations, by permitting one who is considering a contractual transaction to delay committing herself to the contemplated exchange without fearing that such delay will cost her the ability to enter into that contract, should she eventually decide to accept it.

In the absence of an option contract, however, classical contract law provided no protection to an offeree who relied on an offer she had not yet accepted. The offeror remained free to revoke his offer at any time until acceptance took place.

Sometimes an offeree who has not specifically sought the protection of a purchased option will expend resources or otherwise substantially change her position in the belief that the offer will remain open for her to accept, only to have the offeror revoke his offer before she has made an acceptance. What effect, if any, should an offeree's pre-acceptance conduct have on the offeror's power to withdraw his offer at will? The materials that follow explore this question.

James Baird Co. v. Gimbel Bros., Inc.
United States Court of Appeals
64 F.2d 344 (2d Cir. 1933)

L. HAND, Circuit Judge.

The plaintiff sued the defendant for breach of a contract to deliver linoleum under a contract of sale; the defendant denied the making of the contract; the parties tried the case to the judge under a written stipulation and he directed judgment for the defendant. The facts as found, bearing on the making of the contract, the only issue necessary to discuss, were as follows: The defendant, a New York merchant, knew that the Department of Highways in Pennsylvania had asked for bids for the construction of a public building. It sent an employee to the office of a contractor in Philadelphia, who had possession of the specifications, and the employee there computed the amount of the linoleum which would be required on the job, underestimating the total yardage by about one-half the proper amount. In ignorance of this mistake, on December twenty-fourth the defendant sent to some twenty or thirty contractors, likely to bid on the job, an offer to supply all the linoleum required by the specifications at two different lump sums, depending upon the quality used. These offers concluded as follows: "If successful in being awarded this contract, it will be absolutely guaranteed, . . . and . . . we are offering these prices for reasonable" (sic), "prompt acceptance after the general contract has been awarded." The plaintiff, a contractor in Washington, got one of these on the twenty-eighth, and on the same day the defendant learned its mistake and telegraphed all the contractors to whom it had sent the offer, that it withdrew it and would substitute a new one at about double the amount of the old. This withdrawal reached the plaintiff at Washington on the afternoon of the same day, but not until after it had put in a bid at Harrisburg at a lump sum, based as to linoleum upon the prices quoted by the defendant. The public authorities accepted the plaintiff's bid on December thirtieth, the defendant having meanwhile written a letter of confirmation of its withdrawal, received on the thirty-first. The plaintiff formally accepted the offer on January second, and, as the defendant persisted in declining to recognize the existence of a contract, sued it for damages on a breach.

Unless there are circumstances to take it out of the ordinary doctrine, since the offer was withdrawn before it was accepted, the acceptance was too late. Restatement of Contracts, §35. To meet this the plaintiff argues as follows: It was a reasonable implication from the defendant's offer that it should be irrevocable in case the plaintiff acted upon it, that is to say, used the prices quoted in making its bid, thus putting itself in a position from which it could not withdraw without great loss. While it might have withdrawn its bid after receiving the revocation, the time had passed to submit another, and as the item of linoleum was a very trifling part of the cost of the whole building, it would have been an unreasonable hardship to expect it to lose the contract on that account, and probably forfeit its deposit. While it is true that the plaintiff might in advance have secured a contract conditional upon the success of its bid, this was not what the defendant suggested. It understood that the contractors would use its offer in their bids, and would thus in fact commit themselves to supplying the linoleum at the proposed prices. The inevitable implication from all this was that when the contractors acted upon it, they accepted the offer and promised to pay for the linoleum, in case their bid were accepted.

It was of course possible for the parties to make such a contract, and the question is merely as to what they meant; that is, what is to be imputed to the words they used. Whatever plausibility there is in the argument, is in the fact that the defendant must have known the predicament in which the contractors would be put if it withdrew its offer after the bids went in. However, it seems entirely clear that the contractors did not suppose that they accepted the offer merely by putting in their bids. If, for example, the successful one had repudiated the contract with the public authorities after it had been awarded to him, certainly the defendant could not have sued him for a breach. If he had become bankrupt, the defendant could not prove against his estate. It seems plain therefore that there was no contract between them. And if there be any doubt as to this, the language of the offer sets it at rest. The phrase, "if successful in being awarded this contract," is scarcely met by the mere use of the prices in the bids. Surely such a use was not an "award" of the contract to the defendant. Again, the phrase, "we are offering these prices for . . . prompt acceptance after the general contract has been awarded," looks to the usual communication of an acceptance, and precludes the idea that the use of the offer in the bidding shall be the equivalent. It may indeed be argued that this last language contemplated no more than an early notice that the offer had been accepted, the actual acceptance being the bid, but that would wrench its natural meaning too far, especially in the light of the preceding phrase. The contractors had a ready escape from their difficulty by insisting upon a contract before they used the figures; and in commercial transactions it does not in the end promote justice to seek strained interpretations in aid of those who do not protect themselves.

Part of Plaintiff's argument

But the plaintiff says that even though no bilateral contract was made, the defendant should be held under the doctrine of "promissory estoppel." This is to be chiefly found in those cases where persons subscribe to a venture, usually charitable, and are held to their promises after it has been completed. It has been applied much more broadly, however, and has now been generalized in section 90, of the Restatement of Contracts. We may arguendo accept it as it there reads, for it does not apply to the case at bar. Offers are ordinarily made in exchange for a consideration, either a counter-promise or some other act which the promisor wishes to secure. In such cases they propose bargains; they presuppose that each promise or performance is an inducement to the other. Wisconsin, etc., Ry. v. Powers, 191 U.S. 379, 386, 387, 24 S. Ct. 107, 48 L. Ed. 229; Banning Co. v. California, 240 U.S. 142, 152, 153, 36 S. Ct. 338, 60 L. Ed. 569. But a man may make a promise without expecting an equivalent; a donative promise, conditional or absolute. The common law provided for such by sealed instruments, and it is unfortunate that these are no longer generally available. The doctrine of "promissory estoppel" is to avoid the harsh results of allowing the promisor in such a case to repudiate, when the promisee has acted in reliance upon the promise. Siegel v. Spear & Co., 234 N.Y. 479, 138 N.E. 414, 26 A.L.R. 1205. Cf. Allegheny College v. National Bank, 246 N.Y. 369, 159 N.E. 173, 57 L.R.A. 980. But an offer for an exchange is not meant to become a promise until a consideration has been received, either a counter-promise or whatever else is stipulated. To extend it would be to hold the offeror regardless of the stipulated condition of his offer. In the case at bar the defendant offered to deliver the linoleum in exchange for the plaintiff's acceptance, not for its bid, which was a matter of indifference to it. That offer could become a promise to deliver only when the equivalent was received; that is, when the plaintiff promised to take and pay for it. There is no room in such a situation for the doctrine of "promissory estoppel."

Holding

Nor can the offer be regarded as of an option, giving the plaintiff the right seasonably to accept the linoleum at the quoted prices if its bid was accepted, but not binding it to take and pay, if it could get a better bargain elsewhere. There is not the least reason to suppose that the defendant meant to subject itself to such a one-sided obligation. True, if so construed, the doctrine of "promissory estoppel" might apply, the plaintiff having acted in reliance upon it, though, so far as we have found, the decisions are otherwise. Ganss v. Guffey Petroleum Co., 125 App. Div. 760, 110 N.Y.S. 176; Comstock v. North, 88 Miss. 754, 41 So. 374. As to that, however, we need not declare ourselves.

Judgment affirmed. — *Judgment*

Notes and Questions

1. *Bilateral contract analysis.* Judge Hand admits that if the plaintiff had become bound to the defendant by virtue of its use of defendant's bid, then the plaintiff might have a case; he rejects that possibility, however, stating that

"it seems entirely clear that the contractors did not suppose that they accepted the [defendant's] offer merely by putting in their bids." Most courts that have considered similar cases have on this point agreed with Judge Hand: Mere use by a general contractor of one particular subcontractor's bid does not constitute acceptance of that bid, forming a bilateral contract binding both parties. See, e.g., Electrical Construction & Maintenance Co. v. Maeda Pacific Corp., 764 F.2d 619 (9th Cir. 1985); Electro-Lab of Aiken, Inc. v. Sharp Constr. Co. of Sumter, Inc., 593 S.E.2d 170 (S.C. Ct. App. 2004). If in the *Baird* case such a bilateral contract had been formed and then the general contract had been awarded to someone else, would Baird have been stuck with a buildingful of Gimbel Bros. linoleum?

2. *Option contract.* We have noted that an offeree can be protected against the effect of a surprise revocation of an offer by an option contract. In *Baird*, Judge Hand rejects the argument that the plaintiff was protected by an option contract. Why? Is his analysis persuasive?

3. *Effect of mistake.* The trial court in *Baird* apparently found as a fact that the defendant had made a serious mistake in computing the amount of square yardage required by the contract on which plaintiff was bidding. Was this mistake material to the outcome of the case? Should it have been? We will return in Chapter 8 to the general problem of mistake.

Drennan v. Star Paving Co.
California Supreme Court
51 Cal. 2d 409, 333 P.2d 757 (1958)

TRAYNOR, Justice.

Defendant appeals from a judgment for plaintiff in an action to recover damages caused by defendant's refusal to perform certain paving work according to a bid it submitted to plaintiff.

On July 28, 1955, plaintiff, a licensed general contractor, was preparing a bid on the "Monte Vista School Job" in the Lancaster school district. Bids had to be submitted before 8:00 P.M. Plaintiff testified that it was customary in that area for general contractors to receive the bids of subcontractors by telephone on the day set for bidding and to rely on them in computing their own bids. Thus on that day plaintiff's secretary, Mrs. Johnson, received by telephone between fifty and seventy-five subcontractors' bids for various parts of the school job. As each bid came in, she wrote it on a special form, which she brought into plaintiff's office. He then posted it on a master cost sheet setting forth the names and bids of all subcontractors. His own bid had to include the names of subcontractors who were to perform one-half of one per cent or more of the construction work, and he had also to provide a bidder's bond of ten per cent of his total bid of $317,385 as a guarantee that he would enter the contract if awarded the work.

Later in the afternoon, Mrs. Johnson had a telephone conversation with Kenneth R. Hoon, an estimator for defendant. He gave his name and telephone number and stated that he was bidding for defendant for the paving work at the Monte Vista School according to plans and specifications and that his bid was $7,131.60. At Mrs. Johnson's request he repeated his bid. Plaintiff listened to the bid over an extension telephone in his office and posted it on the master sheet after receiving the bid form from Mrs. Johnson. Defendant's was the lowest bid for the paving. Plaintiff computed his own bid accordingly and submitted it with the name of defendant as the subcontractor for the paving. When the bids were opened on July 28th, plaintiff's proved to be the lowest, and he was awarded the contract.

On his way to Los Angeles the next morning plaintiff stopped at defendant's office. The first person he met was defendant's construction engineer, Mr. Oppenheimer. Plaintiff testified: "I introduced myself and he immediately told me that they had made a mistake in their bid to me the night before, they couldn't do it for the price they had bid, and I told him I would expect him to carry through with their original bid because I had used it in compiling my bid and the job was being awarded them. And I would have to go and do the job according to my bid and I would expect them to do the same." *[handwritten: where the initial issue arises]*

Defendant refused to do the paving work for less than $15,000. Plaintiff testified that he "got figures from other people" and after trying for several months to get as low a bid as possible engaged L & H Paving Company, a firm in Lancaster, to do the work for $10,948.60.

The trial court found on substantial evidence that defendant made a definite offer to do the paving on the Monte Vista job according to the plans and specifications for $7,131.60, and that plaintiff relied on defendant's bid in computing his own bid for the school job and naming defendant therein as the subcontractor for the paving work. Accordingly, it entered judgment for plaintiff in the amount of $3,817.00 (the difference between defendant's bid and the cost of the paving to plaintiff) plus costs. *[handwritten: trial courts Ruling]*

Defendant contends that there was no enforceable contract between the parties on the ground that it made a revocable offer and revoked it before plaintiff communicated his acceptance to defendant.

There is no evidence that defendant offered to make its bid irrevocable in exchange for plaintiff's use of its figures in computing his bid. Nor is there evidence that would warrant interpreting plaintiff's use of defendant's bid as the acceptance thereof, binding plaintiff, on condition he received the main contract, to award the subcontract to defendant. In sum, there was neither an option supported by consideration nor a bilateral contract binding on both parties. *[handwritten: defendants argument]*

Plaintiff contends, however, that he relied to his detriment on defendant's offer and that defendant must therefore answer in damages for its refusal to perform. Thus the question is squarely presented: Did plaintiff's reliance make defendant's offer irrevocable? *[handwritten: Plaintiff's argument]* *[handwritten: Issue]*

Section 90 of the Restatement of Contracts states: "A promise which the promisor should reasonably expect to induce action or forbearance of a definite and substantial character on the part of the promisee and which does induce such action or forbearance is binding if injustice can be avoided only by enforcement of the promise." This rule applies in this state. . . . *[handwritten: This Rule applies]*

Defendant's offer constituted a promise to perform on such conditions as were stated expressly or by implication therein or annexed thereto by operation of law. (See 1 Williston, Contracts [3d ed.], §24A, p.56, §61, p.196.)

Defendant had reason to expect that if its bid proved the lowest it would be used by plaintiff. It induced "action . . . of a definite and substantial character on the part of the promisee."

Had defendant's bid expressly stated or clearly implied that it was revocable at any time before acceptance we would treat it accordingly. It was silent on revocation, however, and we must therefore determine whether there are conditions to the right of revocation imposed by law or reasonably inferable in fact. In the analogous problem of an offer for a unilateral contract, the theory is now obsolete that the offer is revocable at any time before complete performance. Thus section 45 of the Restatement of Contracts provides: "If an offer for a unilateral contract is made, and part of the consideration requested in the offer is given or tendered by the offeree in response thereto, the offeror is bound by a contract, the duty of immediate performance of which is conditional on the full consideration being given or tendered within the time stated in the offer, or, if no time is stated therein, within a reasonable time." In explanation, Comment *b* states that the "main offer includes as a subsidiary promise, necessarily implied, that if part of the requested performance is given, the offeror will not revoke his offer, and that if tender is made it will be accepted. Part performance or tender may thus furnish consideration for the subsidiary promise. Moreover, merely acting in justifiable reliance on an offer may in some cases serve as sufficient reason for making a promise binding (see §90)."

Whether implied in fact or law, the subsidiary promise serves to preclude the injustice that would result if the offer could be revoked after the offeree had acted in detrimental reliance thereon. Reasonable reliance resulting in a foreseeable prejudicial change in position affords a compelling basis also for implying a subsidiary promise not to revoke an offer for a bilateral contract.

The absence of consideration is not fatal to the enforcement of such a promise. It is true that in the case of unilateral contracts the Restatement finds consideration for the implied subsidiary promise in the part performance of the bargained-for exchange, but its reference to section 90 makes clear that consideration for such a promise is not always necessary. The very purpose of section 90 is to make a promise binding even though there was no consideration "in the sense of something that is bargained for and given in exchange." (See 1 Corbin, Contracts 634 et seq.) Reasonable reliance serves to hold the offeror in lieu of the consideration ordinarily required to make the offer binding. In a case involving similar facts the Supreme Court of South Dakota stated that

> we believe that reason and justice demand that the doctrine [of section 90] be applied to the present facts. We cannot believe that by accepting this doctrine as controlling in the state of facts before us we will abolish the requirement of a consideration in contract cases, in any different sense than an ordinary estoppel abolishes some legal requirement in its application. We are of the opinion, therefore, that the defendants in executing the agreement [which was not supported by consideration] made a promise which they should have reasonably expected would induce the plaintiff to submit a bid based thereon to the Government, that such promise did induce this action, and that injustice can be avoided only by enforcement of the promise.

Northwestern Engineering Co. v. Ellerman, 69 S.D. 397, 408, 10 N.W.2d 879, 884; see also, Robert Gordon, Inc., v. Ingersoll-Rand Co., 7 Cir., 117 F.2d 654, 661; cf. James Baird Co. v. Gimbel Bros., 2 Cir., 64 F.2d 344.

Part of Holding

When plaintiff used defendant's offer in computing his own bid, he bound himself to perform in reliance on defendant's terms. Though defendant did not bargain for this use of its bid neither did defendant make it idly, indifferent to whether it would be used or not. On the contrary it is reasonable to suppose that defendant submitted its bid to obtain the subcontract. It was bound to realize the substantial possibility that its bid would be the lowest, and that it would be included by plaintiff in his bid. It was to its own interest that the contractor be awarded the general contract; the lower the subcontract bid, the lower the general contractor's bid was likely to be and the greater its chance of acceptance and hence the greater defendant's chance of getting the paving subcontract. Defendant had reason not only to expect plaintiff to rely on its bid but to want him to. Clearly defendant had a stake in plaintiff's reliance on its bid. Given this interest and the fact that plaintiff is bound by his own bid, it is only fair that plaintiff should have at least an opportunity to accept defendant's bid after the general contract has been awarded to him.

It bears noting that a general contractor is not free to delay acceptance after he has been awarded the general contract in the hope of getting a better price. Nor can he reopen bargaining with the subcontractor and at the same time claim a continuing right to accept the original offer. See, R. J. Daum Const. Co. v. Child, Utah, 247 P.2d 817, 823. In the present case plaintiff promptly informed defendant that plaintiff was being awarded the job and that the subcontract was being awarded to defendant.

Defendant contends, however, that its bid was the result of mistake and that it was therefore entitled to revoke it. It relies on the rescission cases of M. F. Kemper Const. Co. v. City of Los Angeles, 37 Cal. 2d 696, 235 P.2d 7, and Brunzell Const. Co. v. G. J. Weisbrod, Inc., 134 Cal. App. 2d 278, 285 P.2d 989. See also, Lemoge Electric v. San Mateo County, 46 Cal. 2d 659, 662, 297 P.2d 638. In those cases, however, the bidder's mistake was known or should have been known to the offeree, and the offeree could be placed in status quo. Of course, if plaintiff had reason to believe that defendant's bid was in error, he could not justifiably rely on it, and section 90 would afford no basis for enforcing it. Robert Gordon, Inc. v. Ingersoll-Rand, Inc., 7 Cir., 117 F.2d 654, 660. Plaintiff, however, had no reason to know that defendant had made a mistake in submitting its bid, since there was usually a variance of 160 per cent between the highest and lowest bids for paving in the desert around Lancaster. He committed himself to performing the main contract in reliance on defendant's figures. Under these circumstances defendant's mistake, far from relieving it of its obligation, constitutes an additional reason for enforcing it, for it misled plaintiff as to the cost of doing the paving. Even had it been clearly understood that defendant's offer was revocable until accepted, it would not necessarily follow that defendant had no duty to exercise reasonable care in preparing its bid. It presented its bid with knowledge of the substantial possibility that it would be used by plaintiff; it could foresee the harm that would ensue from an erroneous underestimate of the cost. Moreover, it was motivated by its own business interest. Whether or not these considerations alone would justify recovery for negligence had the case been tried on that theory (see Biakanja v. Irving, 49 Cal. 2d 647, 650, 320 P.2d 16), they are persuasive that defendant's mistake should not defeat recovery under the rule of section 90 of the Restatement of Contracts. As between the subcontractor who made the bid and the general contractor who reasonably relied on it, the loss resulting from the mistake should fall on the party who caused it.

Leo F. Piazza Paving Co. v. Bebek & Brkich, 141 Cal. App. 2d 226, 296 P.2d 368, 371, and Bard v. Kent, 19 Cal. 2d 449, 122 P.2d 8, 139 A.L.R. 1032, are not to the contrary. In the *Piazza* case the court sustained a finding that defendants intended, not to make a firm bid, but only to give the plaintiff "some kind of an idea to use" in making its bid; there was evidence that the defendants had told plaintiff they were unsure of the significance of the specifications. There was thus no offer, promise, or representation on which the defendants should reasonably have expected the plaintiff to rely. The *Bard* case held that an option not supported by consideration was revoked by the death of the optionor. The issue of recovery under the rule of section 90 was not pleaded at the trial, and it does not appear that the offeree's reliance was "of a definite and substantial character" so that injustice could be avoided "only by the enforcement of the promise."

There is no merit in defendant's contention that plaintiff failed to state a cause of action, on the ground that the complaint failed to allege that plaintiff attempted to mitigate the damages or that they could not have been mitigated. Plaintiff alleged that after defendant's default, "plaintiff had to procure the services of the L & H Co. to perform said asphaltic paving for the sum of $10,948.60." Plaintiff's uncontradicted evidence showed that he spent several months trying to get bids from other subcontractors and that he took the lowest bid. Clearly he acted reasonably to mitigate damages. In any event any uncertainty in plaintiff's allegation as to damages could have been raised by special demurrer. Code Civ. Proc. §430, subd. 9. It was not so raised and was therefore waived. Code Civ. Proc. §434.

The judgment is affirmed.

GIBSON C. J., and SHENK, SCHAUER, SPENCE and McCOMB, JJ., concur.

Notes and Questions

1. *Introduction to promissory estoppel.* In his opinion Justice Traynor first discusses Restatement of Contracts §45, which provides protection to the offeree against revocation of an offer to enter into a unilateral contract when the offeree has relied on the offer by beginning the requested performance. We previously discussed §45 in connection with Cook v. Coldwell Banker, above. While *Drennan* involves an offer to enter into a bilateral contract, Justice Traylor concludes that protection against revocation of an offer should also apply in that situation when the offeree has reasonably relied resulting in foreseeable prejudice. Justice Trayor bases his analysis on Restatement of Contracts §90, which is now commonly referred to as *promissory estoppel*. Promissory estoppel is not limited, however, to reliance on offers. We will explore in subsequent chapters a number of other situations in which the

doctrine may be applicable to protect a party's reliance interest when a contract has not been formed.

2. ***Drennan vs. Baird.*** In *James Baird,* Judge Hand pointed out that promissory estoppel deals with reliance on "promises" and argued that an "offer" is not the same as a donative promise but is rather "not meant to become a promise until a consideration has been received." He also declared that "in commercial transactions it does not in the end promote justice to seek strained interpretations in aid of those who do not protect themselves." Does Justice Traynor in his *Drennan* opinion effectively counter those arguments? How would you counter them, if called on to defend the *Drennan* result?

Despite the coyness of the "cf." signal used by Justice Traynor to introduce his reference to the *James Baird* case, most commentators have viewed the *James Baird* and *Drennan* decisions as being squarely in conflict. If so, *Drennan* has clearly prevailed. Since that case was decided, the overwhelming majority of courts that have considered this type of case have accepted Justice Traynor's analysis (frequently quoting him at length). Examples include Preload Technology, Inc. v. A.B. & J. Construction Co., 696 F.2d 1080 (5th Cir. 1983) (Texas law); Janke Construction Co. v. Vulcan Materials Co., 527 F.2d 772 (7th Cir. 1976) (Wisconsin law); Double AA Builders, Ltd. v. Grand State Constr. L.L.C., 114 P.3d 835 (Ariz. Ct. App. 2005); contra Home Electric Co. v. Hall & Underdown Heating & Air Cond. Co., 358 S.E.2d 539 (N.C. Ct. App. 1987), *aff'd,* 366 S.E.2d 441 (1988) (per curiam). Judge Hand's *James Baird* analysis, apparently quoted verbatim in large chunks by the defendant, got particularly short shrift in James King & Son, Inc. v. De Santis Construction No. 2 Corp., 413 N.Y.S.2d 78 (Sup. Ct. 1977) (*James Baird* case "decided 44 years ago, pre-dating the theory of promissory estoppel in bidding"). The revised Restatement also endorses the *Drennan* analysis, in §87(2). See Comment *e* and Illustration 6. Although the essence of promissory estoppel might seem to be a case-by-case examination of all the factors that could cause the court's sense of injustice to be aroused, in practice the *Drennan* line of cases appears to have matured to the point where establishment of the basic facts will entitle the plaintiff general contractor to judgment more or less automatically, unless the defendant subcontractor can take the case out of the ordinary run by demonstrating some additional factor in its favor. E.g., Crook v. Mortenson-Neal, 727 P.2d 297 (Alaska 1986) (despite some post-award bargaining over terms of proposed subcontract, defendant subcontractor's defense properly characterized by trial court as so "weak" and "incredible" as to be "bordering on bad faith," justifying award of attorney fees to plaintiff general contractor).

3. *Limitations on the **Drennan** rule.* In *Drennan* the court indicated in dictum several situations in which the general contractor would not be allowed to invoke the protections of promissory estoppel. If the defendant's bid had "expressly stated or clearly implied that it was revocable at any time before acceptance," the court would have "treat[ed] it accordingly." Even such language might not be sufficient to preserve for the offeror the power of free revocability, however. In Lyon Metal Products, Inc. v. Hagerman Construction Corp., 391 N.E.2d 1152 (Ind. Ct. App. 1979), the defendant subcontractor's offer was in response to specifications that required (with respect to the general contract) that all bids submitted by general contractors remain open

for 120 days. Defendant's bid was on a quotation form that stated (on the reverse side, in small print), "This quotation may be withdrawn and is subject to change without notice after 15 days from the date of quotation." Judgment in favor of the plaintiff general contractor on the basis of promissory estoppel was affirmed by the Indiana Court of Appeals. In response to the defendant's argument based on the above language, the court held that the trial court could have inferred that Lyon did not intend the 15-day clause to be the controlling time period but rather the 120-day period found in the specifications.

In addition, inequitable conduct by the general contractor may preclude the use of promissory estoppel. Two such situations involve "bid shopping," the practice of trying to find another subcontractor who will do the work more cheaply while continuing to claim that the original bidder is bound, and "bid chopping," the attempt to renegotiate with the bidder to reduce the price. See Lahr Construction Corp. v. J. Kozel & Son, Inc., 640 N.Y.S.2d 957 (Sup. Ct. 1996).

4. *Liability of general contractor to subcontractor.* In his opinion in the *James Baird* case, Judge Hand rejected the possibility that the general contractor had in effect received an "option," giving it the right to buy from the subcontractor at the offered price while reserving the freedom to buy from another supplier "if it could get a better bargain elsewhere." There was, Judge Hand asserted, "not the least reason to suppose that the defendant meant to subject itself to such a one-sided obligation." By invoking promissory estoppel to protect the plaintiff in *Drennan,* the California Supreme Court is of course creating just such an obligation, since promissory estoppel is inherently a doctrine that gives rise not to reciprocally binding relationships but to "one-way" liability. Could a subcontractor ever claim successfully that it had relied on the prospect that the general would accept its bid, providing a basis for holding the *general* on a §90 theory? Occasional cases indicate that this could be possible, with special enough facts. See, e.g., R. S. Bennett & Co. v. Economy Mechanical Industries, Inc., 606 F.2d 182 (7th Cir. 1979) (plaintiff lowered its bid to defendant and other general contractors in reliance on promise that it would get subcontract if defendant was awarded general contract).

It is also possible that in some cases the subcontractor may be able to establish a contract with the general contractor. In *James Baird,* Judge Hand ruled that mere use by the general of the subcontractor's bid did not amount to acceptance of the bid. But, if the subcontractor agrees to submit a bid only because of the general's assurances that the sub will be awarded the contract, conditioned on the general being awarded the prime contract, then the general is bound contractually. E.g., Electrical Construction & Maintenance Co. v. Maeda Pacific Corp., 764 F.2d 619 (9th Cir. 1985).

5. *Bidding statutes.* Some states have enacted statutes to protect subcontractors from bid shopping by general contractors in connection with government contracts. Such statutes commonly restrict the general contractor's freedom to substitute other subcontractors for those listed by it in the bid on the general contract without the approval of the granting authority. E.g., Cal. Pub. Contract Code §4107 (Supp. 2006). See E. F. Brady Co. v. M. H. Golden Co., 67 Cal. Rptr. 2d 886 (Ct. App. 1997) (subcontractor had no cause of action under statute because sub was not listed in bid and had not been

approved as substitute). Compare Clark Pacific v. Krump Construction, Inc., 942 F. Supp. 1324 (D. Nev. 1996) (Nevada statute requires listing of sub-contractors in public works projects and prevents general contractors from refusing to use listed sub except on statutory grounds). But see Mitchell v. Siqueiros, 582 P.2d 1074 (Idaho 1978) (Idaho naming statute not construed to change long-standing contractual principles). Absent such a statute, it seems generally true that under the theory of decision employed in *Drennan,* the subcontractor will be bound (at least for a reasonable time) to its bid, while the general will incur no liability if instead it chooses to "shop around" (although this might cost it the ability to accept the original offer, as suggested in *Drennan*). Does this lack of protection for the subcontractor cast doubt on the wisdom of the *Drennan* decision? The policy problems raised by the construction-bidding cases are further explored in the Comment that follows.

6. *Scholarly commentary. James Baird* and *Drennan* continue to invoke con-siderable scholarly commentary. For an in-depth examination and comparison of the cases that includes insights gathered from trial records, the appellate briefs, and the preconference memoranda circulated among the judges in the cases, see Alfred S. Konefsky, Freedom and Interdependence in Twentieth-Century Contract Law: Traynor and Hand and Promissory Estoppel, 65 U. Cin. L. Rev. 1169 (1997). Other recent scholarship has approached the cases from the perspective of economic analysis. See Richard Craswell, Offer, Acceptance, and Efficient Reliance, 48 Stan. L. Rev. 481 (1996); Sidney W. Delong, The New Requirement of Enforcement Reliance in Commercial Promissory Estoppel: Section 90 as Catch-22, 1997 Wis. L. Rev. 943; Avery Katz, When Should an Offer Stick? The Economics of Promissory Estoppel in Preliminary Negotia-tions, 105 Yale L.J. 1249 (1996).

Comment: Contract Law and Business Practice

Throughout these materials we have used the term "classical contract law" as a short-hand expression for a particular approach to contract law. The classical system represented an attempt to develop reasonably clear rules on the various issues the courts faced in contract cases. Concern with the impact of these rules on commercial behavior, or with reform of the rules to bring them into conformity with the needs of businesses and consumers, was not considered to be an issue for contract law to address.

In the 1920s and 1930s the movement known as legal realism became a significant force in academia. One of the fundamental teachings of the realists was that rules do not decide cases, judges do. Understanding of judicial decisionmaking, therefore, required an analysis of the factors influencing judges. This focus on judicial motivation led the realists along many different paths, including economics, psychology, and social policy. See the discussion and bibliography of works on Legal Realism in Chapter 1.

A natural development of the realist philosophy was to broaden the focus of inquiry beyond judges to include the behavior of people affected by the law. The approach to scholarship that is today usually referred to as the "sociology of law" or "law and society" represents this extension of the realist agenda. Since the sociological approach to law focuses on behavior, a fundamental aspect of its program is empirical research into the impact of law on human behavior. See John Henry Schlegel, American Legal Realism and Empirical Social Science (1995). The University of Wisconsin has been an important center of the law and society movement, so much so that the movement is often referred to as the "Wisconsin School," much as the Law and Economics movement is often described as the "Chicago School." See Stewart Macaulay, Willard's Law School?, 1997 Wis. L. Rev. 1163 (attributing the interdisciplinary culture of the school to the work of J. Willard Hurst).

Probably the seminal work in the sociological approach to contract law was Professor Stewart Macaulay's article, Non-Contractual Relations in Business: A Preliminary Study, 28 Am. Soc. Rev. 55 (1963). Based on interviews with officials of manufacturing companies and with law firms, Macaulay's article challenged central assumptions about contract law. In particular, Macaulay argued that preservation of business relationships rather than legal doctrine was the predominant factor in the behavior of business people. See also David Charny, Nonlegal Sanctions in Commercial Relationships, 104 Harv. L. Rev. 373 (1990) (description and economic analysis of role of nonlegal sanctions). As a result, a fundamental gap existed between the academic view of contract law and the way the world actually works. In 1985 Macaulay updated his study; while he largely reaffirmed his earlier conclusions, he tempered to some degree his original skepticism of the role of contract law. In the later article he stressed that relational considerations often did not produce cooperation, particularly when the amount of money involved in a dispute was substantial. Stewart Macaulay, An Empirical View of Contract, 1985 Wis. L. Rev. 465, 471. For Professor Macaulay's appraisal of the current status of empirical scholarship see Contracts, New Legal Realism, and Improving the Navigation of the Yellow Submarine, 80 Tul. L. Rev. 1161 (2006). Despite the efforts of Professor Macaulay and others, empirical studies of contract law are relatively rare. See Russell Korobkin, Empirical Scholarship in Contract Law: Possibilities and Pitfalls, 2002 U. Ill. L. Rev. 1033, 1036 (2002) ("there is extremely little empirical contract law scholarship being produced in the legal academy today"). Professor Korobkin's article contains a list of empirical studies published from 1985 to 2000. It also appears that the limited empirical scholarship that is being produced has had a relatively minor impact on court decisions. Gregory S. Crespi, The Influence of Two Decades of Contract Law Scholarship on Judicial Rulings: An Empirical Analysis, 57 S.M.U. L. Rev. 105 (2004).

It might be supposed that the influence of the Uniform Commercial Code would have served to counter what might be viewed as the "ivory tower" aspect of contract law; the Code puts a strong emphasis on conforming law to business practice, and Professor Llewellyn, its principal architect, was himself widely viewed as a leading exponent of the Legal Realist point of view. Certainly the Code does direct the courts to inform their decisions by reference to trade custom and business practice. (See, e.g., UCC §§1-205, 2-208.) The rules of the Code were not, however, drafted generally with an eye toward a body of supporting empirical data; in most instances, the drafters appear to have relied generally on their own knowledge of business practices. In light of this overall tendency to reach legal results independent of empirical data, it is perhaps not surprising if decisions in contract cases often seem to have been made "in a vacuum." See generally Thomas P. Lambert, Comment, Bid Shopping and Peddling in the Subcontract Construction Industry, 18 UCLA L. Rev. 389, 409 (1970).

In the area of construction-bidding law, however, academic writers have not been indifferent to the need for empirical research. Scholarly writing on construction-bidding issues dates back at least to 1952 (pre-*Drennan*), when Professor Franklin Schultz published his article, The Firm Offer Puzzle: A Study of Business Practice in the Construction Industry, 19 U. Chi. L. Rev. 237 (1952). Focusing on the problem exemplified by the facts of *Baird* (and on UCC §2-205 — discussed in the following section of this chapter — as a possible solution to that problem), Professor Schultz conducted an empirical survey of the attitudes and practices of contracting firms (both general and sub) in Indiana. After reporting in detail on the findings of that investigation, he concluded that general contractors place relatively little importance on the "firmness" of offers and questioned the wisdom of adding to the imbalance of power already existing in favor of general contractors with a rule making firm offers legally irrevocable.

A similar study was conducted in 1967 for the Virginia Law Review; its findings were reported in Joe C. Creason, Jr., Note, Another Look at Construction Bidding and Contracts at Formation, 53 Va. L. Rev. 1720 (1967). The results of this survey, generally consistent with those of Professor Schultz, led the author to conclude that the best legal solution would be a rule that binds *both* the sub and the general to a contract at the time the sub's bid is used, provided two conditions are met: (1) the sub-bid is responsive to the plans and specifications for the general contract and (2) the sub-bidder is financially and otherwise responsible and capable of performance. See also Margaret N. Kniffin, Innovation or Aberration: Recovery for Reliance on a Contract Offer, as Permitted by the New Restatement (Second) of Contracts, 62 U. Det. L. Rev. 23 (1984). On the other hand, the problem of "nonmutuality" explored by Schultz and the Virginia study led another commentator to propose that the *Drennan* rule be rejected in favor of a rule that bound neither party until the stage of formal contract was reached. Kenneth L. Schriber, Note, Construction Contracts — The Problem of Offer and Acceptance in the General Contractor-Subcontractor Relationship, 37 U. Cin. L. Rev. 798 (1968). For a description of the construction industry and a call for reform of the applicable rules, see Thomas J. Stipanowich, Reconstructing Construction Law: Reality And Reform in a Transactional System, 1998 Wis. L. Rev. 463.

Despite the arguments advanced in favor of a symmetrical, "both-parties-are-bound-or-neither-is-bound" approach, the decisions have continued to invoke promissory estoppel to protect the general contractor against subcontractor withdrawal while declining to find the general contractor bound to a particular sub merely because its sub-bid was used. In Holman Erection Co. v. Orville E. Madsen & Sons, Inc., 330 N.W.2d 693 (Minn. 1983), the Minnesota Supreme Court reviewed the case law and the arguments of various commentators summarized above. The court noted that a number of policy arguments had been advanced for binding the general contractor at the point of bid-use, including the desire to put general and subcontractors on an "equal footing" in any subsequent negotiation, and the avoidance of post-award bid-shopping. The court elected to retain the traditional approach, however. A general contractor inevitably relies in a very substantial way on the bids it receives from subcontractors; failure to enforce them, the court asserted, would subject the general to financial detriment. On the other hand, the subcontractor does not rely on the general and suffers no injury from nonenforcement. Moreover, the court continued, the general contractor is entitled to a certain amount of flexibility in its post-award dealing with potential subcontractors, because of the hectic, last-minute way in which bids on a general contract are typically compiled; that results in large measure from the last-minute submission of bids by potential subcontractors, who adopt this procedure to prevent pre-award bid-shopping.

Berryman v. Kmoch
Supreme Court of Kansas
221 Kan. 304, 559 P.2d 790 (1977)

FROMME, Justice:

Wade Berryman, a landowner, filed this declaratory judgment action to have an option contract declared null and void. Norbert H. Kmoch, the optionee, answered and counter-claimed seeking damages for Berryman's failure to convey the land. After depositions were taken and discovery proceedings completed both parties filed separate motions for summary judgment. The trial court entered a summary judgment for plaintiff and held the option was granted without consideration, was in effect an offer to sell subject to withdrawal at any time prior to acceptance and was withdrawn in July, 1973, prior to its being exercised by Kmoch. Kmoch has appealed.

The option agreement dated June 19, 1973, was signed by Wade Berryman of Meade, Kansas, and was addressed to Mr. Norbert H. Kmoch, 1155 Ash Street, Denver, Colorado. The granting clause provided:

For $10.00 and other valuable consideration, I hereby grant unto you or your assigns an option for 120 days after date to purchase the following described real estate: [Then followed the legal description of 960 acres of land located in Stanton County, Kansas.]

The balance of the option agreement sets forth the terms of purchase including the price for the land and the growing crops, the water rights and irrigation equipment included in the sale, the time possession was to be delivered to the purchaser, and other provisions not pertinent to the questions presented here on appeal.

Before examining the questions raised on appeal it will be helpful to set forth a few of the facts admitted and on which there is no dispute. Berryman was the owner of the land. Kmoch was a Colorado real estate broker. A third person, Samuel M. Goertz, was a Nebraska agricultural consultant. Goertz learned that Berryman was interested in selling the land and talked to Berryman about obtaining an option on the land for Kmoch. Goertz talked to Kmoch and Kmoch prepared the option contract dated June 19, 1973. Goertz and Kmoch flew to Johnson, Kansas, where a meeting with Berryman had been arranged. At this meeting the option agreement was signed by Berryman. Although the agreement recited the option was granted "for $10.00 and other valuable consideration," the $10.00 was not paid.

The next conversation between Berryman and Kmoch occurred during the latter part of July, 1973. Berryman called Kmoch by telephone and asked to be released from the option agreement. Nothing definite was worked out between them. Berryman sold the land to another person. In August, Kmoch decided to exercise the option and went to the Federal Land Bank representative in Garden City, Kansas, to make arrangements to purchase the land. He was then informed by the bank representative that the land had been sold by Berryman. Kmoch then recorded the option agreement in Stanton County. After a telephone conversation with Berryman was unproductive, Kmoch sent a letter to Berryman in October, 1973, attempting to exercise his option on the land. Berryman responded by bringing the present action to have the option declared null and void.

Appellant, Kmoch, acknowledges that the $10.00 cash consideration recited in the option agreement was never paid. However, he points out the agreement included a provision for "other valuable consideration" and that he should have been permitted to introduce evidence to establish time spent and expenses incurred in an effort to interest others in joining him in acquiring the land. He points to the deposition testimony of Goertz and another man by the name of Robert Harris, who had examined the land under option. Their services were sought by Kmoch to obtain a farm report on the land which might interest other investors. In addition appellant argues that promissory estoppel should have been applied by the trial court as a substitute for consideration.

An option contract to purchase land to be binding must be supported by consideration the same as any other contract. If no consideration was given in the present case the trial court correctly found there was no more than a continuing offer to sell. An option contract which is not supported by consideration is a mere offer to sell which may be withdrawn at any time prior to acceptance. . . .

We turn next to appellant's contention that the option contract should have been enforceable under the doctrine of promissory estoppel. This doctrine has been discussed in Marker v. Preferred Fire Ins. Co., 211 Kan. 427, 506 P.2d 1163. . . . In *Marker* it is held:

> In order for the doctrine of promissory estoppel to be invoked the evidence must show that the promise was made under circumstances where the promisor intended and reasonably expected that the promise would be relied upon by the promisee and further that the promisee acted reasonably in relying upon the promise. Furthermore promissory estoppel should be applied only if a refusal to enforce it would be virtually to sanction the perpetration of fraud or would result in other injustice.

211 Kan. 427, Syl. 4, 506 P.2d 1163. . . .

In order for the doctrine of promissory estoppel to be invoked as a substitute for consideration the evidence must show (1) the promise was made under such circumstances that the promisor reasonably expected the promisee to act in reliance on the promise, (2) the promisee acted as could reasonably be expected in relying on the promise, and (3) a refusal by the court to enforce the promise must be virtually to sanction the perpetration of fraud or must result in other injustice.

The requirements are not met here. This was an option contract promising to sell the land to appellant. It was not a contract listing the real estate with Kmoch for sale to others. Kmoch was familiar with real estate contracts and personally drew up the present option. He knew no consideration was paid for the same and that it had the effect of a continuing offer subject to withdrawal at any time before acceptance. The acts which appellant urges as consideration conferred no special benefit on the promisor or on his land. The evidence which appellant desires to introduce in support of promissory estoppel does not relate to acts which could reasonably be expected as a result of extending the option promise. It relates to time, effort, and expense incurred in an attempt to interest other investors in this particular land. The appellant chose the form of the contract. It was not a contract listing the land for sale with one entrusted with duties and obligations to produce a buyer. The appellant was not obligated to do anything and no basis for promissory estoppel could be shown by the evidence proposed.

An option contract can be made binding and irrevocable by subsequent action in reliance upon it even though such action is neither requested nor given in exchange for the option promise. An option promise is no different from other promises in this respect but cases are rare in which an option holder will be reasonably induced to change his position in reliance upon an option promise that is neither under seal nor made binding by a consideration, or in which the option promisor has reason to expect such change of position. (1A Corbin on Contracts, §263, pp. 502-504.)

When an option is conditioned upon a performance of certain acts, the performance of the acts may constitute a consideration to uphold a contract for option; but there is no such condition imposed if the acts were not intended to benefit nor were they incurred on behalf of the optionor.

The appellant argues that to assume Berryman gave the option without expecting something from him in return is to avoid the realities of the business world and that consideration was encompassed by a promise for a promise. The difficulty with that argument is apparent. Appellant did not promise to purchase the land. He was required to do nothing and any assertion that Berryman expected him to raise and pay money for the land as consideration for the option confuses motive with consideration.

In 17 Am. Jur. 2d, Contracts, §93, pp.436, 437, it is said:

> The motive which prompts one to enter into a contract and the consideration for the contract are distinct and different things. . . . These inducements are not . . . either legal or equitable consideration, and actually compose no part of the contract. . . .

In 1 Williston on Contracts, 3d ed., §111, p.439, it is stated:

> Though desire to obtain the consideration for a promise may be, and ordinarily is, the motive inducing the promisor to enter into a contract, yet this is not essential nor, on the other hand, can any motive serve in itself as consideration. . . .

Appellant here confuses Berryman's possible motives — to sell the land — with consideration given. The fact Berryman expected appellant to expend time and money to find a buyer is really irrelevant because he was not bound to do so. He made no promise legally enforceable by Berryman to that effect. To be sufficient consideration, a promise must impose a legal obligation on the promisor. (17 Am. Jur. 2d, Contracts, §105, pp. 450-451.) As stated in 1A Corbin on Contracts, §263, p. 505: "... So, if the only consideration is an illusory promise, there is no contract and no binding option, although there may still be an operative offer and a power of acceptance."

Time and money spent by a party in trying to sell property for which he holds an option cannot be construed as a consideration to the party from whom he has secured the option. . . .

Two cases relied on by appellant to support his position are Talbott v. Nibert, supra, and Steel v. Eagle, 207 Kan. 146, 483 P.2d 1063. They are not persuasive and are readily distinguishable on the facts.

In *Talbott* the plaintiff had acquired an option to purchase majority stock interests in an oil drilling company from another stockholder. In reliance on the option plaintiff personally obtained valuable drilling contracts for the company, paid off a $23,000.00 mortgage on a drilling rig and pulled the company out of financial straits. During this time the stock had increased in value from $90.00 per share to $250.00 per share, largely as a result of plaintiff's efforts. It was plaintiff's intention to acquire a controlling interest in the company by exercising the option, this the optionor knew. The court found the option-offer was duly accepted and the purchase price was tendered before revocation. In our present case the option-offer was withdrawn before acceptance. We will discuss the withdrawal of the option later in this opinion.

In *Steel* the option was for the sale of a milling company. The option agreement stated that the optionee promised to place $5,000.00 with an escrow agent no later than a specified time in the future and that if the option was not exercised according to its terms the $5,000.00 would be forfeited. It was held that the option was adequately supported by consideration, a promise for a promise. The optionor granted the option and promised to transfer title to the company. The optionee promised to pay $5,000.00 as evidence of good faith, said sum to be forfeited in event the option was not exercised. This is not the case here. Our present option recited a completed payment of $10.00, even though it had not been paid. Payment during the option period was not contemplated by either party and the tender of the $10.00 was not made by defendant-appellant in his counter-claim when that pleading was filed.

Now we turn to the question of revocation or withdrawal of the option-promise before acceptance.

Where an offer is for the sale of an interest in land or in other things, if the offeror, after making the offer, sells or contracts to sell the interest to another person, and the offeree acquires reliable information of that fact, before he has exercised his power of creating a contract by acceptance of the offer, the offer is revoked.

In Restatement of the Law, Second, Contracts, §42, p. 96, it is said:

> An offeree's power of acceptance is terminated when the offeror takes definite action inconsistent with an intention to enter into the proposed contract and the offeree acquires reliable information to that effect.

The appellant in his deposition admitted that he was advised in July, 1973, by telephone that Berryman no longer wanted to be obligated by the option. Appellant further admitted that he was advised in August, 1973, by a representative of the Federal Land Bank, which held a substantial mortgage on the land, that Berryman had disposed of this land. The appellant's power of acceptance was terminated thereby and any attempted exercise of the option in October came too late when you consider the appellant's own admissions.

Summary judgment was therefore proper and the judgment is affirmed.

Notes and Questions

1. *Restatement's suggested rule for reliance on an offer.* In §87(2), the Restatement (Second) has adopted the *Drennan* rule, abstracted so as to be potentially applicable to any case where there has been substantial and reasonably foreseeable reliance on an offer before its acceptance. So far, however, only a few cases have applied promissory estoppel to unaccepted offers outside of the construction bidding situation exemplified by *Drennan* itself. Compare First National Bankshares of Beloit, Inc. v. Geisel, 853 F. Supp. 1344 (D. Kan. 1994) (under Kansas law as established by Berryman v. Kmoch, promissory estoppel available to enforce option to sell stock in bank, but summary judgment granted for defendants because plaintiffs failed to establish detrimental reliance) with Strata Production Co. v. Mercury Exploration Co., 916 P.2d 822 (N.M. 1996) (promissory estoppel applied to make oil and gas "farmout" agreement irrevocable for period of time stated in option plus extension; §87(2) cited with approval). Is there something about the construction industry setting that would account for this difference in the use of promissory estoppel?

Professor Margaret Kniffin has argued that the *Drennan* decision is an "aberration," because it insufficiently recognizes the distinction between a "promise" and the mere "conditional promise" reflected in an "offer"; she goes on to assert that in most cases Restatement (Second) §87(2) ought not to be followed. Margaret N. Kniffin, Innovation or Aberration: Recovery for Reliance on a Contract Offer, as Permitted by the New Restatement (Second) of Contracts, 62 U. Det. L. Rev. 23 (1984). But see Rhode Island Hospital Trust National Bank v. Varadian, 647 N.E.2d 1174 (Mass. 1995) (offer and promise treated as equivalent because both represent commitment). The *Berryman* decision illustrates some of the objections that might be raised to the extension of promissory estoppel to other cases of pre-acceptance reliance. Was the court in *Berryman* right to reject the application of promissory estoppel urged by the plaintiff?

2. *Nominal consideration.* If the $10 payment recited in the Berryman-Kmoch option agreement had actually been paid to Berryman, should the outcome of the *Berryman* case have been different? The cases generally appear

to hold that even a very small amount of money can serve as sufficient consideration for an "option contract"—that is, to make an offer irrevocable. See Board of Control of Eastern Michigan University v. Burgess, 206 N.W.2d 256 (Mich. Ct. App. 1973) ($1, if paid or at least tendered, could be sufficient consideration for 60-day option to buy house for $14,000); Keaster v. Bozik, 623 P.2d 1376 (Mont. 1981) ($5 could be sufficient consideration to bind one-year option to purchase land for $200,000). The court in *Bozik* refers to the mentioned sum as "nominal consideration." What does the word *nominal* mean in this context? Is this a departure from the bargain theory of consideration?

3. *Restatement's suggested rule of form for options.* If the payment of a sum as small as $5 or $10 can be enough consideration to bind an option contract, could such a contract be enforced even if the recited payment was not actually made? Some courts have implied a promise on the part of the option holder to pay the consideration. See, e.g, Smith v. Wheeler, 210 S.E.2d 702 (Ga. 1974) (recital of consideration "gives rise to an implied promise to pay which can be enforced by the other party"). The Restatement (Second) in §87(1)(a) goes even further: An offer made in a signed writing is binding "as an option contract" if it "proposes an exchange on fair terms within a reasonable time" and "recites a purported consideration" for its making. Comment *c* to §87 frankly refers to this rule as one that sanctions enforcement on the basis of a "false recital of nominal consideration." The comment explains that the rule is based on form rather than the implication of a promise: The signed writing has "vital significance as a formality," and therefore its recital of consideration should not be open to invalidation by "oral testimony which is easily fabricated." After an extensive review of the history, case law, and academic commentary on the issue, the Texas Supreme Court in 1464-Eight, Ltd. v. Joppich, 154 S.W.3d 101 (Tex. 2004), adopted the position of Restatement (Second) §87(1)(a). The court recognized, however, that its view was the minority position, citing, among other decisions, Berryman v. Kmoch. Note, however, that §87(1)(a) could not be used to make a donative promise enforceable because a donative promise does not propose "an exchange on fair terms" as required by the Restatement.

4. *Services as consideration.* Should the actions of defendant Kmoch in seeking a purchaser for the Berryman land have constituted sufficient consideration to bind Berryman to an option contract? Some courts in similar cases have given effect to language stating expressly that the purchaser's efforts to obtain a loan to finance the purchase are to constitute consideration for the option. Mack v. Coker, 523 P.2d 1342 (Ariz. Ct. App. 1974); Coulter & Smith, Ltd. v. Russell, 966 P.2d 852 (Utah 1998) (purchaser's promise to vendor in written option agreement that purchaser would "proceed posthaste" to annex and develop purchaser's and vendor's tracts jointly constituted consideration for option). Recall again Williston's "tramp" example quoted in connection with Pennsy Supply, Inc. v. American Ash. In Ragosta v. Wilder, 592 A.2d 367 (Vt. 1991), purchasers' efforts to obtain financing to buy defendant's realty were held not to be bargained-for consideration, sufficient to bind defendant to an option contract, but the Vermont Supreme Court also held (remanding the case for reconsideration on this point) that their actions in undertaking to obtain financing (assertedly including payment of $7500 in loan closing costs) might have constituted

reliance sufficient to justify relief based on promissory estoppel. Discussion of this and other issues raised by Berryman v. Kmoch can be found in Charles L. Knapp, Rescuing Reliance: The Perils of Promissory Estoppel, 49 Hastings L.J. 1191, 1266-1274 (1998).

5. *Application of the mailbox rule to options.* Should an option contract be an exception to the "deposited-acceptance" rule, so that even if use of the mail is contemplated, an acceptance to be effective must be *received* by the offeror within the time limit specified? The Restatement (Second) takes this position, in §63(b); Comment *f* explains the suggested rule as resting on the fact that the offeree in such a case already has in the option a "dependable basis for reliance," removing the justification for the rule of convenience applied in ordinary nonoption cases. Some courts have followed the Restatement's position on this issue. See, e.g., Maloney v. Atlantique Condominium Complex, Inc., 399 So. 2d 1111 (Fla. Dist. Ct. App. 1981); Santos v. Dean, 982 P.2d 632 (Wash. Ct. App. 1999). Not all courts agree, however. In Worms v. Burgess, 620 P.2d 455 (Okla. Ct. App. 1980), the court rejected the Restatement position, on the ground that the "mailbox rule" is so widely known that the parties to an option contract should be presumed to have contracted with reference to that rule unless they have expressly provided otherwise. Accord Pennsylvania Academy of Fine Arts v. Grant, 590 A.2d 9 (Pa. Super. Ct. 1991).

6. *Effectiveness of revocation.* At the risk of stating the obvious, it should be recalled here that even if the offer is held to have been revocable, acceptance of that offer will ordinarily still bind the offeror to a contract unless a valid revocation was received by the offeree before acceptance. See, e.g., I. R. Kirk Farms, Inc. v. Pointer, 897 S.W.2d 183 (Mo. Ct. App. 1995) (even if option is unenforceable due to lack of consideration, offer reflected in option may be accepted prior to revocation). In *Berryman,* the seller apparently did not make an unequivocal revocation of his offer, but the buyer's power of acceptance was held to have terminated when he learned that the seller had sold the land to someone else. This rule of indirect communication of revocation, currently expressed in Restatement (Second) §43, was established by the venerable English case of Dickinson v. Dodds, 2 Ch. Div. 463 (1876). See, e.g., Wilson v. Sand Mountain Funeral Home, 739 So.2d 1123 (Ala. Civ. App. 1999) (corporation's offer to repurchase stock from employee was effectively revoked when it sued employee for, inter alia, conspiring to devalue corporation's stock). You may recall that we first encountered the *Dickinson* rule in Normile v. Miller, when the broker told Normile that "you snooze, you lose."

Pop's Cones, Inc. v. Resorts International Hotel, Inc.
Superior Court of New Jersey, Appellate Division
307 N.J. Super. 461, 704 A.2d 1321 (1998)

KLEINER, J.A.D.

Plaintiff, Pop's Cones, Inc., t/a TCBY Yogurt, ("Pop's"), appeals from an order of the Law Division granting defendant, Resorts International, Inc. ("Resorts"), summary judgment and dismissing its complaint seeking damages predicated on a theory of promissory estoppel. . . . In reversing summary judgment, we rely upon principles of promissory estoppel enunciated in Section 90 of the Restatement (Second) of Contracts, and recent cases which, in order to avoid injustice, seemingly relax the strict requirement of "a clear and definite promise" in making a prima facie case of promissory estoppel.

Pop's is an authorized franchisee of TCBY Systems, Inc. ("TCBY"), a national franchisor of frozen yogurt products. Resorts is a casino hotel in Atlantic City that leases retail space along "prime Boardwalk frontage," among other business ventures.

From June of 1991 to September 1994, Pop's operated a TCBY franchise in Margate, New Jersey. Sometime during the months of May or June 1994, Brenda Taube ("Taube"), President of Pop's, had "a number of discussions" with Marlon Phoenix ("Phoenix"), the Executive Director of Business Development and Sales for Resorts, about the possible relocation of Pop's business to space owned by Resorts. During these discussions, Phoenix showed Taube one location for a TCBY vending cart within Resorts Hotel and "three specific locations for the operation of a full service TCBY store."

According to Taube, she and Phoenix specifically discussed the boardwalk property occupied at that time by a business trading as "The Players Club." These discussions included Taube's concerns with the then-current rental fees and Phoenix's indication that Resorts management and Merv Griffin personally[2] were "very anxious to have Pop's as a tenant" and that "financial issues . . . could easily be resolved, such as through a percentage of gross revenue." In order to allay both Taube's and Phoenix's concerns about whether a TCBY franchise at The Players Club location would be successful, Phoenix offered to permit Pop's to operate a vending cart within Resorts free of charge during the summer of 1994 so as to "test the traffic flow." This offer was considered and approved by Paul Ryan, Vice President for Hotel Operations at Resorts.

These discussions led to further meetings with Phoenix about the Players Club location, and Taube contacted TCBY's corporate headquarters about a possible franchise site change. During the weekend of July 4, 1994, Pop's opened the TCBY cart for business at Resorts pursuant to the above stated offer. On July 6, 1994, TCBY gave Taube initial approval for Pop's change in franchise site. In late July or early August of 1994, representatives of TCBY personally visited the Players Club location, with Taube and Phoenix present.

Based on Pop's marketing assessment of the Resorts location, Taube drafted a written proposal dated August 18, 1994, addressing the leasing of Resorts' Players Club location and hand-delivered it to Phoenix. Taube's proposal offered Resorts "7% of net monthly sales (gross less sales tax) for the duration of the [Player's Club] lease . . . [and] [i]f this proposal is acceptable, I'd need a 6 year lease, and a renewable option for another 6 years."

In mid-September 1994, Taube spoke with Phoenix about the status of Pop's lease proposal and "pressed [him] to advise [her] of Resorts' position. [Taube] specifically advised [Phoenix] that Pop's had an option to renew the lease for its Margate location and then needed to give notice to its landlord of

---

2. Merv Griffin was the Chief Executive Officer and a large shareholder of Resorts.

whether it would be staying at that location no later than October 1, 1994." Another conversation about this topic occurred in late September when Taube "asked Phoenix if [Pop's] proposal was in the ballpark of what Resorts was looking for." He responded that it was and that "we are 95% there, we just need Belisle's[3] signature on the deal." Taube admits to having been advised that Belisle had "ultimate responsibility for signing off on the deal" but that Phoenix "assured [her] that Mr. Belisle would follow his recommendation, which was to approve the deal, and that [Phoenix] did not anticipate any difficulties." During this conversation, Taube again mentioned to Phoenix that she had to inform her landlord by October 1, 1994, about whether or not Pop's would renew its lease with them. Taube stated: "Mr. Phoenix assured me that we would have little difficulty in concluding an agreement and advised [Taube] to give notice that [Pop's] would not be extending [its] Margate lease and 'to pack up the Margate store and plan on moving.'"

Relying upon Phoenix's "advice and assurances," Taube notified Pop's landlord in late-September 1994 that it would not be renewing the lease for the Margate location.

In early October, Pop's moved its equipment out of the Margate location and placed it in temporary storage. Taube then commenced a number of new site preparations including: (1) sending designs for the new store to TCBY in October 1994; and (2) retaining an attorney to represent Pop's in finalizing the terms of the lease with Resorts.

By letter dated November 1, 1994, General Counsel for Resorts forwarded a proposed form of lease for The Players Club location to Pop's attorney. The letter provided:

> Per our conversation, enclosed please find the form of lease utilized for retail outlets leasing space in Resorts Hotel. You will note that there are a number of alternative sections depending upon the terms of the deal.
>
> As I advised, I will contact you . . . to inform you of our decision regarding TCBY. . . .

By letter dated December 1, 1994, General Counsel for Resorts forwarded to Pop's attorney a written offer of the terms upon which Resorts was proposing to lease the Players Club space to Pop's. The terms provided:

> [Resorts is] willing to offer the space for an initial three (3) year term with a rent calculated at the greater of 7% of gross revenues or: $50,000 in year one; $60,000 in year two; and $70,000 in year three . . . [with] a three (3) year option to renew after the initial term . . .

The letter also addressed a "boilerplate lease agreement" provision and a proposed addition to the form lease. The letter concluded by stating:

> *This letter is not intended to be binding upon Resorts.* It is intended to set forth the basic terms and conditions upon which Resorts would be willing to negotiate a lease and is subject to those negotiations and the execution of a definitive agreement.

---

3. The reference to Belisle is John Belisle, then-Chief Operating Officer of Resorts.

... [W]e think TCBY will be successful at the Boardwalk location based upon the terms we propose. We look forward to having your client as part of ... Resorts family of customer service providers and believe TCBY will benefit greatly from some of the dynamic changes we plan.

... [W]e would be pleased ... to discuss this proposal in greater detail. (Emphasis added.)

In early-December 1994, Taube and her attorney met with William Murtha, General Counsel of Resorts, and Paul Ryan to finalize the proposed lease. After a number of discussions about the lease, Murtha and Ryan informed Taube that they desired to reschedule the meeting to finalize the lease until after the first of the year because of a public announcement they intended to make about another unrelated business venture that Resorts was about to commence. Ryan again assured Taube that rent for the Players Club space was not an issue and that the lease terms would be worked out. "He also assured [Taube] that Resorts wanted TCBY ... on the boardwalk for the following season."

Several attempts were made in January 1995 to contact Resorts' representatives and confirm that matters were proceeding. On January 30, 1995, Taube's attorney received a letter stating: "This letter is to confirm our conversation of this date wherein I advised that Resorts is withdrawing its December 1, 1994 offer to lease space to your client, TCBY."[4]

According to Taube's certification, "As soon as [Pop's] heard that Resorts was withdrawing its offer, we undertook extensive efforts to reopen [the] franchise at a different location. Because the Margate location had been re-let, it was not available." Ultimately, Pop's found a suitable location but did not reopen for business until July 5, 1996.

On July 17, 1995, Pop's filed a complaint against Resorts seeking damages. The complaint alleged that Pop's "reasonably relied to its detriment on the promises and assurances of Resorts that it would be permitted to relocate its operation to [Resorts'] Boardwalk location. . . ."

After substantial pre-trial discovery, defendant moved for summary judgment. After oral argument, the motion judge, citing Malaker Corp. Stockholders Protective Comm. v. First Jersey Nat. Bank, 163 N.J. Super. 463, 395 A.2d 222 (App. Div. 1978), certif. denied, 79 N.J. 488, 401 A.2d 243 (1979) [granted the defendant's motion — EDS.].

. . . .

The doctrine of promissory estoppel is well-established in New Jersey. *Malaker,* supra, 163 N.J. Super. at 479, 395 A.2d 222 ("Suffice it to say that given an appropriate case, the doctrine [of promissory estoppel] will be enforced."). A promissory estoppel claim will be justified if the plaintiff satisfies its burden of demonstrating the existence of, or for purposes of summary judgment, a dispute as to a material fact with regard to, four separate elements which include:

4. Apparently, in late January 1995, Resorts spoke with another TCBY franchise, Host Marriott, regarding the Players Club's space. Those discussions eventually led to an agreement to have Host Marriott operate a TCBY franchise at the Players Club location. That lease was executed in late May 1995, and TCBY opened shortly thereafter.

(1) a clear and definite promise by the promisor; (2) the promise must be made with the expectation that the promisee will rely thereon; (3) the promisee must in fact reasonably rely on the promise, and (4) detriment of a definite and substantial nature must be incurred in reliance on the promise.

The essential justification for the promissory estoppel doctrine is to avoid the substantial hardship or injustice which would result if such a promise were not enforced. Id. at 484, 395 A.2d 222.

In *Malaker,* the court determined that an implied promise to lend an unspecified amount of money was not "a clear and definite promise" justifying application of the promissory estoppel doctrine. Id. at 478-81, 395 A.2d 222. Specifically, the court concluded that the promisor-bank's oral promise in October 1970 to lend $150,000 for January, February and March of 1971 was not "clear and definite promise" because it did not describe a promise of "sufficient definition." Id. at 479, 395 A.2d 222.

It should be noted that the court in *Malaker* seems to have heightened the amount of proof required to establish a "clear and definite promise" by searching for "*an express promise* of a 'clear and definite' nature." Id. at 484, 395 A.2d 222 (emphasis added). This sort of language might suggest that New Jersey Courts expect proof of most, if not all, of the essential legal elements of a promise before finding it to be "clear and definite."

Although earlier New Jersey decisions discussing promissory estoppel seem to greatly scrutinize a party's proofs regarding an alleged "clear and definite promise by the promisor," see, e.g., id. at 479, 484, 395 A.2d 222, as a prelude to considering the remaining three elements of a promissory estoppel claim, more recent decisions have tended to relax the strict adherence to the *Malaker* formula for determining whether a prima facie case of promissory estoppel exists. This is particularly true where, as here, a plaintiff does not seek to enforce a contract not fully negotiated, but instead seeks damages resulting from its detrimental reliance upon promises made during contract negotiations despite the ultimate failure of those negotiations.

. . .

Further, the Restatement (Second) of Contracts §90 (1979), "Promise Reasonably Inducing Action or Forbearance," provides, in pertinent part:

(1) A promise which the promisor should reasonably expect to induce action or forbearance on the part of the promisee or a third person and which does induce such action or forbearance is binding *if injustice can be avoided only by enforcement of the promise.* The remedy granted for breach may be limited as justice requires.

[Ibid. (emphasis added).]

The Restatement approach is best explained by illustration 10 contained within the comments to Section 90, and based upon Hoffman v. Red Owl Stores, Inc., 26 Wis. 2d 683, 133 N.W.2d 267 (1965):

10. A, who owns and operates a bakery, desires to go into the grocery business. He approaches B, a franchisor of supermarkets. B states to A that for $18,000 B will establish A in a store. B also advises A to move to another town and buy a small grocery to gain experience. A does so. Later B advises A to sell the grocery, which A

does, taking a capital loss and foregoing expected profits from the summer tourist trade. B also advises A to sell his bakery to raise capital for the supermarket franchise, saying "Everything is ready to go. Get your money together and we are set." A sells the bakery taking a capital loss on this sale as well. Still later, B tells A that considerably more than an $18,000 investment will be needed, and the negotiations between the parties collapse. At the point of collapse many details of the proposed agreement between the parties are unresolved. The assurances from B to A are promises on which B reasonably should have expected A to rely, and A is entitled to his actual losses on the sales of the bakery and grocery and for his moving and temporary living expenses. Since the proposed agreement was never made, however, A is not entitled to lost profits from the sale of the grocery or to his expectation interest in the proposed franchise from B.

[Restatement (Second) of Contracts §90 cmt. *d*, illus. 10 (1979).]
. . .

As we read the Restatement, the strict adherence to proof of a "clear and definite promise" as discussed in *Malaker* is being eroded by a more equitable analysis designed to avoid injustice. . . .

The facts as presented by plaintiff by way of its pleadings and certifications filed by Taube, which were not refuted or contradicted by defendant before the motion judge or on appeal, clearly show that when Taube informed Phoenix that Pop's option to renew its lease at its Margate location had to be exercised by October 1, 1994, Phoenix instructed Taube to give notice that it would not be extending the lease. According to Phoenix, virtually nothing remained to be resolved between the parties. Phoenix indicated that the parties were "95% there" and that all that was required for completion of the deal was the signature of John Belisle. Phoenix assured Taube that he had recommended the deal to Belisle, and that Belisle would follow the recommendation. Phoenix also advised Pop's to "pack up the Margate store and plan on moving."

It is also uncontradicted that based upon those representations that Pop's, in fact, did not renew its lease. It vacated its Margate location, placed its equipment and personalty into temporary storage, retained the services of an attorney to finalize the lease with defendant, and engaged in planning the relocation to defendant's property. Ultimately, it incurred the expense of relocating to its present location. That plaintiff . . . relied to its detriment on defendant's assurances seems unquestionable; the facts clearly at least raise a jury question. Additionally, whether plaintiff's reliance upon defendant's assurances was reasonable is also a question for the jury.

Conversely, following the Section 90 approach, a jury could conclude that Phoenix, as promisor, should reasonably have expected to induce action or forbearance on the part of plaintiff to his precise instruction "not to renew the lease" and to "pack up the Margate store and plan on moving." In discussing the "character of reliance protected" under Section 90, comment *b* states:

> The principle of this Section is flexible. The promisor is affected only by reliance which he does or should foresee, and enforcement must be necessary to avoid injustice. Satisfaction of the latter requirement may depend on the reasonableness of the promisee's reliance, on its definite and substantial character in relation to the remedy sought, on the formality with which the promise is made, on

the extent to which evidentiary, cautionary, deterrent and channeling functions of form are met by the commercial setting or otherwise, and on the extent to which such other policies as the enforcement of bargains and the prevention of unjust enrichment are relevant. . . .

[Restatement (Second) of Contracts §90 cmt. *b* (1979) (citations omitted).]

Plaintiff's complaint neither seeks enforcement of the lease nor speculative lost profits which it might have earned had the lease been fully and successfully negotiated. Plaintiff merely seeks to recoup damages it incurred, including the loss of its Margate leasehold, in reasonably relying to its detriment upon defendant's promise. Affording plaintiff all favorable inferences, its equitable claim raised a jury question. . . . Plaintiff's complaint, therefore, should not have been summarily dismissed.

Reversed and remanded for further appropriate proceedings.

Notes and Questions

1. *Requirement of a promise.* In *Pop's Cones* the court dispensed with the requirement indicated by some prior New Jersey decisions that promissory estoppel must be based on a "clear and definite promise." Sections 90 and 87 (2) of the Restatement are in accord that a promise or offer will be sufficient without any heightened requirements of proof. Some courts, however, continue to adhere to this increased standard. See Jensen v. Taco John's International, Inc., 110 F.3d 525 (8th Cir. 1997). Would Resorts's promise have met even the greater standard of a "clear and definite promise"?

Even if a court rejects the standard of a clear and definite promise, not every assurance will be sufficient to invoke promissory estoppel. Compare Security Bank & Trust Co. v. Bogard, 494 N.E.2d 965 (Ind. Ct. App. 1986) (assurances by defendant bank's branch manager that plaintiff's application would go to loan committee and "within two or three days, we ought to have something here, ready for you to go with" held to be merely an "expression of intention" coupled with a "prediction" which were not sufficient to invoke promissory estoppel) with Twin City Fire Insurance Co. v. Philadelphia Life Insurance Co., 795 F.2d 1417 (9th Cir. 1986) (quote by defendant insurance broker of cost of annuity that plaintiff relied on in settlement of personal injury claim amounted to sufficient commitment to invoke promissory estoppel).

2. *The **Hoffman** case.* The court cites with approval Hoffman v. Red Owl Stores, Inc., 133 N.W.2d 267 (Wis. 1967), a leading decision holding that assurances made during negotiations that a contract will be forthcoming amount to a promise sufficient to invoke promissory estoppel, when the promisee has relied to its detriment by giving up another business location and by incurring out-of-pocket expenses in preparation for the new location. As the court notes, the facts of *Hoffman* form the basis of illustration 10 to Restatement (Second) §90. We earlier saw that in the construction bidding cases most courts and the Restatement have adopted the holding of Drennan v. Star Paving, allowing a general contractor to recover on the basis of promissory estoppel against a subcontractor who attempts to revoke a bid.

Does the fact pattern presented by *Pop's Cones* and *Hoffman* present a stronger or weaker basis for invoking promissory estoppel than the type of situation illustrated by *Drennan*?

3. *Nature of the parties.* To what extent do cases like *Pop's Cones* and *Hoffman* turn on the plaintiffs' relative lack of business sophistication, as compared to the agents of the defendants? In Gruen Industries, Inc. v. Biller, 608 F.2d 274 (7th Cir. 1979), the court considered a claim for breach of an asserted promise to sell to plaintiff a controlling block of stock in a business corporation. Since Wisconsin law applied, the principles of Hoffman v. Red Owl governed the case. After finding that the agreement between the parties was not intended to be binding until negotiations were complete, the court went on to hold also that promissory estoppel did not apply. The court distinguished *Hoffman* on a number of points: Any promises were conditional; plaintiffs were represented by sophisticated agents (banker and attorney); both parties had made expenditures in reliance on the likelihood of agreement; the defendants were not in any way enriched by plaintiffs' reliance. It then concluded as follows:

> In summary, the plaintiffs' promissory estoppel argument seeks to transform these complex negotiations into a "no lose" situation. Every business man faces the risk that the substantial transaction costs necessary to bring about a mutually beneficial contract will be lost if the negotiations fail to yield a satisfactory agreement. It is difficult to find the degree of injustice necessary for recovery in estoppel when the promises incorporate so many contingencies and complexities and as a matter of sound business practice are to be formalized before the parties carry them out. We conclude on this basis that the losses are best left where they have fallen, because it is clear that no injustice will result from not enforcing the alleged promise.

Id. at 282. On the other hand, in United Parcel Service Co. v. Rickert, 996 S.W.2d 464 (Ky. 1999), plaintiff pilot was permitted to recover both in fraud and in promissory estoppel against defendant, on the basis that he had been assured continuing employment with defendant if he remained for the time being in the employ of Orion, a contract air carrier with which defendant had maintained an ongoing relationship. The court summarized plaintiff's case as follows:

> The evidence indicates that Rickert was concerned about his job security at Orion when he learned that UPS was terminating its contract with them. He then began to prepare his resume and circulated it to other airlines. He immediately stopped his job search preparations in reliance on what he believed to be the offer by UPS and thereby gave up his option of being employed during the transitional time by another airline. Rickert did not resume his job search until . . . he realized that UPS was probably not going to hire him.

Id. at 469.

4. *Plaintiff's damages.* Pop's Cones sought to recover what are usually referred to as "reliance" damages: the loss of income from the Margate location that it gave up in reliance on receiving a lease for the Resorts location coupled with its out-of-pocket expenses preparing for the Resorts lease. Pop's could have attempted to recover "expectation" damages, the loss in income

that it would have received from the Resorts location during the life of the lease. We will see in Chapter 12 that an issue that has divided the courts is whether a plaintiff in a promissory estoppel case is limited to its reliance damages or may recover its expectation damages, which are usually greater in amount.

5. *Scholarly commentary.* A number of scholars have addressed the question of whether and the extent to which legal obligations should flow from assurances made during preliminary negotiations. In one of the earliest treatments of this subject, Professor Knapp suggested that assurances of a deal made during negotiations should in some cases give rise to a duty to bargain in good faith in an effort to conclude the negotiations. Charles L. Knapp, Enforcing the Contract to Bargain, 44 N.Y.U. L. Rev. 673, 686-689 (1969). See Quake Construction, Inc. v. American Airlines, Inc., below, and its accompanying Notes.

By contrast, Professor Juliet Kostritsky finds doctrines such as promissory estoppel and good faith too vague as standards for regulating representations and assurances made during preliminary negotiations. Instead, she argues that parties who enter into negotiations should be treated as making implied promises to inform the other party of any change in willingness to enter into a contract. Under Kostritsky's approach, a party would be liable for any reliance damages incurred prior to notice of change in willingness to contract. Juliet P. Kostritsky, Bargaining with Uncertainty, Moral Hazard, and Sunk Costs: A Default Rule for Precontractual Negotiations, 44 Hastings L.J. 621 (1993). For a comprehensive review of various theories that could be used to establish liability for conduct during preliminary negotiations, see E. Allan Farnsworth, Precontractual Liability and Preliminary Agreements: Fair Dealing and Failed Negotiations, 87 Colum. L. Rev. 217 (1987).

Some commentators have suggested that conduct like that exhibited by Resorts and by Red Owl Stores could be more properly characterized as tortious, rather than as merely a breach of promise. See Ian Ayres & Gregory Klass, Insincere Promises: The Law of Misrepresented Intent 148-149 (2005); Randy E. Barnett & Mary E. Becker, Beyond Reliance: Promissory Estoppel, Contract Formalities, and Misrepresentations, 15 Hofstra L. Rev. 443, 489-491 (1987) ("negligent promissory representation"); Mark P. Gergen, Liability for Mistake in Contract Formation, 64 So. Cal. L. Rev. 1, 34 (1990) ("negligent misrepresentation").

PROBLEM 2-1

The City of Cantonville is a medium-sized southern town with a population of approximately 350,000. Located near the center of the city is the First Denominational Church, established over 100 years ago. For several years the church has needed to expand its facilities but was unable to do so in its present location because no land was available. Reluctantly, church officials began considering a move to the suburbs and ultimately acquired an option to purchase property there.

Next door to the church is the Cantonville Public Library, housed in an old, crowded building. While the library desperately needs to move to a larger structure, it has been unable to do so because the city council, which is responsible for the library, has been unwilling to appropriate sufficient funds.

Aware of the problems facing both the library and the church, several prominent business leaders, led by Robert McSwain, chairman of the church's board of elders, devised a plan to meet the needs of both the church and the library. Under the plan, the church would purchase the present library property for $200,000, using the property for its expansion. At the same time, the business group would organize a fund-raising campaign designed to raise $1 million, which would be used to finance a new, larger library.

The business leaders discussed the plan informally with the director of the library and with city officials, receiving enthusiastic support. In June 2006, McSwain, acting on behalf of the church and business group, formally presented the plan to the city council at its regular monthly meeting. The plan immediately received "first reading" approval. Two months later the plan obtained final approval, with one major change. The original proposal called for sale of the property to the church when the city received pledges of $1 million in donations to the library. Fearful that some pledges might not be honored, the council's final approval provided that the sale of the property would take place only after donations totaling $1 million had been deposited with the city. The resolution stated that the city's agreement to sell the property would remain open until June 1, 2007, and would be automatically withdrawn unless the sale were concluded by that date. The resolution expressed pleasure that sale would allow the church to remain in the city rather than moving to the suburbs, because the church had been a "good citizen." In particular, the resolution noted, the church had assisted the city in providing housing and food for the needy when welfare was reduced in the 1990s. In fact, in 1998, the church was voted "Citizen of the Year" by the city council.

In September, Ivy Cannon, the public affairs reporter for the Cantonville Star, wrote an article about the city's decision to sell the library property to the church. In the article, Cannon pointed out that, according to real estate experts, the property was worth more than the purchase price. As a result, donations to the library were, in effect, partial subsidies to the church. Because of this article, citizens who had at first supported sale of the library began to question its wisdom, and even its propriety. The next city council meeting was packed with irate citizens, who demanded reconsideration of the decision to sell the property to the church. While several people spoke in favor of the sale, it was clear to the council that sentiment was running strongly against the transaction. At the end of the meeting, by a four-to-one vote, the council rescinded its resolution authorizing the sale of the library property. The one dissenting member argued that the council was bound contractually to sell the property and could not validly rescind the resolution.

Church officials are irate about the turn of events, especially because the church's option to acquire its suburban property has now expired. They have asked your advice about whether the city could rescind the resolution authorizing the sale or whether it was bound contractually to sell the property to the church. What advice would you give?

2. Irrevocability by Statute: The "Firm Offer"

Restatement (Second) §87 states several ways in which an offer may become "binding as an option contract," in addition to the obvious possibility that the offeror's promise of irrevocability may have been purchased by the offeree with some legally effective consideration. One of these (§87(1)(b)) is that the offer may be "made irrevocable by statute." Of course a valid statute does not need the blessing of any Restatement to be effective, so the reference to statutory irrevocability is in a sense both unnecessary and irrelevant to the Restatement's professed mission of restating the common law. It serves as a reminder, however, that this area is one in which statutes are likely to play an important role. One common example is in the public contracting process. In order to protect what is seen as a public interest in orderly and fully competitive bidding on public construction projects, statutes or regulations often provide that bids may not be withdrawn for a period of time, typically running from the time when the bids are first opened. (Would the existence of such a statute or regulation have been relevant to the resolution of Drennan v. Star Paving Co., or similar cases?) See generally Michael L. Closen & Donald G. Weiland, The Construction Industry Bidding Cases: Application of Traditional Contract, Promissory Estoppel, and Other Theories to the Relations between General Contractors and Subcontractors, 13 J. Mar. L. Rev. 565, 571-573 (1980). By court decision, such a rule is applied generally to bids submitted to the federal government. See Refining Associates, Inc. v. United States, 109 F. Supp. 259 (Ct. Cl. 1953).

As Comment d to Restatement (Second) §87 points out, the Uniform Commercial Code also has some provisions making certain offers irrevocable (despite the absence of any consideration). One of these is UCC §2-328(3), restricting the seller's freedom to withdraw from sale goods being offered in an auction in which the right to withdraw is not reserved. More important for our purposes, however, is the UCC's "Firm Offer" provision, §2-205. In this section, the drafters have made a fundamental shift from traditional common law doctrine, by providing that at least some offers will be irrevocable despite the absence of any consideration. What do you think impelled this radical change of policy? As we noted at the beginning of this section, the CISG takes an even more expansive attitude toward the possibility of "firm offers," giving legal effect to the apparent intention to make an offer binding, without the restrictions imposed by §2-205. CISG Art. 16(2)(a). (Unlike UCC Article 2, however, the CISG does not apply to the purchase of goods by a consumer. See CISG Art. 2(a).)

Section 2-205 applies by its terms to "offers," a term which the Code does not define; accordingly on this point general common law principles apply. See I & R Mechanical, Inc. v. Hazelton Mfg. Co., 817 N.E.2d 799 (Mass. Ct. App. 2004) (price quotation not an offer under UCC §2-205). But note that many of the other terms employed in §2-205, even those with everyday meanings, have specialized definitions in the Code. E.g., "merchant," §2-104(1); "goods," §2-105(1); "signed," §1-201(39), and "writing," §1-201(46). Revised Article 2 uses similar but somewhat modified terms. In particular, revised Article 2 adopts the concept of a "record," §2-103(1)(m), to reflect modern electronic transactions. Note also that §2-205 applies to offers made by buyers as well as by sellers. E.g., City University of New York v. Finalco, Inc., 514 N.Y.S.2d 244 (App. Div. 1987) (buyer's offer to purchase used computers from university not revocable during period stated). And of course the section only applies to an offer that is "firm" — i.e., that meets the description in the section of giving "assurance that it will be held open."

Two other aspects of §2-205 may be important in applying it to a given situation. One is the length of the period of irrevocability that it creates. Clearly if the offer merely states that it is "firm," but without saying for how long, the "reasonable" period of irrevocability created might be less than three months, but in any event would not *exceed* that time. What if the offer does specify a period of firmness, but one which is greater than three months? Will the stated time period govern, or will irrevocability be limited to three months? See comment 3. (On this point compare CISG Art. 16(2)(a), which contains no similar time limitation.) The other point to be noted is §2-205's requirement that any "term of assurance [i.e., of 'firmness'] on a form supplied by the offeree must be separately signed by the offeror." What abuse were the drafters seeking here to avoid? Comment 4 indicates this provision offers protection "against the inadvertent signing of a firm offer." Comment 2 elaborates on the requirement of a "signed writing," and notes that a "signature" for this purpose would typically consist at minimum of an "initialing of the clause involved." If a given "offeror" would indeed "inadvertently sign" a firm offer, would it be likely also to "inadvertently" initial a "firmness" clause? (Have you ever signed or initialed something without reading it?) Comment 4 suggests that in such cases §2-302 might possibly be applied to prevent an "unconscionable result."

Finally, what is the relationship, if any, between UCC §2-205 and the principle of reliance-protection exemplified by Restatement (Second) §§90 and 87(2)? Unlike the *Drennan*-based case law and the cited Restatement provisions, §2-205 appears to impose no requirement that the offeree demonstrate reliance on the offer in order to claim the right to accept despite an attempted revocation. Does §2-205 nonetheless serve to protect offeree reliance? Conversely, does the presence of §2-205 in the UCC indicate that a court should not enforce a "firm" *oral* offer for the sale of goods, even if foreseeably relied on? In an article based on extensive research in the "legislative history" of the Code and the writings of Professor Karl Llewellyn, Professor Michael Gibson contended that Llewellyn had little enthusiasm for the principle of promissory estoppel, at least in business affairs, and that he preferred to bring the law in line with the expectations of business people, not by protecting reliance but by expanding the concept of agreement, free from many of the technicalities that had plagued the common law. On the other hand, as Gibson demonstrated, Llewellyn had high regard for the evidentiary safeguard provided by writing requirements, such as the Statute of Frauds. (See UCC §2-201, which we will address in Chapter 4.) For those reasons, Gibson suggested, §2-205 and its comments should be read as precluding any pre-acceptance protection for an *oral* firm offer to buy or sell goods, even if substantially relied on. Michael T. Gibson, Promissory Estoppel, Article 2 of the U.C.C., and the Restatement (Third) of Contracts, 73 Iowa L. Rev. 659, 696-706 (1988). On the other hand, Gibson conceded that many courts and commentators have seen in UCC §1-103 an invitation to apply the principles of "estoppel" under the Code unless "displaced" and have not viewed §2-205 as such a displacement. The strength of the *Drennan*-based case law is such, Gibson concluded, that even in subcontractor-bidding cases involving only (or primarily) the sale of goods, where the provisions of Article 2 should presumably have been applicable, §2-205 and its comments have been "almost completely ignored" in favor of *Drennan*-style promissory estoppel. Id. at 705. See, e.g., E. A. Coronis Assoc. v. M. Gordon Construction Co., 216 A.2d 246 (N.J. Sup. Ct. App. Div. 1966) (subcontractor's bid not binding as firm offer because did not give assurance that it would be held open, but contractor states cause of action under theory of promissory estoppel). See Henry Mather, Firm Offers under the UCC and the CISG, 105 Dick. L. Rev. 31 (2000) (application of promissory estoppel to firm offers that do not comply with UCC §2-205 remains unclear even under the revisions to Article 2; suggesting that states could adopt nonuniform amendments to the section to clarify the issue).

Recall the cases we encountered earlier in this chapter, in which promissory estoppel was argued (sometimes successfully, sometimes not) on behalf of one party who was disappointed by the other's withdrawal from a proposed transaction. Some of those cases — *James Baird, Drennan* — were decided before the advent of Article 2; if they had arisen after the adoption of Article 2 in the relevant jurisdictions, should that factor have affected either the result or the reasoning? In the *Berryman* and *Pop's Cones* cases, could §2-205 have been relevant?

PROBLEM 2-2

After retiring from the practice of law in Chicago, Wallace Branch purchased a tract of land in Kentucky and began to buy and breed thoroughbred racehorses. Although this was initially merely a hobby for Branch, many of his horses did very well, and it has turned into a profitable business. In June of this year, Dorothy Gale comes to Branch's property to have a look at Branch's racehorse, "Tinman," which she has heard might be for sale. Branch tells Gale that Tinman can be purchased for $500,000. After watching the horse in action over a two-day period, Gale tells Branch that she is indeed interested in buying the animal, but will not be in a position to do so unless and until she can assemble a group of investors to go in with her on the purchase, which will take some time. Branch asks her how long she would need, and Gale replies that four months should be ample. At Gale's request, Branch signs the following:

Dear Ms. Gale:

For valuable consideration, I hereby grant unto you or your assigns an option for 120 days after date to purchase my horse "Tinman" for the price of $500,000. If this offer is accepted, the horse will be warranted sound as of the date of delivery but no warranty will be made as to his performance on the track or at stud.

Dated: June 19, 2006   *(signed) Wallace Branch*

Gale takes the above writing (leaving a copy with Branch) to her home in Greensboro, NC, where she proceeds to attempt to interest investors in joining her in the purchase. By mid-September, she has enough commitments from investors to enable her to accept Branch's offer. She is about to do so when she receives the following fax:

Dear Ms. Gale:

Not having heard anything from you, I have decided to sell Tinman to another buyer. Thank you for your interest.

All best wishes,
Wallace Branch

As of the time when she receives the above letter, what if any rights does Gale have against Branch? If you represented her, what course of action would you advise her to take, and why? Would your answers to these questions (or the reasoning behind your answers) be any different if Gale's home were not in North Carolina, but in Ontario, Canada?

PROBLEM 2-3

Marsha Boyston is an investor who specializes in acquiring income producing real estate, such as office buildings and apartment projects. In the typical transaction, Boyston does the following: locates desirable property, assembles a group of individuals who will invest in the project (these investors usually put up 20 percent of the purchase price), and obtains bank financing for the remaining 80 percent of the purchase price. For her services Boyston usually receives 10 percent ownership in the project.

Recently, Boyston negotiated a contract with Herbert Smith, the owner of the Village Garden Apartments, to acquire the property for $1.5 million. She paid Smith $25,000 down. The contract contains a standard "financing contingency" clause, which provides that Boyston will not be obligated to purchase the property if she is unable to obtain financing. If she cannot obtain financing, however, she forfeits the $25,000 down payment.

After signing the contract, Boyston went to the National Bank of City and applied for a loan of $1.2 million (80 percent of the purchase price). On September 24, 2006, she received the following loan commitment letter from Andrea Wilson, the loan officer at National:

September 24, 2006

Ms. Marsha Boyston
219 Olive St.
City, SC 29205

Re: Village Garden Apartments
Dear Marsha:

National Bank of City is pleased to offer a loan commitment to you for the purpose of financing the acquisition of the Village Garden apartments located at 1919 Downing Street, on the following terms and conditions:

1. Borrower—Village Garden Limited Partnership. You are the sole general partner. Other investors will be limited partners.

2. Amount — $1,200,000.
3. Purpose — to purchase the land and buildings known as the Village Garden Apartments.
4. Terms — 15-year amortization.
5. Interest rate — 6.75% fixed.
6. Commitment fee — none.
7. Collateral — first mortgage on the Village Garden apartment project located at 1919 Downing Street.
8. Expiration date of this commitment — This commitment is valid for 30 days from the date of this letter.
9. The Village Garden Partnership must furnish evidence of its organization and its authority to enter into this transaction.
10. Opinion of Counsel — The note and all other documents with regard to this transaction shall be in a form that is satisfactory to counsel for the Bank.
11. Closing Expenses — All legal and other expenses incurred by National Bank will be paid by the borrower.

If the terms of this commitment are acceptable to you, please sign and date this letter and return it to me in the enclosed envelope. If you have any questions, please let me know.

Sincerely,
Andrea Wilson
Loan Officer
National Bank of City

Accepted by:

_____

(date)

While the bank was evaluating the loan, Boyston had been busy contacting business acquaintances who had invested in her previous projects. By the time she received the commitment letter, she had obtained promises from investors for $200,000 of the $300,000 that she needed. After receiving the above letter, she continued her efforts, and by October 1, she had put together a group of eight investors willing to put up $300,000. She immediately contacted Herbert Smith, the owner of the Village Garden apartments, and informed him that she had obtained financing. They agreed to a closing date of October 28, 2006. She also called Ms. Wilson at the bank to tell her that she wished to accept the terms of the bank's loan. Boyston told Wilson that she would personally deliver the signed commitment letter the next day. Later that afternoon, however, Wilson called Boyston and told her that she had just received word from her boss that the bank was withdrawing its commitment letter. Boyston was shocked. She pointed out that she had already told Wilson that she had agreed to the loan. Wilson was very apologetic. Wilson said that she didn't even know the reason why the bank was withdrawing its commitment. Boyston then contacted Smith to inform him of the problem. She asked Smith if he would be willing to agree to an extension of the closing. Smith said he would, but only for two weeks. During that time Boyston tried to obtain other bank financing, but was unable to do so. She finally had to tell Smith that she was unable to go forward with the sale. As a result she forfeited her $25,000 deposit.

Boyston has asked your advice about whether she has any legal rights against the bank because of its withdrawal of the commitment letter. Be prepared to present your analysis of her legal rights and to outline the advice that you would give.

3. Qualified Acceptance: The "Battle of Forms"

If our experience is any guide, it may be that for law students in general, the notion of a "contract" conjures up the image of a sort of all-purpose document, full of legal jargon — whereases, heretofores, and parties of the first and second part — that experienced lawyers know by heart. In fact, the "legal ritual" part of most contracts is negligible or nil; the heart of a written contract is an accurate description of the particular exchange of performances to which the parties are agreeing, plus an identification of the principal risks entailed for one or both parties, with specification of the parties' rights should any of those risk-events occur.

This is not to say there are not "legal forms" for contract lawyers to employ; models can be found in "form books" in law libraries and many companies publish computer software with forms for various types of transactions. But the suggested forms vary with each type of transaction, and the language used in such forms reflects the practicalities of the business in question as well as the rules of law that govern it. Most lawyers who practice extensively in a particular commercial area develop their own set of forms, or "precedents" — model contracts that are used over and over in substantially the same form. Typically these contain at least some language that is almost always repeated verbatim (often referred to as "boilerplate"); other parts will be varied to suit the particular transaction. Of course, no careful lawyer would use a prior contract as a precedent without reviewing it to see what changes might be required. A cautious reliance on precedents is standard practice, however, and for good reason: It saves the lawyer's time and labor; it thereby helps keep down the cost of legal services to the client; and it provides the attorney with a checklist of things to watch out for in the transaction at hand. The advent of computers with word processing programs has made the adaptation of standard forms to the specifics of each transaction much easier.

For many clients, this use of prototype contracts can be carried a step further. Most businesses enter into a large number of substantially similar transactions — sales of goods, for instance, in which the only variants are the type, number, and price of the items sold, the name of the buyer, and the time and place agreed on for delivery. For such multiple transactions, use of a series of hand-tailored contracts (even if prepared with the time-saving help of precedents) would be inefficient. What is needed is a "standard form," a preprinted document that gives all the legal protection required in a particular type of transaction, with blanks for selling personnel to fill in the small amount of information that varies from sale to sale. Today, many companies are reducing their reliance on paper documents and sales personnel. Increasingly, orders are being placed and accepted using electronic forms and "electronic agents."

From the lawyer's point of view, such forms are important principally as a means of bringing legal counsel to bear in multiple transactions that would otherwise have to be conducted without it. To the client, however, the forms have additional utility. Because they serve as efficient organizers of information, they facilitate storage and retrieval of the data important to particular transactions. Standard forms also permit relatively error-free dissemination of identical information to the various persons within and without the organization who have responsibility for different aspects of the completed exchange. On the other hand, we all know from experience that the efficiency gained from the use of standardized forms is likely to be purchased at the cost of some depersonalizing of the individual transaction. If the forms do not completely replace personal contact and negotiation, but only supplement it, their use creates an additional potential risk: that the transaction as recorded will differ from the transaction-in-fact, perhaps in important ways.

We noted earlier in this chapter that the rules of classical contract law were fashioned on the assumption that the parties would deal with each other in the conventional manner: An offer would be made; it would be either accepted or rejected; if the latter, perhaps a counteroffer would be made; that in turn would be accepted or rejected; and so on. Certainly that mode of contracting may still be employed today. But for most businesses, such a leisurely approach to contracting is too expensive and time-consuming to be taken for any but the most important and idiosyncratic of transactions. Most deals will be made — or at least recorded — on forms, either paper or electronic. Courts and legislatures have therefore had to fashion new rules for determining when sufficient agreement has been reached to justify a finding that a contract has been made and for deciding in light of the various communications between the parties what the terms of that contract are.

The materials in this section will be devoted to the situation where the parties are business enterprises utilizing paper forms of the type described above. The first case, Princess Cruises, Inc. v. General Electric Co., although it involves issues of federal law, turns in the end on a pair of common law principles established in the heyday of classical contract law: the "mirror image" and "last shot" rules, as they are often called. The next case, *Brown Machine*, illustrates the different approach taken by UCC Article 2 to the question of nonmatching forms, as spelled out in UCC §2-207.

Princess Cruises, Inc. v. General Electric Co.
United States Court of Appeals
143 F.3d 828 (4th Cir. 1998)

Before ERVIN and WILLIAMS, Circuit Judges, and GOODWIN, United States District Judge for the Southern District of West Virginia, sitting by designation.

OPINION

GOODWIN, District Judge:
This suit arises out of a maritime contract between General Electric Company (GE) and Princess Cruises, Inc. (Princess) for inspection and repair services relating to Princess's cruise ship, the SS *Sky Princess*. In January 1997, a

jury found GE liable for breach of contract and awarded Princess $4,577,743.00 in damages. J.A. at 1876. On appeal, GE contends that the district court erred in denying its renewed motion for judgment as a matter of law, which requested that the court vacate the jury's award of incidental and consequential damages. Specifically, GE argues that the district court erroneously applied Uniform Commercial Code principles, rather than common-law principles, to a contract primarily for services. We agree and hold that when the predominant purpose of a maritime or land-based contract is the rendering of services rather than the furnishing of goods, the U.C.C. is inapplicable, and courts must draw on common-law doctrines when interpreting the contract. Accordingly, we reverse the district court's decision denying GE's renewed motion for judgment as a matter of law and remand for modification of the judgment consistent with this opinion.

I. Factual Background

Princess scheduled the SS *Sky Princess* for routine inspection services and repairs in December 1994 and requested that GE, the original manufacturer of the ship's main turbines, perform services and provide parts incidental to the ship's inspection and repair. Princess issued a Purchase Order in October 1994. The Purchase Order included a proposed contract price of $260,000.00 and contained a brief description of services to be performed by GE. The reverse side of the Purchase Order listed terms and conditions which indicated that Princess intended the Purchase Order to be an offer. These terms and conditions also stated that GE could accept the Purchase Order through acknowledgment or performance; that the terms and conditions could not be changed unilaterally; and that GE would provide a warranty of workmanlike quality and fitness for the use intended. J.A. at 75-76.

On the same day that GE received the Purchase Order, GE faxed a Fixed Price Quotation to Princess. The Fixed Price Quotation provided a more detailed work description than Princess's Purchase Order and included a parts and materials list, an offering price of $201,888.00, and GE's own terms and conditions. When GE reviewed Princess's Purchase Order, it discovered that Princess requested work not contemplated by GE in its Fixed Price Quotation. GE notified Princess of GE's error. On October 28, 1994, GE faxed a Final Price Quotation to Princess. In the Final Price Quotation, GE offered to provide all services, labor, and materials for $231,925.00. Attached to both GE Quotations were GE's terms and conditions, which: (1) rejected the terms and conditions set forth in Princess's Purchase Order; (2) rejected liquidated damages; (3) limited GE's liability to repair or replacement of any defective goods or damaged equipment resulting from defective service, exclusive of all written, oral, implied, or statutory warranties; (4) limited GE's liability on any claims to not more than the greater of either $5000.00 or the contract price; and (5) disclaimed any liability for consequential damages, lost profits, or lost revenue. J.A. at 106-13. During an October 31, 1994 telephone call, Princess gave GE permission to proceed based on the price set forth in GE's Final Price Quotation. J.A. at 825, 1850.

On November 1, 1994, GE sent a confirmatory letter to Princess acknowledging receipt of Princess's Purchase Order and expressing GE's intent to perform the services. J.A. at 115. The letter also restated GE's $231,925.00

offering price from its Final Price Quotation and specified that GE's terms and conditions, attached to the letter, were to govern the contract. Id.

When the SS *Sky Princess* arrived for inspection, GE noted surface rust on the rotor and recommended that it be taken ashore for cleaning and balancing. The parties agree that during the cleaning, good metal was removed from the rotor, rendering the rotor unbalanced. Although GE attempted to correct the imbalance, Princess canceled a ten-day Christmas cruise as a result of delays caused by the repair. At trial, Princess alleged that the continued vibration and high temperatures caused damage to the ship, forcing additional repairs and the cancellation of a ten-day Easter cruise. It was undisputed, however, that Princess paid GE the full amount of the contract: $231,925.00. J.A. at 1008.

On April 22, 1996, Princess filed a four-count complaint against GE, alleging breach of contract, breach of express warranty, breach of implied maritime warranty, and negligence. The district court granted GE's motion for summary judgment as to the negligence claim. Following Princess's presentation of evidence at trial, GE made a motion for judgment as a matter of law, which the district court denied. At the conclusion of the defendant's presentation of evidence, the district court denied GE's second motion for judgment as a matter of law. In instructing the jury, the district court drew on principles set forth in U.C.C. §2-207 and allowed the jury to imply the following terms as part of the contract: (1) the warranty of merchantability; (2) the warranty of fitness for a particular purpose; (3) the warranty of workmanlike performance; (4) Princess's right to recover damages for GE's alleged breach of the contact; and (5) Princess's right to recover incidental and consequential damages, as well as lost profits, proximately caused by GE's alleged breach. On January 24, 1997, the jury returned a $4,577,743.00 verdict in favor of Princess. On February 3, 1997, GE renewed its motion for judgment as a matter of law requesting that the court vacate the jury's award of incidental and consequential damages. The district court heard oral argument on May 6, 1997. Following oral argument, the district court denied GE's renewed motion for judgment as a matter of law and issued an opinion clarifying its ruling.

II. STANDARD OF REVIEW

The Court reviews de novo the district court's denial of GE's renewed motion for judgment as a matter of law. . . . In reviewing the district court's decision, we consider the evidence in the light most favorable to the nonmovant to determine whether the evidence presented at trial was sufficient to allow a reasonable jury to render a verdict in the nonmovant's favor. . . .

III. TO APPLY U.C.C. PRINCIPLES TO A MARITIME CONTRACT FOR SERVICES WOULD HINDER ADMIRALTY LAW'S GOALS OF UNIFORMITY AND PREDICTABILITY

Although GE contended that the district court was required to determine whether goods or services predominated before applying U.C.C. principles to the GE-Princess contract, the district court found it "unnecessary for the Court to determine whether the contract is primarily one for goods or services.

In either case, the UCC is regarded as a source of admiralty law." J.A. at 2024. We respectfully disagree.

One of the primary concerns of admiralty law is uniformity and predictability. See American Dredging Co. v. Miller, 510 U.S. 443, 450-51 (1994). . . . To avoid the creation of multiple and conflicting rules of decision in admiralty, the Fourth Circuit has stated that, "Absent reason to do otherwise, we prefer to adopt rules in admiralty that accord with, rather than diverge from, standard commercial practice." Finora Co. v. Amitie Shipping, Ltd., 54 F.3d 209, 213-14 (4th Cir. 1995). As discussed in more detail below, standard commercial practice requires that a transaction be predominantly for the sale of goods before the U.C.C. applies. See Coakley & Williams, Inc. v. Shatterproof Glass Corp., 706 F.2d 456, 460 (4th Cir. 1983); Bonebrake v. Cox, 499 F.2d 951, 960 (8th Cir. 1974).

In its May 13, 1997 opinion, the district court correctly noted that U.C.C. principles inform admiralty law. See Southworth Mach. Co. v. F/V Corey Pride, 994 F.2d 37, 40 n.3 (1st Cir. 1993); Clem Perrin Marine Towing, Inc. v. Panama Canal Co., 730 F.2d 186, 189 (5th Cir. 1984). However, we are unpersuaded by cases cited to support the district court's legal determination that U.C.C. §2-207 applies to maritime transactions regardless of the nature of the transaction. . . .

Given admiralty law's goals of uniformity and predictability, we find that mixed maritime contracts for goods and services are subject to the same inquiry as land-based mixed contracts. Therefore, a court must first determine whether the predominant purpose of the transaction is the sale of goods. Once this initial analysis has been performed, the court then may properly decide whether the common law, the U.C.C., or other statutory law governs the transaction. Cf. Little Beaver Enters. v. Humphreys Rys., 719 F.2d 75, 79 n.7 (4th Cir. 1983) (noting that maritime contract for services was not covered by U.C.C.); In re American Export Lines, Inc., 620 F.Supp. 490, 515 (S.D.N.Y. 1985). This method accords with standard commercial practice and lends predictability to maritime contracts.

IV. THE GE-PRINCESS CONTRACT WAS PREDOMINANTLY FOR SERVICES

In its order denying GE's renewed motion for judgment as a matter of law, the district court addressed GE's contention that the district court erroneously included U.C.C. principles in its jury instructions. J.A. at 2021. Both by motion and at trial, GE argued that the district court was required to find that the sale of goods predominated in the GE-Princess contract before employing U.C.C. principles in its instructions.

Although the U.C.C. governs the sale of goods, the U.C.C. also applies to certain mixed contracts for goods and services. Whether a particular transaction is governed by the U.C.C., rather than the common law or other statutory law, hinges on the predominant purpose of the transaction, that is, whether the contract primarily concerns the furnishing of goods or the rendering of services. See Coakley & Williams, 706 F.2d at 458 ("Whether the U.C.C. applies turns on a question as to whether the contract . . . involved principally a sale of goods, on the one hand, or a provision of services, on the other."). . . . Thus, before applying the U.C.C., courts generally examine the transaction to determine whether the sale of goods predominates. See Coakley & Williams, 706 F.2d at 458. Because the facts in this case are sufficiently developed and undisputed, it is proper for the Court to determine on appeal whether the GE-Princess transaction was a contract for the sale of goods within the scope of the U.C.C. Cf. Cambridge Plating Co. v. Napco, Inc., 991 F.2d 21, 24 (1st Cir. 1993).

In determining whether goods or services predominate in a particular transaction, we are guided by the seminal case of Bonebrake v. Cox, 499 F.2d 951 (8th Cir. 1974). In holding the U.C.C. applicable, the *Bonebrake* court stated:

> The test for inclusion or exclusion is not whether they are mixed but, granting that they are mixed, whether their predominant factor, their thrust, their purpose, reasonably stated, is the rendition of service, with goods incidentally involved (e.g., contract with artist for painting) or is a transaction of sale, with labor incidentally involved (e.g., installation of a water heater in a bathroom).

Bonebrake, 499 F.2d at 960. The Fourth Circuit has deemed the following factors significant in determining the nature of the contract: (1) the language of the contract, (2) the nature of the business of the supplier, and (3) the intrinsic worth of the materials. See Coakley & Williams, 706 F.2d at 460 (applying Maryland law).

It is plain that the GE-Princess transaction principally concerned the rendering of services, specifically, the routine inspection and repair of the SS *Sky Princess,* with incidental — albeit expensive — parts supplied by GE. Although Princess's standard fine-print terms and conditions mention the sale of goods, J.A. at 76, Princess's actual purchase description requests a GE "service engineer" to perform service functions: the opening of valves for survey and the inspection of the ship's port main turbine. J.A. at 75. GE's Final Price Quotation also contemplates service functions, stating in large print on every page that it is a "Quotation for Services." J.A. at 107-09. The Final Price Quotation's first page notes that GE is offering a quotation for "engineering services." J.A. at 106. GE's Quotation further specifies that the particular type of service offered is "Installation/Repair/Maintenance." J.A. at 107. The Final Price Quotation then lists the scope of the contemplated work — opening, checking, cleaning, inspecting, disassembling — in short, service functions. J.A. at 110; see also J.A. at 1862-68 (listing service tasks actually performed by GE). Although GE's materials list shows that GE planned to manufacture a small number of parts for Princess, Princess appeared to have had most of the needed materials onboard. J.A. at 111. Thus, the language of both the Purchase Order and the Final Price Quotation indicates that although GE planned to supply certain parts, the parts were incidental to the contract's predominant purpose, which was inspection, repair, and maintenance services.

As to the second *Coakley* factor — the nature of the business of the supplier — although GE is known to manufacture goods, GE's correspondence and Quotations came from GE's Installation and Service Engineering Department. J.A. at 97, 106, 115. Evidence at trial showed that GE's Installation and Service Engineering division is comprised of twenty-seven field engineers who perform service functions, such as overhauls and repairs. J.A. at 1076. Finally, the last *Coakley* factor—the intrinsic worth of the materials supplied—cannot be determined because neither Princess's Purchase Order nor GE's Final Price Quotation separately itemized the value of the materials. Instead, both the Purchase Order and the Final Price Quotation blend the cost of the materials into the final price of a services contract, thereby confirming that services rather than materials predominated in the transaction. Although not a *Coakley* factor, it is also telling that, during oral argument, Princess's counsel admitted that the gravamen of Princess's complaint did not arise out of GE's furnishing of deficient parts, but rather out of GE's deficient services. See J.A. at 23-27 (Princess's Complaint stating that Princess's damages arose out of "GE's inspection, supervision . . . recommendation . . . reinstallation and realignment of the turbine unit."). . . . Accordingly, we find as a matter of law that services rather than goods predominated in the GE-Princess contract.

V. UNDER COMMON LAW, GE'S FINAL PRICE QUOTATION WAS A
   COUNTEROFFER ACCEPTED BY PRINCESS

The parties do not dispute that a contract was formed by their exchange of documents. J.A. at 2020. And there is no dispute that the GE-Princess contract for ship inspection and repair is maritime in nature and governed by the substantive law of admiralty. . . . However, the issue here—whether courts should draw on U.C.C. principles or on common-law doctrines when assessing the formation of a maritime services contract—is undecided. When no federal statute or well-established rule of admiralty exists, admiralty law may look to the common law or to state law, either statutory or decisional, to supply the rule of decision. Byrd v. Byrd, 657 F.2d 615, 617 (4th Cir. 1981) (admiralty may look to state law to supply rule of decision). . . . Because the majority of states refer to common-law principles when assessing contracts predominantly for services, we choose to do the same.

Under the common law, an acceptance that varies the terms of the offer is a counteroffer which rejects the original offer. RESTATEMENT (SECOND) OF CONTRACTS §59 (1981) ("A reply to an offer which purports to accept it but is conditional on the offeror's assent to terms additional to or different from those offered is not an acceptance but is a counter-offer."). Virginia follows the same rule. See Chang v. First Colonial Savs. Bank, 242 Va. 388, 410 S.E.2d 928, 931 (1991). Here, GE's Final Price Quotation materially altered the terms of Princess's Purchase Order by offering a different price, limiting damages and liability, and excluding warranties. Thus, GE's Final Price Quotation was a counteroffer rejecting Princess's Purchase Order. Although Princess could have rejected GE's counteroffer, Princess accepted the Final Price Quotation by giving GE permission to proceed with the repair and maintenance services, by not objecting to the confirmatory letter sent by GE, and by paying the amount set forth in GE's Final Price Quotation, $231,925.00, rather than the $260,000.00 price term set forth in Princess's Purchase Order. At common law, an offeror who proceeds under a contract after receiving the counteroffer can accept the terms of the counteroffer by performance. See Diamond Fruit Growers, Inc. v. Krack Corp., 794 F.2d 1440, 1443 (9th Cir. 1986) (citing C. Itoh & Co. (America) v. Jordan Intl. Co.,

552 F.2d 1228, 1236 (7th Cir. 1977)); Durham v. National Pool Equip. Co. of Va., 205 Va. 441, 138 S.E.2d 55, 58 (1964) ("Assent may be inferred from the acts and conduct of the parties.") (citations omitted). Although GE and Princess never discussed the Purchase Order's and the Final Price Quotation's conflicting terms and conditions, both Princess's actions and inaction gave GE every reason to believe that Princess assented to the terms and conditions set forth in GE's Final Price Quotation. See RESTATEMENT (SECOND) OF CONTRACTS §19(1) (1981) ("The manifestation of assent may be made wholly or partly by written or spoken words or by other acts or by failure to act."); Wells v. Weston, 229 Va. 72, 326 S.E.2d 672, 676 (1985) ("The mental assent of [contracting] parties is not requisite for the formation of a contract. . . . In evaluating a party's intent . . . we must examine his outward expression rather than his secret, unexpressed intention.") (citations omitted). Accordingly, we find that the terms and conditions of GE's Final Price Quotation control liability and damages in the GE-Princess transaction.

VI. THE VERDICT DEMONSTRATES THAT THE JURY IMPERMISSIBLY
RELIED ON A CONTRACT
OTHER THAN GE'S FINAL PRICE QUOTATION

For the reasons stated above, the jury could only have considered one contract in awarding damages: GE's Final Price Quotation. The Quotation restricted damages to the contract price, $231,925.00, and eliminated liability for incidental or consequential damages and lost profits or revenue. Moreover, GE's Final Price Quotation controlled the warranties available to its customers. Yet the jury awarded $4,577,743.00 in damages to Princess. This verdict demonstrates that the jury relied on Princess's Purchase Order or some other contract when awarding damages. See J.A. at 2025 (district court opinion noting that "the jury either found that Princess'[s] Purchase Order governed or that neither parties' document established the complete contract"). As a matter of law, the jury could only have awarded damages consistent with the terms and conditions of GE's Final Price Quotation and could not have awarded incidental or consequential damages. By requesting that the Court award Princess the maximum amount available under the Final Price Quotation, see Appellant's Brief at 39-40; Appellant's Reply Brief at 20, GE concedes that it breached its contract with Princess and that damages consistent with its Final Price Quotation are appropriate. Accordingly, we find it unnecessary to remand for a new trial on this issue. We reverse the district court's decision denying GE's motion for judgment as a matter of law and remand for entry of judgment against GE in the amount of $231,925.00, interest to accumulate from the date of the original judgment.

Reversed and Remanded.

Notes and Questions

1. *Applicability of common law or UCC Article 2.* The *Princess Cruises* case is first and foremost a dispute governed by federal admiralty law, as the court indicates. Nevertheless, the court still finds it appropriate to determine whether the dispute is of a type which would otherwise be governed by Article 2

of the UCC, or by the common law of contract. The court's discussion of this issue well sets out the approach that courts have applied to this "scope" question, and its conclusion that the predominant thrust of the contract would be properly seen as "services" rather than a "sale of goods" seems in line with most of the case law in this area. The debate over various proposed revisions of Article 2 in recent years has turned for the most part on the possible application of Article 2 to electronic software and other new subjects of commerce. On the issue of contracts for mixed goods and services, the revision of §2-102, adopted in 2003, does not appear to resolve the issue, leaving courts pretty much where they were before in terms of flexibility in this area.

2. *Application of common law — the "mirror-image" rule.* Having concluded that the common law of contract should apply, rather than the UCC (or, more precisely, that the admiralty law applicable to this case should be informed by common law rather than by UCC Article 2 principles), the court proceeds to apply what it views as the common law rules of offer and acceptance. Classical contract law employed the "mirror-image" rule and the "last shot" rule. The first of these gives a "varying" acceptance the effect of only a counter-offer, preventing the contract from being made on the terms of the original offer. E.g., Poel v. Brunswick-Balke-Callender Co., 110 N.E. 619 (1915). In *Princess Cruises,* the court applies the classical mirror-image rule in a contemporary setting. In support, the court cites Restatement (Second) §59, which merely echoes the classical rule of the first Restatement §60. The court fails, however, to quote comment *a* to Restatement (Second) §59, which provides as follows:

> *a. Qualified acceptance.* A qualified or conditional acceptance proposes an exchange different from that proposed by the original offeror. Such a proposal is a counter-offer and ordinarily terminates the power of acceptance of the original offeree. See §39. The effect of the qualification or condition is to deprive the purported acceptance of effect. But a definite and seasonable expression of acceptance is operative despite the statement of additional or different terms if the acceptance is not made to depend on assent to the additional or different terms. See §61; UCC §2-207(1). The additional or different terms are then to be construed as proposals for modification of the contract. See UCC §2-207(2). Such proposals may sometimes be accepted by the silence of the original offeror. See §69.

The Restatement (Second) on the "varying acceptance" issue thus attempts to steer a course somewhat closer to the UCC than indicated in the court's opinion. In the case that follows, we will compare UCC §2-207 with the common law on this point.

3. *Application of common law — the "last shot" rule.* Classical courts followed the last shot rule to determine when a counter-offer was accepted. Under that rule, a party impliedly assented to and thereby accepted a counter-offer by conduct indicating lack of objection to it. In addition to being based on a questionable notion of implied assent, the last shot rule tended in practice to favor sellers over buyers, because sellers normally "fire the last shot" — i.e., send the last form. Professor John Murray has well described the working of the common law rule; as his analysis shows (and as *Princess Cruises* continues to demonstrate), the favored party was typically — though not always — the seller.

A typical variation of the problem occurs in innumerable contracts between buyers and sellers of goods. The buyer sends its offer through its standardized purchase order form. The seller replies and purportedly accepts the offer through its standardized acknowledgment (acceptance) form. Usually, the only written or typewritten terms on either form set forth the description, price and quantity of the goods. The buyer's form which contains the offer may or may not indicate the quality of the goods ordered. If no quality term is contained in the form, the buyer is entitled to goods of fair average quality or merchantable goods. This is an implied warranty of merchantability which is set forth in the U.C.C. Often, the seller's form will contain a disclaimer of that implied warranty of merchantability. The disclaimer will be contained in a printed provision among many others somewhere on the form. The forms are exchanged, the goods are shipped and, perhaps, even paid for by the purchaser. When the buyer attempts to use the goods, he finds them to be of inferior, nonmerchantable quality. The buyer brings an action for breach of contract, specifically, breach of the implied warranty of merchantability. The seller argues that since his acknowledgment form did not exactly match the terms of the buyer's offer, the form was not an acceptance of the offer. Rather, it was a counter-offer which created a new power of acceptance in the original offeror. When the goods were accepted and received by the purchaser, the counter-offer was accepted. Therefore, the contract or deal was made on the terms set forth in the seller's form. In effect, the seller had the "last shot" since his form created the last power of acceptance which the buyer exercised presumably by accepting and receiving the goods on the terms set forth in the seller's form. Under the matching acceptance rule, this analysis was clearly correct. Yet, the buyer never read the seller's form, the seller never read the buyer's form and neither read their own forms. The printed forms were simply a convenient means of expressing assent to the "dickered" terms, i.e., the written or typewritten terms which described the goods, their quantity and their price. Quaere: did the parties intend to be bound by the terms on the forms and, even if they did, which terms did they intend as binding? The question scarcely survives its statement. In the typical exchange, the parties manifested no intention whatsoever as to the printed provisions of their forms. Yet, they did physically exchange them and the forms constituted the only written evidence of their deal. The traditional judicial reaction was that the forms could not be ignored and since the terms thereon did not match, the last form had to be a counter-offer permitting the seller to have his "last shot" and to prevail.

John Edward Murray, Jr., Contracts §54, at 112-113 (2d ed. 1974).

The court in *Princess Cruises* applies the classical last shot rule. Having concluded that GE's response should be viewed as a counter-offer under the mirror image rule, the court then goes on to hold that Princess Cruises accepted that counter-offer by conduct: by not objecting to its terms; by accepting the services performed by GE; and by paying the price stated in GE's counter-offer. In support, the court cites Restatement (Second) of Contracts §19(1), along with case law to the same effect. See Sharp Electronics Corp. v. Deutsche Financial Services Corp., 216 F.3d 388 (4th Cir. 2000) (manufacturer effectively accepted financer's revised version of financing arrangement re customer's purchases of inventory by continuing to ship inventory to customer with knowledge of terms of financer's counter-offer).

4. *Approach of the CISG.* Unlike UCC Article 2, discussed in the following Note, the Convention on Contracts for the International Sale of Goods appears to follow essentially the common law approach, as Professor Dodge has explained:

The CISG . . . adopts what is essentially a mirror-image rule. Article 19(1) provides: "A reply to an offer which purports to be an acceptance but contains additions, limitations or other modifications is a rejection of the offer and constitutes a counter-offer." Article 19(2) attempts to soften this rule a little by providing that if the additional or different terms are not material *and* the offeror does not object to them, then the purported acceptance is an acceptance and the additional or different terms become part of the contract. But Article 19(3) defines materiality so broadly that it is hard to imagine a change that the CISG would not consider material. This means that, in almost every case, an acceptance that varies the terms of the offer will be a counteroffer which will be accepted by the other party's conduct.

William S. Dodge, Teaching the CISG in Contracts, 50 J. Leg. Ed. 72, 82-83 (2000).

5. *Contrast with UCC Article 2.* On both points — the effect of a varying or qualified acceptance; the effect of performance on the issue of acceptance — the UCC takes a fundamentally different tack. The Code's original approach to the problem of the battle of the forms in UCC §2-207 proved to be both difficult to apply and controversial, as you will see in your study of the following case. The 2003 revisions to Article 2 substantially changed §2-207. The revised Code's approach to the battle of the forms is found in two sections: §2-206(3) and §2-207. However, the original version of §2-207 is likely to remain the law in many states for a number of years, so understanding of its provisions remains important. The following case and problem explore the Code's original approach. The comment following the problem discusses the approach of revised Article 2 to the battle of the forms.

Before you study the next case, read through the original version of §2-207, and its comments. (No, it's not easy going; we are well aware of that. Many courts have found this provision difficult to understand and apply.) Note that in Comment 1 to §2-207, the drafters identify two different situations which (somewhat awkwardly) they have attempted to cover in this single section. The first one mentioned in that comment, the use of "written confirmations," involves an oral agreement between the parties (by telephone, typically), followed by written confirmations sent by one or both of the parties. The *Harlow & Jones* case discussed earlier in this chapter involved an oral agreement followed by written confirmations by the buyer and the seller. The second situation mentioned in Comment 1 is the "varying acceptance" case. (*Princess Cruises* would fall into this general category, although of course that was not regarded as a sale of goods.) The following case, Brown Machine, Inc. v. Hercules, Inc., well illustrates the UCC's handling of the "varying acceptance" situation under the original §2-207.

Brown Machine, Inc. v. Hercules, Inc.
Missouri Court of Appeals
770 S.W.2d 416 (1989)

STEPHAN, Judge.

Hercules Inc. ("Hercules") appeals from the judgment of the trial court awarding respondent Brown Machine $157,911.55 plus interest after a jury verdict in favor of Brown Machine in its action against Hercules for indemnification. We reverse.

In early 1976 Brown Machine had sold appellant Hercules a T-100 trim press. The trim press was a piece of equipment apparently used in manufacturing Cool Whip bowls. The initial sales negotiations between the two companies for the trim press began in October 1975. Bruce Boardman, an engineer at Hercules, asked Jim Ryan, Brown Machine's district sales manager, to send Hercules a quote for a trim press. On November 7, 1975, Brown Machine submitted its original proposal No. 51054 for the model T-100 trim press to Hercules. The proposal set out sixteen numbered paragraphs describing the machine to be sold. Attached to the proposal was a printed form of fifteen paragraphs in boilerplate style captioned "TERMS AND CONDITIONS OF SALE." The eighth paragraph provided as follows:

> 8. LIABILITY: The purchaser agrees to pay in behalf of BROWN all sums which BROWN becomes legally obligated to pay because of bodily injury or property damage caused by or resulting from the use or misuse of the IOS [item of sale], including reasonable attorneys fees and legal expenses. The purchaser agrees to indemnify and hold BROWN harmless from all actions, claims, or demands arising out of or in any way connected with the IOS, its operation, use or misuse, or the design construction or composition of any product made or handled by the IOS, including all such actions, claims, or demands based in whole or in part on the default or negligence of BROWN.

Tim Wilson, Hercules' purchasing agent, reviewed the proposal submitted by Brown Machine. On January 7, 1976, he telephoned Jim Ryan at Brown Machine. Mr. Ryan's call report reflected that Hercules had prepared its purchase order No. 03361 in response to Brown Machine's proposal but that Hercules had objected to the payment term requiring a twenty percent deposit be paid with the order. After talking with Mr. Fassett, Brown Machine's product manager, Mr. Ryan told Mr. Wilson that Brown Machine could not waive the deposit and that an invoice for payment would be forwarded to Hercules.

Mr. Fassett issued a work order that day giving the shop instructions concerning the trim press equipment, followed by a written order the next day. The written order noted that "customer gave verbal P.O. [purchase order] for this stock machine. Will issue revision when formal purchase order received."

On January 19, 1976, Brown Machine received Hercules' written purchase order No. 03361 dated January 6, 1976. The order was for a "Brown T-100 Trimpress in accordance with Brown Machine quote # 51054. All specifications cited within quote except item # 6.1.1 which should read: 'Reverse trim' instead of 'Standard regular forward trim.'" In a blue box on the bottom left of the purchase order form in bold print appeared "THIS ORDER EXPRESSLY LIMITS ACCEPTANCE TO THE TERMS STATED HEREIN INCLUDING THOSE PRINTED ON THE REVERSE SIDE. ANY ADDITIONAL OR DIFFERENT TERMS PROPOSED BY THE SELLER ARE REJECTED UNLESS EXPRESSLY AGREED TO IN WRITING." The reverse side of Hercules' purchase order, captioned "TERMS AND CONDITIONS" contained sixteen boilerplate paragraphs, the last of which provided:

16. OTHER TERMS: No oral agreement or other understanding shall in any way modify this order, or the terms or the conditions hereof. Seller's action in (a) accepting this order, (b) delivering material; or (c) performing services called for hereunder shall constitute an acceptance of the above terms and conditions.

The purchase order contained no indemnity provision.

Brown Machine received two copies of the purchase order. One had been stamped "Vendor's Copy" at the bottom; the other was marked "ACKNOWLEDG-MENT," with a space labeled "accepted by" for signature by Brown Machine. Brown Machine did not return this prepared acknowledgment to Hercules.

The next day, on January 20, 1976, Mr. Fassett issued his second machine order to the shop revising his description to reflect that Brown Machine had received Hercules' formal purchase order and that the machine was no longer inventoried as a Brown stock item. On January 21, 1976, Brown Machine sent Hercules an invoice requesting payment of $4,882.00, the twenty percent deposit for the trim press.

Rather than returning the acknowledgment of the purchase order prepared by Hercules, Mr. Fassett of Brown Machine sent Hercules an "ORDER ACKNOWLEDGEMENT" dated February 5, 1976. This letter stated as follows:

> Below in detail are the specifications covering the equipment ordered, and the equipment will be manufactured to meet these specifications. If these specifications and terms and conditions of Sale are not in accordance with your understanding, please ADVISE US WITHIN SEVEN (7) DAYS OF RECEIPT OF THIS ACKNOWL-EDGEMENT. If we do not hear from you within this period of time, we are proceeding with the construction of the equipment as per these specifications and terms as being agreed; and any changes occurring later may result in additional charges.
>
> *ONE T-100 TRIM PRESS AS FOLLOWS . . .*

The paragraphs following set out the same sixteen specifications contained in Brown Machine's original proposal. Paragraph 6.1.1 of the specifications again provided for "Standard-regular forward trim." Page four of the acknowledgment contained the same "TERMS AND CONDITIONS OF SALE" which had accompanied Brown Machine's earlier proposal of November 7, 1975, including paragraph eight on liability and indemnity. Only two minor changes had been penned in on page four, neither of which has any bearing on the issues presented for appeal.

Hercules responded with a letter on February 9, 1976, to Mr. Fassett that "This is to advise you that Provision 6.1 of your order acknowledgment dated 2/5/76 should read 'Reverse Trim' instead of 'Standard-regular forward trim.' All other specifications are correct." On February 16, 1976, Mr. Fassett confirmed the change in provision 6.1.1 and informed the shop that same day of the requested modification to be made.

Hercules never paid the twenty percent deposit. Brown Machine sent Hercules an invoice dated April 14, 1976, requesting final payment of the total purchase price. Brown eventually shipped the trim press to Hercules and Hercules paid the agreed-upon purchase price.

Sometime later, James Miller, an employee of Hercules, and his wife sued Brown Machine because of injuries he sustained while operating the trim press at Hercules' plant in Union, Missouri. Brown Machine demanded that Hercules defend the Miller lawsuit, but Hercules refused. Brown Machine eventually settled the Millers' lawsuit. Brown Machine later initiated this action against Hercules for indemnification of the settlement amount paid the Millers. Brown Machine claimed a condition of the original sales contract for the trim press required Hercules to indemnify Brown Machine for any claims arising from operation or misuse of the trim press.

Hercules' four points on appeal challenge the submissibility of Brown Machine's case, the verdict director given by Brown Machine, admission of certain allegedly prejudicial testimony and, finally, an instructional error. The dispositive issue on appeal is whether the parties had agreed to an indemnification provision in their contract for the sale of the T-100 trim press.

Hercules' first point disputes Brown Machine's contention that its initial proposal on November 7, 1975, constitutes the offer and that Hercules verbally accepted the offer by the telephone call on January 7, 1976, followed by its written purchase order dated January 6, 1976, which Brown Machine received January 19, 1976.

Article 2 of the Uniform Commercial Code governs transactions involving the sale of goods. UCC §2-102 (1977). Because the term "offer" is not defined in the code, the common law definition remains relevant. UCC §1-103. An offer is made when the offer leads the offeree to reasonably believe that an offer has been made. Gilbert & Bennett Manufacturing Co. v. Westinghouse Electric Corp., 445 F. Supp. 537, 545[3] (D. Mass. 1977). Restatement (Second) of Contracts §24 (1981) defines "offer" as "the manifestation of willingness to enter into a bargain, so made as to justify another person in understanding that his assent to that bargain is invited and will conclude it."

The general rule is that a price quotation is not an offer, but rather is an invitation to enter into negotiations or a mere suggestion to induce offers by others. Maurice Electrical Supply Co. v. Anderson Safeway Guard Rail Corp., 632 F. Supp. 1082, 1087[3] (D.D.C. 1986); USEMCO, Inc. v. Marbro Co., 60 Md. App. 351, 483 A.2d 88, 93[1] (1984). However, price quotes, if detailed enough, can amount to an offer creating the power of acceptance; to do so, it must reasonably appear from the price quote that assent to the quote is all that is needed to ripen the offer into a contract. Quaker State Mushroom Co. v. Dominick's Finer Foods, Inc., 635 F. Supp. 1281, 1284[3] (N.D. Ill. 1986); see Boese-Hilburn Co. v. Dean Machinery Co., 616 S.W.2d 520, 524-25 (Mo. App. 1981).

In this case Hercules could not have reasonably believed that Brown Machine's quotation was intended to be an offer, but rather an offer to enter into negotiations for the trim press. The cover letter accompanying the proposal mentioned that Brown Machine's sales representative would contact Hercules "to discuss this quote" and that the quotation was submitted for Hercules "approval." The sale price as quoted also included the notation "We have included a mechanical ejector (item 9.1.2) because we understand this unit may be used for development of many items that would require this option. However, if you decide this is not necessary $2,575.00 could be deducted from the above price for a total of $21,835.00." Most importantly, paragraph three of the terms and conditions of sale attached to the proposal expressly provided: "No order, sale, agreement for sale, accepted proposal, offer to sell and/or contract of sale shall be binding upon BROWN unless accepted by BROWN . . . on BROWN standard 'Order Acknowlegment' [sic] form." Thus, because the quotation reasonably appeared to be an offer to enter into negotiations for the sale of a trim press with a mechanical ejector for $24,410.00 with acceptance conditioned upon Brown's order acknowledgment form, no firm offer existed. Accord, Quaker State Mushroom, Inc., 635 F. Supp. at 1285. Brown's price quote was merely a proposal, not an offer, because of its provision that Hercules' acceptance was not binding upon Brown until Brown acknowledged the acceptance.

Even if we were to accept Brown Machine's characterization of its proposal as an offer, the quotation by its own terms and conditions expired thirty days after its issuance ("All quoted prices are subject to change without notice except those written proposals which shall expire without notice . . . thirty (30) calendar days from date issued . . ."). Hercules' written purchase order was dated January 6, 1976, and their telephone conversation of January 7, 1976, were both well beyond the expiration of the quote. Thus, even if the quotation were construed as an offer, there was no timely acceptance. See Gilbert & Bennett, 445 F. Supp. at 545[4].

If the acceptance of a price quotation, sufficiently detailed to constitute an offer, is not binding on the seller because the time within which it could have been accepted has lapsed, the purchase order, not the price quotation, is treated as the offer since the purchase order did not create an enforceable contract. McCarty v. Verson Allsteel Press Co., 89 Ill. App. 3d 498, 44 Ill. Dec. 570, 411 N.E.2d at 936, 943[5] (1980). Thus, we believe Hercules' purchase order constitutes the offer. As a general rule, orders are considered as offers to purchase. Aaron E. Levine & Co. v. Calkraft Paper Co., 429 F. Supp. 1039, 1048[15] (E.D. Mich. 1976).

The question then arises whether Brown Machine's acknowledgment containing the indemnity provision constitutes a counter offer or an acceptance of Hercules' offer with additional or different terms. Section 400.2-207, RSMo 1986, which mirrors §2-207 of the Uniform Commercial Code provides the workable rule of law addressing the problem of the discrepancies in the independently drafted documents exchanged between the two parties. . . .

Under subsection (1) an offeree's response to an offer operates as a valid acceptance of the offer even though it contains terms additional to, or different from, the terms of the offer unless the "acceptance is expressly made conditional" on the offeror's assent to the additional or different terms. Where the offeree's acceptance is made "expressly conditional" on the offeror's assent, the response operates not as an acceptance but as a counter offer which must be accepted by the original offeror. Falcon Tankers, Inc. v. Litton Systems, Inc., 355 A.2d 898, 906[7] (Del. Super. 1976). Restatement (Second) of Contracts §59 (1981) expresses it succinctly: "[A]n offeree's reply which purports to accept an offer but makes acceptance conditional on the offeror's assent to terms not contained in the original offer is effective as a counteroffer rather than acceptance."

The general view held by the majority of states is that, to convert an acceptance to a counter offer under UCC §2-207(1), the conditional nature of the acceptance must be clearly expressed in a manner sufficient to notify the offeror that the offeree is unwilling to proceed with the transaction unless the additional or different terms are included in the contract. See Annot., "What Constitutes Acceptance 'Expressly Made Conditional' Converting it to Rejection and Counteroffer under UCC §2-207(1)," 22 A.L.R. 4th 939, 948-49 (1983) and cases cited therein. The conditional assent provision has been construed narrowly to apply only to an acceptance which clearly shows that the offeree is unwilling to proceed absent assent to the additional or different terms. Id.; see Challenge Machinery Co. v. Mattison Machine Works, 138 Mich. App. 15, 359 N.W.2d 232, 235[3] (1984) citing Idaho Power Co. v. Westinghouse Electric Corp., 596 F.2d 924 (9th Cir. 1979); Dorton v. Collins & Aikman Corp., 453 F.2d 1161 (6th Cir. 1972).

We find nothing in Brown Machine's acknowledgment of February 5, 1976, which reflects its unwillingness to proceed unless it obtained Hercules' assent to the additional and different terms in Brown Machine's acknowledgment, that is, page four of the acknowledgment styled "TERMS AND CONDITIONS OF SALE" which contained the indemnity provision. Brown Machine's acknowledgment was not "expressly made conditional" on Hercules' assent to the additional or different terms as provided for under §2-207(1). Acceptance will be considered a counteroffer only if the acceptance is expressly made conditional on assent to the additional terms. Clifford-Jacobs Forging Co. v. Capital Engineering & Mfg. Co., 107 Ill. App. 3d 29, 62 Ill. Dec. 785, 787, 437 N.E.2d 22, 24 (1982). We conclude Brown Machine's acknowledgment did not operate as a counter offer within the scope of §2-207(1).

Having determined that Brown Machine's order acknowledgment is not a counter offer, we believe that Brown Machine's acknowledgment operates as acceptance with additional or different terms from the offer, since the purchase order contained no indemnity provision. Under §2-207(2), additional terms become a part of the contract between merchants unless (a) the offer expressly limits acceptance to the terms of the offer; (b) they materially alter it; or (c) notification of objection to them has already been given or is given within a reasonable time after notice of them is given. Hercules' purchase order here expressly limited acceptance to the terms of its offer. Given such an express limitation, the additional terms, including the indemnification provision, failed to become part of the contract between the parties.

We can conclude Hercules intended the indemnity provision to become a part of the parties' contract only if Hercules, as offeror, expressly assented to the additional terms, and, thus, effectively waived its condition that acceptance be limited to the terms of its offer, the purchase order. While the text of §2-207 does not incorporate such a provision, Official Comment 3 to §2-207 states: "Whether or not additional or different terms will become part of the agreement depends upon the provisions of subsection (2). If they are such as materially to alter the original bargain, they will not be included unless expressly agreed to by the other party." The indemnification provision was clearly a material alteration to the parties' agreement.

The evidence does not establish that Hercules expressly assented to the additional terms contained in Brown Machine's order acknowledgment. Brown Machine's order acknowledgment of February 5, 1976, indicated that "[i]f these specifications and terms and conditions of Sale are not in accordance with your understanding, please ADVISE US WITHIN SEVEN (7) DAYS OF RECEIPT OF THIS ACKNOWLEDGMENT." Hercules replied by letter four days later advising Brown Machine that provision 6.1.1 should provide for reverse trim instead of standard regular forward trim, followed by "all other specifications are correct." Hercules' use of the term "specifications" is unambiguous and clearly refers only to the protocol for the machine's manufacture. Nothing in its response can be construed as express assent to Brown Machine's additional "terms and conditions of sale." Express assent under §2-207(2) cannot be presumed by silence or mere failure to object. N & D Fashions, Inc. v. DHJ Industries, Inc., 548 F.2d 722, 726-27[5] (8th Cir. 1977).

We believe it is clear as a matter of law that the indemnification clause cannot be held to be part of the contract agreed upon by the parties. The judgment of the trial court is reversed. We need not address the remaining points raised by Hercules.

Reversed.

SMITH, P.J., and SATZ, J., concur.

Notes and Questions

1. *The Code's treatment of the "varying acceptance."* Courts and commentators frequently begin discussion of UCC §2-207 by noting that it appears to have as one of its principal purposes the amelioration of a strict "mirror image" approach to contract formation, by permitting nonmatching communications to form a contract if the parties apparently intended that they should. E.g., Northrop Corp. v. Litronic Industries, 29 F.3d 1173 (7th Cir. 1994) (§2-207 has jettisoned mirror image rule); Superior Boiler Works, Inc. v. R. J. Sanders, Inc., 711 A.2d 628 (R.I. 1998) (§2-207 effects "radical departure" from common law rule). The Code's rejection of the mirror-image rule is stated in §2-207(1): "A definite and seasonable expression of acceptance . . . operates as an acceptance even though it states terms additional to or different from those offered. . . ." (If this seems to be merely a tautology, it may help to read the first use of the term *acceptance* as meaning, essentially, *assent,* and the second as meaning *legal acceptance.*)

2. *Finding the first offer.* Under §2-207, as in the classical approach to agreement-formation, the first step is to ascertain at what point an "offer" was first made by one party to the other. (Section 2-207(1) does not use the term "offer," but note §2-207(2)(a) and Comment 1.) The court in *Brown Machine* thus begins by examining the communications between the parties and concludes that the first offer was the buyer's purchase order of January 6; the seller's "proposal" (or "quote") of November 7 was not an offer, but merely an invitation to the buyer to submit an offer. Although a price quotation is often held to be only a preliminary negotiation, it may in some cases amount to an offer. The *Brown Machine* court recognizes this possibility but concludes that in this case the buyer could not have reasonably understood that the seller was making an offer. In reaching that conclusion, however, the court relies in part on the language of the seller's form regarding the need for further acceptance

by the seller. This is of course "boilerplate," about which §2-207 might suggest we should be somewhat skeptical. (Do you think the buyer read that language?) If the seller's initial proposal had not contained that provision, would the court's characterization of it as a mere invitation for an offer still be persuasive?

3. *Testing the response.* Having established that the buyer's purchase order was the first operative offer, the court then proceeds to apply the test of §2-207(1) to the seller's reply. If the seller had (as requested) merely signed and returned the buyer's form, then presumably the offer-and-acceptance analysis would cease at this point, and the terms of the purchase order would constitute the contract. But — as in *Princess Cruises* — each party preferred to use its own forms, so the seller responded with a form of its own, an "Order Acknowledgment." Assuming that this form demonstrated sufficient assent to the buyer's order to be regarded as potentially an "acceptance," the next issue under §2-207(1) is whether the seller's acceptance was "expressly conditional" (in which case, as the court declares, it functions not as an acceptance, but as a "counter-offer").

Courts have differed on when an acceptance should be treated as "expressly conditional" and therefore function as a counter-offer. An early case, Roto-Lith, Ltd. v. F.P. Bartlett & Co., 297 F.2d 497 (1st Cir. 1962), held that an acceptance with terms that were materially different from the offer amounted to an expressly conditional acceptance. Courts and commentators criticized this view because it effectively reestablished the common law mirror image rule, contrary to the intentions of the drafters of §2-207. E.g., White & Summers, Uniform Commercial Code §1-3 (5th ed. 2000). In Ionics, Inc. v. Elmwood Sensors, Inc., 110 F.3d 184 (1st Cir. 1997), the First Circuit recognized its error in *Roto-Lith* and overruled the decision.

Since *Roto-Lith* has been overruled, it now seems well established that an acceptance does not amount to an expressly conditional acceptance simply because it contains terms that materially differ from the terms of the offer. But when is an acceptance expressly conditional? Most courts have focused on the language of the acceptance. If the acceptance uses very clear language indicating that the offeree's assent is expressly conditional on the offeror's agreement to the terms of the offeree's document, then the acceptance will be treated as expressly conditional, even if the language is essentially boilerplate. E.g., Diamond Fruit Growers, Inc. v. Krack Corp., 794 F.2d 1440, 1444 (9th Cir. 1986) (seller's response expressly conditional; its "form tracks the language of the section"). The language, however, must be very clear. If the offeree simply states that its acceptance is "subject to the following terms and conditions" or equivalent conditional language, that is generally held not to be sufficient to treat the acceptance as expressly conditional. See Dorton v. Collins & Aikman Corp., 453 F.2d 1161, 1167 (6th Cir. 1972) ("subject to all of the terms and conditions on the face and reverse side hereof, including arbitration, all of which are accepted by buyer" held not to be an expressly conditional acceptance). Under this test Brown's order acknowledgment was not an expressly conditional acceptance. How could you redraft Brown's form to turn it into an expressly conditional acceptance?

It should be noted that a few courts go beyond the language of the acceptance to determine whether it should be treated as expressly conditional, examining all the facts and circumstances, including trade usage and course of dealings between the parties. See Gardner Zemke Co. v. Dunham Bush, Inc., 850 P.2d 319 (N.M. 1993). See also John E. Murray, Jr., The Chaos of the "Battle of the Forms": Solutions, 39 Vand. L. Rev. 1307, 1330-1343 (1986) (acceptance should be regarded as "conditional" and therefore as a counteroffer based on reasonable understanding of response to offer — not merely because it contains boilerplate language). Which test for an expressly conditional acceptance do you find more persuasive?

4. *Have the additional terms been expressly assented to?* If it concludes that the offeree's response was indeed an "acceptance" but not a "conditional" one, the court must in most cases go on to determine whether the additional terms in that acceptance have become part of the parties' agreement under §2-207. At this point, the §2-207 analysis proceeds to §2-207(2), which declares that the additional terms are to be viewed as "proposals for addition to the contract." The logical first question under §2-207(2) would be, therefore: Has the offeror assented to the offeree's proposed additional terms? In *Brown Machine*, the seller argued that the buyer had in effect accepted the seller's terms by indicating (in writing) that, with one exception, "all other specifications are correct." Was the court right to reject that argument? In another case involving a similar seller-indemnification clause, the seller contended that a "course of dealing" between the parties established that the clause had indeed been assented to by the buyer, the parties having "exchanged the same forms on prior occasions." The court rejected that argument because there was no showing that any employee of the buyer had ever read such a form, or that a previous dispute had called the clause at issue to the buyer's attention. The mere use or even repeated use of forms implies nothing about the parties' awareness of their contents, the court asserted, because such forms are never read. Maxon Corp. v. Tyler Pipe Industries, Inc., 497 N.E.2d 570, 575-576 (Ind. Ct. App. 1986). As the *Brown Machine* opinion puts it, "*express* assent under §2-207(2) cannot be presumed by silence or mere failure to object" (emphasis supplied).

5. *Do the additional terms become part of the contract anyway?* If the additional terms have not been expressly assented to, might they nevertheless in some cases become part of the contract? Section 2-207(2) provides for this possibility, in a case where the parties are both merchants. This will happen, however, only if the terms in question have not been objected to (either in advance — through language in the offer or otherwise — or thereafter) *and* if the terms in question are not "material." The comments to §2-207 provide examples of clauses that typically do amount to a material alteration of the offer (comment 4) and those that do not (comment 5). For example, a clause negating standard warranties would normally be treated as a material alteration under comment 4. Relying on the language of comment 4, many courts examine whether the clause will involve "surprise or hardship" in determining whether the clause involves a material alternation. See Dale R. Horning Co. v. Falconer Glass Industries, Inc., 730 F. Supp. 962 (S.D. Ind. 1990) (clause in glass supplier's confirmation of contract excluding liability for consequential damages was a material alteration of contract with subcontractor; sub failed to show that clause involved "surprise" because suppliers in glass industry routinely limit liability to replacement of defective class; however,

clause involved "hardship" when supplier knew or had reason to know that sub would face substantial liability for delays necessitated by replacing defective glass). Did the buyer in *Brown Machine* sufficiently object to the seller's additional terms? In the absence of such an objection, could the seller's indemnification clause have become part of the contract under §2-207(2)? Or was it "material"?

6. *Has a counter-offer (conditional acceptance) been accepted?* Because it finds the seller's response not to be a conditional acceptance, the court in *Brown Machine* does not have to face the other tough issue frequently raised in §2-207 cases: What constitutes effective assent to a counter-offer expressed in the form of a "conditional acceptance?" When will the additional terms it contains be binding on the other party? It is possible, of course, that the offeror could expressly agree to the terms of the offeree's counter-offer. E.g., In re Mostek Corp., 502 N.Y.S.2d 181 (App. Div. 1986) (seller had signed buyer's purchase order form with arbitration clause). In the absence of such express assent, can agreement be found in the offeror's subsequent conduct? Section 2-207 itself gives no clear answer to that question. The clear consensus of courts and commentators, however, is that conduct alone should not be sufficient to amount to assent to an expressly conditional acceptance. To find assent to a counter-offer in mere performance is to continue in effect the common law's "last shot" approach, which the drafters of §2-207 clearly were attempting to abrogate. See, e.g., Diamond Fruit Growers, Inc. v. Krack Corp., 794 F.2d 1440, 1445 (9th Cir. 1986) (buyer did not agree to terms of conditional acceptance containing disclaimer of warranties and limitation of consequential damages by continuing to receive and pay for goods; policy of Code requires "specific and unequivocal expression of assent"); White & Summers, Uniform Commercial Code §1-3, at 39-40 (5th ed. 2000). In the absence of real assent to the proposed additional terms, what then? In that case, even if the documents of the parties have not formed a contract, their actions (shipment and receipt of the goods) may establish a contractual relationship under §2-207(3), and Comment 7 to §2-207. If the seller in *Brown Machine* had by tracking the statutory language succeeded in making only a "conditional acceptance" (and thus in effect a counter-offer), would its proposed indemnification clause have become part of the contract under §2-207(3)?

7. *What are "supplementary terms" under §2-207(3)?* If an offeree's response is deemed to be at most an "expressly conditional" acceptance, and thus in effect a counter-offer, but the parties proceed to performance without an express acceptance of the counter-offer's terms, what then? Under §2-207(3), the contract will consist of those terms on which the writings of the parties agree, "together with any supplementary terms incorporated under any other provisions of this act [i.e., the UCC]." Clearly those "supplementary terms" would include such implied terms under Article 2 as the implied warranties of merchantibility and fitness (§§2-314 and 2-315) and the damages provisions, including seller liability for consequential damages (§2-715), along with more innocuous "gap-filler" provisions of Article 2 (§§2-307, 2-308, etc.). They also may include terms that are deemed part of the parties' agreement by virtue of the Code's provisions regarding "course of performance," "course of dealing," and "usage of trade" (§§1-205, 2-208). See Coastal & Native Plant Specialties, Inc., v. Engineered Textile Products, Inc., 139 F. Supp.2d 1326, 1337

(N.D. Fla. 2001). But mere receipt of forms without objection may not be held to constitute a course of dealing or course of performance sufficient to establish assent to the terms of those forms, under §2-207, even where forms are repeatedly sent over time:

> . . . [A] course of dealing may become part of an agreement, via a type of estoppel, when one party fails to object to the manner in which the other party performs under the agreement. Terms and conditions contained in a form continually sent by one party do not constitute performance and cannot become binding as a course of dealing. . . . The reason for this distinction between (a) a repeated manner of performance and (b) the repeated sending of forms is pragmatic. A party will certainly be cognizant of the manner in which the other side continually performs under the agreement, and if there is no objection to that performance by the first party, over a sufficient period of time, the first party is assumed to have acquiesced to the second party's manner of performance. The same cannot be said of forms continually sent by one party to the other, which are often not read until a dispute arises.

Premix-Marbletite Mfg. Corp. v. SKW Chemicals, Inc., 145 F. Supp.2d 1348, 1356 (S.D. Fla. 2001), citing and quoting Step-Saver Data Systems, Inc. v. Wyse Tech., 939 F.3d 91 (3d Cir. 1991). In later sections of these materials we will return to a closer examination of the concepts of course of performance, course of dealing, and usage of trade.

8. *Lawyering issues — the effect of "different" terms.* As many commentators have pointed out, the structure of §2-207 makes it likely that the "well-counseled" buyer will include in its "order" (offer) form a provision requiring the seller's acceptance of all of the buyer's terms and objecting in advance to any and all different and additional terms in the seller's response, while an equally well-counseled seller will respond with an "acknowledgement" (acceptance) form that is expressly conditional on the buyer's assent to all its terms. What will be the result of such a strategy if the parties proceed to performance without stopping to iron out the differences between their forms? To the extent that the seller's form has additional provisions not found in the buyer's order, those provisions will be tested by §2-207, particularly as to whether they materially alter the buyer's offer. If the seller's form contains provisions that negate clauses contained in the buyer's form (for example, the buyer's order requires an express warranty by the seller, while the seller's form negates all warranties), the prevailing view is to treat these "different" terms as "knocked out" by each other. See Daitom, Inc. v. Pennwalt Corp., 741 F.2d 1569 (10th Cir. 1984). In that case §2-207(3) determines the terms of the contract.

PROBLEM 2-4

How would the following dispute be resolved under original UCC §2-207?

Mendoza Construction Company is a general contractor that handles major commercial construction projections. Mendoza is the general contractor for the construction of several buildings on the "campus" of Wintel, Inc., a major communications company that is consolidating its operations outside of Columbus.

G&P Industries is a supplier of various industrial products, including roofing materials and compounds.

On September 15, Margaret Navell, the Mendoza supervisor for the Wintel project, called Frank Park at G&P to determine the price, availability, and delivery schedule for various roofing materials and compounds for the Wintel project. Park provided Navell with the information she requested and told her that if she wished to place an order she should do so as soon as possible because demand for the company's products was very brisk. On the morning of October 1 Navell sent a fax to Park. The fax stated that Mendoza wished to place an order for various roofing products and compounds. The price and delivery schedule stated in Navell's fax were as quoted by Park in the conversation on September 15. Delivery of all materials was to be made by November 15.

On the afternoon of October 1, Park sent a fax back to Navell confirming receipt of Navell's order. In addition to confirming the basic terms of Navell's order, the fax also stated:

Acceptance of Your Order Is Subject to the Following Terms and Conditions

1. 10% payment due in 10 days. Payment in full of balance due 7 days after completion of delivery.
2. Any unpaid amounts accrue interest at the rate of 1% per month.
3. Purchaser agrees to pay reasonable attorneys fees and costs of collection should that be necessary.
4. All disputes under this order shall be submitted to arbitration under the Commercial Arbitration Rules of the American Arbitration Association.
5. G&P will supply purchaser with the manufacturer's warranty on all materials sold to purchaser.
6. G&P will notify purchaser of any delays in delivery. If for any reason delivery cannot be made within 60 days of scheduled date, purchaser shall have the right to cancel this contract. G&P will not otherwise be liable for delays in delivery that are beyond its control.

On October 7, Mendoza sent G&P a check for $35,643.20, which represented 10 percent of its order.

On November 4 Park sent a fax to Navell informing her that he had just learned from the manufacturer that supplied G&P with roofing materials that the manufacturer's next delivery would be delayed. Park informed Navell that G&P anticipated that the materials would be delivered in 30-45 days. Navell called Park to complain about the delay, but Park informed her that there was simply nothing he could do. Navell told Park that the delay would subject Mendoza to damages to Wintel under a liquidated damages provision of the contract between Wintel and Mendoza, and that Mendoza would hold G&P responsible for the damages. Park replied that G&P was not responsible for any delays beyond its control. Park also said that if Mendoza refused to honor the contract, G&P would retain the deposit and seek other damages. The telephone conversation ended without resolution of the issue.

Navell then contacted other suppliers of roofing materials and learned that another company could meet Mendoza's needs in a timely fashion. Navell attempted to negotiate cancellation of the contract with G&P, but Park stubbornly refused to make any concessions.

(a) Navell comes to you seeking advice as to whether Mendoza has the legal right to cancel the contract with G&P and enter into a substitute contract. Later in the course we will examine various legal doctrines, such as impossibility or impracticability, that might excuse a party such as G&P from performance even in the absence of a contractual provision providing some form of excuse. Assuming that none of these doctrines would apply to this situation, what advice would you give to Navell?

(b) Assume that Navell decided to cancel the contract with G&P; she sent written notice to that effect, which G&P promptly objected to in writing. G&P has now filed a demand for arbitration seeking damages from Mendoza for breach of contract. You are an associate with a law firm representing Mendoza. The senior attorney responsible for the case, who is also a "shareholder" in your firm, has asked you to research and analyze the issues of Mendoza's contractual liability to G&P. Be prepared for a meeting with the shareholder to discuss these issues and any additional factual information that you think is necessary to analyze the issues involved in the case.

(c) How would your analysis in (a) or (b) above be affected if either of the following provisions had been included in the documents:

- Navell's fax of October 1 on behalf of Mendoza contained the following provision: "Supplier shall be responsible for any penalties or damages incurred by Mendoza as a result of any delays in delivery by Supplier."
- G&P's response to Navell's of October 1 contained the following provision: "Acceptance of your order is expressly conditional on your assent to the terms of this document pursuant to UCC §2-207(1)."

Comment: Battle of the Forms under Revised Article 2

As you can see from our analysis of *Brown Machine*, §2-207 suffered from a number of flaws, principally the complexity and ambiguity of several of its provisions. See James J. White, Contracting under Amended 2-207, 2004 Wis. L. Rev. 723, 724 (identifying six flaws with old §2-207 and quoting a letter from Professor Grant Gilmore characterizing the section as "arguably the greatest statutory mess of all time"). Indeed, commentators have been clamoring for years for revision of the section. See Symposium, Ending "The Battle of the Forms": A Symposium on the Revision of Section 2-207 of the Uniform Commercial Code, 49 Bus. Law. 1019 (1994).

Revised Article 2, adopted in 2003, makes significant changes in former §2-207. Like former §2-207, the revised Article 2 deals with two issues: (1) Has a contract been formed when the parties exchange documents or use confirmations that have different or additional terms? (2) If a contract has been formed, what are the terms of the contract?

1. *Contract formation under revised Article 2.* The issue of contract formation, formerly covered by the first part of §2-207(1), has been moved up into new §2-206(3), which reads: "A definite and seasonable expression of acceptance in a record operates as an acceptance even if it contains terms additional to or different from the offer." Thus, like the former §2-207(1), revised §2-206(3) rejects the common law "mirror image rule" for contract formation.

Comments 2 and 3 to §2-206 deal with the difficult issue of "expressly conditional acceptances" (and expressly conditional offers as well). Comment 2 to §2-206 states:

> The mirror image rule is rejected in subsection (3), but any responsive record must still be reasonably understood as an "acceptance" and not as a proposal for a different transaction. *See* Official Comment 2 to Section 2-207.

Comment 3 to §2-206 makes it clear that to operate as an acceptance an offeree's response must be a "definite acceptance." If the offeree clearly states that it is only willing to do business if the offeror assents to the offeree's terms, the offeree has not made a definite acceptance. The comment states that this result is "consistent with the final clause of former Section 2-207(1)." Similarly, if the offer states that the offeror is only willing to enter into a contract on its terms, a purported acceptance with additional or different terms is not a definite acceptance within the meaning of the section. It is important to note, however, that even if the exchange of documents does not result in the formation of a contract, because of the absence of a definite acceptance under comment 3, a contract may still be formed if the parties proceed to perform. See UCC §2-204(1), which states: "A contract for sale of goods may be made in any manner sufficient to show agreement, including offer and acceptance, conduct by both parties which recognizes the existence of a contract . . ." See also §2-207(i).

2. *Terms of the contract under revised Article 2.* Revised §2-207 deals with the issue of the terms of a contract once a contract has been formed under either §2-204 or §2-206:

> Subject to Section 2-202 [the Code's parol evidence rule, discussed in Chapter 5 — EDS.], if (i) conduct by both parties recognizes the existence of a contract although their records do not otherwise establish a contract, (ii) a contract is formed by an offer and acceptance, or (iii) a contract formed in any manner is confirmed by a record that contains terms additional to or different from those in the contract being confirmed, the terms of the contract are:
>
> (a) terms that appear in the records of both parties;
> (b) terms, whether in a record or not, to which both parties agree; and
> (c) terms supplied or incorporated under any provision of this Act.

Present §2-207(2), with its three-pronged formula for dealing with additional terms as between merchant parties, would simply vanish into oblivion (taking with it, presumably, several decades' worth of student- or faculty-generated flow charts). Revised §2-207 is instead a restated and somewhat expanded version of the present §2-207(3). Comments provide some illustrations and guidance for courts in sorting through various types of communications.

The intent of new §2-207 is to avoid favoring either the first or the last shot in determining the terms of the contract, as stated in new comment 2:

> When forms are exchanged before or during performance, the result from the application of this section differs from the prior Section 2-207 of this Article and the

common law in that this section gives no preference to either the first or the last form; the same test is applied to the terms in each. Terms in a record that insist on all of that record's terms and no other terms as a condition of contract formation have no effect on the operation of this section. When one party insists in that party's record that its own terms are a condition to contract formation, if that party does not subsequently perform or otherwise acknowledge the existence of a contract, if the other party does not agree to those terms, the record's insistence on its own terms will keep a contract from being formed under Sections 2-204 or 2-206, and this section is not applicable. As with original Section 2-207, the courts will have to distinguish between "confirmations" that are addressed in this section and "modifications" that are addressed in Section 2-209.

The difference in approach between the old and new versions of §2-207 (plus the new §2-206(3)) can also be glimpsed in the following statement at the end of comment 3 to the new version: "There is a variety of verbal and nonverbal behavior that may suggest agreement to another's record. This section leaves the interpretation of that behavior to the discretion of the courts."

To summarize some conclusions that can be drawn from these new provisions: If a party, whether offeror or offeree, wishes to refuse to enter into a contract except on its own terms, the party may do so by clear language in its document coupled with a refusal to perform or other acknowledgement of a contractual relationship. See comment 2 to §2-207. However, if a party insists in its document that it will not enter into a contract except on its terms, but that party then proceeds to perform even though the other party has issued a document with different or additional terms, a contract will be formed under §2-204(1) and the terms of the contract will be determined by §2-207. Terms of insistence in a party's document have no application once a contract is formed by performance or otherwise. Comment 2 to §2-207. See White, Contracting under Amended 2-207, 2004 Wis. L. Rev. at 731-732 (discussing effect of "mine only" terms under old and revised section).

How do you think the *Brown Machine* case and Problem 2-4 would be decided under the rules of new §2-206 and §2-207?

4. Postponed Bargaining: The "Agreement to Agree"

In the typical "battle of forms" dispute, as discussed in the previous section of this chapter, the parties have negotiated the terms they regarded as necessary to settle by agreement and have left unresolved the conflicts between the different terms on their respective forms. In some cases the parties may simply have been unaware of any conflict because they never read or compared the forms; in others, it may be that they did not regard the matters dealt with by those conflicting terms as being of any real importance. Or, it may be that the costs of continued bargaining (in time, money, and the risk of losing the deal) could not be justified in light of the relative infrequency with which disputes involving such matters actually arise. It may even be that in some cases one party's failure to pursue the bargaining will stem from a belief that should a dispute arise, the terms of its own form will govern (or else that a similar term will be implied by law).

In the material that follows, however, the parties appear to have completed their bargaining, or at least to have reached an agreement. There are no conflicting forms, no "different or additional" terms to contend with. And yet their agreement may appear to be incomplete, either because some matters usually dealt with in such agreements have not been explicitly covered or because the parties themselves have designated certain matters for postponed decision — agreement at some future time. Such an incomplete bargain posed serious problems under the classical system, as the following excerpt from Professor Corbin's treatise indicates:

> Communications that include mutual expressions of agreement may fail to consummate a contract for the reason that they are not complete, some essential term not having been included. Frequently agreements are arrived at piecemeal, different terms and items being discussed and agreed upon separately. As long as the parties know that there is an essential term not yet agreed on, there is no contract; the preliminary agreements on specific items are mere preliminary negotiation building up the terms of the final offer that may or may not be made. Even though one of the parties may believe that the negotiation has been concluded, all items agreed upon, and the contract closed, there is still no contract unless he is reasonable in his belief and the other party ought to have known that he would so believe. . . .
>
> Further illustrations are to be found in the cases of a so-called contract to make a contract. It is quite possible for parties to make an enforceable contract binding them to prepare and execute a subsequent documentary agreement. In order that such may be the effect, it is necessary that agreement shall have been expressed on all essential terms that are to be incorporated in the document. That document is understood to be a mere memorial of the agreement already reached. If the document or contract that the parties agree to make is to contain any material term that is not already agreed on, no contract has yet been made; and the so-called "contract to make a contract" is not a contract at all.

1 Corbin on Contracts §29. The rules and principles discussed by Professor Corbin have not disappeared from the scene; they can be and are employed by courts today. But they have been supplemented and in some cases substantially modified by new rules and principles, particularly those enunciated in the Uniform Commercial Code and echoed in the Restatement (Second) of Contracts. The materials that follow explore some of these developments.

Walker v. Keith
Kentucky Court of Appeals
382 S.W.2d 198 (1964)

CLAY, Commissioner.

In this declaratory judgment proceeding the plaintiff appellee sought an adjudication that he had effectively exercised an option to extend a lease, and a further determination of the amount of rent to be paid. The relief prayed was granted by the Chancellor. The principal issue is whether the option provision in the lease fixed the rent with sufficient certainty to constitute an enforceable contract between the parties.

In July 1951 appellants, the lessors, leased a small lot to appellee, the lessee, for a 10-year term at a rent of $100 per month. The lessee was given an option to extend the lease for an additional 10-year term, under the same terms and conditions except as to rental. The renewal option provided: "rental will be fixed in such amount as shall actually be agreed upon by the lessors and the lessee with the monthly rental fixed on the comparative basis of rental values as of the date of the renewal with rental values at this time reflected by the comparative business conditions of the two periods."

The lessee gave the proper notice to renew but the parties were unable to agree upon the rent. Preliminary court proceedings finally culminated in this lawsuit. Based upon the verdict of an advisory jury, the Chancellor fixed the new rent at $125 per month.

The question before us is whether the quoted provision is so indefinite and uncertain that the parties cannot be held to have agreed upon this essential rental term of the lease. There have been many cases from other jurisdictions passing on somewhat similar lease provisions and the decisions are in hopeless conflict. We have no authoritative Kentucky decision.

At the outset two observations may be made. One is that rental in the ordinary lease is a very uncomplicated item. It involves the number of dollars the lessee will pay. It, or a method of ascertaining it, can be so easily fixed with certainty. From the standpoint of stability in business transactions, it should be so fixed.

Secondly, as an original proposition, uncomplicated by subtle rules of law, the provision we have quoted, on its face, is ambiguous and indefinite. The language used is equivocal. It neither fixes the rent not furnishes a positive key to its establishment. The terminology is not only confusing but inherently unworkable as a formula.

The above observations should resolve the issue. Unfortunately it is not that simple. Many courts have become intrigued with the possible import of similar language and have interpolated into it a binding obligation. The lease renewal option has been treated as something different from an ordinary contract. The law has become woefully complicated. For this reason we consider it necessary and proper to examine this question in depth.

The following basic principles of law are generally accepted:

> It is a necessary requirement in the nature of things that an agreement in order to be binding must be sufficiently definite to enable a court to give it an exact meaning. Williston on Contracts (3d ed.) Vol. 1, section 37 (page 107).
>
> Like other contracts or agreements for a lease, the provision for a renewal must be certain in order to render it binding and enforceable. Indefiniteness, vagueness, and uncertainty in the terms of such a provision will render it void unless the parties, by their subsequent conduct or acts supplement the covenant and thus remove an alleged uncertainty. The certainty that is required is such as will enable a court to determine what has been agreed upon. 32 Am. Jur., Landlord and Tenant, section 958 (page 806).
>
> The terms of an extension or renewal, under an option therefor in a lease, may be left for future determination by a prescribed method, as by future arbitration or appraisal; but merely leaving the terms for future ascertainment, without providing a method for their determination, renders the agreement unenforceable for uncertainty. 51 C.J.S. Landlord and Tenant 56b (2), page 597.

A renewal covenant in a lease which leaves the renewal rental to be fixed by future agreement between the parties has generally been held unenforceable and void for uncertainty and indefiniteness. Also, as a general rule, provisions for renewal rental dependent upon future valuation of premises without indicating when or how such valuation should be made have been held void for uncertainty and indefiniteness. 32 Am. Jur., Landlord and Tenant, section 965 (page 810).

Many decisions supporting these principles may be found in 30 A.L.R. 572; 68 A.L.R. 157; 166 A.L.R. 1237.

The degree of certainty is the controlling consideration. An example of an appropriate method by which a non-fixed rental could be determined appears in Jackson v. Pepper Gasoline Co., 280 Ky. 226, 133 S.W.2d 91, 126 A.L.R. 1370. The lessee, who operated an automobile service station, agreed to pay "an amount equal to one cent per gallon of gasoline delivered to said station." Observing that the parties had created *a definite objective standard* by which the rent could with certainty be *computed,* the court upheld the lease as against the contention that it was lacking in mutuality. (The Chancellor cited this case as authoritative on the issue before us, but we do not believe it is. Appellee apparently agrees because he does not even cite the case in his brief.)

On the face of the rent provision, the parties had not agreed upon a rent figure. They left the amount to future determination. If they had agreed upon a specific method of making the determination, such as by computation, the application of a formula, or the decision of an arbitrator, they could be said to have agreed upon whatever rent figure emerged from utilization of the method. This was not done.

It will be observed the rent provision expresses two ideas. The first is that the parties agree to agree. The second is that the future agreement will be based on a comparative adjustment in the light of "business conditions." We will examine separately these two concepts and then consider them as a whole.

The lease purports to fix the rent at such an amount as shall "actually be agreed upon." It should be obvious that an agreement to agree cannot constitute a binding contract. Williston on Contracts (3d ed.) Vol. 1, section 45 (page 149); Johnson v. Lowery, Ky., 270 S.W.2d 943; National Bank of Kentucky v. Louisville Trust Co., 6 Cir., 67 F.2d 97. . . .

As said in Williston on Contracts (3d ed.) Vol. 1, section 45 (page 149):

Although a promise may be sufficiently definite when it contains an option given to the promisor, yet if an essential element is reserved for the future agreement of both parties, the promise gives rise to no legal obligation until such future agreement. Since either party, by the very terms of the agreement, may refuse to agree to anything the other party will agree to, it is impossible for the law to fix any obligation to such a promise.

We accept this because it is both sensible and basic to the enforcement of a written contract. We applied it in Johnson v. Lowery, Ky., 270 S.W.2d 943, page 946, wherein we said:

To be enforceable and valid, a contract to enter into a future covenant must specify all material and essential terms and leave nothing to be agreed upon as a result of future negotiations.

This proposition is not universally accepted as it pertains to renewal options in a lease. Hall v. Weatherford, 32 Ariz. 370, 259 P. 282, 56 A.L.R. 903; Rainwater v. Hobeika, 208 S.C. 433, 38 S.E.2d 495, 166 A.L.R. 1228. We have examined the reasons set forth in those opinions and do not find them convincing. The view is taken that the renewal option is for the benefit of the lessee; that the parties intended something; and that the lessee should not be deprived of his right to enforce his contract. This reasoning seems to overlook the fact that a party must have an enforceable contract before he has a right to enforce it. We wonder if these courts would enforce an *original* lease in which the rent was not fixed, but agreed to be agreed upon.

Surely there are some limits to what equity can or should undertake to compel parties in their private affairs to do what the court thinks they should have done. See Slayter v. Pasley, Or., 199 Or. 616, 264 P.2d 444, 449; and dissenting opinion of Judge Weygandt in Moss v. Olson, 148 Ohio 625, 76 N.E.2d 875. In any event, we are not persuaded that renewal options in leases are of such an exceptional character as to justify emasculation of one of the basic rules of contract law. An agreement to agree simply does not fix an enforceable obligation.

As noted, however, the language of the renewal option incorporated a secondary stipulation. Reference was made to "comparative business conditions" which were to play some part in adjusting the new rental. It is contended this provides the necessary certainty, and we will examine a leading case which lends support to the argument.

In Edwards v. Tobin, 132 Or. 38, 284 P. 562, 68 A.L.R. 152, the court upheld and enforced a lease agreement which provided that the rent should be "determined" at the time of renewal, "said rental to be *a reasonable rental* under the then existing conditions." (Our emphasis.) Significance was attached to the last quoted language, the court reasoning that since the parties had agreed upon a reasonable rent, the court would hold the parties to the agreement by fixing it.

All rents tend to be reasonable. When parties are trying to reach an agreement, however, their ideas or claims of reasonableness may widely differ. In addition, they have a right to bargain. They cannot be said to be in *agreement* about what is a reasonable rent until they specify a figure or an exact method of determining it. The term "reasonable rent" is itself indefinite and uncertain. Would an original lease for a "reasonable rent" be enforceable by either party? The very purpose of a rental stipulation is to remove this item from an abstract area.

It is true courts often must *imply* such terms in a contract as "reasonable time" or "reasonable price." This is done when the parties fail to deal with such matters in an otherwise enforceable contract. Here the parties were undertaking to fix the terms rather than leave them to implication. Our problem is not what the law would imply if the contract did not purport to cover the subject matter, but whether the parties, in removing this material term from the field of implication, have fixed their mutual obligations.

We are seeking what the agreement actually was. When dealing with such a specific item as rent, to be payable in dollars, the area of possible agreement is quite limited. If the parties did not agree upon such an unequivocal item or upon a definite method of ascertaining it, then there is a clear case of nonagreement. The court, in fixing an obligation under a non-agreement, is not enforcing the contract but is binding the parties to something they were patently unable to agree to when writing the contract.

The opinion in the *Tobin* case, which purportedly was justifying the enforcement of a contractual obligation between the lessor and lessee, shows on its face the court was doing something entirely different. This question was posed in the opinion: "What logical reason is there for equity to refuse to act when the parties themselves *fail to agree* on the rental?" (Our emphasis.) The obvious logical answer is that even equity cannot enforce as a contract a nonagreement. No distortion of words can hide the fact that when the court admits the parties "fail to agree," then the contract it enforces is one it makes for the parties.

It has been suggested that rent is not a material term of a lease. It is said in the *Tobin* case: "The method of determining the rent pertains more to form than to substance. It was not the essence of the contract, but was merely incidental and ancillary thereto." This seems rather startling. Nothing could be more vital in a lease than the amount of rent. It is the price the lessee agrees to pay and the lessor agrees to accept for the use of the premises. Would a contract to buy a building at a "reasonable price" be enforceable? Would the method of determining the price be a matter of "form" and "incidental and ancillary" to the transaction? In truth it lies at the heart of it. This seems to us as no more than a grammatical means of sweeping the problem under the rug. It will not do to say that the establishment of the rent agreed upon is not of the essence of a lease contract. . . .

We do not think our problem can be solved by determining which is the "majority" rule and which is the "minority" rule. We are inclined, however, to adhere to a sound basic principle of contract law unless there are impelling reasons to depart from it, particularly so when the practical problems involved in such departure are so manifest. Let us briefly examine those practical problems.

What the law requires is an adequate key to a mutual agreement. If "comparative business conditions" afforded sufficient certainty, we might possibly surmount the obstacle of the unenforceable agreement to agree. This term, however, is very broad indeed. Did the parties have in mind local conditions, national conditions, or conditions affecting the lessee's particular business?

That a controversy, rather than a mutual agreement, exists on this very question is established in this case. One of the substantial issues on appeal is whether the Chancellor properly admitted in evidence the consumer price index of the United States Labor Department. At the trial the lessor was attempting to prove the change in local conditions and the lessee sought to prove changes in national conditions. Their minds to this day have never met on a criterion to determine the rent. It is pure fiction to say the court, in deciding upon some figure, is enforcing something the parties agreed to.

One aspect of this problem seems to have been overlooked by courts which have extended themselves to fix the rent and enforce the contract. This is the Statute of Frauds. The purpose of requiring a writing to evidence an agreement is to assure certainty of the essential terms thereof and to avoid controversy and litigation. See 49 Am. Jur., Statute of Frauds, section 313 (page 629); section 353 (page 663); section 354 (page 664). This very case is living proof of the difficulties encountered when a court undertakes to supply a missing essential term of a contract.

In the first place, when the parties failed to enter into a new agreement as the renewal option provided, their rights were no longer *fixed* by the contract. The determination of what they were was automatically shifted to the courtroom. There the court must determine the scope of relevant evidence to establish that certainty which obviously cannot be culled from the contract. Thereupon extensive proof must be taken concerning business conditions, valuations of property, and reasonable rentals. Serious controversies develop concerning the admissibility of evidence on the issue of whether "business conditions" referred to in the lease are those on the local or national level, or are those particularly affecting the lessee's business. An advisory jury is impaneled to express its opinion as to the proper rental figure. The judge then must decide whether the jury verdict conforms to the proof and to his concept of equity. On appeal the appellate court must examine alleged errors in the trial. Assuming some error in the trial (which appears likely on this record), the case may be reversed and the whole process begun anew. All of this time we are piously clinging to a concept that the contract itself fixed the rent with some degree of certainty.

We realize that litigation is oft times inevitable and courts should not shrink from the solution of difficult problems. On the other hand, courts should not expend their powers to establish contract rights which the parties, with an opportunity to do so, have failed to define. As said in Morrison v. Rossingnol, 5 Cal. 64, quoted in 30 A.L.R. at page 579:

> A court of equity is always chary of its power to decree specific performance, and will withhold the exercise of its jurisdiction in that respect, unless there is such a degree of certainty in the terms of the contract as will enable it at one view to do complete equity.

That cannot be done in this case.

Stipulations such as the one before us have been the source of interminable litigation. Courts are called upon not to enforce an agreement or to determine what the agreement was, but to write their own concept of what would constitute a proper one. Why this paternalistic task should be undertaken is difficult to understand when the parties could so easily provide any number of workable methods by which rents could be adjusted. As a practical matter, courts sometimes must assert their right not to be imposed upon. This thought was thus summed up in Slayter v. Pasley, Or., 264 P.2d 444, page 449:

> We should be hesitant about completing an apparently legally incomplete agreement made between persons sui juris enjoying freedom of contract and dealing at arms' length by arbitrarily interpolating into it our concept of the parties' intent merely to validate what would otherwise be an invalid instrument, lest we inadvertently commit them to an ostensible agreement which, in fact, is contrary to the deliberate design of all of them. It is a dangerous doctrine when examined in the light of reason. Judicial paternalism of this character should be as obnoxious to courts as is legislation by judicial fiat. Both import a quality of jural ego and

superiority not consonant with long-accepted ideas of legistic propriety under a democratic form of government. If, however, we follow the urgings of the lessee in the instant matter, we will thereby establish a precedent which will open the door to repeated opportunities to do that which, in principle, courts should not do and, in any event, are not adequately equipped to do.

We think the basic principle of contract law that requires substantial certainty as to the material terms upon which the minds of the parties have met is a sound one and should be adhered to. A renewal option stands on the same footing as any other contract right. Rent is a material term of a lease. If the parties do not fix it with reasonable certainty, it is not the business of courts to do so.

The renewal provision before us was fatally defective in failing to specify either an agreed rental or an agreed method by which it could be fixed with certainty. Because of the lack of agreement, the lessee's option right was illusory. The Chancellor erred in undertaking to enforce it.

The judgment is reversed.

Notes and Questions

1. *Factors favoring the tenant.* It is clear that the court that decided Walker v. Keith could, if it wished, have determined a "reasonable" rental for the renewal term and upheld the plaintiff tenant's right to renew on that basis. What factors impelled its refusal to do so? In the course of its opinion, the *Walker* court concedes that courts have often enforced lease-extension agreements substantially similar to the one at issue in *Walker*, despite incompleteness of the parties' agreement ("decisions are in hopeless conflict"). What considerations might lead a court to decide such a case in favor of enforcement? Should those factors have outweighed the ones that apparently actuated the court in *Walker?* In Cassinari v. Mapes, 542 P.2d 1069 (Nev. 1975), plaintiff tenant sought damages for wrongful eviction from the premises on which he operated a restaurant business. The renewal option provision that plaintiff sought to enforce stated that the five-year renewal term should be on "the same terms and conditions" as the original term, but "at a monthly rental to be determined" at the time of renewal. The court upheld the tenant's claim, on the following reasoning:

> It is appropriate to enforce such a provision since the clause for renewal constitutes part of the consideration for the original lease, and was without question intended by the parties to have meaning and to be effective. Surely we may not presume that one of the signatories agreed to the provision only in the secret belief that it would prove unenforceable. It is proper, then, to imply that the parties intended a reasonable rent for the extended period. If [they are] unable to agree, a court should be allowed to fix the rental since economic conditions are ascertainable with sufficient certainty to make the clause capable of enforcement. This view, we think, carries out the true intention of the parties, and does not constitute a making of a lease by the court in opposition to the desire of lessor and lessee.

Id. at 1071. Is this argument persuasive? Is it equally applicable to the *Walker* case?

2. *Other decisions.* A number of courts have enforced lease-renewal option agreements despite the failure of the parties to agree on a rental figure in advance. See, e.g., Berrey v. Jeffcoat, 785 P.2d 20 (Alaska 1990) ("rent shall be renegotiated and determined according to existing conditions and cost of living increases as of that time"); Little Caesar Enterprises, Inc., v. Bell Canyon Shopping Center, L.C., 13 P.3d 600 (Utah 2000) ("When a bargained-for term of a renewal provision sets a range within which negotiations for a rental rate must take place, the lessor may not render the renewal provision unenforceable simply by refusing to negotiate within the specified range and insisting on rent exceeding the maximum allowed by the contract."). Other courts have disagreed, however, and continue to take the same position as the court in *Walker.* See, e.g., Joseph Martin, Jr., Delicatessen, Inc. v. Schumacher, 417 N.E.2d 541, 544 (N.Y. 1981) ("annual rentals to be agreed upon"); Davis v. Cleve Marsh Hunt Club, 405 S.E.2d 839 (Va. 1991) ("mutually agreed rent").

3. *Open price term agreements under the UCC.* Although *Walker* and the other cases cited in the Notes above involved leases, the common law has generally been resistant in all areas to the notion that an enforceable contract could result from an agreement in which the parties failed to agree on either a specific price or at least a method (specific formula, designated arbitrator, extrinsic market source, et cetera) by which price could be ascertained. On this point, the Uniform Commercial Code takes a diametrically opposite position. Section 2-305 of the Code provides that an "open price term" will not prevent enforcement of a contract for sale, if the parties intended to be bound by their agreement. Whether the parties leave price for their later mutual determination or agree in advance that one of them shall have the power to fix a price, the court in either case may enforce the contract. If the parties later fail to agree on price, the court may enforce a "reasonable price"; if one party has the power to fix price, he must do so "in good faith." Why did the drafters of the Code adopt this position so at odds with the common law tradition? See the Comments to §2-305. The drafters of the Code have obviously assumed that when parties reach an agreement for the sale of goods in which the price is left to be fixed by agreement in the future, they may in fact have intended nevertheless to be presently bound. If so, should the law enforce their agreement, as provided in §2-305? Or are the factors that actuated the decision in Walker v. Keith equally important in sale of goods cases?

On the other hand, it should not be supposed merely from the existence of UCC §2-305 that every sale-of-goods agreement in which price is not fixed will necessarily be valid and enforceable despite that omission. The court may still conclude, as expressly contemplated by §2-305(4), that the parties did not intend to be bound unless the price was fixed by agreement. In that event, failure to reach agreement on price will mean that no enforceable contract of sale has been made, and the court will not fix a "reasonable" price for the parties. In Bethlehem Steel Corp. v. Litton Industries, Inc., 468 A.2d 748 (Pa. Super. Ct. 1983), *aff'd,* 488 A.2d 581 (1984), a closely divided court (4-3) held that the plaintiff could not enforce its option to buy five ore vessels from defendant because the parties had failed to agree on a detailed price escalation clause, which was of crucial importance to both parties; a vigorous dissent argued strongly that an intent to be bound was manifested by both parties and should have been given effect.

4. *Open price term agreements outside the UCC.* If §2-305 makes sense in the context of Article 2, should the courts apply similar principles to "open price" contracts of other types? The Restatement (Second) in Comment *e* to §33 appears to endorse the notion that the principle of UCC §2-305 could be applied to contracts other than the sale of goods (although the remedy might be limited to protection of the reliance or restitution interests). For example, in Arbitron, Inc. v. Tralyn Broadcasting, Inc., 400 F.3d 130 (2d Cir. 2005), the Second Circuit distinguished earlier New York cases, including *Joseph Martin*, note 2 above, and held that an escalation clause in a licensing agreement that allowed the licensor to adjust the monthly fee if the licensee acquired additional radio stations was not impermissibly vague even though it did not contain a definite price. The court held that the clause was not an unenforceable "agreement to agree," but instead allowed the licensor to set the price when stated conditions arose. The court noted that UCC §2-305, which had been adopted in New York, would permit a court to enforce such an agreement. See also Automatic Vending Co. v. Wisdom, 6 Cal. Rptr. 31 (Ct. App. 1960) (agreement for placement of plaintiff's cigarette vending machine on defendant's premises not rendered fatally illusory or void for lack of mutuality by provision giving plaintiff right to set commission rates; power could be exercised only "in good faith and in accordance with fair dealing").

In Oglebay Norton Co. v. Armco, Inc., 556 N.E.2d 515 (Ohio 1990), plaintiff operator of a fleet of ore-carrying vessels sought to enforce a long-term contract with defendant steel producer for the transport of iron ore on the Great Lakes from the mines to the defendant's manufacturing plants. The contract had been in force since 1957, with modifications, and had been extended to run until 2010. The parties had a "close and long-standing business relationship," and both understood that performance of the contract would involve substantial capital investment by the plaintiff to purchase, maintain, and upgrade sufficient vessels to handle defendant's ongoing requirements. The contract provided that the price for plaintiff's shipping services would be set by reference to the rate currently charged by the "leading iron ore shippers" in a given season; failing that, price was to be set by mutual agreement of the parties, "taking into consideration" the rate being charged for similar transportation by leading independent ore shippers. For reasons described in the opinion, both methods of fixing price became ineffective, and the parties failed to agree on a rate. Relying on Restatement (Second) §33 and Comment *e* thereto (which in large part tracks UCC §2-305), the Ohio Supreme Court unanimously affirmed a lower court decision declaring the contract effective, fixing a rate for the current season, and further ordering the parties to negotiate (or, in the failure of negotiation, to mediate) a price for each season through the remaining term of the contract—that is, until the year 2010. The outcome appears traceable in large measure to the long-term nature of the contract and the close relationship of the parties for over 25 years; so viewed, the case seems to represent in effect an application of the "relational contract" approach advocated by Professor Ian Macneil and others.

Quake Construction, Inc. v. American Airlines, Inc.
Supreme Court of Illinois
141 Ill.2d 281, 152 Ill. Dec. 308, 565 N.E.2d 990 (1990)

Justice CALVO delivered the opinion of the court:

Plaintiff, Quake Construction, Inc. (Quake), filed a four-count, third-amended complaint against defendants, American Airlines, Inc. (American), and Jones Brothers Construction Corporation (Jones). . . .

Quake alleged in its complaint the following facts. In February 1985, American hired Jones to prepare bid specifications, accept bids, and award contracts for construction of the expansion of American's facilities at O'Hare International Airport. Quake received an invitation to bid on the employee facilities and automotive maintenance shop project (hereinafter referred to as the project), and in April 1985 submitted its bid to Jones. Jones orally notified Quake that Quake had been awarded the contract for the project. Jones then asked Quake to provide the license numbers of the subcontractors Quake intended to use on the project. Quake notified Jones that the subcontractors would not allow Quake to use their license numbers until Quake submitted a signed subcontract agreement to them. Jones informed Quake that Quake would shortly receive a written contract for the project prepared by Jones. To induce Quake to enter into agreements with its subcontractors and to induce the subcontractors to provide Quake and Jones with their license numbers, Jones sent Quake the following letter of intent dated April 18, 1985:

> We have elected to award the contract for the subject project to your firm as we discussed on April 15, 1985. A contract agreement outlining the detailed terms and conditions is being prepared and will be available for your signature shortly.
>
> Your scope of work as the general contractor includes the complete installation of expanded lunchroom, restroom and locker facilities for American Airlines employees as well as an expansion of American Airlines existing Automotive Maintenance Shop. The project is located on the lower level of 'K' Concourse. A sixty (60) calendar day period shall be allowed for the construction of the locker room, lunchroom and restroom area beginning the week of April 22, 1985. The entire project shall be complete by August 15, 1985.
>
> Subject to negotiated modifications for exterior hollow metal doors and interior ceramic floor tile material as discussed, this notice of award authorizes the work set forth in the following documents at a lump sum price of $1,060,568.00.
>
> (a) Jones Brothers Invitation to Bid dated March 19, 1985.
> (b) Specifications as listed in the Invitation to Bid.
> (c) Drawings as listed in the Invitation to Bid.
> (d) Bid Addendum # 1 dated March 29, 1985.
>
> Quake Construction Inc. shall provide evidence of liability insurance in the amount of $5,000,000 umbrella coverage and 100% performance and payment bond to Jones

Brothers Construction Corporation before commencement of the work. The contract shall include MBE, WBE and EEO goals as established by your bid proposal. Accomplishment of the City of Chicago's residency goals as cited in the Invitation to Bid is also required. As agreed, certificates of commitment from those MBE firms designated on your proposal modification submitted April 13, 1985, shall be provided to Jones Brothers Construction Corporation.

Jones Brothers Construction Corporation reserves the right to cancel this letter of intent if the parties cannot agree on a fully executed subcontract agreement.

Jones and Quake thereafter discussed and orally agreed to certain changes in the written form contract. Handwritten delineations were made to the form contract by Jones and Quake to reflect these changes. Jones advised Quake it would prepare and send the written contract to Quake for Quake's signature. No such formal written contract, however, was entered into by the parties.

At a preconstruction meeting on April 25, 1985, Jones told Quake, Quake's subcontractors, and governmental officials present that Quake was the general contractor for the project. On that same date, immediately after the meeting, American informed Quake that Quake's involvement with the project was terminated. Jones confirmed Quake's termination by a letter dated April 25, 1985. The damages Quake allegedly suffered included the money it spent in procuring the contract and preparing to perform under the contract, and its loss of anticipated profit from the contract.

The main issue is whether the letter of intent from Jones to Quake is an enforceable contract such that a cause of action may be brought by Quake. This court has previously set forth the principles of law concerning the enforceability of letters of intent:

> The fact that parties contemplate that a formal agreement will eventually be executed does not necessarily render prior agreements mere negotiations, where it is clear that the ultimate contract will be substantially based upon the same terms as the previous document. [Citation.] If the parties . . . intended that the . . . document be contractually binding, that intention would not be defeated by the mere recitation in the writing that a more formal agreement was yet to be drawn. However, parties may specifically provide that negotiations are not binding until a formal agreement is in fact executed. [Citation.] If the parties construe the execution of a formal agreement as a condition precedent, then no contract arises unless and until that formal agreement is executed. Chicago Investment Corp. v. Dolins (1985), 107 Ill. 2d 120, 126-27, 89 Ill. Dec. 869, 481 N.E.2d 712.

See Ceres Illinois, Inc. v. Illinois Scrap Processing, Inc. (1986), 114 Ill. 2d 133, 143-44, 102 Ill. Dec. 379, 500 N.E.2d 1. . . . Thus, although letters of intent may be enforceable, such letters are not necessarily enforceable unless the parties intend them to be contractually binding. . . .

A circuit court must initially determine, as a question of law, whether the language of a purported contract is ambiguous as to the parties' intent. . . . If no ambiguity exists in the writing, the parties' intent must be derived by the circuit court, as a matter of law, solely from the writing itself. . . . If the terms of an alleged contract are ambiguous or capable of more than one interpretation, however, parol evidence is admissible to ascertain the parties' intent. (Borg-Warner Corp. v. Anchor Coupling Co. (1958), 16 Ill. 2d 234,

242, 156 N.E.2d 513; Interway, 85 Ill. App. 3d at 1098, 41 Ill. Dec. 117, 407 N.E.2d 615.) If the language of an alleged contract is ambiguous regarding the parties' intent, the interpretation of the language is a question of fact which a circuit court cannot properly determine on a motion to dismiss. . . .

In determining whether the parties intended to reduce their agreement to writing, the following factors may be considered: whether the type of agreement involved is one usually put into writing, whether the agreement contains many or few details, whether the agreement involves a large or small amount of money, whether the agreement requires a formal writing for the full expression of the covenants, and whether the negotiations indicated that a formal written document was contemplated at the completion of the negotiations. (*Ceres*, 114 Ill. 2d at 144, 102 Ill. Dec. 379, 500 N.E.2d 1; *Chicago*, 107 Ill. 2d at 124, 89 Ill. Dec. 869, 481 N.E.2d 712.) Other factors which may be considered are: "where in the negotiating process that process is abandoned, the reasons it is abandoned, the extent of the assurances previously given by the party which now disclaims any contract, and the other party's reliance upon the anticipated completed transaction." A/S Apothekernes Laboratorium for Specialpraeparater v. I.M.C. Chemical Group, Inc. (N.D. Ill. 1988), 678 F. Supp. 193, 196, *aff'd* (7th Cir. 1989), 873 F.2d 155.

. . .

The circuit court in the case at bar dismissed Quake's complaint, relying principally on the following sentence in the letter: "Jones Brothers Construction Corporation reserves the right to cancel this letter of intent if the parties cannot agree on a fully executed subcontract agreement" (hereinafter referred to as the cancellation clause). . . . The circuit court determined, based on the cancellation clause, that the parties agreed not to be bound until they entered into a formal written contract. Consequently, the circuit court held that the letter was not an enforceable contract and accordingly dismissed the complaint.

The appellate court, however, found the letter ambiguous. . . .

We agree with the appellate court majority's analysis and its conclusion that the letter was ambiguous. Consequently, we affirm the decision of the appellate court. The letter of intent included detailed terms of the parties' agreement. The letter stated that Jones awarded the contract for the project to Quake. The letter stated further "this notice of award authorizes the work." Moreover, the letter indicated the work was to commence approximately 4 to 11 days after the letter was written. This short period of time reveals the parties' intent to be bound by the letter so the work could begin on schedule. We also agree with the appellate court that the cancellation clause exhibited the parties' intent to be bound by the letter because no need would exist to provide for the cancellation of the letter unless the letter had some binding effect. The cancellation clause also implied the parties' intention to be bound by the letter at least until they entered into the formal contract. We agree with the appellate court that all of these factors evinced the parties' intent to be bound by the letter.

On the other hand, the letter referred several times to the execution of a formal contract by the parties, thus indicating the parties' intent not to be bound by the letter. The cancellation clause could be interpreted to mean that the parties did not intend to be bound until they entered into a formal agreement. Therefore, the appellate court correctly concluded that the letter was ambiguous regarding the parties' intent to be bound by it.

Defendants contend the letter of intent did not contain all of the terms necessary for the formation of a construction contract. Defendants assert construction contracts typically include terms regarding payment, damages and termination. Defendants argue the detail in the contract is usually extensive if the value and complexity of the construction project are great. Defendants also note the letter stated the contract would include the detailed terms and conditions of the parties' agreement. The letter indicated the contract would include the MBE, WBE and EEO (Minority Business Enterprise, Women's Business Enterprise, and Equal Employment Opportunity, respectively) goals established by Quake's bid proposal. Defendants point out the letter stated certain terms of the agreement still had to be negotiated. Without the formal contract, defendants assert, the parties could not have continued toward the completion of the project because the letter excluded many terms of the agreement which would have been included in the contract. Defendants thus argue the absence in the letter of all the terms of the agreement reveals the parties' intent not to be bound by the letter.

The appellate court stated the number and extent of the terms in the letter can indicate the parties' intent to be bound by the letter. The final contract only need be substantially based on the terms in the letter as long as the parties intended the letter to be binding. (Chicago, 107 Ill. 2d at 126-27, 89 Ill. Dec. 869, 481 N.E.2d 712.) Many of the details regarding the project were included in the letter. The letter adopted by reference the contents of certain documents which included even further details concerning the project. We agree Jones accepted the MBE, WBE and EEO goals established by Quake. The letter merely indicated that those goals would be reiterated in the contract. We acknowledge that the absence of certain terms in the letter indicates the parties' intent not to be bound by the letter. This only confirms our holding that the letter is ambiguous as to the parties' intent.

. . .

Defendants contend even if the letter contained all of the essential terms of a contract, the cancellation clause negated any inference that the parties intended to be bound by the letter. The clause, according to defendants, clearly established the parties' intent not to be so bound. . . .

We do not find defendants' argument persuasive. The appellate court stated that, in addition to the detailed terms of the parties' agreement, the letter also contained a sentence in which Jones said it awarded the contract for the project to Quake. Moreover, the letter stated "this notice of award *authorizes* the work." (Emphasis added.) Furthermore, the appellate court pointed out, the letter was dated April 18, while at the same time the letter indicated that Quake was to begin work the week of April 22 and complete the work by August 15. We agree with the appellate court's conclusion that a "reasonable inference from these facts is that the parties intended that work on the Project would begin prior to execution of a formal contract and would be governed by the terms of the 'Letter of Intent.'" (181 Ill. App. 3d at 914, 130 Ill. Dec. 534, 537 N.E.2d 863.) All of these factors indicate the negotiations were more than merely preliminary and the parties intended the letter to be binding. The factors muddle whatever otherwise "clear" intent may be derived from the cancellation clause.

Defendants acknowledge the letter was dated April 18 and it stated the work would commence the week of April 22. Defendants point out that the letter also indicated Jones would submit a formal contract to Quake "shortly." Defendants argue a contract could conceivably have been written and signed within that period of time. Defendants conclude the appellate court's assumption regarding the date of the letter and the commencement of the work was invalid. While defendants' interpretation of these facts is plausible, we believe it only lends credence to our conclusion the letter is ambiguous concerning the parties' intent. Thus, the trier of fact should decide which interpretation is valid.

. . .

Defendants further contend that the cancellation clause is not ambiguous. Defendants assert parties may agree, in a letter of intent, to the course of, and discontinuance of, their negotiations. Defendants argue the letter of intent in the case at bar merely reflects the parties' agreement regarding the course of their negotiations.

We, like the appellate court, find the cancellation clause itself ambiguous as to the parties' intent. We do not agree with defendants' assertion that the cancellation clause so clearly indicates the parties' intent not to be bound by the letter that the clause negates other evidence in the letter of the parties' intent to be bound. The clause can be construed as a condition precedent to the formation of a contract. The clause, however, also states that Jones can "cancel" the letter. As the appellate court noted, if the parties did not intend to be bound by the letter, they had no need to provide for its cancellation. We also agree with the appellate court that the cancellation clause "implies that the parties could be bound by the 'Letter of Intent' in the absence of a fully executed subcontract agreement." (181 Ill. App. 3d at 914, 130 Ill. Dec. 534, 537 N.E.2d 863.) Thus, the ambiguity within the cancellation clause itself enhances the other ambiguities in the letter.

. . .

Defendants allege that the appellate court's decision puts the continued viability of letters of intent at risk. Defendants contend if we uphold the appellate court's decision finding the cancellation clause ambiguous, negotiating parties will have difficulty finding limiting language which a court would unquestionably consider unambiguous. We disagree. Courts have found letters of intent unambiguous in several cases referred to in this opinion. . . . Thus, the existence or absence of particular language or words will not ensure that a letter of intent is unambiguous. Our decision here follows the settled law in Illinois concerning letters of intent: The intent of the parties is controlling.

Neither we nor the appellate court have decided whether in fact a contract exists, that is, whether the parties intended to be bound by the letter. We merely hold that the parties' intent, based on the letter alone, is ambiguous. Therefore, upon remand, the circuit court must allow the parties to present other evidence of their intent. The trier of fact should then determine, based on the evidence and the letter, whether the parties intended to be bound by the letter.

...

For the foregoing reasons, we affirm the decision of the appellate court. Affirmed.

Justice STAMOS, specially concurring:

Because dismissal is unwarranted unless clearly no set of facts can be proved under the pleadings that will entitle a plaintiff to recover, I agree with the majority that the circuit court should not have dismissed ... Quake's complaint. ...

However, even though the Jones letter of intent is just ambiguous enough for Quake's complaint to survive a motion to dismiss, I consider that any interpretation of the letter's language as potentially establishing an underlying construction contract is far less plausible than the majority implies. ...

Instead of weighing as heavily for as against a construction contract, in my judgment the cancellation clause powerfully militates against any finding of such contract. ...

The cancellation clause refers expressly to cancelling the *letter*, not to cancelling the construction contract that the letter anticipates. A construction contract certainly would bind the parties to that contract's terms, but upon acceptance by Quake the letter here would much more plausibly be viewed as, at most, only binding the parties to efforts at achieving a construction contract on the terms outlined. See, e.g., Evans, Inc. v. Tiffany & Co. (N.D. Ill. 1976), 416 F. Supp. 224 (obligation to negotiate derived from unclear letter of intent); see also Farnsworth, Precontractual Liability, 87 Colum. L. Rev. at 250-69 (discussing letters of intent classified as "agreements with open terms" and "agreements to negotiate"); Knapp, Enforcing the Contract to Bargain, 44 N.Y.U. L. Rev. 673 (1969) (discussing need for recognizing good-faith bargaining duty as intermediate stage between ultimate contract and none); cf. Shell, Substituting Ethical Standards for Common Law Rules in Commercial Cases: An Emerging Statutory Trend, 82 Nw. U.L. Rev. 1198, 1199 & n. 7 (1988) (noting case law on duty of good-faith negotiation pursuant to letters of intent).

...

Hence, the letter itself, as distinguished from the anticipated construction contract, may be regarded as a contract in its own right: a contract to engage in negotiations. If so, it was this contract, not the anticipated construction contract, that might be canceled by Jones pursuant to the cancellation clause. Indeed, the notion of cancelling a construction contract not yet entered into lacks meaning.

...

... Yet, one might ask in reply: If the letter required only an effort to achieve a construction contract, and if failure of the effort would necessarily prevent any such contract from arising to bind the parties, how could the issue of cancelling a mere letter ever take on enough significance to explain inclusion of the cancellation clause? ...

...

[S]everal hypotheses suggest themselves for explaining the present letter of intent's cancellation clause:

> Because the letter can be regarded as creating an obligation on Jones to attempt to achieve a construction contract, existence of the clause might be explained as a device by which Jones could put an end to its obligation to negotiate.
>
> The fact that this letter, like many others, was intended to induce action by third parties furnishes another possible explanation for including the cancellation clause: It would give Jones a way to put an end to any further inducement based on Jones' once-expressed intention.
>
> A third possible explanation lies in the possibility that, as a result of the parties' subsequent conduct (such as commencement of construction work by Quake), an uncancelled letter of intent might become a link in a chain leading to a finding of contract.
>
> Still another possible explanation lies in the fact that, commercially if not legally, letters of intent have a certain weight as trustworthy indicators of business decisions; accordingly, an issuer might wish to cancel a letter once a decision had changed, in order not to mislead those who might otherwise rely on it.

Any or all of these possibilities would adequately explain the clause, without any need whatever to conclude that the clause betokens an intent to be bound to a construction contract thought to be embodied in the letter. See also Precontractual Liability, 87 Colum. L. Rev. at 257-58 (discussing other possible rationales for clause).

If letters of intent are to be used, their drafters would be well advised to avoid ambiguity on the point of whether the issuers are bound. As ever, obscurantist language can produce desired practical effects in the short term, but can well lead eventually to litigation and undesired contractual obligations. Extreme examples exist. (See, e.g., Note, The $10.53 Billion Question—When Are the Parties Bound?: Pennzoil and the Use of Agreements in Principle in Mergers and Acquisitions, 40 Vand. L. Rev. 1367 (1987).) Some counsel and clients may opt for ambiguity on grounds of expediency and may account for the probability of resultant litigation costs in the clients' overall business decisionmaking, but many others could benefit from more precision. In turn, counsel for recipients of such letters should remain alert to the likelihood that the instruments lack contractual force.

• • •

Notes and Questions

1. *A lawyering question.* Both the majority and concurring opinions bemoan the lack of clarity in the letter of intent. How would you have drafted the letter of intent to avoid the ambiguity found by the court?

2. *Incomplete bargains: intention to be bound.* Analytically, it is useful to distinguish two situations of incomplete bargaining. In one type of case, the "agreement to agree," the parties have reached agreement on a number of matters but have left for future agreement one or more terms. Walker v. Keith is such a case. In the second type of case, the "formal contract contemplated,"

the parties have reached agreement in principle on at least the major provisions of their agreement, but they contemplate the execution of a formal written contract. When the parties contemplate the execution of a formal contract, they often reduce their agreement in principle to a written letter of intent. It is, of course, possible that a fact pattern could involve both an agreement to agree and a formal contract contemplated. For example, the parties might reach agreement on all material terms of contract, except for delivery dates, which would be left for future agreement; the parties could express their agreement in principle in a letter of intent which contemplates the execution of a formal contract. Is *Quake Construction* an example of an agreement to agree, a formal contract contemplated, or both?

Both the UCC and the Restatement recognize that parties may be bound contractually when they have reached agreement in principle, even though they contemplate either further negotiations ("agreement to agree") or the execution of a formal written contract ("formal contract contemplated"). UCC §2-204(3) states: "Even if one or more terms are left open a contract for sale does not fail for indefiniteness if the parties have intended to make a contract and there is a reasonably certain basis for giving an appropriate remedy." Section 27 of the Restatement (Second) states: "Manifestations of assent that are in themselves sufficient to conclude a contract will not be prevented from so operating by the fact that the parties also manifest an intention to prepare and adopt a written memorial thereof; but the circumstances may show that the agreements are preliminary negotiations." Both the UCC and the Restatement are in accord with the court's decision in *Quake*, holding that whether a contract is formed in cases of an agreement to agree or formal contract contemplated turns on the factual question of whether the parties intended to be bound when they agreed in principle or only after further negotiations prove successful. The court in *Quake* identified a number of factors that are relevant to a determination of the parties' intention. Restatement (Second) §27, Comment *c* contains a similar list. The *Quake* court remanded the case for trial on this factual issue. Based on the facts set forth in the opinion, how would you resolve the factual question of whether the parties intended to be bound when they executed the letter of intent?

3. *A middle ground: the contract to bargain in good faith.* According to the majority's analysis only two possibilities exist: Either the parties intended to be bound to a construction contract when they signed the letter of intent or they didn't. As concurring Justice Stamos indicates, a third possibility is that the execution of the letter of intent bound the parties to negotiate in good faith to attempt to reach agreement on a construction contract, but the parties reserved the right to terminate the negotiations should they be unsuccessful in reaching agreement. Professor Knapp, in his 1969 article cited by Justice Stamos in his concurrence, was one of the earliest proponents of judicial recognition of the contract to bargain in good faith:

> In the typical "formal contract contemplated" case, the parties have clearly intended a bargain; they have also reached the stage of agreement on at least a number of the material terms of the proposed exchange. However, for some reason, they both apparently contemplate the later execution of a full, formal written document. At this stage of the negotiations, there are once again a number of

possible views which the parties may entertain as to the extent to which each of them is "bound," by good business ethics, to the proposed exchange of performances:

(1) Each may regard himself as not bound to anything at all unless and until a formal writing is signed by him, and, further, as being free to refuse to sign that writing for any reason whatsoever. This is one possible view which the law may take as to the extent of the obligation created by the negotiations to date — none at all. A legal conclusion of this sort, which will be presented as the reflection of the parties' intention, is made more likely by the presence of factors such as the following: a) the contract is of a type which requires writing for enforceability under the Statute of Frauds; b) the contract contemplated involves large sums of money; c) the contract has many details; d) the contract is an unusual one, for which a standard form is not available or appropriate; e) the parties were apparently unwilling to proceed with any performance until the formal document was prepared and signed. There are many cases in which it is impossible to believe that the parties intended any liability to attach to either side until final execution of the contemplated formal document.

(2) Each party may really feel that the "formal" document is only a "formality" — some sort of ritual, desirable for one or more reasons, but in no sense a prerequisite to a "binding" agreement.

This second view is, again, not an unlikely one for the law to adopt on the issue of whether in a particular case a binding legal obligation has been created. The likelihood of such an outcome is increased where: a) no independent policy of the law requires a writing for enforceability, or, if it does, the parties have exchanged letters, telegrams or other writings in which the agreed-upon terms are sufficiently reflected; b) the proposed contract appears relatively simple, and does not involve long-term obligations; c) the contemplated "formal" contract is a standard-form document, which itself contains the details necessary for a contract of this sort; or d) the parties themselves, without waiting for the formality of execution, have proceeded to perform, in a way that suggests they believed full and binding agreement to have been reached.

In each of the two preceding characterizations of the "formal contract contemplated" situation, the parties may have actually reached agreement on every detail of their proposed exchange. In any such case where at the relevant point in negotiation there remain terms on which agreement has not been expressly reached, there is yet a third possibility.

(3) It is possible that the principals have carried the "deal" as far as they can, and that they are relying on their agents (almost always including lawyers, but possibly also accountants and other experts) to complete the process of agreement. In this view of the facts, the purpose of preparing the formal document is not simply to postpone creation of an obligation, or even to provide evidence of its existence or terms, but rather to afford these experts an opportunity to add to the total agreement such protection against various risks as they think necessary or prudent. On this assumption, the principals are likely to feel ethically bound to the outlines of the deal as they have hammered it out, the withdrawal of either one based simply on dissatisfaction with those outlines being regarded by both as admittedly unjustified. The principals, however, are likely to consider themselves still morally free to withdraw if and when it should appear that the "second team" of bargainers have raised a substantial issue on which they are unable to agree and which the principals, when apprised of the difficulty, are likewise unable to resolve.

Charles L. Knapp, Enforcing the Contract to Bargain, 44 N.Y.U. L. Rev. 673, 682-684 (1969). The article goes on to argue that where the true state of mind of the parties is the third of those described above — if a court is to be faithful to its professed regard for the true "intention" of the parties—it should regard them as bound by a contract to bargain in good faith. That contract should be potentially enforceable by damages or specific relief, if appropriate. However, if good faith bargaining should fail to yield a complete agreement, then each party should be free to withdraw from the transaction. In other words, the legal effect of the "agreement to agree" or "formal contract contemplated" should more closely reflect the actual intention of the parties: They should be neither completely free (to withdraw for any reason whatever), nor completely bound (should they later be unable to agree).

In a 1987 article (also cited by Justice Stamos), Professor E. Allan Farnsworth explores various types of intermediate agreements that may be reached in the course of moving toward a complete and final agreement. Like Professor Knapp, Professor Farnsworth sees a middle ground between pure negotiation on the one hand and complete agreement on the other. He identifies two forms of agreement in this middle area. One of these, which he calls the "agreement with open terms," is a contract that the court should if necessary enforce by supplying the open term if the parties have not done so. (In Professor Knapp's analytic framework, this would be a variation of the "parties are completely bound" category, although it does envision further bargaining by the parties.) The other, which Farnsworth dubs an "agreement to negotiate," is the equivalent of Professor Knapp's "contract to bargain." Farnsworth asserts that an agreement to negotiate should be viewed as creating a potentially enforceable duty to bargain in good faith (he prefers to use the rubric of "fair dealing"), but not as giving rise to a duty to reach ultimate agreement. E. Allan Farnsworth, Precontractual Liability and Preliminary Agreements: Fair Dealing and Failed Negotiations, 87 Colum. L. Rev. 217 (1987). The Farnsworth article contains a useful discussion of various bargaining tactics viewed through the lens of "fair dealing," and, in an Appendix, describes several common types of preliminary agreement, such as real estate binders, mortgage commitment letters, and letters of intent in mergers and acquisitions, indicating how each might be characterized using his mode of analysis.

4. *Judicial response to the contract to bargain.* A number of courts have recognized the concept of a contract to bargain in good faith. See Brown v. Cara, 420 F.3d 148 (2d Cir. 2005) (recognizing two types of preliminary agreements under New York law: Type I agreements that are complete and binding and Type II agreements with open terms obligating parties to bargain in good faith); Channel Home Centers v. Grossman, 795 F.2d 291 (3d Cir. 1986) (letter of intent to lease space in shopping center being developed by defendants created duty to negotiate lease in good faith); Copeland v. Baskin Robbins U.S.A., 117 Cal. Rptr.2d 875 (Ct. App. 2002) (court holds that California will recognize a contractual duty to bargain in good faith, but plaintiff failed to show any reliance damages resulting from defendant's withdrawal from proposed ice cream sale agreement, and expectation damages not available). Other courts have been skeptical of the theory. See Ohio Calculating, Inc. v. CPT Corp., 846 F.2d 497 (8th Cir. 1988) (provision in dealership agreement calling for "good faith negotiations" looking toward purchase by defendant of plaintiff's business if its dealership should be terminated was "unenforceable agreement to negotiate"); Racine & Laramie, Ltd., Inc. v. California Dept. of Parks & Recreation, 14 Cal. Rptr. 2d 335

(Ct. App. 1993) (commencement of negotiations in and of itself does not create duty to bargain in good faith, but duty can arise from preexisting agreements, from execution of letter of intent, or from other conduct during negotiations).

Of course, even if courts recognize a duty to bargain in good faith, it will still be necessary for the plaintiff to establish a breach of that duty. E.g., see Venture Associates Corp. v. Zenith Data Systems Corp., 96 F.3d 275, 279 (7th Cir. 1996) (defendant was free to negotiate for new terms not mentioned in the letter of intent, or for changes in terms mentioned in the letter, including the price, so long as it "was not trying to scuttle the deal"); International Minerals & Mining Corp. v. Citicorp North America, Inc., 736 F. Supp. 587 (D.N.J. 1990) (commitment letter issued by defendant bank did obligate it to bargain in good faith with plaintiffs toward the possibility of funding possible acquisition of mining property, but defendant fulfilled its duties in that regard). How does the cause of action for breach of the duty to bargain in good faith differ from the cause of action for breach of the underlying construction contract itself? If the court in *Quake* had recognized a cause of action for breach of the duty to bargain in good faith, should Jones have been held to have breached the duty? If so, what should Quake's remedy have been?

5. *Protection of reliance.* The court in *Quake* recognized the possibility that promises contained in a letter of intent could give rise to reliance-based protection. Other courts have also accepted this theory of recovery. In Arcadian Phosphates, Inc. v. Arcadian Corp., 884 F.2d 69 (2d Cir. 1989), the plaintiff sought to enforce what it asserted was a contract to bargain in good faith toward the purchase by plaintiff of the defendant's phosphate fertilizer business. The parties had entered into a short memorandum of agreement, outlining the principal terms of the proposed purchase; some of the terms were definite but others were not, and the memorandum included provisions for certain reimbursements to plaintiff if the deal failed to go through. The appellate court affirmed the trial court's previous summary dismissal of the plaintiff's breach of contract claim. The parties' memorandum clearly contemplated the possibility that the parties would not reach a full and final agreement, which the court regarded as expressing their intent not to be bound by the memorandum. However, the *Arcadian Phosphates* court continued, the evidence did indicate that the defendants insisted on a substantial change in the deal when market conditions altered, and that the defendants might have violated a promise to bargain in good faith. Such a promise might not be "binding" in the breach-of-contract sense and yet still give rise to a duty to compensate the plaintiff on a promissory estoppel basis — particularly since the remedy for promissory estoppel could appropriately be limited to compensation of the plaintiff's out-of-pocket costs. Id. at 74, n.2. See also Budget Marketing, Inc. v. Centronics Corp., 927 F.2d 421 (8th Cir. 1991), subsequent appeal, 979 F.2d 1333 (8th Cir. 1992) (promissory estoppel recognized as basis for recovery even when letter of intent stated not binding, but no recovery on facts of case) and Vigoda v. Denver Urban Renewal Authority, 646 P.2d 900 (Colo. 1982) (en banc) (defendant's promise to negotiate in good faith only with plaintiff for ninety days actionable in promissory estoppel). This trend toward the use of promissory estoppel in cases of incomplete bargaining is the subject of approving comment in an article by Jonathan O. Hafen, Arcadian Phosphates, Inc. v. Arcadian

Corp.—Taming *Texaco's* Agreement in Principle, 1990 B.Y.U. L. Rev. 1045. The reference in the title is to the Pennzoil v. Texaco case (also mentioned by Justice Stamos in his *Quake* concurrence), discussed in the Comment that follows.

Comment: The Pennzoil/Texaco Case

In January 1984, following complicated negotiations, the Board of Directors of Getty Oil Company voted to accept an offer from Pennzoil Company to merge Getty with Pennzoil. Getty promptly issued a press release declaring the existence of an "agreement in principle" between Pennzoil, Getty, and certain principal Getty shareholders. Drafting of implementation agreements between the parties proceeded expeditiously. At the same time, however, the Getty interests pursued the possibility of a better offer elsewhere, and in a few days announced their agreement to sell all the shares of Getty to Texaco, Inc., at a higher price than Pennzoil had agreed to pay. A flurry of litigation ensued: Pennzoil attempted unsuccessfully to enjoin in Delaware the consummation of the Texaco-Getty merger, after which it sued Texaco in the Texas courts for tortious interference with Pennzoil's asserted contractual right to acquire the Getty shares. A Texas civil jury found for Pennzoil, and awarded it actual damages of $7.53 billion, plus an additional $3 billion in punitive damages—a judgment that was said at the time to be "the largest civil judgment in history." Wall St. J., Nov. 20, 1985, at 3, col. 1. The lower court's judgment was affirmed by the Texas Court of Appeals, in a 99-page opinion, in 729 S.W.2d 768 (Tex. Ct. App. 1987). After other litigation in the federal courts, culminating in Pennzoil Co. v. Texaco, Inc., 481 U.S. 1 (1987) (federal abstention doctrine prevented federal courts from giving Texaco relief from the Texas requirement that it post a $12 billion dollar appeal bond), followed by a federal bankruptcy reorganization by Texaco, the case was finally closed by the payment to Pennzoil by Texaco of $3 billion in cash.

If only because of the sheer magnitude of the dollar amounts at stake, Pennzoil v. Texaco was the focus of much attention, not merely from the business community but from the public in general. From a legal point of view, the case was just as notable for the variety and complexity of the legal issues it raised. These included not merely issues of contract and tort but complex questions of federal procedure, federalism, and constitutional law, as well as the federal regulation of trading in securities (plus, in the final stages, federal bankruptcy procedure). For us at this point, however, the most interesting legal question is the threshold one faced by the Texas trial jury: Were the Getty interests bound by an agreement to sell their stock to Pennzoil?

In submitting the case to the jury, the trial judge framed several special issues with accompanying instructions. The first issue was presumably the most crucial.

Special Issue No. 1

Do you find from a preponderance of the evidence that at the end of the Getty Oil board meeting of January 3, 1984, Pennzoil and each of the Getty entities, to wit, the Getty Oil Company, the Sarah C. Getty Trust and the J. Paul Getty Museum, intended to bind themselves to an agreement that included the following terms:

> a. All Getty Oil shareholders except Pennzoil and the Sarah C. Getty Trust were to receive $110 per share, plus the right to receive a deferred cash consideration from the sale of ERC corporation of at least $5 per share within five years;
>
> b. Pennzoil was to own 3/7ths of the stock of Getty Oil and the Sarah C. Getty Trust was to own the remaining 4/7ths of the stock of Getty Oil; and
>
> c. Pennzoil and the Sarah C. Getty Trust were to endeavor in good faith to agree on a plan for restructuring Getty Oil on or before December 31, 1984, and if they were unable to reach such agreement then they would divide the assets of Getty Oil between them also on a 3/7ths-4/7ths basis.

In his instructions to the jury accompanying Special Issue No. 1, the judge stated as follows:

Instructions

1. An agreement may be partly oral, it may be written or it may be partly written and partly oral. Where an agreement is fully or partially in writing, the law provides that persons may bind themselves to that agreement even though they do not sign it, where their assent is otherwise indicated.

2. In answering Issue No. 1, you should look to the intent of Pennzoil and the Getty entities as outwardly or objectively demonstrated to each other by their words and deeds. The question is not determined by the parties' secret, inward, or subjective intentions.

3. Persons may intend to be bound to an agreement even though they plan to sign a more formal and detailed document at a later time. On the other hand, parties may intend not to be bound until such a document is signed.

4. There is no legal requirement that parties agree on all the matters incidental to their agreement before they can intend to be bound. Thus, even if certain matters were left for future negotiations, those matters may not have been regarded by Pennzoil and the Getty entities as essential to their agreement, if any, on January 3. On the other hand, you may find that the parties did not intend to be bound until each and every term of their transaction was resolved.

5. Every binding agreement carries with it a duty of good faith performance. If Pennzoil and the Getty entities intended to be bound at the end of the Getty Oil board meeting on January 3, they were obliged to negotiate in good faith the terms of the definitive merger agreement and to carry out the transaction.

6. Modification or discussions to modify an agreement do not defeat or nullify a prior intention to be bound. Parties may always, by mutual consent and understanding, add new provisions spelling out additional terms that were not included in their original agreement.

In their appeal to the Texas Court of Appeals, the attorneys for appellant Texaco attacked the trial judge's framing of the issues and accompanying instructions (as well his conduct of the trial) on a variety of grounds. One strongly contested area was the proper application of New York law, which concededly governed the case; Texaco argued that New York law as to existence of a contract and also on the issue of tortious interference was more favorable to it than the rules stated by the trial court in its instructions to the jury. The Texas Court of Appeals' response to those arguments can be found in its 1987 opinion, cited above. Assuming that the general principles of law we have studied thus far should govern, was the jury in Texaco, Inc. v. Pennzoil Co. properly instructed on the issue of a binding agreement between the Getty interests and Pennzoil?

Fuller accounts of the Pennzoil/Texaco dispute can be found in Thomas Petzinger, Jr., Oil & Honor: The Texaco-Pennzoil Wars (1987); James Shannon, Texaco and the $10 Billion Jury (1988); see also Steven Brill, Trial by Jury 287 (1989). Discussions of the effect of Pennzoil/Texaco on the general law applying to preliminary agreements of various kinds can be found in numerous articles, including Robert H. Mnookin & Robert B. Wilson, Rational Bargaining and Market Efficiency: Understanding *Pennzoil v. Texaco,* 75 Va. L. Rev. 295 (1989); Theodore H. Oldham, Letters of Intent in Business Transactions, 68 Mich. Bus. L.J. 524 (1989); Harvey L. Temkin, When Does the "Fat Lady" Sing? An Analysis of "Agreements in Principle" in Corporate Acquisitions, 55 Fordham L. Rev. 125 (1986); see also Harris Ominsky, Counseling the Client on "Gentleman's Agreements," 36 Prac. Law. No. 8, at 25 (1990) (short, practical treatment of perils and pitfalls in use of "letters of assurance," "comfort letters," et al.).

PROBLEM 2-5

You are vice-president and general counsel of Super Comics, Inc., a company that publishes several popular comic magazines featuring a variety of comic and super-hero characters. Super's publications are of course copyrighted, and their principal recurring characters are also registered trademarks, which Super licenses to numerous manufacturers for use on merchandise of various kinds designed for the teen and pre-teen market. Recently Super has been engaged in a negotiation with JayRan Products, Inc., a maker of various toys and novelties, looking to the licensing of JayRan to use the names and pictures of "The Ribbets," a family of comic frogs featured in one of Super's publications, on a line of lunchboxes and related items (thermos bottles, plastic plates and utensils, etc.) for the back-to-school market. You recently met with the vice-president and the chief legal counsel of JayRan to discuss this transaction. (Although Diana Hunter, the president of Super, customarily approves and signs such licensing agreements on behalf of Super, she usually delegates to you the task of negotiating and drafting the agreements.) At that meeting, you and they agreed on the essential terms of the proposed licensing agreement—the rate of royalty payments to be made by JayRan, the products on which the Ribbets would be featured, the length of time the licensing agreement would run (one year, commencing next June 1), the technical and design assistance to be provided by Super, the sales reports and other data to be provided by JayRan from which their royalty payments would be computed, and the circumstances under which one party or the other would have the right to terminate the agreement. At the conclusion of that meeting, it was agreed that you as counsel for Super would prepare a written agreement in form satisfactory to Super and forward it to JayRan's attorney, for approval and — if satisfactory to him — signing by Jay Randolph, the president of JayRan.

Three days ago you completed a draft of the agreement between Super and JayRan. (The drafting task was for you an easy one; the agreement is of a type entered into by Super many times every year and contains many — from your point of view — "standard" clauses.) You then sent (by messenger) four unsigned copies of the draft agreement to Marion Gerber, attorney for JayRan, along with the following letter (signed by you):

Dear Marion:

Here is the draft of our proposed license agreement, as promised. I think it fully incorporates our discussions, and contains (I hope) no surprises. If you and Mr. Randolph find it satisfactory, please return to me the enclosed four copies, signed by him. I will return to you two copies signed also by our president, Diana Hunter.

You have as yet received no reply from Gerber. This morning you have been called to Ms. Hunter's office. She informs you that she has just received from Octopus, Inc., owner of the national chain of "Octopus Garden" seafood restaurants, a proposal to use the Ribbet family on a series of novelty premiums to be given away with children's meals at the Octopus Garden restaurants, beginning next September. The Octopus proposal would require that Super grant it an exclusive license for a one-year period to feature the Ribbets in any manner on, connected with, or related to, food or food products. Hunter tells you she is very anxious to pursue the Octopus deal, which appears likely to be financially very attractive, but that she views the exclusivity clause that they have requested as inconsistent with the proposed licensing of the Ribbets for JayRan's lunchboxes. She asks you whether there is any reason at this point why the negotiations with JayRan cannot be suspended or simply broken off entirely with no liability on Super's part.

What do you tell her?

PROBLEM 2-6

Marigold Realty Corp. ("Marigold") is a corporation that owns a large tract of land in your city, on which is located a large shopping center known as Marigold Plaza. (Marigold has also developed Marigold Manor and Marigold Mountain, residential subdivisions that surround the land occupied by Marigold Plaza.) In Marigold Plaza are two retail shoe stores. One of these is operated by a local merchant; the other is currently occupied by a store that is part of a national chain of retail shoe stores. The local shoe merchant has recently decided to close out his business and retire at the expiration of his current lease. StepRite, Inc., the proprietor of another national shoe store chain, is interested in opening a store in the premises to be vacated, and is actively negotiating with Marigold to that end. Marigold has submitted to StepRite the form of lease used for the present tenant, and StepRite has concurred generally with its treatment of such issues as utilities, insurance, security, hours of operation, obligations of maintenance, and the like.

The amount of the rent has yet to be agreed on, however. If the rent is to be a fixed monthly sum, Marigold has yet to agree to anything less than $10,000 per month, while StepRite has yet to offer more than $7,500. (Both parties agree that if the rent is to be a fixed sum per month, there will be an escalator clause for an annual percentage increase in rent; the amount of that percentage is as yet undetermined — the numbers discussed have ranged from 3 to 6%.) As an alternative, the parties have considered a rental based in part on a percentage of the tenant's gross receipts from sales; StepRite has suggested a fixed rental of $3,500 per month (again, subject to an annual percentage increase) plus 3 percent of the gross.

Besides the rental, several other terms remain to be agreed on. One is the duration of the lease. StepRite would like a five-year term with an option on its part to extend for another five years; Marigold is generally amenable to this, but would probably insist on some provision for renegotiation of the rent at the end of the first five-year term. Another point remaining to be settled relates to renovation of the leased premises. Ordinarily the lessee of such a store would itself bear the cost of whatever renovation might be needed, even though at the end of the lease term nonremovable improvements (such as painting, carpeting, lighting fixtures) would inure to the benefit of the landlord. StepRite is arguing, however, that because the store has been previously occupied, the cost of interior decoration will be higher than it would be in a new building, and that some of that cost should be absorbed in some manner by Marigold. While all these points remain the subject of active discussion and negotiation, StepRite and Marigold appear genuinely anxious to reach agreement with each other and to believe that such agreement is only a matter of time and some effort on their respective parts.

Until now, the negotiations between Marigold and StepRite have proceeded at a rather leisurely pace, because the expiration of the present tenant's lease is several months away. However, StepRite has just been presented with the opportunity to open a store in another local shopping center, in premises which have unexpectedly become vacant on short notice. StepRite has been given only a few days to consider whether it wants to avail itself of this other opportunity, after which that landlord will probably make arrangements with another tenant (one slightly less attractive than StepRite but ready to move quickly). StepRite would prefer to be in Marigold Plaza, and has no desire to operate more than one store in your city. However, it does not want to let this new opportunity go by unless it has assurances that the negotiations with Marigold are going to reach fruition.

(a) As attorney for StepRite, could you draft a "Memorandum of Intent" to be entered into by your client and Marigold, which would give StepRite the assurance it needs at this time? Would that memorandum, if executed, be legally binding on Marigold? On StepRite?

(b) As attorney for Marigold, would you advise your client to sign the memorandum prepared by StepRite's client pursuant to (a), above? Would you advise your client to insist on changes before signing? If so, what would they be? Would you advise your client not to sign *any* such memorandum? If so, what course of action would you propose?

PROBLEM 2-7

Herbert Ventor is a freelance scientist who owns numerous patents. One of his recently obtained patents is for a chemical additive (known as TZ 211) that increases the durability of exterior paint.

Ventor has agreed to grant DuraKote, a national paint manufacturer, an exclusive right for a period of one year to market paint containing his additive. DuraKote will pay Ventor $100,000 for this right. The parties have also agreed that DuraKote will have an option to market the additive on a long-term basis. Royalties and other terms of a long-term contract will be agreed on by the parties if DuraKote elects to exercise the option. DuraKote has asked you to draft a letter from it to Ventor setting forth the agreement of the parties. Prepare a draft of the letter.

5. Electronic Contracting

The classical model of contract formation was based on two major assumptions: The contracting parties had relatively equal bargaining power, and they engaged in a bargaining process, perhaps by mail, but often in person. For more than a century the assumptions upon which the classical model were based have been breaking down. Although many commercial contracts still conform to the classical model, most modern contracts do not. The vast majority of modern contracts involve parties with radically unequal bargaining power; the contracts consist of standard forms and involve little, if any, negotiation; and the contracts are often formed through electronic transactions rather than person-to-person communications.

In the past decade courts have begun to confront issues involving contracts made over the Internet or by other electronic means. Naturally and as a matter of judicial duty, courts have turned to existing legal sources to deal with these issues. At the same time, courts and commentators have developed a new terminology to describe the types of transactions the courts are encountering. The case law and literature involving electronic contracts refer to three types of terms: shrinkwrap terms; clickwrap (or clickthrough) terms; and browsewrap terms. (We use the word "terms" rather than "contracts" or "agreements" because the legal issue is whether these terms have contractual significance.) For a variety of legal and business reasons, when the product is software, the terms are usually presented in the form of a license agreement. See Robert L. Oakley, Fairness in Electronic Contracting: Minimum Standards for Non-negotiated Contracts, 42 Hous. L. Rev. 1041, 1048-1050 (2005).

In a transaction involving *shrinkwrap terms*, the purchaser orders a product (for example, a computer, a home appliance, or software). The order could take place by telephone, over the Internet, or at a store. When the purchaser receives the product, it is wrapped in plastic. Often, but not always, a warning on the outside of the package informs the purchaser that the product contains the seller's contract terms and that use of the product constitutes the purchaser's agreement with those terms. After removing the wrapping, the purchaser has an opportunity to inspect the product and review the contract terms. The contract terms typically, but again not in every situation, state that if the purchaser is dissatisfied with the product or with the contract terms, the purchaser may return the product to the seller within a certain number of days. The contract terms also state that if the purchaser does not return the product within that period of time, the purchaser agrees to the seller's contract terms. The seller may, but will not necessarily, pay for the cost of shipment back to the seller. Transactions involving shrinkwrap terms are sometimes referred to as "rolling contracts," "layered contracts," or "money now, terms later" contracts.

In the typical transaction involving *clickwrap terms*, before completing the purchase of the product, the purchaser must scroll through the seller's terms of sale and click an "I agree" button. For example, if the purchaser is buying the product over the Internet, the purchaser must click the "I agree" button before completing the sale. Some sellers may go further and require the purchaser to put his or her initials in a box to signify agreement with the seller's terms of sale. If the purchaser refuses to do so, the seller will not complete the sale. Clickwrap contracts over the Internet can involve either software or tangible products. If the purchaser buys software or a tangible product at a store in a box, the box will typically have a shrinkwrap contract and any software will be subject to a clickwrap contract to which the purchaser must agree before being able to use the software.

Finally, transactions with *browsewrap terms* typically involve information made available by Internet providers on their websites often, but not necessarily, free of charge, and often, although not necessarily, involving information that the user accesses but does not always download. In the typical browsewrap transaction, the Internet provider has established terms of use of its website. The terms of use state that by using the site the user agrees to the provider's terms of use. The browsewrap and the clickwrap transactions have a fundamental difference. In the clickwrap transaction the purchaser must scroll through the terms of sale and click an agreement button. In the browsewrap transaction the terms of use are normally accessible from the provider's home page by clicking a button, but the user is not required or even encouraged, to scroll through the terms of use and is not required to click any agreement button. The user's purported agreement to the provider's terms of use comes simply from the user's actions in browsing the site. For example, Dell Computer's website has the following browsewrap provision:

> The following are terms of a legal agreement between you and Dell Inc ("Dell"). By accessing, browsing and/or using this site ("Site"), you acknowledge that you have read, understood, and agree, to be bound by these terms and to comply with all applicable laws and regulations, including U.S. export and re-export control laws and regulations. If you do not agree to these terms, do not use this Site. The material provided on this Site is protected by law, including, but not limited to, United States Copyright Law and international treaties. This Site is controlled and operated by Dell from its offices within the United States. Dell makes no representation that materials in the Site are appropriate or available for use in other locations, and access to them from territories where their contents are illegal is prohibited. Those who choose to access this Site from other locations do so on their own initiative and are responsible for compliance with applicable local laws.

Any claim relating to, and the use of, this Site and the materials contained herein is governed by the laws of the state of Texas.

With this background in mind, consider the following cases.

Brower v. Gateway 2000, Inc.
New York Supreme Court, Appellate Division
676 N.Y.S.2d 569 (1998)

MILONAS, J.P., NARDELLI, MAZZARELLI and SAXE, JJ.
MILONAS, Justice Presiding.

Appeal from an order of the Supreme Court (Beatrice Shainswit, J.), entered October 21, 1997 in New York County, which, to the extent appealed from, granted defendants' motion to dismiss the complaint on the ground that there was a valid agreement to arbitrate between the parties.

Appellants are among the many consumers who purchased computers and software products from defendant Gateway 2000 through a direct-sales system, by mail or telephone order. As of July 3, 1995, it was Gateway's practice to include with the materials shipped to the purchaser along with the merchandise a copy of its "Standard Terms and Conditions Agreement" and any relevant warranties for the products in the shipment. The Agreement begins with a "NOTE TO CUSTOMER," which provides, in slightly larger print than the remainder of the document, in a box that spans the width of the page: "This document contains Gateway 2000's Standard Terms and Conditions. By keeping your Gateway 2000 computer system beyond thirty (30) days after the date of delivery, you accept these Terms and Conditions." The document consists of 16 paragraphs, and, as is relevant to this appeal, paragraph 10 of the agreement, entitled "DISPUTE RESOLUTION," reads as follows:

> Any dispute or controversy arising out of or relating to this Agreement or its interpretation shall be settled exclusively and finally by arbitration. The arbitration shall be conducted in accordance with the Rules of Conciliation and Arbitration of the International Chamber of Commerce. The arbitration shall be conducted in Chicago, Illinois, U.S.A. before a sole arbitrator. Any award rendered in any such arbitration proceeding shall be final and binding on each of the parties, and judgment may be entered thereon in a court of competent jurisdiction.

Plaintiffs commenced this action on behalf of themselves and others similarly situated for compensatory and punitive damages, alleging deceptive sales practices in seven causes of action, including breach of warranty, breach of contract, fraud, and unfair trade practices. In particular, the allegations focused on Gateway's representations and advertising that promised "service when you need it," including around-the-clock free technical support, free software technical support and certain on-site services. According to plaintiffs, not only were they unable to avail themselves of this offer because it was virtually impossible to get through to a technician, but also Gateway continued to advertise this claim notwithstanding numerous complaints and reports about the problem.

Insofar as is relevant to appellants, who purchased their computers after July 3, 1995, Gateway moved to dismiss the complaint based on the arbitration clause in the Agreement. Appellants argued that the arbitration clause is invalid under UCC 2-207, unconscionable under UCC 2-302 and an unenforceable contract of adhesion. Specifically, they claimed that the provision was obscure; that a customer could not reasonably be expected to appreciate or investigate its meaning and effect; that the International Chamber of Commerce ("ICC") was not a forum commonly used for consumer matters; and that because ICC headquarters were in France, it was particularly difficult to locate the organization and its rules. To illustrate just how inaccessible the forum was, appellants advised the court that the ICC was not registered with the Secretary of State, that efforts to locate and contact the ICC had been unsuccessful and that apparently the only way to attempt to contact the ICC was through the United States Council for International Business, with which the ICC maintained some sort of relationship.

In support of their arguments, appellants submitted a copy of the ICC's Rules of Conciliation and Arbitration and contended that the cost of ICC arbitration was prohibitive, particularly given the amount of the typical consumer claim involved. For example, a claim of less than $50,000 required advance fees of $4,000 (more than the cost of most Gateway products), of which the $2000 registration fee was nonrefundable even if the consumer prevailed at the arbitration. Consumers would also incur travel expenses disproportionate to the damages sought, which appellants' counsel estimated would not exceed $1,000 per customer in this action, as well as bear the cost of Gateway's legal fees if the consumer did not prevail at the arbitration; in this respect, the ICC rules follow the "loser pays" rule used in England. Also, although Chicago was designated as the site of the actual arbitration, all correspondence must be sent to ICC headquarters in France.

The IAS [Individual Assignment System of cases used in New York under which a case is assigned to a judge for its life — Eds.] court dismissed the complaint as to appellants based on the arbitration clause in the Agreements delivered with their computers. We agree with the court's decision and reasoning in all respects but for the issue of the unconscionability of the designation of the ICC as the arbitration body.

First, the court properly rejected appellants' argument that the arbitration clause was invalid under UCC 2-207. Appellants claim that when they placed their order they did not bargain for, much less accept, arbitration of any dispute, and therefore the arbitration clause in the agreement that accompanied the merchandise shipment was a "material alteration" of a preexisting oral agreement. Under UCC 2-207(2), such a material alteration constitutes "proposals for addition to the contract" that become part of the contract only upon appellants' express acceptance. However, as the court correctly concluded, the clause was not a "material alteration" of an oral agreement, but, rather, simply one provision of the sole contract that existed between the parties. That contract, the court explained, was formed and acceptance was manifested not when the order was placed but only with the retention of the merchandise beyond the 30 days specified in the Agreement enclosed in the shipment of merchandise. Accordingly, the contract was outside the scope of UCC 2-207.

In reaching its conclusion, the IAS court took note of the litigation in Federal courts on this very issue, and, indeed, on this very arbitration clause. In Hill v. Gateway 2000, Inc., 105 F.3d 1147, cert. denied 522 U.S. 808, 118 S. Ct. 47, 139 L.Ed.2d 13, plaintiffs in a class action contested the identical Gateway contract in dispute before us, including the enforceability of the arbitration clause. As that court framed the issue, the "[t]erms inside Gateway's box stand or fall together. If they constitute the parties contract because the Hills had an opportunity to return the computer after reading them, then all must be enforced" (Id. at 1148). The court then concluded that the contract was not formed with the placement of a telephone order or with the delivery of the goods. Instead, an enforceable contract was formed only with the consumer's decision to retain the merchandise beyond the 30-day period specified in the agreement. Thus, the agreement as a whole, including the arbitration clause, was enforceable.

This conclusion was in keeping with the same court's decision in ProCD, Inc. v. Zeidenberg, 86 F.3d 1447, where it found that detailed terms enclosed within the packaging of particular computer software purchased in a retail outlet constituted the contract between the vendor and the consumer who retained the product. In that case, the Seventh Circuit held that UCC 2-207 did not apply and indeed was "irrelevant" to such transactions, noting that the section is generally invoked where multiple agreements have been exchanged between the parties in a classic "battle of the forms," whereas *ProCD* (as well as *Hill* and this case) involves but a single form (Id. at 1452).

The *Hill* decision, in its examination of the formation of the contract, takes note of the realities of conducting business in today's world. Transactions involving "cash now, terms later" have become commonplace, enabling the consumer to make purchases of sophisticated merchandise such as computers over the phone or by mail–and even by computer. Indeed, the concept of "[p]ayment preceding the revelation of full terms" is particularly common in certain industries, such as air transportation and insurance (Id. at 1149; ProCD v. Zeidenberg, supra, at 1451).

While *Hill* and *ProCD*, as the IAS court recognized, are not controlling (although they are decisions of the United States Court of Appeals for the circuit encompassing the forum state designated for arbitration), we agree with their rationale that, in such transactions, there is no agreement or contract upon the placement of the order or even upon the receipt of the goods. By the terms of the Agreement at issue, it is only after the consumer has affirmatively retained the merchandise for more than 30 days–within which the consumer has presumably examined and even used the product(s) and read the agreement–that the contract has been effectuated. In this respect, the case is distinguishable from S & T Sportswear v. Drake Fabrics, 190 A.D.2d 598, 593 N.Y.S.2d 799, cited by appellants, where this Court found that an arbitration clause found on the reverse side of defendant's draft sales contract did constitute a "material alteration" where the parties did in fact have a pre-existing oral agreement.

While appellants argue that *Hill* is contrary to the law of New York in that it departs from the holding of cases such as Matter of Marlene v. Carnac

Textiles, 45 N.Y.2d 327, 408 N.Y.S.2d 410, 380 N.E.2d 239, and its progeny, we disagree with their interpretation of both cases: *Hill* not only involves one form only, as distinguished from the "battle of the forms" scenario of the cases appellants cite, but these cases are simply inapplicable because, as explained, no contract was formed here or in *Hill* until the merchandise was retained beyond the 30-day period. The disputed arbitration clause is simply one provision of the sole contract "proposed" between the parties.

Second, with respect to appellants' claim that the arbitration clause is unenforceable as a contract of adhesion, in that it involved no choice or negotiation on the part of the consumer but was a "take it or leave it" proposition (see, e.g., Matter of State v. Ford Motor Company, 74 N.Y.2d 495, 503, 549 N.Y.S.2d 368, 548 N.E.2d 906), we find that this argument, too, was properly rejected by the IAS court. Although the parties clearly do not possess equal bargaining power, this factor alone does not invalidate the contract as one of adhesion. As the IAS court observed, with the ability to make the purchase elsewhere and the express option to return the goods, the consumer is not in a "take it or leave it" position at all; if any term of the agreement is unacceptable to the consumer, he or she can easily buy a competitor's product instead–either from a retailer or directly from the manufacturer–and reject Gateway's agreement by returning the merchandise (see, e.g., Carnival Cruise Lines v. Shute, 499 U.S. 585, 593-594 Fidelity and Deposit Company of Maryland v. Altman, 209 A.D.2d 195, 618 N.Y.S.2d 286, lv. denied 91 N.Y.2d 805). The consumer has 30 days to make that decision. Within that time, the consumer can inspect the goods and examine and seek clarification of the terms of the agreement; until those 30 days have elapsed, the consumer has the unqualified right to return the merchandise, because the goods or terms are unsatisfactory or for no reason at all.

While returning the goods to avoid the formation of the contract entails affirmative action on the part of the consumer, and even some expense, this may be seen as a trade-off for the convenience and savings for which the consumer presumably opted when he or she chose to make a purchase of such consequence by phone or mail as an alternative to on-site retail shopping. That a consumer does not read the agreement or thereafter claims he or she failed to understand or appreciate some term therein does not invalidate the contract any more than such claim would undo a contract formed under other circumstances (see, e.g., Morris v. Snappy Car Rental, Inc., 84 N.Y.2d 21, 30, 614 N.Y.S.2d 362, 637 N.E.2d 253). . . .

Finally, we turn to appellants' argument that the IAS court should have declared the contract unenforceable, pursuant to UCC 2-302, on the ground that the arbitration clause is unconscionable due to the unduly burdensome procedure and cost for the individual consumer. The IAS court found that while a class-action lawsuit, such as the one herein, may be a less costly alternative to the arbitration (which is generally less costly than litigation), that does not alter the binding effect of the valid arbitration clause contained in the agreement (see, Harris v. Shearson Hayden Stone, 82 A.D.2d 87, 92-93, 441 N.Y.S.2d 70, affd. 56 N.Y.2d 627, 450 N.Y.S.2d 482, 435 N.E.2d 1097 for reasons stated below. . . .

As a general matter, under New York law, unconscionability requires a showing that a contract is "both procedurally and substantively unconscionable when made" (Gillman v. Chase Manhattan Bank, 73 N.Y.2d 1, 10, 537 N.Y.S.2d 787, 534 N.E.2d 824). That is, there must be "some showing of 'an absence of meaningful choice on the part of one of the parties together with contract terms which are unreasonably favorable to the other party' [citation omitted]" (Matter of State of New York v. Avco Financial Service, 50 N.Y.2d 383, 389, 429 N.Y.S.2d 181, 406 N.E.2d 1075). The *Avco* court took pains to note, however, that the purpose of this doctrine is not to redress the inequality between the parties but simply to ensure that the more powerful party cannot "surprise" the other party with some overly oppressive term (Id., at 389, 429 N.Y.S.2d 181, 406 N.E.2d 1075).

As to the procedural element, a court will look to the contract formation process to determine if in fact one party lacked any meaningful choice in entering into the contract, taking into consideration such factors as the setting of the transaction, the experience and education of the party claiming unconscionability, whether the contract contained "fine print," whether the seller used "high-pressured tactics" and any disparity in the parties' bargaining power (Gillman v. Chase Manhattan Bank, supra, at 11, 537 N.Y.S.2d 787, 534 N.E.2d 824). None of these factors supports appellants' claim here. Any purchaser has 30 days within which to thoroughly examine the contents of their shipment, including the terms of the Agreement, and seek clarification of any term therein (e.g., Matter of Ball, supra, at 161, 665 N.Y.S.2d 444). The Agreement itself, which is entitled in large print "STANDARD TERMS AND CONDITIONS AGREEMENT," consists of only three pages and 16 paragraphs, all of which appear in the same size print. Moreover, despite appellants' claims to the contrary, the arbitration clause is in no way "hidden" or "tucked away" within a complex document of inordinate length, nor is the option of returning the merchandise, to avoid the contract, somehow a "precarious" one. We also reject appellants' insinuation that, by using the word "standard," Gateway deliberately meant to convey to the consumer that the terms were standard within the industry, when the document clearly purports to be no more than Gateway's "standard terms and conditions."

With respect to the substantive element, which entails an examination of the substance of the agreement in order to determine whether the terms unreasonably favor one party (Gillman v. Chase Manhattan Bank, supra, 73 N.Y.2d, at 12, 537 N.Y.S.2d 787, 534 N.E.2d 824), we do not find that the possible inconvenience of the chosen site (Chicago) alone rises to the level of unconscionability. We do find, however, that the excessive cost factor that is necessarily entailed in arbitrating before the ICC is unreasonable and surely serves to deter the individual consumer from invoking the process (see, Matter of Teleserve Systems, 230 A.D.2d 585, 594, 659 N.Y.S.2d 659, lv. denied . . .). Barred from resorting to the courts by the arbitration clause in the first instance, the designation of a financially prohibitive forum effectively bars consumers from this forum as well; consumers are thus left with no forum at all in which to resolve a dispute. In this regard, we note that this particular claim is not mentioned in the *Hill* decision, which upheld the clause as part of an enforceable contract. While it is true that, under New York law, unconscionability is generally predicated on the presence of both the procedural and substantive elements, the substantive element alone may be sufficient to render the terms of the provision at issue unenforceable (see, Gillman v. Chase Manhattan Bank, supra, at 12, 537 N.Y.S.2d 787, 534 N.E.2d 824 . . .) Excessive fees, such as those incurred under the ICC procedure, have been grounds for finding an arbitration provision unenforceable or commercially unreasonable (see, e.g., Matter of Teleserve Systems, supra, at 593-594, 659 N.Y.S.2d 659).

[Gateway offered to arbitrate before the American Arbitration Association (AAA) in substitution for the ICC. Plaintiffs argued that the AAA's costs were also excessive because a consumer would be required to pay a nonrefundable $500 filing fee and could incur expenses to arbitrate of over $1000. The court remanded to the trial court for "appropriate substitution of an arbitrator pursuant to the Federal Arbitration Act (9 U.S.C. § 1 et seq.), which provides for such court designation of an arbitrator upon application of either party, where, for whatever reason, one is not otherwise designated (9 U.S.C. § 5)."].

Notes and Questions

1. *Offer and acceptance under ProCD and Hill.* The opinions in *ProCD* and *Hill,* relied on by the court in *Brower,* both authored by Judge Frank Easterbrook of the United States Court of Appeals for the Seventh Circuit, are based on two propositions about offer and acceptance. First, when a purchaser places an order for either software (*ProCD*) or hardware (*Hill*) in person, by telephone, or over the Internet, the purchaser has *not* made an offer. Instead, the vendor makes the offer by shipping the product to the purchaser with the vendor's terms of sale included. Second, the vendor is the "master of the offer." If the vendor's offer states that the purchaser accepts the offer by retaining the product beyond the period of time set forth in the vendor's terms of sale, the purchaser is bound by the vendor's terms if he does not return the product within that period. Judge Easterbrook stated in *ProCD*:

> What then does the current version of the UCC have to say? We think that the place to start is §2-204(1): "A contract for sale of goods may be made in any manner sufficient to show agreement, including conduct by both parties which recognizes the existence of such a contract." A vendor, as master of the offer, may invite acceptance by conduct, and may propose limitations on the kind of conduct that constitutes acceptance. A buyer may accept by performing the acts the vendor proposes to treat as acceptance. And that is what happened. ProCD proposed a contract that a buyer would accept by using the software after having an opportunity to read the license at leisure. This Zeidenberg did. He had no choice, because the software splashed the license on the screen and would not let him proceed without indicating acceptance. So although the district judge was right to say that a contract can be, and often is, formed simply by paying the price and walking out of the store, the UCC permits contracts to be formed in other ways. ProCD proposed such a different way, and without protest Zeidenberg agreed. Ours is not a case in which a consumer opens a package to find an insert saying "you owe us an extra $10,000" and the seller files suit to collect. Any buyer finding such a demand can prevent formation of the contract by returning the package, as can any consumer who concludes that the terms of the license make the software worth less than the purchase price. Nothing in the UCC requires a seller to maximize the buyer's net gains. *ProCD*, 86 F.3d at 1452.

Other courts, in addition to the New York Supreme court in *Brower,* have accepted this reasoning. See I. Lan Systems, Inc., v. Netscout Service Level Corp., 183 F. Supp. 2d 328 (D. Mass. 2002) (clickthrough license terms enforceable; *ProCD* followed, and also additional terms not material); M.A. Mortenson Co., Inc. v. Timberline Software Corp., 998 P.2d 305 (Wash. 2000) (following *Hill* and *ProCD* that contract was formed under UCC §2-204 to find enforceable limitation of consequential damages in defendant's shrinkwrap license).

Scholarly commentators, however, have generally been highly critical of Judge Easterbrook's reasoning. See William H. Lawrence, Rolling Contracts Rolling over Contract Law, 41 San Diego L. Rev. 1099, 1109 n.51 (2004) (citing authorities). Among other criticisms, they point out that Judge Easterbrook failed to explain why the vendor rather than the purchaser is the offeror, especially when the natural understanding of the transaction is that the purchaser is offering to buy the product and the vendor accepts by charging the purchaser for the product and by shipping the goods. This alternative view of the transaction finds support in UCC §2-206, which provides that an offer may be accepted by prompt shipment of goods. For a detailed criticism of Judge Easterbrook's reasoning see Lawrence, Rolling Contracts Rolling Over Contract Law, above. But see Randy E. Barnett, Consenting to Form Contracts, 71 Fordham L. Rev. 627 (2002).

2. *Offer and acceptance under Klocek v. Gateway, Inc.* The leading case rejecting Judge Easterbrook's reasoning in *ProCD* and *Hill,* is Klocek v. Gateway, Inc., 104 F. Supp.2d 1332 (D. Kan. 2000). In that case the court held that it was the purchaser rather than the vendor who made the offer:

> [T]he Seventh Circuit provided no explanation for its conclusion that "the vendor is the master of the offer." See *ProCD,* 86 F.3d at 1452 (citing nothing in support of proposition); *Hill,* 105 F.3d at 1149 (citing ProCD). In typical consumer transactions, the purchaser is the offeror, and the vendor is the offeree. See Brown Mach., Div. of John Brown, Inc. v. Hercules, Inc., 770 S.W.2d 416, 419 (Mo. App.1989) (as general rule orders are considered offers to purchase). . . . While it is possible for the vendor to be the offeror, see *Brown Machine,* 770 S.W.2d at 419 (price quote can amount to offer if it reasonably appears from quote that assent to quote is all that is needed to ripen offer into contract), Gateway provides no factual evidence which would support such a finding in this case. The Court therefore assumes for purposes of the motion to dismiss that plaintiff offered to purchase the computer (either in person or through catalog order) and that Gateway accepted plaintiff's offer (either by completing the sales transaction in person or by agreeing to ship and/or shipping the computer to plaintiff). 104 F. Supp. 2d at 1340.

Under this reasoning, shrinkwrap terms found in the box containing the vendor's product were proposals for additions to the contract governed by UCC §2-207(2). In a transaction involving a consumer purchaser and a merchant seller, the merchant's terms would not become part of the contract unless agreed to by the consumer. If the transaction were between two merchants, the terms would not become part of the contract if any of the three situations set forth in §2-207(2) applied. In particular, any terms by the vendor that materially altered the contract would not become part of the contract. Several courts agree with this approach. See Step-Saver Data Systems Inc. v. Wyse Tech., 939 F.2d 91 (3d Cir. 1991); Licitra v. Gateway, Inc., 734

N.Y.S.2d 389 (Civ. Ct. 2001) (buyer not precluded from recourse to small claims court by arbitration clause in seller's form; form acts as confirmation under §2-207 and arbitration clause is material addition).

3. *Policy considerations.* Judge Easterbrook based his legal analysis on the policy that contracting through standard forms was efficient and socially desirable. By making the vendor the offeror and the purchaser's conduct as acceptance, he promoted these policies:

> Payment preceding the revelation of full terms is common for air transportation, insurance, and many other endeavors. Practical considerations support allowing vendors to enclose the full legal terms with their products. Cashiers cannot be expected to read legal documents to customers before ringing up sales. If the staff at the other end of the phone for direct-sales operations such as Gateway's had to read the four-page statement of terms before taking the buyer's credit card number, the droning voice would anesthetize rather than enlighten many potential buyers. Others would hang up in a rage over the waste of their time. And oral recitation would not avoid customers' assertions (whether true or feigned) that the clerk did not read term X to them, or that they did not remember or understand it. Writing provides benefits for both sides of commercial transactions. Customers as a group are better off when vendors skip costly and ineffectual steps such as telephonic recitation, and use instead a simple approve-or-return device. Competent adults are bound by such documents, read or unread. *Hill,* 105 F.3d at 1149.

But important policy considerations support the decision in *Klocek.* Contract law is based on mutual consent. To claim that a purchaser who receives a product and then is informed of the terms of sale has consented to those terms simply by keeping the product strains the concept of consent to the breaking point. In addition, Judge Easterbrook's approach enables vendors to dictate the terms of the transaction. It is interesting to note that when referring to an unreasonable term that a vendor might include — payments of an additional $10,000 for the product — Judge Easterbrook would apparently still require the purchaser to return the product to prevent being bound by this term of sale.

4. *Is Klocek good for consumers?* While the decision in *Klocek* may appear to give purchasers, particularly consumer purchasers, greater rights than the decisions in *Hill* and *ProCD,* that may not be the case. Under *Hill* and *ProCD* purchasers are not bound contractually until they receive the product and the seller's terms of sale, inspect them (if they choose to do so) for a period of time, and decide whether to keep the product or return it. Under *Klocek* purchasers are bound when the vendor accepts payment. If *Klocek* were to become controlling law, purchasers might lose the right to in essence cancel the sale within the period of time specified by the vendor for return of the product. As a consumer, which would you prefer: (1) A contract in which the seller dictates the terms, subject to some limitations discussed below, but in which you have the right to cancel the sale within a specified period after receiving the product, or (2) A contract that consists of the terms on which you actually agree with the vendor plus the implied-in-law terms that apply in the absence of agreement, but in which you do not have the right to cancel within a designated period after receiving the product? As the preceding analysis indicates, contract formation in rolling contracts involves competing legal and policy arguments over which reasonable people could disagree.

In addition, even if the reasoning used in *Klocek* were to prevail, vendors could respond to avoid the consequences of the decision and bind purchasers to their terms. Indeed, the court in *Klocek* gave vendors directions as to what they should do:

> The Court is mindful of the practical considerations which are involved in commercial transactions, but it is not unreasonable for a vendor to clearly communicate to a buyer—at the time of sale—either the complete terms of the sale or the fact that the vendor will propose additional terms as a condition of sale, if that be the case. 104 F. Supp. 2d at 1341, n. 14.

5. *Regulation of unfair terms. Brower* is a good example of a vendor overreaching to include terms in its standard form document that are unreasonable and effectively deny purchasers the opportunity for a hearing before even an arbitration tribunal. While the court in *Brower* held that a contract was formed on the vendor's terms, it also held that those terms are not insulated from judicial scrutiny. In *Brower* the court found that Gateway's arbitration provision was unconscionable. We will examine the doctrine of unconscionability in greater detail in Chapter 7. Other legal doctrines discussed in later chapters can also be used by courts to invalidate unreasonable terms found in vendors' terms of sale, even if those terms of sale govern the transaction. See Robert A. Hillman & Jeffrey J. Rachlinski, Standard-Form Contracting in the Electronic Age, 77 N.Y.U. L. Rev. 429 (2002) (arguing that existing law regarding standard form contracts provides sufficient protection for purchasers). It is interesting to note that other countries have adopted a more regulatory approach to standard form contracts than the United States. For example, in the European Union standard form contracts are subject to several directives issued by the European Commission that invalidate particularly oppressive provisions. See Robert A. Oakley, Fairness in Electronic Contracting: Minimum Standards for Non-Negotiated Contracts, 42 Hous. L. Rev. 1041 (2005); Jane K. Winn & Brian H. Bix, Diverging Perspectives on Electronic Contracting in the U.S. and E.U., 54 Clev. St. L. Rev. 175 (2006).

6. *Does the UCC apply?* Contracts for the sale of consumer durables, such as refrigerators or washing machines, that come with shrinkwrap terms are clearly subject to the UCC because such products are "goods" under the Code. UCC §2-105(1) ("all things . . . moveable at the time of identification to the contract for sale"). The status of software, on the other hand, is unclear. For many years software was sold on disks; the disks were goods, but the disk itself was not the product and its value was an inconsequential portion of the overall value of the transaction. Today most software is downloaded over the Internet so even a disk may not be present. Computers constitute goods under Article 2 because they are tangible moveable things, but computers typically come loaded with software, producing uncertainty regarding the application of the UCC. Most courts that have dealt with the issue have either applied the UCC to all of these transactions or have indicated that the result would be the same even if common law principles applied. See, e.g. Specht v. Netscape Communication Corp., 306 F.3d 17, 29 n. 13 (2nd Cir. 2002).

With regard to the issue of whether Article 2 of the UCC applies to shrinkwrap, clickwrap, and browsewrap transactions, revised Article 2 has the following definition of goods:

"Goods" means all things that are movable at the time of identification to a contract for sale. The term includes future goods, specially manufactured goods, the unborn young of animals, growing crops, and other identified things attached to realty as described in Section 2-107. *The term does not include information*, the money in which the price is to be paid, investment securities under Article 8, the subject matter of foreign exchange transactions, or choses in action. (emphasis added)

Comment 7 elaborates on this definition:

The definition of "goods" in this article has been amended to exclude information not associated with goods. Thus, this article does not directly apply to an electronic transfer of information, such as the transaction involved in Specht v. Netscape, 150 F. Supp. 2d 585 (S.D.N.Y. 2001), aff'd, 306 F.3d 17 (2d. Cir. 2002). However, transactions often include both goods and information: some are transactions in goods as that term is used in Section 2-103, and some are not. For example, the sale of "smart goods" such as an automobile is a transaction in goods fully within this article even though the automobile contains many computer programs. On the other hand, an architect's provision of architectural plans on a computer disk would not be a transaction in goods. When a transaction includes both the sale of goods and the transfer of rights in information, it is up to the courts to determine whether the transaction is entirely within or outside of this article, or whether or to what extent this article should be applied to a portion of the transaction. While this article may apply to a transaction including information, nothing in this Article alters, creates, or diminishes intellectual property rights.

Assuming the Code applies to an electronic transaction, comment 5 to revised §2-207 states:

The section omits any specific treatment of terms attached to the goods, or in or on the container in which the goods are delivered. This article takes no position on whether a court should follow the reasoning in Step-Saver Data Systems, Inc. v. Wyse Technology, 939 F.2d 91 (3d Cir. 1991) and Klocek v. Gateway, Inc. 104 F. Supp. 2d 1332 (D. Kan. 2000) (original 2-207 governs) or the contrary reasoning in Hill v. Gateway 2000, 105 F. 3d 1147(7th Cir. 1997) (original 2-207 inapplicable).

See Jean Braucher, Amended Article 2 and the Decision to Trust the Courts: The Case Against Enforcing Delayed Mass-Market Terms, Especially for Software, 2004 Wis. L. Rev. 753. Suppose revised Article 2 applied to the transaction in *Brower*. Would the reasoning or result in the case be different?

‖ Register.com, Inc. v. Verio, Inc.
United States Court of Appeals
356 F.3d 393 (2d Cir. 2004)

LEVAL, Circuit Judge.
. . .

BACKGROUND

This plaintiff Register is one of over fifty companies serving as registrars for the issuance of domain names on the world wide web. As a registrar,

Register issues domain names to persons and entities preparing to establish web sites on the Internet. Web sites are identified and accessed by reference to their domain names.

Register was appointed a registrar of domain names by the Internet Corporation for Assigned Names and Numbers, known by the acronym "ICANN." ICANN is a private, non-profit public benefit corporation which was established by agencies of the U.S. government to administer the Internet domain name system. To become a registrar of domain names, Register was required to enter into a standard form agreement with ICANN, designated as the ICANN Registrar Accreditation Agreement, November 1999 version (referred to herein as the "ICANN Agreement").

Applicants to register a domain name submit to the registrar contact information, including at a minimum, the applicant's name, postal address, telephone number, and electronic mail address. The ICANN Agreement, referring to this registrant contact information under the rubric "WHOIS information," requires the registrar, under terms discussed in greater detail below, to preserve it, update it daily, and provide for free public access to it through the Internet as well as through an independent access port, called port 43. See ICANN Agreement §II.F.1.

Section II.F.5 of the ICANN Agreement (which furnishes a major basis for the appellant Verio's contentions on this appeal) requires that the registrar "not impose terms and conditions" on the use made by others of its WHOIS data "except as permitted by ICANN-adopted policy." In specifying what restrictions may be imposed, the ICANN Agreement requires the registrar to permit use of its WHOIS data "for any lawful purposes except to: . . . support the transmission of mass unsolicited, commercial advertising or solicitations *via email (spam);* [and other listed purposes not relevant to this appeal]." (emphasis added).

Another section of the ICANN Agreement (upon which appellee Register relies) provides as follows,

> No Third-Party Beneficiaries: This Agreement shall not be construed to create any obligation by either ICANN or Registrar to any non-party to this Agreement. . . .

ICANN Agreement §II.S.2. Third parties could nonetheless seek enforcement of a registrar's obligations set forth in the ICANN Agreement by resort to a grievance process under ICANN's auspices.

In compliance with §II.F.1 of the ICANN Agreement, Register updated the WHOIS information on a daily basis and established Internet and port 43 service, which allowed free public query of its WHOIS information. An entity making a WHOIS query through Register's Internet site or port 43 would receive a reply furnishing the requested WHOIS information, captioned by a legend devised by Register, which stated,

> By submitting a WHOIS query, you agree that you will use this data only for lawful purposes and that under no circumstances will you use this data to . . . support the transmission of mass unsolicited, commercial advertising or solicitation via email.

The terms of that legend tracked §II.F.5 of the ICANN Agreement in specifying the restrictions Register imposed on the use of its WHOIS data.

Subsequently, as explained below, Register amended the terms of this legend to impose more stringent restrictions on the use of the information gathered through such queries.

In addition to performing the function of a registrar of domain names, Register also engages in the business of selling web-related services to entities that maintain web sites. These services cover various aspects of web site development. In order to solicit business for the services it offers, Register sends out marketing communications. Among the entities it solicits for the sale of such services are entities whose domain names it registered. However, during the registration process, Register offers registrants the opportunity to elect whether or not they will receive marketing communications from it.

The defendant Verio, against whom the preliminary injunction was issued, is engaged in the business of selling a variety of web site design, development and operation services. In the sale of such services, Verio competes with Register's web site development business. To facilitate its pursuit of customers, Verio undertook to obtain daily updates of the WHOIS information relating to newly registered domain names. To achieve this, Verio devised an automated software program, or robot, which each day would submit multiple successive WHOIS queries through the port 43 accesses of various registrars. Upon acquiring the WHOIS information of new registrants, Verio would send them marketing solicitations by email, telemarketing and direct mail. To the extent that Verio's solicitations were sent by email, the practice was inconsistent with the terms of the restrictive legend Register attached to its responses to Verio's queries.

At first, Verio's solicitations addressed to Register's registrants made explicit reference to their recent registration through Register. This led some of the recipients of Verio's solicitations to believe the solicitation was initiated by Register (or an affiliate), and was sent in violation of the registrant's election not to receive solicitations from Register. Register began to receive complaints from registrants. Register in turn complained to Verio and demanded that Verio cease and desist from this form of marketing. Register asserted that Verio was harming Register's goodwill, and that by soliciting via email, was violating the terms to which it had agreed on submitting its queries for WHOIS information. Verio responded to the effect that it had stopped mentioning Register in its solicitation message.

In the meantime, Register changed the restrictive legend it attached to its responses to WHOIS queries. While previously the legend conformed to the terms of §II F.5, which authorized Register to prohibit use of the WHOIS information for mass solicitations "via email," its new legend undertook to bar mass solicitation "via direct mail, electronic mail, or by telephone."[2] Section II.F.5 of Register's ICANN Agreement, as noted above, required Register to permit use of the WHOIS data "for any lawful purpose except to . . . support the transmission of mass unsolicited solicitations via email (spam)." Thus, by

---

2. The new legend stated:

By submitting a WHOIS query, you agree that . . . under no circumstances will you use this data to . . . support the transmission of mass unsolicited . . . advertising or solicitations via direct mail, electronic mail, or by telephone.

undertaking to prohibit Verio from using the WHOIS information for solicitations "via direct mail . . . or by telephone," Register was acting in apparent violation of this term of its ICANN Agreement.

Register wrote to Verio demanding that it cease using WHOIS information derived from Register not only for email marketing, but also for marketing by direct mail and telephone. Verio ceased using the information in email marketing, but refused to stop marketing by direct mail and telephone.

Register brought this suit on August 3, 2000, and moved for a temporary restraining order and a preliminary injunction. Register asserted, among other claims, that Verio was (a) causing confusion among customers, who were led to believe Verio was affiliated with Register; (b) accessing Register's computers without authorization, a violation of the Computer Fraud and Abuse Act, 18 U.S.C. § 1030; and, (c) trespassing on Register's chattels in a manner likely to harm Register's computer systems by the use of Verio's automated robot software programs. On December 8, 2000, the district court entered a preliminary injunction. . . .

DISCUSSION

[Verio first argued that Register's restrictions on Verio's use of WHOIS data for direct mail and telemarketing purposes violated the ICANN agreement. However, ICANN intervened in the case and supported Register's argument that the "no third party beneficiary" clause prevented Verio from asserting any violation of the ICANN agreement. Chapter 9 examines when a person has the status of a third party beneficiary and the rights and duties of such beneficiaries. In connection with this position, both ICANN and Register argued that ICANN provides an internal procedure for resolution of such disputes and that Verio should raise its concerns through that procedure. ICANN contended that, because of the technical and fast changing nature of the Internet, use of its internal procedures was vital to development of well informed and sound Internet policy. The court agreed with this argument.—EDS.]

(b) Verio's assent to Register's contract terms

Verio's next contention assumes that Register was legally authorized to demand that takers of WHOIS data from its systems refrain from using it for mass solicitation by mail and telephone, as well as by email. Verio contends that it nonetheless never became contractually bound to the conditions imposed by Register's restrictive legend because, in the case of each query Verio made, the legend did not appear until after Verio had submitted the query and received the WHOIS data. Accordingly, Verio contends that in no instance did it receive legally enforceable notice of the conditions Register intended to impose. Verio therefore argues it should not be deemed to have taken WHOIS data from Register's systems subject to Register's conditions.

Verio's argument might well be persuasive if its queries addressed to Register's computers had been sporadic and infrequent. If Verio had submitted only one query, or even if it had submitted only a few sporadic queries, that would give considerable force to its contention that it obtained the WHOIS data without being conscious that Register intended to impose conditions, and without being deemed to have accepted Register's conditions. But Verio was daily submitting numerous queries, each of which resulted in its receiving notice of the terms Register exacted. Furthermore, Verio admits that it knew perfectly well what terms Register demanded. Verio's argument fails.

The situation might be compared to one in which plaintiff P maintains a roadside fruit stand displaying bins of apples. A visitor, defendant D, takes an apple and bites into it. As D turns to leave, D sees a sign, visible only as one turns to exit, which says "Apples — 50 cents apiece." D does not pay for the apple. D believes he has no obligation to pay because he had no notice when he bit into the apple that 50 cents was expected in return. D's view is that he never agreed to pay for the apple. Thereafter, each day, several times a day, D revisits the stand, takes an apple, and eats it. D never leaves money.

P sues D in contract for the price of the apples taken. D defends on the ground that on no occasion did he see P's price notice until after he had bitten into the apples. D may well prevail as to the first apple taken. D had no reason to understand upon taking it that P was demanding the payment. In our view, however, D cannot continue on a daily basis to take apples for free, knowing full well that P is offering them only in exchange for 50 cents in compensation, merely because the sign demanding payment is so placed that on each occasion D does not see it until he has bitten into the apple.

Verio's circumstance is effectively the same. Each day Verio repeatedly enters Register's computers and takes that day's new WHOIS data. Each day upon receiving the requested data, Verio receives Register's notice of the terms on which it makes the data available — that the data not be used for mass solicitation via direct mail, email, or telephone. Verio acknowledges that it continued drawing the data from Register's computers with full knowledge that Register offered access subject to these restrictions. Verio is no more free to take Register's data without being bound by the terms on which Register offers it, than D was free, in the example, once he became aware of the terms of P's offer, to take P's apples without obligation to pay the 50 cent price at which P offered them.

Verio seeks support for its position from cases that have dealt with the formation of contracts on the Internet. An excellent example, although decided subsequent to the submission of this case, is Specht v. Netscape Communications Corp., 306 F.3d 17 (2d Cir. 2002). The dispute was whether users of Netscape's software, who downloaded it from Netscape's web site, were bound by an agreement to arbitrate disputes with Netscape, where Netscape had posted the terms of its offer of the software (including the obligation to arbitrate disputes) on the web site from which they downloaded the software. We ruled against Netscape and in favor of the users of its software because the users would not have seen the terms Netscape exacted without scrolling down their computer screens, and there was no reason for them to do so. The evidence did not demonstrate that one who had downloaded Netscape's software had necessarily seen the terms of its offer.

Verio, however, cannot avail itself of the reasoning of *Specht*. In *Specht*, the users in whose favor we decided visited Netscape's web site one time to download its software. Netscape's posting of its terms did not compel the conclusion that its downloaders took the software subject to those terms because there was no way to determine that any downloader had seen the terms of the offer. There was no basis for imputing to the downloaders of

Netscape's software knowledge of the terms on which the software was offered. This case is crucially different. Verio visited Register's computers daily to access WHOIS data and each day saw the terms of Register's offer; Verio admitted that, in entering Register's computers to get the data, it was fully aware of the terms on which Register offered the access.

Verio's next argument is that it was not bound by Register's terms because it rejected them. Even assuming Register is entitled to demand compliance with its terms in exchange for Verio's entry into its systems to take WHOIS data, and even acknowledging that Verio was fully aware of Register's terms, Verio contends that it still is not bound by Register's terms because it did not agree to be bound. In support of its claim, Verio cites a district court case from the Central District of California, Ticketmaster Corp. v. Tickets.com, Inc., No. CV99-7654, 2000 WL 1887522 (C.D.Cal. Aug.10, 2000), in which the court rejected Ticketmaster's application for a preliminary injunction to enforce posted terms of use of data available on its website against a regular user. Noting that the user of Ticketmaster's web site is not required to check an "I agree" box before proceeding, the court concluded that there was insufficient proof of agreement to support a preliminary injunction. Id. at *5.

We acknowledge that the *Ticketmaster* decision gives Verio some support, but not enough. In the first place, the Ticketmaster court was not making a definitive ruling rejecting Ticketmaster's contract claim. It was rather exercising a district court's discretion to deny a preliminary injunction because of a doubt whether the movant had adequately shown likelihood of success on the merits.

But more importantly, we are not inclined to agree with the *Ticketmaster* court's analysis. There is a crucial difference between the circumstances of *Specht*, where we declined to enforce Netscape's specified terms against a user of its software because of inadequate evidence that the user had seen the terms when downloading the software, and those of *Ticketmaster*, where the taker of information from Ticketmaster's site knew full well the terms on which the information was offered but was not offered an icon marked, "I agree," on which to click. Under the circumstances of *Ticketmaster*, we see no reason why the enforceability of the offeror's terms should depend on whether the taker states (or clicks), "I agree."

We recognize that contract offers on the Internet often require the offeree to click on an "I agree" icon. And no doubt, in many circumstances, such a statement of agreement by the offeree is essential to the formation of a contract. But not in all circumstances. While new commerce on the Internet has exposed courts to many new situations, it has not fundamentally changed the principles of contract. It is standard contract doctrine that when a benefit is offered subject to stated conditions, and the offeree makes a decision to take the benefit with knowledge of the terms of the offer, the taking constitutes an acceptance of the terms, which accordingly become binding on the offeree. See, e.g., Restatement (Second of Contracts §69(1)(a) (1981) ("[S]ilence and inaction operate as an acceptance . . . [w]here an offeree takes the benefit of offered services with reasonable opportunity to reject them and reason to know that they were offered with the expectation of compensation."); 2 Richard A. Lord, Williston on Contracts §6:9 (4th ed. 1991) ("[T]he acceptance of the benefit of services may well be held to imply a promise to pay for them if at the time of acceptance the offeree has a reasonable opportunity to reject the service and knows or has reason to know that compensation is expected."); Arthur Linton Corbin, Corbin on Contracts § 71 (West 1 vol. ed. 1952) ("The acceptance of the benefit of the services is a promise to pay for them, if at the time of accepting the benefit the offeree has a reasonable opportunity to reject it and knows that compensation is expected."); Jones v. Brisbin, 41 Wash.2d 167, 172, 247 P.2d 891 (1952) ("Where a person, with reasonable opportunity to reject offered services, takes the benefit of them under circumstances which would indicate, to a reasonable man, that they were offered with the expectation of compensation, a contract, complete with mutual assent, results."); Markstein Bros. Millinery Co. v. J.A. White & Co., 151 Ark. 1, 235 S.W. 39 (1921) (buyer of hats was bound to pay for hats when buyer failed to return them to seller within five days of inspection as seller requested in clear and obvious notice statement).

Returning to the apple stand, the visitor, who sees apples offered for 50 cents apiece and takes an apple, owes 50 cents, regardless whether he did or did not say, "I agree." The choice offered in such circumstances is to take the apple on the known terms of the offer or not to take the apple. As we see it, the defendant in *Ticketmaster* and Verio in this case had a similar choice. Each was offered access to information subject to terms of which they were well aware. Their choice was either to accept the offer of contract, taking the information subject to the terms of the offer, or, if the terms were not acceptable, to decline to take the benefits.

We find that the district court was within its discretion in concluding that Register showed likelihood of success on the merits of its contract claim. . . .

Notes and Questions

1. *Analysis of Register.* The court in *Register* holds that Verio had assented and was contractually bound by the terms of use of Register's Web site because Verio had used the site many times and was well aware of Register's restrictions on use. The court analogizes the situation to the visitor to an apple stand who continues to bite into apples even though the visitor knows of a sign stating the price of apples. The court seems to say that a first time user (and maybe even a user for a few times) would not be bound by the restrictions unless the user were actually aware of the restrictions: "P sues D in contract for the price of the apples taken. D defends on the ground that on no occasion did he see P's price notice until after he had bitten into the apples. *D may well prevail as to the first apple taken.*" (Emphasis added.) Do you agree?

2. *Mutual assent in browsewrap transactions.* The court rejects the argument that clicking an "I agree" button is essential to contract formation on the Internet. Do you agree? Or should courts hold that users are not contractually bound by the terms of use of a Web site unless they click an "I agree" button?

In a survey of case law and policy arguments involving browsewrap agreements, the authors (Christina L. Kunz, John E. Ottaviani, Elaine D. Ziff, Juliet M. Moringiello, Kathleen M. Porter, and Jennifer C. Debrow) contend that browsewrap agreements should be enforceable even if the user has not clicked an agreement button, if four requirements are met:

(i) The user is provided with adequate notice of the existence of the proposed terms.
(ii) The user has a meaningful opportunity to review the terms.
(iii) The user is provided with adequate notice that taking a specified action manifests assent to the terms.
(iv) The user takes the action specified in the latter notice.

Christina L. Kunz et al, Browse-wrap Agreements: Validity of Implied Assent in Electronic Form Agreements, 59 Bus. Law. 279 (2003). On the other hand, in Online Boilerplate: Would Mandatory Website Disclosure of E-standard Terms Backfire?, 104 Mich. L. Rev. 837 (2006), Professor Robert Hillman argues that mandatory disclosure of terms of use on Web sites might backfire "because it may not increase reading or shopping for terms or motivate businesses to draft reasonable ones, but instead, may make heretofore suspect terms more likely enforceable." Id at 839. In particular, mandated disclosure might make it more difficult for consumers to claim that terms were unconscionable because the mandated disclosure would make it more difficult for consumers to establish unfair surprise or procedural unconscionability. Id. at 840. Professor Hillman's article is part of a symposium published in the Michigan Law Review on the enforceability of "boilerplate" provisions in standard form documents.

3. *Mutual assent in clickwrap transactions. Register* deals with a browsewrap transaction, but the court seems to say that if a user had reasonably adequate notice of Register's terms of use and clicked an "I agree" button, the user would be contractually bound by those terms. If so, the court would be implicitly validating clickwrap agreements. Validity of clickwrap agreements is also implicit in the Second Circuit's holding in Specht v. Netscape Communications Corp., 306 F.3d 17 (2d Cir. 2002), which the court distinguished in *Register*. In *Specht* the plaintiffs had downloaded from Netscape's site certain software to enhance the performance of Netscape's basic browser software. The downloads were not accompanied by an "I agree" button and Netscape was unable to show that the plaintiffs were actually aware of or had reasonably adequate notice of the terms under which it permitted downloading, which included an arbitration provision. The court held that the plaintiffs had not assented to the arbitration provision. Implicit in the decision, however, is the proposition that if the plaintiffs had received reasonably adequate notice of the terms of a transaction and had clicked an agreement button, they would have been bound contractually by Netscape's contract terms.

In Caspi v. Microsoft Network, L.L.C., 732 A.2d 528 (N.J. Super. 1999), the court held that residents of New Jersey and other states who subscribed to Microsoft's network service were bound by the terms of a forum selection clause contained on Microsoft's Web site, which required them to litigate disputes in the state of Washington, when they clicked the "I agree" button. The court ruled that users had reasonable notice of the clause because they could review the terms of the contract online:

The plaintiffs in this case were free to scroll through the various computer screens that presented the terms of their contracts before clicking their agreement. Also, it seems clear that there was nothing extraordinary about the size or placement of the forum selection clause text. By every indication we have, the clause was presented in exactly the same format as most other provisions of the contract. It was the first item in the last paragraph of the electronic document. We note that a few paragraphs in the contract were presented in upper case typeface, presumably for emphasis, but most provisions, including the forum selection clause, were presented in lower case typeface. We discern nothing about the style or mode of presentation, or the placement of the provision, that can be taken as a basis for concluding that the forum selection clause was proffered unfairly, or with a design to conceal or de-emphasize its provisions. To conclude that plaintiffs are not bound by that clause would be equivalent to holding that they were bound by no other clause either, since all provisions were identically presented. Plaintiffs must be taken to have known that they were entering into a contract; and no good purpose, consonant with the dictates of reasonable reliability in commerce, would be served by permitting them to disavow particular provisions or the contract as a whole. Id. at 532.

Other courts have upheld clickwrap terms when the purchaser has reasonable notice of the terms and clicks an agreement button. See Seibert v. Amateur Athletic Union of U.S., Inc., 422 F.Supp.2d 1033 (D.Minn. 2006); Forrest v. Verizon Communications, Inc., 805 A.2d 1007 (D.C. 2002). But see Mark E. Budnitz, Consumers Surfing for Sales in Cyberspace: What Constitutes Acceptance and What Legal Terms and Conditions Bind the Consumer?, 16 Ga. St. U.L. Rev. 741 (2000) (diversity of transaction completion buttons used by online vendors creates consumer uncertainty regarding significance of clicking on button).

Is reasonable notice of contract terms coupled with the affirmative act of clicking on an agreement button sufficient to show assent to the seller's terms? Consider the following comment by Professor White:

> The buyer will understand that his click on the "I agree" clause is a proper acceptance of the seller's terms, but now the seller's offer is coercive. The buyer has received and spent all evening setting up his computer, and he is sitting in his study in International Falls, Minnesota, in his underwear with a beer when he has to decide whether to agree to the new terms or go out in the negative-thirty-degree temperature and return the computer. This offer is more objectionable than a predelivery e-mail because it is coercive. James J. White, Contracting Under Amended 2-207, 2004 Wis. L. Rev. 723, 748.

Do you agree that clickwrap transactions are or can be coercive? If so, should that be sufficient reason to find that a clickwrap transaction does not amount to a contract?

PROBLEM 2-8

David Copperfield is a resident of a midwestern city, where he lives in and operates a bed-and-breakfast inn, which he calls "Merlin's Castle." The inn is comfortably and attractively furnished with antique furniture, oil paintings, and oriental rugs. Recently David saw on television an "infomercial" program advertising the "CarpetWizard" (TM), a machine for vacuuming and steam-cleaning carpets and rugs. In that program, the CarpetWizard was advertised for sale at the price of $399.95, for which sum the buyer would also receive "absolutely free" a lightweight carpet sweeper and a device for dusting blinds, shades, and ceiling fixtures. In the course of the program, in which the product was demonstrated repeatedly by enthusiastic actors, the spokesperson also stated several times that if a buyer was not entirely satisfied with the CarpetWizard after using it for two weeks, the entire purchase price would be "cheerfully refunded," and the buyer could keep the sweeper and duster.

Watching the program, David was persuaded that the CarpetWizard and its accompanying devices would be useful in keeping his inn clean and neat. The program listed a Web site where David could purchase the CarpetWizard: *http://www.morek.com/carpetwizard*. When David accessed the Web site, he saw pictures of various vacuum cleaners and similar devices, with specifications for each of the products. Immediately below the pictures of all the products in fairly large type was a button where David could "place an order." Several other buttons, in somewhat smaller type, were located at the bottom of the page. One of these buttons was labeled, "contract terms and warranty." David clicked on the button and found a long document with some provisions in all caps while others were in regular type. David quickly scrolled through the document. At the end he found a button which stated, "return to product page." David clicked on this button and was returned to the page with the pictures of the products. He then clicked on the "place an order" button and moved to a page that asked for credit card and delivery information. David entered this information and clicked the button at the bottom of the page which stated "complete order." A page appeared confirming David's entry of credit card and delivery information. At the bottom of the page appeared another button which stated: "Confirm order. Your order is not complete until you click here." David clicked this button and a message appeared on the screen with his order confirmation number. He was told that he would receive an email when his order was shipped. He received the confirming email the next day.

Two weeks later, the merchandise he had ordered was delivered to David. In the packing box, in addition to the CarpetWizard itself plus the sweeper and duster, was a booklet entitled "INSTRUCTION MANUAL," the contents of which consisted mostly of instructions for operating those products. However, the last two pages of that booklet (which David did not read at the time) were entitled "BUYER'S WARRANTY," and contained several para-graphs of text. Included on those two pages were: (1) a disclaimer of any liability on CWI's part for any consequential damage resulting from the use or misuse of any CWI products; (2) a provision that any claim for refund must be made within 5 days of the buyer's receipt of the merchandise, and must be accompanied by *all* of the merchandise in the original packing case, sent postage prepaid and insured to the seller's factory in Florida; and (3) a statement that any and all disputes arising out of the buyer's purchase of any CWI product must be submitted to arbitration in Florida.

Attached to the last page of the Instruction Manual was a tear-off card entitled "WARRANTY REGISTRATION." The card stated "Please fill out and return so that we may have a record of your purchase, to ensure that you receive the full protection of your Buyer's Warranty." The card provided a space for the buyer to fill in the place and date of the purchase and the serial number of the CarpetWizard purchased. The card then asked several questions about the buyer's purchasing habits, followed by a space for the buyer's signature, name and address. David filled out the card, signed it, and mailed it back to CWI.

A week after receiving the CarpetWizard, David got around to trying it out. After reading the instructions in the manual to be sure he was operating the machine correctly, David used the CarpetWizard to clean the rugs in his inn, starting with those in his own personal apartment. When it appeared to work as promised, he went on to use the machine on the rugs in the guest rooms and common areas of the inn. Within a few hours, several of the rugs appeared discolored and worn as a result of its operation. When David attempted to go over the affected areas again, in an effort to improve the result, the CarpetWizard short-circuited and caught fire. The machine itself was damaged beyond repair, as was the rug that David was cleaning at the time.

For the purpose of this question, ignore any possible application of tort law to these facts, and also ignore the possibility that statutes or regulations (federal, state, or local) we have not studied might provide various types of protection for David in this case. Assuming that the damage to the CarpetWizard itself as well as to David's rugs could be characterized as "consequential damage," answer the following questions on the basis of general contract law and UCC Article 2.

Is David entitled to a full refund of the price he paid for the CWI products?

Is he entitled to compensation for any injury to his rugs that resulted from his use of the CarpetWizard?

If CWI declines to make compensation as David requests it to, will David have to initiate an arbitration proceeding in Florida to recover any money from CWI?

3 Liability in the Absence of Bargained-for Exchange: Promissory Estoppel and Restitution

A. PROTECTION OF PROMISEE RELIANCE: THE DOCTRINE OF PROMISSORY ESTOPPEL

If one were to define classical contract law as a system of abstract, formal rules, self-contained and logically consistent, based on principles enunciated in the first instance by Professor Langdell and brought to fruition by the labors of Professor Williston, then one might appear to be describing the first (and probably foremost) of the Restatements: the original Restatement of Contracts, officially adopted by the American Law Institute in 1932. During the preparation of the first Restatement, however, Professor Arthur Corbin showed that courts often used reliance as a basis of contractual obligation. His work led to the inclusion of the reliance principle in §90 of the first Restatement. (One version of the history of §90 is recounted in Grant Gilmore, The Death of Contract 62-64 (1974).) Corbin also drafted the remedies chapter of the first Restatement, which contained a number of sections based on the principle of unjust enrichment. In his 1974 disquisition on what he perceived as "The Death of Contract," Professor Grant Gilmore put forth the thesis that the Restatement was "schizophrenic." In §90 of the Restatement, he declared, the drafters had embraced a principle that was as antithetical to §75—which encapsulated the bargain theory of consideration—as antimatter would be to the universe we know. In the end, he concluded, the two could not live side by side: "one must swallow up the other." Grant Gilmore, The Death of Contract 60-61 (1974).

To understand and evaluate Gilmore's prophecy, we must consider some of the developments leading up to the adoption of §90 and examine also the effect that it in turn has had on subsequent case law. In his 1952 articles detailing the history of §90, Professor Benjamin Boyer described the various strands of case law that were woven to form the abstract principle expressed in §90. Benjamin F. Boyer, Promissory Estoppel: Principle from Precedents (Pts. 1-2), 50 Mich. L. Rev. 639, 873 (1952). Some of the categories he

215

identified are reflected in the material that follows. Perhaps the most significant aspect of §90, however, is not its accuracy as a summation of the case law that had gone before, but its influence on the case law that was to come. It is difficult to think of a better example of the complementary operation of the processes of induction and deduction than the creation of §90 and its subsequent effect on American law.

Section 90 of the original Restatement was both short and deceptively simple. The section was entitled "Promise Reasonably Inducing Definite and Substantial Action." (Although the principle is commonly called "promissory estoppel," that term was not used in §90.) Its text provided as follows:

> A promise which the promisor should reasonably expect to induce action or forbearance of a definite and substantial character on the part of the promisee and which does induce such action or forbearance is binding if injustice can be avoided only by enforcement of the promise.

Section 90 did not place any limitations on the subject matter of the "promise" it envisioned, or on the types of persons who might benefit from its application. Nor did it specify any particular reason why the promise in question might otherwise have been nonbinding, although there is some indication in Restatement §19(b) that the drafters considered §90 as an exception to the requirement of consideration and perhaps to that of mutual assent as well. We have already seen the application of promissory estoppel to prevent revocation of an offer when the offeree has detrimentally relied on the offer. In later chapters we will consider its effect on other classical doctrines, such as the statute of frauds. At this point, however, we focus on the earliest legal role for "unbargained-for reliance," namely, as a substitute for consideration.

1. Promises Within the Family

On its face, the system of classical contract law would appear to apply as readily to dealings between two family members as it would to any other transaction. The Restatement of Contracts in its examples constantly speaks of dealings between *"A"* and *"B,"* often without more particular description of those ubiquitous characters. Upon reflection, however, it should be obvious that the nature of the bargain theory excluded from its sphere most of the dealings between family members. Of course, relatives can, and sometimes do, enter into formal contracts with each other, but most promises in the family context are likely to be actuated by feelings of affection and altruism rather than by the expectation of a quid pro quo in return. To the extent that the law imposes legal obligations in the family context, these obligations are, for the most part, based on the relationship of the parties—the parental duty of support, for example—rather than contract. Courses on domestic relations or family law examine such duties. We will see in the second part of this chapter, however, that some contemporary courts have used the doctrine of restitution to create legal obligations in the family context when justice seems to demand it. As the following cases show, promissory estoppel provides an additional tool for courts to reach what they consider to be equitable decisions.

Kirksey v. Kirksey
Alabama Supreme Court
8 Ala. 131 (1845)

Assumpsit by the defendant, against the plaintiff in error. The question is presented in this Court, upon a case agreed, which shows the following facts:

The plaintiff was the wife of defendant's brother, but had for some time been a widow, and had several children. In 1840, the plaintiff resided on public land, under a contract of lease, she had held over, and was comfortably settled, and would have attempted to secure the land she lived on. The defendant resided in Talladega county, some sixty, or seventy miles off. On the 10th October, 1840, he wrote to her the following letter:

> Dear sister Antillico — Much to my mortification, I heard, that brother Henry was dead, and one of his children. I know that your situation is one of grief, and difficulty. You had a bad chance before, but a great deal worse now. I should like to come and see you, but cannot with convenience at present. . . . I do not know whether you have a preference on the place you live on, or not. If you had, I would advise you to obtain your preference, and sell the land and quit the country, as I understand it is very unhealthy, and I know society is very bad. If you will come down and see me, I will let you have a place to raise your family, and I have more open land than I can tend; and on the account of your situation, and that of your family, I feel like I want you and the children to do well.

Within a month or two after the receipt of this letter, the plaintiff abandoned her possession, without disposing of it, and removed with her family, to the residence of the defendant, who put her in comfortable houses, and gave her land to cultivate for two years, at the end of which time he notified her to remove, and put her in a house, not comfortable, in the woods, which he afterwards required her to leave.

A verdict being found for the plaintiff, for two hundred dollars, the above facts were agreed, and if they will sustain the action, the judgment is to be affirmed, otherwise it is to be reversed.

ORMOND, J. — The inclination of my mind, is, that the loss and inconvenience, which the plaintiff sustained in breaking up, and moving to the defendant's, a distance of sixty miles, is a sufficient consideration to support the promise, to furnish her with a house, and land to cultivate, until she could raise her family. My brothers, however think, that the promise on the part of the defendant, was a mere gratuity, and that an action will not lie for its breach. The judgment of the Court below must therefore be reversed, pursuant to the agreement of the parties.

Notes and Questions

1. *Analyzing* **Kirksey.** In light of cases like Hamer v. Sidway, does it appear that the plaintiff in *Kirksey* suffered a "legal detriment?" Is it also possible that her brother-in-law, the defendant, received from her actions a "benefit" — at least a legal one, and possibly a real one as well? If either of these questions should be answered affirmatively, could the court have held that the defendant's promise was supported by consideration? Perhaps because he disagrees with the majority, the writer of the opinion does not shed much light on the question of why the court refused to find that the defendant's promise was supported by consideration. (If nothing else, *Kirksey* demonstrates the wisdom of the more usual practice of having a proponent of the decision write the opinion explaining it.) Recall Professor Williston's discussion of the "tramp hypothetical," quoted in the *Pennsy Supply* case in Chapter 2. Could Professor Williston's reasoning provide a rationale for the decision in *Kirksey?*

2. *Questions about* **Kirksey**. *Kirksey* raises a number of questions. Why did plaintiff's brother-in-law invite her to move to his part of the state? Was his promise to her altruistic or did he expect something in return? Why did the defendant evict plaintiff from the property? Since there were good arguments for both sides of the case, why did the court decide for what appears to be the less sympathetic party? Was there perhaps gender bias on their part? See Amy Kastely, Cogs or Cyborgs: Blasphemy and Irony in Contract Theories, 90 Nw. U. L. Rev. 132 (1995) (citing *Kirksey* as an example of the differential application of contract law to women). What happened to the parties after the case was over? For the answers to these and many more questions, see William R. Casto & Val D. Ricks, "Dear Sister Antillico . . . ": The Story of *Kirksey v. Kirksey,* 94 Geo. L.J. 321 (2006).

Greiner v. Greiner
Kansas Supreme Court
131 Kan. 760, 293 P. 759 (1930)

BURCH, J.

Maggie Greiner commenced an action of forcible detention against her son, Frank Greiner, to recover possession of a quarter section of land, and an additional tract of 80 acres. Frank answered that his mother had given him the 80-acre tract under such circumstances that she not only could not reclaim it, but that she should execute a conveyance to him. The district court ordered plaintiff to execute a deed conveying the 80-acre tract to defendant, and plaintiff appeals.

Peter Greiner died testate, leaving a widow — the plaintiff — and sons and daughters. His sons Henry, Frank, and Nicholas and his daughter, Kate, were disinherited — were given $5 apiece. Henry died in June, 1925, unmarried and intestate, and his mother inherited considerable property from him. She then concluded to place the other two disinherited sons on an equal footing with those who had been favored in the will, and she took active measures to accomplish her purpose. At first she intended to give Frank and Nicholas land, about 90 acres apiece. Later, she entered into a written contract to pay Nicholas $2,000. Frank had gone to Logan county, had homesteaded a quarter section of land, and had lived there sixteen or seventeen years. Mrs. Greiner lived in Mitchell county, and the land in controversy lies in Mitchell county, not far from her home. The brief for plaintiff says she inherited from Henry only a three-sevenths interest in the 80-acre tract. The brief for defendant says she inherited the entire interest, and Mrs. Greiner so testified. In any event, some deeds were to be executed, and in July, 1926, Mrs. Greiner had Nicholas write to Frank and tell Frank to come down, she was going to make settlement with him and Nicholas. Frank came to Mitchell county and had a conversation with his mother. At that time there was a house on the quarter section. In the conversation, Mrs. Greiner told Frank she was going to pay him and Nicholas. Frank told her he did not want money, he wanted a home — a little land for a home. She said all right, she had the land, and she wanted him to move into the house, and they would divide up later. He said that would be all right, and he would move back. . . .

A. Diebolt, cashier of the Home State Bank of Tipton, prepared the contract between Mrs. Greiner and Nicholas. He testified as follows:

> In the summer or fall of 1926 I had a conversation with Maggie Greiner about Frank coming back to Mitchell county. As near as I can say, it was before wheat sowing time. If I recall correctly, Frank was in the bank with her. The substance of the conversation was that she brought Frank back to Mitchell county, he wasn't doing any good out there, did not have enough to come. I do not know the town, it was in the western part. She said there was plenty of land there; that Frank had been disinherited by his father, and she was going to give him an interest in the land. As I recall, she was going to give him 92 or 97 acres.

Referring to an incident occurring in the fall of 1926, Louis [Greiner, one of the sons favored in the will — EDS.] testified as follows:

> At that time I don't remember whether I had a conversation with mother about Frank moving on that eighty, but that was a settled fact at that time, that he was going to move there at that time. Oh, I had several conversations during the year. I was there several times in 1926. I had several conversations with her in the fall of 1926.

Q. Well, do you remember what she said at any one of those conversations about Frank Greiner?
A. I heard about him moving back, and she gave him that place as his share. . . .
Q. That eighty acres?
A. Yes, sir. . . .
Q. And did she say why she was going to give him that eighty?
A. Yes, sir.
Q. What did she say?
A. Because the rest of us, there were four of them disinherited in the will of my father; he was one of those disinherited.

Frank moved back on September 20, 1926. Mrs. Greiner then determined to move the house from the quarter section to the 80-acre tract, and give that specific tract to Frank. Frank testified as follows:

Q. You were asked about what was said about this house, moving this house over onto this eighty, was there any conversation about that, when you had this talk with your mother about moving on this place?

A. Yes, sir, there was.

Q. All right now, I don't think you told regarding that; what was that, please?

A. Well, she said we would move that house over there, and the buildings, and said, "That will be a home for you."

. . .

The buildings were moved from the quarter section to the 80-acre tract, and Frank commenced to occupy the 80-acre tract in the spring of 1927. Mrs. Greiner testified as follows:

> I remember of Frank living in Logan county up to 1926. I remember of his coming back that fall, and at different times. He did not then move on this place. He moved on after we had things arranged and the house fixed. I fixed the house and everything, and had it fixed for him. Then he moved on, and has lived there ever since.

The manner of assuring title to Frank came up. At first a will was contemplated. Louis Greiner testified as follows:

Q. Now did she say anything about this place, any arrangement, after those deeds were made here, and so on?

A. Well, we had fixed a date she was going to make a will to that effect, come to Beloit.

Q. Yes?

A. And in the meantime, she had signed some papers with Diebolt to pay Nick $2,000, and she called me up, and wanted me to come up one morning, and she told me what she had done.

Q. Yes?

A. Said Gustie had been raising so much storm about it, she wanted me to come and see if I couldn't get that paper back, and she would go to Beloit and make a will in favor of Frank and Nick; and so I went to Tipton with her, and we got this paper, and fixed a date to go to Beloit the next week; and the next week came, and I came there, and she absolutely wouldn't go, wouldn't do a thing.

Q. Did she say why?

A. She said Gustie told her if she would make a will they would move her off the place, that if she would make a will, she would be moved off the place at once.

Q. Then what was done about this place?

A. Well, she said that she would let Frank have it the way it was, and she wouldn't make a will.

Later, Mrs. Greiner said she was going to give Frank a deed.

August Greiner, "Gustie," a son favored in the will, lives with his mother. He returned from California a few days after she had made the written contract to pay Nicholas $2,000. The money has not yet been paid. August had a fight with Frank and Albert, and brought an action against them on account of it. He testified he helped move the house from the quarter section to the 80-acre tract, but he testified he never heard that his mother intended to give the 80-acre tract to Frank. A crystal gazer could tell why no deed to Frank has been executed.

An omission is noted in the testimony of Louis Greiner quoted above. Louis testified it was a settled fact that Frank was to move on the eighty, and his mother gave him that place as his share. The matter omitted consisted of a single question and answer as follows: "Q. That she was going to give him that? A. Yes, sir." In that way the learned counsel for plaintiff adroitly turned a settled fact into a matter of future intention, and the appeal is based chiefly on that legal distinction. The contention is that Maggie Greiner was going to settle with the disinherited boys; she was going to give Frank land; she was going to give Frank the 80-acre tract; she was going to move the buildings; she was going to make a will; she was going to give Frank a deed; and these expressions of future intention did not make a contract with Frank that she would give him the 80-acre tract if he would move from Logan county to Mitchell county.

A promise for breach of which the law gives a remedy, or recognizes as creating a legal duty, is a contract. The promise need not be in any crystallized form of words: "I promise," "I agree," etc. Ritual scrupulousness is not required and, generally, any manifestation, by words or conduct or both, which the promisee is justified in understanding as an expression of intention to make a promise, is sufficient. Restatement Law of Contracts, Am. Law Inst., §§1, 2, 5. In this instance, there is no doubt whatever respecting the intention of Maggie Greiner, either before or after she first sent for Frank to come to Mitchell county. Indeed, she fulfilled her intention up to the point of the formal matter of executing and delivering a deed. The only question is whether the untutored woman — she could not write — sufficiently expressed a promise to Frank when he came down to see her in response to the letter from Nicholas. The court has no hesitation in saying that Mrs. Greiner did promise to give Frank land for a home if he would move back to Mitchell county. Just at that point the promise was unenforceable because of indefiniteness. No particular land was specified. But the offer was later made perfectly definite. The 80-acre tract was segregated for Frank, Mrs. Greiner fitted it for his occupancy as a home, and she gave him possession of it. Restatement Law of Contracts, Am. Law Inst., §32, Comment *c*.

Plaintiff says there was no consideration for Maggie Greiner's promise; she did everything for Frank, and he did nothing for her. Section 90 of the American Law Institute's Restatement of the Law of Contracts reads as follows:

> Section 90. Promise reasonably inducing definite and substantial action is binding. A promise which the promisor should reasonably expect to induce action or forbearance of a definite and substantial character on the part of the promisee and which does induce such action or forbearance, is binding if injustice can be avoided only by enforcement of the promise.

In this instance, Frank did give up his homestead in Logan county, did move to Mitchell county, did establish himself and his family on the 80-acre tract, made some lasting and valuable improvements upon it and made other expenditures, relying on his mother's promise; and he lived on the land for nearly a year before he was served with notice to quit.

It is not necessary to review the conflicting evidence in detail. The evidence satisfied the district court that Mrs. Greiner should execute a deed to Frank. On the evidence favorable to him, and the inferences derivable from the evidence favorable to him, this court cannot say it would not be unjust to deny him a deed and to put him off, and cannot say a money judgment would afford him adequate relief.

The judgment of the district court is affirmed.

Notes and Questions

1. *The evolution of promissory estoppel.* While Restatement §90 is usually referred to as "promissory estoppel," you will note that the text of the section does not use that term. In addition to providing a convenient label, the term "promissory estoppel" is useful in distinguishing promissory estoppel from its doctrinal forerunner, equitable estoppel. The doctrine of equitable estoppel (sometimes called "estoppel in pais") is generally said to apply where one party has made a misstatement of fact, rather than a promise. In its traditional form, equitable estoppel can be seen at work in cases like Colonial Theatrical Enterprises v. Sage, 237 N.W. 529 (Mich. 1931) (owner of leasehold interest in property estopped to assert ownership against bona fide purchaser who had relied on owner's disclaimer of interest) and Hetchler v. American Life Insurance Co., 254 N.W. 221 (Mich. 1934) (insurance company estopped to assert true expiration date of life insurance policy where the insured relied on company's statement of later date by failing to extend term of policy before his death). Prior to the solidification of promissory estoppel as a doctrine in the 1930s, some courts expanded the doctrine of equitable estoppel to enforce promises made between family members. See Ricketts v. Scothorn, 77 N.W. 365 (Neb. 1898) (promissory note given by grandfather to induce grand-daughter to stop work enforced under doctrine of equitable estoppel).

2. *When is reliance detrimental?* Although the text of Restatement §90 speaks only of enforcement in order to avoid "injustice," the section is routinely referred to as protecting "detrimental reliance." Do we know if Frank Greiner "detrimentally" relied on his mother's promise — that is, that he was worse off as a result of his reliance on that promise than he otherwise would have been? What facts would be relevant to that question?

3. *Moral obligation.* Although the facts of *Greiner* are somewhat sketchy, one can glimpse between the lines a picture of sibling rivalry, generational conflict, greed, envy, and all the other standard features of life in a large and propertied family, all of which are familiar to television "soap" viewers. Do you think Mrs. Greiner might have made her promises to Frank and his brother Nicholas out of feelings of "moral obligation"? If so, could that factor have affected the application of §90?

Wright v. Newman
Georgia Supreme Court
266 Ga. 519, 467 S.E.2d 533 (1996)

CARLEY, Justice.

Seeking to recover child support for her daughter and her son, Kim Newman filed suit against Bruce Wright. Wright's answer admitted his paternity only as to Newman's daughter and DNA testing subsequently showed that he is not the father of her son. The trial court nevertheless ordered Wright to pay child support for both children. As to Newman's son, the trial court based its order upon Wright's "actions in having himself listed on the child's birth certificate, giving the child his surname and establishing a parent-child relationship. . . . " According to the trial court, Wright had thereby

> allow[ed] the child to consider him his father and in so doing deterr[ed Newman] from seeking to establish the paternity of the child's natural father [,] thus denying the child an opportunity to establish a parent-child relationship with the natural father.

We granted Wright's application for a discretionary appeal so as to review the trial court's order requiring that he pay child support for Newman's son.

Wright does not contest the trial court's factual findings. He asserts only that the trial court erred in its legal conclusion that the facts authorized the imposition of an obligation to provide support for Newman's son. If Wright were the natural father of Newman's son, he would be legally obligated to provide support. OCGA §19-7-2. Likewise, if Wright had formally adopted Newman's son, he would be legally obligated to provide support. OCGA §19-8-19(a)(2). However, Wright is neither the natural nor the formally adoptive father of the child and "the theory of 'virtual adoption' is not applicable to a dispute as to who is legally responsible for the support of minor children." Ellison v. Thompson, 240 Ga. 594, 596, 242 S.E.2d 95 (1978).

Although Wright is neither the natural nor the formally adoptive father of Newman's son and the theory of "virtual adoption" is inapplicable, it does not necessarily follow that, as a matter of law, he has no legal obligation for child support. A number of jurisdictions have recognized that a legally enforceable obligation to provide child support can be "based upon parentage *or* contract. . . . " (Emphasis supplied.) Albert v. Albert, 415 So. 2d 818, 819 (Fla. App. 1982). See also Anno., 90 A.L.R.2d 583 (1963). Georgia is included among those jurisdictions. Foltz v. Foltz, 238 Ga. 193, 194, 232 S.E.2d 66 (1977). Accordingly, the issue for resolution is whether Wright can be held liable for child support for Newman's son under this state's contract law.

There was no formal written contract whereby Wright agreed to support Newman's son. Compare Foltz v. Foltz, supra. Nevertheless, under this state's contract law,

> [a] promise which the promisor should reasonably expect to induce action or forbearance on the part of the promisee or a third person and which does induce such action or forbearance is binding if injustice can be avoided only by enforcement of the promise. The remedy granted for breach may be limited as justice requires.

OCGA §13-3-44(a). This statute codifies the principle of promissory estoppel. Insilco Corp. v. First Nat. Bank of Dalton, 248 Ga. 322(1), 283 S.E.2d 262 (1981). In accordance with that principle,

[a] party may enter into a contract invalid and unenforceable, and by reason of the covenants therein contained and promises made in connection with the same, wrongfully cause the opposite party to forego a valuable legal right to his detriment, and in this manner by his conduct waive the right to repudiate the contract and become estopped to deny the opposite party any benefits that may accrue to him under the terms of the agreement.

Pepsi Cola Bottling Co. of Dothan, Ala., Inc. v. First Nat. Bank of Columbus, 248 Ga. 114, 116-117(2), 281 S.E.2d 579 (1981).

The evidence authorizes the finding that Wright promised both Newman and her son that he would assume all of the obligations and responsibilities of fatherhood, including that of providing support. As the trial court found, this promise was evidenced by Wright's listing of himself as the father on the child's birth certificate and giving the child his last name. Wright is presumed to know "the legal consequences of his actions. Since parents are legally obligated to support their minor children, [he] accepted this support obligation by acknowledging paternity." Marshall v. Marshall, 386 So. 2d 11, 12 (Fla. App. 1980). There is no dispute that, at the time he made his commitment, Wright knew that he was not the natural father of the child. Compare NPA v. WBA, 8 Va. App. 246, 380 S.E.2d 178 (1989). Thus, he undertook his commitment knowingly and voluntarily. Moreover, he continued to do so for some 10 years, holding himself out to others as the father of the child and allowing the child to consider him to be the natural father.

The evidence further authorizes the finding that Newman and her son relied upon Wright's promise to their detriment. As the trial court found, Newman refrained from identifying and seeking support from the child's natural father. Had Newman not refrained from doing so, she might now have a source of financial support for the child and the child might now have a natural father who provided emotional, as well as financial, support. If, after 10 years of honoring his voluntary commitment, Wright were now allowed to evade the consequences of his promise, an injustice to Newman and her son would result. Under the evidence, the duty to support which Wright voluntarily assumed 10 years ago remains enforceable under the contractual doctrine of promissory estoppel and the trial court's order which compels Wright to discharge that obligation must be affirmed. Nygard v. Nygard, 156 Mich. App. 94, 401 N.W.2d 323 (1986); Marshall v. Marshall, supra; In re Marriage of Johnson, 88 Cal. App. 3d 848, 152 Cal. Rptr. 121 (1979); Hartford v. Hartford, 53 Ohio App. 2d 79, 7 O.O.3d 53, 371 N.E.2d 591 (1977).

Judgment affirmed.

All the Justices concur, except BENHAM, C.J., who dissents.

SEARS, Justice, concurring.

I concur fully with the majority opinion. I write separately only to address the dissenting opinion's misperception that Newman has not relied upon Wright's promise to her detriment.

It is an established principle in Georgia that a promise which the promisor should reasonably expect to induce action or forbearance on the part of the promisee or a third person and which does induce such action or forbearance is binding if injustice can be avoided only by enforcement of the promise. This doctrine, known as "promissory estoppel," prevents a promisor from reneging on a promise, when the promisor should have expected that the promisee would rely upon the promise, and the promisee does in fact rely upon the promise to her detriment. Sufficient consideration to enforce a contractual promise pursuant to promissory estoppel may be found in any benefit accruing to the promisor, or any reliance, loss, trouble, disadvantage, or charge imposed upon the promisee.

Bearing these principles in mind, and as explained very well in the majority opinion, it is clear that Wright's commitment to Newman to assume the obligations of fatherhood as regards her son are enforceable. Specifically, it is abundantly clear that Wright should have known that Newman would rely upon his promise, especially after he undertook for ten years to fulfill the obligations of fatherhood. In this regard, it could hardly have escaped Wright's notice that Newman refrained from seeking to identify and obtain support from the child's biological father while Wright was fulfilling his commitment to her. Moreover, Newman did in fact rely upon Wright's promise, to her detriment when, ten years after he undertook the obligations of fatherhood, Wright reneged on his promise.

Promissory estoppel requires only that the reliance by the injured party be reasonable. In this case, it cannot seriously be argued that Newman's reliance was anything other than reasonable, as she had absolutely no indication that Wright would ever renege, especially after he fulfilled his promise for such a long time. Moreover, contrary to the dissent's implicit assertion, promissory estoppel does not require that the injured party exhaust all other possible means of obtaining the benefit of the promise from any and all sources before being able to enforce the promise against the promisor. In this regard, it is illogical to argue that Newman, after reasonably relying upon Wright's promise for ten years, can now simply seek to determine the identity of the biological father and collect support from him. First, there is nothing in the case law that requires Newman to do so before being entitled to have Wright's promise enforced. Second, this requirement would be an imposing, if not an impossible, burden, and would require Newman not only to identify the father (if possible), but also to locate him, bring a costly legal action against him, and to succeed in that action. Imposing this requirement would effectively penalize Newman for no reasons other than (1) her reasonable reliance upon a promise that was not kept, and (2) for allowing herself to be dissuaded by Wright from seeking the identity of the biological father. As noted, nowhere does the case law support imposing such a requirement, and none of the facts in this case support doing so now.

Finally, there can be no doubt that, unless Wright's promise to Newman is enforced, injustice will result. Given the approximately ten years that have passed since the child's birth, during which time Wright, for all purposes, was the child's father, it likely will be impossible for Newman to establish the identity of the child's biological father, bring a successful paternity action, and obtain support from that individual. Consequently, if Wright is allowed to renege on his obligation, Newman likely will not receive any support to assist in the cost of raising her son, despite having been promised the receipt of such by Wright. Furthermore, an even greater injustice will be inflicted upon the boy himself. A child who has been told by any adult, regardless of the existence of a biological relationship, that he will always be able to depend upon the adult for parenting and sustenance, will suffer a great deal when that commitment is broken. And when a child suffers under those circumstances, society-at-large suffers as well.[5]

Because Wright's promise is capable of being enforced under the law, and because I believe that Wright's promise must be enforced in order to prevent a grave miscarriage of justice, I concur fully in the majority opinion.

BENHAM, Chief Justice, dissenting.

I respectfully dissent. While I agree with the majority opinion's statement that liability for child support may be based on promissory estoppel in a case where there is no statutory obligation or express contract, I first note that this issue was not brought by either of the parties. Further, there is a critical element that must be shown for promissory estoppel to apply. In addition to making a showing of expectation and reasonable reliance, a person asserting liability on the theory of promissory estoppel must show that she relied on the promise to her detriment. Nickell v. IAG Federal Credit Union, 213 Ga. App. 516, 445 S.E.2d 335 (1994); Lake Tightsqueeze, Inc. v. Chrysler First Financial Services Corp., 210 Ga. App. 178, 435 S.E.2d 486 (1993). The majority states that Newman and her son incurred detriment by refraining from identifying and seeking support from the child's natural father. However, the record is completely bereft of any evidence that Newman met her burden of proof as to promissory estoppel, and the majority fails to state how she is prevented from now instituting a child support action against the natural father. Newman has not alleged, nor does the record reveal, that she does not know the identity of the natural father, nor does she show that the natural father is dead or unable to be found. Consequently, Newman has not shown that she is now unable to do what she would have had to do ten years ago — seek support from the natural father.

In fact, Wright contends, and Newman does not refute, that Newman severed the relationship and all ties with Wright when the child was approximately three years old. For approximately the next five years, until the child was eight, Newman and Wright did not communicate. Only for the past two years has Wright visited with the child. Importantly, Wright contends that during the past seven years he did not support the child. Thus, taking Wright's undisputed contentions as true, any prejudice incurred by Newman because of the passage of ten years in time is not due to Wright's actions, since, at least for the past seven years, Newman has been in the same situation — receiving no support payments from Wright. Thus, although Wright may be morally obligated to support the ten-year-old child, he is not legally obligated to do so because Newman has failed to show that she or the child incurred any detriment by Wright's failure to fulfill his promise made ten years ago.

For the foregoing reasons, I dissent.

---

5. Wright is also morally obligated to provide support for Newman's son. Merely because an obligation may not be capable of legal enforcement, one is not necessarily free to act in any way that he might choose. In addition to our legal duties, we are also bound by a consciousness of duty that is based upon fundamental values such as honor, truth, and responsibility. The "non-legal" obligations that we undertake are no less sacrosanct merely because they may not be capable of legal enforcement. The moral (as opposed to the legal) dilemma faced by Wright lies within his conscience, heart, and soul. He need have looked no further than there to determine what he must do in this case.

Notes and Questions

1. *Codification of common law.* As the court indicates, the Georgia legislature has adopted the doctrine of promissory estoppel by statute. In most jurisdictions, promissory estoppel, like other principles of contract law, has been recognized by common law court decision. Georgia is one of the few states that has attempted to codify significant principles of common law. Codification of the common law was a significant movement in the nineteenth century. Proponents of codification sought to simplify the law and to make the law more democratic by reducing the power of lawyers. See Mark D. Rosen, What Has Happened to the Common Law? — Recent American Codifications, and Their Impact on Judicial Practice and the Law's Subsequent Development, 1994 Wis. L. Rev. 1119. In the twentieth century, both the Restatement movement and the preparation of the Uniform Commercial Code represent attempts to bring order to the law, although the antilawyer aspects of earlier codification movements have not been as significant in these efforts. See generally Nathan M. Crystal, Codification and the Rise of the Restatement Movement, 54 Wash. L. Rev. 239 (1979). What advantages to statutory enactment of doctrines like promissory estoppel can you identify? What disadvantages might result?

2. *Implied promise as basis for promissory estoppel.* Wright apparently did not make an express promise to support the child. Instead, his promise to provide support was implied from the fact that he had listed himself as the father on the birth certificate and from the fact that he had given the child his last name. Courts seem to have generally recognized that an estoppel, whether promissory or equitable, can be based on conduct as well as an express promise. E.g., Division of Labor Law Enforcement v. Transpacific Transportation Co., 137 Cal. Rptr. 855 (Ct. App. 1977) (recognizing possibility of implied promise but finding no liability on facts of case); Nappi v. Nappi Distributors, 691 A.2d 1198 (Me. 1997) (promise may be implied from conduct). But see Simpson v. Murkowski, 129 P.3d 435 (Alaska 2006) (promissory estoppel requires actual promise that is very clear). Do you agree with the view that promissory estoppel can be based on an implied promise? Were the facts in *Wright* sufficient to establish an implied promise?

3. *Hypothetical variations of **Wright**.* Would it affect the result or the reasoning in *Wright* if

(a) Wright had been able to show who the actual father was and that the actual father was financially incapable of providing support?

(b) The majority and concurring opinions had accepted the dissent's asserted facts that Wright had not paid child support for seven years and had not seen the child during a period of five years?

(c) When he gave the child his name, Wright mistakenly believed that he was the child's father? See Smith v. Department of Human Resources, 487 S.E.2d 94 (Ga. Ct. App. 1997).

4. *Policy considerations.* Since Wright knew he was not the child's father, does the decision penalize him for beneficence? Will this decision discourage

people from voluntarily assuming support obligations for children they did not conceive?

We have previously discussed the justifications for the law imposing formal requirements as a condition of achieving a certain status or incurring certain obligations. See the excerpt from Lon Fuller's article, Consideration and Form, quoted in Note 7 following *Pennsy Supply* in Chapter 2. One of the purposes of legal formalities is to protect a party against making inadvertent or ill-considered commitments (the "cautionary" function). Suppose after the *Wright* case was decided, a member of the Georgia legislature introduced a bill that provides as follows: "A promise by a person to pay child support is not enforceable unless the person is the child's parent or the promise is made in writing under oath before a notary public or other official authorized to administer oaths." Would you favor such legislation? Why?

5. *The province of contract law. Wright* raises larger social issues of responsibility for out-of-wedlock children. To what extent should courts be concerned about these larger social problems when they render decisions? As a result of the *Wright* decision, principles of contract law can determine support obligations even when family law does not provide for such an obligation. Do you agree that support obligations should be based either on contract or family law principles, or should such obligations be limited to family law? Why? We will reencounter this issue in connection with our discussion of surrogate parent contracts in Chapter 7.

6. *Morality as a basis for legal obligation.* Justice Sears (concurring) in footnote 5 states that Wright is morally obligated to provide for Newman's son, and even dissenting Justice Benham appears to agree that Wright had this moral obligation. Do you agree? Should a judge's view of the morality of a party's actions affect the judge's legal analysis? Is such an effect on judicial decisionmaking inevitable whether the judge says so or not? Would it be proper for a judge to cite a religious text, such as the Bible or the Qur'an, in support of a moral proposition? In the next section we will consider when a promise may be enforceable because of a "moral obligation."

2. Charitable Subscriptions

If the bargain theory of consideration has as a principal function distinguishing exchanges from gifts (with enforcement to be accorded only to the former), then obviously charitable gifts will generally fall on the nonenforcement side of the line. In scores of charitable cases, courts have sought consideration for the subscriber's promise, but the consensus of legal commentators appears to be that such efforts are often unconvincing, reflecting more a desire to uphold the gift than a genuine finding that a bargain has been made. In his study of the roots of promissory estoppel, Professor Boyer discussed at length the charitable subscription cases, suggesting that the use of promissory estoppel in this area has afforded courts a measure of relief from the vexing problem of whether and how promises of charitable contributions should be legally enforced. Benjamin F. Boyer, Promissory Estoppel: Principle from Precedents

(Pt. 1), 50 Mich. L. Rev. 639, 644-653 (1952). The following case is a recent example.

King v. Trustees of Boston University
Supreme Judicial Court of Massachusetts
420 Mass. 52, 647 N.E.2d 1196 (1995)

ABRAMS, Justice.

A jury determined that Dr. Martin Luther King, Jr., made a charitable pledge to Boston University (BU) of certain papers he had deposited with BU. The plaintiff, Coretta Scott King, in her capacity as administratrix of the estate of her late husband, and in her individual capacity, appeals from that judgment. The plaintiff sued BU for conversion, alleging that the estate and not BU held title to Dr. King's papers, which have been housed in BU's library's special collection since they were delivered to BU at Dr. King's request in July, 1964.

The case was submitted to the jury on theories of contract, charitable pledge, statute of limitations, and laches. In response to special questions the jury determined that Dr. King made a promise to give absolute title to his papers to BU in a letter signed by him and dated July 16, 1964, and that the promise to give the papers was enforceable as a charitable pledge supported by consideration or reliance. The jury also determined that the letter promising the papers was not a contract. The jury accordingly did not reach BU's additional statute of limitations and laches defenses. The trial judge denied the plaintiff's motion for judgment notwithstanding the verdict or for a new trial. The plaintiff appealed. We granted the plaintiff's application for direct appellate review. We affirm.

I. *Facts.* In reviewing the judge's denial of the plaintiff's motion for directed verdict on the affirmative defense of charitable pledge, we summarize the evidence in a light favorable to the nonmoving party, BU. . . . In 1963, BU commenced plans to expand its library's special collections. Once plans for construction of a library to house new holdings were firm, the newly appointed director of special collections, Dr. Howard Gotlieb, began his efforts to obtain Dr. King's papers. Dr. King, an alumnus of BU's graduate school program, was one of the first individuals BU officials sought to induce to deposit documents in the archives.

Around the same time, Dr. King was approached regarding his papers by other universities, including his undergraduate alma mater, Morehouse College. Mrs. King testified that, although her late husband thought "Boston seemed to be the only place, the best place, for safety," he was concerned that depositing his papers with BU would evoke criticism that he was "taking them away from a black institution in the South." However, the volatile circumstances during the 1960s in the South led Dr. King to deposit some of his papers with BU pursuant to a letter, which is the centerpiece of this litigation and is set forth herewith:

563 Johnson Ave. NE
Atlanta, Georgia
July 16, 1964

Boston University Library
725 Commonwealth Ave.
Boston 15, Massachusetts

Dear Sirs:

On this 16th day of July, 1964, I name the Boston University Library the Repository of my correspondence, manuscripts and other papers, along with a few of my awards and other materials which may come to be of interest in historical or other research.

In accordance with this action I have authorized the removal of most of the above-mentioned papers and other objects to Boston University, including most correspondence through 1961, at once. It is my intention that after the end of each calendar year, similar files of materials for an additional year should be sent to Boston University.

All papers and other objects which thus pass into the custody of Boston University remain my legal property until otherwise indicated, according to the statements below. However, if, despite scrupulous care, any such materials are damaged or lost while in custody of Boston University, I absolve Boston University of responsibility to me for such damage or loss.

I intend each year to indicate a portion of the materials deposited with Boston University to become the absolute property of Boston University as an outright gift from me, until all shall have been thus given to the University. In the event of my death, all such materials deposited with the University shall become from that date the absolute property of Boston University.

Sincerely yours,
Martin Luther King, Jr. /s/

At issue is whether the evidence at trial was sufficient to submit the question of charitable pledge to the jury. BU asserts that the evidence was sufficient to raise a question of fact for the jury as to whether there was a promise by Dr. King to transfer title to his papers to BU and whether any such promise was supported by consideration or reliance by BU. We agree.

II. *Evidence of an enforceable charitable pledge.*[3] Because the jury found that BU had acquired rightful ownership of the papers via a charitable pledge, but not a contract, we review the case on that basis. We note at the outset that there is scant Massachusetts case law in the area of charitable pledges and subscriptions.

A charitable subscription is "an oral or written promise to do certain acts or to give real or personal property to a charity or for a charitable purpose." See generally E.L. Fisch, D.J. Freed, & E.R. Schacter, Charities and Charitable Foundations §63, at 77 (1974). To enforce a charitable subscription or a charitable pledge in Massachusetts, a party must establish that there was a

3. The term "subscription" and "pledge" are frequently used interchangeably. . . . See generally Annot., Lack of Consideration as Barring Enforcement of Promise to Make Charitable Contribution or Subscription-Modern Cases, 86 A.L.R.4th 241 (1991). We note that, because of the bailor-bailee relationship between the donor and charitable institution, the transaction here technically is a charitable pledge. See R.A. Brown, Personal Property §15.1, at 469 (3d ed. 1975) (defining a pledge as "a bailment of personal property to secure an obligation of the bailor").

promise to give some property to a charitable institution and that the promise was supported by consideration or reliance. Congregation Kadimah Toras-Moshe v. DeLeo, 405 Mass. 365, 367 & n. 3, 540 N.E.2d 691 (1989), and cases cited therein.[4] See In re Morton 1200 Shoe Co., 40 B.R. 948 (Bankr. D. Mass. 1984) (discussing Massachusetts law of charitable subscriptions).

The jurors were asked two special questions regarding BU's affirmative defense of rightful ownership by way of a charitable pledge: (1) "Does the letter, dated July 16, 1964, from Martin Luther King, Jr., to [BU], set forth a promise by Dr. King to transfer ownership of his papers to [BU]?"; and (2) "Did [BU] take action in reliance on that promise or was that promise supported by consideration?" In determining whether the case properly was submitted to the jury, we consider first, whether the evidence was sufficient to sustain a conclusion that the letter contained a promise to make a gift and second, whether the evidence was sufficient to support a determination that any promise found was supported by consideration or reliance.

III(A). *Evidence of a promise to make a gift.* The plaintiff argues that the terms of the letter promising "to indicate a portion of the materials deposited with [BU] to become the absolute property of [BU] as an outright gift . . . until all shall have been thus given to [BU]," could not as a matter of basic contract law constitute a promise sufficient to establish an inter vivos charitable pledge because there is no indication of a bargained for exchange which would have bound Dr. King to his promise. The plaintiff asserts that the above-quoted excerpt (hereinafter "first statement") from the letter merely described an unenforceable "unilateral and gratuitous mechanism by which he might" make a gift of the papers in the future but by which he was not bound. In support of her position that Dr. King did not intend to bind himself to his statement of intent to make a gift of the papers he deposited with BU, the plaintiff points to the language which appears above the promise to make gifts of the deposited papers that "[a]ll papers and other objects which thus pass into the custody of [BU] remain my legal property until otherwise indicated,

4. In Congregation Kadimah Toras-Moshe v. DeLeo, 405 Mass. 365, 540 N.E.2d 691 (1989), the Congregation sued the estate of a decedent who had made an oral gratuitous promise to give $25,000 to the synagogue. The Congregation planned to spend the $25,000 on renovation of a storage room in the synagogue into a library. The oral promise was never memorialized in a writing or consummated by delivery before the decedent died intestate. Noting that "[a] hope or expectation, even though well founded, is not equivalent to either legal detriment or reliance," id. at 366-367, 540 N.E.2d 691, we affirmed the judgment of the trial court that the oral charitable subscription was not enforceable because it was oral, not supported by consideration, and without evidence of reliance.

By requiring that a promise to make a charitable subscription be supported by consideration or reliance, we declined to adopt the standard for enforceable charitable subscriptions set forth in the Restatement (Second) of Contracts §90 (1981). See id. at 368, 540 N.E.2d 691. Section 90(1), as modified for charitable subscriptions by subsection (2), provides that, "[a] promise which the promisor should reasonably expect to induce action or forbearance on the part of the promisee or a third person . . . is binding if injustice can be avoided only by enforcement of the promise. . . ." We noted that, although §90 thus dispenses with a strict requirement of consideration or reasonable reliance for a charitable subscription to be enforceable, the official comments to the Restatement make clear that consideration and reliance remain relevant to whether the promise must be enforced to avoid injustice. Id. See Arrowsmith v. Mercantile-Safe Deposit & Trust Co., supra 313 Md. at 353-354, 545 A.2d 674 (rejecting argument that court should adopt Restatement [Second] of Contracts §90[2]); Jordan v. Mount Sinai Hosp. of Greater Miami, Inc., supra at 108 ("Courts should act with restraint in respect to the public policy arguments endeavoring to sustain a mere charitable subscription. To ascribe consideration where there is none, or to adopt any other theory which affords charities a different legal rationale than other entities, is to approve fiction").

according to the statements below." According to the plaintiff, because of Dr. King's initial retention of legal ownership, BU could not reasonably rely on the letter's statements of intent to make a gift of the papers. We do not agree.

The letter contains two sentences which might reasonably be construed as a promise to give personal property to a charity or for a charitable purpose. The first statement, quoted above, is that Dr. King intended in subsequent installments to transfer title to portions of the papers in BU's custody until all the papers in its custody became its property. The second statement immediately follows the first, expressing an intent that "[i]n the event of [Dr. King's] death, all . . . materials deposited with [BU] shall become from that date the absolute property of [BU]" (hereinafter "second statement"). BU claims that these two sentences should be read together as a promise to make a gift of all of the papers deposited with it at some point between the first day of deposit and at the very latest, on Dr. King's death.

Before analyzing the first and second statements, we note the considerations governing our review. A primary concern in enforcing charitable subscriptions, as with enforcement of other gratuitous transfers such as gifts and trusts, is ascertaining the intention of the donor. . . . If donative intent is sufficiently clear, we shall give effect to that intent to the extent possible without abandoning basic contractual principles, such as specificity of the donor's promise, consideration, and reasonableness of the charity's reliance. *DeLeo*, supra 405 Mass. at 368 n. 5, 540 N.E.2d 691. In determining the intention of Dr. King as expressed in the letter and the understanding BU had of that letter, we look first to the language of the letter, in its entirety, but also consider the circumstances and relationship of the parties with respect to the papers.

III(A)(1). *First statement.* Regarding the first statement, the plaintiff contends that it is not a promise but a mere statement of intent to do something in the future. . . . However, our interpretation of that first statement is strongly influenced by the bailor-bailee relationship the letter unequivocally establishes between Dr. King and BU.

A bailment is established by "delivery of personalty for some particular purpose, or on mere deposit, upon a contract, express or implied, that after the purpose has been fulfilled it shall be redelivered to the person who delivered it, or otherwise dealt with according to his directions, or kept until he reclaims it, as the case may be." 9 S. Williston, Contracts §1030 (3d ed. 1967), quoting State v. Warwick, 48 Del. 568, 576, 108 A.2d 85 (1954). . . . The terms of the letter establish a bailment in which certain "correspondence, manuscripts and other papers, along with a few of [Dr. King's] awards" were placed in "the custody of [BU]." The bailed papers were to "remain [Dr. King's] legal property until otherwise indicated." By accepting delivery of the papers, BU assumed the duty of care as bailee set forth in the letter, that of "scrupulous care." . . .

Generally there will be a case for the jury as to donative intent if property allegedly promised to a charity or other eleemosynary institution is placed by the donor in the custody of the donee.[5] The bailor-bailee relationship

---

5. We do not suggest that bailment of property allegedly promised to a bailee-charity creates an irrebuttable presumption of donative intent on the part of the bailor. Nor do we suggest that we would weigh bailment more heavily than evidence that the parties agreed to conditions or terms of a bailment that express a lack of donative intent.

established in the letter could be viewed by a rational factfinder as a security for the promise to give a gift in the future of the bailed property, and thus as evidence in addition to the statement in the letter of an intent of the donor to be bound. Furthermore, while we have been unwilling to abandon fundamental principles of contract law in determining the enforceability of charitable subscriptions, see *DeLeo*, supra 405 Mass. at 368 n. 4, 540 N.E.2d 691, second par. (declining to adopt Restatement [Second] of Contracts rule that charitable subscriptions enforceable without consideration or reliance where justice so requires), we do recognize that the "meeting of minds" between a donor and a charitable institution differs from the understanding we require in the context of enforceable arm's-length commercial agreements. Charities depend on donations for their existence, whereas their donors may give personal property on conditions they choose, with or without imposing conditions or demanding consideration. In re Field's Will, 15 Misc. 2d 950, 951, 181 N.Y.S.2d 922 (1959), modified, 11 A.D.2d 774, 204 N.Y.S.2d 947 (1960) ("Charitable subscription agreements can rarely be regarded as part of a bargaining agreement that provide for a quid pro quo"). In combination with the letter and in the context of a disputed pledge to a charity, the bailment of Dr. King's letters provided sufficient evidence of donative intent to submit to the jury the questions whether there was a promise to transfer ownership of the bailed property and whether there was consideration or reliance on that promise.[6]

III(A)(2). *Second statement.* [The second statement in Dr. King's letter — "In the event of my death, all such materials deposited with the University shall become from that date the absolute property of Boston University" — posed an additional legal issue because it did not take effect until his death. The plaintiff argued that this statement amounted to a will and that it was therefore unenforceable because it failed to comply with the statutory formalities for a will, including the requirement of at least two subscribing witnesses. The court rejected this argument. It found that the statute of wills did not prevent a person from making a contract or a promise to take effect at his death, and that was what Dr. King had done. — Eds.]

III(B). *Evidence of consideration or reliance.* The judge did not err in submitting the second question on charitable pledge, regarding whether there was consideration for or reliance on the promise, to the jury. "It may be found somewhat difficult to reconcile all the views which have been taken, in the various

---

Intent is our primary concern and a bailment may be evidence of donative intent. However, a bailor and a bailee-charity may agree to a contractual bailment in terms that make clear that the bailed property is not being pledged as a future gift or that the bailed property may remain in the custody of the charity or become the charity's property only if certain conditions are met. . . .

6. The jury could have found on that evidence alone that the first statement in the letter expressing an intent to give all papers in BU's custody to it at some future date was not a mere statement of future intent when the bailment relationship is considered. However, there was evidence in addition to the bailor-bailee relationship which justified submission of the special questions on whether there was a charitable pledge to the jury. First, there was evidence the papers would be appraised for (Dr. King's) tax purposes. Second, as promised in the letter, Dr. King delivered additional papers after the initial boxes of papers were delivered. This evidence could be considered by a jury in determining whether Dr. King intended to be bound by his promise. Thus, the trial judge did not err in submitting to the jury the first special question on charitable pledge. There was evidence which the jury could weigh in determining whether the statement of intent to give a gift of portions of the papers was an expression of an intent to be bound.

cases that have arisen upon the validity of promises, where the ground of defence has been that they were gratuitous and without consideration." Ives v. Sterling, 6 Met. 310, 315 (1843). There was evidence that BU undertook indexing of the papers, made the papers available to researchers, and provided trained staff to care for the papers and assist researchers. BU held a convocation to commemorate receipt of the papers. Dr. King spoke at the convocation. In a speech at that time, he explained why he chose BU as the repository for his papers.

As we explained above, the letter established that so long as BU, as bailee, attended the papers with "scrupulous care," Dr. King, as bailor, would release them from liability for "any such materials . . . damaged or lost while in [its] custody." The jury could conclude that certain actions of BU, including indexing of the papers, went beyond the obligations BU assumed as a bailee to attend the papers with "scrupulous care" and constituted reliance or consideration for the promises Dr. King included in the letter to transfer ownership of all bailed papers to BU at some future date or at his death. Trustees of Amherst Academy v. Cowls, 6 Pick. 427, 431 (1828) ("It seems that an actual benefit to the promisor, or an actual loss or disadvantage to the promisee, will be a sufficient consideration to uphold a promise deliberately made. Whether the consideration received is equal in value to the sum promised to be paid, seems not to be material to the validity of a note . . . "); *Ives*, supra at 317-319; Ladies' Collegiate Inst. v. French, 16 Gray 196, 202 (1860).

The issue before us is not whether we agree with the jury's verdict but whether the case was properly submitted to the jury. We conclude that the letter could have been read to contain a promise supported by consideration or reliance; "[t]he issue [of whether transfer of ownership to BU was transferred by way of a charitable pledge by Dr. King] was, therefore, properly submitted to the jury, and their verdicts, unless otherwise untenable, must stand." Carr v. Arthur D. Little, Inc., 348 Mass. 469, 474, 204 N.E.2d 466 (1965) (evidence sufficient as matter of contract law to raise question of fact for jury as to existence of common employment). . . .

Judgment affirmed.

Notes and Questions

1. *Analyzing the **King** case.* Dr. King's letter had two statements expressing his intention regarding his papers. Was it necessary for the court to find both statements legally enforceable? Why? Note that the *King* case was brought in Massachusetts and decided by a Massachusetts jury. Do you think a Georgia jury would have been more sympathetic to the claim of Dr. King's estate? Why? Why was the case brought in Massachusetts rather than Georgia? What happens to Dr. King's papers that were not on deposit with BU at his death?

2. *The Restatement's proposed rule for charitable subscriptions.* As finally adopted by the American Law Institute, Restatement (Second) §90(2) provides, "A charitable subscription or a marriage settlement is binding under Subsection (1) without proof that the promise induced action or forbearance." A handful of courts have considered whether to adopt the approach of §90(2), jettisoning

entirely the requirement of either consideration or reliance for enforcement of charitable subscriptions. Only one has done so. See Salsbury v. Northwestern Bell Telephone Co., 221 N.W.2d 609 (Iowa 1974). The *Salsbury* court offered the following rationale for its decision: "Charitable subscriptions often serve the public interest by making possible projects which otherwise could never come about. . . . [In addition,] where a subscription is unequivocal the pledgor should be made to keep his word." Id. at 613.

In *King* the Supreme Judicial Court of Massacusetts joins several other courts that have rejected §90(2), but it does not offer any reasons for refusing to accept the Restatement recommendation. In Maryland National Bank v. United Jewish Appeal Federation, 407 A.2d 1130 (Md. 1979), the Maryland court justified its rejection of §90(2) on the following grounds:

> UJA would have us "view traditional contract law requirements of consideration liberally" in order to maintain what it believes to be a judicial policy of favoring charities. We deeply appreciate the fact that private philanthropy serves a highly important function in our society. . . . But we are not persuaded that we should, by judicial fiat, adopt a policy of favoring charities at the expense of the law of contracts which has been long established in this state. We do not think that this law should be disregarded or modified so as to bestow a preferred status upon charitable organizations and institutions. It may be that there are cases in which judgments according to the law do not appear to subserve the purposes of justice, but this, ordinarily, the courts may not remedy. "It is safer that a private right should fail, or a wrong go unredressed, than that settled principles should be disregarded in order to meet the equity of a particular case." . . . If change is to be made it should be by legislative enactment, as in the matter of the tax status of charitable organizations.

Id. at 1135-1136. Would a shift in the law to the approach set forth in Restatement §90(2) be desirable? What effect do you think it would have on charitable organizations and their potential financial supporters?

3. *Other case examples.* Of course, even the adoption of Restatement §90(2) does not necessarily mean that a charitable subscription will be enforceable. See Congregation Kadimah Toras-Moshe v. DeLeo, 540 N.E.2d 691 (Mass. 1989) (even if court were to adopt Restatement §90(2), there is no injustice in refusing to enforce decedent's oral promise made shortly before his death to donate $25,000; congregation's allocation of gift to its budget was insufficient reliance on the promise). How does Boston University's reliance in *King* compare to the plaintiff's reliance in *Congregation Kadimah Toras-Moshe*?

While courts have generally refused to adopt Restatement §90(2), they have on the whole been sympathetic to the claims of charitable organizations to enforce pledges. In the leading case of Allegheny College v. National Chautauqua County Bank, 159 N.E.173 (1927), Justice Cardozo of the New York Court of Appeals held that a pledge to the plaintiff college by a donor, later deceased, was binding contractually on the ground that the college made an "implied promise" to memorialize the donor's name, thus creating an enforceable bilateral contract. In "dictum" (statements by a court not necessary to the decision of the case) Cardozo also indicated that the doctrine of promissory estoppel could be used to enforce donative promises that had been relied on by charities. Cardozo suggested that the willingness of courts to find liability on the basis of either a contract or promissory estoppel rested on public policy. In a later New York case, Woodmere

Academy v. Steinberg, 363 N.E.2d 1169 (N.Y. 1977), the New York Court of Appeals enforced Mr. Steinberg's pledge in the unpaid amount of $200,000. Steinberg decided not to honor the pledge because he had moved from the community, his children were no longer attending the Academy, and he had decided to redirect the funds to support the State of Israel. The Court rejected Steinberg's argument that the Academy had failed to honor various conditions to the pledge, noting that "as a matter of public policy, pledge agreements calculated to enforce eleemosynary enterprises are enforceable." Id. at 1172. On the facts of the case, Steinberg's pledge was probably enforceable either on the basis of consideration or promissory estoppel because the Academy had renamed its library in honor of Steinberg's wife.

4. *Practical and legal constraints.* The authors of a comprehensive study of the enforceability of charitable pledges conclude that although courts have generally been willing to enforce pledges on any of a variety of legal theories, "[w]hen it comes to enforcing pledges, charities have demonstrated a timidity not characteristic of their solicitation practices." Mary Frances Budig et al., Pledges to Non-Profit Organizations: Are They Enforceable and Must They Be Enforced? at 3 (1993) (Program on Philanthropy and the Law, N.Y.U. Law School). The study concludes that changes in financial and accounting practices of charities in recent years are "forcing charities to deal more responsibly in pursuing pledges." Id. at 4. In particular, Financial Accounting Standard (FAS) 116 now requires charities to treat pledges as assets on their financial statements. As the report notes: "An 'asset' is more tangible than a 'pledge', and directors will have a stronger and more immediate duty to protect a pledge/asset." Id. at 83.

Comment *b* to Restatement (Second) §90 suggests generally that whether a promise should be enforced may depend in part on "the extent to which the evidentiary, cautionary, deterrent and channeling functions of form are met." In In re Payson, N.Y.L.J., July 26, 1978, at 14, a New York Surrogate's Court enforced a promise to donate nearly $1.5 million (the unpaid balance of a $5 million gift promised during the decedent's lifetime) to the Metropolitan Museum of Art. Although there was substantial evidence that the promise was in fact made and adhered to by the decedent during her lifetime, the original promise was oral and informally made. While upholding the enforceability of the gift, the court cautioned both donors and charities against treating such gifts casually. Urging charities to adhere to "prudent business methods," the court noted that informality exposes donors (or their estates) to the risk of unforeseen tax problems. And, the court observed, even charities that are successful in obtaining court enforcement of casually made pledges may suffer harm: Potential donors could become more reticent about making gifts. In connection with the court's admonition about the dangers of informal practices by charities, consider the following problem.

PROBLEM 3-1

You are a legislative aide to a member of your state legislature. Another member of the legislature has introduced the following act dealing with charitable subscriptions:

Charitable Subscription Act

Section 1. Preamble. The legislature finds that uncertainty exists in this state as to the binding effect of charitable subscriptions or pledges. To protect the interests of charities and donors, and to reduce litigation, the legislature hereby adopts the following act, which shall be known as the "Charitable Subscription Act."

Section 2. Binding Charitable Subscription. A donor may make a charitable subscription or pledge that is legally binding against the donor or his estate, even though not supported by consideration, and not otherwise enforceable as a completed gift or contract, if it satisfies either of the following requirements:

(a) If the subscription is on a written form supplied by the charity, it must contain in bold face type, at least 10 point in size, on the front of the form, the following statement: **Legally Binding Pledge.**

(b) If the subscription is not on a form supplied by the charity, it must be in writing, signed by the donor, and contain clear language showing that the donor intends to make a legally binding subscription or pledge.

An oral pledge, not evidenced by a writing, shall be conclusively presumed to be nonbinding and may be revoked by the donor at any time until the gift is completed. In construing this act, in case of doubt, a court shall construe a pledge or subscription as nonbinding.

Section 3. Effective Date. This Act shall take effect for all charitable pledges or subscriptions made after _____.

Your boss has asked you the following questions:

(a) What changes in the law would be made by the adoption of this act?
(b) As a matter of policy, would adoption of the act be wise?

Prepare a memorandum that addresses these questions.

3. Promises in a Commercial Context

Although significant amounts of money or property were often at stake, the cases examined earlier in this section did not involve transactions of the sort one ordinarily thinks of as commercial. Of course, one might view the operation of modern charitable organizations as commercial in every sense other than profitmaking; many of them receive and pay millions of dollars each year and in the course of their activities enter into all kinds of contracts for goods and services. (Cf. the suggestion in UCC §2-104, Comment 2 that for some purposes a university — and, presumably, other nonprofit entities such as a hospital or even a church — should be considered a "merchant," as that term is used in the Code.) But the promises of contributions made to charities have generally been viewed by donor and donee alike as essentially gratuitous, made from altruistic motives rather than for the purpose of reciprocal financial gain.

In its early days, the principle of promissory estoppel was often viewed as appropriately confined to the noncommercial sphere, with one significant exception: employee benefit or pension cases. But see Kevin M. Teeven, Origins of Promissory Estoppel: Justifiable Reliance and Commercial

Uncertainty Before Williston's Restatement, 34 U. Mem. L. Rev. 499 (2004) (arguing that beginning in the 1860s, during periods of economic uncertainty, courts protected justifiable reliance on commercial promises). You will recall from the *Plowman* case that an employer's promise to pay a pension or other benefit at or after retirement might not satisfy the requirement of bargained-for exchange. Professor Boyer's history of promissory estoppel showed that employee bonus and pension plan cases made an important contribution to the genesis of §90. In fact, one of the few illustrations to the original Restatement §90 presented such a case:

> 2. *A* promises *B* to pay him an annuity during *B's* life. *B* thereupon resigns a profitable employment, as *A* expected that he might. *B* receives the annuity for some years, in the meantime becoming disqualified from again obtaining good employment. *A's* promise is binding.

In his 1960 survey of the case law under §90, however, Professor Stanley Henderson concluded that promissory estoppel had outgrown any earlier limitations and that protection of unbargained-for reliance on commercial promises had become its principal application. Stanley D. Henderson, Promissory Estoppel and Traditional Contract Doctrine, 78 Yale L.J. 343, 343-344 (1960). In the previous chapter we saw situations in which courts have employed the doctrine of promissory estoppel to enforce promises in a commercial context where mutual assent is absent or incomplete. Here we examine a few situations in which courts have employed the doctrine to enforce commercial promises even in the absence of consideration.

Katz v. Danny Dare, Inc.
Missouri Court of Appeals
610 S.W.2d 121 (1980)

TURNAGE, Presiding Judge.

I. G. Katz filed three suits in the Associate Division of the Circuit Court seeking pension payments for three separate time periods alleged to be due from Danny Dare, Inc. Two suits resulted in judgment in favor of Katz, but a request for a trial de novo was filed and those cases were assigned to a circuit judge for trial. The other suit pending in the Associate Division was transferred to the same circuit judge and all the cases were consolidated for trial without a jury. Judgment was entered in favor of Dare in all cases. On this appeal Katz contends the promise of pension payments made to him by Dare is binding under the Doctrine of Promissory Estoppel. Reversed and remanded.

There is little or no dispute as to the facts in this case. Katz began work for Dare in 1950 and continued in that employ until his retirement on June 1, 1975. The president of Dare was Harry Shopmaker, who was also the brother of Katz's wife. Katz worked in a variety of positions including executive vice president, sales manager, and a member of the board of directors, although he was not a member of the board at the time of his retirement. In February

1973, Katz was opening a store, operated by Dare, for business and placed a bag of money on the counter next to the cash register. A man walked in, picked up the bag of money and left. When Katz followed him and attempted to retrieve the money, Katz was struck in the head. He was hospitalized and even though he returned to work he conceded he had some difficulties. His walk was impaired and he suffered some memory loss and was not able to function as he had before. Shopmaker and others testified to many mistakes which Katz made after his return at considerable cost to Dare. Shopmaker reached the decision that he would have to work out some agreeable pension to induce Katz to retire because he did not feel he could carry Katz as an employee. At that time Katz's earnings were about $23,000 per year.

Shopmaker began discussions with Katz concerning retirement but Katz insisted that he did not want to retire but wanted to continue working. Katz was 65 at the time of his injury and felt he could continue performing useful work for Dare to justify his remaining as an employee. However, Shopmaker persisted in his assessment that Katz was more of a liability than an asset as an employee and continued negotiating with Katz over a period of about 13 months in an effort to reach an agreement by which Katz would retire with a pension from Dare. Shopmaker first offered Katz $10,500 per year as a pension but Katz refused. Thereafter, while Katz was on vacation, Shopmaker sent Katz a letter to demonstrate how Katz could actually wind up with more take-home pay by retiring than he could by continuing as an employee. In the letter Shopmaker proposed an annual pension payable by Dare of $13,000, added the Social Security benefit which Katz and his wife would receive after retirement, and added $2,520 per year which Katz could earn for part-time employment, but not necessarily from Dare, to demonstrate that Katz would actually realize about $1,000 per year more in income by retiring with the Dare pension over what he would realize if he continued his employment. Shopmaker testified that he sent this letter in an effort to persuade Katz to retire.

Katz acceded to the offer of a pension of $13,000 per year for life, and on May 22, 1975, the board of directors of Dare unanimously approved the following resolution:

> WHEREAS, I. G. Katz has been a loyal employee of Danny Dare, Inc. and its predecessor companies for more than 25 years; and,
> WHEREAS, the said I. G. Katz has requested retirement because of failing health; and,
> WHEREAS, it has been the custom in the past for the company to retire all executives having loyally served the company for many years with a remuneration in keeping with the sum received during their last five years of employment;
> NOW THEN BE IT RESOLVED, that Danny Dare, Inc. pay to I. G. Katz the sum of $500.00 bi-weekly, or a total of $13,000.00 per year, so long as he shall live.

Katz retired on June 1, 1975, at age 67, and Dare began payment of the pension at the rate of $500 every other week. Katz testified that he would not have retired without the pension and relied on the promise of Dare to pay the pension when he made his decision to retire. Shopmaker testified that at the time the board resolution was passed, the board intended for Katz to rely on the resolution and to retire, but he said Katz would have been fired had he not elected to retire.

In the Fall of 1975, Katz began working for another company on 3 to 4 half-days per week. At the end of that year Shopmaker asked Katz if he could do part-time work for Dare and Katz told him he could work one-half day on Wednesdays. For the next two and one-half years Katz continued to work for Dare one-half day per week.

In July, 1978, Dare sent a semi-monthly check for $250 instead of $500. Katz sent the check back and stated he was entitled to the full $500. Thereafter Dare stopped sending any checks. Shopmaker testified that he cut off the checks to Katz because he felt Katz's health had improved to the point that he could work, as demonstrated by the part-time job he held. Katz testified the decrease was made after Shopmaker told him he would have to work one-half day for five days a week for Dare or his pension would be cut in half. Katz testified, without challenge, that he was not able to work 40 hours per week in 1978 at age 70.

The trial court entered a judgment in which some findings of fact were made. The court found that Katz based his claim on the Doctrine of Promissory Estoppel as applied in Feinberg v. Pfeiffer Company, 322 S.W.2d 163 (Mo. App. 1959). The court found that Katz was not in the same situation as Feinberg had been because Katz faced the prospect of being fired if he did not accept the pension offer whereas there was no such evidence in the *Feinberg* case. The court found the pension from Dare did not require Katz to do anything and he was in fact free to work for another company. The court found Katz did not give up anything to which he was legally entitled when he elected to retire. The court found that since Katz had the choice of accepting retirement and a pension or being fired, that it could not be said that he suffered any detriment or significant change of position when he elected to retire. The court further found that it could not find any injustice resulting to Katz because by the time payments had been terminated, he had received about $40,000 plus a paid vacation for his wife and himself to Hawaii. The court found these were benefits he would not have received had he been fired.

Katz contends he falls within the holding in *Feinberg* and Dare contends that because Katz faced the alternative of accepting the pension or being fired that he falls without the holding in *Feinberg*.

At the outset it is interesting to note in view of the argument made by Dare that the court in *Feinberg* stated at p.165:

> It is clear from the evidence that there was no contract, oral or written, as to plaintiff's length of employment, and that she was free to quit, and the defendant to discharge her, at any time.

In *Feinberg* the board of directors passed a resolution offering Feinberg the opportunity to retire at any time she would elect with retirement pay of $200 per month for life. Feinberg retired about two and one-half years after the resolution was passed and began to receive the retirement pay. The pay continued for about seven years when the company sent a check for $100 per month, which Feinberg refused and thereafter payments were discontinued.

The court observed that Section 90 of the Restatement of the Law of Contracts had been adopted by the Supreme Court in In Re Jamison's Estate, 202 S.W.2d 879 (Mo. 1947). The court noted that one of the illustrations under §90 was strikingly similar to the facts in *Feinberg*. The court applied the Doctrine of Promissory Estoppel, as articulated in §90, and held that Feinberg had relied upon the promise of the pension when she resigned a paying position and elected to accept a lesser amount in pension. The court held it was immaterial as to whether Feinberg became unable to obtain other employment before or after the company discontinued the pension payment. The court held the reliance by Feinberg was in giving up her job in reliance on the promise of a pension. Her subsequent disability went to the prevention of injustice which is part of the Doctrine of Promissory Estoppel.

There are three elements to be satisfied to invoke the Doctrine of Promissory Estoppel. These are: (1) a promise; (2) a detrimental reliance on such promise; and (3) injustice can be avoided only by enforcement of the promise.

This court is not convinced that the alternative Shopmaker gave to Katz of either accepting the pension and retiring or be fired takes this case out of the operation of Promissory Estoppel. The fact remains that Katz was not fired, but instead did voluntarily retire, but only after the board of directors had adopted the resolution promising to pay Katz a pension of $13,000 per year for life. Thus, the same facts are present in this case as were present in *Feinberg*. When Katz elected to retire and give up earnings of about $23,000 per year to accept a pension of $13,000 per year, he did so as a result of a promise made by Dare and to his detriment by the loss of $10,000 per year in earnings. It is conceded Dare intended that Katz rely on its promise of a pension and Dare does not contend Katz did not in fact rely on such promise. The fact that the payments continued for about three years and that Katz at age 70 could not work full-time was unquestioned. Thus, the element that injustice can be avoided only by enforcement of the promise is present, because Katz cannot now engage in a full-time job to return to the earnings which he gave up in reliance on the pension.

Dare's argument that the threat of being fired removes this case from the operation of Promissory Estoppel is similar to an argument advanced in Trexler's Estate, 27 Pa. Dist. & Co. Rep. 4 (1936), cited with approval in Fried v. Fisher, 328 Pa. 497, 196 A. 39 (1938). In *Trexler* the depression had forced General Trexler to decide whether to fire several employees who had been with him for many years or place them on a pension. The General decided to promise them a pension of $50 per month and at his death, the employees filed a claim against his estate for the continuation of the payments. The court observed that the General could have summarily discharged the employees, but was loath to do this without making some provision for their old age. This was shown by the numerous conferences which the General had with his executives in considering each employee's financial situation, age and general status. The court said it was clear that the General wanted to reduce overhead and at the same time wanted to give these faithful employees some protection. The court stated it as an open question of what the General would have done if the men had not accepted his offer of a lifetime pension. The court said it would not speculate on that point but it was sufficient to observe that the men accepted the offer and received the pension. The court applied §90 of the

Restatement and held that under the Doctrine of Promissory Estoppel the estate was bound to continue the payments.

The facts in this case are strikingly similar to *Trexler*. Shopmaker undoubtedly wanted to reduce his overhead by reducing the amount being paid to Katz and it is true that Katz could have been summarily discharged. However, it is also true that Shopmaker refused to fire Katz, but instead patiently negotiated for about 13 months to work out a pension which Katz did agree to accept and voluntarily retired.

While Dare strenuously urges that the threat of firing effectively removed any legitimate choice on the part of Katz, the facts do not bear this out. The fact is that Katz continued in his employment with Dare until he retired and such retirement was voluntary on the part of Katz. Had Shopmaker desired to terminate Katz without any promise of a pension he could have done so and Katz would have had no recourse. However, the fact is that Shopmaker did not discharge Katz but actually made every effort to induce Katz to retire voluntarily on the promise of a pension of $13,000 per year.

Dare appears to have led the trial court into error by relying on Pitts v. McGraw-Edison Co., 329 F.2d 412 (6th Cir. 1964). Pitts was informed that the company had retired him and would pay him a certain percentage of sales thereafter. Thus, the main distinction between this case and *Pitts* is that Pitts did not elect to retire on the promise of any payment, but was simply informed that he had been retired by the company and the company would make payment to him. There was no promise made to Pitts on which he acted to his detriment. In addition, the court was applying the law of Tennessee and the court stated that Tennessee had not adopted §90 of the Restatement. The court in *Pitts* found that Pitts had not given up anything to which he was legally entitled and was not restricted in any way in his activities after being placed in retirement by his company.

The facts in *Pitts* would not enable Pitts to recover under Promissory Estoppel in Missouri because there was no action taken by Pitts in reliance on a promise. The test to be applied in this case is not whether Katz gave up something to which he was legally entitled, but rather whether Dare made a promise to him on which he acted to his detriment. The legally entitled test could never be met by an employee such as Katz or Feinberg because neither could show any legal obligation on the company to promise a pension. The Doctrine of Promissory Estoppel is designed to protect those to whom a promise is made which is not legally enforcible until the requirements of the doctrine are met. *Pitts* is not applicable either on the facts or the law.

The trial court misapplied the law when it held that Katz was required to show that he gave up something to which he was legally entitled before he could enforce the promise of a pension made by Dare. The elements of Promissory Estoppel are present: a promise of a pension to Katz, his detrimental reliance thereon, and injustice can only be avoided by enforcing that promise. The judgment is reversed and the case is remanded with directions to enter judgment in all suits in favor of Katz for the amount of unpaid pension.

All concur.

Notes and Questions

1. *Analyzing the **Katz** case.* The trial court in *Katz* found that Katz "did not give up anything to which he was legally entitled when he elected to retire." Was the trial court simply (and mistakenly) applying the test for consideration? Or did it have something else in mind? In the Court of Appeals' opinion, Judge Turnage states, "The legally entitled test could never be met by an employee such as Katz or Feinberg because neither could show any legal obligation on the company to promise a pension." Of course, if Danny Dare had already been obligated to pay Katz a pension, then Katz wouldn't have needed to rely on the doctrine of promissory estoppel to enforce the company's promise. Can the trial court really have meant something that obvious? Or is the Court of Appeals unfairly representing the trial court's position? What do you think the trial court probably meant by the "not legally entitled" explanation of its decision? Is its position persuasive?

2. *When is reliance detrimental?* Although Restatement §90 does not use the term "detrimental reliance," that phrase has often been used to refer to the section's requirement that the promise induce "action or forbearance" by the promisee. In many actions in which promissory estoppel is involved, the plaintiff will have made actual expenditures in reliance on the promise. Such conduct not only satisfies the requirement of "action or forebearance" in reliance on the promise but also constitutes reliance that is detrimental to the plaintiff. As the *Katz* case indicates, however, a change of position will often be sufficient to invoke promissory estoppel even if the conduct does not involve an expenditure of funds. Further, in some cases a change of position that might be viewed as financially beneficial can nonetheless support an action for promissory estoppel. A case illustrative of such a situation is Vastoler v. American Can Co., 700 F.2d 916 (3d Cir. 1983). Vastoler accepted a promotion to a supervisory position in part because of the employer's promise of certain pension benefits. When the employer subsequently denied making the promise, Vastoler brought suit on the basis of promissory estoppel. The trial court granted summary judgment for the employer on the ground that Vastoler did not suffer financial loss because he was better off economically having accepted the supervisory position. In reversing that decision, the Court of Appeals made the following remarks on the issue of detrimental reliance:

> The second error in the district court's reasoning involves an even more fundamental deficiency. It failed to consider the human dynamics and anxieties inherent in supervisory positions. All jobs are not the same, and work involves more than one's "daily bread" and the weekly paycheck. Certain jobs have higher levels of stress and anxiety. Often, increased responsibilities torture the mind as well as the body. The different levels of stress associated with different jobs explains why some qualified people do not want to be President of Fortune 500 corporations, nominee for the Presidency of the United States, or foreman of their plants. Some privates do not want the decision-making burdens of majors and generals. . . .
>
> A jury could certainly find that when Vastoler changed his position from an hourly worker responsible for his individual tasks to a salaried supervisor responsible for approximately fifty subordinate employees he was forced to absorb additional stress and emotional trauma. As a supervisor, he would have had the additional responsibility for assigning jobs to workers, disciplining workers, and perhaps recommending that

some be fired or laid off. The stress and emotional trauma inherent in such a supervisory position cannot be measured in purely financial terms. Therefore, the presence of detrimental reliance in this case is a sufficiently disputed issue for the trier of fact that summary judgment cannot be granted to American Can Company.

Id. at 919.

3. *Katz* **compared with** *Hayes.* Not all employees have been as successful as Mr. Katz. In Hayes v. Plantations Steel Co., 438 A.2d 1091 (R.I. 1982), the plaintiff Hayes, after 25 years of employment, announced his decision to retire, effective in six months. One week before his actual date of retirement, Hayes met with an officer of the defendant company, who promised him that the company "would take care" of him. After Hayes's retirement, the company paid him a pension for four years but stopped doing so because of financial conditions and a change of ownership. The trial court ruled that the company was contractually bound to pay Hayes his pension, but the Supreme Court reversed. The Court first held that even if the company had made a promise, the promise was not supported by consideration. Citing the classical requirement of consideration as bargained-for exchange, the Court concluded that Hayes's retirement could not constitute consideration because he announced his decision before the company made its promise. For similar reasons the court rejected Hayes's promissory estoppel theory. Under that theory Hayes was required to show that the promise induced detrimental reliance, and he could not do so because his decision to retire preceded the promise. Do you think the factual differences between *Katz* and *Hayes* warrant different legal results? For further discussion and comparison of *Katz* and *Hayes*, see Charles L. Knapp, Rescuing Reliance: The Perils of Promissory Estoppel, 49 Hastings L.J. 1191, 1254-1261 (1998).

4. *Federal law governing benefit plans.* In 1974 Congress enacted the Employee Retirement Income Security Act of 1974 (commonly known as ERISA), 29 U.S.C. §1001 et seq. ERISA is a highly specialized body of law, but for our purpose it is sufficient to know that the act applies to an "employee benefit plan," a term that is broadly defined to include both retirement benefits and welfare benefits, such as medical insurance. Id. at §1002. Danny Dare's promise to Katz would not have been covered by ERISA because it did not amount to a "plan." To be an ERISA plan, the obligation requires the creation of an ongoing administrative program. A one-time obligation is not sufficient to amount to a plan. See Fort Halifax Packing Co. v. Coyne, 482 U.S. 1, 12 (1987).

Shoemaker v. Commonwealth Bank
Pennsylvania Superior Court
700 A.2d 1003 (1997)

JOHNSON, Judge:

We are asked to determine whether a mortgagor who is obligated by a mortgage to maintain insurance on the mortgaged property can establish a cause of action in promissory estoppel based upon an oral promise made by the mortgagee to obtain insurance. We find no merit in those portions of the instant case sounding in fraud and breach of contract. We conclude, nevertheless, that a mortgagee's promise to obtain insurance can be actionable on a theory of promissory estoppel. Accordingly, on this appeal from the order granting summary judgment to the mortgagee, we affirm in part, reverse in part and remand for further proceedings.

Lorraine and Robert S. Shoemaker obtained a $25,000 mortgage on their home from Commonwealth Bank (Commonwealth). The mortgage agreement provided that the Shoemakers were required to "carry insurance" on the property. By January 1994, the Shoemakers had allowed the home-owners' insurance policy covering their home to expire. In 1995, the Shoemakers' home, still uninsured, was destroyed by fire. The parties disagree as to the series of events that occurred after the insurance had lapsed.

The Shoemakers allege that Commonwealth sent a letter to them, dated January 20, 1994, that informed them that their insurance had been cancelled and that if they did not purchase a new insurance policy, Commonwealth might "be forced to purchase [insurance] and add the premium to [their] loan balance." The Shoemakers further allege that Mrs. Shoemaker received a telephone call from a representative of Commonwealth in which the representative informed her that if the Shoemakers did not obtain insurance, Commonwealth would do so and would add the cost of the premium to the balance of the mortgage. The Shoemakers assert that they assumed, based on the letter and phone conversation, that Commonwealth had obtained insurance on their home. They also contend that they received no further contact from Commonwealth regarding the insurance and that they continued to pay premiums as a part of their loan payments. Only after the house burned, the Shoemakers allege, did they learn that the house was uninsured.

Commonwealth, on the other hand, admits that it sent the letter of January 20, but denies the Shoemakers' allegations regarding the contents of the alleged conversation between its representative and Mrs. Shoemaker. Commonwealth further claims that it obtained insurance coverage for the Shoemakers' home and notified them of this fact by a letter dated February 4, 1994. Commonwealth also asserts that it elected to allow this coverage to expire on December 1, 1994, and that, by the letter dated October 25, 1994, it informed the Shoemakers of this fact and reminded them of their obligation under the mortgage to carry insurance on the property. The Shoemakers deny receiving any letter from Commonwealth regarding the insurance other than the letter dated January 20, 1994, that informed them that their policy had expired.

After the house burned down, Mrs. Shoemaker sued Commonwealth, alleging causes of action in fraud, promissory estoppel and breach of contract; the basis for all three causes of action was Commonwealth's alleged failure to obtain insurance coverage for the Shoemaker home. By order of the court, Mr. Shoemaker was joined as an involuntary plaintiff. Commonwealth then filed a motion for summary judgment.

The trial court granted Commonwealth's motion. The court noted that, even if Commonwealth had promised to obtain insurance on the Shoemakers' home, it made no representation regarding the duration of that coverage. The court concluded that because Commonwealth had actually obtained insurance, even though the policy later expired, it had fulfilled its promise to the Shoemakers. Thus, the court reasoned that because Commonwealth had made no misrepresentation and breached no promise, the Shoemakers could not prevail on any of their causes of action. Mrs. Shoemaker now appeals. . . .

[The court first ruled that the trial court was correct in granting summary judgment for the bank on the Shoemakers' fraud claim. While Mrs. Shoemaker testified that the bank's representative had "said that they would acquire insurance for me," summary judgment was proper because as a matter of law "the breach of a promise to do something in the future is not actionable in fraud." — EDS.]

Mrs. Shoemaker next argues that the trial court erred by granting summary judgment on their promissory estoppel claim. The doctrine of promissory estoppel allows a party, under certain circumstances, to enforce a promise even though that promise is not supported by consideration. See Thatcher's Drug Store of West Goshen, Inc. v. Consolidated Supermarkets, Inc., 535 Pa. 469, 476, 636 A.2d 156, 160 (1994); Restatement (Second) of Contracts §90. To establish a promissory estoppel cause of action, a party must prove that: (1) the promisor made a promise that he should have reasonably expected would induce action or forbearance on the part of the promisee; (2) the promisee actually took action or refrained from taking action in reliance on the promise; and (3) injustice can be avoided only by enforcing the promise. Holewinski v. Children's Hospital of Pittsburgh, 437 Pa. Super. 174, 178, 649 A.2d 712, 714 (1994), appeal denied, 540 Pa. 641, 659 A.2d 560 (1995); Cardamone v. University of Pittsburgh, 253 Pa. Super. 65, 74, 384 A.2d 1228, 1233 (1978).

In their complaint, the Shoemakers allege that Commonwealth promised that it would purchase "adequate insurance" and add the cost of the premium to the cost of their loan. They further allege that they relied on this promise by not purchasing the insurance on their own and that injustice can be avoided only by enforcing Commonwealth's promise. Commonwealth, on the other hand, argues that the Shoemakers cannot enforce their claim through promissory estoppel because of the Shoemakers' contractual obligation to maintain insurance under the mortgage. Further, Commonwealth argues that even if such a promise was actionable, the facts alleged by the Shoemakers are insufficient to support their claim because they have not alleged that Commonwealth promised to maintain such insurance for a particular duration.

Our research has not discovered any Pennsylvania cases that have addressed the question of whether a mortgagor who is obligated by a mortgage to maintain insurance on their property can establish a cause of action in promissory estoppel based upon an oral promise made by the mortgagee to obtain insurance. We have, however, discovered cases from other jurisdictions that have addressed this question, and the weight of this authority holds that such promises are actionable.

In Graddon v. Knight, 138 Cal. App. 2d 577, 292 P.2d 632 (1956), a California appellate court considered whether homeowners, who were obligated under a deed of trust to procure and maintain fire insurance on their home, could establish a cause of action based upon an oral promise by a bank to obtain the insurance on the homeowners' behalf. The court first considered whether the bank's promise to obtain fire insurance was inconsistent with the term of the deed of trust that required the homeowners to [maintain the insurance. The court] concluded that the bank's promise was not inconsistent with the homeowners' obligation under the deed of trust because the deed required only that the homeowners procure and maintain insurance; the deed did not bar them from making a separate agreement under which another party would procure the insurance on their behalf. Id. at 635-36. The court then held that the evidence presented by the plaintiffs was sufficient to establish a cause of action in promissory estoppel because the plaintiffs relied to their detriment on the bank's promise to obtain insurance. Id. at 636-37. . . . In accord with these cases, illustration 13 to comment e of section 90 of the Restatement (Second) of Contracts provides:

> A, a bank, lends money to B on the security of a mortgage on B's new home. The mortgage requires B to insure the property. At the closing of the transaction A promises to arrange for the required insurance, and in reliance on the promise B fails to insure. Six months later the property, still uninsured, is destroyed by fire. The promise is binding.

Restatement (Second) of Contracts §90, cmt. e, illus. 13. See also Murphy v. Burke, 454 Pa. 391, 398, 311 A.2d 904, 908 (1973) (adopting section 90 as Pennsylvania law). We find this authority persuasive and thus we reject Commonwealth's claim that the Shoemakers cannot maintain a cause of action because of their obligation under the mortgage to maintain insurance on the property.

We must next determine whether the Shoemakers' allegations and the evidence that they have presented are sufficient to create genuine issues of material fact with regard to each element of a promissory estoppel cause of action and thus survive Commonwealth's motion for summary judgment. The first element of a promissory estoppel cause of action is that the promisor made a promise that he should reasonably have expected to induce action or forbearance on the part of the promisee. *Holewinski,* supra, at 178, 649 A.2d at 714. The Shoemakers have alleged that the bank promised to obtain insurance on their behalf and that it would add this cost to their mortgage payment. Mrs. Shoemaker testified in her deposition and swore in an affidavit that a representative from Commonwealth stated that the bank would acquire insurance if she did not and that she instructed the representative to take that action. Because the Shoemakers claim that Commonwealth's promise to obtain insurance was, essentially, conditioned upon the Shoemakers' course of conduct, i.e., that Commonwealth would obtain insurance if they did not, we conclude that this evidence, if believed, would be sufficient to allow a jury to find that Commonwealth made a promise upon which it reasonably should have expected the Shoemakers to rely. See *Holewinski,* supra.

The second element of a promissory estoppel cause of action is that the promisee actually relied upon the promise. Id. at 178, 649 A.2d at 714. The Shoemakers allege that they actually relied upon Commonwealth's promise and, thus, failed to obtain insurance. In support of this allegation, Mrs. Shoemaker testified in her deposition and swore in her affidavit that she instructed Commonwealth's representative to acquire insurance on her behalf.

We conclude that this evidence, if believed, would be sufficient to allow a jury to find that the Shoemakers relied upon Commonwealth's promise to obtain insurance. See *Holewinski,* supra.

The final element of a promissory estoppel cause of action is that injustice can be avoided only by enforcement of the promise. Id. at 178, 649 A.2d at 714. One of the factors that a court may consider in determining whether a promisee has satisfied this element is "'the reasonableness of the promisee's reliance.'" *Thatcher's Drug Store,* supra, at 477, 636 A.2d at 160, quoting Restatement (Second) of Contracts §90, cmt. b. Mrs. Shoemaker testified that she and her husband received no communication from Commonwealth regarding their insurance after her conversation with a Commonwealth representative in early 1994. Commonwealth, on the other hand, asserts that it sent the Shoemakers letters informing them that their house would be uninsured after December 1, 1994. We conclude that this evidence is sufficient to create a genuine issue of material fact regarding the reasonableness of the Shoemakers' reliance. Accordingly, we hold that the trial court erred by granting summary judgment on the Shoemakers' promissory estoppel claim.

. . .

We therefore reverse that portion of the trial court's order that granted summary judgment on the Shoemakers' promissory estoppel claim and remand for trial on that claim. We affirm the grant of summary judgment on the Shoemakers' fraud and breach of contract claims.

. . .

Notes and Questions

1. *Analyzing **Shoemaker**.* Consider the following questions:

(a) Although the court does not focus on this fact, Mrs. Shoemaker testified at her deposition that she could not have gotten home-owners' insurance on her own: "I told them go ahead and do so because at that point I was in no financial situation to do so on my own." 700 A.2d at 1006. Is this fact legally significant? Why?

(b) The court mentions but does not address the bank's argument that a cause of action for promissory estoppel did not lie because, even if the bank made a promise to obtain insurance for the Shoemakers, the promise did not have a duration. What response would you give to this argument?

(c) A significant issue in the case revolves around the alleged letter from the bank dated October 25, 1994. The bank claims that in this letter it informed the Shoemakers that they would be required to maintain insurance on their home after December 1, 1994. Mrs. Shoemaker testified that she never received this letter. What lawyering lessons can you learn from this factual dispute?

(d) Suppose the mortgage documents signed by the Shoemakers stated that no agreement or modification would be legally binding on the bank unless set forth in a writing signed by the bank. Should such a provision have been relevant to the Shoemakers' claim? Why? Should it have been conclusive? Why?

2. *Promissory fraud.* The court states that the Shoemakers' allegations against the bank were legally insufficient to establish fraud because they had alleged nothing more than a breach of promise by the bank to do something in the future. As the court states, while a breach of promise may be actionable under either a contract or promissory estoppel theory, it is not normally actionable as fraud because fraud requires a misrepresentation of a present fact rather than a promise to do something in the future. In some cases, however, a breach of promise may be fraudulent—if the promisor did not intend to perform the promise at the time the promise was made. In such a case the promisor has misrepresented a present fact, namely the promisor's intention to perform the promise. Restatement (Second) of Torts §530 provides as follows: "A representation of the maker's own intention to do or not to do a particular thing is fraudulent if he does not have that intention." See, e.g., Gerhardt v. Harris, 934 P.2d 976 (Kan. 1997) (client stated cause of action for fraud against lawyer when client alleged that lawyer promised to abide by decision of fee dispute board without intention of doing so).

3. *The functions of form.* Recall Professor Fuller's suggestion that legal "forms" (in which category he suggested "consideration" might be placed) serve a variety of functions in a legal system, among them the "cautionary" function of "acting as a check against inconsiderate action," and also the "channeling" function of distinguishing conduct that has legal consequences from conduct that does not. Does the promissory estoppel cause of action as applied by the court in *Shoemaker* serve these purposes?

4. *Other commercial cases.* Since its promulgation in the 1930s, §90 has been applied to enforce a wide variety of promises in commercial situations. See, e.g., Cohen v. Cowles Media Co., 479 N.W.2d 387 (Minn. 1992) (news source allowed to recover on promissory estoppel theory from newspaper that breached promise of confidentiality); Chesus v. Watts, 967 S.W.2d 97 (Mo. Ct. App. 1998) (homeowners association had standing to bring promissory estoppel claim against developers to enforce promise to turn over common areas in good repair).

On the other hand, it should not be thought that the mere mention of promissory estoppel will cause a court to roll over and play dead. Courts have typically denied recovery when the defendant *failed to make a promise* on which liability could be based or when the plaintiff *failed to establish detrimental reliance.* See, e.g., Creative Demos, Inc. v. Wal-Mart Stores, Inc., 142 F.3d 367 (7th Cir. 1998) (food demonstration contractor failed to establish detrimental reliance element of promissory estoppel claim against grocery store chain for refusal to honor promise to retain contractor's services through specific date when contractor continued to earn substantial profit after promise was made); Jones v. Best, 950 P.2d 1 (Wash. 1998) (en banc) (vendor's promissory estoppel defense against real estate agent failed because evidence showed that real estate agent did not make promise to accept reduced commission).

5. *The Restatement (Second) view of promissory estoppel.* In light of the widespread acceptance of promissory estoppel as enunciated in §90 of the first Restatement, it is not surprising that the drafters of the Restatement (Second)

chose to retain and expand the doctrine. As we noted earlier, the new §90 has an additional subsection providing for enforcement of charitable subscriptions even without a showing of detrimental reliance. In addition, the drafters revised the text of §90 by adding a reference to the possibility of third-party reliance, by indicating that the remedy to be awarded "may be limited as justice requires," and by deleting the requirement that reliance to be protectible must be "definite and substantial." Various aspects of the Restatement (Second) approach to promissory estoppel are considered in Charles L. Knapp, Reliance in the Revised *Restatement:* The Proliferation of Promissory Estoppel, 81 Colum. L. Rev. 52 (1981). On the issue of third-party recovery, see Michael B. Metzger & Michael J. Phillips, Promissory Estoppel and Third Parties, 42 Sw. L.J. 931 (1988).

6. *The CISG and promissory estoppel.* In Geneva Pharmaceuticals Technology Corp. v. Barr Laboratories, 201 F. Supp.2d 236 (S.D.N.Y. 2002), plaintiff pharmaceutical manufacturer asserted a variety of claims against defendant competitor and raw material supplier, including antitrust, breach of contract, and tort. Because the plaintiff was an American corporation and the defendant Canadian, the CISG governed their contractual relations, and preempted the plaintiff's state law contract claims. Plaintiff's tort claims, on the other hand, were clearly not preempted. The plaintiff also asserted a promissory estoppel claim, however, and the court had to decide whether that was preempted along with the contract claim. Noting that the CISG in Article 16(2)(b) recognizes reliance, the court indicated that perhaps a reliance claim intended to establish a "firm offer" would be preempted by that provision. (Compare CISG Art. 16(2)(b) to Restatement (Second) §87(2), which we considered in the previous chapter.) Here, however, the plaintiff's claim of promissory estoppel was a more general one asserted to make a promise binding, and the court held such a claim not to be preempted by the CISG.

Comment: The Status and Future of Promissory Estoppel

In its infancy, promissory estoppel was generally regarded as a principle to which the court should resort only after conventional contract analysis had failed to produce recovery; its function was to serve as a "substitute" for some element of the classical system that was insufficiently satisfied by the case at hand. As the doctrine developed over the years, it came to have an independent significance, to be viewed not just as a subcategory of "contract," but as a distinct theory of action — one not necessarily grounded in the principles of contract or circumscribed by its limitations. An exploration of this development can be found in an article by Professors Michael Metzger and Michael Phillips, The Emergence of Promissory Estoppel as an Independent Theory of Recovery, 35 Rutgers L. Rev. 472 (1983). See also Kevin M. Teeven, A History of Promissory Estoppel: Growth in the Face of Doctrinal Resistance, 72 Tenn. L. Rev. 1111 (2005).

The remarkable growth and expansion of promissory estoppel since its incorporation in the first Restatement led Professor Knapp to conclude in 1981 that promissory estoppel had become "perhaps the most radical and expansive development of this century in the law of promissory liability." Charles L. Knapp, Reliance in the Revised *Restatement:* The Proliferation of Promissory Estoppel, 81 Colum. L. Rev. 52, 53 (1981). In a comprehensive review of the status of promissory estoppel almost two decades later, however, Professor Knapp suggested that a "reassessment appears to be in order," and that "1980 may have been the high-water mark for promissory estoppel." Charles L. Knapp, Rescuing Reliance: The Perils of Promissory Estoppel, 49 Hastings L.J. 1191, 1192 (1998). See also E. Allan Farnsworth, Developments in Contract Law During the 1980's: The Top Ten, 41 Case W. Res. L. Rev. 203, 219-220 (1990) (failure of promissory estoppel to make headway in overcoming formal barriers to contract enforcement included as one of top ten developments). Two factors support Professor Knapp's more cautious appraisal of the current status of promissory estoppel: critical scholarly commentary and relative lack of success of promissory estoppel claims in the courts.

Since the early 1980s many scholars have questioned the intellectual foundations of promissory estoppel. Some writers have been directly critical of the doctrine. Professor Jay Feinman has criticized promissory estoppel as outmoded and has instead argued for courts to focus on relational principles in contract cases. Jay M. Feinman, The Last Promissory Estoppel Article, 61 Fordham L. Rev. 303 (1992). See also Jay M. Feinman, Promissory Estoppel and Judicial Method, 97 Harv. L. Rev. 678, 718 (1984) (finding that none of the various modes of decisionmaking used by judges in promissory estoppel cases produce either certainty or objectivity). Professor Michael Gibson has contended that Karl Llewellyn, the principal architect of the UCC, strongly believed that reliance should play no role in enforcing commercial promises. Michael Gibson, Promissory Estoppel, Article 2 of the U.C.C., and the Restatement (Third) of Contracts, 73 Iowa L. Rev. 659 (1988).

More significant than outright criticism, however, has been the rise of "assent-based" theories of liability. In a highly influential article written in 1985, Professors Daniel Farber and John Matheson studied more than 200 promissory estoppel cases decided during a ten-year period. They concluded that courts are enforcing promises seriously made in a commercial context *even in the absence of reliance:*

> The traditional view of contract law divides promissory liability into two categories. By far the larger category involves the bargained-for exchange of promises for other consideration. These bargains are enforced, even in the absence of reliance, in order to protect the parties' expectation that future conduct will be governed by present commitments. The other, much smaller category, is that of promissory estoppel. Here, liability is imposed to remedy the injury to promisees who have relied on promises in vain.
>
> Based on our survey of recent promissory estoppel cases, we believe that promissory estoppel is losing its link with reliance. In key cases promises have been enforced with only the weakest showing of any detriment to the promisee. Reliance-based damages are the exception, not the rule. With the decline of reliance, promissory estoppel is moving away from tort law. It has become a means of enforcing promises differing in doctrinal detail from traditional contract law but sharing a common goal. That goal, we have argued, is to foster trust between economic actors. Trust is a moral good, but it is also an economic asset. It allows

coordination and planning between economic actors and fosters the formation of valuable economic institutions.

Daniel A. Farber & John H. Matheson, Beyond Promissory Estoppel: Contract Law and the "Invisible Handshake," 52 U. Chi. L. Rev. 903, 945 (1985). Subsequently, Professors Yorio and Thel seconded the Farber/Matheson conclusion that courts were basing liability on assent. Edward Yorio & Steve Thel, The Promissory Basis of Section 90, 101 Yale L.J. 111 (1991). Other articles adopting the assent-based approach to contractual liability include the following: Randy E. Barnett, The Death of Reliance, 46 J. Legal Ed. 518 (1996); Randy E. Barnett & Mary E. Becker, Beyond Reliance: Promissory Estoppel, Contract Formalities, and Misrepresentations, 15 Hofstra L. Rev. 443 (1987); Juliet P. Kostritsky, A New Theory of Assent-Based Liability Emerging Under the Guise of Promissory Estoppel: An Explanation and Defense, 33 Wayne L. Rev. 895 (1987).

In one sense, the assent-based scholars could be seen as strengthening promissory estoppel, by finding liability even in the absence of detrimental reliance. But, as Professor Knapp argues in his Hastings Law Journal article, at a more fundamental level, eliminating or reducing the focus on reliance undermines the equitable foundations that are at the heart of promissory estoppel. Rescuing Reliance: The Perils of Promissory Estoppel, 49 Hastings L.J. at 1333-1334 (1998).

The second factor that seems to have contributed to the decline of promissory estoppel is the relative lack of success of the doctrine in the courts. While virtually every jurisdiction has accepted the doctrine, see Eric Mills Holmes, Restatement of Promissory Estoppel, 32 Willamette L. Rev. 263 (1996), promissory estoppel claims are rarely successful. In an empirical study of promissory estoppel cases during the period from July 1, 1994 through June 30, 1996, Professor Robert Hillman concludes that promissory estoppel has been successful in less than 10 percent of the cases in which it has been asserted. Robert A. Hillman, Questioning the "New Consensus" on Promissory Estoppel: An Empirical and Theoretical Study, 98 Colum. L. Rev. 580, 589 (1998) (tables 1.1 and 1.2). See also Robert A. Hillman, The Unfulfilled Promise of Promissory Estoppel in the Employment Setting, 31 Rutgers L.J. 1 (1999). Accord Sidney W. DeLong, The New Requirement of Enforcement Reliance in Commercial Promissory Estoppel: Section 90 as Catch-22, 1997 Wis. L. Rev. 943 (arguing that promissory estoppel has not become a major source of commercial obligation). But see Juliet P. Kostritsky, The Rise and Fall of Promissory Estoppel or Is Promissory Estoppel Really as Unsuccessful as Scholars Say It Is: A New Look at the Data, 37 Wake Forest L. Rev. 531 (2002) (based on a five-year survey of cases, concluding that promissory estoppel remains a vital theory in contract law, especially when qualitative factors rather than win/loss ratios are considered).

Interestingly, however, Professor Hillman also concludes, contrary to the assent-based theorists, that in those recent cases in which promissory estoppel has been successfully asserted as a basis of recovery, the factor of actual reliance has played a significant role. 98 Colum. L. Rev. at 597 (table 4.1). He reaches the same conclusion about the earlier cases discussed by Farber and Matheson: "The promise theorists' assertion of the relative unimportance of reliance," Hillman asserts, "seems much less persuasive after reviewing the cases and arguments to support it." The cases they rely on "are not impressive in number and can be read in more than one way." An "alternative reading" of those cases, he concludes, "suggests the importance of both promise and reliance." 98 Colum. L. Rev. at 618.

In his wide-ranging review of the history and scholarship on promissory estoppel, Professor Knapp argues that much is at stake in the debate over the role of reliance:

> And this, finally, is what it all comes down to. For our contract law system to work properly, it cannot consist only of law, any more than it could consist only of equity. Equity without law would be tyranny indeed — shapeless, unpredictable, reflecting nothing more than the judge's personal predilections. But in the contract area, as we have seen, law without equity can be tyranny, too: cold and unforgiving; rewarding wealth and power with still greater wealth and power; repaying trust with betrayal; and finally — tritely but truly — adding insult to injury. With the aid of equitable doctrines like promissory estoppel to counter-balance the weight of legal rules, the courts in this area can continue the never-ending process of tightrope-walking that is contract decision-making. Without them, we are back where we were a century ago.

Rescuing Reliance: The Perils of Promissory Estoppel, 49 Hastings L.J. at 1334 (1998).

B. LIABILITY FOR BENEFITS RECEIVED: THE PRINCIPLE OF RESTITUTION

The material in this section introduces you to a body of law now known as "restitution." In its inception, the law of restitution had contractual roots. Beginning in the latter part of the eighteenth century, however, judges and scholars began to think of restitutionary actions as distinct from contract law. During the twentieth century, restitution broke away from its contractual origins and became a separate body of law. Although restitution has achieved independence from contract law, the concept of restitution is still extremely important to contract law because many restitutionary actions arise out of contractual relationships.

One of the most perplexing problems that students face in trying to understand the concept of restitution is a confusing array of terms: *implied contract, implied-in-fact contract, implied-in-law contract, quasi contract, common counts, quantum meruit,* and *quantum valebat,* to mention a few. The text that follows attempts to clarify this muddle by focusing on the historical development of the right to restitution. (Even if the textual material helps to clarify your understanding of these terms, do not be surprised if court opinions you read confuse the terms or use them loosely.)

As we saw earlier, in our discussion of the history of consideration, before Slade's Case, 76 Eng. Rep. 1074 (1602), the common law courts drew the boundary between the action of assumpsit and the action of debt on the basis of whether an express promise was made. If a person sold goods or provided services to another on request, the action of debt would lie against the recipient. If the recipient, in addition, expressly promised to pay for the goods or services after they were received, assumpsit was available. In Slade's Case, the Exchequer Chamber held that every executory contract implied a promise. As a result, assumpsit would lie even in the absence of an express promise. Because it was more favorable procedurally than debt, assumpsit soon replaced debt as the action to recover the price of goods or services.

After Slade's Case, standardized forms of pleading, called "common counts," were developed for use in typical cases arising under assumpsit, such as actions to recover the promised price of goods sold, services performed, or money loaned. At about the same time, common counts were also developed for recovery of the reasonable value of goods delivered ("quantum valebat") or services performed ("quantum meruit"). Technically, these actions were separate from assumpsit because the claim was for an unliquidated sum rather than a sum certain. Eventually, however, these new forms of action were absorbed into the general action of assumpsit. In all of these actions, liability was originally based on a consensual transaction. Soon, however, the courts expanded liability to nonconsensual situations by making use of the concept of an "implied promise." Thus, by the end of the seventeenth century, an action in assumpsit was also available in many nonconsensual situations. For example, if a bank or other commercial party made an overpayment by mistake, the amount of the overpayment could be recovered in an action of assumpsit. See A.W.B. Simpson, A History of the Common Law of Contract 489-505 (1987); James B. Ames, The History of Assumpsit (Pt. II), 2 Harv. L. Rev. 53, 63-69 (1888) (history of common law developments).

Ultimately, the nonconsensual basis of some of the situations in which assumpsit was available was recognized and expressed. In 1760, Lord Mansfield, in Moses v. Macferlan, 97 Eng. Rep. 676, faced the question of whether assumpsit could be used in an action for money had and received when no express agreement had been made and it was impossible under the facts to imply an agreement. Mansfield stated,

> If the defendant be under an obligation, from the ties of natural justice, to refund; the law implies a debt, and gives this action, founded in the equity of the plaintiff's case, as it were upon a contract ("quasi ex contractu," as the Roman law expresses it).

97 Eng. Rep. at 678. After that time, it became common to speak of two types of implied contracts that were actionable in assumpsit, one being "implied-in-fact" and the other "implied-in-law" (quasi contract).

In the United States, the concept of quasi-contractual liability founded on unjust enrichment was widely accepted, but the scope of liability remained unclear. During the last 100 years, scholars have begun to pay increasing attention to this developing field of law. In 1937 the American Law Institute (ALI) published its Restatement of Restitution a major attempt at systematic treatment of the field. The reporters for the Restatement consciously rejected the term *quasi contract*, selecting instead the label *restitution*, which was broader in at least two ways. First, while the term *quasi contract* implies a relationship to contract law, the modern law of restitution is based on unjust enrichment and has no particular relationship to contract. Although some restitutionary situations arise in a contractual context, many do not. For example, restitution is available when a person has wrongfully obtained property from another by fraud or conversion. Second, at common law, the remedy in a quasi-contractual action was damages. In restitutionary actions, modern courts can fashion equitable remedies such as a "constructive trust" or "accounting." Warren A. Seavey & Austin W. Scott, Restitution, 54 L.Q. Rev. 29, 38-39 (1938) (discussing relationship between restitution and common law quasi-contractual actions).

More recently, Professor George Palmer published a four-volume treatise, Law of Restitution (1978); other scholars have been focusing their attention on explicating the underlying rationale for restitution and arguing for the importance of this body of law. See Andrew Kull, Rationalizing Restitution, 83 Cal. L. Rev. 1191 (1995); Christopher T. Wonnell, Replacing The Unitary Principle of Unjust Enrichment, 45 Emory L.J. 153 (1996). A recent issue of the Texas Law Review contains a collection of articles on Restitution, including pieces by Professors Daniel Friedmann, Andrew Kull, and Mark Gergen. Symposium: Restitution and Unjust Enrichment, 79 Tex. L. Rev. 1763 (2001). With Professor Kull serving as Reporter, the American Law Institute is currently preparing a revised Restatement of Restitution and Unjust Enrichment. See Andrew Kull, Rescission and Restitution, 61 Bus. Law. 569 (2006).

The Restatement of Restitution succinctly states the basis of liability as follows: "A person who has been unjustly enriched at the expense of another is required to make restitution to the other." Restatement of Restitution §1. This formula identifies two elements that are central to restitutionary recovery: enrichment under circumstances where the retention of benefits would be unjust. But what is "enrichment"? And when is enrichment "unjust"? The materials that follow address these questions.

1. Restitution in the Absence of a Promise

In the preceding materials, we have focused on the reasons why the law might choose to enforce an apparently seriously intended promise. Suppose one party has received a benefit from another, but has made no promise to pay for that benefit. Ordinarily, classical contract law would find no basis for imposing a promissory obligation in those circumstances. Might there still be some legal obligation, based on principles of restitution? The following cases explore that question.

‖ Credit Bureau Enterprises, Inc. v. Pelo

Supreme Court of Iowa
608 N.W.2d 20 (2000)

Considered en banc.

McGiverin, Chief Justice.

In this appeal of a small claims decision, defendant Russell N. Pelo contends the district court erred by entering judgment against him for payment of a hospital bill.

Upon our review, we agree with the district court's conclusion and judgment that defendant Pelo is personally liable for the hospital bill.

I. BACKGROUND FACTS AND PROCEEDINGS.

On Sunday January 8, 1995, at 3:00 a.m., the Hardin County Magistrate was contacted by Dr. Gude from the Ellsworth Municipal Hospital in Iowa Falls in regard to a patient, Russell N. Pelo. The record indicates that Pelo left his marital residence, after having an argument with his wife, and checked into a motel in Iowa Falls. Pelo later telephoned his wife "making threats of self harm" and purchased a shotgun. While the record is silent regarding the subsequent events, Pelo was apparently taken to the Ellsworth Municipal Hospital by the police, who had been advised of his threats.

Pursuant to the emergency hospitalization procedures set forth in Iowa Code section 229.22(3) and (4) (1995), the magistrate found probable cause that Pelo was seriously mentally impaired and likely to physically injure himself. The magistrate thus entered an emergency hospitalization order on January 8, requiring that Pelo be detained in custody at the hospital's psychiatric unit for examination and care for a period not to exceed forty-eight hours.

During admission to the hospital, Pelo was given a hospital release form to sign which would have made either Pelo or his insurance company responsible for the hospital bill. Pelo refused to sign the form. According to Pelo, at approximately five o'clock that morning, a nurse awakened him and demanded that he sign the hospital release form or the hospital could not insure the safety or return of his personal items. Pelo eventually read and signed the form. The form stated that Pelo understood he remained liable for any charges not covered by insurance.

Thereafter, Pelo's wife filed an application for involuntary hospitalization of Pelo pursuant to Iowa Code section 229.6 and apparently an order for immediate hospitalization was entered by a hospitalization referee under Iowa Code section 229.11.

An evidentiary hearing was held before the judicial hospitalization referee on January 13, concerning Pelo's commitment status. Medical reports and testimony were received by the referee. Pursuant to a written order, the hospitalization referee found that Pelo suffers from mental illness described as bipolar disorder, an illness from which Pelo has suffered for many years. In addition, the referee concluded "that although the Respondent [Pelo] clearly is in need of and would benefit from treatment for a serious mental illness, the required elements for involuntary hospitalization are lacking," and that further involuntary hospitalization was not authorized. Pelo was released from the hospital and court jurisdiction as of January 13, 1995.

The hospital later sought compensation from Pelo in the amount of $2,775.79 for medical services provided to him from January 8 to January 13, 1995. Pelo refused to pay the bill or authorize his health insurance carrier to do so. The hospital later assigned its claim against Pelo concerning the hospital bill to plaintiff Credit Bureau Enterprises, Inc., for collection. Plaintiff Credit Bureau filed a petition against Pelo on the small claims docket in district court, seeking judgment on the hospital bill. Credit Bureau later also named Cerro Gordo county as a defendant, based on the theory that the county, Pelo's county of legal settlement, would be liable for mental health services provided to Pelo. See Iowa Code §§230.1, 230.2.

At a hearing concerning plaintiff's small claims petition, Pelo admitted that he was hospitalized from January 8 through January 13, 1995, but argued that he made no agreement to pay for services provided to him. Pelo explained that upon being admitted to the hospital, he refused to complete the hospital release form so that his health insurance carrier could be contacted for payment because he believed that he did not need evaluation or treatment. Pelo argued he later signed the release form under duress and that he did not agree to pay for medical services provided. Pelo stated he had health insurance and was not indigent at the time he was hospitalized.

The district associate judge concluded that there was no statutory requirement that Cerro Gordo county pay for medical services provided to Pelo during his hospitalization because Pelo was hospitalized at a private hospital and not a state hospital. See Iowa Code §230.1. The court further concluded, however, that as a matter of public policy and under a reasonable interpretation of the involuntary commitment and mentally ill support statutes in Iowa Code chapters 229 and 230, Pelo could not be permitted to receive court-ordered services and then choose to ignore his responsibility to pay for those services. The court therefore entered judgment in favor of plaintiff Credit Bureau and against Pelo in the amount of $2,775.79, plus interest. The court also dismissed Credit Bureau's claim against Cerro Gordo county.

Under Iowa Code section 631.13, Pelo appealed to a district court judge the district associate court's decision that he was personally liable for the hospital bill. However, neither Pelo nor the plaintiff appealed that portion of the decision dismissing plaintiff's claim against Cerro Gordo county. The county is therefore not involved in this appeal and is out of the case.

On Pelo's appeal, the district court judge affirmed. The court concluded that by signing the hospital form, Pelo had entered into a valid, enforceable contract to be financially responsible for the hospital bill. In doing so, the court rejected Pelo's contention that the agreement was not enforceable because he allegedly signed the form under duress. In the alternative, the court concluded that Pelo was liable for payment of the hospital bill under a theory of contract implied in law or quasi-contract, based on the court's conclusion that Pelo benefited from his hospitalization for which he should pay.

We granted Pelo's application for discretionary review. See Iowa Code §631.16.

II. STANDARD OF REVIEW.

On discretionary review of a small claims action, see Iowa Code §631.16, our standard of review depends on the nature of the case. Hyde v. Anania, 578 N.W.2d 647, 648 (Iowa 1998). If the action is a law case, we review the district judge's ruling on error. Id. This small claims case began as an action to collect on account, which is a law action. In such cases, we review the judgment of the district court for correction of errors at law. Iowa R.App. P. 4; Meier v. Sac & Fox Indian Tribe, 476 N.W.2d 61, 62 (Iowa 1991).

III. DEFENDANT'S LIABILITY.

The issue we must decide is who pays for mental health medical services provided to a patient who is involuntarily committed to a private hospital. To answer this question, we first examine the applicable statutes governing involuntary hospitalization procedures for persons with mental illness. [The court concludes that under statutory law, there is no clear requirement that the county of a patient's residence pay for the cost of treatment at a private, as opposed to a public, hospital. Later statutory changes addressed the problem revealed in this case. — EDS.]

B. LIABILITY UNDER IMPLIED CONTRACT THEORY.

The district court judge concluded that Pelo was liable for payment of the private hospital bill under a contract implied in law or quasicontract theory.

1. Applicable law.

"A contract implied in law is an obligation imposed by the law without regard to either party's expressions of assent either by words or acts." Irons v. Community State Bank, 461 N.W.2d 849, 855 (Iowa App. 1990) (citing Corbin on Contracts §19 (1952)). Such contracts do not arise from the traditional bargaining process, but rather "rest on a legal fiction arising from considerations of justice and the equitable principles of unjust enrichment." Hunter v. Union State Bank, 505 N.W.2d 172, 177 (Iowa 1993). As such, they are not real contracts and the general rules of contracts therefore do not apply to them. Id.; accord 1 Samuel Williston, A Treatise on the Law of Contracts §1:6, at 27 (Richard A. Lord ed., 4th ed. 1990) (hereinafter "Williston"). More specifically, the contracts clause of article I, section 10 of the United States Constitution does not apply to quasi-contracts. Williston, §1:6, at 27.

"Restitution and unjust enrichment are modern designations for the older doctrine of quasi contracts or contracts implied in law, sometimes called constructive contracts." Robert's River Rides v. Steamboat Dev. Corp., 520 N.W.2d 294, 302 (Iowa 1994) (citations omitted). The term " 'unjust enrichment is an equitable principle mandating that one shall not be permitted to unjustly enrich oneself at the expense of another or to receive property or benefits without making compensation for them.' " Id. (quoting West Branch State Bank v. Gates, 477 N.W.2d 848, 851-52 (Iowa 1991)). Under these principles, where a person acts to confer benefits on another in a setting in which the actor is not acting officiously, the benefited party may be required to make restitution to the actor. Okoboji Camp Owners Coop. v. Carlson, 578 N.W.2d 652, 654 (Iowa 1998) (citing Restatement of Restitution §§1, 2 (1936)). Thus, where a person performs services for another which are known to and accepted by the latter, the law implies a promise to pay for those services. Patterson v. Patterson's Estate, 189 N.W.2d 601, 604 (Iowa 1971); Snyder v. Nixon, 188 Iowa 779, 781, 176 N.W. 808, 809 (1920) ("The general rule is that where one renders services of value to another with his knowledge and consent, the presumption is that the one rendering the services expects to be compensated, and that the one to whom the services are rendered intends to pay for the same, and so the law implies a promise to pay.").

The Restatement of Restitution states that "[a] person who officiously[2] confers a benefit upon another is not entitled to restitution therefor." Restatement of Restitution §2. Under this rule, recovery is denied so that one will not have to pay for a benefit forced upon one against one's will, see 1 E. Allan Farnsworth, Farnsworth on Contracts §2.20, at 173 (2d ed. 1998), or for which one did not request or knowingly accept. See Nursing Care Servs. v. Dobos, 380 So. 2d 516, 518 (Fla. Dist. Ct. App. 1980) (referring to rule as the "officious intermeddler doctrine").

In certain circumstances, however, restitution for services performed will be required even though the recipient did not request or voluntarily consent to receive such services. For example, section 116 of the Restatement of Restitution provides:

> A person who has supplied things or services to another, although acting without the other's knowledge or consent, is entitled to restitution therefor from the other if
> (a) he acted unofficiously and with intent to charge therefor, and
> (b) the things or services were necessary to prevent the other from suffering serious bodily harm or pain, and
> (c) the person supplying them had no reason to know that the other would not consent to receiving them, if mentally competent; and
> (d) *it was impossible for the other to give consent or,* because of extreme youth or *mental impairment, the other's consent would have been immaterial.*

(Emphasis added.) Comment b to section 116 states:

> Knowledge of dissent. There can be no restitution for services or things rendered to a person who *refuses to accept the services and who is of sufficient mental capacity to understand the necessity of receiving them. . . . If, however, the person is insane, or if he is otherwise not fully mentally competent,* . . . a person rendering necessaries or professional services is entitled to recover from such person under the conditions stated in this Section, *although the person expresses an unwillingness to accept the things or services.*[3]

(Emphasis added.)

In addition to the principles set forth in the Restatement of Restitution discussed above, cases from other jurisdictions have concluded that a patient is liable for the reasonable value of medical services rendered by a hospital based on an implied in law contract theory. See *Nursing Care Servs.,* 380 So. 2d at 518 (concluding that provider of nursing care services was entitled to value of services provided to patient based on emergency aid quasicontract theory);

---

2. "Officiousness means interference in the affairs of others not justified by the circumstances under which the interference takes place." Restatement of Restitution §2 cmt. a.

3. Another illustration explains:

A is seriously hurt in an accident. Becoming hysterical with pain, he fights his rescuers and refuses to permit anyone to touch him. Over his protests, B, a surgeon, renders first aid services in stopping a hemorrhage which soon would have caused A's death. B is entitled to compensation from A.

Restatement of Restitution §116 cmt. b, illus. 4.

Galloway v. Methodist Hosps., Inc., 658 N.E.2d 611, 614 (Ind. Ct. App. 1995) (holding that equity demanded that patients pay for medical services rendered by hospital in birth of child to prevent unjust enrichment); Heartland Health Sys. v. Chamberlin, 871 S.W.2d 8, 11 (Mo. Ct. App. 1993) (affirming on appeal judgment entered in favor of hospital against patient for payment of medical services under quantum meruit theory). . . .

2. *Application of law to facts.*

The district court concluded that Pelo benefitted by his hospitalization and that Pelo was liable for medical services rendered to him. Upon our review, we agree with the district court's decision.

We first point out that Pelo does not challenge the factual basis for his hospitalization. Nor is it likely that such a challenge would be successful given the fact that the necessary probable cause findings concerning emergency hospitalization by the magistrate, see Iowa Code §229.22(3), and involuntary commitment procedures by the hospitalization referee, see Iowa Code §229.11, were made. These factfinding requirements are in place to guarantee a patient's liberty and due process interests when the state exercises its authority through emergency hospitalization and involuntary commitment proceedings. This authority is based on the standard for commitment, "serious mental impairment" as defined in section 229.1(14), which "melds the important elements of the police power and parens patriae doctrine." B.A.A. v. University of Iowa Hosps., 421 N.W.2d 118, 122-23 (Iowa 1988) (discussing historical background of state's authority in involuntary commitment proceedings).

Pelo also does not challenge the hospitalization referee's finding that he suffers from mental illness described as bipolar disorder. Nor does Pelo challenge the district court's finding that $2,775.79 was the reasonable cost of services provided to him during his hospitalization. Pelo contends, however, that he has no duty to pay for those services because he did not ask to be hospitalized and derived no benefit from his hospitalization. Pelo bases his argument, in part, on the hospitalization referee's finding made after the commitment hearing that further hospitalization was not authorized (based on a finding that there was not clear and convincing evidence that Pelo was seriously mentally impaired, see Iowa Code §229.13). Pelo apparently interprets the referee's decision to mean that he should not have been hospitalized in the first place and that he therefore derived no benefit from his hospitalization.

We find no merit in these contentions. First, the hospitalization referee's final decision is not relevant to Pelo's duty to pay for services previously rendered to him by the hospital. The referee's decision only addressed the propriety of any *future* hospitalization, not whether there was an adequate basis for hospitalization of Pelo in the first place or whether he medically benefited from his hospitalization.

Second, Pelo's opinion as to whether he needed or consented to medical services provided to him during his hospitalization is essentially irrelevant. This is because the emergency hospitalization order, which was based on the magistrate's probable cause finding that Pelo was seriously mentally impaired, see Iowa Code §229.22(3), establishes that Pelo lacked sufficient judgment to make responsible decisions concerning hospitalization and lacked the ability to consent to treatment. See Iowa Code §229.1(14) (defining "seriously mentally impaired").

Additionally, like the district court, we find that Pelo's hospitalization was indeed of medical benefit to him. The hospital provided services to Pelo from January 8 to 13, 1995, in good faith and not gratuitously. Such services were provided for Pelo's benefit, pursuant to court orders based on probable cause findings that Pelo was seriously mentally impaired and likely to injure himself or others if not immediately detained in the hospital. Based on the later reports of the physicians who examined and evaluated Pelo during his hospitalization, the referee found that Pelo "clearly is in need of and would benefit from treatment for a serious mental illness." This finding, we believe, would at a minimum alert Pelo to the seriousness of his mental illness and the need for further treatment, a fact that would surely be of medical benefit to him. The fact that Pelo was involuntarily hospitalized in order that this evaluation and finding could be made, and the fact that he may disagree with whether this finding is of medical benefit to him, does not eliminate the medical benefit he received from such hospitalization.

We conclude that plaintiff is entitled to recover the value of those medical services provided to Pelo. See Restatement of Restitution §116 cmt. b (if a person is otherwise not fully mentally competent, a person rendering necessaries or professional services is entitled to recover from such person although the person expresses an unwillingness to accept the services). The district court therefore properly determined that Pelo was legally obligated to pay for those services based on an implied in law contract theory. See Heartland Health Sys., 871 S.W.2d at 11 (affirming on appeal judgment entered in favor of hospital against patient for payment of medical services under quantum meruit theory).

Because we conclude that Pelo is legally obligated to pay for medical services provided to him under an implied contract in law or quasicontract theory, we need not consider whether an express contract was formed based on Pelo's later signature on the hospital admission form. See Johnson v. Dodgen, 451 N.W.2d 168, 175 (Iowa 1990) (the existence of a contract generally precludes the application of the doctrine of unjust enrichment); Chariton Feed & Grain, Inc. v. Harder, 369 N.W.2d 777, 791 (Iowa 1985) (an express and an implied contract cannot be found to exist on the same subject matter).

C. CONSTITUTIONAL CLAIMS.

Pelo further contends that to require him to pay for medical services he did not want or ask for violates either his constitutional right to due process under article I, section 9 of the Iowa Constitution, or his right to contract under article I, section 21 of the Iowa Constitution. These contentions have no merit. First, quasi-contracts are not true contracts and therefore the general rules of contract, including the constitutional provisions concerning the right to contract, do not apply to them. See Williston, §1:6, at 27.

Additionally, we point out that Pelo does not assert that the emergency hospitalization or involuntary commitment proceedings are constitutionally invalid. Based on this fact, and the preliminary factual probable cause findings of the magistrate and hospitalization referee that Pelo was seriously mentally impaired, we assume that Pelo's involuntary hospitalization complied with the requisite procedural due process safeguards. Having established these facts, holding Pelo liable for payment of the medical services provided to him during his hospitalization does not violate his constitutional right to due process or his right to contract under the Iowa Constitution.

IV. DISPOSITION.

We conclude that the district court properly determined that defendant Pelo was liable for payment of mental health medical services provided to him during his hospitalization at Ellsworth Municipal Hospital under a quasi-contract theory. The court therefore properly entered judgment in favor of plaintiff Credit Bureau against defendant Pelo for the amount of the hospital bill.

We affirm the judgment of the district court.

AFFIRMED.

All justices concur except CARTER, J., who takes no part.

Notes and Questions

1. *Analyzing* **Pelo.** Because the court is satisfied that Pelo's apparent need for care was clear and the procedural protections afforded him were adequate, it never has to reach the issue of whether true contractual liability could have been imposed on the basis of the form he signed while under the hospital's care. Do you think that other claim should have succeeded? Consider Restatement (Second) of Contract §§174-177, "Duress and Undue Influence"; consider also §15, "Mental Illness or Defect." We will consider those topics in Chapter 7, but at this point note that Pelo might well have had one or more effective defenses to contractual liability, given his apparent mental condition at the time he signed the form. In particular, regardless of whether the hospital is seen as having applied an "improper" threat to obtain his assent, the mere fact that the hospital was clearly aware of his mental state might well prevent its enforcement of any contractual obligation on his part.

2. *Restitutionary liability for emergency services rendered.* As the court in *Pelo* points out, the Restatement of Restitution §116 provides for restitution in favor of one furnishing emergency services in a situation where serious bodily harm or pain will otherwise result, provided the plaintiff acted "unofficiously." Sometimes, as in In re Estate of Crisan, 107 N.W.2d 907 (Mich. 1961), the patient is unconscious when the care is rendered, and dies without ever regaining consciousness. Even more than in *Pelo*, there can be no question of "real" assent in such a case; to talk of an "implied contract" is clearly a legal fiction. Moreover, since in *Crisan* the patient did not recover, it is possible that the services ultimately did not "benefit" her. The restitutionary obligation will presumably lie anyway, however, based on the "reasonable value" of the services received. Cf. Doe v. HCA Health Services of Tennessee, Inc., 46 S.W.2d 191, 198-199 (Tenn. 2001) (price term in agreement between patient and hospital too indefinite for contract to be enforceable, but patient liable for

the reasonable value of services rendered, based on the costs of the hospital's operation and the prices charged for similar services by other hospitals in the area). In other cases, however, the patient was conscious and could have entered into an agreement, and perhaps the issue of payment was even discussed, but no definite agreement was reached. In such a case, the provider will be able to recover the reasonable value of the care furnished, not under the rubric of Restatement of Restitution §116, but on the more general restitutionary principle that one who receives services, with the knowledge that the person furnishing them reasonably expects to be paid, will be liable for the reasonable value of those services. See, e.g., the *Doe* case cited above, and Galloway v. Methodist Hospitals, Inc., cited by the court in *Pelo*. As mentioned previously, the Restatement of Restitution is being revised. Proposed §20 provides as follows:

§20. Protection Of Another's Life Or Health

A person who performs, supplies, or obtains professional services reasonably necessary for the protection of another's life or health has a claim in restitution against the other if the circumstances justify the claimant's decision to intervene without a prior agreement for payment or reimbursement. Restitution under this Section is measured by a reasonable charge for the services provided. Restatement (Third) of Restitution (T.D. #2 2002)

What changes if any would this section make from §116 of the First Restatement? Would application of this revised section have affected the result in *Pelo*?

3. *Contrast between contract and "pure" restitution (or "quasi-contract").* The court in *Pelo* is at great pains to make clear that the liability of the defendant is based in restitution, not pursuant to a contract, and that these are two quite separate bases of obligation. Contracts "implied in law" are "not real contracts," the court declares; they "do not arise from the traditional bargaining process," and "general rules of contracts . . . do not apply to them." Despite the theoretical separation between "true" contract and "quasi" contract, they do have some potential overlap, as the Restatement of Restitution recognizes in the following provision:

§107. Effect of Existence of Bargain upon Right to Restitution

(1) A person of full capacity who, pursuant to a contract with another, has performed services or transferred property to the other or otherwise has conferred a benefit upon him, is not entitled to compensation therefor other than in accordance with the terms of such bargain, unless the transaction is rescinded for fraud, mistake, duress, undue influence or illegality, or unless the other has failed to perform his part of the bargain.

(2) In the absence of circumstances indicating otherwise, it is inferred that a person who requests another to perform services for him or to transfer property to him thereby bargains to pay therefor.

As Restatement of Restitution §107(2) states, when a person "requests another to perform services for him or to transfer property to him," the law will infer a bargain to pay. Such cases are usually referred to as "implied-in-fact" contracts. Implied-in-fact contracts, like express contracts, are "true" contracts. While the distinction between implied-in-fact contracts and restitution claims may be hazy, the crucial factor will often be whether the party receiving the benefit of services or property had "requested" it. See Candace S. Kovacic, A Proposal to Simplify Quantum Meruit Litigation, 35 Am. U.L. Rev. 547, 550-551 (1986). If so, a claim based on implied-in-fact contract will lie. The distinction between implied-in-fact and implied-in-law contracts is discussed in more detail in the two cases that follow *Pelo*.

Frequently the distinction between express contract, implied-in-fact contract, and restitution will be immaterial. See Restatement of Restitution §107, cmt. *b*. However, sometimes the distinction will be important. In *Pelo*, for example, the court states that constitutional claims regarding the right to contract do not apply to restitutionary claims. Many procedural or evidentiary rules applicable to contracts will also not apply when restitution is the basis for recovery. In In re Estate of Etherton, 671 N.E.2d 364 (Ill. App. 1996), the plaintiff was held entitled to "quantum meruit" payment for service performed in harvesting crops during the decedent's illness; evidentiary rules (a "Dead Man's Act") prevented proof of an express contract between plaintiff and the decedent, but the court held he could recover on the basis of work performed by someone not related to the recipient, with the intention of receiving payment, knowingly and voluntarily received.

> The facts that petitioner was a friend of decedent and that it is "not unheard of" for farmers sometimes to help each other out for free are insufficient to erase this presumption [of expectation of payment]. The services provided were not trivial, and petitioner's heavy farm equipment cost money to operate. Although the presumption of nongratuity may burst if the friendship is of such a quality as to be nearly familial . . . , the evidence here does not suggest that petitioner and decedent shared anything more than a casual friendship.

Id. at 368.

4. *Restitutionary liability for preservation of goods.* In a companion provision to §116, the Restatement of Restitution also provides for restitutionary recovery in a case where the plaintiff has acted to preserve things belonging to the plaintiff:

Section 117. Preservation of another's things or credit.

(1) A person who, although acting without the other's knowledge or consent, has preserved things belonging to another from damage or destruction, is entitled to restitution for services rendered or expenditures incurred therein, if

(a) he was in lawful possession or custody of the things or if he lawfully took possession thereof, and the services or expenses were not made necessary by his breach of duty to the other, and

(b) it was reasonably necessary that the services should be rendered or the expenditures incurred before it was possible to communicate with the owner by reasonable means, and

(c) he had no reason to believe that the owner did not desire him so to act, and

(d) he intended to charge for such services or to retain the things as his own if the identity of the owner were not discovered or if the owner should disclaim, and

(e) the things have been accepted by the owner. . . .

Illustration:

. . .

2. In a storm, *A's* boat is cast adrift on a river and is being broken by the current. *B* engages the assistance of others and after several hours' work removes the boat to a place of safety from which *A*, with knowledge of the facts, subsequently takes it. Assuming *B's* intent to charge for his services and expenses, he is entitled to restitution from *A*.

Note that here, as in §116, the Restatement of Restitution stresses the point that in situations where the services were performed without the consent of the person receiving them, the party seeking restitution must in effect negate the possibility that the services were performed "officiously," that is, thrust upon the recipient without any reason for believing that the person would have wanted them or would have expected to pay for them. Proposed §21 of the revised Restatement would rewrite the section as follows:

§21. Protection Of Another's Property

A person who takes effective action to protect another's property or economic interests has a claim in restitution against the other if
(a) the circumstances justify the claimant's decision to intervene without a prior agreement for payment or reimbursement, and
(b) it is reasonable for the claimant to assume that the defendant would wish the action performed.
Restitution under this Section is measured by (i) the loss avoided by the defendant or (ii) a reasonable charge for the services provided, whichever is less. (T.D. #2 2002).

How does this section compare to §117 of the original Restatement?

5. *Economic analysis of restitutionary claims.* Professor (now Judge) Richard Posner, the leading advocate for the application of economic analysis to legal problems, has offered the following economic justification for the modern rule allowing restitutionary recovery for benefits conferred to preserve life, health, or property:

A doctor chances on a stranger lying unconscious on the street, treats him, and later demands a fee. Has he a legal claim? The law's answer is yes. The older legal terminology spoke of an implied contract between the physician and the stranger for medical assistance. This idea has been attacked as a fiction, and modern writers prefer to base the physician's legal right on the principle of unjust enrichment. This term smacks of morality, but the cases are better explained in economic terms. The concept of an implied contract is a useful shorthand for an economic approach; it underscores the continuity between issues in express contracts and the issues nowadays treated under the rubric of unjust enrichment.

In the case of the doctor, the costs of a voluntary transaction would be prohibitive. The cause of high transaction costs in that case is incapacity. In other cases it might be time (e.g., the stranger is conscious but bleeding profusely and there is no time to discuss terms). In such cases, the law considers whether, had transaction costs not been prohibitive, the parties would have come to terms, and if so what (approximately) the terms would have been. If a court is reasonably confident both that there would have been a transaction and what its essential terms would have been (that the doctor use his best efforts and that the patient pay the doctor's normal fee for treatment of the sort rendered), it does not hesitate to write a contract between the parties after the fact. . . .

But now suppose that a man stands under my window, playing the violin beautifully, and when he has finished knocks on my door and demands a fee for his efforts. Though I enjoyed his playing I nonetheless refuse to pay anything for it. The court would deny the violinist's claim for a fee—however reasonable the fee might appear to be—on the ground that, although the violinist conferred a benefit on me (and not with the intent that it be gratuitous), he did so officiously. Translated from legal into economic terminology, this means he conferred an unbargained-for benefit in circumstances where the costs of a voluntary bargain would have been low. In such cases the law insists that the voluntary route be followed—and is on firm economic grounds in doing so.

Richard A. Posner, Economic Analysis of Law 135-136 (6th ed. 2002). What does Posner mean by "transaction costs"? When transaction costs are low, why should the law insist that obligations be dependent on an actual bargain rather than being imposed by law? According to Posner, when is it permissible for a court to impose an obligation to pay for benefits received even in the absence of an actual bargain?

Commerce Partnership 8098 Limited Partnership v. Equity Contracting Co.
Florida District Court of Appeal, En Banc
695 So. 2d 383 (1997)

GROSS, Judge.

Equity Contracting Company, Inc. ("Equity") filed a one-count complaint against Commerce Partnership 8098 Limited Partnership ("Commerce"). The count was set forth under the heading "Quantum Meruit." The complaint contained the following allegations:

> Commerce was the owner of an office building. Commerce contracted with a general contractor, World Properties, Inc., to perform improvements on its property. Equity was the stucco and surfacing subcontractor for the job, having contracted with the general contractor to perform the work. Because it inspected the job on a weekly basis, Commerce was aware of Equity's work. Equity completely performed its subcontract and the reasonable value of its work was $17,100. Commerce failed to pay the general contractor the full amounts due for the job. The general contractor did not pay Equity. Commerce was unjustly enriched because it had accepted Equity's services without paying any entity for them.

In its answer, Commerce asserted that it had paid the general contractor in full.

At the non-jury trial, Equity presented its direct case in under 30 minutes. Equity's president testified that his company had contracted with the general contractor to stucco Commerce's property for $17,100. He indicated that at the start of the job he expected payment only from the general contractor and not from Commerce. Both the general contractor and a representative from Commerce inspected the work as it progressed. After the work was completed, Commerce gave Equity a punch list of remedial work. When Equity's president asked for at least partial payment from Commerce, the latter's representative indicated that "he couldn't do it." Having received no payment, Equity did not complete the punch list. Equity brought suit against the general contractor, who later declared bankruptcy. Equity adduced no evidence regarding Commerce's payments to the general contractor under the construction contract or to any other party for work covered by the contract.

After Equity rested, Commerce moved for an involuntary dismissal, arguing that the evidence did not establish a contract implied in fact. Commerce's attorney contended that the term "quantum meruit" was synonymous with a contract implied in fact. The trial court denied the motion. During closing argument, Equity asserted that it had established a claim for quantum meruit, which it interpreted to mean unjust enrichment. Arguing that a quasi contract claim had first been injected into the case during closing argument, Commerce's attorney obtained permission to reopen his case. By this point in the trial, there was no agreement as to the cause of action at issue or the requirements of proof. The trial judge observed, "[w]e are in equity and I have some difficulty with wondering what the issues are and who is going to prove what."

Commerce's witness testified that the contract price it had negotiated with the general contractor for the improvements was $256,894. He identified three payments totalling $223,065.04 that Commerce made to the general contractor—$173,088.07 in progress payments, $24,976.97 in response to application for payment number 8, and $25,000 in final settlement of the general contractor's lawsuit against Commerce. Commerce also sought to introduce evidence that it had paid $64,097 directly to three subcontractors who had performed work on the building, who were not paid by the general contractor, and who had perfected mechanics' liens. The trial court sustained Equity's objection to this testimony on the ground of relevance.

Relying on Zaleznik v. Gulf Coast Roofing Co., Inc., 576 So. 2d 776 (Fla. 2d DCA 1991), the trial court entered judgment in favor of Equity for $17,100.

CONTRACT IMPLIED IN FACT AND QUASI CONTRACT

This case is a paradigm for the confusion that often surrounds the litigation of implied contracts.

A contract implied in fact is one form of an enforceable contract; it is based on a tacit promise, one that is inferred in whole or in part from the parties' conduct, not solely from their words. 17 Am. Jur. 2d "Contracts" §3 (1964); 1 Arthur Linton Corbin, Corbin on Contracts §§1.18-1.20 (Joseph M. Perillo ed. 1993). Where an agreement is arrived at by words, oral or written, the contract is said to be "express." 17 Am. Jur. 2d "Contracts" at §3. A contract implied in fact is not put into promissory words with sufficient clarity, so a fact finder must examine and interpret the parties' conduct to give definition to their unspoken agreement. Id.; 3 Corbin on Contracts §562 (1960). . . .

Common examples of contracts implied in fact are where a person performs services at another's request, or "where services are rendered by one person for another without his expressed request, but with his knowledge, and under circumstances" fairly raising the presumption that the parties understood and intended that compensation was to be paid. . . . In these circumstances, the law implies the promise to pay a reasonable amount for the services. . . .

A contract implied in law, or quasi contract, is not based upon the finding, by a process of implication from the facts, of an agreement between the parties. A contract implied in law is a legal fiction, an obligation created by the law without regard to the parties' expression of assent by their words or conduct. 1 Corbin on Contracts §1.20;. . . . The fiction was adopted to provide a remedy where one party was unjustly enriched, where that party received a benefit under circumstances that made it unjust to retain it without giving compensation. . . .

The elements of a cause of action for a quasi contract are that: (1) the plaintiff has conferred a benefit on the defendant; (2) the defendant has knowledge of the benefit; (3) the defendant has accepted or retained the benefit conferred and (4) the circumstances are such that it would be inequitable for the defendant to retain the benefit without paying fair value for it. Hillman Const. Corp. v. Wainer, 636 So. 2d 576, 577 (Fla. 4th DCA 1994); Henry M. Butler, Inc. v. Trizec Properties, Inc., 524 So. 2d 710, 711-12 (Fla. 2d DCA 1988). Because the basis for recovery does not turn on the finding of an enforceable agreement, there may be recovery under a contract implied in law even where the parties had no dealings at all with each other. . . . This is unlike a contract implied in fact which must arise from the interaction of the parties or their agents.

To describe the cause of action encompassed by a contract implied in law, Florida courts have synonymously used a number of different terms—"quasi contract," "unjust enrichment," "restitution," "constructive contract," and "quantum meruit." This profusion of terminology has its roots in legal history. Concerned about the confusion between contracts implied in law and fact, two legal scholars sought to "extirpate the term 'contract implied in law' from legal usage and to substitute for it the term 'quasi contract'." 1 Corbin on Contracts §1.20. As Corbin explains, although the term "quasi contract" took hold, "the older term successfully resisted extirpation to the further confusion of law students and lawyers." Id. . . .

At trial in this case, Commerce's attorney understood "quantum meruit" to mean a contract implied in fact. Equity and the trial court were proceeding under a theory of quasi contract. This confusion over "quantum meruit" is understandable, since there are cases to support both positions. . . .

The blurring of the distinction between contract implied in fact and quasi contract has been exacerbated by the potential for both theories to apply to the same factual setting. For example, a common form of contract implied in fact is where one party has performed services at the request of another without discussion of compensation. These circumstances justify the inference of a promise to pay a reasonable amount for the service. The enforceability of this obligation turns on the implied promise, not on whether the defendant has received something of value. A contract implied in fact can be enforced even where a defendant has received nothing of value.

However, where there is no enforceable express or implied in fact contract but where the defendant has received something of value, or has otherwise benefitted from the service supplied, recovery under a quasi contractual theory may be appropriate. See Lamborn v. Slack, 107 So. 2d 277 (Fla. 2d DCA 1958) (in which the court found a contract implied in fact but discussed the issue using quasi contractual principles). When properly raised in the pleadings, this overlapping of theories may require a fact finder to view the facts as they might apply to both. 3 Corbin on Contracts §561 (1960).

Contrary to Commerce's belief at trial, Equity was asserting a quasi contract claim against it, not a contract implied in fact.

A SUBCONTRACTOR'S QUASI CONTRACT ACTION AGAINST AN OWNER

In [Maloney v. Therm Alum Industries Corp., 636 So. 2d 767 (Fla. Dist. Ct. App. 1994)], this court considered the availability of a quasi contract theory to a construction subcontractor seeking recovery against an owner of property, where there had been no dealings between the owner and the subcontractor. Pursuant to a contract with the general contractor, the subcontractor in *Maloney* furnished glass walls, windows and doors for the construction of an office building. The subcontractor was not paid in full for its work. The general contractor and subcontractor submitted their claims against each other to arbitration. In the circuit court action, the subcontractor sought to recover damages against the owner on a quasi contract theory. Id. at 768. Relying on two out-of-state cases, this court held that a subcontractor could maintain a quasi contract action against an owner, provided that it pled and proved two elements to establish that the enrichment of the owner was unjust — that the subcontractor had exhausted all remedies against the general contractor and still remained unpaid and that the owner had not given consideration to any person for the improvements furnished by the subcontractor. Id. at 769-70. We quoted the following passage from Paschall's Inc. v. Dozier, 219 Tenn. 45, 407 S.W.2d 150, 155 (1966):

> The most significant requirement for a recovery on quasi contract is that the enrichment to the defendant be unjust. Consequently, if the landowner has given any consideration to any person for the improvements, it would not be unjust for him to retain the benefit without paying the furnisher. Also, we think that before recovery can be had against the landowner on an unjust enrichment theory, the furnisher of the materials and labor must have exhausted his remedies against the person with whom he had contracted, and still has not received the reasonable value of his services.

Id. 636 So. 2d at 770. *Maloney* reversed the judgment for the contractor based upon quasi contract because the status of the subcontractor's arbitration claim with the general contractor was not established at trial. Under these circumstances, we held that it was "premature and therefore improper to permit the subcontractor to pursue" a quasi contract claim against the owner. Id. at 769.

In *Gene B. Glick Co.*, 651 So. 2d at 190, we affirmed a judgment in favor of a property owner who had been sued by a subcontractor on a quasi contract theory. We held that an unjust enrichment cannot exist "where payment has been made for the benefit conferred." The payment to which we referred was the owner's payment to the general contractor on the construction contract. . . .

There is language in *Maloney* which can be read to suggest that we imposed a third limitation on the ability of a subcontractor to maintain a quasi contract claim against an owner. *Maloney* quotes two paragraphs from Construction and Design Law §8.8C.1(1989), which include the following sentence:

> First, the subcontractor may not recover an equitable remedy if he has failed his legal remedies, such as a statutory mechanic's lien.

636 So. 2d at 770. We expressly recede from this statement in *Maloney* because it is without support in Florida law.

Florida's construction lien statute does not purport to be the exclusive remedy for a lienor, such as a subcontractor, against an owner. Section 713.30, Florida Statutes (1995), provides that the construction lien part of Chapter 713 "shall be cumulative to other existing remedies." The plain language of the statute does not supersede any remedies available to a party seeking payment. St. Regis Paper Co. v. Quality Pipeline, Inc., 469 So. 2d 820, 822-23 (Fla. 2d DCA 1985). Applying section 713.30, the third district rejected the argument that a materialman's failure to perfect a statutory lien left it without any remedy to recover for materials which it had furnished to a construction project. Peninsular Supply Co. v. C.B. Day Realty of Florida, Inc., 423 So. 2d 500, 501-502 (Fla. 3d DCA 1982). As the *Peninsular Supply* court observed:

> The purpose of the Mechanics' Lien Law is to prevent an owner from being obligated to pay for an improvement more than once. It was not intended, nor shall we interpret it to permit an unjust enrichment.

Id. at 503 (citations omitted).

. . .

. . . [T]wo requirements that *Maloney* imposes on a subcontractor's quasi contract action against an owner—exhaustion of remedies against the contractor and the owner's receipt of the benefit conferred without paying consideration to anyone—limit the cause of action to those situations where the enrichment of the owner is truly unjust when compared to the uncompensated subcontractor. The contractor with whom the subcontractor is in privity is always the pocket of first resort. Moreover, the owner can be liable only where it received a windfall benefit, something for nothing.

. . .

REVERSAL IS REQUIRED UNDER THE FACTS OF THIS CASE

In this case, Equity did not prove at trial that Commerce had not made payment to any party for the benefits conferred on the property by Equity.

This was not an affirmative defense, but an essential element of a quasi contract claim by a subcontractor against an owner. . . . Had Commerce moved for an involuntary dismissal on this ground, the motion should have been granted. Contrary to the trial court's evidentiary ruling, Commerce's attempt to prove that it had paid $64,097 directly to subcontractors for work on the building was relevant to issues in this case. What Commerce expended on this project was central to Equity's cause of action. Commerce contended that these payments were for work covered under the construction contract for which the subcontractors had not been paid by the general contractor. If the $64,097 is added to the $256,894 [sic; $223,065.04?] that Commerce paid to the general contractor, then the total amount Commerce spent on the project exceeded the contract price for the improvements. As we have observed, where an owner has given consideration for the subcontractor's work by paying out the contract price for the work, an unpaid subcontractor's claim that the owner has been unjustly enriched must fail.

The trial court's reliance on *Zaleznik* was misplaced. In that case it was undisputed that the owner received over $70,000 in construction work for which it paid no one. What Commerce paid out on this project was not fully litigated below, so whether its "enrichment" was "unjust" is an open question.

The judgment appealed is reversed, and the cause is remanded to the trial court to take additional evidence from the parties on whether Commerce made payment to or on behalf of its general contractor covering the benefits Equity conferred on the subject property. Equity shall have the burden of proving its claim of a contract implied in law that Commerce has failed to make such payment by the greater weight of the evidence. If the court shall determine that Commerce has not paid anyone for the benefits conferred by Equity, then it shall enter judgment for Equity; correspondingly, if the court shall determine that Equity has failed to prove that Commerce did not make such payment, then the court shall enter judgment for Commerce.

GUNTHER, C.J., and GLICKSTEIN, DELL, STONE, WARNER, POLEN, FARMER, KLEIN, PARIENTE, STEVENSON and SHAHOOD, JJ., concur.

Notes and Questions

1. *Owner's liability in restitution.* The court in *Commerce Partnership* holds that a subcontractor may recover in restitution from an owner when the owner has not paid the general contractor for the work performed and the subcontractor has exhausted its remedies against the general contractor. In Lucent Technologies, Inc. v. Mid-West Electronics, Inc., 49 S.W.2d 236 (Mo. Ct. App. 2001), an air conditioning contractor was able to recover in quantum meruit from the owner of the property for renovation of an air conditioning system pursuant to a contract with a prospective buyer of property, when the purchaser was unable to close the deal and the owner ultimately sold the property to another buyer. The owner benefitted from work done by the plaintiff, presumably by an increase in the purchase price to the ultimate buyer. Not all courts accept the restitutionary principle applied in *Commerce*

Partnership, however. E.g., Bennett Heating & Air Conditioning, Inc. v. NationsBank of Maryland, 674 A.2d 534, 540-541 (Md. 1996). The question is discussed in detail and the various policy arguments pro and con are weighed in Doug Rendleman, Quantum Meruit for the Subcontractor: Has Restitution Jumped Off Dawson's Dock?, 79 Tex. L. Rev. 2055 (2001). What are the principal arguments that you would make in favor of allowing such claims by subcontractors? What arguments would you make against such claims? Which view do you support? Why?

2. *Factual questions.* In *Commerce Partnership,* the court of appeals remanded the case for a new trial, with instructions that Equity bears the burden of proving that Commerce did not pay the general contractor, World Properties, for the stucco work done by Equity. If you were counsel for Equity, what fact investigation would you do to determine whether Commerce had or had not made payment to World Properties for Equity's work?

3. *Restitutionary liability of lessors.* Restitutionary claims have also been brought by contractors against lessors of property when the lessee has contracted but has not paid for improvements to the leased property. Courts have commonly denied recovery for such claims, on the ground that the owner has not been unjustly enriched, where there has been no showing that the owner needed or wanted the improvements contracted for by the tenant. E.g., Graves v. Berkowitz, 15 S.W.3d 59 (Mo. Ct. App. 2000) (not inequitable for defendant owner to retain benefit of construction work without paying for it; landlord knew of work but was only "passive beneficiary"); Puttkammer v. Minth, 266 N.W.2d 361 (Wis. 1978) (contractor does not state cause of action for unjust enrichment when complaint alleges only that owner knew that improvements were being made). Some courts, however, will allow restitutionary recovery if such a showing can be made. E.g., Idaho Lumber, Inc. v. Buck, 710 P.2d 647 (Idaho Ct. App. 1985) (contractor allowed to recover from landlord on restitutionary basis for remodeling work done for tenant); Webcon Group, Inc. v. S.M. Properties, L.P., 1 S.W.3d 538 (Mo. Ct. App. 1999) (property owner liable in restitution for improvements contracted for by prior lessee where property subsequently leased to another; even though present tenant not using improvements, they were necessary for use of property during prior lease and owner benefitted therefrom). See generally 2 George E. Palmer, Law of Restitution §10.7, at 422-425 (1978). Even if a contractor cannot recover from a landlord in restitution, a variety of other legal theories may provide a basis for recovery. See Elaine Marie Tomko, Annotation, Landlord's Liability to Third Party for Repairs Authorized by Tenant, 46 A.L.R.5th 1 (1997).

4. *The mechanic's lien.* The statutory law of virtually every jurisdiction includes provisions for "mechanic's liens." A mechanic's lien is a statutory encumbrance (as opposed to a contractual encumbrance like a mortgage) on real property for the value of improvements made to the property by a laborer or supplier of materials pursuant to contract. These statutes require the laborer or supplier to take certain steps to assert the lien. Typically, the lien must be filed in the public records and suit must be brought to enforce the lien within a set period. Failure to meet these requirements results in loss of the lien. Owners of property on which improvements are being made (along with banks and other institutions that finance construction) typically protect

themselves from mechanic's liens by releasing funds only when all subcontractors have signed "lien waivers." If an owner has released funds based on a lien waiver by a subcontractor, the subcontractor will almost certainly be unable to maintain a claim for restitution. See George M. Morris Construction Co. v. Four Seasons Motor Inn, Inc., 567 P.2d 965 (N.M. 1977) (lien waivers precluded action by laborers against owner who had made payments in reliance on waivers). If the subcontractor has failed to take advantage of the protection of the lien statute, some courts have denied restitutionary relief. See Season Comfort Corp. v. Ben A. Borenstein Co., 655 N.E.2d 1065 (Ill. Ct. App. 1995). Why does the *Commerce Partnership* court reject this view? The result in other states may turn on the precise wording of the lien statute. See Donnybrook Building Supply Co. v. Alaska National Bank of the North, 736 P.2d 1147, 1154 (Alaska 1987) (subcontractor may not obtain restitutionary relief because lien statute preserves rights of lienor "under a contract").

Watts v. Watts
Supreme Court of Wisconsin
137 Wis. 2d 506, 405 N.W.2d 303 (1987)

SHIRLEY S. ABRAHAMSON, Justice.

This is an appeal from a judgment of the circuit court for Dane County, William D. Byrne, Judge, dismissing Sue Ann Watts' amended complaint, pursuant to sec. 802.06(2)(f), Stats. 1985-86, for failure to state a claim upon which relief may be granted. This court took jurisdiction of the appeal upon certification by the court of appeals under sec. (Rule) 809.61, Stats. 1985-86. For the reasons set forth, we hold that the complaint states a claim upon which relief may be granted. Accordingly, we reverse the judgment of the circuit court and remand the cause to the circuit court for further proceedings consistent with this opinion.

The case involves a dispute between Sue Ann Evans Watts, the plaintiff, and James Watts, the defendant, over their respective interests in property accumulated during their nonmarital cohabitation relationship which spanned 12 years and produced two children. The case presents an issue of first impression and comes to this court at the pleading stage of the case, before trial and before the facts have been determined.

The plaintiff asked the circuit court to order an accounting of the defendant's personal and business assets accumulated between June 1969 through December 1981 (the duration of the parties' cohabitation) and to determine plaintiff's share of this property. The circuit court's dismissal of plaintiff's amended complaint is the subject of this appeal. The plaintiff rests her claim for an accounting and a share in the accumulated property on the following legal theories: (1) she is entitled to an equitable division of property under sec. 767.255, Stats. 1985-86; (2) the defendant is estopped to assert as a defense to plaintiff's claim under sec. 767.255, that the parties are not married; (3) the plaintiff is entitled to damages for defendant's breach of an express contract or an implied-in-fact contract between the parties; (4) the defendant holds the accumulated property under a constructive trust based upon unjust enrichment; and (5) the plaintiff is entitled to partition of the parties' real and personal property pursuant to the partition statutes, secs. 820.01 and 842.02(1), 1985-86, and common law principles of partition.

The circuit court dismissed the amended complaint, concluding that sec. 767.255, Stats. 1985-86, authorizing a court to divide property, does not apply to the division of property between unmarried persons. Without analyzing the four other legal theories upon which the plaintiff rests her claim, the circuit court simply concluded that the legislature, not the court, should provide relief to parties who have accumulated property in non-marital cohabitation relationships. The circuit court gave no further explanation for its decision.

We agree with the circuit court that the legislature did not intend sec. 767.255 to apply to an unmarried couple. We disagree with the circuit court's implicit conclusion that courts cannot or should not, without express authorization from the legislature, divide property between persons who have engaged in nonmarital cohabitation. Courts traditionally have settled contract and property disputes between unmarried persons, some of whom have cohabited. Nonmarital cohabitation does not render every agreement between the cohabiting parties illegal and does not automatically preclude one of the parties from seeking judicial relief, such as statutory or common law partition, damages for breach of express or implied contract, constructive trust and quantum meruit where the party alleges, and later proves, facts supporting the legal theory. The issue for the court in each case is whether the complaining party has set forth any legally cognizable claim. . . .

We test the sufficiency of the plaintiff's amended complaint by first setting forth the facts asserted in the complaint and then analyzing each of the five legal theories upon which the plaintiff rests her claim for relief.

I.

The plaintiff commenced this action in 1982. The plaintiff's amended complaint alleges the following facts, which for purposes of this appeal must be accepted as true. The plaintiff and the defendant met in 1967, when she was 19 years old, was living with her parents and was working full time as a nurse's aide in preparation for a nursing career. Shortly after the parties met, the defendant persuaded the plaintiff to move into an apartment paid for by him and to quit her job. According to the amended complaint, the defendant "indicated" to the plaintiff that he would provide for her.

Early in 1969, the parties began living together in a "marriage-like" relationship, holding themselves out to the public as husband and wife. The plaintiff assumed the defendant's surname as her own. Subsequently, she gave birth to two children who were also given the defendant's surname. The parties filed joint income tax returns and maintained joint bank accounts asserting that they were husband and wife. The defendant insured the plaintiff as his wife on his medical insurance policy. He also took out a life insurance policy on her as his wife, naming himself as the beneficiary. The parties purchased real and personal property as husband and wife. The plaintiff executed documents and obligated herself on promissory notes to lending institutions as the defendant's wife.

During their relationship, the plaintiff contributed childcare and home making services, including cleaning, cooking, laundering, shopping, running errands, and maintaining the grounds surrounding the parties' home. Additionally, the plaintiff contributed personal property to the relationship which she owned at the beginning of the relationship or acquired through gifts or purchases during the relationship. She served as hostess for the defendant for social and business-related events. The amended complaint further asserts that periodically, between 1969 and 1975, the plaintiff cooked and cleaned for the defendant and his employees while his business, a landscaping service, was building and landscaping a golf course.

From 1973 to 1976, the plaintiff worked 20-25 hours per week at the defendant's office, performing duties as a receptionist, typist, and assistant bookkeeper. From 1976 to 1981, the plaintiff worked 40-60 hours per week at a business she started with the defendant's sister-in-law, then continued and managed the business herself after the dissolution of that partnership. The plaintiff further alleges that in 1981 the defendant made their relationship so intolerable that she was forced to move from their home and their relationship was irretrievably broken. Subsequently, the defendant barred the plaintiff from returning to her business.

The plaintiff alleges that during the parties' relationship, and because of her domestic and business contributions, the business and personal wealth of the couple increased. Furthermore, the plaintiff alleges that she never received any compensation for these contributions to the relationship and that the defendant indicated to the plaintiff both orally and through his conduct that he considered her to be his wife and that she would share equally in the increased wealth.

The plaintiff asserts that since the breakdown of the relationship the defendant has refused to share equally with her the wealth accumulated through their joint efforts or to compensate her in any way for her contributions to the relationship.

II.

The plaintiff's first legal theory to support her claim against the property accumulated during the cohabitation is that the plaintiff, defendant, and their children constitute a "family," thus entitling the plaintiff to bring an action for property division under sec. 767.02(1)(h), Stats. 1985-86, and to have the court "divide the property of the parties and divest and transfer the title of any such property" pursuant to sec. 767.255, 1985-86.

The plaintiff asserts that the legislature intended secs. 767.02(1)(h) and 767.255, which usually govern division of property between married persons in divorce or legal separation proceedings, to govern a property division action between unmarried cohabitants who constitute a family. The plaintiff points out that secs. 767.02(1)(h) and 767.255 are part of chapter 767, which is entitled "Actions Affecting the Family," and that in 1979 the legislature deliberately changed the title of the chapter from "Actions Affecting Marriage" to "Actions Affecting the Family." The legislature has failed to provide any definition for "family" under ch. 767, or for that matter under any chapter of the Family Code.

The plaintiff relies on Warden v. Warden, 36 Wash. App. 693, 676 P.2d 1037 (1984), to support her claim for relief under secs. 767.02(1)(h) and 767.255. In *Warden*, the Washington court of appeals held that the statute providing guidelines for property division upon dissolution of marriage, legal separation, etc., could also be applied to divide property acquired by unmarried cohabitants in what was "tantamount to a marital family except for a legal marriage." *Warden*, 36 Wash. App. at 698, 676 P.2d at 1039. *Warden* is remarkably similar on its facts to the instant case. The parties in *Warden* had lived together for 11 years, had two children, held themselves out as husband and wife, acquired property together, and filed joint tax returns. On those facts, the Washington court of appeals held that the trial court correctly treated the parties as a "family" within the meaning of the Washington marriage dissolution statute. In addition, the trial court had considered such statutory factors as the length and purpose of the parties' relationship, their two children, and the contributions and future prospects of each in determining their respective shares of the property.

Although the *Warden* case provides support for the plaintiff's argument, most courts which have addressed the issue of whether marriage dissolution statutes provide relief to unmarried cohabitants have either rejected or avoided application of a marriage dissolution statute to unmarried cohabitants. See, e.g., Marvin v. Marvin, 18 Cal. 3d 660, 681, 134 Cal. Rptr. 815, 557 P.2d 106 (1976); Metten v. Benge, 366 N.W.2d 577, 579-80 (Iowa 1985); Glasgo v. Glasgo, 410 N.E.2d 1325, 1331 (Ind. Ct. App. 1980); Kozlowski v. Kozlowski, 80 N.J. 378, 383, 403 A.2d 902, 905 (1979).

The purpose of statutory construction is to ascertain the intent of the legislature and give effect to that intent. If the language of the statute is unclear, the court will endeavor to discover the legislature's intent as disclosed by the scope, history, context, subject matter and purpose of the statute. Ball v. District No. 4, Area Bd., 117 Wis. 2d 529, 538, 345 N.W.2d 389 (1984).

While we agree with the plaintiff that some provisions in ch. 767 govern a mother, father, and their children, regardless of marriage,[7] upon our analysis of sec. 767.255 and the Family Code, we conclude that the legislature did not intend sec. 767.255 to extend to unmarried cohabitants.

When the legislature added what is now sec. 767.255 in 1977 as part of the no fault divorce bill, it stated that its "sole purpose" was "to promote an equitable and reasonable adjudication of the economic and custodial issues involved in *marriage* relationships." (emphasis supplied) Moreover, the unambiguous language of sec. 767.255 and the criteria for property division listed in sec. 767.255 plainly contemplate that the parties who are governed by that section are or have been married. Finally, secs. 767.02(1)(h) and 767.255 were both in existence before the 1979 legislature changed the title of ch. 767 from "Marriage" to "Family." A change in the title of the chapter would not change the import of these statutory provisions.

Furthermore, the Family Code emphasizes marriage. The entire Family Code, of which ch. 767 is an integral part, is governed generally by the

---

7. The plaintiff correctly points out that ch. 767 includes actions for determining paternity, which are not dependent upon the marital status of the parents. See secs. 767.45-767.53, Stats. 1985-86.

provisions of sec. 765.001(2), which states in part that "[i]t is the intent of chs. 765 to 768 to promote the stability and best interests of *marriage and the family. . . . Marriage* is the institution that *is the foundation of family and of society.* Its stability is basic to morality and civilization, and of vital interest to society and the state." (emphasis supplied) Section 765.001(3) further states that "[c]hapters 765 to 768 shall be liberally construed to effect the objectives of sub. (2)." The conclusion is almost inescapable from this language in sec. 765.001 (2)(3) that the legislature not only intended chs. 765-768 to protect and promote the "family," but also intended "family" to be within the "marriage" context.[10]

The statutory prohibition of marriages which do not conform to statutory requirements, sec. 765.21, Stats. 1985-86,[11] further suggests that the legislature intended that the Family Code applies, for the most part, to those couples who have been joined in marriage according to law.

On the basis of our analysis of sec. 767.255 and the Family Code which revealed no clear evidence that the legislature intended sec. 767.255 to apply to unmarried persons, we decline the invitation to extend the application of sec. 767.255 to unmarried cohabitants. We therefore hold that the plaintiff has not stated a claim for property division under sec. 767.255.

III.

The plaintiff urges that the defendant, as a result of his own words and conduct, be estopped from asserting the lack of a legal marriage as a defense against the plaintiff's claim for property division under sec. 767.255. . . .

Although the defendant has not discussed this legal theory, we conclude that the doctrine of "marriage by estoppel" should not be applied in this case. We reach this result primarily because we have already concluded that the legislature did not intend sec. 767.255 to govern property division between unmarried cohabitants. We do not think the parties' conduct should place them within the ambit of a statute which the legislature did not intend to govern them.

IV.

The plaintiff's third legal theory on which her claim rests is that she and the defendant had a contract to share equally the property accumulated during their relationship. The essence of the complaint is that the parties had a contract, either an express or implied in fact contract, which the defendant breached.

Wisconsin courts have long recognized the importance of freedom of contract and have endeavored to protect the right to contract. A contract will not be enforced, however, if it violates public policy. A declaration that the contract is against public policy should be made only after a careful balancing,

---

10. When the legislature abolished criminal sanctions for cohabitation in 1983, it nevertheless added a section to the criminal code stating that while the state does not regulate private sexual activity of consenting adults, the state does not condone or encourage sexual conduct outside the institution of marriage. . . .

11. Common law marriages were abolished in 1917. Laws of 1917, ch. 218, sec. 21. Sec. 765.21, Stats. 1985-86, provides that marriages contracted in violation of specified provisions of ch. 765 are void.

in the light of all the circumstances, of the interest in enforcing a particular promise against the policy against enforcement. Courts should be reluctant to frustrate a party's reasonable expectations without a corresponding benefit to be gained in deterring "misconduct" or avoiding inappropriate use of the judicial system. . . . ; Restatement (Second) of Contracts Section 178 comments b and e (1981).

The defendant appears to attack the plaintiff's contract theory on three grounds. First, the defendant apparently asserts that the court's recognition of plaintiff's contract claim for a share of the parties' property contravenes the Wisconsin Family Code. Second, the defendant asserts that the legislature, not the courts, should determine the property and contract rights of unmarried cohabiting parties. Third, the defendant intimates that the parties' relationship was immoral and illegal and that any recognition of a contract between the parties or plaintiff's claim for a share of the property accumulated during the cohabitation contravenes public policy.

The defendant rests his argument that judicial recognition of a contract between unmarried cohabitants for property division violates the Wisconsin Family Code on Hewitt v. Hewitt, 77 Ill. 2d 49, 31 Ill. Dec. 827, 394 N.E.2d 1204, 3 A.L.R.4th 1 (1979). In *Hewitt* the Illinois Supreme Court concluded that judicial recognition of mutual property rights between unmarried cohabitants would violate the policy of the Illinois Marriage and Dissolution Act because enhancing the attractiveness of a private arrangement contravenes the Act's policy of strengthening and preserving the integrity of marriage. The Illinois court concluded that allowing such a contract claim would weaken the sanctity of marriage, put in doubt the rights of inheritance, and open the door to false pretenses of marriage. *Hewitt*, 77 Ill. 2d at 65, 31 Ill. Dec. at 834, 394 N.E.2d at 1211.

We agree with Professor Prince and other commentators that the *Hewitt* court made an unsupportable inferential leap when it found that cohabitation agreements run contrary to statutory policy and that the *Hewitt* court's approach is patently inconsistent with the principle that public policy limits are to be narrowly and exactly applied.[14]

Furthermore, the Illinois statutes upon which the Illinois supreme court rested its decision are distinguishable from the Wisconsin statutes. The Illinois supreme court relied on the fact that Illinois still retained "fault" divorce and that cohabitation was unlawful. By contrast, Wisconsin abolished "fault" in divorce in 1977 and abolished criminal sanctions for nonmarital cohabitation in 1983.

The defendant has failed to persuade this court that enforcing an express or implied in fact contract between these parties would in fact violate the Wisconsin Family Code. The Family Code, chs. 765-68, Stats. 1985-86, is intended to promote the institution of marriage and the family. We find no indication, however, that the Wisconsin legislature intended the Family Code to restrict in any way a court's resolution of property or contract disputes between unmarried cohabitants.

14. Prince, Public Policy Limitations in Cohabitation Agreements: Unruly Horse or Circus Pony, 70 Minn. L. Rev. 163, 189-205 (1985).

The defendant also urges that if the court is not willing to say that the Family Code proscribes contracts between unmarried cohabiting parties, then the court should refuse to resolve the contract and property rights of unmarried cohabitants without legislative guidance. The defendant asserts that this court should conclude, as the *Hewitt* court did, that the task of determining the rights of cohabiting parties is too complex and difficult for the court and should be left to the legislature. We are not persuaded by the defendant's argument. Courts have traditionally developed principles of contract and property law through the case-by-case method of the common law. While ultimately the legislature may resolve the problems raised by unmarried cohabiting parties, we are not persuaded that the court should refrain from resolving such disputes until the legislature gives us direction. Our survey of the cases in other jurisdictions reveals that *Hewitt* is not widely followed.

We turn to the defendant's third point, namely, that any contract between the parties regarding property division contravenes public policy because the contract is based on immoral or illegal sexual activity. . . . [A]t oral argument defendant's attorney indicated that he did not find this argument persuasive in light of the current community mores, the substantial number of unmarried people who cohabit, and the legislature's abolition of criminal sanctions for cohabitation. . . . Because illegal sexual activity has posed a problem for courts in contract actions, we discuss this issue even though the defendant did not emphasize it.

Courts have generally refused to enforce contracts for which the sole consideration is sexual relations, sometimes referred to as "meretricious" relationships. See In Matter of Estate of Steffes, 95 Wis. 2d 490, 514, 290 N.W.2d 697 (1980), citing Restatement of Contracts Section 589 (1932). Courts distinguish, however, between contracts that are explicitly and inseparably founded on sexual services and those that are not. This court, and numerous other courts,[17] have concluded that "a bargain between two people is not illegal merely because there is an illicit relationship between the two so long as the bargain is independent of the illicit relationship and the illicit relationship does not constitute any part of the consideration bargained for and is not a condition of the bargain." *Steffes*, supra, 95 Wis. 2d at 514, 290 N.W.2d 697.

While not condoning the illicit sexual relationship of the parties, many courts have recognized that the result of a court's refusal to enforce contract and property rights between unmarried cohabitants is that one party keeps all or most of the assets accumulated during the relationship, while the other party, no more or less "guilty," is deprived of property which he or she has helped to accumulate. . . .

The *Hewitt* decision, which leaves one party to the relationship enriched at the expense of the other party who had contributed to the acquisition of the property, has often been criticized by courts and commentators as being unduly harsh.[18] Moreover, courts recognize that their refusal to enforce what

17. See, e.g., Glasgo v. Glasgo, 410 N.E.2d 1325, 1331 (Ind. App. 1980); Tyranski v. Piggins, 44 Mich. App. 570, 573-74, 205 N.W.2d 595, 598-99 (1973); Kozlowski v. Kozlowski, 80 N.J. 378, 387, 403 A.2d 902, 907 (1979); Latham v. Latham, 274 Or. 421, 426-27, 547 P.2d 144, 147 (1976); Marvin v. Marvin, 18 Cal. 3d 660, 670-71, 134 Cal. Rptr. 815, 822, 557 P.2d 106, 113 (1976).

18. See Prince, Public Policy Limitations on Cohabitation Agreements: Unruly Horse or Circus Pony, 70 Minn. L. Rev. 163, 189-205 (1985); Oldham & Caudill, A Reconnaissance of Public Policy

are in other contexts clearly lawful promises will not undo the parties' relationship and may not discourage others from entering into such relationships. Tyranski v. Piggins, 44 Mich. App. 570, 577, 205 N.W.2d 595 (1973). A harsh, per se rule that the contract and property rights of unmarried cohabiting parties will not be recognized might actually encourage a partner with greater income potential to avoid marriage in order to retain all accumulated assets, leaving the other party with nothing. See Marvin v. Marvin, supra, 18 Cal. 3d at 683, 134 Cal. Rptr. at 831, 557 P.2d at 122. . . .

The plaintiff has alleged that she quit her job and abandoned her career training upon the defendant's promise to take care of her. A change in one party's circumstances in performance of the agreement may imply an agreement between the parties. *Steffes*, supra, 95 Wis. 2d at 504, 290 N.W.2d 697; *Tyranski*, supra, 44 Mich. App. at 574, 205 N.W.2d at 597.

In addition, the plaintiff alleges that she performed housekeeping, childbearing, childrearing, and other services related to the maintenance of the parties' home, in addition to various services for the defendant's business and her own business, for which she received no compensation. Courts have recognized that money, property, or services (including housekeeping or childrearing) may constitute adequate consideration independent of the parties' sexual relationship to support an agreement to share or transfer property. . . . *Steffes*, supra 95 Wis. 2d at 501, 290 N.W.2d 697.[19]

According to the plaintiff's complaint, the parties cohabited for more than twelve years, held joint bank accounts, made joint purchases, filed joint income tax returns, and were listed as husband and wife on other legal documents. Courts have held that such a relationship and "joint acts of a financial nature can give rise to an inference that the parties intended to share equally." Beal v. Beal, 282 Or. 115, 122, 577 P.2d 507, 510 (1978). The joint ownership of property and the filing of joint income tax returns strongly implies that the parties intended their relationship to be in the nature of a joint enterprise, financially as well as personally. See *Beal*, 282 Or. at 122, 577 P.2d at 510; Warden v. Warden, supra, 36 Wash. App. at 696-97, 676 P.2d at 1038.

. . . Accordingly, we conclude that the plaintiff in this case has pleaded the facts necessary to state a claim for damages resulting from the defendant's breach of an express or an implied in fact contract to share with the plaintiff the property accumulated through the efforts of both parties during their relationship. Once again, we do not judge the merits of the plaintiff's claim; we merely hold that she be given her day in court to prove her claim.

Restrictions upon Enforcement of Contracts between Cohabitants, 18 Fam. L.Q. 93, 132 (Spring 1984); Comment, Marvin v. Marvin: Five Years Later, 65 Marq. L. Rev. 389, 414 (1982).

19. Until recently, the prevailing view was that services performed in the context of a "family or marriage relationship" were presumed gratuitous. However, that presumption was rebuttable. See *Steffes*, 95 Wis. 2d at 501, 290 N.W.2d at 703-704. In *Steffes*, we held the presumption to be irrelevant where the plaintiff can show either an express or implied agreement to pay for those services, even where the plaintiff has rendered them "with a sense of affection, devotion and duty." Id., 95 Wis. 2d at 503, 290 N.W.2d at 703-704. For a discussion of the evolution of thought regarding the economic value of homemaking services by cohabitants, see Bruch, Property Rights of De Facto Spouses Including Thoughts on the Value of Homemakers' Services, 10 Fam. L.Q. 101, 110-14 (Summer 1976).

V.

The plaintiff's fourth theory of recovery involves unjust enrichment. Essentially, she alleges that the defendant accepted and retained the benefit of services she provided knowing that she expected to share equally in the wealth accumulated during their relationship. She argues that it is unfair for the defendant to retain all the assets they accumulated under these circumstances and that a constructive trust should be imposed on the property as a result of the defendant's unjust enrichment. In his brief, the defendant does not attack specifically either the legal theory or the factual allegations made by the plaintiff.

Unlike claims for breach of an express or implied in fact contract, a claim of unjust enrichment does not arise out of an agreement entered into by the parties. Rather, an action for recovery based upon unjust enrichment is grounded on the moral principle that one who has received a benefit has a duty to make restitution where retaining such a benefit would be unjust. Puttkammer v. Minth, 83 Wis. 2d 686, 689, 266 N.W.2d 361, 363 (1978).

Because no express or implied in fact agreement exists between the parties, recovery based upon unjust enrichment is sometimes referred to as "quasi contract," or contract "implied in law" rather than "implied in fact." Quasi contracts are obligations created by law to prevent injustice. Shulse v. City of Mayville, 223 Wis. 624, 632, 271 N.W. 643 (1937).

In Wisconsin, an action for unjust enrichment, or quasi contract, is based upon proof of three elements: (1) a benefit conferred on the defendant by the plaintiff, (2) appreciation or knowledge by the defendant of the benefit, and (3) acceptance or retention of the benefit by the defendant under circumstances making it inequitable for the defendant to retain the benefit. *Puttkammer*, supra, 83 Wis. 2d at 689, 266 N.W.2d 361; Wis. J.I. Civil No. 3028 (1981).

The plaintiff has cited no cases directly supporting actions in unjust enrichment by unmarried cohabitants, and the defendant provides no authority against it. . . .

The *Steffes* case, however, does provide . . . support for the plaintiff's position. Although *Steffes* involved a claim for recovery in contract by an unmarried cohabitant for the value of services she performed for the decedent, the same equitable principles that governed that case would appear to apply in a case where the plaintiff is seeking recovery based upon unjust enrichment. In *Steffes*, the court cited with approval a statement by the trial judge that "[t]he question I have in mind is why should the estate be enriched when that man was just as much a part of the illicit relationship as she was and not let her have her fair dues. I don't understand that law that would interpret unjust enrichment that way and deprive one and let the other benefit and do it on the basis that there was an illicit relationship but not equally held against the both. . . . " *Steffes*, supra, 95 Wis. 2d at 508, 290 N.W.2d 697.

As part of his general argument, the defendant claims that the court should leave the parties to an illicit relationship such as the one in this case essentially as they are found, providing no relief at all to either party. For support, the defendant relies heavily on Hewitt v. Hewitt, supra, and the dissent in *Steffes*, to argue that courts should provide no relief whatsoever to unmarried cohabitants until the legislature provides specifically for it. See *Steffes*, supra, 95 Wis. 2d at 521-22, 290 N.W.2d 697 (Coffey, J., dissenting).

As we have discussed previously, allowing no relief at all to one party in a so-called "illicit" relationship effectively provides total relief to the other, by leaving that party owner of all the assets acquired through the efforts of both. Yet it cannot seriously be argued that the party retaining all the assets is less "guilty" than the other. Such a result is contrary to the principles of equity. Many courts have held, and we now so hold, that unmarried cohabitants may raise claims based upon unjust enrichment following the termination of their relationships where one of the parties attempts to retain an unreasonable amount of the property acquired through the efforts of both.

In this case, the plaintiff alleges that she contributed both property and services to the parties' relationship. She claims that because of these contributions the parties' assets increased, but that she was never compensated for her contributions. She further alleges that the defendant, knowing that the plaintiff expected to share in the property accumulated, "accepted the services rendered to him by the plaintiff" and that it would be unfair under the circumstances to allow him to retain everything while she receives nothing. We conclude that the facts alleged are sufficient to state a claim for recovery based upon unjust enrichment. . . .

VI.

The plaintiff's last alternative legal theory on which her claim rests is the doctrine of partition. The plaintiff has asserted in her complaint a claim for partition of "all real and personal property accumulated by the couple during their relationship according to the plaintiff's interest therein and pursuant to Chapters 820 and 842, Wis. Stats." . . .

In Wisconsin partition is a remedy under both the statutes and common law. Partition applies generally to all disputes over property held by more than one party. . . .

In this case, the plaintiff has alleged that she and the defendant were engaged in a joint venture or partnership, that they purchased real and personal property as husband and wife, and that they intended to share all the property acquired during their relationship. . . . We do not, of course, presume to judge the merits of the plaintiff's claim. Proof of her allegations must be made to the circuit court. We merely hold that the plaintiff has alleged sufficient facts in her complaint to state a claim for relief statutory or common law partition.

In summary, we hold that the plaintiff's complaint has stated a claim upon which relief may be granted. We conclude that her claim may not rest on sec. 767.255, Stats. 1985-86, or the doctrine of "marriage by estoppel," but that it may rest on contract, unjust enrichment or partition. Accordingly, we reverse the judgment of the circuit court, and remand the cause to the circuit court for further proceedings consistent with this opinion.

The judgment of the circuit court is reversed and the cause remanded.

Notes and Questions

1. *Measure of recovery.* Assuming that a court recognizes a right to quantum meruit recovery on behalf of a cohabitant, how is such recovery to be measured? On trial following remand in *Watts*, a jury awarded the plaintiff $113,000 on her unjust enrichment claim. The evidence showed that the defendant's net worth had increased by $1,113,900.88, during the 11 years the parties cohabited, so the jury's award amounted to about 10 percent of the defendant's increase in net worth. The Wisconsin Court of Appeals affirmed. 448 N.W.2d 292 (Wis. Ct. App. 1989). By contrast, in Waage v. Borer, 525 N.W.2d 96 (Wis. Ct. App. 1994), the court distinguished *Watts* and held that uncompensated services rendered during a cohabitation period of eight years were not sufficient to establish a claim for unjust enrichment because the claimant had failed to show that the defendant's wealth had been increased during the period of cohabitation. The court also ruled that the claimant's forgone employment opportunities were not relevant to her unjust enrichment claim.

Although the Wisconsin courts appear to focus on the increase in the defendant's net worth in measuring quantum meruit recovery in claims between cohabitants, courts in other jurisdictions will not necessarily agree, particularly in cases in which the increase in the defendant's wealth has been substantial. For example, in Maglica v. Maglica, 78 Cal. Rptr. 2d 101 (Ct. App. 1998), the California Court of Appeals reversed a jury verdict awarding one cohabitant $84 million on a quantum meruit theory. The court ruled that the trial judge had committed reversible error by instructing the jury to measure recovery by the amount by which the defendant had benefited from the plaintiff's services. The court held that the proper measure of recovery was the reasonable value of the plaintiff's services. What do you think the proper measure of recovery should be in such cases? Why?

2. *The **Marvin** case.* If parties are legally married, either by a "ceremonial" marriage, or by a "common law" marriage (recognized in a minority of jurisdictions), and subsequently separate or divorce, the spouse who sacrificed income while rendering services to the other may obtain court-ordered awards of support or alimony. In addition, in many jurisdictions courts have the power to order an equitable division of marital assets. Beginning with the leading case of Marvin v. Marvin, 557 P.2d 106 (Cal. 1976) (en banc), a number of jurisdictions have allowed a party to a nonmarital relationship who makes substantial contributions to the other party to obtain some form of recovery from the other. Such courts have relied on a number of legal theories, including express contract, implied-in-fact contract, and restitution based on unjust enrichment. The court in *Marvin* indicated that the opinion did "not preclude the evolution of additional equitable remedies to protect the expectations of the parties to a nonmarital relationship in cases in which existing remedies prove inadequate. . . . " Id. at 123 n.25. See generally, Symposium, Unmarried Partners and the Legacy of *Marvin v. Marvin*, 76 Notre Dame L. Rev. 1261 (2001).

Courts in a few states, however, have found contracts between unmarried cohabitants unenforceable. For example, Hewitt v. Hewitt, 394 N.E.2d 1204 (Ill. 1979), discussed by the court in *Watts*, denied recovery to a plaintiff who had lived with the defendant for 15 years in a nonmarital relationship to which three children were born. For a discussion of the current state of the law, see Allen M. Parkman, The Contractual Alternative to Marriage, 32 N. Ky. L. Rev. 125, 147-154 (2005). What are the principal arguments against recognition of a contractual or restitutionary recovery by a party to a nonmarital relationship who makes substantial contributions to the other? Does the opinion in *Watts* adequately address the arguments?

3. *Legislative reactions to **Marvin**.* Some states have adopted "antipalimony statutes," which allow cohabitants to enter into written agreements defining their economic relationship, but which preclude other theories of recovery, such as unjust enrichment. Do you think such a statute would be desirable as a matter of policy? Why? Depending on the judicial attitude toward such statutes, they may receive either a broad or a narrow construction. See, e.g., In re Estate of Eriksen, 337 N.W.2d 671 (Minn. 1983) (allowing claim for constructive trust in absence of written contract, construing statute to apply only if sexual relations were sole consideration for contract).

4. *Same-sex couples.* In *Watts*, the court considers the effect on plaintiff's claim of both legislation and case law establishing a public policy in favor of marriage as a legal and social institution. Plaintiffs in cases like *Watts* have had the historic burden of finding some viable basis for justifying recovery despite their failure to utilize the available option of a legal marriage, which would have given each partner specified legal rights. Until recently, same-sex couples have been uniformly denied access to such a legal status. However, in Goodridge v. Department of Public Health, 798 N.E.2d 941 (Mass. 2003), the Massachusetts Supreme Judicial Court held that the state's statutory prohibitions against marriage by same-sex couples lacked a rational basis and violated the state constitutional provision guaranteeing equal protection of the law. Efforts to overrule *Goodridge* by constitutional amendment have to date been unsuccessful. As a result thousands of gay couples have legally married in Massachusetts. See also Lewis v. Harris, 908 A.2d 196 (N.J. 2006) (finding violation of equal protection clause of New Jersey constitution and requiring legislature within 180 days to amend marriage statutes or enact appropriate statutory structure to afford same-sex couples the same rights and benefits accorded opposite-sex couples). But see Andersen v. King County, 138 P.3d 963 (Wash. 2006) (upholding state's Defense of Marriage Act under rational basis standard of review). For a discussion of American and Canadian cases, see Robin C. Miller & Jason Binimow, Marriage Between Persons of Same Sex–United States and Canadian Cases, 1 A.L.R. Fed. 2d 1 (2005).

Several jurisdictions have adopted "domestic partnership" statutes or ordinances of various types, perhaps the broadest of which is California's Domestic Partnership Act. Cal. Code Ann. §297 (West 2004). The most noteworthy such action to date, however, is Vermont's creation of a new partnership status, the "civil union," in response to the Vermont Supreme Court's 1999 ruling that the state's refusal to issue marriage licenses to same-sex couples violated the Vermont Constitution's "common benefits" clause. Baker v. State, 744 A.2d 864 (1999); see generally Lewis A. Silverman, Vermont Civil Unions, Full Faith and Credit, and Marital Status, 89 Ky. L.J. 1075 (2000-2001).

In the absence of legal protection for their relationships, some gay and lesbian couples have attempted to use traditional contract and property doctrines to protect their interests. Several court decisions have upheld the validity of cohabitation and property agreements between same-sex couples. See Whorton v. Dillingham, 248 Cal. Rptr. 405 (Ct. App. 1988) (validity of cohabitation agreement recognized); Posik v. Layton, 695 So.2d 759 (Fla. Dist. Ct. App. 1997) (support agreement between unmarried female cohabitants enforceable); Crooke v. Gilden, 414 S.E.2d 645 (Ga. 1992) (contract to share expenses for real property upheld because supported by legal consideration, even though defendant offered parol evidence to show that the parties were living in an "illegal and immoral" relationship); see also Silver v. Starrett, 674 N.Y.S.2d 915 (N.Y. Sup. Ct. 1998) (although New York courts have rejected *Marvin* implied-contract approach, express "separation agreement" between female cohabitants will be enforced). See Craig W. Christensen, Legal Ordering of Family Values: The Case of Gay and Lesbian Families, 18 Cardozo L. Rev. 1299 (1997); Ruthann Robson & S. E. Valentine, Lov(h)ers: Lesbians as Intimate Partners and Lesbian Legal Theory, 63 Temp. L. Rev. 511 (1990). Professor Kellye Testy has argued that the general feminist critique of contract law has been overbroad and that contract law includes a commitment to "fairness and connectivity" which can be harnessed to benefit women in general and lesbians in particular. Kellye Y. Testy, An Unlikely Resurrection, 90 Nw. U. L. Rev. 219, 220 (1995). Testy refers specifically to cohabitation contracts as one situation in which contract law could be used to protect the interests of lesbian couples. She recognizes, however, the dangers of such an approach:

> First, aspirations that lesbians may have for a new and better way of creating relations may be stunted by reliance on a patriarchal contractual model, thus domesticating or colonizing lesbian relationships. Second, relationship contracts also invite the state into lesbian relations, which means that patriarchy is also invited to the extent state power is patriarchal power.

Id. at 226.

5. *Intra-family claims.* Another common family situation in which restitutionary claims have been asserted involves cases in which one family member has cared for an aged parent or relative and then asserts a restitutionary claim against the estate of the deceased parent or relative. The effect of allowing such claims is to enable the family member asserting the claim to obtain a larger share of the estate than would otherwise be received under either the deceased person's will or the state's intestacy law (if no will is involved). Underlying such claims may be family tensions resulting from feelings that the family member providing services has made a personal sacrifice while the others (often siblings of the claimant) have not done their fair share in caring for the aged parent. The general rule followed in deciding such claims is that services rendered by family members to each other are presumed to be gratuitous, while services rendered between individuals who are not members of the same family are presumed to be for compensation. Whether the parties are part of the same family depends on the facts and circumstances rather than simply kinship. Consider for example Adams v. Underwood, 470 S.W.2d 180 (Tenn. 1971), where the Tennessee Supreme Court stated:

where, as in this case, an adult or emancipated child, by pre-arrangement with a parent, gives up an established home and moves into the home of the parent, not for the purposes of reestablishing a family relationship, but for the purpose of rendering services of an extraordinarily burdensome nature, over a long period of time, the presumption of gratuity need not apply.

Id. at 186. See also In re Estate of Bush (Fuller v. Terrell), 908 S.W.2d 809 (Mo. 1995) (plaintiff allowed to recover for services rendered to sister-in-law without having to overcome presumption that services were rendered gratuitously).

Even if the presumption that the services were rendered gratuitously applies, the presumption can be overcome, but courts differ on what the party seeking recovery must establish. See In re Grossman's Estate, 27 N.W.2d 365 (Wis. 1947) (presumption overcome when adult daughter left her home three times for extended periods to move 100 miles to care for ailing parents). Other courts may require a stronger showing to allow recovery between family members. Some courts have held that the one who renders services may recover only if she proves an express contract. West v. West, 229 S.W.2d 451 (Ky. 1950). Other courts will allow recovery based on either an express or implied contract but will demand proof by "clear and convincing evidence," a standard that is more demanding than the normal civil standard of the "preponderance of the evidence." Harrison v. Harrison, 75 So. 2d 620 (Ala. 1954). Which approach would you favor? Why? What factors should a court take into account in deciding whether to allow such a restitutionary claim?

2. Promissory Restitution

In the preceding section we examined situations in which one party sought a restitutionary recovery for benefits conferred on another where the other party never expressly promised to pay for those benefits. Suppose the recipient of services does make an express promise to pay for them, but only after the benefits are received? As we saw in the *Plowman* case in the previous chapter, classical theory would hold that a promise for benefits previously received was not binding because the benefits constituted "past consideration." Even classical theory recognized some exceptions to the past consideration doctrine; as we will see, additional exceptions are being created or explored by contemporary courts and the Restatement (Second). The following cases examine these developments.

Mills v. Wyman
Massachusetts Supreme Judicial Court
20 Mass. (3 Pick.) 207 (1825)

This was an action of assumpsit brought to recover a compensation for the board, nursing, &c., of Levi Wyman, son of the defendant, from the 5th to the 20th of February, 1821. The plaintiff then lived at Hartford, in Connecticut; the defendant, at Shrewsbury, in this county. Levi Wyman, at the time when the services were rendered, was about 25 years of age, and had long ceased to be a member of his father's family. He was on his return from a voyage at sea, and being suddenly taken sick at Hartford, and being poor and in distress, was relieved by the plaintiff in the manner and to the extent above stated. On the 24th of February, after all the expenses had been incurred, the defendant wrote a letter to the plaintiff, promising to pay him such expenses. There was no consideration for this promise, except what grew out of the relation which subsisted between Levi Wyman and the defendant, and Howe J., before whom the cause was tried in the Court of Common Pleas, thinking this not sufficient to support the action, directed a non-suit. To this direction the plaintiff filed exceptions.

PARKER, C.J. General rules of law established for the protection and security of honest and fair-minded men, who may inconsiderately make promises without any equivalent, will sometimes screen men of a different character from engagements which they are bound in foro conscientiae to perform. This is a defect inherent in all human systems of legislation. This rule that a mere verbal promise, without any consideration, cannot be enforced by action, is universal in its application, and cannot be departed from to suit particular cases in which a refusal to perform such a promise may be disgraceful.

The promise declared on in this case appears to have been made without any legal consideration. The kindness and services towards the sick son of the defendant were not bestowed at his request. The son was in no respect under the care of the defendant. He was twenty-five years old, and had long left his father's family. On his return from a foreign country, he fell sick among strangers, and the plaintiff acted the part of the good Samaritan, giving him shelter and comfort until he died. The defendant, his father, on being informed of this event, influenced by a transient feeling of gratitude, promises in writing to pay the plaintiff for the expenses he had incurred. But he has determined to break this promise, and is willing to have his case appear on record as a strong example of particular injustice sometimes necessarily resulting from the operation of general rules.

It is said a moral obligation is a sufficient consideration to support an express promise; and some authorities lay down the rule thus broadly; but upon examination of the cases we are satisfied that the universality of the rule cannot be supported, and that there must have been some preexisting obligation, which has become inoperative by positive law, to form a basis for an effective promise. The cases of debts barred by the statute of limitations, of debts incurred by infants, of debts of bankrupts, are generally put for illustration of the rule. Express promises founded on such preexisting equitable obligations may be enforced; there is a good consideration for them; they merely remove an impediment created by law to the recovery of debts honestly due, but which public policy protects the debtors from being compelled to pay. In all these cases there was originally a quid pro quo; and according to the principles of natural justice the party receiving ought to pay; but the legislature has said he shall not be coerced; then comes the promise to pay the debt that is barred, the promise of the man to pay the debt of the infant, of the discharged bankrupt to restore to his creditor what by the law he had lost. In all these cases there is a moral obligation founded upon an antecedent valuable consideration. These promises therefore have a sound legal basis. They are not promises to pay something for nothing; not naked pacts; but the voluntary revival or creation of obligation which before existed in natural law, but which had been dispensed with, not for the benefit of the party obliged solely, but principally for the public convenience. If moral obligation, in its fullest sense, is a good substratum for an express promise, it is not easy to perceive why it is not equally good to support an implied promise. What a man ought to do, generally he ought to be made to do, whether he promise or refuse. But the law of society has left most of such obligations to the *interior* forum, as the tribunal of conscience has been aptly called. Is there not a moral obligation upon every son who has become affluent by means of the education and advantages bestowed upon him by his father, to relieve that father from pecuniary embarrassment, to promote his comfort and happiness, and even to share with him his riches, if thereby he will be made happy? And yet such a son may, with impunity, leave such a father in any degree of penury above that which will expose the community in which he dwells, to the danger of being obliged to preserve him from absolute want. Is not a wealthy father under strong moral obligation to advance the interest of an obedient, well disposed son, to furnish him with the means of acquiring and maintaining a becoming rank in life, to rescue him from the horrors of debt incurred by misfortune? Yet the law will uphold him in any degree of parsimony, short of that which would reduce his son to the necessity of seeking public charity.

Without doubt there are great interests of society which justify withholding the coercive arm of the law from these duties of imperfect obligation, as they are called; imperfect, not because they are less binding upon the conscience than those which are called perfect, but because the wisdom of the social law does not impose sanctions upon them.

A deliberate promise, in writing, made freely and without any mistake, one which may lead the party to whom it is made into contracts and expenses, cannot be broken without a violation of moral duty. But if there was nothing paid or promised for it, the law, perhaps wisely, leaves the execution of it to the conscience of him who makes it. It is only when the party making the promise gains something, or he to whom it is made loses something, that the law gives the promise validity. And in the case of the promise of the adult to pay the debt of the infant, of the debtor discharged by the statute of limitations or bankruptcy, the principle is preserved by looking back to the origin of the transaction, where an equivalent is to be found. An exact equivalent is not required by the law; for there being a consideration, the parties are left to estimate its value: though here the courts of equity will step in to relieve from gross inadequacy between the consideration and the promise.

These principles are deduced from the general current of decided cases upon the subject, as well as from the known maxims of the common law. The general position, that moral obligation is a sufficient consideration for an express promise, is to be limited in its application, to cases where at some time or other a good or valuable consideration has existed.

A legal obligation is always a sufficient consideration to support either an express or an implied promise; such as an infant's debt for necessaries, or a father's promise to pay for the support and education of his minor children. But when the child shall have attained to manhood, and shall have become his own agent in the world's business, the debts he incurs, whatever may be their nature, create no obligation upon the father; and it seems to follow, that his promise founded upon such a debt has no legally binding force.

The cases of instruments under seal and certain mercantile contracts, in which considerations need not be proved, do not contradict the principles above suggested. The first import a consideration in themselves, and the second belong to a branch of the mercantile law, which has found it necessary to disregard the point of consideration in respect to instruments negotiable in their nature and essential to the interests of commerce. . . .

It has been attempted to show a legal obligation on the part of the defendant by virtue of our statute, which compels lineal kindred in the ascending or descending line to support such of their poor relations as are likely to become chargeable to the town where they have their settlement. But it is a sufficient answer to this position, that such legal obligation does not exist except in the very cases provided for in the statute, and never until the party charged has been adjudged to be of sufficient ability thereto. We do not know from the report any of the facts which are necessary to create such an obligation. Whether the deceased had a legal settlement in this commonwealth at the time of his death, whether he was likely to become chargeable had he lived, whether the defendant was of sufficient ability, are essential facts to be adjudicated by the court to which is given jurisdiction on this subject. The legal liability does not arise until these facts have all been ascertained by judgment, after hearing the party intended to be charged.

For the foregoing reasons we are all of opinion that the nonsuit directed by the Court of Common Pleas was right, and that judgment be entered thereon for costs for the defendant.

Notes and Questions

1. *Hypothetical variations of* **Mills.** Suppose the plaintiff had written the defendant about his son's illness on February 5 and the defendant had promptly written back promising to pay his son's expenses. Would the result have been different? Suppose instead that Levi Wyman was a 16-year-old boy, living at home with his parents, when he became ill while on a short trip away from home. Would the result have been different? On the latter assumed facts, would it have mattered whether the father had written the letter of February 24, promising to pay for his son's care?

2. *Moral obligation.* Cases like Mills v. Wyman are often referred to as involving enforcement of a "moral obligation." It is useful, however, to refine this point. The court in *Mills* clearly holds that the law will not necessarily enforce every promise, regardless of the morality of failing to honor a promise seriously made. In stating the general rule, the court notes that "there are great interests of society which justify withholding the coercive arm of the law from these duties of imperfect obligation." What interests do you suppose the court had in mind? Charles Fried, a noted philosopher and contract scholar, argues that this view is

wrong and that the law should follow morality, enforcing a promise seriously made. Recall the material following the *Plowman* case in Chapter 2.

The court in *Mills* also declares that a moral obligation can give rise to a legal obligation in certain specific situations: If a person was subject to a legal obligation that has become unenforceable (either because of passage of time, such as the statute of limitations, or for some other reason), a subsequent promise to honor or revive the legal obligation will be enforceable at law. Is it accurate to characterize this liability as being based on "moral obligation"?

3. *Debts barred by time.* The court states that promises to pay debts barred by the statute of limitations are enforceable because the debt is a preexisting legal obligation. A modern statement of this rule can be found in Restatement (Second) §82. As the Restatement provides in §82(2), a promise to pay a debt barred by the statute of limitations can be express or it may be implied from the conduct of the obligor. Case law has recognized a number of situations in which an implied promise to pay may be found: voluntary acknowledgment of the debt, part payment of principal or interest on the debt, delivery of a note reflecting the debt, and transfer to the creditor of security for the debt. See 4 Williston on Contracts §8.22, at 350 (4th ed. 1992). As the Restatement indicates, such conduct does not necessarily mean that a promise should be implied; other factors may indicate a different intention. Today, in most jurisdictions, statutes regulate the enforceability of promises to pay debts barred by the statute of limitations. Such statutes often define the type of conduct that constitutes an implied promise to pay the debt. See, e.g., S.C. Code Ann. §15-3-120 (Law. Co-op. 1977) (part payment of principal or interest equivalent of written promise); see generally 4 Williston on Contracts §8.22, at 353-354 n.15 (4th ed. 1992) (listing statutes).

4. *Debts discharged in bankruptcy.* Promises to pay debts previously discharged in bankruptcy are also legally enforceable. Restatement (Second) §83. Unlike promises to pay debts barred by the statute of limitations, promises to pay debts discharged in bankruptcy will not be judicially implied. Restatement (Second) §83 provides that the promise must be "express." See also E. Allan Farnsworth, Farnsworth on Contracts §2.8, at 59 (4th ed. 2004); 4 Williston on Contracts §8.19, at 321-322 (4th ed. 1992). Can this difference in treatment be justified? Consider the following comment from the Restatement: "In modern times discharge in bankruptcy has been thought to reflect a somewhat stronger public policy than the statute of limitations, and a promise implied from acknowledgment or part payment does not revive a debt discharged in bankruptcy." Restatement (Second) §83 comment *a.*

5. *Statutory restrictions on promises to revive debts.* At common law a promise to pay a debt barred by the statute of limitations or discharged in bankruptcy was binding even though made orally. Early in the nineteenth century, however, the English Parliament passed legislation requiring such promises to be in writing in order to be enforceable. 6 Geo. IV, ch. 16, Section CXXXI (debts discharged in bankruptcy); Lord Tenterden's Act, 9 Geo. IV, ch. 14 (debts barred by the statute of limitations). Many states have enacted similar legislation. 3 Corbin on Contracts §9.14 (rev. ed. 1996). What is the purpose of such legislation? Recall Professor Fuller's discussion of the function of legal formalities quoted in the Notes following the *Pennsy Supply* case in Chapter 2.

Under the United States Constitution, Congress has the power to establish "uniform Laws on the subject of Bankruptcies throughout the United States." Art. I, §8. Under §524(c), (d) of the Bankruptcy Code, Congress has imposed a number of limitations on the ability of debtors to reassume by agreement debts discharged in bankruptcy.

6. *Obligations of minors.* The court in *Mills* also refers to "debts incurred by infants" as a situation in which the law will enforce a promise for benefits previously received. The court's statement requires some elaboration. Contracts made by a minor prior to the time the minor reaches the legal age of majority (now 18) are unenforceable unless they are for "necessaries," goods and services needed by the minor. After reaching the age of majority a minor becomes legally liable on any contracts made during minority that the minor elects to "affirm." A minor may affirm a contract either expressly or by failure to "disaffirm" the contract within a reasonable time after reaching the age of majority. Restatement (Second) §85 reflects the rule that a minor's promise when he reaches the age of majority to perform a contract made during minority is legally binding. Section 85 has broader scope, however, applying to a promise to honor any "voidable" obligation. We will return in Chapter 7 to the subject of minors' capacity to contract.

7. *Scholarly commentary.* In recent years a number of scholars have conducted extensive historical research into leading contract cases. Professor Geoffrey Watson's inquiry into Mills v. Wyman has led him to reach some surprising conclusions:

> A close reading of the historical record reveals a starkly different version of the facts of Mills v. Wyman. . . . Seth Wyman never made the promise that the court said he made, and . . . young Levi Wyman did not meet the untimely death that the court said he had met. Thus the court rightly absolved Seth Wyman, but for the wrong reasons. . . . [O]ther records from the period, including evidence of Seth Wyman's considerable wealth, . . . raise new questions about the motivations of the parties.

In the Tribunal of Conscience: *Mills v. Wyman* Reconsidered, 71 Tul. L. Rev. 1749, 1751 (1997). In his article Professor Watson goes beyond historical research to propose reform of the moral obligation doctrine. Finding the various explanations of the doctrine unpersuasive, he argues that promises made with an intention to be bound should be enforceable because such a rule would increase "allocational efficiency" and would link "legal liability more closely to moral responsibility." Id. at 1805.

▌ **Webb v. McGowin**
Alabama Court of Appeals
27 Ala. App. 82, 168 So. 196 (1935), cert. denied,
232 Ala. 374, 168 So. 199 (1936)

BRICKEN, Presiding Judge.

This action is in assumpsit. The complaint as originally filed was amended. The demurrers to the complaint as amended were sustained, and because of this adverse ruling by the court the plaintiff took a nonsuit, and the assignment of errors on this appeal are predicated upon said action or ruling of the court.

A fair statement of the case presenting the questions for decision is set out in appellant's brief, which we adopt.

> On the 3d day of August, 1925, appellant while in the employ of the W. T. Smith Lumber Company, a corporation, and acting within the scope of his employment, was engaged in clearing the upper floor of mill No. 2 of the company. While so engaged he was in the act of dropping a pine block from the upper floor of the mill to the ground below; this being the usual and ordinary way of clearing the floor, and it being the duty of the plaintiff in the course of his employment to so drop it. The block weighed about 75 pounds.
>
> As appellant was in the act of dropping the block to the ground below, he was on the edge of the upper floor of the mill. As he started to turn the block loose so that it would drop to the ground, he saw J. Greeley McGowin, testator of the defendants, on the ground below and directly under where the block would have fallen had appellant turned it loose. Had he turned it loose it would have struck McGowin with such force as to have caused him serious bodily harm or death. Appellant could have remained safely on the upper floor of the mill by turning the block loose and allowing it to drop, but had he done this the block would have fallen on McGowin and caused him serious injuries or death. The only safe and reasonable way to prevent this was for appellant to hold to the block and divert its direction in falling from the place where McGowin was standing and the only safe way to divert it so as to prevent its coming into contact with McGowin was for appellant to fall with it to the ground below. Appellant did this, and by holding to the block and falling with it to the ground below, he diverted the course of its fall in such a way that McGowin was not injured. In thus preventing the injuries to McGowin appellant himself received serious bodily injuries, resulting in his right leg being broken, the heel of his right foot torn off and his right arm broken. He was badly crippled for life and rendered unable to do physical or mental labor.
>
> On September 1, 1925, in consideration of appellant having prevented him from sustaining death or serious bodily harm and in consideration of the injuries appellant had received, McGowin agreed with him to care for and maintain him for the remainder of appellant's life at the rate of $15 every two weeks from the time he sustained his injuries to and during the remainder of appellant's life; it being agreed that McGowin would pay this sum to appellant for his maintenance. Under the agreement McGowin paid or caused to be paid to appellant the sum so agreed on up until McGowin's death on January 1, 1934. After his death the payments were continued to and including January 27, 1934, at which time they were discontinued. Thereupon plaintiff brought suit to recover the unpaid installments accruing up to the time of the bringing of the suit.
>
> The material averments of the different counts of the original complaint and the amended complaint are predicated upon the foregoing statement of facts.

In other words, the complaint as amended averred in substance: (1) That on August 3, 1925, appellant saved J. Greeley McGowin, appellee's testator, from death or grievous bodily harm; (2) that in doing so appellant sustained bodily injury crippling him for life; (3) that in consideration of the services rendered and the injuries received by appellant, McGowin agreed to care for him the remainder of appellant's life, the amount to be paid being $15 every two weeks; (4) that McGowin complied with this agreement until he died on

January 1, 1934, and the payments were kept up to January 27, 1934, after which they were discontinued.

The action was for the unpaid installments accruing after January 27, 1934, to the time of the suit.

The principal grounds of demurrer to the original and amended complaint are: (1) It states no cause of action; (2) its averments show the contract was without consideration; (3) it fails to allege that McGowin had, at or before the services were rendered, agreed to pay appellant for them; (4) the contract declared on is void under the statute of frauds.

1. The averments of the complaint show that appellant saved McGowin from death or grievous bodily harm. This was a material benefit to him of infinitely more value than any financial aid he could have received. Receiving this benefit, McGowin became morally bound to compensate appellant for the services rendered. Recognizing his moral obligation, he expressly agreed to pay appellant as alleged in the complaint and complied with this agreement up to the time of his death; a period of more than 8 years.

Had McGowin been accidentally poisoned and a physician, without his knowledge or request, had administered an antidote, thus saving his life, a subsequent promise by McGowin to pay the physician would have been valid. Likewise, McGowin's agreement as disclosed by the complaint to compensate appellant for saving him from death or grievous bodily injury is valid and enforceable.

Where the promisee cares for, improves, and preserves the property of the promisor, though done without his request, it is sufficient consideration for the promisor's subsequent agreement to pay for the service, because of the material benefit received. . . .

In Boothe v. Fitzpatrick, 36 Vt. 681, the court held that a promise by defendant to pay for the past keeping of a bull which had escaped from defendant's premises and been cared for by plaintiff was valid, although there was no previous request, because the subsequent promise obviated that objection; it being equivalent to a previous request. On the same principle, had the promisee saved the promisor's life or his body from grievous harm, his subsequent promise to pay for the services rendered would have been valid. Such service would have been far more material than caring for his bull. Any holding that saving a man from death or grievous bodily harm is not a material benefit sufficient to uphold a subsequent promise to pay for the service, necessarily rests on the assumption that saving life and preservation of the body from harm have only a sentimental value. The converse of this is true. Life and preservation of the body have material, pecuniary values, measurable in dollars and cents. Because of this, physicians practice their profession charging for services rendered in saving life and curing the body of its ills, and surgeons perform operations. The same is true as to the law of negligence, authorizing the assessment of damages in personal injury cases based upon the extent of the injuries, earnings, and life expectancies of those injured.

In the business of life insurance, the value of a man's life is measured in dollars and cents according to his expectancy, the soundness of his body, and his ability to pay premiums. The same is true as to health and accident insurance.

It follows that if, as alleged in the complaint, appellant saved J. Greeley McGowin from death or grievous bodily harm, and McGowin subsequently agreed to pay him for the service rendered, it became a valid and enforceable contract.

2. It is well settled that a moral obligation is a sufficient consideration to support a subsequent promise to pay where the promisor has received a material benefit, although there was no original duty or liability resting on the promisor. . . . State ex rel. Bayer v. Funk, 105 Or. 134, 199 P. 592, 209 P. 113, 25 A.L.R. 625, 634. . . . In the case of State ex rel. Bayer v. Funk, supra, the court held that a moral obligation is a sufficient consideration to support an executory promise where the promisor has received an actual pecuniary or material benefit for which he subsequently expressly promised to pay.

The case at bar is clearly distinguishable from that class of cases where the consideration is a mere moral obligation or conscientious duty unconnected with receipt by promisor of benefits of a material or pecuniary nature. . . . Here the promisor received a material benefit constituting a valid consideration for his promise.

3. Some authorities hold that, for a moral obligation to support a subsequent promise to pay, there must have existed a prior legal or equitable obligation, which for some reason had become unenforceable, but for which the promisor was still morally bound. This rule, however, is subject to qualification in those cases where the promisor, having received a material benefit from the promisee, is morally bound to compensate him for the services rendered and in consideration of this obligation promises to pay. In such cases the subsequent promise to pay is an affirmance or ratification of the services rendered carrying with it the presumption that a previous request for the service was made. . . .

Under the decisions above cited, McGowin's express promise to pay appellant for the services rendered was an affirmance or ratification of what appellant had done raising the presumption that the services had been rendered at McGowin's request.

4. The averments of the complaint show that in saving McGowin from death or grievous bodily harm, appellant was crippled for life. This was part of the consideration of the contract declared on. McGowin was benefited. Appellant was injured. Benefit to the promisor or injury to the promisee is a sufficient legal consideration for the promisor's agreement to pay. Fisher v. Bartlett, 8 Greenl. (Me.) 122, 22 Am. Dec. 225; State ex rel. Bayer v. Funk, supra.

5. Under the averments of the complaint the services rendered by appellant were not gratuitous. The agreement of McGowin to pay and the acceptance of payment by appellant conclusively shows the contrary.

6. The contract declared on was not void under the statute of frauds (Code 1923, §8034). The demurrer on this ground was not well taken. 25 R.C. L. 456, 457 and 470, §49. . . .

From what has been said, we are of the opinion that the court below erred in the ruling complained of; that is to say, in sustaining the demurrer, and for this error the case is reversed and remanded.

Reversed and remanded.

SAMFORD, Judge (concurring).

The questions involved in this case are not free from doubt, and perhaps the strict letter of the rule, as stated by judges, though not always in accord, would bar a recovery by plaintiff, but following the principle announced by Chief Justice Marshall in Hoffman v. Porter, Fed. Cas. No. 6,577, 2 Brock. 156, 159, where he says, "I do not think that law ought to be separated from justice, where it is at most doubtful," I concur in the conclusions reached by the court.

Notes and Questions

1. *Promissory restitution principle.* The above case is often cited as an example of the "material benefit" rule, which holds that if a person receives a material benefit from another, other than gratuitously, a subsequent promise to compensate the person for rendering such benefit is enforceable. For further discussion of the background of Webb v. McGowin, see Richard Danzig & Geoffrey Watson, The Capability Problem in Contract Law: Further Readings on Well-Known Cases ch. V (2d ed. 2004). Restatement (Second) §86 adopts the material benefit rule. Professor Stanley Henderson has referred to §86 as "promissory restitution." Stanley D. Henderson, Promises Grounded in the Past: The Idea of Unjust Enrichment and the Law of Contracts, 57 Va. L. Rev. 1115, 1118 (1971). Is this a proper characterization of the section? If the receipt of material benefit alone is not enough to give rise to a right of recovery, why does the additional fact of the subsequent promise justify imposing an obligation?

Note that promissory restitution cases can be seen as occupying a middle ground between classical contracts and the pure restitution cases discussed in the previous section of this chapter. The promissory restitution cases bear a similarity to classical contract because the obligation rests on the assent of the person subject to liability. On the other hand, the promissory restitution cases involve liability even though no bargained-for exchange has occurred. In addition, as discussed in Note 2 below, the measure of recovery is based on restitutionary principles. For a recent examination of the application of §86 see Clay B. Tousey III, Exceptional Circumstances: The Material Benefit Rule in Practice and Theory, 28 Campbell L. Rev. 153 (2006). See also Kevin M. Teeven, Moral Obligation Promise for Harm Caused, 39 Gonz. L. Rev. 349 (2004).

Not all courts agree with the material benefit rule. In Harrington v. Taylor, 36 S.E.2d 227 (N.C. 1945), a wife after being assaulted by her husband took refuge in the plaintiff's house. The next day the husband gained entry to the plaintiff's house. In the ensuing struggle, the wife knocked her husband down and was about to strike him with an ax when the plaintiff intervened and was struck by the ax, receiving a severely mutilated hand, but saving the husband's life. Subsequently, the husband orally promised to pay the plaintiff for her damages. When the husband later refused to honor the promise, the plaintiff brought suit. The North Carolina Supreme Court affirmed the lower court's decision to sustain the demurrer to the complaint. The court stated that "however much the defendant should be impelled by common gratitude to alleviate the plaintiff's misfortune, a humanitarian act of this kind, voluntarily performed, is not such consideration as would entitle her to recover at law." Id. at 227. For further discussion of Harrington v. Taylor, see Richard Danzig & Geoffrey Watson, The Capability Problem in Contract Law: Further Readings on Well-Known Cases ch. VI (2d ed. 2004). Are *Webb* and *Harrington* in direct conflict or can the two cases be reconciled?

2. *The Restatement (Second) version of the principle.* Would the promise in Mills v. Wyman be enforceable under Restatement (Second) §86? Consider the following illustration to that section:

> 1. *A* gives emergency care to *B's* adult son while the son is sick and without funds far from home. *B* subsequently promises to reimburse *A* for his expenses. The promise is not binding under this Section.

Is this illustration consistent with the text of §86?

How would Webb v. McGowin be decided under §86? In particular, how would you respond to an argument that recovery should be denied because Webb rendered his services gratuitously in that he did not expect to receive compensation?

The text, comments, and illustrations to Restatement (Second) §86 recognize other limitations on the availability of promissory restitution. If enforcement of the promise would be disproportionate to the reasonable value of the benefit received, enforcement may be limited to that value. Restatement (Second) §86 comment *i*. The Restatement gives the following illustrations of this principle:

> 12. *A*, a married woman of sixty, has rendered household services without compensation over a period of years for *B*, a man of eighty living alone and having no close relatives. *B* has a net worth of three million dollars and has often assured *A* that she will be well paid for her services, whose reasonable value is not in excess of $6,000. *B* executes and delivers to *A* a written promise to pay *A* $25,000 "to be taken from my estate." The promise is binding.
>
> 13. The facts being otherwise as stated in Illustration 12, *B's* promise is made orally and is to leave *A* his entire estate. *A* cannot recover more than the reasonable value of her services.

In Comment *f* to §86, the Restatement also suggests that a promise to pay an additional sum for benefits received under a preexisting bargain is not enforceable:

> By virtue of the policy of enforcing bargains, the enrichment of one party as a result of an unequal exchange is not regarded as unjust, and this Section has no application to a promise to pay or perform more or to accept less than is called for by a pre-existing bargain between the same parties.

3. *Legislation.* New York has enacted legislation making promises based on moral obligation enforceable provided the promise complies with certain formal requirements:

A promise in writing and signed by the promisor or by his agent shall not be denied effect as a valid contractual obligation on the ground that consideration for the promise is past or executed, if the consideration is expressed in the writing and is proved to have been given or performed and would be a valid consideration but for the time when it was given or performed.

N.Y. Gen. Oblig. Law §5-1105 (McKinney 2001). New York courts have applied the statute in a number of cases to enforce promises that met the statutory requirements even though a bargained-for exchange had not occurred. See, e.g., Braka v. Travel Assistance Int'l., 807 N.Y.S.2d 372 (App. Div. 2006) (finding that son's written promise to repay father for expenses incurred by father when son was injured while traveling in Fiji was enforceable under statute, thus allowing son to recover from travel insurance company). However, the statute has been criticized as "too broad in scope and too restrictive in formal requirements." Robert Braucher, Freedom of Contract and the Second Restatement, 78 Yale L.J. 598, 605 (1969). What do you think Professor Braucher had in mind?

4. *Scholarly commentary.* Professors Lon Fuller and Richard Posner have both attempted to justify the doctrine that certain promises based on moral obligation are enforceable. Fuller relies on principles of morality, while Posner offers an economic justification. Which of these do you find the more persuasive?

> *Moral Obligation as Consideration.* — Courts have frequently enforced promises on the simple ground that the promisor was only promising to do what he ought to have done anyway. These cases have either been condemned as wanton departures from legal principle, or reluctantly accepted as involving the kind of compromise logic must inevitably make at times with sentiment. I believe that these decisions are capable of rational defense. When we say the defendant was morally obligated to do the thing he promised, we in effect assert the existence of a substantive ground for enforcing the promise. In a broad sense, a similar line of reasoning justifies the special status accorded by the law to contracts of exchange. Men *ought* to exchange goods and services; therefore when they enter contracts to that end, we enforce those contracts. On the side of form, concern for formal guaranties justifiably diminishes where the promise is backed by a moral obligation to do the thing promised. What does it matter that the promisor may have acted without great deliberation, since he is only promising to do what he should have done without a promise? For the same reason, can we not justifiably overlook some degree of evidentiary insecurity?
>
> In refutation of the notion of "moral consideration" it is sometimes said that a moral obligation plus a mere promise to perform that obligation can no more create legal liability than zero plus zero can have any other sum than zero. But a mathematical analogy at least equally appropriate is the proposition that one-half plus one-half equals one. The court's conviction that the promisor ought to do the thing, plus the promisor's own admission of his obligation, may tilt the scales in favor of enforcement where neither standing alone would be sufficient. If it be argued that moral consideration threatens certainty, the solution would seem to lie, not in rejecting the doctrine, but in taming it by continuing the process of judicial exclusion and inclusion already begun in the cases involving infants' contracts, barred debts, and discharged bankrupts.

Lon L. Fuller, Consideration and Form, 41 Colum. L. Rev. 799, 821-822 (1941).

Among the exceptions to the general principle that gratuitous promises will not be enforced are several which are grouped under the rubric of "past consideration." A subsequent promise to pay a debt barred by the statute of limitations, or to pay a debt discharged in bankruptcy, or to pay a debt that is uncollectable because the debtor was a minor at the time the debt was contracted, is legally enforceable even though there is no fresh consideration for the promise. There are classes of promise in which the utility of the promise to the promisor is often great and the costs of enforcement low. First, as regards utility, it should be noted not only that the stakes are often substantial (these are formal debts after all) but that the *incremental* gain in utility from the enforceable character of the promise may be great. The legal promise conveys information (which a mere stated intention to pay would not) about the promisor's attitude toward the payment of debts barred by a technicality. The information conveyed enhances the promisor's reputation for credit-worthiness and may induce people — not necessarily the promisee himself, which is why the promise itself may not be bilateral — to extend credit to him in the future. And enforcement costs are likely to be low or at least no higher than in conventional bilateral-contract cases because the underlying obligation — the original debt — is fully bilateral. The original debt is not directly enforceable only because of a condition which in the case of the statute of limitations slightly, and in the case of discharge in bankruptcy or voidability by reason of minority not at all, increases the likelihood of error compared to what it would have been in a suit on the original bilateral contract that gave rise to the debt.

The foregoing are cases where, although the promise is not bilateral, the promisor's intent is not donative, that is, not motivated by interdependence between the promisor's and the promisee's utility functions. Another class of "past consideration" cases, however, is best understood on the premise of the law's (implicit) recognition of the existence of interdependent utility functions. These are cases involving promises to compensate rescuers or others who have rendered an unbargained but valuable service to the promisor. . . .

The facts of a leading rescue past-consideration case, Webb v. McGowin, illustrate the benefits that may accrue to the promisor in such cases if the promise is legally enforceable, over and above the benefits of the transfer itself. The rescued person promised to pay his rescuer $15 every two weeks for the rest of the rescuer's life. This was a generous gift to the extent that the promise was enforceable but a much less generous one to the extent it was not. Had the promisor believed that such a promise was unenforceable, he might have decided instead to make a one-time transfer that might have had a much lower present value than that of the annuity which he in fact promised. Both parties would have been made worse off by this alternative. Hence, it is not surprising that the court held the promise to be enforceable.

Lon Fuller in a well-known article suggested a different rationale for the past-consideration doctrine. Proceeding from the premise that the requirement of consideration is designed in part to prevent people from making promises on the spur of the moment — promises they do not really mean to make and therefore should not be forced to honor (the "cautionary" function of consideration) — he argues that where the promise is to do what the promisor is morally obligated to do anyway, we need not worry whether he is acting deliberately or not — he *should* have made the promise and that is all that is important. This paternalistic approach is both difficult to square with the basic premises of contract law and an unnecessary embellishment to a theory of the enforcement of gratuitous promises. Fuller is aware of the relevance of economic considerations in explaining the pattern of enforcement and only fails to see that economic analysis can also explain the past-consideration cases.

Richard A. Posner, Gratuitous Promises in Economics and Law, 6 J. Legal Stud. 411, 418-419 (1977). What does Posner mean by "utility?" How can enforceability of a promise based on a past benefit increase utility?

5. *Recovery in the absence of a promise.* Suppose McGowin had *not promised* to care for Webb. Could he have still been held liable to Webb on pure restitutionary principles? Recall the *Pelo* case and its discussion of Restatement of Restitution §116. The difficulty facing Webb in such an action would be having to show that the services were not rendered gratuitously (i.e., were rendered with an "intent to charge" under Restatement §116). In cases involving professional providers of services, modern courts have been willing to find an intent to charge and have allowed recovery for the reasonable value of the services rendered. The courts have refused, however, to allow recovery by nonprofessionals even for out-of-pocket losses involved in rescues. In a similar vein, section 20 of the tentative draft of the Restatement (Third) of Restitution (quoted in the notes following *Pelo*) follows this case law by limiting restitutionary recovery to protect the life or health of another to providers of "professional services." However, comment *b*, after discussing various justifications for this limitation, states that this restriction is not "logically inevitable. On the contrary, a claim in restitution based on an emergency rescue by a nonprofessional would be entirely consistent with the rule of this Section, in any case in which the court was satisfied *(inter alia)* that the claimant had not acted gratuitously, and that the benefit conferred was capable of valuation."

A student comment criticizes the limitations of recovery to professional providers of services:

> The current general rule against such a recovery is all the more reprehensible since viable models of systems that recompense rescuers are provided by civil and maritime law. Key civil and maritime law concepts should be incorporated into the common law to ensure a rescuer's just compensation. Under the proposed model, fairness to the successful nonnegligent rescuer is achieved by requiring a rescuee unjustly enriched by the rescuer's actions to reimburse the rescuer for out-of-pocket expenses. Fairness to the rescuee, who may also be nonnegligent, is achieved by allowing a trial court to consider certain equitable factors. Most important among those factors is the rescuee's ability to pay, so that the rescuee's liability will not be excessive. . . . This Comment acknowledges that imposing a possibly heavy liability upon a nonnegligent rescuee may well be thought onerous. But this objection lacks force, because the rescuee is undoubtedly better off as a result of the rescuer's efforts. The common law was justifiably wary of externally imposed private liabilities, but in the rescue situation, personal autonomy is outweighed by other compelling societal values. Justice requires that a rescuee who has enjoyed the benefits of a rescuer's efforts bear the costs of that benefit to the extent the rescuee is financially able.

Ross A. Albert, Comment, Restitutionary Recovery for Rescuers of Human Life, 74 Cal. L. Rev. 85, 124-125 (1986). Do you agree or disagree? Why?

PROBLEM 3-2

Alliance Aviation, Inc., a large manufacturer of military aircraft, employs a number of pilots to test fly its experimental aircraft. Because of the riskiness of the work, test pilots command substantial salaries, in many cases well over $250,000 per year.

Several years ago one of the pilots employed by Alliance, William "Buck" Rogers, made a test flight of the prototype of Alliance's A-1 bomber. During the flight a fire broke out in the cockpit. While Rogers could have avoided injury to himself by ejecting from the aircraft, had he done so the A-1 would have crashed, possibly into a nearby residential community. Under company policy, which was incorporated into Rogers's employment contract, test pilots were required to use their best efforts to avoid the risk of harm to civilians. Instead of ejecting, Rogers flew the crippled plane back to its base, where he made an emergency crash landing; unfortunately, Rogers suffered serious injuries resulting in partial paralysis and ending his career as a test pilot.

Because of the severity of his injuries, Rogers was hospitalized for several months. While recuperating, he received frequent visits from co-workers at Alliance, including Tom Agnew, the president of the company. During one of the visits, after expressing regret that Rogers had suffered permanent injury, Agnew told Rogers that the company planned to provide for him financially. A few weeks later Rogers received the following letter from Agnew:

Dear Buck:

Everyone at Alliance is so glad to hear that you are making such fine progress and that you'll be home soon. I know Mary and the kids will be over-joyed to have you home again.

Buck, you have worked for Alliance for almost ten years and if my memory is correct you have test flown every major military plane that the company now manufactures. During this time, your safety record is unblemished. Now, because of your professionalism, your career as a pilot is over. But we at Alliance want you to know that we haven't forgotten your efforts over these last ten years. I am enclosing a check for $7500. You'll receive checks in this amount every month so long as the company's financial condition continues to be solid.

Sincerely,
Tom

Over the next few years, the company regularly sent these monthly checks to Buck. Buck in turn often visited the company; at Agnew's request, he even met on occasion with some of the company's test pilots to discuss their work and give them advice.

During this same period of time, Buck was the subject of an interview and series of newspaper stories by Ruth Tarbell, a reporter for a nationally known daily. As a result of this project, an idea emerged for Buck and Ruth to collaborate on a book about the military aircraft industry. Although Buck began work on the book as a staunch supporter of both the military and private industry, his research first led to surprise and then anger. In the end,

Buck and Ruth produced a best-selling exposé of the military aircraft industry: "The Wrong Stuff: The Government and the Military Aircraft Industry."

Although the book contains only a few unfavorable portions about Alliance, Agnew is furious, feeling that Buck betrayed the company. At best, he thinks the book will lead to more government red tape, at worst, loss of government contracts. Agnew has asked you whether the company can legally terminate Rogers's pension. What advice would you give?

PROBLEM 3-3

On November 1, Ronald Chang, a wealthy businessman, died suddenly of a heart attack. Ronald left a will in which he appointed the National Bank of City as his personal representative. Melinda O'Shea is the trust officer at National Bank who is in charge of Ronald's estate. The bank has retained the law firm in which you are an associate to provide legal services in connection with the administration of the estate. Today Ms. O'Shea called Edna Prinkley, the partner with whom you work, to ask for advice. The matter deals with Ronald's sister, Patricia Chang. Patricia has presented to Ms. O'Shea the following handwritten letter to her from her brother:

December 26

Dear Pat:

It was wonderful spending Christmas with you and mother. I can't believe it's been ten years since we had Christmas dinner together, but it seems like every year something urgent keeps me away. Anyway, I can't tell you how much I enjoyed the few hours we had together.

It's hard for me to believe that it's been 15 years since dad died. You have sacrificed in so many ways living with and taking care of mother. I guess your decision to move back home to live with mother pretty much ended your relationship with James; I know it put any thought of an academic career on hold, at least for the time being. I wish I could have contributed more financially to help you out, but it's only been in the last couple of years that I have really come into my own.

Anyway, this is more than a thank you note for Christmas and an apology for my failings. I have thought about the situation for some time, and I want to compensate you for what you have done and are continuing to do for mother and for me. I am making arrangements to transfer to you 1 million dollars in shares that I have in a mutual fund. I hope this gift will ease any concern you may have about your financial future.

With love,
Ron

Ronald did not transfer the $1 million in mutual fund shares to Patricia Chang before his death. Under his will, his estate, which is valued at approximately $10 million, passes to his wife and his children. The will makes no mention of any bequest to Patricia. Ms. O'Shea wants to know whether the letter from Ronald to Patricia Chang legally obligates the estate to pay Patricia the $1 million mentioned in the letter. What advice would you give? If you think there are additional facts that might affect your answer to Ms. O'Shea's question, indicate what they would be, and why they might be relevant.

4 | **The Statute of Frauds**

Early in our study, we encountered the rule — now of only limited importance — that a promise might be made enforceable merely by virtue of its expression in a sealed writing. At this point we turn our attention to a different kind of legal "formality": the statute of frauds. Unlike use of the seal (in the few situations where that device is still effective), a promisor's compliance with the formality imposed by the statute of frauds will not by itself make her promise enforceable. If a promise is not supported by consideration (or some substitute), then compliance with the statute of frauds will not be sufficient for enforcement. *Failure* to comply with the statute of frauds, however, has the reverse effect: The promise, even if it is supported by consideration, will be *unenforceable*.

The original statute of frauds (actually titled "An act for prevention of frauds and perjuries") was passed by the English parliament in 1677. It covered a variety of subjects, including some questions of civil procedure and succession to property, but the major part of the statute consisted of provisions requiring *certain types of contracts* to be in writing to be legally effective. "No action shall be brought," the statute declared, to enforce any such agreement, "unless that agreement . . . or some memorandum or note thereof, shall be in writing, and signed by the party to be charged therewith . . ." (i.e., the person against whom enforcement is sought).

The statute of frauds remained a part of English law for nearly three centuries. (Most of its provisions were repealed by Parliament in 1954.) During this time it became, either by legislative imitation or in a few cases by judicial decision, part of the law of every American state. The American statutes vary in their wording and today are likely to apply to other types of contracts beyond those originally covered by the English statute. Today any statute that requires a transaction to be memorialized in writing for legal efficacy is likely to be referred to as a "statute of frauds." In fact, it is a misnomer to refer to the statute of frauds as a single statute. Most states have a general statutory provision referred to as the statute of frauds but also a number of other statutory sections scattered in different parts of the state's code of statutory law requiring various types of contracts to be in writing.

In section 110, the Restatement (Second) of Contracts describes the coverage of the typical American statute of frauds:

§110. Classes of Contracts Covered

(1) The following classes of contracts are subject to a statute, commonly called the Statute of Frauds, forbidding enforcement unless there is a written memorandum or an applicable exception:

(a) a contract of an executor or administrator to answer for a duty of his decedent (the executor-administrator provision);

(b) a contract to answer for the duty of another (the suretyship provision);

(c) a contract made upon consideration of marriage (the marriage provision);

(d) a contract for the sale of an interest in land (the land contract provision);

(e) a contract that is not to be performed within one year from the making thereof (the one-year provision).

In addition, the original English statute of frauds applied to contracts for the sale of goods. This aspect of the statute of frauds is now covered by UCC §2-201, which requires contracts for the sale of goods in excess of $500 ($5000 under revised Article 2) to be evidenced by a writing signed by the party against whom enforcement is sought, unless some exception to the statute applies. The second part of this chapter examines §2-201. Note that the statute of frauds provisons of the Uniform Commercial Code are separate from the general statute of frauds. Note also that the Restatement refers to the possibility of special statutory provisions in each state requiring certain classes of contracts to be in writing. See, e.g., N.Y. Gen. Oblig. Law §5-701(a)(10) (McKinney 2001) (contracts to pay compensation for services rendered in sale or purchase of business opportunities); Tex. Bus. & Com. Code Ann. §26.01(b)(3) (West 2002) (agreement made in consideration of nonmarital conjugal cohabitation). It should also be recalled that statutes commonly require that a testamentary disposition must be in writing to be given legal effect. Additional formalities, such as attestation by witnesses, are also usually required.

Despite their statutory character, the original sections of the English statute have been so commonly reproduced and so frequently given judicial construction that they have acquired a distinct common law flavor. It is therefore possible to generalize in common law fashion about the construction of the statute of frauds—indeed, not merely possible, but *necessary*. The statute of frauds as a living rule of law cannot now be understood froms statutory language alone; the body of court decisions applying the statute form an essential part of its substance. (This is why the Restatement (Second) of Contracts, which ordinarily confines itself to restating the rules of common law, devotes a whole chapter (§§110-150) to explicating the application of the various traditional provisions of the statute of frauds, as listed in §110, quoted above.)

This is not to suggest that decisions under the various local statutes of frauds have been uniform or that courts have been unusually consistent in their approach to the statute. To some extent, the reverse is true. Although the statute was styled "an act for prevention of frauds and perjuries," it does not by its terms deal directly with perjury or fraud; it merely requires a writing as a means of avoiding the potential enforcement of spurious claims. If stringently followed, this approach would obviously have the effect of eliminating or at least minimizing the likelihood of such fraud being successful; however, it also has the potential for denying enforcement of many *non*perjured and *non*fraudulent claims as well, whenever the formal requirement has not been complied with. The courts have therefore been continuously faced with the necessity of choosing between the injustice of enforcing a possibly fraudulent claim and the injustice of refusing to enforce a possibly honest one. In these circumstances, it is hardly surprising that the courts have vacillated between strict and lenient enforcement of the rules that require a writing for enforceability. By and large, the courts have been rather more lenient than less, as will be evident from the body of case law that has grown up around the statute of frauds.

Some of this case law has resulted in the imposition of limitations on the scope of the statute not dictated by the statutory language itself. Thus, a promise "to answer for the debt of another person" is usually held not to be within the statute unless it was made to the creditor to whom that debt is owed (as opposed to being made to the debtor himself or to someone else) (see Restatement (Second) §112); even then the promise will probably not be subject to the statute if the creditor, in return for the making of the new promise, discharged the original debtor from his obligation (§115). The "debt of another" provision has also been held to be inapplicable when the promisor who has guaranteed payment of another's debt did so mainly for his own economic advantage, rather than out of solicitude for the debtor's well-being (§116). E.g., Walder, Sondak, Berkeley & Brogan v. Lipari, 692 A.2d 68 (N.J. Super. Ct. 1997) (closely held corporations held liable on oral guarantee of principal shareholder's legal fees for criminal defense; defendants' main purpose was protection of their business reputation); Thomas A. Armbruster, Inc. v. Barron, 491 A.2d 882 (Pa. Super. Ct. 1985) (oral promise made by one-third shareholder to guarantee corporation's contract for construction of bowling alley not subject to statute of frauds because "main purpose" of guarantee was to protect shareholder's investment of money).

Although statutes in many jurisdictions have restricted or abolished it, breach of a promise to marry was once a valid cause of action in most jurisdictions; nevertheless, mutual promises to marry have consistently been held not to constitute a "Contract Made Upon Consideration of Marriage" (§124). Such judicial constructions obviously have the effect of narrowing the scope of the statute, thus widening the potential enforceability of oral agreements.

The first section of this chapter will examine the judicial treatment of contracts subject to the general statute of frauds, while the second section addresses contracts governed by §2-201 of the UCC.

A. GENERAL PRINCIPLES: SCOPE AND APPLICATION

Whenever the statute of frauds is asserted as a defense against the enforcement of an alleged contract, a series of questions is likely to be raised.

First, is the contract at issue one of the types to which the statute of frauds applies, so that a signed memorandum will be required for its enforcement? (Or, as courts often put it, is this contract "within" the statute?) If the answer to that question is *No*, then the statute of frauds has no application to the case, and the plaintiff is free to prove her contract by any combination of relevant evidence, written or oral, direct or circumstantial. If, however, the answer to that first question is *Yes*, then a second question must be addressed: Is the statute of frauds "satisfied"? That is, is there some sort of written statement ("some memorandum or note") of its terms, signed by the defendant (the "party to be charged"), that is sufficient to meet the statute's requirements? If the answer to this second question is *Yes*, then the statute again presents no bar to enforcement, and the case may proceed in normal fashion. (Note that the plaintiff will still have the burden of persuading the trier of fact that the agreement was made as she alleges; the existence of a signed writing may help the plaintiff prove that the asserted contract was actually made, but it will not necessarily be conclusive on that issue.) Suppose, however, that the answers to the first two questions are *Yes* and *No*: Yes, the contract sued on is within the statute; no, there is not a writing sufficient to satisfy the statutory requirement. Does this end the case? Not necessarily. A third question must still be answered: Are there other factors in the case, such as performance or reliance by the plaintiff, which might invoke an exception to the statutory bar?

Crabtree v. Elizabeth Arden Sales Corp.
New York Court of Appeals
305 N.Y. 48, 110 N.E.2d 551 (1953)

FULD, Judge.

In September of 1947, Nate Crabtree entered into preliminary negotiations with Elizabeth Arden Sales Corporation, manufacturers and sellers of cosmetics, looking toward his employment as sales manager. Interviewed on September 26th, by Robert P. Johns, executive vice-president and general manager of the corporation, who had apprised him of the possible opening, Crabtree requested a three-year contract at $25,000 a year. Explaining that he would be giving up a secure well-paying job to take a position in an entirely new field of endeavor—which he believed would take him some years to master—he insisted upon an agreement for a definite term. And he repeated his desire for a contract for three years to Miss Elizabeth Arden, the corporation's president. When Miss Arden finally indicated that she was prepared to offer a two-year contract, based on an annual salary of $20,000 for the first six months, $25,000 for the second six months and $30,000 for the second year, plus expenses of $5,000 a year for each of those years, Crabtree replied that that offer was "interesting." Miss Arden thereupon had her personal secretary make this memorandum on a telephone order blank that happened to be at hand:

EMPLOYMENT AGREEMENT WITH

NATE CRABTREE   Date Sept. 26-1947
   At 681 — 5th Ave   6:PM

                    Begin   20000.
                    6 months   25000.
                    6 months   30000.

                    5000. — per year
                    Expense money
                    [2 years to make good]

   Arrangement with Mr. Crabtree
      By Miss Arden
      Present Miss Arden
               Mr. Johns
               Mr. Crabtree
               Miss O'Leary

A few days later, Crabtree 'phoned Mr. Johns and telegraphed Miss Arden; he accepted the "invitation to join the Arden organization," and Miss Arden wired back her "welcome." When he reported for work, a "pay-roll change" card was made up and initialed by Mr. Johns, and then forwarded to the payroll department. Reciting that it was prepared on September 30, 1947, and was to be effective as of October 22d, it specified the names of the parties, Crabtree's "Job Classification" and, in addition, contained the notation that:

This employee is to be paid as follows:

   First six months of employment $20,000. per annum
   Next six months of employment   25,000. per annum
   After one year of employment   30,000. per annum

Approved by *RPJ* [initialed]

After six months of employment, Crabtree received the scheduled increase from $20,000 to $25,000, but the further specified increase at the end of the year was not paid. Both Mr. Johns and the comptroller of the corporation, Mr. Carstens, told Crabtree that they would attempt to straighten out the matter with Miss Arden, and, with that in mind, the comptroller prepared another "pay-roll change" card, to which his signature is appended, noting that there was to be a "Salary increase" from $25,000 to $30,000 a year, "per contractual arrangements with Miss Arden." The latter, however, refused to approve the increase and, after further fruitless discussion, plaintiff left defendant's employ and commenced this action for breach of contract.

At the ensuing trial, defendant denied the existence of any agreement to employ plaintiff for two years, and further contended that, even if one had been made, the statute of frauds barred its enforcement. The trial court found against defendant on both issues and awarded plaintiff damages of about $14,000, and the Appellate Division, two justices dissenting, affirmed. Since the contract relied upon was not to be performed within a year, the primary question for decision is whether there was a memorandum of its terms, subscribed by defendant, to satisfy the statute of frauds, Personal Property Law, §31.

Each of the two payroll cards — the one initialed by the defendant's general manager, the other signed by its comptroller — unquestionably constitutes a memorandum under the statute. That they were not prepared or signed with the intention of evidencing the contract, or that they came into existence subsequent to its execution, is of no consequence, see Marks v. Cowdin, 226 N.Y. 138, 145, 123 N.E. 139, 141; Spiegel v. Lowenstein, 162 App. Div. 443, 448-449, 147 N.Y.S. 655, 658; see, also, Restatement, Contracts, §§209, 210, 214; it is enough, to meet the statute's demands, that they were signed with intent to authenticate the information contained therein and that such information does evidence the terms of the contract. See . . . Corbin on Contracts [1951], pp.732-733, 763-764; 2 Williston on Contracts [Rev. ed., 1936], pp.1682-1683. Those two writings contain all of the essential terms of the contract — the parties to it, the position that plaintiff was to assume, the salary that he was to receive — except that relating to the duration of plaintiff's employment. Accordingly, we must consider whether that item, the length of the contract, may be supplied by reference to the earlier unsigned office memorandum, and, if so, whether its notation, "2 years to make good," sufficiently designates a period of employment.

The statute of frauds does not require the "memorandum . . . to be in one document. It may be pieced together out of separate writings, connected with one another either expressly or by the internal evidence of subject-matter and occasion." Marks v. Cowdin, supra, 226 N.Y. 138, 145, 123 N.E. 139, 141, see, also, 2 Williston, op. cit., p.1671; Restatement, Contracts, §208, subd. [a]. Where each of the separate writings has been subscribed by the party to be charged, little if any difficulty is encountered. See, e.g., Marks v. Cowdin, supra, 226 N.Y. 138, 144-145, 123 N.E. 139, 141. Where, however, some writings have been signed, and others have not — as in the case before us — there is basic disagreement as to what constitutes a sufficient connection permitting the unsigned papers to be considered as part of the statutory memorandum. The courts of some jurisdictions insist that there be a reference, of varying degrees of specificity, in the signed writing to that unsigned, and, if there is no such reference, they refuse to permit consideration of the latter in determining whether the memorandum satisfies the statute. . . . That conclusion is based upon a construction of the statute which requires that the connection between the writings and defendant's acknowledgement of the one not subscribed, appear from examination of the papers alone, without the aid of parol evidence. The other position — which has gained increasing support over the years — is that a sufficient connection between the papers is established simply by a reference in them to the same subject matter or transaction. . . . The statute is not pressed "to the extreme of a literal and rigid logic," Marks v. Cowdin, supra, 226 N.Y. 138, 144, 123 N.E. 139, 141, and oral testimony is admitted to show the connection between the documents and to establish the acquiescence, of the party to be charged, to the contents of the one unsigned. See Beckwith v. Talbot, 95 U.S. 289, 24 L. Ed. 496; . . . 2 Corbin, op. cit., §§512-518; cf. Restatement, Contracts, §208, subd. [b], par. [iii].

The view last expressed impresses us as the more sound, and, indeed — although several of our cases appear to have gone the other way . . . — this court has on a number of occasions approved the rule, and we now definitively adopt it, permitting the signed and unsigned writings to be read together, provided that they clearly refer to the same subject matter or transaction. . . .

The language of the statute — "Every agreement . . . is void, unless . . . some note or memorandum thereof be in writing, and subscribed by the party to be charged," Personal Property Law, §31 — does not impose the requirement that the signed acknowledgment of the contract must appear from the writings alone, unaided by oral testimony. The danger of fraud and perjury, generally attendant upon the admission of parol evidence, is at a minimum in a case such as this. None of the terms of the contract are supplied by parol. All of them must be set out in the various writings presented to the court, and at least one writing, the one establishing a contractual relationship between the parties, must bear the signature of the party to be charged, while the unsigned document must on its face refer to the same transaction as that set forth in the one that was signed. Parol evidence — to portray the circumstances surrounding the making of the memorandum — serves only to connect the separate documents and to show that there was assent, by the party to be charged, to the contents of the one unsigned. If that testimony does not convincingly connect the papers, or does not show assent to the unsigned paper, it is within the province of the judge to conclude, as a matter of law, that the statute has not been satisfied. True, the possibility still remains that, by fraud or perjury, an agreement never in fact made may occasionally be enforced under the subject matter or transaction test. It is better to run that risk, though, than to deny enforcement to all agreements, merely because the signed document made no specific mention of the unsigned writing. As the United States Supreme Court declared, in sanctioning the admission of parol evidence to establish the connection between the signed and unsigned writings, "There may be cases in which it would be a violation of reason and common sense to ignore a reference which derives its significance from such [parol] proof. If there is ground for any doubt in the matter, the general rule should be enforced. But where there is no ground for doubt, its enforcement would aid, instead of discouraging, fraud." Beckwith v. Talbot, supra, 95 U.S. 289, 292, 24 L. Ed. 496; see also, . . . 2 Corbin, op. cit. §512, and cases there cited.

Turning to the writings in the case before us — the unsigned office memo, the payroll change form initialed by the general manager Johns, and the paper signed by the comptroller Carstens — it is apparent, and most patently, that all three refer on their face to the same transaction. The parties, the position to be filled by plaintiff, the salary to be paid him, are all identically set forth; it is hardly possible that such detailed information could refer to another or a different agreement. Even more, the card signed by Carstens notes that it was prepared for the purpose of a "Salary increase per contractual arrangements with Miss Arden." That certainly constitutes a reference of sorts to a more comprehensive "arrangement," and parol is permissible to furnish the explanation.

The corroborative evidence of defendant's assent to the contents of the unsigned office memorandum is also convincing. Prepared by defendant's agent, Miss Arden's personal secretary, there is little likelihood that the paper was fraudulently manufactured or that defendant had not assented to its contents. Furthermore, the evidence as to the conduct of the parties at the time it was prepared persuasively demonstrates defendant's assent to its terms. Under such circumstances, the courts below were fully justified in finding that the three papers constituted the "memorandum" of their agreement within the meaning of the statute.

Nor can there be any doubt that the memorandum contains all of the essential terms of the contract. . . . Only one term, the length of the employment, is in dispute. The September 26th office memorandum contains the notation, "2 years to make good." What purpose, other than to denote the length of the contract term, such a notation could have, is hard to imagine. Without it, the employment would be at will, see Martin v. New York Life Ins. Co., 148 N.Y. 117, 121, 42 N.E. 416, 417, and its inclusion may not be treated as meaningless or purposeless. Quite obviously, as the courts below decided, the phrase signifies that the parties agreed to a term, a certain and definite term, of two years, after which, if plaintiff did not "make good," he would be subject to discharge. And examination of other parts of the memorandum supports that construction. Throughout the writings, a scale of wages, increasing plaintiff's salary periodically, is set out; that type of arrangement is hardly consistent with the hypothesis that the employment was meant to be at will. The most that may be argued from defendant's standpoint is that "2 years to make good," is a cryptic and ambiguous statement. But, in such a case, parol evidence is admissible to explain its meaning. See Martocci v. Greater New York Brewery, 301 N.Y. 57, 63, 92 N.E.2d 887, 889; Marks v. Cowdin, supra, 226 N.Y. 138, 143-144, 123 N.E. 139, 140, 141; 2 Williston, op. cit., §576; 2 Corbin, op. cit., §527. Having in mind the relations of the parties, the course of the negotiations and plaintiff's insistence upon security of employment, the purpose of the phrase — or so the trier of the facts was warranted in finding — was to grant plaintiff the tenure he desired.

The judgment should be affirmed, with costs.

LOUGHRAN, C.J., and LEWIS, CONWAY, DESMOND, DYE and FROESSEL, JJ., concur.

Judgment affirmed.

Notes and Questions

1. *The "one year" clause.* The contract in *Crabtree* was governed by the "one year" provision of the statute of frauds, which requires a contract "not to be performed within one year" from the date the contract is made to be in writing. What is the rationale for subjecting contracts of a longer duration to the statute of frauds, while exempting shorter contracts from that provision?

Courts on the whole have been quite lenient in interpreting the one-year provision of the statute of frauds. The standard view is that a contract is not subject to the statutory provision if it is *possible to be performed* within a year, even though the prospect of such performance is remote. Thus, in Freedman v. Chemical Construction Corp., 372 N.E.2d 12 (N.Y. 1977), plaintiff alleged that defendant had orally promised to pay him a commission for procuring a contract for the construction of a chemical plant in Saudi Arabia, plaintiff's fee to be payable on completion of the plant. Some nine years in fact passed between the making of the alleged promise and the plant's completion, but the court nevertheless held the contract not to be within the one-year clause; the whole process *could* have taken place within a year, said the court, even if that would have been "unlikely or improbable." Accord Griffith v. One Investment Plaza Associates, 488 A.2d 182 (Md. 1985) (agreement to pay commissions for procuring tenants for defendant's building enforceable; no showing that plaintiff could not have procured sufficient tenants within a year). In *Freedman*, however, the plaintiff's claim was barred by another provision of the New York statute of frauds, which applies to certain claims for brokerage commissions and finder's fees (N.Y. Gen. Oblig. Law §5-701(a)(10) (McKinney 2001).

In applying the one-year provision courts typically distinguish between the possibility of *performance* within one year and *termination* within one year. The fact that a contract may be terminated within a year is not sufficient to remove the contract from the requirements of the statute; only performance will do. (Without this distinction, the one-year provision of the statute of frauds would be judicially negated because any contract can be terminated within one year due to breach.) Thus, a contract for a definite duration (like five years) is subject to the statute of frauds even though it might be terminated within one year because of breach by one party or because of some excusing event, such as impossibility of performance. Restatement (Second) §130, Comment *b*.

The distinction between performance and termination is often a fine one, however. Compare D & N Boening, Inc. v. Kirsch Beverages, Inc., 472 N.E.2d 992 (N.Y. 1984) (oral contract for beverage distributorship to continue for as long as products were "satisfactorily distributed" was subject to statute of frauds; contract could only end within year because of termination on account of breach), with Ohanian v. Avis Rent A Car Systems, Inc., 779 F.2d 101 (2d Cir. 1985) (oral employment agreement interpreted by court as providing for termination by defendant employer only for "just cause"; held not within one-year clause because some events that might have constituted proper basis for termination under that provision would not have amounted to an unexcused breach by plaintiff employee).

2. *Lifetime contracts.* Sometimes an employee will allege that her employer has orally agreed to a contract of "permanent" or "lifetime" employment. If the employer asserts the statute of frauds one-year clause as a defense to enforcement, the court is likely to hold it inapplicable, on the basis that contracts measured by a lifetime are inherently capable of termination by full performance in less than a year, if the measuring lifetime should end before a year is up, as of course is always a possibility. Perhaps reacting to the expansion of employee rights in the employment-at-will area, some judges and commentators in recent years have urged reconsideration of this issue, arguing that such an agreement is really a contract for a term of years, and should be regarded as falling within the statute. E.g., McInerney v. Charter Golf, Inc., 680 N.E.2d 1347 (Ill. 1997) (employee who allegedly gave up existing employment in exchange for oral offer of permanent employment from defendant barred from asserting claim by one-year statute of frauds

because relationship of more than one year clearly contemplated; strong three-judge dissent argued majority's holding contrary to both the statute and the great weight of authority, and poor policy as well); Wior v. Anchor Industries, Inc., 669 N.E.2d 172 (Ind. 1996) (statute of frauds bars suit on employer's promise of permanent employment until retirement; court treats as in effect a 20-year contract, rather than a lifetime one). See also Frank Vickory, The Erosion of the Employment-at-Will Doctrine and the Statute of Frauds: Time to Amend the Statute, 30 Am. Bus. L. J. 97 (1992), arguing that recent erosion of the at-will doctrine coupled with traditional willingness to enforce oral agreements puts employers in this area at an unfair disadvantage. We will return in Chapter 6 to a fuller consideration of the various issues at stake in the law's treatment of employment agreements.

3. *Requirements for linking documents. Crabtree* allows the memorandum requirement of the statute of frauds to be satisfied by linking several documents through oral testimony even though the documents do not expressly refer to each other. Other issues may arise with regard to linking documents: Is assent to the unsigned writing necessary? In *Crabtree* the court stated: "If that testimony does not convincingly connect the papers, *or does not show assent to the unsigned paper,* it is within the province of the judge to conclude, as a matter of law, that the statute has not been satisfied" (emphasis supplied). The Restatement (Second) is to the same effect, although perhaps somewhat more generous. Section 132 provides that a memorandum may consist of several writings if one is signed and the others clearly relate to the same transaction. Comment *c* states: "Even if there is no internal reference or physical connection, the documents may be read together if in the circumstances they clearly relate to the same transaction *and the party to be charged has acquiesced in the contents of the unsigned writing*" (emphasis supplied).

It seems likely that the more persuasive the evidence that plaintiff's story is true, the readier a court will be to combine the writings in *Crabtree* fashion. See, e.g., Gregerson v. Jensen, 617 P.2d 369 (Utah 1980) (check endorsed by defendant vendor of land contained reference to "deed"; held sufficient when taken with later-drafted deed containing sufficient description of property, apparently prepared at direction of defendant but never signed by him). Suppose the memorandum quoted in the *Crabtree* opinion had been made not by Arden's secretary but by Crabtree himself, during his meeting with the Arden executives. Would the contract have been enforced?

Must the signed writing show the existence of a contract? In Horn & Hardart Co. v. Pillsbury Co., 888 F.2d 8 (2d Cir. 1989), the court stated:

> . . . [T]he rule fashioned in *Crabtree* to permit satisfaction of the Statute of Frauds by a series of signed and unsigned writings contains two strict threshold requirements. First, the signed writing must itself establish "a contractual relationship between the parties." . . . Second, the unsigned writing must "on its face refer to the same transaction as that set forth in the one that was signed." . . . Compliance with these two threshold requirements may be decided by the district court as a matter of law, and must be considered without the introduction of parol evidence.

Id. at 11. Here again, the Restatement seems more liberal. As discussed in the next Note, under Restatement (Second) §133 and its illustrations, it is not necessary for the signed writing to establish a contractual relationship; the memorandum may consist of an informal writing (even a letter that is not sent), an offer, or a document that attempts to repudiate contractual liability.

4. *Alternate analysis of **Crabtree**.* Could the court in *Crabtree* have reached the same outcome on other grounds? Restatement (Second) §133 states that a memorandum sufficient to satisfy the statute of frauds need *not* have been "made as a memorandum of a contract." The comments to that section amplify this rule by suggesting that the memorandum may consist of "an entry in a diary or in the minutes of a meeting," a "communication to or from an agent of the party [to be charged]," or "an informal letter to a third person" (Comment *b*). A memorandum may even be sufficient even though it "repudiates or cancels the contract, or asserts that it is not binding because not in writing" (Comment *c*). Section 133 is accompanied by the following illustrations:

> 1. *A* and *B* enter into an oral contract for the sale of Blackacre. *A* writes and signs a letter to his friend *C* containing an accurate statement of the contract. The letter is a sufficient memorandum to charge *A* even though it is never mailed.
> 2. *A* writes to *B* the following letter:
>
>> Dear *B*: I will employ you as superintendent of my mill for a term of three years from date, at a salary of $28,000 a year. Let me know if you wish to accept this offer. [Signed] *A*.
>
> *B* accepts the offer orally. The letter is a sufficient memorandum to charge *A*. . . .
> 4. *A* and *B* enter into an oral contract by which *A* promises to sell and *B* promises to buy Blackacre for $5,000. *A* writes and signs a letter to *B* in which he states accurately the terms of the bargain, but adds "our agreement was oral. It, therefore, is not binding upon me, and I shall not carry it out." The letter is a sufficient memorandum to charge *A*.

Could any of the principles illustrated above have been applied in *Crabtree*?

5. *The requirement of a "signed writing."* Although the requirements of a writing and a signature are commonly referred to as legal "formalities," it is clear that neither the writing itself nor the signature need be "formal" in order to satisfy the statutory requirement. Both the Restatement and the Uniform Commercial Code take a lenient view of what may constitute a "writing" and a "signature" for purposes of the statute of frauds. Restatement (Second) §§131-137; UCC §1-201(39), (46), and comments thereto. Revised Article 2 uses the term "record." See, e.g., Rosenfeld v. Basquiat, 78 F.3d 84 (2d Cir. 1996) (short memo written and signed by artist in crayon on large piece of paper could be sufficient memo for enforcement of asserted contract for sale of three paintings—eventually worth over $350,000—for total price of $12,000); Owen v. Kroger Co., 936 F. Supp. 579 (S.D. Ind. 1996) (preprinted wording on memos, showing corporate logo and indicating memos were "from the desk of" named agents of defendant, could serve as signature; jury question whether by using pad writers intended to "authenticate" information stated). Recall Professor Fuller's discussion of the various functions that legal formalities may serve (quoted in the Notes following the *Pennsy Supply* case, in Chapter 2). Fuller identified and described three such functions: cautionary, channeling, and evidentiary. Which ones are served by the statute of frauds? Would it be appropriate to permit enforcement of contracts covered

by the statute where the evidence of genuine agreement was strongly credible, even if it was not a "signed writing" in the usual sense?

In recent years, developments in communications technology have posed problems for courts attempting to reconcile modern means of recording and storing information with traditional requirements of formality. Compare Parma Tile Mosaic & Marble Co. v. Est. of Short, 663 N.E.2d 633 (N.Y. 1996) (automatic printing of sender's name at top of transmitted fax message not a signature for statute of frauds purposes), with Cloud Corp. v. Hasbro, Inc., 2002 WL 31873610 (7th Cir. Ill.) (e-mail message sent by defendant's employee to plaintiff satisfied both writing and signature requirements of UCC as well as contractual requirement that modification be in writing). In 2000, Congress adopted the Electronic Signatures in Global and National Commerce Act (E-Sign Act), requiring states to recognize electronic signatures in many transactions. States may elect to adopt measures of their own in this area, for which the Uniform Electronic Transactions Act (UETA) may serve as a model, so long as those are not inconsistent with the E-Sign Act. The effect of these statutes is described in an Editors' Note in the Supplement. See the *Cloud Corp.* case, supra (stating in dictum that if case had arisen after adoption of E-Sign Act, statute would require court to hold that e-mail satisfied writing and signature requirement).

Winternitz v. Summit Hills Joint Venture
Court of Special Appeals of Maryland
73 Md. App. 16, 532 A.2d 1089 (1987),
cert. denied, 312 Md. 127, 538 A.2d 778 (1988)

WILNER, Judge.

Appellant operated a pharmacy and convenience store in the Summit Hills Shopping Center under a lease that expired on January 31, 1983. In an action filed in the Circuit Court for Montgomery County, he contended that (1) the landlord orally agreed to renew that lease and to permit him to assign it to a purchaser of his business, (2) the landlord and its agents thereafter breached both the renewed lease and the assignment agreement, and (3) as a result of their conduct, he was required to reduce significantly the sale price of his business. A jury apparently credited his story, for it awarded him $45,000 in damages for breach of lease (Count I), breach of an assignment agreement (Count II), and malicious interference with his contract to sell the business (Count III).

The court nullified that award by granting judgment N.O.V., principally on the basis that the Statute of Frauds (Md. Code Ann. Real Prop. art., §5-103) made the alleged lease renewal unenforceable, leaving nothing to assign. The correctness of that ruling is the issue in this appeal.

The relevant facts, taken in a light most favorable to appellant, are as follows.

Appellant was operating his pharmacy under a six-year lease that expired January 31, 1983. The rent was $1,658 per month. Paragraph 24 of the lease obliged appellant to deliver possession of the premises at the end of the term, but paragraph 25 provided that, if he continued in possession thereafter, he would become a month-to-month tenant, at a rental of $1,658 per month.

That extended month-to-month tenancy was subject to termination by either party upon 30 days written notice.

The landlord, since 1979, was Summit Hills Joint Venture. It employed Southern Management Corporation to manage the shopping center. Ronald Frank, a partner in the Joint Venture, was an officer of Southern Management; Bonita Harris was employed by Southern Management as a property manager.

In October, 1982, appellant met with Mr. Frank to discuss a renewal of the lease. He informed Frank that he might want to sell his pharmacy business and asked if there would be any objection to his transferring the lease. Frank, according to appellant, agreed to renew the lease and indicated that there would be no objection to an assignment if the assignee was financially sound. In mid-January, 1983, Ms. Harris delivered to appellant a proposed two-year lease, with a conditional option to renew for an additional eight years, the condition being that appellant make certain renovations to the premises by October 31, 1984. The rent for the first two years was to be $1,700 per month, subject to escalation during the optional eight-year extension. After some clarification by Ms. Harris with respect to the renovations, appellant said that he accepted the lease and asked when it could be signed.

The signature lines on the proposed new lease showed that appellant would sign as tenant and that Ms. Harris, as property manager, would sign for the landlord. On the front and last pages, however, someone had written the word "SAMPLE." Appellant stated that that marking was on the lease when he received it. Despite the fact that both appellant and Ms. Harris were apparently authorized to sign the lease at that time, it was not in fact signed; indeed, Ms. Harris told appellant that "there was nobody available to sign [the lease] at that time." She instructed appellant to pay the new rent—$1,700—rather than the existing rent—$1,658—for February in the expectation that, at some point, a new lease would be signed. He did so.

In the belief that he had a renewal of the lease and permission to assign it, appellant listed the business for sale in mid-January. His agent quickly found a buyer, and, on February 2, 1983, appellant signed a contract with the Suh family to sell the business for $70,000 plus the "full wholesale price" of the inventory. The contract made specific mention of the lease. Paragraph 1(c) stated: "Purchaser to assume the following obligations of Seller as part of purchase price: Lease on the premises for two years @ $1,700 per month plus an option for 8 yrs at rent plus CPI not to exceed 12% per yr."

A further provision near the bottom of the contract stated: "This contract is contingent on seller procuring lease as stated in 1(c) otherwise this contract is null and void and purchasers deposit returned."

Settlement was to occur on March 7, 1983.

On February 5, appellant, the Suhs, and the Suhs' accountant met with Ms. Harris, who reviewed the Suhs' financial affairs and, according to appellant, said that she "foresaw no foreseeable problem" with a transfer of the lease. Several days later, appellant called Mr. Frank and was again assured that "as far as I know everything is okay." On February 21, however, Frank informed appellant that he had changed his mind and intended to "negotiate his own lease." Frank confirmed that two days later, telling appellant that he would neither transfer the lease nor renew it. He said that he would regard the extra amount already paid for the February rent (the difference between $1,658 and $1,700) as an overpayment that would be refunded. Later that day, Ms. Harris delivered a 30-day eviction notice directing appellant to vacate the premises by the end of March.

Faced with this turn of events, appellant was forced to renegotiate his contract with the Suhs. On March 7, 1983, a new contract was signed, calling for a purchase price of $15,000 (rather than $70,000) plus the inventory at appellant's cost. Appellant vacated the premises on March 25. The "overpayment" for February was credited against his March rent.

(1) BREACH OF CONTRACT

Count I of appellant's amended complaint stated two alternative causes of action — one, that the landlord had effectively renewed the lease which it then breached, and, two, that appellant became a holdover tenant under the prior lease and that, somehow, the landlord breached that lease. The only remedy sought was money damages for the breach. In response to a special verdict sheet, the jury found that appellant had a contract of lease with the landlord, that the landlord breached that contract, and that appellant sustained damage as a result. In Count II, appellant asserted that the landlord had agreed to permit the renewed lease to be assigned to a qualified buyer, that that agreement was supported by consideration (appellant's renewal of the lease), that appellant produced a qualified buyer whom the landlord found acceptable, and that the landlord thereafter breached that agreement by declining to renew the lease and permit an assignment. As with Count I, the only remedy sought was money damages. The jury specifically found that there *was* a contract to assign the lease and that the landlord breached it.

It is evident, from both the amended complaint and the evidence, that these two counts are related. The key to both is whether the landlord, through its agents, effectively *and enforceably* renewed the lease, other than on a monthly basis, beyond January 31, 1983. If not, as the landlord contends, not only would Count I fall but Count II as well, for absent an enforceable renewal, there would be nothing that appellant could assign.

The evidence viewed in a light favorable to appellant clearly suffices to establish an agreement between the parties to renew the lease on the terms set forth in the document delivered to appellant in mid-January. Because neither that document nor any other pertaining to it was ever signed by the landlord, however, the Statute of Frauds is implicated. Md. Code Ann. Real Prop. art., §§5-101 and 5-102 provide that a leasehold interest in land for a term of one year or more that is not in writing and signed by the party creating it "has the force and effect of an estate or interest at will only, and has no other or greater force or effect, either in law or equity." See also §5-103, providing that a leasehold estate may not be granted unless in writing signed by the grantor, and §5-104 precluding any action brought on a contract for the disposition of any interest in land unless the contract or some memorandum of it is in writing signed by the party to be charged.

Appellant relies on the doctrine of "part performance" to escape the bar of these provisions. That doctrine is succinctly stated in Restatement (Second) of Contracts §129:

A contract for the transfer of an interest in land may be specifically enforced notwithstanding failure to comply with the Statute of Frauds if it is established that the party seeking enforcement, in reasonable reliance on the contract and on the continuing assent of the party against whom enforcement is sought, has so changed his position that injustice can be avoided only by specific enforcement.

As pointed out in Comment *a* to §129, application of the doctrine and thus enforcement of a contract declared unenforceable by the statute,

> has . . . been justified on the ground that repudiation after "part performance" amounts to a "virtual fraud." A more accurate statement is that courts with equitable powers are vested by tradition with what in substance is a dispensing power based on the promisee's reliance, a discretion to be exercised with caution in light of all the circumstances.

Where the "defense" of part performance is raised, the dispute often concerns the nature and quality of the performance — whether it so relates to and furnishes evidence of the oral agreement as to justify a court in effectively excusing compliance with the statute. . . . Beall v. Beall, 291 Md. 224, 434 A.2d 1015 (1981). . . . That is how the dispute is portrayed here, appellant contending that his payment of $1,700 in rent for February constitutes sufficient part performance, appellees contending that it does not. In point of fact, however, that issue is quite irrelevant in this case.

The law is clear and well established that "part performance" is an equitable doctrine available only where the principal relief sought is specific performance of the oral agreement. It has no application in an action at law for money damages. . . . Restatement (Second) of Contracts §129, Comment *c*. Nor has the recent merger of law and equity *procedure* in this State changed that principle. As Professor Corbin states, 2 Corbin on Contracts §422, at 456:

> The rule that part performance may make a contract for the sale of land specifically enforceable was the creation of the courts of equity and was not recognized at common law. The result of this is, *even in jurisdictions where law and equity are combined,* that a suit solely for damages, or other purely common law remedy, for breach of the express contract is generally not maintainable, however greatly the plaintiff may have changed his position in reliance on the contract and however unjust it may be for the defendant to make use of the statute in defense. (Emphasis added.)[1]

As Counts I and II of the amended complaint sought only money damages and not any equitable relief, the part performance asserted by appellant, whether or not it would suffice to justify specific performance or ancillary equitable relief, does not bar application of the Statute of Frauds in this case. For that reason, we conclude that the trial court did not err in granting judgment N.O.V. on those two counts.

---

1. We are aware of no case in any State that has merged its law and equity procedure holding that the doctrine of part performance applies in an action solely for money damages and thus have no basis for concluding that Professor Corbin's statement is not correct.

(2) MALICIOUS INTERFERENCE WITH CONTRACTUAL RELATIONSHIP

In Count III of his amended complaint, appellant contended that, in wrongfully breaching its agreement to permit appellant to assign the renewed lease to the Suhs, the landlord (and its agents) intentionally and maliciously interfered with appellant's existing contract with the Suhs. Although the count was scantily drawn, the theory seemed to be that, by reneging on the agreement to renew and permit assignment of the lease, the defendants deliberately and wrongfully precluded appellant from satisfying the contingency in his first contract with the Suhs, to his ultimate economic disadvantage.

There was evidence sufficient to support those allegations. Again, taken in a light most favorable to appellant, the evidence showed that (1) the landlord had in fact agreed to renew the lease and to permit its assignment by appellant to the Suhs, (2) through Mr. Frank it then breached those agreements, and (3) that action was taken maliciously and with intent to injure appellant.

The evidence supporting that last element came primarily from Milton Korn, the broker who found the Suhs and helped negotiate the contract between them and appellant. Korn stated that, upon learning from appellant that a problem had developed in obtaining the new lease, he called Mr. Frank, who informed him "that under no circumstances would he give [appellant] a lease. He wants that man to walk out of that store without a dime." Korn continued:

> Then I spoke to Mr. Frank from the standpoint of giving the new — the purchasers a lease — them taking over the space, and at first he wouldn't do it, and I called him many, many times. Generally he was on vacation, or he was somewhere else. I tried to get ahold of his partner or associate, Mr. Hillman, and they wouldn't let me speak to him. It was almost a daily affair trying to get in touch with him.
>
> Finally, I got ahold of Mr. Frank, and I asked him point blank — I said "They [sic] people qualify. You have already qualified them. Will you give them a lease?"
>
> "As long as Mr. Winternitz walks out with nothing."[2]

The tort at issue "as it exists in Maryland, has been described thusly: 'a third party who, without legal justification, intentionally interferes with the right of a party to a contract, or induces a breach thereof, is liable in tort to the injured contracting party.'" Orfanos v. Athenian, Inc., 66 Md. App. 507, 520, 505 A.2d 131 (1986), quoting from Wilmington Trust Co. v. Clark, 289 Md. 313, 329, 424 A.2d 744 (1981). This description, we said, is not substantially different than that stated in the Restatement (Second) of Torts §§766-67. In that regard, §§766A and 767 are particularly instructive.

Section 766A provides:

One who intentionally and improperly interferes with the performance of a contract (except a contract to marry) between another and a third person, by preventing the

---

2. There was also some evidence of a number of disagreements between Messrs. Winternitz and Frank over various aspects of the landlord-tenant relationship. Winternitz had at one point also operated a liquor store in the shopping center, which Frank found objectionable and forced Winternitz to discontinue. He also made Winternitz discontinue his State lottery agency.

other from performing the contract or causing his performance to be more expensive or burdensome, is subject to liability to the other for the pecuniary loss resulting to him.

Section 767 continues:

In determining whether an actor's conduct in intentionally interfering with a contract or a prospective contractual relation of another is improper or not, consideration is given to the following factors:

(a) the nature of the actor's conduct,
(b) the actor's motive,
(c) the interests of the other with which the actor's conduct interferes,
(d) the interests sought to be advanced by the actor,
(e) the social interests in protecting the freedom of action of the actor and the contractual interests of the other,
(f) the proximity or remoteness of the actor's conduct to the interference and
(g) the relations between the parties.

In examining these principles in the context of this case, several things seem clear. First, §766A, on its face, does not purport either to define or to limit the method of interference necessary to constitute that aspect of the tort. We see no reason why the refusal by the defendant to perform a legal duty owed to the plaintiff, including a contractual obligation, could not suffice in this regard. . . . The key element is the fact of intentional and improper conduct that prevents or burdens performance by the plaintiff; the precise form of that conduct, including whether it independently constitutes a breach of a separate contract between the plaintiff and defendant is important only in determining whether the conduct is of that quality. See §767(a). . . .

That said, however, the law does not permit the conversion of every breach of contract into a tort action, merely because one effect of the breach is to prevent or hinder the plaintiff in carrying out his obligations under other contracts. The losses sustained as a result of that may, if foreseeable, be an element of damage in a breach of contract action, but that collateral effect does not, of itself, establish the tort. The other elements of the tort enumerated in §767 that bear on the perniciousness of the defendant's conduct must also be taken into account.

Although conceding that a contract unenforceable by reason of the Statute of Frauds can be the subject of malicious interference (see Daugherty v. Kessler, 264 Md. 281, 286 A.2d 95 (1972)), appellees seem to base their defense of Count III on the notion that the breach of an unenforceable contract between the parties cannot constitute the kind of impermissible conduct required for the tort. They assume that, as the agreement to renew the lease was unenforceable, appellant had nothing to assign and that, after January 31, he had merely a month-to-month tenancy which the landlord was free to terminate on 30 days' notice.

That defense overlooks, or at least disregards, the fact that, on competent evidence, a jury found that the parties did in fact agree to renew the lease and permit its assignment. There was, in other words, a valid contract to those effects which cannot be swept entirely aside. In *Daugherty*, though focusing on the contract that was interfered with, the Court made the point, at 285, 286 A.2d 95.

> An oral contract, like that before us, may be unenforceable as between the parties but between them and as to third parties may in various aspects have life, force and effect. 2 Corbin on Contracts, §279, The Legal Operation of the Statute of Frauds, pp.20-21, says: "A contract where the parties have not complied with the requirements of the statute is neither void nor voidable; it has much effect upon the legal relations of the contracting parties with each other and with third persons."

That principle, we think, has significance in this context as well. That appellant is precluded from collecting damages for breach of his contract with the landlord does not authorize the landlord to breach it, much less to breach it with the deliberate and malicious intent of sabotaging appellant's contract with the Suhs. The breach itself is culpable, though not directly remediable. What is both culpable and remediable is effecting the breach not for its own sake, to end the contractual relationship between appellant and the landlord, but for the deliberate, independent, and successful purpose of interfering with appellant's contract with the Suhs. As appellees do not challenge the existence of the other requisite elements of the tort or the instructions given by the court, we think that the jury was entitled to find the verdict it did on Count III and that the court erred in nullifying it.

Judgment on Counts I and II affirmed; judgment N.O.V. on Count III reversed and judgment entered on original verdict in accordance with Md. rule 2-532(f)(1)(A); appellees to pay the costs.

Notes and Questions

1. *Interests in land.* When the statute of frauds was enacted in England in the seventeenth century, land was the basis of the English economy. It is not surprising, therefore, that contracts for the transfer of an interest in land were one of the types of contracts subject to the original English statute of frauds. While land may be of less relative significance in modern times, contracts involving the sale of land do typically involve fairly large sums of money. Note that the land provision of the statute of frauds is not limited to contracts for the sale of land but can apply to the transfer of other interests in land, such as easements, mortgages, and leases. E.g., Presten v. Sailer, 542 A.2d 7 (N.J. Super. Ct. App. Div. 1988) (purchase of cooperative apartment proprietary lease held subject to the statute of frauds); contra Firth v. Lu, 49 P.3d 117 (Wash. 2002) (sale of stock in corporation that operates housing cooperative, not interest in real property for purpose of statute of frauds; *Presten* discussed and distinguished). The statutes in many jurisdictions, like the one in Maryland, limit its application to "long-term" leases, for example, ones lasting more than a year. (It should be noted, however, that the land clause and the one-year clause of the statute of frauds are independent provisions; if an agreement is within either one it will be subject to the statutory requirements.) On the scope of the land contract provision of the statute of frauds, see generally Farnsworth, Contracts §6.5 (4th ed. 2004).

2. *The "part performance" doctrine.* After the statute of frauds was enacted in the seventeenth century, the English courts soon encountered cases in which one party claimed to have taken possession of land pursuant to an oral agreement that the other party denied making — hardly surprising during an era in which literacy was not widespread. The English "equity" courts recognized an exception to the statute in the case of "part performance." Butcher v. Stapley, 23 Eng. Rep. 524 (Ch. 1685). As the court in *Winternitz* points out in footnote 1, however, the part performance exception has traditionally applied only to actions at "equity" rather than at "law." See, e.g. Collier v. Brooks, 632 So.2d 149 (Fla. Dist. Ct. App. 1994) (part performance exception to statute of frauds could apply in action for specific performance, but not in action at law for damages). The Restatement (Second) continues this limitation in §129, comment *c*. A brief history of the distinction between law and equity is set forth in the Comment following these Notes; it may help you understand this part of the court's analysis on this point. Can the limitation of the part performance exception to equity cases be defended as a matter of policy? Or is this purely a historical distinction that should be abolished? It should be noted, however, that the Restatement does recognize in §139 (examined in Alaska Democratic Party v. Rice, the next case in these materials) the possibility that promissory estoppel may be used to avoid the application of the statute of frauds.

What type of part performance will be sufficient to make an oral promise to transfer an interest in land enforceable? (The terminology that is often used is "to take the contract out of the statute.") Most courts accept transfer of possession of the property coupled with the making of valuable improvements as sufficient part performance; mere payment of money is unlikely to be enough, however. See Farnsworth, Contracts §6.9, at 396-397 (4th ed. 2004). Beyond that area of agreement the courts of different states take a variety of approaches, some quite strict, others more liberal, in the application of the exception. Cardozo's often-cited formulation is that the performance must be "unequivocally referable" to the alleged oral agreement. Burns v. McCormick, 135 N.E. 273, 273 (N.Y. 1922). Is this a useful test?

3. *Tort analysis.* Even if the plaintiff in *Winternitz* had not been selling his business, wouldn't the landlord's breach of the oral agreement to renew the lease have interfered with a variety of contractual relationships, such as sales agreements with customers or employment agreements with employees? More generally, in the modern business world doesn't the breach of one contract almost always affect other contracts? If this is accurate, will a plaintiff almost always be able to state a claim for tortious interference with contractual relationships when the other party breaches an agreement that is unenforceable because of the statute of frauds? Or can you articulate a principle that would distinguish *Winternitz* from such cases?

4. *Result-oriented jurisprudence.* In reading *Winternitz*, were you surprised when the court, after appearing to be on the verge of leaving the plaintiff remediless, upheld his action for wrongful interference? Able attorneys are aware that there is often more than one way to get from point A to point B, and that if one road to relief is blocked by doctrine or precedent, a judge persuaded that injustice will otherwise result may be willing to open up another — even if, as suggested in the preceding note, the result seems open

to criticism. "Hard cases" may, as often asserted, make "bad law," but sometimes — as, perhaps, in *Winternitz* — the reverse may also be true: bad law makes hard cases.

Comment: The Historical Development of Law and Equity

The English origins of our modern legal system began in the thirteenth century with the establishment of a centralized court system. 1 William S. Holdsworth, A History of English Law 194-264 (1982). To obtain relief in court a party had to show that his situation fit within one of the well established "writs" for granting relief. The writ system was, of course, not static; new writs were recognized over time, and old writs were redefined to deal with changing circumstances. (Recall the discussion of the development of the writ of assumpsit, in the Comment on the History of the Consideration Doctrine, in Chapter 2.)

Not every litigant could obtain relief through the writ system, and over the years many subjects petitioned the King for help when they were unable to find a remedy in the law courts. These petitions ultimately became the basis for an independent Court of Chancery, administered by one of the King's assistants, the Chancellor. Id. at 401-402. As time passed tension developed between the law courts and the Court of Chancery, but in the seventeenth century, the power of the Court of Chancery to act became firmly established. Id. at 461. Originally discretionary in its decisionmaking, the Court of Chancery gradually developed a more legalistic, precedent-based method of decision. Id. at 465-469. One principle followed by the Court of Chancery was that equity would act only when the remedy at law (typically damages) was "inadequate" to compensate the plaintiff. Id. at 456-457. Since land was fundamental to the English economy, and each piece of land was deemed "unique," a damage remedy for breach of a contract to transfer an interest in land was necessarily considered inadequate. The equity courts took jurisdiction in such cases and would award a decree of specific performance. (The remedy of specific performance is discussed in more detail in Chapter 12.) Thus, disputes involving land typically came before the equity courts rather than the law courts, and it was in the equity courts that the exception to the statute of frauds for part performance developed.

When America achieved its independence, each of the American states in its original constitution adopted or "received" the English common law as the basis for the law of that state. (Americans did not see themselves as revolting against the English system but against its King. Indeed, Americans relied on the fundamental rights of Englishmen as the basis of the revolution. For a history of these developments, see Gordon S. Wood, The Creation of the American Republic 1776-1787 (1972).) In the nineteenth century, under the intellectual influence of David Dudley Field, procedural reform swept the United States. One of the major aspects of this reform was the "merger" of the law and equity courts. Rather than dual court systems as in the orginal English system, a single court of general jurisdiction was granted the power to provide any form of relief, whether traditionally given at law or in equity. See generally Daun van Ee, David Dudley Field and the Reconstruction of the Law (1986).

Despite this procedural merger, the historical distinction between law and equity continues to have some modern significance. For example, in your course in civil procedure, you will learn that a litigant has a right to a jury trial if the matter was one that historically was decided by the law courts rather than the equity courts. Beacon Theatres, Inc. v. Westover, 359 U.S. 500 (1958). When we discuss remedies later on in this course, we will see that the basic remedy for breach of contract is damages. If a party wishes to obtain in personam relief, such as an injunction or specific performance (remedies that traditionally were awarded by the equity courts), the litigant must show that the damage remedy is "inadequate." The limitation of the part performance exception to the statute of frauds, as discussed in *Winternitz*, is another example of the continued influence of the distinction between law and equity.

In a famous speech, Justice Oliver Wendell Holmes bemoaned the influence of history on the law:

> It is revolting to have no better reason for a rule of law than that so it was laid down in the time of Henry IV. It is still more revolting if the grounds upon which it was laid down have vanished long since, and the rule simply persists from blind imitation of the past.

Oliver Wendell Holmes, The Path of the Law, 10 Harv. L. Rev. 457, 469 (1897). Keep Justice Holmes's observation in mind as your study of the rules of contract law progresses.

Alaska Democratic Party v. Rice
Supreme Court of Alaska
934 P. 2d 1313 (1997)

Before COMPTON, C.J., and RABINOWITZ, MATTHEWS, EASTAUGH and FABE, JJ.

OPINION

RABINOWITZ, Justice.

I. INTRODUCTION

Kathleen Rice (Rice) contended that Greg Wakefield, in his capacity as chair-elect of the Alaska Democratic Party (Party), offered her a two-year position as executive director of the Party. When the job failed to materialize, Rice sued on the alleged oral contract. She was awarded damages after a jury trial. The Party and Wakefield now appeal. We affirm.

II. FACTS AND PROCEEDINGS

Rice worked for the Party in one capacity or another from approximately 1987 to 1991. In 1991, she was fired from her position as executive director by Rhonda Roberts, the then current chair of the Party. In 1991, Rice began working for the Maryland Democratic Party. While she was in Maryland, Greg Wakefield contacted her regarding his potential candidacy for the Party chair and the possibility of Rice serving as his executive director.

In May 1992, Wakefield was in fact elected to chair the Party. His term was set to begin the following February. Rice claims that sometime during the summer after Wakefield had been elected, he "confirmed his decision" to hire her as executive director on the following specific terms: "$36,000.00 a year for at least two years and an additional two years if . . . Wakefield is re-elected; and approximately $4,000.00 a year in fringe benefits."

In August 1992, Nathan Landau, the chair of the Maryland Democratic Party, resigned and asked Rice to come work for him in his new capacity as co-finance chair of the Gore vice-presidential campaign. She accepted this offer. Rice asserts that later, in either September or October, she accepted Wakefield's offer to work for the Party in Alaska. In November, Rice moved to Alaska, resigning her position with Landau, which she claims "could have continued indefinitely . . . at a pay scale the same as that offered by Wakefield." No written contract was entered into between Rice and Wakefield or between Rice and the Party.

In a closed-door meeting on February 5, 1993, the executive committee of the Party advised Wakefield that he could not hire Rice as executive director. Rice alleges that even after this meeting, Wakefield continued to assure her that she had the job. However, on February 15, Wakefield informed her that she could not have the job. Rice filed suit.

On cross-motions for summary judgment, the superior court dismissed all counts except those based on the theories of promissory estoppel and misrepresentation. After a trial by jury, Rice was awarded $28,864 in damages on her promissory estoppel claim and $1,558 in damages on her misrepresentation claim. The superior court denied the Party's and Wakefield's motions for directed verdicts and judgment N.O.V. This appeal followed.

III. DISCUSSION

A. THE SUPERIOR COURT DID NOT ERR IN DENYING THE PARTY'S MOTION FOR SUMMARY JUDGMENT ON RICE'S PROMISSORY ESTOPPEL CLAIM.

The question of whether the doctrine of promissory estoppel can be invoked to enforce an oral contract that falls within the Statute of Frauds presents a question of first impression. In order to resolve this question, the policy concerns behind both the Statute of Frauds and the doctrine of promissory estoppel must be examined. The purpose of the Statute of Frauds is to prevent fraud by requiring that certain categories of contracts be reduced to writing. However, "it is not intended as an escape route for persons seeking to avoid obligations undertaken by or imposed upon them." Eavenson v. Lewis Means, Inc., 105 N.M. 161, 730 P.2d 464, 465 (1986), overruled on other grounds by Strata Prod. Co. v. Mercury Exploration Co., 121 N.M. 622, 916 P.2d 822 (1996).

In its ruling on cross summary judgment motions in this case, the superior court addressed some of the conflicting case law on this question and ultimately concluded that as between the Statute of Frauds and promissory estoppel, the latter would prevail. It based this conclusion, in large part, on section 139 of the Restatement (Second) of Contracts which provides that

[a] promise which the promisor should reasonably expect to induce action or forbearance on the part of the promisee or a third person and which does induce the action or forbearance is enforceable *notwithstanding the Statute of Frauds* if injustice can be avoided only by enforcement of the promise. . . .

Restatement (Second) of Contracts §139 (1981) (emphasis added). Section 139(2) then goes on to enumerate factors to consider in making the determination of "whether injustice can be avoided only by enforcement of the promise." Id.

In reaching its decision on this issue, the superior court reasoned:

The Restatement test referenced herein provides an appropriate balance between the competing considerations supporting strict enforcement of the Statute, on the one hand, and prevention of a miscarriage of justice, on the other. Plaintiff's burden in overriding the Statute *is to establish the promise's existence by clear and convincing evidence.* This heightened burden, along with the other criteria imposed by Section 139, insure that the polices which gave rise to the Statute of Frauds will not, in fact, be nullified by application of the Restatement exception.

(Emphasis added.) Commentators have noted that "there is no question that many courts are now prepared to use promissory estoppel to overcome the requirements of the statute of frauds." 2 Arthur L. Corbin, Corbin on Contracts §281A (1950 & Supp. 1996). We join those states which endorse the Restatement approach in employment disputes such as this one.[2]

Concerning the applicability of section 139,[3] the requisites for a claim must be met, as the jury reasonably found they were here. The Party and

---

2. See McIntosh v. Murphy, 52 Haw. 29, 469 P.2d 177 (1970); Eavenson v. Lewis Means, Inc., 105 N.M. 161, 730 P.2d 464 (1986), overruled by Strata Prod. Co. v. Mercury Exploration Co., 121 N.M. 622, 916 P.2d 822, 828 (1996) (recasting elements of promissory estoppel), and Glasscock v. Wilson Constructors, Inc., 627 F.2d 1065 (10th Cir. 1980).

Numerous decisions have rejected the Restatement approach both implicitly and explicitly. See, e.g., Venable v. Hickerson, Phelps, Kirtley & Assoc., Inc., 903 S.W.2d 659 (Mo. App. 1995), Greaves v. Medical Imaging Sys., Inc., 124 Wash. 2d 389, 879 P.2d 276 (1994), Collins v. Allied Pharmacy Management, Inc., 871 S.W.2d 929 (Tex. App. 1994), Dickens v. Quincy College Corp., 245 Ill. App. 3d 1055, 185 Ill. Dec. 822, 615 N.E.2d 381 (1993), Stearns v. Emery-Waterhouse Co., 596 A.2d 72 (Me. 1991), Sales Serv., Inc. v. Daewoo Int'l (America) Corp., 770 S.W.2d 453 (Mo. App. 1989), Whiteco Indus., Inc. v. Kopani, 514 N.E.2d 840 (Ind. App. 1987), Cunnison v. Richardson Greenshields Securities, Inc., 107 A.D.2d 50, 485 N.Y.S.2d 272 (N.Y. App. Div. 1985), Moran v. NAV Servs., 189 Ga. App. 825, 377 S.E.2d 909 (1989), Munoz v. Kaiser Steel Corp., 156 Cal. App. 3d 965, 203 Cal. Rptr. 345 (1984).

3. In reviewing a jury's determination, this court views the evidence in the light most favorable to the judgment. It does not "weigh the evidence or judge the credibility of the witnesses," but instead, "determine[s] whether there is room for diversity of opinion among reasonable people. If so, the question is one for the jury." Levar v. Elkins, 604 P.2d 602, 604 (Alaska 1980).

In denying the Party's and Wakefield's motions for judgment N.O.V., the superior court stated in part:

Rice, however, testified that Caroline Covington had told her that the Chair makes the decision regarding employment of executive directors. Rice claimed Wakefield told her it was his decision who to hire. He allegedly said that if everyone was mad, he and Kathleen would work together through May and then both quit, suggesting again that the decision would be his, notwithstanding opposition. Plaintiff said that when John Pugh was chair, he had communicated that it was within his discretion to fire executive director Bob Speed. And the Party Plan did not give the executive committee authority over such hiring decisions. This was sufficient evidence for the jury to decide that Rice relied on Wakefield's implicit promise that the executive committee could not derail his selection for executive or finance director. While

Wakefield reasonably could have expected to induce Rice's action by their promise. Rice did in fact resign from her job, move from Maryland, and lose money as a result of her reliance on the Party and Wakefield, which amounted to a substantial worsening of her position. In addition, her reliance on the oral representations was reasonable.

Nonetheless, the promise is only enforceable where injustice can only be avoided by enforcement of the promise. The following circumstances are relevant to this inquiry:

a) the availability and adequacy of other remedies, particularly cancellation and restitution;

b) the definite and substantial character of the action or forbearance in relation to the remedy sought;

c) the extent to which the action or forbearance corroborates evidence of the making and terms of the promise, *or the making and terms are otherwise established by clear and convincing evidence;*

d) the reasonableness of the action or forbearance;

e) the extent to which the action or forbearance was foreseeable by the promisor.

Restatement (Second) of Contracts §139(2). In the context of this factual record, the jury could reasonably find that Rice would be a victim of injustice without an award of damages, considering her induced resignation, her move from Maryland, and her loss of money and position.

The Statute of Frauds represents a traditional contract principle that is largely formalistic and does not generally concern substantive rights. The extent to which a reliance exception would undermine this principle is minimal and the rights that it would protect are significant. The need to satisfy the clear and convincing proof standard with respect to the subsection 139(2)(c) factor also reassures us that promissory estoppel will not render the statute of frauds superfluous in the employment context. Accordingly, we affirm the superior court's treatment of this issue and adopt section 139 as the law of this jurisdiction.[4]

B. THE SUPERIOR COURT DID NOT COMMIT AN ERROR BY NOT INCORPORATING THE PHRASE "DEFINITE AND SUBSTANTIAL" INTO JURY INSTRUCTION NUMBER 12.

In regard to Rice's section 139 claim, one aspect of Jury Instruction 12 directed the jury to decide whether Rice "took action in reliance upon the

---

the Party focuses on the reasonableness of Rice's reliance, that is only one factor for the jury to evaluate in deciding whether injustice could be avoided only by enforcing the contract.

Our review of the record persuades us that there is ample evidence supporting the superior court's analysis.

4. The Party and Wakefield present further arguments as to why they should prevail on the promissory estoppel claim. They argue first that "[t]here was no substantial change of position, no reliance, and no foreseeability of reliance." And second, that " '[t]he interests of justice' do not require enforcement of the alleged 'promise.'"

These arguments were not included in the points on appeal submitted at filing, nor were they presented anywhere in the body of the opening brief; they are only argued in the reply brief. As such, they will not be considered by this court. Alaska Rule of Appellate Procedure 204(e). See also Swick v. Seward School Bd., 379 P.2d 97 (Alaska 1963). The arguments are, in any event, without merit. They involve issues that were appropriately resolved against the Party and Wakefield by the jury. . . .

promise. . . ." The Party and Wakefield claim that section 139 of the Restatement (Second) of Contracts requires more than that "action" be taken; they contend that the action must be of a "definite and substantial" character. As such, they argue that "instruction 12 omitted a crucial component of the section 139 factors."

The Restatement lists "the definite and substantial character of the action or forbearance in relation to the remedy sought" as a significant "circumstance [ ]" to consider when applying the doctrine of promissory estoppel. Restatement (Second) of Contracts §139. The Party and Wakefield are wrong to characterize this language as creating a "requirement[ ]." Further, the "definite and substantial" language was given to the jury in Instruction 13.[6]

When read as a whole, the instructions clearly direct the jury to consider the definite and substantial character of Rice's action before concluding that an injustice could be avoided only by enforcing the promise. As such, the instructions are compatible with the Restatement, and it was not error to omit this modifier from the text of Instruction 12.

C. THE EVIDENTIARY RECORD SUPPORTS THE JURY'S VERDICT

1. Agency

The Party argues that Wakefield, as chair-elect, had neither implied nor apparent authority to contract on behalf of the party. Consequently, they conclude that "the Party is not vicariously liable to Rice under the law of agency." The jury, after being properly instructed on the law of agency, apparently concluded that Wakefield was acting as an agent for the Party when he allegedly offered Rice the job.

The superior court declined to reverse the jury's implied determination of this issue. In denying the Party's motion for a judgment N.O.V. on this issue, the superior court concluded that it would have been reasonable for the jury to find that Wakefield had implied authority, apparent authority, or both. In this respect, the superior court observed that "[t]he Party elected Greg Wakefield as its new Chair. In so doing, the Party arguably cloaked Wakefield with apparent authority to conduct business on behalf of his incoming administration." The superior court also concluded, after discussing the Party Plan and comments allegedly made by Party officials, that the "evidence provides a sufficient basis for a finding of the Chair's implied general authority to make hiring decisions regarding executive personnel."

In addition to its more general complaints on this topic, the Party specifically claims that "even if Wakefield, as chair-elect, had the implied or

---

6. Instruction 13 reads in full as follows:

In determining whether injustice can be avoided only by enforcement of a promise, you may consider, among others, the following circumstances:
    (a) the definite and substantial character of the plaintiff's action in relation to the remedy sought;
    (b) the extent to which plaintiff's action corroborates evidence of the making and terms of the promise, or the making and terms are otherwise established by clear and convincing evidence;
    (c) the reasonableness of plaintiff's action;
    (d) the extent to which plaintiff's action was foreseeable by the promisor.

apparent authority to hire someone, he lacked the authority to hire Rice at all, and most especially for a set term employment contract of two or more years, as opposed to an employment contract at will." The superior court properly refuted both branches of this argument. In response to the first branch, the superior court concluded that "[b]ecause the evidence supported a finding of general authority, there was no need to adduce evidence of a specific intention to authorize Rice's hiring in particular." With respect to whether Wakefield had the authority to hire someone for a term of years, the superior court held that since the question had not been raised at trial or on motion for directed verdict, it was accordingly waived.

The question of whether Wakefield had implied or apparent authority to retain an executive director during the term of his chairmanship was properly submitted to the jury for resolution.

2. Misrepresentation

The Party and Wakefield do not, in this appeal, dispute the fact that the jury instructions covering Rice's misrepresentation claim accurately set forth the correct legal standards. The only legal contention that they raise with this claim is that since at the time that the alleged representations were made "Wakefield was a volunteer, not speaking in his business or professional capacity," his representations cannot provide a basis for recovery. This argument is derived from the text of subsection 552(1) of the Restatement (Second) of Torts (1977). That section would allow recovery against "[o]ne who, in the course of his business, profession or employment, or in any other transaction in which he has a pecuniary interest, supplies false information. . . ." Id.

The Party and Wakefield argue that this language constitutes a "prerequisite for claiming negligent misrepresentation." However, the comment to Subsection 552(1) explains that it is designed primarily to distinguish cases where "the information is given purely gratuitously. . . ." That is not this case. Wakefield had a significant stake in Rice's acceptance of his alleged offer; he apparently wanted her to serve as his executive director. Despite the fact that his term had not yet commenced when the representations were made, they were clearly made in the course of the business of running a political party. As such, even if the Restatement (Second) of Torts does create a prerequisite, that prerequisite was functionally met in this case. . . .

Both legal and factual support for the jury's verdict on the misrepresentation claim are found in this record. The Party's and Wakefield's arguments to the contrary are without merit.

D. THE DAMAGE AMOUNT WAS NOT EXCESSIVE IN LIGHT OF THE EVIDENCE.

1. Section 139 claim

According to the special verdict form, Rice was awarded $28,864.00 in damages for lost earnings and benefits on her section 139 claim. The salary that Rice claims to have been offered was $36,000.00 per year plus $4,200.00 in employee benefits. The Party and Wakefield do not seem to dispute the fact that the $28,864.00 amount is a fair measure of Rice's lost wages based upon the salary figures she alleges. The gist of their argument on the promissory estoppel claim is rather that the full "benefit of the bargain [was] not necessary to avoid injustice."

As discussed in section III.A., supra, a proven section 139 claim has the effect of rendering the oral contract, which would have been invalid under the Statute of Frauds, legally enforceable on the terms established by Rice. The superior court correctly instructed the jury as to the proper method of calculating damages.

Further, since this jury was specifically instructed not to find for Rice on this claim unless "[i]njustice can be avoided only be enforcement of the promise," it can be inferred that the jury concluded that the damages award was "necessary to avoid injustice." This question was properly reserved for the jury, and there is nothing unreasonable or outrageous about their award. The Party's and Wakefield's contentions to the contrary are without merit.

2. Misrepresentation

The special verdict forms indicate that the jury awarded Rice $1,558.00 on her misrepresentation claim. This amount represents what Rice claims to have spent on moving expenses. As a result of this award, the Party and Wakefield complain that "under the judgment, [Rice] gets both her travel costs . . . and damages calculated with reference to the terms of the promise," giving her more than she would have received even if the alleged contract had been honored.

This argument would have been valid if the superior court had actually awarded this damage item to Rice. It did not. The final judgment order reduced the total award of the jury, which would have been $30,422.00 with the misrepresentation award, to the $28,864.00 amount that represents only lost wages and benefits.[12] Consequently, we reject the Party and Wakefield's contention that the damage award is excessive on this ground.

IV. CONCLUSION

We affirm the judgment of the superior court.

Notes and Questions

1. *Reliance on the promise of a writing, under the first Restatement.* The first Restatement envisioned two distinct situations in which enforcement of an oral contract could be based on an estoppel to assert the statute of frauds. In the first situation, the plaintiff detrimentally relied on the defendant's misrepresentation that a writing had been created that would comply with the statute. In the second, the plaintiff similarly relied on a promise by the defendant to create such a memorandum. Restatement (First) of Contracts §178, comment *f*. Numerous courts have applied promissory estoppel to overcome the statute of frauds in cases where the defendant was shown to have

---

12. In its jury instructions on the misrepresentation claim, the superior court explicitly noted its intention to "make any adjustments that may be necessary to insure that there is no double recovery."

promised the plaintiff a signed memorandum of their agreement, as suggested by Comment *f.* See, e.g., Alaska Airlines, Inc. v. Stephenson, 217 F.2d 295 (9th Cir. 1954) (plaintiff quit a job in California and moved to Alaska on strength of defendant's promise to employ him as general manager; written contract repeatedly promised but never delivered); Klinke v. Famous Recipe Fried Chicken, Inc., 616 P.2d 644 (Wash. 1980) (plaintiff quit his job and moved to Washington on strength of defendant's promise to enter into written ten-year franchise contract). What is there in such cases that would justify overriding the principle of requiring a writing signed by the defendant? Is the evidentiary function of the statute sufficiently protected?

2. *Reliance on oral promises of performance, under Restatement (Second).* In adopting the rule of §139, the drafters of the revised Restatement have moved a considerable distance (at least in theory) beyond the estoppel applications suggested in Comment *f* to §178. As the court in the above case indicates, a number of courts have expressed their approval of §139 and applied it to permit enforcement of asserted oral contracts within the statute of frauds. See, e.g., Kolkman v. Roth, 656 N.W.2d 148 (Iowa 2003) (recognizing promissory estoppel exception to statute of frauds to enforce oral agreement for lease of farmland in excess of one year) and the cases cited by the court in *Alaska Democratic Party* in the first paragraph of footnote 2. On the other hand, some courts still refuse to recognize a promissory estoppel exception to the statute of frauds. E.g., Whiteco Industries, Inc. v. Kopani, 514 N.E.2d 840 (Ind. Ct. App. 1987) (any change in statute of frauds should be made by the legislature); Stearns v. Emery-Waterhouse Co., 596 A.2d 72 (Me. 1991) (rejecting application of §139 in context of employment contracts; employees allowed to recover only if they can establish employer's fraudulent conduct by clear and convincing evidence); Stangl v. Ernst Home Center, Inc., 948 P.2d 356 (Utah Ct. App. 1997) (landlord's claim against prospective tenant for breach of agreement to lease barred by statute of frauds; to permit promissory estoppel in such a case would "eviscerate" the statute of frauds); and the cases cited by the court in *Alaska Democratic Party* in the second paragraph of footnote 2. Finally, still other courts have expressed the view that any estoppel exception to the statute of frauds should be limited to the two situations described in Comment *f* to former §178. See the *Klinke* case, cited in Note 1 above; Arnold & Assocs., Inc. v. Misys Healthcare Sys., 275 F. Supp. 2d 1013, 1024 (D. Ariz. 2003) (under Arizona law promissory estoppel bars application of statute of frauds only when there has been: (1) a misrepresentation that statute's requirements have been met, or (2) a promise to put agreement in writing). Which approach seems preferable to you: §139 of the revised Restatement (promissory estoppel generally available to overcome statute of frauds), Comment *f* of the original Restatement (promissory estoppel available only where defendant has promised to create a sufficient writing), or rejection of any promissory estoppel exception to the statute of frauds? Why?

3. *Application of §139.* Even if a deciding court accepts the principle of §139, enforcement of the oral contract will not necessarily follow. See D & S Coal Co. v. USX Corp., 678 F. Supp. 1318 (E.D. Tenn. 1988) (based on analysis of factors set forth in §139 court refuses to enforce defendant's alleged promise to lease land for coal mining). Besides listing several factors

commonly associated with claims based on reliance, §139 directs the court also to consider whether other remedies, such as restitution, might be available and adequate in the circumstances. Where the plaintiff has rendered partial performance to the defendant pursuant to a contract unenforceable because of the statute of frauds, the court will ordinarily grant plaintiff a remedy in restitution for the reasonable value of that partial performance. Such an award is not viewed as contravening the statute, since the theory of recovery is not enforcement of the contract but prevention of unjust enrichment. See, e.g., Montanaro Brothers Builders, Inc. v. Snow, 460 A.2d 1297 (Conn. 1983) (recognizing right to restitution of payment for real estate option that was unenforceable due to the statute of frauds) and Restatement (Second) §139, Illustration 4, based on Chevalier v. Lane's, Inc., 213 S.W.2d 530 (Tex. 1948) (employee entitled to payment for services performed, but not to damages for wrongful discharge). As Restatement (Second) §375 points out, sometimes even a restitutionary recovery will not be available, because the relevant statute of frauds specifically forbids it. See, e.g., N.Y. Gen. Oblig. Law §5-701(a)(10) (McKinney 2001) (broker's commissions; statute also applies to contract "implied in fact or in law to pay reasonable compensation" for such services).

For the plaintiff to obtain enforcement of the oral contract under §139, it may thus be necessary for him to demonstrate that by virtue of his reliance he has suffered injury that will not be compensable on any other basis. In Munoz v. Kaiser Steel Corp., 203 Cal. Rptr. 345 (Ct. App. 1984), the plaintiff employee alleged that he had left Texas and moved to California in reliance on defendant's promise to employ him as a plant foreman for at least three years. Plaintiff asserted that to make the move he had sold his house in Texas (albeit at a substantial profit over the original purchase price) and bought a house in California for an even higher price, which he subsequently "lost" because he could not keep up the mortgage payments after being fired by defendant. The California appellate court upheld the trial court's grant of summary judgment for the defendant on plaintiff's claim for breach of contract. Citing numerous cases, the court held that estoppel to overcome the statute of frauds could only rest on either unjust enrichment of the defendant or unconscionable injury to the plaintiff. The former did not apply, the court found, because the plaintiff had been adequately compensated for all his services to the defendant. As for unconscionable injury, the court noted that the plaintiff had wished to return to California (his childhood home) and had been unemployed at the time he accepted the defendant's offer of work. Without expressly adopting or rejecting Restatement (Second) §139, the court merely observed that the outcome would have been the same in any event, because that section's standard of "injustice" appeared to be substantially the same as the rule of decision employed by the court.

4. *Tort claim.* As indicated by the success of the fraud claim in the *Alaska Democratic Party* case, the borderline between promissory estoppel and claims for fraud or misrepresentation is a thin one — so thin, in fact, that some commentators have advocated shunting at least some of what we traditionally regard as promissory estoppel cases over to the area of tort law. See, e.g., Randy Barnett & Mary Becker, Beyond Reliance: Promissory Estoppel, Contract Formalities, and Misrepresentations, 15 Hofstra L. Rev.

443, 489-491 (1987) ("negligent promissory representations"). Although we ordinarily think of actionable misrepresentation as involving a misstatement of fact, the making of a promise with the intention not to keep it has also traditionally been regarded as a species of "fraud" in Anglo-American law. If justifiably relied on to the promisee's detriment, such a promise could be the basis of a tort action for fraud, as it was in *Alaska Democratic Party*. Should such a tort claim be barred if the fraudulent promise was made as part of an oral agreement that would have been unenforceable as a contract because of the statute of frauds principles? See, e.g., Hurwitz v. Bocian, 670 N.E.2d 408 (Mass. Ct. App. 1996). Plaintiff Hurwitz claimed that defendant Bocian had promised to marry her when his divorce became final, and had also promised to make her a partner in his advertising agency if she would remain at her job with his company and help him see it through "hard times." Her story was supported by credible evidence that he had not intended to keep those promises when he made them (for one thing, he had never applied for a divorce). In affirming a lower court judgment for plaintiff on her fraud claim, the appellate court considered authority from other jurisdictions denying such an action unless the statute of frauds is complied with, but nevertheless held that the action could be allowed on an estoppel basis.

PROBLEM 4-1

You are a judge of the General Trial Court of Madison County, in the southern state of Madison. An action was recently commenced in your court by Elizabeth Ross against Aaron Burr School of Law, a private law school located in Colonial City, in the state of Madison. The plaintiff's complaint in that action alleges the following facts:

1. Plaintiff is a June 2003 magna cum laude graduate of Hamilton Law School, in Franklin City, capital city of the eastern state of Franklin. From August 2003 through July 2004, plaintiff served as clerk to Judge Brandex of the United States Court of Appeals for the Twelfth Circuit. From August 2004 through July 2005, plaintiff served as clerk to Justice Marshall Law of the United States Supreme Court, in Washington, D.C.

2. On or about December 14, 2004, plaintiff was interviewed for employment by defendant. Defendant at that time offered to employ plaintiff as an assistant professor of law, a tenure-track position, at an annual salary starting at $84,000 per year, to commence in August 2005.

3. At the time defendant made the offer referred to in paragraph 2 above, plaintiff asked defendant for some assurance that her employment would continue for a substantial period of time, stating that if she were to accept his offer she would have to move herself and her belongings to Colonial City, leaving behind friends and family in Washington, D.C., and would be embarking on a career in teaching without having prior experience in teaching at the university level. Defendant responded that because faculty members were sometimes requested to assist students in the school's clinical programs with certain legal responsibilities, plaintiff's continued employment past the first year would be contingent on her taking and passing the Madison State Bar Examination during that time.

Except for that contingency, however, defendant asserted that its practice was to evaluate entry-level faculty hires (such as plaintiff would be) for promotion during their third year of teaching, so her position with defendant would be secure for at least a three-year period, through July of 2008.

4. On January 5, 2005, plaintiff received the following signed letter, dated January 2, 2005, from Arnold Benedict, dean of defendant law school:

Dear Elizabeth:

I hope you have had time since our conversation of two weeks ago to consider further our offer of a teaching position commencing with the coming academic year. As we discussed, your salary for the academic year 2005-2006 would be $84,000 per year, to be adjusted in subsequent years, plus the health and retirement benefits enjoyed by our faculty members generally. Your teaching load would be worked out between you and our associate dean for academic affairs. All of us here are looking forward to welcoming you as a colleague, and I hope you will see fit to accept this offer.

All best wishes,
[signed] *Arnold Benedict*
Dean, Aaron Burr School of Law

5. On January 10, 2005, plaintiff sent the following signed letter to Dean Benedict:

Dear Dean Benedict:

Thank you for your letter of January 2. Although it will be difficult for me to leave my friends and family here in Washington, I am strongly attracted by your offer to join the Aaron Burr faculty. I have therefore decided to accept your offer of a position as an assistant professor on your faculty. I understand that my starting salary in this position will be $84,000 per year upon commencement of work in August 2005, with possible adjustment upward in the second and third year. I also understand that my employment will be for at least a three-year period, provided I take and pass the Madison State Bar Exam, with my retention beyond that period being dependent on your evaluation of my performance during that period.

Thank you again for your offer. I am excited at the prospect of joining you and your colleagues at Aaron Burr, and I hope that I can justify your faith in my ability.

Sincerely,
[signed] *Elizabeth Ross*

6. Plaintiff moved to Colonial City in July of 2005, and in August she commenced her work as a member of defendant's faculty. In July 2005 she took the Madison State Bar Examination, and was notified in November 2005 that she had passed that exam.

7. On March 15, 2006, plaintiff was told by Dean Benedict that her appointment would be terminated as of the end of the current academic year. Plaintiff completed her teaching and other responsibilities over the remainder

of the spring semester at defendant, and was paid her salary through the end of July 2006.

8. At the time plaintiff was discharged, she asked defendant for a statement of the reasons for her discharge, and was informed that defendant's budgetary problems made it necessary to reduce expenses. Plaintiff did at all times between August 1, 2005, and July 31, 2006, satisfactorily perform her services as an assistant professor on defendant's faculty, to the best of her knowledge and belief.

9. After her discharge by defendant, plaintiff was unable to find employment as as law professor for the academic year 2006-2007. On February 1, 2007, she accepted a job as an associate attorney with the Colonial City law firm of Dewey, Wyndham & Howe, at an annual salary of $60,000, where she continues to be employed at the present time.

Plaintiff's complaint goes on to ask for damages in the amount of lost wages at the rate of $7,000 per month from August 1, 2006 through January 31, 2007, and at the rate of $2,000 per month for the eighteen-month period thereafter, plus interest.

In its answer to plaintiff's complaint, defendant admits the truth of plaintiff's allegations numbered 1, 2, 4, 5, 6, 7, and 8, above, and of the first and second sentences of the plaintiff's allegation numbered 3. With respect to the third paragraph of plaintiff's complaint, defendant admits that Dean Benedict did tell plaintiff that tenure-track faculty assistant professors were evaluated for promotion during their third year of teaching, but denies that Dean Benedict or any other representative of defendant ever assured plaintiff that she would have three years of employment with defendant, or that her employment by defendant during that period would be "secure." Defendant asserts that all its untenured faculty members are hired on a one-year contract basis, renewable at the pleasure of the defendant, and that plaintiff was or should have been aware of that fact. Defendant's answer also denies any knowledge of the truth or falsity of plaintiff's allegation numbered 9.

As an affirmative defense, the answer alleges that if there was any contract for three years' employment of plaintiff by defendant, as alleged in plaintiff's complaint, such contract is not evidenced by any note or memorandum signed by the defendant and thus is unenforceable because of the statute of frauds. Defendant also moves that summary judgment be entered for it on plaintiff's complaint on the ground that plaintiff's action is barred by the statute of frauds.

The statutes of your state include a modern version of the old English statute of frauds, providing as follows:

> No contract which . . . by its terms is not to be performed within one year from the date of making thereof . . . shall be enforceable unless the contract or some note or memorandum thereof shall be in writing and signed by the party to be charged.

The statutes of the state of Franklin contain a substantially similar provision.

How will you rule on defendant's motion? What reasons will you give for that ruling?

B. THE SALE OF GOODS STATUTE OF FRAUDS: UCC §2-201

By the time the Uniform Commercial Code was drafted, it was obvious that not everyone viewed the statute of frauds as an unmixed blessing. Courts often regarded it as an obstacle to the doing of justice, rather than an aid. Some commentators flatly advocated its abolition on the ground that changes in the law of procedure and evidence since the statute's adoption had mooted its original purpose, with the result that the statute was not only unpredictable and exception-riddled, but also unnecessary. See, e.g., Hugh E. Willis, The Statute of Frauds — A Legal Anachronism, 3 Ind. L.J. 427 (1928). As we have already noted, Parliament substantially repealed the English statute of frauds in 1954. Nevertheless, instead of eliminating the formal writing requirement, the UCC recodified the notion of a sale of goods statute of frauds in §2-201.

This renewed fealty to the concept of a writing requirement may have stemmed in part from the views of Professor Karl Llewellyn, principal author of UCC Article 2, who had earlier in his career declared the statute of frauds to be "an amazing product . . . after two centuries and a half . . . better adapted to our needs than when it first was passed." Karl N. Llewellyn, What Price Contract? — An Essay in Perspective, 40 Yale L.J. 704, 747 (1931). And much of the Code is devoted to business documents of various types, which by their very nature entail at least a writing and typically an authenticating signature as well. See, e.g., UCC §§3-104 (negotiable instruments), 5-104 (letters of credit), 7-202 (warehouse receipts), and §9-203 (security interests). When it came to the sale of goods, however, the drafters of the Code took a fresh look at the statute of frauds. In some minor respects they slightly tightened up its requirements. In several important ways, however, UCC §2-201 made substantial inroads on the notion of a writing requirement by recognizing the practicalities of both making and enforcing contracts for the sale of goods.

The 2003 revisions to Article 2 continue the statute of frauds with only minor changes. Early in the revision process, it appeared that the drafting committee would recommend the complete elimination of any statute of frauds from the new Article 2, on the grounds that even the Code's more modern version of that statute still produced anomalous and unpredictable results, and that business people did not really need or benefit from its presence in the statute. See, e.g., Michael Braunstein, Remedy, Reason, and the Statute of Frauds: A Critical Economic Analysis, 1989 Utah L. Rev. 383 (arguing for repeal of the statute because the costs exceed its benefits). But some felt strongly otherwise. E.g., Morris G. Shanker, In Defense of the Sales Statute of Frauds and Parole [sic] Evidence Rule: A Fair Price of Admission to the Courts, 100 Com. L.J. 259 (1995). As a result, the issue was revisited, and the proponents of the statute of frauds prevailed. The revised version retains the text of section 2-201 virtually unchanged, except for the addition of a new subsection (4) clarifying the relationship between the Article 2 statute of frauds and the traditional one year clause of the general statute of frauds, and an increase in the threshold amount for coverage from $500 to $5,000.

The Convention for the International Sale of Goods contains no provision similar to the statute of frauds. Instead, in Article 11, the CISG expressly negates any requirement of writing or other formality, and provides that a contract for sale may be proved by witnesses.

Buffaloe v. Hart
North Carolina Court of Appeals
114 N.C. App. 52, 441 S.E.2d 172 (1994)

GREENE, Judge.

Patricia Hart and Lowell Thomas Hart (defendants) appeal from the trial court's denial of their motions for directed verdict and judgment notwithstanding the verdict in this action brought by Homer Buffaloe (plaintiff) for breach of contract.

Plaintiff filed a complaint for breach of contract and damages in Franklin County Superior Court on 13 November 1989. Defendants, in their answers, denied the existence of the contract and contended the alleged contract was unenforceable because it violated the statute of frauds. The case was tried with a jury during the 28 September 1992 term of Franklin County Superior Court. Plaintiff presented evidence that tended to show that he is a tobacco farmer in Franklin County, North Carolina, has known defendants for about ten years and rented tobacco from them in 1988 and 1989. Plaintiff rented from defendants, pursuant to an oral agreement, five "roanoke box [tobacco] barns" (the barns) located on their farm for use in his tobacco farming operations during the 1988 farming year. The agreement with defendants for rental of the tobacco and the barns was not reduced to writing and was based on a "handshake, oral" agreement. Plaintiff stated, "I had bought some equipment prior to then, and we always done it on a handshake agreement, cash basis. That's the way it was." Defendants agreed to provide insurance coverage for the barns in 1988. On 20 October 1988, plaintiff paid the $2,000.00 rent owed for the barns and the $992.64 owed to Patricia Hart (Mrs. Hart) for the tobacco rent.

Plaintiff began negotiating with defendants several days later about purchasing the barns. Plaintiff offered to pay $20,000.00 for the five barns in annual installments of $5,000.00 over a four year period, but did not offer any interest payments. The offer was made in Mrs. Hart's front yard with only defendants and plaintiff present. Defendants accepted the offer, and both parties shook hands. Plaintiff already had possession of the barns under the rental agreement. Plaintiff did not remove the barns from defendants' land because he agreed to farm their land in 1989 with tobacco he rented from defendants.

On 3 January 1989, plaintiff applied for a loan with Production Credit Association in order to pay for the barns. He informed Lowell Thomas Hart (Mr. Hart) that he would pay for all the barns if the loan came through. Mr. Hart responded that it "would be fine with us." On the financial statement portion of the application, he listed the barns, but his loan was denied. Plaintiff and Mr. Hart then reconfirmed that plaintiff was to pay four yearly installments of $5,000.00 for the barns. Because he was unsuccessful in obtaining insurance coverage for the barns, defendants agreed to provide insurance for the five barns for 1989 if plaintiff would reimburse them for the cost. On 20 October 1989, plaintiff promptly reimbursed defendants in full for the insurance coverage. Plaintiff testified that "[a]fter I bought the barns was the only time I agreed to pay insurance" and when he rented the barns in 1988, Mrs. Hart "was supposed to pay" the insurance.

During the 1989 tobacco farming season, plaintiff decided to sell the barns and placed a "for sale" ad which expired 23 October 1989 under farm equipment saying "five roanoke box barns, gas, [plaintiff's] phone number" in The News and Observer. The ad ran two lines for four days and resulted in several calls, including contact with Ashley P. Mohorn (Mr. Mohorn), Ronald E. Stainback (Mr. Stainback), and Lawrence Elliot (Mr. Elliot). Plaintiff received a $500.00 check dated 22 October 1989 as a down payment from Mr. Mohorn for two of the barns after quoting a price of $8,000.00 each. Mr. Stainback met with plaintiff, informed him that he would take two barns, and Mr. Elliot would take one. Mr. Stainback wrote plaintiff a check for $1,000.00 dated 25 October 1989, representing a deposit on the three barns.

Mrs. Hart called plaintiff in the fall of 1989 and asked if he could "straighten up with her," and he "told her it would be in the next two or three days" and that he was going to sell the barns. She responded that would "be fine with her." On the morning of 22 or 23 October 1989, plaintiff delivered a check in person to her for the first $5,000.00 due defendants. The payment was in the form of plaintiff's personal check number 1468, dated 23 October 1989, payable to Patricia Hart, signed by plaintiff, and with written words on the "for" line indicating the check was for payment for the five barns. When plaintiff gave her the check, she asked him if he wanted a receipt, but he said "no, the check would be the receipt." The next night after plaintiff delivered the check, she called him and told him "she didn't want to sell [him] the barns; she'd already sold them" to somebody else. Plaintiff received a letter, postmarked 26 October 1989, with the check in it. "She had torn . . . [the check] so bad you couldn't hardly put it back together," and "had tore off [plaintiff's] name—tore off her name, the 'for' line, and the date." Plaintiff was able to piece the check back together to see his signature and the five thousand dollars. He later discovered that defendants sold the five barns to "the same guys" plaintiff had agreed to sell them to.

Randy Baker (Baker) testified that plaintiff told him he had bought the barns and had him repair boxes on the barns. Plaintiff paid Baker for this work. J.R. Fowler, Jr. testified that plaintiff told him he had bought the five barns in 1989, was going to pay five thousand dollars a year until they were paid for, was going to sell them, and had run an ad in the paper. Jack Stone (Stone), an auctioneer for the State of North Carolina, testified that "[plaintiff] approached me and said that he had some bulk barns," "said that he had purchased the barns," and "asked if [Stone] could sell them." Stone received a $41,000.00 check for the five barns and held it in escrow until he could inform plaintiff; however, plaintiff told Stone "he thought he already had them sold." After Stone informed plaintiff to let him know if he had already sold the barns, "[plaintiff] calls back and said that the lady had backed out on him and he couldn't sell the barns to nobody 'til he got this straight." At the close of plaintiff's evidence, defendants moved for a directed verdict which was denied.

Defendants presented evidence tending to show that "[plaintiff] agreed to pay [Mr. Hart] twenty thousand dollars for the five barns, and he agreed to pay it over a four year period of time"; however, plaintiff later called Mr. Hart and wished to make a new arrangement in that plaintiff would secure a loan and pay for the barns all at one time. When the loan was not approved, plaintiff contacted Mr. Hart and "wanted to know if he could continue the rental agreement that he had had the previous year." When Mr. Hart's wife told him that plaintiff "had come over and brought the rent check, and left the five thousand dollars as an enticement to buy the barns, [he] told her that it just wasn't sufficient considering the fact that there had been a tremendous acreage increase in the tobacco poundage." He instructed Mrs. Hart to call plaintiff and "tell him we weren't interested." His wife tore up the check, put it in an envelope, and mailed it to plaintiff. At the close of all the evidence, defendants moved for a directed verdict which was denied.

The jury answered the questions submitted to them as follows:

WAS THERE A CONTRACT BETWEEN THE PLAINTIFF, HOMER BUFFA-LOE, AND THE DEFENDANTS, LOWELL THOMAS HART AND PATRICIA HART?

ANSWER: <u>YES</u>

....

IF SO, DID HOMER BUFFALOE ACCEPT THE TOBACCO BARNS UNDER THE TERMS AND CONDITIONS OF THE CONTRACT?

ANSWER: <u>YES</u>

...

IF THERE WAS A CONTRACT, DID PATRICIA HART AND LOWELL THOMAS HART ACCEPT A PAYMENT FOR THE TOBACCO BARNS UNDER THE TERMS AND CONDITIONS OF THE CONTRACT?

ANSWER: <u>YES</u>

...

IF THERE WAS A CONTRACT, DID LOWELL THOMAS HART AND PATRICIA HART BREACH THIS CONTRACT?

ANSWER: <u>YES</u>

...

WAS THERE A RENTAL CONTRACT FOR THE TOBACCO BARNS FOR THE YEAR 1989 BETWEEN THE PLAINTIFF, HOMER BUFFALOE, AND THE DEFENDANTS, LOWELL THOMAS HART AND PATRICIA HART?

ANSWER: <u>NO</u>

The jury awarded plaintiff damages of $21,000.00. Defendants filed a motion for judgment notwithstanding the verdict which was denied.

_____

The issues presented are whether (I) a personal check signed by plaintiff, describing the property involved and containing an amount representing partial payment is sufficient to constitute a writing under the statute of frauds; and (II) there is substantial relevant evidence that plaintiff "accepted" the barns and defendants "accepted" plaintiff's check, taking the contract out of the statute of frauds.

Because the barns, the subject of this dispute, are "goods" within the meaning of the Uniform Commercial Code, N.C.G.S. §25-2-105 (1986), and because the price for the barns is at least $500.00, the provisions of N.C. Gen. Stat. §25-2-201 apply. . . .

I

Defendants argue in their brief that the check delivered by plaintiff to Mrs. Hart fails to meet the requirements of N.C. Gen. Stat. §25-2-201(1), commonly referred to as a statute of frauds, because the check "was not negotiated or endorsed by the Defendants and therefore the signature of the Defendants did not appear on the check." A check may constitute a writing sufficient to satisfy the requirements of Section 25-2-201(1) provided it (1) contains a writing sufficient to indicate a contract of sale between the parties; (2) is signed by the party or his authorized agent against whom enforcement is sought; and (3) states a quantity. See N.C.G.S. §25-2-201 official cmt.; Harper v. Battle, 180 N.C. 375, 376, 104 S.E. 658, 659 (1920) (check collected by defendant with her written endorsement thereon, in which property is described as "Watts Street House" is sufficient writing within statute of frauds); Burriss v. Starr, 165 N.C. 657, 661, 81 S.E. 929, 931 (1914) (note drawn up by defendant, signed by plaintiff, not sufficient to satisfy statute of frauds because it did not obligate defendant to perform); Arthur Linton Corbin, Corbin on Contracts §508, at 734 (1950).

The only writing in this case is a personal check which, although specifying the quantity of "five barns" on the "for" line, addressed to Patricia Hart, signed by plaintiff, and containing an amount of $5,000.00, is not sufficient to satisfy Section 25-2-201. Defendants, the parties "against whom enforcement is sought," did not endorse the check, and therefore, their handwriting does not appear anywhere on the check. In fact, the name of defendant, Mr. Hart, is totally absent from the check. Therefore, because the requirement of Section 25-2-201(1) that the writing be "signed by the party against whom enforcement is sought or by his authorized agent or broker" is absent from the check, the alleged oral contract between plaintiff and defendants is unenforceable under that section. See Manyon v. Graser, 66 A.D.2d 1012, 411 N.Y.S.2d 746 (1978) (check for $100 on which was stated "deposit on purchase of nine-foot strip" which was not endorsed and letter stating "not feasible to sell property" were not sufficient memoranda to take oral agreement to sell land out of statute of frauds).

II

Defendants further argue that the part performance exception in Section 25-2-201(3)(c) does not apply because "there was no overt action by the plaintiff, purported buyer, in fact no change from the rental period and therefore no basis for a finding of part performance," "[t]here is no overt action of the Defendants in giving up possession of the tobacco barns," and "the delivery of the check by the Plaintiff to the Defendant, Patricia Hart, did not constitute partial payment of the contract because the check was never accepted legally by the Defendants." We disagree.

To qualify under Section 25-2-201(3)(c), the seller must deliver the goods and have them accepted by the buyer. "Acceptance must be voluntary and unconditional" and may "be inferred from the buyer's conduct in taking physical possession of the goods or some part of them." Howse v. Crumb, 143 Colo. 90, 352 P.2d 285, 288 (Colo. 1960). The official comment to Section 25-2-201 explains that for the buyer, he is required to deliver "something . . . that is accepted by the seller as such performance. Thus, part payment may be made by money or check, accepted by the seller." N.C.G.S. §25-2-201 official cmt. Under this standard, Section 25-2-201(3)(c) presents questions of fact, which are questions for the jury, on the issue of acceptance. See Sass v. Thomas, 90 N.C. App. 719, 724, 370 S.E.2d 73, 76 (1988); Coffman v. Fleming, 226 S.W. 67 (Mo. App. 1920), aff'd, 301 Mo. 313, 256 S.W. 731 (1923) (question of whether plaintiff accepted check as part payment one of fact to be determined by jury).

In this case, the evidence, in the light most favorable to plaintiff, establishes that plaintiff told several people about purchasing the barns, reimbursed defendants for insurance on the barns, paid for improvements, took possession, enlisted the aid of an auctioneer and the paper to sell the barns, and received deposits from three buyers on the barns. The evidence, in the light most favorable to plaintiff, also establishes that plaintiff delivered a check for $5,000.00 on 22 October 1989 to defendants, and the check was not returned to plaintiff until 26 October 1989. Under the standards for deciding motions for directed verdict and judgment notwithstanding the verdict, Guyther v. Nationwide Mut. Fire Ins. Co., 109 N.C. App. 506, 513-14, 428 S.E.2d 238, 242 (1993), this evidence represents substantial relevant evidence that a reasonable mind might accept as adequate to support the conclusions reached by the jury that there was a "contract between the plaintiff, Homer Buffaloe, and the defendants," plaintiff "accept[ed] the tobacco barns under the terms and conditions of the contract," and defendants "accept[ed] a payment for the tobacco barns under the terms and conditions of the contract." See Kaufman v. Solomon, 524 F.2d 501 (3d Cir. 1975) (whether possession by seller of check from buyer for 30 days is "acceptance" poses issue for resolution by fact finder); Fournier v. Burby, 121 Vt. 88, 148 A.2d 362 (1959) (enforceable contract where plaintiff delivered check to defendant on 21 July 1957 and defendant returned it unendorsed by letter postmarked 6 August 1957); Maryatt v. Hubbard, 33 Wash. 2d 325, 205 P.2d 623 (1949) (enforceable contract where plaintiff delivered check to defendant on 23 December 1946 and defendant marked through her endorsement on check and returned it to plaintiff on 17 January 1947); Miller v. Wooters, 131 Ill. App. 3d 682, 86 Ill. Dec. 835, 476 N.E.2d 11 (1985) (oral contract within exception to statute of frauds where buyer gave check to seller in payment for truck even though buyer stopped payment on check the next day). Therefore, the trial court did not err in denying defendants' motions for directed verdict or motion for judgment notwithstanding the verdict.

No error.

COZORT and ORR, JJ., concur.

Notes and Questions

1. *A variation of* **Buffaloe**. The court in Buffaloe v. Hart first considers the possibility that the buyer's check could constitute a memorandum sufficient to satisfy the statute, but rejects that possibility because the sellers never signed it. If Mr. Buffaloe had delivered his check to the Harts, then changed his mind and immediately stopped payment on it, could the Harts have enforced against him the agreement to purchase the barns?

2. *UCC writing requirements.* By reducing the required contents of the writing to a bare minimum, §2-201(1) makes enforcement possible on the basis of very fragmentary notations of terms, authenticated perhaps by only initials or even a printed letterhead (see §1-201(39) and Comment), so long as the court is persuaded that the writing does "indicate a contract for sale has been made" (or that "the offered oral evidence rests on a real transaction," in the words of Comment 1 to §2-201). The drafters have stated in §2-201(1) that "a term agreed upon" may be omitted from the memorandum, thereby implicitly allowing enforcement even in the absence of a writing stating the price term. Comment 1 to §2-201 makes this explicit, observing that parties often contract on the basis of a published price list or a market price, which provides a safeguard against fraud. Section 2-201 also states, however, that enforcement will be limited to the quantity "shown" in the writing; this initially proved problematic in cases involving requirements or output contracts, where obviously the parties at the outset cannot set a fixed quantity (although they may set a maximum or minimum), but the courts have generally permitted enforcement so long as the term "requirements" or "output" or some functional equivalent appears in the writing. E.g., Advent Systems Ltd. v. Unisys Corp., 925 F.2d 670 (3d Cir. 1991) (exclusive requirements contract for supply of computer software satisfies UCC statute of frauds even though it failed to specify quantity). Revised Article 2 uses the term "record" rather than "writing" but otherwise makes only minor changes in §2-201.

3. *Partial performance.* In permitting enforcement on the basis of "payment . . . made and accepted" or "goods . . . which have been received and accepted," the Code might appear simply to be repeating the original statute's provision regarding partial performance of a sale of goods contract. However, as amplified by Comment 2, §2-201(3)(c) appears not to go quite so far as the English statute, which validated the *entire* contract on the basis of only partial performance. After some initial authority to the contrary, the courts have generally taken the view that where the asserted contract is for one unit of the goods in question, even a payment of only part of the price will be sufficient under §2-201(3)(c) to validate the entire contract (since the goods cannot be apportioned). See, e.g., Sedmak v. Charlie's Chevrolet, Inc., 622 S.W.2d 694 (Mo. Ct. App. 1981) ($500 payment sufficient for enforcement of purchase of one Corvette auto); Songbird Jet Ltd. v. Amax Inc., 581 F. Supp. 912 (S.D.N.Y. 1984) ($250,000 payment sufficient for enforcement of contract to buy jet plane for over $9 million). In its opinion, the court in *Buffaloe* never directly addresses the issue of whether Buffaloe's partial payment might be insufficient to enable him to enforce the agreement for all five barns. In light of the discussion above, should that factor have

prevented the plaintiff from prevailing? Or can the decision be explained consistently with that aspect of §2-201(3)(c)

4. *The "admissions" exception.* In its approach to the writing requirement and the possibility of part performance, §2-201 was patterned on existing law, even if it did depart from precedent in some respects. The "admissions" provision of §2-201(3)(b), however, was not generally reflected in the pre-Code law. See Peter J. Shedd, Statute of Frauds: Judicial Admission Exception—Where Has It Gone? Is It Coming Back?, 6 Whittier L. Rev. 1 (1984). In the early days of the statute of frauds, it appears that the defendant was not permitted to assert the statutory defense if in fact he admitted making the agreement; later, however, the rule developed that even oral admissions in court would not preclude the defendant's raising the statutory bar. One reason appears to have been that such admissions are merely oral (although they will be embodied in a writing produced by a court reporter or other official) and in any event are not "signed." More fundamentally, it was felt that the defendant should not be deprived of his statutory "right" by anything but a "voluntary" admission (an admission made under the compulsion of legal process being not truly voluntary). Does this development reflect a view that the judicial process is a "sporting" affair, rather than a search for the truth? Its emergence is traced in detail (and vigorously criticized) in Robert S. Stevens, Ethics and the Statute of Frauds, 37 Cornell L.Q. 355 (1952).

A question raised under §2-201(3)(b) is the issue of what constitutes an admission: If the defendant denies that he made a contract with the plaintiff, but admits facts that in the court's view establish that such a contract was indeed made, should the statute of frauds defense be lost? To the effect that it should, see, e.g., Wehry v. Daniels, 784 N.E.2d 532 (Ind. Ct. App. 2003) (defendant's testimony as to facts sufficient to form contract constitutes admission even if defendant denies that contract was created); Nebraska Builders Products Co. v. The Industrial Erectors, Inc., 478 N.W.2d 257 (Neb. 1992) (defendant sufficiently admitted facts to justify application of admissions exception; question is not witness's possibly inadvertent use of legal terminology, but the nature of facts admitted); but cf. DF Activities Corp. v. Brown, 851 F.2d 920 (7th Cir. 1988) (in light of defendant's sworn affidavit that there was no contract between the parties, motion to dismiss should be granted; possibility of admission on deposition too remote).

5. *The "special manufacture" exception.* Section 2-201(3)(a) establishes an exception to the statute of frauds for "specially manufactured goods." Under this subsection the goods must be specially manufactured for the buyer and "not suitable for sale to others in the ordinary course of the seller's business." Compare LTV Aerospace Corp. v. Bateman, 492 S.W.2d 703 (Tex. Ct. App. 1973) (agreement for sale of 8000 shipping containers for all-terrain vehicles manufactured by defendant for export to Southeast Asia enforceable under exception since containers were made pursuant to defendant's specifications and were not suitable for sale to others), with Colorado Carpet Installation, Inc. v. Palermo, 668 P.2d 1384 (Colo. 1983) (contract for sale of carpeting not subject to exception because carpeting was standard item, not specially cut; nothing in character of carpet required basic changes to make it marketable to other purchasers).

6. *The "record" and "signature" requirements under revised Article 2.* We noted earlier in this chapter that both the general law of contract and the UCC have taken a rather lenient approach to the requirement of a "signed writing." The 2003 revision of Article 2 goes another step in this direction, changing the requirement of a "signed writing" to a "signed record." This provision and the related definitional sections make plain the drafters' intention to accommodate the modern predilection for communicating and storing data by electronic means. As recently revised, UCC §1-201(31) defines "record" as "information that is inscribed on a tangible medium or that is stored in an electronic or other medium and is retrievable in perceivable form." As part of an expanded definitional section in Article 2, revised §2-103(1)(p) defines "sign" to mean either "to execute or adopt a tangible symbol" or "to attach to or logically associate with the record an electronic sound, symbol, or process." Comment 10 points out that this definition is intended to be consistent with the requirements both of the Uniform Electronic Transactions Act §2(8) and also the federal Electronic Signatures in Global and National Commerce Act, 15 U.S.C. §7001 et seq. (These statutes are discussed in the Supplement.)

As the commercial world becomes more and more accustomed to doing without "hard copies" of many documents that in earlier times would have been seen as important, it may be wondered whether in the long run the formal requirements of a statute of frauds will endure in anything like their present form. In this connection, it should be remembered that the Convention for the International Sale of Goods explicitly rejects any such formal requirement; as mentioned earlier, under CISG Article 11 a contract for sale need not be evidenced by any writing, and may be proved by witnesses. See also UCC §8-113, and Comment (no statute of frauds applies to contract for sale of securities; "unsuited to the realities of the securities business" in light of "increasing use of electronic means of communication").

7. *Promissory estoppel.* As we have seen, many courts are disposed to accept the suggestion of Restatement (Second) §139 that the principle of promissory estoppel may justify enforcement of an oral contract despite the one-year clause of the statute of frauds. Suppose an oral agreement subject to UCC §2-201 has not been memorialized (even by a plaintiff's confirmation) but has been substantially relied on by the plaintiff—perhaps by performance or preparation for performance, perhaps in other ways. Should the principle of Restatement (Second) §139 be applicable to such a case? The majority view is that promissory estoppel can operate as an exception to §2-201 by virtue of §1-103. However, a substantial minority of decisions have concluded that the exceptions specifically listed in §2-201 "displace" any common law exceptions, including estoppel. See Vitauts M. Gulbis, Annotation, Promissory Estoppel as Basis for Avoidance of UCC Statute of Frauds (UCC §2-201), 29 A.L.R.4th 1006 (1984 and Supp.). Revised §2-201 does not specifically mention the possibility of reliance, but a new Comment 2 indicates that there is no intention on the drafters' part to foreclose the possibility of an estoppel-based exception, thus leaving the issue open for courts to resolve on extra-Code principles.

8. *The CISG.* We have earlier mentioned that the CISG has no provision in the nature of a statute of frauds. As Professor William Dodge has observed, American lawyers need to be knowledgeable about the CISG or risk making

costly errors for their clients. See William S. Dodge, Teaching the CISG in Contracts, 50 J. Leg. Ed. 72, 74-77 (2000) (recommending that contracts teachers and casebook editors make greater efforts to acquaint students with the applicability and effect of the CISG). As an example of the possible effect of such ignorance, he cites GPL Treatment, Ltd. v. Louisiana-Pacific Corp., 894 P.2d 470 (Or. Ct. App. 1995), aff'd, 914 P.2d 682 (Or. 1996) (en banc). In that case, the plaintiff, with considerable effort, was able to overcome the defendant's statute of frauds defense by invoking the merchant's exception in §2-201(2), discussed in the following Comment; the case was decided for the plaintiff at both the intermediate appellate and Supreme Court levels by sharply divided courts. But, as Professor Dodge points out:

> There was an easier way. Because the plaintiffs had their places of business in Canada and the defendant had its in the United States, and because both Canada and the United States have ratified the CISG, the CISG rather than the UCC was applicable to this transaction. . . . [T]he CISG does not have a statute of frauds and would have allowed the plaintiffs to submit their evidence of an oral contract for the sale of cedar shakes to the jury without the need to produce a writing of any sort. Apparently the plaintiffs raised [that] argument, but . . . so late that the trial judge ruled the argument had been waived. The result was that the plaintiffs gave up an argument that was a sure winner, . . . presumably costing the plaintiffs a good deal more in attorney's fees. 50 J. Leg. Ed. at 75.

Comment: The Merchant Confirmation Exception

Section 2-201(2) creates another exception to the UCC statute of frauds not found in other versions of the statute of frauds. Unlike the other exceptions, which apply regardless of the nature of the parties, §2-201(2) applies only if the transaction is "between merchants." The term "merchant" is defined in §2-104(1) as:

> a person who deals in goods of the kind or otherwise by his occupation holds himself out as having knowledge or skill peculiar to the practices or goods involved in the transaction or to whom such knowledge or skill may be attributed by his employment of an agent or broker or other intermediary who by his occupation holds himself out as having such knowledge or skill.

If the transaction is between merchants, then the confirmation exception of §2-201 could apply. For the section to apply, one of the merchants must send a "confirmation of the contract" in writing within a reasonable period of time after the contract was formed. The paradigm case for application of the section is an oral contract between two merchants, either in person or by telephone, which one or perhaps both of the parties confirms in writing (an e-mail, for example). The confirmation must be received by the other party, who must have reason to know its contents. Presumably an organization that actually receives a confirmation would have reason to know its contents (although perhaps not if the confirmation was sent to the wrong department). However, a confirmation that was misdelivered by the sender or by an Internet provider would not comply with the section.

The confirmation must be "sufficient against the sender." In other words, the sender's confirmation must satisfy the requirements of §2-201(1) as to the sender. It must show the existence of a contract, must be signed by the sender, and must show the quantity of goods. If the sender's confirmation does not meet these requirements, then the merchant confirmation exception does not apply. For example, a writing clearly indicating that it is nothing but an offer or that negotiations are still going on will not do. In the leading case of Bazak International Corp. v. Mast Industries, Inc., 535 N.E.2d 633 (N.Y. 1989), the New York Court of Appeals held that a buyer's purchase order forms met the requirements of §2-201(2) and were sufficient against the sender even though the documents were ambiguous as to whether they confirmed a contract or were mere offers. The court rejected the seller's arguments that the documents must contain explicit language showing that they were in confirmation of a contract. The court concluded that the Code intended to place the burden of dealing with an ambiguous document on the "receiving merchant because there is less unfairness in requiring it to disavow than in denying the sending merchant who has failed to use any magic words an opportunity to prove the existence of a contract." Id. at 639. Accord GPL Treatment, Ltd. v. Louisiana-Pacific Co., 914 P.2d 682 (Or. 1996) (en banc); but see Kline Iron & Steel Co. v. Gray Communications Consultants, Inc., 715 F. Supp. 135 (D.S.C. 1989) (writing that required buyer to sign and return copy to indicate acceptance was only an offer, not a "confirmation" under UCC §2-201(2)).

If the confirmation meets the requirements of §2-201(2), it is treated as sufficient to comply with the statute of frauds against the recipient merchant *even though the recipient has not signed any writing showing the existence of a contract*. See comment 3. The rationale for the exception is that "the practice of objecting to an improper confirmation ought to be familiar to any person in business." See comment 4 to revised §2-201(2). If the receiving merchant fails to object, there is sufficient evidence to conclude that a real transaction may have occurred between the parties.

It is important to note that compliance with the merchant confirmation exception does not necessarily mean that a contract has been formed. For example, suppose a telephone conversation occurs between a merchant seller and a merchant buyer. After the telephone conversation, the seller, believing that a contract has been formed, sends the buyer a confirmation of a contract that meets the requirements of §2-201(1). The buyer fails to object to the confirmation within ten days. The buyer will be unable to raise the statute of frauds defense because the merchant confirmation exception has been satisfied. However, the buyer can still argue to the trier of fact that the telephone conversation did not result in the formation of a contract. Of course, the seller will claim that the buyer's failure to object to the confirmation is evidence that a contract was formed; while this argument may well be persuasive, it would not be conclusive on the issue of contract formation. Comment 3 makes this point explicit: "The only effect, however, is to take away from the party who fails to answer the defense of the Statute of Frauds; the burden of persuading the trier of fact that a contract was in fact made orally prior to the record confirmation is unaffected."

Outside the UCC, a party who receives a confirmation of a contract could preserve its defense of the statute of frauds by not responding to the confirmation, because other versions of the statute of frauds do not recognize a confirmation exception like §2-201(2). Indeed, in a transaction outside the UCC a response could be dangerous, because a court might find that a writing denying the existence of a contract was in law a sufficient writing. See Note 4 following the *Crabtree* case above. Under the UCC, however, a merchant cannot preserve the defense of the statute of frauds without making a written "objection" to a confirmation. Drafting an objection under §2-201(2) can be tricky. See, e.g., Simmons Oil Corp. v. Bulk Sales Corp., 498 F. Supp. 457 (D.N.J. 1980) (telex stating that terms proposed by seller were "not acceptable" and proposing alternative terms was not a sufficient objection under UCC §2-201(2) because it "volunteers too much"; to be sufficient objection, response must deny existence of transaction).

In our previous study of contract formation we encountered the concept of a "confirmation" under UCC §2-207. Section 2-207 deals with contract formation and the terms of a contract. It recognizes that parties can enter into a contract in any manner, including orally, followed by a confirmation in a writing by one or both parties. Under the original version of §2-207, section 2 determines whether any additional or different terms in a confirmation become part of the contract. Under revised §2-207 confirmations of previous agreements have little significance; any confirmation cannot add or modify terms agreed on (or implied as a matter of law) unless the confirmations agree on those terms or the parties otherwise agree to those additional or different terms. While a confirmation has relatively limited importance under revised §2-207, a confirmation will continue to have importance as an exception to the statute of frauds if the transaction is between merchants and the other requirements of §2-201(2) discussed above are met.

PROBLEM 4-2

Machine Tools, Inc. manufactures a variety of tools for business and consumers. The company is owned equally by three individuals: Ellen Gilchrist, Sue Miller, and Tom Wolfe. In late February 2006, Gilchrist, Miller, and Wolfe were approached by the representatives of a large tobacco company, which has been engaged in a program of diversification through acquisitions. After some negotiations, the parties agreed in principle to the sale of the assets of Machine Tools. The parties also agreed that their lawyers would prepare a formal, written contract reflecting the terms of their agreement. On March 2, 2006, Helen Franklin, an attorney for the tobacco company, wrote the following letter to the owners of Machine Tools:

> Dear Ms. Gilchrist, Ms. Miller, and Mr. Wolfe:
>
> This letter will confirm the agreement that was reached last week between my client, Tobacco National, Inc., and the three of you, who are the only shareholders of Machine Tools, Inc. of New City.
>
> 1. *Agreement of Sale.* You agree to sell and Tobacco National agrees to purchase all of the assets of Machine Tools, Inc. on the terms set forth below. These assets

consist of the company's land and building located in New City, the equipment used in the company's operations, and all inventory of raw materials and finished tools. Accounts receivable shall be retained by you. All debt including accounts payable shall be paid by you at or before closing.

2. *Purchase Price.* The purchase price is ten million dollars ($10,000,000), subject to adjustment as follows: An inventory of raw materials and finished tools shall be made as of the date of closing. The purchase price shall be adjusted up or down to the extent the cost of the inventory, based on your current accounting practices, exceeds or is less than $1,000,000. The purchase price shall be payable at closing $1 million in cash and $9 million in the common stock of Tobacco National. Sale or other disposition of your common stock shall be subject to regulations and restrictions of the Securities & Exchange Commission and applicable state law.

3. *Closing.* The closing will be held no sooner than January 2, 2007, and no later than January 31, 2007, the exact time and place to be agreed by the parties.

4. *Other Documents; Arbitration.* A formal, written contract containing customary warranties and representations of the seller will be prepared by Tobacco National and submitted for review by you and your counsel. You agree to execute any documents necessary to effect the transfer of assets from Machine Tools, Inc. to Tobacco National. It is the intention of the parties that a final binding agreement has already been reached and that execution of any other documents is a mere formality. The parties agree to negotiate in good faith to resolve any disputes over the provisions of these documents and to submit to arbitration any dispute that cannot be resolved by negotiation. Arbitration shall be governed by the rules of the American Arbitration Association.

Each of you should sign the original of this letter, and return it to me, retaining a copy for your files. I look forward to meeting you as this transaction proceeds.

> Sincerely,
> *Helen Franklin, Esq.*

Gilchrist, Miller, and Wolfe received the letter on March 3 and immediately consulted with their attorney to discuss the details of the transaction. During the next week they began to have "cold feet" about the sale, principally because so much of the purchase price was payable in restricted stock of Tobacco National, and ultimately decided that they did not want to go forward with the transaction. On March 8, they asked their lawyer whether they were legally bound to the sale, and how they should proceed. If you were their lawyer, what advice would you give?

5 | The Meaning of the Agreement: Principles of Interpretation and the Parol Evidence Rule

At this point in our studies, we have seen enough to realize that issues affecting the outcome of contractual disputes can be divided roughly into questions of "substance" and "form." To the extent that contract law is concerned with the actual assent of the parties to an asserted contract, one might characterize this as concern with the "substance" of their agreement. Questions such as "Was an offer truly made?" or "Was an acceptance manifested?" would seem to fall into this category. By contrast, the various "statutes of frauds" discussed in the preceding chapter seem to be requirements not of substance, but only of "form" — the expression of an agreement in a particular medium and with a particular indicium of assent. Of course, this distinction between substance and form tends (like many others) to blur somewhat on closer examination: The requirement of "definiteness," for instance, seems (for some courts at least) to be an issue of form as well as substance; thoughtful application of the statute of frauds is likely to be concerned not merely with the minimum requirements of form but also with the issue of real agreement. And commentators have debated whether the requirement of consideration is truly one of form or of substance (or both). Nevertheless, the distinction between form and substance has appeared to many to be a useful one, and it persists in the literature. E.g., Lon Fuller, Consideration and Form, 41 Colum. L. Rev. 799 (1941); Duncan Kennedy, Form and Substance in Private Law Adjudication, 89 Harv. L. Rev. 1685 (1976). See generally P.S. Atiyah & Robert S. Summers, Form and Substance in Anglo-American Law (1987).

Chapter 5 continues this parallel and to some extent overlapping examination of form and substance in contract law. The first section of this chapter will be devoted to the methods employed by courts to interpret the parties' expressions of assent. Even where the parties have initially agreed on particular words and phrases to describe their contemplated exchange of performances, they may disagree later about the meaning that should be attached to those manifestations of agreement. In such a case, before deciding whether one party or the other has fallen short in its performance of the obligations imposed by their agreement, it will be necessary for the court first to figure out just what the performance obligations of each party really are — what those words and phrases should be taken to mean in the context of that agreement.

349

In the second section of this chapter we shall examine the particular problems of interpretation that arise when the parties have chosen to memorialize their agreement in a written document. As we have seen, the law does not require all types of contracts to be in writing in order to be enforceable, and even those that are within the scope of a statute of frauds usually do not have to be written out in complete and exhaustive detail in order to satisfy the minimal requirements of the statute. But for various reasons, parties often do choose to express their agreements in written form, often a writing of some length, complexity, and formality. Where this has been done, one of the parties may later contend that this writing does not accurately or completely express their "true" agreement — that there were additional agreements made between them not contained in the writing, or even that the writing in some respect describes their agreement in an inaccurate or misleading fashion. Courts over the years have worked out a method of screening evidence of such "extrinsic" matters, through the application of the so-called parol evidence rule. The meaning and application of that rule will be examined in the latter part of this chapter. As we shall see, courts and commentators differ among themselves, sometimes sharply, about the application of the parol evidence rule — whether it is a question of form or of substance, and what its proper role should be in the resolution of contract disputes.

A. PRINCIPLES OF INTERPRETATION

Language is a system of symbols by which we express ideas. But, as we all know, language as a medium for expression of ideas is far from perfect. The words a person uses may not fully express the ideas that the person was trying to convey. Even when people appear to be using the same words, they may attribute different meaning to those words. Contracts, like other linguistic expressions, suffer from these problems of meaning. In these materials we use the term *interpretation* to refer to the process by which a court gives meaning to contractual language when the parties attach materially different meanings to that language. Some courts and writers have drawn a distinction between interpretation — the process of determining the meaning that the parties attributed to contractual language — and *construction,* which is the judicial role in determining the legal effect of that language. These materials will ordinarily use the term *interpretation* to include construction, a usage favored by modern contract theorists because the distinction between interpretation and construction is both cumbersome and usually unnecessary. See E. Allan Farnsworth, Contracts §7.7 (4th ed. 2004).

Over the first three-quarters of the nineteenth century, English and American courts adopted a "subjective" approach to problems of interpretation. Under the subjectivist view, if the parties attributed materially different meanings to contractual language, no contract was formed. Courts reasoned that the formation of a contract required a "meeting of the minds."

The leading example of the subjectivist approach to contractual interpretation is the case of Raffles v. Wichelhaus, 159 Eng. Rep. 375 (1864), often referred to as the "Peerless Case." In *Raffles,* two merchants entered into a contract for the sale of cotton to arrive "ex Peerless from Bombay." In fact there were two ships named Peerless that were sailing from Bombay, one leaving in October, the other in December. The seller contemplated making delivery by the December Peerless, while the buyer expected the cotton to be shipped on the October Peerless. When the buyer refused to take delivery in December, the seller brought suit for breach of contract. The Court of Exchequer held for the buyer, accepting his plea that because "the defendant meant one Peerless and the plaintiff another . . . there was no consensus ad idem, and therefore no binding contract." Id. at 376. Commenting on the case, Professor Gilmore remarked that the subjectivist approach represented a deeper philosophical idea: "the untrammeled autonomy of the individual will." Grant Gilmore, The Death of Contract 40 (1974). See generally A.W. Brian Simpson, Contracts for Cotton to Arrive: The Case of the Two Ships Peerless, 11 Cardozo L. Rev. 287 (1989).

In his lectures on the common law, given in 1881, Holmes criticized the subjective theory, arguing that courts should instead adopt an "external" approach to contractual interpretation. In a later article Holmes defended his theory of interpretation on two grounds: (1) The subjective approach made enforcement of contracts too difficult; (2) The external method was fair because a speaker should always expect his words to be understood in accordance with their normal usage. Oliver Wendell Holmes, The Theory of Legal Interpretation, 12 Harv. L. Rev. 417, 419 (1899). Professor Williston, both in his treatise and in the original Restatement, presented a systematic, "objective" theory of contractual interpretation. Under this theory, words and conduct should be interpreted in accordance with the standard of a reasonable person familiar with the circumstances, rather than in accordance with the subjective intention of either of the parties. Restatement §§230, 233. This objective approach, however, led to the striking conclusion that contractual language could be given a meaning that *neither* of the parties intended. Restatement §230, Comment *b*. Consider Illustration 1 to §230 of the first Restatement:

> 1. In an integrated agreement *A* promises to sell, and *B* promises to buy certain patents. *A* intends to sell only English patents on a certain invention. *B* understands that *A* promises to sell the English, French, and American patents on the invention. If a reasonably intelligent person . . . would understand the agreement to state a promise to sell the English and American patents, but not the French patents, there is a contract and *A* and *B* are bound by that meaning.

Modern contract law has departed from the extreme objectivist approach, adopting instead what could be characterized as a modified objective approach. Professor Corbin laid the foundation of the modern approach in his treatise. According to Corbin, in interpreting a contract, a court should answer two questions: (1) Whose meaning controls the interpretation of the contract? (2) What was that party's meaning? 3 Corbin on Contracts §536, at 31-32. Corbin thought that it would be absurd for a court to give a contract a meaning that neither of the parties intended.

> If a court says that parties are bound by this meaning even though neither one of them held it, it is very probable that the court believes, either that both of them did in fact hold it, or that one of them did and the other had reason to know that he did. But to hold that, although *A* intends to sell Blackacre and *B* intends to buy Whiteacre, *A* must convey and

> *B* must accept Greenacre because their "integration" would so be understood by *C* or by a large community of third persons, is to hold justice up to ridicule.

3 Corbin on Contracts §539, at 81.

The Restatement (Second) follows Corbin's view. Section 200 states that the purpose of interpretation is the determination of meaning of contractual language. Under §201(1), if both parties do in fact attach the same meaning to a provision, that meaning will govern. Thus, the mutual understanding of the parties controls, even if it is different from the interpretation that would be given to the contract by a reasonable person. Restatement (Second) §203, Comment *c*. As the Seventh Circuit Court of Appeals said:

> [P]arties, like Humpty Dumpty, may use words as they please. If they wish the symbols "one Caterpillar D9G tractor" to mean "500 railroad cars full of watermelons," that's fine — provided [the] parties share this weird meaning.

TKO Equipment Co. v. C & G Coal Co., 863 F.2d 541, 545 (7th Cir. 1988) (in case involving issue of whether transaction should be characterized as "sale" or "lease," even if parties shared meaning that transaction was lease, this meaning may not operate to detriment of creditors, who were strangers to transaction and had no way of knowing shared meaning). If the parties attach different meanings to their contractual language, however, the agreement is to be interpreted in accordance with the meaning of one party if the other party either knew or had reason to know of the meaning attached by the former. Restatement (Second) §201(2).

In many cases, therefore, the crucial issue in interpreting a contract is whether one party knew (or had reason to know) of the meaning attached to the contract by the other. If so, the party having knowledge or reason to know is bound by the meaning of the other. Restatement (Second) §201(2)(b); 3 Corbin on Contracts §543, at 140.

What if a court should conclude that the parties did indeed attach different meanings to a material term of the contract, but neither party knew or had reason to know the meaning of the other? Then, even under the modern approach of the Restatement (Second), the result in *Raffles* would still follow: No contract exists because of the absence of mutual assent. Restatement (Second) §201(3) and Comment *d*; see also Hill-Shafer Partnership v. Chilson Family Trust, 799 P.2d 810 (Ariz. 1990) (en banc) (no contract formed for sale of real estate when buyer and seller had different reasonable understandings of property being sold); William F. Young, Jr., Equivocation in the Making of Agreements, 64 Colum. L. Rev. 619 (1964) (arguing that *Raffles* should only apply when there is no sensible basis for choosing between the conflicting meanings of the parties).

Joyner v. Adams
North Carolina Court of Appeals
87 N.C. App. 570, 361 S.E.2d 902 (1987)

This is an action for rents allegedly due under the terms of a lease. Plaintiff, Marguerite B. Joyner, owns real property known as Waters Edge Office Park. To develop the property into an office park, plaintiff and her husband, William T. Joyner, Jr., contracted with Brown Investment Company (Brown) in 1972. Brown agreed, under the "Base Lease," to lease the property from plaintiff at an annual rent, increased each year to correspond with the increase in the Wholesale Price Index, published by the United States Department of Labor. The parties contemplated that Brown would remove all existing buildings, regrade the property, prepare an appropriate land plan, and subdivide the area into individual lots. When each lot was subdivided, the lease called for the execution of individual "Lot Leases" to take the place of the Base Lease. The rent due under the Lot Leases was based, in part, on the occupancy of buildings planned for each lot.

Due to financial difficulties suffered by Brown, the lease was amended in 1975 to substitute defendant, J. R. Adams, as the lessee/developer. The amendment also suspended the annual rent increases. Instead, defendant agreed to pay a fixed rate until 30 September 1980, at which time he was obligated to have subdivided "all of the undeveloped land . . . whereby all portions are deemed lots and eligible for the execution of a [Lot Lease]." If defendant failed to comply with that provision, the amendment required him to pay, retroactively, the amount of rent which would have been due under the terms of the Base Lease. As of 30 September 1980, defendant had executed separate lot leases and had built buildings on all lots except one. Defendant had, however, subdivided the remaining lot, graded it, installed water and sewer lines on it, and built all planned roads and driveways leading to the lot. A building was not built on the lot and a Lot Lease was not executed until late 1982.

Plaintiff filed this action on 27 September 1983, claiming that defendant failed to comply with the requirements of the lease for developing the property and seeking to recover the difference between the actual, fixed rent paid by defendant and the rent recomputed under the terms of the Base Lease. On 5 July 1985, summary judgment was granted for defendant. In an unpublished opinion, 80 N.C. App. 166, 341 S.E.2d 619, this court reversed, holding that the provision of the 1975 amendment relating to the conditions upon which the retroactive rent escalation would occur was ambiguous. Consequently, the case was remanded for a factual determination of the parties' intent.

On remand, the trial court, sitting without a jury, found that plaintiff intended the escalation clause to require defendant to complete, or at least be ready to begin, construction of all buildings planned for the lot. It also found, however, that defendant intended the clause to require only the subdivision of all lots or, at most, whatever development was necessary to prepare the lot for building construction. The court concluded there was "no meeting of the minds" on the question of what conditions would trigger the rent escalation. The court also concluded that, although the parties had different intentions, the ambiguity should be resolved against defendant, who was "the party that drafted the 1975 amended lease." Accordingly, the court awarded plaintiff damages in the stipulated amount of $93,695.75. Defendant appeals. . . .

EAGLES, Judge.

I

Both parties argue that the trial court erred in concluding that there was no "meeting of the minds" on the rent escalation provision. Each contends that there is no evidentiary basis for finding the other party had a contrary intention. A trial court's findings of fact, however, are conclusive on appeal if supported by competent evidence, Hill v. Town of Hillsborough, 48 N.C. App. 553, 269 S.E.2d 303 (1980), and there is evidence here to support the trial court's findings.

Plaintiff introduced three memoranda written during the negotiation process. One, written to Mr. Joyner by Mr. Mark Lynch, an accountant negotiating on behalf of the Joyners, stated that defendant "would agree" that completion of all buildings within five years would be required to avoid retroactive recomputation of the rent under the Base Lease. The other two memoranda, one written by defendant's negotiator, Mr. Ed Clark, referred to the "completed development" of the property as a possible condition to avoiding rent escalation. Mr. Lynch testified that he and Mr. Joyner interpreted "completed development" to mean the construction of all buildings. In addition, plaintiff testified that she expressed to defendant her wish that the contract contain a more specific provision regarding the construction of buildings on the lots. This evidence is sufficient to support the trial court's finding that plaintiff intended the provision in question to require defendant at least to have begun construction of all buildings on the lots.

Defendant argues that, when read in conjunction with the terms of the Base Lease, his interpretation is the only reasonable interpretation of the rent escalation provision. That argument was rejected in this court's previous decision in this case. The law of the case is that the language in the amendment is ambiguous and susceptible to more than one reasonable meaning, even when considered with the terms of the Base Lease.

Contrary to plaintiff's contention, there is also evidence that defendant attributed a different meaning to the disputed provision. The evidence indisputably shows that both parties intended the rent escalation clause to require defendant to develop all the property by 30 September 1980. Defendant's evidence showed that, in the local real estate market, a lot is considered "developed" when water and sewer lines are installed and the lot is otherwise ready for the construction of a building. Defendant also established that he was an experienced commercial real estate developer and that Mr. Joyner had personal experience in the real estate business. There is, therefore, competent evidence to support the trial court's finding that defendant intended the provision to require, at most, what he actually accomplished by 30 September 1980.

In arguing that her meaning was the only one intended by the parties, plaintiff specifically cites evidence of her purpose in entering the lease with defendant as well as evidence of the conduct of the parties after the lease was executed. Evidence of the parties' purposes in entering a contract and their conduct after the agreement is some evidence of their intent. See Century Communications v. Housing Authority of City of Wilson, 313 N.C. 143, 326 S.E.2d 261 (1985). However, much of the evidence relied on by plaintiff, as well as other evidence in the record, can support more than one inference. Which among those possible inferences should be deemed credible and worthy of belief is a decision for the trial court. See Williams v. Insurance Co., 288 N.C. 338, 218 S.E.2d 368 (1975). The evidence here does not show, as a matter of law, what effect the parties intended the language in the rent escalation provision to have. Therefore, while the evidence and applicable rules of interpretation would have permitted the trial court to find plaintiff's meaning was intended by both parties, they clearly did not compel that finding. It is not the province of this court to reweigh the evidence. . . .

II

It is axiomatic that where parties have attributed different meanings to a term within a contract, there is no "meeting of the minds" on that provision and a court will not enforce either party's meaning. See O'Grady v. Bank, 296 N.C. 212, 250 S.E.2d 587 (1978); Elliott v. Duke University, 66 N.C. App. 590, 311 S.E.2d 632, *disc. rev. denied,* 311 N.C. 754, 321 S.E.2d 132 (1984); Restatement (Second) of Contracts, sections 20, 201 (1979) (difference must be "material"); Frigaliment Importing Co. v. B.N.S. International Sales Corp., 190 F. Supp. 116 (S.D.N.Y. 1960). Consequently, having found divergent meanings between the parties, the trial court did not err in concluding there was no meeting of the minds on the question of what conditions would trigger the retroactive rent escalation.

It is also well-established, although not often enunciated in North Carolina cases, that, where one party knows or has reason to know what the other party means by certain language and the other party does not know or have reason to know of the meaning attached to the disputed language by the first party, the court will enforce the contract in accordance with the innocent party's meaning. See Insurance Agency v. Leasing Corp., 31 N.C. App. 490, 229 S.E.2d 697 (1976); Restatement (Second) of Contracts, sections 20, 201(2) (1979); 3 Corbin, Contracts, section 537 (1960 and Supp. 1984). In fact, it seems that a determination of whether either or both parties knew or had reason to know of a different meaning attributed by the other is essential in almost every case where the court finds a lack of mutual assent. Id. Here, much of the evidence of the negotiations reflects directly on each party's knowledge of what the other party intended the provision to require. Since the trial court failed to make findings of fact on that crucial question, this case must be remanded.

. . . In this case, whether the parties knew or had reason to know of the other's meaning of the disputed language is essential to the proper determination of the contract's enforceability. Accordingly, we remand for findings of fact on that issue.

In remanding, we necessarily find that the trial court erred in awarding judgment for plaintiff based on the rule that ambiguity in contract terms must be construed most strongly against the party which drafted the contract. See Root v. Insurance Co., supra; Restatement (Second) of Contracts, section 206 (1979). The rule is essentially one of legal effect, of "construction" rather than "interpretation," since "it can scarcely be said to be designed to ascertain the meanings attached by the parties." Farnsworth, Contracts, section 7.11, page 500 (1982). The rule's application rests on a public policy theory that the party who chose the word is more likely to have provided more carefully for the protection of his own interests, is more likely to have had reason to know of uncertainties, and may have even left the meaning deliberately obscure. Id.; Restatement (Second) Contracts, section 206, comment a (1979); 3 Corbin supra, section 559. Consequently, the rule is usually applied in cases involving an adhesion contract or where one party is in a stronger bargaining position, although it is not necessarily limited to those situations. Id. In this case, where the parties were at arms length and were equally sophisticated, we believe the rule was improvidently invoked.

Before this rule of construction should be applied, the record should affirmatively show that "the form of expression in words was actually chosen by one [party] rather than by the other." 3 Corbin supra, section 559 at 266. The only evidence admitted regarding who drafted the 1975 amendment is Mr. Joyner's testimony that no one in his law firm had anything to do with it. Even assuming this is sufficient to support an inference that defendant or his agent wrote the provision, it does not establish that defendant can be charged with having chosen its language.

The record reveals that both parties are experienced in the real estate business and that they bargained from essentially equal positions of power. The record also shows the parties engaged in a fairly protracted negotiation process, with the provision in question undergoing particular scrutiny. Nothing in the record shows that it was defendant, rather than plaintiff, who "drafted" the provision. Instead, it appears that the language was assented to by parties who had both the knowledge to understand its import and the bargaining power to alter it. Therefore, the policy behind the rule is not served in its application here and the trial court erred in using the rule to award judgment for plaintiff. . . .

If, on remand, the trial court finds that defendant knew or had reason to know what meaning plaintiff attached to the disputed terminology and that plaintiff did not know or have reason to know of the meaning attached to the disputed language by defendant, the trial court should conclude that there is a contract as to the plaintiff's meaning. Otherwise, plaintiff's claim does not prevail.

Affirmed in part, reversed and remanded in part.

WELLS and MARTIN, JJ., concur.

Notes and Questions

1. *Whose meaning prevails?* In remanding the *Joyner* case for findings of fact, the court declares that the plaintiff can prevail only if the trial court concludes that the defendant knew or at least had reason to know of the meaning she intended while she did *not* know (or have reason to know) of the meaning he intended. Why is this particular combination of findings necessary to the plaintiff's case? Suppose the court were to find that *neither* party knew or had reason to know of the meaning intended by the other: Who would prevail, and why? Suppose instead that the lower court on remand were to find that the defendant actually did know of the meaning intended by the plaintiff, but also that the plaintiff, although she did not actually know of defendant's meaning, did at least have "reason to know" of that meaning. What then?

The rule of Restatement (Second) §201(2)(b) has been generally approved by the courts. E.g., Centron DPL Co. v. Tilden Financial Corp., 965 F.2d 673 (8th Cir. 1992) (in dispute between lender and borrower about meaning of prepayment term of note, case remanded for factual determination of whether lender knew or had reason to know of borrower's meaning);

Sprucewood Investment Corp. v. Alaska Housing Finance Corp., 33 P.3d 1156 (Alaska 2001) (where both contractor and owner shared the same meaning of term requiring demolition of building or contractor knew of owner's meaning at time contract was made, that meaning would apply even if term could reasonably have a different meaning).

2. *Subsequent proceedings in Joyner.* When the *Joyner* case was heard again on remand, the trial court found that the defendant neither knew nor had reason to know of the plaintiff's meaning, and therefore it held for the defendant. In affirming this decision, the court of appeals referred to the following evidence to support the trial court's finding of fact regarding the defendant's lack of knowledge or reason to know of the plaintiff's meaning:

> We determine that at least four instances of competent evidence exist to support the trial court's finding. First, plaintiff's testimony reveals two versions of her meaning of the conditions triggering the recomputation agreement. Her initial testimony was that "completed building" was the condition for avoiding recomputation. However, her subsequent testimony was that the condition meant "completed buildings" *and* tenant occupation of the buildings. Plaintiff also testified about her inexperience and unfamiliarity with commercial real estate transactions.
>
> Second, even if plaintiff did not have more than one meaning, plaintiff's lack of direct communication with defendant during negotiations was insufficient to give defendant reason to know that either version of plaintiff's meaning of the conditions triggering the recomputation provision differed from defendant's meaning. In negotiations, plaintiff did not meet with defendant; she was represented by her husband-attorney and several accountants. Nowhere does the record show that plaintiff's negotiators conveyed either version of plaintiff's meaning to defendant.
>
> The third instance is the lack of evidence that defendant assented to the contract in reliance on a "completed building" meaning of the recomputation conditions. The record shows that plaintiff's negotiators recommended a "completed building" clause for the recomputation provision without stating whether it was plaintiff who requested the recommendation. The record also shows that defendant flatly rejected plaintiff's negotiators' recommendation that the agreement recomputation provision include "completed building" language. Subsequent to defendant's rejection, the record shows that none of plaintiff's negotiators informed defendant that plaintiff knew of defendant's rejection, that plaintiff disagreed with defendant's rejection, or that defendant's rejection was to have no effect.
>
> The fourth instance is defendant's evidence showing that his previous extensive business knowledge and experience with commercial real estate transactions led him to attribute meanings to the recomputation terms "subdivision," "development," and "construction" different from plaintiff's meanings. Defendant offered this evidence to show that he did not have reason to know that the recomputation provision should have been understood to include "completed buildings."
>
> Based on the record before us, we determine that a reasonable lessee in defendant's position would not have been reasonably induced to believe that he must complete all buildings by the recomputation provision deadline. Thus, the trial court properly found that defendant had no knowledge or reason to know plaintiff's meaning that would allow plaintiff to prevail.

Joyner v. Adams, 387 S.E.2d 235, 239 (N.C. Ct. App. 1990).

3. *Construction against drafter.* In the trial court's second decision in the *Joyner* case (the one reversed by the above-reproduced appellate decision), the trial court broke the tie resulting from its finding that no "meeting of

the minds" had occurred and found for plaintiff Joyner by invoking the principle that a contractual ambiguity should generally be resolved against the party who drafted the language in question (sometimes known as the maxim of interpretation *contra proferentem* — see item 5 in the text below). As the court indicates, this maxim is frequently employed in cases involving "adhesion contracts" but is by no means limited to such cases. See St. Charles Foods, Inc. v. America's Favorite Chicken Co., 198 F.3d 815 (11th Cir. 1999) (letter agreement between franchisor and franchisee that was ambiguous about scope of right of first refusal construed against franchisor that drafted language); Guerrant v. Roth, 777 N.E.2d 499 (Ill. App. Ct. 2002) (ambiguity in contingency fee agreement written by attorney particularly subject to rule requiring construction against drafter). Does the appellate court adequately justify its refusal to apply this maxim in *Joyner?* Other courts have agreed that the maxim should be limited in its application to cases where one party can fairly be regarded as solely responsible for the language in question. E.g., Western Sling & Cable Co. v. Hamilton, 545 So. 2d 29, 32 (Ala. 1989) ("[w]here both parties to a contract are sophisticated business persons advised by counsel and the contract is a product of negotiations at arm's length between the parties, . . . no reason to automatically construe ambiguities in the contract against the drafter").

Over the years, courts have developed a number of principles of interpretation to aid them in giving meaning to expressions of contractual agreement. The following useful list was compiled by Professor Edwin Patterson:

> In this brief treatment we can only quote a list of standard maxims, which may not be complete. The ones most often phrased in Latin are given first:
>
> 1. *Noscitur a sociis.* The meaning of a word in a series is affected by others in the same series; or, a word may be affected by its immediate context. The example for the next maxim may be taken to illustrate this one.
>
> 2. *Ejusdem generis.* A general term joined with a specific one will be deemed to include only things that are like (of the same genus as) the specific one. This one if applied usually leads to a restrictive interpretation. E.g., *S* contracts to sell *B* his farm together with the "cattle, hogs, and other animals." This would probably not include *S*'s favorite house-dog, but might include a few sheep that *S* was raising for the market.
>
> 3. *Expressio unius exclusio alterius.* If one or more specific items are listed, without any more general or inclusive terms, other items although similar in kind are excluded. E.g., *S* contracts to sell *B* his farm together with "the cattle and hogs on the farm." This language would be interpreted to exclude the sheep and *S*'s favorite house-dog.
>
> 4. *Ut magis valeat quam pereat.* By this maxim an interpretation that makes the contract valid is preferred to one that makes it invalid.
>
> 5. *Omnia praesumuntur contra proferentem.* This maxim states that if a written contract contains a word or phrase which is capable of two reasonable meanings, one of which favors one party and the other of which favors the other, that interpretation will be preferred which is less favorable to the one by whom the contract was drafted. This maxim favors the party of lesser bargaining power, who has little or no

opportunity to choose the terms of the contract, and perforce accepts one drawn by the stronger party. . . . However, the maxim is commonly invoked in cases that do not reveal any disparity of bargaining power between the parties.

6. *Interpret contract as a whole.* A writing or writings that form part of the same transaction should be interpreted together as a whole, that is, every term should be interpreted as a part of the whole and not as if isolated from it. This maxim expresses the contextual theory of meaning, which is, perhaps, a truism.

7. *"Purpose of the parties."* "The principal apparent purpose of the parties is given great weight in determining the meaning to be given to manifestations of intention or to any part thereof." This maxim must be used with caution. In fact, the two parties to a (bargain) contract necessarily have different purposes, and if these are apparent, then the court can construe a principal or common purpose from the two as a guide to the interpretation of language or the filling of gaps. Thus a contract to sell, buy, and export scrap copper was construed to make the buyer's obtaining of an export license a condition of the seller's promise to deliver. However, if the purposes of the parties are obscure the court may well fall back upon "plain meaning."

8. *Specific provision is exception to a general one.* If two provisions of a contract are inconsistent with each other and if one is "general" enough to include the specific situation to which the other is confined, the specific provision will be deemed to qualify the more general one, that is, to state an exception to it. A lease of a truck-trailer provided that the lessee should be absolutely liable for loss or damage to the vehicle, yet another clause stated that no party's liability should be increased by this contract. It was held that the former was more specific and therefore controlled the general provision, hence the lessee was liable. A careful draftsman would have stated the former as an exception to the latter, and the court in effect does it for him.

9. *Handwritten or typed provisions control printed provisions.* Where a written contract contains both printed provisions and handwritten or typed provisions, and the two are inconsistent, the handwritten or typed provisions are preferred. This maxim is based on the inference that the language inserted by handwriting or by typewriter for this particular contract is a more recent and more reliable expression of their intentions than is the language of a printed form. While this maxim is used in interpreting insurance contracts and other contracts of adhesion, it is also applicable to all contracts drawn up on a printed form.

10. *Public interest preferred.* If a public interest is affected by a contract, that interpretation or construction is preferred which favors the public interest. The proper scope of application of this rule seems doubtful. It may have some appropriate uses in construing contracts between private parties. However, as applied to government contracts it would, if applied, be used to save the taxpayers' money as against those contracting with the government. But this is not, it is believed, a standard of interpretation or construction uniformly applied to government contracts.

This battery of maxims is never fired all together. The judge or other interpreter-construer of a contract may, by making prudent choices, possibly obtain some useful guides for his reasoning and justifications for his conclusion.

Edwin W. Patterson, The Interpretation and Construction of Contracts, 64 Colum. L. Rev. 833, 853-855 (1964). Courts will not necessarily view these maxims as controlling, however. In Ortega Rock Quarry v. Golden Eagle Ins. Corp., 46 Cal. Rptr. 3d 517 (Ct. App. 2006), an insurance policy excluded from coverage liability for damage caused by "pollutants," which were defined as "any solid, liquid, gaseous or thermal irritant or contaminant, including smoke, vapor, soot, fumes, acids, alkalis, chemicals and waste." Plaintiff insured, the subject of an EPA enforcement action for allegedly dumping rocks and fill into a creek bed, argued that the exception from coverage should be limited by the principle of *ejusdem generis* to the enumerated items, man-made pollutants, rather than "natural" substances such as rocks and dirt. The court disagreed, however, noting that even such natural elements are considered "pollutants" under the Clean Water Act, a principal motivation for the policy language at issue.

One maxim omitted from Professor Patterson's list is reflected in Restatement (Second) §203(a). The section provides that in interpreting an agreement, a court should prefer an interpretation that makes an agreement reasonable, lawful, and effective to one that produces an unreasonable or unlawful result or that renders the agreement ineffective. The Restatement gives the following example:

> 1. *A* licenses *B* to manufacture pipes under *A*'s patents, and *B* agrees to pay "a royalty of 50 cents per 1,000 feet for an output of 5,000,000 or less feet per year, and for an output of over 5,000,000 per year at the rate of 30 cents per thousand feet." The 50 cent rate is payable on the first 5,000,000 feet, the 30 cent rate only on the excess. The more literal reading is unreasonable, since it would involve a smaller payment for 6,000,000 feet than for 4,000,000 feet.

Restatement (Second) §203, Illustration 1. See also Fishman v. LaSalle National Bank, 247 F.3d 300 (1st Cir. 2001) (loan agreement term setting amount of prepayment premium would be interpreted to produce rational result rather than apply implausible meaning that would come from literal reading); Cadle Co. v. Vargas, 771 N.E.2d 179 (Mass. App. Ct. 2002) (loan guarantee agreement would not be interpreted to lead to absurd result; "common sense is as much a part of contract interpretation as . . . the arsenal of canons"). Judge Richard A. Posner has cited the *Fishman* case as an example of a judicial technique he calls the "Best Guess" rule, in which a court combines common sense and some practical knowledge of the ways of the business world to reach results that are both commercially efficient and generally within the realm of what either party could reasonably have expected the contract to mean. Richard A. Posner, The Law and Economics of Contract Interpretation, 83 Tex. L. Rev. 1581, 1603 (2005).

The possibility exists that even after applying the array of interpretive principles, a court may conclude that parties failed to agree upon a material term. Depending on the posture of the case, it may be appropriate for a court to conclude that the parties did not make an enforceable agreement. See Restatement (Second) §33, Comment *a*. In other cases, however, the evidence of intent to be bound or the degree of performance already rendered may cause rescission to be inappropriate. Restatement (Second) §204 recommends that in those situations the courts should supply a term that is reasonable under the circumstances. Professor Prince has addressed the topic of omitted terms and noted that gaps in the contract may result from lack of foresight, incomplete bargaining, or excessive initial optimism about performance of the contract. Harry G. Prince, Contract Interpretation in California: Plain Meaning, Parol Evidence and Use of the "Just Result" Principle, 31 Loy. L.A.L. Rev. 557, 619-620 (1998). Professor Prince argues that in such cases, courts should not strain to apply principles of interpretation to fill the gap, but should instead strive to achieve a just outcome:

> A tremendously better approach would be to simply recognize that, in such cases of *lacunae* within the contract terms, the courts are empowered to weigh a number of equitable factors and attempt to reach a just result. Those equitable factors would include addressing public interests and public good, allowing for sharing of unanticipated losses and gains, avoiding the award of a windfall to one party at the cost of denying recovery to the other side, and considering the parties' good or bad faith behavior.

Id. at 650. See Acme Investments, Inc. v. Southwest Tracor, Inc., 911 F. Supp. 1261 (D. Neb. 1995) (relying on §204 and community standards of fairness in supplying term setting time to exercise option to repurchase property); Weston Investments, Inc. v. Domtar Industries, Inc., 2002 W.L. 31011141 (Del. Super. Ct.) (relying on §204 in supplying omitted term where parties consciously failed to agree on provision with large tax consequences but still intended to be bound; in rare circumstances courts will provide terms consistent with good faith and reasonable expectations).

Frigaliment Importing Co. v. B.N.S. International Sales Corp.
United States District Court
190 F. Supp. 116 (S.D.N.Y. 1960)

FRIENDLY, Circuit Judge.

The issue is, what is chicken? Plaintiff says "chicken" means a young chicken, suitable for broiling and frying. Defendant says "chicken" means any bird of that genus that meets contract specifications on weight and quality, including what it calls "stewing chicken" and plaintiff pejoratively terms "fowl." Dictionaries give both meanings, as well as some others not relevant here. To support its [interpretation], plaintiff sends a number of volleys over the net; defendant essays to return them and adds a few serves of its own. Assuming that both parties were acting in good faith, the case nicely illustrates Holmes' remark "that the making of a contract depends not on the agreement of two minds in one intention, but on the agreement of two sets of external signs — not on the parties' having *meant* the same thing but on their having *said* the same thing." The Path of the Law, in Collected Legal Papers, p. 178. I have concluded that plaintiff has not sustained its burden of persuasion that the contract used "chicken" in the narrower sense.

The action is for breach of the warranty that goods sold shall correspond to the description, New York Personal Property Law, McKinney's Consol. Laws, c.41, §95. Two contracts are in suit. In the first, dated May 2, 1957, defendant, a New York sales corporation, confirmed the sale to plaintiff, a Swiss corporation, of

U.S. Fresh Frozen Chicken, Grade A, Government Inspected, Eviscerated

2 1/2-3 lbs. and 1 1/2-2 lbs. each

all chicken individually wrapped in cryovac, packed in secured fiber cartons or wooden boxes, suitable for export

75,000 lbs. 2 1/2-3 lbs.	@$33.00
25,000 lbs. 1 1/2-2 lbs.	@$36.50

per 100 lbs. FAS New York

scheduled May 10, 1957 pursuant to instructions from Penson & Co., New York.

The second contract, also dated May 2, 1957, was identical save that only 50,000 lbs. of the heavier "chicken" were called for, the price of the smaller birds was $37 per 100 lbs., and shipment was scheduled for May 30. The initial shipment under the first contract was short but the balance was shipped on May 17. When the initial shipment arrived in Switzerland, plaintiff found, on May 28, that the 2 1/2-3 lbs. birds were not young chicken suitable for broiling and frying but stewing chicken or "fowl"; indeed, many of the cartons and bags plainly so indicated. Protests ensued. Nevertheless, shipment under the second contract was made on May 29, the 2 1/2-3 lbs. birds again being stewing chicken. Defendant stopped the transportation of these at Rotterdam.

This action followed. Plaintiff says that, notwithstanding that its acceptance was in Switzerland, New York law controls under the principle of Rubin v. Irving Trust Co., 1953, 305 N.Y. 288, 305, 113 N.E.2d 424, 431; defendant does not dispute this, and relies on New York decisions. I shall follow the apparent agreement of the parties as to the applicable law.

Since the word "chicken" standing alone is ambiguous, I turn first to see whether the contract itself offers any aid to its interpretation. Plaintiff says the 1 1/2-2 lbs. birds necessarily had to be young chicken since the older birds do not come in that size, hence the 2 1/2-3 lbs. birds must likewise be young. This is unpersuasive — a contract for "apples" of two different sizes could be filled with different kinds of apples even though only one species come in both sizes. Defendant notes that the contract called not simply for chicken but for "U.S. Fresh Frozen Chicken, Grade A, Government Inspected." It says the contract thereby incorporated by reference the Department of Agriculture's regulations, which favor its interpretation; I shall return to this after reviewing plaintiff's other contentions.

The first hinges on an exchange of cablegrams which preceded execution of the formal contracts. The negotiations leading up to the contracts were conducted in New York between defendant's secretary, Ernest R. Bauer, and a Mr. Stovicek, who was in New York for the Czechoslovak government at the World Trade Fair. A few days after meeting Bauer at the fair, Stovicek telephoned and inquired whether defendant would be interested in exporting poultry to Switzerland. Bauer then met with Stovicek, who showed him a cable from plaintiff dated April 26, 1957, announcing that they "are buyer" of 25,000 lbs. of chicken 2 1/2-3 lbs. weight, Cryovac packed, grade A Government inspected, at a price up to 33¢ per pound, for shipment on May 10, to be confirmed by the following morning, and were interested in further offerings. After testing the market for price, Bauer accepted, and Stovicek sent a confirmation that evening. Plaintiff stresses that, although these and subsequent cables between plaintiff and defendant, which laid the basis for the additional quantities under the first and for all of the second contract, were predominantly in German, they used the English word "chicken"; it claims this was done because it understood "chicken" meant young chicken whereas the German word, "Huhn," included both "Brathuhn" (broilers) and "Suppenhuhn" (stewing chicken), and that defendant, whose officers were thoroughly conversant with German, should have realized this. Whatever force this argument might otherwise have is largely drained away by Bauer's testimony that he asked Stovicek what kind of chickens were wanted, received the answer "any kind of chickens," and then, in German, asked whether the cable meant "Huhn" and received an affirmative response. . . .

Plaintiff's next contention is that there was a definite trade usage that "chicken" meant "young chicken." Defendant showed that it was only beginning in the poultry trade in 1957, thereby bringing itself within the principle that "when one of the parties is not a member of the trade or other circle, his acceptance of the standard must be made to appear" by proving either that he had actual knowledge of the usage or that the usage is "so generally known in the community that his actual individual knowledge of it may be inferred." 9 Wigmore, Evidence (3d ed. 1940) §2464. Here there was no proof of actual knowledge of the alleged usage; indeed, it is quite plain that defendant's belief was to the contrary. In order to meet the alternative requirement, the law of New York demands a showing that "the usage is of so long continuance, so well established, so notorious, so universal and so reasonable in itself, as that the presumption is violent that the parties contracted with reference to it, and made it a part of their agreement." Walls v. Bailey, 1872, 49 N.Y. 464, 472-473.

Plaintiff endeavored to establish such a usage by the testimony of three witnesses and certain other evidence. Strasser, resident buyer in New York for a large chain of Swiss cooperatives, testified that "on chicken I would definitely understand a broiler." However, the force of this testimony was considerably weakened by the fact that in his own transactions the witness, a careful businessman, protected himself by using "broiler" when that was what he wanted and "fowl" when he wished older birds. Indeed, there are some indications, dating back to a remark of Lord Mansfield, Edie v. East India Co., 2 Burr. 1216, 1222 (1761), that no credit should be given "witnesses to usage, who could not adduce instances in verification." 7 Wigmore, Evidence (3d ed. 1940), §1954; see McDonald v. Acker, Merrall & Condit Co., 2d Dept. 1920, 192 App. Div. 123, 126, 182 N.Y.S. 607. While Wigmore thinks this goes too far, a witness' consistent failure to rely on the alleged usage deprives his opinion testimony of much of its effect. Niesielowski, an officer of one of the companies that had furnished the stewing chicken to defendant, testified that "chicken" meant "the male species of the poultry industry. That could be a broiler, a fryer or a roaster," but not a stewing chicken; however, he also testified that upon receiving defendant's inquiry for "chickens," he asked whether the desire was for "fowl or frying chickens" and, in fact, supplied fowl, although taking the precaution of asking defendant, a day or two after plaintiff's acceptance of the contracts in suit, to change its confirmation of its order from "chickens," as defendant had originally prepared it, to "stewing chickens." Dates, an employee of Urner-Barry Company, which publishes a daily market report on the poultry trade, gave it as his view that the trade meaning of "chicken" was "broilers and fryers." In addition to this opinion testimony, plaintiff relied on the fact that the Urner-Barry service, the Journal of Commerce, and Weinberg Bros. & Co. of Chicago, a large supplier of poultry, published quotations in a manner which, in one way or another, distinguish between "chicken," comprising broilers, fryers and certain other categories, and "fowl," which, Bauer acknowledged, included stewing chickens. This material would be impressive if there were nothing to the contrary. However, there was, as will now be seen.

Defendant's witness Weininger, who operates a chicken eviscerating plant in New Jersey, testified "Chicken is everything except a goose, a duck, and a turkey. Everything is a chicken, but then you have to say, you have to specify which category you want or that you are talking about." Its witness Fox said that in the trade "chicken" would encompass all the various classifications. Sadina, who conducts a food inspection service, testified that he would consider any bird coming within the classes of "chicken" in the Department of Agriculture's regulations to be a chicken. The specifications approved by the General Services Administration include fowl as well as broilers and fryers under the classification "chickens." Statistics of the Institute of American Poultry Industries use the phrases "Young chickens" and "Mature chickens," under the general heading "Total chickens," and the Department of Agriculture's daily and weekly price reports avoid use of the word "chicken" without specification.

Defendant advances several other points which it claims affirmatively support its construction. Primary among these is the regulation of the Department of Agriculture, 7 C.F.R. §70.300-70.370, entitled, "Grading and Inspection of Poultry and Edible Products Thereof," and in particular §70.301 which recited:

Chickens. The following are the various classes of chickens:

(a) Broiler or fryer . . .
(b) Roaster . . .
(c) Capon . . .
(d) Stag . . .
(e) Hen or stewing chicken or fowl . . .
(f) Cock or old rooster . . .

Defendant argues, as previously noted, that the contract incorporated these regulations by reference. Plaintiff answers that the contract provision related simply to grade and Government inspection and did not incorporate the Government definition of "chicken," and also that the definition in the Regulations is ignored in the trade. However, the latter contention was contradicted by Weininger and Sadina; and there is force in defendant's argument that the contract made the regulations a dictionary, particularly since the reference to Government grading was already in plaintiff's initial cable to Stovicek.

Defendant makes a further argument based on the impossibility of its obtaining broilers and fryers at the 33¢ price offered by plaintiff for the 2 1/2-3 lbs. birds. There is no substantial dispute that, in late April, 1957, the price for 2 1/2-3 lbs. broilers was between 35 and 37¢ per pound, and that when defendant entered into the contracts, it was well aware of this and intended to fill them, by supplying fowl in these weights. It claims that plaintiff must likewise have known the market since plaintiff had reserved shipping space on April 23, three days before plaintiff's cable to Stovicek, or, at least, that Stovicek was chargeable with such knowledge. It is scarcely an answer to say, as plaintiff does in its brief, that the 33¢ price offered by the 2 1/2-3 lbs. "chickens" was closer to the prevailing 35¢ price for broilers than to the 30¢ at which defendant procured fowl. Plaintiff must have expected defendant to make some profit — certainly it could not have expected defendant deliberately to incur a loss.

Finally, defendant relies on conduct by the plaintiff after the first shipment had been received. On May 28 plaintiff sent two cables complaining that the larger birds in the first shipment constituted "fowl." Defendant answered with a cable refusing to recognize plaintiff's objection and announcing "We have today ready for shipment 50,000 lbs. chicken 2 1/2-3 lbs. 25,000 lbs. broilers 1 1/2-2 lbs.," these being the goods procured for shipment under the second contract, and asked immediate answer "whether we are to ship this merchandise to you and whether you will accept the merchandise." After several other cable exchanges, plaintiff replied on May 29 "Confirm again that merchandise is to be shipped since resold by us if not enough pursuant to contract chickens are shipped the missing quantity is to be shipped within ten days stop we resold to our customers pursuant to your contract chickens grade A you have to deliver us said merchandise we again state that we shall make you fully responsible for all resulting costs."[2] Defendant argues that if plaintiff was sincere in thinking it was entitled to young chickens, plaintiff would not have allowed the shipment under the second contract to go forward, since the distinction between broilers and chickens drawn in defendant's cablegram must have made it clear that the larger birds would not be broilers. However, plaintiff answers that the cables show plaintiff was insisting on delivery of young chickens and that defendant shipped old ones at its peril. Defendant's point would be highly relevant on another disputed issue — whether if liability were established, the measure of damages should be the difference in market value of broilers and stewing chicken in New York or the larger difference in Europe, but I cannot give it weight on the issue of interpretation. Defendant points out also that plaintiff proceeded to deliver some of the larger birds in Europe, describing them as "poulets"; defendant argues that it was only when plaintiff's customers complained about this that plaintiff developed the idea that "chicken" meant "young chicken." There is little force in this in view of plaintiff's immediate and consistent protests.

When all the evidence is reviewed, it is clear that defendant believed it could comply with the contracts by delivering stewing chicken in the 2 1/2-3 lbs. size. Defendant's subjective intent would not be significant if this did not coincide with an objective meaning of "chicken." Here it did coincide with one of the dictionary meanings, with the definition in the Department of

---

2. These cables were in German; "chicken," "broilers" and, on some occasions, "fowl," were in English.

Agriculture Regulations to which the contract made at least oblique reference, with at least some usage in the trade, with the realities of the market, and with what plaintiff's spokesman had said. Plaintiff asserts it to be equally plain that plaintiff's own subjective intent was to obtain broilers and fryers; the only evidence against this is the material as to market prices and this may not have been sufficiently brought home. In any event it is unnecessary to determine that issue. For plaintiff has the burden of showing that "chicken" was used in the narrower rather than in the broader sense, and this it has not sustained.

This opinion constitutes the Court's findings of fact and conclusions of law. Judgment shall be entered dismissing the complaint with costs.

Notes and Questions

1. *Whose meaning prevails? Joyner* illustrates the application of the principles of the modified objective theory of contract interpretation: A party is bound by the other party's meaning if the first party either knew or had reason to know of the second party's meaning while the second party did not know or have reason to know of the first party's interpretation. Consider the effect of these principles in *Frigaliment*. Does the court hold that a contract was formed and that the word *chicken* is to be interpreted in accordance with the defendant's meaning, or does the court hold that no contract was formed because there was no reasonable basis for choosing between the conflicting meanings of the word *chicken?* Does it make any difference to the result in the case? Would the choice between these theories have made a difference if Frigaliment had refused to accept the "chickens" and B.N.S. had brought suit for breach of contract?

2. *Ambiguity and "plain meaning."* More extensively than *Joyner, Frigaliment* examines the various types of evidence that each party can introduce to convince the trier of fact that its meaning should prevail. Before proceeding to an examination of the circumstances surrounding the making of the contract, the court notes that the word *chicken* is ambiguous. Is it necessary for a court to make a preliminary determination that the contract is ambiguous before receiving evidence of surrounding circumstances? Courts often state that the "plain meaning" of the language of a contract should govern and that extrinsic evidence is admissible only if the court concludes that the contract is ambiguous. E.g., Bangor Publishing Co. v. Union Street Market, 706 A.2d 595 (Me. 1998) (trial court erroneously admitted extrinsic evidence when advertising contract was unambiguous and plainly imposed personal liability on corporate officer).

Contract scholars (including both objectivists and advocates of a more flexible, modern approach to interpretation) have consistently rejected the idea that words can have only one precise meaning. As Holmes said, "It is not true that in practice (and I know no reason why theory should disagree with the facts) a given word or even a given collocation of words has one meaning and no other. A word generally has several meanings, even in a dictionary." Oliver Wendell Holmes, The Theory of Legal Interpretation, 12 Harv. L. Rev. 417 (1899). See also 4 Williston on Contracts §609, at 403. Professor Corbin argued that a court should admit all relevant evidence in order to determine the intention of the parties, including evidence of subjective intent. 3 Corbin on Contracts §538, at 73. See also 3 Corbin on Contracts §542, at 101-103. The Restatement adopts Corbin's view on the admissibility of extrinsic evidence. Restatement (Second) §202; see also 3 Corbin on Contracts §543. UCC §2-202 clearly rejects any requirement of ambiguity as a prerequisite to evidence of trade usage in Comment 1(c) to that section, but fails to take a clear position as to other types of extrinsic evidence. Cf. Golden Peanut Co. v. Bass, 563 S.E.2d 116 (Ga. 2002) (UCC §2-202 was meant to liberalize parol evidence rule and allow extrinsic evidence without showing of ambiguity).

Although contract theorists have been practically unanimous in their rejection of the plain meaning rule, some (perhaps most) courts will nonetheless rely on the rule and refuse to receive extrinsic evidence of meaning unless the court first concludes that the agreement is ambiguous. Joseph M. Perillo, Calamari & Perillo on Contracts §3-10, at 151 n.10 (5th ed. 2003).

3. *Patent and latent ambiguity.* Assuming a court requires the contract to be ambiguous before admitting extrinsic evidence, when is an agreement ambiguous? Courts and scholars have identified two types of ambiguity: patent or intrinsic ambiguity and latent or extrinsic ambiguity. In Bohler-Uddeholm America, Inc. v. Bohler-Uddeholm Corp., 247 F.3d 79 (3d Cir. 2001), a case involving the dissolution of a joint venture for the manufacture of steel ingots, the court was faced with a disputed term concerning the sharing of certain profits. The defendant appealed after a jury returned a verdict against it for $4.1 million, asserting that the contract had a plain meaning that favored its position and that the trial court had erred in admitting extrinsic evidence to uncover a latent ambiguity. The Third Circuit Court of Appeals, faced with apparently conflicting Pennsylvania precedents, first noted that the state's courts have often held that where a written contract is facially clear a court should not look for its meaning beyond its "four corners." Nevertheless, Pennsylvania decisions also permit the court to receive and consider extrinsic evidence to determine whether there may be in the agreement a "latent ambiguity," one not apparent from the words alone (at least in their common meanings) but visible in the light of surrounding circumstances. Such evidence should consist of more than the parties' own declarations of their "intentions" at the time of contracting, however, and it should not seek to impose on the writing a meaning beyond any reasonable understanding of its terms. The cases thus resolve the apparent tension between "plain meaning" and "latent ambiguity" analyses, the court concluded,

> . . . by allowing only extrinsic evidence of a certain nature to establish latent ambiguity in a contract; a court should determine whether the type of extrinsic evidence offered could be used to support a reasonable alternative interpretation under the precepts of Pennsylvania law on contract interpretation. . . . Once the court determines that a party has offered extrinsic evidence capable of establishing latent ambiguity, a decision as to which of the competing interpretations of the contract is the correct one is reserved for the factfinder, who would examine the content of the extrinsic evidence (along with all the other evidence) in order to make this determination. . . .

247 F.3d at 92-94. The Third Circuit Court thus upheld the trial court finding of a latent ambiguity based on permissible extrinsic evidence, but remanded the case on other grounds.

In a similar approach, the Seventh Circuit Court of Appeals has made a distinction between objective and subjective extrinsic evidence. Objective evidence, testimony of disinterested third parties or trade usage or the like, is deemed permissible to establish latent ambiguity because such evidence cannot be easily fabricated. Subjective evidence, testimony about what the parties believed the contract meant, is not acceptable for that purpose because it tends to be self-serving. AM International, Inc. v. Graphic Management Associates, Inc., 44 F.3d 572, 574-576 (7th Cir. 1995). Would you classify the term "chicken" as involving patent or latent ambiguity? If the *Frigaliment* court had applied the Pennsylvania approach, would extrinsic evidence of the meaning of the word "chicken" have been admitted? Why?

4. *Contextual approach to interpretation.* Under the modern theory of interpretation, a court should examine all relevant circumstances in interpreting the agreement, including preliminary negotiations and communications between the parties. Restatement (Second) §202(1); 3 Corbin on Contracts §543. We will see in the second part of this chapter that this broad principle of admissibility is counterbalanced by the parol evidence rule, which sometimes acts to exclude evidence offered to contradict or to supplement a writing that the parties intend to be a final expression of their agreement. The parol evidence rule would probably not have applied in *Frigaliment* because the parties did not enter into a writing that they intended to be a final expression of their agreement.

5. *Effect of relevant statute.* What effect does the court give to the Department of Agriculture regulation defining the classes of chickens? The modern view is that definitions of terms contained in statutes or administrative regulations are not determinative of the meaning of such terms in contracts. Restatement (Second) §201, Comment *c;* 3 Corbin on Contracts §551. What is the justification for this approach?

6. *Relevance of trade usage.* The plaintiff buyer in *Frigaliment* attempted to show the existence of a trade usage by which the term "chicken" would be understood to mean a young chicken. While ultimately rejecting that contention as not sufficiently established by the testimony of the plaintiff's witnesses, the court appears to have regarded evidence of this type as admissible and relevant to the disputed issue of interpretation. Indeed, the existence of a relevant trade usage can overcome even the apparently unambiguous, "plain meaning" of contract language. See Southern Pacific Trans. Co. v. Santa Fe Pacific Pipelines, Inc., 88 Cal. Rptr. 2d 777 (Ct. App. 1999) (parties are presumed to contract pursuant to established usage and custom of trade even when instrument appears plain and unambiguous on its face); Hurst v. W. J. Lake & Co. 16 P.2d 627 (Or. 1932) (reversing trial court's grant of defendant's motion for judgment on the pleadings, holding that plaintiff should have been allowed to show that written contract for the sale of horsemeat scraps of "minimum 50 percent protein" was performable by delivery of horsemeat scraps containing as little as 49.5 percent protein in light of trade custom).

In §1-205, the Uniform Commercial Code defines "usage of trade" and generally provides that evidence of trade usage should be relevant to the interpretation of the parties' agreement. The Comments to that section elaborate on the meaning and application of the Code's concept of trade usage and contrast it with the somewhat more restrictive view of "custom" as developed in the earlier common law. See generally Amy H. Kastely, Stock Equipment for the Bargain in Fact: Trade Usage, "Express Terms," and Consistency under Section 1-205 of the Uniform Commercial Code, 64 N.C.L. Rev. 777 (1986). Section 1-205 also defines a "course of dealing" between the parties that may reflect a shared understanding regarding a later agreement, and §2-208 addresses the possibility of a "course of performance" that reflects the parties' understanding of the contract. See Putnam Park Assocs. v. Fahnestock & Co., 807 A.2d 991 (Conn. 2002) (course of performance in accepting late delivery of documents given great weight in interpretation). (Usage of trade and related concepts are addressed by Revised UCC §1-303.) Of course, under the Code (as in *Frigaliment*, decided under the common law) the court may receive evidence of an asserted trade usage and yet ultimately find that the contended usage has not been sufficiently established as a fact. E.g., Williams v. Curtin, 807 F.2d 1046 (D.C. Cir. 1986) (evidence failed to establish trade usage that "slaw cabbage" referred to cabbage of a certain minimum size). Later in this chapter we shall examine more closely the role of trade usage and related concepts under the UCC, particularly in light of the Code's version of the parol evidence rule (§2-202).

7. *Scholarly commentary.* Professor Lisa Bernstein is skeptical about the weight that decisionmakers should give to general standards, such as trade usage. Professor Bernstein has drawn a distinction between cases in which the parties wish to preserve their relationship and "end game" situations in which the relationship has collapsed and the parties are attempting to maximize their gains or minimize their losses. She argues that norms such as trade usage, course of dealing, and course of performance are relationship preserving, but parties to a dispute do not usually want a dispute-resolution body to apply these norms. Bernstein contends that parties often rationally prefer that relationship-preserving norms be left to the nonlegal realm:

> [This article suggests] that transactors do not necessarily want the relationship-preserving norms they follow in performing contracts and cooperatively resolving disputes among themselves to be used by third-party neutrals to decide cases when they are in an end-game situation. After presenting evidence that merchants implicitly recognize the distinction between relationship-preserving and end-game norms, it suggests that when courts apply the Code's usage of trade, course of dealing, and course of performance provisions, they will often be using relationship-preserving norms to resolve end-game disputes. It then explores the effects of this aspect of the Code's adjudicative approach on contracting relationships, and demonstrates that this approach both prevents transactors from selecting their preferred mix of legal and extralegal terms and makes them less willing to flexibly adjust their contracting relationships. It also suggests that this approach may undermine transactors' attempts to create the contracting framework that will best promote successful renegotiation and long-term cooperation. [The article also explores] the reasons that the Code's adjudicative approach may inhibit the "expansion of commercial practices."

Lisa Bernstein, Merchant Law in a Merchant Court: Rethinking the Code's Search for Immanent Business Norms, 144 U. Pa. L. Rev. 1765, 1770-1771

(1996). See also Lisa Bernstein, Opting Out of the Legal System: Extralegal Contractual Relations in the Diamond Industry, 21 J. Legal Stud. 115 (1992) (extralegal enforcement system based on reputational bonds within the diamond industry is more efficient than traditional legal system).

Other commentators have considered issues of contract interpretation from an economic perspective. Professors Alan Schwartz and Robert Scott have argued that courts, in interpreting written contracts between firms, should adopt a strict formalist approach rather than a contextual one because this is what firms themselves prefer. Alan Schwartz & Robert E. Scott, Contract Theory and the Limits of Contract Law, 113 Yale L. J. 541 (2003). Further discussion of this proposition can be found in James W. Bowers, Murphy's Law and the Elementary Theory of Contract Interpretation: A Response to Schwartz and Scott, 57 Rutgers L. Rev. 587 (2005); and Avery Wiener Katz, The Economics of Form and Substance in Contract Interpretation, 104 Colum. L. Rev. 496 (2004).

C & J Fertilizer, Inc. v. Allied Mutual Insurance Co.
Supreme Court of Iowa
227 N.W.2d 169 (1975)

REYNOLDSON, Justice.

This action to recover for burglary loss under two separate insurance policies was tried to the court, resulting in a finding plaintiff had failed to establish a burglary within the policy definitions. Plaintiff appeals from judgment entered for defendant. We reverse and remand.

Trial court made certain findings of fact in support of its conclusion reached. Plaintiff operated a fertilizer plant in Olds, Iowa. At time of loss, plaintiff was insured under policies issued by defendant and titled "BROAD FORM STOREKEEPERS POLICY" and "MERCANTILE BURGLARY AND ROBBERY POLICY." Each policy defined "burglary" as meaning,

> ... the felonious abstraction of insured property (1) from within the premises by a person making felonious entry therein by actual force and violence, of which force and violence there are visible marks made by tools, explosives, electricity or chemicals upon, or physical damage to, the exterior of the premises at the place of such entry. ...

On Saturday, April 18, 1970, all exterior doors to the building were locked when plaintiff's employees left the premises at the end of the business day. The following day, Sunday, April 19, 1970, one of plaintiff's employees was at the plant and found all doors locked and secure. On Monday, April 20, 1970, when the employees reported for work, the exterior doors were locked, but the front office door was unlocked.

There were truck tire tread marks visible in the mud in the driveway leading to and from the plexiglas door entrance to the warehouse. It was demonstrated this door could be forced open without leaving visible marks or physical damage.

There were no visible marks on the exterior of the building made by tools, explosives, electricity or chemicals, and there was no physical damage to the exterior of the building to evidence felonious entry into the building by force and violence.

Chemicals had been stored in an interior room of the warehouse. The door to this room, which had been locked, was physically damaged and carried visible marks made by tools. Chemicals had been taken at a net loss to plaintiff in the sum of $9,582. Office and shop equipment valued at $400.30 was also taken from the building.

Trial court held the policy definition of "burglary" was unambiguous, there was nothing in the record "upon which to base a finding that the door to plaintiff's place of business was entered feloniously, by actual force and violence," and, applying the policy language, found for defendant.

Certain other facts in the record were apparently deemed irrelevant by trial court because of its view the applicable law required it to enforce the policy provision. Because we conclude different rules of law apply, we also consider those facts.

The "BROAD FORM STOREKEEPERS POLICY" was issued April 14, 1969; the "MERCANTILE BURGLARY AND ROBBERY POLICY" on April 14, 1970. Those policies are in evidence. Prior policies apparently were first purchased in 1968. The agent, who had power to bind insurance coverage for defendant, was told plaintiff would be handling farm chemicals. After inspecting the building then used by plaintiff for storage he made certain suggestions regarding security. There ensued a conversation in which he pointed out there had to be visible evidence of burglary. There was no testimony by anyone that plaintiff was then or thereafter informed the policy to be delivered would define burglary to require "visible marks made by tools, explosives, electricity or chemicals upon, or physical damage to, the exterior of the premises at the place of . . . entry."

The import of this conversation with defendant's agent when the coverage was sold is best confirmed by the agent's complete and vocally-expressed surprise when defendant denied coverage. From what the agent saw (tire tracks and marks on the interior of the building) and his contacts with the investigating officers " . . . the thought didn't enter my mind that it wasn't covered. . . . " From the trial testimony it was obvious the only understanding was that there should be some hard evidence of a third-party burglary vis-à-vis an "inside job." The latter was in this instance effectively ruled out when the thief was required to break an interior door lock to gain access to the chemicals.

The agent testified the insurance was purchased and "the policy was sent out afterwards." The president of plaintiff corporation, a 37-year-old farmer with a high school education, looked at that portion of the policy setting out coverages, including coverage for burglary loss, the amounts of insurance, and the "location and description." He could not recall reading the fine print defining "burglary" on page three of the policy. . . .

I. Revolution in Formation of Contractual Relationships

Many of our principles for resolving conflicts relating to written contracts were formulated at an early time when parties of equal strength negotiated in the historical sequence of offer, acceptance, and reduction to writing. The concept that both parties assented to the resulting document had solid footing in fact.

Only recently has the sweeping change in the inception of the document received widespread recognition:

> Standard form contracts probably account for more than ninety-nine percent of all contracts now made. Most persons have difficulty remembering the last time they contracted other than by standard form; except for casual oral agreements, they probably never have. But if they are active, they contract by standard form several times a day. Parking lot and theater tickets, package receipts, department store charge slips, and gas station credit card purchase slips are all standard form contracts. . . .
>
> The contracting still imagined by courts and law teachers as typical, in which both parties participate in choosing the language of their entire agreement, is no longer of much more than historical importance.

> —W. Slawson, Standard Form Contracts and Democratic Control of Lawmaking Power, 84 Harv. L. Rev. 529 (1971).

With respect to those interested in buying insurance, it has been observed that:

> His chances of successfully negotiating with the company for any substantial change in the proposed contract are just about zero. The insurance company tenders the insurance upon a "take it or leave it" basis. . . .
>
> Few persons solicited to take policies understand the subject of insurance or the rules of law governing the negotiations, and they have no voice in dictating the terms of what is called the contract. They are clear upon two or three points which the agent promises to protect, and for everything else they must sign ready-made applications and accept ready-made policies carefully concocted to conserve the interests of the company. . . . The subject, therefore, is *sui generis,* and the rules of a legal system devised to govern the formation of ordinary contracts between man and man cannot be mechanically applied to it.

> —7 Williston on Contracts §900, pp.29-30 (3d ed. 1963).

See also 3 Corbin on Contracts §559, p.266 (1960); 6A Corbin on Contracts §1376, p.21; Grismore on Contracts §294, pp.505-507 (rev. ed. J. E. Murray, Jr. 1965); R. Keeton, Insurance Law Rights At Variance With Policy Provisions, 83 Harv. L. Rev. 961, 966-967 (1970); F. Kessler, Contracts of Adhesion — Some Thoughts About Freedom of Contract, 43 Colum. L. Rev. 629 (1943); C. Oldfather, Toward a Usable Method of Judicial Review of the Adhesion Contractor's Lawmaking, 16 Kansas L. Rev. 303 (1968).

It is generally recognized the insured will not read the detailed, cross-referenced, standardized, mass-produced insurance form, nor understand it if he does. 7 Williston on Contracts §906B, p.300 ("But where the document thus delivered to him is a contract of insurance the majority rule is that the insured is not bound to know its contents"); 3 Corbin on Contracts §559, pp.265-266 ("One who applies for an insurance policy . . . may not even read the policy, the number of its terms and the fineness of its print being such as to discourage him"); Note, Unconscionable Contracts: The Uniform Commercial Code, 45 Iowa L. Rev. 843, 844 (1960) ("It is probably a safe assertion that most involved standardized form contracts are never read by the party who 'adheres' to them. In such situations, the proponent of the form is free to dictate terms most advantageous to himself"). . . .

The concept that persons must obey public laws enacted by their own representatives does not offend a fundamental sense of justice: an inherent element of assent pervades the process.

But the inevitable result of enforcing all provisions of the adhesion contract, frequently, as here, delivered subsequent to the transaction and containing provisions never assented to, would be an abdication of judicial responsibility in face of basic unfairness and a recognition that persons' rights shall be controlled by private lawmakers without the consent, express or implied, of those affected. See Grismore, supra §294 at p.506; K. Llewellyn, What Price Contract? — An Essay in Perspective, 40 Yale L.J. 704, 731 (1931); Meyer, Contracts of Adhesion and the Doctrine of Fundamental Breach, 50 Va. L. Rev. 1178, 1179 (1964); C. Oldfather, supra at 303-304. A question is also raised whether a court may constitutionally allow that power to exist in private hands except where appropriate safeguards are present, including a right to meaningful judicial review. See W. Slawson, supra at 553.

The statutory requirement that the form of policies be approved by the commissioner of insurance, §515.109, The Code, neither resolves the issue whether the fineprint provisions nullify the insurance bargained for in a given case nor ousts the court from necessary jurisdiction. . . . In this connection it has been pertinently stated:

> Insurance contracts continue to be contracts of adhesion, under which the insured is left little choice beyond electing among standardized provisions offered to him, even when the standard forms are prescribed by public officials rather than insurers. Moreover, although statutory and administrative regulations have made increasing inroads on the insurer's autonomy by prescribing some kinds of provisions and proscribing others, most insurance policy provisions are still drafted by insurers. Regulation is relatively weak in most instances, and even the provisions prescribed or approved by legislative or administrative action ordinarily are in essence adoptions, outright or slightly modified, of proposals made by insurers' draftsmen.
>
> Under such circumstances as these, judicial regulation of contracts of adhesion, whether concerning insurance or some other kind of transaction, remains appropriate.
>
> — R. Keeton, supra at 966-967.

See also 3 Corbin on Contracts §559, p.267.

The mass-produced boiler-plate "contracts," necessitated and spawned by the explosive growth of complex business transactions in a burgeoning population left courts frequently frustrated in attempting to arrive at just results by applying many of the traditional contract-construing stratagems. As long as fifteen years ago Professor Llewellyn, reflecting on this situation in his book "The Common Law Tradition — Deciding Appeals," pp.362-371 wrote,

> What the story shows thus far is first, scholars persistently off-base while judges grope over well-nigh a century in irregular but dogged fashion for escape from a

recurring discomfort of imbalance that rests on what is in fact substantial *non*agreement despite perfect semblance of agreement. (pp.367-368). . . .

The answer, I suggest, is this: Instead of thinking about "assent" to boiler-plate clauses, we can recognize that so far as concerns the specific, there is no assent at all. What has in fact been assented to, specifically, are the few dickered terms, and the broad type of transaction, and but one thing more. That one thing more is a blanket assent (not a specific assent) to any not unreasonable or indecent terms the seller may have on his form, which do not alter or eviscerate the reasonable meaning of the dickered terms. The fine print which has not been read has no business to cut under the reasonable meaning of those dickered terms which constitute the dominant and only real expression of agreement, but much of it commonly belongs in. (p.370)

In fairness to the often-discerned ability of the common law to develop solutions for changing demands, it should be noted appellate courts take cases as they come, constrained by issues the litigants formulated in trial court — a point not infrequently overlooked by academicians. Nor can a lawyer in the ordinary case be faulted for not risking a client's cause on an uncharted course when there is a reasonable prospect of reaching a fair result through familiar channels of long-accepted legal principles, for example, those grounded on ambiguity in language, the duty to define limitations or exclusions in clear and explicit terms, and interpretation of language from the viewpoint of an ordinary person, not a specialist or expert. . . .

Plaintiff's claim it should be granted relief under the legal doctrines of reasonable expectations, implied warranty and unconscionability should be viewed against the above backdrop.

II. REASONABLE EXPECTATIONS

This court adopted the doctrine of reasonable expectations in Rodman v. State Farm Mutual Ins. Co., 208 N.W.2d 903, 905-908 (Iowa 1973). The *Rodman* court approved the following articulation of that concept:

> The objectively reasonable expectations of applicants and intended beneficiaries regarding the terms of insurance contracts will be honored even though painstaking study of the policy provisions would have negated those expectations.

208 N.W.2d at 906.

See Gray v. Zurich Insurance Company, 65 Cal. 2d 263, 54 Cal. Rptr. 104, 107-108, 419 P.2d 168, 171-172 (1966); Allen v. Metropolitan Life Ins. Co., 44 N.J. 294, 305, 208 A.2d 638, 644 (1965); Restatement (Second) of Contracts, supra, §237, Comments *e* and *f*, pp.540-541; 1 Corbin on Contracts §1, p.2 ("That portion of the field of law that is classified and described as the law of contracts attempts the realization of reasonable expectations that have been induced by the making of a promise"); 7 Williston on Contracts §900, pp.33-34 ("Some courts, recognizing that very few insureds even try to read and understand the policy or application, have declared that the insured is justified in assuming that the policy which is delivered to him has been faithfully prepared by the company to provide the protection against the risk which he had asked for. . . . Obviously this judicial attitude is a far cry from the old motto 'caveat emptor.' ").

At comment *f* to §237 of Restatement (Second) of Contracts, supra pp.540-541, we find the following analysis of the reasonable expectations doctrine:

> Although customers typically adhere to standardized agreements and are bound by them without even appearing to know the standard terms in detail, they are not bound to unknown terms which are beyond the range of reasonable expectation. A debtor who delivers a check to his creditor with the amount blank does not authorize the insertion of an infinite figure. Similarly, a party who adheres to the other party's standard terms does not assent to a term if the other party has reason to believe that the adhering party would not have accepted the agreement if he had known that the agreement contained the particular term. Such a belief or assumption may be shown by the prior negotiations or inferred from the circumstances. Reason to believe may be inferred from the fact that the term is bizarre or oppressive, from the fact that it eviscerates the non-standard terms explicitly agreed to, or from the fact that it eliminates the dominant purpose of the transaction. The inference is reinforced if the adhering party never had an opportunity to read the term, or if it is illegible or otherwise hidden from view. This rule is closely related to the policy against unconscionable terms and the rule of interpretation against the draftsman.

Nor can it be asserted the above doctrine does not apply here because plaintiff knew the policy contained the provision now complained of and cannot be heard to say it reasonably expected what it knew was not there. A search of the record discloses no such knowledge.

The evidence does show, as above noted, a "dicker" for burglary insurance coverage on chemicals and equipment. The negotiation was for what was actually expressed in the policies' "Insuring Agreements": the insurer's promise "To pay for loss by burglary or by robbery of a watchman, while the premises are not open for business, of merchandise, furniture, fixtures and equipment within the premises. . . ."

In addition, the conversation included statements from which the plaintiff should have understood defendant's obligation to pay would not arise where the burglary was an "inside job." Thus the following exclusion should have been reasonably anticipated:

> Exclusions
>
> This policy does not apply: . . .
>
> (b) to loss due to any fraudulent, dishonest or criminal act by any Insured, a partner therein, or an officer, employee, director, trustee or authorized representative thereof. . . .

But there was nothing relating to the negotiations with defendant's agent which would have led plaintiff to reasonably anticipate defendant would bury within the definition of "burglary" another exclusion denying coverage when, no matter how extensive the proof of a third-party burglary, no marks were left on the exterior of the premises. This escape clause, here triggered by the burglar's talent (an investigating law officer, apparently acquainted with the current modus operandi, gained access to the steel building without leaving any marks by leaning on the overhead plexiglas door while simultaneously turning the locked handle), was never read to or by plaintiff's personnel, nor was the substance explained by defendant's agent.

Moreover, the burglary "definition" which crept into this policy comports neither with the concept a layman might have of that crime, nor with a legal interpretation. See State v. Murray, 222 Iowa 925, 931, 270 N.W. 355, 358 (1936) ("We have held that even though the door was partially open, by opening it farther, in order to enter the building, this is a sufficient breaking to comply with the demands of the statute"); State v. Ferguson, 149 Iowa 476, 478-479, 128 N.W. 840, 841-842 (1910) ("It need not appear that this office was an independent building, for it is well known that it is burglary for one to break and enter an inner door or window, although the culprit entered through an open outer door. . . . "); see State v. Hougland, 197 N.W.2d 364, 365 (Iowa 1972).

The most plaintiff might have reasonably anticipated was a policy requirement of visual evidence (abundant here) indicating the burglary was an "outside" not an "inside" job. The exclusion in issue, masking as a definition, makes insurer's obligation to pay turn on the skill of the burglar, not on the event the parties bargained for: a bona-fide third party burglary resulting in loss of plaintiff's chemicals and equipment.

The "reasonable expectations" attention to the basic agreement, to the concept of substance over form, was appropriately applied by this court for the insurer's benefit in Central Bearings Co. v. Wolverine Insurance Company, 179 N.W.2d 443 (Iowa 1970), a case antedating *Rodman*. We there reversed a judgment for the insured which trial court apparently grounded on a claimed ambiguity in the policy. In denying coverage on what was essentially a products liability claim where the insured purchased only a "Premises-Operations" policy (without any misrepresentation, misunderstanding or overreaching) we said at page 449 of 179 N.W.2d:

> In summation we think the insured as a reasonable person would understand the policy coverage purchased meant the insured was not covered for loss if the "accident" with concomitant damage to a victim occurred away from the premises and after the operation or sale was complete.

The same rationale of reasonable expectations should be applied when it would operate to the advantage of the insured. Appropriately applied to this case, the doctrine demands reversal and judgment for plaintiff. . . .

Reversed and remanded.

HARRIS and McCORMICK, JJ., concur.

MASON and RAWLINGS, JJ., concur in Divisions I, II and IV and the result.

LeGRAND, J., MOORE, C.J., and REES and UHLENHOPP, JJ., dissent.

LeGRAND, Justice (dissenting).

I dissent from the result reached by the majority because it ignores virtually every rule by which we have heretofore adjudicated such cases and affords plaintiff ex post facto insurance coverage which it not only did not buy but which it *knew* it did not buy. . . .

While it may be very well to talk in grand terms about "mass advertising" by insurance companies and "incessant" assurances as to coverage which mislead the "unwary," particularly about "fine-print" provisions, such discussion should somehow be related to the case under review. Our primary duty, after all, is to resolve *this* dispute for *these* litigants under *this* record.

There is total silence in this case concerning any of the practices the majority finds offensive; nor is there any claim plaintiff was beguiled by such conduct into believing it had more protection than it actually did.

The record is even stronger against the majority's fine-print argument, the stereotype accusation which serves as a coup de grace in all insurance cases. Except for larger type on the face sheet and black (but not larger) print to designate divisions and sub-headings, the entire policies are of one size and style of print. To compare the *face* sheet with the body of the policy is like comparing a book's jacket cover with the narrative content; and the use of black type or other means of emphasis to separate one part of an instrument from another is an approved editorial expedient which serves to *assist*, not *hinder*, readability. In fact many of our opinions, including that of the majority in the instant case, resort to that device.

Tested by any objective standard, the size and style of type used cannot be fairly described as "fine print." The majority's description, right or wrong, of the plight of consumers generally should not be the basis for resolving the case now before us.

Like all other appeals, this one should be decided on what the record discloses — a fact which the majority concedes but promptly disregards.

Crucial to a correct determination of this appeal is the disputed provision of each policy defining burglary as "the felonious abstraction of insured property ... by a person making felonious entry ... by actual force and violence, of which force and violence there are visible marks made by tools, explosives, electricity or chemicals upon, or physical damage to, the exterior of the premises at the place of such entry. ... " The starting point of any consideration of that definition is a determination whether it is ambiguous. Yet the majority does not even mention ambiguity.

The purpose of such a provision, of course, is to omit from coverage "inside jobs" or those resulting from fraud or complicity by the assured. The overwhelming weight of authority upholds such provisions as legitimate in purpose and unambiguous in application. Annot. 99 A.L.R.2d 129, 134 (1965); 44 Am. Jur. 2d Insurance §1400, §1401 (1969); 10 Couch Cyclopedia of Insurance Law (2d ed.) 42:128-42:130 (1962); 5 Appleman Insurance Law and Practice §3176, §3177. ...

Once this indisputable fact is recognized, plaintiff's arguments virtually collapse. We may not — at least we *should* not — by any accepted standard of construction meddle with contracts which clearly and plainly state their meaning simply because we dislike that meaning, even in the case of insurance policies. ...

... Here we have affirmative and unequivocal testimony from an officer and director of the plaintiff corporation that he knew the disputed provision was in the policies because "it was just like the insurance policy I have on my farm."

I cannot agree plaintiff may now assert it reasonably expected from these policies something it knew was not there. ...

Notes and Questions

1. *Reasonable expectation of coverage in C & J case.* Does the court in *C & J Fertilizer* adequately justify its determination that the "reasonable expectations" of the insured included coverage on the facts of that case? In Atwater Creamery Co. v. Western National Mutual Insurance Co., 366 N.W.2d 271 (Minn. 1985), the insured sought a declaratory judgment that the loss from a burglary from its chemical storage building was covered by its policy with defendant, despite the absence of visible marks of physical damage to the exterior of plaintiff's building. The policy language on this point was identical to that employed in the *C & J Fertilizer* case, and the Minnesota Supreme Court upheld a trial court determination that the doctrine of reasonable expectations applied to permit recovery on the policy. Investigators including local, county, and state police personnel had determined that none of plaintiff's employees were involved in the burglary. Calling this definition of "burglary" a "classic example of a policy provision that should be, and has been, interpreted according to the reasonable expectations of the insured" (id. at 277), the appellate court went on to observe as follows:

> There are, of course, fidelity bonds which cover employee theft. The creamery had such a policy covering director and manager theft. The fidelity company, however, does not undertake to insure against the risk of third-party burglaries. A business that requests and purchases burglary insurance reasonably is seeking coverage for loss from third-party burglaries whether a break-in is accomplished by an inept burglar or by a highly skilled burglar. . . . [Plaintiff] could reasonably have expected the burglary policy to cover this burglary where the police, as well as the trial court, found that it was an "outside job."

Id. at 278.

2. *Development of reasonable expectations doctrine.* The doctrine of reasonable expectations as applied to insurance policies has been adopted by more than half the states. See Eugene R. Anderson & James J. Fournier, Why Courts Enforce Insurance Policyholder's Objectively Reasonable Expectations of Insurance Coverage, 5 Conn. Ins. L.J. 335, 356 n.57 (1998) (listing 34 jurisdictions that had accepted the doctrine in some form) and Roger C. Henderson, The Doctrine of Reasonable Expectations in Insurance Law After Two Decades, 51 Ohio St. L.J. 823 (1990) (inventory of jurisdictions that have adopted concept). Recent examples include UPMC Health Sys. v. Metrop. Life Ins. Co., 391 F.3d 497 (3d Cir. 2004) (where insured had reasonable expectation that coverage under plan would be extended for second year at original rates, based on insurer's original proposal accepted by plaintiff insured, even unambiguous later contrary provision would not be given effect under Pennsylvania law where included in policy application but not signaled to insured); MacKinnon v. Truck Ins. Exch., 73 P. 3d 1205 (Cal. 2003) (landlord had reasonable expectation that recovery for tenant's injury from pesticide sprayed to control yellow jackets would not be precluded by "pollution" exclusion aimed primarily at "environmental" pollution). The court in UPMC specifically noted that the doctrine of reasonable expectations should not be confined to adhesion contracts or non-sophisticated insureds. 391 F.3d at 503-504.

Many jurisdictions have substantially limited the reasonable expectations doctrine by requiring a presence of ambiguity or have otherwise displayed a reluctance to adopt it as a broad rule. See, e.g., Aguiar v. Generali Assicurrazioni Ins. Co., 715 N.E.2d 1046 (Mass. App. Ct. 1999) (Massachusetts cases have "smiled upon" though not wholly embraced doctrine; likely to apply to ambiguous provision rather than unambiguous term whose meaning is not in dispute); Andersen v. Highland House Co., 757 N.E.2d 329 (Ohio 2001) (declining to adopt the reasonable expectations doctrine, but noting in dicta that it would support construing ambiguous term in favor of the insured). Indeed, even the court that decided the *C & J Fertilizer* case appears to have restricted the application of the doctrine in later decisions. See, e.g., Monroe County v. International Ins. Co., 609 N.W.2d 522 (Iowa 2000) (exclusion for claims in litigation before effective date of policy held not inconsistent with insured's reasonable expectations; the "narrow doctrine" applies primarily when written policy "eviscerates terms explicitly agreed to or is manifestly inconsistent with purpose of transaction").

Some courts resist application of the doctrine even in modified form. The Florida Supreme Court declined to adopt the reasonable expectations doctrine in a case involving a question whether ammonia fumes came within an exclusion from insurance coverage for harm resulting from "escape of pollutants." Deni Associates of Florida, Inc. v. State Farm Fire & Casualty Insurance Co., 711 So. 2d 1135 (Fla. 1998). After noting that some jurisdictions apply the reasonable expectations doctrine only when the contract term is ambiguous and other courts apply the doctrine even when the meaning of the term is clear and unambiguous, the Florida court declined to apply the concept in either situation. The court stated:

> We decline to adopt the doctrine of reasonable expectations. There is no need for it if the policy provisions are ambiguous because in Florida ambiguities are construed against the insurer. To apply the doctrine to an unambiguous provision would be to rewrite the contract and the basis upon which the premiums are charged. . . .
>
> Constructing insurance policies upon a determination as to whether the insured's subjective expectations are reasonable can only lead to uncertainty and unnecessary litigation.

711 So. 2d at 1140.

3. *Ambiguity and interpretation of insurance contracts.* We have seen that many courts require a contract to be ambiguous before they will admit extrinsic evidence to interpret the contract. In the context of insurance policies, the ambiguity doctrine takes on added significance. Most courts have held that not only is extrinsic evidence admissible to show the meaning of an ambiguous insurance policy, but that an ambiguous policy should be construed against the insurer and in favor of the insured as indicated in the above excerpt from the *Deni Associates* opinion. Some scholars have questioned the wisdom of this approach to interpretation of insurance policies. See Michael B. Rappaport, The Ambiguity Rule and Insurance Law: Why Insurance Contracts Should Not Be Construed Against the Drafter, 30 Ga. L. Rev. 171 (1995). Accord David S. Miller, Note, Insurance as Contract: The Argument for Abandoning the Ambiguity Doctrine, 88 Colum. L. Rev. 1849 (1988). The California courts indicate that the rule of construing language against the insurer is resorted to

only after other basic rules of interpretation fail to resolve an ambiguity. See *Golden Eagle Ins. Co. v. Insurance Company of the West*, 121 Cal. Rptr. 2d 682 (Ct. App. 2002).

Should the doctrine of reasonable expectations depend for its application on a determination by the court that the provision in question is ambiguous? Many courts have so indicated. E.g, *Max True Plastering Co. v. United States Fidelity & Guaranty Co.*, 912 P.2d 861 (Okla. 1996). But as *C & J Fertilizer* and other cases applying the doctrine of reasonable expectations suggest, it goes beyond a mere resolution of ambiguity against the drafter. In his 1970 article, which appears to have played a key part in the burgeoning interest in this doctrine, Professor Robert Keeton stated the principle thus:

> The objectively reasonable expectations of applicants and intended beneficiaries regarding the terms of insurance contracts will be honored even though painstaking study of the policy provisions would have negated those expectations.

Robert E. Keeton, Insurance Law Rights at Variance with Policy Provisions, 83 Harv. L. Rev. 961, 967 (1970). In other words, the doctrine may involve the court's refusing to apply an exclusion unambiguously stated in the policy or negating some other clearly phrased term. See also Eugene R. Anderson & James J. Fournier, Why Courts Enforce Insurance Policyholders' Objectively Reasonable Expectations of Insurance Coverage, 5 Conn. Ins. L.J. 335 (1998) (noting at least three variations on applying the doctrine: when there is ambiguity, when the "fine print" undermines more prominent expectations, and when overall circumstances or premium charged suggest reasonable expectations are negated); Roger C. Henderson, The Doctrine of Reasonable Expectations in Insurance Law After Two Decades, 51 Ohio St. L.J. 823, 827 (1990) (if doctrine involves a new principle, it applies without regard to whether policy is ambiguous).

4. *Scholarly commentary.* Many commentators support the doctrine of reasonable expectations, in varying degrees. Professor Roger Henderson concludes his 1990 study of the development of the doctrine as follows:

> It has evolved over the past two decades into a doctrine that balances the needs of insureds against those of insurers, as it continues to further the overriding goal of fair and equitable allocation of costs of accidents and sickness in this society. Although it has matured in many respects, it appears that it has not stopped growing, nor should it.

Roger C. Henderson, The Doctrine of Reasonable Expectations in Insurance Law After Two Decades, 51 Ohio St. L.J. 823, 853 (1990). See Symposium, The Insurance Law Doctrine of Reasonable Expectations after Three Decades, 5 Conn. Ins. L.J. 1 (1998). See also William A. Mayhew, Reasonable Expectations: Seeking a Principled Application, 13 Pepp. L. Rev. 267 (1986); Mark C. Rahdert, Reasonable Expectations Reconsidered, 18 Conn. L. Rev. 323 (1986). But see Stephen J. Ware, Comment, A Critique of the Reasonable Expectations Doctrine, 56 U. Chi. L. Rev. 1461, 1493 (1989). Despite the misgivings of some critics and the somewhat more cautious mood of the courts, it appears that this doctrine will continue to play a role in the resolution of disputes over insurance coverage.

5. *Restatement approach to reasonable expectations.* The court in *C & J Fertilizer* cites with approval Restatement (Second) of Contracts §211, Comment *f* (numbered as §237 in tentative draft). Professor Henderson notes, however, that §211 is narrower than a full-fledged version of the doctrine of reasonable expectations:

> The "black letter" formulation of the Restatement reflects the American Law Institute's conservative approach in its recognition of an exception to the rule that standardized agreements will be enforced as written. The exception was narrowly drawn so as to assess the situation from the drafter's perspective: "Where the other party has reason to believe that the party manifesting such assent would not do so if he knew that the writing contained a particular term, the term is not part of the agreement." Only where a party has "reason to believe" that the other party, one who understands that a typical form contract is being used, would not have assented to a particular term is that term to be ignored. . . . [A]pplication of the exception requires taking the perspective of the insurer. As it is almost always the insured who will want to avoid a term of the policy or form contract, the decision maker asked to apply the exception must focus on information that was available to the insurer, i.e., what the insurer had reason to believe. If adhered to faithfully, this approach could disclose a significantly different "reasonable belief" from that derived by application of the Keeton formulation — the objectively determinable reasonable expectations of the insured.

Roger C. Henderson, The Doctrine of Reasonable Expectations in Insurance Law After Two Decades, 51 Ohio St. L.J. 823, 846-847 (1990). See Sutton v. Banner Life Insurance Co., 686 A.2d 1045 (D.C. 1996) (§211(3) applied to insurer's defense of suicide to claim under life insurance policy; question of fact exists as to whether insurer should have known that insured would not have agreed to running of new two-year suicide period when insured applied for increase in coverage). Do you agree with the Restatement formulation or do you favor the Keeton version of the doctrine?

6. *Defining "adhesion contract."* Although developed in the case law as a doctrine relating specifically to insurance contracts, the doctrine of reasonable expectations appears to apply to adhesion contracts generally. The Restatement formulation, although it narrows the doctrine by focusing on the expectations of the drafter, broadens the principle to cover all standardized contracts, not just insurance agreements. The court in *C & J Fertilizer* cites and quotes from a number of the leading articles discussing contracts of adhesion, including Professor Kessler's classic 1943 essay. Attempts to define the adhesion contract usually include references to the employment of a standardized form and some degree of imbalance of bargaining power, involving a "take-it-or-leave-it" approach, that is to say: "a standardized contract, which, imposed and drafted by the party of superior bargaining strength, relegates to the subscribing party only the opportunity to adhere to the contract or reject it." Neal v. State Farm Insurance Cos., 10 Cal. Rptr. 781, 784 (Ct. App. 1961) (Tobriner, J.).

Professor Todd Rakoff offers the following analysis of what constitutes a contract of adhesion:

> The term "contract of adhesion" has acquired many significations and therefore needs definition. One of the factors that intuitively lie at the core of the concept is the

use of standard form documents. But that element is certainly not sufficient; two parties could employ standard forms as the basis for a negotiating session, and no one would be concerned. Another of the central factors is the presentation of demands on a take-it-or-leave-it basis. That too, considered alone, is not enough; sellers quote prices on a nonnegotiable basis in many quite unobjectionable contexts. It is the combination of the two elements that characterizes the problem. More precisely spelled out, the following seven characteristics define a model "contract of adhesion":

(1) The document whose legal validity is at issue is a printed form that contains many terms and clearly purports to be a contract.

(2) The form has been drafted by, or on behalf of, one party to the transaction.

(3) The drafting party participates in numerous transactions of the type represented by the form and enters into these transactions as a matter of routine.

(4) The form is presented to the adhering party with the representation that, except perhaps for a few identified items (such as the price term), the drafting party will enter into the transaction only on the terms contained in the document. This representation may be explicit or may be implicit in the situation, but it is understood by the adherent.

(5) After the parties have dickered over whatever terms are open to bargaining, the document is signed by the adherent.

(6) The adhering party enters into few transactions of the type represented by the form—few, at least, in comparison with the drafting party.

(7) The principal obligation of the adhering party in the transaction considered as a whole is the payment of money.

Todd D. Rakoff, Contracts of Adhesion: An Essay in Reconstruction, 96 Harv. L. Rev. 1173, 1176-1177 (1983). Professor Rakoff argues that underlying the issue of enforceability of contracts of adhesion is the allocation of power and freedom between commercial organizations and individuals. Viewed from this perspective, Rakoff concludes, contrary to the overwhelming body of court decisions and scholarly analysis, that contracts of adhesion should be presumptively unenforceable. Rakoff goes on to propose a specific framework by which judges could implement the general principles he advocates, including imposition of the burden of proof on the drafter of an adhesion contract to show the reasonableness of the provision in question. Id. at 1248-1261.

7. *Relationship to unconscionability doctrine.* As we shall see in Chapter 7, the employment of standardized forms and the absence of bargaining over terms may also be the first step toward application of the doctrine of unconscionability. Unconscionability goes beyond interpretation and involves either judicial invalidation of provisions of a written contract or imposition of terms different from those stated in the contract without requiring ambiguity or departure from reasonable expectations.

B. THE PAROL EVIDENCE RULE

We saw in Chapter 2 that from a very early time the common law established a link between the enforceability of a promise and compliance by the promisor with certain formalities when the promise was made. (Recall the action of covenant, which was used to enforce written promises made under seal.) Over time the seal has declined in importance, but contract law continues in a number of ways to attach significance to the execution of an agreement in writing. One of these is, of course, the policy embodied in the statute of frauds, which we surveyed in Chapter 4. Another is the preference for agreement expressed in a formal writing, over various other modes of expression, both oral and written. This preference is implemented by a rule of contract law commonly referred to as the "parol evidence rule." (Note: *parol,* not *parole,* which is a different legal term.) As use of the word "parol" suggests, this rule is usually thought of as involving the admissibility of evidence of oral agreements, but it may apply as well to various types of written evidence. In order to understand the function of the rule, it may be helpful first to think in a more general fashion about the body of law that applies generally to the admission of evidence into court.

Unless the parties to a legal dispute are able to reduce their differences to ones solely of law rather than fact, resolution of that dispute by the litigation process will require a trial on the merits, at which the disputed issues of fact can be considered and decided by the trier of fact (which may be a jury or a judge). In the course of that trial, the parties are likely to offer a wide variety of evidence on those issues. Some of this evidence will be in the form of oral testimony by persons who have firsthand knowledge of the facts at issue, while some of it will be evidence in written form — letters or memoranda, perhaps. Under the rules of evidence commonly applied in American courts, any evidence to be prima facie admissible into court must be "relevant" — rationally probative of some fact material to the parties' dispute. (Thus, in a contract dispute, the plaintiff's testimony that she had a conversation with the defendant in which they mutually agreed to an exchange of performances would ordinarily be relevant and admissible in a case where the plaintiff sought to enforce that agreement while the defendant denied making it.) Relevant evidence may, however, be excluded by some other rule of evidence based on the likelihood that evidence of a given type will be misleading or otherwise untrustworthy. (Thus, testimony by the plaintiff's spouse that she later told him about her agreement with the defendant would probably be viewed as inadmissible hearsay, if offered to establish the fact of the defendant's assent to that agreement.) And evidence of potential relevance may also be excluded by other rules of evidence, having to do not with its likely probative value but with some other policy of the law. (Thus, communications between the defendant and his attorney about defendant's transaction with the plaintiff might be highly relevant to the disputed issues of fact but would probably not be admissible because those communications are protected by the attorney-client privilege.)

The rules of evidence are of considerable theoretical difficulty and immense practical importance, and even a nodding acquaintance with them involves considerable study, as you will probably discover later in your law school career. The law of evidence can be found in detail in the major treatises on the subject, most notably the ten-volume set by Professor John Henry Wigmore (later revised first by Professor James H. Chadbourn and then Peter

Tillers) and McCormick on Evidence (edited in its present version by Professor John William Strong). The rules of evidence may also be embodied in official versions, such as the Federal Rules of Evidence, which are applied in federal courts throughout the United States. Despite its commonly employed appellation, however, the "parol evidence rule" is considered by authorities on evidence and contracts alike to be not a rule of evidence, but a rule of "substantive" law. E. Allan Farnsworth, Contracts §7.2 (4th ed. 2004). This distinction is for our purposes not very important, although it does have some practical consequences. For example, under ordinary rules of evidence, the right to object to inadmissible evidence is lost if not asserted at the time when the evidence is offered. This is not necessarily the case with evidence admitted in violation of the parol evidence rule, however. See Estate of Parker v. Dorchak, 673 So. 2d 1379 (Miss. 1996) (since parol evidence rule is matter of substantive law, evidence admitted in violation of rule, even though without objection, should be disregarded if objection is made before case submitted to trier of fact). Similarly, federal courts, which are required to follow state substantive law but apply federal procedural law in cases involving diversity of citizenship, are bound to apply state versions of the parol evidence rule. AM International, Inc. v. Graphic Management Associates, Inc., 44 F.3d 572 (7th Cir. 1995).

The parol evidence rule can be found in various sources, and the wordings may differ somewhat. E.g., Restatement (Second) of Contracts §§209-218; Uniform Commercial Code §2-202. The gist of it can be stated thus: When the parties to a contract have mutually agreed to incorporate (or "integrate") a final version of their entire agreement in a writing, neither party will be permitted to contradict or supplement that written agreement with "extrinsic" evidence (written or oral) of prior agreements or negotiations between them. When the writing is intended to be final only with respect to a part of their agreement, the writing may not be contradicted, but it may be supplemented by such extrinsic evidence. Excellent discussions of the parol evidence rule can be found in E. Allan Farnsworth, Contracts §§7.2 -7.6 (4th ed. 2004), and in Joseph M. Perillo, Calamari & Perillo on Contracts §§3.2-3.8 (5th ed. 2003). An interesting account of the historical origins of the rule, as well as a provocative exploration of its implications for present-day contract law, can be found in Hila Keren, Textual Harassment: A New Historicist Reappraisal of the Parol Evidence Rule with Gender in Mind, 13 Am. U. J. Gender Soc. Pol'y & L. 251 (2005).

In order to understand the working of the parol evidence rule, it is necessary first to apprehend its basic function: The rule does not define what evidence is affirmatively admissible, it only operates to *exclude* evidence — evidence that would otherwise be admissible as rationally probative of some fact at issue. If the parol evidence rule applies at all in a given situation, it has the effect of preventing one party from introducing into court extrinsic (or "collateral") evidence of matters not contained in the written agreement between the parties (hence, "extrinsic" to it), where that evidence is offered to supplement or contradict the written agreement. If the parol evidence rule does not apply (either because the parties have not executed such a written agreement or because the offered evidence comes within some exception to that rule), then admission of the evidence will turn on the body of rules that collectively make up the law of evidence. Of course, even if the offered parol evidence is ruled admissible and received into evidence, that alone may not prove decisive: Like any other evidence, it may still be rejected as not credible by the trier of fact.

To begin our examination of the parol evidence rule in action, let us first envision the procedural setting in which a parol evidence issue arises. Suppose the owner of an apartment project enters into a written contract with a painting contractor calling for the painting of the "interior of the building, including walls, ceilings, and trim." Later, a dispute develops about whether the contract requires the contractor to paint the common areas (hallways, etc.). When the parties are unable to resolve the dispute through negotiation, the owner discharges the contractor, who then brings suit against the owner claiming that the discharge constitutes a breach of contract. At trial the contractor offers to introduce evidence (either oral testimony or correspondence) that the owner was informed (at or before the time of contracting) that the contractor's bid for the work did not include common areas, and the owner agreed to that. The owner objects to such evidence being considered by the fact finder because of the parol evidence rule. If the matter were being tried before a jury, the judge would hold an "in camera" hearing, that is, out of the presence of the jury, in which the party offering parol evidence would outline what the evidence would show, both parties would make legal arguments about the application of the parol evidence rule, and the judge would decide if the evidence were admissible under the rule. (Such in camera hearings are not unique to contract law but are employed whenever evidence of doubtful admissibility is being offered by one of the parties; another common example is the determination of the admissibility of an alleged confession by a defendant in a criminal case.) If the matter were being tried by a judge sitting without a jury, the in camera hearing would be unnecessary, but the judge would still be required to rule on the admissibility of the evidence. You may wonder why in nonjury cases the judge must rule on the admissibility of the evidence since the judge will have heard the evidence no matter how he rules. Even in nonjury cases, however, the admissibility of evidence can be important. If a judge reaches a decision based on evidence that was not properly admitted, the judge's decision could be reversed on appeal under the "clearly erroneous" rule for appellate review of trial court factual determinations.

We will see that both courts and commentators differ widely over the scope and application of the parol evidence rule. The following case illustrates the classical approach.

┃ **Thompson v. Libby**
Minnesota Supreme Court
34 Minn. 374, 26 N.W. 1 (1885)

MITCHELL, J. The plaintiff being the owner of a quantity of logs marked "H. C. A.," cut in the winters of 1882 and 1883, and lying in the Mississippi river, or on its banks, above Minneapolis, defendant and the plaintiff, through his agent, D. S. Mooers, having fully agreed on the terms of a sale and purchase of the logs referred to, executed the following written agreement:

AGREEMENT.

Hastings, Minn., June 1, 1883.

I have this day sold to R. C. Libby, of Hastings, Minn., all my logs marked "H. C. A.," cut in the winters of 1882 and 1883, for ten dollars a thousand feet, boom scale at Minneapolis, Minnesota. Payments cash as fast as scale bills are produced.

[Signed] *J. H. Thompson,*
Per *D. S. Mooers.*
R. C. Libby.

This action having been brought for the purchase-money, the defendant — having pleaded a warranty of the quality of the logs, alleged to have been made at the time of the sale, and a breach of it — offered on the trial oral testimony to prove the warranty, which was admitted, over the objection of plaintiff that it was incompetent to prove a verbal warranty, the contract of sale being in writing. This raises the only point in the case.

No ground was laid for the reformation of the written contract, and any charge of fraud on part of plaintiff or his agent in making the sale was on the trial expressly disclaimed. No rule is more familiar than that "parol contemporaneous evidence is inadmissible to contradict or vary the terms of a valid written instrument," and yet none has given rise to more misapprehension as to its application. It is a rule founded on the obvious inconvenience and injustice that would result if matters in writing, made with consideration and deliberation, and intended to embody the entire agreement of the parties, were liable to be controlled by what Lord Coke expressively calls "the uncertain testimony of slippery memory." Hence, where the parties have deliberately put their engagements into writing in such terms as to import a legal obligation, without any uncertainty as to the object or extent of such engagement, it is conclusively presumed that the whole engagement of the parties, and the manner and extent of their undertaking, was reduced to writing. 1 Greenl. Ev. §275. Of course, the rule presupposes that the parties intended to have the terms of their complete agreement embraced in the writing, and hence it does not apply where the writing is incomplete on its face and does not purport to contain the whole agreement, as in the case of mere bills of parcels, and the like.

But in what manner shall it be ascertained whether the parties intended to express the whole of their agreement in writing? It is sometimes loosely stated that where the whole contract be not reduced to writing, parol evidence may be admitted to prove the part omitted. But to allow a party to lay the foundation for such parol evidence by oral testimony that only part of the agreement was reduced to writing, and then prove by parol the part omitted, would be to work in a circle, and to permit the very evil which the rule was designed to prevent. The only criterion of the completeness of the written contract as a full expression of the agreement of the parties is the writing itself. If it imports on its face to be a complete expression of the whole agreement, — that is, contains such language as imports a complete legal obligation, — it is to be presumed that the parties have introduced into it every material item and term; and parol evidence cannot be admitted to add another term to the agreement, although the writing contains nothing on the particular one to which the parol evidence is directed. The rule forbids to add by parol where the writing is silent, as well as to vary where it speaks, — 2 Phil. Evidence, (Cow. & H. Notes,) 669; Naumberg v. Young, 44 N.J. Law, 331; Hei v. Heller, 53 Wis. 415, — and the law controlling the operation of a written contract becomes a part of it, and cannot be varied by parol any more than what is written. 2 Phil. Ev. (Cow. & H. Notes,) 668; La Farge v. Rickert, 5 Wend. 187; Creery v. Holly, 14 Wend. 26; Stone v. Harmon, 31 Minn. 512.

The written agreement in the case at bar, as it appears on its face, in connection with the law controlling its construction and operation, purports to be a complete expression of the whole agreement of the parties as to the sale and purchase of these logs, solemnly executed by both parties. There is nothing on its face (and this is a question of law for the court) to indicate that it is a mere informal and incomplete memorandum. Parol evidence of extrinsic facts and circumstances would, if necessary, be admissible, as it always is, to apply the contract to its subject-matter, or in order to a more perfect understanding of its language. But in that case such evidence is used, not to contradict or vary the written instrument, but to aid, uphold, and enforce it as it stands. The language of this contract "imports a legal obligation, without any uncertainty as to its object or the extent of the engagement," and therefore "it must be conclusively presumed that the whole engagement of the parties, and the manner and extent of the undertaking, was reduced to writing." No new term, forming a mere incident to or part of the contract of sale, can be added by parol. . . .

. . . [W]e are referred to a few cases which seem to hold that parol evidence of a warranty is admissible on the ground that a warranty is collateral to the contract of sale, and that the rule does not exclude parol evidence of matters collateral to the subject of the written agreement. It seems to us that this is based upon a misapprehension as to the sense in which the term "collateral" is used in the rule invoked. There are a great many matters that, in a general sense, may be considered collateral to the contract; for example, in the case of leases, covenants for repairs, improvements, payment of taxes, etc., are, in a sense, collateral to a demise of the premises. But parol evidence of these would not be admissible to add to the terms of a written lease. So, in a sense, a warranty is collateral to a contract of sale, for the title would pass without a warranty. It is also collateral in the sense that its breach is no ground for a rescission of the contract by the vendor [sic; vendee?], but that he must resort to his action on the warranty for damages. But, when made, a warranty is a part of the contract of sale. The common sense of men would say, and correctly so, that when, on a sale of personal property, a warranty is given, it is one of the terms of the sale, and not a separate and independent contract. To justify the admission of a parol promise by one of the parties to a written contract, on the ground that it is collateral, the promise must relate to a subject distinct from that to which the writing relates. Dutton v. Gerrish, 9 Cush. 89; Naumberg v. Young, supra; 2 Taylor, Ev. §1038. See Lindley v. Lacey, 34 Law J., C. P., 7.

We have carefully examined all the cases cited in the quite exhaustive brief of counsel for defendant, and find but very few that are at all in conflict with the views already expressed, and these few do not commend themselves to our judgment. Our conclusion therefore is that the court erred in admitting parol evidence of a warranty, and therefore the order refusing a new trial must be reversed.

Notes and Questions

1. *Rationale for parol evidence rule.* The court states that the parol evidence rule is "founded on the obvious inconvenience and injustice" that would result if extrinsic evidence were admissible to contradict or vary the terms of a written agreement. What specific "inconvenience" and "injustice" can result from the introduction of extrinsic evidence?

2. *Meaning of "integration."* As the *Thompson* court indicates, at the core of the parol evidence rule is the concept that parties typically arrive at contract terms through a process of preliminary negotiations and then produce a writing containing the final terms that have been mutually adopted. (As you are well aware, however, adhesion contracts do not fit this pattern.) The final writing is then considered the best evidence of the contract and displaces any earlier agreement or proposals, whether oral or written. See E. Allan Farnsworth, Contracts §7.2, at 418 (4th ed. 2004) (the useful purpose of parol evidence rule is to replace negotiations and superseded understandings with a final authoritative statement of the agreement). Both classical and modern contract law use the term *complete integration* to refer to a writing that is intended to be a final and exclusive expression of the agreement of the parties. First Restatement §228; Restatement (Second) §210. Both classical and modern contract law also recognize the possibility of a *partial integration,* a writing that is intended to be final but not complete because it deals with some but not all aspects of a transaction between the parties. The correct application of the parol evidence rule thus requires that the court first determine whether the writing in question is intended to be a final expression of the parties agreement and, if so, whether it is a complete or partial statement of the contract terms. How would you assess the writing in *Thompson* in light of these standards?

3. *Determining integration.* The *Thompson* court states that the written contract does not appear on its face to be either an "informal or incomplete" memorandum, and therefore the court concludes that the writing is a completely integrated agreement. The court's determination is based on an approach often identified with Professor Williston who argued that the question of integration must be determined from the "four corners" of the writing without resort to extrinsic evidence. 4 Williston on Contracts §633, at 1015. Moreover, Williston asserted that the inclusion in the writing of a "merger clause" would conclusively establish that the writing was integrated. 4 Williston on Contracts §633, at 1014. A merger clause states that the writing is intended to be final and complete; all prior understandings are deemed to have been "merged" into or superseded by the final writing. The following is an example of a typical merger clause:

> *Entire Agreement.* This document constitutes the entire agreement of the parties and there are no representations, warranties, or agreements other than those contained in this document.

A substantial number of jurisdictions still generally adhere to the "four corners" approach to determining integration and accord conclusive or nearly conclusive weight to the presence of a merger clause. See, e.g., ADR North America, L.L.C. v. Agway, Inc., 303 F.3d 653 (6th Cir. 2002) (under Michigan law written integration clause is conclusive evidence that the parties intended the document to be the final and complete expression of their agreement); Kassebaum v. Kassebaum, 42 S.W.3d 685 (Mo. Ct. App. 2001) (contract that appears complete on its face is conclusively presumed to be final and complete); Fontbank, Inc. v. CompuServe, Inc., 742 N.E.2d 674 (Ohio Ct. App. 2000) (contract which appears complete and unambiguous on its face will be presumed final and complete expression of agreement; presumption is strongest where writing contains merger or integration clause). What policy considerations could be used to justify the "four corners" approach to the parol evidence rule?

Not surprisingly, perhaps, many other courts have adopted an alternative method to determining integration which more readily looks beyond the contents of the writing. The central precept for this contextual approach is reflected in Restatement (Second) §210, Comment *b*: "[A] writing cannot of itself prove its own completeness, and wide latitude must be allowed for inquiry into circumstances bearing on the intention of the parties." This approach is also frequently identified with Professor Corbin. A finding of integration should always depend on the actual intent of the parties, according to Corbin, and a court should consider evidence of all the facts and circumstances surrounding the execution of the contract, as well as the writing, in uncovering that intent. 3 Corbin on Contracts §§578, 582, at 411-412, 448-450. After hearing this evidence, the court should determine (in camera, in jury cases) whether the agreement was integrated. 3 Corbin on Contracts §588, at 528-530. In this approach, a merger clause will not be solely determinative of the issue of integration. See, e.g., Sierra Diesel Injection Service, Inc. v. Burroughs Corp., Inc. 890 F.2d 108 (9th Cir. 1989) (merger clause not dispositive of complete integration in contract between unsophisticated customer and merchant with pre-printed forms and multiple documents); I.C.C. Protective Coatings v. A.E. Staley Mfg. Co., 695 N.E.2d 1030 (Ind. Ct. App. 1998) (question of integration depends on all relevant evidence; weight given to merger clause will depend on facts and circumstances of each particular case). See also Restatement (Second) §216, Comment *e* (merger clause does not control question of integration); UCC §2-202, Comment 1(a) (rejects any assumption that writing that is final on some terms is exclusive). Professor Farnsworth reports that the trend among courts favors the Corbin-Restatement (Second) approach to determining integration. E. Allan Farnsworth, Contracts §7.3, at 419 (4th ed. 2004).

Adherents of the "four corners" approach (like the *Thompson* court) argue that to permit consideration of extrinsic evidence on the threshold question of integration is to do exactly what the parol evidence rule is designed to avoid; proponents of the other view argue that one cannot know the intent of the parties simply by looking at the document, and that even when applied in this more permissive fashion the rule can still perform its function of keeping extrinsic evidence from the jury if the judge rules that the writing is indeed an integration of their agreement. Thus, even under the contextual approach to integration, courts may find that a merger clause does accurately reflect the parties' intent that the writing constitute a complete integration. E.g., Globe Metallurgical, Inc. v. Hewlett-Packard Co., 953 F. Supp. 876 (S.D. Ohio 1994) (though not dispositive alone, merger clause in contract between sophisticated parties with relatively equal bargaining power held effective to bar parol evidence). For a comparison of the approaches of Professors Williston and Corbin, see John D. Calamari & Joseph M. Perillo, A Plea for a Uniform Parol Evidence Rule and Principles of Contract Interpretation, 42 Ind. L.J. 333 (1967).

The court in Thompson v. Libby indicated that not all extrinsic evidence would be subject to the parol evidence rule, even in the case of a fully integrated written agreement. Such evidence would be admissible, the court indicated, "if necessary . . . to apply the contract to its subject-matter, or in order to a more perfect understanding of its language." In addition, the *Thompson* court alluded in passing to the existence of certain exceptions to that rule. "No ground was laid for the reformation of the written contract, and any charge of fraud on part of plaintiff or his agent in making the sale was . . . expressly disclaimed." In order to understand and appreciate the effect of the parol evidence rule, it is necessary not only to understand the scope of the rule — what types of evidence it generally purports to exclude from consideration — but also the numerous exceptions to its operation. Even during the classical period, courts recognized a number of exceptions to the parol evidence rule; those exceptions have if anything tended to expand in recent years. Although the various exceptions have not yet reached the point where they "swallow up" the rule, they at least are so numerous and collectively so broad that the parol evidence rule has become — even more than the statute of frauds — a rule that can be understood only in light of its exceptions.

The parol evidence rule does not apply to evidence offered to explain the meaning of the agreement. To begin with, the parol evidence rule as we have seen applies only to written agreements that are in some sense "integrated," either "partially" or "completely." Restatement (Second) §210; UCC §2-202 (writing may be intended by parties "as a final expression of their agreement with respect to such terms as are included therein" and may also be "intended . . . as a complete and exclusive statement of the terms of the agreement"). If found to be a partial integration, the writing may not be contradicted by extrinsic evidence. Restatement (Second) §213, Comment *b* ("inconsistent terms"); UCC §2-202 ("may not be contradicted"). It may, however, be supplemented by additional *consistent* terms. If the writing is a complete integration, then not only may it not be contradicted, it may not even be supplemented. Restatement (Second) §213(2), Comment *c* ("consistent additional terms are superseded"); UCC §2-202(b). Whatever the degree of integration, however — partial, complete, or not at all — a written agreement may, as the *Thompson* court suggested, always be *explained* by extrinsic evidence. Restatement (Second) §214(c).

To illustrate these principles in application, let us return to the facts of Thompson v. Libby. Given the written agreement which existed in that case, extrinsic evidence would not have been admissible to prove that the agreed-on price for the wood was $8 a thousand feet, rather than $10, for this would have been regarded as a "contradictory" term. Nor would it have been permissible to show by extrinsic evidence that the seller was obliged not only to deliver the logs but also to mill them into planks; even if this were seen as a "consistent additional term," rather than a contradictory one, the Thompson-Libby agreement was apparently regarded by the court as fully integrated, thus precluding the showing of additional terms (whether contradictory or not). It should, however, have been permissible to show by extrinsic evidence of the parties' agreement what periods of time were intended to be included in the phrase "winters of 1882 and 1883," or what was meant by the term "boom scale," because such evidence would have served merely to "explain" the agreement. (On those points, evidence of trade usage might have been relevant as well.) Classical and modern courts might differ, however, on the scope of this latter exception. Classical courts generally admitted parol evidence for explanatory purposes only if the writing appeared on its face to be ambiguous, while modern courts are more likely to admit parol evidence to show that the language used in the agreement has a special meaning, even if that language does not appear unclear merely from an inspection of the writing. Restatement (Second) §214, Comment *b*. (Recall our discussion of patent and latent ambiguity after the *Frigaliment* case above.)

Explanation of the agreement may be in practice the most important of the reasons why extrinsic evidence may be admitted despite the parol evidence rule, but it only begins the catalog of that rule's exceptions. The following are some of the other commonly accepted ones:

The parol evidence rule does not apply to agreements, whether oral or written, made after the execution of the writing. Litman v. Massachusetts Mutual Life Insurance Co., 739 F.2d 1549, 1558 (11th Cir. 1984) (evidence of subsequent oral modification of plaintiff's written employment contract not barred by parol evidence rule; later written amendments not fully integrated so as to exclude proof of asserted oral agreement); 4 Williston on Contracts §632, at 978; 3 Corbin on Contracts §574, at 373. Suppose Thompson and Libby had orally agreed in August 1883 that payment for the logs would be made partly in cash and partly by promissory notes. In the event of subsequent litigation between them, the parol evidence rule would not bar testimony as to this later oral agreement.

The parol evidence rule does not apply to evidence offered to show that effectiveness of the agreement was subject to an oral condition precedent. Wickenheiser v. Ramm Vending Promotion, Inc., 560 So. 2d 350 (Fla. Dist. Ct. App. 1990) (despite execution of formal agreement for purchase of pizza distributorship, evidence that agreement was orally agreed to be conditional on approval by buyer's family within two weeks was admissible, precluding summary judgment in favor of seller); Restatement (Second) §217. Suppose Libby had told Thompson (or his agent) when the contract was signed that the agreement was contingent upon the local bank's approval of a loan for which Libby had applied, and about which he would hear within a week. If the bank had denied the loan, the parol evidence rule would not bar evidence of Libby's oral statement, even though the writing was absolute on its face, because the evidence would establish an oral condition to the effectiveness of the agreement.

The parol evidence rule does not apply to evidence offered to show that the agreement is invalid for any reason, such as fraud, duress, undue influence, incapacity, mistake, or illegality. Restatement (Second) §214(d). This exception can be justified theoretically on the basis that such invalidating factors result in what is apparently a contract being in legal contemplation not a "contract" at all and thus not entitled to the benefit of the parol evidence rule. It also can be justified on the practical ground that while a written agreement may in fact be "a forgery, a joke, a sham, or an agreement without consideration, or it may be voidable for fraud, duress, mistake, or the like, or it may be illegal," none of these things is likely to appear on the face of the document. Restatement (Second) §214, Comment *c*. To apply the parol evidence rule to exclude such evidence would in effect create a roadblock to the application of many important policies of the law. To continue our series of illustrations, suppose that Thompson and Libby had entered into their contract believing that 20,000 feet of logs had been cut when in fact the true number was closer to 5000. In that case, evidence of their discussions about the quantity to be sold should be admissible as bearing on the possible defense of mistake of fact.

The case of fraud is a little more problematic, however. Some courts would limit the fraud exception to cases of "fraud in the execution" — for example, if Thompson asks Libby to sign what he says is a receipt for logs delivered, but it's really a "contract" for the sale of more logs. See HCB Contractors v. Liberty Place Hotel Assoc., 652 A.2d 1278 (Pa. 1995) (parol evidence rule barred evidence offered by general contractor that it had been falsely induced to enter into construction contract and lien waivers based on representations by owners that they would continue to own property; plaintiff failed to allege that owners fraudulently omitted provision from contract). Most courts, however, will extend the fraud exception also to instances of "fraud in the inducement" — misrepresentations of fact that induce the other party to enter into the contract. Miles Excavating, Inc. v. Rutledge Backhoe & Septic Tank Services, Inc., 927 P.2d 517 (Kan. Ct. App. 1996) (parol evidence admissible to show fraud in inducement of contract even when it contains provision stating that parties have not relied on any oral representations). As yet a further limitation, some courts will prohibit the introduction of parol evidence to support a claim of fraud in the inducement if the alleged misrepresentation directly contradicts a term in the writing. This limitation is discussed in the *Sherrodd* case later in this chapter and in the section on misrepresentation in Chapter 7. Suppose Libby sought to show that in order to induce him to sign the contract, Thompson had represented that to his own personal knowledge at least half of the cut logs were good quality hardwood, while it later appeared that only a quarter or less met that description. Many courts would view evidence of that statement by Thompson as admissible under the fraud exception, even though as you can see it comes very close to the claim that Libby tried unsuccessfully to make in the actual case.

The parol evidence rule does not apply to evidence that is offered to establish a right to an "equitable" remedy, such as "reformation" of the contract. Restatement (Second)

§214(e). If one party can establish that a part of the agreement was inadvertently omitted from the writing due to some mistake (perhaps the error of a "scrivener," a secretary, or even a computer printer), that party may seek judicial reformation of the agreement—a court order declaring that the mistakenly omitted provision will be treated in law as part of the agreement. Generally, however, a writing may be reformed in this fashion only if it is shown by "clear and convincing evidence" that the parties really did intend their written agreement to contain the term in question. Thompson v. Estate of Coffield, 894 P.2d 1065 (Okla. 1995) (parol evidence rule does not apply in action to reform deed to reflect oral agreement that sale of property was subject to unrecorded coal leases, but plaintiff must prove oral agreement by clear and convincing evidence). See generally George E. Palmer, Reformation and the Parol Evidence Rule, 65 Mich. L. Rev. 833 (1967). In *Thompson,* the defendant Libby might have sought to have the agreement reformed to include the warranty of quality, but he probably would have been unable to meet this higher standard of proof—indeed, the court's opinion suggests he did not even attempt to do so.

The parol evidence rule does not apply to evidence introduced to establish a "collateral" agreement between the parties. In Thompson v. Libby the court held that evidence of an oral warranty as to quality was not admissible under the collateral agreement exception because that exception only applied to an agreement about a "subject distinct from that to which the writing relates." By the time the first Restatement was drafted in the 1930s, a growing number of courts were adopting a more flexible approach to the parol evidence rule than that illustrated by the court in Thompson v. Libby. 3 Corbin on Contracts §584, at 477. Frequently, these courts relied on the collateral agreement exception to justify the admission of parol evidence, even when the evidence did not relate to a separate or distinct transaction. The revised Restatement continues the collateral agreement exception, but with a slightly different approach, in §216(2), which provides that an agreement will not be regarded as fully integrated if the parties have made a consistent additional agreement which is either agreed to for separate consideration or is "such a term as in the circumstances might naturally be omitted from the writing."

The Uniform Commercial Code Comments express a similar rule, but tilted somewhat more in the direction of admissibility: Comment 3 to §2-202 indicates that "consistent additional terms" should be excluded under §2-202(b) only where the court concludes that if such terms had actually been agreed upon they would "certainly have been included in the document." If the Thompson-Libby contract were made today it would as a sale of goods be subject to Article 2 of the Uniform Commercial Code; on the facts of Thompson v. Libby, would buyer Libby have fared better under §2-202? Suppose that Libby were also to allege that Thompson had promised at the time their written agreement was signed that if Libby would buy the logs, Thompson would mill them into planks for Libby at Thompson's sawmill for a discounted price (two-thirds of Thompson's usual charge for that service), and that Thompson had later refused to honor that promise. Libby might assert that breach by Thompson in an action for damages for breach of contract (based on the higher amount Libby had to pay to have the logs milled elsewhere), or even as justification for a refusal by Libby to accept the logs at all. Would evidence of the oral milling agreement be barred by the parol evidence rule?

Taylor v. State Farm Mutual Automobile Insurance Co.
Supreme Court of Arizona, en banc
175 Ariz. 148, 854 P.2d 1134 (1993)

FELDMAN, Chief Justice.

Bobby Sid Taylor petitions us to review a decision reversing a jury verdict in his favor in a bad faith claim against State Farm Mutual Automobile Insurance Co. He argues that the court of appeals erroneously held that his bad faith claim was barred by a release he signed in 1981. We granted review because the case raises important issues in the area of contract and insurance law. . . .

FACTS AND PROCEDURAL HISTORY

This insurance bad faith action arises out of an accident that occurred approximately sixteen years ago. Many of the facts are undisputed. The accident involved three vehicles — one occupied by Anne Ring and passenger James Rivers, the second by Douglas Wistrom, and the third by Bobby Sid Taylor. Ring, Rivers, and Taylor all were injured. The facts surrounding the accident are set forth in Ring v. Taylor, 141 Ariz. 56, 59, 685 P.2d 121, 124 (Ct. App. 1984). Ring, her husband, and Rivers filed actions against Taylor and Wistrom. These actions were consolidated before trial. Taylor's insurer, State Farm, retained attorney Leroy W. Hofmann to defend Taylor. Taylor also personally retained attorney Norman Bruce Randall, who filed a counterclaim against Ring for Taylor's damages. Taylor, therefore, was represented by both Randall and Hofmann in the matter. Because the Rings and Rivers agreed with Wistrom to a stipulated judgment and covenant not to execute, Taylor was the only party vulnerable to the Ring/Rivers claims. At trial, the Rings and Rivers obtained combined verdicts against Taylor for approximately $2.5 million in excess of his insurance policy limits. The court of appeals affirmed these judgments. *Taylor*, 141 Ariz. at 59, 71, 685 P.2d at 124, 136.

The Rings eventually settled with State Farm. Taylor, however, sued State Farm for bad faith seeking damages for the excess Rivers judgment, claiming, among other things, that State Farm improperly failed to settle the Rivers matter within policy limits. State Farm moved for summary judgment, asserting that Taylor relinquished his bad faith claim when, in 1981, he signed a release drafted by attorney Randall in exchange for State Farm's payment of $15,000 in uninsured motorist benefits.[1] Taylor also moved for partial

---

1. Because Wistrom was uninsured, Randall believed that Taylor might be entitled to recover for his injuries under the uninsured motorist provisions of Taylor's policy. State Farm, however, disputes Taylor's entitlement to these benefits. In any event, Randall prepared a release as part of the transaction. It is this release that is at issue. The extent of State Farm's participation in its drafting is disputed.

summary judgment, seeking a ruling that, as a matter of law, the release did not preclude his bad faith claim. The judge denied both motions, finding that the release was ambiguous and that therefore parol evidence was admissible at trial to aid in interpreting the release. A second judge, who presided at trial, also denied State Farm's motion for directed verdict based on the release. Having been instructed on the interpretation of the release, the jury returned a verdict in favor of Taylor for compensatory damages of $2.1 million. The court also awarded Taylor $300,000 in attorney fees.

The court of appeals reversed, holding that the release agreement was not ambiguous and therefore the judge erred by admitting parol evidence to vary its terms. Taylor v. State Farm Mut. Auto. Ins. Co., No. 1 CA-CV 9908 (Sep. 17, 1991) (mem. dec.). Based on the agreement's "four corners," the court held that "it clearly release[d] all policy contract rights, claims, and causes of action that Taylor has or may have against State Farm." Id. at 20. According to the court, because the release should have been strictly enforced, there was no basis for Taylor's bad faith claim. Id. We believe the court's decision both incorrectly applies settled legal principles and raises unsettled issues of contract interpretation.

DISCUSSION

Much of the dispute in this case centers on the events that surround the drafting of the release and the inferences that can be drawn from those events. As noted, the trial court found that the release was ambiguous and admitted extrinsic evidence to aid in its interpretation. The court of appeals found no ambiguity. *Taylor,* mem. dec. at 20, 23. In resolving this issue, we must address the scope and application of the parol evidence rule in Arizona and decide whether, under these facts, the trial court properly admitted extrinsic evidence to interpret the release.

A. LEGAL PRINCIPLES

The application of the parol evidence rule has been the subject of much controversy and scholarly debate. . . . "When two parties have made a contract and have expressed it in a writing to which they have both assented as the complete and accurate integration of that contract, evidence, whether parol or otherwise, of antecedent understandings and negotiations will not be admitted for the purpose of varying or contradicting the writing." 3 Arthur L. Corbin, Corbin on Contracts §573, at 357 (1960) ("Corbin"). . . . Antecedent understandings and negotiations may be admissible, however, for purposes other than varying or contradicting a final agreement. 3 Corbin §576, at 384. Interpretation is one such purpose. 3 Corbin §579, at 412-13; Restatement (Second) of Contracts §214(c) & cmt. b (1979) ("Restatement").

Interpretation is the process by which we determine the meaning of words in a contract. See Restatement §200. Generally, and in Arizona, a court will attempt to enforce a contract according to the parties' intent. . . . "The primary and ultimate purpose of interpretation" is to discover that intent and to make it effective. 3 Corbin §572B, at 421 (1992 Supp.). The court must decide what evidence, other than the writing, is admissible in the interpretation process, bearing in mind that the parol evidence rule prohibits extrinsic evidence to vary or contradict, but not to interpret, the agreement. See 3 Corbin §543, at 130-34. These substantive principles are clear, but their application has been troublesome.

1. Restrictive view

Under the restrictive "plain meaning" view of the parol evidence rule, evidence of prior negotiations may be used for interpretation only upon a finding that some language in the contract is unclear, ambiguous, or vague. E. Allan Farnsworth, Farnsworth on Contracts §7.12, at 270 (1990) ("Farnsworth"). Under this approach, "if a writing, or the term in question, appears to be plain and unambiguous on its face, its meaning must be determined from the four corners of the instrument without resort to extrinsic evidence of any nature." Calamari & Perillo, supra §3-10, at 166-67. . . . Thus, if the judge finds from the face of a document that it conveys only one meaning, parol evidence is neither considered nor admitted for any purpose. The danger here, of course, is that what appears plain and clear to one judge may not be so plain to another (as in this case), and the judge's decision, uninformed by context, may not reflect the intent of the parties.

2. Corbin view

Under the view embraced by Professor Corbin and the Second Restatement, there is no need to make a preliminary finding of ambiguity before the *judge considers* extrinsic evidence. 3 Corbin §542, at 100-05 (1992 Supp.); Restatement §212 cmt. b; Farnsworth §7.12, at 272. . . . Instead, the court considers all of the proffered evidence to determine its relevance to the parties' intent and then applies the parol evidence rule to exclude from the fact finder's consideration only the evidence that contradicts or varies the meaning of the agreement. 3 Corbin §542, at 100-01 (1992 Supp.). According to Corbin, the court cannot apply the parol evidence rule without first understanding the meaning the parties intended to give the agreement. Id. To understand the agreement, the judge cannot be restricted to the four corners of the document. Again, even under the Corbin view, the court can admit evidence for *interpretation* but must stop short of *contradiction*. See 3 Corbin §574, at 371-72. . . .

3. Arizona view

Writing for a unanimous court in Smith v. Melson, Inc., 135 Ariz. 119, 121-22, 659 P.2d 1264, 1266-67 (1983), Chief Justice Holohan expressly committed Arizona to the Corbin view of contract interpretation. . . . We have held that a court may consider surrounding circumstances, including negotiation, prior understandings, and subsequent conduct, but have not elaborated much further. . . .

According to Corbin, the proper analysis has two steps. First, the court *considers* the evidence that is alleged to determine the extent of integration, illuminate the meaning of the contract language, or demonstrate the parties' intent. See 3 Corbin §542, at 100-01 (1992 Supp.). The court's function at this stage is to eliminate the evidence that has no probative value in determining the parties' intent. Id. The second step involves "finalizing" the court's understanding of the contract. Id. at 100. Here, the parol evidence rule applies and *precludes admission* of the extrinsic evidence that would vary or contradict the meaning of the written words. Id.

Even during the first step, the judge may properly decide not to consider certain offered evidence because it does not aid in interpretation but, instead, varies or contradicts the written words. See id. at 101. This might occur when the court decides that the asserted meaning of the contract language is so unreasonable or extraordinary that it is improbable that the parties actually subscribed to the interpretation asserted by the proponent of the extrinsic evidence. See id. "The more bizarre and unusual an asserted interpretation is, the more convincing must be the testimony that supports it." 3 Corbin §579, at 420. At what point a judge stops "listening to testimony that white is black and that a dollar is fifty cents is a matter for sound judicial discretion and common sense." Id.

When interpreting a contract, nevertheless, it is fundamental that a court attempt to "ascertain and give effect to the intention of the parties at the time the contract was made if at all possible." . . . If, for example, parties use language that is mutually intended to have a special meaning, and that meaning is proved by credible evidence, a court is obligated to enforce the agreement according to the parties' intent, even if the language ordinarily might mean something different. See Restatement §212 cmt. b, illus. 3 & 4. The judge, therefore, must avoid the often irresistible temptation to automatically interpret contract language as he or she would understand the words. This natural tendency is sometimes disguised in the judge's ruling that contract language is "unambiguous." See 3 Corbin §543A, at 159 (1992 Supp.). Words, however, are seldom so clear that they "apply themselves to the subject matter." Restatement §214 cmt. b. On occasion, exposition of the evidence regarding the intention of the parties will illuminate plausible interpretations other than the one that is facially obvious to the judge. See id. Thus, ambiguity determined by the judge's view of "clear meaning" is a troublesome concept that often obstructs the court's proper and primary function in this area — to enforce the meaning intended by the contracting parties. See 3 Corbin §542, at 122-24. . . .

Recognizing these problems, we are hesitant to endorse, without explanation, the often repeated and usually over-simplified construct that ambiguity must exist before parol evidence is admissible. We have previously criticized the ambiguity prerequisite in the context of non-negotiated agreements. See State Farm Mut. Auto. Ins. Co. v. Wilson, 162 Ariz. 251, 257, 782 P.2d 727, 733 (1989) (recognizing the lack of logic in requiring ambiguity, which may be fortuitous, to prove the true terms of an agreement). . . . Moreover, a contract may be susceptible to multiple interpretations and therefore truly ambiguous yet, given the context in which it was negotiated, not susceptible to a clearly contradicting and wholly unpersuasive interpretation asserted by the proponent of extrinsic evidence. In such a case, it seems clear that a court should exclude that evidence as violating the parol evidence rule despite the presence of some contract ambiguity. Finally, and most important, the ambiguity determination distracts the court from its primary objective — to enforce the contract as intended by the parties. Consequently, although relevant, contract ambiguity is not the only linchpin of a court's decision to admit parol evidence.

The better rule is that the judge first considers the offered evidence and, if he or she finds that the contract language is "reasonably susceptible" to the interpretation asserted by its proponent, the evidence is admissible to determine the meaning intended by the parties. See Restatement §215 cmt. b; see also Pacific Gas & Elec. Co. v. G.W. Thomas Dray. & Rigging Co., 69 Cal. 2d 33, 69 Cal. Rptr. 561, 564, 566, 567-68, 442 P.2d 641, 644, 645-46 (1968). . . . The meaning that appears plain and unambiguous on the first reading of a document may not appear nearly so plain once the judge considers the evidence. In such a case, the parol evidence rule is not violated because the evidence is not being offered to contradict or vary the meaning of the agreement. To the contrary, it is being offered to explain what the parties truly may have intended. We believe that this rule embodies the concepts endorsed by Corbin and adopted by this court ten years ago in *Melson*. Other courts more recently have expressed approval of the position taken by Corbin and the Restatement (Second) of Contracts. See, e.g., C.R. Anthony Co. v. Loretto Mall Partners, 817 P.2d 238, 241-44 & n. 3 (N.M. 1991); Isbrandtsen v. North Branch Corp., 150 Vt. 575, 556 A.2d 81, 83-85 (1988); Berg v. Hudesman, 115 Wash.2d 657, 801 P.2d 222, 227-30 (1990); see also 3 Corbin §542, at 105-112 (Supp. 1992) (citing cases).

A judge may not always be in a position to rule on a parol evidence objection at first blush, having not yet heard enough relevant evidence on the issue. If this occurs, the judge might, for example, admit the extrinsic evidence conditionally, reserve ruling on the issue until enough relevant evidence is presented, or, if the case is being tried to a jury, consider the evidence outside the jury's presence. See, e.g., Ariz. R. Evid. 103(c), 104(b), 104(c), 105. Because the judge is in the best position to decide how to proceed, we leave this decision to his or her sound discretion. As noted also, the judge need not waste much time if the asserted interpretation is unreasonable or the offered evidence is not persuasive. A proffered interpretation that is highly improbable would necessarily require very convincing evidence. In such a case, the judge might quickly decide that the contract language is not reasonably susceptible to the asserted meaning, stop listening to evidence supporting it, and rule that its admission would violate the parol evidence rule. See 3 Corbin §542, at 112; §579, at 420.

We now apply these principles to the facts of this case.

B. WAS THE RELEASE SO CLEAR THAT THE TRIAL JUDGE ERRED IN ADMITTING EXTRINSIC EVIDENCE TO INTERPRET IT?

Taylor released "all *contractual* rights, claims, and causes of action he ha[d] or may have against STATE FARM under the policy of insurance . . . in connection with the collision . . . *and all subsequent matters.*" See Appendix (emphasis added). Taylor argued that the bad faith claim sounds in tort and was therefore neither covered nor intended to be covered by the language releasing "all contractual" claims. The trial court found that

[p]arts of the document suggest that the parties contemplated the question of the insurer's settlement of claims within policy limits. Yet on page 2 of the document, the release satisfies "all contractual rights, claims, and causes of action." As a matter of statutory or contract construction, the word "contractual" modifies the words

"rights," "claims," and the words "causes of action." Although the breach of the duty of good faith and fair dealing arises out of contract, the action itself is a tort claim. Thus, there is ambiguity here. Where there is an ambiguity, parol evidence will be admitted on this issue.

Minute Entry, Jan. 12, 1987 at 1-2 (citations omitted). The court of appeals held that Taylor's bad faith action was purely contractual and therefore, unlike the trial judge, found no ambiguity in the release language. *Taylor,* mem. dec. at 16.[3] We must decide whether the release language is reasonably susceptible to Taylor's proffered interpretation in light of the evidence relevant to the parties' intent. If it is, admission of extrinsic evidence supporting his interpretation did not violate the parol evidence rule.

> *1. Was the release language reasonably susceptible to differing interpretations, including that the bad faith claim was not released despite the contractual quality of such a claim?*

First, we address the court of appeals' holding that Taylor's bad faith claim was only contractual and that the trial court erred by finding that the release language, which indisputably covered contractual matters, was unclear, requiring extrinsic evidence for interpretation. *Taylor,* mem. dec. at 16, 23.

. . .

It is true that bad faith has its genesis in contract. . . . Our cases show, however, that the precise legal character of a bad faith claim may depend on the context of the discussion. . . .

Because the legal character of bad faith was and is not universally established, the release reasonably could be interpreted as Taylor asserts. The trial court, therefore, did not err in concluding that the text of the release did not necessarily cover claims for bad faith.

> *2. Was there extrinsic evidence to support the conclusion that the release language was reasonably susceptible to Taylor's interpretation?*

At the time the parties made the agreement, it was obvious that Taylor had a sizable potential claim for bad faith. The release was agreed to months after the jury returned verdicts against Taylor and less than six months after this court recognized the tort of bad faith in *Noble.* Most of the alleged conduct that is the basis for Taylor's bad faith claim had already occurred. In fact, although occurring later, the Rings garnished State Farm seeking to satisfy their entire judgment, including the excess above the policy limits, based on State Farm's liability to Taylor for alleged bad faith. Ring v. State Farm Mut. Auto. Ins., 147 Ariz. 32, 33, 708 P.2d 457, 458 (Ct. App. 1985). There was

---

3. These conflicting rulings illustrate the problems inherent in finding ambiguity. Two trial judges found the agreement ambiguous, that is, "doubtful or uncertain . . . [or] capable of being understood in two or more possible senses or ways." Webster's Ninth New Collegiate Dictionary 77 (1989). Three court of appeals judges, reading the same agreement, found the meaning clear beyond all question. At one time, this court held that if one court found a contract ambiguous and another found it clear, it must be ambiguous. See Federal Ins. Co. v. P.A.T. Homes, Inc., 113 Ariz. 136, 138-39, 547 P.2d 1050, 1052-53 (1976). For obvious reasons, we should discard such doctrine and have done so. See *Wilson,* 162 Ariz. at 256-58, 782 P.2d at 732-34.

some evidence that Hofmann, on behalf of State Farm, directed that "general release language" be used in the agreement without expressly mentioning "bad faith." The document's cryptic language supports this. Such a direction, in light of the obvious nature of the claim, supports Taylor's interpretation.

Also, State Farm internally designated the $15,000 payment to Taylor as being for uninsured motorist ("UM") coverage. Although State Farm denies its importance, its ultimate significance was for the fact finder to determine. State Farm's subsequent conduct may shed light on its understanding of what was covered by the agreement. See *Darner,* 140 Ariz. at 393, 682 P.2d at 398. This, too, supports the idea that the release is reasonably susceptible to Taylor's interpretation.

The potential size of the bad faith claim also cannot be ignored. At the time the parties entered into the release agreement, a jury had already rendered verdicts against Taylor far exceeding his insurance policy limits. Thus, the potential size of Taylor's bad faith claim was obvious. We recognize that, with few exceptions, parties are free to structure a deal in any way they wish. Nevertheless, it is arguably reasonable to conclude that Taylor and his counsel would seek something more than just the payment of a potentially bona fide $15,000 UM claim to release a bad faith claim possibly worth millions of dollars.

Finally, and perhaps most telling, is the fact that the parties used limiting language in the release. It is reasonable to believe that if the parties had agreed to release the bad faith claim, they would not have drawn the release so narrowly — confining it to "contractual" and "subsequent" matters, with *no* mention of tort claims or bad faith. Surely, State Farm knew what language would effectively release it from Taylor's potential bad faith claim. It can be inferred that sophisticated parties in the business of settling insurance claims, faced with the task of releasing a claim as large as Taylor's, would have used more specific or at least broader[7] language if that was their agreement. This is especially true in light of the conspicuous nature of the claim, the parties' obvious knowledge of its existence, and the very recent supreme court authority characterizing the claim as a tort. . . . For these reasons, we hold that extrinsic evidence produces support for Taylor's contention that the release language was not intended to release his bad faith claim.

This is *not* to say, however, that the release language excluded bad faith as a matter of law. Substantial evidence supports State Farm's interpretation as well. The release language is broad enough to release something more than just the contractual UM claim.[8] Also, the recitals refer to matters that may not pertain to UM coverage but are relevant to Taylor's bad faith claim.[9] Finally,

---

7. State Farm apparently did not insist that the release contain the broad language usually found in insurance company forms — releasing all claims of whatever nature, known or unknown.

8. There was evidence that Randall believed that at least one claim other than UM and bad faith remained — a medical payment claim — that was released by the agreement. At oral argument, it was conceded that any medical payment claim would have been released by the agreement. Whether or not that claim was valid, Randall's belief dispels the notion that bad faith was the only claim other than UM that could have been contemplated by the breadth of the release language.

9. We recognize, as did the court of appeals, that a contract should be interpreted, if at all possible, in a way that does not render parts of it superfluous. *Taylor,* mem. dec. at 18. State Farm, however, strenuously argued this very point to the jury, which nevertheless remained unconvinced — a permissible result. Cf. Restatement §203 cmts. a & b. Also, State Farm argues that any uncertainty in the language should be construed against the drafter. This rule, however, is subordinate to the rule

there was credible evidence that both parties contemplated that bad faith would be covered by the release. All of the evidence, however, does not render the release language impervious to Taylor's interpretation. Instead, it demonstrates that there were three reasonable, but conflicting, interpretations of the language used in the agreement: (1) the parties agreed to release the bad faith claim; (2) the parties agreed to exclude the bad faith claim; and (3) the parties did not reach any agreement regarding release of the bad faith claim (in which case, of course, the claim would not be released). In light of this, the trial judge correctly concluded that the release could not as a matter of law be interpreted to include or exclude Taylor's bad faith claim.

C. WAS THE PAROL EVIDENCE FOR THE JURY?

Whether contract language is reasonably susceptible to more than one interpretation so that extrinsic evidence is admissible is a question of law for the court. See Leo Eisenberg & Co., Inc. v. Payson, 162 Ariz. 529, 532-33, 785 P.2d 49, 52-53 (1989). We have concluded in the preceding section that the language of the agreement, illuminated by the surrounding circumstances, indicates that either of the interpretations offered was reasonable. Because interpretation was needed and because the extrinsic evidence established controversy over what occurred and what inferences to draw from the events, the matter was properly submitted to the jury. See *Burkons*, 168 Ariz. at 351, 813 P.2d at 716; *Leo Eisenberg*, 162 Ariz. at 533, 785 P.2d at 53. The trial judge, therefore, instructed the jury as follows:

> . . . [State Farm] has alleged the affirmative defense of release. In this regard, [State Farm] contends that the agreement . . . was intended by the parties thereto to, among other things, release [State Farm] from all bad faith claims.
> . . . Whether the parties intended the bad faith claims to be released is for you to determine. If you find that the parties to said agreement intended thereby that [State Farm] be released from bad faith claims, then your verdict must be for [State Farm].
> . . .
>
> A release is to be construed according to the intent of the parties to it. This intention is to be determined by what was within the contemplation of the parties when the release was executed, which, in turn, is to be resolved in the light of all of the surrounding facts and circumstances under which the parties acted.

Reporter's Transcript, Mar. 12, 1987, at 184-85. The instruction states the issue quite clearly. So instructed, the jury resolved the release issue in Taylor's favor. We leave that resolution undisturbed.

CONCLUSION

The trial court properly considered and then admitted extrinsic evidence to interpret the release and determine whether it included Taylor's bad faith claim. That question, in this case, was appropriately left to the trier of fact.

---

that the intent of the parties should govern. *Polk*, 111 Ariz. at 495, 533 P.2d at 662. In any event, it is the *missing* language of "bad faith" that makes this agreement unclear. Although Randall drafted the agreement, he alleges that State Farm is responsible for the omission. Thus, it is unclear who, if anyone, the rule should be applied against.

There remain other issues not resolved by the court of appeals. We are aware of the frustration that additional delay imposes on all involved, especially in a case as old as this. Nevertheless, because the other issues were initially and fully presented to the court of appeals, prudence dictates that the court of appeals complete its review of this case as expeditiously as possible. The decision of the court of appeals pertaining to the release is vacated and the matter is remanded to the court of appeals for resolution of the remaining issues.

MOELLER, V.C.J., ZLAKET, J., and JAMES D. HATHAWAY, Judge, concur.

Justice FREDERICK J. MARTONE did not participate in this matter; pursuant to riz. Const. art. VI, §3, Judge JAMES D. HATHAWAY of the Court of Appeals, Division Two, was designated to sit in his stead.

CORCORAN, Justice, specially concurring:

I concur with the opinion — but without enthusiasm. It is certainly true that wavering and overlapping lines of interpretation, rather than bright straight borders prevail in this area of contract interpretation. I don't know whether our opinion helps.

The canon of interpretation which we propound today is amorphous. The problem with an amorphous rule is that in the end, only *this* court can make a *final* determination in construing any contract. Our interpretation will be based upon which parol evidence impresses us the most. That ultimately means that this court *must* decide every contract dispute subject to this analysis. As the history of this case shows, the trial court may go one way and the court of appeals another and this court yet another.

I fear that this opinion makes this court the supreme court of arguments "that white is black and that a dollar is fifty cents" — to use the colorful words of Professor Corbin.

APPENDIX
Full Text of Release:

AGREEMENT

This Agreement made and entered into this 4th day of August, 1981, by and between BOBBY SID TAYLOR and the STATE FARM MUTUAL AUTOMOBILE INSURANCE COMPANY, (hereinafter referred to as STATE FARM), by and through its agent undersigned.

WHEREAS, BOBBY SID TAYLOR was covered by an automobile insurance policy issued by STATE FARM, which was in effect on the 9th day of April, 1977, providing liability and uninsured motorist coverage to him, and

WHEREAS, an automobile collision occurred on April 9, 1977 between vehicles operated by BOBBY SID TAYLOR, DOUGLAS ALAN WISTROM and ANNE L. RING, and

WHEREAS, a trial took place in the Superior Court of Maricopa County, State of Arizona in consolidated causes C-382960 and C-383090, resulting in a jury verdict against BOBBY SID TAYLOR in the total amount of $2,621,000, and judgments having been entered against BOBBY SID TAYLOR in accordance with said jury verdicts, and

WHEREAS, having been fully apprised of all settlement offers made by the plaintiffs in the consolidated cases referred to above, during the discovery process, prior to trial, during the trial, and subsequently, BOBBY SID TAYLOR maintained and does now maintain that the operation of his motor vehicle on April 9, 1977 did not contribute to the injuries sustained by the plaintiffs, and at no time has he insisted, demanded, or even encouraged his insurer to settle the plaintiffs' claims within his policy limits, and

WHEREAS, one of the drivers of an automobile involved in the collision on April 9, 1977, to wit: DOUGLAS ALAN WISTROM, was uninsured on the date of said collision, and BOBBY SID TAYLOR having a bona fide belief that the negligence of DOUGLAS ALAN WISTROM contributed to his bodily injuries sustained in that collision, and

WHEREAS, BOBBY SID TAYLOR has demanded compensation from STATE FARM under the uninsured motorist coverage afforded to him, and

WHEREAS, BOBBY SID TAYLOR desires to settle the uninsured motorist claim, and to relieve STATE FARM of any and all other contractual claims, interests, or causes of action he has or may have against STATE FARM, and

WHEREAS, STATE FARM has agreed that uninsured motorist coverage is available to BOBBY SID TAYLOR and appropriate under the facts surrounding the collision on April 9, 1977, and STATE FARM having been fully apprised in the premises,

THEREFORE, in consideration of the mutual [cov]enants contained herein, STATE FARM agrees to pay the sum of $15,000 to BOBBY SID TAYLOR in full satisfaction of all contractual rights, claims, and causes of action he has or may have against STATE FARM under the policy of insurance referred to herein, in connection with the collision on April 9, 1977, and all subsequent matters, and BOBBY SID TAYLOR hereby accepts that sum pursuant to the recitals contained herein.

[SIGNATURES]

Notes and Questions

1. *Claims of insurer bad faith.* The *Taylor* opinion raises several significant points about insurance law and practice. The court indicates that Arizona recognizes a cause of action in tort against an insurance company for bad faith refusal to settle a policy claim. The issue of tort liability of insurers and other contracting parties for breach of contract is explored in a comment in Chapter 11 on the availability of punitive damages. For now it is probably sufficient for you to know that throughout the country courts have generally recognized that insurance companies can be liable when they refuse in bad faith to defend or settle claims brought under their policies. See generally Douglas R. Richmond, An Overview of Insurance Bad Faith Law and Litigation, 25 Seton Hall L. Rev. 74 (1994). Cases of bad faith refusal to defend or settle fall into two broad categories: third-party and first-party claims. In a third-party claim, the insured seeks to recover damages from her insurer because the insurer failed in bad faith to defend or settle a claim brought by a third party against the insured (for example, a claim covered by an automobile insurance policy). The significance of a bad faith claim is that the insurer can be held liable even for amounts in excess of the policy limit because of its bad faith conduct. In a first-party claim, the insured seeks to recover damages because the insurance company refused to settle in bad faith a claim brought by the insured rather than a third party (for example, under a health or fire

insurance policy). Courts have been somewhat more resistant to first-party than to third-party claims perhaps because damage to the insured in a third-party claim is clear and substantial (the amount in excess of the policy limit), while damage in a first-party claim (often emotional distress and punitive damages) may be more problematic. Nonetheless, a growing number of jurisdictions have recognized first-party bad faith tort claims. See Universe Life Ins. Co. v. Giles, 950 S.W.2d 48 (Tex. 1997) (indicating that approximately half the jurisdictions have clearly recognized first-party bad faith tort claims, while only a handful has explicitly rejected this cause of action).

Note also that Taylor was represented by two lawyers. Taylor's insurer, State Farm, retained one lawyer to defend him. In addition, Taylor personally retained attorney Randall, who filed a counterclaim against Ring for Taylor's damages. Insurance companies are required under what is known as the "duty to defend" provision of the typical third-party liability insurance policy to pay for defense counsel when a claim is brought against the insured. Given the high cost of legal services, the duty to defend provision of the policy is as important, if not more important, than the liability provision of the policy. When the insured has an interest that differs from that of the insurer, however, the insured may find it necessary to hire separate counsel. One example of such a situation is when the insured has a counterclaim for damages, as was the case in *Taylor*. Moreover, conflicts of interest can sometimes arise between insurer and insured. If the insurer contests coverage under the policy or if the plaintiff is seeking damages in excess of the policy limit, the insured may need to retain separate counsel. For a discussion of the many difficult conflict of interest issues facing insurance defense counsel, see Nathan M. Crystal, An Introduction to Professional Responsibility 134-143 (1998). Suppose State Farm had been successful in its claim that the release agreement barred Taylor's bad faith claim. Would Taylor have had any other avenue of relief?

2. *Contrasting **Thompson** with **Taylor**. Thompson* dealt with what is sometimes referred to as "supplementation" of the written agreement. In a case of supplementation one party offers extrinsic evidence to show that the contracting parties entered into an agreement that was not expressed in the writing. Recall that in *Thompson* the defendant claimed that the plaintiff's agent had made an oral warranty about the quality of the logs. By contrast, *Taylor* involves a case of interpretation rather than supplementation. The extrinsic evidence offered in *Taylor* did not show a separate agreement, but rather conduct and other background circumstances that Taylor claimed were relevant to the issue of whether the release should be interpreted to cover a claim in tort against State Farm for bad faith refusal to settle. For discussion of the distinction between supplementation and interpretation, see Harry G. Prince, Contract Interpretation in California: Plain Meaning, Parol Evidence and Use of the "Just Result" Principle, 31 Loy. L.A. L. Rev. 557, 605-613 (1998). What was the extrinsic evidence that Taylor offered to interpret the agreement? Are the legal principles applicable to admission of extrinsic evidence in cases of interpretation different from those involved in cases of supplementation? If not, should they be?

Thompson and *Taylor* also illustrate the ongoing tension between two opposing views of the parol evidence rule. These could be labeled "classical" and "modern"; they could also fairly be called "Willistonian" and "Corbinian," since the views of Professor Williston tended more to a conservative approach giving great weight to a formal writing (both to the parol evidence rule and to questions of interpretation generally), while the views of Professor Corbin would considerably restrict the effect of the parol evidence rule and thereby allow much greater use of extrinsic evidence in determining the completeness and meaning of written contracts. Do not be mistaken in thinking, however, that the classical or Willistonian approach to the parol evidence rule is outmoded and no longer used by the courts. See, e.g., Hershon v. Gibraltar Building & Loan Ass'n., Inc., 864 F.2d 848 (D.C. Cir. 1989) (applying Maryland law, which rejects Corbin's view of parol evidence rule, to exclude extrinsic evidence offered to show that parties who signed general release did not intend it to apply to mortgage loan made by defendant to plaintiffs). Cf. Eichengreen v. Rollins, Inc., 757 N.E.2d 952 (Ill. App. Ct. 2001) (stating Illinois courts have considered but declined to adopt modern approaches to interpretation and integration in non-UCC cases; UCC may require modern approach in sale of goods cases).

3. *Plain meaning, ambiguity, and the parol evidence rule.* The facts in *Taylor* point to the relationship between the "four corners" approach to determining integration of a writing under the parol evidence rule (as in *Thompson*) and the "plain meaning" approach to interpreting written terms (as used by the intermediate appellate court in *Taylor*). Courts that rely on the facial completeness of a written contract to conclude that it is fully integrated are likely to rely on the apparent plain meaning of words to bar use of extrinsic evidence to aid interpretation, and the presence of a merger clause may further impel such courts to assign a plain meaning to words. This tendency continues even though the usual formulation of the parol evidence rule, as reflected in both *Thompson* and *Taylor*, explicitly states that the parol evidence rule does not bar the use of extrinsic evidence to explain or interpret a writing.

While all courts will allow use of extrinsic evidence to interpret a contract with a patent or facial ambiguity, the point of difference is that "plain meaning" adherents will not allow use of extrinsic evidence to uncover a latent ambiguity. (Recall the discussion in the notes after the *Frigaliment* case on patent and latent ambiguity.) By contrast, the modern approach used by the Arizona Supreme Court in *Taylor* allows use of extrinsic or parol evidence if the disputed language of the contract is "reasonably susceptible" to the different proffered meanings advanced by the parties. In making the determination of whether the language is susceptible of more than one meaning, the court will consider at least preliminarily the extrinsic evidence and need not find the agreement to be patently ambiguous. As the *Taylor* opinion states, the Restatement (Second) adopts generally the Corbin or modern approach. See particularly Restatement (Second) §214(c) and Comment *b* thereto ("[e]ven though words seem on their face to have only a single possible meaning, other meanings often appear when the circumstances are disclosed"). The release agreement in *Taylor* did not contain a merger clause. If it had, do you think the outcome would have been affected? Would you draft a release to include a merger clause? Why or why not?

4. *Continuing debate on use of parol evidence.* While the *Taylor* court and many others have adopted the Restatement or Corbin approach to use of extrinsic evidence in the process of interpretation, some judges have expressed vigorous criticism. In Trident Center v. Connecticut General Life Ins. Co., 847 F.2d 564 (9th Cir. 1988), Judge Kozinski of the Ninth Circuit had this to say about the California Supreme Court's adoption of the modern approach to the plain meaning rule:

> Two decades ago the California Supreme Court in Pacific Gas & Electric Co. v. G.W. Thomas Drayage & Rigging Co., 69 Cal. 2d 33, 442 P.2d 641, 69 Cal. Rptr. 561 (1968), turned its back on the notion that a contract can ever have a plain meaning discernible by a court without resort to extrinsic evidence. The court reasoned that contractual obligations flow not from the words of the contract, but from the intention of the parties. "Accordingly," the court stated, "the exclusion of relevant, extrinsic, evidence to explain the meaning of a written instrument could be justified only if it were feasible to determine the meaning the parties gave to the words from the instrument alone." 69 Cal. 2d at 38, 442 P.2d 641, 69 Cal. Rptr. 561. This, the California Supreme Court concluded, is impossible: "If words had absolute and constant referents, it might be possible to discover contractual intention in the words themselves and in the manner in which they were arranged. Words, however, do not have absolute and constant referents." Id. . . .
>
> *Pacific Gas* casts a long shadow of uncertainty over all transactions negotiated and executed under the law of California. As this case illustrates, even when the transaction is very sizeable, even if it involves only sophisticated parties, even if it was negotiated with the aid of counsel, even if it results in contract language that is devoid of ambiguity, costly and protracted litigation cannot be avoided if one party has a strong enough motive for challenging the contract. While this rule creates much business for lawyers and an occasional windfall to some clients, it leads only to frustration and delay for most litigants and clogs already overburdened courts.
>
> It also chips away at the foundation of our legal system. By giving credence to the idea that words are inadequate to express concepts, *Pacific Gas* undermines the basic principle that language provides a meaningful constraint on public and private conduct. . . .

847 F.2d 568-569. For a criticism of Judge Kozinski's characterization of California law, see Cole Taylor Bank v. Truck Insurance Exchange, 51 F.3d 736, 737-738 (7th Cir. 1995).

In his comprehensive review of principles of interpretation and the parol evidence rule in California, Professor Prince contends that Judge Kozinski's characterization of *Pacific Gas* is an "exaggerated misreading" and that Judge Kozinski's own opinion shows that application of the *Pacific Gas* approach does not lead to the extreme consequences he asserts will occur:

> Judge Kozinski made three significant observations in his opinion, including two footnotes, that severely undercut his criticism of *Pacific Gas.* First, the judge clearly and expressly concluded that the loan contract was not reasonably susceptible to the interpretation proffered by the debtor. Under the rule enunciated in *Pacific Gas,* if the trial court, after a preliminary look at the extrinsic evidence, reaches the same conclusion as it did before reviewing the evidence, then exclusion of the extrinsic evidence would be proper and dismissal or other summary disposal of the case would be appropriate. *Pacific Gas* only requires the trial court to take a

preliminary look at the proffered interpretation and related extrinsic evidence before reaching a conclusion about the apparent "plain meaning" of the contract. This precaution is not unreasonable considering the procedural history of *Pacific Gas*, in which the trial and appellate courts deemed the same contract to have two conflicting plain meanings. Nevertheless, if the court concludes that the contract is not reasonably susceptible to the proposed interpretation, then dismissal is proper at an early point in the proceedings.

In his footnotes, Judge Kozinski also stated that the lender might obtain summary judgment after completion of discovery unless Trident could present some extrinsic evidence to raise a triable issue of interpretation — a dubious proposition given the relatively clear language of the contract. The extreme nature of his criticism seems inappropriate given that Judge Kozinski recognized that the action could still be disposed of early in the proceedings. Finally, the judge stated that sanctions might even be appropriate for parties "urging an interpretation lacking any objectively reasonable basis in fact" for "facially unambiguous contracts." The import of Judge Kozinski's latter suggestions is that a party may indeed offer a proposed interpretation of an agreement that is so inconsistent with the express terms, once context is considered pursuant to *Pacific Gas*, that the court would be proper in summarily disposing of the case without going further in the proceedings. Indeed, that may well have been the case in *Trident Center* had Judge Kozinski not been so determined to use it as a springboard for his criticism of *Pacific Gas*.

Harry G. Prince, Contract Interpretation in California: Plain Meaning, Parol Evidence and Use of the "Just Result" Principle, 31 Loy. L.A. L. Rev. 557, 584-585 (1998).

5. *Scholarly commentary.* As the *Taylor* opinion and the preceding notes suggest, the ferment over the parol evidence rule still continues and has led to widely divided views among academic writers. Some scholars call for a return to the traditional approach to the rule because it gives parties the incentive to negotiate written agreements carefully and because it reduces the cost of litigation. See Olivia W. Karlin & Louis W. Karlin, The California Parol Evidence Rule, 21 Sw. U. L. Rev. 1361 (1992). Other writers defend the modern approach because the intention of the parties can only be determined in context, not from the words of a document. E.g., Margaret N. Kniffin, a New Trend in Contract Interpretation: The Search for Reality as Opposed to Virtual Reality, 74 Or. L. Rev. 643 (1995). Some authors conclude that evaluation of the benefits of the traditional and modern approaches depends on the level of transaction costs and the competency of the judiciary to evaluate extrinsic evidence. Eric A. Posner, The Parol Evidence Rule, The Plain Meaning Rule, and The Principles of Contractual Interpretation, 146 U. Pa. L. Rev. 533 (1998). A number of scholars have even called for complete abolition of the rule because it is so complex and riddled with exceptions. Susan J. Martin-Davidson, Yes, Judge Kozinski, There Is a Parol Evidence Rule in California — The Lessons of a Pyrrhic Victory, 25 Sw. U. L. Rev. 1 (1995-1996). Others have called for recasting the rule in various ways. See, e.g., Justin Sweet, Contract Making and Parol Evidence: Diagnosis and Treatment of a Sick Rule, 53 Cornell L. Rev. 1036 (1968); John E. Murray, Jr., The Parol Evidence Process and Standardized Agreements under the *Restatement (Second) of Contracts*, 123 U. Pa. L. Rev. 1342 (1975); Nicholas R. Weiskopf, Supplementing Written Agreements: Restating the Parol Evidence Rule in Terms of Credibility and Relative Fault, 34 Emory L.J. 93 (1985).

Probably the most forceful argument for its abolition was presented over a half century ago by Judge Jerome Frank, a prominent Legal Realist, in his opinion written for the court in Zell v. American Seating Co., 138 F.2d 641 (2d Cir. 1943). Offering a rare but refreshing insight into the judicial process, Judge Frank candidly admitted, "that, were we enthusiastic devotees of [the parol evidence] rule, we might so construe the record as to bring this case within the rule's scope. . . . " Id. at 644. Judge Frank refused to apply the rule, however, because he doubted that the rule was "so beneficent, so promotive of the administration of justice, and so necessary to business stability, that it should be given the widest possible application." Id. In discussing the rule, Judge Frank made the following observations:

> Although seldom mentioned in modern decisions, the most important motive for perpetuation of the rule is distrust of juries, fear that they cannot adequately cope with, or will be unfairly prejudiced by, conflicting "parol" testimony. If the rule were frankly recognized as primarily a device to control juries, its shortcomings would become obvious. . . . [Numerous] exceptions have removed most of that insulation of the jury from "oral" testimony which the rule is said to provide. . . . Perjury, of course, is pernicious and doubtless much of it is used in our courts daily with unfortunate success. The problem of avoiding its efficacious use should be met head on. Were it consistently met in an indirect manner — in accordance with the viewpoint of the adulators of the parol evidence rule — by wiping out substantive rights provable only through oral testimony, we would have wholesale destruction of familiar causes of action such as, for instance, suits for personal injury and for enforcement of wholly oral agreements.

Id. at 644-646.

6. *Interpretation and the parol evidence rule under the CISG.* Article 8 of the CISG sets forth general principles of contract interpretation:

> (1) For the purposes of this Convention statements made by and other conduct of a party are to be interpreted according to his intent where the other party knew or could not have been unaware what that intent was.
>
> (2) If the preceding paragraph is not applicable, statements made by and conduct of a party are to be interpreted according to the understanding a reasonable person of the same kind as the other party would have had in the same circumstances.
>
> (3) In determining the intent of a party or the understanding a reasonable person would have had, due consideration is to be given to all relevant circumstances of the case including the negotiations, any practices which the parties have established between themselves, usages and any subsequent conduct of the parties.

CISG, art. 8. Thus, the CISG takes a modified objective approach to interpretation which focuses on what the parties knew or had reason to know about each other's intent, consistent with the Restatement (Second) §201, and permits use of all relevant extrinsic evidence in arriving at that interpretation, an approach that also appears largely consistent with the Restatement (Second) Contracts §§212, 214, as discussed in *Taylor*. See William S. Dodge, Teaching the CISG in Contracts, 50 J. Leg. Ed. 72, 87-88 (2000) (observing that the CISG approach to interpretation is "barely distinguishable" from the approach of the Restatement (Second)).

Given that the CISG does not have a statute of frauds and in Article 11 allows a contract to be proved by witnesses, as discussed in Chapter 4, it is not surprising that the CISG also fails to include a parol evidence rule. The 11th Circuit Court of Appeals addressed the interaction of the parol evidence rule and the CISG in MCC-Marble Ceramic Center, Inc. v. Ceramica Nuova d'Agostino, S.p.A., 144 F.3d 1384 (11th Cir. 1998). The president of MCC, a Florida corporation, traveled to Italy and entered into a contract to purchase ceramic tiles from D'Agostino, an Italian corporation. The parties initially negotiated an oral agreement (through a translator) on the crucial terms of price, quality, quantity, delivery and payment and then signed one of D'Agostino's standard, pre-printed order forms which was written in Italian. The front side of the form contained a clause stating that additional provisions were on the reverse side, but the MCC president did not speak or read Italian. After a quantity of tile had been delivered, the parties fell into a dispute about the quality of tile, whether MCC had properly paid for the delivered tile, and whether D'Agostino was justified in ceasing further delivery. D'Agostino relied on reverse-side provisions of the order form which required that MCC give notice of any defects within 10 days of receiving the goods and that allowed D'Agostino to cease delivery if MCC defaulted in payment. MCC responded that the parties had never intended to have the reverse-side terms apply to their contract. In support of its position, MCC offered affidavits stating that it did not intend to be bound by the reverse-side terms and that D'Agostino was aware of that intent. The court framed the key question as whether the evidence of the earlier oral contract would be barred under the parol evidence rule since the parties later adopted a writing. Acknowledging the competing arguments in favor of and against the concept, the court concluded that the drafters of the CISG intended to reject the parol evidence rule and that Article 8(3) "is a clear instruction to admit and consider parol evidence regarding the negotiations to the extent they reveal the parties's subjective intent." 144 F.3d at 1389. The court thus reversed a grant of summary judgment in favor of D'Agostino and remanded the case.

Notwithstanding the clear support for the *MCC-Marble* court's decision found in the text of the CISG and scholarly commentary, Professor Dodge observes that the court expressed some "discomfort" with the prospect of oral negotiations undermining a subsequent writing. William S. Dodge, Teaching the CISG in Contracts, 50 J. Leg. Ed. 72, 86-89 (2000). The court suggested that parties could avoid this outcome by adopting a merger clause, but Professor Dodge questions whether this would be true.

> *MCC-Marble* suggests in dictum that the parties to a contract could create a private parol evidence rule by inserting a merger clause in their contract, but it is not clear that this is so. A merger clause works under the common law and UCC because it states that the writing is a completely integrated agreement, and the parol evidence rule states that such an agreement should not be contradicted by extrinsic evidence. Under the CISG, by contrast, there is no parol evidence rule for a merger clause to invoke, and Article 8(3) states that a court should give "due consideration . . . to all relevant circumstances of the case including the negotiations," without any apparent exception for agreements that state that they are complete and final. . . . CISG Article 6 allows the parties to derogate from (almost) any provision of the CISG, but such derogation may have to be express rather than implied, and it is not clear that a standard merger clause would do the trick.

Id. at 89 (footnotes omitted). Based on the provisions in Article 8, what effect do you believe a merger clause should have under the CISG?

Sherrodd, Inc. v. Morrison-Knudsen Co.
Supreme Court of Montana
249 Mont. 282, 815 P.2d 1135 (1991)

TURNAGE, Chief Justice.

This action arises out of a construction contract on which plaintiff Sherrodd, Inc., was a subcontractor. Sherrodd, Inc., appeals from a summary judgment entered for defendants by the District Court for the Thirteenth Judicial District, Yellowstone County. We affirm.

The issue is whether the entry of summary judgment for defendants was proper.

Sherrodd, Inc. (Sherrodd), is a family-owned Montana construction corporation. Sherrodd subcontracted with COP Construction (COP) to do certain earth-moving work involved in the construction of fifty family housing units in Forsyth, Montana, for the Army Corps of Engineers. COP itself was a subcontractor to the general contractors Morrison-Knudsen Company, Inc. (Morrison-Knudsen), and Schlekeway Construction, Inc. (Schlekeway). Safeco Insurance Company of America (Safeco) provided COP's payment bond on the job.

Sherrodd contends that while its officer William Sherrodd was examining the building site in preparation for submitting a bid on this project, a representative of Morrison-Knudsen told him that there were 25,000 cubic yards of excavation to be performed on the job. It claims that its bid of $97,500 on the subcontract was made in reliance on that representation, based on $3.90 per cubic yard for 25,000 cubic yards. Morrison-Knudsen denies that its representative made any such statement to William Sherrodd.

Sherrodd's bid, and, in turn, COP's bid including Sherrodd's bid, were submitted and accepted. Sherrodd began work before a written contract was signed. While performing the earthwork, Sherrodd discovered that the quantity of work far exceeded 25,000 cubic yards.

The written contract between Sherrodd and COP provided that Sherrodd would perform earthwork in the quantity "LS" for the consideration of $97,500. The parties agree that the letters "LS" mean lump sum. Sherrodd contends that its officers signed the contract, even though by then they knew that the job involved more than 25,000 cubic yards of earthwork, because a COP officer threatened to withhold payment for work already done unless the contract was signed. Sherrodd further contends that the COP officer verbally represented that a deal would be worked out wherein Sherrodd would be paid more than the sum provided for in the contract. COP's position is that it only agreed to assist Sherrodd in presenting a claim for additional compensation to the Army Corps of Engineers, based on differences in the moisture content of the soil from that stated in the bid proposal. That was done, but the claim was denied.

In its "Standard Subcontract Provisions," the contract entered between Sherrodd and COP also provided that

> the Subcontractor has, by examination, satisfied himself as to the . . . character, quantity and kind of materials to be encountered . . . No verbal agreement with any agent either before or after the execution of this Subcontract shall affect or modify any of the terms or obligations herein contained and this contract shall be conclusively considered as containing and expressing all of the terms and conditions agreed upon by the parties hereto. No changes . . . shall be valid . . . unless reduced to writing and signed by the parties hereto.

Sherrodd was paid the $97,500 provided for in the contract, less approximately $9,750 for work left uncompleted. It brought this suit to set aside the price provisions in the contract and to recover quantum meruit plus tort damages. Its legal theories were fraud, both actual and constructive, and breach of the covenant of good faith and fair dealing. Defendants moved for summary judgment, which was granted based on the parol evidence rule regarding modification of written contracts.

Summary judgment is proper when the pleadings, depositions, answers to interrogatories, and admissions on file, together with the affidavits, if any, show that there are no genuine issues of material fact and that the moving party is entitled to judgment as a matter of law. Rule 56(c), M.R. Civ. P. The District Court held that, under the parol evidence rule, Sherrodd could not introduce evidence of the alleged oral misrepresentations by either the Morrison-Knudsen representative or the COP officer. Therefore, it concluded that even taking the evidence in the light most favorable to Sherrodd, summary judgment for defendants was proper.

The parol evidence rule is codified in Montana statutes. Section 28-2-904, MCA, provides that:

> The execution of a contract in writing, whether the law requires it to be written or not, supersedes all the oral negotiations or stipulations concerning its matter which preceded or accompanied the execution of the instrument.

Section 28-2-905, MCA, provides that when an agreement has been reduced to writing by the parties, there can be no evidence of the terms of the agreement other than the contents of the writing except when a mistake or imperfection of the writing is claimed or when the validity of the agreement is the fact in dispute.

Although it mentions mutual mistake in its brief to this Court, Sherrodd did not rely on that theory in the proceedings below, as evidenced in the pretrial order and in the District Court's memorandum on the summary judgment. We will not consider on appeal a theory not raised at the trial court level. Morse v. Cremer (1982), 200 Mont. 71, 81, 647 P.2d 358, 363.

A further exception is made to the parol evidence rule when fraud is alleged. Section 28-2-905(2), MCA. However, that exception only applies when the alleged fraud does not relate directly to the subject of the contract. Where an alleged oral promise directly contradicts the terms of an express written contract, the parol evidence rule applies. Continental Oil Co. v. Bell (1933), 94 Mont. 123, 133, 21 P.2d 65, 67. Accord, Superior Oil Company v. Vanderhoof (D. Mont. 1969), 297 F. Supp. 1086.

Here, any reliance on the alleged fraudulent statement of the Morrison-Knudsen representative is contradicted by the terms of the written contract that Sherrodd has, "by examination, satisfied himself as to the . . . character, quantity and kind of materials to be encountered." The contention that the $97,500 covered only 25,000 cubic yards of earthwork contradicts the terms of the written agreement that all "negotiations and agreements" prior to the date of the contract are merged in the writing and that the work to be done is "lump sum." We conclude that the parol evidence rule applies. Because the written agreement supersedes all previous oral agreements, the rule prohibits admission of any evidence of the representation by the Morrison-Knudsen representative.

Next we consider Sherrodd's claim that COP officers induced Sherrodd officers to sign the contract with the promise that more money would be paid than the contract provided. Section 28-2-1602, MCA, provides that a written contract may be altered only by a subsequent contract in writing or by an executed oral agreement. Also, Sherrodd's subcontract provided that "No changes . . . shall be valid . . . unless reduced to writing and signed by the parties hereto." As the District Court noted, there is no allegation of a subsequent contract in writing, and if there had been an executed oral agreement to pay additional sums for the work, there would have been no reason for this lawsuit.

Because of the inadmissibility of Sherrodd's evidence as to alleged misrepresentations, the claim of breach of the covenant of good faith and fair dealing also fails. There is no allegation of any violation of the express terms of the written contract, as would be required in this arms-length contract under our opinion in Story v. City of Bozeman (1990), 242 Mont. 436, 791 P.2d 767.

As we have stated,

> Commercial stability requires that parties to a contract may rely upon its express terms without worrying that the law will allow the other party to change the terms of the agreement at a later date.

Baker v. Bailey (1989), 240 Mont. 139, 143, 782 P.2d 1286, 1288.

The parol evidence rule is the public policy of Montana and it is clearly established by statute and the decisions of this Court. If this public policy and rule is not upheld, contracting parties that include lawful provisions in written contracts would be under a cloud of uncertainty as to whether or not their written contracts may be relied upon. The public policy and law does not permit such uncertainty to occur.

We conclude that the compensation of Sherrodd is governed exclusively by the written contract and that Sherrodd's claims are barred under the parol evidence rule. We hold that the District Court did not err in granting summary judgment for defendants.

Affirmed.

HARRISON, GRAY, McDONOUGH and WEBER, JJ., concur.

TRIEWEILER, Justice, dissenting.

I dissent from the opinion of the majority.

If the facts are as alleged by the plaintiff (and for purposes of this proceeding we must assume that they are), then the result of this case is that no party can be held accountable for its fraudulent conduct so long as it is in a sufficiently superior bargaining position to compel its victim to sign a document relieving it of liability.

The facts, as alleged by the plaintiff, offend any reasonable sense of fairness. No court should be so bound by a 58-year-old precedent that it cannot adapt to circumstances such as those presented in this case.

The plaintiff was informed by Lou Castino, the construction manager for Schlekeway and Associates, that the project he was being asked to bid on involved moving 25,000 cubic yards of dirt. It was based on that information that he submitted his bid. It was based on his bid that he was given an oral request to proceed with the work.

After commencing work on the project, plaintiff realized that the amount of earth that had to be moved greatly exceeded 25,000 cubic yards, and was actually more than twice that amount. He had conversations with representatives of both COP Construction and Schlekeway and Associates, during which it was agreed that the amount of work to be performed would be recalculated, and during which the defendants agreed to compensate plaintiff on the basis of the actual amount of work done, rather than the price which was originally agreed upon.

By May 22, 1985, plaintiff had already been working on the project and had incurred substantial expenses and obligations to his own employees. He had not been paid for his work, and was still operating without a written agreement. It was on that date that he was requested by COP Construction's superintendent to sign the written contract which the defendants now assert as a bar to his cause of action. He was advised that if he did not sign the agreement he would not receive the progress payment in the amount of $70,372.80 which was due. Without the progress payment he would not have been able to pay his current expenses and payroll.

He was further advised that he would not be bound by the terms of the written agreement, but that he would be paid for the actual work done at the rate of $3.90 per cubic yard.

Thereafter, the amount of earth work to be done was recalculated at approximately 50,000 cubic yards. On that basis, plaintiff tried to recover the full amount due, but payment was refused. Instead, the defendants raised the written agreement as a bar to any further payment to the plaintiff.

Because of the defendants' failure to pay the plaintiff the additional $100,000 to $120,000 which they owed him, plaintiff's business lost its ability to borrow money, lost its bonding, and was unable to complete additional contracts because of a lack of operating capital. Plaintiff was unable to bid on contracts that required bonding, and completely lost its ability to carry on business as it had in the past. As a direct result of the defendants' failure to pay the amounts due, plaintiff was unable to continue in business as a construction company, which it had done for the previous 30 years.

If the plaintiff's allegations are true, then defendant COP Construction Company's conduct, at least, satisfies the elements of fraud. See Poulsen, et al. v. Treasure State Industries, 192 Mont. 69, 626 P.2d 822 (1981). COP's employees represented to the plaintiff that he would be paid for the full amount of work done, regardless of the written terms of the contract. That representation was untrue and material, and COP's superintendent either knew it was untrue or had no reason to believe that it was true. COP Construction intended that the plaintiff act in reliance upon that representation. Plaintiff did rely on it, and had no reason to believe that COP's superintendent would mislead him. As a result, plaintiff has sustained the total loss of his business and substantial damages.

The majority has affirmed the dismissal of plaintiff's claim based solely on the parol evidence rule found at §28-2-904, MCA. That rule provides that a written agreement supersedes all oral negotiations which preceded or accompanied the execution of the instrument. Furthermore, §28-2-905, MCA, provides that the terms of a written agreement cannot be proven by evidence other than what is contained in the written document.

However, an important exception is found at §28-2-905(2), MCA, which provides, in relevant part, as follows:

> This section does not exclude other evidence of the circumstances under which the agreement was made or to which it relates . . . or other evidence to explain . . . fraud.

In addition, §28-2-1611, MCA, provides as follows:

> When, through *fraud* or a mutual mistake of the parties or a mistake of one party while the other at the time knew or suspected, a written contract does not truly express the intention of the parties, it may be revised on the application of a party aggrieved so as to express that intention, so far as it can be done without prejudice to rights acquired by third persons in good faith and for value. (Emphasis added.)

In this case, in spite of the exceptions to the parol evidence rule set forth by statute above, the majority has chosen to rely on this Court's 58-year-old decision in Continental Oil v. Bell, 94 Mont. 123, 133, 21 P.2d 65, 68 (1933). In that case, this Court held that parol evidence of fraud was not admissible when the oral promise directly contradicts a provision of the written contract.

I would not follow this Court's previous decision in *Continental Oil* for two reasons:

1. That decision made no specific reference to the statute which is controlling, and yet adds qualifications to the statute which were not included by the legislature. The legislature provided that parol evidence could be offered to establish that a contract was induced by fraud. It made no exception where evidence of the fraudulent oral agreement contradicted a term in the written agreement.

2. To follow the decision in *Continental Oil* creates a terrible injustice, rewards fraudulent parties who are in a superior bargaining position, and totally defeats the purpose for which the fraud exception was provided to the parol evidence rule.

Based on this decision, and our previous decision in *Continental Oil,* all that a fraudulent party needs to do in order to avoid accountability for fraudulent conduct is to obtain the signature of his defrauded victim on a written agreement.

The majority expresses concern that but for this decision general contractors would not be able to rely on written agreements with their subcontractors. However, general contractors who induce subcontractors to enter into a written agreement by fraudulent representations should find no security in the piece of paper which resulted from their culpable conduct. Furthermore, a justice system worth its salt should have equal compassion for Montana's many subcontractors who, while operating without the benefit of legal advice, sign whatever is necessary in order to keep their operations afloat and their crews at work. When what they have signed results from an obvious misrepresentation and causes them the kind of substantial damages and hardship that have resulted in this case, those subcontractors are entitled to the protection of Montana's laws and its courts.

For these reasons, I dissent from the majority opinion. I would reverse the judgment of the District Court and remand for a jury trial to determine the merits of the plaintiff's claim. That is really all the protection that Montana's general contractors need.

HUNT, J., concurs with the foregoing dissent of Justice Trieweiler.

Notes and Questions

1. *Alleged fraud, merger clauses, and disclaimers.* The parol evidence rule, as typically stated, recognizes a general exception for fraud. See Restatement (Second) §214(d). Consistent with the dissent in *Sherrodd,* a number of courts take the view that not even the combination of a merger clause and a specific disclaimer can shield a party from a claim of fraud. See Pancakes of Hawaii, Inc. v. Pomare Properties Corp., 944 P.2d 97 (Haw. Ct. App. 1997) (merger clause with disclaimer of oral representations would not bar parol evidence to support allegation of false statements about occupancy level of new shopping center); Snyder v. Lovercheck, 992 P.2d 1079 (Wyo. 1999) (considering contrary authority but holding that a claim of fraud will not be barred by merger clause and specific disclaimer). On the other hand, many courts agree with the majority in *Sherrodd* that a party cannot base a claim of fraud upon the very type of a representation that is disclaimed in the writing. See Circle Centre Development Co. v. Y/G Indiana, L.P., 762 N.E.2d 176 (Ind. Ct. App. 2002) (specific disclaimer of reliance in writing would bar proof of fraud based on alleged misrepresentation about dollar amount of sales by other stores in mall); Schlumberger Technology Corp. v. Swanson, 959 S.W.2d 171 (Tex. 1997) (considering contrary position before concluding that specific disclaimer of reliance on representations will bar proof of fraud). This topic is also discussed in the section in Chapter 7 on misrepresentation.

2. *Policy implications of **Sherrodd**.* The majority and dissenting opinions in *Sherrodd* obviously differ on the application of the fraud exception to the parol evidence rule, but at a deeper level the opinions reflect a fundamental disagreement about values. In his analysis of the role of reliance in modern contract law, Professor Knapp offers the following view of *Sherrodd:*

> Each party has a reliance story to tell, and each story — if true — is compelling. If Sherrodd is telling the truth, he has at least been misled, possibly been consciously lied to, and in any event been bullied and ultimately betrayed by the defendant's agents. In reliance on their assurances, he has completed his performance while at the same time binding himself to the very written document that may prevent him

from recovering the full payment that he was promised, which he has honestly earned. To deny him his claim in these circumstances is clearly an injustice.

But what if Sherrodd's story is a lie? Then COP is being asked to pay more than Sherrodd had agreed to accept for his services, even though COP has bound itself in turn to Morrison-Knudsen, relying on Sherrodd's willingness to render his performance at the originally agreed upon figure. And all this in the teeth of Sherrodd's signing of a written contract that expressly binds him to the agreement he now repudiates. If these are indeed the true facts, then surely to allow Sherrodd his claim would also be an injustice. How should this dilemma be resolved?

Professor Knapp goes on to suggest that the judge should hear evidence of these conflicting stories and determine whether Sherrodd's story is sufficiently credible to be considered by the trier of fact. In support of the modern, Corbinian view of the parol evidence rule, Professor Knapp argues that this approach should be used because the stricter view of the parol evidence rule represented by *Sherrodd* embodies a flawed world view:

> Proponents of a strong parol evidence rule may see [the conflict between approaches to the parol evidence rule] simply as the difference between tidiness and sloppiness, or as the difference between prudence and heedlessness, and those factors surely play a part. But at the most basic level, it's the difference between a world that runs on paper, and a world that runs on face-to-face communication — between a world that says "I don't believe it unless I see it in writing, and I won't *do* it unless a writing tells me to," and a world that says, "If you assure me this is so, I will take you at your word, and rely on that, as you well know."
>
> Each one of us lives, simultaneously, in both of those worlds. We have no choice in the matter. If the parol evidence rule forces a court to envision our world as being one where *only* paper matters, or — the slightly weaker version — a world where paper *always* prevails over face-to-face communication, then that rule forces the court (along with the rest of us) to deny something we know to be true. And that something is simply this: There are situations where it is, truly, more reasonable to rely on a spoken word of commitment than on a piece of paper, signed or not. And there should be.

Charles L. Knapp, Rescuing Reliance: The Perils of Promissory Estoppel, 49 Hastings L. J. 1191, 1322-1323, 1325 (1998).

Similarly, Professor James Mooney laments what he calls the "new conceptualism" in contract law:

> Just as they have in contract formation disputes, American courts recently have embraced far more conceptualist approaches to contract interpretation issues. They invoke the parol evidence rule more frequently today, exalting the written word over the parties' actual, parol agreement. They exercise their pre-modern faith in the objectivity of language, and overturn jury verdicts, by applying classical interpretive rules like "plain meaning," "four corners," and interpretation as a "matter of law." In general, American courts the past dozen years have moved noticeably away from the most fundamental theorem of contract interpretation, that the law should enforce the parties' intention, toward a more abstract, disembodied inquiry, resembling, what should the parties have meant when they signed this form contract?
>
> In addition, this intellectual regression once again has had important political consequences. The cases just described are reasonably representative. Notice that, as in formation cases, it is almost invariably a seller, a bank, an employer, or (most

often) an insurer that benefits from the New Conceptualism in contract interpretation. This judicial tilt away from underdogs, back toward the privileged beneficiaries
of classical contract law, is, of course, the New Conceptualism's most troubling feature
of all.

Ralph James Mooney, The New Conceptualism in Contract Law, 74 Or. L.
Rev. 1131, 1170-1171 (1995). See also Jay M. Feinman, Un-Making Law: The
Classical Revival in the Common Law, 28 Seattle U. L. Rev. 1, 22-26 (2004).

3. *Other exceptions to the parol evidence rule.* Sherrodd could have asserted
legal theories other than fraud in an effort to convince the court to admit
parol evidence. The court mentions the possibility of mutual mistake, but
rejects this contention because the plaintiff did not raise the issue at the trial
court. Another theory not mentioned in the opinion is the possibility that the
agreement was unenforceable because of economic duress. Sherrodd claimed
that he signed the agreement when the defendant threatened to refuse to
make a progress payment for work that was already done, without which
Sherrodd could not pay his employees or meet current expenses. We will
discuss duress further in Chapter 7 and mistake in Chapter 8. Based on your
studies thus far, does it seem to you that Sherrodd might have had more
success if he had attempted to proceed on either a mistake or a duress theory?
Why? At the very least the possible applicability of these doctrines shows how
the quality of lawyering may have an impact on the outcome of a case.

4. *Promissory estoppel and the parol evidence rule.* In earlier chapters, we saw
the doctrine of promissory estoppel being used by courts in a variety of ways:
as a substitute for consideration, permitting recovery for detrimental reliance
on a gratuitous promise; as a basis for holding an offer open despite the
offeror's attempt to revoke; as a basis for enforcing an oral agreement within
the statute of frauds despite the lack of a memorandum signed by the
defendant. In light of these and other similar developments, Professor Knapp
observed in 1981, "it seems inevitable that another bastion of form-over-
substance, the parol evidence rule, eventually will fall under similar attack."
Charles L. Knapp, Reliance in the Revised *Restatement:* The Proliferation of
Promissory Estoppel, 81 Colum. L. Rev. 52, 78 (1981). See also Michael B.
Metzger, The Parol Evidence Rule: Promissory Estoppel's Next Conquest, 36
Vand. L. Rev. 1383 (1983).

Indeed, there are a handful of cases that appear to hold that the parol
evidence rule does not bar a showing of extrinsic evidence that the plaintiff
detrimentally relied on promises or assurances not contained in an integrated
written contract, for the purpose of applying the promissory estoppel
principle. The leading case is Prudential Insurance Co. of America v. Clark,
456 F.2d 932 (5th Cir. 1972) (insurance agent's promise to obtain life
insurance without war risk exclusion). A more recent example is Starr v. O-I
Brockway Glass, Inc., 637 A.2d 1371 (Pa. Super. Ct. 1994). See Eric Mills
Holmes, The Four Phases of Promissory Estoppel, 20 Seattle U. L. Rev. 45,
59-62 (1996). Most cases, however, have rejected the use of promissory
estoppel to avoid the parol evidence rule. See, e.g, Banbury v. Omnitrition
International Inc., 533 N.W.2d 876 (Minn. Ct. App. 1995); Ed Schory & Sons,
Inc. v. Society National Bank, 662 N.E.2d 1074 (Ohio 1996); Highlands
Management Co. v. First Interstate Bank of Texas, N.A., 956 S.W.2d 749 (Tex.

Ct. App. 1997, *writ denied*). It seems, therefore, that Professor Farnsworth was right in his observation that the earlier movement toward protecting reliance at the expense of formal requirements has not continued, and if anything may have reversed itself. E. Allan Farnsworth, Developments in Contract Law During the 1980's: The Top Ten, 41 Case W. Res. L. Rev. 203, 219-220 (1990). Can you offer any explanation for this development? The relationship between the parol evidence rule and promissory estoppel is further discussed in Charles L. Knapp, Rescuing Reliance: The Perils of Promissory Estoppel, 49 Hastings L. J. 1191, 1325-1330 (1998).

Nanakuli Paving & Rock Co. v. Shell Oil Co.
United States Court of Appeals
664 F.2d 772 (9th Cir. 1981)

HOFFMAN, District Judge:

Appellant Nanakuli Paving and Rock Company (Nanakuli) initially filed this breach of contract action against appellee Shell Oil Company (Shell) in Hawaiian State Court in February, 1976. Nanakuli, the second largest asphaltic paving contractor in Hawaii, had bought all its asphalt requirements from 1963 to 1974 from Shell under two long-term supply contracts; its suit charged Shell with breach of the later 1969 contract. The jury returned a verdict of $220,800 for Nanakuli on its first claim, which is that Shell breached the 1969 contract in January, 1974, by failing to price protect Nanakuli on 7200 tons of asphalt at the time Shell raised the price for asphalt from $44 to $76. Nanakuli's theory is that price-protection, as a usage of the asphaltic paving trade in Hawaii, was incorporated into the 1969 agreement between the parties, as demonstrated by the routine use of price protection by suppliers to that trade, and reinforced by the way in which Shell actually performed the 1969 contract up until 1974. Price protection, appellant claims, required that Shell hold the price on the tonnage Nanakuli had already committed because Nanakuli had incorporated that price into bids put out to or contracts awarded by general contractors and government agencies. The District Judge set aside the verdict and granted Shell's motion for judgment n.o.v., which decision we vacate. . . .

Nanakuli offers two theories for why Shell's failure to offer price protection in 1974 was a breach of the 1969 contract. First, it argues, all material suppliers to the asphaltic paving trade in Hawaii followed the trade usage of price protection and thus it should be assumed, under the U.C.C., that the parties intended to incorporate price protection into their 1969 agreement. This is so, Nanakuli continues, even though the written contract provided for price to be "Shell's Posted Price at time of delivery," F.O.B. Honolulu. Its proof of a usage that was incorporated into the contract is reinforced by evidence of the commercial context, which under the U.C.C. should form the background for viewing a particular contract. The full agreement must be examined in light of the close, almost symbiotic relations between Shell and Nanakuli on the island of Oahu, whereby the expansion of Shell on the island was intimately connected to the business growth of

Nanakuli. The U.C.C. looks to the actual performance of a contract as the best indication of what the parties intended those terms to mean. Nanakuli points out that Shell had price protected it on the two occasions of price increases under the 1969 contract other than the 1974 increase. In 1970 and 1971 Shell extended the old price for four and three months, respectively, after an announced increase. This was done, in the words of Shell's agent in Hawaii, in order to permit Nanakuli's to "chew up" tonnage already committed at Shell's old price.[4]

Nanakuli's second theory for price protection is that Shell was obliged to price protect Nanakuli, even if price protection was not incorporated into their contract, because price protection was the commercially reasonable standard for fair dealing in the asphaltic paving trade in Hawaii in 1974. Observance of those standards is part of the good-faith requirement that the Code imposes on merchants in performing a sales contract. Shell was obliged to price protect Nanakuli in order to act in good faith, Nanakuli argues, because such a practice was universal in that trade in that locality.

Shell presents three arguments for upholding the judgment n.o.v. or, on cross appeal, urging that the District Judge erred in admitting certain evidence. First, it says, the District Court should not have denied Shell's motion in limine to define trade, for purposes of trade usage evidence, as the sale and purchase of asphalt in Hawaii, rather than expanding the definition of trade to include other suppliers of materials to the asphaltic paving trade. Asphalt, its argument runs, was the subject matter of the disputed contract and the only product Shell supplied to the asphaltic paving trade. Shell protests that the judge, by expanding the definition of trade to include the other major suppliers to the asphaltic paving trade, allowed the admission of highly prejudicial evidence of routine price protection by all suppliers of aggregate. Asphaltic concrete paving is formed by mixing paving asphalt with crushed rock, or aggregate, in a "hot-mix" plant and then pouring the mixture onto the surface to be paved. Shell's second complaint is that the two prior occasions on which it price protected Nanakuli, although representing the only other instances of price increases under the 1969 contract, constituted mere waivers of the contract's price term, not a course of performance of the contract. A course of performance of the contract, in contrast to a waiver, demonstrates how the parties understand the terms of their agreement. Shell cites two U.C.C. Comments in support of that argument: (1) that, when the meaning of acts is ambiguous, the preference is for the waiver interpretation, and (2) that one act alone does not constitute a relevant course of performance. Shell's final argument is that, even assuming its prior price protection constituted a course of performance and that the broad trade definition was correct and evidence of trade usages by aggregate suppliers was admissible, price protection could not be construed as reasonably consistent with the express price term in the contract, in which case the Code provides that the express term controls. . . .

---

4. Price protection was practiced in the asphaltic paving trade by either extending the old price for a period of time after a new one went into effect or charging the old price for a specified tonnage, which represented work committed at the old price. In addition, several months' advance notice was given of price increases.

I

[Until 1963 Nanakuli was the smaller of two major paving contractors in Hawaii and was unable to compete with the larger contractor, Hawaiian Bitumuls (H.B.), for government contracts. In 1963 Nanakuli negotiated a five-year contact with Shell, which provided Nanakuli with a guaranteed supply of asphalt at reduced prices. The new agreement enabled Shell to increase its presence as an asphalt supplier in Hawaii and allowed Nanakuli to expand its paving business.

In 1968 Shell and Nanakuli entered into further negotiations. Nanakuli wished to expand its cement plant at a cost of approximately $300,000. Nanakuli and Shell originally discussed Shell's financing of the expansion, but the parties finally agreed on indirect financing through a $2 discount on all sales of asphalt over 5000 tons. In 1969 Nanakuli borrowed funds from its bank to finance the expansion. At the same time Nanakuli and Shell executed several agreements, including a long-term supply contract to run until 1976.

Nanakuli offered evidence from its president, Lennox, and its vice president, Smith, that the 1969 contract included a commitment by Shell never to charge Nanakuli more than Chevron charged H.B., but the trial court ruled this evidence inadmissible as parol evidence because the court found that the price term of the 1969 contract was not ambiguous. — EDS.]

II

The key to price protection being so prevalent in 1969 that both parties would intend to incorporate it into their contract is found in one reality of the Oahu asphaltic paving market: the largest paving contracts were let by government agencies and none of the three levels of government — local, state, or federal — allowed escalation clauses for paving materials. If a paver bid at one price and another went into effect before the award was made, the paving company would lose a great deal of money, since it could not pass on increases to any government agency or to most general contractors. Extensive evidence was presented that, as a consequence, aggregate suppliers routinely price protected paving contractors in the 1960's and 1970's, as did the largest asphaltic supplier in Oahu, Chevron. . . .

III

The Code considers actual performance of a contract as the most relevant evidence of how the parties interpreted the terms of that contract. In 1970 and 1971, the only points at which Shell raised prices between 1969 and 1974, it price protected Nanakuli by holding its old price for four and three months, respectively, after announcing a price increase. . . .

IV

Two important factors form the backdrop for the 1974 failure by Shell to price protect Nanakuli: the Arab oil embargo and a complete change of command and policy in Shell's asphalt management. The jury was read a page or so from the World Book about the events and effect of the partial oil embargo, which shortened supplies and increased the price of petroleum, of which asphalt is a byproduct. The federal government imposed direct price controls on petroleum, but not on asphalt. Despite the international importance of those events, the jury may have viewed the second factor as of more direct significance to this case. The structural changes at Shell offered a possible explanation for why Shell in 1974 acted out of step with, not only the trade usage and commercially reasonable practices of all suppliers to the asphaltic paving trade on Oahu, but also with its previous agreement with, or at least treatment of, Nanakuli. . . .

V

The validity of the jury verdict in this case depends on four legal questions. First, how broad was the trade to whose usages Shell was bound under its 1969 agreement with Nanakuli: did it extend to the Hawaiian asphaltic paving trade or was it limited merely to the purchase and sale of asphalt, which would only include evidence of practices by Shell and Chevron? Second, were the two instances of price protection of Nanakuli by Shell in 1970 and 1971 waivers of the 1969 contract as a matter of law or was the jury entitled to find that they constituted a course of performance of the contract? Third, could the jury have construed an express contract term of Shell's posted price at delivery as reasonably consistent with a trade usage and Shell's course of performance of the 1969 contract of price protection, which consisted of charging the old price at times of price increases, either for a period of time or for specific tonnage committed at a fixed price in non-escalating contracts? Fourth, could the jury have found that good faith obliged Shell to at least give advance notice of a $32 increase in 1974, that is, could they have found that the commercially reasonable standards of fair dealing in the trade in Hawaii in 1974 were to give some form of price protection?

We approach the first issue in this case mindful that an underlying purpose of the U.C.C. as enacted in Hawaii is to allow for liberal interpretation of commercial usages. The Code provides, "This chapter shall be liberally construed and applied to promote its underlying purposes and policies." Haw. Rev. Stat. §490:1-102(1). Only three purposes are listed, one of which is "[t]o permit the continued expansion of commercial practices through custom, usage and agreement of the parties. . . . " Id. §490:1-102(2)(b). . . .

The Code defines usage of trade as "any practice or method of dealing having such regularity of observance in a *place, vocation or trade* as to justify an expectation that it will be observed with respect to the transaction in question." Id. §490:1-205(2) (emphasis supplied). We understand the use of the word "or" to mean that parties can be bound by a usage common to the *place* they are in business, even if it is not the usage of their particular vocation or trade. That reading is borne out by the repetition of the disjunctive "or" in subsection 3, which provides that usages "in the vocation or trade in which they are engaged *or* of which they are or should be aware give particular meaning to and supplement or qualify terms of an agreement." Id. §490:1-205(3). The drafters' Comments say that trade usage is to be used to reach the " . . . commercial meaning of the agreement. . . . " by interpreting the language "as meaning what it may fairly be expected to mean to parties involved in the particular transaction *in a given locality or* in a given *vocation or trade.*" Id., Comment 4 (emphasis supplied). The inference of the two subsections and the Comment, read together, is that a usage need not necessarily be one practiced by members of the party's own trade or vocation to be binding *if* it is so commonly practiced in a locality that a party should be aware of it. . . . This language indicates that Shell would be bound not only by usages of sellers of asphalt but by more general usages on Oahu, as long as those usages were so regular in their observance that Shell should have been aware of them. This reading of the Code, in our opinion, achieves an equitable result. A party is always held to conduct generally observed by members of his chosen trade because the other party is justified in so assuming unless he indicates otherwise. He is held to more general business practices to the extent of his actual knowledge of those practices or to the degree his ignorance of those practices is not excusable: they were so generally practiced he should have been aware of them.

[The court then cites two leading treatises — Corbin on Contracts and White & Summers, Uniform Commercial Code — to support its interpretation. — EDS.]. [Thus,] even if Shell did not "regularly deal" with aggregate supplies, it did deal constantly and almost exclusively on Oahu with one asphalt paver. It therefore should have been aware of the usage of Nanakuli and other asphaltic pavers to bid at fixed prices and therefore receive price protection from their materials suppliers due to the refusal by government agencies to accept escalation clauses. Therefore, we do not find the lower court abused its discretion or misread the Code as applied to the peculiar facts of this case in ruling that the applicable trade was the asphaltic paving trade in Hawaii. . . .

Shell argued not only that the definition of trade was too broad, but also that the practice itself was not sufficiently regular to reach the level of a usage and that Nanakuli failed to show with enough precision how the usage was carried out in order for a jury to calculate damages. The extent of a usage is ultimately a jury question. The Code provides, "The existence and scope of such a usage are to be proved as facts." Haw. Rev. Stat. §490:1-205(2). The practice must have "such regularity of observance . . . as to justify an expectation that it will be observed. . . . " Id. The Comment explains:

> The ancient English tests for "custom" are abandoned in this connection. Therefore, it is not required that a usage of trade be "ancient or immemorial," "universal" or the like. . . . [F]ull recognition is thus available for new usages and for usages currently observed by the great majority of decent dealers, even though dissidents ready to cut corners do not agree.

Id., Comment 5. The Comment's demand that "not universality but only the described 'regularity of observance' " is required reinforces the provision only giving "effect to usages of which the parties 'are or should be aware.' . . . " Id., Comment 7. A "regularly observed" practice of protection, of which Shell "should have been aware," was enough to constitute a usage that Nanakuli had reason to believe was incorporated into the agreement.[28]

Nanakuli went beyond proof of a regular observance. It proved and offered to prove that price protection was probably a universal practice by suppliers to the asphaltic paving trade in 1969. It had been practiced by H.C. & D. since at least 1962, by P.C. & A. since well before 1960, and by Chevron routinely for years, with the last specific instance before the contract being March, 1969, as shown by documentary evidence. The only usage evidence missing was the behavior by Shell, the only other asphalt supplier in Hawaii, prior to 1969. That was because its only major customer was Nanakuli and the judge ruled prior course of dealings between Shell and Nanakuli inadmissible. Shell did not point in rebuttal to one instance of failure to price protect by any supplier to an asphalt paver in Hawaii before its own 1974 refusal to price protect Nanakuli. Thus, there clearly was enough proof for a jury to find that the practice of price protection in the asphaltic paving trade existed in Hawaii in 1969 and was regular enough in its observance to rise to the level of a usage that would be binding on Nanakuli and Shell.

Shell next argues that, even if such a usage existed, its outlines were not precise enough to determine whether Shell would have extended the old price for Nanakuli for several months or would have charged the old price on the volume of tonnage committed at that price. The jury awarded Nanakuli damages based on the specific tonnage committed before the price increase of 1974. Shell says the jury could not have ascertained with enough certainty how price protection was carried out to calculate such an award for Nanakuli. The argument is not persuasive. The Code provides, "The remedies provided by this chapter shall be liberally administered to the end that the aggrieved party may be put in as good a position as if the other party had fully performed. . . . " Id. §490:1-106(1). The Comments list as one of three purposes of this section "to reject any doctrine that damages must be calculable with mathematical accuracy. Compensatory damages are often at best approximate: they have to be proved with whatever definiteness and accuracy the facts permit, but no more." Id., Comment 1. Nanakuli got advance notices of each but the disputed increase by Shell, as well as an extension of several months at the old price in 1970, 1971, 1977, and 1978. Shell protests that in 1970 and 1971 Nanakuli's protected tonnage only amounted to 3,300 and 1,100 tons, respectively. Chevron's price protection of H.B. in 1969 however, is also part of the trade usage; H.B.'s protection amounted to 12,000 tons. The increase in Nanakuli's tonnage by 1974 is explained by its growth since the 1970 and 1971 increases.

---

28. White and Summers write that Code requirements for proving a usage are "far less stringent" than the old ones for custom. "A usage of trade need not be *well known,* let alone 'universal.'" It only needs to be regular enough that the parties expect it to be observed. White & Summers, supra §3-3 at 87 (emphasis supplied). "Note particularly [in 1-205(1) & (2)] that it is not necessary for both parties to be consciously aware of the trade usage. It is enough if the trade usage is such as to 'justify an expectation' of its observance." Id. at 84.

In addition, the scope of protection offered by a particular usage is left to the jury. . . . The manner in which the usage of price protection was carried out was presented with sufficient precision to allow the jury to calculate damages at $220,800.

VI

WAIVER OR COURSE OF PERFORMANCE

Course of performance under the Code is the action of the parties in carrying out the contract at issue, whereas course of dealing consists of relations between the parties *prior* to signing that contract. Evidence of the latter was excluded by the District Judge; evidence of the former consisted of Shell's price protection of Nanakuli in 1970 and 1971. Shell protested that the jury could not have found that those two instances of price protection amounted to a course of performance of its 1969 contract, relying on two Code comments. First, one instance does not constitute a course of performance. "A single occasion of conduct does not fall within the language of this section. . . . " Haw. Rev. Stat. §490:2-208, Comment 4. Although the Comment rules out one instance, it does not further delineate how many acts are needed to form a course of performance. The prior occasions here were only two, but they constituted the only occasions before 1974 that would call for such conduct. In addition, the language used by a top asphalt official of Shell in connection with the first price protection of Nanakuli indicated that Shell felt that Nanakuli was entitled to some form of price protection. On that occasion in 1970 Blee, who had negotiated the contract with Nanakuli and was familiar with exactly what terms Shell was bound to by that agreement, wrote of the need to "bargain" with Nanakuli over the extent of price protection to be given, indicating that some price protection was a legal right of Nanakuli's under the 1969 agreement.

Shell's second defense is that the Comment expresses a preference for an interpretation of waiver. . . . Id., Comment 3. The preference for waiver only applies, however, where acts are ambiguous. It was within the province of the jury to determine whether those acts were ambiguous, and if not, whether they constituted waivers or a course of performance of the contract. The jury's interpretation of those acts as a course of performance was bolstered by evidence offered by Shell that it again price protected Nanakuli on the only two occasions of post-1974 price increases, in 1977 and 1978.

VII

EXPRESS TERMS AS REASONABLY CONSISTENT
WITH USAGE AND COURSE OF PERFORMANCE

Perhaps one of the most fundamental departures of the Code from prior contract law is found in the parol evidence rule and the definition of an agreement between two parties. Under the U.C.C., an agreement goes beyond the written words on a piece of paper. " 'Agreement' means the bargain of the parties in fact as found in their language or by implication from other circumstances including course of dealing or usage of trade or course of performance as provided in this chapter (sections 490:1-205 and 490:2-208)." Id. §490:1-201(3). Express terms, then, do not constitute the entire agreement, which must be sought also in evidence of usages, dealings, and performance of the contract itself. The purpose of evidence of usages, which are defined in the previous section, is to help to understand the entire agreement. . . . Id. §490: 1-205, Comment 4. Course of dealing is more important than usages of the trade, being specific usages between the two parties to the contract. "[C]ourse of dealing controls usage of trade." Id. §490:1-205(4). It "is a sequence of previous conduct between the parties to a particular transaction which is fairly to be regarded as establishing a common basis of understanding for interpreting their expressions and other conduct." Id. §490:1-205(1). Much of the evidence of prior dealings between Shell and Nanakuli in negotiating the 1963 contract and in carrying out similar earlier contracts was excluded by the court.

A commercial agreement, then, is broader than the written paper and its meaning is to be determined not just by the language used by them in the written contract but "by their action, read and interpreted in the light of commercial practices and other surrounding circumstances. The measure and background for interpretation are set by the commercial context, which may explain and supplement even the language of a formal or final writing." Id., Comment 1. Performance, usages, and prior dealings are important enough to be admitted always, even for a final and complete agreement; only if they cannot be reasonably reconciled with the express terms of the contract are they not binding on the parties. "The express terms of an agreement and an applicable course of dealing or usage of trade shall be construed wherever reasonable as consistent with each other; but when such construction is unreasonable express terms control both course of dealing and usage of trade and course of dealing controls usage of trade." Id. §490:1-205(4).

Of these three, then, [i.e., course of performance, course of dealing, and usage of trade — EDS.] the most important evidence of the agreement of the parties is their actual performance of the contract. Id. The operative definition of course of performance is as follows: "Where the contract for sale involves repeated occasions for performance by either party with knowledge of the nature of the performance and opportunity for objection to it by the other, any course of performance accepted or acquiesced in without objection shall be relevant to determine the meaning of the agreement." Id. §490:2-208(1). "Course of dealing . . . is restricted, literally, to a sequence of conduct between the parties previous to the agreement. However, the provisions of the Act on course of performance make it clear that a sequence of conduct after or under the agreement may have equivalent meaning (Section 2-208)." Id. 490:1-205, Comment 2. The importance of evidence of course of performance is explained: "The parties themselves know best what they have meant by their words of agreement and their action under that agreement is the best indication of what that meaning was. This section thus rounds out the set of factors which determines the meaning of the 'agreement.' . . . " Id. §490:2-208, Comment 1. "Under this section a course of performance is always relevant to determine the meaning of the agreement." Id., Comment 2.[33]

---

33. Section 2-208, much like 1-205, provides "[t]he express terms of the agreement and any such course of performance, as well as any course of dealing and usage of trade, shall be construed whenever reasonable as consistent with each other; but when such construction is unreasonable, express terms shall control course of performance and course of performance shall control both course of dealing and usage of trade (section 490:1-205)." Id. §490:2-208(2).

Our study of the Code provisions and Comments, then, form the first basis of our holding that a trade usage to price protect pavers at times of price increases for work committed on nonescalating contracts could reasonably be construed as consistent with an express term of seller's posted price at delivery. Since the agreement of the parties is broader than the express terms and includes usages, which may even add terms to the agreement,[34] and since the commercial background provided by those usages is vital to an understanding of the agreement, we follow the Code's mandate to proceed on the assumption that the parties have included those usages unless they cannot reasonably be construed as consistent with the express terms. . . .

[The Court then reviews a number of federal and state decisions holding that trade usage, course of dealing, and course of performance should be freely admitted. — EDS.]

Some guidelines can be offered as to how usage evidence can be allowed to modify a contract.[44] First, the court must allow a check on usage evidence by demanding that it be sufficiently definite and widespread to prevent unilateral post-hoc revision of contract terms by one party. The Code's intent is to put usage evidence on an objective basis. J. H. Levie, Trade Usage and Custom Under the Common Law and the Uniform Commercial Code, 40 N.Y.U.L. Rev. 1101 (1965), states:

> When trade usage adds new terms to cover matters on which the agreement is silent the court is really making a contract for the parties, even though it says it only consulted trade usage to find the parties' probable intent. There is nothing wrong or even unusual about this practice, which really is no different from reading constructive conditions into a contract. Nevertheless the court does create new obligations, and perhaps that is why the courts often say that usage . . . must be proved by clear and convincing evidence. . . .

Id. at 1102. Although the Code abandoned the traditional common law test of nonconsensual custom and views usage as a way of determining the parties'

---

34. "The agreement of the parties includes that part of their bargain found in course of dealing, usage of trade, or course of performance. These sources are relevant not only to the interpretation of express contract terms, but may themselves constitute contract terms." White & Summers, supra, §3-3 at 84.

44. White and Summers write that usage and dealings evidence "may not only supplement or qualify express terms, but in appropriate circumstances may even override express terms." White & Summers, supra, §3-3 at 84. "[T]he provision that express terms control inconsistent course of dealing and [usages and performance evidence] really cannot be taken at face value." Id. at 86. That reading, although at odds with the actual wording of the Code, is a realistic reading of what some of the cases allow. A better formulation of the Code's mandate is offered by R. W. Kirst, Usage of Trade and Course of Dealing: Subversion of the UCC Theory, 1977 [U. Ill.] Law Forum 811:

> The need to determine whether the parties intended a usage . . . to be part of the contract does not end if the court finds that the commercial practice is inconsistent with or contradicts the express language of the writing. If an inconsistency exists, the intention of the parties remains unclear. The parties may have intended either to include or exclude the practice. Determining the intent of the parties requires that the court attempt to construe the written term consistently with the commercial practice, if that is reasonable. If consistent construction is unreasonable the Code directs that the written term be taken as expressing the parties' intent. Before concluding that a jury could not reasonably find a consistent construction, the judge must understand the commercial background of the dispute.

Id. at 824.

probable intent, id. at 1106-07, thus abolishing the requirement that common law custom be universally practiced, trade usages still must be well settled, id. at 1113. . . .

Evidence of a trade usage does not need to be protected against perjury because, as one commentator has written, "an outside standard does exist to help judge the truth of the assertion that the parties intended the usage to control the particular dispute: the existence and scope of the usage can be determined from other members of the trade." Kirst, supra, at 839. Kirst sets out guards on jury determination of usage evidence:

> Questions of the parties' intentions concerning an asserted trade usage or course of dealing will not always require a jury determination. If the evidence fails to show a practice is regularly observed, the judge can exclude the evidence because it does not show a course of dealing or usage of trade as defined in the Code. If the members of the trade confirm an actual usage but do not support the assertion that the usage applies to the particular facts in litigation, the judge will exclude evidence of the usage as irrelevant. If the parties used new and different language to convey their agreed intention to abandon the past practice, the court will recognize that practice under the old language is irrelevant to the contract containing the new language and, consequently, will exclude the evidence.

. . . That formulation of relevance of the usage evidence seems a fair one to follow in this case. Here the evidence was overwhelming that all suppliers to the asphaltic paving trade price protected customers under the same types of circumstances. Chevron's contract with H.B. was a similar long-term supply contract between a buyer and seller with very close relations, on a form supplied by the seller, covering sales of asphalt, and setting the price at seller's posted price, with no mention of price protection. The same commentator offers a second guideline:

> Because the stock printed forms cannot always reflect the changing methods of business, members of the trade may do business with a standard clause in the forms that they ignore in practice. If the trade consistently ignores obsolete clauses at variance with actual trade practices, a litigant can maintain that it is reasonable that the courts also ignore the clauses. Similarly, members of a trade may handle a particular subset of commercial transactions in a manner consistent [sic: inconsistent?] with written terms because the writing cannot provide for all variations or contingencies. Thus, if the trade regards an express term and a trade usage as consistent because the usage is not a complete contradiction but only an occasional but definite exception to a written term, the courts should interpret the contract according to the usage.

Kirst, supra, at 824. Levie, supra, at 1112, writes, "Astonishing as it will seem to most practicing attorneys, under the Code it will be possible in some cases to use custom to contradict the written agreement. . . . Therefore usage may be used to 'qualify' the agreement, which presumably means to 'cut down' express terms although not to negate them entirely." Here, the express price term was "Shell's Posted Price at time of delivery." A total negation of that term would be that the buyer was to set the price. It is a less than complete negation of the term that an unstated exception exists at times of price increases, at which times the old price is to be charged, for a certain period or for a specified tonnage, on work already committed at the lower price on nonescalating contracts. Such a usage forms a broad and important exception to the express term, but does not swallow it entirely. Therefore, we hold that, under these particular facts, a reasonable jury could have found that price protection was incorporated into the 1969 agreement between Nanakuli and Shell and that price protection was reasonably consistent with the express term of seller's posted price at delivery.

VIII

GOOD FAITH IN SETTING PRICE

Nanakuli offers an alternative theory why Shell should have offered price protection at the time of the price increases of 1974. Even if price protection was not a term of the agreement, Shell could not have exercised good faith in carrying out its 1969 contract with Nanakuli when it raised its price by $32 effective January 1 in a letter written December 31st and only received on January 4, given the universal practice of advance notice of such an increase in the asphaltic paving trade. The Code provides, "A price to be fixed by the seller or by the buyer means a price for him to fix in good faith," Haw. Rev. Stat. §490:2-305(2). For a merchant good faith means "the observance of reasonable commercial standards of fair dealing in the trade." Id. 490:2-103 (1)(b). The comment to Section 2-305 explains, "[I]n the normal case a 'posted price' . . . satisfies the good faith requirement." Id., Comment 3. However, the words "in the normal case" mean that, although a posted price will usually be satisfactory, it will not be so under all circumstances. In addition, the dispute here was not over the amount of the increase — that is, the price that the seller fixed — but over the manner in which that increase was put into effect. It is true that Shell, in order to observe the good faith standards of the trade in 1974, was not bound by the practices of aggregate companies, which did not labor under the same disabilities as did asphalt suppliers in 1974. However, Nanakuli presented evidence that Chevron, in raising its price to $76, gave at least six weeks' advance notice, in accord with the long-time usage of the asphaltic paving trade. Shell, on the other hand, gave absolutely no notice, from which the jury could have concluded that Shell's manner of carrying out the price increase of 1974 did not conform to commercially reasonable standards. In both the timing of the announcement and its refusal to protect work already bid at the old price, Shell could be found to have breached the obligation of good faith imposed by the Code on all merchants. "Every contract or duty within this chapter imposes an obligation of good faith in its performance or enforcement," id. §490:1-203, which for merchants entails the observance of commercially reasonable standards of fair dealing in the trade. The Comment to 1-203 reads:

> This section sets forth a basic principle running throughout this Act. The principle involved is that in commercial transactions good faith is required in the performance and enforcement of all agreements or duties. Particular applications of this general principle appear in specific provisions of the Act. . . . It is further implemented by Section 1-205 on course of dealing and usage of trade.

Id. §490:1-203, Comment. Chevron's conduct in 1974 offered enough relevant evidence of commercially reasonable standards of fair dealing in the asphalt trade in Hawaii in 1974 for the jury to find that Shell's failure to give sufficient advance notice and price protect Nanakuli after the imposition of the new price did not conform to good faith dealings in Hawaii at that time.

Because the jury could have found for Nanakuli on its price protection claim under either theory, we reverse the judgment of the District Court and reinstate the jury verdict for Nanakuli in the amount of $220,800, plus interest according to law.

Reversed and remanded with directions to enter final judgment.

KENNEDY, Circuit Judge, concurring specially:

The case involves specific pricing practices, not an allegation of unfair dealing generally. Our opinion should not be interpreted to permit juries to import price protection or a similarly specific contract term from a concept of good faith that is not based on well-established custom and usage or other objective standards of which the parties had clear notice. Here, evidence of custom and usage regarding price protection in the asphaltic paving trade was not contradicted in major respects, and the jury could find that the parties knew or should have known of the practice at the time of making the contract. In my view, these are necessary predicates for either theory of the case, namely, interpretation of the contract based on the course of its performance or a finding that good faith required the seller to hold the price. With these observations, I concur.

Notes and Questions

1. *Defining usage of trade and related concepts.* In its opinion the court discusses usage of trade, course of dealing, and course of performance. See UCC §§1-205(2) (trade usage); 1-205(1) (course of dealing); and 2-208 (course of performance). (All three concepts are defined in Revised UCC §1-303.) The Restatement contains provisions that are similar to these Code provisions. Restatement (Second) §§222 (trade usage), 223 (course of dealing), and 202(4) (course of performance). How are these concepts different from one another? Which is most important in interpreting a contract? Why?

2. *Burden of proof.* As *Nanakuli* indicates, evidence of trade usage is only admissible if the party offering the evidence establishes that the usage exists. What is the burden of proof necessary to establish the existence of a trade usage? Who makes the determination of whether the usage exists? On these points, compare *Nanakuli* with *Frigaliment* (section A of this chapter).

3. *Scope of relevant trade.* How did the court define the trade to whose usages Shell was bound? Was Shell a member of that trade? What test does the court employ to decide when a party to a contract is bound by a trade usage? In Flower City Painting Contractors, Inc. v. Gumina Construction Co., 591 F.2d 162 (2d Cir. 1979), the Second Circuit Court of Appeals held that a painting subcontractor, a newcomer to the painting business, was not bound by a trade usage that the term "units" included not only apartment interiors but exteriors and common buildings as well. Is *Flower City Painting* consistent

with *Nanakuli?* Professor Elizabeth Warren, relying on principles of economic analysis, has argued that if both parties to a contract are members of a trade, both should be bound by usages of the trade, even if one of the parties did not know of the usage. Elizabeth Warren, Trade Usage and Parties in the Trade: An Economic Rationale for an Inflexible Rule, 42 U. Pitt. L. Rev. 515 (1981).

4. *Consistency between trade usage and express terms.* Courts are divided on the issue of when evidence of trade usage, course of dealing, or course of performance is admissible. Some courts adopt a restrictive view, holding that such evidence is inadmissible if it appears to contradict the terms of the written agreement between the parties. Southern Concrete Services, Inc. v. Mableton Contractors, Inc., 407 F. Supp. 581 (N.D. Ga. 1975), *aff'd per curiam,* 569 F.2d 1154 (5th Cir. 1978) (evidence of trade usage showing that quantity term of contract was not binding on either buyer or seller was inadmissible); Trent Partners and Associates, Inc. v. Digital Equipment Corp., 120 F. Supp. 2d 84 (D. Mass. 1999) (trade usage must be construed as consistent with express terms if possible; express terms must control any inconsistent trade usage).

Other courts have gone to the opposite extreme, holding that such evidence is almost always admissible, even if it appears, as suggested by the *Nanakuli* court, that the trade usage "cuts down" the express terms. Tigg Corp. v. Dow Corning Corp., 822 F.2d 358 (3d Cir. 1987) (evidence of trade usage admissible to show that agreement should be regarded as contract for buyer's requirements, despite stated minimums in writing; no requirement that written contract be found ambiguous before such evidence admitted); Chase Manhattan Bank v. First Marion Bank, 437 F.2d 1040 (5th Cir. 1971) (evidence of trade usage or course of dealing between banks showing that duration of subordination agreements extended until repayment of lead lender was admissible even though express terms of subordination agreement provided for duration of only 18 months; such evidence was necessary to understand the context in which the agreement was made); Hayter Trucking, Inc., v. Shell Western E & P, Inc., 22 Cal. Rptr. 2d 229 (Ct. App. 1993) (extrinsic evidence of custom and practice in oil industry to permit termination of vacuum truck service contracts only "for cause" was admissible to explain or supplement terms of integrated agreement, even though agreement contained broad termination provision). The all-or-nothing approach to such evidence reflected in these cases has been criticized by Professor Roger Kirst in an article cited extensively by the court in *Nanakuli.* What is the approach that Professor Kirst advocates and how does it differ from the methods used by the courts that he criticizes?

5. *"Careful negation" of trade usage.* Can parties to a contract negate the effect of a trade usage or a prior course of dealing by express contractual language? Professor Kirst argues that mere "boilerplate" language generally negating the effect of trade usage or course of dealing should not be conclusive; to give it that effect would elevate form over the actual intent of the parties. Roger W. Kirst, Usage of Trade and Course of Dealing: Subversion of the UCC Theory, 1977 U. Ill. L.F. 811, 863-868; accord, Amy H. Kastely, Stock Equipment for the Bargain in Fact: Trade Usage, "Express Terms," and Consistency under Section 1-205 of the Uniform Commercial Code, 64 N.C.L. Rev. 777 (1986). Professor Kirst

would agree, however, that a clause that specifically negates a particular trade usage or course of dealing may be given effect. Consider Allapattah Services, Inc. v. Exxon Corp., 61 F. Supp. 2d 1308 (S.D. Fla. 1999) (typical merger clause does not suffice to negate importance of trade usage and course of dealing); A&A Mechanical, Inc. v. Thermal Equipment Sales, Inc., 998 S.W.2d 505 (Ky. Ct. App. 1999) (typical merger clause will not bar evidence of trade usage, course of dealing and course of performance; excluding term must specifically refer to such evidence); and UCC §2-202, Comment 2 (course of performance, course of dealing, and usage of trade part of agreement unless "carefully negated"); but see Madison Industries, Inc. v. Eastman Kodak Co., 581 A.2d 85 (N.J. Super. Ct. App. Div. 1990) (evidence of trade usage excluded where contract provided in general language that no course of dealing, course of performance, or usage of trade should be effective unless in a writing signed by authorized agents of both parties).

6. *The **Nanakuli** case as an exemplar of "modern" contract law.* The *Nanakuli* case was decided in 1981, a time that can with hindsight be seen as a highwater mark for the kind of "modern" contract law developed over roughly the middle half of the twentieth century. See generally Charles L. Knapp, An Offer You Can't Revoke, 2004 Wis. L. Rev. 309, 316-319 (listing some characteristics of "modern" contract law). The seeming modern consensus formed by the convergence of UCC Article 2 and the Restatement (Second) of Contracts has since splintered, however, under the dual onslaught of Critical Legal Studies from the left and Law and Economics from the right. Professor DiMatteo has characterized *Nanakuli* as displaying for the most part an embrace of full "contextualism"—the interpretation and enforcement of contracts in light of the commercial setting of the transaction, the aims of the parties and the real-world context of the case, as advocated by Karl Llewellyn and other legal realists. Larry A. DiMatteo, Reason and Context: A Dual Track Theory of Interpretation, 109 Penn. St. L. Rev. 397, 471-474 (2004). Others have seen in the *Nanakuli* case an illustration of the kind of "relational" contract law advocated by Ian Macneil. Peter Linzer, Uncontracts: Context, Contorts and the Relational Approach, 1988 Ann. Surv. of Amer. L. 139, 155-160, 182-185.

7. *Other scholarly commentary.* Professor Eyal Zamir has called on courts to reverse their traditional approach to contract interpretation. Eyal Zamir, The Inverted Hierarchy of Contract Interpretation and Supplementation, 97 Colum. L. Rev. 1710 (1997). According to Zamir, the traditional approach involves a hierarchy in which courts give the greatest weight to the language practices. Zamir argues that the hierarchy should be reversed to give preference to standards of reasonableness and good faith, default rules (gap fillers), and trade usages. The reversal of the hierarchy is warranted, Zamir claims, for several reasons; First, the reversed hierarchy conforms better to the intention of the parties than a literalistic enforcement of the words of any document the parties may have executed.

> In many cases, the contract document is drafted by lawyers. Whether it is drafted by the lawyers of both parties, or by one party's lawyer, it is usually phrased in legal language, using terminology that laypersons—consumers and merchants alike—do not fully understand. In the case of detailed standard-form contracts, customers

frequently do not bother to read most of the provisions of the form, focusing instead on a few central issues such as price and time of delivery. . . .

. . . [I]f it is true that typically there is a gap between the words of the formal contract and the actual understandings and intentions of the parties — a claim sustained by empirical findings — then the interpreter's concentration on the formal contract may actually frustrate the goal of realizing these intentions and understandings.

Id. at 1771-1773.

Second, contract law should properly be viewed, Zamir argues, as public rather than private law because it involves the use of the power of the state to coerce a party into performance of an agreement that the party no longer wishes to honor. Viewed from this public perspective, social principles, such as good faith and fair dealing, should be primary factors in resolving contractual disputes. Id at 1777–1778. Finally, a proper application of principles of economic analysis supports a reversal of the traditional approach to contract interpretation. From an economic prespective, the law should attempt to maximize social utility, not necessarily promote individual preferences. Id at 1801.

PROBLEM 5-1

A & B Tax Preparers, Inc. is a corporation engaged in the nationwide business of preparing state and federal income tax returns. In 2003 Herbert Keynes, a resident of Minneapolis, answered A & B's advertisement seeking a local manager for its Neville, California office. After investigating Keynes's background and interviewing him personally, A & B offered Keynes the position of manager of the Neville office. Keynes signed one of the company's printed forms it uses for hiring managers. (A copy of the contract follows this problem; portions in italic are handwritten.)

After signing the contract, Keynes resigned his job in Minneapolis and moved to Neville. Over the next several years the Neville office became very successful. Keynes's share of profits increased from approximately $30,000 in 2004 to over $90,000 for the year ending January 31, 2006.

In September 2006, Keynes received a letter from A & B in which the company stated that effective February 1, 2007, his percentage of net profits would be reduced from 50 percent to 40 percent. The letter referred to paragraph 6.1 of the policy manual of the company, which provided as follows:

6.1 Compensation of Managers. Profit percentages for managers are guaranteed only for the first two years of employment. The Company reserves the right to adjust percentages in subsequent years based on the profitability of the local branch.

The letter stated that Keynes should sign and return the letter to A & B by October 15, 2006. Keynes telephoned Henry Adams, the president of the company, to complain about this change, saying that he understood that the company would not unilaterally change his profit percentage.

Adams responded that Keynes had received a copy of the policy manual and that he assumed Keynes had read and understood it. Adams also said that considering the growth in profits of the Neville branch, Keynes's income should continue to increase, even though Keynes would be receiving a lower percentage of the profits. Keynes wasn't satisfied with these answers and told Adams that he wouldn't agree to the change. Adams said that Keynes did not have a choice and that if he did not return the letter by October 15, the company would be forced to terminate the agreement.

Keynes ignored Adams's threats and refused to sign the letter. On October 20, 2006, Keynes received a letter from A & B informing him that the company was terminating his contract as manager effective immediately. The company has now brought suit against Keynes seeking an injunction to prevent him from using the company's name and property; Keynes has filed counterclaims for damages and injunctive relief.

During the direct examination of Mr. Keynes at trial the following takes place:

Keynes's lawyer:	Mr. Keynes, did you have a telephone conversation with Mr. Adams on December 14, 2003?
A & B's lawyer:	Objection, your honor. Parol evidence rule.
Judge:	Bailiff, please escort the jury out of the courtroom. [After the jury leaves] All right, counsel, what will the testimony show?
Keynes's lawyer:	Your honor, Mr. Keynes will testify that he called Mr. Adams on December 14, 2003 and the parties discussed paragraph 6.1 of the manual. Mr. Keynes will testify that he told Mr. Adams that he did not think that it would be fair for him to resign his job, move to Neville, build up the business, and then have the company arbitrarily increase its share of the profits. Mr. Keynes will also testify that Adams told him that if he did a good job he didn't need to worry about the company increasing its share of profits. He said that the company had only increased its percentage of profits in the past when a manager had not met company projections of profitability. Mr. Keynes will also testify that he asked Adams to put that in writing but that Adams refused because he said the company's lawyers had told him not to have any side agreements.
Judge:	[Speaking to counsel for A & B] I'll hear you now, counsel.

As counsel for A & B, what arguments would you make against admissibility of the evidence? As counsel for Keynes, what arguments would you make to admit the evidence? As judge, how would you rule on A & B's objection?

MANAGER'S CONTRACT

Agreement made and entered into this *17th* day of *December, 2003*, by and between *Herbert Keynes* (hereinafter referred to as "Manager") and A & B Tax Preparers, Inc. (hereinafter referred to as "Company").

In consideration of the mutual covenants contained in this document, the parties hereby agree as follows:

1. **Employment and Duties.** Company hereby employs Manager to manage its office at *Neville, California*. Manager agrees to operate the office in accordance with the provisions of the Company's policy manual, a copy of which has previously been

given to Manager. Company reserves the right to change the provisions of the manual at any time. The provisions of the manual, as modified from time to time, are incorporated by reference as part of this contract.

2. **Compensation.** As compensation for his services, Manager shall be entitled to 50% of the net profits of the office, after deduction of all expenses of the office.

3. **Accounting and Inspection of Records.** Manager shall remit to the Company on the fifteenth and last days of each month the Company's share of profits of the office, along with an income statement for such period certified by the Manager to be correct. The Company reserves the right to audit the books and records of the office at any time.

4. **Termination.** This agreement shall continue for a two-year period from *January 31, 2004* until *January 31, 2006*. The agreement shall automatically renew for additional two-year periods until either party gives written notice of termination at least ninety days prior to the end of any such two-year period. The Company reserves the right to terminate this agreement at any time for cause.

5. **Entire Agreement.** This document constitutes the entire agreement of the parties. The Company makes no representations, warranties, or guarantees of any kind whatsoever.

6. **Additional Provisions.**

The Company agrees to pay Keynes's moving expenses to Neville, California in an amount not to exceed $7,000.

In witness whereof, the parties have executed this agreement on the day and year first above written.

A & B Tax Preparers, Inc.

By: */s/ Henry Adams*
Henry Adams, Pres.

By: */s/ Herbert Keynes*
Signature of Manager

PROBLEM 5-2

Pursuant to an urban redevelopment plan, the city of Northeast "condemned" property located at 1416 F Street for $2.5 million, the fair market value of the property at the time of the condemnation. (In condemnation proceedings, either a government agency or someone acting pursuant to governmental authority acquires privately owned property to be used for a public purpose. The owner is entitled to receive fair market value for her property. Although the condemnor and owner frequently reach agreement for a voluntary transfer of the property, the property may be taken against the owner's will. Condemnation proceedings are controlled by statutory provisions which vary from state to state.)

At the time of the taking, the property was owned by Janice N. Owens, a local real estate developer, and was under a 30-year lease (expiring October 31, 2020) to Metropolitan Parking, Inc., which used the property for a parking garage.

Owens claims that the entire condemnation award properly belongs to her as owner of the property, while Metropolitan claims that it is entitled to a portion of the award measured by the fair market value of its leasehold interest. Because of the dispute between Owens and Metropolitan, the city has paid the condemnation award into court for a judicial determination of the distribution of the condemnation award.

The lease between Owens and Metropolitan does not specifically mention condemnation; it contains the following clauses:

ARTICLE I

Definitions

For the purposes hereof, unless the context otherwise requires: . . .

Section 1.04. Any reference herein to the termination of this lease shall be deemed to include any termination hereof by expiration, default, or otherwise. . . .

ARTICLE XX

Section 20.01. Upon termination of this lease by default, lapse of time, or for any reason, all of the right, title, and interest of Lessee in and to the premises and the leasehold estate created hereby shall automatically vest in Lessor without the execution of any further instrument.

(1) Assume you are a lawyer representing Metropolitan. What fact investigation would you undertake in preparing your case? Be prepared to explain why the factual questions you would investigate would be significant.

(2) Assume you know no facts other than those stated above. What arguments would you make in support of Metropolitan's claim to a share of the condemnation award?

(3) Assume you represent Owens. What arguments would you make in support of her claim to the entire condemnation award?

(4) Assume you represent a tenant who is negotiating a lease of property. Draft a clause to include in the agreement that would protect the tenant against the risk of loss resulting from condemnation.

6 | Supplementing the Agreement: Implied Terms, the Obligation of Good Faith, and Warranties

Up to this point, we have generally concentrated on the problem of discovering and applying the agreement of the parties. As Chapter 5 demonstrated, the parties' true "agreement" may involve more than their formal written expressions of agreement; it may be found as well in their informal writings and in their conversations, or even in their actions. And all of these may be interpreted in the light of the parties' own dealings, past and present, and of the customs and mores of the community in which they were acting. In this chapter we will widen our field of vision still further, to take in the possibility that the "contract" (meaning, here, set of legal obligations) that the court enforces in a given case will include not merely those terms on which the parties have thus "agreed," but also other terms, which the court finds to be "implied" in that agreement.

A. THE RATIONALE FOR IMPLIED TERMS

The phrase *implied term* is itself ambiguous, of course. In one sense, any term that the court finds to be "implicit" in the parties' words or conduct even though not literally expressed by them is an implied term—implied, in fact, by the parties themselves. In this chapter, we will be using the notion of an implied term to refer also to a term that the court does not find in the parties' agreement, even as broadly viewed, but that the court holds should be "implied by law"—made a part of that agreement by operation of the rules of law rather than by the agreement of the parties themselves. Sometimes a term will be implied (in this latter sense) because a statute so provides; sometimes because common law precedents dictate, or because the court concludes that in the particular case its implication is appropriate.

By the time our survey of this area has been completed, you may well conclude that the borderline between terms that are implied-in-fact (i.e., agreed to in some meaningful sense by the parties themselves) and implied-in-law

437

(imposed by the court) is not an easy one to draw. Certainly one of the reasons militating in favor of an implied-by-law term may be its apparent consistency with the intention of the parties, as evinced by those terms to which they did agree. Nevertheless, the process of implication is somewhat more complicated than this, and the goals this area of contract law may serve are more varied than merely an effectuating of the parties' own intent, as the following materials will demonstrate.

Wood v. Lucy, Lady Duff-Gordon
New York Court of Appeals
222 N.Y. 88, 118 N.E. 214 (1917)

Appeal from a judgment entered April 24, 1917, upon an order of the Appellate Division of the Supreme Court ... which reversed an order of Special Term denying a motion by defendant for judgment in her favor upon the pleadings and granted said motion. ...

CARDOZO, J. The defendant styles herself "a creator of fashions." Her favor helps a sale. Manufacturers of dresses, millinery and like articles are glad to pay for a certificate of her approval. The things which she designs, fabrics, parasols and what not, have a new value in the public mind when issued in her name. She employed the plaintiff to help her to turn this vogue into money. He was to have the exclusive right, subject always to her approval, to place her indorsements on the designs of others. He was also to have the exclusive right to place her own designs on sale, or to license others to market them. In return, she was to have one-half of "all profits and revenues" derived from any contracts he might make. The exclusive right was to last at least one year from April 1, 1915, and thereafter from year to year unless terminated by notice of ninety days. The plaintiff says that he kept the contract on his part, and that the defendant broke it. She placed her indorsement on fabrics, dresses and millinery without his knowledge, and withheld the profits. He sues her for the damages, and the case comes here on demurrer.

The agreement of employment is signed by both parties. It has a wealth of recitals. The defendant insists, however, that it lacks the elements of a contract. She says that the plaintiff does not bind himself to anything. It is true that he does not promise in so many words that he will use reasonable efforts to place the defendant's indorsements and market her designs. We think, however, that such a promise is fairly to be implied. The law has outgrown its primitive stage of formalism when the precise word was the sovereign talisman, and every slip was fatal. It takes a broader view to-day. A promise may be lacking, and yet the whole writing may be "instinct with an obligation," imperfectly expressed (Scott, J., in McCall Co. v. Wright, 133 App. Div. 62; Moran v. Standard Oil Co., 211 N.Y. 187, 198). If that is so, there is a contract.

The implication of a promise here finds support in many circumstances. The defendant gave an *exclusive* privilege. She was to have no right for at least a year to place her own indorsements or market her own designs except through the agency of the plaintiff. The acceptance of the exclusive agency was an assumption of its duties (Phoenix Hermetic Co. v. Filtrine Mfg. Co.,

164 App. Div. 424; W. G. Taylor Co. v. Bannerman, 120 Wis. 189; Mueller v. Bethesda Mineral Spring Co., 88 Mich. 390). We are not to suppose that one party was to be placed at the mercy of the other (Hearn v. Stevens & Bro., 111 App. Div. 101, 106; Russell v. Allerton, 108 N.Y. 288). Many other terms of the agreement point the same way. We are told at the outset by way of recital that "the said Otis F. Wood possesses a business organization adapted to the placing of such indorsements as the said Lucy, Lady Duff-Gordon has approved."

The implication is that the plaintiff's business organization will be used for the purpose for which it is adapted. But the terms of the defendant's compensation are even more significant. Her sole compensation for the grant of an exclusive agency is to be one-half of all the profits resulting from the plaintiff's efforts. Unless he gave his efforts, she could never get anything. Without an implied promise, the transaction cannot have such business "efficacy as both parties must have intended that at all events it should have" (Bowen, L.J., in The Moorcock, 14 P.D. 64, 68). But the contract does not stop there. The plaintiff goes on to promise that he will account monthly for all moneys received by him, and that he will take out all such patents and copyrights and trademarks as may in his judgment be necessary to protect the rights and articles affected by the agreement. It is true, of course, as the Appellate Division has said, that if he was under no duty to try to market designs or to place certificates of indorsement, his promise to account for profits or take out copyrights would be valueless. But in determining the intention of the parties, the promise *has* a value. It helps to enforce the conclusion that the plaintiff *had* some duties. His promise to pay the defendant one-half of the profits and revenues resulting from the exclusive agency and to render accounts monthly, was a promise to use reasonable efforts to bring profits and revenues into existence. For this conclusion, the authorities are ample. . . .

The judgment of the Appellate Division should be reversed, and the order of the Special Term affirmed, with costs in the Appellate Division and in this court.

CUDDEBACK, MCLAUGHLIN and ANDREWS, JJ., concur; HISCOCK, Ch. J., CHASE and CRANE, JJ., dissent.

Judgment reversed, etc.

Notes and Questions

1. *Factual context.* The historical and economic context of the *Wood* case is discussed by Professor Walter F. Pratt, Jr., in his article, American Contract Law at the Turn of the Century, 39 S.C. L. Rev. 415 (1988). Professor Pratt explains that Lady Duff-Gordon rose from a meager start in business to become one of the preeminent designers of her time and that she breached her exclusive marketing contract with Wood by directly entering into a very "innovative" arrangement to sell her designer dresses through the Sears, Roebuck and Company mail order catalogue. Id. at 429-430, 438-439. Professor Pratt identifies a number of other imaginative business measures taken by Lady Duff-Gordon and observes that she is also remembered for having survived the sinking of the Titanic. Id. at 419 n.14, 429-432.

2. *Implied terms and illusory promises.* In the course of his opinion for the court in *Wood,* Judge Cardozo declares that the implication of a promise on Wood's part is necessary to give the parties' agreement "business efficacy." "We are not to suppose," he declares, "that one party was to be placed at the mercy of the other." Do you agree? Is it conceivable that Lady Duff-Gordon might have regarded even an agreement that did *not* impose such obligations on Wood as having sufficient "business efficacy" from her point of view to make it worth entering into? Suppose the agreement between them had generally been as described in the above case, but that it had in addition expressly provided that while Wood was free to make efforts on her behalf (from which, if successful, he and she would both profit), he was not *obligated* to do so. Would such an agreement have been enforceable by Lady Duff-Gordon? By Wood? In an article discussing generally the requirement of consideration, Professor Melvin Eisenberg takes the position that agreements in which one party makes only a nonbinding, "illusory" promise frequently reflect a rational bargain and ought to be enforceable according to their terms. The party making the *non*illusory promise, he asserts, has in effect bargained for a "chance": the chance to show that his performance is attractive. (As an analogy, Eisenberg cites the "money-back" guarantee, by which the seller demonstrates his own confidence in his product by promising to refund the buyer's money if she is not satisfied for any reason. See UCC §2-326, defining the "sale on approval.") If one party was deceived into believing that he had indeed received a true promise in return, then Eisenberg suggests that the parties' promise should go unenforced on grounds of unconscionability. However, where the party who purchases an illusory promise knew what she was bargaining for — as Lady Duff-Gordon presumably would have known, in the above-assumed hypothetical variation of *Wood* — Eisenberg sees no reason to withhold enforcement of that party's genuine promise merely because the return promise is lacking in substance. Melvin A. Eisenberg, The Principles of Consideration, 67 Cornell L. Rev. 640, 649-651 (1982).

Recent decisions continue to follow the principle recognized in *Wood* that an implied obligation to use reasonable efforts will prevent a somewhat indefinite promise from being illusory. See Emerson Radio Corp. v. Orion Sales, Inc., 253 F.3d 159 (3rd Cir. 2001) (noting widespread adoption of reasoning in *Wood* by courts to impose implied obligation of reasonable efforts in exclusive license contracts); Magruder Quarry & Co., L.L.C. v. Briscoe, 83 S.W.3d 647 (Mo. Ct. App. 2002) (citing *Wood* in finding implied obligation to use reasonable efforts to mine and sell rock under quarry lease).

3. *When should a promise to use "reasonable" or "best efforts" be implied?* The *Wood* case is generally regarded as the genesis of the provision in UCC §2-306(2) that imposes a "best efforts" obligation in cases where the contract for sale calls for "exclusive dealing." See MDC Corp. v. John H. Harland Co., 228 F.Supp. 387, 393 n.3 (S.D.N.Y. 2002). In *Wood,* the defendant claimed that although their agreement obligated her to market her designs only through Wood, it left him apparently free to do nothing on her behalf, while at the same time representing whomever else he pleased. Such an arrangement would have lacked "business efficacy," according to Judge Cardozo, because it

would have effectively placed one party (Lucy) at the mercy of another (Wood), and therefore the court implied a duty on Wood's part to use reasonable efforts on Lucy's behalf. Cases under the Code have explored the extent to which an arrangement must be "exclusive" to trigger the best efforts obligation of §2-306(2). In *MDC*, the contract permitted a requirements seller to maintain certain other existing relationships with particular customers; the parties' relationship was nevertheless held to be sufficiently "exclusive" to obligate the requirements buyer to use its best efforts to generate a market for the seller's goods. MDC Corp, 228 F.Supp. at 394; see also Tigg Corp. v. Dow Corning Corp., 962 F.2d 1119, 1125 (3d Cir. 1992) (contract permitting supplier to sell to others if buyer failed to buy stated minimum amounts nevertheless held to be "exclusive dealing arrangement" invoking §2-306(2); once minimum was reached seller could sell only to buyer under their contract). Other aspects of the law's treatment of requirements contracts are discussed in the Comment that follows Seidenberg v. Summit Bank in the next section of this chapter.

4. *Assessing best or reasonable efforts.* In *Wood*, Lady Duff-Gordon made a promise to the plaintiff, which she subsequently failed to perform. (The *Wood* case came up on demurrer, so the truth of the plaintiff's allegations of fact had of course been assumed for the purpose of decision.) The potential barrier to enforcement of the exclusive arrangement inhered not in the lack of a commitment by Lady Duff-Gordon but in the asserted failure of Wood to make any commitment in return. Once Judge Cardozo and his colleagues had concluded that the plaintiff Wood did indeed assume an obligation, albeit an "implied" one, the court could proceed to enforcement of the defendant's express commitment. Suppose that the plaintiff in this case had instead been Lady Duff-Gordon, asserting that defendant Wood should respond in damages because allegedly he had failed to use reasonable efforts to promote the sale of her designs and endorsements. In that case, would the implied obligation assumed by Wood under their agreement have been sufficient to enable her complaint to survive defendant Wood's demurrer? If so, what obstacle would she still have faced before achieving her goal of recovering a judgment?

Parties frequently define an express obligation in terms of "best efforts" or "reasonable efforts." The court in *Wood* found an implied promise to use "reasonable efforts," while the UCC in §2-306(2) implies a duty to use "best efforts." Do the two different wordings suggest different levels of obligation? Some courts have suggested that either phrasing should be read to impose an obligation of due diligence or reasonable efforts. See Permanence Corp. v. Kennametal, Inc., 908 F.2d 98, 100 n.2 (6th Cir. 1990); Trecom Business Systems, Inc. v. Prasad, 980 F.Supp. 770, 774 n.1 (D.N.J. 1997). But see Daniel J. Coplan, When Is "Best Efforts" Really "Best Efforts": An Analysis of the Obligation to Exploit in Entertainment Licensing Agreements, 31 Sw. U. L. Rev. 725 (2002) (stating that express "best efforts" terms in licenses tend to impose a higher burden that rises to near fiduciary level of obligation). However, finding that such an obligation exists—whether expressly or impliedly—is easier than determining in a given case whether it has been *breached.* For illustrative discussions, see Zilg v. Prentice-Hall, Inc., 717 F.2d 671 (2d Cir. 1983) (publisher had met obligation to promote sales of author's book);

Bloor v. Falstaff Brewing Corp., 601 F.2d 609 (2d Cir. 1979) (beer distributor had breached obligation to promote sales of brewer's products). These cases are discussed in the course of Professor Farnsworth's article, On Trying to Keep One's Promises: The Duty of Best Efforts in Contract Law, 46 U. Pitt. L. Rev. 1 (1984).

5. *Implied-in-fact or in-law?* Would you characterize the promise to use reasonable efforts in *Wood* as implied-in-law or implied-in-fact? Both? Does it make any difference? The connection between implication from facts and implication by law is further illustrated by the following cases.

Leibel v. Raynor Manufacturing Co.
Kentucky Court of Appeals
571 S.W.2d 640 (1978)

HOWERTON, Judge.

This is an appeal from a summary judgment dismissing Count I of appellant's three-count complaint. The dismissal of Count I was deemed to be a final, appealable judgment. With this we agree and accept jurisdiction.

The essential facts are that the parties entered into an oral agreement whereby appellant was to have an exclusive dealer-distributorship for appellee's garage doors in a territory extending for a 50-mile radius from Lexington, Kentucky. The agreement was entered into on or about March 1, 1974. The appellee agreed to sell and deliver to the appellant its garage doors, operators and parts at the factory distributor price, and the appellant agreed to sell, install and service Raynor products exclusively, thereby establishing a relationship of dealer-distributor and manufacturer-supplier. There is no real dispute concerning the nature of the relationship.

As a result of the agreement, the appellant borrowed substantial sums of money in order to make certain capital expenditures, purchase an inventory, and to provide working capital for starting the business, including the rental of storage and office space, employment of personnel, and the purchase of a service truck, tools and equipment.

After two years of what appears to have been decreasing sales of Raynor products in the Lexington area, appellee notified the appellant on or about June 30, 1976, that as of that date the relationship was terminated. Appellant was also notified that Helton Overhead Door Sales had been established by the appellee as the new dealer-distributor for the area, and that the appellant would be required to order all future doors, operators and parts from the new dealer-distributor.

Appellee's motion for a summary judgment was based on the ground that the agreement was for an indefinite duration, and that it could be terminated at will by either party. The appellant resisted the motion on the theory that he was entitled to reasonable notice of appellee's intention to terminate the agreement.

On April 20, 1977, the circuit court granted the summary judgment and entered its memorandum opinion, setting forth its four reasons for the judgment. Appellant had relied in part upon the provisions regarding sales in the Uniform

Commercial Code, and specifically subsections (2), (3) of KRS 355.2-309. The trial court concluded that the Code, as it applies to the sale of goods, was not intended to apply to the situation in this case. Secondly, the court concluded that even if the Uniform Commercial Code did apply, KRS 355.2-309(2), (3) means merely that actual notice of the termination must be given. Written notice had been given. The court concluded that the additional requirement of "reasonable notification" was not necessary. . . . Finally, the court concluded that if it required reasonable notification for termination of the agreement, it would be making a contract for the parties by stating a time for the duration of the contract.

We disagree with the conclusions of the trial court and hold that reasonable notification is required in order to terminate an on-going oral agreement for the sale of goods in a relationship of manufacturer-supplier and dealer-distributor or franchisee. The summary judgment must therefore be set aside and a determination must be made on the factual issue of whether or not the notification of termination given in this case was reasonable under the circumstances.

Appellant argues that this contract is now controlled by Article II of the Uniform Commercial Code. The opinion of the trial court provided only that, "It is the opinion of the court that the Uniform Commercial Code applies to the sale of goods and is not intended to apply to the type of situation we have in this case." The rule for application of Article II in Kentucky was stated in Buttorff v. United Electronic Laboratories, Inc., Ky., 459 S.W.2d 581 (1970). According to the opinion in *Buttorff*, supra, we are to look to the real nature of the agreement, the real purpose, and what the parties really intended. It appears that the case sub judice can be distinguished from *Buttorff*, supra, on its facts. The relationship in *Buttorff*, supra, was found to be a contract for personal services, not for the sale of goods or merchandise. Buttorff was actually a commissioned salesman for United Electronics Laboratories' cameras and related equipment.

We must now consider the provisions of the Uniform Commercial Code in order to determine whether or not the article on sales is applicable to the situation at bar. This question has not yet been decided by a Kentucky court.

Article II of the Uniform Commercial Code applies to transactions involving goods and merchandise. "A contract between an automobile manufacturer and an automobile dealer is a contract of sale since it is apparent that its over all purpose and object is to effect the sale of the automobiles manufactured by the manufacturer, and the fact that it may speak in terms of franchises does not change its true character." 1 Anderson, UCC §2-101:5, p.201 (2d ed.) "When a manufacturer sells its product to the public through a local dealer, the transaction is a sale, and the application of the Code is not avoided by describing the relationship as a 'sales distribution' plan." Id., at 202. In relation to the same section of the Code, Anderson also cites a Pennsylvania case which held that, "A dealership contract for the sale of automobile parts is a contract for the sale of goods, even though the contract declares that it is a personal service contract." Cum. Supp., Anderson, UCC, p.174 (2d ed.) Anderson also cites a California case holding that, "Where a supplier of milk agreed with a distributor that the latter would resell milk purchased from the supplier to wholesalers, the relationship between the supplier and the distributor was a sale of goods, and not a contract for services." Id.

In the case at bar, we have a clear situation where the dealer-distributor was to sell the "goods" of the manufacturer-supplier. Appellant was not a commissioned salesman, and the agreement appears to be for the sale of goods.

We conclude that the time has come to recognize that a distributorship agreement must be recognized as an agreement for the sale of goods and subject to the provisions of Article II of the Uniform Commercial Code, which has been adopted by Kentucky in Chapter 355 of the Kentucky Revised Statutes. The amount of money being invested pursuant to distributorship agreements is ever increasing. Often there are no formal written agreements, and it may be that the manufacturer's policy is to have no written agreements. By not establishing a length of time for the contract to exist, either party may terminate the relationship at will, but without a requirement for good faith and fair play, either party may be severely damaged. When sales are the primary essence of the distributorship agreement, the dealer is compelled to keep a large inventory on hand. If the distributorship is terminated without allowing the dealer sufficient time to sell his remaining inventory, substantial damages may result, even if the manufacturer agrees to repurchase the inventory. Reasonable notification should be the minimum amount of protection afforded to either party upon the termination of an ongoing sales agreement. When such reasonable notice is not given, a cause of action for damages may exist.

Having concluded that the Code is applicable to the relationship between the appellant and appellee, we must look at the specific requirements of KRS 355.2-309, "Absence of Specific Time Provisions—Notice of Termination." Subsection (2) reads, "Where the contract provides for successive performances, but is indefinite in duration, it is valid for a reasonable time but unless otherwise agreed may be terminated at any time by either party." Subsection (3) goes on to provide, "Termination of a contract by one (1) party except on the happening of an agreed event requires that reasonable notification be received by the other party and an agreement dispensing with notification is invalid if its operation would be unconscionable." There can be no doubt that reasonable notice is now required. . . . Today, in Kentucky, if the provisions of Article II of the Uniform Commercial Code apply to the relationship, reasonable notice of the intention to terminate the agreement must be given. In some cases, it would be required even if a written agreement provided for dispensing with notification. We therefore find additional error in the trial court's opinion when it concluded that even if the provisions of the Code were applicable, only actual notice of termination would be required.

Comment 8 to §2-309 in 1 Anderson, supra, at p.445 reads:

> Subsection (3) recognizes that the application of principles of good faith and sound commercial practice normally call for such notification of the termination of a going contract relationship as will give the other party reasonable time to seek a substitute arrangement. An agreement dispensing with notification, or limiting the time for the seeking of a substitute arrangement, is of course valid under this subsection unless the results of putting it into operation would be the creation of an unconscionable state of affairs.

It is also quite clear that the requirement of a reasonable notification does not relate to the method of giving notice, but to the circumstances under which the notice is given and the extent of advanced warning of termination that the notification gives.

Anderson, supra, in the cumulative supplement volume at p.282, cites two Minnesota cases relating to the time which might be needed for recoupment of investment. McGinnis Piano and Organ Co. v. Yamaha International Corporation, 480 F.2d 474 (8th Cir. 1973) is cited for the proposition that "in some states, it is implied that a dealership contract which may be terminated upon notice must be allowed to continue for a sufficient period to enable the franchisee to recoup his investment." The case of O. M. Droney Beverage Co. v. Miller Brewing Co., 365 F. Supp. 1067 (D. Minn. 1973), is cited for the proposition that "under Minnesota law 'a reasonable duration will be implied in franchise agreements where a dealer has made substantial investments in reliance on the agreement.' "

The distributorship agreement existing between appellant and appellee is one in which the essence was the sale of goods. Appellant was certainly not an employee or commissioned salesman of appellee. Appellant purchased the products of the appellee at wholesale prices, and marketed them in the Lexington area. The appellant does not dispute the fact that the agreement was terminable at will, but he contends, and the law so holds, that the appellee was required to give reasonable notification of intent to terminate the contract. What length of time constitutes reasonable notice is a question of material fact which remains to be decided. We cannot say that the written notice given in this case was "reasonable" as a matter of law.

The summary judgment granted by the trial court must therefore be vacated, and the case remanded for further proceedings.

All concur.

Notes and Questions

1. *"Gap-Filling" provisions of Article 2.* Article 2 of the Code provides many terms — like those stated in §2-309 — that will as a matter of law be implied in contracts for the sale of goods unless otherwise agreed by the parties. (Other examples are §§2-308 (place of delivery), 2-310 (time of payment), 2-509 (risk of loss), and 2-513 (buyer's right of inspection).) Rules of law that supply implied terms for the parties may be supported on the basis that the terms they provide are "fair" or "just." Indeed, some of the implied-by-law obligations imposed by the UCC are mandatory and may not be varied even if the parties expressly agree otherwise. (See, e.g., §§2-309(3), 2-719(3); see generally UCC §1-102 and Comments 2 and 3; Revised UCC §1-302.) For the most part, however, such rules are regarded merely as "gap-fillers," subject to preemption by the parties' express agreement. (Sometimes the form of an agreement varying the Code rule is itself prescribed by a Code provision; see, e.g., UCC §2-316, regulating disclaimers of implied warranties.)

The Code's system of implied terms has been justified on grounds not only of fairness but also of economic efficiency: If the terms that the law would supply are indeed those most parties would voluntarily choose for themselves, then the process of agreement-making will in general be less costly because contracting parties will have fewer terms to bargain out. We have seen that parties may employ standardized forms for this reason; implied terms that are standardized by law can serve the same purpose. "Off-the-rack" terms, like ready-made suits, are less costly than custom-tailored ones. See Selcke v. New England Insurance Co., 995 F.2d 688, 690 (7th Cir. 1993) (noting that the law could require that parties specify every right or duty, "but then contracts would be very long"). Additionally, it would be extremely inefficient for parties to bargain over terms to address situations that are not likely to occur. David Charny, Hypothetical Bargains: The Normative Structure of Contract Interpretation, 89 Mich. L. Rev. 1815 (1991).

2. *Implied terms as default rules.* The general approach of the courts has been to devise implied terms, often called "default rules," that reflect a "hypothetical bargain," the agreement that the parties probably would have made had they bargained over the issue. Lisa Bernstein, Social Norms and Default Rules Analysis, 3 S. Cal. Interdisc. L.J. 59, 62-63 (1993). Many writers have suggested other bases for supplying default rules. Some observers assert that default rules should be premised on relational aspects of repeated or long-term transactions between the same parties. See, e.g., Jay M. Feinman, Relational Contract and Default Rules, 3 S. Cal. Interdisc. L.J. 43 (1993). Another theorist advocates a consent theory which looks for some form of assent to implied terms. See Randy E. Barnett, The Sound of Silence: Default Rules and Contractual Consent, 78 Va. L. Rev. 821 (1992). Professors Ayres and Gertner argue that in determining the proper default rule it is important to understand the reason for contractual incompleteness. Some contracts are incomplete because one of the parties has more information than the other and engages in strategic behavior. In such cases Ayres and Gertner argue that efficiency-minded courts should consider adopting what they refer to as "penalty default rules," ones that penalize parties for strategic behavior and thereby create incentives for knowledgeable parties to reveal information in the course of bargaining with the other side. Ian Ayres & Robert Gertner, Filling Gaps in Incomplete Contracts: An Economic Theory of Default Rules, 99 Yale L.J. 87, 94 (1989). Professor W. David Slawson, however, takes the position that "default rule analysis" is merely a new name for an old process of courts adopting preemptible rules and further asserts that the various theories make little worthwhile contribution to the process. See W. David Slawson, The Futile Search for Principles for Default Rules, 3 S. Cal. Interdisc. L.J. 29 (1993). On what basis would you justify the default rule in §2-309(3)?

3. *Enforcing distributorship agreements.* The enforceability of exclusive distributorship agreements was problematic under the common law. If the agreement failed to impose definite obligations on the dealer, or if it was of indefinite duration (so that either party was free to terminate the agreement at any time), the agreement could be held unenforceable for lack of consideration or lack of mutuality of obligation. A classic example is Du Pont v. Claiborne-Reno Co., 64 F.2d 224 (8th Cir. 1933). Although Reno served from 1924 to 1930 as the exclusive distributor in Iowa of certain Du Pont products, the contract did not expressly provide that Reno was committed for a specific period of time. Applying the same presumption used in employment

contracts of indefinite duration, the court deemed Reno free to terminate at will. Moreover, because Reno was deemed not bound, the court held that the contract could not be enforced against Du Pont. Id. at 232-233.

As *Leibel* demonstrates, distributorship agreements today are likely to fall within the general scope of Article 2, as "transactions in goods." If so, the implied obligations found in UCC §§2-306 and 2-309 should eliminate most problems of lack of consideration or lack of mutuality. E.g., Thermal Systems of Alabama, Inc. v. Sigafoose, 533 So. 2d 567 (Ala. 1988) (rejecting arguments of lack of mutuality and indefiniteness against enforceability of a distributorship agreement, based on UCC §§2-306 and 2-309). A distributorship contract of indefinite duration, however, will still be subject to termination at-will upon reasonable notice. See, e.g., WMTC, Inc. v. G.A. Braun, Inc., 247 F.3d 114 (4th Cir. 2001) (applying South Carolina law).

4. *Assessing reasonable notice.* Discussing whether Raynor had given Leibel "reasonable notification" of its intention to terminate their arrangement, the *Leibel* opinion refers to some possibly relevant factors: the distributor's need to sell off its remaining inventory and the question whether it still has substantial unrecouped investment made in reliance on the agreement. See, e.g., Sofa Gallery, Inc. v. Stratford Co., 872 F.2d 259 (8th Cir. 1989) (reasonable notice of termination without cause takes into account time needed to recoup reasonable initial or continuing investment, close out product line, and minimize losses). Some courts have made a distinction between cases involving an investment by a distributor and those without startup or similar costs. See Italian & French Wine Co. v. Negociants USA, Inc. 842 F. Supp. 693 (W.D.N.Y. 1993) (distributorship agreements without an investment may be merely a type of employment or personal services contract that is properly terminable at will). Comment 8 to UCC §2-309 refers to a related factor: whether there has been sufficient or "reasonable time" to find a "substitute arrangement."

The determination whether notice is reasonable may also be affected by the terms contained in the parties' present or prior agreement and by industry standards. See Retail Associates, Inc. v. Macy's East, Inc., 245 F.3d 694 (8th Cir. 2001) (ninety days' notice for termination of consignment contract to place maternity clothes in department stores was reasonable given that consignor had virtually no capital investment, that inventory would turn over in six-month seasons, and that consignor had other outlets to sell any remaining inventory).

5. *Effect of express termination provisions.* Unlike *Leibel,* most modern commercial contracts will specify events of termination. Suppose Leibel and Raynor had entered into a written agreement that provided for immediate termination on written notice by Raynor. What result? Suppose the written agreement provided that Raynor could terminate the agreement on written notice to Leibel if its sales declined for two consecutive years. Compare Delta Services & Equipment, Inc. v. Ryko Manufacturing Co., 908 F.2d 7 (5th Cir. 1990) (distributorship contract that specified various grounds for termination, including minimum sales provision, was not thereby terminable only on the occurrence of one of those agreed-upon events; instead, contract was for indefinite duration, terminable either on reasonable notice under UCC §2-309(3) or on happening of one of agreed events), with Viking Supply v. National Cart Co., Inc., 310 F.3d 1092 (8th Cir. 2002) (agreement that

provided for termination by manufacturer of shopping cart corrals if distributor lost key sales contract with Target stores was not at-will and was terminable upon the occurrence of the specified event).

B. THE IMPLIED OBLIGATION OF GOOD FAITH

In this section, we will survey a variety of situations in which one party to a contract claimed to be acting in ways either expressly permitted or at least not forbidden by its terms, but the other party complained that such conduct was somehow improper and actionable. In such cases, courts have frequently employed the notion of "good faith" as an aid to decision. Similarly, the Uniform Commercial Code declares in revised §1-304 (formerly §1-203) that "every contract or duty" within its scope "imposes an obligation of good faith in its performance or enforcement." Although the first Restatement did not address this point directly, Restatement (Second) §205 echoes the above UCC provision, extending the "duty of good faith and fair dealing" to "every contract."

We saw in Chapter 3 that occasionally parties will be held to a duty to bargain in good faith when negotiating toward a contract. Once a contract has been concluded, however, the above authorities are unanimous in declaring that its terms will be deemed to include an obligation of good faith that is binding on both parties. To say that generally an obligation of good faith will be implied does not, of course, answer the harder question of what that obligation requires of each party in the context of their particular agreement.

The UCC originally offered two definitions of good faith. In §1-201(19) it was defined simply as "honesty in fact," suggesting that at a minimum lying and other kinds of deception should be regarded as "bad faith" conduct and proscribed. In the context of Article 2, §2-103(1)(b) of the Code also defined good faith, at least where merchants are concerned, as requiring not merely honesty but also "the observance of reasonable commercial standards of fair dealing in the trade." The revisions to Articles 1 and 2 now both adopt the same definition which combines the elements of the two original provisions, stating that good faith "means honesty in fact and the observance of reasonable commercial standards of fair dealing." See Revised UCC §1-201(b)(20); Revised UCC §2-103(j). With the exception of a more narrow provision in Article 5, the UCC would thus generally apply to all parties (both merchant and nonmerchant) the complementary concepts of "subjective honesty" and "objective reasonableness" in determining good faith. See Official Comment to Revised UCC §1-201(b)(20). While the revised official version of Article 1 appears to be on its way to general adoption, not all jurisdictions adopting the new Article have acquiesced in its expanded definition of "good faith." Several states have chosen instead to retain the more minimal standard of "honesty in fact," at least for parties who are not Article 2 "merchants."

In his pioneering survey of this subject, Professor Robert Summers suggested that the concept of good faith does not have—and indeed cannot have—a single definition of its own. Instead, he argued, it must be understood as an "excluder," a phrase without general meaning of its own that serves to exclude a wide range of heterogeneous conduct, which we call "bad faith." Observing that a judge who uses the phrase *good faith* typically is most concerned with ruling out certain conduct, and less with formulating "the positive conduct of a standard," Summers offered the following analysis and illustrative examples:

> Good faith, then, takes on specific and variant meanings by way of contrast with the specific and variant forms of bad faith which judges decide to prohibit. From the cases it would be possible to compile a list of forms of bad faith, with an opposite for each listed as the corresponding specific meaning of good faith. The beginnings of such a list might look like this:

Form of bad faith conduct	*Meaning of good faith*
1. seller concealing a defect in what he is selling	fully disclosing material facts
2. builder willfully failing to perform in full, though otherwise substantially performing	substantially performing without knowingly deviating from specifications
3. contractor openly abusing bargaining power to coerce an increase in the contract price	refraining from abuse of bargaining power
4. hiring a broker and then deliberately preventing him from consummating the deal	acting cooperatively
5. conscious lack of diligence in mitigating the other party's damages	acting diligently
6. arbitrarily and capriciously exercising a power to terminate a contract	acting with some reason
7. adopting an overreaching interpretation of contract language	interpreting contract language fairly
8. harassing the other party for repeated assurances of performance	accepting adequate assurances

Robert S. Summers, "Good Faith" in General Contract Law and the Sales Provisions of the Uniform Commercial Code, 54 Va. L. Rev. 195, 202-203 (1968). See also Robert S. Summers, The General Duty of Good Faith — Its Recognition and Conceptualization, 67 Cornell L. Rev. 810 (1982).

In a 1933 decision, the New York Court of Appeals declared,

> In every contract there is an implied covenant that neither party shall do anything which will have the effect of destroying or injuring the right of the other party to receive the fruits of the contract, which means that in every contract there is an implied obligation of good faith and fair dealing.

Kirke La Shelle Co. v. Paul Armstrong Co., 188 N.E. 163, 167 (N.Y. 1933). Commentators have pursued this "fruits of the contract" approach. Thus, Professor Steven Burton has suggested that bad faith consists of attempts by one party to recapture "forgone opportunities" — occasions for the realization of gain that (in light of any applicable business practices or the course of dealing between the parties) he should have understood to be precluded by the contract at issue. Steven J. Burton, Breach of Contract and the Common Law Duty to Perform in Good Faith, 94 Harv. L. Rev. 369 (1980); Steven J. Burton, Good Faith Performance of a Contract Within Article 2 of the Uniform Commercial Code, 67 Iowa L. Rev. 1 (1981); see also Steven J. Burton & Eric G. Andersen, Contractual Good Faith (1995). Professor Timothy Muris, in a somewhat similar vein, has advanced the thesis that the notion of good faith is one of the concepts used in law to police against "opportunistic behavior." Timothy J. Muris, Opportunistic Behavior and the Law of Contracts, 65 Minn. L. Rev. 521 (1981). Arguing more generally and criticizing Summers's excluder analysis, Professor Dennis Patterson claims that good faith has substantive content. He argues that good faith should be seen as protecting the "reasonable expectations" of the contracting parties considered in light of the background practices and customs in which the agreement arose. Dennis M. Patterson, Good Faith and Lender Liability 7 (1990).

Professor Michael Van Alstine, writing more recently, reported that beginning in the 1990s courts have moved toward "a new textualist approach," giving a near absolute priority to express terms and rendering the implied duty of good faith irrelevant in many situations. Michael P. Van Alstine, Of Textualism, Party Autonomy, and Good Faith, 40 Wm. & Mary L. Rev. 1223 (1999). Professor Van Alstine's study gives evidence that while nearly all courts recognize the implied duty of good faith, at least in principle, not all will give that concept a broad application. Other recent commentators have sounded a similar skeptical note. See generally Teri J. Dobbins, Losing Faith: Extracting the Implied Covenant of Good Faith from (Some) Contracts, 84 Or. L. Rev. 227 (2005); Harold Dubroff, The Implied Covenant of Good Faith in Contract Interpretation and Gap-Filling: Reviling a Revered Relic, 80 St. John's L. Rev. 559 (2006); Emily M.S. Houh, The Doctrine of Good Faith in Contract Law: A (Nearly) Empty Vessel?, 2005 Utah L. Rev. 1 (2005). Perhaps reflecting this more recent tendency to approach "good faith" with caution, the drafters of the revised UCC Article 1 have added to their Comment on the new §1-304 the following language, not found in the previous version:

> This section does not support an independent cause of action for failure to perform or enforce in good faith. Rather, this section means that a failure to perform or enforce, in good faith, a specific duty or obligation under the contract, constitutes a breach of that contract or makes unavailable, under the particular circumstances, a remedial right or power. This distinction makes it clear that the doctrine of good faith merely directs courts towards interpreting contracts within the commercial context in which they are created, performed, and enforced, and does not create a separate duty of fairness and reasonableness which can be independently breached.

In one way or another, most courts and writers who have spoken of an obligation of good faith do appear at least to share the view that this concept should be employed in cases where one party's actions were such as to undermine the "spirit" of the contract—either by enabling that party to realize gains that in making that contract he had implicitly agreed to surrender, or by unfairly denying to the other party the fruits of the contract that she reasonably expected to receive. (Often, of course, the two will go together, but that need not always be the case.) In this sense, the obligation of good faith can be viewed as a device for protecting the bargain that the parties themselves have made against later attempts by one side to undermine it. The following cases illustrate the process by which the abstract obligation of good faith may be given concrete application.

Seidenberg v. Summit Bank

Superior Court of New Jersey, Appellate Division.
348 N.J. Super. 243, 791 A.2d 1068 (2002)

Before Judges KING, WINKELSTEIN and CLARKSON S. FISHER, Jr.
The opinion of the court was delivered by
CLARKSON S. FISHER, Jr., J.S.C. (temporarily assigned).

After settling all their disputes concerning the express terms of their commercial transaction, plaintiffs filed a second amended complaint alleging a breach of the implied covenant of good faith and fair dealing. The Law Division dismissed the action, finding that plaintiffs failed to state a claim upon which relief may be granted. Because we conclude the assessment of the validity of the claim was both erroneous and premature, we reverse.

. . .

II

Plaintiffs Richard Seidenberg and Eric Raymond formed two Pennsylvania corporations—Corporate Dynamics and Philadelphia Benefits Corporation—in 1971 and 1985, respectively. These entities marketed, provided consultation services and sold health insurance benefit plans to employers. Plaintiffs were the sole shareholders of the two entities.

In 1997, plaintiffs sold their stock in Corporate Dynamics and Philadelphia Benefits Corporation (hereafter collectively referred to as "the brokerage firms") to defendant Summit Bank ("Summit") in exchange for 445,000 shares of the common stock of Bancorp Corporation, Summit's parent corporation[1]; in addition, plaintiffs agreed to place 49,500 shares of Bancorp Corporation into escrow until December 12, 2001, as security for any existing but unknown or undisclosed liabilities. As part of the transaction, plaintiffs retained their positions as executives of the brokerage firms and also were to be placed in charge of the daily operations of any other employee benefits insurance business which might be acquired by Summit.

Plaintiffs' employment agreements with Summit acknowledged the parties' joint obligation to work together with respect to the future performance of the brokerage firms:

Summit and [plaintiffs] shall work together to formulate joint marketing programs which will give [the brokerage firms] access to the market resources of Summit to the extent permitted by applicable laws, regulations and administrative policies and

---

1. As of the date of closing, the stock had a value of $43.50 per share.

guidelines, including but not limited to those relating to customer privacy, issued by Federal or state regulatory authorities or agencies or self-regulatory organizations or financial industry trade groups.

In the second amended complaint, plaintiffs contend, among other things, that Summit (a) failed to allow for the creation of a close working relationship between the entities, (b) failed to create an effective cross-selling structure to generate leads, (c) failed to introduce the brokerage firms to vendors doing business with Summit as a way of increasing their potential customer base, (d) failed to develop existing relationships (referred to in the pleadings as "low hanging fruit") which could easily be picked and turned into clients for the brokerage firms, (e) failed to provide plaintiffs with information necessary to provide full advice concerning health and other employee benefits, thereby precluding plaintiffs from quoting coverage to Summit, (f) unreasonably delayed a direct mail campaign, (g) thwarted an agreed-upon joint marketing campaign, and (h) failed to advise of Summit's pursuit of the acquisition of another entity which plaintiffs claim would fall within their ambit and right to operate.

Plaintiffs claimed that Summit's lack of performance in these areas impacted their reasonable expectations of compensation and future involvement. For example, plaintiffs' salaries were reduced in exchange for a bonus to which they would be entitled based on the growth of the brokerage firms. They claim this was agreeable due to the anticipation of a substantial bonus upon the growth of the business. Accordingly, the allegations contained in the second amended complaint, briefly outlined above, are linked to plaintiffs' compensation. In addition, plaintiffs claim there was an expectation of continued employment since their employment agreements contained a minimum term of five years and provided also that, in the absence of termination by Summit, employment would continue until each reached the age of 70.

Plaintiffs assert that these allegations give rise to an inference of bad faith. They claim that these circumstances demonstrate that Summit "never had any intention to perform to begin with," and that Summit "from the start, . . . never [was] committed to developing the business with [plaintiffs], but rather simply wanted to acquire the business and seek out their own broker to run it or grow it." In December 1999, Summit terminated plaintiffs from their positions, triggering this lawsuit.

III

On February 10, 2000, plaintiffs filed a complaint in the Chancery Division. After the joinder of issue, the parties reached a partial settlement of their disputes and, on July 25, 2000, a consent order was entered which eliminated all claims except plaintiffs' claim of a breach of the implied covenant of good faith and fair dealing. With the resolution of the equity claims, the Chancery judge, as was his prerogative, transferred the matter to the Law Division. On August 16, 2000, plaintiffs filed a second amended complaint and defendants quickly filed a motion to dismiss for failure to state a claim upon which relief may be granted. . . .

The motion was granted. In essence, the Law Division judge held that plaintiffs were not claiming a breach of the implied covenant of good faith and fair dealing but were seeking to prove the existence (and obtain enforcement) of an oral agreement allegedly made beyond the four corners of the written agreements in violation of the parol evidence rule:

> I am satisfied that the facts as pled do not allege as a matter of law and cannot allege as a matter of law a breach of the covenant of good faith and fair dealing. Because in fact what the complaint is alleging is that there were agreements made orally outside of the written agreements that the bank would do certain things. And, that because the bank didn't do certain things, the plaintiffs were deprived of certain income.

The ruling under review also placed emphasis on the bargaining power of the parties:

> We are not dealing with unsophisticated people. [Plaintiffs], from the record it would appear, are very sophisticated businessmen, developed very successful businesses. And, with the assistance of very able counsel entered into certain contracts with the bank that set out the framework for the way they would act as president and vice-president of [the brokerage firms]. . . . [They] leaned back in reliance on things that were said to them during the course of the negotiations by the people from the bank, then they certainly had the opportunity to have those representations and considerations put into the written agreement and they weren't done — that just simply wasn't done.

Based upon these observations as to the meaning of plaintiffs' allegations, the motion to dismiss was granted. We find the Law Division judge's conclusions misapprehend the nature of the cause of action and represent an erroneous interpretation of the evolving implied covenant of good faith and fair dealing.

IV

We start with the premise that in New Jersey the covenant of good faith and fair dealing is contained in all contracts and mandates that "neither party shall do anything which will have the effect of destroying or injuring the right of the other party to receive the fruits of the contract." Sons of Thunder v. Borden, Inc., 148 N.J. 396, 420, 690 A.2d 575 (1997); Palisades Properties, Inc. v. Brunetti, 44 N.J.117, 130, 207 A.2d 522 (1965). While this general statement represents the guiding principle in such matters, determining whether the present action may be maintained requires closer examination.

The implied covenant of good faith and fair dealing has evolved to the point where it permits the adjustment of the obligations of contracting parties in a number of different ways. Some cases have focused on a plaintiff's inadequate bargaining power or financial vulnerability in order to avoid an inequitable result otherwise permitted by a contract's express terms. See e.g., *Sons of Thunder*. Other decisions have revolved around the expectations of the parties, generating a need to contrast those expectations with the absence of any express terms. See e.g., Onderdonk v. Presbyterian Homes, 85 N.J. 171, 425 A.2d 1057 (1981). And still others have emphasized the defendant's bad faith or outright dishonesty. See e.g., Pickett v. Lloyd's, 131 N.J. 457, 621 A.2d 445 (1993). Yet, as the implied covenant of good faith and fair dealing continues to develop, and in light of the covenant's essential factors as discerned from the existing case law, we cannot say, in examining the unadorned record in this case, that an actionable claim cannot be found in plaintiffs' allegations.

In granting defendant's motion to dismiss, we understand the Law Division to have relied on two points: the parties' equal strength at the time the contract was formed and plaintiffs' assertion of oral discussions unreflected by the written contract. We find erroneous both the undue emphasis placed on the absence of plaintiffs' financial vulnerability and the misperceived importance of the parol evidence rule, particularly when viewed at the pleading stage.

A

Sons of Thunder — often viewed as a watershed event in the course of the implied covenant of good faith and fair dealing — is, perhaps, the best example of how a plaintiff's unequal bargaining power will bring the implied covenant to the forefront even if defendant acted in conformity with the express terms of the contract. In the wake of *Sons of Thunder,* it certainly would have been fair to conclude that bargaining power is a critical aspect of any application of the implied covenant to a contractual dispute.

In *Sons of Thunder,* the Court emphasized the parties' unequal bargaining power as one factor in finding a breach of the implied covenant of good faith and fair dealing. *Sons of Thunder* involved an operator of a vessel which contracted to supply clams to Borden. Even though the contract's term was for one year and was also terminable on 90 days' notice, the Court found that Borden could still be found to have violated the implied covenant because it had preyed on Sons of Thunder's lack of sophistication and desperate financial straits. The Court stressed the importance of protecting and vindicating plaintiff's expectations particularly in light of the significant investments made by Sons of Thunder in anticipation of Borden's good faith performance. The Court also emphasized this feature in the earlier case of Bak-A-Lum Corp. v. Alcoa Bldg. Prods., Inc., 69 N.J. 123, 130, 351 A.2d 349 (1976). That these two seminal cases in the growth of the implied covenant stressed economic dependency and financial strength understandably suggests the importance of this factor. Nevertheless, while disparate strength may sometimes be a prominent feature, it is not the *sine qua non* of such a cause of action. It is merely one factor among many to be considered. . . .

In this case, it is undisputed that the parties are all sophisticated and financially strong; it appears undisputed that plaintiffs possessed sufficient bargaining power during the formation of their agreement with Summit. According to their own contentions, plaintiffs have been in the insurance industry for several years and built two very successful brokerage firms. Furthermore, the record reflects that both parties were assisted by able counsel in negotiating their agreement. But equal bargaining power and the advice of competent counsel at the formation of the contract are not determinative. Rather, we conclude that while the bargaining power and sophistication of the parties must be viewed as significant, and should be considered in the analysis of any such dispute, it is not the sole criterion by which this claim must be resolved.

B

We also discern from her oral opinion that the Law Division judge believed plaintiffs would be unable to substantiate their claim because, in reality, they seek to prove some oral agreement dehors the written contract. In short, the Law Division judge appears to have found the parol evidence rule an insurmountable obstacle to plaintiffs' claim. We find this erroneous.

The parol evidence rule prohibits the introduction of oral promises which tend to alter or vary an integrated written instrument. . . . Parol evidence may, however, be admitted in order to provide understanding into the parties' intentions. . . .

Put in the present context, it must first be observed that the parol evidence rule does not even come into play "until it is first determined what the true agreement of the parties is." *Ibid.* Accordingly, the rule cannot inhibit the application of the implied covenant of good faith and fair dealing because that covenant is contained in all contracts made in New Jersey by operation of law. Sons of Thunder, 148 N.J. at 420, 690 A.2d 575. Moreover, the central premise of the implied covenant is the enhanced status of the parties' reasonable expectations. If the parol evidence rule is vigorously applied in such situations, the opportunity to pursue such a claim would be extremely limited. The manner in which our courts have defined the scope of the covenant demonstrates the fallacy of such a broad application of the parol evidence rule.

The implied covenant of good faith and fair dealing has been applied in three general ways, each largely unaffected by the parol evidence rule. First, the covenant permits the inclusion of terms and conditions which have not been expressly set forth in the written contract. The earlier cases, such as *Bak-A-Lum* . . . and *Onderdonk* . . . provide examples of the imposition of absent terms and conditions. The covenant acts in such instances to include terms "the parties must have intended . . . because they are necessary to give business efficacy" to the contract. New Jersey Bank v. Palladino, 77 N.J. 33, 46, 389 A.2d 454 (1978). . . . Second, the covenant has been utilized to allow redress for the bad faith performance of an agreement even when the defendant has not breached any express term, as in *Sons of Thunder*. And third, the covenant has been held, in more recent cases, to permit inquiry into a party's exercise of discretion expressly granted by a contract's terms. See Wilson v. Amerada Hess Corporation, 168 N.J. 236, 250, 773 A.2d 1121 (2001); R.J. Gaydos Ins. Agency, Inc. v. National Consumer Ins. Co., 168 N.J. 255, 281, 773 A.2d 1132 (2001); Emerson Radio, 253 F.3d at 170-72.

The second aspect, exemplified by *Sons of Thunder*, and the third, represented by cases such as *Wilson*, are implicated in this case. In both these situations, the parol evidence rule has a potential for coming into play. For, while the implied covenant has gone far in altering the way in which contractual performance will be weighed, our Supreme Court has consistently held that the "implied covenant of good faith and fair dealing cannot override an express term in a contract." *Wilson*, 168 N.J. at 244, 773 A.2d 1121; *Sons of Thunder*, 148 N.J. at 419, 690 A.2d 575. But, instead of altering or overriding an express term, the implied covenant requires that a contracting party act in good faith when exercising either discretion in performing its contractual obligations . . . or its right to terminate. . . . Accordingly, it may occur that a party will be found to have breached the implied covenant even if the action complained of does not violate a "pertinent express term." *Wilson*, 168 N.J. at 244, 773 A.2d 1121. By staying within those parameters, the implied covenant—while necessarily "vague and amorphous" . . . — remains faithful to the purposes of the parol evidence rule.

Accordingly, it can readily be seen that the parol evidence rule appears to have no present application in the case at hand. By concluding that plaintiffs seek to prove an oral agreement outside the bounds of a fully integrated written contract, the Law Division judge misapprehended the scope of the implied covenant of good faith and fair dealing and overly-expanded the importance of the parol evidence rule. The parol evidence rule is not impacted because the obligation to act with good faith and fair dealing is, by its very nature, "implied." The prohibition on parol evidence to alter or vary a written contract relates, in the present context, only to the creation of the contract. Because the covenant of good faith and fair dealing is implied by operation of law, the view that the parol evidence rule somehow inhibits plaintiffs' claim is erroneous. And, because plaintiffs do not seek to contradict or alter any express term in their written contract, but rather question Summit's *bona fides* in both its performance and termination of the contract, there presently appears to be no concern that the particular manner in which plaintiffs would have the implied covenant applied would run afoul of the parol evidence rule.

To determine what is considered a good faith performance, the court must consider the expectations of the parties and the purposes for which the contract was made. It would be difficult, if not impossible, to make that determination without considering evidence outside the written memorialization of the parties' agreement. Therefore, in determining whether a breach of the covenant has occurred, a court must allow for parol evidence and the Law Division's determination that the need for parol evidence is fatal to the second amended complaint is erroneous.

C

The guiding principle in the application of the implied covenant of good faith and fair dealing emanates from the fundamental notion that a party to a contract may not unreasonably frustrate its purpose:

> [W]here a party alleges frustration of its expectation or fundamental purpose in entering the contract, the question of what interest will be protected by the implied duty answers itself; the plaintiff's interest is internal to the understanding of the parties and good faith requires the defendant not exercise such discretion as it may have under the literal terms of the contract to thwart plaintiff's expectation or purpose.

[Emerson Radio Corp. v. Orion Sales Inc., 80 F.Supp.2d 307, 314 (D.N.J.2000), *rev'd in part on other grounds*, 253 F.3d 159 (3d Cir. 2001), cited with approval in *Wilson*, 168 N.J. at 250, 773 A.2d 1121.]

See also . . . Restatement (Second) of Contracts, §205, comment a (1979) ("Good faith performance . . . emphasizes faithfulness to an agreed common purpose and consistency with the justified expectations of the other party").

As discussed earlier, the application of the implied covenant of good faith and fair dealing has addressed three distinct type of situations: (1) when the contract does not provide a term necessary to fulfill the parties' expectations, . . . (2) when bad faith served as a pretext for the exercise of a contractual right to terminate, . . . and (3) when the contract expressly provides a party with discretion regarding its performance, *see e.g., Wilson*, 168 N.J. 236, 773 A.2d 1121. . . .

Here, plaintiffs appear to urge an application of both the second and third facets of the implied covenant. The Law Division judge's decision to dismiss the second amended complaint constituted a mistaken understanding of the covenant in these areas.

Faced with a motion to dismiss pursuant to R. 4:6-2(e), the court below was required to determine only whether the second amended complaint sufficiently outlined a cause of action consistent with any of these categories. In this case, the second amended complaint alleges circumstances which, if proven, might support a claim based upon Summit's termination of their relationship. To some extent, plaintiffs alleged there was an expectation — despite the express contractual right of Summit to terminate — that the relationship would last until they reached retirement age. This contention would, on its face, fall within that type of implied covenant claim prohibiting a party from terminating a contractual relationship in bad faith notwithstanding the expressed right to do so.

The second amended complaint also alleges that Summit used insufficient energy in discretionary areas. That is, plaintiffs allege that Summit failed to pursue or create leads, frustrated or delayed marketing efforts, and deprived plaintiffs of information which might improve their benefits under the contract, thus sufficiently alleging a cause of action under the discretionary tranche of the multi-faceted implied covenant of good faith and fair dealing.

D

The last element of a maintainable cause of action based upon the implied covenant of good faith and fair dealing is bad faith or ill motive. Courts have described this element in various ways. Most importantly, our Supreme Court has recently emphasized the level of bad faith and improper motive which will be required in a party's exercise of the discretion permitted by the contract:

[A] party exercising its right to use discretion in setting price under a contract breaches the duty of good faith and fair dealing if that party exercises its discretionary authority arbitrarily, unreasonably, or capriciously, with the objective of preventing the other party from receiving its reasonably expected fruits under the contract.

. . . In that setting, an allegation of bad faith or unfair dealing should not be permitted to be advanced in the abstract and absent improper motive. Without bad motive or intention, discretionary decisions that happen to result in economic disadvantage to the other party are of no legal significance.

[*Wilson*, 168 N.J. at 251, 773 A.2d 1121 (citations omitted).]

While *Wilson*'s description of good faith relates to price setting, we fail to see why it would not be similarly applied in examining the type of performance (or lack thereof) as alleged by plaintiffs.

Before finding a breach of the implied covenant, care must be taken that the bad faith element is fully realized. Recognizing a concern for an overly ambitious application of the implied covenant, the Court in *Wilson* — in defining the level of bad faith required in such matters — charted a careful course between implying a promise to avoid an apparent unjust result and requiring parties to adhere to the bargain they freely and voluntarily made. Referencing one federal court of appeal's holdings that the covenant is not intended to supplant the prohibition on judicial rewriting of contracts or provide undue protection to contracting parties who can protect themselves,[4] the *Wilson* decision represents an increased emphasis on the importance of this factor:

> [A]n allegation of bad faith or unfair dealing should not be permitted to be advanced in the abstract and absent improper motive.
>
> Because the implied covenant of good faith and fair dealing applies to the parties' performance under the contract notwithstanding [a] provision in the contract permitting [the exercise of discretion in setting prices] . . . the issue is whether . . . [the defendant] acted in bad faith or violated any commercially reasonable standard thereby depriving plaintiffs of their right to make a reasonable profit.

[168 N.J. at 251, 253, 773 A.2d 1121.]

Providing a more precise definition of bad faith in the context of this, or any other similar case, is unrealistic. *See e.g.,* Wade v. Kessler Institute, 343 N.J.Super. 338, 346-48, 778 A.2d 580 (App.Div.2001). We recognize that expressions such as "bad faith," "improper motive," and other similar words and phrases used to describe this requisite state of mind provide little guidance. While the particular defining words chosen will inherently be of "little assistance to the trial judge who must distinguish bad faith from mere sharp commercial practice," *Emerson Radio*, 80 F.Supp.2d at 311, it is best to entrust the drawing of such a line to trial judges and juries with the admonition that an unduly expansive version of bad faith, as Judge Greenberg cautioned in *Northview Motors,* "could become an all-embracing statement of the parties' obligations under contract law, imposing unintended obligations upon parties and destroying the mutual benefits created by legally binding agreements." 227 F.3d at 92. In the final analysis, bad faith must be judged not only in light of the proofs regarding the defendant's state of mind but also in the context from which the claim arose. The Court in *Wilson* coupled the element of bad faith with a requirement that the plaintiff demonstrate a violation of "any commercially reasonable standard." 168 N.J. at 253, 773 A.2d 1121. Accordingly, this element may be determined, at least in part, by

---

4. "Contract law does not require parties to behave altruistically toward each other; it does not proceed on the philosophy that I am my brother's keeper." Original Great Am. Chocolate Chip Cookie Co. v. River Valley Cookies, Ltd., 970 F.2d 273, 280 (7th Cir. 1992) (quoted with approval in *Wilson,* 168 N.J. at 251-52, 773 A.2d 1121). *See also,* Kham & Nate's Shoes No. 2, Inc. v. First Bank of Whiting, 908 F.2d 1351, 1357 (7th Cir. 1990) (the covenant of good faith and fair dealing "does not imply a general duty of 'kindness' in performance").

the nature of the parties' undertaking and the standards applicable to the business or industry in which they have engaged. Ultimately, however, the presence of bad faith is to be found in the eye of the beholder or, more to the point, in the eye of the trier of fact. Any attempt to provide greater definition is to expect some "delusive exactness" which, as Justice Holmes said, is "a source of fallacy throughout the law." Truax v. Corrigan, 257 U.S. 312, 342, 42 S.Ct. 124, 133, 66 L.Ed. 254, 267 (1921) (dissenting opinion).

Even though the order of dismissal was not based upon some insufficiency in regard to its allegations of bad faith, we lastly pause, in providing guidance for future proceedings in this case, to observe that the second amended complaint was adequate in this regard, alleging that plaintiffs "suffered as a result of . . . Summit's bad faith" and that Summit's actions were "wanton and willful and without privilege or right." Whether plaintiffs' proofs will meet the bad faith standard defined in *Wilson*, or even survive summary judgment, remains to be seen. This question, however, certainly cannot be resolved until the parties are at least given a full and fair opportunity for further investigation and discovery.

V

To summarize, plaintiffs' claim of a breach of the implied covenant of good faith and fair dealing is not precluded merely because the parties possessed equal bargaining power, or because plaintiffs were not financially vulnerable during the contract's formation, or even if the plaintiffs negotiated the contract with the assistance of highly competent counsel. These are factors which the trier of fact may consider in weighing the sufficiency of plaintiffs' claim but they are not the only factors. Also, we conclude that the parol evidence rule presently appears to have no impact upon the ability of plaintiffs to substantiate either their claim that they had a reasonable expectation of a continued relationship (notwithstanding the expressed right of Summit to terminate), or their claim that Summit failed to perform its contractual obligations in good faith. And lastly, while the appropriate level of bad faith may be difficult to define and may also vary depending upon the nature of the alleged breach and the type of business engaged in by the parties, we find plaintiffs' allegations of bad faith and ill motives are sufficient to survive dismissal.

. . . Whether those allegations can be substantiated remains to be seen after the parties have been afforded a full and fair opportunity for further investigation and discovery.

The order of dismissal is reversed and the matter remanded for further proceedings in conformity herewith. We do not retain jurisdiction.

Notes and Questions

1. *Applications of the good faith principle.* In the course of its discussion, the *Seidenberg* court gives us an overview of the ways in which the doctrine of good faith may come into play in the course of adjudicating a contract dispute. First, a court may be persuaded that in order for the contract between the parties to

have "business efficacy," it is necessary to imply terms not expressly incorporated in the agreement. (Wood v. Lucy, Lady Duff-Gordon is probably the best-known example of such a case, but as discussed in Note 3 after *Wood*, UCC §2-306(2) and the cases applying it also exemplify that principle.) The court is careful to add, as have many other courts and commentators, that the court will not imply any term that conflicts with the express terms of the parties' agreement. (Of course whether there is indeed such a conflict will often be a matter of judgment. Recall the *Nanakuli* case in Chapter 5, in which the appellate court upheld the lower court's determination that Shell's failure to price-protect Nanakuli was not only a breach of their agreement, properly understood in the light of course of performance and trade usage, but also a breach of the duty of good faith.) Second, the court in *Seidenberg* indicates that the covenant of good faith may permit a finding of breach even where no express term of the agreement has been violated. *Seidenberg* itself appears to be, potentially, an example of such as a case; so also are the *Sons of Thunder* and *Mathis* cases, discussed in the following notes. (*Nanakuli* could also be so described.) And finally, the notion of good faith has often been applied to judge the appropriateness of a party's exercise of some type of discretion expressly granted to it by the terms of a contract. The next two principal cases, Morin Bldg. Products Co. v. Baystone Constr. Inc., and Locke v. Warner Bros. Inc., exemplify this latter type of analysis in two very different settings.

2. *Application of the parol evidence rule.* In light of the recent tendency of some courts toward a higher regard for the "formalism" reflected in the parol evidence rule, note the *Seidenberg* court's treatment of that issue. While conceding that the parol evidence rule might apply in a case where the offered evidence appears to directly contradict an express term in the contract, the appellate court asserts that because the obligation of good faith is an implied term rather than an express one, the parol evidence rule will ordinarily be irrelevant to the issue of its existence and application. Do you agree that the parol evidence rule should not be relevant to resolution of the plaintiff's claims in *Seidenberg*?

3. *The **Sons of Thunder** case.* The court in *Seidenberg* describes Sons of Thunder v. Borden, Inc., 690 A.2d 575 (N.J. 1997), as a case that is "often viewed as a watershed event in the course of the implied covenant of good faith and fair dealing," demonstrating as it does a situation where, in light of all the circumstances, the court may apply the covenant of good faith and fair dealing even where the defendant has apparently "acted in conformity with the express terms of the contract." In that case, the plaintiffs invested large amounts of funds in clam-fishing vessels, based on assurances of purchases to be made by the defendant Borden. Borden, however, consistently failed to perform in accordance with the contracts and eventually exercised an express right to terminate the contracts with 60 and 90 days' notice. The New Jersey Supreme Court agreed with the defendent that the implied covenant of good faith could not override the express right to terminate, but also held that Borden could have breached the implied covenant of good faith in its *performance* before exercising the right to terminate. The court stated that Borden "destroyed Sons of Thunder's reasonable expectations and right to receive the fruits of the contract" by never buying the required amount of clams. 690 A.2d at 589.

4. *Good faith and open price terms.* As we have noted earlier, the definition of good faith incorporated in Revised UCC §1-201(b)(20) recognizes the obligations of both subjective honesty in fact and objective commercially reasonable behavior. The distinction between those two standards was highlighted in Mathis v. Exxon Corp., 302 F.3d 448 (5th Cir. 2002). A group of 54 plaintiff franchisees alleged that Exxon breached the duty of good faith in setting gasoline prices for the purpose of driving the franchisees out of business and then replacing them with stores owned directly by Exxon. The Fifth Circuit noted that the contract expressly allowed Exxon to set the prices at which it would sell gasoline to the franchisees, that Comment 3 to §2-305 suggested that a "posted price" set by a merchant would "normally" meet the requirements of good faith, and that the prices charged by Exxon were comparable to its competitors. Id. at 453-54. Nevertheless, the court upheld a jury verdict against Exxon for $5.7 million on the strength of substantial evidence that Exxon set its prices to the franchisees at a level that was intended to make the franchises unprofitable and drive them out of business. Thus, a breach of the duty of good faith could be shown through the improper motive even though the prices set might appear to be objectively reasonable. Id at 458-59. Accord Wilson v. Amerada Hess Corp., 773 A.2d 1121 (N.J. 2001) (reversing summary judgment on dealers' claim of breach of duty of good faith by franchisor; dealers should be allowed discovery to show franchisor's intent to set prices that would make the businesses unprofitable and allow replacement with franchisor's stores).

5. *The duty of good faith in loan agreements.* "Lender liability" is a term commonly used to refer to one category of cases involving interaction between express terms and proposed limits derived from the implied obligation of good faith. Those cases generally involve an express grant of authority to the lender to terminate credit or demand immediate repayment, weighed against a claim by the debtor that the lender must exercise the authority in good faith. Courts have been divided on the effect of the duty of good faith in these situations. In K.M.C. Co., Inc. v. Irving Trust Co., 757 F.2d 752 (6th Cir. 1985), the court held that the duty of good faith limited a lender's express right to terminate a financing agreement with and demand repayment from a grocery business, especially since the lender also had control of the grocery business's bank account with its operating funds. Other courts have also imposed an obligation of good faith on lenders in similar circumstances. See Reid v. Key Bank of Southern Maine, Inc., 821 F.2d 9 (1st Cir. 1987); Quality Automotive Co. v. Signet Bank/Maryland, 775 F. Supp. 849 (D. Md. 1991). In contrast, however, many subsequent decisions have been critical of *K.M.C.* on the ground that the court effectively overrode the express terms of the contract. See Kham & Nate's Shoes No. 2, Inc. v. First Bank, 908 F.2d 1351 (7th Cir. 1990) (holding that the implied covenant of good faith cannot limit express contract rights, even if the conduct appears opportunistic). The courts giving priority to the express provisions in loan agreements find support in the official comment to Revised UCC §1-309, which states that the obligation of good faith "has no application to demand instruments . . . whose very nature permits call at any time with or without reason." See Oak Rubber Co. v. Bank One, N.A., 214 F. Supp. 2d 820 (N.D. Ohio 2002); Solar Motors, Inc. v. First National Bank of Chandron, 545 N.W.2d 714 (Neb. 1996). See generally

Steven J. Burton & Eric G. Andersen, Contractual Good Faith, 150-159 (1995) (criticizing *K.M.C.* for not adhering closely enough to the parties' justifiable expectations and allowing the jury to second-guess business judgment, but also criticizing *Kham,* for a literal contract reading that allowed the lender to recapture a forgone opportunity); Dennis M. Patterson, A Fable from the Seventh Circuit: Frank Easterbrook on Good Faith, 76 Iowa L. Rev. 503 (1991) (criticizing *Kham* for being regressively formalistic).

Comment: Requirements and Output Contracts

Although a contract to buy and sell goods, even a long-term one, may be very precise in stating the quantity of goods to be delivered, often the parties choose instead to leave that term flexible. Sometimes the parties will agree that the seller undertakes to supply all goods of a given type that the buyer may "require" during the term of their contract; in other cases, the buyer will be obligated to buy all the seller's "output" of a given commodity. Such arrangements, likely to stretch over a period of months or even years, may be commercially advantageous to both parties. On the one hand, they provide the output seller with a guaranteed market for its goods, and the requirements buyer with an assured source for its needs. They do involve some risk for the other party, to be sure, but if the output buyer is confident that it can use as much as the seller is likely to produce, the risk may appear small; conversely, the requirements seller may see little chance that the buyer's requirements will exceed its capacity to supply. Those risks may of course be further controlled by contractual provisions imposing some maximum on the output buyer's obligation to buy, or the requirements seller's obligation to supply.

Initially, "requirements" contracts got a cold reception from American courts (similar to that accorded to distributorship agreements such as those in *Leibel*). They were frequently held invalid on various grounds: as lacking in consideration (the buyer was felt to have made only an illusory promise to buy); as lacking in mutuality (the seller was bound, but the buyer in effect was not); as too vague or indefinite for enforcement (the quantity that buyer was bound to purchase could not be precisely ascertained). Such agreements continued to be made, however, and answers to the objections described above were developed. The theoretical problem of lack of consideration was effectively met by Professor Corbin, who asserted that consideration existed because of the commitment by the buyer to either buy goods from the designated seller or *not buy at all.* See 1A Corbin on Contracts §156; Restatement (Second) §77. The buyer's performance of such an agreement does therefore entail sufficient legal "detriment" to constitute consideration because each alternative would have been sufficient consideration if bargained for separately. See Restatement (Second) §77, Comment *b.*

The second objection to enforcement of requirements contracts, their lack of mutuality, was met by a growing willingness (which we have already noted in Chapter 2) on the part of courts and commentators to demote mutuality of obligation to the status of a mere corollary of the consideration rule, with no independent force of its own. And the indefiniteness problem in many cases was overcome by the fact that sufficient information to allow for enforcement can often be gleaned from the buyer's past history, estimates by the parties, a prior course of dealing between them, or their course of performance under the agreement at issue. See, e.g., Eastern Air Lines, Inc. v. Gulf Oil Corp., 415 F. Supp. 429, 436-437 (S.D. Fla. 1975) (obligation of Eastern to purchase fuel exclusively from Gulf, but only at certain cities, was enforceable and would be construed in light of extensive past dealings between the parties and industry practices).

Thus, by the time the Uniform Commercial Code was drafted, the requirements contract had a long legal history. In §2-306, the drafters of the Code apparently attempted to continue the trend toward validation of such agreements in general, and also to provide assistance to any court that must decide whether a particular "requirements buyer" or "output seller" has failed to perform its obligation. See generally Elliot Axelrod, The Requirements Contract—What Is Required?, 31 Drake L. Rev. 83 (1981); John C. Weistart, Requirements and Output Contracts: Quantity Variations under the UCC, 1973 Duke L.J. 599; Paulette K. Zisk, Note, Requirements Contracts, "More or Less," Under the Uniform Commercial Code, 33 Rutgers L. Rev. 105 (1980).

Early judicial hostility to the requirements contract appears to have been based in part on the difficulty of distinguishing between agreements that truly bound the buyer to buy all of its needs of an item from the particular seller, at least in a particular market or region, and agreements in which the buyer merely promised to buy whatever it might want or choose to buy from that seller. The latter promise was viewed as illusory: in substance, no promise at all. Even today, under the UCC, an agreement that does not to some appreciable degree bind the buyer to buy *only* from the particular seller is likely to be viewed as invalid and unenforceable, because lacking in consideration or mutuality of obligation. See, e.g., Brooklyn Bagel Boys, Inc., v. Earthgrains Refrigerated Dough Products, Inc., 212 F.3d 373 (7th Cir. 2000) (contract which contained price structure and required buyer's "non-binding" forecast of needs every three months held not to be requirements contract because buyer was not required to buy all of its bagels or any specified quantity from seller); Orchard Group, Inc. v. Konica Medical Corp., 135 F.3d 421 (6th Cir. 1998) (letter agreement with buying group of health care providers which established discount rate on x-ray film prices and stated term of 36 months held unenforceable because it failed either to provide an estimated quantity or to require plaintiff to purchase exclusively from Konica). Sometimes, however, courts will find an implied promise of exclusivity that renders the contract binding. See, e.g., Essco Geometric v. Harvard Industries, 46 F.3d 718 (8th Cir. 1995) (extrinsic evidence established that both buyer and seller understood arrangement to be exclusive even though not expressly stated in letter agreement); Pepsi-Cola Co. v. Steak 'N Shake, Inc., 981 F. Supp. 1149 (S.D. Ind. 1997) (contract must be read as a whole to determine parties' intent; exclusivity may be implied). Or, the court may find consideration apart from the buyer's executory promise. Famous Brands, Inc. v. David Sherman Corp., 814 F.2d 517 (8th Cir. 1987) (UCC requirement of good faith in filling requirements is deemed sufficient consideration to support contract to distribute grain alcohol; in the alternative, promissory estoppel may be used to enforce bottler's promise). The requirement of exclusivity is sharply criticized in Allen Blair, "You Don't Have to Be Ludwig Wittgenstein": How Llewellyn's Concept of Agreement Should Change the Law of Open-Quantity Contracts, 37 Seton Hall L. Rev. 67 (2006).

The UCC attempts in §2-306 to assist in the enforcement of requirements and output contracts by focusing on the general requirement of good faith and stressing the likelihood that the parties themselves may have furnished an estimate against which performance may be measured. The Comments to §2-306 furnish further suggestions, including the possibility (Comment 3) that the agreement may contain a "maximum or minimum." Comment 2 indicates that the seller in a requirements contract is to be protected against increases in demand that exceed the bounds of "good faith." A "ballooning" of demand by a requirements buyer has often been held to be in bad faith, both at common law and under the Code. See, e.g., A&A Mechanical, Inc. v. Thermal Equipment Sales, Inc., 998 S.W. 2d 505 (Ky. Ct. App. 1999) (assuming contract for ductwork came under §2-306, 29% increase in quantity would be unreasonable deviation from estimate).

The Code also protects the requirements seller against a bad faith reduction in the buyer's demand, but this has proven somewhat more problematic for the courts. Generally courts have held that a requirements buyer may reduce its level of purchases even to zero, so long as it acts in good faith. See MDC Corp. v. John H. Harland Co., 228 F. Supp. 2d 387 (S.D.N.Y. 2002) (noting that most authorities hold that a requirements buyer may decrease its orders as long as it does so in good faith). This may be the case even where the contract contains an estimate of the buyer's level of demand. See Empire Gas Corp. v. American Bakeries, Inc., 840 F.2d 1333 (7th Cir. 1988) (holding that requirements buyer may reduce its level of demand even to zero so long as it acts in good faith); but see Simcala, Inc. v. American Coal Trade, Inc., 821 So. 2d 197 (Ala. 2001) (holding that principles of statutory interpretation require that decreases not be disproportionate to any estimate under plain meaning of §2-306(1); buyer's decrease in purchases from estimate of 17,500 tons of coal to 7200 tons would be a breach even if buyer acted in good faith).

Assuming that a court applies the test of good faith to a substantial reduction in purchases by a requirements buyer, how is breach established? The cases in these area are not altogether clear, but the reduction will probably be in good faith if resulting directly from reasons beyond the buyer's control. E.g., R. A. Weaver & Associates, Inc. v. Asphalt Construction, Inc., 587 F.2d 1315 (D.C. Cir. 1978) (defendant buyer not liable for breach after construction project was altered to eliminate use of limestone that plaintiff had contracted to supply). In contrast, a buyer that attempts to procure its requirements more cheaply elsewhere or with intent to harm the seller is clearly acting in bad faith. See Chemical Distributors, Inc. v. Exxon Corp., 1 F.3d 1478 (5th Cir. 1993) (jury finding of bad faith justified by evidence that buyer bypassed seller to purchase requirements directly and more inexpensively from manufacturer and in effort to eliminate seller as competitor in related market).

Section 2-306 also addresses "output" contracts, agreements to sell exclusively to a buyer all the goods that the seller may produce. Termination of output by a seller is likely to be judged by a standard very similar to that generally applied in evaluating reduction of requirements by a buyer. See Feld v. Henry S. Levy & Sons, Inc., 335 N.E.2d 320 (N.Y. 1975) (while bankruptcy or imperilment of the company's existence would justify termination of bread crumb production, mere yield of less profit would not be a good faith reason). The good faith standard applies even if the output contract contains an estimated quantity. See Canusa Corp. v. A&R Lobosco, Inc., 986 F. Supp. 723 (E.D.N.Y. 1997) (cessation of output would be judged by good faith of the reason rather than the amount of variation from the contract estimate; cessation because performance was more costly than expected was not a good faith reason).

Morin Building Products Co. v. Baystone Construction, Inc.
United States Court of Appeals
717 F.2d 413 (7th Cir. 1983)

POSNER, Circuit Judge.

This appeal from a judgment for the plaintiff in a diversity suit requires us to interpret Indiana's common law of contracts. General Motors, which is not a party to this case, hired Baystone Construction, Inc., the defendant, to build an addition to a Chevrolet plant in Muncie, Indiana. Baystone hired Morin Building Products Company, the plaintiff, to supply and erect the aluminum walls for the addition. The contract required that the exterior siding of the walls be of "aluminum type 3003, not less than 18 B & S gauge, with a mill finish and stucco embossed surface texture to match finish and texture of existing metal siding." The contract also provided "that all work shall be done subject to the final approval of the Architect or Owner's [General Motors'] authorized agent, and his decision in matters relating to artistic effect shall be final, if within the terms of the Contract Documents"; and that "should any dispute arise as to the quality or fitness of materials or workmanship, the decision as to acceptability shall rest strictly with the Owner, based on the requirement that all work done or materials furnished shall be first class in every respect. What is usual or customary in erecting other buildings shall in no wise enter into any consideration or decision."

Morin put up the walls. But viewed in bright sunlight from an acute angle the exterior siding did not give the impression of having a uniform finish, and General Motors' representative rejected it. Baystone removed Morin's siding and hired another subcontractor to replace it. General Motors approved the replacement siding. Baystone refused to pay Morin the balance of the contract price ($23,000) and Morin brought this suit for the balance, and won.

The only issue on appeal is the correctness of a jury instruction which, after quoting the contractual provisions requiring that the owner (General Motors) be satisfied with the contractor's (Morin's) work, states: "Notwithstanding the apparent finality of the foregoing language, however, the general rule applying to satisfaction in the case of contracts for the construction of commercial buildings is that the satisfaction clause must be determined by objective criteria. Under this standard, the question is not whether the owner was satisfied in fact, but whether the owner, as a reasonable person, should have been satisfied with the materials and workmanship in question." There was much evidence that General Motors' rejection of Morin's exterior siding had been totally unreasonable. Not only was the lack of absolute uniformity in the finish of the walls a seemingly trivial defect given the strictly utilitarian purpose of the building that they enclosed, but it may have been inevitable; "mill finish sheet" is defined in the trade as "sheet having a nonuniform finish which may vary from sheet to sheet and within a sheet, and may not be entirely free from stains or oil." If the instruction was correct, so was the judgment. But if the instruction was incorrect — if the proper standard is not whether a reasonable man would have been satisfied with Morin's exterior siding but whether General Motors' authorized representative in fact was — then there must be a new trial to determine whether he really was dissatisfied, or whether he was not and the rejection therefore was in bad faith.

Some cases hold that if the contract provides that the seller's performance must be to the buyer's satisfaction, his rejection — however unreasonable — of the seller's performance is not a breach of the contract unless the rejection is in bad faith. See, e.g., Stone Mountain Properties, Ltd. v. Helmer, 139 Ga. App. 865, 869, 229 S.E.2d 779, 783 (1976). But most cases conform to the position stated in section 228 of the Restatement (Second) of Contracts (1979): if "it is practicable to determine whether a reasonable person in the position of the obligor would be satisfied, an interpretation is preferred under which the condition [that the obligor be satisfied with the obligee's performance] occurs if such a reasonable person in the position of the obligor would be satisfied." See Farnsworth, Contracts 556-59 (1982); Annot., 44 A.L.R.2d 1114, 1117, 1119-20 (1955). Indiana Tri-City Plaza Bowl, Inc. v. Estate of Glueck, 422 N.E.2d 670, 675 (Ind. App. 1981) . . . adopts the majority position as the law of Indiana.

We do not understand the majority position to be paternalistic; and paternalism would be out of place in a case such as this, where the subcontractor is a substantial multistate enterprise. The requirement of reasonableness is read into a contract not to protect the weaker party but to approximate what the parties would have expressly provided with respect to a contingency that they did not foresee, if they had foreseen it. Therefore the requirement is not read into every contract, because it is not always a reliable guide to the parties' intentions. In particular, the presumption that the performing party would not have wanted to put himself at the mercy of the paying party's whim is overcome when the nature of the performance contracted for is such that there are no objective standards to guide the court. It cannot be assumed in such a case that the parties would have wanted a court to second-guess the buyer's rejection. So "the reasonable person standard is employed when the contract involves commercial quality, operative fitness, or mechanical utility which other knowledgeable persons can judge. . . . The standard of good faith is employed when the contract involves personal aesthetics or fancy." Indiana Tri-City Plaza Bowl, Inc. v. Estate of Glueck, supra, 422 N.E.2d at 675; see also Action Engineering v. Martin Marietta Aluminum, 670 F.2d 456, 460-61 (3d Cir. 1982).

We have to decide which category the contract between Baystone and Morin belongs in. The particular in which Morin's aluminum siding was found wanting was its appearance, which may seem quintessentially a matter of "personal aesthetics," or as the contract put it, "artistic effect." But it is easy to imagine situations where this would not be so. Suppose the manager of a steel plant rejected a shipment of pig iron because he did not think the pigs had a pretty shape. The reasonable-man standard would be applied even if the contract had an "acceptability shall rest strictly with the Owner" clause, for it would be fantastic to think that the iron supplier would have subjected his contract rights to the whimsy of the buyer's agent. At the other extreme would be a contract to paint a portrait, the buyer having reserved the right to reject the portrait if it did not satisfy him. Such a buyer wants a portrait that will please him rather than a jury, even a jury of connoisseurs, so the only question would be his good faith in rejecting the portrait, Gibson v. Cranage, 39 Mich. 49 (1878).

This case is closer to the first example than to the second. The building for which the aluminum siding was intended was a factory — not usually intended to be a thing of beauty. That aesthetic considerations were decidedly secondary to considerations of function and cost is suggested by the fact that the contract specified mill-finish aluminum, which is unpainted. There is much debate in the record over whether it is even possible to ensure a uniform finish within and among sheets, but it is at least clear that mill finish usually is not uniform. If General Motors and Baystone had wanted a uniform finish they would in all likelihood have ordered a painted siding. Whether Morin's siding achieved a reasonable uniformity amounting to satisfactory commercial quality was susceptible of objective judgment; in the language of the Restatement, a reasonableness standard was "practicable."

But this means only that a requirement of reasonableness would be read into this contract if it contained a standard owner's satisfaction clause, which it did not; and since the ultimate touchstone of decision must be the intent of the parties to the contract we must consider the actual language they used. The contract refers explicitly to "artistic effect," a choice of words that may seem deliberately designed to put the contract in the "personal aesthetics" category whatever an outside observer might think. But the reference appears as number 17 in a list of conditions in a general purpose form contract. And the words "artistic effect" are immediately followed by the qualifying phrase, "if within the terms of the Contract Documents," which suggests that the "artistic effect" clause is limited to contracts in which artistic effect is one of the things the buyer is aiming for; it is not clear that he was here. The other clause on which Baystone relies, relating to the quality or fitness of workmanship and materials, may seem all-encompassing, but it is qualified by the phrase, "based on the requirement that all work done or materials furnished shall be first class in every respect" — and it is not clear that Morin's were not. This clause also was not drafted for this contract; it was incorporated by reference to another form contract (the Chevrolet Division's "Contract General Conditions"), of which it is paragraph 35. We do not disparage form contracts, without which the commercial life of the nation would grind to a halt. But we are left with more than a suspicion that the artistic-effect and quality-fitness clauses in the form contract used here were not intended to cover the aesthetics of a mill-finish aluminum factory wall.

If we are right, Morin might prevail even under the minority position, which makes good faith the only standard but presupposes that the contract conditioned acceptance of performance on the buyer's satisfaction in the particular respect in which he was dissatisfied. Maybe this contract was not intended to allow General Motors to reject the aluminum siding on the basis of artistic effect. It would not follow that the contract put Morin under no obligations whatsoever with regard to uniformity of finish. The contract expressly required it to use aluminum having "a mill finish . . . to match finish . . . of existing metal siding." The jury was asked to decide whether a reasonable man would have found that Morin had used aluminum sufficiently uniform to satisfy the matching requirement. This was the right standard if, as we believe, the parties would have adopted it had they foreseen this dispute. It is unlikely that Morin intended to bind itself to a higher and perhaps unattainable standard of achieving whatever perfection of matching that General Motors' agent insisted on, or that General Motors would have required Baystone to submit to such a standard. Because it is difficult — maybe impossible — to achieve a uniform finish with mill-finish aluminum, Morin would have been running a considerable risk of rejection if it had agreed to such a condition, and it therefore could have been expected to demand a compensating increase in the contract price. This would have required General Motors to pay a premium to obtain a freedom of action that it could not have thought terribly important, since its objective was not aesthetic. If a uniform finish was important to it, it could have gotten such a finish by specifying painted siding.

All this is conjecture; we do not know how important the aesthetics were to General Motors when the contract was signed or how difficult it really would have been to obtain the uniformity of finish it desired. The fact that General Motors accepted the replacement siding proves little, for there is evidence that the replacement siding produced the same striped effect, when viewed from an acute angle in bright sunlight, that Morin's had. When in doubt on a difficult issue of state law it is only prudent to defer to the view of the district judge, Murphy v. White Hen Pantry Co., 691 F.2d 350, 354 (7th Cir. 1982), here an experienced Indiana lawyer who thought this the type of contract where the buyer cannot unreasonably withhold approval of the seller's performance.

Lest this conclusion be thought to strike at the foundations of freedom of contract, we repeat that if it appeared from the language or circumstances of the contract that the parties really intended General Motors to have the right to reject Morin's work for failure to satisfy the private aesthetic taste of General Motors' representative, the rejection would have been proper even if unreasonable. But the contract is ambiguous because of the qualifications with which the terms "artistic effect" and "decision as to acceptability" are hedged about, and the circumstances suggest that the parties probably did not intend to subject Morin's rights to aesthetic whim.

Affirmed.

Notes and Questions

1. *Interpretation of conditions of satisfactory performance.* Contracts frequently contain express terms that obligate one party to perform to the "satisfaction" of the other, or condition one party's duty of performance on his "satisfaction"

with the performance of the other party. As Judge Posner's opinion in *Morin* illustrates, such provisions are unlikely to be interpreted as conferring on the party whose satisfaction is at issue an unlimited power to determine and declare his own dissatisfaction, without external check. Indeed, if pure unbridled discretion were the test, the party whose performance was so conditioned might be held to have made only an "illusory" promise, defeating the contract as a whole. Instead, one of the two approaches described in *Morin* will ordinarily be used: Either the obligor's declaration of dissatisfaction will be judged by a standard of reasonableness; or at minimum he will be held to the standard of "honest" dissatisfaction. As Judge Posner states, the "objective" standard has been traditionally employed in cases where "commercial quality, operative fitness, or mechanical utility" are in question, while the "subjective" standard is likely to be employed where "personal aesthetics or fancy" are at issue.

In an extensive survey of the "satisfaction" cases, Conditions of Personal Satisfaction in the Law of Contract, 27 N.Y.L. Sch. L. Rev. 103 (1981), Professor James Brook pointed out that early decisions did not make the objective/subjective distinction; all cases, whether involving "mechanical utility" or not, were judged by the same, subjective standard of the promisee's honest dissatisfaction. Following later case law, Restatement (Second) §228 declares that the objective test should be preferred when it is "practicable to determine whether a reasonable person in the position of the obligor would be satisfied." Comment *a* to §228 indicates that the subjective standard should be used only where "the agreement leaves no doubt that it is only honest dissatisfaction that is meant and no more." See Able Distributing Co. v. Lampe, 773 P.2d 504 (Ariz. Ct. App. 1989) (objective standard applied to determine whether there had been "satisfactory" completion of subcontract for plumbing work on apartment complex). Where personal services are involved, the court may be more likely to approve the use of a subjective test. E.g., Beasley v. St. Mary's Hospital of Centralia, 558 N.E.2d 677 (Ill. App. Ct. 1990) (contract obligating doctor to remain "satisfactory" to hospital in performance of his duties held to permit discharge upon subjective dissatisfaction with his performance).

Where the contract conditions performance by one party on the other's performance to the satisfaction of some independent third party, such as an architect or engineer, the Restatement (Second) indicates a greater tolerance for the application of a subjective test, on the assumption that a third party is less likely to be affected by the "selfish interests" of the obligor. See Restatement, Contracts (Second) §227, Comment *b*, Illustration 3, and §228, Comment *b*. Accord Hanscom v. Gregorie, 562 A.2d 1232 (Me. 1989) (defendants freed from purchase obligation where their building inspector determined that plaintiff's building was not free from "defects of a substantial nature," even though trial court concluded that defects in question, though expensive to remedy, were not "substantial"; contract left that question to honest judgment of defendant's expert).

2. *Judge Posner's analysis.* Does Judge Posner adequately justify the court's choice of an objective standard in *Morin?* Comment *b* to Restatement (Second) §228 indicates that a preference for the objective test may be justified in part by the desire to avoid "forfeiture," which the Restatement defines elsewhere

(Comment *b* to §229) as "the denial of compensation that results when the obligee loses his right to the agreed exchange after he has relied substantially, as by preparation or performance on the expectation of that exchange." Was this factor at work in *Morin?* (You will recall, incidentally, that Judge Posner as an academic was the leader of the so-called Chicago School of "efficiency" theorists. In that light, it is interesting to note in the *Morin* opinion his careful disclaimer of "paternalism" and his expression of solicitude for the "foundations of freedom of contract.")

3. *Effect of standard of interpretation.* Even where the court does agree with the defendant that only the subjective test of "honest dissatisfaction" should be employed, one ought not to assume that the defendant will therefore ultimately prevail. Although the plaintiff's burden of establishing that defendant was not honestly dissatisfied may be a difficult one, it is not necessarily impossible. E.g., Forman v. Benson, 446 N.E.2d 535 (Ill. App. Ct. 1983) (seller's rejection of buyer's credit report held pretextual, an attempt to renegotiate price and interest rate). Conversely, application of the objective, reasonableness standard will not necessarily produce a victory for the plaintiff. See, e.g., Kennedy Associates, Inc. v. Fischer, 667 P.2d 174 (Alaska 1983) (even under objective test mortgage lender could reasonably disapprove property in question after conducting agreed inspection).

Locke v. Warner Bros., Inc.
California Court of Appeal
57 Cal. App. 4th 354, 66 Cal. Rptr. 2d 921 (1997), review denied
(Nov. 19, 1997)

KLEIN, Presiding Judge.

Plaintiffs and appellants Sondra Locke (Locke) and Caritas Films, a California corporation (Caritas) (sometimes collectively referred to as Locke) appeal a judgment following a grant of summary judgment in favor of defendant and respondent Warner Bros., Inc. (Warner).

The essential issue presented is whether triable issues of material fact are present which would preclude summary judgment.

We conclude triable issues are present with respect to whether Warner breached its development deal with Locke by categorically refusing to work with her, and whether Warner fraudulently entered into said agreement without the intention to work with Locke. The judgment therefore is reversed as to the second and fourth causes of action and otherwise is affirmed.

FACTUAL AND PROCEDURAL BACKGROUND

1. LOCKE'S DISPUTE WITH EASTWOOD.

In 1975, Locke came to Warner to appear with Clint Eastwood in *The Outlaw Josey Wales* (Warner Bros. 1976). During the filming of the movie, Locke and Eastwood began a personal and romantic relationship. For the next dozen years, they lived in Eastwood's Los Angeles and Northern California homes. Locke also appeared in a number of Eastwood's films. In 1986, Locke made her directorial debut in *Ratboy* (Warner Bros. 1986).

In 1988, the relationship deteriorated, and in 1989 Eastwood terminated it. Locke then brought suit against Eastwood, alleging numerous causes of action. That action was resolved by a November 21, 1990, settlement agreement and mutual general release. Under said agreement, Eastwood agreed to pay Locke additional compensation in the sum of $450,000 "on account of past employment and Locke's contentions" and to convey certain real property to her.

2.   LOCKE'S DEVELOPMENT DEAL WITH WARNER.

According to Locke, Eastwood secured a development deal for Locke with Warner in exchange for Locke's dropping her case against him. Contemporaneously with the Locke/Eastwood settlement agreement, Locke entered into a written agreement with Warner, dated November 27, 1990. It is the Locke/Warner agreement which is the subject of the instant controversy.

The Locke/Warner agreement had two basic components. The first element states Locke would receive $250,000 per year for three years for a "non-exclusive first look deal." It required Locke to submit to Warner any picture she was interested in developing before submitting it to any other studio. Warner then had 30 days either to approve or reject a submission.

The second element of the contract was a $750,000 "pay or play" directing deal. The provision is called "pay or play" because it gives the studio a choice: It can either "play" the director by using the director's services, or pay the director his or her fee.

Unbeknownst to Locke at the time, Eastwood had agreed to reimburse Warner for the cost of her contract if she did not succeed in getting projects produced and developed. Early in the second year of the three-year contract, Warner charged $975,000 to an Eastwood film, *Unforgiven* (Warner Bros. 1992).

Warner paid Locke the guaranteed compensation of $1.5 million under the agreement. In accordance with the agreement, Warner also provided Locke with an office on the studio lot and an administrative assistant. However, Warner did not develop any of Locke's proposed projects or hire her to direct any films. Locke contends the development deal was a sham, that Warner never intended to make any films with her, and that Warner's sole motivation in entering into the agreement was to assist Eastwood in settling his litigation with Locke.

3.   LOCKE'S ACTION AGAINST WARNER.

On March 10, 1994, Locke filed suit against Warner, alleging four causes of action.

The first cause of action alleged sex discrimination in violation of public policy. Locke alleged Warner denied her the benefit of the bargain of the development deal on account of her gender.

The third cause of action, captioned "Tortious Breach of the Implied Covenant of Good Faith and Fair Dealing in Violation of Public Policy," alleged a similar claim. Locke pled that in denying her the benefits of the

Warner/Locke agreement, Warner was "motivated by [its] discriminatory bias against women in violation of . . . public policy."

The second cause of action alleged that Warner breached the contract by refusing to consider Locke's proposed projects and thereby deprived her of the benefit of the bargain of the Warner/Locke agreement.

Lastly, the fourth cause of action alleged fraud. Locke pled that at the time Warner entered into the agreement with her, it concealed and failed to disclose it had no intention of honoring the agreement.

Warner answered, denied each and every allegation and asserted various affirmative defenses.

4. WARNER'S MOTION FOR SUMMARY JUDGMENT AND
   OPPOSITION THERETO.

On January 6, 1995, Warner filed a motion for summary judgment. Warner contended it did not breach its contract with Locke because it did consider all the projects she presented, and the studio's decision not to put any of those projects into active development or "hand" Locke a script which it already owned was not a breach of any express or implied contractual duty. Warner asserted the odds are slim a producer can get a project into development and even slimmer a director will be hired to direct a film. During the term of Locke's deal, Warner had similar deals with numerous other producers and directors, who fared no better than Locke.

As for Locke's sex discrimination claims, Warner averred there was no evidence it ignored Locke's projects or otherwise discriminated against her on account of her gender. Finally, Warner urged the fraud claim was meritless because Locke had no evidence that when Warner signed the contract, it did not intend to honor the deal, and moreover, Warner had fulfilled its contractual obligations to Locke.

In opposing summary judgment, Locke contended Warner breached the agreement in that it had no intention of accepting any project regardless of its merits. Locke also asserted Warner committed fraud by entering into the agreement without any intention of approving any project with Locke or allowing Locke to direct another film.

Locke's opposition papers cited the deposition testimony of Joseph Terry, who recounted a conversation he had with Bob Brassel, a Warner executive, regarding Locke's projects. Terry had stated to Brassel: "'Well, Bob, this woman has a deal on the lot. She's a director that you want to work with. You have a deal with her. . . . I've got five here that she's interested in.' And then I would get nothing. . . . I was told [by Brassel], 'Joe, we're not going to work with her,' and then, 'That's Clint's deal.' And that's something I just completely did not understand."

Similarly, the declaration of Mary Wellnitz stated: She worked with Locke to set up projects at Warner, without success. Shortly after she began her association with Locke, Wellnitz submitted a script to Lance Young, who at the time was a senior vice-president of production at Warner. After discussing the script, Young told Wellnitz, "Mary, I want you to know that I think Sondra is a wonderful woman and very talented, but, if you think I can go down the hall and tell Bob Daly that I have a movie I want to make with her he would tell me to forget it. They are not going to make a movie with her here."

5. TRIAL COURT'S RULING.

On February 17, 1995, the trial court granted summary judgment in favor of Warner. Thereafter, the trial court signed an extensive order granting summary judgment. The order stated:

> Under the contract, Warner had no obligation either to put into development any of the projects submitted to the studio for its consideration, or to "hand off" to Locke any scripts for her to direct that it previously had acquired from someone else. The implied covenant of good faith and fair dealing cannot be imposed to create a contract different from the one the parties negotiated for themselves. Warner had the option to pass on each project Locke submitted. Warner was not required to have a "good faith" or "fair" basis for declining to exercise its right to develop her material. Such a requirement would be improper and unworkable. A judge or jury cannot and should not substitute its judgment for a film studio's when the studio is making the creative decision of whether to develop or produce a proposed motion picture. Such highly subjective artistic and business decisions are not proper subjects for judicial review. Moreover, Warner had legitimate commercial and artistic reasons for declining to develop the projects Locke submitted.

With respect to Locke's claim she was defrauded by Warner when it entered into the agreement with the undisclosed intention not to honor its contractual obligations, the trial court ruled that because Warner did not breach its contractual obligations to Locke, the fraud claim was meritless. Also, it could not be inferred from the statements by Young and Brassel that two years earlier, when Warner entered into agreement, it had no intention of working with Locke.

As for the two causes of action alleging sex discrimination, the trial court found no evidence Warner declined to develop the projects Locke submitted, and declined to use her directing services, on account of her gender.

Locke filed a timely notice of appeal from the judgment.

CONTENTIONS

Locke contends: The trial court erred by granting Warner's motion for summary judgment based on its conclusion there were no disputed issues of material fact; the trial court erred in weighing the evidence, resolving doubts against Locke, the nonmoving party, and adopting only those inferences favorable to Warner where the evidence supported contrary inferences; and the trial court committed reversible error first by failing to make any findings or evidentiary rulings and then by adopting Warner's defective ruling.

DISCUSSION

1. STANDARD OF APPELLATE REVIEW.

. . .

2. A TRIABLE ISSUE EXISTS AS TO WHETHER WARNER BREACHED ITS CONTRACT WITH LOCKE BY FAILING TO EVALUATE LOCKE'S PROPOSALS ON THEIR MERITS.

As indicated, the second cause of action alleged Warner breached the contract by "refusing to consider the projects prepared by [Locke] and depriving [Locke] of the benefit of the bargain of the Warner-Locke agreement."

In granting summary judgment on this claim, the trial court ruled "[a] judge or jury cannot and should not substitute its own judgment for a film studio's when the studio is making the creative decision of whether to develop or produce a proposed motion picture. Such highly-subjective artistic and business decisions are not proper subjects for judicial review."

The trial court's ruling missed the mark by failing to distinguish between Warner's right to make a subjective creative decision, which is not reviewable for reasonableness, and the requirement the dissatisfaction be bona fide or genuine.

a. General principles.

" '[W]here a contract confers on one party a discretionary power affecting the rights of the other, a duty is imposed to exercise that discretion in good faith and in accordance with fair dealing.' [Citations.]" (Perdue v. Crocker National Bank (1985) 38 Cal. 3d 913, 923 [216 Cal. Rptr. 345, 702 P.2d 503]; accord, Kendall v. Ernest Pestana, Inc. (1985) 40 Cal. 3d 488, 500 [220 Cal. Rptr. 818, 709 P.2d 837].) It is settled that in "'every contract there is an implied covenant that neither party shall do anything which will have the effect of destroying or injuring the right of the other party to receive the fruits of the contract. . . .'" (Kendall, supra, at p.500; accord, Waller v. Truck Ins. Exchange, Inc., supra, 11 Cal. 4th at p.36.)

Therefore, when it is a condition of an obligor's duty that he or she be subjectively satisfied with respect to the obligee's performance, the subjective standard of *honest satisfaction* is applicable. (1 Witkin, Summary of Cal. Law (9th ed. 1987) Contracts, §729, p.659; Rest. 2d Contracts, §228, coms. a, b, pp.182-183.) "Where the contract involves matters of fancy, taste or judgment, the promisor is the sole judge of his satisfaction. If he asserts *in good faith* that he is not satisfied, there can be no inquiry into the reasonableness of his attitude. [Citations.] Traditional examples are employment contracts . . . and agreements to paint a portrait, write a literary or scientific article, or produce a play or vaudeville act. [Citations.]" (1 Witkin, Summary of Cal. Law, supra, §730, p.660; accord, Schuyler v. Pantages (1921) 54 Cal. App. 83, 85-87 [201 P.137].) In such cases, "the promisor's determination that he is not satisfied, *when made in good faith*, has been held to be a defense to an action on the contract. [Citations.]" (Mattei v. Hopper (1958) 51 Cal. 2d 119, 123 [330 P.2d 625], italics added.)

Therefore, the trial court erred in deferring entirely to what it characterized as Warner's "creative decision" in the handling of the development deal. If Warner acted in bad faith by categorically rejecting Locke's work and refusing to work with her, irrespective of the merits of her proposals, such conduct is not beyond the reach of the law.

b. Locke presented evidence from which a trier of fact reasonably could infer Warner breached the agreement by refusing to consider her proposals in good faith.

Merely because Warner paid Locke the guaranteed compensation under the agreement does not establish Warner fulfilled its contractual obligation. As pointed out by Locke, the value in the subject development deal was not merely the guaranteed payments under the agreement, but also the opportunity to direct and produce films and earn additional sums, and most importantly, the opportunity to promote and enhance a career.

Unquestionably, Warner was entitled to reject Locke's work based on its subjective judgment, and its creative decision in that regard is not subject to being second-guessed by a court. However, bearing in mind the requirement that subjective dissatisfaction must be an honestly held dissatisfaction, the evidence raises a triable issue as to whether Warner breached its agreement with Locke by not considering her proposals on their merits.

As indicated, the deposition testimony of Joseph Terry recounted a conversation he had with Bob Brassel, a Warner executive, regarding Locke's projects. In that conversation, Brassel stated " 'Joe, we're not going to work with her,' and then, 'That's Clint's deal.' "

Similarly, the declaration of Mary Wellnitz recalled a conversation she had with Lance Young, a senior vice-president of production at Warner. After discussing the script with Wellnitz, Young told her: "Mary, I want you to know that I think Sondra is a wonderful woman and very talented, but, if you think I can go down the hall and tell Bob Daly that I have a movie I want to make with her he would tell me to forget it. They are not going to make a movie with her here."

The above evidence raises a triable issue of material fact as to whether Warner breached its contract with Locke by categorically refusing to work with her, irrespective of the merits of her proposals. While Warner was entitled to reject Locke's proposals based on its subjective dissatisfaction, the evidence calls into question whether Warner had an honest or good faith dissatisfaction with Locke's proposals, or whether it merely went through the motions of purporting to "consider" her projects.

c. No merit to Warner's contention Locke seeks to rewrite the instant agreement to limit Warner's discretionary power.

Warner argues that while the implied covenant of good faith and fair dealing is implied in all contracts, it is limited to assuring compliance with the express terms of the contract and cannot be extended to create obligations not contemplated in the contract. (Racine & Laramie, Ltd. v. Department of Parks & Recreation (1992) 11 Cal. App. 4th 1026, 1032 [14 Cal. Rptr. 2d 335].)

This principle is illustrated in Carma Developers (Cal.), Inc. v. Marathon Development California, Inc. (1992) 2 Cal. 4th 342, 351-352 [6 Cal. Rptr. 2d 467, 826 P.2d 710], wherein the parties entered into a lease agreement which stated that if the tenant procured a potential sublessee and asked the landlord for consent to sublease, the landlord had the right to terminate the lease, enter into negotiations with the prospective sublessee, and appropriate for itself all profits from the new arrangement. *Carma* recognized "[t]he covenant of good faith finds particular application in situations where one party is invested with a discretionary power affecting the rights of another." (Id., at p.372.) The court expressed the view that "[s]uch power must be exercised in good faith." (Ibid.) At the same time, *Carma* upheld the right of the landlord under the express terms of the lease to freely exercise its discretion to terminate the lease in order to claim for itself—and deprive the tenant of—the appreciated rental value of the premises. (Id., at p.376.)

In this regard, *Carma* stated: "We are aware of no reported case in which a court has held the covenant of good faith may be read to prohibit a party from doing that which is expressly permitted by an agreement. On the contrary, as a general matter, implied terms should never be read to vary express terms. 'The general rule [regarding the covenant of good faith] is plainly subject to the exception that the parties may, by express provisions of the contract, grant the right to engage in the very acts and conduct which would otherwise have been forbidden by an implied covenant of good faith and fair dealing. . . . This is in accord with the general principle that, in interpreting a contract "an implication . . . should not be made when the contrary is indicated in clear and express words." 3 Corbin, Contracts, §564, p.298 (1960). . . . *As to acts and conduct authorized by the express provisions of the contract,* no covenant of good faith and fair dealing can be implied which forbids such acts and conduct. And if defendants were given the right to do what they did by the express provisions of the contract there can be no breach.' [Citation.]" (Carma Developers (Cal.), Inc. v. Marathon Development California, Inc., supra, 2 Cal. 4th at p.374, italics added.)

In Third Story Music, Inc. v. Waits (1995) 41 Cal. App. 4th 798, 801 [48 Cal. Rptr. 2d 747], the issue presented was "whether a promise to market music, or to refrain from doing so, at the election of the promisor is subject to the implied covenant of good faith and fair dealing where substantial consideration has been paid by the promisor."

In that case, Warner Communications obtained from Third Story Music (TSM) the worldwide right to manufacture, sell, distribute and advertise the musical output of singer/songwriter Tom Waits. (Third Story Music, Inc. v. Waits, supra, 41 Cal. App. 4th at pp.800-801.) The agreement also specifically stated that Warner Communications "'may at our election refrain from any or all of the foregoing.'" (Id., at p.801.) TSM sued Warner Communications for contract damages based on breach of the implied covenant of good faith and fair dealing, claiming Warner Communications had impeded TSM's receiving the benefit of the agreement. (Id., at p.802.) Warner Communications demurred to the complaint, alleging the clause in the agreement permitting it to "'at [its] election refrain' from doing anything to profitably exploit the music is controlling and precludes application of any implied covenant." (Ibid.) The demurrer was sustained on those grounds. (Ibid.)

The reviewing court affirmed, holding the implied covenant was unavailing to the plaintiff. (Third Story Music, Inc. v. Waits, supra, 41 Cal. App. 4th at pp.808-809.) Because the agreement expressly provided Warner Communications had the right to refrain from marketing the Waits recordings, the implied covenant of good faith and fair dealing did not limit the discretion given to Warner Communications in that regard. (Ibid.; Carma Developers (Cal.), Inc. v. Marathon Development California, Inc., supra, 2 Cal. 4th at p.374.)

Warner's reliance herein on *Third Story Music, Inc.,* is misplaced. The Locke/Warner agreement did not give Warner the express right to refrain from working with Locke. Rather, the agreement gave Warner *discretion* with respect to developing Locke's projects. The implied covenant of good faith and fair dealing obligated Warner to exercise that discretion honestly and in good faith.

In sum, the Warner/Locke agreement contained an implied covenant of good faith and fair dealing, that neither party would frustrate the other party's right to receive the benefits of the contract. (Comunale v. Traders & General Ins. Co., supra, 50 Cal. 2d at p.658; Waller v. Truck Ins. Exchange, Inc., supra, 11 Cal. 4th at p.36.) Whether Warner violated the implied covenant and breached the contract by categorically refusing to work with Locke is a question for the trier of fact.

3. A TRIABLE ISSUE EXISTS AS TO WHETHER WARNER MADE A FRAUDULENT PROMISE.

In the fourth cause of action, Locke pled at the time Warner entered into the agreement with her, it concealed and failed to disclose it had no intention of honoring the agreement.

The trial court held that because Warner did not breach any express or implied obligations owed to Locke, she could not prevail on the fraud claim. However, as explained above, a triable issue exists as to whether Warner breached the agreement with Locke. Therefore, the trial court's rationale for disposing of the fraud claim is undermined.

The trial court also ruled Locke could not prevail on the fraud claim because there was no evidence Warner had a fraudulent intent at the time the parties entered into the contract. The trial court acknowledged Locke "filed a declaration of her development assistant, Mary Wellnitz, in which Ms. Wellnitz states that a Warner Bros. executive, Lance Young, remarked in late 1992 that Warner Bros. was 'not going to make a movie' with Ms. Locke. [Locke] also offered the deposition testimony of a third party, Joe Terry, in which he recalled a 1993 conversation with another Warner Bros. production executive, Bob Brassel, in which Mr. Brassel said that the studio was not going to work with Ms. Locke. However, the Court does not believe that these statements would permit a jury to infer that two years earlier, when plaintiffs and the defendant entered into their contract, Warner Bros. intended to breach its obligations."

We disagree. Fraudulent intent must often be established by circumstantial evidence, and may be "inferred from such circumstances as defendant's . . . failure even to attempt performance, . . . " (Tenzer v. Superscope, Inc., supra, 39 Cal. 3d at p.30.) Based on the above evidence that Warner had expressed an absolute unwillingness to work with Locke, a trier of fact reasonably could infer Warner never intended to give Locke's proposals a good faith evaluation and that Warner entered into the agreement with Locke solely as an accommodation to Eastwood, who had promised to reimburse Warner for any losses under the agreement. The trial court erred in concluding such an inference could not be drawn from the evidence. We conclude the issue of fraudulent intent is one for the trier of fact.

4. LOCKE WAIVED ANY ERROR IN THE TRIAL COURT'S RULING WITH RESPECT TO HER CAUSES OF ACTION ALLEGING GENDER BIAS.

Locke's opening brief does not assert any error in the trial court's disposition of her two causes of action alleging sex discrimination. Accordingly, this court may treat the claims as having been waived.

Belatedly, Locke's reply brief contends she presented evidence which raised the inference she was discriminated against because of her gender. "Ordinarily, [appellants'] failure to raise an issue in their opening brief waives the issue on appeal. [Citation.]" (Tisher v. California Horse Racing Bd. (1991) 231 Cal. App. 3d 349, 361 [282 Cal. Rptr. 330]; accord, 1119 Delaware v. Continental Land Title Co. (1993) 16 Cal. App. 4th 992, 1004 [20 Cal. Rptr. 2d 438]; Regency Outdoor Advertising, Inc. v. Carolina Lanes, Inc. (1995) 31 Cal. App. 4th 1323, 1333 [37 Cal. Rptr. 2d 552].) Locke has not shown good cause for the untimely contention. Therefore, we disregard Locke's argument the trial court erred in granting summary judgment on the first and third causes of action.

5. REMAINING ISSUES NOT REACHED.

Because we find triable issues are present with respect to the second and fourth causes of action, it is unnecessary to address Locke's remaining contentions.

DISPOSITION

The judgment is reversed with respect to the second and fourth causes of action and is otherwise affirmed. Locke to recover costs on appeal.

KITCHING, J., and ALDRICH, J., concurred.

Notes and Questions

1. *Standards for the exercise of discretion.* In *Morin*, we saw the court choosing between an "objective" and a "subjective" standard for the good faith exercise of discretion — between a "reasonable person" standard and one of mere "honesty in fact." In the *Locke* case, it appears that defendant Warner Brothers argued that the contract with Locke gave it an absolute right to refrain from developing any of Locke's proposals, so long as it paid her the minimum amounts required by their agreement. Locke on the other hand took the position, accepted by the appellate court, that while their contract gave Warner Brothers discretion in deciding whether to proceed with any of her projects, the implied obligation of good faith required at a minimum that it exercise that discretion honestly — that it judge her various proposals on their merits, not simply refuse "categorically" to work with her. Do you agree with the court's view? What other evidence should Locke be required to produce at trial to establish bad faith on the part of Warner Brothers? Should Warner be required to produce evidence of objective, rational bases for rejecting all of Locke's proposals?

2. *Factual context for* **Locke.** As the court indicated, the *Locke* case had its beginning in the intimate and professional relationship between actors Sondra Locke and Clint Eastwood. News accounts indicate that the relationship came to an abrupt end when Eastwood had locks changed on the shared home and packed Locke's belongings while she was away. See generally Ann W. O'Neill, Locke Feels Vindicated After Lawsuit, L.A. Times, Sept. 29, 1996, at A1. Locke originally brought suit against Eastwood in 1989

for a share in the real property and on other theories in what is commonly called a "palimony" lawsuit, similar to that in the *Watts* case in Chapter 2. As part of a 1990 settlement of the 1989 lawsuit, Eastwood facilitated the $1.5 million three-year development contract between Locke and Warner. In 1994 Locke sued Warner for breach after all her proposals were rejected under the development contract. While pursuing the case against Warner, Locke discovered evidence of the "side-deal" between Warner and Eastwood that required Eastwood to reimburse Warner for its payments to Locke. Locke then initiated a second lawsuit against Eastwood for fraud relating to the Warner contract, seeking recovery for the damage allegedly done to her career. The second Locke-Eastwood lawsuit was settled in 1996 for an undisclosed amount after the jury in the case had begun deliberations. Id. Thus, this action by Locke against Warner constituted the remaining part of the litigation. Note that Restatement (Second) §205, Comment *d* states that "[s]ubterfuges and evasions violate the obligation of good faith even though the actor believes his conduct to be justified." Suppose the court had accepted Warner's contention that the contract (and perhaps industry practice as well) gave it a completely unfettered right to accept or reject Locke's proposals for whatever reason it chose — indeed, to act for "a good reason, a bad reason, or no reason at all," as the freedom to be completely arbitrary is often described. Would it necessarily follow that Locke's suit should fail?

3. *Gender or racial discrimination as breach of duty of good faith.* Locke's complaint also alleged that Warner denied her the benefits of the contract because of gender bias against women, but Locke's appellate briefs failed to make a timely challenge to the trial court's grant of summary judgment on this issue. If Locke had been able to prove that Warner rejected her proposals because of her gender, would that constitute a breach of the implied covenant of good faith? What sort of evidence might Locke have been able to produce to prove gender discrimination? Similar questions could be raised whether discrimination in contract performance on the basis of race, ethnicity, sexual orientation, or disability would amount to a breach of the duty of good faith, apart from perhaps violating federal or state antidiscrimination statutes. Cf. Doe v. Kohn Nast & Graf, 862 F. Supp. 1310 (E.D. Pa. 1994) (plaintiff alleged discrimination covered by Americans with Disabilities Act on the basis of HIV-infected status and separate claim for breach of implied duty of good faith after being barred from his office; court refused to dismiss good faith issue); Ricci v. Key Bancshares of Maine, Inc., 662 F. Supp. 1132 (1987) (court upheld jury finding of discrimination based on national origin under federal statute and separate claim for breach of implied covenant of good faith in abrupt termination of credit agreement).

Professor Steven Burton has taken the position that, while other contract law doctrine may prevent race discrimination in performance of contracts, the implied duty of good faith cannot be used to rule out racially discriminatory conduct. Burton bases this conclusion on the theory that implied terms should rest on the agreement of the parties and, realistically, parties in an "unjust society" might not rule out racial discrimination. Steven J. Burton, Racial Discrimination in Contract Performance: *Patterson* and a State Law Alternative, 25 Harv. C.R.-C.L. L. Rev. 431, 464 n.116 (1990). In response, Professor

Neil Williams asserted that society has reached a consensus, reflected in a number of civil rights laws, that racial discrimination is wrong. In Williams' view, construing the implied duty of good faith to prohibit racial discrimination would give "effect to the reasonable expectations of the parties that they will not be treated in a manner offensive to prevailing community norms." Neil G. Williams, Offer, Acceptance, and Improper Considerations: A Common Law Model for the Prohibition of Racial Discrimination in the Contracting Process, 62 Geo. Wash. L. Rev. 183, 214 (1994). In a similar vein, Professor Emily Houh has recently argued that the concept of good faith could be productively applied in the employment context to reach certain types of invidious discriminatory treatment based on factors such as race or gender but not cognizable under existing statutory law. Emily M.S. Houh, Critical Race Realism: Re-Claiming the Antidiscrimination Principle through the Doctrine of Good Faith in Contract Law, 66 U. Pitt. L. Rev. 455 (2005). Would it be consistent with the express terms and implicit understanding of the parties in *Locke* to imply a term that Warner would not reject Locke's movie proposals based on her gender?

Donahue v. Federal Express Corp.
Superior Court of Pennsylvania
753 A.2d 238 (2000)

Judges: Before: MCEWEN, President Judge, LALLY-GREEN, J., and CIRILLO, President Judge Emeritus.

LALLY-GREEN, J.:

In this employment case, Appellant Brion O. Donahue appeals from the order dated April 29, 1999, granting preliminary objections in the nature of a demurrer filed by Defendants/Appellees Federal Express Corporation ("FedEx") and Robert W. Marshall and entering judgment in Appellees' favor. We affirm.

On January 22, 1999, Appellant filed a complaint against FedEx and Marshall, alleging the following. Appellant was a FedEx employee from November 1979 until January 1997. Complaint, Docket Entry 1, P 4. Appellant's final position was Commercial MX Service Administrator. Id. Marshall was Appellant's immediate supervisor. Id., P 3.

Appellant questioned numerous invoices which did not comport with repair orders in his department. Id., P 6. Appellant also called FedEx's attention to other improprieties, such as FedEx's failure to pay invoices and Marshall's practice of directing auto body work to a Cleveland auto body shop owned by a person with whom Marshall vacationed. Id., P 12. After Appellant complained to Marshall about the invoice-discrepancy issue, Marshall accused Appellant of gross misconduct. Id., P 6. Specifically, Appellant was accused of making a racial remark in front of another FedEx employee, and was accused of making derogatory remarks about Marshall to vendors and others. Id., P 7. In the months leading to his discharge, FedEx management denied Appellant the clerical assistance that he requested, gave Appellant additional duties of tire purchasing and file maintenance, and ordered Appellant to falsify data to meet administrative requirements. Id., P 8.

FedEx has a Guaranteed Fair Treatment Procedure ("GFTP") for employee grievances. Id., P 5. Appellant appealed his termination through Step 1 of the GFTP. Id. FedEx management upheld the termination, concluding that Appellant violated FedEx's Acceptable Conduct Policy. Id., P 10 & Exhibit D. Appellant appealed through Step 2 of the GFTP, alleging that Marshall was seeking retribution for exposing the vendor non-payment issue. Id., P 11 and Exhibit E. FedEx management again upheld the termination. Id., P 13. Finally, Appellant appealed through Step 3 of the GFTP, alleging that FedEx accused him of making unprofessional remarks, "but did not identify the purported comments, nor give [Appellant] the opportunity to deny the same." Id., P 14. Again, FedEx management upheld the termination. Id., P 16.

In Count 1 of his complaint, labeled "Wrongful Termination," Appellant alleges: (1) FedEx breached the implied covenant of good faith and fair dealing in at-will employment contracts; (2) FedEx violated public policy insofar as the termination violates the Pennsylvania Human Relations Act ("PHRA"), 43 P.S. §951 et seq.; (3) Appellant supplied sufficient additional consideration to remove his status from that of an at-will employee; and (4) FedEx violated public policy by retaliating against him for lodging complaints against Marshall. Id., P 19.

Count 2 of the complaint alleges that FedEx violated the PHRA. Id., PP 21-26. Count 3 alleges that Marshall intentionally interfered with Appellant's contractual relations with FedEx, and that Marshall and FedEx defamed Appellant. Id., PP 27-35. Count 4 alleges that FedEx breached its implied employment contract with Appellant. Id., PP 36-38.[1]

On March 17, 1999, FedEx and Marshall filed preliminary objections in the nature of a demurrer. Docket Entry 3. Appellant filed a responsive brief. Docket Entry 5. On April 29, 1999, the esteemed trial court, the Honorable Eugene Strassburger, granted the preliminary objections and entered judgment in favor of FedEx and Marshall. This appeal followed.[2]

Appellant raises four issues on appeal:

I. Whether the court below erred in granting Preliminary Objections where appellant raised [the] breach of the duty of good faith and fair dealing exception to [the] at-will employment rule.

II. Whether the court below erred in granting Preliminary Objections where [the] doctrine of necessary implication dictated that parties in an employment relationship do and perform those things that according to reason and justice they should do in order to carry out the employment relationship.

---

1. On appeal, Appellant raises no challenge to the dismissal of his PHRA, intentional interference, and defamation claims.

2. In his Concise Statement of Matters Complained of on Appeal, Appellant contended that the court erred by: (1) dismissing his wrongful termination claim; (2) finding that the law does not impose an implied duty of good faith and fair dealing in an at-will employment relationship; (3) ruling that no statute or public policy was implicated by his termination; (4) failing to find additional consideration to rebut the presumption of at-will employment; (5) failing to find that Marshall specifically intended to harm Appellant; and (6) failing to find an implied employment contract arising from the GFTP. Docket Entry 12.

III. Whether the court below erred in granting Preliminary Objections where [the] Guaranteed Fair Treatment Procedure of employer created a promise to dismiss only for cause.

IV. Whether the court below erred in granting Preliminary Objections where appellant alleges employer specifically intended to harm appellant.

Appellant's Brief at 3.

Our standard and scope of review are well settled.

> Our standard of review mandates that on an appeal from an order sustaining preliminary objections which would result in the dismissal of suit, we accept as true all well-pleaded material facts set forth in the Appellant['s] complaint and all reasonable inferences which may be drawn from those facts. . . .

Ellenbogen v. PNC Bank N.A., 1999 PA Super 131, 731 A.2d 175, 181 (Pa. Super. 1999) (citations and footnote omitted).

First, Appellant argues that the trial court erred by dismissing his claim for breach of the implied duty of good faith and fair dealing. Specifically, Appellant claims that FedEx breached this duty "by terminating him in contravention of its GFTP and engaging in a sham review of his conduct in the GFTP." Appellant's Brief at 10.

Every contract in Pennsylvania imposes on each party a duty of good faith and fair dealing in its performance and its enforcement. Kaplan v. Cablevision of Pa., Inc., 448 Pa. Super. 306, 671 A.2d 716, 722 (Pa. Super. 1996), appeal denied, 546 Pa. 645, 683 A.2d 883 (1996), citing, inter alia, Somers v. Somers, 418 Pa. Super. 131, 613 A.2d 1211, 1213 (Pa. Super. 1992), appeal denied, 533 Pa. 652, 624 A.2d 111 (1993). Good faith has been defined as "honesty in fact in the conduct or transaction concerned." Kaplan, 671 A.2d at 722. Appellant relies on Somers for the proposition that the implied duty of good faith and fair dealing applies to at-will employment relationships.

In that case, plaintiff Somers entered into an at-will employment relationship (as a consultant) with a corporation. The consulting contract further provided that if net profits were realized from a particular project, Somers would receive 50% of the profits. Somers, 613 A.2d at 1212. In order for profits to be realized, it was necessary for the corporation to resolve a claim with a third party. Id. Somers and the corporation disagreed as to how to handle this claim; as a result, Somers was fired. Id. Moreover, Somers alleged that the corporation showed a lack of good faith and due diligence in resolving its dispute with the third party, and in settling the claim for significantly less than was owed, thereby depriving him of approximately $3 million as his share of the proceeds. Id. at 1215. The trial court dismissed Somers' claim for breach of the implied duty of good faith and fair dealing.

This Court reversed, stating that "the duty to perform contractual obligations in good faith does not evaporate merely because the contract is an employment contract, and the employee has been held to be an employee at will." Id. at 1213, citing Baker v. Lafayette College, 350 Pa. Super. 68, 504

A.2d 247 (Pa. Super. 1986), *affirmed*, 516 Pa. 291, 532 A.2d 399 (1987), and Jacobs v. Kraft Cheese Co., 310 Pa. 75, 164 A. 774 (1933).[4] We concluded that Somers should have the opportunity to establish that the corporation acted in bad faith when it settled the claim in such a manner as to deprive him of his fair share of the profits related to the project. *Somers*, 613 A.2d at 1215.

Somers and the cases cited therein provide that, in an at-will employment relationship, the duty of good faith and fair dealing applies to those contractual terms that exist beyond the at-will employment relationship. For example, the plaintiff in *Somers* could recover for breach of implied duties connected to the profit sharing provision, but could not recover for the termination per se.

Baker involved a two-year employment contract between a college and a professor. The college's faculty handbook, which was explicitly made part of the contract itself, obliged the college to conduct an honest and meaningful evaluation of the professor's performance before deciding whether or not to extend the contract beyond its original term. *Baker*, 504 A.2d at 255.

The Court affirmed the grant of summary judgment in favor of the college and held that the implied duty of good faith and fair dealing applied to this reevaluation provision.[5] Id. Thus, the college was contractually obligated "to render a sincere and substantial performance of these contractual undertakings, complying with the spirit as well as the letter of the contract." Id. The *Baker* Court stressed that its holding was narrowly tailored to the facts of that case:

> We emphasize that our holding is a narrow one. This case does not present the more difficult issue whether an obligation of good faith and fair dealing should be implied into any employer-employee relationship, including at-will employment. Consequently, we do not decide that issue. We hold only that when an employer such as the College here expressly provides in an employment contract for a comprehensive evaluation and review process, we may look to the employer's good faith to determine whether the employer has in fact performed those contractual obligations.

Id.

In the years since *Baker* was decided, it appears that no Pennsylvania appellate court has held that an implied duty of good faith and fair dealing applies to termination of a pure at-will employment relationship. Indeed, our Supreme Court has held that "an at will employee has no cause of action against his employer for termination of the at-will relationship except where that termination threatens clear mandates of public policy." Pipkin v.

---

4. In *Jacobs*, plaintiff Jacobs approached Kraft with a new method for making cream cheese. Kraft hired Jacobs for a fixed term of 78 weeks. The employment contract expressly stated that Jacobs' employment was conditioned on his producing a cream cheese "satisfactory to the market," as measured by sales. After nine weeks, Kraft fired Jacobs, declaring that the cheese was unmarketable. Kraft had not attempted to market the product. A jury found in Jacobs' favor. Our Supreme Court affirmed the verdict, holding that, under the circumstances, Kraft had an implied duty to attempt to market the cheese before firing Jacobs.

5. In *Baker*, the trial court had granted summary judgment to Lafayette College on Baker's breach of contract/bad faith claim. We affirmed, holding that the record contained no evidence tending to establish that the College's review procedures were a sham or otherwise undertaken in bad faith. *Baker*, 504 A.2d at 256. Our Supreme Court affirmed. *Baker*, 516 Pa. 291, 532 A.2d 399 (1987).

Pennsylvania State Police, 548 Pa. 1, 5, 693 A.2d 190, 191 (1997). See also Werner v. Zazyczny, 545 Pa. 570, 579, 681 A.2d 1331, 1335 (1996); Paul v. Lankenau Hosp., 524 Pa. 90, 95, 569 A.2d 346, 348 (1990). In keeping with the above authority, we hold that Appellant cannot as a matter of law maintain an action for breach of the implied duty of good faith and fair dealing, insofar as the underlying claim is for termination of an at-will employment relationship.

Appellant suggests that he can maintain a cause of action for breach of the implied duty of good faith and fair dealing arising out of his claim that he was not treated fairly under the GFTP. Appellant's Brief at 10. If the GFTP were expressly incorporated into Appellant's employment contract, his claim would be analogous to *Baker*, which held that such a claim is viable. Appellant's complaint, however, points to no specific provision of the GFTP indicating that its provisions imposed separate contractual duties on FedEx.[7] In fact, the GFTP expressly states that "the policies and procedures set forth by the Company provide guidelines for management and other employees during employment but do not create contractual rights regarding termination or otherwise." Docket Entry 1 (Complaint), Exhibit A, page 3. Because Appellant has failed to allege facts indicating that the GFTP imposes any additional contractual duties on FedEx, Appellant's first claim lacks merit.

Appellant also argues that his termination violates public policy because he was fired for "blowing the whistle" on FedEx's failure to pay invoices and other unscrupulous practices. Appellant's Brief at 11-12. Generally, as noted above, no cause of action exists for termination of an at-will employment relationship unless the termination violates public policy. See *Pipkin*, supra. For example, "an employer (1) cannot require an employee to commit a crime, (2) cannot prevent an employee from complying with a statutorily imposed duty, and (3) cannot discharge an employee when specially prohibited from doing so by statute." Spierling v. First Am. Home Health Servs., Inc., 1999 PA Super 222, 737 A.2d 1250, 1252 (Pa. Super. 1999), quoting Hennessy v. Santiago, 708 A.2d 1269, 1273 (Pa. Super. 1998). In an appropriate case, the courts may announce that a particular practice violates public policy, even in the absence of a legislative pronouncement to that effect. Shick v. Shirey, 552 Pa. 590, 602, 716 A.2d 1231, 1237 (1998). On the other hand, a court's power to announce public policy is limited: "public policy is to be ascertained by reference to the laws and legal precedents and not from general considerations of supposed public interest." Id. (citations omitted).

Our Courts have repeatedly rejected claims that a private employer violated public policy by firing an employee for whistleblowing, when the employee was under no legal duty to report the acts at issue. See Geary v. United States Steel Corp., 456 Pa. 171, 183, 319 A.2d 174, 180 (1974) (no wrongful discharge claim where employee complained to superiors about

---

7. In this respect, Appellant's claim is more analogous to Banas v. Matthews Int'l Corp., 348 Pa. Super. 464, 502 A.2d 637, 647-648 (Pa. Super. 1985) (en banc). In that case, Banas was fired for using company materials for personal projects without permission. Banas alleged that he had permission, and pointed to sections of the employee handbook which stated that employees could use company materials for certain personal projects so long as they had permission. We found that the handbook was immaterial to the case, and that Banas could be fired at will regardless of the handbook because it did not create any contractual promise of job security.

substandard and potentially unsafe quality of employer's product); *Spierling,* 737 A.2d at 1254 (no wrongful discharge claim where employee was fired after searching discarded files for evidence of Medicare fraud and reporting such fraud to investigators). . . .

Appellant contends that employees should not be fired from private companies for reporting unscrupulous practices.[8] Appellant has failed to identify any relevant statutes or legal precedents indicating that such retaliation violates public policy. Accordingly, Appellant's claim for wrongful discharge under the public policy exception cannot stand.

Next, Appellant argues that the trial court failed to recognize duties imposed on FedEx by the "doctrine of necessary implication." Appellant's Brief at 13-15. According to Appellant, contracting parties have a duty to do those things that reason and justice dictate are necessary to ensure that the other party is not deprived of the fruits of the contract. Id. Upon review of this claim, we find that it is indistinguishable from Appellant's arguments concerning the implied duty of good faith and fair dealing. For the reasons set forth above, this claim lacks merit.

Next, Appellant argues that he furnished sufficient additional consideration to overcome the presumption that he is an at-will employee. An employee can defeat the at-will presumption by establishing that he gave his employer additional consideration other than the services for which he was hired. Cashdollar v. Mercy Hosp. of Pittsburgh, 406 Pa. Super. 606, 595 A.2d 70, 72-73 (Pa. Super. 1991). Additional consideration exists "when an employee affords his employer a substantial benefit other than the services which the employee is hired to perform, or when the employee undergoes a substantial hardship other than the services which he is hired to perform." 595 A.2d at 73 (citation omitted). For example, in *Cashdollar,* we found sufficient additional consideration where the employee, in response to the employer's persistent recruitment efforts, gave up a stable position in another state, sold his house, and relocated to a new city with his pregnant wife, only to be fired after sixteen days on the job. Id. On the other hand, our Courts have found no additional consideration where the employee "has suffered detriments, in the course of his or her employment, that are 'commensurate with those incurred by all manner of salaried professionals.'" Id., citing Veno v. Meredith, 357 Pa. Super. 85, 515 A.2d 571, 580 (Pa. Super. 1986) (no additional consideration when employee was fired after eight years over a difference of opinion with his employer, even though employee had originally moved from Newark to Pennsylvania and had foregone other employment opportunities over the years), *appeal denied,* 532 Pa. 665, 616 A.2d 986 (1992).

Appellant argues that he gave additional consideration by conferring "substantial, superior job performance." Appellant's Brief at 17. A general allegation of superior work performance is insufficient to establish additional consideration. First, performing well on the job does not generally confer a substantial benefit on his employer beyond that which the employee is paid to do. Moreover, performing well on the job does not generally constitute a detriment beyond that which is incurred by all manner of salaried

---

8. Unlike Appellant, public employees are protected by Pennsylvania's Whistleblower Law. *Holewinski,* 649 A.2d at 715; 43 P.S. §1421 et seq.

professionals. After reviewing Appellant's complaint as a whole, we conclude that Appellant has alleged no facts tending to establish that he conferred additional consideration. This claim fails.

Finally, Appellant argues that the trial court erred in granting preliminary objections because Appellant alleged that FedEx specifically intended to harm him. In *Krasja*, 622 A.2d at 360, we held an employee cannot maintain a cause of action for wrongful discharge based on a "specific intent to harm" theory. We reasoned that such a theory was no longer viable in light of our Supreme Court's decision in *Paul*, supra, which held that an at-will employee has no cause of action for wrongful discharge unless the termination violates public policy. Id. Accordingly, Appellant's "specific intent to harm" claim fails as a matter of law.

Order affirmed.

McEwen, President Judge, Concurs in the Result.

Notes and Questions

1. *Presumption of employment at-will.* The "at-will" doctrine is a concept that we have encountered before. You should recall from the Leibel v. Raynor Manufacturing Co. case earlier in this chapter that a franchise contract of indefinite duration is presumed to be at-will, meaning that either party is free to terminate the contract at any time and without a requirement of good or just cause. Application of the at-will doctrine to employment contracts in the United States has been traced back to the nineteenth century and it is widely recognized as "the prevailing rule throughout the country." Fitzgerald v. Salsbury Chemical, Inc., 613 N.W.2d 275, 280 (Iowa 2000). As one court put it, the doctrine "provides a heavy presumption that a contract for employment, unless otherwise expressly stated, is at-will in nature, with duration indefinite." Merrill v. Crothall-American, Inc., 606 A.2d 96, 102 (Del. 1992).

By definition, the at-will doctrine does not apply to a contract with a specified duration, e.g., a one-year or five-year contract. A contract that includes a specified duration is construed to mean that the employee may be terminated only for just or good cause. Era Aviation, Inc. v. Seekins, 973 P.2d 1137 (Alaska 1999); Wilder v. Cody Country Chamber of Commerce, 868 P.2d 211 (Wyo. 1994). The presumption of at-will employment, however, cannot be easily overcome and therefore an agreement for a term must be specific. See Bernard v. IMI Systems, Inc., 618 A.2d 338 (N.J. 1993) (overruling judicial precedent that salary stated in annual terms would implicitly create a year-long contract; more required to overcome at-will presumption); Booth v. McDonnell Douglas Truck Services, Inc., 585 A.2d 24 (Pa. Super. Ct. 1991) (fact that salary, evaluations, and benefits were described on annual basis is not enough to overcome at-will presumption and to imply a year term). But see Rooney v. Tyson, 697 N.E.2d 571 (N.Y. 1998) (agreement to employ fight trainer "for as long as [defendant] fought professionally" established legally cognizable duration and was not contract subject to termination at-will).

Another possibility is that the employee and the employer have an agreement that, although for an indefinite period, the employment contract can be terminated only with just or good cause. The parties may have an explicit agreement to this effect or the employee might allege that the commitment took the form of a promise of "permanent employment." Courts steeped in the traditional approach to at-will employment contracts have routinely denied such claims, holding that permanent employment does not mean employment "for life," merely that the employee's position will be of indefinite duration. Joseph M. Perillo, Calamari & Perillo on Contracts §2.9, at 59 (5th ed. 2003). Even if interpreted literally, promises of "permanent" employment have customarily been held to be unenforceable unless supported by some additional consideration beyond the employee's performance of her duties on the job. See, e.g., Worley v. Wyoming Bottling Co., 1 P.3d 615 (Wyo. 2000).

2. *The implied duty of good faith and at-will employment.* The *Donahue* court recognizes, as have the other cases in this section, that the implied covenant of good faith and fair dealing applies to every contract and identifies at least two situations in which the implied duty might be breached in an at-will employment contract. First, the court cites its earlier decision in Somers v. Somers, 613 A.2d 1211 (Pa. Super. Ct. 1992), in which an at-will employee sufficiently stated a claim for breach of the duty of good faith in alleging that the employer deprived him of compensation that appeared to have already been earned before termination. Other courts have recognized similar claims that termination which deprives the at-will employee of earned compensation would violate the duty of good faith. See, e.g., Trent Partners and Assoc., Inc. v. Digital Equipment Corp., 120 F. Supp. 2d 84 (D. Mass. 1999) (breach of duty of good faith to deprive at-will employee of commission by termination on the brink of a sale, but principle does not extend to generalized expectations of future orders that are not certain); Fortune v. National Cash Register Co., 364 N.E.2d 1251 (Mass. 1977) (discharge motivated by desire to deny plaintiff the benefit of a sales commission that had been earned in full would be breach of duty of good faith). Second, the *Donahue* court allows for the possibility that the implied duty of good faith may apply with regard to the manner in which an at-will employee is terminated, holding that a promised evaluation must be conducted in good faith. See also E. I. DuPont de Nemours & Co. v. Pressman, 679 A.2d 436 (Del. 1996) (breach of the implied covenant of good faith would be established by proving that employer created false grounds and fictitious basis for termination of at-will employee but not by the termination itself). Cf. Schuster v. Derocili, 775 A.2d 1029 (Del. 2001) (termination based on resistance to sexual harassment in workplace would violate implied covenant of good faith); Monge v. Beebe Rubber Co., 316 A.2d 549 (N.H. 1974) (alleged retaliatory discharge for plaintiff's rejection of foreman's sexual advances would breach implied duty of good faith).

The *Donahue* court and many others, however, have emphatically rejected the proposition that the implied covenant of good faith will transform an at-will employment relationship into one that generally requires good cause for discharge. See MacKay v. Rayonier, Inc., 75 F. Supp. 2d 22 (D. Conn. 1999); Wilder v. Cody Country Chamber of Commerce, 868 P.2d 211 (Wyo. 1994). Some courts have gone even further and held that the implied covenant of good faith imposes no limit on at-will employment contracts. E.g., Kerrigan v. Britches of Georgetowne, Inc., 705 A.2d 624 (D.C. 1997) (implied covenant of good faith is not relevant to employment at-will); Breen v. Dakota Gear & Joint Co., 433 N.W.2d 221 (S.D. 1988) (Restatement (Second) concept of good faith is overly broad and should not be applicable to at-will employment contracts).

3. *Other exceptions to at-will doctrine.* The *Donahue* court and other jurisdictions have recognized a number of other possible limitations on the ability of an employer to terminate an at-will employee:

Public policy. A clear majority of jurisdictions recognize a public policy exception to the at-will employment doctrine and often treat such claims as sounding in tort. See Wholey v. Sears, Roebuck & Co., 803 A.2d 482, 488-89 (Md. 2002) (citing 30 jurisdictions recognizing public policy exception in nonexhaustive listing). The decision usually regarded as the leading case applying the public policy limitation is Petermann v. International Brotherhood of Teamsters, 344 P.2d 25 (Cal. Ct. App. 1959), which held that an at-will employee would be entitled to relief for wrongful discharge if he were fired because he refused to commit perjury at the request of his employer. See also Thompson v. St. Regis Paper Co., 685 P.2d 1081 (Wash. 1984) (employee's discharge would be tortious if based on steps taken to comply with antibribery measures in Foreign Corrupt Practices Act). As indicated in *Donahue,* however, courts generally restrict this theory to circumstances involving a "clear mandate" of public policy founded on constitutional, legislative, administrative, or established judicial authority. See Thibodeau v. Design Group One Architects, LLC, 802 A.2d 731 (Conn. 2002) (public policy exception adopted by courts in effort to balance competing interests of employees and employers, but claim must be predicated on employer's violation of important and clearly articulated public policy; statute established policy against discrimination based on pregnancy, but it did not apply to businesses with fewer than three employees). Some jurisdictions have rejected the public policy limitation altogether. See Salter v. Alfa Insurance Co., Inc., 561 So. 2d 1050 (Ala. 1990) (refusing to adopt public policy limit because it would overrule nearly 70 years of precedent and because "public policy" standard is too nebulous); De Petris v. Union Settlement Ass'n., Inc., 657 N.E.2d 269 (N.Y. 1995) (confirming that New York does not recognize a tort of wrongful discharge in at-will employment). What is the nature of the public policy argument raised in *Donahue?* Do you agree with the court's decision on that issue?

Additional consideration as basis of implied "for cause" term. The employee in *Donahue* argued that he gave additional consideration to the employer. The court recognized that, if proved, such consideration would defeat the at-will presumption and require just cause for termination. The *Donahue* court referred to precedent holding that the additional consideration can be found in the employee's relinquishment of another job, at least in circumstances where there are persistent recruitment efforts by the employer and the employee incurs expense and other hardship in relocating. For such courts the role of extra consideration is to indicate the parties' intent to have a more lasting relationship than a presumed at-will contract. See, e.g., Rabago-Alvarez v. Dart Industries, Inc., 127 Cal. Rptr. 222 (Ct. App. 1976); Greene v. Oliver Realty, Inc., 526 A.2d 1192 (Pa. 1987). What claim of additional consideration does Donahue make?

Employee handbook as basis of implied "for cause" term. Yet another exception to the at-will presumption is found in cases recognizing a cause of action for breach of contract when the defendant employer had committed itself, by public statements in personnel manuals or otherwise, to refrain from terminating employees except for good cause. A leading decision in this area is Toussaint v. Blue Cross & Blue Shield, 292 N.W.2d 880 (Mich. 1980), in which the employee received assurance of job security before accepting employment and the company manual stated there would be dismissal only for cause. The court deemed the company's statement to create an "implied-in-fact" term that the employee would be discharged only for cause. Id. at 894. See also Weiner v. McGraw-Hill, Inc., 443 N.E.2d 441 (N.Y. 1982) (employer's promise in handbook to discharge only for cause supported by consideration in employee's acceptance and continuation of employment); Woolley v. Hoffmann-La Roche, Inc., 491 A.2d 1257 (N.J.), *modified*, 499 A.2d 515 (N.J. 1985) (concern that employee claims of implied terms might be sustained on inadequate proof is largely overcome when the employer's manuals are in evidence). See generally Julia Barnhart, Comment, The Implied-in-Fact Contract Exception to At-Will Employment: A Call for Reform, 45 UCLA L. Rev. 817 (1998) (reviewing the evolution of the implied-in-fact limitation in California).

Not all courts agree, however, that statements of job security made in policy manuals are contractually binding. See, e.g., Fleming v. AT&T Information Services, Inc., 878 F.2d 1472, 1474 (D.C. Cir. 1989) (company's written policies of treating employees fairly and of providing post-termination counseling are "irrelevant" in determining whether the employee is hired at-will); Williams v. Wal-Mart Stores, Inc., 882 F. Supp. 612, 615-616 (S.D. Tex. 1995) (Texas law makes it clear that for manual to alter at-will relationship it must "specifically and expressly limit" employer's right to terminate employee; unsigned manuals may also fail to satisfy the statute of frauds). As indicated by the *Donahue* court, the inclusion of a disclaimer in an employee manual stating that the document does not create a binding obligation may preclude a claim on that basis, but the disclaimer will not necessarily be effective. Compare Farnum v. Brattleboro Retreat, Inc., 671 A.2d 1249, 1254 (Vt. 1995) ("mere inclusion of boilerplate language" that employment is at-will cannot negate implied contract; disclaimers must be evaluated in context of other manual provisions and employment circumstances), with Lincoln v. Wackenhut Corp., 867 P.2d 701, 703-704 (Wyo. 1994) (handbook disclaimer found effective when disclaimer was in bold print, large type, capitalized, conspicuously placed, unambiguous, and reserved employer's right to change its terms).

Promissory estoppel. Some courts have also held that detrimental reliance by a discharged employee may serve as a basis for relief. See Sheppard v. Morgan-Keegan, 266 Cal. Rptr. 784 (Ct. App. 1990) (employee who resigned a position and moved across country would not expect to be terminated before he had a chance to perform in job; summary judgment for employer reversed, citing promissory estoppel as well as the implied covenant of good faith); Peck v. IMEDIA, 679 A.2d 745 (N.J. 1996) (promissory estoppel may protect preperformance reliance in connection with at-will employment; failure to promptly notify new employee of intent to rescind position might be breach of duty of good faith); Worley v. Wyoming Bottling Co., 1 P.3d 615 (Wyo. 2000) (at-will employee pled sufficient case for promissory estoppel in alleging employer's promise of job security induced procurement of home refinance loan). But see Geiger v. AT&T Corp., 962 F. Supp. 637 (E.D. Pa. 1997) (promissory estoppel is not recognized in Pennsylvania as a limit on at-will doctrine); Slate v. Saxon, Marquoit, Bertoni & Todd, 999 P.2d 1152 (Or. 2000) (associate attorney terminated after taking state bar exam but before beginning work under indefinite duration contract with law firm could not bring promissory estoppel claim; at-will nature of employment precluded possibility of reasonable or substantial reliance).

4. *At-will doctrine and personnel actions other than discharge.* The plaintiff in *Donahue* appeared to allege that retaliatory personnel actions were taken against him before his actual discharge. If a court recognizes restrictions on an employer's right to discharge an at-will employee, will such limitations also apply to demotions or other changes in employment conditions? Compare Scott v. Pacific Gas & Electric Co., 904 P.2d 834 (Cal. 1995) (extending policy manual exception to demotions), with White v. State of Washington, 929 P.2d 396 (Wash. 1997) (refusing to extend public policy exception to employer's personnel actions that are less than discharge).

5. *At-will employment and ethical duties of lawyers.* Termination of at-will employees may raise additional questions when the party terminated is an attorney. In Wieder v. Skala, 609 N.E.2d 105 (N.Y. 1992), the New York Court of Appeals ruled that an associate attorney's employment contract with a law firm should be read to implicitly incorporate certain ethical standards of the profession, such as the duty to report suspected unfitness of other attorneys. Thus, the court found a termination wrongful when the plaintiff associate was discharged for reporting another attorney's misconduct. But see Bohatch v. Butler & Binion, 977 S.W.2d 543 (Tex. 1998) (law firm could not be held liable in damages for wrongful expulsion of partner who alleged in good faith that another partner engaged in unethical conduct). *Wieder* and *Bohatch* both involved lawyers in private firms who were discharged because they reported misconduct by other attorneys. Lawyers employed by private corporations rather than law firms have also brought wrongful discharge claims. Compare General Dynamics Corp. v. Superior Court, 876 P.2d 487 (Cal. 1994) (recognizing right of in-house counsel to bring claim for wrongful discharge based on public policy and implied contract theories), with Balla v. Gambro, Inc., 584 N.E.2d 104 (Ill. 1991) (in-house counsel did not have cause of action against employer for wrongful discharge when employer fired him after he threatened to take whatever action was necessary to prevent company from selling defective kidney dialysis machines).

6. *Scholarly analysis.* What interests are at stake in a decision like *Donahue*? Many legal scholars have advocated a change in the at-will doctrine to benefit employees based on the individual's interest in freedom from unjust discharge, along with the public's interest in a securely employed labor force. See, e.g., Cynthia L. Estlund, Wrongful Discharge Protections in an At-Will World, 74 Tex. L. Rev. 1655 (1996); Pauline T. Kim, Bargaining with Imperfect Information: A Study of Worker Perceptions of Legal Protection in an At-Will World, 83 Cornell L. Rev. 105 (1997); David Millon, Default Rules,

Wealth Distribution, and Corporate Law Reform: Employment At Will Versus Job Security, 146 U. Pa. L. Rev. 975 (1998).

Other writers have argued in favor of the employment at-will rule on grounds of efficiency. Limitations on an employer's right of discharge increase litigation costs and may harm employees as a class by making employers more reluctant to hire risky employees. See Richard A. Epstein, In Defense of the Contract At Will, 51 U. Chi. L. Rev. 947 (1984). See also John P. Frantz, Market Ordering Versus Statutory Control of Termination Decisions: A Case for the Inefficiency of Just Cause Dismissal Requirements, 20 Harv. J.L. & Pub. Poly. 555 (1997); Andrew P. Morriss, Bad Data, Bad Economics, and Bad Policy: Time to Fire the Wrongful Discharge Law, 74 Tex. L. Rev. 1901 (1996).

A rebuttal to the efficiency arguments can be found in Peter Linzer, The Decline of Assent: At-Will Employment as a Case Study of the Breakdown of Private Law Theory, 20 Ga. L. Rev. 323, 409-415 (1986). Professor Linzer asserts that many of the recent attempts by the courts to ground relief against wrongful discharge on one of the traditional common law bases — contract or tort — are not entirely convincing and that the traditional subject-area divisions should not be controlling. Id. at 335-369. Relying on a variety of strands of theory (including modern notions of "the firm" and the "relational contract" theories of Professor Ian Macneil), Linzer argues that relief from improper discharge in many cases is appropriate and, moreover, that the courts, and not merely the legislatures, are appropriate organs for creating such rules of relief.

> I think it can even be argued that courts are institutionally at least as capable as legislatures to apply community values to problems of private law. Courts — at least Anglo-American courts — have done this as long as there have been courts. Certainly they can easily get out of touch, and in any event we are not speaking of a Gallup Poll. But judges seeking a policy basis will be affected by the attitudes of the time, as well as by their own ethical, economic, social and political biases. Legislators hear from constituents and lobbyists, but with many private law matters they are likely to be importuned more loudly, and to hear more clearly, after the courts have acted rather than while the issue is "abstract" and unresolved.

Id. at 423. Noting that "inaction" is action that preserves the employer-dominant power regime, Linzer concludes by calling on courts to return to "common law creativity" by discerning and applying community values in this and other areas where traditional common law rules appear inadequate. Id. at 424. Linzer also urges courts to recognize that "all contributors to an enterprise deserve some security and some share of the enterprise itself." Id. at 425. Would it be feasible or wise to reverse the at-will presumption and require that employers have good cause to discharge an employee with a contract of indefinite duration?

PROBLEM 6-1

Ed Evers owned an accounting company in Santa Carlita, your city. Last January, Ed was approached by Fran Farmer of Acme Accountants, a large accounting firm with a number of branch offices in Santa Carlita and neighboring communities. Fran suggested that Ed come to work for Acme as a manager. "You'll be paid a salary plus commissions," Fran told Ed, "and I'm sure you'll make more money than you're making now." "That's tempting," Ed responded, "I plan to retire in five years or so, and it sure would be nice to get rid of the headache of running my own business in the meantime. But I averaged $5,000 per month in profits over the last five years. Can you match that?" Fran said, "Come with us and you should do even better than that, no question about it."

Ed then notified his clients that he was closing his business and would start work for Acme on February 1. On his first day at Acme, Ed completed a one-page employment form that stated that he would be on "probation status" for three months and then would become a "permanent employee." Just above the signature block was a clause that read, "This form is the entire employment agreement of the parties." The personnel officer told Ed the form was mandatory and was used only to initiate company benefit programs.

Ed was assigned to manage the largest Acme branch office in downtown Santa Carlita. Business at the branch grew steadily as Ed's old clients brought their work to that location. Ed was paid a base salary of $5,000 and commissions of about $3,000 each month during the first three months. Although pleased with his income, Ed also became concerned because Acme charged a 20 percent fee to customers who took "instant payment" of their income tax refunds. Ed told Fran on April 30 that this fee was too high, as the market rate was only 10 percent for that service; clients might be put off, he argued, and go elsewhere. Fran said she would reconsider the fee.

Shortly after joining Acme, Ed also began to have lunch on a regular basis and go out on dates after hours with a coworker, Andy Lee. On May 1, Fran stopped Ed as he returned from lunch with Andy and told Ed that intraoffice romantic relationships were strictly forbidden. Ed responded that he had meticulously avoided socializing with Andy during business hours and would continue to do so, but that he intended to continue to see Andy for lunch and on his own time. One week later Ed received Acme's "Manager of the Month" award for April. On May 15, Fran gave notice to Ed that he was being reassigned to a small Acme branch in the suburbs as a tax preparer, and would receive a $3,000 monthly base salary plus commissions.

Ed comes to your office today very upset. He believes Fran reassigned him either because of his complaint about the "instant payment" fee or because of his relationship with Andy. Ed tells you that although he is a new Acme employee, he is familiar with Acme practices over the past ten years, and that over that time period only two managers have been demoted or terminated, both of whom were found to have inflated their monthly commissions with false numbers. Ed wants to know whether he has any claim against Fran or Acme, and what issues would likely arise in an action against them. Besides your knowledge of basic contract law, you know that your state's constitution has an article which protects "freedom of association" in language similar to the First Amendment of the U.S. Constitution. What is your assessment?

PROBLEM 6-2

You are an attorney in Center City, a small midwestern town. One of your longtime clients is Marjorie Glazier, the owner of a local gift shop and a lifelong resident of Center City. Ms. Glazier's sister, Ruth, was married several years ago to Francis Fallon; Ruth and her husband have recently returned to Center City to live, following his retirement from the United States Navy. Although Mr. Fallon retired with full pension rights, he is still a relatively young man (48), with two children aged 13 and 16, and wants to establish himself in some business enterprise in order to meet the expenses (which he foresees as substantial) of his children's education and also to hedge against inflation and consequent devaluation in the purchasing power of his pension payments. He has saved a substantial sum from his Navy pay over the years and is willing to invest all or most of it in a promising opportunity.

Recently Mr. Fallon purchased, at a favorable price, a corner lot on Maple Avenue, near the city limits, with a small building on it in which the previous owner had operated a food market. Believing this location to be ideal for the operation of a small luncheonette/bakery shop, Fallon has been discussing with representatives of Captain Donut, Inc. (a nationwide franchisor of doughnut shops) the possibility of opening a Captain Donut shop in the building on his Maple Avenue lot. He has, he tells you, been assured by them that his store building can be converted to the standard Captain Donut format with remodeling and equipment costs of probably no more than $80,000, and that (based on figures from comparable locations in your state) a shop at that location should—after an initial period of operation, and with efficient management—earn for its owner a net profit of $85,000 a year, or more. In his purchase of the Maple Avenue lot, Fallon was not represented by a lawyer. At the urging of Ms. Glazier, however, he has now consulted you about his proposed entry into a franchise agreement with Captain Donut, Inc. He submits for your examination and advice the following form, which—he has been assured—is the standard agreement between Captain Donut, Inc. and its franchisees:

FRANCHISE AGREEMENT

AGREEMENT dated, _____, between CAPTAIN DONUT, INC., a Delaware corporation with its principal offices at 493 E. Martindale Rd., Pittsburgh, Pennsylvania (herein called "Franchisor") and _____ ("Franchisee").

WHEREAS, Franchisor has originated and developed a plan for operating retail establishments for the preparation and sale of doughnuts, pastry, cakes, pies, and related food items; and

The distinguishing characteristics of Franchisor's above-mentioned plan (herein called the "Captain Donut system") include the trade name "Captain Donut" and the registered trademark of a cartoon figure bearing the name "Captain Donut," a unique and standardized color scheme and layout for the place where such retail business is conducted (herein called a "Captain Donut shop"), and the recipes and secret formulas from which Franchisor's unique types of doughnuts and other pastry foods can be prepared (herein called "the secret formulas"), together with such other trademarks, trade names, design and layout schemes, and secret formulas as may from time to time be developed by Franchisor and incorporated into the Captain Donut system; and

Franchisor's Captain Donut shops have an established national reputation for high-quality and distinctive doughnuts and pastry products, prepared and sold in conditions of convenience, cleanliness, and attractiveness, all of which Franchisor has fostered through advertising in various national media and through its enforcement of the contractual obligations of Captain Donut franchisees to operate their Captain Donut shops according to the quality standards set forth in Franchisor's Manual of Operations; and

Franchisor has developed a course for training qualified persons to operate a Captain Donut shop according to the Captain Donut system, and is willing to train franchisees in such methods of operation, and to assist them in the establishment and initial operation of their Captain Donut shops; and

Franchisee has applied to be granted a franchise for operation of a Captain Donut shop at the following premises: _____, and Franchisor is willing to grant such a franchise upon the terms and conditions set forth below.

Now, THEREFORE, the parties hereby agree as follows:

1. *Franchise.* Franchisor hereby grants to Franchisee, upon the terms and conditions herein set forth, a franchise to operate a Captain Donut shop upon the above-specified premises (herein called "the Premises"), and in connection therewith a license to use in the operation of Franchisee's shop (herein called "the Shop") the trade name "Captain Donut," the trademark figure of Captain Donut, and such other trade name, trademarks, layout and color schemes, secret formulas, and other information as shall now or during the term of this Agreement constitute a part of the Captain Donut system, as communicated to Franchisee by Franchisor.

2. *Term.* Except as provided in Paragraph 11 hereof, the term of Franchisee's license hereunder shall be ten years from the date of this Agreement, but may be renewed thereafter for such period or periods, and upon such terms, as Franchisor and Franchisee shall then find mutually agreeable.

3. *Exclusive License.* Franchisor agrees that it will not, while Franchisee's license hereunder is in force, grant to any other person the right to open or operate a Captain Donut shop within five miles of the Premises. Except as stated in the preceding sentence, Franchisor's right to use and/or license the trade name and trademark of Captain Donut and the other components of the Captain Donut system during the term of this Agreement is acknowledged by Franchisee to be unimpaired hereby.

4. *Training.* Before the opening of the Shop, Franchisor will make available to one representative of Franchisee, at the Franchisor's headquarters in Pittsburgh, Pa., a five-day training course in the operation of a Captain Donut shop. There shall be no charge to Franchisee for such training other than the fees specified in Paragraphs 7 and 8 hereof, but Franchisee shall bear the cost of all such representative's traveling and living expenses in connection with the training course.

5. *Uniformity of Operations.* Franchisee agrees that in order to preserve the distinctive value of the Captain Donut system to the parties hereto and to all other franchisees thereunder, the Franchisor must establish and maintain uniform standards of quality, cleanliness, appearance, and efficiency of operation. In furtherance thereof, Franchisor shall furnish to Franchisee hereunder one or more copies of its Manual of Operations, together with such supplements and amendments thereto as may be issued by it from time to time (herein called collectively "the Manual"). Franchisee agrees that it shall forthwith erect upon the Premises such distinctive signs bearing the trademarks or other emblems of the Captain Donut system as shall be therein specified, and shall decorate the exterior and interior of the Shop in accordance therewith, shall acquire

such bakery and kitchen equipment as shall be required thereby in order to produce doughnuts and other pastry of sufficient quantity and quality, shall prepare the doughnuts and other foods to be sold in the Shop according to the secret formulas of Franchisor as contained therein, using only approved ingredients as specified in Paragraph 6, below, and shall in all respects conform its operation of the Shop to the system as outlined in the Manual, all to the satisfaction of Franchisor. Franchisor shall have the right to inspect the Premises and the Shop from time to time hereunder, at any time during regular business hours, to assure itself that the provisions of this Agreement and of this Paragraph 5 are being observed. In connection with the initial public opening of the Shop, Franchisor shall conduct such advertising and promotional activities as may appear to it advisable, and will furnish to Franchisee for one week, at Franchisor's expense, one or more of Franchisor's advisory personnel to assist in such campaign and in the opening and initial operation of the Shop. Franchisee acknowledges that the Manual contains much secret and confidential information, the continued confidentiality of which is necessary for the continued success of the Captain Donut system, and agrees not to divulge such information to any person other than its own authorized employees, agrees not to copy or permit any other person to copy the Manual or any portion thereof, and agrees that the Manual delivered to it hereunder shall be and remain the sole and exclusive property of Franchisor, and shall be redelivered to Franchisor upon the termination of Franchisee's license hereunder.

6. *Purchases.* In order further to assure the uniform quality of the items to be sold at the Shop, Franchisee agrees that it will purchase all food products sold or used in the Shop from Franchisor or from suppliers listed in the Manual or otherwise approved in writing by Franchisor as authorized suppliers of products meeting its specifications; provided, further, that Franchisor will upon Franchisee's request approve for purchases by Franchisee hereunder any supplier whose products in Franchisor's judgment conform to the specifications and standards of Franchisor for use in the Captain Donut system; provided, however, that all doughnuts sold by Franchisee during the entire period of this Agreement shall be made from Franchisor's own secret-formula mix, and Franchisee shall purchase all of its requirements of such mix from Franchisor itself, at such prices as shall be set from time to time by Franchisor.

7. *Initial Franchise Fee.* In consideration of the rights acquired by it hereunder, including without limitation the franchise granted herein, the license of rights, the training course provided, and the communication to it of the Manual and other information necessary for the operation of the Shop, Franchisee hereby agrees to pay to Franchisor upon the execution of this Agreement an initial nonrefundable franchise fee of Twenty-five Thousand ($25,000) Dollars.

8. *Weekly Franchise Fee.* During the entire term of this Agreement, as further consideration for the rights acquired hereunder, Franchisee shall pay to Franchisor a weekly franchise fee of Five (5%) Percent of Franchisee's gross sales in the Shop. Such fees shall be payable on Tuesday of each week with respect to the gross sales of the preceding week, and shall be accompanied by weekly financial reports in such form as Franchisor shall prescribe. Franchisee shall maintain financial records in such form as Franchisor shall require (which records shall be available for inspection and copy by Franchisor at any time during regular business hours), and shall furnish Franchisor on or before the 15th day of April in each year with a certified profit and loss statement for the preceding year and balance sheet as of the end of such year.

9. *Competition with Franchisor.* Franchisee shall during the term of this Agreement devote substantially its full time to the operation of the Shop. Franchisee shall not, directly or indirectly, own, engage in, be interested in, or be associated with any doughnut shop, pastry shop, "convenient" market, or other food shop within a

ten-mile radius of the Premises, both for the duration of the rights granted to the Franchisee hereunder (except for Franchisee's operation of the Shop itself) and for a period of five years after their termination for any reason whatsoever.

10. *Insurance.* Franchisee shall at its own expense maintain liability insurance with personal injury coverage of not less than $200,000 per person and $500,000 per accident, and property damage coverage of not less than $50,000. Such insurance policies shall name Franchisor as an additional insured, and shall be in form and with insurers satisfactory to Franchisor; Franchisor shall receive copies of all such policies, together with satisfactory evidence of premium payment. Franchisee shall indemnify Franchisor and save it harmless from all loss, liability, and expense (including attorneys' fees) arising from any occurrence in or in connection with Franchisee's operation of the Shop.

11. *Termination for Cause.* If Franchisee shall fail to pay Franchisor any monies owed it hereunder when due, or fail to operate the Shop to the satisfaction of Franchisor as required by Paragraph 5 hereof, or in any other respect whatsoever fail to comply with the terms and provisions of this Agreement, or cease to do business at the Premises, or make an assignment for the benefit of creditors, or be the subject of a receivership, bankruptcy, or insolvency proceeding, then unless Franchisee shall cure such default within ten (10) days after written notice thereof is sent to it by Franchisor, Franchisor shall have the right forthwith to terminate this Agreement and all of Franchisee's rights hereunder. In the event of such termination, Franchisee shall remain liable to Franchisor for any sums then owed and for any damages incurred by Franchisor by reason of such termination, and the provisions of this Agreement relating to termination shall apply.

12. *Events upon Termination.* Upon the expiration or termination of its license hereunder for any reason, Franchisee shall immediately discontinue use of the trade name and trademark licenses hereunder, and the secret formulas and other information contained in the Manual, and all signs, emblems, advertising matter, distinctive layout, color scheme, or other materials indicative of or identified with the Captain Donut system, and shall thereafter do nothing to indicate that it or any food products sold by it have any connection with the Captain Donut system, and shall return to Franchisor all copies of the Manual theretofore furnished hereunder. Franchisee will immediately refrain from selling any doughnuts prepared from Franchisor's mix (Paragraph 6); provided, that Franchisor will upon such termination repurchase any unopened bags of such mix at the price previously paid to it by Franchisee therefor. The provisions of Paragraph 9 shall continue to be applicable to Franchisee in the event of such termination, and Franchisor shall be entitled to specific enforcement, by injunctive relief, of the provisions of this Paragraph 12 and of Paragraph 9, above.

13. *Relationship of Parties.* In all respects the relation of the parties hereto shall be that of independent contractors. Nothing herein shall be deemed to create a partnership, joint venture, or agency between them, and no employee of one shall be deemed an employee of the other.

14. *Transfer of Rights.* Neither this Agreement nor any of Franchisee's rights or privileges hereunder shall be assigned or transferred, by operation of law or otherwise in any manner, by Franchisee without the prior written consent of Franchisor. Without limitation of the foregoing sentence, the words "Franchisor" and "Franchisee" as used herein shall wherever appropriate refer to the parties hereto and their respective heirs, executors, administrators, successors, and assigns.

15. *Notices.* Any notice to be given hereunder shall be deemed given when sent by registered or certified mail, return receipt requested, to Franchisor at its address first above given and to Franchisee at the following address: _____.

16. *Miscellaneous Provisions.* This Agreement contains the entire agreement between the parties, and may not be modified except by a writing signed by both parties. Franchisee acknowledges that in entering into this Agreement it is relying on no promises, representations, or warranties made by Franchisor other than those stated herein. No waiver by Franchisor of any breach or default by Franchisee in any of its obligations hereunder shall be deemed a waiver of any subsequent breach by Franchisee of the same or any other provision of this Agreement. The invalidity or unenforceability of any term or provision of this Agreement shall not affect the remaining terms and provisions, which shall remain in full force and effect, and any court which finds that any provision hereto would be unenforceable because overly broad is hereby authorized and requested to reform such provision to the extent necessary to reduce it to the point where it would be enforceable, and to enforce such provision as reformed.

IN WITNESS WHEREOF, the parties have executed this Agreement on the day and year first above written.

Franchisor: CAPTAIN DONUT, INC.

By: _____

Franchisee: _____

1. Answer the following questions based on the agreement:

   (a) What rights would Mr. Fallon have under the agreement if he is unable to remodel and equip his shop for the $80,000 projected by the company?
   (b) Suppose Mr. Fallon's wife decides to open a restaurant in Center City. Would that cause any problem for Mr. Fallon under the franchise agreement?
   (c) Suppose Mr. Fallon negotiates an agreement to supply local hotels with doughnuts for their restaurants. These doughnuts will be sold under each hotel's label, without use of Captain Donut's name or trademark. Is Mr. Fallon permitted to do this under the agreement? If so, would such sales be subject to the weekly franchise fee?

2. Review the agreement and prepare a list of issues that you would raise for discussion with Mr. Fallon.

C. WARRANTIES

In the seventeenth century the English courts first adopted what has since come to be known as the principle of "caveat emptor": "let the buyer beware." This doctrine meant that the seller bore no responsibility at all for the quality of the product he was selling unless he expressly guaranteed it or gave a "warranty" to the buyer. The leading case for this doctrine was Chandelor v. Lopus, 79 Eng. Rep. 3, decided by the Court of Exchequer-Chamber in 1603.

In *Chandelor* the defendant, a goldsmith, sold a stone to the plaintiff. Although the defendant had "affirmed" that the stone was a "bezar-stone," this representation turned out to be false, and the plaintiff brought suit. The court held for the defendant because "the bare affirmation that it was a bezar-stone, without warranting it to be so, is no cause of action. . . . " Moreover, the court held that the declaration did not state a cause of action even if the defendant knew that his statements were false, because "every one in selling his wares will affirm that his wares are good, or the horse which he sells is sound; yet if he does not warrant them to be so, it is no cause of action. . . . " (A "bezar-stone" was not a precious jewel but instead "an object somewhat similar to a gall stone, but formed in the intestines of goats, and was thought at the time to possess medicinal value." Alfred W. B. Simpson, A History of the Common Law of Contract 536 (1975). Does this fact affect your view of the holding in *Chandelor*?)

American courts embraced the doctrine of caveat emptor in the nineteenth century. For example, in Seixas v. Woods, 2 Caine R. 48 (N.Y. 1804), the defendant, a middleman, sold certain wood, advertised as "brazilletto," to the plaintiff. Unknown to either the buyer or the seller, the wood was "peachum," a much less valuable type of wood. In an action by the buyer seeking a refund of the price, the New York Court of Errors held for the seller because no warranty was made. See generally Walton H. Hamilton, The Ancient Maxim Caveat Emptor, 40 Yale L.J. 1133 (1931).

In the last quarter of the nineteenth century, American courts, responding to changing market conditions, gradually reversed the rule of caveat emptor by imposing obligations on the seller as to the quality of goods sold. These obligations, or "implied warranties," were not based on actual agreement of the parties but were instead imposed by law on the seller. By 1906 the arguments for imposing warranty obligations on sellers had become generally accepted, and enough particular instances had been sanctioned by case law that the National Conference of Commissioners on Uniform State Laws felt justified in including in its newly promulgated Uniform Sales Act several provisions for implied warranties in the sale of goods. See, e.g., §§14 (implied warranty in sale by description); 15 (implied warranties of quality); 16 (implied warranties in sale by sample). See generally Karl N. Llewellyn, On Warranty of Quality, and Society (Pts. I, II), 36 Colum. L. Rev. 699 (1936), 37 Colum. L. Rev. 341 (1937); William L. Prosser, The Implied Warranty of Merchantable Quality, 27 Minn. L. Rev. 117 (1943); Timothy J. Sullivan, Innovation in the Law of Warranty: The Burden of Reform, 32 Hastings L.J. 341 (1980).

The Uniform Commercial Code continues this statutory treatment of warranties. UCC §2-313 deals with creation of "express warranties." Notably, the section does not require that the seller have the intent to create an express warranty, and thus represents a substantial change from the days of *Chandelor* described above. The most common application of this section is the written or oral express warranty given by a seller or manufacturer of a consumer product (an automobile or a washing machine, for example), concerning the quality or nature of the goods (for example, "the car will get at least 25 miles per gallon of gas" or "this tractor is a 1999 model").

UCC §2-314 sets forth a second type of warranty — the "implied warranty of merchantability." Under this warranty a "merchant" (see UCC §2-104) who regularly sells goods of a particular kind impliedly warrants to the buyer that the goods are of good quality and are fit for the ordinary purposes for which they are used.

Section 2-315 defines a third type of warranty, the "implied warranty of fitness for a particular purpose." This warranty differs from the implied warranty of merchantability in several respects. To begin with, the warranty is created only when the buyer relies on the seller's skill or judgment to select suitable goods and the seller has reason to know of this reliance. Further, breach of the warranty does not require a showing that the goods are defective in any way — merely that the goods are not fit for the buyer's particular purpose.

Claims of implied warranty, however, are often made in non-UCC transactions. For example, in the leading case of Javins v. First National Realty Corp., 428 F.2d 1071 (D.C. Cir.), *cert. denied*, 400 U.S. 925 (1970), the United States Court of Appeals for the District of Columbia held that a warranty of habitability would be implied into leases of urban dwelling units. In his opinion, Judge J. Skelly Wright observed that the common law rule absolving the lessor of all obligation to repair had developed during the early Middle Ages in an era when the land was more important than the simple structure that might be included in the leasehold, and at a time when tenants were deemed fully capable of making repairs. Judge Wright then asserted that in more modern times, with more complex structures, tenants are primarily interested in having a dwelling that is suitable for occupation and are more dependent on landlords to maintain the condition of a building. Finally, Judge Wright noted that there exists a well-documented inequality in bargaining power between landlord and tenant that tends to leave tenants with "little leverage" in negotiating for better housing. Id. at 1077-1080.

The overwhelming majority of states now recognizes an implied warranty of habitability in residential leases, by virtue of legislative or judicial action. See Barbara Jo Smith, Note: Tenants in Search of Parity with Consumers: Creating a Reasonable Expectations Warranty, 72 Wash. U.L.Q. 475 (1994). Many of the statutory provisions have been influenced by the Uniform Residential Landlord Tenant Act adopted by the American Law Institute in 1972. Section 2.104 of that Act accepts the concept of the warranty of habitability and defines the landlord's obligation as follows:

> (a) A landlord shall
>
> (1) comply with the requirements of applicable building and housing codes materially affecting health and safety;
>
> (2) make all repairs and do whatever is necessary to put and keep the premises in a fit and habitable condition;
>
> (3) keep all common areas of the premises in a clean and safe condition;
>
> (4) maintain in good and safe working order and condition all electrical, plumbing, sanitary, heating, ventilating, air-conditioning, and other facilities and appliances, including elevators, supplied or required to be supplied by him;
>
> (5) provide and maintain appropriate receptacles and conveniences for the removal of ashes, garbage, rubbish, and other waste incidental to the occupancy of the dwelling unit and arrange for their removal; and

(6) supply running water and reasonable amounts of hot water at all times and reasonable heat [between [October 1] and [May 1]] except where the building that includes the dwelling unit is not required by law to be equipped for that purpose, or the dwelling unit is so constructed that heat or hot water is generated by an installation within the exclusive control of the tenant and supplied by a direct public utility connection.

As you read the following cases and notes consider and analyze the policy reasons for judicial and legislative action imposing express and implied warranty liability.

Bayliner Marine Corp. v. Crow
Supreme Court of Virginia
257 Va. 121, 509 S.E.2d 499 (1999)

Present: All the Justices.
KEENAN, Justice.

In this appeal, the dispositive issue is whether there was sufficient evidence to support the trial court's ruling that the manufacturer of a sport fishing boat breached an express warranty and implied warranties of merchantability and fitness for a particular purpose.

In the summer of 1989, John R. Crow was invited by John Atherton, then a sales representative for Tidewater Yacht Agency, Inc. (Tidewater), to ride on a new model sport fishing boat known as a 3486 Trophy Convertible, manufactured by Bayliner Marine Corporation (Bayliner). At that time, Tidewater was the exclusive authorized dealer in southeastern Virginia for this model Bayliner boat. During an excursion lasting about 20 minutes, Crow piloted the boat for a short period of time but was not able to determine its speed because there was no equipment on board for such testing.

When Crow asked Atherton about the maximum speed of the boat, Atherton explained that he had no personal experience with the boat or information from other customers concerning the boat's performance. Therefore, Atherton consulted two documents described as "prop matrixes," which were included by Bayliner in its dealer's manual.

Atherton gave Crow copies of the "prop matrixes," which listed the boat models offered by Bayliner and stated the recommended propeller sizes, gear ratios, and engine sizes for each model. The "prop matrixes" also listed the maximum speed for each model. The 3486 Trophy Convertible was listed as having a maximum speed of 30 miles per hour when equipped with a size "20 × 20" or "20[×]19" propeller. The boat Crow purchased did not have either size propeller but, instead, had a size "20 × 17" propeller.

At the bottom of one of the "prop matrixes" was the following disclaimer: "This data is intended for comparative purposes only, and is available without reference to weather conditions or other variables. All testing was done at or near sea level, with full fuel and water tanks, and approximately 600 lb. passenger and gear weight."

Atherton also showed Crow a Bayliner brochure describing the 1989 boat models, including the 3486 Trophy Convertible. The brochure included a picture of that model fully rigged for offshore fishing, accompanied by the statement that this model "delivers the kind of performance you need to get to the prime offshore fishing grounds."

In August 1989, Crow entered into a written contract for the purchase of the 3486 Trophy Convertible in which he had ridden. The purchase price was $120,000, exclusive of taxes. The purchase price included various equipment to be installed by Tidewater including a generator, a cockpit cover, a "Bimini top," a winch, a spotlight, radar, a navigation system, an icemaker, fishing outriggers, an automatic pilot system, extra fuel gauges, a second radio, and air conditioning and heating units. The total weight of the added equipment was about 2,000 pounds. Crow did not test drive the boat after the additional equipment was installed or at any other time prior to taking delivery.

When Crow took delivery of the boat in September 1989, he piloted it onto the Elizabeth River. He noticed that the boat's speed measuring equipment, which was installed in accordance with the contract terms, indicated that the boat's maximum speed was 13 miles per hour. Crow immediately returned to Tidewater and reported the problem.

During the next 12 to 14 months, while Crow retained ownership and possession of the boat, Tidewater made numerous repairs and adjustments to the boat in an attempt to increase its speed capability. Despite these efforts, the boat consistently achieved a maximum speed of only 17 miles per hour, except for one period following an engine modification when it temporarily reached a speed of about 24 miles per hour. In July 1990, a representative from Bayliner wrote Crow a letter stating that the performance representations made at the time of purchase were incorrect, and that 23 to 25 miles per hour was the maximum speed the boat could achieve.

In 1992, Crow filed a motion for judgment against Tidewater, Bayliner, and Brunswick Corporation, the manufacturer of the boat's diesel engines.[1] Crow alleged, among other things, that Bayliner breached express warranties, and implied warranties of merchantability and fitness for a particular purpose.

At a bench trial in 1994, Crow, Atherton, and Gordon W. Shelton, III, Tidewater's owner, testified that speed is a critical quality in boats used for offshore sport fishing in the Tidewater area of Virginia because of the distance between the coast and the offshore fishing grounds. According to these witnesses, a typical offshore fishing site in that area is 90 miles from the coast. Therefore, the speed at which the boat can travel to and from fishing sites has a major impact on the amount of time left in a day for fishing.

Crow testified that because of the boat's slow speed, he could not use the boat for offshore fishing, that he had no other use for it, and that he would not have purchased the boat if he had known that its maximum speed was 23 to 25 miles per hour. Crow testified that he had not used the boat for fishing since 1991 or 1992. He admitted, however, that between September 1989, and

---

1. Crow nonsuited his claim against Tidewater prior to trial. The negligence claim against Brunswick was dismissed in the trial court's final judgment order.

September 1994, the boat's engines had registered about 850 hours of use. Bob Schey, Bayliner's manager of yacht testing, testified that a pleasure boat in a climate such as Virginia's typically would register 150 engine hours per year.

The trial court entered judgment in favor of Crow against Bayliner on the counts of breach of express warranty and breach of implied warranties of merchantability and fitness for a particular purpose. The court awarded Crow damages of $135,000, plus prejudgment interest from June 1993. The court explained that the $135,000 award represented the purchase price of the boat, and about $15,000 in "damages" for a portion of the expenses Crow claimed in storing, maintaining, insuring, and financing the boat.

On appeal, we review the evidence in the light most favorable to Crow, the prevailing party at trial. Tuomala v. Regent University, 252 Va. 368, 375, 477 S.E.2d 501, 505 (1996); W.S. Carnes, Inc. v. Board of Supervisors of Chesterfield County, 252 Va. 377, 385, 478 S.E.2d 295, 301 (1996). We will uphold the trial court's judgment unless it is plainly wrong or without evidence to support it. Code §8.01-680; Horton v. Horton, 254 Va. 111, 115, 487 S.E.2d 200, 203 (1997).

Crow argues that the "prop matrixes" he received created an express warranty by Bayliner that the boat he purchased was capable of a maximum speed of 30 miles per hour. We disagree.

Code §8.2-313 provides, in relevant part:

Express warranties by the seller are created as follows:

(a) Any affirmation of fact or promise made by the seller to the buyer which relates to the goods and becomes part of the basis of the bargain creates an express warranty that the goods shall conform to the affirmation or promise.

(b) Any description of the goods which is made a part of the basis of the bargain creates an express warranty that the goods shall conform to the description.

The issue whether a particular affirmation of fact made by the seller constitutes an express warranty is generally a question of fact. See id., Official Comment 3; Daughtrey v. Ashe, 243 Va. 73, 78, 413 S.E.2d 336, 339 (1992). In *Daughtrey*, we examined whether a jeweler's statement on an appraisal form constituted an express warranty. We held that the jeweler's description of the particular diamonds being purchased as "v.v.s. quality" constituted an express warranty that the diamonds were, in fact, of that grade. Id. at 77, 413 S.E.2d at 338.

Unlike the representation in *Daughtrey*, however, the statements in the "prop matrixes" provided by Bayliner did not relate to the particular boat purchased by Crow, or to one having substantially similar characteristics. By their plain terms, the figures stated in the "prop matrixes" referred to a boat with different sized propellers that carried equipment weighing substantially less than the equipment on Crow's boat. Therefore, we conclude that the statements contained in the "prop matrixes" did not constitute an express warranty by Bayliner about the performance capabilities of the particular boat purchased by Crow.

Crow also contends that Bayliner made an express warranty regarding the boat's maximum speed in the statement in Bayliner's sales brochure that this model boat "delivers the kind of performance you need to get to the prime offshore fishing grounds." While the general rule is that a description of the goods that forms a basis of the bargain constitutes an express warranty, Code §8.2-313(2) directs that "a statement purporting to be merely the seller's opinion or commendation of the goods does not create a warranty."

The statement made by Bayliner in its sales brochure is merely a commendation of the boat's performance and does not describe a specific characteristic or feature of the boat. The statement simply expressed the manufacturer's opinion concerning the quality of the boat's performance and did not create an express warranty that the boat was capable of attaining a speed of 30 miles per hour. Therefore, we conclude that the evidence does not support the trial court's finding that Bayliner breached an express warranty made to Crow.

We next consider whether the evidence supports the trial court's conclusion that Bayliner breached an implied warranty of merchantability. Crow asserts that because his boat was not capable of achieving a maximum speed of 30 miles per hour, it was not fit for its ordinary purpose as an offshore sport fishing boat. Bayliner contends in response that, although the boat did not meet the needs of this particular sport fisherman, there was no evidence from which the trial court could conclude that the boat generally was not merchantable as an offshore fishing boat. We agree with Bayliner's argument.

Code §8.2-314 provides that, in all contracts for the sale of goods by a merchant, a warranty is implied that the goods will be merchantable. To be merchantable, the goods must be such as would "pass without objection in the trade" and as "are fit for the ordinary purposes for which such goods are used." Code §8.2-314(2)(a), (c). The first phrase concerns whether a "significant segment of the buying public" would object to buying the goods, while the second phrase concerns whether the goods are "reasonably capable of performing their ordinary functions." Federal Signal Corp. v. Safety Factors, Inc., 125 Wash. 2d 413, 886 P.2d 172, 180 (Wash. 1994). In order to prove that a product is not merchantable, the complaining party must first establish the standard of merchantability in the trade. Laird v. Scribner Coop, Inc., 237 Neb. 532, 466 N.W.2d 798, 804 (Neb. 1991). Bayliner correctly notes that the record contains no evidence of the standard of merchantability in the offshore fishing boat trade. Nor does the record contain any evidence supporting a conclusion that a significant portion of the boat-buying public would object to purchasing an offshore fishing boat with the speed capability of the 3486 Trophy Convertible.

Crow, nevertheless, relies on his own testimony that the boat's speed was inadequate for his intended use, and Atherton's opinion testimony that the boat took "a long time" to reach certain fishing grounds in the Gulf Stream off the coast of Virginia. However, this evidence did not address the standard of merchantability in the trade or whether Crow's boat failed to meet that standard. Thus, we hold that Crow failed to prove that the boat would not "pass without objection in the trade" as required by Code §8.2-314(2)(a).

We next consider whether the record supports a conclusion that Crow's boat was not fit for its ordinary purpose as an offshore sport fishing boat. Generally, the issue whether goods are fit for the ordinary purposes for which they are used is a factual question. See Federal Ins. Co. v. Village of Westmont, 271 Ill. App. 3d 892, 649 N.E.2d 986, 990, 208 Ill. Dec. 626 (App. Ct. Ill. 1995);

Tallmadge v. Aurora Chrysler Plymouth, Inc., 25 Wash. App. 90, 605 P.2d 1275, 1278 (Wash. Ct. App. 1979). Here, the evidence is uncontroverted that Crow used the boat for offshore fishing, at least during the first few years after purchasing it, and that the boat's engines were used for 850 hours. While Crow stated that many of those hours were incurred during various repair or modification attempts and that the boat was of little value to him, this testimony does not support a conclusion that a boat with this speed capability is generally unacceptable as an offshore fishing boat. Thus, considered in the light most favorable to Crow, the evidence fails to establish that the boat was not fit for the ordinary purpose for which it was intended.

We next address Crow's claim that Bayliner breached an implied warranty of fitness for a particular purpose. Code §8.2-315 provides that when a seller "has reason to know any particular purpose for which the goods are required and that the buyer is relying on the seller's skill or judgment to select or furnish suitable goods, there is . . . an implied warranty that the goods shall be fit for such purpose." See also Medcom, Inc. v. C. Arthur Weaver Co., Inc., 232 Va. 80, 84-85, 348 S.E.2d 243, 246 (1986). This statute embodies a long-standing common law rule in Virginia. Layne-Atlantic Co. v. Koppers Co., 214 Va. 467, 471, 201 S.E.2d 609, 613 (1974). The question whether there was an implied warranty of fitness for a particular purpose in a sale of goods is ordinarily a question of fact based on the circumstances surrounding the transaction. Stones v. Sears, Roebuck & Co., 251 Neb. 560, 558 N.W.2d 540, 547 (Neb. 1997).

Crow contends that the "particular purpose" for which the boat was intended was use as an offshore fishing boat capable of traveling at a maximum speed of 30 miles per hour. However, to establish an implied warranty of fitness for a particular purpose, the buyer must prove as a threshold matter that he made known to the seller the particular purpose for which the goods were required. See Medcom, 232 Va. at 84, 348 S.E.2d at 246. The record before us does not support a conclusion that Crow informed Atherton of this precise requirement. Although Crow informed Atherton that he intended to use the boat for offshore fishing and discussed the boat's speed in this context, these facts did not establish that Atherton knew on the date of sale that a boat incapable of travelling at 30 miles per hour was unacceptable to Crow. Thus, we conclude that the evidence fails to support the trial court's ruling that Bayliner breached an implied warranty of fitness for a particular purpose.

For these reasons, we will reverse the trial court's judgment and enter final judgment in favor of Bayliner.

Reversed and final judgment.

Notes and Questions

1. *Elements of an express warranty.* Under UCC §2-313, a seller may provide the basis for an express warranty in several ways: making a representation about the goods, giving a description, or displaying a sample or model. The *Bayliner Marine* court cited the earlier case of Daughtrey v. Ashe, 413 S.E.2d 336 (Va. 1992), as providing an example of an affirmation of fact about goods

(the statement about the quality of diamonds) that served as basis for an express warranty. See also Redmac, Inc. v. Computerland of Peoria, 489 N.E.2d 380 (Ill. App. Ct. 1986) (express warranty based on statement that computer would be defect free or repaired within warranty period); Goodwin v. Durant Bank & Trust Co., 952 P.2d 41 (Okla. 1998) (description of backhoe equipment as 1990 model amounted to express warranty; equipment actually was 1987 model). The *Bayliner Marine* court also noted, however, the need to distinguish between a type of factual representation about the quality of goods that may give rise to an express warranty and "mere puffery" or sales talk that will not serve as a basis for a binding commitment. See Boud v. SDNCO, Inc., 54 P.3d 1131 (Utah 2002) (affirmation of fact must be objective and capable of being proven true or false; statement that boat was "best in class" or "superb" would be puffery but statement that boat was "fastest in class" could be verified). How would you assess the seller's statements or conduct in *Bayliner Marine* with regard to this aspect of an express warranty?

As a second element, pre-Code law required that a buyer prove reliance on a representation about the quality of the goods to establish that an express warranty had been created. See Uniform Sales Act §12; White & Summers, Uniform Commercial Code §9-5, 350 (5th ed. 2000). Whether reliance is required under the Code is unclear. The text of §2-313 provides that an affirmation, promise, description, sample, or model will amount to an express warranty if it is part of the "basis of the bargain" but does not define that concept. Some courts have held that reliance is still required to establish an express warranty, as under pre-Code law. Other courts, however, have adopted a substantially different interpretation of UCC §2-313. In a leading case on the question, the California Court of Appeals ruled in Keith v. Buchanan, 220 Cal. Rptr. 392, 398 (Ct. App. 1985), that "a warranty statement made by a seller is presumptively part of the basis of the bargain, and the burden is on the seller to prove that the resulting bargain does not rest at all on the representation." Thus, the *Keith* approach does not require an affirmative showing of reliance by the buyer. The approach of the *Keith* and similar courts finds support in Comment 3 to §2-313, which provides that once a seller has made an affirmation of fact about the goods, "no particular reliance on such statements need be shown in order to weave them into the fabric of the agreement. Rather, any fact which is to take such affirmations, once made, out of the agreement requires clear affirmative proof."

2. *Implied warranty of merchantability.* The buyer in *Bayliner Marine* also sought recovery based on the implied warranty of merchantability in UCC §2-314. For this warranty to arise, the buyer must establish that the seller is a "merchant" with respect to the goods sold. A merchant is defined in the Code as a party who regularly deals in goods of the kind or holds itself out as having particular knowledge about the kind of goods. UCC §2-104(1). If the seller is a merchant, §2-314(2) includes several alternative bases for assessing the merchantability of goods, including the two most frequently applied tests: whether the goods would "pass without objection in the trade" and "are fit for the ordinary purposes for which such goods are used." The range of cases involving the implied warranty of merchantability is vast, from the sale of very expensive equipment to the purchase of a hamburger.

See, e.g., Frantz v. Cantrell, 711 N.E.2d 856 (Ind. Ct. App. 1999) (roof shingles that were curled up at the edges and failed to seal cannot be said to "pass without objection in the trade"); Goodman v. Wenco Foods, Inc., 423 S.E.2d 444 (N.C. 1992) (bone in hamburger would constitute breach of implied warranty of merchantability if it would not be reasonably expected by consumer). Do you think the buyer in *Bayliner Marine* could have made a better case for the proposition that the boat was not merchantable? What evidence should the buyer have offered?

3. *Implied warranty of fitness for a particular purpose.* The implied warranty of fitness for a particular purpose under §2-315 differs from the implied warranty of merchantability in several respects. First, liability under this warranty is not limited to merchant sellers. Second, the warranty is created only when the buyer relies on the seller's skill or judgment to select suitable goods for the buyer's particular purpose and the seller has reason to know of this reliance. Third, breach of the warranty does not require a showing that the goods are defective in any way — merely that the goods are not fit for the buyer's particular purpose. See, e.g., Neilson Business Equipment Center, Inc. v. Monteleone, 524 A.2d 1172 (Del. 1987) (computer equipment did not meet needs of buyer who relied on seller to select goods and customize software). Most courts also hold that the buyer's particular purpose must be one other than the ordinary use of the goods. Compare Jackson v. Thomas, 21 P.3d 1007 (Kan. Ct. App. 2001) (use of solvent for ordinary cleaning purpose barred any claim for fitness warranty), with Soaper v. Hope Industries, Inc., 424 S.E.2d 493 (S.C. 1992) (purchaser of film processing equipment who made known particular needs could sue on fitness warranty even though use was ordinary use).

4. *Disclaimers of express warranties.* Warranty obligations arise as a matter of contract, and the Code also allows sellers to eliminate or modify the Code's warranties by agreement. The validity of disclaimers of warranties is governed by §2-316 of the UCC. Under §2-316(1), a disclaimer of an express warranty is inoperative if the disclaimer cannot be construed as "consistent" with terms in the contract that would create the express warranty. UCC §2-316(1), Comment 1. See, e.g., Consolidated Data Terminals v. Applied Digital Data Systems, Inc., 708 F.2d 385 (9th Cir. 1983) (manufacturer's specifications about speed of computer constituted express warranty and were not disclaimed by language in contract providing that the manufacturer "makes no warranty, express or implied"). Since express warranties may be created orally or by one of several writings, the existence of an express warranty may turn on the application of the parol evidence rule. Indeed, §2-316(1) states that it is "subject to" the provisions of UCC §2-202, the parol evidence rule. See, e.g., Hoover Universal, Inc. v. Brockway Imco, Inc., 809 F.2d 1039 (4th Cir. 1987) (evidence regarding seller's earlier representations about machine's capacity was inadmissible since subsequent written contract was intended by parties to be final expression of their agreement). Some courts, however, have found grounds to permit evidence of express warranties despite the parol evidence rule. See, e.g., L.S. Heath & Son, Inc. v. AT&T Information Systems, Inc., 9 F.3d 561 (7th Cir. 1993) (when earlier written representation was claimed to be inconsistent with subsequent written disclaimer, parol evidence was admissible to determine if later writing was intended to be final expression of parties' agreement even though writing contained merger clause).

5. *Disclaimers and implied warranties.* The implied warranties of merchantability and fitness for a particular purpose can be disclaimed in several ways under UCC §2-316(2) and (3). To disclaim the implied warranty of *merchantability* under §2-316(2), "the language must mention merchantability and in the case of a writing must be conspicuous." In contrast, the Code provides that a disclaimer of the implied warranty of *fitness* for a particular purpose must be in a conspicuous writing and will be effective if it states that "[t]here are no warranties which extend beyond the description on the face hereof." UCC §2-316(2). Thus, the disclaiming language for the fitness warranty can be less specific than that required for the implied warranty of merchantability, but it must be in a writing. Moreover, additional methods of excluding the implied warranties are found in §2-316(3), probably the most common of which is the "as is" disclaimer. Section 2-316(3), unlike §2-316(2), does not include a conspicuousness requirement, but most courts agree that one should be implied to carry out the section's purpose of avoiding surprise to buyers. See, e.g., Lumber Mut. Ins. Co. v. Clarklift of Detroit, Inc., 569 N.W.2d 681 (Mich. Ct. App. 1997) ("as is" disclaimer must be conspicuous to be effective); but see DeKalb Agresearch, Inc. v. Abbott, 391 F. Supp. 152 (N.D. Ala. 1974) (applying the statutory language literally and holding that "as is" disclaimer need not be conspicuous), *aff'd,* 511 F.2d 1162 (5th Cir. 1975). Notably, some states have enacted nonuniform versions of §2-316, making all disclaimers of the implied warranty of merchantability ineffective in consumer transactions. See, e.g., Wolfe v. Welton, 558 S.E.2d 363 (W. Va. 2001).

PROBLEM 6-3

In February 2006 Frank McCarty began a business that involved the home delivery of pet food and supplies at prices substantially lower than those in grocery and pet stores. The business prospered immediately, and by April, Frank was making a profit of $1,000 per week.

Beginning in March 2006, and for several months thereafter, Firebrand Tire Company engaged in an extensive national advertising campaign for its new "Roadsafe Steel Belted X-10 Tire." The typical advertisement contained the following:

> Concerned about tire safety? The new steel belted X-10 from Firebrand has been designed and tested especially for protection against road hazards. No tire on the market is more reliable than the X-10. When you think of safety, think of Firebrand.

In June 2006 McCarty went to an independent local tire dealer to purchase tires for the van that he used in his business. When a salesman asked McCarty if he could be of help, McCarty told him that he wished to buy a reliable, heavy-duty tire for his van. The salesman recommended the X-10. After some discussion McCarty agreed to purchase the tires. The salesman gave him a brochure that described the tires and asked McCarty to sign it. While McCarty was waiting for his tires to be installed, he thumbed through the brochure, which contained the following warranty provision:

Limited One-Year Warranty

Firebrand warrants to the purchaser that the tires which he has purchased will be free from defects in materials and workmanship for a period of one year from the date of purchase. This warranty will be honored by any authorized Firebrand dealer. Firebrand will repair or replace any such defective tire. In no event, however, will Firebrand be liable for actual or consequential damages, purchaser's sole remedy being limited to repair or replacement of any defective tire.

There are no express warranties, whether oral or written, other than in this document. The IMPLIED WARRANTIES OF MERCHANTABILITY AND FITNESS FOR A PARTICULAR PURPOSE are hereby LIMITED to a period of ONE YEAR from the date of purchase.

In March 2007 McCarty's van swerved off the road when the left front tire blew out. Evidence indicates that the tire failed when pierced by a large piece of metal lying in the road. The van, which had a value of $25,000, was totally destroyed. McCarty was injured and required hospitalization for several weeks. His total medical and hospital bills were approximately $100,000. Because of McCarty's absence, the business could not continue and subsequently it failed. An expert is prepared to testify that his business had a fair market value of $150,000. McCarty has brought suit against Firebrand and the retailer. Analyze McCarty's rights against Firebrand and the dealer based on both breach of warranty and tort theories.

Caceci v. Di Canio Construction Corp.
Court of Appeals of New York
72 N.Y.2d 521, 526 N.E.2d 266 (1988)

BELLACOSA, J.:

As another building block in our common-law judicial process, this court recognizes the "Housing Merchant" warranty, imposing by legal implication a contractual liability on a homebuilder for skillful performance and quality of a newly constructed home the defendant builder contracted for and sold to plaintiffs. The doctrine that the buyer must beware (caveat emptor) may not be invoked in these circumstances by the appellant-defendant builder-seller against the plaintiffs purchasers, whose affirmed award of damages after a nonjury trial should also be upheld by our court.

On November 29, 1976, plaintiffs Mary and Thomas Caceci entered into a contract with defendant Di Canio Construction Corp. for the sale and conveyance of a parcel of land in Suffolk County on which a one-family ranch home was to be constructed by the defendant builder. The contract price was $55,000. DiCanio guaranteed "for one year from title closing, the plumbing, heating, and electrical work, roof and basement walls against seepage and defective workmanship," but added that "[liability] under this guarantee shall be limited to replacement or repair of any defects or defective parts." The contract also provided that the dwelling "shall be constructed in accordance with the requirements as to materials and workmanship of the Municipality . . . with the requirements of the lending institution which shall make the mortgage loan [and] with the approved plans and specifications." Paragraph (24) concluded: "It is further agreed that none of the terms hereof except those specifically made to survive title closing shall survive such title closing."

On October 14, 1977, title closed. Four years later in December 1981, Mary Caceci noticed a dip in the kitchen floor. The condition was brought to defendant's attention and an attempt to repair the house was made by jacking up the basement ceiling and inserting shims to close the gap. The area was spackled over and sealed. These repairs did not solve the problem and the floor soon began to dip again. In November 1982, defendant made another attempt to repair the house, while assuring plaintiff that the cracks and dips were the result of a normal settling process. Unconvinced, plaintiffs hired a firm experienced in structural and concrete repairs to do test borings and analysis of soil samples. The results showed the cause of the sinking foundation was its placement on top of soil composed of deteriorating tree trunks, wood and other biodegradable materials. The repair work to cure the problem, which took seven months, included digging up the entire slab foundation, removing the wood and tree trunks, and pouring a new foundation.

In May 1983, plaintiffs commenced this action, alleging six causes of action. A nonjury trial was held and, prior to the close of proof, the court dismissed three causes of action based on fraud and negligent repair. The claims which went to verdict were based on breach of contract (rejected), negligent construction (upheld) and breach of implied warranty of workman-like construction (upheld). The trial court noted that photographs and testimony established that defendant, in pouring the original concrete footing and slab, became aware of the substances in the soil and thus breached duties in negligence and in implied warranty. A judgment of $57,466, representing the reasonable cost of correcting defendant's slipshod performance, was entered in plaintiffs' favor together with costs and interest from December 1981.

The Appellate Division affirmed solely on the implied warranty theory, confirming that there was sufficient evidence from which the trier of fact could infer that defendant knew the house was being erected on poor soil.

We, too, affirm, holding that there is an implied term in the express contract between the builder-vendor and purchasers that the house to be constructed would be done in a skillful manner free from material defects. Contrary to the view expressed by the lower courts in this case, however, the builder-seller's knowledge of the defect, however relevant in a fraud claim, is not decisive under this implied contractual warranty theory. Further, the contract's standard merger clause is of no legal effect in these circumstances of an implied warranty with respect to latent defects. Plaintiffs' claim based on a breach of implied warranty could only arise at closing of title when the builder-vendor conveyed a house which suffered from latent material defects. To hold, in a case such as this, that the closing itself, the very act which triggers the claim, also served to extinguish it is self-contradictory, illusory and against public policy. Finally, the contention that Real Property Law §251 prohibits this "Housing Merchant" warranty by legal implication also is not persuasive, since that statute is expressly limited to deeds of conveyance and has no application to contracts for the construction and sale of new homes.

Traditionally, the doctrine that the buyer must beware (caveat emptor) governed the sale of personal property and real property. The rationale for the judicially created doctrine was an outgrowth of the 19th century political philosophy of laissez-faire; namely, that a "buyer deserved whatever he got if he relied on his own inspection of the merchandise and did not extract an express warranty from the seller" (Roberts, The Case of the Unwary Home Buyer: The Housing Merchant Did It, 52 Cornell L.Q. 835, 836-837). Thus, the law treated express warranty or negligence or fraud as providing a purchaser of chattel or of real property with a surfeit of remedies.

As the industrial revolution roared into the era of mass produced goods, the law governing the sale of personal property started to relax the rigid results of the caveat emptor rule, culminating in the recognition of an implied warranty of merchantability (see, Uniform Sales Act §15, 1 ULA; UCC §§2-314, 2-315). This change in attitude as to chattels had little effect upon sales of real property, because prior to World War II there was no corresponding marketing or production transformation in the home construction industry. The post-World War II boom in housing, however, produced a building industry revolution and a growing awareness of the relative helplessness of would-be homeowners in the face of poor or deficient quality.

Since law usually reflects society's conflicts and developments, it started to catch up to the changes in home building and purchasing practices by bringing fresh and sharp scrutiny to the doctrine of caveat emptor in these circumstances. One commentator even pointed to the irony of a system of law which "[offered] greater protection to the purchaser of a seventy-nine cent dog leash than it [did] to the purchaser of a 40,000-dollar house" (Haskell, The Case for an Implied Warranty of Quality in Sales of Real Property, 53 Geo. L.J. 633 [1965]; see also, Roberts, The Case of the Unwary House Buyer: The Housing Merchant Did It, 52 Cornell L.Q. 835 [1967]; Bearman, Caveat Emptor in Sales of Realty — Recent Assaults Upon the Rule, 14 Vand. L Rev 541 [1961]).

To harmonize the legal inconsistency and to soften the harsh effect of the caveat emptor doctrine, many jurisdictions recognized an implied warranty of skillful construction in connection with the sale of newly constructed houses. In fact, English courts, the originators of the caveat emptor rule, were the first to qualify it with the recognition of the implied warranty theory (Miller v. Cannon Hill Estates, [1931] 2 KB 113). Likewise, lower courts of our State have over the last three decades recognized and joined the legal trend. This case presents the first opportunity, however, for this court to address the continued appropriateness of the caveat emptor doctrine in these circumstances.

...

The justification in cases which have relaxed the doctrine of caveat emptor with respect to homes contracted for sale prior to construction is that the two parties involved in the purchase of such a home generally do not bargain as equals in relation to potential latent defects from faulty performance. When a buyer signs a contract prior to construction of a house, inspection of premises is an impossibility, especially and obviously with respect to latent defects. Thus, the purchaser has no meaningful choice but to rely on the builder-vendor to deliver what was bargained for — a house reasonably fit for the purpose for which it was intended. The builder-vendor, on the other hand, maintains a superior position and is the only one who can prevent the occurrence of major defects. We hold that responsibility and liability in cases such as the instant one should, as a matter of sound contract principles, policy and fairness, be placed on the party best able to prevent and bear the loss.

Defendant argues that departure from the rule of caveat emptor involves far-reaching policy considerations and, therefore, the decision to supplant it or modify it in these circumstances with an implied contractual warranty of skillful construction must be left to the Legislature. The court's role is not so limited. Defendant fails to appreciate that we are presented with what was in the first instance a court-made rule. Moreover, significant growth in many diverse areas of the law has emerged from this court's application of the common-law process to developing, changing and even outdated doctrines.

The mid-19th century well-established principle that the original seller of goods was not liable for damages caused by defects in the product with respect to anyone except the immediate purchaser or one in privity to that purchaser (see, Winterbottom v. Wright, 10 Mees & W 109, 152 Eng Rep 402 [1842]), evolved into an almost grudging exception that a seller could be liable to a third person for negligence in the preparation and sale of an article "imminently dangerous" to human safety (Thomas v. Winchester, 6 NY 397, 408 [1852]). Then, Judge Cardozo, in MacPherson v. Buick Motor Co. (217 NY 382), significantly extended the class of inherently dangerous articles to anything which becomes dangerous because it was negligently made. The underlying rationale for the extension of the court-made rule was that the manufacturer, by placing a product on the market, assumed responsibility to the ultimate purchaser and user.

. . .

Chief Judge Cardozo's preeminent work The Nature of Judicial Process captures our role best: "If judges have woefully misinterpreted the mores of their day, or if the mores of their day are no longer those of ours, they ought not to tie, in helpless submission, the hands of their successors" (Cardozo, Nature of Judicial Process, at 152; see also, at 109-110, 150-152). These cases and these views are especially apt in the area of contractual relations where it has long been the law in New York that courts will imply a covenant of good faith where the implied terms are consistent with other mutually agreed upon terms (Wood v. Duff-Gordon, 222 NY 88; see also, Park W. Mgt. Corp. v. Mitchell, 47 N.Y.2d 316, 325). Here, the implication that the builder must construct a house free from material defects and in a skillful manner is wholly consistent with the express terms of the contract and with the reasonable expectation of the purchasers. Common sense dictates that the purchasers were entitled to expect, without necessarily expressly stating the obvious in this contract, that the house being purchased was to be a habitable place. The law ought to fulfill that commonsense expectation.

Defendant's claims with respect to the sufficiency of the evidence, to the exclusion of expert witness proof and to the measure of damages, have been reviewed and are without merit.

Accordingly, the order of the Appellate Division should be affirmed, with costs.

BELLACOSA, J. Judges SIMONS, KAYE, ALEXANDER, TITONE and HANCOCK, JR., concur; Chief Judge WACHTLER taking no part.

Notes and Questions

1. *Implied warranties of quality in new home sales.* A clear majority of jurisdictions has recognized an implied warranty of quality in the sale of a new home by a builder-vendor. See Jeff Sovern, Toward a Theory of Warranties in Sales of New Homes: Housing the Implied Warranty Advocates, Law and Economics Mavens, and Consumer Psychologists Under One Roof, 1993 Wis. L. Rev. 13, 15-21 (citing over 30 states that have recognized an implied warranty of quality and only a few that have expressly rejected it). The warranty may be called an implied warranty of skillful construction, as in *Caceci,* or by a variety of other names including warranty of habitability, workmanlike performance, or merchantability. Id. For example, the New Jersey Supreme Court held that an implied warranty of "reasonable workmanship and habitability" attaches to the sale of a new home by the builder-vendor in McDonald v. Mianecki, 398 A.2d 1283, 1292-1293 (N.J. 1979). The *McDonald* court observed that "[c]learly every builder-vendor holds himself out, expressly or impliedly, as having the expertise necessary to construct a livable dwelling. It is equally as obvious that almost every buyer acts upon these representations and expects that the new house he is buying, whether already constructed or not yet built, will be suitable for use as a home. Otherwise, there would be no sale." Id.

2. *Habitability versus skillful construction.* The *Caceci* court states that the builder-vendor must construct a house "free from material defect and in a skillful manner." As the law concerning the implied warranty of quality has developed, it has become clear that it may have two separable components — a warranty of habitability and a warranty of skillful or sound construction — though the courts have not been consistent or clear in recognizing the distinction. See Albrecht v. Clifford, 767 N.E.2d 42 (Mass. 2002) (reviewing development of the law and noting that courts have blurred the distinction between the implied warranties of habitability and good workmanship, using different labels for similar concepts). Professor Timothy Davis concludes that the difference between the implied warranty of skillful construction and the implied warranty of habitability is that the former warranty focuses on the manner in which the work is performed while the latter reflects the "end result" expectation that the home will not have any major defects which render it unsuitable for habitation. Timothy Davis, The Illusive Warranty of Workmanlike Performance: Constructing a Conceptual Framework, 72 Neb. L. Rev. 981, 1013-1020 (1993). Thus, Professor Davis concludes that the implied warranty of skillful or workmanlike performance may include defects that do not render the house uninhabitable. In the *McDonald* case noted above, the New Jersey Supreme Court held that the implied warranty of habitability would extend to potable water in circumstances where the builder was obligated to construct a well to provide water for a house not serviced by a public water system. 398 A.2d at 1293-1294. By contrast, in Aronsohn v.

Mandara, 484 A.2d 675 (N.J. 1984), the New Jersey Supreme Court held that a patio which was added to a preexisting home would not come within the implied warranty of habitability because it did not fall within the scope of necessities to make a home suitable for living; however, the court did hold that a builder could be held liable for breach of an implied warranty that the patio would be constructed in a good quality manner. Do you agree that courts should imply a warranty of skillful construction in addition to a warranty of habitability? If so, what would the implied warranty of skillful construction include?

3. *Legislative action.* Some states have enacted legislation providing for implied warranties of quality in the sale of new homes. See Jeff Sovern, Toward a Theory of Warranties in Sales of New Homes: Housing the Implied Warranty Advocates, Law and Economics Mavens, and Consumer Psychologists Under One Roof, 1993 Wis. L. Rev. 13, 22-23 (listing states that have adopted statutes providing an implied warranty of quality for new homes). For example, within weeks after the *Caceci* decision was rendered, the New York legislature enacted a housing merchant warranty law, New York Gen. Bus. §§777-777b (McKinney 1996). See Amy L. McDaniel, Note, The New York Housing Merchant Warranty Statute: Analysis and Proposals, 75 Cornell L. Rev. 754 (1990). The New York law creates three types of warranties: a one-year warranty of skillful construction; a two-year warranty on major systems such as plumbing, electrical, and heating and cooling; and a six-year warranty on latent, material defects. The statute also eliminates any "privity" requirement that would limit the warranty to initial purchasers. Notably, however, the law also has the effect of protecting the builder by narrowing the scope of the implied warranty through its definition of the terms "skillful" and "material defect," and by excluding from its scope any obvious defects. Id. at 767-774. The New York Court of Appeals has ruled that the statutory enactment codifies and supplants the *Caceci* implied housing merchant warranty. Fumarelli v. Marsam Development, Inc., 703 N.E.2d 251 (N.Y. 1998).

4. *Effectiveness of disclaimers.* Can the builder-vendor contractually modify or "disclaim" the implied warranty of habitability? The prevailing view is that the implied warranty of habitability may be modified or disclaimed. Many courts, however, view disclaimers with suspicion and will refuse to enforce a disclaimer unless it is conspicuous, specific, and the result of mutual agreement. E.g., Petersen v. Hubschman Construction Co., 389 N.E.2d 1154 (Ill. 1979). A related question is what effect a disclaimer will have on the seller's duty to disclose. Compare Mackintosh v. Jack Matthews & Co., 855 P.2d 549 (Nev. 1993) ("as is" disclaimer ineffective when seller had duty to disclose information not accessible to diligent buyer), with Richey v. Patrick, 904 P.2d 798 (Wyo. 1995) ("as is" clause barred claim for nondisclosure by purchaser who failed to exercise right to conduct expert inspections). See generally David L. Abney, Disclaiming the Implied Real Estate Common-Law Warranties, 17 Real Est. L.J. 141 (1988); Frona M. Powell, Disclaimers of Implied Warranty in the Sale of New Homes, 34 Vill. L. Rev. 1123 (1989). The New York legislation cited above permits exclusion or modification of the implied warranty if the seller provides a written warranty that complies with certain requirements as to form, but it also provides that a disclaimer is

void as against public policy if it attempts to disclaim compliance with applicable building codes or if it permits the home to be unsafe. Should builder-vendors be able to disclaim the implied warranty of habitability? Is the sale of a new home analogous to the sale of goods, where sellers are allowed to disclaim implied warranties under UCC §2-316? Can you imagine circumstances in which both buyer and seller might wish to have an effective disclaimer?

5. *Liability of party other than a professional builder-vendor.* As indicated by the *Caceci* court, the implied warranty of quality in new home sales has roots in the implied warranty of merchantability in the sale of goods. Should a buyer of a home be able to maintain an action against a seller other than a merchant or professional builder-vendor? Most courts have refused to apply the warranty to a nonmerchant owner who sells a used home. See, e.g., Choung v. Iemma, 708 N.E.2d 7 (Ind. Ct. App. 1999) (implied warranty applies only to a "builder-vendor," a person in the business of building and selling homes for profit); Everts v. Parkinson, 555 S.E.2d 667 (N.C. Ct. App. 2001) (implied warranty not applicable to casual seller who would have no advantage in knowledge over purchaser); but see Andreychak v. Lent, 607 A.2d 1346 (N.J. Super. Ct. App. Div. 1992) (allowing implied warranty action against non-builder owner by the purchaser of used home when the septic system failed). Cf. Morris v. Rush, 69 S.W.3d 876 (Ark. Ct. App. 2002) (holding that implied warranty would not attach to nonprofessional individual who builds his own home, lives in it, and then sells it).

A buyer may have more success in assigning liability for the implied warranty of quality to a commercial lender, rather than an earlier occupant. In Connor v. Great Western Savings & Loan Assn., 447 P.2d 609 (Cal. 1968), the California Supreme Court held that a savings and loan association could be held liable to a purchaser of a single-family home for a defective foundation when the savings and loan was found to have failed to exercise ordinary care. Great Western's role in the project went far beyond that of the usual lender to the point where it became an active participant in the construction project. Subsequently, the California legislature enacted a statute limiting the liability of financial institutions to situations in which they act beyond the role of a lender of money. Cal. Civ. Code §3434 (West 1997). Courts in other jurisdictions seem to follow a similar approach, limiting the liability of lenders to situations in which they have become in essence joint venturers. See Terrace Condominium Assn. v. Midlantic National Bank, 633 A.2d 1060 (N.J. Super. Ct. Law Div. 1993) (bank became more than lender when it took over condominiums in foreclosure from defaulting developer and assumed the builder-vendor's responsibilities, including the implied warranties of habitability and reasonable workmanship).

6. *Implied warranties and commercial buildings.* Should the courts imply a warranty of habitability in the sale of commercial rather than residential real estate? The courts are divided. Compare, e.g., Conklin v. Hurley, 428 So. 2d 654 (Fla. 1983) (developer of waterfront building lots not liable to investors for breach of implied warranty of habitability), with Tusch Enterprises v. Coffin, 740 P.2d 1022 (Idaho 1987) (investor could recover from vendor of three duplexes for breach of the implied warranty of habitability). See Frona M. Powell & Jane P. Mallor, The Case for an Implied Warranty of Quality in

Sales of Commercial Real Estate, 68 Wash. U.L.Q. 305 (1990); Kathleen McNamara Tomcho, Note, Commercial Real Estate Buyer Beware: Sellers May Have the Right to Remain Silent, 70 S. Cal. L. Rev. 1571 (1997). Do you think the implied warranty of habitability should apply to sale of commercial property? Why? Could a useful distinction be drawn between residential property held for investment purposes and purely commercial property, such as an office building, implying a warranty in the first situation but not the second?

7

Avoiding Enforcement: Incapacity, Bargaining Misconduct, Unconscionability, and Public Policy

In Chapter 4 we saw that, under the statute of frauds, the failure of the parties to execute a writing renders an agreement unenforceable unless some exception to the statute is applicable. The requirement of *form* expressed by the statute of frauds (and by such other formalities as the parol evidence rule) reflects certain policies. (Recall the evidentiary, cautionary, and channelling functions of formalities discussed by Professor Fuller, reprinted after the *Pennsy Supply* case in Chapter 2.) In this chapter we turn our attention to other grounds for avoiding enforcement of an agreement. The doctrines examined in this chapter reflect policies somewhat different from those on which the statute of frauds is based: a concern with the *competency* of parties to make an agreement, with the *bargaining process* by which an agreement is reached, and with the *substance* of any resulting agreement.

We have seen that modern courts have shown an increasing willingness to expand the scope of contractual obligation, both to rectify unjust enrichment and to redress injury resulting from detrimental reliance. Similarly, courts have broadened their role in interpreting agreements and in implying contractual provisions, to produce what the courts consider to be just outcomes. We will see a similar trend in the following materials, a widening of the grounds for avoiding enforcement of an agreement from those that existed during the classical period. As you study these materials, consider whether this expansion is desirable, or whether, as some critics contend, it is likely to produce arbitrary results that threaten the efficiency of the market system.

A. MINORITY AND MENTAL INCAPACITY

Quite early, the common law declared that certain classes of persons lacked "capacity" to contract. Alfred W. B. Simpson, A History of the Common Law of Contract 539-557 (1987). In the case of minors (also commonly referred to as "infants"), this restriction could be justified on the ground that they did not have the judgment to protect themselves in the marketplace. The same justification was not applicable to married women, however, who were also denied the right to contract at common law. Instead, the theory behind this restriction was that marriage resulted in the union of husband and wife into a single legal personality, that of the husband. As Professor Lawrence Friedman has put it, "husband and wife were one flesh; but the man was the owner of that flesh." Lawrence M. Friedman, A History of American Law (3d ed. 2005). During the nineteenth century, this legal disability was removed by the passage of Married Women's Property Acts. See Richard H. Chused, Married Women's Property Law: 1800-1850, 71 Geo. L.J. 1359 (1983); Peggy Rabkin, The Origins of Law Reform: The Social Significance of the Nineteenth Century Codification Movement and Its Contribution to the Passage of the Early Married Women's Property Acts, 24 Buff. L. Rev. 683 (1975).

Statutory restrictions have also been imposed on the capacity of other persons to make contracts. During the period of legalized slavery in this country, many states enacted "Slave Codes," which denied enslaved persons legal capacity to contract for themselves. See Anthony R. Chase, Race, Culture, and Contract Law: From the Cottonfield to the Courtroom, 28 Conn. L. Rev. 1 (1995). During the same period, some states restricted the ability of free African-Americans to enter into certain types of contracts and exercise other civil rights. See John Hope Franklin and Alfred A. Moss, Jr., From Slavery to Freedom 141 (8th ed. 2000); Steven A. Siegel, The Federal Government's Power to Enact Color-Conscious Laws: An Originalist Inquiry, 92 Nw. U. L. Rev. 477 (1998). Even after the Civil War and the end of legalized slavery, many states enacted "Black Codes," which continued to restrict the ability of African-Americans to make and enforce contracts. See John Hope Franklin and Alfred A. Moss, Jr., From Slavery to Freedom 250-251 (8th ed. 2000). Restrictions on contract and property rights have also been placed on other people of color, including Asian-Americans. See Angelo N. Ancheta, Race, Rights and the Asian American Experience (2d ed. 2006); Natsu Taylor Saito, Alien and Non-Alien Alike: Citizenship, "Foreignness," and Racial Hierarchy in American Law, 76 Or. L. Rev. 261 (1997). Some writers have discussed such restrictions on contract and property rights as part of a broader denial of "economic personality." See Adrienne D. Davis, The Private Law of Race and Sex: An Antebellum Perspective, 51 Stan. L. Rev. 221 (1999); Thomas W. Joo, New "Conspiracy Theory" of the Fourteenth Amendment: Nineteenth Century Chinese Civil Rights Cases and the Development of Substantive Due Process Jurisprudence, 29 U.S.F. L. Rev. 353 (1995). While such formal legal restrictions on the capacity to contract were largely removed with the enactment of federal and state civil rights laws, informal cultural and social barriers have been much more difficult to overcome. See Keith Aoki, Direct Democracy, Racial Group Agency, Local Government Law and Residential Racial Segregation: Some Reflections on Radical and Plural Democracy, 33 Cal. W. L. Rev. 185 (1997); Neil G. Williams, Offer, Acceptance, and Improper Consideration: A Common Law Model for the Prohibition of Racial Discrimination in the Contracting Process, 62 Geo. Wash. L. Rev. 183 (1994).

The removal of race- and gender-based restrictions on the ability to contract reflected a new societal consensus that such laws were designed to oppress, rather than protect, the affected groups. The following cases and notes explore contemporary limitations on contractual capacity. While these restrictions on capacity appear less controversial than limitations based on race and gender, some may question whether these restrictions, too, are unwarranted or overbroad.

PROBLEM 7-1

You have an appointment with new clients, James and Mary Swan, owners of Swan's Used Auto Sales. The Swans told you over the telephone that they have a problem with a young man, Bob Byers, to whom they sold a car twelve months ago. They tell you that Bob is trying to cancel the deal because he was only seventeen at the time that he purchased the car in August 2006. The Swans tell you that they have checked their records and Bob completed a portion of the purchase agreement by indicating that his date of birth was March 1, 1988. Bob is now stating that his date of birth is March 1, 1989, and he is demanding return of the sales price of $6000. At the same time, Bob has told the Swans that the car is no longer operable and that the Swans should have the car towed from the street in front of Bob's home. Read the following case and accompanying notes and identify the factual questions and legal issues that you will need to pursue in advising the Swans. Your professor may elect to provide you with further instructions.

Dodson v. Shrader
Supreme Court of Tennessee
824 S.W.2d 545 (1992)

O'BRIEN, Justice.

This is an action to disaffirm the contract of a minor for the purchase of a pick-up truck and for a refund of the purchase price. The issue is whether the minor is entitled to a full refund of the money he paid or whether the seller is entitled to a setoff for the decrease in value of the pick-up truck while it was in the possession of the minor.

In early April of 1987, Joseph Eugene Dodson, then 16 years of age, purchased a used 1984 pick-up truck from Burns and Mary Shrader. The Shraders owned and operated Shrader's Auto Sales in Columbia, Tennessee. Dodson paid $4,900 in cash for the truck, using money he borrowed from his girlfriend's grandmother. At the time of the purchase there was no inquiry by the Shraders, and no misrepresentation by Mr. Dodson, concerning his minority. However, Mr. Shrader did testify that at the time he believed Mr. Dodson to be 18 or 19 years of age.

In December 1987, nine (9) months after the date of purchase, the truck began to develop mechanical problems. A mechanic diagnosed the problem as a burnt valve, but could not be certain without inspecting the valves inside the engine. Mr. Dodson did not want, or did not have the money, to effect these repairs. He continued to drive the truck despite the mechanical problems. One month later, in January, the truck's engine "blew up" and the truck became inoperable.

Mr. Dodson parked the vehicle in the front yard at his parents' home where he lived. He contacted the Shraders to rescind the purchase of the truck and requested a full refund. The Shraders refused to accept the tender of the truck or to give Mr. Dodson the refund requested.

Mr. Dodson then filed an action in general sessions court seeking to rescind the contract and recover the amount paid for the truck. The general sessions court dismissed the warrant and Mr. Dodson perfected a de novo appeal to the circuit court. At the time the appeal was filed in the circuit court Mr. Shrader, through counsel, declined to accept the tender of the truck without compensation for its depreciation. Before the circuit court could hear the case, the truck, while parked in Dodson's front yard, was struck on the left front fender by a hit-and-run driver. At the time of the circuit court trial, according to Shrader, the truck was worth only $500 due to the damage to the engine and the left front fender.

The case was heard in the circuit court in November 1988. The trial judge, based on previous common-law decisions and, under the doctrine of stare decisis reluctantly granted the rescission. The Shraders were ordered, upon tender and delivery of the truck, to reimburse the $4,900 purchase price to Mr. Dodson. The Shraders appealed.

The Court of Appeals, per TODD, J., affirmed; CANTRELL, J., concurring separately, KOCH, J., dissenting.

The earliest recorded case in this State, on the issue involved, appears to be in Wheaton v. East, 13 Tenn. 35 (5 Yeager 41) (1833). In pronouncing the rule to apply governing infant's contracts, the court [quoted]:

> . . . "that when the court can pronounce the contract to be to the infant's prejudice, it is void, and when to his benefit, as for necessaries, it is good; and when the contract is of any uncertain nature, as to benefit or prejudice, it is voidable only, at the election of the infant."

The law on the subject of the protection of infant's rights has been slow to evolve. However, in Human v. Hartsell, 24 Tenn. App. 678, 148 S.W.2d 634, 636 (1940) the Court of Appeals noted:

> . . . In Tuck v. Payne, 159 Tenn. 192, 17 S.W.2d 8, in an opinion by Mr. Justice McKinney, the modern rule that contracts of infants are not void but only voidable and subject to be disaffirmed by the minor either before or after attaining majority appears to have been favored.
>
> Under this rule the efforts of early authorities to classify contracts as beneficial or harmful and determine whether they are void or only voidable upon the basis of such classification are abandoned in favor of permitting the infant himself when he has become of age to determine what contracts are and what are not to his interest and liking. He is thus permitted to assume the burden of a contract, clearly disadvantageous to him, if he deems himself under a moral obligation to do so.
>
> The adoption of this rule does not lead to any retrenchment of the infant's rights but gives him the option of invoking contracts found to be advantageous but which, if held void, could not be enforced against the other party to the contract.

Thus the minor can secure the advantage of contracts advantageous to himself and be relieved of the effect of an injudicious contract.

. . .

As noted by the Court of Appeals, the rule in Tennessee, as modified, is in accord with the majority rule on the issue among our sister states. This rule is based upon the underlying purpose of the "infancy doctrine" which is to protect minors from their lack of judgment and "from squandering their wealth through improvident contracts with crafty adults who would take advantage of them in the marketplace." Halbman v. Lemke, 99 Wis. 2d 241, 245, 298 N.W.2d 562, 564 (1980).

There is, however, a modern trend among the states, either by judicial action or by statute, in the approach to the problem of balancing the rights of minors against those of innocent merchants. As a result, two (2) minority rules have developed which allow the other party to a contract with a minor to refund less than the full consideration paid in the event of rescission.

The first of these minority rules is called the "Benefit Rule." E.g., Hall v. Butterfield, 59 N.H. 354 (1879); Johnson v. Northwestern Mut. Life Insurance Co., 56 Minn. 365, 59 N.W. 992 (1894); Berglund v. American Multigraph Sales Co., 135 Minn. 67, 160 N.W. 191 (1916); Porter v. Wilson, 106 N.H. 270, 209 A.2d 730 (1965); Valencia v. White, 134 Ariz. 139, 654 P.2d 287 (Ariz. App. 1982). The rule holds that, upon rescission, recovery of the full purchase price is subject to a deduction for the minor's use of the merchandise. This rule recognizes that the traditional rule in regard to necessaries has been extended so far as to hold an infant bound by his contracts, where he failed to restore what he has received under them to the extent of the benefit actually derived by him from what he has received from the other party to the transaction. . . .

The other minority rule holds that the minor's recovery of the full purchase price is subject to a deduction for the minor's "use" of the consideration he or she received under the contract, or for the "depreciation" or "deterioration" of the consideration in his or her possession. See . . . Pettit v. Liston, 97 Or. 464, 191 P. 660 (1920).

We are impressed by the statement made by the Arizona Appeals Court in Valencia v. White, supra, citing the Court of Appeals of Ohio in Haydocy Pontiac Inc. v. Lee, 19 Ohio App. 2d 217, 250 N.E.2d 898 (1969):

> At a time when we see young persons between 18 and 21 years of age demanding and assuming more responsibilities in their daily lives; when we see such persons emancipated, married, and raising families; when we see such persons charged with the responsibility for committing crimes; when we see such persons being sued in tort claims for acts of negligence; when we see such persons subject to military service; when we see such persons engaged in business and acting in almost all other respects as an adult, it seems timely to re-examine the case law pertaining to contractual rights and responsibilities of infants to see if the law as pronounced and applied by the courts should be redefined.

. . . Upon serious reflection we are convinced that a modified form of the Oregon rule should be adopted in this State concerning the rights and responsibilities of minors in their business dealings. . . .

We state the rule to be followed hereafter, in reference to a contract of a minor, to be where the minor has not been overreached in any way, and there has been no undue influence, and the contract is a fair and reasonable one, and the minor has actually paid money on the purchase price, and taken and used the article purchased, that he ought not to be permitted to recover the amount actually paid, without allowing the vendor of the goods reasonable compensation for the use of, depreciation, and willful or negligent damage to the article purchased, while in his hands. If there has been any fraud or imposition on the part of the seller or if the contract is unfair, or any unfair advantage has been taken of the minor inducing him to make the purchase, then the rule does not apply. Whether there has been such an overreaching on the part of the seller, and the fair market value of the property returned, would always, in any case, be a question for the trier of fact. This rule will fully and fairly protect the minor against injustice or imposition, and at the same time it will be fair to a business person who has dealt with such minor in good faith.

This rule is best adapted to modern conditions under which minors are permitted to, and do in fact, transact a great deal of business for themselves, long before they have reached the age of legal majority. Many young people work and earn money and collect it and spend it oftentimes without any oversight or restriction. The law does not question their right to buy if they have the money to pay for their purchases. It seems intolerably burdensome for everyone concerned if merchants and business people cannot deal with them safely, in a fair and reasonable way. Further, it does not appear consistent with practice of proper moral influence upon young people, tend to encourage honesty and integrity, or lead them to a good and useful business future, if they are taught that they can make purchases with their own money, for their own benefit, and after paying for them, and using them until they are worn out and destroyed, go back and compel the vendor to return to them what they have paid upon the purchase price. Such a doctrine can only lead to the corruption of principles and encourage young people in habits of trickery and dishonesty. . . .

We note that in this case, some nine (9) months after the date of purchase, the truck purchased by the plaintiff began to develop mechanical problems. Plaintiff was informed of the probable nature of the difficulty which apparently involved internal problems in the engine. He continued to drive the vehicle until the engine "blew up" and the truck became inoperable. Whether or not this involved gross negligence or intentional conduct on his part is a matter for determination at the trial level. It is not possible to determine from this record whether a counterclaim for tortious damage to the vehicle was asserted. After the first tender of the vehicle was made by plaintiff, and refused by the defendant, the truck was damaged by a hit-and-run driver while parked on plaintiff's property. The amount of that damage and the liability for that amount between the purchaser and the vendor, as well as the fair market value of the vehicle at the time of tender, is also an issue for the trier of fact.

The case is remanded to the trial court for further proceedings in accordance with this judgment. The costs on appellate review are assessed equally between the parties.

REID, C.J. and DROWOTA, DAUGHTREY and ANDERSON, JJ., concur.

Notes and Questions

1. *Traditional infancy or minority doctrine.* The *Dodson* court begins its analysis by recognizing the traditional rule that allows a minor to disaffirm or avoid a contract, even if there has been full performance and the minor cannot return to the adult what was received in the exchange. See E. Allan Farnsworth, Contracts §§4.4-4.5, at 222-227 (4th ed. 2004). Thus, if the minor received services that cannot be returned or the minor received goods that have since lost value, courts have allowed disaffirmance and required the minor to return only what the minor still possesses or any identifiable proceeds. The court in Halbman v. Lemke, 298 N.W.2d 562 (Wis. 1980), cited by the *Dodson* court, applied the traditional rule in holding that a minor who disaffirmed a contract for the purchase of an automobile was not required to make restitution to the seller for the substantial diminution in value of the vehicle, absent a showing that the minor misrepresented his age or willfully destroyed the property. The Court stated: "[W]e believe that to require a disaffirming minor to make restitution for diminished value is, in effect, to bind the minor to a part of the obligation which by law he is privileged to avoid." Id. at 567.

The *Dodson* court, however, departs from the traditional rule and adopts an approach that requires a disaffirming minor to make restitution for either the benefit received under the contract or the depreciation in the value of the property, at least when the minor is seeking to recover payment made to the adult. Some of the cases cited by the *Dodson* court have gone even further in requiring minors generally to pay for the value of all benefit received. See, e.g., Valencia v. White, 654 P.2d 287 (Ariz. App. 1982) (minor who owned and operated trucking business required to make restitution to adult who provided repair services); Porter v. Wilson, 209 A.2d 730 (N.H. 1965) (minor could disaffirm contract for legal services but required to make restitution to adult for benefit received). Are you persuaded that the traditional rule has become outdated and that a disaffirming minor should be obligated to pay for any benefit received?

2. *Liability for "necessaries" and tortious conduct.* Even under the traditional rule, the right of a minor to avoid a contract has been subject to an important limitation: The minor is liable for the reasonable value of "necessaries." The recovery for the adult allowed in these cases, however, is based on restitution rather than enforcement of the contract. See Garay v. Overholtzer, 631 A.2d 429 (Md. 1993); Restatement (Second) §12, Comment f. Necessaries usually have been limited to items that one needs to live, such as food, clothing, and shelter. See, e.g., Yale Diagnostic Radiology v. Estate of Fountain, 838 A.2d 179 (Conn. 2003) (medical services rendered to minor were necessaries and minor is liable when payment cannot be collected from parent); Young v. Weaver, 883 So. 2d 234 (Ala. Civ. App. 2003) (while housing is generally a necessity, apartment leased by minor was not because minor could have returned home to live). Some courts have been willing to construe the concept more broadly. See Zelnick v. Adams, 561 S.E.2d 711 (Va. 2002) (contract for legal services may be a necessary if needed to protect rights of minor; legal services to protect inheritance rights could be a necessary depending on facts).

As suggested by the materials in Note 1, the minor's ability to disaffirm may also be restricted if the minor engages in tortious conduct such as misrepresentation of age or willful destruction of goods. See Del Bosco v. U.S. Ski Association, 839 F. Supp. 1470, 1475 n.3 (D. Colo. 1993) (misrepresentation of age might preclude assertion of minority defense); Monahan v. Friederick, 455 N.W.2d 914 (Wis. Ct. App. 1990) (willful destruction of car would lead to tort liability of minor, but trial court made no such finding). Mere ignorance of the minor's age, however, is no defense to the minor's disaffirmance. See Iverson v. Scholl, Inc., 483 N.E.2d 893 (Ill. App. Ct. 1985). Cf. Joseph M. Perillo, Calamari & Perillo on Contracts §8.7, at 297-298 (5th ed. 2003) (majority view is that minor who misrepresents age can still disaffirm but may be liable in tort for fraud).

3. *Ratification after reaching majority.* Even if a minor enters into a contract that does not involve necessaries, the contract is not void but only "voidable" at the election of the minor. Restatement (Second) §14. Once the minor reaches the age of majority, she has the power to affirm or ratify the contract, in which event the minor is bound. Moreover, on reaching the age of majority, the minor must act within a reasonable period of time to disaffirm the contract or she will be deemed to have affirmed the transaction. E.g., In re The Score Board, Inc., 238 B.R. 585 (Bankr. D.N.J. 1999) (professional basketball player Kobe Bryant, who signed contract while a minor but accepted payment and performed autograph signing duties for more than 18 months after reaching majority, held to have ratified contract); Muller v. CES Credit Union, 832 N.E.2d 80 (Ohio Ct. App. 2005) (minor must disaffirm within a reasonable time after reaching majority; delay of four years was too long).

4. *Statutory limits on the minority doctrine.* Legislative reduction of the age of majority from 21 to 18 in many states has, of course, curtailed the amount of litigation involving minors' contracts. Other statutory provisions may also apply to validate specific types of contracts made by a person even before reaching the age of majority. See, e.g., Sharon v. City of Newton, 769 N.E.2d 738 (Mass. 2002) (detailing Massachusetts state laws allowing minors to contract for education financing, life insurance, motor vehicle liability insurance, drug dependency treatment, and medical or dental care). Cf. Lane v. MRA Holdings, LLC, 242 F. Supp. 2d 1205 (M.D. Fla. 2002) (because Florida statute restricted the ability of minors to consent only to "compensated" use of photos, seventeen-year-old woman who posed partially nude for "Girls Gone Wild" video could not disaffirm her uncompensated consent); Douglass vs. Pflueger Hawaii, Inc., 135 P.3d 129 (Haw. 2006) (statutory provisions allowing for employment of sixteen- and seventeen-year-old persons meant that contract could not be disaffirmed on basis of minority doctrine).

5. *Avoidance of employment contract provisions.* In a number of cases raising issues similar to those in *Dodson,* courts have been divided on the question whether a minor should be allowed to disaffirm an employment agreement after the minor has received benefits derived from being employed. Compare Robinson v. Food Service, 415 F. Supp. 2d 1227 (D. Kan. 2005) (holding Kansas state courts would not allow minors to disaffirm employment contract that on the whole had been beneficial) and Sheller v. Frank's Nursery & Crafts, Inc., 957 F. Supp. 150 (N.D. Ill. 1997) (holding that minors suing

for sexual discrimination could not disaffirm employment contract with arbitration agreement while retaining benefits of the employment), with Stroupes v. The Finish Line, Inc., 2005 U.S. Dist. LEXIS 6975 (E.D. Tenn. 2005) (holding that minor suing for sexual harassment could disaffirm employment contract with arbitration agreement and bring suit in court). You should note that a minor may allege that an arbitration agreement is unenforceable for other reasons that will be discussed further in section D of this chapter on the unconscionability doctrine.

6. *Pre- and postinjury release agreements.* Sponsors of youth recreational activities such as soccer, little league baseball, gymnastics, or skiing, frequently require releases from liability for personal injury as a precondition to children being permitted to participate. Many courts have held that minors are able to disaffirm such preinjury exculpatory agreements signed by the parent. See, e.g., Cooper v. Aspen Skiing Co., 48 P.3d 1229 (Colo. 2002) (minor could disaffirm prospective release and bring action for skiing injuries); Hojnowski v. Vans Skate Park, 901 A.2d 381 (N.J. 2006) (parent's execution of pre-injury release for minor's use of commercial recreational facility was unenforceable). On the other hand, the court in Zivich v. Mentor Soccer Club, Inc., 696 N.E.2d 201 (Ohio 1998), held that the minor could not disaffirm a release agreement signed by his parent before engaging in soccer play. In deciding to allow the parent to bind the minor to a preinjury release, the Ohio Supreme Court asserted that enforcement of the release supports two policy concerns: encouraging volunteer programs that promote organized recreational activities for children and recognition of the liberty interest of parents in making life choices for children. Id. at 205-206. Accord Sharon v. City of Newton, 769 N.E.2d 738 (Mass. 2002) (court will not disturb fundamental right of parent to sign release and thereby allow child to participate in cheerleading activity; decision supported by state public policy of encouraging athletic activities for youth).

Postinjury settlement agreements on behalf of minors will typically involve the execution of a release of the minor's claims. In most jurisdictions, settlements by minors must be approved by a court and may not be later disaffirmed. See, e.g., Wreglesworth v. Arctco, Inc., 738 N.E.2d 964 (Ill. App. Ct. 2000); White v. Allied Mutual Ins. Co., 31 P.3d 328 (Kan. Ct. App. 2001). If the settlement agreement is not approved by a court, the minor will probably be allowed to avoid the postinjury release. See Villalobos v. Cicero School District 99, 841 NE. 2d 87 (Ill. App. Ct. 2005); Mitchell v. Mitchell, 963 S.W.2d 222 (Ky. Ct. App. 1998).

7. *Effect of marriage.* Should a minor automatically attain contractual capacity upon emancipation by virtue of marriage? Compare Lay v. Suggs, 559 So. 2d 740 (Fla. Dist. Ct. App. 1990) (under Florida statute minor's marriage results in emancipation and dissolves inability to contract; once the parent is no longer able to command obedience, the parent should not be responsible for the child), with Mitchell v. Mitchell, 963 S.W.2d 222 (Ky. Ct. App. 1998) (emancipation through marriage does not confer capacity to contract; minor's marriage frequently may indicate lack of wisdom and maturity). Notably, the minority doctrine is a personal defense and the fact that one spouse may disaffirm will offer no relief to the other spouse. See, e.g., H & S Homes, L.L.C. v. McDonald, 823 So. 2d 627 (Ala. 2001) (husband's

status as a minor raised possible basis for his avoidance of arbitration agreement; wife, who was not a minor, held bound by provision).

Hauer v. Union State Bank of Wautoma
Court of Appeals of Wisconsin
192 Wis. 2d 576, 532 N.W.2d 456 (1995)

SNYDER, Judge.

The issues in this case arise out of a loan made by Union State Bank of Wautoma to Kathy Hauer. The Bank appeals from a judgment which (1) voided the loan on the grounds that Hauer lacked the mental capacity to enter into the loan, (2) required the Bank to return Hauer's collateral and (3) dismissed the Bank's counterclaim which sought to recover the proceeds of the loan from Hauer. Because we conclude that there is evidence in the record to support the jury's findings that Hauer was mentally incompetent at the time of the loan and that the Bank failed to act in good faith in granting the loan, we affirm.

I. FACTS

In order to place the loan in context, we must first set forth the relevant events giving rise to the loan. The following facts are taken from court documents and undisputed testimony at trial.

In 1987, Hauer suffered a brain injury in a motorcycle accident. She was subsequently adjudicated to be incompetent, resulting in a guardian being appointed by the court. On September 20, 1988, Hauer's guardianship was terminated based upon a letter from her treating physician, Kenneth Viste. Viste opined that Hauer had recovered to the point where she had ongoing memory, showed good judgment, was reasonable in her goals and plans and could manage her own affairs. Her monthly income after the accident was $900, which consisted of social security disability and interest income from a mutual fund worth approximately $80,000.

On October 18, 1988, the Bank loaned Ben Eilbes $7600 to start a small business. In December, Eilbes requested but was denied an additional $2000 loan from the Bank. By June of 1989, Eilbes was in default on the loan. Around this time, Eilbes met Hauer through her daughter, who told Eilbes about the existence of Hauer's mutual fund. Eilbes subsequently discussed his business with Hauer on several occasions and Hauer expressed an interest in becoming an investor in the business. Because Hauer could only sell her stocks at certain times, Eilbes suggested that she take out a short-term loan using the stocks as collateral. Eilbes told Hauer that if she loaned him money, he would give her a job, pay her interest on the loan and pay the loan when it came due. Hauer agreed.

Eilbes then contacted Richard Schroeder, assistant vice president of the Bank, and told Schroeder that Hauer wanted to invest in his business but that she needed short-term financing and could provide adequate collateral. Eilbes told Schroeder that he would use the money invested by Hauer in part to either bring the payments current on his defaulted loan or pay the loan off in full. Schroeder then called Hauer's stockbroker and financial consultant, Stephen Landolt, in an effort to verify the existence of Hauer's fund. Landolt told Schroeder that Hauer needed the interest income to live on and that he wished the Bank would not use it as collateral for a loan. Schroeder also conceded that it was possible that Landolt told him that Hauer was suffering from brain damage, but did not specifically recall that part of their conversation.

At some later date Eilbes met personally with Schroeder in order to further discuss the potential loan to Hauer, after which Schroeder indicated that the Bank would be willing to loan Hauer $30,000. Schroeder gave Eilbes a loan application to give to Hauer to fill out. On October 26, 1989, Hauer and Eilbes went to the Bank to meet with Schroeder and sign the necessary paperwork. Prior to this date, Schroeder had not spoken to or met with Hauer. During this meeting Schroeder explained the terms of the loan to Hauer — that she would sign a consumer single-payment note due in six months and give the Bank a security interest in her mutual fund as collateral. Schroeder did not notice anything that would cause him to believe that Hauer did not understand the loan transaction.

On April 26, 1990, the date the loan matured, Hauer filed suit against the Bank and Eilbes. Hauer subsequently amended her complaint three times. The Bank filed a counterclaim for judgment on the defaulted loan after Hauer's first amended complaint. In Hauer's third amended complaint, she alleged the following specific causes of action: (1) the Bank knew or should have known that she lacked the mental capacity to understand the loan, (2) the Bank intentionally misrepresented, negligently misrepresented, or misrepresented the circumstances surrounding the loan on which she relied, and (3) the Bank breached a fiduciary duty owed to her.

On January 7, 1992, the Bank moved for summary judgment on the grounds that Hauer failed to state any claim for which relief could be granted. The trial court granted summary judgment in part by dismissing Hauer's misrepresentation claims. However, the court held that the pleadings stated the following causes of action which required factual determinations: (1) Hauer lacked the mental capacity to enter into the loan agreement and the Bank knew or should have known about her condition, (2) the Bank breached its duty of good faith and fair dealing under §401.203, Stats., and (3) the Bank had a fiduciary duty to Hauer and breached that duty.

Prior to trial and over the Bank's objection, Hauer dismissed Eilbes because he appeared to be judgment proof and was filing bankruptcy. A twelve-person jury subsequently found that Hauer lacked the mental capacity to enter into the loan and that the Bank failed to act in good faith toward Hauer in the loan transaction. The trial court denied the Bank's motions after verdict and entered judgment voiding the loan contract, dismissing the Bank's counterclaim and ordering the Bank to return Hauer's collateral. The Bank appeals.

In addition to voiding the contract, Hauer also sought damages arising out of the Bank's conduct for punitive damages and actual attorney's fees. The trial court refused to submit questions to the jury regarding punitive damages. Further, the trial court ruled postverdict that Hauer was not entitled to actual attorney's fees. Hauer cross-appeals from these adverse rulings. We will discuss further facts as we discuss the appellate issues.

II. MENTAL CAPACITY TO CONTRACT

Over the Bank's objection, the jury was presented with the following special verdict question: Did the plaintiff, Kathy Hauer, lack the mental capacity to enter into the loan transaction at the time of that transaction? The jury answered this question, "Yes." In denying the Bank's motions after verdict, the trial court held that based on this finding, the note and security agreement were "void or voidable." Further, the court ruled that Hauer was not liable for repayment of the $30,000 loan because she no longer possessed the funds.

The Bank in its motions after verdict and on appeal argues that the jury's verdict as to mental incompetency is invalid. The Bank contends that Hauer failed to state a claim upon which relief can be granted or, in the alternative, that the evidence does not support the jury's verdict.

A. MENTAL INCOMPETENCE—CAUSE OF ACTION

We first address the Bank's argument that Hauer's claim of mental incompetence fails to state a claim for which relief can be granted. This presents a question of law which we review independently. Peterman v. Midwestern Nat'l Ins. Co., 177 Wis. 2d 682, 697, 503 N.W.2d 312, 318 (Ct. App. 1993). The Bank contends that a claim of mental incompetence is an affirmative defense to an action to enforce a contract only and that Hauer cannot avail herself of such a defense because she failed to plead any affirmative defenses. We disagree.

We have previously recognized that the vast majority of courts have held that an incompetent person's transactions are voidable—the incompetent has the power to void the contract entirely. See Production Credit Ass'n v. Kehl, 148 Wis. 2d 225, 229-30, 434 N.W.2d 816, 818 (Ct. App. 1988); see also 5 Samuel Williston, Williston on Contracts §10:3 (4th ed. 1993). Further, Wisconsin has long recognized a cause of action to rescind a contract or conveyance based upon the lack of mental competency at the time of the transaction. See, e.g., First Nat'l Bank v. Nennig, 92 Wis. 2d 518, 521, 285 N.W.2d 614, 616 (1979). Accordingly, we conclude that Hauer properly stated a cause of action to void the loan contract.

B. SUFFICIENCY OF THE EVIDENCE

The Bank argues that even if Hauer has a cause of action to void the contract based upon the lack of mental capacity, the record is devoid of credible evidence to sustain the jury's verdict. In reviewing a jury's verdict, we will sustain the verdict if there is any credible evidence to support it. Fehring v. Republic Ins. Co., 118 Wis. 2d 299, 305, 347 N.W.2d 595, 598 (1984). The weight and credibility of the evidence are left to the province of the jury. Id. When the evidence permits more than one inference, this court must accept the inference that favors the jury's verdict. Id. at 305-06, 347 N.W.2d at 598.

The law presumes that every adult person is fully competent until satisfactory proof to the contrary is presented. First Nat'l Bank, 92 Wis. 2d at

529-30, 285 N.W.2d at 620. The burden of proof is on the person seeking to void the act. Nyka v. State, 268 Wis. 644, 646, 68 N.W.2d 458, 460 (1955). The test for determining competency is whether the person involved had sufficient mental ability to know what he or she was doing and the nature and consequences of the transaction. First Nat'l Bank, 92 Wis. 2d at 530, 285 N.W.2d at 620; see also Restatement (Second) of Contracts §15(1)(a) (1979). Almost any conduct may be relevant, as may lay opinions, expert opinions and prior and subsequent adjudications of incompetency. Restatement, supra, at §15 cmt. *c*.

Our review of the record reveals that there is credible evidence which the jury could have relied on in reaching its verdict. First, it is undisputed that Hauer was under court-appointed guardianship approximately one year before the loan transaction. Second, Hauer's testimony indicates a complete lack of understanding of the nature and consequences of the transaction.[2] Third, Hauer's psychological expert, Charles Barnes, testified that when he treated her in 1987, Hauer was "very deficient in her cognitive abilities, her abilities to remember and to read, write and spell . . . she was very malleable, gullible, people could convince her of almost anything." Barnes further testified that because Hauer's condition had not changed in any significant way by 1990 when he next evaluated her, she was "incompetent and . . . unable to make reasoned decisions" on the date she made the loan.

The Bank argues that Barnes's testimony was irrelevant and erroneously admitted because Viste, Hauer's treating neurologist, informed the court that in his opinion Hauer was no longer in need of a guardian and could manage her own affairs a year prior to the loan.[3] The Bank contends that Hauer should be judicially estopped from asserting incompetence at the time of the loan after convincing the court the previous year that she was competent. However, competency must be determined on the date the instrument was executed. *Production Credit,* 148 Wis. 2d at 230, 434 N.W.2d at 818.

The Bank further points out that both Eilbes and Schroeder testified that Hauer was much different at trial than she was on the day the loan was executed. Nevertheless, the weight and credibility of the evidence are for the jury to decide, not this court. The jury apparently gave more credence to Hauer's and Barnes's testimony than Schroeder's testimony and Viste's 1988 opinion. In sum, while we agree that there is evidence which the jury could have relied on to find that Hauer was competent, we must accept the inference that favors the jury's verdict when the evidence permits more than one inference. *Fehring,* 118 Wis. 2d at 305-06, 347 N.W.2d at 598.

III. Effect of Incompetence

Having concluded that Hauer stated a claim for relief and that sufficient credible evidence was presented to sustain the jury's verdict, we now turn to

---

2. For example, Hauer testified that she believed that she was merely cosigning a loan for Eilbes and that he was responsible for paying it back.

3. Over the Bank's objection, a portion of Viste's deposition was read at trial, where Viste concluded that based on Barnes's opinion, he had erred in finding that Hauer was competent and no longer in need of a guardian in 1988.

the unresolved problem regarding the rights and responsibilities of the parties relative to the disposition of the consideration exchanged in the loan transaction. We must decide the legal question of whether Hauer may recover her collateral without liability for the loan proceeds. We review questions of law independently of the trial court. State v. Jason J.C., 181 Wis. 2d 868, 872-73, 512 N.W.2d 522, 524 (Ct. App. 1994).

Postverdict, the trial court ruled that Hauer's action to void the contract required the Bank to return her collateral and Hauer to return any loan proceeds in her possession. However, it is undisputed that Hauer loaned the entire $30,000 to Eilbes and that the money had long since disappeared. On appeal, the Bank contends that equity dictates that the proper remedy upon voiding the loan transaction is to return the parties to their preloan status — the Bank must return Hauer's stocks and Hauer must be held liable to the Bank for $30,000.

The trial court offered two explanations for voiding the contract but not holding Hauer liable for repayment of the loan: (1) the law and policy of the "infancy doctrine" set forth in Halbman v. Lemke, 99 Wis. 2d 241, 298 N.W.2d 562 (1980), and (2) the jury's finding that the Bank failed to act in good faith. We will address each in turn.

A. INFANCY DOCTRINE

In *Halbman*, our supreme court held that a minor who disaffirms a contract may recover the purchase price without liability for use, depreciation or other diminution in value. Id. at 251, 298 N.W.2d at 567. As a general rule, a minor who disaffirms a contract is expected to return as much of the consideration as remains in the minor's possession. However, the minor's right to disaffirm is permitted even where the minor cannot return the property. Id. at 245-46, 298 N.W.2d at 565. The trial court ruled that the infancy doctrine was analogous and applies when the voidness arises from mental incapacity to contract. We disagree.

The purpose of the infancy doctrine is to protect "minors from foolishly squandering their wealth through improvident contracts with crafty adults who would take advantage of them in the marketplace." Id. at 245, 298 N.W.2d at 564. The common law has long recognized this policy to protect minors. Id. However, "[a] contract made by a person who is mentally incompetent requires the reconciliation of two conflicting policies: the protection of justifiable expectations and of the security of transactions, and the protection of persons unable to protect themselves against imposition." Restatement, supra, §15 cmt. *a*.

The trial court's analogy fails given the fact that the two types of incapacity are essentially dissimilar. Williston, supra, §10:3. "An infant is often mentally competent in fact to understand the force of his bargain, but it is the policy of the law to protect the minor. By contrast, the adult mental incompetent may be subject to varying degrees of infirmity or mental illness, not all equally incapacitating." Id. This difference in part accounts for the majority of jurisdictions holding that absent fraud or knowledge of the incapacity by the other contracting party, the contractual act of an incompetent is voidable by the incompetent only if avoidance accords with equitable principles. Id.

Accordingly, we conclude that the infancy doctrine does not apply to cases of mental incompetence.

B. GOOD FAITH

The jury was presented with the following special verdict question: "Did the defendant, Union State Bank of Wautoma, fail to act in good faith toward [Hauer] in the loan transaction?" The jury answered that question, "Yes." In denying the Bank's motions after verdict, the court concluded that even if the infancy doctrine did not apply, the jury's finding that the Bank failed to act in good faith in the loan transaction distinguished this case from the "general rule" providing that the person seeking relief from a contract must return the consideration paid. We agree. Before we address this issue, however, we must first deal with the Bank's preliminary arguments concerning the applicability of "good faith."

1. *Tort v. contract*

At the outset, we note that there was much confusion among the parties and the trial court over what theory of law Hauer was basing her claim for recovery on,[4] and this confusion extends to the parties' arguments on appeal. This is due in large part to the parties' intermingling of tort and contract principles.

Wisconsin law recognizes differences between civil actions for breach of contract and tort. Autumn Grove Joint Venture v. Rachlin, 138 Wis. 2d 273, 281, 405 N.W.2d 759, 763 (Ct. App. 1987). Where a contract is involved, in order for a claim in tort to exist, a duty must exist independently of the duty to perform under the contract, such as a fiduciary relationship. Id. at 281 & n. 6, 405 N.W.2d at 763. Although Hauer alleged in her pleadings that the Bank had a fiduciary relationship, this claim was dismissed upon the Bank's motion for directed verdict after Hauer presented her evidence. Hauer does not challenge this ruling on appeal, and we are therefore left solely with contract issues.
. . . .

2. *Section 401.203, Stats.*

The question of good faith was further complicated in this case by the trial court's ruling on summary judgment that Hauer's complaint stated a cause of action based on the Bank's duty of good faith and fair dealing pursuant to §401.203 [UCC §1-203], Stats. We will address this claim next.

Section 401.203, Stats., is a general provision of Wisconsin's Uniform Commercial Code. According to §401.203, "[e]very contract or duty within [the Uniform Commercial Code] imposes an obligation of good faith in its *performance or enforcement*." (Emphasis added.) However, at issue in this case is the Bank's good faith in the *formation* of the contract with Hauer. Because the general requirement of good faith under this section applies only to the performance or enforcement of a contract, it does not impose a duty of good faith in the negotiation and formation of contracts. See Robert S. Summers,

---

4. The trial court lamented this fact in motions after verdict: "I think it is fair to say any case in which the attorneys [do] not have the same theories the day before trial is likely to be a disaster throughout and that seems to have been the situation in this one."

"Good Faith" in General Contract Law and the Sales Provisions of the Uniform Commercial Code, 54 Va. L. Rev. 195, 220 (1968).

The trial court, therefore, erroneously created a cause of action under §401.203, Stats. . . .

3. *Mental incompetency and common law duty of good faith*

Based on the above discussion, we agree with the Bank that Hauer did not have a *separate* cause of action for lack of good faith in tort or in contract under §401.203, Stats. However, we disagree with the Bank that this ends the analysis. Rather, the concept of good faith is relevant to the effect of Hauer's successful claim to void the contract based on mental incompetence.

Wisconsin common law, like other states, reads the duty of good faith into every contract. See Market Street Assocs. Ltd. Partnership v. Frey, 941 F.2d 588, 592 (7th Cir. 1991) (citing Wisconsin law). The great weight of authority from other jurisdictions provides that the unadjudicated mental incompetence of one of the parties is not a sufficient reason for setting aside an executed contract if the parties cannot be restored to their original positions, provided that the contract was made in good faith, for a fair consideration and without knowledge of the incompetence. Williston, supra, §10:3.

Stated differently, if the contract is made on fair terms and the other party has no reason to know of the incompetency, the contract ceases to be voidable where performance in whole or in part changes the situation such that the parties cannot be restored to their previous positions. Restatement, supra, §15 cmt. f.[8] If, on the other hand, the other party knew of the incompetency or took unfair advantage of the incompetent, consideration dissipated without benefit to the incompetent need not be restored. Id. at cmt. *e*.

The Bank asserts that "[i]f a contract is entered into between two adults, each of whom has no actual knowledge of incompetence about the other, it would produce profound, unfair and inequitable results if that contract . . . becomes void and leaves one party with absolutely no remedy or recourse to be returned to their precontract condition." We agree with this statement on its face. However, the Bank's argument assumes a material fact at issue — whether the Bank knew that Hauer was mentally incompetent at the time of the loan. Further, the question of knowledge is not limited to "actual knowledge," but also includes whether the Bank had reason to know of the incompetence. See Restatement, supra, §15(1)(b); see also *Casson*, 166 Wis. at 406, 166 N.W. at 24 (cause of action existed where mental incompetence was "known or ought to have been known by the defendants").

Whether the Bank knew or had reason to know that Hauer was incompetent is a question of fact for the jury to decide. Inexplicably, the Bank neither requested a special verdict question regarding its knowledge nor

---

8. RESTATEMENT (SECOND) OF CONTRACTS §15(2) (1979) provides:

Where the contract is made on fair terms and the other party is without knowledge of the mental illness or defect, the power of avoidance [based on mental incompetency] terminates to the extent that the contract has been so performed in whole or in part or the circumstances have so changed that avoidance would be unjust.

objected to the form of the special verdict on the grounds that it lacked a question pertaining to knowledge. This is true despite the fact that Hauer in her proposed special verdict submitted a question regarding the Bank's knowledge,[10] and that the trial court concluded at the summary judgment stage that there was a dispute of material fact as to whether the Bank had knowledge of Hauer's incompetence.

. . .

The Bank argues that it does not have an affirmative duty to inquire into the mental capacity of a loan applicant to evaluate his or her capacity to understand a proposed transaction. We agree. However, a contracting party exposes itself to a voidable contract where it is put on notice or given a reason to suspect the other party's incompetence such as would indicate to a reasonably prudent person that inquiry should be made of the party's mental condition. See Hedgepeth v. Home Savs. and Loan Ass'n, 87 N.C. App. 610, 361 S.E.2d 888, 889-90 (1987). As the trial court aptly stated: "I did not say there's any duty to make an investigation, but the bank takes a risk the contract will be . . . voidable if they know of facts which support the claim of inability to contract."

We agree that ideally the knowledge question should have been given to the jury as suggested in Hauer's proposed special verdict. However, we are bound by the record as it comes to us. Fiumefreddo v. McLean, 174 Wis. 2d 10, 26, 496 N.W.2d 226, 232 (Ct. App. 1993). We conclude that the finding that the Bank knew or had reason to know that Hauer was mentally incompetent to understand the nature of the loan at the time it was entered into is inherent and intertwined in the jury's finding that the Bank failed to act in good faith. This is necessarily true because the Bank could not have been found to have lacked good faith as a matter of law absent knowledge of the incompetency. The two findings are inseparable.[12]

4. Sufficiency of the evidence

The last question we must address is whether there was any credible evidence to sustain the jury's verdict that the Bank failed to act in good faith. If there is, we are bound to sustain the jury's verdict. Fehring, 118 Wis. 2d at 305, 347 N.W.2d at 598.

The Bank contends that "[t]he record is devoid of any evidence that the Bank had knowledge of any facts which created a suspicion that it should not enter the loan." We agree with the trial court's summary that there is evidence

---

10. Hauer's proposed special verdict form stated in part:

QUESTION NO. 1: Was the plaintiff, Kathy Hauer, at the time of the loan, suffering from diminished mental capacity?

QUESTION NO. 2: If your answer to Question No. 1 was "yes," then answer this question: Did the Union State Bank of Wautoma, through its officers or employees, know or should have known that the plaintiff, Kathy Hauer, was suffering from diminished mental capacity?

12. In this regard, we agree with the trial court's analysis that:

[To] the extent [the bank] had knowledge of a problem alleged to have existed, that may have some impact on their duty of good faith as opposed to an affirmative duty to look. . . . To the extent they knew of special conditions existing, that may bear on the good faith matter. . . .

in the record "that there were flags up that would prompt a reasonable banker to move more slowly and more carefully in the transaction."

For example, the Bank knew that Eilbes was in default of his loan at the Bank. Eilbes approached the Bank and laid all the groundwork for a loan to be given to a third-party investor, Hauer, whom the Bank did not know. Eilbes told Schroeder that he would make his defaulted loan current or pay it off entirely with Hauer's investment. Schroeder testified that upon investigating the matter initially, Hauer's stockbroker told him not to use Hauer's fund as collateral because she needed the fund to live on and Hauer could not afford to lose the fund. He further testified that it was possible that the stockbroker told him that Hauer suffered a brain injury. In addition, Hauer's banking expert opined that the Bank should not have made the loan. Accordingly, we conclude that the evidence and reasonable inferences that can be drawn from the evidence support the jury's conclusion that the Bank failed to act in good faith.

...

Judgment affirmed.

Notes and Questions

1. *Restoration of consideration by disaffirming party.* The law concerning mental incapacity has a great deal in common with the minority doctrine concerning matters such as liability for necessaries and the possibility of disaffirmance or ratification. See E. Allan Farnsworth, Contracts §§4.7-4.8, at 231-234 (4th ed. 2004). Regarding the obligation to make restoration of consideration upon disaffirmance, however, the *Hauer* court highlights an important distinction between the traditional rules on minority doctrine and mental incompetency: the minor generally can disaffirm even if restoration cannot be made, but the mentally incompetent person is required to make restoration to the other party unless special circumstances are present. See Restatement (Second) §15(2). In *Hauer,* of course, the court finds special circumstances in the purported lack of good faith of the other party. Compare Pappert v. Sargent, 847 P.2d 66 (Alaska 1993) (party who contracted with mentally incompetent person in good faith, without actual or constructive knowledge of condition, is entitled to restitution). Are you persuaded that there is good justification for the different approaches to restitution in minority and mental incompetency cases?

2. *Effect of court-decreed guardianship.* A second elemental difference between the minority doctrine and cases of mental incompetency is the ability to determine a party's status, both by parties at the time of contracting and by the court upon the occurrence of a dispute. The car dealer in *Dodson* obviously could have required proof of age before agreeing to sell the car and thereby ascertained whether the buyer had reached majority. Determining mental competency is sure to be more difficult, both at the time of contracting and later in court. As suggested by the *Hauer* facts, statutory law in each state establishes procedures by which a court on petition of a family member or other interested party can declare a person legally incompetent and appoint a guardian or conservator to care for the incompetent's person or property.

E.g., Unif. Prob. Code, §§5-301 (guardian of person of incompetent), 5-401 (conservator of property of incompetent). The general rule is that a person does not have capacity to enter into contracts if the person's property is under conservatorship. Restatement (Second) §13. See Sun Trust Bank v. Harper, 551 S.E.2d 419 (Ga. Ct. App. 2002) (after being placed under guardianship by court, decedent lacked capacity to modify terms of retirement account notwithstanding alleged lucid moments); Huntington National Bank v. Toland, 594 N.E.2d 1103 (Ohio Ct. App. 1991) (though decedent maintained "sparkling" record in dealings with bank for four-year period before death, adjudication of mental incompetency 35 years earlier still rendered contract voidable unless ratified by guardian). The *Hauer* case is unusual in that the plaintiff had been judicially declared to be incompetent at a prior time, but had been relieved of the guardianship by the time the contract was made. Should this fact make any difference in deciding the case and, if so, which side does it favor? Is one party likely to know that another has been adjudged mentally incompetent?

3. *Cognitive and volitional tests for incapacity.* Even without a formal adjudication of incompetency, contract law provides that a person may lack mental capacity to enter into a contract, as recognized by the court in *Hauer* and by the Restatement. How is mental competency to be determined? The court in *Hauer* uses the traditional "cognitive" test for contractual capacity. Under this approach a person lacks capacity to enter into a contract if the person is unable to understand the nature of the transaction or its consequences. In §15, the Restatement (Second) has gone beyond the cognitive standard to adopt an alternative "volitional" test for incapacity. Under this view a person lacks capacity to contract if the person is unable to act in a reasonable manner in the transaction and the other party has reason to know of the condition. The Restatement (Second) includes the following illustration, based on Ortelere v. Teachers' Retirement Board, 250 N.E.2d 460 (N.Y. 1969):

> A, a school teacher, is a member of a retirement plan and has elected a lower monthly benefit in order to provide a benefit to her husband if she dies first. At age 60 she suffers a "nervous breakdown," takes a leave of absence, and is treated for cerebral arteriosclerosis. When the leave expires she applies for retirement, revokes her previous election, and elects a larger annuity with no death benefit. In view of her reduced life expectancy, the change is foolhardy, and there are no other circumstances to explain the change. She fully understands the plan, but by reason of mental illness is unable to make a decision based on the prospect of her dying before her husband. The officers of the plan have reason to know of her condition. Two months after the changed election she dies. The change of election is voidable.

Restatement (Second) §15, Illustration 1. A dissenting judge in *Ortelere* expressed concern, however, that any benefit gained by use of the volitional test would be "outweighed by frivolous claims which will burden our courts and undermine the security of contracts." Ortelere v. Teachers' Retirement Board, 250 N.E.2d 460, 468 (N.Y. 1969) (Jasen, J., dissenting). See also Estate of McGovern v. State Employees' Retirement Board, 517 A.2d 523 (Pa. 1986) (on facts similar to *Ortelere,* court rejected new volitional test of §15 and adhered to traditional cognitive test of mental capacity); but see In re Davis & Davis, 89 P.3d 1206, 1211-1212 (Ore. Ct. App. 2004) (concurring opinion) (volitional test reflects a more up-to-date understanding of human behavior and mental health). Further understanding of the *Ortelere* case can be gained from Richard Danzig & Geoffrey R. Watson, The Capability Problem in Contract Law 242-306 (2d ed. 2004), which includes excerpts from the *Ortelere* trial transcript.

4. *Vulnerability to misconduct by other parties.* *Hauer* is representative of a type of case in which a party asserts not only lack of capacity but also a claim that the other party engaged in overreaching or other improper conduct. In such cases claims of incapacity are often combined with allegations of fraud, duress, or undue influence. Another example is Farnum v. Silvano, 540 N.E.2d 202 (Mass. App. Ct. 1989), which involved a sale by an elderly plaintiff, Viola Farnum, of her home to the defendant for a price of $65,000 when the home had a fair market value of $115,000 and at a time when she had a growing need for income. The defendant, who did yard work for the plaintiff, knew of the plaintiff's unstable mental condition, which manifested itself in a variety of ways, including the following:

> She would lament not hearing from sisters who were dead. She would wonder where the people upstairs in her house had gone, but there was no upstairs to her house. . . . She became abnormally forgetful. Frequently, she locked herself out of her house and broke into it, rather than calling on a neighbor with whom she had left a key. . . . She hid her cat to protect it from "the cops . . . looking for my cat." She would express a desire to return to Cape Cod although she was on Cape Cod. . . .

Id. at 203. Finding that the plaintiff lacked the mental capacity to enter into the contract and that the defendant was aware of this condition, the Court of Appeals ordered rescission of the contract. In light of this conclusion, the court found it unnecessary to consider the claims of fraud, undue influence, and constructive trust that Farnum had also advanced.

5. *Burden of proof and relevant time for determining capacity.* You should not conclude from the outcome in *Hauer* that courts will too readily find that a party lacked mental capacity at the time of contract formation. As stated in *Hauer,* there is a presumption of competency and the burden of proof is on the party seeking to avoid a contract. This burden may be difficult to carry. See In re Estate of Obermeier, 540 N.Y.S.2d 613 (App. Div. 1989) (fact that decedent resided in nursing home, was often confused, suffered from dementia, and was on sedatives did not prove lack of capacity at time of signing contract to sell real property); Rawlings v. John Hancock Mutual Life Ins. Co., 78 S.W.3d 291 (Tenn. Ct. App. 2001) (evidence that decedent was an alcoholic and suffered from depression and dementia was insufficient to prove that she did not have capacity to understand consequences or act in reasonable manner at particular time transaction was made).

6. *Mental incapacity in other areas of law.* The issue of mental incapacity arises in other fields of law. For example, in criminal cases, the traditional standard for mental capacity has been the M'Naghten test. M'Naghten's Case, 8 Eng. Rep. 718 (1843). Under this test a defendant lacks mental

capacity to commit a crime if the defendant is unable to distinguish right from wrong. Rollin M. Perkins & Ronald Boyce, Criminal Law 958-963 (1982). The Model Penal Code recognizes incapacity as consisting of inability to either "appreciate the criminality" of conduct or "conform his conduct to the requirements of law." Model Penal Code §4.01 (1962). How do these standards compare to the standard for contractual capacity as expressed in §15 of the Restatement (Second)? Should it be easier or more difficult to establish incapacity in criminal prosecutions or breach of contract cases? Why?

7. *Incapacity resulting from intoxication.* The Restatement (Second) §16 provides that a contract is voidable if a party has reason to know that because of intoxication the other person is unable to either understand the transaction or act in a reasonable manner. Comment *a* to the section states that "compulsive alcoholism" may be a form of mental illness but also recognizes that intoxication may be "voluntary." Should intoxication that is a temporary, self-induced condition affect a person's ability to disaffirm a contract? See Hakimoglu v. Trump Taj Mahal Assocs., 876 F. Supp. 625 (D.N.J. 1994) *aff'd on other grounds*, 70 F.3d 291 (3d Cir. 1995) (recognizing possibilty under common law that patron could defend against collection of gambling debts based on incapacity due to intoxication); Miller v. Rhode Island Hospital, 625 A.2d 778 (R.I. 1993) (reversing trial court and holding intoxication can render a patient incompetent to give consent to treatment).

B.   DURESS AND UNDUE INFLUENCE

At a very early time the common law recognized that some agreements should not be legally enforceable because of the process by which they were made. In the thirteenth century, agreements made while one party was under physical imprisonment or threat of physical harm were unenforceable at law because made under "duress." While such relief at law was limited to cases involving actual or threatened physical harm, over time the courts of equity recognized a right to relief against other types of coercion, under the doctrine of "undue influence." The equitable doctrine of undue influence, however, was not unlimited in its application. Generally, a court of equity would not act unless the undue influence arose between family members or in some other confidential or "fiduciary" relationship, such as between lawyer and client or between trustee and beneficiary.

Since these early days, the doctrines of duress and undue influence have undergone a dramatic expansion. Courts have gradually broadened the types of threats that are considered improper under the defense of duress, first to threats to a person's property (known as "duress of goods") and later to "economic duress." Similarly, the defense of undue influence has been extended to situations that do not involve a confidential relationship. The history of these developments is traced in John P. Dawson, Economic

Duress—An Essay in Perspective, 45 Mich. L. Rev. 253 (1947). The materials that follow illustrate this more modern approach.

Totem Marine Tug & Barge, Inc. v. Alyeska Pipeline Service Co.

Supreme Court of Alaska
584 P.2d 15 (1978)

BURKE, Justice.

This appeal arises from the superior court's granting of summary judgment in favor of defendants-appellees Alyeska Pipeline Services, et al., in a contract action brought by plaintiffs-appellants Totem Marine Tug & Barge, Inc., Pacific, Inc., and Richard Stair.

The following summary of events is derived from the materials submitted in the summary judgment proceedings below.

Totem is a closely held Alaska corporation which began operations in March of 1975. Richard Stair, at all times relevant to this case, was vice-president of Totem. In June of 1975, Totem entered into a contract with Alyeska under which Totem was to transport pipeline construction materials from Houston, Texas, to a designated port in southern Alaska, with the possibility of one or two cargo stops along the way. In order to carry out this contract, which was Totem's first, Totem chartered a barge (the "Marine Flasher") and an ocean-going tug (the "Kirt Chouest"). These charters and other initial operations costs were made possible by loans to Totem from Richard Stair individually and Pacific, Inc., a corporation of which Stair was principal stockholder and officer, as well as by guarantees by Stair and Pacific.

By the terms of the contract, Totem was to have completed performance by approximately August 15, 1975. From the start, however, there were numerous problems which impeded Totem's performance of the contract. For example, according to Totem, Alyeska represented that approximately 1,800 to 2,100 tons of regular uncoated pipe were to be loaded in Houston, and that perhaps another 6,000 or 7,000 tons of materials would be put on the barge at later stops along the west coast. Upon the arrival of the tug and barge in Houston, however, Totem found that about 6,700 to 7,200 tons of coated pipe, steel beams and valves, haphazardly and improperly piled, were in the yard to be loaded. This situation called for remodeling of the barge and extra cranes and stevedores, and resulted in the loading taking thirty days rather than the three days which Totem had anticipated it would take to load 2,000 tons. The lengthy loading period was also caused in part by Alyeska's delay in assuring Totem that it would pay for the additional expenses, bad weather and other administrative problems.

The difficulties continued after the tug and barge left Houston. It soon became apparent that the vessels were travelling more slowly than anticipated because of the extra load. In response to Alyeska's complaints and with its verbal consent, on August 13, 1975, Totem chartered a second tug, the "N. Joseph Guidry." When the "Guidry" reached the Panama Canal, however,

Alyeska had not yet furnished the written amendment to the parties' contract. Afraid that Alyeska would not agree to cover the cost of the second tug, Stair notified the "Guidry" not to go through the Canal. After some discussions in which Alyeska complained of the delays and accused Totem of lying about the horsepower of the first tug, Alyeska executed the amendment on August 21, 1975.

By this time the "Guidry" had lost its preferred passage through the Canal and had to wait two or three additional days before it could go through. Upon finally meeting, the three vessels encountered the tail of a hurricane which lasted for about eight or nine days and which substantially impeded their progress.

The three vessels finally arrived in the vicinity of San Pedro, California, where Totem planned to change crews and refuel. On Alyeska's orders, however, the vessels instead pulled into port at Long Beach, California. At this point, Alyeska's agents commenced off-loading the barge, without Totem's consent, without the necessary load survey, and without a marine survey, the absence of which voided Totem's insurance. After much wrangling and some concessions by Alyeska, the freight was off-loaded. Thereafter, on or about September 14, 1975, Alyeska terminated the contract. Although there was talk by an Alyeska official of reinstating the contract, the termination was affirmed a few days later at a meeting at which Alyeska officials refused to give a reason for the termination.

Following termination of the contract, Totem submitted termination invoices to Alyeska and began pressing the latter for payment. The invoices came to something between $260,000 and $300,000. An official from Alyeska told Totem that they would look over the invoices but that they were not sure when payment would be made — perhaps in a day or perhaps in six to eight months. Totem was in urgent need of cash as the invoices represented debts which the company had incurred on 10-30 day payment schedules. Totem's creditors were demanding payment and according to Stair, without immediate cash, Totem would go bankrupt. Totem then turned over the collection to its attorney, Roy Bell, directing him to advise Alyeska of Totem's financial straits. Thereafter, Bell met with Alyeska officials in Seattle, and after some negotiations, Totem received a settlement offer from Alyeska for $97,500. On November 6, 1975, Totem, through its president Stair, signed an agreement releasing Alyeska from all claims by Totem in exchange for $97,500.

On March 26, 1976, Totem, Richard Stair, and Pacific filed a complaint against Alyeska, which was subsequently amended. In the amended complaint, the plaintiffs sought to rescind the settlement and release on the ground of economic duress and to recover the balance allegedly due on the original contract. In addition, they alleged that Alyeska had wrongfully terminated the contract and sought miscellaneous other compensatory and punitive damages.

Before filing an answer, Alyeska moved for summary judgment against the plaintiffs on the ground that Totem had executed a binding release of all claims against Alyeska and that as a matter of law, Totem could not prevail on its claim of economic duress. In opposition, plaintiffs contended that the purported release was executed under duress in that Alyeska wrongfully terminated the contract; that Alyeska knew that Totem was faced with large debts and impending bankruptcy; that Alyeska withheld funds admittedly owed knowing the effect this would have on plaintiffs and that plaintiffs had no alternative but to involuntarily accept the $97,500 in order to avoid bankruptcy. Plaintiffs maintained that they had thus raised genuine issues of material fact such that trial was necessary, and that Alyeska was not entitled to judgment as a matter of law. Alyeska disputed the plaintiffs' assertions.

On November 30, 1976, the superior court granted the defendant's motion for summary judgment. This appeal followed. . . .

II

As was noted above, a court's initial task in deciding motions for summary judgment is to determine whether there exist genuine issues of material fact. In order to decide whether such issues exist in this case, we must examine the doctrine allowing avoidance of a release on grounds of economic duress.

This court has not yet decided a case involving a claim of economic duress or what is also called business compulsion. At early common law, a contract could be avoided on the ground of duress only if a party could show that the agreement was entered into for fear of loss of life or limb, mayhem or imprisonment. 13 Williston on Contracts, §1601 at 649 (3d ed. Jaeger 1970). The threat had to be such as to overcome the will of a person of ordinary firmness and courage. Id., §1602 at 656. Subsequently, however, the concept has been broadened to include myriad forms of economic coercion which force a person to involuntarily enter into a particular transaction. The test has come to be whether the will of the person induced by the threat was overcome rather than that of a reasonably firm person. Id., §1602 at 657.

At the outset it is helpful to acknowledge the various policy considerations which are involved in cases involving economic duress. Typically, those claiming such coercion are attempting to avoid the consequences of a modification of an original contract or of a settlement and release agreement. On the one hand, courts are reluctant to set aside agreements because of the notion of freedom of contract and because of the desirability of having private dispute resolutions be final. On the other hand, there is an increasing recognition of the law's role in correcting inequitable or unequal exchanges between parties of disproportionate bargaining power and a greater willingness to not enforce agreements which were entered into under coercive circumstances.

There are various statements of what constitutes economic duress, but as noted by one commentator, "The history of generalization in this field offers no great encouragement for those who seek to summarize results in any single formula." Dawson, Economic Duress—An Essay in Perspective, 45 Mich. L. Rev. 253, 289 (1947). Section 492(b) of the Restatement of Contracts defines duress as:

> any wrongful threat of one person by words or other conduct that induces another to enter into a transaction under the influence of such fear as precludes him from exercising free will and judgment, if the threat was intended or should reasonably have been expected to operate as an inducement.

Professor Williston states the basic elements of economic duress in the following manner:

> 1. The party alleging economic duress must show that he has been the victim of a wrongful or unlawful act or threat, and
> 2. Such act or threat must be one which deprives the victim of his unfettered will.

13 Williston on Contracts, §1617 at 704 [footnotes omitted].

Many courts state the test somewhat differently, eliminating use of the vague term "free will," but retaining the same basic idea. Under this standard, duress exists where: (1) one party involuntarily accepted the terms of another, (2) circumstances permitted no other alternative, and (3) such circumstances were the result of coercive acts of the other party. . . . W. R. Grimshaw Co. v. Nevil C. Withrow Co., 248 F.2d 896, 904 (8th Cir. 1957). . . . The third element is further explained as follows:

> In order to substantiate the allegation of economic duress or business compulsion, the plaintiff must go beyond the mere showing of reluctance to accept and of financial embarrassment. There must be a showing of acts on the part of the defendant which produced these two factors. The assertion of duress must be proven by evidence that the duress resulted from defendant's wrongful and oppressive conduct and not by the plaintiff's necessities.

W. R. Grimshaw Co., supra, 248 F.2d at 904.

As the above indicates, one essential element of economic duress is that the plaintiff show that the other party by wrongful acts or threats, intentionally caused him to involuntarily enter into a particular transaction. Courts have not attempted to define exactly what constitutes a wrongful or coercive act, as wrongfulness depends on the particular facts in each case. This requirement may be satisfied where the alleged wrongdoer's conduct is criminal or tortious but an act or threat may also be considered wrongful if it is wrongful in the moral sense. Restatement of Contracts §492, Comment *g*. . . .

In many cases, a threat to breach a contract or to withhold payment of an admitted debt has constituted a wrongful act. . . . Austin Instrument, Inc. v. Loral Corp., 29 N.Y.2d 124, 324 N.Y.S.2d 22, 25, 272 N.E.2d 533, 535 (1971); . . . see also 13 Williston, supra, §1616A at 701. Implicit in such cases is the additional requirement that the threat to breach the contract or withhold payment be done in bad faith. . . . Restatement (Second) of Contracts §318, Comment *e*.

Economic duress does not exist, however, merely because a person has been the victim of a wrongful act; in addition, the victim must have no choice but to agree to the other party's terms or face serious financial hardship. Thus, in order to avoid a contract, a party must also show that he had no reasonable alternative to agreeing to the other party's terms, or, as it is often stated, that he had no adequate remedy if the threat were to be carried out. First National Bank of Cincinnati v. Pepper, 454 F.2d 626, 632-33 (2d Cir. 1972); *Austin Instrument*, supra, 324 N.Y.S.2d at 25, 272 N.E.2d at 535; . . . Tri-State Roofing Company of Uniontown v. Simon, 187 Pa. Super. 17, 142 A.2d 333,

335-36 (1958). What constitutes a reasonable alternative is a question of fact, depending on the circumstances of each case. An available legal remedy, such as an action for breach of contract, may provide such an alternative. *First National Bank of Cincinnati,* supra; *Austin Instrument,* supra; *Tri-State Roofing,* supra. Where one party wrongfully threatens to withhold goods, services or money from another unless certain demands are met, the availability on the market of similar goods and services or of other sources of funds may also provide an alternative to succumbing to the coercing party's demands. *Austin Instrument,* supra; *Tri-State Roofing,* supra. Generally, it has been said that "[t]he adequacy of the remedy is to be tested by a practical standard which takes into consideration the exigencies of the situation in which the alleged victim finds himself." Ross Systems [v. Linden Dari-Delite, Inc., 35 N.J. 329, 173 A.2d 258, 262 (1961)]. See also *First National Bank of Cincinnati,* supra at 634; Dalzell, Duress By Economic Pressure I, 20 N.C.L. Rev. 237, 240 (1942).

An available alternative or remedy may not be adequate where the delay involved in pursuing that remedy would cause immediate and irreparable loss to one's economic or business interest. For example, in *Austin Instrument,* supra, and Gallagher Switchboard Corp. v. Heckler Electric Co., 36 Misc. 2d 225, 232 N.Y.S.2d 590 (N.Y. Sup. Ct. 1962), duress was found in the following circumstances: A subcontractor threatened to refuse further delivery under a contract unless the contractor agreed to modify the existing contract between the parties. The contractor was unable to obtain the necessary materials elsewhere without delay, and if it did not have the materials promptly, it would have been in default on its main contract with the government. In each case such default would have had grave economic consequences for the contractor and hence it agreed to the modifications. In both, the courts found that the alternatives to agreeing to the modification were inadequate (i.e., suing for breach of contract or obtaining the materials elsewhere) and that modifications therefore were signed under duress and voidable.

Professor Dalzell, in Duress By Economic Pressure II, 20 N.C.L. Rev. 340, 370 (1942), notes the following with regard to the adequacy of legal remedies where one party refuses to pay a contract claim:

> Nowadays, a wait of even a few weeks in collecting on a contract claim is sometimes serious or fatal for an enterprise at a crisis in its history. The business of a creditor in financial straits is at the mercy of an unscrupulous debtor, who need only suggest that if the creditor does not care to settle on the debtor's own hard terms, he can sue. This situation, in which promptness in payment is vastly more important than even approximate justice in the settlement terms, is too common in modern business relations to be ignored by society and the courts.

This view finds support in Capps v. Georgia Pacific Corporation, 253 Or. 248, 453 P.2d 935 (1969). There, the plaintiff was owed $157,000 as a commission for finding a lessee for defendant's property but in exchange for $5,000, the plaintiff signed a release of his claim against defendant. The plaintiff sued for the balance of the commission, alleging that the release had been executed under duress. His complaint, however, was dismissed. On appeal, the court held that the plaintiff had stated a claim where he alleged that he had accepted the grossly inadequate sum because he was in danger of immediately losing his home by mortgage foreclosure and other property by foreclosure and repossession if he did not obtain immediate funds from the defendant. One basis for its holding was found in the following quote by a leading commentator in the area of economic duress:

> The most that can be claimed [regarding the law of economic duress] is that change has been broadly toward acceptance of a general conclusion — that in the absence of specific countervailing factors of policy or administrative feasibility, restitution is required of any excessive gain that results, in a bargain transaction, from impaired bargaining power, whether the impairment consists of economic necessity, mental or physical disability, or a wide disparity in knowledge or experience.

Dawson, Economic Duress — An Essay In Perspective, 45 Mich. L. Rev. 253, 289 (1947).

III

Turning to the instant case, we believe that Totem's allegations, if proved, would support a finding that it executed a release of its contract claims against Alyeska under economic duress. Totem has alleged that Alyeska deliberately withheld payment of an acknowledged debt, knowing that Totem had no choice but to accept an inadequate sum in settlement of that debt; that Totem was faced with impending bankruptcy; that Totem was unable to meet its pressing debts other than by accepting the immediate cash payment offered by Alyeska; and that through necessity, Totem thus involuntarily accepted an inadequate settlement offer from Alyeska and executed a release of all claims under the contract. If the release was in fact executed under these circumstances,[5] we think that under the legal principles discussed above that this would constitute the type of wrongful conduct and lack of alternatives that would render the release voidable by Totem on the ground of economic duress. We would add that although Totem need not necessarily prove its allegation that Alyeska's termination of the contract was wrongful in order to sustain a claim of economic duress, the events leading to the termination would be probative as to whether Alyeska exerted any wrongful pressure on Totem and whether Alyeska wrongfully withheld payment from Totem.[6] . . .

Our examination of the materials presented by Totem in opposition to Alyeska's motion for summary judgment leads us to conclude that Totem has made a sufficient factual showing as to each of the elements of economic duress to withstand that motion. There is no doubt that Alyeska disputes many of the factual allegations made by Totem[7] and drawing all inferences in favor of Totem, we believe that genuine issues of material fact exist in this case such

---

5. By way of clarification, we would note that Totem would not have to prove that Alyeska admitted to owing the precise sum Totem claimed it was owed upon termination of the contract but only that Alyeska acknowledged that it owed Totem approximately that amount which Totem sought.

6. We make no comment as to whether Alyeska's termination of the contract was wrongful nor as to the truth of Totem's other allegations.

7. For example, Alyeska has denied that it ever admitted to owing any particular sum to Totem and has disputed the truthfulness of Totem's assertions of impending bankruptcy. Other factual issues which remain unresolved include whether or not Alyeska knew of Totem's financial situation after termination of the contract and whether Alyeska did in fact threaten by words or conduct to withhold payment unless Totem agreed to settle.

that trial is necessary. Admittedly, Totem's showing was somewhat weak in that, for example, it did not produce the testimony of Roy Bell, the attorney who represented Totem in the negotiations leading to the settlement and release. At trial, it will probably be necessary for Totem to produce this evidence if it is to prevail on its claim of duress. However, a party opposing a motion for summary judgment need not produce all of the evidence it may have at its disposal but need only show that issues of material fact exist. 10 C. Wright and A. Miller, Federal Practice and Procedure: Civil, §2727 at 546 (1973). Therefore, we hold that the superior court erred in granting summary judgment for appellees and remand the case to the superior court for trial in accordance with the legal principles set forth above. . . .

Reversed and remanded.

Notes and Questions

1. *Void vs. voidable contracts.* As noted by the *Totem Marine* court, duress had its origin in cases of physical compulsion in which a party manifested assent as a result of a threat to life or limb. Restatement (Second) §174 recognizes that a contract is void if made under coercion involving a physical threat. Cf. Radford v. Keith, 584 S.E.2d 815 (N.C. Ct. App. 2003) (plaintiff properly stated claim for duress where contractor berated plaintiff for two hours, placed a guard at the door to his office during meeting, and refused to allow her to leave his office until plaintiff signed agreement to pay additional $25,000 for home). But see Schultz v. Schultz, 867 So. 2d 745 (La. Ct. App. 2003) (reversing trial court and finding duress was not established in signing child support reduction agreement where claimant feared ex-husband as violent man and wanted to avoid argument but there was no evidence of use of force or threats).

It is presently more common that a party claims to be the victim of economic coercion, as in *Totem Marine*. Contracts made under economic duress, rather than physical compulsion, are deemed voidable rather than void. Thus, such contracts will be binding unless disaffirmed and may be expressly or implicitly ratified by the purported victim. See, e.g., Hyman v. Ford Motor Co., 142 F. Supp. 2d 735 (D.S.C. 2001) (contract executed under duress may be ratified by acceptance of benefits, remaining silent after opportunity to disavow, or rendering performance).

2. *Wrongful or improper threat.* Faced with a question of first impression, the *Totem Marine* court cited a number of authorities in arriving at a definition of economic duress. Consistent with the Restatement (Second) §175, the court's test can be viewed as requiring three elements: a wrongful or improper threat, a lack of reasonable alternative, and actual inducement of the contract by the threat. Restatement (Second) §§175 and 176 use the term "improper threat" while courts such as *Totem Marine* will often use the term "wrongful" to describe an actionable threat. More important than the use of either particular term is the fact the threat need not be "illegal" in order to give rise to a claim of duress. See Quigley v. KPMG Peat Marwick, LLP, 749 A.2d 405 (N.J. Super. Ct. App. Div. 2000) (threat that establishes duress may be wrongful in moral or equitable sense even if not illegal). But see Farm Credit Services of

Michigan's Heartland, P.C.A. v. Weldon, 591 N.W.2d 438 (Mich. Ct. App. 1998) (illegality is still an element of duress under Michigan law).

When is a threat wrongful or improper? The Restatement (Second) §176 definition includes threats to commit a crime or tort and threats of criminal prosecution. While threats to engage in litigation or to refuse to honor a contractual obligation are not per se improper, such threats may be improper if the circumstances show that the threat was made in "bad faith." Id. §176(1)(c), (d). See also Kelso v. McGowan, 604 So. 2d 726 (Miss. 1992) (threat to breach enforceable contract can constitute "wrongful" act); but cf. Professional Service Network, Inc. v. American Alliance Holding Co., 238 F.3d 897 (7th Cir. 2001) (not an improper threat for seller of stock to insist on settlement of dispute under the contract before cooperating in tax filing worth $5 million to buyer; seller had "colorable case" and its position was not frivolous). What was the threat in the *Totem Marine* case? How could the plaintiff establish that the threat was made in bad faith?

3. *Threat of criminal proceedings.* A threat by an attorney to institute criminal proceedings in order to aid a client in a civil dispute may not only render any resulting agreement unenforceable because of duress but may also subject the attorney to discipline because of professional misconduct. In 1969 the American Bar Association issued its Model Code of Professional Responsibility for attorneys; the Code was widely adopted throughout the country. Disciplinary Rule 7-105 of the Code of Professional Responsibility states, "A lawyer shall not present, participate in presenting, or threaten to present criminal charges solely to obtain an advantage in a civil matter." In 1983 the ABA issued the Model Rules of Professional Conduct to succeed the Code of Professional Responsibility. The Model Rules have been adopted in more than 40 states. In 2002 the ABA issued a revised version of the Model Rules. Both the 1983 and 2002 versions of the Model Rules delete the specific ethical prohibition against a lawyer's threatening criminal prosecution. Nevertheless, such threats may amount to extortion under state criminal statutes and could also be found to be unethical under general ethical concepts. E.g., Model Rules of Professional Conduct, Rule 1.2(d) (lawyer may not counsel or assist a client in conduct that is criminal or fraudulent); Model Rule 4.4 (respect for rights of third persons). In addition, some states have modified the ABA's Model Rules to continue the prohibition against threats of criminal proceedings to obtain an advantage in a civil matter.

4. *Lack of reasonable alternative.* Even if a threat is improper, the resulting agreement is enforceable unless the party who submitted to the agreement had no reasonable alternative but to accept the agreement. Comment *b* to §175 of the Restatement (Second) indicates a number of possible reasonable alternatives: the availability of legal action if, in the circumstances, that course presents a viable option; alternative sources of goods, services, or funds when there is a threat to withhold such things; and toleration if the threat involves only a minor vexation. Compare Uniwill v. City of Los Angeles, 21 Cal. Rptr. 3d 464 (Ct. App. 2004) (developer of shopping mall stated viable claim for economic duress in alleging that city and electric company wrongfully threatened to stop project unless easement was granted and resort to legal proceedings would have led to financial ruin), with Dunes Hospitality, L.L.C. v. Country Kitchen Int'l, Inc., 623 N.W.2d 484 (S.D. 2001) (no duress where

claimant company included sophisticated principals, had assistance of counsel, and had reasonable alternative of filing lawsuit rather than signing settlement agreement).

5. *Inducement of involuntary assent.* The *Totem Marine* court would also require a showing that the wrongful threat "caused" the victim to involuntarily enter into the transaction. Consistently, Comment *c* to Restatement (Second) of Contracts §175 states that "the improper threat must induce the making of the contract," meaning that the threat must "substantially contribute" to the manifestation of assent. (This requirement suggests, at least implicitly, that the victim of the threat might have additional reasons for manifesting assent to the agreement.) Despite earlier standards that required the threat be "such as to overcome the will of a person of ordinary firmness and courage," as stated in *Totem Marine,* the standard is now a subjective one that asks whether the particular victim was induced by the threat. Comment *c* goes on to state that "[a]ll attendant circumstances must be considered, including such matters as the age, background and relationship of the parties." See Holler v. Holler, 612 S.E.2d 469 (S.C. Ct. App. 2005) (immigrant wife who spoke little English, had no means of financial self support, was pregnant, and had visa that was about to expire stated good claim for duress in signing prenuptial agreement as demanded by husband before marriage).

6. *Must threatening party cause hardship?* A question which frequently arises is the role that an alleged victim's financial difficulty plays in the determination of economic duress. In Selmer Co. v. Blakeslee-Midwest Co., 704 F.2d 924 (7th Cir. 1983), Judge Posner stated that the fact a party agreed to a settlement because of a desperate need for cash could not be the basis for duress unless the other side had caused the financial hardship. The judge further observed that the inability of parties in dire straits to enter into enforceable agreements could cause other parties to refuse to settle even when both sides wanted to do so, thus ultimately working to the detriment of the alleged victim. Id. at 928. Most courts that have faced the issue agree with *Selmer.* Indeed, the Alaska Supreme Court that decided *Totem Marine* later adopted this view. Northern Fabrication Co. v. UNOCAL, 980 P.2d 958 (Alaska 1999) (for economic duress there must be a causal link between coercive acts and circumstances of economic duress). See also Spradling v. Blackburn, 919 F. Supp. 969 (S.D. W. Va. 1996) (citing split of authority, but deciding that duress is not proved merely by showing that financial necessity caused one party to make agreement).

On the other hand, a few courts have held, sometimes implicitly, that it is enough that one party takes advantage of the other side's dire circumstances without having caused the financial hardship. See, e.g., Rich & Whillock, Inc. v. Ashton Development, Inc., 204 Cal. Rptr. 86 (Ct. App. 1984) (finding economic duress in settlement agreement because dominant party *knew* that victim was new company, overextended to its creditors and subcontractors, and faced imminent bankruptcy if not paid); Butitta v. First Mortgage Corp., 578 N.E.2d 116 (Ill. App. Ct. 1991) (duress may consist of taking undue advantage of the business or financial stress of the other party).

7. *Role of duress in contract settlement or modification.* Claims of duress frequently arise in connection with releases executed to settle contractual disputes — the situation illustrated by the principal case. The defense of

duress can also be used to avoid enforcement of a contractual "modification" of an executory contract. The validity of such a modification may also depend on whether the requirement of consideration has been satisfied; sometimes it is also necessary to determine whether the original contract has become "impracticable" to perform as a result of some changed circumstances since the making of the contract. The doctrine of impracticability and the enforcement of contractual modifications are discussed in Chapter 8.

8. *Rationale for duress doctrine.* In a ground-breaking article quoted in the *Totem Marine* case, Professor John Dawson traced the history of the modern law of duress and argued that the doctrine was based on the principle of prevention of excessive gain resulting from exploitation of impaired bargaining power. John P. Dawson, Economic Duress—An Essay in Perspective, 45 Mich. L. Rev. 253, 289 (1947). Accepting this foundation of the doctrine, the revised Restatement makes a threat improper if the threat was for an illegitimate end and the resulting agreement did not involve a fair exchange. Id. §176(2).

The unavoidable lack of clear standards in economic duress cases was noted in an often-cited article by one of the leading scholars of the Critical Legal Studies movement, Professor Roberto Unger. He argued that the emergence of the modern doctrine of economic duress illustrates an inherent contradiction in modern law:

> According to this doctrine, a contract may be voidable for economic duress whenever a significant inequality of bargaining power exists between the parties. Gross inequalities of bargaining power, however, are all too common in the current forms of market economy, a fact shown not only by the dealings between individual consumers and large corporate enterprises, but also by the huge disparities of scale and market influence among enterprises themselves. Thus, the doctrine of economic duress must serve as a roving commission to correct the most egregious and overt forms of an omnipresent type of disparity. But the unproven assumption of the doctrine is that the amount of corrective intervention needed to keep a contractual regime from becoming a power order will not be so great that it destroys the vitality of decentralized decisionmaking through contract. If this assumption proved false, no compromise between correction and abstention could achieve its intended effect. The only solution would be the one that every such compromise is meant to avoid: the remaking of the institutional arrangements that define the market economy. The doctrinal manifestation of this problem is the vagueness of the concept of economic duress. The cost of preventing the revised duress doctrine from running wild and from correcting almost everything is to draw unstable, unjustified, and unjustifiable lines between the contracts that are avoidable and those that are not.

Roberto Mangabeira Unger, The Critical Legal Studies Movement, 96 Harv. L. Rev. 561, 629 (1983). A more recent study reports that the longstanding "conflict and confusion" about the elements of duress continues and that consequently only a small fraction of duress claims are successful. Grace M. Giesel, A Realistic Proposal for the Contract Duress Doctrine, 107 W. Va. L. Rev. 443, 463-465 (2005). Professor Giesel proposes a formulation of the duress doctrine that would first emphasize whether there was lack of reasonable alternatives for the victim and would also group wrongful threats into four categories: threat of criminal or tortious conduct, threat of criminal prosecution, bad faith use of civil process, and bad faith conduct within an existing contract.

Odorizzi v. Bloomfield School District
California District Court of Appeals
246 Cal. App. 2d 123, 54 Cal. Rptr. 533 (1966)

FLEMING, Justice.

Appeal from a judgment dismissing plaintiff's amended complaint on demurrer.

Plaintiff Donald Odorizzi was employed during 1964 as an elementary school teacher by defendant Bloomfield School District and was under contract with the District to continue to teach school the following year as a permanent employee. On June 10 he was arrested on criminal charges of homosexual activity, and on June 11 he signed and delivered to his superiors his written resignation as a teacher, a resignation which the District accepted on June 13. In July the criminal charges against Odorizzi were dismissed under Penal Code, section 995, and in September he sought to resume his employment with the District. On the District's refusal to reinstate him he filed suit for declaratory and other relief.

Odorizzi's amended complaint asserts his resignation was invalid because obtained through duress, fraud, mistake, and undue influence and given at a time when he lacked capacity to make a valid contract. Specifically, Odorizzi declares he was under such severe mental and emotional strain at the time he signed his resignation, having just completed the process of arrest, questioning by the police, booking, and release on bail, and having gone for forty hours without sleep, that he was incapable of rational thought or action. While he was in this condition and unable to think clearly, the superintendent of the District and the principal of his school came to his apartment. They said they were trying to help him and had his best interests at heart, that he should take their advice and immediately resign his position with the District, that there was no time to consult an attorney, that if he did not resign immediately the District would suspend and dismiss him from his position and publicize the proceedings, his "aforedescribed arrest" and cause him "to suffer extreme embarrassment and humiliation"; but that if he resigned at once the incident would not be publicized and would not jeopardize his chances of securing employment as a teacher elsewhere. Odorizzi pleads that because of his faith and confidence in their representations they were able to substitute their will and judgment in place of his own and thus obtain his signature to his purported resignation. A demurrer to his amended complaint was sustained without leave to amend.

By his complaint plaintiff in effect seeks to rescind his resignation pursuant to Civil Code, section 1689, on the ground that his consent had not been real or free within the meaning of Civil Code, section 1567, but had been obtained through duress, menace, fraud, undue influence, or mistake. A pleading under these sections is sufficient if stripped of its conclusions, it sets forth sufficient facts to justify legal relief. . . . In our view the facts in the amended complaint are insufficient to state a cause of action for duress, menace, fraud, or mistake, but they do set out sufficient elements to justify rescission of a consent because of undue influence. We summarize our conclusions on each of these points.

1. No duress or menace has been pleaded. Duress consists in unlawful confinement of another's person, or relatives, or property, which causes him to consent to a transaction through fear. (Civ. Code, §1569.) Duress is often used interchangeably with menace . . . but in California menace is technically a threat of duress or a threat of injury to the person, property, or character of another. (Civ. Code, §1570; Restatement, Contracts, §§492, 493.) We agree with respondent's contention that neither duress nor menace was involved in this case, because the action or threat in duress or menace must be unlawful, and a threat to take legal action is not unlawful unless the party making the threat knows the falsity of his claim. (Leeper v. Beltrami, 53 Cal. 2d 195, 204, 1 Cal. Rptr. 12, 347 P.2d 12, 77 A.L.R.2d 803.) The amended complaint shows in substance that the school representatives announced their intention to initiate suspension and dismissal proceedings under Education Code, sections 13403, 13408 et seq. at a time when the filing of such proceedings was not only their legal right but their positive duty as school officials. (Educ. Code, §13409; Board of Education, etc. v. Weiland, 179 Cal. App. 2d 808, 4 Cal. Rptr. 286.) Although the filing of such proceedings might be extremely damaging to plaintiff's reputation, the injury would remain incidental so long as the school officials acted in good faith in the performance of their duties. (Schumm by Whymer v. Berg, 37 Cal. 2d 174, 185-186, 231 P.2d 39, 21 A.L.R.2d 1051.) Neither duress nor menace was present as a ground for rescission.

2. Nor do we find a cause of action for fraud, either actual or constructive. (Civ. Code, §§1571 to 1574.) Actual fraud involves conscious misrepresentation, or concealment, or non-disclosure of a material fact which induces the innocent party to enter the contract. (Civ. Code, §1572; Pearson v. Norton, 230 Cal. App. 2d 1, 7, 40 Cal. Rptr. 634; Restatement, Contracts, §471.) A complaint for fraud must plead misrepresentation, knowledge of falsity, intent to induce reliance, justifiable reliance, and resulting damage. (Sixta v. Ochsner, 187 Cal. App. 2d 485, 489, 9 Cal. Rptr. 617; Zinn v. Ex-Cell-O Corp., 148 Cal. App. 2d 56, 68, 306 P.2d 1017.) While the amended complaint charged misrepresentation, it failed to assert the elements of knowledge of falsity, intent to induce reliance, and justifiable reliance. A cause of action for actual fraud was therefore not stated. . . .

Constructive fraud arises on a breach of duty by one in a confidential or fiduciary relationship to another which induces justifiable reliance by the latter to his prejudice. (Civ. Code, §1573.) Plaintiff has attempted to bring himself within this category, for the amended complaint asserts the existence of a confidential relationship between the school superintendent and principal as agents of the defendant, and the plaintiff. Such a confidential relationship may exist whenever a person with justification places trust and confidence in the integrity and fidelity of another. . . . Plaintiff, however, sets forth no facts to support his conclusion of a confidential relationship between the representatives of the school district and himself, other than that the parties bore the relationship of employer and employee to each other. Under prevailing judicial opinion no presumption of a confidential relationship arises from the bare fact that parties to a contract are employer and employee; rather, additional ties must be brought out in order to create the presumption of a confidential relationship between the two. . . . The absence of a confidential relationship between employer and employee is especially apparent where, as here, the parties were negotiating to bring about a termination of their relationship. In such a situation each party is expected to look after his own interests, and a lack of confidentiality is implicit in the subject matter of their dealings. We think the allegations of constructive fraud were inadequate.

3. As to mistake, the amended complaint fails to disclose any facts which would suggest that consent had been obtained through a mistake of fact or of law. The material facts of the transaction were known to both parties. Neither party was laboring under any misapprehension of law of which the other took advantage. The discussion between plaintiff and the school district representatives principally attempted to evaluate the probable consequences of plaintiff's predicament and to predict the future course of events. The fact that their speculations did not forecast the exact pattern which events subsequently took does not provide the basis for a claim that they were acting under some sort of mistake. The doctrine of mistake customarily involves such errors as the nature of the transaction, the identity of the parties, the identity of the things to which the contract relates, or the occurrence of collateral happenings. (Restatement, Contracts §502, Comment *e*.) Errors of this nature were not present in the case at bench.

4. However, the pleading does set out a claim that plaintiff's consent to the transaction had been obtained through the use of undue influence.

Undue influence, in the sense we are concerned with here, is a shorthand legal phrase used to describe persuasion which tends to be coercive in nature, persuasion which overcomes the will without convincing the judgment. (Estate of Ricks, 160 Cal. 467, 480-482, 117 P. 539.) The hallmark of such persuasion is high pressure, a pressure which works on mental, moral, or emotional weakness to such an extent that it approaches the boundaries of coercion. In this sense, undue influence has been called overpersuasion. (Kelly v. McCarthy, 6 Cal. 2d 347, 364, 57 P.2d 118.) Misrepresentations of law or fact are not essential to the charge, for a person's will may be overborne without misrepresentation. By statutory definition undue influence includes "taking an unfair advantage of another's weakness of mind; or . . . taking a grossly oppressive and unfair advantage of another's necessities or distress." (Civ. Code, §1575.) While most reported cases of undue influence involve persons who bear a confidential relationship to one another, a confidential or authoritative relationship between the parties need not be present when the undue influence involves unfair advantage taken of another's weakness or distress. . . .

We paraphrase the summary of undue influence given the jury by Sir James P. Wilde in Hall v. Hall, L.R. 1, P & D 481, 482 (1868): To make a good contract a man must be a free agent. Pressure of whatever sort which overpowers the will without convincing the judgment is a species of restraint under which no valid contract can be made. Importunity or threats, if carried to the degree in which the free play of a man's will is overborne, constitute undue influence, although no force is used or threatened. A party may be led but not driven, and his acts must be the offspring of his own volition and not the record of someone else's.

In essence undue influence involves the use of excessive pressure to persuade one vulnerable to such pressure, pressure applied by a dominant subject to a servient object. In combination, the elements of undue susceptibility in the servient person and excessive pressure by the dominating person make the latter's influence undue, for it results in the apparent will of the servient person being in fact the will of the dominant person.

Undue susceptibility may consist of total weakness of mind which leaves a person entirely without understanding (Civ. Code, §38); or, a lesser weakness which destroys the capacity of a person to make a contract even though he is not totally incapacitated (Civ. Code, §39; Peterson v. Ellebrecht, 205 Cal. App. 2d 718, 721-722, 23 Cal. Rptr. 349); or, the first element in our equation, a still lesser weakness which provides sufficient grounds to rescind a contract for undue influence (Civ. Code, §1575; . . .) Such lesser weakness need not be longlasting nor wholly incapacitating, but may be merely a lack of full vigor due to age, . . . physical condition, . . . emotional anguish, . . . or a combination of such factors. The reported cases have usually involved elderly, sick, senile persons alleged to have executed wills or deeds under pressure. (Malone v. Malone, 155 Cal. App. 2d 161, 317 P.2d 65 [constant importuning of a senile husband]; Stewart v. Marvin, 139 Cal. App. 2d 769, 294 P.2d 114 [persistent nagging of elderly spouse].) In some of its aspects this lesser weakness could perhaps be called weakness of spirit. But whatever name we give it, this first element of undue influence resolves itself into a lessened capacity of the object to make a free contract.

In the present case plaintiff has pleaded that such weakness at the time he signed his resignation prevented him from freely and competently applying his judgment to the problem before him. Plaintiff declares he was under severe mental and emotional strain at the time because he had just completed the process of arrest, questioning, booking, and release on bail and had been without sleep for forty hours. It is possible that exhaustion and emotional turmoil may wholly incapacitate a person from exercising his judgment. As an abstract question of pleading, plaintiff has pleaded that possibility and sufficient allegations to state a case for rescission.

Undue influence in its second aspect involves an application of excessive strength by a dominant subject against a servient object. Judicial consideration of this second element in undue influence has been relatively rare, for there are few cases denying persons who persuade but do not misrepresent the benefit of their bargain. Yet logically, the same legal consequences should apply to the results of excessive strength as to the results of undue weakness. Whether from weakness on one side, or strength on the other, or a combination of the two, undue influence occurs whenever there results "that kind of influence or supremacy of one mind over another by which that other is prevented from acting according to his own wish or judgment, and whereby the will of the person is overborne and he is induced to do or forbear to do an act which he would not do, or would do, if left to act freely." (Webb v. Saunders, 79 Cal. App. 2d 863, 871, 181 P.2d 43, 47.) Undue influence involves a type of mismatch which our statute calls unfair advantage. (Civ.

Code, §1575.) Whether a person of subnormal capacities has been subjected to ordinary force or a person of normal capacities subjected to extraordinary force, the match is equally out of balance. If will has been overcome against judgment, consent may be rescinded.

The difficulty, of course, lies in determining when the forces of persuasion have overflowed their normal banks and become oppressive flood waters. There are second thoughts to every bargain, and hindsight is still better than foresight. Undue influence cannot be used as a pretext to avoid bad bargains or escape from bargains which refuse to come up to expectations. A woman who buys a dress on impulse, which on critical inspection by her best friend turns out to be less fashionable than she had thought, is not legally entitled to set aside the sale on the ground that the saleswoman used all her wiles to close the sale. A man who buys a tract of desert land in the expectation that it is in the immediate path of the city's growth and will become another Palm Springs, an expectation cultivated in glowing terms by the seller, cannot rescind his bargain when things turn out differently. If we are temporarily persuaded against our better judgment to do something about which we later have second thoughts, we must abide the consequences of the risks inherent in managing our own affairs. (Estate of Anderson, 185 Cal. 700, 706-707, 198 P. 407.)

However, overpersuasion is generally accompanied by certain characteristics which tend to create a pattern. The pattern usually involves several of the following elements: (1) discussion of the transaction at an unusual or inappropriate time, (2) consummation of the transaction in an unusual place, (3) insistent demand that the business be finished at once, (4) extreme emphasis on untoward consequences of delay, (5) the use of multiple persuaders by the dominant side against a single servient party, (6) absence of third-party advisers to the servient party, (7) statements that there is no time to consult financial advisers or attorneys. If a number of these elements are simultaneously present, the persuasion may be characterized as excessive. The cases are illustrative:

Moore v. Moore, 56 Cal. 89, 93, and 81 Cal. 195, 22 P. 589, 874. The pregnant wife of a man who had been shot to death on October 30 and buried on November 1 was approached by four members of her husband's family on November 2 or 3 and persuaded to deed her entire interest in her husband's estate to his children by a prior marriage. In finding the use of undue influence on Mrs. Moore, the court commented: "It was the second day after her late husband's funeral. It was at a time when she would naturally feel averse to transacting any business, and she might reasonably presume that her late husband's brother would not apply to her at such a time to transact any important business, unless it was of a nature that would admit of no delay. And as it would admit of delay, the only reason which we can discover for their unseemly haste is, that they thought that she would be more likely to comply with their wishes then than at some future time, after she had recovered from the shock which she had then so recently experienced. If for that reason they selected that time for the accomplishment of their purpose, it seems to us that they not only took, but that they designed to take, an unfair advantage of her weakness of mind. If they did not, they probably can explain why they selected that inappropriate time for the transaction of business which might have been delayed for weeks without injury to any one. In the absence of any explanation, it appears to us that the time was selected with reference to just that condition of mind which she alleges that she was then in.

"Taking an unfair advantage of another's weakness of mind is undue influence, and the law will not permit the retention of an advantage thus obtained." (Civ. Code, §1575.)

Weger v. Rocha, 138 Cal. App. 109, 32 P.2d 417. Plaintiff, while confined in a cast in a hospital, gave a release of claims for personal injuries for a relatively small sum to an agent who spent two hours persuading her to sign. At the time of signing plaintiff was in a highly nervous and hysterical condition and suffering much pain, and she signed the release in order to terminate the interview. The court held that the release had been secured by the use of undue influence. . . .

The difference between legitimate persuasion and excessive pressure, like the difference between seduction and rape, rests to a considerable extent in the manner in which the parties go about their business. For example, if a day or two after Odorizzi's release on bail the superintendent of the school district had called him into his office during business hours and directed his attention to those provisions of the Education Code compelling his leave of absence and authorizing his suspension on the filing of written charges, had told him that the District contemplated filing written charges against him, had pointed out the alternative of resignation available to him, had informed him he was free to consult counsel or any adviser he wished and to consider the matter overnight and return with his decision the next day, it is extremely unlikely that any complaint about the use of excessive pressure could ever have been made against the school district.

But, according to the allegations of the complaint, this is not the way it happened, and if it had happened that way, plaintiff would never have resigned. Rather, the representatives of the school board undertook to achieve their objective by overpersuasion and imposition to secure plaintiff's signature but not his consent to his resignation through a high-pressure carrot-and-stick technique — under which they assured plaintiff they were trying to assist him, he should rely on their advice, there wasn't time to consult an attorney, if he didn't resign at once the school district would suspend and dismiss him from his position and publicize the proceedings, but if he did resign the incident wouldn't jeopardize his chances of securing a teaching post elsewhere.

Plaintiff has thus pleaded both subjective and objective elements entering the undue influence equation and stated sufficient facts to put in issue the question whether his free will had been overborne by defendant's agents at a time when he was unable to function in a normal manner. It was sufficient to pose ". . . the ultimate question . . . whether a free and competent judgment was merely influenced, or whether a mind was so dominated as to prevent the exercise of an independent judgment." (Williston on Contracts, §1625 [rev. ed.]; Restatement, Contracts §497, Comment c.) The question cannot be resolved by an analysis of pleading but requires a finding of fact.

We express no opinion on the merits of plaintiff's case, or the propriety of his continuing to teach school (Educ. Code, §13403), or the timeliness of his rescission (Civ. Code, §1691). We do hold that his pleading, liberally construed, states a cause of action for rescission of a transaction to which his apparent consent had been obtained through the use of undue influence.

The judgment is reversed.

ROTH, P.J., and HERNDON, J., concur.

Notes and Questions

1. *Defining undue influence.* The *Odorizzi* court identifies the essence of undue influence as involving the use of excessive pressure by a dominant party in overcoming the will of a vulnerable person. Similarly, the Restatement (Second) §177(1) describes undue influence as involving "unfair persuasion of a party who is under the domination of the person exercising the persuasion or who by virtue of the relation between them is justified in assuming that that person will not act in a manner inconsistent with his welfare." Although neither the *Odorizzi* court or the Restatement (Second) require the presence of a special relationship, such a finding will often be a significant factor in a court's assessment of undue influence. See, e.g., Sepulveda v. Aviles, 762 N.Y.S. 2d 358 (App. Div. 2003) (normally burden of proving undue influence will rest on party asserting it, but presence of confidential relationship will shift burden to beneficiary of transaction to prove that it was fair and free from undue influence). The mere fact that parties have a close relationship, however, or that some influence is exerted, will not necessarily prove undue influence. See, e.g., Robertson v. Robertson, 15 S.W.3d 407 (Mo. Ct. App. 2000) (even though defendant held special relationship of confidence and trust as farm manager for elderly grantor and the challenged deed recited price of $100 paid for land worth between $100,000 and $250,000, plaintiffs raised only suspicion of undue influence and presented no actual proof).

2. *Factors indicating undue influence.* As an aid to applying the general concept of undue influence, the *Odorizzi* court identifies seven characteristics that are often found in such cases. Should all of the seven elements be required to find a contract tainted by undue influence? In Keithley v. Civil Service Board, 89 Cal. Rptr. 809 (Ct. App. 1970), a police officer's resignation from the force was held to have been coerced, and therefore unlawful, despite the absence of the factors numbered (4) and (7) in the *Odorizzi* opinion. The officer had been charged with rape by a woman—not his wife—with whom he admitted having intercourse, but with her consent, not by force. The court's opinion, affirming a judgment of the Civil Service Board (which had been set aside by the lower court in this action), observed that the officer had not slept for 24 hours, that he was called to police headquarters for three successive days, and that on the third day was questioned by a superior officer who emphasized that the charges should not be made public. The court concluded that there was substantial evidence of undue influence. Id. at 815.

3. *Assessing **Odorizzi** for possible duress.* You will note that duress as defined by the court in *Odorizzi* is substantially narrower than the second Restatement's concept of duress. Subsequent California decisions indicate that the doctrine has evolved under state law to now encompass wrongful threats that leave the victim without reasonable alternatives. See Rich & Whillock v. Ashton Development, Inc., 204 Cal. Rptr. 86, 89 (Ct. App. 1984). Could the

plaintiff's resignation in *Odorizzi* have been rescinded under a more contemporary definition of duress? In what respect could undue influence be easier to establish than duress? How might it be more difficult?

4. *Role of bad faith.* Does the decision in *Odorizzi* depend on whether the school officials honestly believed the charges were likely to be upheld? The court's opinion indicates that the charges originally lodged against Odorizzi were dropped the following month, but the court does not state the reasons for that action. Suppose when the school officials urged Odorizzi to resign, they had proceeded as the court in *Odorizzi* indicates they should have, giving him time to consider their proposition and advising him to seek legal counsel before deciding. If you had been consulted by Odorizzi at that time, what advice would you have given?

5. *Undue influence and duress in agreements related to marriage.* In a category of cases that combine economic interests and personal relationships, claims of duress and undue influence have been used to challenge prenuptial as well as marriage dissolution agreements. A notable example is In re Bonds, 5 P.3d 815 (Cal. 2000), in which Sun Bonds, the former wife of professional baseball player Barry Bonds, challenged the validity of their premarital agreement which provided that each party waived any interest in the earnings made by the other party during the marriage. The contract was signed the day before the marriage, only Barry had assistance of counsel, and English was not Sun's first language. Nevertheless, the trial court held that the agreement was enforceable, basing its decision on findings that Sun had not been subject to any threat or coercion, that she had been advised that she could seek counsel, and that there was substantial evidence that she understood the agreement. Id. at 834-36. The California Supreme Court upheld the trial court's decision, noting that the applicable Family Code provisions placed the burden of proof on Sun to demonstrate that the agreement was not voluntarily made and that the absence of counsel was not decisive. Id. at 829. Notably, the California Legislature responded to the *Bonds* decision by amending the statute to provide that a premarital agreement is not voluntary if a party is not represented by counsel when signing the agreement, unless that party waives the right to independent counsel "in a separate writing." See Cal. Fam. Code §1615(c)(1) (West 2002). But see In re Marriage of Matson, 730 P.2d 668 (Wash. 1986) (prenuptial agreement held invalid; timing of contract discouraged use of counsel, wife thought husband would protect her interests, there was great disparity in business experience, and wife was not advised about effect of agreement). For a general discussion of the enforceability of premarital agreements, see Brian Bix, Bargaining in the Shadow of Love: The Enforcement of Premarital Agreements and How We Think About Marriage, 40 Wm. & Mary L. Rev. 145, 193-200 (1998).

In cases raising somewhat similar issues, a number of courts have upheld challenges to divorce settlement agreements on finding duress exerted by one former spouse against another. E.g., In re Marriage of Baltins, 260 Cal. Rptr. 403 (Ct. App. 1989) (settlement agreement was voidable on grounds of duress based on husband's threats to file for bankruptcy, to dissipate wife's share in property and to refuse to see their adopted child; husband also acted to prevent wife from receiving legal counsel); Golding v. Golding, 581 N.Y.S.2d 4 (App. Div. 1992) (settlement agreement was voidable on basis of duress in light of husband's threat not to grant "Get" or Jewish divorce and wife's fears based on sister's failure to obtain "Get" in earlier divorce).

6. *Revisiting the **Batsakis** case.* Recall Batsakis v. Demotsis, in Chapter 2, the case in which a wartime agreement to exchange a loan of drachmas for later repayment in dollars was upheld over a lack-of-consideration defense. Could the principles applied in *Totem Marine* or *Odorizzi* have been relevant to the decision of that case?

C. MISREPRESENTATION AND NONDISCLOSURE

Early in the history of the common law, with rare exceptions, the English courts did not generally recognize fraud as a defense to an action in assumpsit. The courts did provide indirect relief, however, by allowing recovery for damages flowing from fraud in a separate action, which later came to be known as the tort action of "deceit." The modern tort action for misrepresentation is a descendent of this common law remedy.

Although fraud was not recognized as a defense at law, courts of equity allowed a party who had been a victim of fraud to avoid the contract by way of equitable "rescission." Rescission amounted to a judicial return of the parties to the status quo that existed before the contract was formed. In rescission a court of equity ordered both the wrongdoer and the injured party to return to the other any money or property received from the other. Over time the law courts recognized a legal right of rescission, which was similar to the equitable remedy but differed in some technical respects. In particular, at law in order to obtain rescission, a party had to show that she had made a "tender" of any money or property received before instituting the action, while in equity tender was unnecessary. With the procedural merger of law and equity in the nineteenth century, the difference between legal and equitable rescission has become relatively unimportant, although there are still situations in which the difference can be significant. (For example, if a party complies with the requirements of legal rescission, including tender, she is entitled to avoid the contract; a court could refuse to grant the remedy of equitable rescission if the court concludes that fairness does not warrant rescission of the transaction.)

As a result of these historical developments, under modern law a victim of misrepresentation may have a choice between two significant avenues of redress: a tort action for damages or a right to avoid the enforceability of the contract by way of rescission. (This right of rescission could be exercised either by defense to an action to enforce the contract or in an affirmative action seeking restitution of benefits conferred on the other party.) What factors affect the choice between these two remedies, making one or the other more attractive or, possibly, unavailable as a remedy? One such factor is that the remedy of rescission requires the injured party to return any money or property that he has received; thus, if the defrauded party does not want to do so, rescission is not a desirable remedy. Suppose, for example, that the purchaser of a home receives a "termite letter" from the seller stating that the home is free of wood-boring insects. After purchasing the home, the buyer learns that the home is infested with termites. It turns out that the seller fraudulently procured the termite letter by bribing the termite company. If the buyer does not want to give up the home, a tort action for money damages to compensate the buyer for the termite problem is a more attractive remedy than rescission.

Sometimes rescission may be unavailable even if the defrauded party would prefer this remedy. If the defrauded party is unable to return the property received from the wrongdoer because it has been transferred to a third person, rescission may not be allowed. Restatement of Restitution §66. On the other hand, sometimes a party may be able to obtain rescission even though a tort remedy would be unavailable. A party may rescind a contract for a material misrepresentation even if the misrepresentation was not made with fraudulent intent. Restatement (Second) §164(1) (contract voidable for either fraudulent or material misrepresentation). The law may not recognize a tort action or may limit the scope of the remedy, however, if the misrepresentation was not made with fraudulent intent (often called "scienter"). Compare Restatement (Second) of Torts §549 (damages for fraudulent misrepresentation) with §§552, 552B, and 552C (remedy and damages for negligent and innocent misrepresentation). For discussions of tort and contractual rights based on misrepresentation, see W. Page Keeton et al., Prosser and Keeton on the Law of Torts §§105-110, at 725-770 (5th ed. 1984); Fleming James, Jr. & Oscar S. Gray, Misrepresentation (Pts. I, II), 37 Md. L. Rev. 286, 488 (1977-1978).

The materials that follow address several questions: When is a misrepresentation actionable either by way of rescission or in tort? When does a failure to disclose information amount to misrepresentation? What effect does a contractual disclaimer of representations have on an injured party's right to rescind a contract or recover damages for misrepresentation?

Syester v. Banta
Iowa Supreme Court
257 Iowa 613, 133 N.W.2d 666 (1965)

SNELL, Justice.

This is a law action seeking damages, actual and exemplary, for allegedly false and fraudulent representations in the sale of dancing instruction to plaintiff. From the final judgment entered after a jury verdict for plaintiff in a substantial amount defendants have appealed.

Plaintiff is a lonely and elderly widow who fell for the blandishments and flattery of those who saw some "easy money" available.

Defendants are the owners of the Des Moines Arthur Murray Dance Studio. They have a legitimate service to sell but when their selling techniques transcend the utmost limits of reason and fairness they must expect courts and juries to frown thereon. In this case the jury has done so.

Since the beginning of recorded history men and women have persisted in selling their birthrights for a mess of pottage and courts cannot protect against the folly of bad judgment. We can, however, insist on honesty in selling. The old doctrine of caveat emptor is no longer the pole star for business.

Much of the testimony was uncontradicted. The testimony as to intentional fraud and misrepresentation as well as the motive and credibility of some witnesses was attacked but these were questions for the jury. It was for the jury to say who should be believed.

It is not for us to say who should have prevailed with the jury. It is for us to determine the sufficiency of the admissible evidence to generate a jury question and the correctness of the instructions given the jury. We will mention only as much of the testimony as is necessary for that purpose.

Plaintiff is a widow living alone. She has no family. Her exact age does not appear but a former employee of defendants and a favorite dancing instructor of plaintiff testified "that during the period from 1957 through the fall of 1960 she was 68 years old."

After her husband's death plaintiff worked at Bishop's as a "coffee girl." She first went to the Arthur Murray Studio in 1954 as a gift from a friend. On the first visit there was no attempt to sell her any lessons but she was invited to return a few days later. When she returned she was interviewed by the manager and sold a small course of dancing lessons. From that time on there appears to have been an astoundingly successful selling campaign.

The testimony of defendants' manager and his written summary of payments, received as Exhibit 1, are not in complete accord, but the variation is not vital. By May 2, 1955 defendants sold plaintiff 3222 hours of dancing instruction for which she paid $21,020.50. In all, according to the testimony of defendants' manager plaintiff paid $33,497.00 for 4057 hours of instruction. Because of some refunds and credits defendants' Exhibit 1 shows plaintiff's cost to be only $29,174.30. Defendants' Exhibit 1 is as follows:

Exhibit 1
Summary of Dance Course Purchased by Agnes Syester

Date	Sold by	Hours in Course	Amt Paid
9-27-54	Brick	206	1709.50
10-15-54	Neidt	300	2490.00
11-4-54	Neidt	16	88.00
1-8-55	Bersch	500	3825.00
1-19-55	Bersch	1000	6800.00
5-2-55	Bersch	1200	6000.00
5-24-55	Brick	100	995.00
6-22-55	Brick	10	79.80
5-25-57	Brick-Ziegler	11	130.00
6-22-57	Brick	10	106.00
6-4-58	Carey	10	106.00
9-8-58	Carey	10	99.00
1-6-59	Erickson	4	25.00
5-27-59	Wolf	10	116.00

Date	Sold by	Hours in Course	Amt Paid
6-10-59	Wolf	10	112.50
6-10-59	Wolf	10	112.50
12-2-59	Carey-Kenton	25	290.00
3-2-60	Carey	625	6090.00
		4057	$29174.30

On May 2, 1955 when plaintiff bought 1200 additional hours of instruction for $6,000 she had already bought 2022 hours and had used only 261 hours.

Included in the courses offered were lifetime memberships. With the purchase of 1,000 or 1,200 hours of instruction it was the policy of defendants to give free attendance to weekly dances for life and two hours of instruction or practice a month to keep active on what had been learned. Included in plaintiff's purchases were three lifetime memberships. Plaintiff attended the weekly dances and incidental entertainments and admitted having fun.

Plaintiff testified that defendants' manager sold her the first lifetime membership. She testified "He promised me all the privileges of the studio and I would be a professional dancer." To make such a promise to a lady plaintiff's age was ridiculous. The fact that she was so gullible as to be an easy victim does not justify taking over $29,000 of her money. She may have been willing and easily sold but nevertheless a victim.

The members of defendants' staff were carefully schooled and supervised in the art of high-powered salesmanship. Mr. Carey, a witness for plaintiff, testified at length as to methods and as to his contact with plaintiff. There was evidence that Mr. Carey was a disgruntled former employee and instructor and had expressed hostility toward defendants, but his credibility was for the jury.

Defendants' studio occupies seven rooms consisting of a grand ballroom and six private studios. Each private studio is wired for sound so the manager could monitor conversations between instructor and student and without the student's knowledge correct the instructor's sales technique.

Mr. Carey had received two months training including a course on sales technique taught by the manager. Plaintiff's Exhibit H is a revised edition of defendants' "Eight Good Rules For Interviewing." It is an exhaustive set of instructions, outlines and suggested conversations covering twenty-two typewritten pages. A few pertinent parts are:

1. How to prevent a prospect from consulting his banker, lawyer, wife or friend.

2. Avoid permitting your prospect to think the matter over.

3. Tell the prospect that has never danced before that it is an advantage and tell the prospect that has danced before that it is an advantage.

4. To dance with the prospect and then tell the prospect that the rhythm is very good, their animation or self confidence is good, that their natural ability is very good. That they will be an excellent ballroom dancer in much less time and that if they didn't have natural ability it would take twice as long.

5. To summarize the prospect's ability to learn as follows: "Did you know that the three most important points on this D.A. are: Rhythm, natural ability and animation? You've been graded Excellent in all three."

6. In quoting the price for various courses, the instructor is supposed to say "the trouble with most people is that they dance lifelessly, but as I told you on your analysis, you have animation—vitality in your dancing. No matter what course you decide on you're going to be a really smooth dancer (men would rather be a smooth dancer—women would rather be a beautiful, graceful dancer)."

7. To use "emotional selling" and the instructor is tutored as follows: "This is the warm-up period and is a very important part of your interview. You have proved to him by now that he can learn to dance; now you must appeal to his emotions in such a way that he will want lessons regardless of the cost."

Theoretically, for advancing proficiency in dancing (the jury must have thought that $29,000 had something to do with it), plaintiff was awarded a Bronze Medal, then a Silver Medal and then a Gold Medal. These awards were given plaintiff all in the same year although defendants' manager testified that it takes approximately two to four years to qualify for a Bronze Medal, five to seven years for a Silver Medal and anytime after 1200 hours a student could qualify for the Gold Medal. Finally after considerable thought about new incentives for plaintiff to buy something more she was shown a film on Gold Star dancing. This is a difficult professional type of dancing. "The dancers on the film were brought in from Europe by Mr. Murray. The dancing is English quick step and is the type of dancing done by Ginger Rogers and Fred Astaire only about twice as difficult." This film had been studied 15 to 20 times to determine what parts to stress with plaintiff.

Plaintiff was easily sold a Gold Star course of 625 hours for $6,250. A few days later she came into the ballroom, handed Mr. Carey an envelope and said "Well, it took some doing but here is the money." The money was delivered to the manager.

The Gold Star course was started although even the instructor was "faking it" and had no idea what he was doing.

Mr. Carey testified that from 1957 through the fall of 1960 plaintiff's dancing ability did not improve. "She was 68 years old and had gone as far as she would ever go in dancing, thereon it would be merely repetitious." In his opinion "it would take 200 to 400 hours of instructions to teach her to dance in the manner she was dancing in 1960." He also testified that while he was at the studio none of his students ever failed to qualify for any of the medals. When he questioned plaintiff's ability to do the advanced type of dancing she was being sold he was reminded by defendants' manager that he was an employee and that the manager made the rules.

Mr. Carey testified at length as to the attentions, inducements, promises and lies (he said they were) lavished on plaintiff. He became plaintiff's regular instructor. He was about twenty-five years old and apparently quite charming and fascinating to plaintiff. She gave him a diamond ring for his birthday in 1960.

The testimony is rather fantastic but it would unduly extend this opinion to set it forth in greater detail. It was in our opinion sufficient for the jury to find that plaintiff was the victim of a calculated course of intentional misrepresentations.

The charge for instruction varied somewhat up to $10 per hour. After some refunds, and, according to defendants' computation, plaintiff paid approximately $6.75 per hour for 3425 hours of instruction or about $23,000.

If Mr. Carey's estimate of plaintiff's ability and possibility of progress is accepted plaintiff was knowingly overcharged for 3025 hours or a total sum of $20,418.75.

Mr. Carey was discharged by defendants in the fall of 1960. Plaintiff quit the studio shortly thereafter. She still had 1750 hours of unused time that she had purchased. She testified that she did so because she "was unhappy because things didn't go right and I was through with dancing, and that was the only reason I quit." Defendants' manager testified that plaintiff "became unhappy over the dismissal of Mr. Carey and left the studio." Another witness for defendants said plaintiff complained mostly about losing her instructor, Mr. Carey.

In January 1961 plaintiff employed counsel to represent her in a lawsuit against defendants. Her counsel contacted defendants. Conferences were held. Apparently a divertive campaign was planned by defendants. Mr. Carey testified:

> I next heard from Mr. Theiss in January of 1961 when he called and asked me to come down to the studio to discuss employment. I went to see him and he told me that Mrs. Syester was suing him and wanted to know if I still had any influence over her, to get her to drop the suit. I told him I felt that I still did and I would try to get her to come back in the studio and drop her legal action against him. He said he would reinstate me and pay all of my past due commissions. I accepted the position and went to Bishop's Cafeteria where Mrs. Syester was the coffee girl to see what her feelings were toward the studio. She was very cold toward me and I reported this to Mr. Theiss. He said not to concern myself with the studio, that my job was merely to get her to drop the lawsuit, so I went to Bishop's a couple of times a day to try and talk with Mrs. Syester. Finally I succeeded and told her that I was back in the studio and that Mr. Theiss wanted her back. I told her that there would be no hard feelings on our part if she would just drop the suit and come back but she said she did not want to come back to the studio. I continued talking to her and finally got her to accept coming to a party and told her that I would be out to pick her up and escort her to the studio. This was about a week after I first contacted her, in February of 1961. I told her that I was going to the party and I would save her some waltzes. I knew this was her favorite dance. And I felt that if she would pass up this waltz, she was not interested in dancing. She did not come to the studio so the next day I went down to Bishop's and told her she disappointed me very much. Then I started talking about all of the lessons she and I had had and all of the months we had danced and the fun we had together. I told her how wonderful she had done. I painted word pictures and things so she could see this. I asked her if she remembered about when she got the Bronze. She kept saying that was best but all she wanted was her money back. I finally persuaded her to come to the studio and we danced for about 45 minutes. It was at this time that she called the lawsuit off. . . . When I went to Bishop's Cafeteria to see Mrs. Syester I told her she was a good dancer and that she still had the ability to be a professional, excellent dancer. I told her that she did not need an attorney; after all Mrs. Theiss and myself were her only friends and we wanted her back at the studio to continue with her Gold Star and reminded her of all the waltzes we would do together.

During the month of February several people contacted plaintiff at the instigation of defendants' manager, including Mr. Carey. These efforts were fruitful. Plaintiff made what defendants claim was a complete settlement. Defendants' counsel prepared a written release (defendants' Exhibit 2) and was present during one conference of the parties. Defendants' counsel did not instigate, carry on, nor make the "settlement" with plaintiff. He testified that he "did not want to get that implicated." In any event defendants' manager at plaintiff's home persuaded plaintiff to discharge her counsel by phone and agree to settle for the refund of her March 2, 1960 payment of $6,090. This was reported to defendants' counsel, who in behalf of his client, wrote settlement checks. Plaintiff's counsel received his share although there is no evidence that the settlement was ever pursuant to his advice. There is evidence that defendants were attempting to lead plaintiff away from her own counsel. Their efforts were so far beyond the limits of propriety that their own counsel hesitated to participate.

The release signed by plaintiff is a specific release of her claim based on the March 2, 1960 payment and a general release of all claims. If obtained in good faith it is a bar to all plaintiff's claims. The release was witnessed by Estella M. Smith, whose identity does not appear and by defendants' manager. After signing this release on March 6, 1961 plaintiff's then pending lawsuit was dismissed. Plaintiff returned to the studio and participated in the activities for several months.

A second release dated January 28, 1963 was obtained by defendants' manager. It purports to be a contractual release for $4,000. The $4,000 to be paid was to be evidenced by a note. There is no claim that anything has been paid thereon. The note provided for installment payments but instead of being signed by defendants it is signed by plaintiff. Defendants' manager testified that this was all a mistake and that the studio was to pay.

Accepting defendants' explanation that it was a mistake the most charitable thing that can be said is that plaintiff would sign anything requested, even a note wherein she was the payee.

The present action was filed March 12, 1963. It alleged fraud and misrepresentation in the several sales to plaintiff and in obtaining dismissal of the previous lawsuit and the releases signed by plaintiff.

Defendants denied any fraud or misrepresentations and urged the releases as a complete defense. Defendants offered evidence in support of their position. At the close of plaintiff's evidence and again at the close of all the evidence defendants moved for a directed verdict. The motions were overruled. The jury returned a verdict for plaintiff in the sum of $14,300 actual damages and $40,000 punitive damages. Defendants appealed.

I. The court told the jury to first consider the issues involved in the releases signed by plaintiff and placed on plaintiff the burden of proving by clear, satisfactory and convincing evidence that they were not binding on her. This was proper.

In five instructions, separately numbered but in sequence, the court instructed on fraud, expression of opinion as distinguished from a statement of fact, fraudulent misrepresentation, intent to mislead, consideration for releases, presumption of freedom from fraud, need for prudence in signing and failure of consideration.

On appeal defendants challenged the sufficiency of the evidence to generate a jury question but not the accuracy of the instructions.

Defendants argue in the absence of fraud the execution of a valid release bars a future action based on the rights relinquished. The rule is stated in Kilby v. Charles City Western Railway Company, 191 Iowa 926, 928, 183 N.W. 371 as follows:

> Where a settlement has been had between competent parties, and a release has been fairly entered into, without fraud or overreaching, it becomes binding and effectual, and will be upheld and enforced. It is undoubtedly the law that an instrument of this character can be impeached for fraud in procuring the same or where the same was executed by a party who was mentally incompetent to legally execute such an instrument. The burden of proof is on the party seeking to impeach such written instrument.

Mere failure to read an instrument before signing will not avoid its provisions. Crum v. McCollum, 211 Iowa 319, 233 N.W. 678. These propositions are not in dispute and further citation of authority is unnecessary. . . .

. . . The evidence was such that the jury could find that there was such a concerted effort, lacking in propriety, to obtain the releases as to constitute fraudulent overreaching. The jury obviously concluded that there was a predatory play on the vanity and credulity of an old lady. We find no reason for interfering with that conclusion.

II. Defendants argue that "In an action based upon fraud, certain universally recognized elements must be alleged and shown, and the failure to establish any one or more of such elements is fatal to such action." With this statement we agree and so did the trial court. In Instruction No. 10 the jury was told that to recover the burden was on plaintiff to establish by clear, satisfactory and convincing evidence each of the following propositions:

> 1. That the defendants made one or more of the representations claimed by plaintiff. . . .
> 2. That said statements, or one or more of them, were false.
> 3. That said false statements or representations were as to material matters with reference to the entering into the lesson contracts.
> 4. That the defendants knew the said representations, or one or more of them, were false.
> 5. That said representations were made with intent to deceive and defraud the plaintiff.
> 6. That the plaintiff believed and relied upon said false representations and would not have entered into the lesson contracts, except for believing and relying upon said misrepresentations.
> 7. That the plaintiff was damaged in some amount through relying on said representations.

> If you find that the plaintiff has established each and every one of the foregoing propositions, numbered 1 to 7 inclusive by evidence which is clear, satisfactory and convincing, then your verdict will be for the plaintiff and against the defendants in such amount as you find plaintiff is justly entitled to receive.

If you find, however, that the plaintiff has failed to establish any one or more of the foregoing propositions, numbered 1 to 7 inclusive, then your verdict will be for the defendants.

The instruction was adequate. Here again the problem was factual. Defendants argue that the representations proved by plaintiff were nothing more than mere expressions of opinion or "puffing" and that the only substantial expression of opinion was in fact accomplished.

In Christy v. Heil, supra, we considered statements of fact as distinguished from opinion or puffing. We said "Ordinarily the question of whether the representations made are opinion or fact is for the jury to determine and depends upon the facts and circumstances in each case." (Citations) loc. cit. 608, 123 N.W.2d loc. cit. 411. "We must review the evidence in the light most favorable to the purchasers." loc. cit. 613, 123 N.W.2d loc. cit. 414.

Defendants' review of the authorities is exhaustive and scholarly but the fact remains that in the case at bar there was evidence, which if believed by the jury, would support a finding of fraud.

III. Defendants argue that there was no proof of damage. Although the court's instructions on measure of damage were closer to the "out of pocket" rule than to the "benefit of bargain" rule to which we are committed (see 37 C.J.S. Fraud §143, page 477) defendants make no complaint. The instruction was not prejudicial to defendants. Defendants say that the rule was properly stated but suggest that the statement of the issues including the amount prayed for may have been misleading. The fact that plaintiff asked for something beyond the correct measure of damage is not reversible error if, as defendants say, the court properly instructed the jury.

Defendants argue that there was no evidence from which the jury could find the fair and reasonable value of the instruction received other than the amount paid by plaintiff. Defendants' manager testified that plaintiff still has 899 hours of unused lessons. Mr. Carey's testimony would support a finding that plaintiff was knowingly overcharged for 3025 hours or the sum of $20,418.75. The jury's verdict for $14,300 actual damages was within the evidence. We have no means of knowing just how the jury computed the damage. It was for more than the charge for the unused time according to defendants, but less than would be due for unproductive instruction. In argument defendants have stressed the value of plaintiff's enjoyment. That may have entered into the jury's computation.

The verdict was not beyond the scope of the evidence or the instructions.

IV. In addition to actual damages plaintiff asked for exemplary or punitive damages. The claim was submitted to the jury and a verdict for $40,000 punitive damages was returned.

Defendants argue that the record will not support an award of punitive damages in any amount and that the issue should not have been submitted, but do not challenge the accuracy of the instructions relative thereto.

. . . The jury award of $40,000 was large. However, the evidence of greed and avariciousness on the part of defendants is shocking to our sense of justice as it obviously was to the jury.

The allowance of exemplary damages is wholly within the discretion of the jury where there is a legal basis for the allowance of such damages. We may interfere only where passion and prejudice appear and then only by reversal. . . .

We think the question of exemplary damages was properly submitted to the jury; that there was evidence to support a verdict; that there is no indication of such passion and prejudice as to require a reversal and that the case should be and hereby is affirmed.

GARFIELD, C.J., and HAYS, LARSON, PETERSON, THORNTON, and MOORE, JJ., concur.

THOMPSON and STUART, JJ., concur in result.

Notes and Questions

1. *Fraudulent or material misrepresentation.* Section 164(1) of the Second Restatement provides that a contract is voidable if a party's "manifestation of assent is induced by either a fraudulent or a material misrepresentation by the other party upon which the recipient is justified in relying. . . ." For examples of intentional fraud, see Conway v. Romarion, 557 S.E.2d 54 (Ga. Ct. App. 2001) (false statements and conduct by seller designed to hide extensive pet damage to house would provide basis for rescission of contract by buyers if proved at trial); Sarvis v. Vermont State Colleges, 772 A.2d 494 (Vt. 2001) (college could rescind employment agreement when employee gave false information on resume to hide record of criminal incarceration). Restatement (Second) §162(1)(b) and (c) define "fraudulent" also to include an assertion made as true but without knowledge or confidence by the maker whether it is true or false, and thus may include statements that are made recklessly or negligently. See, e.g., Waste Management of Massachusetts, Inc. v. Carver, 642 N.E.2d 1058 (Mass. App. Ct. 1994) (rescission granted where seller made misrepresentation about extent of land contamination without obtaining current information from consultants hired to test land; seller could not avoid liability by ignoring available information).

Additionally, as noted by the introduction to this chapter, a contract may be subject to rescission because of an innocent but material misrepresentation, see Restatement (Second) §162(2) and Comment *c*. See also Alfa Life Ins. Corp. v. Lewis, 910 So.2d 757 (Ala. 2005) (decedent's presumably innocent failure to disclose heart condition would still amount to material misrepresentation and allow rescission under insurance code); Groothand v. Schlueter, 949 S.W.2d 923 (Mo. Ct. App. 1997) (rescission available for buyers of house with structural problems without showing that sellers knew representations to be false). Was there evidence on which the jury could find that the releases in *Syester* were induced by misrepresentation? Can you think of other bases for avoiding a contract that might be applicable to this case?

2. *Contract or tort claim.* Assuming the jury could properly find that the releases were voidable because induced by misrepresentation, Ms. Syester could then assert a tort claim for damages based on the defendants' fraud in inducing her to enter into the series of contracts for dancing instruction. Could Ms. Syester have also attempted to rescind these contracts rather than attempting to recover damages in tort for fraud? As a tactical matter, should she have done so?

3. *Misrepresentation based on false opinion or prediction.* One of the instructions given by the lower court to the jury dealt with the distinction between statements of opinion and representations of fact. The revised Restatement defines an opinion as the expression of a belief, without certainty, as to the existence of a fact. Typically, opinions deal with matters such as quality or value of property. Restatement (Second) §168(1). The classical rule was that a statement of opinion could not be fraudulent, an approach based on the view that the morals of the marketplace required a certain degree of leeway for "puffing" in bargaining. Under the revised Restatement, however, a statement of opinion amounts to a misrepresentation of fact if the person giving the opinion misrepresented his state of mind (i.e., stated that he held a certain opinion when in fact he did not). Restatement (Second) §159, Comment *d*. See also Bennett v. Coors Brewing Co., 189 F.3d 1221 (10th Cir. 1999) (employees made prima facie case of misrepresentation by showing that employer made false statements about plans to downsize in order to get employees to take severance package). Moreover, under §169 of the revised Restatement, a statement of opinion may also be actionable if the one giving the opinion (a) stands in a relationship of trust or confidence to the recipient (a "fiduciary relationship"), (b) is an expert on matters covered by the opinion, or (c) renders the opinion to one who, because of age or other factors, is peculiarly susceptible to misrepresentation. Which of these rules could apply to the facts of the *Syester* case?

4. *Reasonable reliance.* Assuming that a misrepresentation occurred in *Syester,* is it clear that all the other elements for misrepresentation are present? Was reliance by the plaintiff reasonable? See Schlaifer Nance & Co. v. Estate of Andy Warhol, 119 F.3d 91 (2d Cir. 1997) (purchaser of license to reproduce Andy Warhol's artwork did not reasonably rely on false statements that estate held all property rights in light of overt evidence to contrary); Mehta v. Mehta, 602 N.Y.S.2d 142 (App. Div. 1993) (reliance by one party on other's misrepresentation of the value of jointly owned assets was not reasonable where both parties had equal access to business records). Notably, the fact that the misrepresentation relates to a matter of public record will not necessarily preclude reasonable reliance. See, e.g., Cao v. Nguyen, 607 N.W.2d 528 (Neb. 2000) (false statement that house was a duplex constituted grounds for rescission even though public records revealed that house was legal only for single occupancy; buyers' reliance was reasonable under circumstances).

If Mrs. Syester was not reasonable in relying on representations that she had the ability to become a professional dancer, then what could justify the jury verdict and appellate decision in her favor? The case may have involved enough instances of clear fraud, such as the selling of the "Gold Star" lessons that the instructor had no qualifications to teach, to warrant the decision in Mrs. Syester's favor. Or perhaps the outcome suggests that the common law is in fact imbued with principles of morality and the need to protect those perceived as vulnerable. For an essay including discussion of these aspects of the *Syester* case, see M. Cathleen Kaveny, Between Example and Doctrine: Contract Law and Common Morality, 33 Journal of Religious Ethics 669 (2005). See also Bennett v. Bailey, 597 S.W.2d 532 (Tex. Civ. App. 1980) (upholding award of $78,000 in treble damages to widow under state consumer protection law after dance studio engaged in deceptive practices in selling her almost $30,000 in dance lessons).

5. *Ethical limits on attorney's direct contact with opposing party.* In an effort to get Ms. Syester to sign the releases, the defendants persuaded her to discharge her attorney. At the time the defendants were also represented by counsel. Under the Model Rules of Professional Conduct, it is improper for a lawyer to "communicate about the subject of the representation with a person the lawyer knows to be represented by another lawyer in the matter, unless the lawyer has the consent of the other lawyer or is authorized to do so by law or court order." Model Rules of Professional Conduct, Rule 4.2. What is the purpose of this rule? Did the defendants' lawyer violate the rule?

Hill v. Jones
Arizona Court of Appeals
151 Ariz. 81, 725 P.2d 1115 (1986), review denied
(Oct. 1, 1986)

MEYERSON, Judge.

Must the seller of a residence disclose to the buyer facts pertaining to past termite infestation? This is the primary question presented in this appeal. Plaintiffs Warren G. Hill and Gloria R. Hill (buyers) filed suit to rescind an agreement to purchase a residence. Buyers alleged that Ora G. Jones and Barbara R. Jones (sellers) had made misrepresentations concerning termite damage in the residence and had failed to disclose to them the existence of the damage and history of termite infestation in the residence. The trial court dismissed the claim for misrepresentation based upon a so-called integration clause in the parties' agreement.

Sellers then sought summary judgment on the "concealment" claim arguing that they had no duty to disclose information pertaining to termite infestation and that even if they did, the record failed to show all of the elements necessary for fraudulent concealment. The trial court granted summary judgment, finding that there was "no genuinely disputed issue of material fact and that the law favors the . . . defendants." The trial court awarded sellers $1,000.00 in attorney's fees. Buyers have appealed from the judgment and sellers have cross-appealed from the trial court's ruling on attorney's fees.

I. FACTS

In 1982, buyers entered into an agreement to purchase sellers' residence for $72,000. The agreement was entered after buyers made several visits to the home. The purchase agreement provided that sellers were to pay for and place in escrow a termite inspection report stating that the property was free from evidence of termite infestation. Escrow was scheduled to close two months later.

One of the central features of the house is a parquet teak floor covering the sunken living room, the dining room, the entryway and portions of the halls. On a subsequent visit to the house, and when sellers were present, buyers noticed a small "ripple" in the wood floor on the step leading up to the dining room from the sunken living room. Mr. Hill asked if the ripple could be termite damage. Mrs. Jones answered that it was water damage. A few years previously, a broken water heater in the house had in fact caused water damage in the area of the dining room and steps which necessitated that some repairs be made to the floor. No further discussion on the subject, however, took place between the parties at that time or afterwards.

Mr. Hill, through his job as maintenance supervisor at a school district, had seen similar "ripples" in wood which had turned out to be termite damage. Mr. Hill was not totally satisfied with Mrs. Jones's explanation, but he felt that the termite inspection report would reveal whether the ripple was due to termites or some other cause.

The termite inspection report stated that there was no visible evidence of infestation. The report failed to note the existence of physical damage or evidence of previous treatment. The realtor notified the parties that the property had passed the termite inspection. Apparently, neither party actually saw the report prior to close of escrow.

After moving into the house, buyers found a pamphlet left in one of the drawers entitled "Termites, the Silent Saboteurs." They learned from a neighbor that the house had some termite infestation in the past. Shortly after the close of escrow, Mrs. Hill noticed that the wood on the steps leading down to the sunken living room was crumbling. She called an exterminator who confirmed the existence of termite damage to the floor and steps and to wood columns in the house. The estimated cost of repairing the wood floor alone was approximately $5,000.

Through discovery after their lawsuit was filed, buyers learned the following. When sellers purchased the residence in 1974, they received two termite guarantees that had been given to the previous owner by Truly Nolen, as well as a diagram showing termite treatment at the residence that had taken place in 1963. The guarantees provided for semi-annual inspections and annual termite booster treatments. The accompanying diagram stated that the existing damage had not been repaired. The second guarantee, dated 1965, reinstated the earlier contract for inspection and treatment. Mr. Jones admitted that he read the guarantees when he received them. Sellers renewed the guarantees when they purchased the residence in 1974. They also paid the annual fee each year until they sold the home.

On two occasions during sellers' ownership of the house but while they were at their other residence in Minnesota, a neighbor noticed "streamers" evidencing live termites in the wood tile floor near the entryway. On both occasions, Truly Nolen gave a booster treatment for termites. On the second incident, Truly Nolen drilled through one of the wood tiles to treat for termites. The neighbor showed Mr. Jones the area where the damage and treatment had occurred. Sellers had also seen termites on the back fence and had replaced and treated portions of the fence.

Sellers did not mention any of this information to buyers prior to close of escrow. They did not mention the past termite infestation and treatment to the realtor or to the termite inspector. There was evidence of holes on the patio that had been drilled years previously to treat for termites. The inspector returned to the residence to determine why he had not found evidence of prior treatment and termite damage. He indicated that he had not seen the holes in the patio because of boxes stacked there. It is unclear whether the boxes had been placed there by buyers or sellers. He had not found the damage inside the house because a large plant, which buyers had purchased from sellers, covered the area. After investigating the second time, the inspector found the damage and evidence of past treatment. He acknowledged that this information should have appeared in the report. He complained, however, that he should have been told of any history of termite infestation and treatment before he performed his inspection and that it was customary for the inspector to be given such information.

Other evidence presented to the trial court was that during their numerous visits to the residence before close of escrow, buyers had unrestricted access to view and inspect the entire house. Both Mr. and Mrs. Hill had seen termite damage and were therefore familiar with what it might look like. Mr. Hill had seen termite damage on the fence at this property. Mrs. Hill had noticed the holes on the patio but claimed not to realize at the time what they were for. Buyers asked no questions about termites except when they asked if the "ripple" on the stairs was termite damage. Mrs. Hill admitted she was not "trying" to find problems with the house because she really wanted it.

II. CONTRACT INTEGRATION CLAUSE

We first turn to the trial court's ruling that the agreement of the parties did not give buyers the right to rely on the statement made by Mrs. Jones that the "ripple" in the floor was water damage. We find this ruling to be in error. The contract provision upon which the trial court based its ruling reads as follows:

> That the Purchaser has investigated the said premises, and the Broker and the Seller are hereby released from all responsibility regarding the valuation thereof, and neither Purchaser, Seller, nor Broker shall be bound by any understanding, agreement, promise, representation or stipulation expressed or implied, not specified herein.

In Lufty v. R. D. Roper & Sons Motor Co., 57 Ariz. 495, 506, 115 P.2d 161, 166 (1941), the Arizona Supreme Court considered a similar clause in an agreement and concluded that "any provision in a contract making it possible for a party thereto to free himself from the consequences of his own fraud in procuring its execution is invalid and necessarily constitutes no defense." The court went on to hold that "parol evidence is always admissible to show fraud, and this is true, even though it has the effect of varying the terms of a writing between the parties." 57 Ariz. at 506-507, 115 P.2d at 166; Barnes v. Lopez, 25 Ariz. App. 477, 480, 544 P.2d 694, 697 (1976). In this case, the claimed misrepresentation occurred after the parties executed the contract.[1] Assuming, for the purposes of this decision, that the integration clause would extend

---

1. Buyers' fraud theory is apparently based on the premise that they were not bound under the contract until a satisfactory termite inspection report was submitted.

to statements made subsequent to the execution of the contract, the clause could not shield sellers from liability should buyers be able to prove fraud.

III. Duty to Disclose

The principal legal question presented in this appeal is whether a seller has a duty to disclose to the buyer the existence of termite damage in a residential dwelling known to the seller, but not to the buyer, which materially affects the value of the property. For the reasons stated herein, we hold that such a duty exists.

This is not the place to trace the history of the doctrine of caveat emptor. Suffice it to say that its vitality has waned during the latter half of the 20th century. E.g., Richards v. Powercraft Homes, Inc., 139 Ariz. 242, 678 P.2d 427 (1984) (implied warranty of workmanship and habitability extends to subsequent buyers of homes); see generally Quashnock v. Frost, 299 Pa. Super. 9, 445 A.2d 121 (1982); Ollerman v. O'Rourke Co., 94 Wis. 2d 17, 288 N.W.2d 95 (1980). The modern view is that a vendor has an affirmative duty to disclose material facts where:

> 1. Disclosure is necessary to prevent a previous assertion from being a misrepresentation or from being fraudulent or material;
> 2. Disclosure would correct a mistake of the other party as to a basic assumption on which that party is making the contract and if nondisclosure amounts to a failure to act in good faith and in accordance with reasonable standards of fair dealing;
> 3. Disclosure would correct a mistake of the other party as to the contents or effect of a writing, evidencing or embodying an agreement in whole or in part;
> 4. The other person is entitled to know the fact because of a relationship of trust and confidence between them.

Restatement (Second) of Contracts §161 (1981) (Restatement); see Restatement (Second) of Torts §551 (1977).

Arizona courts have long recognized that under certain circumstances there may be a "duty to speak." Van Buren v. Pima Community College Dist. Bd., 113 Ariz. 85, 87, 546 P.2d 821, 823 (1976); Batty v. Arizona State Dental Bd., 57 Ariz. 239, 254, 112 P.2d 870, 877 (1941). As the supreme court noted in the context of a confidential relationship, "[s]uppression of a material fact which a party is bound in good faith to disclose is equivalent to a false representation." Leigh v. Loyd, 74 Ariz. 84, 87, 244 P.2d 356, 358 (1952); National Housing Indus. Inc. v. E. L. Jones Dev. Co., 118 Ariz. 374, 379, 576 P.2d 1374, 1379 (1978).

Thus, the important question we must answer is whether under the facts of this case, buyers should have been permitted to present to the jury their claim that sellers were under a duty to disclose their (sellers') knowledge of termite infestation in the residence. This broader question involves two inquiries. First, must a seller of residential property advise the buyer of material facts within his knowledge pertaining to the value of the property? Second, may termite damage and the existence of past infestation constitute such material facts?

The doctrine imposing a duty to disclose is akin to the well-established contractual rules pertaining to relief from contracts based upon mistake. Although the law of contracts supports the finality of transactions, over the years courts have recognized that under certain limited circumstances it is unjust to strictly enforce the policy favoring finality. Thus, for example, even a unilateral mistake of one party to a transaction may justify rescission. Restatement §153.

There is also a judicial policy promoting honesty and fair dealing in business relationships. This policy is expressed in the law of fraudulent and negligent misrepresentations. Where a misrepresentation is fraudulent or where a negligent misrepresentation is one of material fact, the policy of finality rightly gives way to the policy of promoting honest dealings between the parties. See Restatement §164(1).

Under certain circumstances nondisclosure of a fact known to one party may be equivalent to the assertion that the fact does not exist. For example "[w]hen one conveys a false impression by the disclosure of some facts and the concealment of others, such concealment is in effect a false representation that what is disclosed is the whole truth." State v. Coddington, 135 Ariz. 480, 481, 662 P.2d 155, 156 (App. 1983). Thus, nondisclosure may be equated with and given the same legal effect as fraud and misrepresentation. One category of cases where this has been done involves the area of nondisclosure of material facts affecting the value of property, known to the seller but not reasonably capable of being known to the buyer.

Courts have formulated this "duty to disclose" in slightly different ways. For example, the Florida Supreme Court recently declared that "where the seller of a home knows of facts materially affecting the value of the property which are not readily observable and are not known to the buyer, the seller is under a duty to disclose them to the buyer." Johnson v. Davis, 480 So. 2d 625, 629 (Fla. 1985) (defective roof in three-year old home). In California, the rule has been stated this way:

> [W]here the seller knows of facts materially affecting the value or desirability of the property which are known or accessible only to him and also knows that such facts are not known to, or within the reach of the diligent attention and observation of the buyer, the seller is under a duty to disclose them to the buyer.

Lingsch v. Savage, 213 Cal. App. 2d 729, 735, 29 Cal. Rptr. 201, 204 (1963); contra Ray v. Montgomery, 399 So. 2d 230 (Ala. 1980); see generally W. Prosser & W. Keeton, The Law of Torts §106 (5th ed. 1984).[2] We find that the Florida formulation of the disclosure rule properly balances the legitimate interests of the parties in a transaction for the sale of a private residence and accordingly adopt it for such cases.

As can be seen, the rule requiring disclosure is invoked in the case of material facts.[3] Thus, we are led to the second inquiry — whether the existence

2. There are variations on this same theme. For example, Pennsylvania has limited the obligation of disclosure to cases of dangerous defects. Glanski v. Ervine, 269 Pa. Super. 182, 191, 409 A.2d 425, 430 (1979).

3. Arizona has recognized that a duty to disclose may arise where the buyer makes an inquiry of the seller, regardless of whether or not the fact is material. Universal Inv. Co. v. Sahara Motor Inn, Inc., 127 Ariz. 213, 215, 619 P.2d 485, 487 (1980). The inquiry by buyers whether the ripple was termite damage imposed a duty upon sellers to disclose what information they knew concerning the existence of termite infestation in the residence.

of termite damage in a residential dwelling is the type of material fact which gives rise to the duty to disclose. The existence of termite damage and past termite infestation has been considered by other courts to be sufficiently material to warrant disclosure. See generally Annotation, 22 A.L.R.3d 972 (1968).

In Lynn v. Taylor, 7 Kan. App. 2d 369, 642 P.2d 131 (1982), the purchaser of a termite-damaged residence brought suit against the seller and realtor for fraud and against the termite inspector for negligence. An initial termite report found evidence of prior termite infestation and recommended treatment. A second report indicated that the house was termite free. The first report was not given to the buyer. The seller contended that because treatment would not have repaired the existing damage, the first report was not material. The buyer testified that he would not have purchased the house had he known of the first report. Under these circumstances, the court concluded that the facts contained in the first report were material. See Hunt v. Walker, 483 S.W.2d 732 (Tenn. App. 1971) (severe damage to the residence by past termite infestation); Mercer v. Woodard, 166 Ga. App. 119, 123, 303 S.E.2d 475, 481-82 (1983) (duty of disclosure extends to fact of past termite damage).

Although sellers have attempted to draw a distinction between live termites[4] and past infestation, the concept of materiality is an elastic one which is not limited by the termites' health. "A matter is material if it is one to which a reasonable person would attach importance in determining his choice of action in the transaction in question." Lynn v. Taylor, 7 Kan. App. 2d at 371, 642 P.2d at 134-35. For example, termite damage substantially affecting the structural soundness of the residence may be material even if there is no evidence of present infestation. Unless reasonable minds could not differ, materiality is a factual matter which must be determined by the trier of fact. The termite damage in this case may or may not be material. Accordingly, we conclude that buyers should be allowed to present their case to a jury.

Sellers argue that even assuming the existence of a duty to disclose, summary judgment was proper because the record shows that their "silence . . . did not induce or influence" the buyers. This is so, sellers contend, because Mr. Hill stated in his deposition that he intended to rely on the termite inspection report. But this argument begs the question. If sellers were fully aware of the extent of termite damage and if such information had been disclosed to buyers, a jury could accept Mr. Hill's testimony that had he known of the termite damage he would not have purchased the house.

Sellers further contend that buyers were put on notice of the possible existence of termite infestation and were therefore "chargeable with the knowledge which [an] inquiry, if made, would have revealed." Godfrey v. Navratil, 3 Ariz. App. 47, 51, 411 P.2d 470 (1966) (quoting Luke v. Smith, 13 Ariz. 155, 162, 108 P. 494, 496 (1910)). It is also true that "a party may . . . reasonably expect the other to take normal steps to inform himself and to draw his own conclusions." Restatement §161, comment *d*. Under the facts of this case, the question of buyers' knowledge of the termite problem (or their

---

4. Sellers acknowledge that a duty of disclosure would exist if live termites were present. Obde v. Schlemeyer, 56 Wash. 2d 449, 353 P.2d 672 (1960).

diligence in attempting to inform themselves about the termite problem) should be left to the jury.[5]

By virtue of our holding, sellers' cross-appeal is moot. Reversed and remanded.

CONTRERAS, P.J., and YALE MCFATE, J. (Retired), concur.

Notes and Questions

1. *Historical perspective: **Laidlaw v. Organ**.* The classical view was that a party to a business transaction could not avoid the transaction because of nondisclosure of material information by the other party. Reflecting the ethic of individualism, courts required a party to protect his own interests by requesting information from the other party or by making an adequate investigation before entering into a transaction. Perhaps the leading example of the nineteenth century approach is Laidlaw v. Organ, 15 U.S. (2 Wheat) 178 (1817). In *Laidlaw* the plaintiff buyer alleged a wrongful refusal by the defendant seller to deliver a quantity of tobacco pursuant to a contract of purchase. The defendant claimed it was privileged to avoid the contract on the ground of fraud by the buyer. The contract was made in New Orleans, at a time when news of the Treaty of Ghent, ending the war with Britain, had not yet reached that city. The buyer's agent was aware of the ending of the war; the seller's agent was not. And when the seller's agent asked if there was any news "calculated to enhance the price or value" of the tobacco, the buyer's agent remained silent, despite the fact that the ending of the war could increase the market value of the tobacco by as much as 50 percent. The judge at trial refused to allow a defense of fraud into the case and directed a verdict for the buyer. On appeal, the Supreme Court reversed and sent the case back for retrial on the issue of whether the buyer had committed actual fraud. The Court, however, agreed with the buyer's argument that liability could not be based on the buyer's failure to disclose any special knowledge it may have had about the end of the war.

> Even if the vendor had been entitled to the disclosure, he waived it by not insisting on an answer to his question; and the silence of the vendee might as well have been interpreted into an affirmative as a negative answer. But, on principle, he was not bound to disclose. . . . There was, in the present case, no circumvention or manoeuvre practiced by the vendee, unless rising earlier in the morning, and obtaining by superior diligence and alertness that intelligence by which the price of commodities was regulated, be such. . . . [I]t would be difficult to circumscribe the contrary doctrine within proper limits, where the means of intelligence are equally accessible to both parties.

Id. at 193-195. For background on the case and its place in early nineteenth century contract law see M. H. Hoeflich, *Laidlaw v. Organ* (15 U.S. 84), Gulian

---

5. Sellers also contend that they had no knowledge of any existing termite damage in the house. An extended discussion of the facts on this point is unnecessary. Simply stated, the facts are in conflict on this issue.

C. Verplanck, and the Shaping of Early Nineteenth Century Contract Law: A Tale of a Case and a Commentary, 1991 U. Ill. L. Rev. 55. Are there any material differences — other than the obvious one of time — that distinguish *Hill* from *Laidlaw*?

2. *Modern approach to nondisclosure.* The facts in the *Hill* case raise the possibilities of actual fraud (as in the *Syester* case), fraud through concealment by taking steps to prevent another party from learning a fact (Restatement (Second) §160), and nondisclosure. The modern view is that in some situations a failure to disclose a material fact may justify rescission of a contract. Restatement (Second) §161. While Restatement §161(a), (c), and (d) provide for rescission because of nondisclosure only in limited situations, §161(b) states a broader basis for relief: when the nondisclosure amounts to a failure to act in accordance with standards of good faith and fair dealing. When should this provision be applied? Professor Page Keeton has suggested several factors that a court should consider in deciding when fairness requires disclosure of material information:

> (1) The difference in the degree of intelligence of the parties to the transaction. This is simply because the community sense of justice demands it;
>
> (2) The relation that the parties bear to each other;
>
> (3) The manner in which the information is acquired. Information which affects the value of the subject matter of a contract may have been acquired by chance, by effort, or by an illegal act. It makes a difference on the ethical quality of non-disclosure;
>
> (4) The nature of the fact not disclosed. In contracts of sale of real property, if the vendor conceals an intrinsic defect not discoverable by reasonable care, there is a much greater likelihood of the existence of a duty to disclose the non-discoverable and intrinsic defect than there would be to disclose something extrinsic likely to affect market value;
>
> (5) The general class to which the person who is concealing the information belongs. It is much more likely that a seller will be required to disclose information than a purchaser;
>
> (6) The nature of the contract itself. In releases, and contracts of insurance, practically all material facts must be disclosed;
>
> (7) The importance of the fact not disclosed;
>
> (8) Any conduct of the person not disclosing something to prevent discovery. The active concealment of any material fact — anything that might prevent the purchaser from buying at the price agreed on is, and should be, as a matter of law fraudulent.

W. Page Keeton et al., Prosser and Keeton on the Law of Torts §106, at 739 (5th ed. 1984), summarizing factors set forth in W. Page Keeton, Fraud — Concealment and Non-disclosure, 15 Tex. L. Rev. 1 (1936). Compare Saxon Mortgage, Inc. v. Mortgage Plus, Inc., 130 F.Supp.2d 1236 (D. Kan. 2001) (mortgage originator breached duty to disclose by failing to inform purchaser of mortgages that the loans had erroneous appraisals, forged papers, and early defaults), and Carpenter v. Carpenter, 449 S.E.2d 502 (Va. Ct. App. 1994) (parties to prenuptial agreement have duty to make full and frank disclosure of facts involving affected property rights), with AKA Distributing Co. v. Whirlpool Corp., 137 F.3d 1083 (8th Cir. 1997) (manufacturer had no duty to disclose to "arms length" distributors that it planned to seek private label contract to sell line of vacuum cleaners that distributors helped design), and Mallen v. Mallen, 622 S.E.2d 812 (Ga. 2005) (while acknowledging that majority of jurisdictions recognize special relationship between engaged parties, court rejects that view and holds that husband did not have duty to make full disclosure of his financial circumstances; wife should have verified husband's statements).

3. *Economic analysis of nondisclosure.* An article by Professor Anthony Kronman presents an economic analysis of the duty of disclosure. Professor Kronman argues that courts should draw a distinction between information that has been casually acquired and information obtained through a deliberate and costly investigation. Disclosure of deliberately acquired information should not be required, he contends, because it is socially desirable to give parties an incentive to acquire information. Nondisclosure protects a party's investment in the acquisition of such information. (Kronman points out that a rule permitting nondisclosure amounts to a legal recognition of a property right in the information.) Casually acquired information, on the other hand, does not reflect an investment of resources. Kronman argues that disclosure of such information should be required when the holder knows that the other party is without such information, because disclosure is the least costly method of reducing mistaken contracts. Anthony T. Kronman, Mistake, Disclosure, Information and the Law of Contracts, 7 J. Legal Stud. 1, 16-18 (1978). Compare Robert L. Birmingham, The Duty to Disclose and the Prisoner's Dilemma: *Laidlaw v. Organ*, 29 Wm. & Mary L. Rev. 249 (1988) (criticism of Kronman's economic analysis of the duty of disclosure). Would Professor Keeton's analysis justify imposing a duty of disclosure in the *Hill* case? What about Professor Kronman's approach? Which approach do you find more persuasive? Why?

4. *Real estate disclosure statutes and common law actions.* The *Hill* case apparently did not involve an increasingly common requirement in transfers of existing residential real estate: the mandatory seller's disclosure form. A clear majority of states have adopted statutory law that supplements or perhaps displaces common law requirements for disclosure. See Stephanie Stern, Temporal Dynamics of Disclosure: The Example of Residential Real Estate Conveyancing, 2005 Utah L. Rev. 57, 60-64. For example, the Iowa Real Estate Disclosure Act, Iowa Code §558A.1 et seq. (1997), requires transferors of real estate to provide a written disclosure statement. Section 558A.3 of the Iowa Code states that "[a]ll information required by this section and rules adopted by the state real estate commission shall be disclosed in good faith" and Section 558A.4 further provides that, "the disclosure statement shall include information relating to the condition and important characteristics of the property and structures located on the property, including significant defects in the structural integrity of the structure . . ." A person who violates the Iowa Act's disclosure requirement is ordinarily liable for the amount of actual damage the buyer suffers but the Act states "the transferor . . . shall not be liable for [any] error, inaccuracy, or omission in information required in a disclosure statement, unless that person has actual knowledge of the inaccuracy, or fails to exercise ordinary care in obtaining the information." Id. §558A.6. Thus, a seller can be liable under the statute even in the absence of actual fraud by failing to exercise ordinary care. See Jensen v. Sattler, 696 N.W.2d 582, 586-587 (Iowa 2005). On the other hand,

the disclosure laws commonly limit the transferor's liability to actual damages or termination of an offer, except if there is willful failure to deliver the disclosures, in which case treble damages may be available. See Stephanie Stern, Temporal Dynamics of Disclosure: The Example of Residential Real Estate Conveyancing, 2005 Utah L. Rev. 57, 63-64.

5. *Innocent or negligent nondisclosure.* In *Hill* the sellers knew that the property had been infested with termites, so their concealment of that fact can be characterized as intentional. Should rescission be available for negligent or even innocent nondisclosure? Several courts have indicated that a party who seeks rescission because of nondisclosure must show actual knowledge by the other party of the undisclosed fact. See San Diego Hospice v. County of San Diego, 37 Cal. Rptr. 2d 501 (Ct. App. 1995) (seller of land could not have committed fraudulent nondisclosure regarding underground tank when seller had no actual knowledge of the tank's existence); Weintraub v. Krobatsch, 317 A.2d 68 (N.J. 1974) (seller failed to disclose severe cockroach infestation; case remanded for trial on several issues, including whether seller deliberately failed to make disclosure because of fear of losing the sale). Under Restatement (Second) §161, may either a negligent or innocent nondisclosure be the basis for rescission? Do you agree with this approach? Why?

6. *Tort liability for nondisclosure. Hill* involves a claim for rescission rather than damages in tort. Could the plaintiffs have recovered in a tort action for damages? The Restatement (Second) of Torts §551 provides that nondisclosure will give rise to liability if the party is "under a duty to the other to exercise reasonable care to disclose the matter in question" and then indicates that the duty arises in a number of situations including when there is a fiduciary or similar relationship, when partial or earlier disclosures would be misleading, and when the other party would reasonably expect disclosure of facts that are basic to the transaction. See also Pearson v. Simmonds Precision Products, Inc., 624 A.2d 1134 (Vt. 1993) (employer liable in tort for negligent failure to disclose that there was a "good chance" that newly recruited employee's position might be terminated). But cf. Underwood v. Risman, 605 N.E.2d 832 (Mass. 1993) (landlord could not be liable in tort for failure to disclose presence of lead-based paint that landlord did not know about; duty of disclosure necessarily implies that fact is known to person expected to disclose it). Is tort liability for nondisclosure more difficult to establish than a right to rescind? Why?

7. *Effect of disclaimer or merger clause.* The court in *Hill* ruled that the contract integration clause did not bar the purchasers' action to rescind the contract on the basis of fraud because "any provision in a contract making it possible for a party thereto to free himself from the consequences of his own fraud in procuring its execution is invalid and necessarily constitutes no defense." The maxim that "fraud vitiates every transaction" has long been part of the common law, e.g., Sabo v. Delman, 143 N.E.2d 906 (N.Y. 1957) (clause in patent assignment agreement disclaiming all verbal representations was ineffective to bar claim to rescind contract due to fraud). However, in the landmark case of Danann Realty Corp. v. Harris, 157 N.E.2d 597 (N.Y. 1959), decided just two years after *Sabo*, the New York Court of Appeals held that when a contract contains a "specific" disclaimer of representations (as opposed to a "general and vague merger clause"), a tort action for fraud will not

lie because the clause shows a lack of justified reliance on any oral representations. In that case a buyer of a leasehold interest in a building brought suit against the seller for damages, alleging that the seller made oral misrepresentations about the expenses and profits of the building, but the contract contained a clause stating that the seller made no representations about expenses or profits. In a vigorous dissent, Judge Fuld argued that the clause in question was not a "specific" disclaimer at all, but a typical general renunciation of any responsibility for oral statements, and that the majority had effectively allowed a party to engage in fraud so long as the contract was carefully drafted. Subsequent courts in New York have continued to apply the *Danann Realty* distinction based on whether a disclaimer is general or specific in nature. Compare Greenfield v. Shapiro, 106 F. Supp. 2d 535 (S.D.N.Y. 2000) (well-settled New York law that a general merger clause will not bar a claim of fraud in action to rescind contract), with Masters v. Visual Building Inspections, Inc., 643 N.Y.S.2d 599 (App. Div. 1996) (specific disclaimer and merger clauses were effective to bar claim of fraud). Do you agree that a "specific" disclaimer should bar a tort action for damages for fraud but not an action to rescind? Why?

Suppose the misrepresentation was made innocently or negligently, rather than knowingly or intentionally. Should a disclaimer be effective in such a case? Compare Wilkinson v. Carpenter, 554 P.2d 512 (Or. 1976) (disclaimer would be effective when alleged misrepresentation was innocent and not intentional), with Bank of Montreal v. Signet Bank, 193 F.3d 818 (4th Cir. 1999) (disclaiming language in contract would not bar claim of intentional, reckless, or even innocent misrepresentation; false representation of material fact is always ground for rescission or action for damages).

8. *Effect of fiduciary relationship.* In Hill v. Jones we saw that under some circumstances a party to a business transaction has a duty to disclose material facts to the other party. More specifically, this duty may arise "because of a relationship of trust and confidence." Restatement (Second) §161(d). Such an association is often called a "fiduciary" relationship and a greater duty is imposed between two contracting parties. See E. Allan Farnsworth, Contracts §4.27, at 297-298 (4th ed. 2004). When a fiduciary relationship exists, not only does this duty of disclosure apply, but the law also imposes additional obligations on the fiduciary: The terms of the transaction must be fair and must be fully explained to the other party. Restatement (Second) §173. Moreover, the fiduciary has the burden of proving compliance with her legal obligations by clear and convincing evidence. See Miller v. Sears, 636 P.2d 1183 (Alaska 1981) (contract for sale of property subject to rescission by client because attorney failed to establish that he had fully disclosed all material terms to client; attorney has burden of proving compliance with fiduciary duties by clear and convincing evidence). What is the justification for these stringent requirements?

Historically, certain relationships — lawyer and client, trustee and beneficiary — have been treated as fiduciary in character. In addition, a fiduciary relationship can exist when one party reposes trust and confidence in another party who, in turn, accepts and fosters the relationship. See, e.g., Lynch v. Cruttenden & Co., 22 Cal. Rptr. 2d 636 (Ct. App. 1993) (fiduciary relationship sufficiently pled based on allegations that broker induced confidence of plaintiffs through close friendship and representation that he was expert in investments); Liebergesell v. Evans, 613 P.2d 1170 (Wash. 1980) (en banc) (financially inexperienced school teacher proved fiduciary relationship with acquaintances to whom loan was made based on confidential relationship, even though not fitting within a classic category of fiduciary relations). Mere friendship standing alone, however, is not sufficient to establish a fiduciary relationship. See Lefkowitz v. Smith Barney, Harris Upham & Co., 804 F.2d 154 (1st Cir. 1986) (allegations of an individual's minimal knowledge of his investments and his reliance on account executive as long-standing personal friend to guide him in business matters were insufficient to establish fiduciary relationship).

9. *Attorney discipline for breach of fiduciary duty.* If a lawyer violates fiduciary duties to a client, the lawyer may be subject to professional discipline as well as liability in either contract or tort. See, e.g., In re James, 452 A.2d 163 (D.C. 1982). In *James* a lawyer purchased a building from his clients. The agreement of purchase provided that on resale by the lawyer, the proceeds would be divided equally between the lawyer and the clients. The agreement, however, did not require the lawyer to sell the property; it also failed to state whether the clients were entitled to any of the rental from the building during the lawyer's ownership. While the lawyer discussed the agreement with his clients for "about an hour," he was found guilty of professional misconduct by failing to make a full disclosure to his clients of the risks and disadvantages of the transaction. See also Beery v. State Bar of California, 739 P.2d 1289 (Cal. 1987) (lawyer disciplined for advising client to invest in financially troubled business in which lawyer held an interest and without advising client to seek independent counsel); In the Matter of Humen, 586 A.2d 237 (N.J. 1991) (lawyer disciplined for advising client to borrow money unnecessarily to purchase home and then providing mortgage without disclosing to client that attorney was the mortgagee; court has repeatedly warned lawyers about dangers of engaging in business with clients). The following Comment discusses ethical obligations of lawyers in more detail.

Comment: Lawyers' Professional Ethics

In each state, the admission of lawyers to the practice of law and the responsibility for their discipline once admitted rest with the highest court of that state. While the rules and procedures vary in different jurisdictions, typically the highest state court (or some board created by the court and acting pursuant to its authority) has promulgated a set of rules of professional conduct. These rules are usually based on Model Rules of Professional Conduct, originally adopted by the American Bar Association in 1983 and revised in 2002.[1] The American Bar Association, a private association of lawyers, has no legal authority over the practice of law but is extremely influential in the area of professional ethics by virtue of its studies and

---

1. Some states still adhere to the Code of Professional Responsibility, the predecessor to the Model Rules of Professional Conduct.

publications. Rules of professional ethics impose restrictions on the conduct of lawyers principally in three areas: (1) the lawyer-client relationship, (2) the lawyer's obligations to the system of justice, and (3) permissible methods of obtaining legal business.

A number of the most important rules of professional ethics focus on the lawyer-client relationship. Generally, these rules reflect three cardinal principles: loyalty, competence, and confidentiality. The duty of loyalty, of course, extends to the avoidance of any conflict of interest arising from the attorney's representation of clients with interests adverse to each other. Thus, a lawyer must refuse to represent multiple clients if a conflict of interest exists between those clients (a husband and wife in a contested divorce case, for example). Model Rule (MR) 1.7. The duty of loyalty also extends to avoidance of a conflict between the clients' interests and those of the attorney. For this reason, a lawyer must protect and account for any client money or property that comes into the lawyer's possession. Further, the lawyer must maintain any client money in a separate "trust account" and not "commingle" client funds with funds belonging to the lawyer. MR 1.15. A lawyer must not violate his obligations as a fiduciary to his client by entering into a business transaction with the client unless the transaction meets a number of requirements, including fairness and full disclosure. MR 1.8(a).

In his representation of a client, a lawyer must handle the matter competently. MR 1.1. A failure to act competently may result in tort liability for malpractice as well as professional discipline. See, e.g., Sierra Fria Corp. v. Evans, 127 F.3d 175 (1st Cir. 1997) (attorney must exercise reasonable care and skill in matter for which attorney was retained); Horne v. Peckham, 158 Cal. Rptr. 714 (Ct. App. 1979) (lawyer who is not a specialist in tax law has a duty either to refer tax matters to a specialist or to conform to the standard expected of a specialist). Finally, subject to certain exceptions, a lawyer must not reveal any confidential information received from a client. MR 1.6.

While the lawyer's relationship with his client is central to his role, lawyers are also officers of the court and as such have obligations to the system of justice. A lawyer must not engage in fraud, deceit, or misrepresentation in his representation of a client. MR 8.4(c). Lawyers are generally required to report professional misconduct by other lawyers to the appropriate disciplinary authorities. MR 8.3. To protect the impartiality of decisionmakers, rules of professional ethics prohibit lawyers from having improper contacts with either judges or jurors. MR 3.5. At times the lawyer's duty to the system of justice may even override the lawyer's duty to his client. Thus, sometimes a lawyer must reveal legal authority that is damaging to his client's case, even though opposing counsel has failed to find the authority. MR 3.3(a)(2). In some situations a lawyer may even be required to reveal confidential information received from a client in order to rectify fraud committed by the client or another person. MR 1.6, 3.3. See Nix v. Whiteside, 475 U.S. 157 (1986) (defendant in criminal case not denied constitutional right to effective assistance of counsel when lawyer informed client that he would report client's intention to commit perjury to the court).

Finally, a number of rules of professional ethics impose restrictions on the ways in which lawyers may obtain business. Traditionally, the legal profession has considered professional advertising or solicitation as ethically improper. In 1976 the United States Supreme Court ushered in a period of dramatic change in the rules dealing with delivery of legal services when it held that advertising of the price and availability of routine legal services (uncontested divorces, for example) was protected under the first amendment and could not be prohibited by rules of professional conduct. Bates & O'Steen v. State Bar, 433 U.S. 350 (1977). Since then, the Court has decided a number of cases that have expanded the first amendment protection for lawyer advertising. A review of such cases can be found in Florida Bar v. Went For It, Inc., 515 U.S. 618 (1995) (holding by 5-4 decision that state could ban attorneys from sending direct-mail solicitations to disaster victims or relatives for 30 days after incident). Because of these cases, the rules of ethics dealing with advertising have been liberalized, although restrictions remain in a number of states. MR 7.1, 7.2, 7.3. Regulation of advertising and solicitation by attorneys will undoubtedly remain a subject of debate and litigation for years to come.

Park 100 Investors, Inc., vs. Kartes
Indiana Court of Appeals
650 N.E.2d 347 (1995)

OPINION
BARTEAU, Judge.

Park 100 appeals the trial court's finding that James and Nancy Kartes are not liable for unpaid rent under a personal guaranty of lease. We affirm.

FACTS

In 1984, James and Nancy Kartes were part-owners of Kartes Video Communications, Inc. (KVC) in Indianapolis. The company was growing rapidly and required larger operating facilities. Robert Scannell, a representative of the Park 100 industrial complex in Indianapolis, contacted the Karteses and marketed facilities in Park 100 that KVC could lease. After discussing the general requirements and terms for the new facilities, James Kartes delegated all of the lease negotiations to David Kaplan, a KVC senior vice-president.

Kaplan and Scannell worked out the details for KVC's lease of Building 107 in Park 100. Park 100 provided a lease agreement form to KVC. The lease did not include any provisions for a personal guaranty of the lease and a personal guaranty was never mentioned during any of the lease negotiations. KVC's attorney approved the lease and Kaplan signed and delivered the lease to Scannell on or before July 27, 1984. KVC made preparations to move its operations into Building 107 over the weekend of July 28-29, 1984.

On Friday, July 27, 1984, the evening before KVC was to move into Building 107, Scannell went to KVC's offices at 5:00 p.m. and found the Karteses getting into their car to leave for the day. Scannell told the Karteses that he had "lease papers" for them to sign. James Kartes explained that they were late for their daughter's wedding rehearsal and asked if the matter could wait until the following Monday. Scannell informed the Karteses that the matter could not wait and that KVC could not move into Building 107 until the papers were signed.

The Karteses and Scannell then went into KVC's building, where Scannell produced a document entitled "Lease Agreement."[1] From the lobby of the building, James Kartes telephoned Kaplan, who was in another part of the building, and asked if the lease agreement had been approved by KVC's lawyer. Scannell remained silent. Upon ending his discussion with Kaplan, James Kartes asked where he was to sign the document. Scannell opened the papers to the signature page and the Karteses both signed the document. The Karteses, being officers of the corporation, did not think it unusual that their signatures would be required on the lease. Scannell never told the Karteses that what they were signing was actually a personal guaranty of lease.

Years later, Park 100 sent the Karteses a "Tenant Agreement" that included an estoppel certificate. At this time the Karteses first learned of the personal guaranty of lease. They immediately disavowed the guaranty and refused to affirm that portion of the "Tenant Agreement."

Eventually, the Kartes sold their interest in KVC to Saffron Associates, which subsequently failed to make rent payments to Park 100. Park 100 brought suit to collect the unpaid rent from the Karteses under the personal guaranty.

ISSUES

Park 100 raises numerous issues and arguments on appeal. We find that one issue is dispositive of this matter: whether the trial court erred in finding that Park 100 used fraudulent means to procure the signatures of the Karteses on the guaranty of lease.

DISCUSSION

Upon the motion of Park 100, the trial court entered thorough and well-reasoned Findings of Facts and Conclusions of Law. When the trial court enters special Findings of Fact and Conclusions of Law pursuant to a motion by a party, this court employs a two-tiered standard of review. First, we must determine whether the findings support the judgment. The second inquiry is whether the conclusions and judgment are clearly erroneous based on the facts as found by the trial court. American Cyanamid Co. v. Stephen (1993), Ind. App., 623 N.E.2d 1065, 1070.

The trial court found that Park 100 obtained the signatures of the Karteses on the personal guaranty of lease through fraudulent means. Under Indiana law, the elements of actual fraud are as follows:

---

1. The parties dispute the size of the document Scannell presented to the Karteses. Mr. Kartes testified that the document included approximately fifteen pages, while Scannell maintained that he only presented the two-page guaranty of lease to the Kartes. Combined, the lease agreement and guaranty total 17 pages. The trial court specifically found that Mr. Kartes's testimony was clear, complete, and highly credible, whereas Scannell's testimony was sketchy, inconsistent at best, and far less credible than Mr. Kartes's testimony.

(1) A material misrepresentation of past or existing fact by the party to be charged, which
(2) was false,
(3) was made with knowledge or in reckless ignorance of the falsity,
(4) was relied upon by the complaining party, and
(5) proximately caused the complaining party injury.

Pugh's IGA v. Super Food Services, Inc. (1988), Ind.App., 531 N.E.2d 1194, 1197, reh'g denied, trans. denied. In its findings and conclusions, the trial court found: (1) The statements made by Scannell, Park 100's agent, that the personal guaranty was "lease papers" and that KVC could not move into the building until the papers were signed, were each misrepresentations of material facts; (2) Scannell knew that the document he presented for the Karteses' signatures was a guaranty and, therefore, knowingly made false misrepresentations; and (3) the Karteses, through the use of ordinary care and diligence, believed that the document they were signing was a lease, and reasonably relied upon Scannell's statements to their detriment.

The evidence and testimony presented at trial supports these findings and conclusions. A guaranty of lease was never discussed during the lease negotiations, and the lease agreement makes no reference to a guaranty. The document that Scannell presented to the Karteses was entitled "Lease Agreement" and Scannell never told the Karteses that they were signing a personal guaranty of lease, even when he overheard the telephone conversation in which Mr. Kartes asked Kaplan if the lease agreement had been approved by KVC's lawyer.[3]

Park 100 argues that the Karteses failed to prove the third element of actual fraud, that of reliance. Park 100 summarily argues that one's reliance upon a material misrepresentation must be justified and, in an arm's-length relationship involving knowledgeable business people such as the Karteses, such reliance is misplaced. Park 100 concludes that the Karteses had a duty to read the document that they signed and cannot avoid their obligations under the agreement by claiming ignorance of its terms.

Generally, parties are obligated to know the terms of the agreement they are signing, and cannot avoid their obligations under the agreement due to a failure to read it. W.T. Rawleigh Co. v. Snider (1935), 207 Ind. 686, 690, 194 N.E. 356, 358; Givan v. Masterson (1898), 152 Ind. 127, 130, 51 N.E. 237, 238. However, where one employs misrepresentation to induce a party's obligation under a contract, one cannot bind the party to the terms of the agreement.

It has many times been held, and is a well-settled rule of law, that a contract of guaranty cannot be enforced by the guarantee, where the guarantor has been

---

3. The trial court also found that Scannell had a duty to inform the Karteses that the document was a guaranty and not a lease, and that his silence was a fraudulent omission of a material fact. Park 100 argues that Scannell had no such duty and that the trial court erred on this point. We need not address this argument because Scannell's express misrepresentations alone support the finding of actual fraud. But see, Midwest Commerce Banking Co. v. Elkhart City Centre (7th Cir. 1993), 4 F.3d 521, 524 and cases cited therein.

induced to enter into the contract by fraudulent misrepresentations or concealment on the part of the guarantee.

Doerr v. Hibben Hollweg & Co. (1926), 84 Ind. App. 239, 241-42, 150 N.E. 795, 796.

Scannell misrepresented the personal guaranty as "lease papers," and in furtherance of this misrepresentation, the personal guaranty was disguised under the title of "Lease Agreement." We are not persuaded by Park 100's argument that the Karteses cannot prove actual fraud because the Karteses should have known better than to rely on Scannell's representations.

"Whether one has the right to rely depends largely on the facts of the case." Fire Ins. Exchange v. Bell (1994), Ind. App., 634 N.E.2d 517, 522, aff'd in part, vacated in part, 643 N.E.2d 310. When Scannell presented the "lease papers," Mr. Kartes telephoned Kaplan. Only upon confirming that KVC's attorney had examined and approved the lease agreement did the Karteses affix their signatures to the document entitled "Lease Agreement." "While a person relying on another's representations must use ordinary care and diligence to guard against fraud, the requirement of reasonable prudence in business transactions is not carried to the extent that the law will ignore an intentional fraud practiced on the unwary." Fire Ins. Exchange, 634 N.E.2d at 521. The evidence supports the trial court's finding that the Karteses acted with ordinary care and diligence.

CONCLUSION

Whether fraud is present in a case is rooted in the surrounding facts and circumstances and is for the trial court to determine. A.G. Edwards & Sons, Inc. v. Hilligoss (1991), Ind. App., 597 N.E.2d 1, 3. We cannot reweigh the evidence and substitute our judgment for that of the trial court, as Park 100 invites us to do. Wolfeld v. Hanika (1932), 95 Ind. App. 44, 179 N.E. 178. The evidence supports the trial court's conclusion that Park 100 obtained the signatures of the Karteses on the personal guaranty of lease through fraudulent means, and the findings support the judgment. The trial court's conclusion and judgment in favor of James and Nancy Kartes are not clearly erroneous.

Affirmed.

RILEY, J. and SHARPNACK, C.J. concur.

Notes and Questions

1. *Fraud in the execution.* The *Park 100* case differs significantly from the two previous cases in this section. In both *Syester* and *Hill*, the party alleging fraud presumably understood the terms of the written contracts that they signed but alleged that they were fraudulently induced to enter the agreements by false statements or material nondisclosures. The Karteses, however, alleged that they were misled regarding the content of the document that they executed or signed. As to the latter type of fraud, Restatement (Second) §166 provides:

> If a party's manifestation of assent is induced by the other party's fraudulent misrepresentation as to the contents or effect of a writing evidencing or embodying in whole or in part an agreement, the court at the request of the recipient may reform the writing to express the terms of the agreement as asserted,
>
> (a) if the recipient was justified in relying on the misrepresentation, . . .

See, e.g., Rosenthal v. Great Western Fin. Securities Corp., 926 P.2d 1061, 1073 (Cal. 1996) (discussing difference between "fraud in the execution" where the party is deceived as to the nature of the writing and "fraud in the inducement" where the party knows what he is signing but does so as the result of misrepresentations). Recall, however, the Ray v. Eurice Brothers case from Chapter 2. Is the availability of relief for fraud in the execution consistent with the notion of a "duty to read" that normally binds parties to signed agreements whether the agreement is read or not?

2. *Hypothetical variations of **Park 100***. Consider whether any of the following changes in the facts might have had any effect on the outcome in *Park 100*, either separately or cumulatively:

(a) When Mr. Kartes phoned Kaplan, he was in a phone booth in the corner of the lobby, where his conversation could not be overheard by Scannell;

(b) Scannell did not claim that when he presented the papers to the Karteses for their signature that it was only a two-page document (see footnote 1 to the court's opinion), but asserted rather that the 15-page document he presented did in fact constitute "lease papers," just as he said it did;

(c) When the Karteses met Scannell in the lobby, they were not hurrying off to their daughter's wedding rehearsal but were headed home at the end of a long day to spend a quiet evening eating dinner and watching television;

(d) Scannell testified that in deals such as this one involving a small, closely held corporation, personal shareholder guarantees were so common that he truly regarded the added provision as a "formality."

D. UNCONSCIONABILITY

In civil law countries, the idea that a grossly unfair bargain should be unenforceable has a long history. Under Roman law, which greatly influenced the development of the civil law, the doctrine of "laesio enormis" provided that a party could rescind a land sale transaction if the disproportion between the values exchanged was greater than two to one. Modern civil law countries, such as Germany and France, recognize a number of doctrines that allow courts to refuse to enforce grossly unfair bargains. John P. Dawson, Duress and the Fair Exchange in French and German Law, 11 Tul. L. Rev. 345, 12 Tul. L. Rev. 42 (1937); John P. Dawson, Unconscionable Coercion: The

German Version, 89 Harv. L. Rev. 1041 (1976). A more recent assessment of French and German law indicates that such doctrines have been tempered on occasion by the desire for more certainty in contracts. See A. H. Angelo & E. P. Ellinger, Unconscionable Contracts: A Comparative Study of Approaches in England, France, Germany and the United States, 14 Loy. L.A. Intl. & Comp. L.J. 455 (1992). The law of Louisiana, which is based on the civil law, includes a concept of "abuse of rights." Glenda M. Redmann, Abuse of Rights: An Overview of the Historical Evolution and the Current Application in Louisiana Contracts, 32 Loy. L. Rev. 946 (1987).

Unlike the civil law, the Anglo-American common law did not develop an explicit doctrine for dealing with unfair bargains, but there were a number of grounds that the common law courts could use to avoid enforcing such agreements. In equity a court could deny specific performance or other equitable relief if the price was inadequate or if the one seeking relief had "unclean hands." See Emily L. Sherwin, Law and Equity in Contract Enforcement, 50 Md. L. Rev. 253 (1991). At law, a court could manipulate doctrines such as consideration, mutual assent, or principles of interpretation to find in favor of a party who was the victim of an unfair bargain. See Joseph M. Perillo, Calamari & Perillo on Contracts, §9.38, at 383-384 (5th ed. 2003).

During the first half of the twentieth century, economic and social changes made the problem of enforceability of unfair bargains more acute than at any previous time. Large commercial enterprises increasingly began using standard form contracts to conduct business transactions. The typical standard form contract contains numerous "boilerplate" provisions that are extremely favorable to the drafting party. Moreover, negotiation of such terms rarely occurs both because the terms are normally not read and also because the form is usually presented on a "take-it-or-leave-it" basis, as exemplified in the *C & J Fertilizer* case in Chapter 5. Thus, the emergence of the standard form brought into question the concept of mutual assent, a pillar of classical contract law. The same period also witnessed a growing public awareness of the problems of the poor and unsophisticated, potential victims for unscrupulous commercial parties.

One judicial tool that emerged for dealing with unfair contracts was the doctrine of "unconscionability," codified in UCC §2-302. Although §2-302 applies strictly only to contracts for the sale of goods, its formulation of the unconscionability standard has been incorporated in the Restatement (Second) §208 and has been regularly applied to all types of contracts. See E. Allan Farnsworth, Contracts §4.28, at 298-299 (4th ed. 2004). The section was drafted to address concerns that the practice of courts' distorting other doctrinal rules to police for unfairness would produce confusion and unpredictability or, as stated by Professor Karl Llewellyn, concern that "[c]overt tools are never reliable tools." Karl Llewellyn, Book Review, 52 Harv. L. Rev. 700, 703 (1939). Thus, §2-302 was designed to allow courts to examine contracts explicitly for bargaining unfairness.

In a seminal article on the doctrine, Professor Arthur Leff traced the drafting history of §2-302 and demonstrated that in its earliest draft the doctrine was intended to apply only to standard form contracts. In subsequent drafts, the scope and purpose of the section became increasingly vague. As a result, Leff argued, the drafters produced a section that was a pure abstraction, devoid of content. Arthur Allen Leff, Unconscionability and the Code — The Emperor's New Clause, 115 U. Pa. L. Rev. 485 (1967). Leff also predicted, however, that the courts would likely cure the faults in §2-302 by applying a "smoothing nacre of more or less reasonable applications." Id. at 558-559. Subsequent writers have concluded that the courts, in fact, have shown considerable restraint in applying the unconscionability doctrine. See, e.g., E. Allan Farnsworth, Developments in Contract Law During the 1980s: The Top Ten, 41 Case W. Res. L. Rev. 203 (1990) (describing unconscionability and related doctrines as an area of "arrested development"); Jeffrey L. Harrison, Class, Personality, Contract, and Unconscionability, 35 Wm. & Mary L. Rev. 445 (1994) (advocating a greater use of the unconscionability doctrine to limit unfair exchanges). During recent drafting of revisions to Article 2, the section on unconscionability was left essentially unchanged. See Carol B. Swanson, Unconscionable Quandary: UCC Article 2 and the Unconscionability Doctrine, 31 N.M.L. Rev. 359 (2001).

A merger of the civil law concepts governing uneven exchanges and the common law doctrine of unconscionability is found in Article 3.10 of the UNIDROIT Principles of International Commercial Contracts, first discussed in Chapter 1 and reprinted in the Supplement. The article provides for avoidance or reformation if, at the time of making, the contract or a term unjustifiably gave an excessive advantage to one party. In addition to the presence of an uneven exchange, Article 3.10(1)(a) provides that courts should have regard for "the fact that the other party has taken advantage of the first party's dependence, economic distress or urgent needs, or of its improvidence, ignorance, inexperience or lack of bargaining skills." For further discussion, see Joseph M. Perillo, UNIDROIT Principles of International Commercial Contracts: The Black Letter Text and a Review, 63 Fordham L. Rev. 281, 293-294 (1994).

The inherent vagueness of the unconscionability concept has resulted in a number of issues for courts to resolve. How should a court determine when an agreement is unconscionable? To what extent does the doctrine allow a court to refuse to enforce a contract simply because the contract is harsh, even if the bargaining process has not otherwise been defective? Does the doctrine apply to commercial as well as consumer transactions?

Williams v. Walker-Thomas Furniture Co.
United States Court of Appeals
350 F.2d 445 (D.C. Cir. 1965)

Before BAZELON, Chief Judge, and DANAHER and WRIGHT, Circuit Judges.
J. SKELLY WRIGHT, Circuit Judge:
Appellee, Walker-Thomas Furniture Company, operates a retail furniture store in the District of Columbia. During the period from 1957 to 1962 each appellant in these cases purchased a number of household items from Walker-Thomas, for which payment was to be made in installments. The terms of each purchase were contained in a printed form contract which set forth the value

of the purchased item and purported to lease the item to appellant for a stipulated monthly rent payment. The contract then provided, in substance, that title would remain in Walker-Thomas until the total of all the monthly payments made equaled the stated value of the item, at which time appellants could take title. In the event of a default in the payment of any monthly installment, Walker-Thomas could repossess the item.

The contract further provided that "the amount of each periodical installment payment to be made by [purchaser] to the Company under this present lease shall be inclusive of and not in addition to the amount of each installment payment to be made by [purchaser] under such prior leases, bills or accounts; *and all payments now and hereafter made by [purchaser] shall be credited pro rata on all outstanding leases, bills and accounts* due the Company by [purchaser] at the time each such payment is made." (Emphasis added.) The effect of this rather obscure provision was to keep a balance due on every item purchased until the balance due on all items, whenever purchased, was liquidated. As a result, the debt incurred at the time of purchase of each item was secured by the right to repossess all the items previously purchased by the same purchaser, and each new item purchased automatically became subject to a security interest arising out of the previous dealings.

On May 12, 1962, appellant Thorne purchased an item described as a Daveno, three tables, and two lamps, having total stated value of $391.10. Shortly thereafter, he defaulted on his monthly payments and appellee sought to replevy all the items purchased since the first transaction in 1958. Similarly, on April 17, 1962, appellant Williams bought a stereo set of stated value of $514.95.[1] She too defaulted shortly thereafter, and appellee sought to replevy all the items purchased since December, 1957. The Court of General Sessions granted judgment for appellee. The District of Columbia Court of Appeals affirmed, and we granted appellants' motion for leave to appeal to this court.

Appellants' principal contention, rejected by both the trial and the appellate courts below, is that these contracts, or at least some of them, are unconscionable and, hence, not enforceable. In its opinion in Williams v. Walker-Thomas Furniture Company, 198 A.2d 914, 916 (1964), the District of Columbia Court of Appeals explained its rejection of this contention as follows:

> Appellant's second argument presents a more serious question. The record reveals that prior to the last purchase appellant had reduced the balance in her account to $164. The last purchase, a stereo set, raised the balance due to $678. Significantly, at the time of this and the preceding purchases, appellee was aware of appellant's financial position. The reverse side of the stereo contract listed the name of appellant's social worker and her $218 monthly stipend from the government. Nevertheless, with full knowledge that appellant had to feed, clothe and support both herself and seven children on this amount, appellee sold her a $514 stereo set.
>
> We cannot condemn too strongly appellee's conduct. It raises serious questions of sharp practice and irresponsible business dealings. A review of the legislation in the District of Columbia affecting retail sales and the pertinent decisions of the

---

1. At the time of this purchase her account showed a balance of $164 still owing from her prior purchases. The total of all the purchases made over the years in question came to $1,800. The total payments amounted to $1,400.

highest court in this jurisdiction disclose, however, no ground upon which this court can declare the contracts in question contrary to public policy. We note that were the Maryland Retail Installment Sales Act, Art. 83 §§128-153, or its equivalent, in force in the District of Columbia, we could grant appellant appropriate relief. We think Congress should consider corrective legislation to protect the public from such exploitive contracts as were utilized in the case at bar.

We do not agree that the court lacked the power to refuse enforcement to contracts found to be unconscionable. In other jurisdictions, it has been held as a matter of common law that unconscionable contracts are not enforceable.[2] While no decision of this court so holding has been found, the notion that an unconscionable bargain should not be given full enforcement is by no means novel. In Scott v. United States, 79 U.S. (12 Wall.) 443, 445, 20 L. Ed. 438 (1870), the Supreme Court stated:

> If a contract be unreasonable and unconscionable, but not void for fraud, a court of law will give to the party who sues for its breach damages, not according to its letter, but only such as he is equitably entitled to. . . .

Since we have never adopted or rejected such a rule, the question here presented is actually one of first impression.

Congress has recently enacted the Uniform Commercial Code, which specifically provides that the court may refuse to enforce a contract which it finds to be unconscionable at the time it was made. 28 D.C. Code §2-302 (Supp. IV 1965). The enactment of this section, which occurred subsequent to the contracts here in suit, does not mean that the common law of the District of Columbia was otherwise at the time of enactment, nor does it preclude the court from adopting a similar rule in the exercise of its powers to develop the common law for the District of Columbia. In fact, in view of the absence of prior authority on the point, we consider the congressional adoption of §2-302 persuasive authority for following the rationale of the cases from which the section is explicitly derived.[5] Accordingly, we hold that where the element of unconscionability is present at the time a contract is made, the contract should not be enforced.

Unconscionability has generally been recognized to include an absence of meaningful choice on the part of one of the parties together with contract terms which are unreasonably favorable to the other party.[6] Whether a meaningful choice is present in a particular case can only be determined by consideration of all the circumstances surrounding the transaction. In many cases the meaningfulness of the choice is negated by a gross inequality of

---

2. Campbell Soup Co. v. Wentz, 3 Cir., 172 F.2d 80 (1948); Indianapolis Morris Plan Corporation v. Sparks, 132 Ind. App. 145, 172 N.E.2d 899 (1961); Henningsen v. Bloomfield Motors, Inc., 32 N.J. 358, 161 A.2d 69, 84-96, 75 A.L.R.2d 1 (1960). Cf. 1 Corbin, Contracts §128 (1963).

5. See Comment, §2-302, Uniform Commercial Code (1962). Compare Note, 45 Va. L. Rev. 583, 590 (1959), where it is predicted that the rule of §2-302 will be followed by analogy in cases which involve contracts not specifically covered by the section. Cf. 1 State of New York Law Revision Commission, Report and Record of Hearings on the Uniform Commercial Code 108-110 (1954) (remarks of Professor Llewellyn).

6. See Henningsen v. Bloomfield Motors, Inc., supra note 2; Campbell Soup Co. v. Wentz, supra note 2.

bargaining power.[7] The manner in which the contract was entered is also relevant to this consideration. Did each party to the contract, considering his obvious education or lack of it, have a reasonable opportunity to understand the terms of the contract, or were the important terms hidden in a maze of fine print and minimized by deceptive sales practices? Ordinarily, one who signs an agreement without full knowledge of its terms might be held to assume the risk that he has entered a one-sided bargain.[8] But when a party of little bargaining power, and hence little real choice, signs a commercially unreasonable contract with little or no knowledge of its terms, it is hardly likely that his consent, or even an objective manifestation of his consent, was ever given to all the terms. In such a case the usual rule that the terms of the agreement are not to be questioned[9] should be abandoned and the court should consider whether the terms of the contract are so unfair that enforcement should be withheld.[10]

In determining reasonableness or fairness, the primary concern must be with the terms of the contract considered in light of the circumstances existing when the contract was made. The test is not simple, nor can it be mechanically applied. The terms are to be considered "in the light of the general commercial background and the commercial needs of the particular trade or case."[11] Corbin suggests the test as being whether the terms are "so extreme as to appear unconscionable according to the mores and business practices of the time and place." 1 Corbin, op. cit. supra note 2.[12] We think this formulation correctly states the test to be applied in those cases where no meaningful choice was exercised upon entering the contract.

Because the trial court and the appellate court did not feel that enforcement could be refused, no findings were made on the possible unconscionability of the contracts in these cases. Since the record is not

---

7. See Henningsen v. Bloomfield Motors, Inc., supra note 2, 161 A.2d at 86, and authorities there cited. Inquiry into the relative bargaining power of the two parties is not an inquiry wholly divorced from the general question of unconscionability, since a one-sided bargain is itself evidence of the inequality of the bargaining parties. This fact was vaguely recognized in the common law doctrine of intrinsic fraud, that is, fraud which can be presumed from the grossly unfair nature of the terms of the contract. See the oft-quoted statement of Lord Hardwicke in Earl of Chesterfield v. Janssen, 28 Eng. Rep. 82, 100 (1751): ". . . [Fraud] may be apparent from the intrinsic nature and subject of the bargain itself; such as no man in his senses and not under delusion would make. . . ." . . .

8. See Restatement, Contracts §70 (1932); Note, 63 Harv. L. Rev. 494 (1950). See also Daley v. People's Building, Loan & Savings Assn., 178 Mass. 13, 59 N.E. 452, 453 (1901), in which Mr. Justice Holmes, while sitting on the Supreme Judicial Court of Massachusetts, made this observation:

. . . Courts are less and less disposed to interfere with parties making such contracts as they choose, so long as they interfere with no one's welfare but their own. . . . It will be understood that we are speaking of parties standing in an equal position where neither has any oppressive advantage or power. . . .

9. This rule has never been without exception. In cases involving merely the transfer of unequal amounts of the same commodity, the courts have held the bargain unenforceable for the reason that "in such a case, it is clear, that the law cannot indulge in the presumption of equivalence between the consideration and the promise." 1 Williston, Contracts §115 (3d ed. 1957).

10. See the general discussion of "Boiler-Plate Agreements" in Llewellyn, The Common Law Tradition 362-371 (1960).

11. Comment, Uniform Commercial Code §2-307. [sic; should be §2-302.]

12. See Henningsen v. Bloomfield Motors, Inc., supra note 2; Mandel v. Liebman, 303 N.Y. 88, 100 N.E.2d 149 (1951). The traditional test as stated in Greer v. Tweed, [N.Y.C.P., 13 Abb. Pr., N.S., 427, 429 (1872)], is "such as no man in his senses and not under delusion would make on the one hand, and as no honest or fair man would accept, on the other."

sufficient for our deciding the issue as a matter of law, the cases must be remanded to the trial court for further proceedings.

So ordered.

DANAHER, Circuit Judge (dissenting):

The District of Columbia Court of Appeals obviously was as unhappy about the situation here presented as any of us can possibly be. Its opinion in the *Williams* case, quoted in the majority text, concludes: "We think Congress should consider corrective legislation to protect the public from such exploitive contracts as were utilized in the case at bar."

My view is thus summed up by an able court which made no finding that there had actually been sharp practice. Rather the appellant seems to have known precisely where she stood.

There are many aspects of public policy here involved. What is a luxury to some may seem an outright necessity to others. Is public oversight to be required of the expenditures of relief funds? A washing machine, e.g., in the hands of a relief client might become a fruitful source of income. Many relief clients may well need credit, and certain business establishments will take long chances on the sale of items, expecting their pricing policies will afford a degree of protection commensurate with the risk. Perhaps a remedy when necessary will be found within the provisions of the "Loan Shark" law, D.C. Code §§26-601 et seq. (1961).

I mention such matters only to emphasize the desirability of a cautious approach to any such problem, particularly since the law for so long has allowed parties such great latitude in making their own contracts. I dare say there must annually be thousands upon thousands of installment credit transactions in this jurisdiction, and one can only speculate as to the effect the decision in these cases will have.

I join the District of Columbia Court of Appeals in its disposition of the issues.

Notes and Questions

1. *Procedural and substantive unconscionability.* The *Williams* court states that unconscionability consists of "an absence of meaningful choice on the part of one of the parties together with contract terms which are unreasonably favorable to the other party" and goes on to note that conspicuousness and intelligibility of a clause will also be relevant. In his very notable assessment of UCC §2-302, Professor Leff coined the terms *procedural unconscionability* and *substantive unconscionability* to identify what he perceived as two key aspects of the new provision. Arthur Allen Leff, Unconscionability and the Code — The Emperor's New Clause, 115 U. Pa. L. Rev. 485, 487-488 (1967). Read together, the Leff article and the *Williams* case indicate that procedural unconscionability may refer to either lack of choice by one party or some defect in the bargaining process (such as quasi-fraud or quasi-duress) and that substantive unconscionability relates to the fairness of the terms of the resulting bargain. Many courts now use these concepts as a framework for analysis of unconscionability problems, generally requiring a showing of both procedural and substantive elements. See, e.g., American Stone Diamond,

Inc. v. Lloyds of London, 934 F. Supp. 839, 844 (S.D. Tex. 1996) (under Texas law party asserting unconscionability has burden of proving both elements); Dean Witter Reynolds v. Superior Court, 259 Cal. Rptr. 789, 795 (Ct. App. 1989) (both elements of unconscionability required under "sliding scale"; if more of one element present, less may be required of the other). But see Maxwell v. Fidelity Financial Services, Inc., 907 P.2d 51, 58 (Ariz. 1995) (agreeing with jurisdictions that accept either procedural or substantive unconscionability alone may be sufficient); Gillman v. Chase Manhattan Bank, N.A., 534 N.E.2d 824, 829 (N.Y. 1988) (suggesting that an "outrageous" substantive provision alone may be enough for unconscionability). This issue is discussed in the Adler v. Fred Lind Manor case late in this section.

While Professor Leff agreed that the contract in *Williams* was procedurally unconscionable, he criticized the court's analysis of the substantive aspect of the transaction as follows:

> How does that test apply to the *Williams* facts? What is it about Mrs. Williams' contract which is "unconscionable?" Surprisingly, the answer is not clear, even about *what* in the contract is bad. It seems, however, that there are two possibilities. First, it may be that the provision by which each item purchased became security for all items purchased was the objectionable feature of the contract. Or it might be that the furniture company sold this expensive stereo set to this particular party which forms the unconscionability of the contract. If the vice is the add-on clause, then one encounters the now-familiar problem: such a clause is hardly such a moral outrage as by itself meets Judge Wright's standard of being "so extreme as to appear unconscionable according to the mores and business practices of the time and place." . . . Of the thirty-seven jurisdictions which have statutes regulating retail installment sales, only one has a provision making add-on clauses impermissible. In such circumstances it does seem a bit much to find "so extreme as to appear unconscionable according to the mores and business practices of the time and place" an add-on clause in the District of Columbia which is used and statutorily permitted almost everyplace else, including contiguous Maryland. One's gorge can hardly be expected to rise with such nice geographic selectivity.
>
> If one is not convinced that the unconscionability inheres in the add-on provision, it may be argued that it inheres in the contract as a whole, in the act of having sold this expensive item to a poor person knowing of her poverty. This is quite clearly the primary significance of the case to some of the commentators. . . .

Arthur Allen Leff, Unconscionability and the Code — The Emperor's New Clause, 115 U. Pa. L. Rev. 485, 554-556 (1967). Do Professor Leff's stated choices exhaust the alternatives? Or is it possible that unfairness lies in selling "this expensive item" (the stereo) and others as well, "to a poor person, knowing of her poverty," *pursuant to a contract with an add-on clause?* Failing to make add-on clauses illegal per se is not necessarily the same as giving them a vote of thanks; for instance, the Uniform Consumer Credit Code (UCCC or U3C), promulgated by the National Conference of Commissioners on Uniform State Laws after the *Williams* decision, permits the use of add-on clauses in consumer credit sales but requires that moneys paid by the buyer be allocated to the goods purchased in the order of their purchase, rather than pro rata to all goods as yet unpaid for. UCCC §§3.302, 3.303.

As an alternative to the procedural/substantive framework for unconscionability analysis, the Uniform Consumer Credit Code §5.108 and some courts have adopted a multifactor balancing approach. UCCC §5.108 calls for assessment of a number of elements including whether the seller believes the consumer is likely to default on the obligation, whether the consumer will receive substantial benefit from the transaction, gross disparity between the contract and market price, and whether the seller has knowingly taken advantage of a consumer's bargaining impairment due to mental impairment, lack of education, or similar factors. The Kansas Supreme Court adopted a balancing test in Wille v. Southwestern Bell Telephone Co., 549 P.2d 903 (Kan. 1976), weighing factors such as the use of a standard form contract, limitation on available remedies for breach, use of inconspicuous or incomprehensible terms, overall imbalance in the bargain, exploitation of a party's lack of experience or education, and inequality of bargaining or economic power. Id. at 906-907.

2. *Factual context for **Williams**.* Is it possible that the judges in *Williams*, and perhaps some current readers of the case, are influenced by stereotypes that may come to mind based on the limited facts that are given in the Court of Appeals opinion? While the court does not reveal Williams's race or ethnicity, educational background, or work experience, the majority opinion reports her monthly income of $218 and the dissent indicates that she received "relief funds." What common assumptions about Williams might be made on the basis of that information and how might they affect the resolution of the case? Would it make a difference to the outcome of the case if Williams happened to be an educated person with business experience who suddenly found herself with seven children to raise as a single parent because of the accidental death of her husband? Professor Muriel Morisey Spence suggests that possible scenario and warns that discussion of the *Williams* case may often reinforce stereotypes concerning gender, race, and class. Muriel Morisey Spence, Teaching Williams v. Walker-Thomas Furniture Co., 3 Temple Pol. & C.R. L. Rev. 89 (1994). Professor Spence highlights the fact that Williams appears to have made timely payments for about five years before defaulting on the account for reasons not revealed. Id. at 96. Moreover, do you think that even a well-educated person would have understood the add-on clause and been able to protect herself against it? (Did you understand the clause the first time you read it?)

Additional background facts about the appellants, Mrs. Williams and the Thornes, can in fact be gathered from the lower court opinions before the cases were consolidated, Williams v. Walker-Thomas Furniture Co., 198 A.2d 914 (D.C. 1964) and Thorne v. Walker-Thomas Furniture Co., 198 A.2d 914 (D.C. 1964). A recent law review article also incorporates much additional information that has surfaced over the years. Eben Colby, What Did the Doctrine of Unconscionability Do to the Walker-Thomas Furniture Company?, 34 Conn. L. Rev. 625 (2002). From those collective sources, it becomes clear that the Thornes and Mrs. Williams did pay their respective accounts faithfully for four to five years before eventually defaulting. While the cause for Mrs. Williams's default is not clear, it appears that illness led to the Thornes' default. The lower court reports that Mrs. Williams was a person of limited education and Colby reports that Mr. Thorne had a third-grade education. Colby also reports that Walker-Thomas was known to have a practice of repossessing goods, having filed "approximately one hundred writs of replevin each year for many years preceding Williams's litigation." 34 Conn. L. Rev. at 652. The lower court opinion also reflects that the store sold most of the goods through door-to-door sales, reporting that Mrs. Williams "testified that most of the purchases were made at her home; that the contracts were signed in blank; that she did not read the instruments; and that she was not provided with a copy. She admitted, however, that she did not ask anyone to read or explain the contracts to her." 198 A.2d at 915. Mrs. Williams's purchases included sheets, curtains, toys, rugs, chairs, a chest of drawers, beds, mattresses, a washing machine, and, finally, the stereo set. Id. Do any of these additional facts affect your opinion about the applicability of the unconscionability doctrine to the cases?

3. *Price term unconscionability and rent-to-own cases.* In *Williams* the court considered whether the doctrine of unconscionability should apply to an "add-on" clause, a part of the contract that consumers are unlikely to read or understand. Should the doctrine also apply to provisions of the contract on which consumers usually do focus their attention, such as the price term in a sales contact or the monthly fee in a rental agreement? Whether the drafters of UCC §2-302 intended the section to be used to police the price term of a contract is unclear from its history. Nonetheless, a number of early cases held consumer contracts unconscionable because of excessive price. E.g., American Home Improvement, Inc. v. MacIver, 201 A.2d 886 (N.H. 1964) (contract for home improvement in the amount of $2,658, which included $809 in interest and $806 for sales commission, was unconscionable); Frostifresh Corp. v. Reynoso, 274 N.Y.S.2d 757 (Dist. Ct. 1966) (sale of refrigerator-freezer costing $348 for price of $1,396.10 held unconscionable where negotiations were conducted in Spanish, contract was written in English, and salesman represented that unit would pay for itself through $25 referral fees when neighbors bought the same item). Moreover, both the Restatement and the Uniform Consumer Credit Code indicate that excessive price may be a basis of unconscionability. Restatement (Second) §208, Comment *c;* UCCC §5.108(4)(c).

Courts have been divided, however, in cases alleging unconscionable price terms in rent-to-own cases. Compare Remco Enterprises v. Houston, 677 P.2d 567 (Kan. Ct. App. 1984) (rent-to-own contract charging twice the retail price for television set if retained until purchased not unconscionable; company provided access to goods otherwise unavailable), with Green v. Continental Rentals, 678 A.2d 759 (N.J. Super. 1994) (rent-to-own contracts resulting in payment of more than twice cash price held unconscionable due to excessive interest charged). Notably, a report of the Federal Trade Commission, Bureau of Economics Staff Report: Survey of Rent-to-Own Customers (April 2000), reveals that rent-to-own customers are more likely to be African-American, younger, less educated, have lower incomes, have children in the household, rent their residence, live in the South, and live in non-suburban areas, and that 70 percent of renters eventually purchase the items. Moreover, forty-six states regulate the rent-to-own industry, but often with laws that have been promoted by the industry and opposed by consumer advocates. The report is available at http://www.ftc.gov/reports/index.htm. For a discussion of rent-to-own contracts, advocating more policing based on whether profits are excessive, see Steven W. Bender, Rate Regulation at the Crossroads of Usury and Unconscionability: The Case for Regulating Abusive Commercial and Consumer Interest Rates Under the Unconscionability Standard, 31 Hous. L. Rev. 721 (1994).

4. *Ahern v. Knecht: Unconscionability in the suburbs?* Many of the price term cases involve basic consumer purchases by persons with limited income and, presumably, relatively limited choices. Should the unconscionability doctrine be equally available to claimants who appear to have more resources and consequently more plentiful contract options? In Ahern v. Knecht, 563 N.E.2d 787 (Ill. App. Ct. 1990), the plaintiff was confronted with a central air conditioner that failed to cool in the middle of a heat wave. Mrs. Ahern selected Knecht's repair company from a telephone book, partly because his advertisement stressed "honesty." Knecht required an initial payment of $154 for the service call and, after his initial survey, told Mrs. Ahern that the total charge would be $762. Mrs. Ahern initially expressed shock at that amount, but eventually complied with Knecht's demand for a check for the full amount before she left home to keep a medical appointment. Upon her return, Mrs. Ahern discovered that Knecht was gone and that the air conditioner was completely inoperative. Another company later made an effective repair for a charge of $72 after Knecht refused to return. The Aherns brought an action to recover the amount paid to Knecht. The trial court determined that Knecht's services had a value of only $150, subtracted the $72 paid to the second company to complete the repair, and gave judgment to the Aherns for the balance of $684 they had paid to Knecht. The appellate court upheld the judgment, noting that while courts normally do not assess the sufficiency of consideration, a finding of gross inadequacy or failure of consideration, combined with other inequitable features, will justify equitable rescission of the agreement. The court stated that "[e]ven where there is no actual fraud, courts will relieve against hard and unconscionable contracts which have been procured by taking advantage of the condition, circumstances or necessity of other parties." Id. at 792. The court noted that Mrs. Ahern stood at a bargaining disadvantage because she had little knowledge about the technology of air conditioners, was committed to the service charge after calling Knecht, and was apparently intimidated by the demand for payment. Many other customers obviously complained about the practices of the Knecht firm, leading to an action by the state attorney general under consumer protection laws, as reflected in the case People ex rel. Hartigan v. Knecht Services, Inc., 575 N.E.2d 1378 (Ill. App. Ct. 1991), briefly discussed in the Comment following these notes. Are you persuaded that the unconscionability doctrine should be applied in a case such as *Ahern?* Could some theory other than fraud or unconscionability have served as a basis for granting relief to the Aherns?

5. *Procedural limits.* The court in *Williams* held that the case must be remanded to the trial court for a determination of whether the clause was unconscionable. Section 2-302 provides that the question of unconscionability is a legal issue to be decided by the court, rather than the trier of fact, but only after providing the parties an opportunity to present evidence relevant to the

disputed provision. See Reznor v. J. Artist Management, Inc., 365 F. Supp. 2d 565, 576 (S.D.N.Y. 2005) (under New York law evidentiary hearing should be held except when there is no doubt about validity of contract term); Schroeder v. Fageol Motors, Inc., 544 P.2d 20, 24-25 (Wash. 1975) (en banc) (trial court erred in determining unconscionability on summary judgment without giving parties opportunity to present evidence). UCC §2-302 and Restatement (Second) §208 further provide that unconscionability is to be judged as of the time that the contract is made. Accordingly, courts generally emphasize that contracts should not be judged based on developments after the contract was formed. See Boston Helicopter Charter, Inc. v. Augusta Aviation Corp., 767 F. Supp. 363, 375 (D. Mass. 1991); Strand v. U. S. Bank National Association ND, 693 N.W.2d 918, 921 (N.D. 2005).

Applying a rather restrictive reading to the language of §2-302, some courts have held that the doctrine of unconscionability is a defensive concept and may not be used to obtain affirmative relief by way of either damages or restitution. This construction is based on the fact the section indicates that courts may "refuse" to enforce or "limit the application" of the unconscionable contract or a clause therein. See, e.g., Arthur v. Microsoft Corp., 676 N.W.2d 29, 38-39 (Neb. 2004) (purchasers could not state claim for money damages under UCC §2-302 based on allegation that price versus cost disparity was unconscionable); Best v. United States National Bank, 714 P.2d 1049, 1055 (Or. Ct. App. 1986), aff'd, 739 P.2d 554 (Or. 1987) (bank entitled to summary judgment on cause of action for restitution claiming that charges for checks drawn with insufficient funds were unconscionable). A few courts have allowed damages or restitution after finding that the contract or one of its clauses was unconscionable. In the *Ahern* case discussed in the preceding note, the court found a contract unconscionable where the plaintiffs had paid $762 to a repair company for services that were worth at most $150. The court set aside the contract and granted restitution of the amount paid in excess of the value of services rendered. 563 N.E.2d at 788. See also Langemeier v. National Oats, Inc., 775 F.2d 975, 977-978 (8th Cir. 1985) (noting that §2-302 allows the court to enforce remainder of contract without the unconscionable term, which may lead to affirmative relief); White & Summers, Uniform Commercial Code §4-8 at 173 (5th ed. 2000) (recognizing the possibility of restitutionary relief).

6. *Scholarly commentary.* Not all commentators agree with the widespread use of the procedural/substantive framework for determining unconscionability. Professor Robert Hillman advocates, in essence, the use of traditional doctrines, such as duress, undue influence, or fraud, whenever applicable, because they are more specific than the unconscionability doctrine and would limit application of the doctrine to extreme cases that truly shock the conscience. Robert A. Hillman, Debunking Some Myths about Unconscionability: A New Framework for U.C.C. Section 2-302, 67 Cornell L. Rev. 1 (1981). In a similar vein, Professor Prince has taken aim specifically at the "lack of meaningful choice" test adopted in *Williams* and widely used by the courts. Harry G. Prince, Unconscionability in California: A Need for Restraint and Consistency, 46 Hastings L. J. 459 (1995). Prince observes that the quasi-fraud form of procedural unconscionability involves terms that are likely hidden or unintelligible if found, and therefore relates to the common law forms of bargaining

misbehavior. Application of the lack of meaningful choice test, Prince suggests, is much more vague and difficult, except in cases of extreme necessity, and results in further obfuscation of an already imprecise concept. Id. at 474-479.

Professor Richard A. Epstein has offered a critique of unconscionability that analyzes the economic consequences of a variety of common contractual provisions such as the add-on clause in *Williams*. He concludes that such clauses normally promote efficiency by reducing transaction costs and benefit both parties. Richard A. Epstein, Unconscionability: A Critical Reappraisal, 18 J.L. & Econ. 293 (1975). Epstein asserts that the add-on clause provides an efficient means for the seller to obtain additional security to make the transaction feasible for both parties and should not be deemed unconscionable. Id. at 307. He does allow, however, that the unconscionability doctrine can serve an economically useful purpose when applied to agreements made under circumstances where coercive behavior (fraud, duress, etc.) was likely but difficult to prove. In such cases, Epstein suggests that the application of the doctrine advances the principle of freedom of contract while reducing judicial costs. Id. at 303-305. See also Russell Korobkin, Bounded Rationality, Standard Form Contracts, and Unconscionability, 70 U. Chi. L. Rev. 1203 (2003) (noting, inter alia, that limited ability of buyers to read and comprehend terms in standard form contracts inhibits operation of market to produce efficient standard terms).

Professor Lee Pizzimenti argues that recognition of the doctrine of unconscionability cannot cure the problem of unfair contracts because parties with inferior bargaining power are unlikely to recognize or enforce their legal rights. She argues that a more effective way to minimize the occurrence of unconscionable contracts is to forbid lawyers from drafting them. She proposes adoption of the following disciplinary rule:

> A lawyer shall not assist in the preparation of a written instrument containing terms which are unconscionable. A lawyer may assist in such preparation where there is a basis for concluding the terms are not unconscionable that is not frivolous, including a good faith argument for an extension, modification or reversal of existing law.

Lee A. Pizzimenti, Prohibiting Lawyers from Assisting in Unconscionable Transactions: Using an Overt Tool, 72 Marq. L. Rev. 151, 174 (1989). Do you agree with this proposal? Why?

Comment: Consumer Protection Legislation

The materials in this chapter examine a variety of judicially developed doctrines for dealing with the problems of coercion in the bargaining process or unfairness of the terms of a bargain. A number of commentators have argued, however, that judicial decisionmaking in individual cases is not the proper way to deal with such problems. To such critics, the judicial process is an inefficient, often ineffective way of attacking contractual abuses. Moreover, because regulation of such conduct involves important and difficult questions of social policy, legislatures rather than courts are said to be the appropriate institutions to determine the need for and scope of any such regulation. See Robert A. Hillman, Debunking Some Myths about Unconscionability: A New Framework for U.C.C. Section 2-302, 67 Cornell L. Rev. 1, 27-29 (1981); Arthur Allen Leff, Unconscionability and the Crowd—Consumers and the Common Law Tradition, 31 U. Pitt. L. Rev. 349, 356-357 (1970).

Since the late 1960s, both Congress and the individual state legislatures have enacted a number of consumer protection statutes. In addition, administrative agencies and regulatory officials at both the federal and state levels have been increasingly active in dealing with consumer protection issues. Because such regulation covers a wide range of activities (such as consumer credit, sales practices, and collection activities), an exhaustive review is impossible. This comment will touch on some of the major statutory and administrative efforts in this area.

In broad terms, consumer protection legislation has aimed at accomplishing three goals. One of these goals has been to require commercial parties to disclose information to consumers in a meaningful fashion. *Disclosure legislation* is based on the theory that increased information gives consumers an opportunity to avoid entering into unfair contracts. Such legislation has undoubtedly improved the functioning of the marketplace to some degree. As a means of controlling unfair contracts, however, disclosure legislation has its limitations because abusive contractual provisions may be found in standard form contracts that are rarely read by consumers and are not subject to negotiation. Thus, some consumer protection legislation has a goal of *substantive regulation* rather than greater disclosure. Under such regulation, particular contractual provisions thought to be unfair are declared unlawful. Finally, since legal changes to protect consumers are meaningful only if enforced, most consumer protection statutes contain provisions designed to *improve enforcement.*

In 1968 Congress enacted the Consumer Credit Protection Act, 15 U.S.C. §1601 et seq., commonly known as the Truth-in-Lending Act. Principally a disclosure statute, the Act requires lenders in consumer credit transactions to disclose by a uniform method the rate of interest on consumer loans (the annual percentage rate or APR) along with various other terms of the loan, such as the scope of any security interest that the creditor would obtain in the debtor's property. To a limited extent, the Act engages in substantive regulation. Consumers are granted a right to rescind within three business days any loan contract that involves a mortgage on the consumer's principal residence. (First mortgage loans to acquire or construct the consumer's dwelling are excepted from this right of rescission.) 15 U.S.C. §1635. In an effort to increase creditor compliance, the Act contains a private cause of action for violation of its provisions, including authorization of class actions and the recovery of attorney's fees. 15 U.S.C. §1640. (Since 1968 the Act has been amended on a number of occasions to include provisions dealing with credit reporting, discrimination in extensions of credit, and collection practices.)

In the same year that Congress passed the Truth-in-Lending Act, the National Conference of Commissioners on Uniform State Laws adopted the Uniform Consumer Credit Code; six years later the Conference issued a revised version of the UCCC. Although the 1968 version of the UCCC contained disclosure provisions similar to those found in the Truth-in-Lending Act, the 1974 version eliminated those provisions on the theory that the federal legislation had as a practical matter preempted the field of disclosure. 7A U.L.A., Prefatory Note at 12 (1999). The principal thrust of the revised UCCC is substantive regulation rather than disclosure. In an effort to protect consumers from exorbitant interest charges, the UCCC sets maximum interest rates for various types of consumer loans. Within the bounds set by these rates, market forces are to determine the cost of credit. In addition, the UCCC prohibits a number of creditor practices, such as assignments of wages and confession of judgment clauses. UCCC §§3.305, 3.306. Interestingly, the UCCC allows (with some modification) the cross-collateral clause that was involved in Williams v. Walker-Thomas Furniture Co. UCCC §3.302. See Note 1 following the *Williams* case. As we have seen, the UCCC also contains a provision outlining factors a court should consider in deciding whether a clause is unconscionable. UCCC §5.108. Only a few states have adopted the UCCC.

In 1975 Congress enacted the Magnuson-Moss Warranty — Federal Trade Commission Improvement Act, 15 U.S.C. §2301 et seq. The portion of the Act dealing with consumer product warranties contains provisions requiring increased disclosure of warranty terms, regulating to some degree the substance of warranty obligations, and improving consumer remedies for breach of warranty. The other portion of the Act grants increased regulatory power to the Federal Trade Commission (FTC). Created by Congress in 1914, the FTC had been inactive in consumer protection until the 1970s, when several critical studies of its activities, along with a growing consumer movement, combined to produce political pressure on the Commission to become more aggressive. The 1975 legislation increased the Commission's power by granting it authority to promulgate rules defining unfair or deceptive acts or practices in or affecting commerce. One of the most significant rules adopted by the Commission is designed to prevent creditors from relying on the "holder-in-due-course doctrine" to overcome various consumer defenses against debt enforcement. 40 Fed. Reg. 53,506 (1975) (codified in 16 C.F.R. pt. 433). The Commission also adopted a rule declaring unlawful a variety of creditor practices: confession of judgment clauses, wage assignments, security interests in household goods, waivers of exemptions of property from creditor remedies, pyramiding of late charges, and cosigner liability. 49 Fed. Reg. 7740 (1984) (codified in 16 C.F.R. pt. 444). See American Financial Services Assn. v. FTC, 767 F.2d 957 (D.C. Cir. 1985), *cert. denied,* 475 U.S. 1011 (1986) (2-1 decision upholding FTC's authority to promulgate the Credit Practices Rule).

A number of states have enacted consumer protection statutes, many of which are modeled on the FTC Act (such statutes are often referred to as "little FTC" or "consumer fraud" acts). These acts typically give some state governmental agency, such as the office of the attorney general or the department of consumer affairs, regulatory power in consumer matters, usually including the right to bring lawsuits to protect consumers from improper conduct by sellers and creditors. See, e.g., In re National Credit Management Group, L.L.C., 21 F. Supp. 2d 424 D.N.J. 1998) (action by attorney general under New Jersey Consumer Fraud Act to enjoin certain practices in connection with the sale of credit monitoring services); People ex rel. Hartigan v. Knecht Services, Inc., 575 N.E.2d 1378 (Ill. App. Ct. 1991) (unconscionably high prices alone do not constitute an unfair practice under the Illinois Consumer Fraud Act, but the combination of an unconscionably large price, little or no service, and the absence of reasonable alternatives does violate the Act). The statutory provisions frequently give consumers a right to recover double or treble damages for willful violations, along with attorney fees. E.g., Mass. Gen. Laws Ann. ch. 93A, §9 (West 2006); S.C. Code Ann. §39-5-140 (West 2002); Texas Bus. & Com. Code Ann. §17.50 (West 1987 & Supp. 2004). For a discussion of the importance of state unfair trade practices statutes, see Stewart Macaulay, Bambi Meets Godzilla: Reflections on Contracts Scholarship and Teaching vs. State Unfair and Deceptive Trade Practices and Consumer Protection Statutes, 26 Hous. L. Rev. 575 (1989).

Higgins v. Superior Court of Los Angeles County
California Court of Appeal
140 Cal. App. 4th 1238; 45 Cal. Rptr. 3d 293 (2006)

RUBIN, Judge.

In this writ proceeding, five siblings who appeared in an episode of the television program *Extreme Makeover: Home Edition* (*Extreme Makeover*) challenge an order compelling them to arbitrate most of their claims against various entities involved with the production and broadcast of the program. Petitioners claim the arbitration clause contained in a written agreement they executed before the program was broadcast is unconscionable. We agree. Accordingly, we grant the petition for writ of mandate.

FACTUAL AND PROCEDURAL BACKGROUND

Petitioners Charles, Michael, Charis, Joshua, and Jeremiah Higgins are siblings. In February 2005, when they executed the agreement whose arbitration provision is at issue, they were 21, 19, 17, 16, and 14 years old, respectively.

Real parties in interest, to whom we refer collectively as the television defendants, are (1) American Broadcasting Companies, Inc., the network that broadcasts *Extreme Makeover*; (2) Disney/ABC International Television, Inc., which asserts it had no involvement with the *Extreme Makeover* program in which petitioners appeared; (3) Lock and Key Productions, the show's producer; (4) Endemol USA, Inc., which is also involved in producing the program; and (5) Pardee Homes, which constructed the home featured in the *Extreme Makeover* episode in which petitioners appeared.

Petitioners' parents died in 2004. The eldest sibling, Charles, became the guardian for the then three minor children. (To avoid confusion with his siblings, we refer to Charles Higgins by his first name.) Shortly thereafter, petitioners moved in with church acquaintances, Firipeli and Lokilani Leomiti, a couple with three children of their own. The Leomitis are defendants in the litigation but are not involved in the present writ proceeding.

According to Charles, after moving in with the Leomitis, he was advised by members of his church that producers of *Extreme Makeover* had contacted the church and had asked to speak to him about the production of a show based on the loss of petitioners' parents and that petitioners were now living with the Leomitis.[4] In July or August 2004, Charles called and spoke with an associate producer of Lock and Key about the program and petitioners' living situation.

Over the next several months, there were additional contacts between petitioners and persons affiliated with the production of the program, including in-person interviews and the filming of a casting tape. By early 2005, petitioners and the Leomitis were chosen to participate in the program in which the Leomitis' home would be completely renovated.

On February 1, 2005, a Lock and Key producer sent by Federal Express to each of the petitioners and to the Leomitis an "Agreement and Release" for their signatures.[5] The Agreement and Release contains 24 single-spaced pages and 72 numbered paragraphs. Attached to it were several pages of exhibits, including an authorization for release of medical information, an emergency medical release, and, as exhibit C, a one-page document entitled "Release." To avoid confusion with the one-page exhibit C Release, we refer to the 24-page Agreement and Release simply as the "Agreement," and to exhibit C as the "Release."

At the top of the first page of the Agreement, the following appears in large and underlined print: "NOTE: DO NOT SIGN THIS UNTIL YOU HAVE READ IT COMPLETELY." The second-to-last numbered paragraph also states in pertinent part: "I have been given ample opportunity to read, and I have carefully read, this entire agreement. . . . I certify that I have made such an investigation of the facts pertinent to this Agreement and of all the matters pertaining thereto as I have deemed necessary. . . . I represent and warrant that I have reviewed this document with my own legal counsel prior to signing (or, IN THE ALTERNATIVE, although I have been given a reasonable opportunity to discuss this Agreement with counsel of my choice, I have voluntarily declined such opportunity)."

The last section of the Agreement, which includes 12 numbered paragraphs, is entitled "MISCELLANEOUS." None of the paragraphs in that section contains a heading or title. Paragraph 69 contains the following arbitration provision:

---

4. Lock and Key's executive producer describes Extreme Makeover as a "'reality' based television series" whose "premise . . . is to find needy and deserving families who live in a home which does not serve their needs. The Program takes the selected families' existing homes and land and radically improves them by demolishing and rebuilding the home."

5. The version of the agreement intended for the three minor petitioners was slightly different than the one intended for the two adult petitioners and the Leomitis. The slight variations between the two versions are not relevant to the issue before us. In this opinion, we quote from, and cite to, the adult version.

69. I agree that any and all disputes or controversies arising under this Agreement or any of its terms, any effort by any party to enforce, interpret, construe, rescind, terminate or annul this Agreement, or any provision thereof, and any and all disputes or controversies relating to my appearance or participation in the Program, shall be resolved by binding arbitration in accordance with the following procedure. . . . All arbitration proceedings shall be conducted under the auspices of the American Arbitration Association. . . . I agree that the arbitrator's ruling, or arbitrators' ruling, as applicable, shall be final and binding and not subject to appeal or challenge. . . . The parties hereto agree that, notwithstanding the provisions of this paragraph, Producer shall have a right to injunctive or other equitable relief as provided for in California Code of Civil Procedure §1281.8 or other relevant laws.

There is nothing in the Agreement that brings the reader's attention to the arbitration provision. Although a different font is used occasionally to highlight certain terms in the Agreement, that is not the case with the paragraph containing the arbitration provision. Six paragraphs in the Agreement contain a box for the petitioners to initial; initialing is not required for the arbitration provision. . . .

The one-page Release is typed in a smaller font than the Agreement. It consists of four, single-spaced paragraphs, the middle of which contains the following arbitration clause: "I agree that any and all disputes or controversies arising under this Release or any of its terms, any effort by any party to enforce, interpret, construe, rescind, terminate or annul this Release, or any provision thereof, shall be resolved exclusively by binding arbitration before a single, neutral arbitrator, who shall be a retired judge of a state or federal court. All arbitration proceedings shall be conducted under the auspices of the American Arbitration Association, under its Commercial Arbitration Rules, through its Los Angeles, California office. I agree that the arbitration proceedings, testimony, discovery and documents filed in the course of such proceedings, including the fact that the arbitration is being conducted, will be treated as confidential. . . ."

There is no evidence that any discussions took place between petitioners and any representative of the television defendants regarding either the Agreement or the Release, or that any of the television defendants directly imposed any deadline by which petitioners were required to execute the documents.

On February 5, 2005, a field producer from Lock and Key and a location manager for the program went to the Leomitis' home and met with the Leomitis. Although physically present at the house, petitioners did not participate in the meeting. During the meeting, one of the Leomitis asked about the documents they had received, and the producer and location manager advised the Leomitis that they should read the documents carefully, call if they had questions, and then execute and return the documents.

According to Charles, after this meeting, the Leomitis emerged with a packet of documents, which they handed to petitioners. Mrs. Leomiti instructed petitioners to "flip through the pages and sign and initial the document where it contained a signature line or box." Charles stated that from the time Mrs. Leomiti "handed the document to us and the time we signed it, approximately five to ten minutes passed." The document contained complex legal terms that he did not understand. He did not know what an arbitration agreement was and did not understand its significance or the legal consequences that could flow from signing it. He did not specifically state whether or not he saw the arbitration provisions contained either in paragraph 69 or the Release before he signed the documents.

Each of the petitioners executed the Agreement and signed all exhibits, including the Release.

On February 16, 2005, representatives from the show appeared and started to reconstruct the Leomitis' home. When the new home was completed, it had nine bedrooms, including one for each of the five petitioners. The existing mortgage was also paid off.

The program featuring petitioners and the Leomitis was broadcast on Easter Sunday, 2005.

Petitioners allege that, after the show was first broadcast, the Leomitis informed petitioners that the home was theirs (the Leomitis'), and the Leomitis ultimately forced petitioners to leave. Charles contacted Lock and Key's field producer and asked for help. The producer responded that he could not assist petitioners. Sometime thereafter, the *Extreme Makeover* episode was rebroadcast.

In August 2005, petitioners filed this action against the television defendants and the Leomitis. According to the record before us, the complaint includes claims for, among other things, intentional and negligent misrepresentation, breach of contract, unfair competition . . . , and false advertising. . . . With respect to the television defendants, the complaint appears to allege that those defendants breached promises to provide petitioners with a home, exploited petitioners, and portrayed petitioners in a false light (by rebroadcasting the episode when they knew the episode no longer reflected petitioners' living situation).

The television defendants petitioned to compel arbitration pursuant to the Federal Arbitration Act (FAA) (9 U.S.C. §1 et seq.). The television defendants maintained that all claims against both them and the Leomitis should be arbitrated. The Leomitis joined in the petition.[5]

Petitioners opposed the petition, claiming, among other things, that the arbitration provision was unconscionable. . . .

After argument, the trial court issued an order granting the petition in most respects, conditioned on the television defendants paying all arbitration costs. . . . The court . . . cited United States and California Supreme Court decisions holding that under the FAA, where a party seeks to avoid application of an arbitration provision on the ground that the agreement in which the provision is contained is unenforceable, that claim must be considered by the arbitrator, not the court. The trial court also stated that "since defendants have shown that plaintiffs signed the releases having had an opportunity to read them, the arbitration provisions are found by this court to be

---

5. The memorandum of points and authorities filed in support of the petition to compel arbitration appears to rely exclusively on the arbitration provision in the Agreement, and not on the arbitration provision in the one-page Release. . . . The fact that two documents contain an arbitration provision does not affect our analysis.

enforceable." The court did not address petitioners' other specific claims of unconscionability, presumably because it construed petitioners' opposition to the petition to compel arbitration as an attack only on the entire Agreement and one-page Release, not on the arbitration provisions contained in those documents.

Petitioners then filed this writ petition challenging the trial court's ruling. We issued an alternative writ, received additional briefing from the parties, and heard oral argument.

DISCUSSION

A. UNCONSCIONABILITY AS A DEFENSE TO ENFORCEMENT OF ARBITRATION PROVISIONS

The trial court ruled, and petitioners do not dispute, that the enforceability of the arbitration clause is governed by the FAA. Federal law applies to arbitration provisions in contracts involving interstate commerce. (See 9 U.S.C. §2; . . . .) Numerous cases observe that arbitration is generally favored under both the FAA and California law. (E.g., Balandran v. Labor Ready, Inc. (2004) 124 Cal. App. 4th 1522, 1527 [22 Cal. Rptr. 3d 441]; . . . .) At the same time, our Supreme Court has emphasized that "although we have spoken of a 'strong public policy of this state in favor of resolving disputes by arbitration' [citation], Code of Civil Procedure §1281 makes clear that an arbitration agreement is to be rescinded on the same grounds as other contracts or contract terms. In this respect, arbitration agreements are neither favored nor disfavored, but simply placed on an equal footing with other contracts." (Armendariz v. Foundation Health Psychcare Services, Inc. (2000) 24 Cal. 4th 83, 126-127 [99 Cal. Rptr. 2d 745, 6 P.3d 669] (*Armendariz*); see also Buckeye Check Cashing, Inc. v. Cardegna (2006) [546 U.S. 440], 163 L. Ed. 2d 1038, 1042, 126 S. Ct. 1204, 1207 (*Buckeye*). . . .

Thus, under both the FAA and California law, "arbitration agreements are valid, irrevocable, and enforceable, save upon such grounds as exist at law or in equity for the revocation of any contract." (*Armendariz*, supra, 24 Cal. 4th at p. 98, fn. omitted.)

One ground is unconscionability, the basis asserted by petitioners below and in this writ proceeding. (See Flores v. Transamerica HomeFirst, Inc. (2001) 93 Cal. App. 4th 846, 856 [113 Cal. Rptr. 2d 376].) "The '"strong public policy of this state in favor of resolving disputes by arbitration'" does not extend to an arbitration agreement permeated by unconscionability." (*Ibid.*) As is frequently the case with inquiries into unconscionability, our analysis begins—although it does not end—with whether the Agreement and Release are contracts of adhesion. (See *Armendariz*, supra, 24 Cal. 4th at p. 113.) Petitioners contend that they are and that the arbitration provisions are unconscionable. A contract of adhesion is a standardized contract that is imposed and drafted by the party of superior bargaining strength and relegates to the other party "'only the opportunity to adhere to the contract or reject it.'" (*Ibid.*, quoting Neal v. State Farm Ins. Cos. (1961) 188 Cal. App. 2d 690, 694 [10 Cal. Rptr. 781].) Adhesion contracts are routine in modern day commerce, and at least one commentator has suggested they are worthy of neither praise nor condemnation, only analysis. (1 Corbin on Contracts (1993) §1.4, p. 14.) If a court finds a contract to be adhesive, it must then determine whether "'other factors are present which, under established legal rules — legislative or judicial — operate to render it'" unenforceable. (*Armendariz, at p. 113*, citing Graham v. Scissor-Tail, Inc. (1981) 28 Cal.3d 807, 820 [171 Cal. Rptr. 604, 623 P.2d 165] (*Graham*).)

One "established rule" is that a court need not enforce an adhesion contract that is unconscionable. (*Graham*, supra, 28 Cal.3d at p. 820.) As our Supreme Court explained in *Armendariz*, the Legislature has now codified the principle, historically developed in case law, that a court may refuse to enforce an unconscionable provision in a contract. (Civ. Code, §1670.5.)[8] . . .

Unconscionability has both a procedural and a substantive element, the former focusing on "oppression" or "surprise" due to unequal bargaining power, the latter on "overly harsh" or "one-sided" results. (*Armendariz*, supra, 24 Cal. 4th at p. 114.) "'The prevailing view is that [procedural and substantive unconscionability] must *both* be present in order for a court to exercise its discretion to refuse to enforce a contract or clause under the doctrine of unconscionability.' [Citation.] But they need not be present in the same degree. . . . [T]he more substantively oppressive the contract term, the less evidence of procedural unconscionability is required to come to the conclusion that the term is unenforceable, and vice versa." (*Ibid*.)

Under the FAA, a court may not consider a claim that an arbitration provision is unenforceable if it is a subterfuge for a challenge that the entire agreement (in which the arbitration clause is only a part) is unconscionable. That contention must be presented to the arbitrator. . . . Our task, therefore, is two-fold: (1) Does the petition here challenge the enforceability of the Agreement and the Release, in toto, or does it contest only the arbitration provision? (2) If it is the latter, is the arbitration provision unconscionable?

B. THE STANDARD OF REVIEW

. . .

C. THE TRIAL COURT INCORRECTLY CONCLUDED
PETITIONERS WERE CHALLENGING THE ENFORCEABILITY
OF THE ENTIRE AGREEMENT AND RELEASE

The trial court offered two reasons for its decision to order arbitration. First, it concluded that petitioners' opposition to arbitration was predicated on a challenge to the Agreement as a whole, not to the arbitration provision in particular. From this premise, the trial court reasoned that, because the enforceability of the entire agreement is to be considered by the arbitrator, not the court . . . , the petition should be granted. The trial court's framing of the issue was seen in its written ruling, where it stated, "Although plaintiffs

---

8. Civil Code §1670.5, subdivision (a), provides: "If the court as a matter of law finds the contract or any clause of the contract to have been unconscionable at the time it was made the court may refuse to enforce the contract, or it may enforce the remainder of the contract without the unconscionable clause, or it may so limit the application of any unconscionable clause as to avoid any unconscionable result."

argue that the 'arbitration agreements' are enforceable, their argument is directed not at the arbitration provisions but at the releases themselves." . . .

Although we agree with the court's legal analysis, its ultimate conclusion was flawed because petitioners' opposition to the petition was that the arbitration clause in particular, not the entire Agreement, was unconscionable. Petitioners devoted considerable attention to paragraph 69 of the Agreement, emphasizing that it "is not set out or made distinguishable in any manner. It is misidentified within the caption as 'miscellaneous.' It is not distinguished in different type font size, bold letters, capital letters, in red, and does not contain any separate waiver notice." The caption of a four-page argument made by petitioners reads: "The Arbitration Agreements Are Procedurally and Substantively Unconscionable Thereby Barring Their Enforcement." And in arguing that the arbitration provision was substantively unconscionable, petitioners quoted from paragraph 69 in an effort to demonstrate that the provision was one-sided, requiring only them, and not the television defendants, to submit to arbitration. The principal thrust of petitioners' oral argument to the trial court was likewise that "the entire arbitration clause was itself one-sided. So only the plaintiffs under that clause have a duty to arbitrate."

. . .

The second justification offered by the trial court for granting the television defendants' petition to compel arbitration was that petitioners had an opportunity to read the Agreement and Release before signing them. While this is factually correct and legally bears on whether the Agreement is procedurally unconscionable, no authority is cited for a supposed rule that if a party reads an agreement he or she is barred from claiming it is unconscionable. Such a rule would seriously undermine the unconscionability defense.

Given the limited scope of the trial court's ruling, we could remand to permit it to decide whether the arbitration provision is unconscionable. Instead, because the case is before us on uncontested facts and our review is de novo, we decide the legal issues in the first instance. . . .

D. THE ARBITRATION PROVISION IS UNCONSCIONABLE

1. The adhesive nature of the parties' agreement

We begin with whether the parties' agreement was adhesive. (See *Armendariz*, supra, 24 Cal. 4th at p. 113.) As discussed above, "'[t]he term [contract of adhesion] signifies a standardized contract, which, imposed and drafted by the party of superior bargaining strength, relegates to the subscribing party only the opportunity to adhere to the contract or reject it.'" (*Ibid.*)

In this case, it is undisputed that the lengthy Agreement was drafted by the television defendants. It is a standardized contract; none of the petitioners' names or other identifying information is included in the body of the document. There is no serious doubt that the television defendants had far more bargaining power than petitioners.

The remaining question is whether petitioners were relegated only to signing or rejecting the Agreement. The television defendants note that there is no evidence petitioners were told they could not negotiate any terms of the Agreement or that petitioners made any attempt to do so. Although literally correct, the uncontested evidence was that on the day petitioners signed the Agreement the television defendants initially met with the Leomitis alone. Inferentially, at the television defendants' urging, immediately after the meeting concluded, the Leomitis gave the Agreement and exhibits to petitioners with directions to "flip through the pages and sign." The documents were returned in five to 10 minutes. One of the producers testified that he told the Leomitis "that these agreements must be executed as a condition to their further participation in the program."

From these facts, we conclude the Agreement was presented to petitioners on a take-it-or-leave-it basis by the party with the superior bargaining position who was not willing to engage in negotiations. Accordingly, we conclude the Agreement and exhibits constitute a contract of adhesion.

2. Procedural unconscionability

"Procedural unconscionability focuses on the factors of surprise and oppression [citations], with surprise being a function of the disappointed reasonable expectations of the weaker party." (Harper v. Ultimo, [(2003) 113 Cal. App. 4th 1402, 1406, 7 Cal. Rptr. 3d 418.])

In this case, the arbitration provision appears in one paragraph near the end of a lengthy, single-spaced document. The entire agreement was drafted by the television defendants, who transmitted copies of it to the petitioners. The television defendants knew petitioners were young and unsophisticated, and had recently lost both parents. Indeed, it was petitioners' vulnerability that made them so attractive to the television defendants. The latter made no effort to highlight the presence of the arbitration provision in the Agreement. It was one of 12 numbered paragraphs in a section entitled "MISCELLA-NEOUS." In contrast to several other paragraphs, no text in the arbitration provision is highlighted. No words are printed in bold letters or larger font; nor are they capitalized. Although petitioners were required to place their initials in boxes adjacent to six other paragraphs, no box appeared next to the arbitration provision.

It is true that the top of the first page advises petitioners to read the entire agreement before signing it and the second-to-last paragraph states that the person signing acknowledges doing so. This language, although relevant to our inquiry, does not defeat the otherwise strong showing of procedural unconscionability.

We now turn to substantive unconscionability, utilizing our Supreme Court's sliding scale approach. (See *Armendariz*, supra, 24 Cal. 4th at p. 114.) Procedural and substantive unconscionability "need not be present in the same degree. . . ." (*Ibid.*)

3. Substantive unconscionability

"Substantively unconscionable terms may 'generally be described as unfairly one-sided.' [Citation.] For example, an agreement may lack 'a modicum of bilaterality' and therefore be unconscionable if the agreement requires 'arbitration only for the claims of the weaker party but a choice of forums for the claims of the stronger party.'" (Fitz v. NCR Corp. (2004) 118 Cal. App. 4th 702, 713 [13 Cal. Rptr. 3d 88], quoting *Armendariz*, supra, 24 Cal. 4th at p. 119.)

In this case, the arbitration provision requires only petitioners to submit their claims to arbitration. The clause repeatedly includes "I agree" language, with the "I" being a reference to the "applicant" (i.e., each of the petitioners). The only time the phrase "the parties" is used is in the last sentence, where "the parties" agree that, notwithstanding the arbitration provision, the producer has the right to seek injunctive or other equitable relief in a court of law as provided for in Code of Civil Procedure §1281.1 or other relevant laws.

The television defendants claim that the arbitration provision is bilateral, because "all disputes or controversies arising under this Agreement or any of its terms, any effort by any party to enforce . . . this Agreement . . . and any and all disputes or controversies relating to my appearance or participation in the Program, shall be resolved by binding arbitration." (P 69.) Thus, "all disputes" are subject to arbitration, and either side may move to compel. But they miss the point: only one side (petitioners) agreed to that clause.[11]

The television defendants also assert that their contractual right to seek injunctive relief shows that they are required to arbitrate since, ordinarily, a party may seek injunctive relief as a matter of civil law. The provision would be meaningless, they argue, if the television defendants were not required to submit their claims to arbitration. We disagree. Under the arbitration provision, the television defendants (though not petitioners) can *compel* arbitration. The injunction clause is significant because the television defendants can compel arbitration without fearing that doing so would preclude them from seeking injunctive or other equitable relief in a court of record.[12]

Additional elements of substantive unconscionability are found in the provision barring only petitioners from seeking appellate review of the arbitrator's decision and, at least insofar as it could impact petitioners' statutory claims, the provision requiring arbitration in accordance with the rules of the American Arbitration Association, which provide that arbitration costs are to be borne equally by the parties. . . .[13] The harsh, one-sided nature of the arbitration provision, combined with the elements of procedural unconscionability earlier discussed, leads us to conclude that the arbitration provision is unconscionable and, therefore, unenforceable. Accordingly, it was error for the trial court to have granted the petition to compel arbitration.

DISPOSITION

The petition for writ of mandate is granted. The respondent court is directed to vacate that part of its December 1, 2005, order granting the

11. Interestingly, petitioners claim the television defendants did not even sign the Agreement until after the motion to compel arbitration was filed, a point not disputed by the television defendants.

12. The fact that the injunction provision is one-sided does not necessarily mean that the clause is substantively unconscionable. A "contracting party with superior bargaining strength may provide 'extra protection' for itself within the terms of the arbitration agreement if 'business realities' create a special need for the advantage. [Citation.] The 'business realities,' creating the special need, must be explained in the terms of the contract or factually established." (Fitz v. NCR Corp., supra, 118 Cal. App.4th at p. 723.) We observe that although the television defendants explained why it was important to deny petitioners injunctive relief, they did not attempt to explain why they needed such remedy.

13. As noted above, the trial court shifted all arbitration costs to the television defendants. (See Gutierrez v. Autowest, Inc. (2003) 114 Cal.App.4th 77, 92-93 [7 Cal. Rptr. 3d 267] [unconscionable requirement for payment of arbitration costs may be severed].)

petition of the television defendants to compel arbitration and staying certain claims, and to thereafter enter a new and different order denying the petition to compel arbitration. Petitioners are entitled to recover their costs in this writ proceeding. . . .

COOPER, P. J., and BOLAND, J., concurred.

Notes and Questions

1. *Enforceability of arbitration agreements.* The court in *Higgins* recognizes that the Federal Arbitration Act and California state law both establish strong policy favoring the enforceability of written arbitration agreements. As the courts often note, however, in order for such agreements to be presumptively enforceable they must meet the basic requirements for formation of a binding contract, including the presence of mutual assent and consideration. See, e.g., Lopez v. Charles Schwab & Co., Inc., 13 Cal. Rptr. 3d 544, 547 (Ct. App. 2004); Holloman v. Circuit City Stores, Inc., 894 A.2d 547 (Md. 2006). Do these fundamental requirements seem to be met in the *Higgins* case? Even if those requirements are satisfied, the arbitration agreement may still be subject to challenge on other grounds, such as the policing doctrines covered in this chapter. (As the *Higgins* court emphasizes, the challenge must be to the arbitration clause itself and not the contract as a whole.) Are there theories other than unconscionability that the Higgins family could have used to argue that the arbitration agreement was unenforceable?

The *Higgins* opinion is concerned only with the forum in which claims will be heard and not the merits of those underlying claims. How do you imagine the Higgins family would state a cause of action for breach of contract, and against which party or parties?

2. *"Adhesion contracts" and procedural unconscionability.* The *Higgins* court begins its discussion of procedural unconscionability by noting that the agreement and release are adhesive, as defined by the court. Recall the discussion of adhesion contracts in note 6 after the *C&J Fertilizer* case in Chapter 5. Although the *Higgins* court does not do so, a number of California decisions have held that the fact that a contract is adhesive is enough of itself to render a contract procedurally unconscionable. See, e.g., Flores v. Transamerica HomeFirst, Inc., 113 Cal. Rptr. 2d 376, 382 (Ct. App. 2001). Other California decisions, as well as those from other jurisdictions, have held that something more most be shown before an adhesion contract can be found to be procedurally unconscionable. See, e.g., Morris v. Redwood Empire Bancorp, 27 Cal. Rptr. 3d 797, 807 (Ct. App. 2005) (noting that some California decisions seem to "reflexively" find adhesion contracts procedurally unconscionable but holding that there must also be a showing of a lack of market alternatives); Cooper v. MRM Investment Company, 367 F.3d 493, 504 (7th Cir. 2002) (mere fact that contract was presented on nonnegotiable basis is not enough to render it procedurally unconscionable if employee had alternatives available). Are there factors beyond the adhesive nature of the contract in *Higgins* sufficient to support the finding of procedural unconscionability?

3. *Substantive unconscionability.* Following the majority view on the question, the appellate court holds that the arbitration agreement must also have an element of substantive unconscionability in order to be rendered unenforceable. Both the trial court and the appellate court agreed that the arbitral costs would be prohibitive for the Higgins family. Many other courts have recognized that the arbitration agreement may be substantively unconscionable if excessive costs of arbitration effectively preclude the claimant from pursing relief. See Adkins v. Labor Ready, Inc., 303 F.3d 496, 502 (4th Cir. 2002). The remedy for such problem, however, may be to sever or reform this portion of the arbitration agreement and enforce the remainder, as done by the trial court in the *Higgins* case. The next case, *Adler v. Fred Lind Manor*, discusses in more detail both the possibilities of excessive costs and severance.

Another possible basis for substantive unconscionability identified by the *Higgins* court is the lack of "bilateral" application of the arbitration agreement. The California Supreme Court in the cited *Armendariz* case concluded that mandatory arbitration agreements must have a "modicum of bilaterality" to avoid substantive unconscionability. The court stated that if the arbitration system is indeed fair, then the party drafting the arbitration agreement should also be willing to submit claims to arbitration. Armendariz v. Foundation Health Psychcare Services, Inc., 6 P.3d 669, 691-692 (Cal. 2000). The arbitration agreement, however, does not need to be completely balanced in the remedies available to each side and the court held open the possibility that a party may explain why it needs the additional protection, rather than simply maximizing its advantage. Id. at 694-695. See also Torrance v. Aames Funding Corp., 242 F. Supp.2d 862, 871-872 (D. Ore. 2002) (noting that numerous courts have enforced arbitration clauses in which one party reserved the right to sue in court and thus obligations were not perfectly reciprocal). Are you persuaded that the arbitration agreement in *Higgins* is sufficiently one-sided as to render it substantively unconscionable?

4. *Questionable proliferation of mandatory arbitration agreements in consumer contracts.* As you read the *Higgins* opinion, you will observe citations to a range of cases involving mandatory arbitration agreements, often in consumer contracts: Buckeye Check Cashing, Inc. v. Cardegna, 546 U.S. 440 (2006) (check cashing services); Gutierrez v. Autowest, Inc., 7 Cal. Rptr. 3d 267 (Ct. App. 2003) (automobile leasing agreement); Harper v. Ultimo, 7 Cal. Rptr. 3d 418 (Ct. App 2003) (home repair contract); Flores v. Transamerica HomeFirst, Inc., 113 Cal. Rptr. 2d 376 (Ct. App. 2001) (home mortgage loan). The ubiquitous spread of mandatory arbitration agreements is not unique to California. See, e.g., Kristian v. Comcast Corp., 446 F.3d 25 (1st Cir. 2006) (cable services contract); Discover Bank v. Vaden, 409 F. Supp. 2d 632 (D. Md. 2006) (credit card contract); Vicksburg Partners, L.P. v. Stephens, 911 So. 2d 507 (Miss. 2005) (contract for nursing home care); Wisconsin Auto Title Loans, Inc. v. Jones, 714 N.W.2d 155 (Wis. 2006) (loans with automobile titles as collateral). See generally Charles L. Knapp, Taking Contracts Private: The Quiet Revolution in Contract Law, 71 Fordham L. Rev. 761, 796, nn.118-19 (2002) (listing cases, many involving consumers, in which arbitration agreements were found unconscionable by state or federal courts).

In an article criticizing the widespread use of arbitration agreements in consumer contracts, Professor Richard M. Alderman summarized his findings:

> The underlying premise of the ADR [Alternative Dispute Resolution] rhetoric was simple: the legal system had become too expensive, too slow, and too inefficient to deal with the myriad of problems it was being asked to resolve. . . . A voluntary, more efficient, less expensive, and more flexible alternative was needed. ADR, consisting of negotiation, mediation, and arbitration, was the panacea for the ills of the legal system, and became the catch phrase of the 80s and 90s.
>
> From a philosophical perspective, it is difficult to find fault with the concept of ADR, specifically the use of arbitration as an alternative to litigation in consumer cases. No one can oppose a system of dispute resolution that is less expensive, more efficient, and more flexible. At first glance, arbitration of consumer disputes would appear to offer substantial benefits over formal litigation. Because the rules of arbitration are less formal, and arbitrators have more freedom to "do the right thing," it should be more likely consumers would fare better in arbitration than before a judge, where they are bound by more formal rules and are subject to appellate review. Additionally, the speed and reduced cost of arbitration should provide prompt resolution. Consumers, if given the choice, would surely favor arbitration over litigation.
>
> Upon further review, however, the realities of pre-dispute mandatory arbitration, as currently employed in American consumer transactions, differ sharply from the idealized process described above. First, the consumer rarely, if ever, chooses arbitration; pre-dispute arbitration is imposed upon the consumer by a contract of adhesion in which the consumer has no real choice. Second, arbitration often is not as prompt or as inexpensive as alternative courts, especially small claims courts. Third, the informal rules, lack of guidelines, and finality of the decision often favor the business organization, due in large part to its significant role as a "repeat-player." Finally, and perhaps most importantly, imposition of mandatory arbitration generally precludes the consumer's freedom to choose to litigate in a class action and eliminates any favorable precedent or law reform that could arise through litigation.

Professor Richard M. Alderman, Pre-Dispute Mandatory Arbitration in Consumer Contracts: A Call for Reform, 38 Hous. L. Rev. 1237 (2001). See also Creola Johnson, Payday Loans: Shrewd Business or Predatory Lending?, 87 Minn. L. Rev. 1 (2002) (noting that abuses in "pay day" lending industry are compounded by growing trend of including mandatory arbitration agreements that prevent consumers from filing class action suits). The equally prevalent use of arbitration agreements in employment contracts is explored in the following case and notes.

Adler v. Fred Lind Manor
Supreme Court of Washington (En Banc.)
153 Wash.2d 331; 103 P.3d 773 (2004)

BRIDGE, J.

Like its companion case, Zuver v. Airtouch Communications, Inc., 153 Wash.2d 293, 103 P.3d 753 (2004), this case requires us to consider the enforceability of a predispute employment arbitration agreement in the context of employment discrimination litigation. Here, after employee Gerald Adler sued his employer Fred Lind Manor, the trial court granted Fred Lind Manor's motion to compel arbitration under the arbitration agreement. Adler asserts that the arbitration agreement is unenforceable because it violates his right to a jury trial, because the Washington Law Against Discrimination (WLAD), chapter 49.60 RCW, entitles him to a judicial forum, and because the arbitration agreement is both procedurally and substantively unconscionable. He also claims that Fred Lind Manor waived its right to arbitration and/or should be equitably estopped from demanding arbitration. We agree with Adler that the agreement's attorney fees and 180-day limitations provisions unreasonably favor Fred Lind Manor and are thus substantively unconscionable. We further conclude that factual disputes preclude resolution of Adler's claims of procedural unconscionability, the substantive conscionability of the fee-splitting provision, and whether his right to a jury trial was violated. We therefore remand these claims to the trial court for further proceedings consistent with this opinion.

I. STATEMENT OF FACTS

Gerald Adler immigrated to the United States from Poland in 1990. On June 4, 1992, Fred Lind Manor, a business that provides housing and services to senior citizens, hired Adler for a maintenance personnel position. Two months later, Fred Lind Manor promoted Adler to maintenance and housekeeper supervisor.

In 1995, Paradigm Senior Living assumed management of Fred Lind Manor and required all current employees to sign an arbitration agreement as a condition of their continued employment. The arbitration agreement provided:

Arbitration Agreement

I hereby agree that any dispute related to my employment relationship shall be resolved exclusively through binding arbitration in Seattle, Washington under the American Arbitration Association's Commercial Arbitration Rules, except as other wise [sic] provided here.

I agree to the following terms of arbitration as part of this agreement to arbitration. The aggrieved party must deliver to the other party a written notice of his/her/its intention to seek arbitration no later than 180 days after the event that first gives rise to the dispute. Otherwise his/her/its rights shall be irrevocably waived. The dispute shall be decided by one arbitrator selected by mutual agreement of the parties, or absent agreement, in accordance with the Rules. The arbitrator's fee and other expenses of the arbitration process shall be shared equally. The parties shall bear their own respective costs and attorneys fees. Washington law, to the extent permitted, shall govern all substantive aspects of the dispute and all procedural issues not covered by the Rules.

Adler signed the agreement as did general manager, Christine Serold.

Adler received another promotion to maintenance and housekeeper director in May 1998. Then on January 16, 2001, general manager Mark Mullen ordered him to move a commercial dryer, and while moving the dryer, Adler hurt his hip and back. On January 17, 2001, Adler visited his doctor who diagnosed him with hip osteoarthritis and advised him to perform "light duty." Id. at 5. On that same day, Adler filed his first claim with the Department of Labor and Industries (DLI).[1] He sustained additional injuries on June 1, 2001, and January 14, 2002, and filed claims with DLI for these injuries.[2] On June 11, 2002, Mullen fired Adler for "'inability to operate all aspects of [the] maintenance department.'" Fred Lind Manor replaced Adler with a younger employee.

On October 2, 2002, Adler filed a complaint with the Equal Employment Opportunity Commission (EEOC) alleging that Fred Lind Manor and Mullen violated the Americans with Disabilities Act of 1990, 42 U.S.C. §12101, the Age Discrimination in Employment Act of 1967, 29 U.S.C. §623, and Title VII of the Civil Rights Act of 1964 (Title VII), as amended, 42 U.S.C. §2000e. In December 2002, Fred Lind Manor responded asserting that it had discharged Adler because of poor attendance, failure to meet productivity standards, Adler's sexual harassment of another employee, unauthorized use of Fred Lind Manor's facilities, and failure to respect residents' rights. Fred Lind Manor did not mention the existence of the arbitration agreement.

On January 9, 2003, the parties attended EEOC mediation. Neither party made reference to the arbitration agreement. Approximately four months after mediation, the EEOC dismissed Adler's complaint stating that "the EEOC is unable to conclude that the information obtained establishes violations of the statutes." . . .

On May 20, 2003, Adler filed a complaint in superior court alleging that Fred Lind Manor violated the WLAD by discriminating against him for his disability, age, and national origin; discharged him for pursuing worker's benefits in violation of Title 51 RCW; committed the tort of wrongful discharge in violation of public policy; committed the tort of intentional infliction of emotional distress; and created a hostile work environment. Fred Lind Manor filed its answer on August 1, 2003, claiming for the first time that Adler must submit his claims to arbitration. Fourteen days later, Fred Lind Manor moved to compel arbitration and stay proceedings. During a telephone conversation with Adler's attorney, Fred Lind Manor indicated that at arbitration, it planned to seek dismissal of Adler's claims pursuant to the 180-day statute of limitations provision of the arbitration agreement.

In response to Fred Lind Manor's motion to compel arbitration, Adler claimed he did not understand that the 1995 agreement required him to arbitrate his future claims nor was he given a copy of the agreement.[3] He requested that the court declare the agreement void as unconscionable or, alternatively, find that Fred Lind Manor had waived arbitration. Without

---

1. Adler claims that he made a request to Mullen that Fred Lind Manor provide him with light duty pursuant to his doctor's orders, but Mullen failed to accommodate his hip injury.

2. Adler also asserts that on other occasions, Mullen criticized Adler's claims to DLI, made fun of his accent, criticized him for hiring "foreigners," and ridiculed him for his Polish origin.

3. Fred Lind Manor disputes Adler's claim that he never received a copy of the arbitration agreement. It notes that within one month of his termination, Adler requested a copy of his personnel file, which contained the arbitration agreement, and that he was permitted to inspect, examine, and copy his file. Fred Lind Manor contends Adler's action is verified by handwritten numbers he placed on the pages of his file while examining it. . . .

holding a hearing, the trial court granted Fred Lind Manor's motion to compel arbitration and stay proceedings.

. . . We granted review.

II ANALYSIS

. . . Section 2 of the FAA provides that written arbitration agreements "shall be valid, irrevocable, and enforceable, save upon such grounds as exist at law or in equity for the revocation of *any* contract." 9 U.S.C. §2 (emphasis added). The United States Supreme Court has stated that "[s]ection 2 is a congressional declaration of a liberal federal policy favoring arbitration agreements, notwithstanding any state substantive or procedural policies to the contrary."[4] Moses H. Cone Mem'l Hosp. v. Mercury Constr. Corp., 460 U. S. 1, 24, 103 S. Ct. 927, 74 L. Ed. 2d 765 (1983). . . .

Although federal and state courts presume arbitrability, "generally applicable contract defenses, such as fraud, duress, or unconscionability, may be applied to invalidate arbitration agreements without contravening §2." Doctor's Assocs., Inc., v. Casarotto, 517 U.S. 681, 687, 116 S. Ct. 1652, 134 L. Ed. 2d 902 (1996). . . .

We engage in de novo review of a trial court's decision to grant a motion to compel or deny arbitration. . . . The party opposing arbitration bears the burden of showing that the agreement is not enforceable. See Green Tree Fin. Corp. v. Randolph, 531 U.S. 79, 92, 121 S. Ct. 513, 148 L. Ed. 2d 373 (2000).

WLAD REQUIREMENTS

Relying on cases holding that an exclusive remedies provision in a collective bargaining agreement does not prevent employees from initiating civil suits in court for violations of the WLAD, Adler argues that the WLAD requires a judicial forum for discrimination claims of employees. . . . The United States Supreme Court . . . has held that in instances where a valid individual employee-employer arbitration agreement exists, the FAA requires that employees arbitrate federal and state law discrimination claims. See Gilmer v. Interstate/Johnson Lane Corp., 500 U.S. 20, 27-28, 111 S. Ct. 1647, 114 L. Ed. 2d 26 (1991) (holding that the FAA requires arbitration of age discrimination claims when a valid arbitration agreement exists). . . . Moreover, the FAA clearly preempts any state law to the contrary. . . . Thus, we reject Adler's claim that the WLAD entitles him to a judicial forum.

UNCONSCIONABILITY

It is black letter law of contracts that the parties to a contract shall be bound by its terms. . . . Adler argues that he should be exempt from the terms of the agreement here because it is both procedurally and substantively unconscionable. "The existence of an unconscionable bargain is a question of law for the courts." Nelson v. McGoldrick, 127 Wash.2d 124, 131, 896 P.2d 1258 (1995). . . . In Washington, we have recognized two categories of unconscionability, substantive and procedural. Id. (citing Schroeder v. Fageol

---

4. Washington State also has a strong public policy favoring arbitration of disputes. See Int'l Ass'n of Fire Fighters, Local 46 v. City of Everett, 146 Wash.2d 29, 51, 42 P.3d 1265 (2002). . . .

Motors, Inc., 86 Wash.2d 256, 260, 544 P.2d 20 (1975)). "Substantive unconscionability involves those cases where a clause or term in the contract is alleged to be one-sided or overly harsh. . . ." *Schroeder*, 86 Wash.2d at 260. "'Shocking to the conscience', 'monstrously harsh', and 'exceedingly calloused' are terms sometimes used to define substantive unconscionability." *Nelson*, 127 Wash.2d at 131. . . . Procedural unconscionability is "the lack of a meaningful choice, considering all the circumstances surrounding the transaction including "'[t]he manner in which the contract was entered," whether each party had "a reasonable opportunity to understand the terms of the contract," and whether "the important terms [were] hidden in a maze of fine print."'" Id. at 131 (alterations in original) (quoting *Schroeder*, 86 Wash.2d at 260 (quoting Williams v. Walker-Thomas Furniture Co., 121 U.S. App. D.C. 315, 350 F.2d 445, 449 (D.C. Cir. 1965))). We have cautioned that "these three factors [should] not be applied mechanically without regard to whether in truth a meaningful choice existed." Id.

We have not explicitly addressed whether a party challenging a contract must show both substantive and procedural unconscionability. However, our decisions in *Nelson*, 127 Wash.2d at 131, and *Schroeder*, 86 Wash.2d at 260, analyze procedural and substantive unconscionability separately without suggesting that courts must find both to render a contract void. . . .

Fred Lind Manor and amicus, Association of Washington Business (AWB), urge us to require proof of both substantive and procedural unconscionability to render a contract void as unconscionable. The AWB asserts that a majority of courts adopt this approach since,

> [i]f, despite grossly unequal bargaining power between the parties or other evidence of lack of meaningful choice, the terms of the contract are nonetheless fair, the weaker party has suffered no injury. Likewise, courts should not interfere with the terms of a contract, however "harsh" or one-sided, where the parties were of equal bargaining power or where there was no unfairness in the manner in which the contract was executed.

Amicus Curiae Br. of AWB at 11. *See also* 8 Samuel Williston, a Treatise on the Law of Contracts §18:10, at 67 (Richard A. Lord, 4th ed. 1998) ("[S]urprise or an inability to bargain with understanding as to the terms of an agreement (procedural unfairness) must culminate in the drafting party's exacting harsh or unreasonable terms from the other party (substantive unfairness) before the concept of unconscionability becomes applicable in the view of perhaps most jurisdictions.").

In Maxwell v. Fidelity Financial Services, Inc., 184 Ariz. 82, 90, 907 P.2d 51 (1995), the Arizona Supreme Court considered an almost identical argument. There the court held that "a claim of unconscionability can be established with a showing of substantive unconscionability alone, especially in cases involving either price-cost disparity or limitation of remedies." Id. The court, however, reserved the question whether procedural unconscionability alone could render a contract void as unconscionable. Id.

We agree with the Arizona Supreme Court. In some instances, individual contractual provisions may be so one-sided and harsh as to render them substantively unconscionable despite the fact that the circumstances surrounding the parties' agreement to the contract do not support a finding of procedural unconscionability. See 2 Restatement (Second) of Contracts §208 cmt. e (1981) ("Particular terms may be unconscionable whether or not the contract as a whole is unconscionable."). Accordingly, we now hold that substantive unconscionability alone can support a finding of unconscionability. However, since Adler has yet to prove a valid claim of procedural unconscionability, we decline to consider whether it alone will support a claim of unconscionability.

PROCEDURAL UNCONSCIONABILITY

. . .

First, Adler asserts that the arbitration agreement is an adhesion contract, which he argues, supports his claim of unconscionability. We have established the following factors to determine whether an adhesion contract exists: "(1) whether the contract is a standard form printed contract, (2) whether it was 'prepared by one party and submitted to the other on a "take it or leave it" basis', and (3) whether there was 'no true equality of bargaining power' between the parties." Yakima County (W. Valley) Fire Prot. Dist. No. 12 v. City of Yakima, 122 Wash.2d 371, 393, 858 P.2d 245 (1993). . . . [T]he fact that an agreement is an adhesion contract does not necessarily render it procedurally unconscionable. . . .

Fred Lind Manor and Adler's agreement is an adhesion contract. Paradigm provided a standard form printed arbitration agreement to all of Fred Lind Manor's employees. . . . Fred Lind Manor's representative, Serold, informed employees that they must sign the agreement as a condition of their continued employment, i.e., on a "take it or leave it basis." Id. Presumably, employees were not free to negotiate the terms of the agreement with Fred Lind Manor. Thus, there was "'no true equality of bargaining power.'" *Yakima County Fire Prot. Dist.*, 122 Wash.2d at 393. . . . Nonetheless, the fact that Fred Lind Manor and Adler's arbitration agreement is an adhesion contract does not end our inquiry. Id.

Adler further asserts that the agreement is procedurally unconscionable because his unequal bargaining power precluded him from negotiating terms of the agreement. . . . However, we have held that while unequal bargaining power may exist between parties, the mere existence of unequal bargaining power will not, standing alone, justify a finding of procedural unconscionability. . . . Rather, the key inquiry for finding procedural unconscionability is whether Adler lacked meaningful choice. *Schroeder*, 86 Wash.2d at 260.

Adler contends he lacked meaningful choice because the manner in which he entered the contract shows that he was forced to sign the agreement under threat that Fred Lind Manor would fire him, and that his financial circumstances, namely his new daughter and new house, placed pressure on him to sign the agreement. He further avers that he "had no idea what an arbitration was or what it meant." Fred Lind Manor, however, disputes Adler's version of the facts asserting that it had no knowledge of Adler's financial circumstances; that it never threatened to fire him if he refused to sign the agreement; that Serold explained that "arbitration was an alternative to going into a lawsuit in court," and that Adler "'did not indicate any reservations or reluctance in signing the document, and prior to signing, he read it, seemed to understand it, and absolutely signed it of his own free will.'" . . .

Adler also contends that he did not have a reasonable opportunity to understand the arbitration agreement since his limited English impaired his ability to fully comprehend its provisions. On the other hand, Fred Lind Manor claims that Serold explained the terms of the agreement and that Adler appeared to understand its terms. Perhaps most importantly, Adler admits that he pondered the arbitration agreement for a week and presumably, had ample opportunity to contact counsel and inquire about the meaning of its terms. We conclude therefore that the evidence here weighs against Adler's claim that he did not have a reasonable opportunity to understand the terms of the agreement.

Further, the important terms were not hidden in a "maze of fine print." First, this short half page agreement is clearly labeled **"Arbitration Agreement"** in boldface type and normal font. The first sentence explicitly states, "I hereby agree that any dispute related to my employment relationship shall be resolved exclusively through binding arbitration." Thus, this circumstance of Adler and Fred Lind Manor's transaction does not support Adler's claim of procedural unconscionability.

Nevertheless, we have cautioned that these factors should "not be applied mechanically without regard to whether in truth a meaningful choice existed." *Nelson*, 127 Wash.2d at 131. Although Fred Lind Manor appears to have provided Adler with a reasonable opportunity to understand the terms of the agreement, and the important terms were not hidden, Adler and Fred Lind Manor offer remarkably different versions of the facts pertaining to the manner in which the contract was entered into. . . . Consequently, we cannot make a determination of procedural unconscionability without further factual findings.

When disputes exist as to the circumstances surrounding an agreement, we remand to the trial court to make additional findings. . . . If Fred Lind Manor's representative threatened to fire him for refusing to sign the agreement despite the fact that Adler raised concerns with its terms or indicated a lack of understanding, the manner of the transaction would lend support to Adler's claim of procedural unconscionability.[9] . . . However, if, as Fred Lind Manor contends, Serold explained the document and/or offered to answer Adler's concerns or questions, such facts will not lend support to Adler's claim of procedural unconscionability. . . . Accordingly, we remand Adler's case to the trial court for further proceedings consistent with this opinion.

SUBSTANTIVE UNCONSCIONABILITY

Adler contends that the agreement's unilateral application renders it substantively unconscionable. He further argues that the arbitration agreement's fee-splitting, attorney fees, and limitations provisions are substantively unconscionable. Fred Lind Manor disputes Adler's claims countering that he improperly relies on California and Ninth Circuit law.

---

9. If the trial court finds that Adler has proved his claim of procedural unconscionability, in accordance with the facts of this particular case such a finding will necessarily lead to a finding that Adler's waiver of his right to a jury was not "knowing, voluntary, and intelligent." If such a finding is ultimately made, the arbitration agreement would be void.

UNILATERAL APPLICATION

Relying on Ingle [v. Circuit City Stores, Inc., 328 F.3d 1165, 1171, 1174 (9th Cir. 2003), cert. denied, 540 U.S. 1160, 124 S. Ct. 1169, 157 L. Ed. 2d 1204 (2004)], Adler argues that the arbitration agreement is substantively unconscionable because it applies only to disputes brought by employees, not to disputes brought by Fred Lind Manor against its employees. Fred Lind Manor, however, claims that the agreement is bilateral since it also requires Fred Lind Manor to arbitrate any of its disputes brought against its employees.

To interpret the meaning of a contract's terms, Washington courts employ the context rule. . . . The context rule requires that we determine the intent of the parties by viewing the contract as a whole, which includes the subject matter and intent of the contract, examination of the circumstances surrounding its formation, subsequent acts and conduct of the parties, the reasonableness of the respective interpretations advanced by the parties, and statements made by the parties during preliminary negotiations, trade usage, and/or course of dealing. . . .

The text of the agreement here, as well as the parties' statements and conduct, support Fred Lind Manor's claim that the agreement also requires it to arbitrate its disputes against employees. First, at the time the arbitration agreements were executed, then-manager Serold informed employees that the arbitration agreement reflected management's policy that all employment disputes, "whether by employer or an employee," be subject to binding arbitration instead of a lawsuit in court. Serold also indisputably acted in her role as Fred Lind Manor's representative when she signed Adler's and other employees' agreements on Fred Lind Manor's behalf. Id. Most importantly, the agreement provides, "[t]he *aggrieved party* must deliver to the other party a written notice of *his/her/its* intention to seek arbitration . . . Otherwise *his/her/its rights* shall be irrevocably waived." . . . (emphasis added). This provision does not single out individual employees' disputes against Fred Lind Manor. Rather, it refers generically to the "aggrieved party," and, by use of the words "his/her/its," clearly contemplates suits brought by Fred Lind Manor against its employees. . . . Thus, we reject Adler's argument that this arbitration agreement applies unilaterally.

FEE-SPLITTING PROVISION

Next, Adler argues that the agreement's fee-splitting provision is substantively unconscionable because the cost of arbitration would effectively bar him from bringing his claims.[11] . . .

As noted in *Zuver,* the United States Supreme Court has acknowledged that arbitration fees may prohibit employees from bringing their discrimination claims but held that "where . . . a party seeks to invalidate an arbitration agreement on the ground that arbitration would be prohibitively expensive, that party bears the burden of showing the likelihood of incurring such costs." *Green Tree Fin. Corp.,* 531 U.S. at 92. In *Zuver* we further held that in order for

---

11. The fee-splitting provision states, "[t]he arbitrator's fee and other expenses of the arbitration process shall be shared equally." . . .

a party opposing arbitration to meet his burden of showing the likelihood of incurring excessive costs, the Court of Appeals decision in Mendez [v. Palm Harbor Homes, Inc., 45 P.3d 594 (2002)] sets forth the proper approach. There the court held that by producing an affidavit describing his personal finances as well as fee information obtained from the American Arbitration Association's Seattle office, the party opposing arbitration, Mendez, had provided sufficient evidence to prove that the fee-splitting provision in his arbitration agreement was substantively unconscionable. Id. at 467-68. Unlike Mendez, Adler has failed to provide any specific information about the arbitration fees he will be required to share and why such fees would effectively prohibit him from bringing his claims. Consequently, he has not met his burden here to show that the agreement's fee-splitting provision is substantively unconscionable.

Although Adler has failed to meet his burden, we hesitate to reach a final decision about the substantive conscionability of the agreement's fee-splitting provision. In similar circumstances, the Third Circuit Court of Appeals has remanded the case to the trial court and permitted limited discovery on the issue of whether such fees would effectively prohibit arbitration. . . . Alexander v. Anthony Int'l, L.P., 341 F.3d 256, 268 (3d Cir. 2003). Like the Third Circuit, we believe that Adler should have the opportunity to prove that the costs of arbitration would prohibit him from vindicating his claims. Therefore, on remand the trial court should provide the parties with the opportunity to engage in limited discovery regarding the costs of arbitration. On remand, "[o]nce prohibitive costs are established, the opposing party [Fred Lind Manor] must present contrary offsetting evidence to enforce arbitration." . . . Such evidence may include an offer to pay all or part of the arbitration fees and costs. . . .

ATTORNEY FEES PROVISION

The arbitration agreement provides that "[t]he parties shall bear their own respective costs and attorneys fees." . . . Adler contends that this provision is substantively unconscionable because it is one-sided and overly harsh requiring him to waive the right to recover his attorney fees and costs under RCW 49.60.030(2).[12] Fred Lind Manor, on the other hand, asserts that this provision,

> provides only that the employer need not pay plaintiff's fees and costs leading up to and during the hearing; it does not hamper a prevailing claimant's right to attorney fees under the WLAD after ultimately prevailing. Both the Agreement and the rules provide that Washington law, including the WLAD, governs.

Resp'ts' Br. at 39.

We do not find Fred Lind Manor's interpretation of this provision persuasive. It is a well-known principle of contract interpretation that "specific terms and exact terms are given greater weight than general language." 2 Restatement (Second) of Contracts §203(c) (1981). While the

---

12. RCW 49.60.030(2) provides that prevailing plaintiffs shall "recover the actual damages sustained by the person, or both, together with the cost of suit including reasonable attorneys' fees."

agreement generally provides that "Washington law, to the extent permitted, shall govern all substantive aspects of the dispute and all procedural issues not covered by the Rules," the agreement's attorney fees provision specifically and unambiguously states that the "parties *shall* bear their own respective costs and attorneys fees." . . . (emphasis added). Moreover, any ambiguity between these arguably conflicting provisions is resolved against the drafter, Fred Lind Manor. . . . Consequently, this provision effectively undermines a plaintiff's rights to attorney fees under RCW 49.60.030(2) and "helps . . . the party with a substantially stronger bargaining position and more resources, to the disadvantage of an employee needing to obtain legal assistance." *Alexander*, 341 F.3d at 267. See also Brooks v. Travelers Ins. Co., 297 F.3d 167, 171 (2d Cir. 2002) (noting that an arbitration agreement which restricts recovery of attorney fees would prevent plaintiffs from vindicating their statutory rights under Title VII). Thus, we hold that the attorney fees provision of the agreement is substantively unconscionable.

LIMITATION ON ACTIONS

Adler also argues the arbitration agreement's 180-day statute of limitations is substantively unconscionable because it provides for a substantially shorter limitations period than he is entitled to under the WLAD. Chapter 49.60 RCW, however, does not expressly provide for a particular statute of limitations for employment discrimination claims. Instead, courts have applied the general three-year statute of limitations in RCW 4.16.080(2) to WLAD claims reasoning that violations of chapter 49.60 RCW amount to an invasion of a person's legal rights.

. . .

. . . Washington courts have established that a contract's limitations provision will "prevail over general statutes of limitations unless prohibited by statute or public policy, or unless they are unreasonable." Ashburn [v. Safeco Ins. Co. of Am., 713 P.2d 742, rev. denied, 105 Wash.2d 1016 (1986). . . . No statute explicitly prohibits Fred Lind Manor and Adler from adopting a shorter limitation provision for WLAD claims in their contract.

Numerous courts have considered whether limitations provisions in arbitration agreements and/or adhesion contracts are substantively unconscionable. Some have held that six-month limitations provisions for Title VII claims are reasonable, but that shorter limitations periods, i.e., 30 days, are substantively unconscionable. Soltani v. W.&S. Life Ins. Co., 258 F.3d 1038, 1044 (9th Cir. 2001) (upholding a six-month limitations provision in an employment contract); Taylor v. W.&S. Life Ins. Co., 966 F.2d 1188, 1206 (7th Cir. 1992) (upholding a six-month limitation period). Cf. *Alexander*, 341 F.3d at 267 (holding that a 30-day limitations provision is substantively unconscionable); Plaskett v. Bechtel Int'l, Inc., 243 F. Supp. 2d 334, 341 (D.V.I. 2003) (holding that a 30-day limitations provision is substantively unconscionable). The Ninth Circuit has held that even one-year limitations provisions are substantively unconscionable because they deprive plaintiffs the benefit of the continuing violation and tolling doctrines under federal and state discrimination laws. *Ingle*, 328 F.3d at 1175; Circuit City Stores, Inc. v. Adams, 279 F.3d 889, 894-95 (9th Cir.), cert. denied, 535 U.S. 1112, 153 L. Ed. 2d 160, 122 S. Ct. 2329 (2002).

We agree with the Ninth Circuit. By limiting the period of time in which its employees may bring discrimination claims, Fred Lind Manor obtains unfair advantages. First, in order to timely pursue his claim against Fred Lind Manor at arbitration, an employee may be forced to forgo the opportunity to file his complaint and have that complaint investigated and mediated by the EEOC or Washington Human Rights Commission (WHRC) . . . Moreover, because the agreement demands that an employee "deliver to the other party a written notice of his/her/its intention to seek arbitration no later than 180 days *after the event that first gives rise to the dispute*," that employee could be barred from seeking those damages for a hostile work environment arising out of discriminatory behavior which occurred outside the limitations period. . . . (emphasis added). The agreement's language requiring written notice within 180 days of "the event that *first* gives rise to the dispute," could be interpreted to insulate the employer from potential liability for violative behavior occurring outside the limitations period by establishing a liability cut-off if notice of the *first* violative behavior is not given within 180 days. Therefore, we hold that the 180-day limitations provision in the agreement unreasonably favors Fred Lind Manor and thus is substantively unconscionable.

SEVERANCE OF THE SUBSTANTIVELY UNCONSCIONABLE PROVISIONS

Fred Lind Manor urges us to sever any provisions we find to be substantively unconscionable arguing that the essential term of the parties' bargain, i.e., arbitration, should be retained. Adler, however, contends that because the substantively unconscionable provisions pervade the entire agreement, we should refuse to sever those provisions and declare the entire agreement void. See *Ingle,* 328 F.3d at 1180 (holding that the employer's "insidious pattern" of seeking to tip the scales in its favor during employment disputes justified a decision to declare the entire agreement unenforceable). The Restatement (Second) of Contracts §208 (1981) provides that:

> If a contract or term thereof is unconscionable at the time the contract is made a court may refuse to enforce the contract, *or may enforce the remainder of the contract without the unconscionable term,* or may so limit the application of any unconscionable term as to avoid any unconscionable result.

(Emphasis added.) For contracts concerning leases, sales, real property, and retail installments, our legislature has adopted the *Restatement* position directing that in cases where these contracts are found to contain an unconscionable provision, courts may "enforce the remainder of the . . . contract without the unconscionable clause." . . .

The *Restatement* position concerning severance of unconscionable provisions should also apply in cases where courts are confronted with substantively unconscionable provisions in employment arbitration agreements. Accord Helstrom v. N. Slope Borough, 797 P.2d 1192, 1200 (Alaska 1990); . . . Application of this rule facilitates the accomplishment of important federal and state public policies favoring arbitration of disputes. . . .

Nonetheless, we acknowledge that in instances where an employer engages in an "insidious pattern" of seeking to tip the scales in its favor in employment disputes by inserting numerous unconscionable provisions in an arbitration agreement, courts may decline to sever the unconscionable provisions. *Ingle*, 328 F.3d at 1180. In this case, however, Adler and Fred Lind Manor's arbitration agreement contains just two substantively unconscionable provisions. The primary thrust of their agreement is the agreement to arbitrate. Consequently, we can sever the unconscionable attorney fees and limitations provisions without disturbing the primary intent of the parties to arbitrate their disputes.[15] . . .

JURY TRIAL RIGHTS

Adler argues that compelling him to arbitrate his disputes violates his jury trial rights under article I, section 21 of the Washington Constitution because he did not "knowing[ly], voluntar[ily], and intelligent[ly]" waive his right to a jury trial. . . .

[A]s discussed supra, disputes still remain about the manner in which Adler entered into the arbitration agreement with Fred Lind Manor. Consequently, we decline to hold here that Adler knowingly and voluntarily entered into the arbitration agreement with Fred Lind Manor. On remand, if the trial court concludes that Fred Lind Manor's representative threatened to fire him if he refused to sign the agreement despite the fact he raised concerns with its terms or indicated a lack of understanding, then the evidence here would not support Fred Lind Manor's claim that Adler knowingly and voluntarily agreed to arbitration, and thus implicitly waived his right to a jury trial. However, if as Fred Lind Manor contends, its representative explained the document and offered to answer Adler's concerns or questions, Adler's claim fails.

WAIVER

Adler also argues that Fred Lind Manor waived its right to compel arbitration by waiting until August 2003 before invoking the arbitration agreement. . . .

Fred Lind Manor has not acted in a manner here which suggests waiver. . . . Fred Lind Manor raised its defense of arbitration in its initial answer to Adler's complaint and promptly moved to compel arbitration after serving its answer. Thus, we conclude that Fred Lind Manor neither commenced litigation nor ignored arbitration.

. . .

III CONCLUSION

We reject Adler's claims that the WLAD entitles him to a judicial forum, that Fred Lind Manor has waived its right to arbitrate this dispute, and/or that Fred Lind Manor should be equitably estopped from asserting arbitration. However, we conclude that the attorney fees and limitations provisions of the arbitration agreement are substantively unconscionable but sever these provisions from the agreement thus preserving the parties' intent to arbitrate their disputes. We remand to the trial court for determination, consistent with this opinion, of Adler's claims of procedural unconscionability, including

---

15. On remand, in the event the trial court finds the fee-splitting provision to be substantively unconscionable, it may likewise sever that provision and still compel arbitration.

whether Adler implicitly waived his right to a jury trial and the substantive conscionability of the fee-splitting provision.

Alexander, C.J., and Johnson, Sanders, Ireland, Chambers, Owens, and Fairhurst, JJ., concur.

Madsen, J. (concurring opinion) [Omitted. – EDS.]

Notes and Questions

1. *Policy orientation of the court.* The *Higgins* court held that the arbitration agreement in that case was unconscionable, whereas the *Adler* opinion reflects the court's strong inclination to enforce the arbitration agreement before it after severing certain substantively unconscionable aspects. Do factual differences between the two cases make them reconcilable? Or would one be justified in concluding that the enforceability of an arbitration clause is often a highly debatable question that is likely to turn on the policy orientation of the court deciding the case?

2. *Procedural and substantive unconscionability.* Consistent with *Higgins*, the *Adler* court frames its discussion of unconscionability as involving questions of procedural and substantive unconscionability. While acknowledging arguments by Fred Lind Manor and amicus curiae that a party should be required to show both procedural and substantive unconscionability to prevail, the *Adler* court departs from that more common approach and holds that substantive unconscionability alone can be enough to render a contract unenforceable. The *Adler* court cites Restatement (Second) of Contracts §208 cmt. *e* in support of its conclusion. Comment *c* to that section, however, may be more relevant. It reads, in part:

> *c. Overall imbalance.* Inadequacy of consideration does not of itself invalidate a bargain, but gross disparity in the values exchanged may be an important factor in a determination that a contract is unconscionable and may be sufficient ground, without more, for denying specific performance. . . . Theoretically it is possible for a contract to be oppressive taken as a whole, even though there is no weakness in the bargaining process and no single term which is in itself unconscionable. Ordinarily, however, an unconscionable contract involves other factors as well as overall imbalance.

Does this comment support the decision in *Adler to* depart from the majority approach that requires both procedural and substantive unconscionability to be shown?

The *Adler* court, of course, remanded the case for additional factual inquiry concerning the circumstances under which Adler signed the arbitration agreement. Which of the alleged facts would be most significant in determining whether there was procedural unconscionability?

3. *Severance of substantively unconscionable terms.* The *Adler* court found that a number of provisions in the agreement were substantively unconscionable but held that the appropriate remedy was to sever those provisions and enforce the remainder of the arbitration agreement. Many courts have taken this approach. See, e.g., Kristian v. Comcast Corp., 446 F.3d 25, 61 (1st Cir.

2006) (terms prohibiting class actions, treble damages and attorney's fees could be severed); Morrison v. Circuit City Stores, 317 F.3d 646, 678 (6th Cir. 2003) (terms splitting arbitration costs and limiting remedy could be severed). But see Ferguson v. Countrywide Credit Indus., 298 F.3d 778, 788 (9th Cir. 2002) (unconscionable terms involving lack of mutuality in scope, payment of fees, and limiting discovery so permeated arbitration agreement that they could not be severed; arbitration agreement held unenforceable); State ex rel. Dunlap v. Berger, 567 S.E.2d 265, 284 (W. Va. 2002) (unconscionable terms that were exculpatory and limited buyer's remedies in arbitration were purposely intended to shield jewelry store from liability and would not be reformed by court).

4. *Prohibitions on class actions.* Arbitration agreements also frequently ban class actions and courts must decide whether such terms should be enforced. The pivotal concern in this area is that claimants in actions for relatively small amounts of damages may not be able to vindicate meritorious claims because the cost of litigation for the individual claimant would be prohibitive. A class action suit, however, in which multiple claimants bring suit jointly, might make the litigation cost effective. The courts have been divided on whether bans on class actions in arbitration agreements should be enforced. Compare Jones v. Deja Vu, Inc., 419 F. Supp. 2d 1146, 1149 (N.D. Cal. 2005) (ban on class actions in employment setting unenforceable where claim was type for which such actions are intended and employer offered no justification for the prohibition), with Hubbert v. Dell Corp., 835 N.E.2d 113, 125-126 (Ill. Ct. App. 2005) (plaintiff failed to prove that consumers would fail to pursue claims without class action available). See generally Jean R. Sternlight and Elizabeth J. Jensen, Mandatory Arbitration: Using Arbitration to Eliminate Consumer Class Actions: Efficient Business Practice or Unconscionable Abuse?, 67 Law & Contemp. Prob. 75 (2004) (asserting that arbitral class action bans effectively insulate companies from liability, that use of the unconscionability doctrine is too expensive and unwieldy to correct this practice, and that federal legislation should be adopted to prohibit bans on consumer arbitral class actions).

5. *Confidentiality clauses.* In a companion case to *Adler*, Zuver v. Airtouch Communications, Inc., 103 P.3d 753 (2004), the Washington Supreme Court held that a confidentiality agreement in an employment arbitration agreement was substantively unconscionable. The *Zuver* court quoted and adopted the following reasoning from Cole v. Burns International Security Services, 105 F.3d 1465, 1477 (D.C. Cir. 1997):

> [W]hile a lack of public disclosure of arbitration awards is acceptable in the collective bargaining context, because both employers and unions monitor such decisions and the awards rarely involve issues of concern to persons other than the parties, in the context of individual statutory claims, a lack of public disclosure may systematically favor companies over individuals.

103 P.3d at 765. The *Zuver* court agreed that the confidentiality provision benefitted the employer by "hamper[ing] an employee's ability to prove a pattern of discrimination or to take advantage of findings in past arbitrations." Id. See also Susan Randall, Judicial Attitudes Toward Arbitration and the

Resurgence of Unconscionability, 52 Buffalo L. Rev. 185, 218-220 (2004) (observing that most courts confronting the issue have held that confidentiality clauses are unconscionable). But see Iberia Credit Bureau, Inc. v. Cingular Wireless LLC, 379 F.3d 159, 175-176 (5th Cir. 2004) (confidentiality clause favored cellular provider but was not so offensive as to be invalid).

6. *Proliferation of arbitration agreements in employment contracts.* Recent cases reflect the widespread use of mandatory arbitration agreements in employment settings, covering a wide range of workers from those involved in professional or managerial activities to those more likely involved primarily in labor or service roles, as in *Adler.* See, e.g., Circuit City Stores, Inc. v. Adams, 279 F.3d 889 (9th Cir. 2002) (holding mandatory arbitration agreement unenforceable against store salesperson); Brown v. Dorsey & Whitney, LLP, 267 F. Supp. 2d 61 (D. D.C. 2003) (holding mandatory arbitration agreement enforceable against attorney-employee); Geiger v. Ryan's Family Steak Houses, Inc., 134 F. Supp. 2d 985 (S.D. Ind. 2001) (finding unconscionable the mandatory arbitration agreements signed by servers at restaurant; court expressed "major doubts" that typical high school graduates would have time to read and understand complex agreement during job application process). For discussions of the prevalent use of arbitration agreements in employment contracts, see Katherine Eddy, Note, To Every Remedy a Wrong: The Confounding of Civil Liberties Through Mandatory Arbitration Clauses in Employment Contracts, 52 Hastings L.J. 771, 791 (2001); Christine M. Reilly, Comment, Achieving Knowing and Voluntary Consent in Pre-Dispute Mandatory Arbitration Agreements at the Contracting Stage of Employment, 90 Cal. L. Rev. 1203 (2002).

7. *Unconscionability in Commercial Cases.* Merchants or other commercial parties frequently allege that they are victims of unconscionable bargains, though the courts usually have been disinclined to give relief to those parties. On appropriate facts, however, courts have occasionally found unconscionability in such cases. A leading example is A & M Produce v. FMC Corp., 186 Cal. Rptr. 114 (Ct. App. 1982) in which a contract for sale of faulty agricultural machinery included a warranty disclaimer and an exclusion of consequential damages. The court found procedural unconscionability on two grounds: first, due to the disparity in size and bargaining power between the buyer, a local though relatively large farming business, and the seller, an international manufacturer; and second, because the objectionable terms were located on the back side of the contract and were not pointed out by the salesperson. The court also found substantive unconscionability because the clauses shifted to the buyer the risk of lost crops due to failure of the machinery. Id. at 124-126. As the case suggests, the merchant who succeeds with an unconscionability claim is likely to assert a bargaining disadvantage in relation to a more powerful party. See, e.g., Construction Associates, Inc. v. Fargo Water Equipment Co., 446 N.W.2d 237 (N.D. 1989) (in contract between local construction company and international seller, clause limiting liability for seller's breach to providing replacement goods held unconscionable); Johnson v. Mobil Oil Co., 415 F. Supp. 264 (E.D. Mich. 1976) (retailer had less than eighth grade education, was practically illiterate, signed the contract while busily engaged with service station, and did not discuss any term other than amount of rent). See also Jane P. Mallor, Unconscionability in Contracts

Between Merchants, 40 Sw. L.J. 1065, 1086-1087 (1986) (asserting that merchants should have a more demanding duty to read and therefore should be unable to assert unfair surprise, and that lack of meaningful choice applies only when the merchant can show necessity or that the other party abuses monopoly-like advantage); Harry G. Prince, Unconscionability in California: A Need for Restraint and Consistency, 46 Hastings L. J. 460 (1995) (criticizing *A&M Produce* and other California decisions finding parties with substantial business experience to be victims of unconscionability, asserting that merchants are more likely to have resort to counsel, to read and understand contracts, and to have the ability to find alternative bargains).

Comment: Commercial, Employment and Consumer Arbitration

For years complaints have raged about the slowness and expense of the judicial process. Because of these concerns, critics of litigation have urged the use of alternative forms of dispute resolution, particularly arbitration. Although courts of an earlier day were extremely hostile to contracts providing for arbitration, regarding this as an attempt to oust them of their rightful jurisdiction, this attitude has given way to one that encourages arbitration as a means of relieving congested court dockets. See generally Ian R. MacNeil, American Arbitration Law: Reformation, Nationalization, Internationalization (1992); Linda R. Hirshman, The Second Arbitration Trilogy: The Federalization of Arbitration Law, 71 Va. L. Rev. 1305 (1985).

To change the restrictive common law rules dealing with arbitration, statutes providing for its use have been enacted at both the federal and state levels. In 1925 Congress enacted the United States Arbitration Act (the Federal Act), which establishes federal substantive law for arbitration of maritime matters or transactions involving interstate commerce. 9 U.S.C. §§1-14. In 1955 the National Conference of Commissioners on Uniform State Laws (NCCUSL) promulgated the Uniform Arbitration Act to govern arbitration to the extent not superseded by the federal legislation. 7 U.L.A. 1 (1997). In 2000 NCCUSL produced a revised Arbitration Act. 7 U.L.A. (Supp. 2002). The initial Uniform Arbitration Act was adopted in more than 35 jurisdictions and similar laws were adopted in most remaining states. As of 2006, the revised Arbitration Act had been adopted in 12 jurisdictions and introduced before legislatures in several other states. The status of adoptions can be found at the NCCUSL website at www.nccusl.org.

Arbitration is now regularly used to resolve disputes arising from many employment contracts (including both unionized and individual employees), securities transactions, construction agreements, and commercial contracts, both domestic and international. See Domke on Commercial Arbitration (3d ed., Larry E. Edmondson ed. 2003); Dennis R. Nolan, Labor and Employment Arbitration in a Nutshell (1998); Jacqueline M. Nolan-Haley, Alternative Dispute Resolution in a Nutshell (2d ed. 2001). Fundamental differences exist, however, with regard to arbitration of commercial disputes between sophisticated entities and arbitration of employment or consumer matters. This comment provides a brief overview of these various types of arbitration.

A dispute is subject to arbitration if the parties have entered into a valid contract calling for arbitration and the dispute is "arbitrable." While some types of disputes may not be subject to arbitration, the courts have greatly broadened the scope of matters subject to arbitration. See Vicki Zick, Comment, Reshaping the Constitution to Meet the Practical Needs of the Day: The Judicial Preference for Binding Arbitration, 82 Marq. L. Rev. 247 (1998).

Commercial Arbitration

The following is a typical contractual provision calling for arbitration of a commercial matter:

> Any controversy or claim arising out of or relating to this contract, or the breach thereof, shall be settled by arbitration administered by the American Arbitration Association under its Commercial Arbitration Rules, and judgment on the award rendered by the arbitrator(s) may be entered in any court having jurisdiction thereof.

The American Arbitration Association (AAA), a private, nonprofit organization based in New York, has published rules on various types of arbitration proceedings. The AAA adopted revised Commercial Dispute Resolution Procedures (hereinafter referred to as CDRP), which became effective July 1, 2003. These rules are available at the AAA's website (www.adr.org). You may recall that the arbitration agreements in both the *Higgins* and *Adler* cases provided that arbitration would take place under AAA commercial arbitration rules.

If a dispute develops under a commercial contract containing an arbitration clause, a party who wishes to arbitrate the matter must file a "demand" for arbitration with the AAA and pay its administrative fee, which is set by a schedule in accordance with the amount involved. Under the CDRP, the initial filing fee for a case depends on the size of the claim. As of December 2006, a claim involving less than $10,000 requires a filing fee of $750; if the case involves $10,000 to $75,000, the filing fee is $950; if the case involves $75,000 to $150,000, the filing fee is $1800. The demand, which is usually much simpler than a complaint filed in court, should contain a statement of the nature of the dispute, the amount involved, the remedy sought, and the hearing locale requested. The demand is served on the opposing party, who has an opportunity to file an answer or counterclaim. CDRP R-4.

If the party receiving a demand refuses to submit to arbitration, court proceedings to compel arbitration may be necessary. The party demanding arbitration could file a court action seeking an order compelling the other party to arbitrate the dispute. On the other hand, the party resisting arbitration could file an action to "stay" the arbitration proceeding, perhaps in response to a lawsuit initiated by the other side. Federal Act §3; Uniform Act §7. In each of these cases, the court must decide whether the parties entered into a valid agreement to arbitrate.

Assuming a matter has been referred to arbitration, either because both parties have voluntarily submitted to arbitration or pursuant to a court order, the next step in the process is the selection of an arbitrator. Sometimes the agreement will designate an arbitrator or provide a method for selection.

CDRP R-12. If the agreement is silent on the selection of an arbitrator, rules of the AAA provide a "list method" of selection. The AAA sends a list of proposed arbitrators, along with their biographical statements, to each of the parties, who are asked to strike unacceptable names from the list and to rank acceptable candidates in order of preference. If possible, the AAA will appoint an arbitrator in accordance with the mutual preferences of the parties; if not, the AAA will choose one. CDRP R-11. Commercial arbitrators are usually not lawyers; typically, they work in the relevant industry. Normally, one arbitrator is used, although the AAA in its discretion can direct the use of three arbitrators. CDRP R-15.

Once the arbitrator is selected, a hearing date will be fixed. CDRP R-22. In most jurisdictions, pretrial discovery is not allowed in arbitration proceedings, although the parties could agree to it informally. At the request of any party, the arbitrator has the power to order the production of documents and other information and the identification of witnesses to be called. At least five days before the hearing, parties are required to exchange exhibits they intend to submit at the hearing. CDRP R-21. The arbitrator has the power to subpoena witnesses or documents for the hearing. Federal Act §7; Uniform Act §17. In addition, under the Uniform Act, the arbitrator may allow the taking of a deposition of a witness who cannot be subpoenaed or is unable to attend. Uniform Act §17. By agreement of the parties, it is also possible for a matter to be submitted to the arbitrator in writing for decision without a hearing. CDRP R-30. If a hearing is held, it is less formal than the typical court proceeding. In particular, the arbitrator may consider any evidence that is relevant and material, even if it does not comply with the rules of evidence. CDRP R-31.

After the close of the hearing, the arbitrator is required to reach a decision within 30 days. CDRP R-41. Except in labor arbitration, the arbitrator's "award" typically states only the result without any reasons. CDRP R-42. (This form of award is recommended in arbitration in order to insulate the award from judicial scrutiny.) Subject to the agreement of the parties, the award may provide for any legal or equitable remedy, including specific performance. See generally Michael F. Hoellering, Remedies in Arbitration, in Arbitration and the Law (1984) (Annual Report of General Counsel of AAA).

In many cases the award will be voluntarily honored by the losing party. While the losing party may seek judicial review, the grounds for "vacating" an award are extremely limited. An arbitration award cannot be overturned on the ground that it is contrary to the law or the evidence. The Federal Act lists the following bases for judicial review of an arbitration award:

(1) Where the award was procured by corruption, fraud, or undue means.
(2) Where there was evident partiality or corruption in the arbitrators, or either of them.
(3) Where the arbitrators were guilty of misconduct in refusing to postpone the hearing, upon sufficient cause shown, or in refusing to hear evidence pertinent and material to the controversy; or of any other misbehavior by which the rights of any party have been prejudiced.

(4) Where the arbitrators exceeded their powers, or so imperfectly executed them that a mutual, final, and definite award upon the subject matter submitted was not made.

Federal Act §10(a). Section 23 of the Uniform Act is similar.

After an award is issued, if the agreement to arbitrate so provides, the prevailing party may seek judicial "confirmation" of the award, the effect of which is to make the award a judgment of a court. Federal Act §9; Uniform Act §25.

Employment Arbitration

One of the areas in which arbitration first found acceptance was unionized employment. Dating back to the 1950s, the courts accepted that employers and unions could enter into binding agreements requiring arbitration of disputes between employers and unions, partly as a way of avoiding extended labor disputes, though in that early period the U.S. Supreme Court held that federal statutorily based antidiscrimination claims could be brought in court notwithstanding the union's arbitration agreement. See Frederick L. Sullivan, Accepting Evolution in Workplace Justice: The Need for Congress to Mandate Arbitration, 26 W. New Eng. L. Rev. 281, 290-293 (2004). Details of the collective-bargaining arbitration process are beyond the scope of this comment.

In recent years, the U.S. Supreme Court has interpreted the FAA in an expansive manner that resulted in the presumptive enforceability of mandatory arbitration agreements between employers and independent (or non-unionized) employees, even in claims concerning federal antidiscrimination laws. See Circuit City Stores, Inc. v. Adams, 532 U.S. 105, 109-10 (2001) (holding that the FAA applied to all employment except a narrow class of interstate transportation workers listed in the Act). As one article described, the application of the pro-arbitration policy of the FAA to a broad range of individual employees has resulted in "a tidal wave of employment contracts containing arbitration clauses." William H. Daughtrey, Jr. & Donnie L. Kidd, Jr., Modifications Necessary for Commercial Arbitration Law to Protect Statutory Rights Against Discrimination in Employment: A Discussion and Proposals for Change, 14 Ohio St. J. on Disp. Resol. 29, 31 (1998). The percentage of employers using arbitration to resolve disputes grew from less than 4 percent in 1993 to 19 percent in 1996, and the AAA caseload of employment arbitrations grew from three million in 1997 to six million in 2002. See Elizabeth Hill, Due Process at Low Cost: An Empirical Study of Employment Arbitration Under the Auspices of the American Arbitration Association, 18 Ohio St. J. on Disp. Resol. 777, 779-780 (2003).

The expansion of the arbitration process to a broad range of employment (and consumer) disputes has engendered great controversy and criticism but it remains the applicable law. See, e.g., Jean R. Sternlight, Rethinking the Constitutionality of the Supreme Court's Preference for Binding Arbitration: A Fresh Assessment of Jury Trial, Separation of Powers, and Due Process Concerns, 72 Tul. L. Rev. 1 (1997); David R. Wade & Curtiss K. Behrens, Opening Pandora's Box: Circuit City v. Adams and the Enforceability of

Compulsory, Prospective Arbitration Agreements, 86 Marq. L. Rev. 1 (2002). Thus, the application of the FAA's pro-arbitration policy to individual employment contracts means that employees will find it difficult to avoid enforcement of an agreement to arbitrate. As the *Adler* case illustrates, for such an employee who does wish to avoid arbitration, the only avenue available is to find some general grounds for invalidating a contract, such as unconscionability, that can be applied specifically to the arbitration agreement. See Susan Randall, Judicial Attitudes Toward Arbitration and the Resurgence of Unconscionability, 52 Buffalo L. Rev. 185 (2004); Jeffrey W. Stempel, Arbitration, Unconscionability, and Equilibrium: The Return of Unconscionability Analysis as a Counterweight to Arbitration Formalism, 19 Ohio St. J. on Disp. Resol. 757 (2004).

Assuming that the dispute between the individual employee and the employer is ultimately submitted to arbitration, the arbitral rules that are likely to be applied are derivative of the commercial arbitration model described above rather than the form of arbitration found in collective bargaining arrangements. See Michael H. LeRoy & Peter Feuille, Reinventing the Enterprise Wheel: Court Review of Punitive Awards in Labor and Employment Arbitrations, 11 Harv. Negotiation L. Rev. 199, 212-213 (2006). In 1996, the AAA issued National Rules for the Resolution of Employment Disputes to govern arbitration in employment settings. These rules are now known as the Employment Arbitration Rules and Mediation Procedures after amendment of selected provisions, effective July 1, 2006. The rules are available at the AAA website (www.adr.org).

The 1996 National Rules for the Resolution of Employment Disputes reflected the "Due Process Protocol for Mediation and Arbitration of Statutory Disputes Arising Out of the Employment Relationship" promulgated in 1995 by a special task force composed of individuals representing management, labor, employment, civil rights organizations, private administrative agencies, government, and the AAA. The Due Process Protocol was designed to promote fairness and equity in resolving workplace disputes and has been endorsed by a broad range of organizations including the AAA, the Judicial Arbitration and Mediation Services, Inc. (JAMS), and the American Bar Association Section on Labor and Employment. See Margaret M. Harding, The Limits of the Due Process Protocols, 19 Ohio St. J. on Disp. Resol. 369, 403-405 (2004). By agreeing to arbitrate only agreements that meet the requirements of the Due Process Protocol, organizations such as AAA and JAMS are offering some procedural protection to the independent employee in arbitration.

A fundamental concern in employment arbitration is whether the employee can afford to pursue the claim. The AAA Employment Arbitration Rules create a division between two types of arbitration arrangements, one for disputes arising out of employer-promulgated plans that are imposed on employees as a condition of employment and the other for disputes arising out of individually-negotiated employment agreements. The AAA categorizes the claim when the arbitration is filed, but appeal can be made to the arbitrator. For arbitration under an employer-promulgated plan, the employee's nonrefundable filing fee is capped in the amount of $150, payable in full when a claim is filed unless the plan provides that the employee pay less. The employer pays the remainder of the initial fee and other expenses of the hearing.

For individually-negotiated employment agreements, the employee must pay filing fees according to a schedule similar to that used in commercial arbitration. A claim involving less than $10,000 requires a filing fee of $750; if the case involves $10,000 to $75,000, the filing fee is $950; if the case involves $75,000 to $150,000, the filing fee is $1800. In addition, other arbitral expenses are generally borne equally by both sides. The AAA also adopted Supplementary Rules for Class Action Arbitration that adjust fees based on that factor. Procedures other than AAA may require that the employee pay a larger share of the costs, and the law in California may require that the employer pay a larger share.

Arbitration may begin either by joint submission of the parties or the submission of a demand by a single party. Employment Arbitration Rules-4. The appointment process contemplates that the parties may have agreed in advance to an arbitrator or a process for naming one, or may agree at the time the dispute arises. Alternatively, the AAA will provide a list of arbitrators and the parties will reach agreement through a process of objecting to some names and ranking the others. Employment Arbitration Rules-12.

The arbitrator has the ability to order such discovery as may appear necessary to the full exploration of the issues. Employment Arbitration Rules-9. Similarly, the parties are permitted to offer evidence deemed relevant and material to the dispute. Employment Arbitration Rules-30. The arbitrator is required to make an award in writing no later than 30 days from the date of closing of the hearing, in most cases, and the awards are made public and are deemed final and binding. The arbitrator is able to grant any remedy or relief that would have been available to the parties had the matter been heard in court including awards of attorney's fees and costs, in accordance with applicable law. Employment Arbitration Rules-39.

Consumer Arbitration

As suggested by the *Higgins* case and the notes following it, there has been a dramatic increase in the use of mandatory arbitration agreements in a wide variety of contracts involving consumers or otherwise noncommercial parties. The AAA describes consumer transactions as those involving goods or services primarily for personal, family, or household use, including:

> among other things, transactions involving: banking, credit cards, home loans and other financial services; health care services; brokerage services; home construction and improvements; insurance; communications; and the purchase and lease of motor vehicles and other personal property.

See Statement of Principles of the National Consumer Disputes Advisory Committee: Introduction, available at the AAA website: (www.adr.org). While there is a variety of fora in which a consumer arbitration procedure could be conducted, the AAA plays a leading role in this area as well. The Due Process Protocol for employment arbitration served as a model for a Consumer Due Process Protocol adopted in 1998 at the instigation of the AAA, and the latter document expands and refines many of the principles set forth in the employment protocol. (The Consumer Protocol is also available at the AAA website.) The Consumer Protocol does not prohibit the use of mandatory pre-dispute arbitration clauses, but it does state that notice of mandatory arbitration should be "clear and adequate," and it preserves for consumers the right to go to the local small claims court instead of arbitration if the claim meets that court's jurisdictional requirements. The stated principles also establish as guidelines the norms that arbitration should be held in a location that is convenient for both parties and in a reasonably prompt fashion.

Similar to the employment protocol, the consumer rules indicate that the AAA will not participate in an arbitration governed by an agreement that does not meet its standards. Unlike the employment protocol, the Consumer Protocol explicitly requires that the any alternative dispute resolution program be independent of the parties. See Margaret M. Harding, The Limits of the Due Process Protocols, 19 Ohio St. J. on Disp. Resol. 369, 405-406 (2004). The AAA Consumer Protocol provides that it applies to standardized non-negotiable contracts between businesses and consumers.

For arbitrations that proceed before the AAA, the applicable rules are the Commercial Dispute Resolution Procedures described above, as altered by the AAA's Supplementary Procedures for Consumer-Related Disputes. The stated goal of the AAA is to provide a low cost, streamlined process to resolve disputes between consumers and businesses. As with the commercial and employment procedures, the consumer process begins with a demand by the claimant. C-2. Unlike the other procedures, the arbitrators for consumer disputes are simply appointed by the AAA, subject to possible objection by the parties. C-4. For claims under $10,000, the expectation is that the arbitrator will decide the case based on submission of documents without a hearing, but the presumption is that a hearing will be conducted if the claim is for more than $10,000. C-5 and C-6. The arbitrator will normally make a written award within 14 days of the close of the hearing or receipt of the final documents, and the arbitrator may award any remedy that would be available under the applicable law. C-7.

A consumer is responsible for one-half the arbitrator's fees up to a maximum of $125 if the claim or counterclaim does not exceed $10,000. If the consumer's claim or counterclaim is greater than $10,000, but does not exceed $75,000, then the consumer is responsible for one-half the arbitrator's fees up to a maximum of $375. If the consumer's claim or counterclaim exceeds $75,000, or if the consumer's claim or counterclaim is non-monetary, then the consumer must pay an Administrative Fee in accordance with the Commercial Fee Schedule. The consumer can apply for a waiver of fees based on financial limitations. The arbitrator's fee is set at $250 for a desk arbitration that is decided on submission of papers or for a telephone hearing. The fees are set at $750 per day for an in-person hearing. The business must pay any administrative fees.

In theory, arbitration should offer consumers a quick and low cost process for resolving disputes. In reality, however, the agreements between consumers and businesses are rarely consensual, and businesses tend to stack the process in their favor by prohibiting consumer class actions, imposing prohibitive costs on individuals, limiting remedies, and setting up discovery rules that favor the business. See Richard M. Alderman, Pre-dispute Mandatory

Arbitration in Consumer Contracts: A Call for Reform, 38 Hous. L. Rev. 1237 (2001); Mark E. Budnitz, Mandatory Arbitration: The High Cost of Mandatory Consumer Arbitration, 67 Law & Contemp. Prob. 133 (2004). Thus, it is likely that for years to come many consumers will continue to struggle to avoid arbitration agreements in consumer contracts.

E. PUBLIC POLICY

For the most part, this chapter has focused on situations in which a party may have a defense against enforceability of a contract because of some bargaining misconduct by the other party. In this section, we examine situations in which, although the process of contract formation is untainted, a contract may still be unenforceable because the contract itself either violates or runs directly contrary to some public policy. Such contracts are often said to be unenforceable because of "illegality," but that term is a misnomer because in many situations the contract itself is not, strictly speaking, illegal. See E. Allan Farnsworth, Contracts §5.1, at 315 (4th ed. 2004).

Judicial refusal to enforce a promise because it violates some standard of public policy has early roots in the common law. Fifteenth and sixteenth century courts refused to enforce contracts that involved usury. Similarly, contracts in "restraint of trade" were held invalid. For example, in John Dyer's Case, 2 Hen. V, f.5, p.26 (1414), an action on a bond, the defendant pleaded by way of defense that he had satisfied his obligation to refrain from engaging in his profession of dyer in a certain town for one-half a year. Commenting on the pleadings, the judge stated that the defendant could have demurred to the bond because the condition was against the common law and thereby void. See Alfred W. B. Simpson, A History of the Common Law of Contract 506-524 (1987). The materials that follow examine some contemporary aspects of public policy limitations on the enforceability of contractual obligations.

PROBLEM 7-2

Ellen Erickson has been employed as a genetic researcher by Neogenetics, Inc., a corporation that is engaged in genetic research and commercial sale of products developed by such research. For some time Erickson has been considering leaving the company and starting her own business. She is concerned, however, about the following provision in her employment contract:

> 8. *Covenant not to compete.* Employee hereby covenants and agrees that during the period of her employment and for a period of two years thereafter, she will not engage, whether directly or indirectly, nor will she have any interest, whether as shareholder, creditor, or otherwise, in any business that is engaged in genetic research or in the marketing of products that are generated by such research.

Erickson has asked your advice about the enforceability of this clause and its potential impact on her if she starts her own genetic research firm. In light of the case and notes that follow, what advice would you give?

Valley Medical Specialists v. Farber
Supreme Court of Arizona
194 Ariz. 363, 982 P.2d 1277 (1999)

OPINION

FELDMAN, Justice.

We granted review to determine whether the restrictive covenant between Dr. Steven Farber and Valley Medical Specialists is enforceable. We hold that it is not. Public policy concerns in this case outweigh Valley Medical's protectable interests in enforcing the agreement. We thus vacate the court of appeals' opinion, affirm the trial court's judgment, and remand to the court of appeals to resolve any remaining issues. We have jurisdiction pursuant to Arizona Constitution article VI, §5(3) and A.R.S. §12-120.24.

FACTS AND PROCEDURAL HISTORY

In 1985, Valley Medical Specialists ("VMS"), a professional corporation, hired Steven S. Farber, D.O., an internist and pulmonologist who, among other things, treated AIDS and HIV-positive patients and performed brachytherapy—a procedure that radiates the inside of the lung in lung cancer patients. Brachytherapy can only be performed at certain hospitals that have the necessary equipment. A few years after joining VMS, Dr. Farber became a shareholder and subsequently a minority officer and director. In 1991, the three directors, including Dr. Farber, entered into new stock and employment agreements. The employment agreement contained a restrictive covenant, the scope of which was amended over time.

In 1994, Dr. Farber left VMS and began practicing within the area defined by the restrictive covenant, which at that time read as follows:

The parties recognize that the duties to be rendered under the terms of this Agreement by the Employee are special, unique and of an extraordinary character. The Employee, in consideration of the compensation to be paid to him pursuant to the terms of this Agreement, expressly agrees to the following restrictive covenants:

  (a) The Employee shall not, directly or indirectly:
    (i) Request any present or future patients of the Employer to curtail or cancel their professional affiliation with the Employer;
    (ii) Either separately, jointly, or in association with others, establish, engage in, or become interested in, as an employee, owner, partner, shareholder or otherwise, or furnish any information to, work for, or assist in any manner, anyone competing with, or who may compete with the Employer in the practice of medicine.
    (iii) Disclose the identity of any past, present or future patients of the Employer to any other person, firm or corporation engaged in a medical

practice the same as, similar to or in general competition with the medical services provided by the Employer.

(iv) Either separately, jointly or in association with others provide medical care or medical assistance for any person or persons who were patients or [sic] Employer during the period that Employee was in the hire of Employer.

...

(d) *The restrictive covenants set forth herein shall continue during the term of this Agreement and for a period of three (3) years after the date of termination, for any reason, of this Agreement. The restrictive covenants set forth herein shall be binding upon the Employee in that geographical area encompassed within the boundaries measured by a five (5) mile radius of any office maintained or utilized by Employer at the time of execution of the Agreement or at any time thereafter.*

(e) The Employee agrees that a violation on his part of any covenant set forth in this Paragraph 17 will cause such damage to the Employer as will be irreparable and for that reason, that Employee further agrees that the Employer shall be entitled, as a matter of right, and upon notice as provided in Paragraph 20 hereof, to an injunction from any court of competent jurisdiction, restraining any further violation of said covenants by Employee, his corporation, employees, partners or agents. Such right to injunctive remedies shall be in addition to and cumulative with any other rights and remedies the Employer may have pursuant to this Agreement or law, including, specifically with regard to the covenants set forth in subparagraph 17(a) above, the recovery of liquidated damages equal to forty percent (40%) of the gross receipts received for medical services provided by the Employee, or any employee, associate, partner, or corporation of the Employee during the term of this Agreement and for a period of three (3) years after the date of termination, for any reason, of this Agreement. The Employee expressly acknowledges and agrees that the covenants and agreement contained in this Paragraph 17 are minimum and reasonable in scope and are necessary to protect the legitimate interest of the Employer and its goodwill.

(Emphasis added.)

VMS filed a complaint against Dr. Farber seeking (1) preliminary and permanent injunctions enjoining Dr. Farber from violating the restrictive covenant, (2) liquidated damages for breach of the employment agreement, and (3) damages for breach of fiduciary duty, conversion of patient files and confidential information, and intentional interference with contractual and/or business relations.

Following six days of testimony and argument, the trial court denied VMS's request for a preliminary injunction, finding that the restrictive covenant violated public policy or, alternatively, was unenforceable because it was too broad. Specifically, the court found that: any covenant over six months would be unreasonable; the five-mile radius from each of the three VMS offices was unreasonable because it covered a total of 235 square miles; and the restriction was unreasonable because it did not provide an exception for emergency medical aid and was not limited to pulmonology.

The court of appeals reversed, concluding that a modified covenant was reasonable. Valley Med. Specialists v. Farber, 190 Ariz. 563, 950 P.2d 1184 (App. 1997). The court noted that there were eight hospitals outside the restricted area where Dr. Farber could practice. Id. at 567, 950 P.2d at 1188. Although the covenant made no exceptions for emergency medicine, the court held that the severability clause permitted the trial court to modify the covenant so Dr. Farber could provide emergency services within the restricted area. Id. (citing Phoenix Orthopaedic Surgeons, Ltd. v. Peairs ("*Peairs*"), 164 Ariz. 54, 61, 790 P.2d 752, 759 (App. 1989)). Moreover, VMS was allowed to stipulate that Dr. Farber could perform brachytherapy and treat AIDS and HIV patients within the restricted area, again even though the covenant contained no such exceptions. *Valley Med. Specialists*, 190 Ariz. at 567, 950 P.2d at 1188.

The court of appeals found the restriction, when so modified, reasonable as to time and place. Although non-emergency patients might be required to travel further to see Dr. Farber, they could continue to see him if they were willing to drive that far. 190 Ariz. at 567-68, 950 P.2d at 1188-89. Three years was reasonable because the record contained testimony that it might take Dr. Farber's replacement three to five years to develop his pulmonary practice referral sources to the level they were when Dr. Farber resigned. Id.

The court found that the restrictive covenant did not violate public policy, believing that courts must not unnecessarily restrict the freedom of contract. Id. at 568, 950 P.2d at 1189. Moreover, the record was void of any evidence that the availability of pulmonologists in the restricted area would be inadequate without Dr. Farber. Id.

DISCUSSION

A. STANDARD OF REVIEW

. . .

B. HISTORY OF RESTRICTIVE COVENANTS

A brief reference to basic principles is appropriate. Historically, covenants not to compete were viewed as restraints of trade and were invalid at common law. Ohio Urology, Inc. v. Poll, 72 Ohio App. 3d 446, 594 N.E.2d 1027, 1031 (Ohio App. 1991); see generally Harlan M. Blake, Employee Agreements not to Compete, 73 Harv. L. Rev. 625 (1960); Serena L. Kafker, Golden Handcuffs: Enforceability of Noncompetition Clauses in Professional Partnership Agreements of Accountants, Physicians, and Attorneys, 31 Am. Bus. L. J. 31, 33 (1993). Eventually, ancillary restraints, such as those incident to employment or partnership agreements, were enforced under the rule of reason. See Restatement (Second) of Contracts §188 (hereinafter "Restatement"). Given the public interest in doctor-patient relationships, the validity of restrictive covenants between physicians was carefully examined long ago in Mandeville v. Harman:

> The rule is not that a limited restraint is good, but that it may be good. It is valid when the restraint is reasonable; and the restraint is reasonable when it imposes no shackle upon the one party which is not beneficial to the other.
>
> The authorities are uniform that such contracts are valid when the restraint they impose is reasonable, and the test to be applied, . . . is this: To consider whether the restraint is such only as to afford a fair protection to the interest of the party in favor of whom it is given, and not so large as to interfere with the interest of the public. Whatever restraint is larger than the necessary protection of the party can be of no

benefit to either; it can only be oppressive, and, if oppressive, it is, in the eye of the law, unreasonable and void, on the ground of public policy, as being injurious to the interests of the public.

42 N.J. Eq. 185, 7 A. 37, 38-39 (N.J. 1886) (citations omitted); see also Karlin v. Weinberg, 77 N.J. 408, 390 A.2d 1161, 1165 (N.J. 1978). To be enforced, the restriction must do more than simply prohibit fair competition by the employee. Bryceland [v. Northey, 160 Ariz. 213, 216, 772 P.2d 36, 39 (App. 1989)]. In other words, a covenant not to compete is invalid unless it protects some legitimate interest beyond the employer's desire to protect itself from competition. Amex Distrib. Co. v. Mascari, 150 Ariz. 510, 518, 724 P.2d 596, 604 (App. 1986). The legitimate purpose of post-employment restraints is "to prevent competitive use, for a time, of information or relationships which pertain peculiarly to the employer and which the employee acquired in the course of the employment." Blake, supra, 73 Harv. L. Rev., at 647. Despite the freedom to contract, the law does not favor restrictive covenants. *Ohio Urology, Inc.,* 594 N.E.2d at 1031. This disfavor is particularly strong concerning such covenants among physicians because the practice of medicine affects the public to a much greater extent. Id. In fact, "for the past 60 years, the American Medical Association (AMA) has consistently taken the position that noncompetition agreements between physicians impact negatively on patient care." Paula Berg, Judicial Enforcement of Covenants not to Compete Between Physicians: Protecting Doctors' Interests at Patients' Expense, 45 Rutgers L. Rev. 1, 6 (1992).

C. LEVEL OF SCRUTINY–PUBLIC POLICY CONSIDERATIONS

We first address the level of scrutiny that should be afforded to this restrictive covenant. Dr. Farber argues that this contract is simply an employer-employee agreement and thus the restrictive covenant should be strictly construed against the employer. See *Amex Distrib. Co.,* 150 Ariz. at 514, 724 P.2d at 600 (noting employer-employee restrictive covenants are disfavored and strictly construed against the employer). This was the approach taken by the trial court. VMS contends that this is more akin to the sale of a business; thus, the noncompete provision should not be strictly construed against it. See id. (courts more lenient in enforcing restrictive covenants connected to sale of business because of need to effectively transfer goodwill). Finding the agreement here not on all fours with either approach, the court of appeals applied a standard "somewhere between" the two. *Valley Med. Specialists,* 190 Ariz. at 566, 950 P.2d at 1187.

Although this agreement is between partners, it is more analogous to an employer-employee agreement than a sale of a business. See Restatement §188 cmt. *h* ("A rule similar to that applicable to an employee or agent applies to a partner who makes a promise not to compete that is ancillary to the partnership agreement or to an agreement by which he disposes of his partnership interest."). Many of the concerns present in the sale of a business are not present or are reduced where, as here, a physician leaves a medical group, even when that physician is a partner. When a business is sold, the value of that business's goodwill usually figures significantly into the purchase price. The buyer therefore deserves some protection from competition from the former owner. See Kafker, supra, 31 Am. Bus. L.J. at 33. A restraint accompanying the sale of a business is necessary for the buyer to get the full goodwill value for which it has paid. Blake, supra, 73 Harv. L. Rev., at 647.

It is true that in this case, unlike typical employer-employee agreements, Dr. Farber may not have been at a bargaining disadvantage, which is one of the reasons such restrictive covenants are strictly construed. See, e.g., Rash v. Toccoa Clinic Med. Assocs., 253 Ga. 322, 320 S.E.2d 170, 172-73 (Ga. 1984). Unequal bargaining power may be a factor to consider when examining the hardship on the departing employee. But in cases involving the professions, public policy concerns may outweigh any protectable interest the remaining firm members may have. Thus, this case does not turn on the hardship to Dr. Farber.

By restricting a physician's practice of medicine, this covenant involves strong public policy implications and must be closely scrutinized. See *Peairs*, 164 Ariz. at 60, 790 P.2d at 758; *Ohio Urology, Inc.*, 594 N.E.2d at 1032 (restrictive covenant in medical context "strictly construed in favor of professional mobility and access to medical care and facilities"). Although stopping short of banning restrictive covenants between physicians, the American Medical Association ("AMA") "discourages" such covenants, finding they are not in the public interest.

> The Council on Ethical and Judicial Affairs discourages any agreement between physicians which restricts the right of a physician to practice medicine for a specified period of time or in a specified area upon termination of employment or a partnership or a corporate agreement. Such restrictive agreements are not in the public interest.

1989 Current Opinions of the Council on Ethical and Judicial Affairs, Section 9.02 (hereinafter "AMA Opinions"). In addition, the AMA recognizes that free choice of doctors is the right of every patient, and free competition among physicians is a prerequisite of optimal care and ethical practice. See AMA Opinions, Section 9.06; *Ohio Urology, Inc.*, 594 N.E.2d at 1030.

For similar reasons, restrictive covenants are prohibited between attorneys. See Dwyer v. Jung, 133 N.J. Super. 343, 336 A.2d 498, 501 (N.J. Super. Ct. Ch. Div.), *aff'd,* 137 N.J. Super. 135, 348 A.2d 208 (N.J. Super. Ct. App. Div. 1975); Cohen v. Lord, Day & Lord, 75 N.Y.2d 95, 550 N.E.2d 410, 410-11, 551 N.Y.S.2d 157 (N.Y. App. 1989). In 1969, the American Bar Association adopted a code of professional conduct that contained a disciplinary rule prohibiting restrictive covenants between attorneys. See Berg, supra, 45 Rutgers L. Rev., at 37. The ethical rules adopted by this court provide:

> A lawyer shall not participate in offering or making:
> (a) a partnership or employment agreement that restricts the rights of a lawyer to practice after termination of the relationship except an agreement concerning benefits upon retirement; or
> (b) an agreement in which a restriction on the lawyers right to practice is part of the settlement of a controversy between private parties.

Ethical Rule ("ER") 5.6, Arizona Rules of Professional Conduct, Rule 42, Ariz. R. Sup. Ct.

Restrictive covenants between lawyers limit not only their professional autonomy but also the client's freedom to choose a lawyer. See ER 5.6 cmt. We do not, of course, enact ethical rules for the medical profession, but given the view of the AMA to which we have previously alluded, we believe the principle behind prohibiting restrictive covenants in the legal profession is relevant.

> Commercial standards may not be used to evaluate the reasonableness of lawyer restrictive covenants. Strong public policy considerations preclude their applicability. In that sense lawyer restrictions are injurious to the public interest. A client is always entitled to be represented by counsel of his own choosing. The attorney-client relationship is consensual, highly fiduciary on the part of counsel, and he may do nothing which restricts the right of the client to repose confidence in any counsel of his choice. No concept of the practice of law is more deeply rooted.

Dwyer, 336 A.2d at 500.

We therefore conclude that the doctor-patient relationship is special and entitled to unique protection. It cannot be easily or accurately compared to relationships in the commercial context. In light of the great public policy interest involved in covenants not to compete between physicians, each agreement will be strictly construed for reasonableness.[1]

D. REASONABLENESS OF COVENANT

Reasonableness is a fact-intensive inquiry that depends on the totality of the circumstances. *Bryceland,* 160 Ariz. at 217, 772 P.2d at 40 ("Each case hinges on its own particular facts."); Olliver/Pilcher Ins. [v. Daniels, 148 Ariz. 530, 532, 715 P.2d 1218, 1220 (1986)]. A restriction is unreasonable and thus will not be enforced: (1) if the restraint is greater than necessary to protect the employer's legitimate interest; or (2) if that interest is outweighed by the hardship to the employee and the likely injury to the public. See Restatement §188 cmt. a.; see also Blake, supra, 73 Harv. L. Rev., at 648-49; Ferdinand S. Tinio, Annotation, Validity and Construction of Contractual Restrictions on Right of Medical Practitioner to Practice, Incident to Partnership Agreement, 62 A.L.R.3d 970, 984 (1975). Thus, in the present case, the reasonableness inquiry requires us to examine the interests of the employer, employee, patients, and public in general. See 62 A.L.R.3d at 976; see also *Peairs,* 164 Ariz. at 57, 790 P.2d at 755; *Amex Distrib. Co.,* 150 Ariz. at 514, 724 P.2d at 600 (accommodating right to work, right to contract, and public's right to competition); see generally Blake, supra. Balancing these competing interests is no easy task and no exact formula can be used. See Restatement §188 cmt. a.

In holding this restrictive covenant enforceable, the court of appeals relied heavily on *Peairs,* noting the restriction here was "very similar to the one in *Peairs,* which restricted a doctor from practicing orthopedic medicine

---

1. Dr. Farber asks us to hold restrictive covenants in the medical profession void per se as against public policy. Finding the present covenant unreasonable and thus unenforceable by injunction, we need not and do not address that contention.

and surgery within a five-mile radius of each of three offices for three years." *Valley Med. Specialists,* 190 Ariz. at 567, 950 P.2d at 1188. As noted, however, each case must be decided on its own unique facts. *Bryceland,* 160 Ariz. at 217, 772 P.2d at 40. Here, the facts are sufficiently distinguishable from *Peairs* to warrant different treatment. For instance, in *Peairs* the three offices were "clustered," and the total restricted area was thus much smaller. 164 Ariz. at 60, 790 P.2d at 758. The *Peairs* restrictive covenant prevented the practice of "orthopedic medicine and surgery." Id. at 56, 790 P.2d at 754. Here, however, the covenant prohibited Dr. Farber from providing any and all forms of "medical care," including not only pulmonology, but emergency medicine, brachytherapy treatment, and HIV-positive and AIDS patient care. Finally, the trial court in *Peairs* granted the preliminary injunction, while the trial court here denied it. Because we review the grant or denial of a preliminary injunction for abuse of discretion, the trial judge's ruling after hearing the evidence in both cases is another factor that distinguishes the two cases.

E. VMS'S PROTECTABLE INTEREST

VMS contends, and the court of appeals agreed, that it has a protectable interest in its patients and referral sources. In the commercial context, it is clear that employers have a legitimate interest in retaining their customer base. See, e.g., *Bryceland,* 160 Ariz. at 217, 772 P.2d at 40. "The employer's point of view is that the company's clientele is an asset of value which has been acquired by virtue of effort and expenditures over a period of time, and which should be protected as a form of property." Blake, supra, 73 Harv. L. Rev. at 654. In the medical context, however, the personal relationship between doctor and patient as well as the patient's freedom to see a particular doctor, affects the extent of the employer's interest. See Ohio Urology Inc., 594 N.E.2d at 1031-32. "The practice of a physician is a thing so purely personal, depending so absolutely on the confidence reposed in his personal skill and ability, that when he ceases to exist it necessarily ceases also. . . ." *Mandeville,* 7 A. at 40-41 (holding medical practice's patient base is not protectable interest); see also Berg, supra, 45 Rutgers L. Rev. at 17.

Even in the commercial context, the employer's interest in its customer base is balanced with the employee's right to the customers. Where the employee took an active role and brought customers with him or her to the job, courts are more reluctant to enforce restrictive covenants. Blake, supra, 73 Harv. L. Rev. at 664, 667. Dr. Farber was a pulmonologist. He did not learn his skills from VMS. Restrictive covenants are designed to protect an employer's customer base by preventing "a skilled employee from leaving an employer and, based on his skill acquired from that employment, luring away the employer's clients or business while the employer is vulnerable — that is — before the employer has had a chance to replace the employee with someone qualified to do the job." *Bryceland,* 160 Ariz. at 217, 772 P.2d at 40. These facts support the trial judge's conclusion that VMS's interest in protecting its patient base was outweighed by other factors.

We agree with VMS, however, that it has a protectable interest in its referral sources. See Medical Specialists, Inc. v. Sleweon, 652 N.E.2d 517, 523 (Ind. App. 1995) ("Clearly, the continued success of [a specialty] practice, which is dependent upon patient referrals, is a legitimate interest worthy of protection."); Ballesteros v. Johnson, 812 S.W.2d 217, 223 (Mo. App. 1991).

F. SCOPE OF THE RESTRICTIVE COVENANT

The restriction cannot be greater than necessary to protect VMS's legitimate interests. A restraint's scope is defined by its duration and geographic area. The frequency of contact between doctors and their patients affects the permissible length of the restraint. Blake, supra, 73 Harv. L. Rev. at 659. The idea is to give the employer a reasonable amount of time to overcome the former employee's loss, usually by hiring a replacement and giving that replacement time to establish a working relationship. Id. Even in the commercial context, "[w]hen the restraint is for the purpose of protecting customer relationships, its duration is reasonable only if it is no longer than necessary for the employer to put a new man on the job and for the new employee to have a reasonable opportunity to demonstrate his effectiveness to the customers." *Amex Distrib. Co.*, 150 Ariz. at 518, 724 P.2d at 604 (quoting Blake, supra, 73 Harv. L. Rev. at 677).

In this case, the trial judge found that the three-year period was an unreasonable duration because

> all of the experts agree that the practice of pulmonology entails treating patients with chronic conditions which require more hospital care than office care and which requires regular contact with the treating physician at least once within each six-month period so that any provision over six months is onerous and unnecessary to protect VMS's economic interests where virtually all of Dr. Farber's VMS patients had an opportunity by late 1994 or early 1995 (Farber left September 12, 1994) to decide which pulmonologist . . . they would consult for their ongoing treatment[.]

On this record, we cannot say this factual finding was clearly erroneous. The three-year duration is unreasonable.

The activity prohibited by the restraint also defines the covenant's scope. The restraint must be limited to the particular speciality of the present employment. See Blake, supra, 73 Harv. L. Rev. at 676. On its face, the restriction here is not limited to internal medicine or even pulmonology. It precludes any type of practice, even in fields that do not compete with VMS. Thus, we agree with the trial judge that this restriction is too broad. Compare *Peairs*, 164 Ariz. at 56, 790 P.2d at 754 (upholding injunction that enforced restrictive covenant preventing doctor from practicing only orthopaedic medicine and orthopaedic surgery).

G. PUBLIC POLICY

The court of appeals held that the restrictive covenant does not violate public policy, pointing out that the record contains nothing to suggest there will be a lack of pulmonologists in the restricted area if Dr. Farber is precluded from practicing there. Even if we assume other pulmonologists will be available to cover Dr. Farber's patients, we disagree with this view. It ignores the significant interests of individual patients within the restricted area. Kafker, supra, 31 Am. Bus. L.J. at 39-40. A court must evaluate the extent to which enforcing the covenant would foreclose patients from seeing the departing physician if they desire to do so. See *Karlin*, 390 A.2d at 1170; see also AMA Opinions, Section 9.06.

Concluding that patients' right to see the doctor of their choice is entitled to substantial protection, VMS's protectable interests here are comparatively minimal. See Berg, supra, 45 Rutgers L. Rev. at 15-36. The geographic scope of this covenant encompasses approximately 235 square miles, making it very difficult for Dr. Farber's existing patients to continue treatment with him if they so desire. After six days of testimony, the trial judge concluded that this restrictive covenant was unreasonably broad and against public policy. Specifically, the judge found:

(1) the three year duration was unreasonable because pulmonology patients typically require contact with the treating physician once every six months. Thus, a restriction over six months is unnecessary to protect VMS's economic interests. Patients would have had opportunity within approximately six months to decide which doctor to see for continuing treatment;

(2) the five mile radius was unreasonable because with the three offices, the restriction covered more than 235 square miles;

(3) the restriction was unreasonable because it did not expressly provide for an exception for emergency medical treatment;

(4) the restriction was overly broad because it is not limited to pulmonology;

(5) the covenant violates public policy because of the sensitive and personal nature of the doctor-patient relationship.

Given the facts and the principles discussed, that finding is well supported factually and legally.

H. SEVERANCE—THE BLUE PENCIL RULE

This contract contains a severance clause.[2] The court of appeals accepted a stipulation by VMS that the restriction would not prohibit Dr. Farber from treating HIV-positive and AIDS patients or from performing brachytherapy. On its face, however, the restriction is broader than that, restricting him from providing "medical care or medical assistance for any person or persons who were patients or [sic] Employer during the period that Employee was in the hire of Employer." Arizona courts will "blue pencil" restrictive covenants, eliminating grammatically severable, unreasonable provisions. See *Amex Distrib. Co.*, 150 Ariz. at 514, 724 P.2d at 600; *Olliver/Pilcher Ins.*, 148 Ariz. at 533, 715 P.2d at 1221 ("If it is clear from its terms that a contract was intended to be severable, the court can enforce the lawful part and ignore the unlawful part."). Here, however, the modifications go further than cutting

---

2. "Since it is the agreement and desire of the parties hereto that the provisions of this Paragraph 17 be enforced to the fullest extent possible under the laws and public policies applied in each jurisdiction in which enforcement is sought, should any particular provision of this Paragraph 17 be deemed invalid or unenforceable, the same shall be deemed reformed and amended to delete herefrom that portion thus adjudicated invalid, and the deletion shall apply only with respect to the operation of said provision and, to the extent a provision of this Paragraph 17 would be deemed unenforceable by virtue of its scope, but may be made unenforceable by limitation thereof, each party agrees that this Agreement shall be reformed and amended so that the same shall be enforceable to the fullest extent permissible under the laws and public policies applied in the jurisdiction in which enforcement is sought, the parties hereto acknowledging that the covenants contained in this Paragraph 17 are an indispensable part of the transactions contemplated herein."

grammatically severable portions. The court of appeals, in essence, rewrote the agreement in an attempt to make it enforceable. This goes too far. "Where the severability of the agreement is not evident from the contract itself, the court cannot create a new agreement for the parties to uphold the contract." *Olliver/Pilcher Ins.*, 148 Ariz. at 533, 715 P.2d at 1221.

Even the blue pencil rule has its critics. For every agreement that makes its way to court, many more do not. Thus, the words of the covenant have an *in terrorem* effect on departing employees. See Blake, supra, 73 Harv. L. Rev. at 682-83. Employers may therefore create ominous covenants, knowing that if the words are challenged, courts will modify the agreement to make it enforceable. Id. Although we will tolerate ignoring severable portions of a covenant to make it more reasonable, we will not permit courts to add terms or rewrite provisions.

In modifying the agreement, the court of appeals cited *Peairs,* which indeed allowed the trial court to alter the restrictive covenant in a contract "between medical professionals whose services are necessary for the welfare of the public." 164 Ariz. at 61, 790 P.2d at 759. We disapprove of the portion of *Peairs* that permits courts to rewrite and create a restrictive covenant significantly different from that created by the parties.

Conclusion

We hold that the restrictive covenant between Dr. Farber and VMS cannot be enforced. Valley Medical Specialists' interest in enforcing the restriction is outweighed by the likely injury to patients and the public in general. See Restatement §188. In so holding, we need not reach the question of the hardship imposed on Dr. Farber. The public policy implications here are enough to invalidate this particular agreement. We stop short of holding that restrictive covenants between physicians will never be enforced, but caution that such restrictions will be strictly construed. The burden is on the party wishing to enforce the covenant to demonstrate that the restraint is no greater than necessary to protect the employer's legitimate interest, and that such interest is not outweighed by the hardship to the employee and the likely injury to the public. Here VMS has not met that burden. The restriction fails because its public policy' implications outweigh the legitimate interests of VMS.

Dr. Farber listed in his petition for review several issues "presented to, but not decided by, the court of appeals." Valley Medical Specialists' response also contained "additional issues if the court accepts review." None of the issues were briefed in this court. We thus remand to the court of appeals for a determination of those issues that are capable of decision and still need to be decided.

Thomas A. Zlaket, Chief Justice, Charles E. Jones, Vice Chief Justice, Frederick J. Martone, Justice, and Ruth V. McGregor, Justice, concur.

Notes and Questions

1. *Public policy limits and freedom of contract.* The Restatement (Second) §179 recognizes a number of categories of contracts which may be unenforceable on grounds of public policy, including agreements in restraint

of trade as in *Valley Medical*. The courts often state, however, that there is a strong public interest in freedom of contract and there must be a well established basis for any public policy that would deny enforcement of a contract. See, e.g., Swavely v. Freeway Ford Truck Sales, 700 N.E.2d 181 (Ill. App. Ct. 1998) (because public policy strongly favors freedom to contract, courts should refuse enforcement only if contract is clearly contrary to public policy found in constitutions, statutes, or court decisions); Beacon Hill Civic Ass'n. v. Ristorante Toscano, Inc., 662 N.E.2d 1015 (Mass. 1996) (freedom of contract is in the public interest; courts should "not go out of their way" to find inconsistency with public policy). Does the court reveal any evidence that the parties in *Valley Medical* did not freely enter into the contract? Would such a finding be relevant to a decision to refuse enforcement of a contract on grounds of public policy?

2. *Ancillary covenants*. Historically, the common law provided that agreements in restraint of trade were unenforceable. The rationale for this prohibition was that such agreements tend to restrain competition and thereby harm the public interest. 6A Corbin on Contracts §1380. However, the common law also recognized a number of exceptions to this prohibition. In United States v. Addyston Pipe & Steel Co., 85 F. 271 (6th Cir. 1898), *aff'd*, 175 U.S. 211 (1899), Judge (later President and Chief Justice) Taft outlined the common law exceptions as follows:

> [C]ovenants in partial restraint of trade are generally upheld as valid when they are agreements (1) by the seller of property or business not to compete with the buyer in such a way as to derogate from the value of the property or business sold; (2) by a retiring partner not to compete with the firm; (3) by a partner pending the partnership not to do anything to interfere, by competition or otherwise, with the business of the firm; (4) by the buyer of property not to use the same in competition with the business retained by the seller; and (5) by an assistant, servant, or agent not to compete with his master or employer after the expiration of his time of service. Before such agreements are upheld, however, the court must find that the restraints attempted thereby are reasonably necessary (1, 2, and 3) to the enjoyment by the buyer of the property, good will, or interest in the partnership bought; or (4) to the legitimate ends of the existing partnership; or (5) to the prevention of possible injury to the business of the seller from use by the buyer of the thing sold; or (6) to protection from the danger of loss to the employer's business caused by the unjust use on the part of the employee of the confidential knowledge acquired in such business.

85 F. at 281-282. As Judge Taft stated, the rationale for these exceptions was to protect the right of the covenantee to the legitimate fruits of the contract.

The revised Restatement preserves the common law rule that a covenant not to compete is unenforceable unless it is "ancillary" to a valid transaction. Restatement (Second) §187. Section 188 defines restraints that are ancillary to a valid transaction or relationship to include the following: a promise by a seller of a business not to compete with the buyer so as to injure the business sold; a promise by an employee or agent not to compete with his employer or principal; and a promise by a partner not to compete with the partnership. The clearest example of a nonancillary covenant is an agreement between competitors to fix prices.

3. *Reasonableness of covenant.* Consistent with Restatement (Second) Contracts §188, Comments *f* and *g*, the *Valley Medical* court recognized the level of scrutiny used in examining an ancillary covenant not to compete will depend on the type of transaction involved. A covenant related to partnership or sale of business contracts will not be scrutinized as strictly or closely as a covenant related to employment because employees are usually at a greater bargaining disadvantage and therefore need more protection from the court. The court also indicates that the assessment of the enforceability of the covenant would depend on the nature of Valley Medical's valid protectible interest, if any. In assessing the reasonableness of the covenant, the court indicates that the general considerations are its scope, the hardship imposed on the promisor, and the public interest. More specifically, the court examines the scope of the covenant with regard to the time period covered, the geographical reach, and the scope of activities prohibited. (See also Comment d to Restatement (Second) §188.) What conclusions does the court reach on these issues? Are you persuaded by the court's analysis?

4. *Covenants restraining medical practice.* Even though the public interest in the practice of medicine is significant, a majority of courts, like the Arizona Supreme Court in *Valley Medical,* have declined to adopt "per se" rules that would invalidate all such covenants. See, e.g., Deutsch v. Barsky, 795 A.2d 669 (D.C. 2002) (stating that court has never held that ancillary covenants between dentists are per se violation of public policy; rule of reason to be applied); Pierson v. Medical Health Centers, P.A., 869 A.2d 901 (N.J. 2005) (rejecting argument that covenants by doctors should be invalid per se). Notwithstanding the majority approach, some state legislatures have enacted statutes that expressly prohibit covenants not to compete among physicians, and courts in other states have construed more general statutory prohibitions on non-compete covenants to apply to physicians. See Murfreesboro Medical Clinic, P.A. v. Udom, 166 S.W.3d 67 (Tenn. 2005) (citing express statutory prohibitions in Colorado, Delaware, and Massachusetts and judicial construction banning covenants not to compete among physicians in six other states; court decided that such prohibitions are per se unenforceable in Tennessee except as specifically allowed by statute).

As *Valley Medical* illustrates, of course, a covenant restraining medical practice may still be unreasonable even though not unenforceable per se. See, e.g., Nalle Clinic Co. v. Parker, 399 S.E.2d 363 (N.C. Ct. App. 1991) (covenant by doctor not to practice medicine or surgery for two years in particular county was invalid because of harm to public when county had only one other pediatric endocrinologist). See also S. Elizabeth Wilborn Malloy, Physician Restrictive Covenants: The Neglect of Incumbent Patient Interests, 41 Wake Forest L. Rev. 189 (2006) (recommending a revision of the reasonableness test to take better account of the interests of patients).

5. *Public policy based on statutes.* As the prior note indicates, some states have enacted statutes that govern covenants not to compete among physicians. The Restatement (Second) §179, Comment *b,* states that "the declaration of public policy has now become largely the province of legislators rather than judges" and courts may refuse to enforce contracts that conflict with statutory law. When statutes explicitly declare that certain contracts are unenforceable or void, courts will obey the legislative mandate. Restatement (Second) §178,

Comment *a*. See, e.g., K&K Services, Inc. v. City of Irwindale, 54 Cal. Rptr. 2d 836 (Ct. App. 1996) (statute provides contractor may not "bring or maintain any action" to enforce a contract unless "duly licensed" at all times during performance). In the more typical situation, the making of the contract violates or is inconsistent with a statute, but the statute is silent on the question of whether the contract is unenforceable. Generally a distinction is drawn between regulatory statutes, which are designed to protect the public, and revenue-raising measures. Violation of the latter will not generally prevent the enforceability of a contract. 6A Corbin on Contracts §1512, at 710-711. Compare Professional Property Services, Inc. v. Agler Green Townhouses, Inc., 998 F. Supp. 831 (S.D. Ohio 1998) (state requirement of license for property managers rendered contract void because statute was designed for "police or regulatory" purposes), with Benjamin v. Koeppel, 650 N.E.2d 829 (N.Y. 1995) (statute requiring that attorneys admitted to practice also register with court office and pay fee was primarily intended to raise revenue; failure to pay fee would not render attorney's contracts unenforceable).

6. *Covenants restraining legal practice.* As recognized by the *Valley Medical* court, covenants by lawyers not to compete with their firms after their departure are a special case because of restrictions found in the rules of professional ethics. See Model Rules of Professional Conduct, Rule 5.6, quoted in the in *Valley Medical* opinion. Courts also tend to disallow provisions which apply a financial penalty to competition without purporting to prohibit practice directly. In Cohen v. Lord, Day & Lord, 550 N.E.2d 410 (N.Y. 1989), the New York Court of Appeals ruled that a partnership agreement that conditioned payment of a departing partner's share of earned but uncollected revenues on noncompetition by the former partner was unenforceable because of the ethical prohibition on restriction of practice by lawyers. The denial of enforcement to lawyers' restrictive covenants usually is based on the strong public interest in allowing clients to retain counsel of their choice. See Stevens v. Rooks Pitts and Poust, 682 N.E.2d 1125 (Ill. App. Ct. 1997) (agreement that reduces departing partner's compensation based on competition with former firm held unenforceable on grounds of public policy because it restricts clients' choice of counsel and lawyer's ability to take on clients); Whiteside v. Griffis & Griffis, P.C., 902 S.W.2d 739 (Tex. App. 1995) (agreement that reduced departing partner's share in law firm goodwill based on competition with firm was void as against public policy in ethics rules).

By contrast, in Howard v. Babcock, 863 P.2d 150 (Cal. 1994), the California Supreme Court held "that an agreement among law partners imposing a reasonable toll on departing partners who compete with the firm is enforceable." Id. at 151. The court acknowledged that it was going against the weight of authority, but remarked:

> "The traditional view of the law firm as a stable institution with an assured future is now challenged by an awareness that even the largest and most prestigious firms are fragile economic units. . . ." (Hillman, Law Firm Breakups (1990) §1.1, at p.1.) Not the least of the changes rocking the legal profession is the propensity of withdrawing partners in law firms to "grab" clients of the firm and set up a competing practice. . . . In response, many firms have inserted noncompetition clauses into their partnership agreements. . . . These noncompetition clauses have grown and

flourished, despite, or in defiance of, the consistent holding of many courts across the nation that a noncompetition clause violates the rules of professional conduct of the legal profession. It is evident that these agreements address important business interests of law firms that can no longer be ignored.

Id. at 157. At least two other courts have agreed with the California approach. See Fearnow v. Ridenour, Swenson, Cleere & Evans, P.C., 138 P.3d 723, 728 (Ariz. 2006); Capozzi v. Latsha & Capozzi, 797 A.2d 314 (Pa. Super. Ct. 2002). See generally Robert M. Wilcox, Enforcing Lawyer Non-Competition Agreements While Maintaining the Profession: The Role of Conflict of Interest Principles, 84 Minn. L. Rev. 915 (2000) (proposing more liberal approach to enforcement of restraints on lawyers).

7. *Covenants restraining nonprofessional employment.* Courts have been willing to enforce reasonable covenants not to compete on employees in a variety of contexts that may not raise the special issues that attach to lawyers and doctors, provided that the employer has a protectible interest and the restraints are reasonable in duration, geographic extent, and restricted activities. See, e.g., Safety-Kleen Systems v. Hennkens, 301 F.3d 931 (8th Cir. 2002) (covenant of salesperson for waste management company not to compete for one year in areas served held enforceable); Advanced Marine Enterprises, Inc. v. PRC Inc., 501 S.E.2d 148 (Va. 1998) (covenant not to compete for eight months within 50 miles of employer's offices was enforceable where entire engineering department resigned, went to work for competitor, and took client information). But see Gateway 2000, Inc. v. Kelley, 9 F. Supp. 2d 790 (E.D. Mich. 1998) (covenant that prohibited manufacturing supervisor for one year from working in any capacity for any computer manufacturer in the world deemed unenforceable); Metro Traffic Control v. Shadow Traffic, 27 Cal. Rptr. 2d 573 (Ct. App. 1994) (under state statute postemployment restraints on profession, trade, or business are void unless necessary to protect trade secrets).

8. *"Blue pencil" reduction of objectionable covenant.* The intermediate appellate court in *Valley Medical* held that the covenant not to compete could be enforced after its scope had been reduced. The Arizona Supreme Court strongly disagreed with this approach, disapproving its earlier decision that seemed to permit such modification of a covenant. At the same time, the Arizona Supreme Court endorsed a mechanical approach to possible reduction of a covenant which allows severance or reduction only if the objectionable term can literally be "lined out" and the remainder enforced. For example, in a covenant that prohibited a former employee from working for competitors in "Stephens or Comanche County," the court could "blue pencil" or line out one of the two counties to make the geographical scope reasonable.

The Reporter's Note to Restatement (Second) §184 makes it clear that the section rejects the mechanical approach and endorses a more flexible method which allows reduction of the effect or scope of a clause to make it reasonable. Comment b to §184 indicates, however, that the court's discretion to reduce a covenant should be exercised only when there is no evidence of overreaching or bad faith by the promisee. This qualified approach to granting partial enforcement allows the courts to guard against the possibility recognized by the *Valley Medical* court that employers may intentionally write overbroad covenants not to compete in anticipation that few employees will have the inclination or ability to challenge them. Notably, however, some courts refuse to use either the traditional or more modern approach to severance to save a covenant not to compete that is flawed. See Ceramic & Metal Coatings Corp. v. Hizer, 529 S.E.2d 160 (Ga. Ct. App. 2000) (completely rejecting the "blue pencil theory of severability" with regard to employment contracts even if contract has severability clause); Moore v. Eggers Consulting Co., Inc., 562 N.E.2d 534 (Neb. 1997) (not role of court to reform unreasonable covenant to make it legally enforceable). Recall the discussion in Note 3 after the *Adler* case in the preceding section of this chapter concerning possible severance of unconscionable terms.

R.R. v. M.H. & another[1]
Supreme Judicial Court of Massachusetts
426 Mass. 501, 689 N.E.2d 790 (1998)

WILKINS, Chief Justice.

[On its own motion, the Supreme Court took jurisdiction of the appeal of a trial court decision that a surrogacy parenting agreement was enforceable. The Supreme Court had not previously dealt with the enforceability of a surrogacy agreement. — EDS.]

...

THE FACTS

The baby girl who is the subject of this action was born on August 15, 1997, in Leominster. The defendant mother and the plaintiff father are her biological parents. The father and his wife, who live in Rhode Island, were married in June, 1989. The wife is infertile. Sometime in 1994, she and the father learned of an egg donor program but did not pursue it because the procedure was not covered by insurance and had a relatively low success rate. Because of their ages (they were both in their forties), they concluded that pursuing adoption was not feasible. In April, 1996, responding to a newspaper advertisement for surrogacy services, they consulted a Rhode Island attorney who had drafted surrogacy contracts for both surrogates and couples seeking surrogacy services. On the attorney's advice, the father and his wife consulted the New England Surrogate Parenting Advisors (NESPA), a for-profit corporation that helps infertile couples find women willing to act as surrogate mothers. They entered into a contract with NESPA in September, 1996, and paid a fee of $6,000.

Meanwhile, in the spring of 1996, the mother, who was married and had two children, responded to a NESPA advertisement. She reported to NESPA that her family was complete and that she desired to allow others less fortunate

---

1. D.H., the husband of M.H.

than herself to have children. The mother submitted a surrogacy application to NESPA. The judge found that the mother was motivated to apply to NESPA by a desire to be pregnant, in order to earn money, and to help an infertile couple.

In October, Dr. Angela Figueroa of NESPA brought the mother together with the father and his wife. They had a seemingly informative exchange of information and views. The mother was advised to seek an attorney's advice concerning the surrogacy agreement. Shortly thereafter, the mother, the father, and his wife met again to discuss the surrogacy and other matters. The mother also met with a clinical psychologist as part of NESPA's evaluation of her suitability to act as a surrogate. The psychologist, who also evaluated the father and his wife, advised the mother to consult legal counsel, to give her husband a chance to air his concerns, to discuss arrangements for contact with the child, to consider and discuss her expectations concerning termination of the pregnancy, and to arrange a meeting between her husband and the father and his wife.[2] The psychologist concluded that the mother was solid, thoughtful, and well grounded, that she would have no problem giving the child to the father, and that she was happy to act as a surrogate. The mother told the psychologist that she was not motivated by money, although she did plan to use the funds received for her children's education. The mother's husband told the psychologist by telephone that he supported his wife's decision.

The mother signed the surrogate parenting agreement and her signature was notarized on November 1. The father signed on November 18. The agreement stated that the parties intended that the "Surrogate shall be inseminated with the semen of Natural Father" and "that, on the birth of the child or children so conceived, Natural Father, as the Natural Father, will have the full legal parental rights of a father, and surrogate will permit Natural Father to take the child or children home from the hospital to live with he [sic] and his wife." The agreement acknowledged that the mother's parental rights would not terminate if she permitted the father to take the child home and have custody, that the mother could at any time seek to enforce her parental rights by court order, but that, if she attempted to obtain custody or visitation rights, she would forfeit her rights under the agreement and would be obligated to reimburse the father for all fees and expenses paid to her under it. The agreement provided that its interpretation would be governed by Rhode Island law.

The agreement provided for compensation to the mother in the amount of $10,000 "for services rendered in conceiving, carrying and giving birth to the Child." Payment of the $10,000 was to be made as follows: $500 on verification of the pregnancy; $2,500 at the end of the third month; $3,500 at the end of the sixth month; and $3,500 at the time of birth "and when delivery of child occurs." The agreement stated that no payment was made in connection with adoption of the child, the termination of parental rights, or consent to surrender the child for adoption. The father acknowledged the mother's right to determine whether to carry the pregnancy to term, but the

2. Her husband had had a vasectomy in 1994 and did not have sexual relations with the mother after October, 1996.

mother agreed to refund all payments if, without the father's consent, she had an abortion that was not necessary for her physical health. The father assumed various expenses of the pregnancy, including tests, and had the right to name the child. The mother would be obliged, however, to repay all expenses and fees for services if tests showed that the father was not the biological father of the child, or if the mother refused to permit the father to take the child home from the hospital. The agreement also provided that the mother would maintain some contact with the child after the birth.

The judge found that the mother entered into the agreement on her own volition after consulting legal counsel. There was no evidence of undue influence, coercion, or duress. The mother fully understood that she was contracting to give custody of the baby to the father. She sought to inseminate herself on November 30 and December 1, 1996. The attempt at conception was successful.

The lawyer for the father sent the mother a check for $500 in December, 1996, and another for $2,500 in February. In May, the father's lawyer sent the mother a check for $3,500. She told the lawyer that she had changed her mind and wanted to keep the child. She returned the check uncashed in the middle of June. The mother has made no attempt to refund the amounts that the father paid her, including $550 that he paid for pregnancy-related expenses.

PROCEDURE

Approximately two weeks after the mother changed her mind and returned the check for $3,500, and before the child was born, the father commenced this action against the mother seeking to establish his paternity, alleging breach of contract, and requesting a declaration of his rights under the surrogacy agreement. Subsequently, the wife's [sic; mother's?] husband was added as a defendant. The judge appointed a guardian ad litem to represent the interests of the unborn child. Proceedings were held on aspects of the preliminary injunction request (now resolved) and on the mother's motion to determine whether surrogacy contracts are enforceable in Massachusetts.

On August 4, 1997, the judge entered an order directing the mother to give the child to the father when it was discharged from the hospital and granting the father temporary physical custody of the child. She did so based on her determination that the father's custody claim was likely to prevail on the merits of the contract claim, and, if not on that claim, then on the basis of the best interests of the child. The mother was granted the right to frequent visits.

On August 13, 1997, the judge reported the propriety of her August 1 order which, as we have said, was based in part on her conclusion that the surrogacy contract was enforceable. She acknowledged that specific questions were not reportable under Mass. R. Dom. Rel. P. 64 (1997) (see Gray v. Commissioner of Revenue, 422 Mass. 666, 667-668, 665 N.E.2d 17 [1996]), but nevertheless set forth the questions that appear in the margin.[3] The judge determined to continue with an inquiry into the best interests of the child,

3. "1. Is a surrogacy contract enforceable, wherein a woman, the egg donor, provides child bearing services to a man, the semen donor, and delivers to him physical custody of their child in exchange for monetary consideration, and which further provides that she retains her constitutional rights to abortion during pregnancy and to parental rights after the birth of the child, but conditions

while appellate proceedings were continuing. She conducted further hearings, and, shortly before the case was argued in this court, she filed a procedural history and supplemental findings dated October 3, 1997.

OTHER JURISDICTIONS

A significant minority of States have legislation addressing surrogacy agreements. Some simply deny enforcement of all such agreements. See Ariz. Rev. Stat. Ann. §25-218(A) (West 1991); D.C. Code Ann. §16-402(a) (1997); Ind. Code Ann. §§31-20-1-1, 31-20-1-2 (Michie 1997); Mich. Comp. Laws Ann. §722.855 (West 1993); N.Y. Dom. Rel. Law §122 (McKinney Supp. 1997); N.D. Cent. Code §14-18-05 (1991); Utah Code Ann. §76-7-204 (1995). Others expressly deny enforcement only if the surrogate is to be compensated. See Ky. Rev. Stat. Ann. §199.590(4) (Michie 1995); La. Rev. Stat. Ann. §9:2713 (West 1991); Neb. Rev. Stat. §25-21,200 (1995); Wash. Rev. Code §§26.26.230, 26.26.240 (1996). Some States have simply exempted surrogacy agreements from provisions making it a crime to sell babies. See Ala. Code §26-10A-34 (1992); Iowa Code §710.11 (1997); W. Va. Code §48-4-16(e)(3) (1996). A few States have explicitly made unpaid surrogacy agreements lawful. See Fla. Stat. ch. 742.15 (1995); Nev. Rev. Stat. §126.045 (1995); N.H. Rev. Stat. Ann. §168-B:16 (1994 & Supp. 1996); Va. Code Ann. §§20-159, 20-160(B)(4) (Michie 1995). Florida, New Hampshire, and Virginia require that the intended mother be infertile. See Fla. Stat. ch. 742.15(2)(a); N.H. Rev. Stat. Ann. §168-B:17(II) (1994); Va. Code Ann. §20-160(B)(8). New Hampshire and Virginia place restrictions on who may act as a surrogate and require advance judicial approval of the agreement. See N.H. Rev. Stat. Ann. §§168-B:16(I)(b), 168-B:17; Va. Code Ann. §§20-159(B), 20-160(B)(6). Last, Arkansas raises a presumption that a child born to a surrogate mother is the child of the intended parents and not the surrogate. Ark. Code Ann. §9-10-201(b), (c) (Michie 1993).

There are few appellate court opinions on the enforceability of traditional surrogacy agreements. The Kentucky Legislature . . . has provided that a compensated surrogacy agreement is unenforceable (Ky. Rev. Stat. Ann. §199.590[4]), thus changing the rule that the Supreme Court of Kentucky announced in Surrogate Parenting Assocs., Inc. v. Commonwealth ex rel. Armstrong, 704 S.W.2d 209 (Ky. 1986). In In re Marriage of Moschetta, 25 Cal. App. 4th 1218, 30 Cal. Rptr. 2d 893 (1994), the court declined to enforce a traditional surrogacy agreement because it was incompatible with California parentage and adoption statutes. Id. at 1222, 30 Cal. Rptr. 2d 893. The surrogate, who was to be paid $10,000, had agreed that (a) the father could obtain sole custody of any resulting child, (b) she would agree to terminate her

---

and limits the exercise of those rights, unless she forgoes the benefits of the contract and/or makes restitution of benefits already received?

"If the answer to the question on contract enforceability is affirmative, secondary questions that derive from the primary question are:

"2. If the surrogate mother has received payment for her services, is specific performance an appropriate remedy for her breach, as to the provision that she relinquish physical custody of the child when born?

parental rights, and (c) she would aid the father's wife in adopting the child. Id. at 1223, 30 Cal. Rptr. 2d 893. The court sent the case back to the trial court for a determination whether the father should be awarded primary physical custody. Id. at 1234, 30 Cal. Rptr. 2d 893.

The best known opinion is that of the Supreme Court of New Jersey in Matter of Baby M., 109 N.J. 396, 537 A.2d 1227 (1988), where the court invalidated a compensated surrogacy contract because it conflicted with the law and public policy of the State. Id. at 411, 537 A.2d 1227. The Baby M surrogacy agreement involved broader concessions from the mother than the agreement before us because it provided that the mother would surrender her parental rights and would allow the father's wife to adopt the child. Id. at 412, 537 A.2d 1227. The agreement, therefore, directly conflicted with a statute prohibiting the payment of money to obtain an adoption and a statute barring enforcement of an agreement to adoption made prior to the birth of the child. Id. at 422, 537 A.2d 1227. The court acknowledged that an award of custody to the father was in the best interests of the child, but struck down orders terminating the mother's parental rights and authorizing the adoption of the child by the husband's wife. Id. at 411, 537 A.2d 1227. The court added that it found no "legal prohibition against surrogacy when the surrogate mother volunteers, without any payment, to act as a surrogate and is given the right to change her mind and to assert her parental rights." Id. at 469, 537 A.2d 1227.

DISCUSSION

1. The governing law. . . . The significance, if any, of the surrogacy agreement on the relationship of the parties and on the child is appropriately determined by Massachusetts law.

2. General Laws c. 46, §4B. The case before us concerns traditional surrogacy, in which the fertile member of an infertile couple is one of the child's biological parents. Surrogate fatherhood, the insemination of the fertile wife with sperm of a donor, often an anonymous donor, is a recognized and accepted procedure.[8] If the mother's husband consents to the procedure, the resulting child is considered the legitimate child of the mother and her husband. G.L. c. 46, §4B. Section 4B does not comment on the rights and obligations, if any, of the biological father, although inferentially he has none. In the case before us, the infertile spouse is the wife. No statute decrees the consequences of the artificial insemination of a surrogate with the sperm of a fertile husband. This situation presents different considerations from surrogate fatherhood because surrogate motherhood is never anonymous and her commitment and contribution is unavoidably much greater than that of a sperm donor.[10]

. . .

---

8. In Adoption of Galen, 425 Mass. 201, 680 N.E.2d 70 (1997), and in Adoption of Tammy, 416 Mass. 205, 619 N.E.2d 315 (1993), each involving the surrogate fatherhood of a child, we upheld the right of a woman to adopt the child of a woman with whom she had a committed relationship.

10. A situation which involves considerations different from those in the case before us arises when the birth mother has had transferred to her uterus an embryo formed through in vitro fertilization of the intended parents' sperm and egg. This latter process in which the birth mother is not genetically related to the child (except coincidentally if an intended parent is a relative) has been called gestational surrogacy. In Johnson v. Calvert, 5 Cal. 4th 84, 96, 19 Cal. Rptr. 2d 494, 851 P.2d

3. *Adoption statutes.* Policies underlying our adoption legislation suggest that a surrogate parenting agreement should be given no effect if the mother's agreement was obtained prior to a reasonable time after the child's birth or if her agreement was induced by the payment of money. Adoption legislation is, of course, not applicable to child custody, but it does provide us with some guidance. Although the agreement makes no reference to adoption and does not concern the termination of parental rights or the adoption of the child by the father's wife, the normal expectation in the case of a surrogacy agreement seems to be that the father's wife will adopt the child with the consent of the mother (and the father). Under G.L. c. 210, §2, adoption requires the written consent of the father and the mother but, in these circumstances, not the mother's husband. Any such consent, written, witnessed, and notarized, is not to be executed "sooner than the fourth calendar day after the date of birth of the child to be adopted." Id. That statutory standard should be interpreted as providing that no mother may effectively agree to surrender her child for adoption earlier than the fourth day after its birth, by which time she better knows the strength of her bond with her child. Although a consent to surrender custody has less permanency than a consent to adoption, the legislative judgment that a mother should have time after a child's birth to reflect on her wishes concerning the child weighs heavily in our consideration whether to give effect to a prenatal custody agreement. No private agreement concerning adoption or custody can be conclusive in any event because a judge, passing on custody of a child, must decide what is in the best interests of the child.[11]

Adoptive parents may pay expenses of a birth parent but may make no direct payment to her. See G.L. c. 210, §11A; 102 Code Mass. Regs. §5.09 (1997). Even though the agreement seeks to attribute that payment of $10,000, not to custody or adoption, but solely to the mother's services in carrying the child, the father ostensibly was promised more than those services because, as a practical matter, the mother agreed to surrender custody of the child. She could assert custody rights, according to the agreement, only if she repaid the father all amounts that she had received and also reimbursed him for all expenses he had incurred. The statutory prohibition of payment for receiving a child through adoption suggests that, as a matter of policy, a mother's agreement to surrender custody in exchange for money (beyond pregnancy-related expenses) should be given no effect in deciding the custody of the child.

4. *Conclusion.* The mother's purported consent to custody in the agreement is ineffective because no such consent should be recognized unless given on or after the fourth day following the child's birth. In reaching this conclusion, we apply to consent to custody the same principle which underlies the statutory restriction on when a mother's consent to adoption may be

---

776, cert. denied, 510 U.S. 874, 114 S. Ct. 206, 126 L. Ed. 2d 163, and cert. dismissed sub nom. Baby Boy J. v. Johnson, 510 U.S. 938, 114 S. Ct. 374, 126 L. Ed. 2d 324 (1993), the Supreme Court of California gave effect to a contract that provided that the mother of a child born as a result of a gestational surrogacy would be the egg donor and not the surrogate. Id.

11. In the case of a divorce, a judge may approve an agreement between parents concerning child custody unless the judge makes specific findings that the agreement would not be in the best interests of the child. G.L. c. 208, §31.

effectively given. Moreover, the payment of money to influence the mother's custody decision makes the agreement as to custody void. Eliminating any financial reward to a surrogate mother is the only way to assure that no economic pressure will cause a woman, who may well be a member of an economically vulnerable class, to act as a surrogate. It is true that a surrogate enters into the agreement before she becomes pregnant and thus is not presented with the desperation that a poor unwed pregnant woman may confront. However, compensated surrogacy arrangements raise the concern that, under financial pressure, a woman will permit her body to be used and her child to be given away.

There is no doubt that compensation was a factor in inducing the mother to enter into the surrogacy agreement and to cede custody to the father. If the payment of $10,000 was really only compensation for the mother's services in carrying the child and giving birth and was unrelated to custody of the child, the agreement would not have provided that the mother must refund all compensation paid (and expenses paid) if she should challenge the father's right to custody. Nor would the agreement have provided that final payment be made only when the child is delivered to the father. We simply decline, on public policy grounds, to apply to a surrogacy agreement of the type involved here the general principle that an agreement between informed, mature adults should be enforced absent proof of duress, fraud, or undue influence.

We recognize that there is nothing inherently unlawful in an arrangement by which an informed woman agrees to attempt to conceive artificially and give birth to a child whose father would be the husband of an infertile wife. We suspect that many such arrangements are made and carried out without disagreement.

If no compensation is paid beyond pregnancy-related expenses and if the mother is not bound by her consent to the father's custody of the child unless she consents after a suitable period has passed following the child's birth, the objections we have identified in this opinion to the enforceability of a surrogate's consent to custody would be overcome. Other conditions might be important in deciding the enforceability of a surrogacy agreement, such as a requirement that (a) the mother's husband give his informed consent to the agreement in advance; (b) the mother be an adult and have had at least one successful pregnancy; (c) the mother, her husband, and the intended parents have been evaluated for the soundness of their judgment and for their capacity to carry out the agreement; (d) the father's wife be incapable of bearing a child without endangering her health; (e) the intended parents be suitable persons to assume custody of the child; and (f) all parties have the advice of counsel. The mother and father may not, however, make a binding best-interests-of-the-child determination by private agreement. Any custody agreement is subject to a judicial determination of custody based on the best interests of the child.

The conditions that we describe are not likely to be satisfactory to an intended father because, following the birth of the child, the mother can refuse to consent to the father's custody even though the father has incurred substantial pregnancy-related expenses. A surrogacy agreement judicially approved before conception may be a better procedure, as is permitted by statutes in Virginia and New Hampshire. A Massachusetts statute concerning surrogacy agreements, pro or con, would provide guidance to judges, lawyers, infertile couples interested in surrogate parenthood, and prospective surrogate mothers.[12]

We do not reach but comment briefly on the mother's argument that the agreement was unconscionable. She actively sought to become a surrogate and entered into the surrogacy agreement voluntarily, advised by counsel, not under duress, and fully informed. Unconscionability is not apparent on this record.

A declaration shall be entered that the surrogacy agreement is not enforceable. Such further orders as may be appropriate, consistent with this opinion, may be entered in the Probate and Family Court.

So ordered.

Notes and Questions

1. *Public policy and family relations.* The courts recognize a general public policy limit on contracts that are deemed to impair or harm family relations. Restatement (Second) §§189, 190 address promises that are unreasonably in restraint of marriage and promises that are detrimental to marital relationships. The Restatement (Second) §191 provides, more specifically, that a contract affecting the custody of a child is unenforceable on grounds of public policy unless it is consistent with the "best interest of the child." This section is consistent with the view that termination of parental rights in exchange for money is against public policy, as commonly reflected in adoption statutes. As suggested by Note 1 after the *Valley Medical* case, however, courts often state that there is a strong public interest in freedom of contract, respecting the ability of parties to bind themselves prospectively to a future performance. Are you persuaded that there are aspects of surrogate parenting contracts that make it inappropriate to apply the normal precept of freedom to contract?

The *R.R. v. M.H.* court cites both legislation and court decisions from other jurisdictions in support of its approach to determining the enforceability of the surrogate parenting contract. Is the question of enforcement of surrogate parenting contracts one that is particularly suited for legislative action or is there a role for the courts in resolving such issues? Does it appear that the *R.R. v. M.H.* court is merely deciding a pending case or is the court essentially adopting legislation? Based on the description of state statutory laws given in *R.R. v. M.H.*, do you favor legislation regarding the validity of surrogacy contracts? If so, what form of legislation would you support? Why?

---

12. The National Conference of Commissioners on Uniform State Laws has approved alternative proposals concerning surrogacy agreements. One alternative simply states that "[a]n agreement in which a woman agrees to become a surrogate or to relinquish her rights and duties as parent of a child thereafter conceived through assisted conception is void." Uniform Status of Children of Assisted Conception Act, Alternative B, §5, 9B U.L.A. 208 (Master ed. Supp. 1997). The other alternative provides for judicial approval of an agreement before conception if various conditions are met and allows the payment of compensation. Id. at 201-207, Alternative A, §§5, 6, 9(a).

2. *The "Baby M" case.* As indicated by the *R.R. v. M.H.* court, the best known decision addressing the enforceability of surrogate parenting contracts is In re Baby M., 537 A.2d 1227 (N.J. 1988). The contract in that case also called for payment of $10,000 to the surrogate and, as noted by the *R.R. v. M.H.* court, stipulated that Mrs. Whitehead, the surrogate, would not "form or attempt to form a parent-child relationship" with the baby she had agreed to bear and would permit Mrs. Stern, the biological father's wife, to become the baby's legal mother. In deciding that the contract was unenforceable, the New Jersey Supreme Court concluded that the agreement was inconsistent with statutory provisions that prohibit payment of money in connection with adoptions, that require proof of parental unfitness or abandonment before termination of parental rights, and that make consent to private adoptions revocable for a period after birth. Id. at 1240. In addition, however, the court ruled that the contract was fundamentally at odds with public policy:

> The surrogacy contract is based on principles that are directly contrary to the objectives of our laws. It guarantees the separation of a child from its mother; it looks to adoption regardless of suitability; it totally ignores the child; it takes the child from the mother regardless of her wishes and her maternal fitness; and it does all of this, it accomplishes all of its goals, through the use of money.
>
> Beyond that is the potential degradation of some women that may result from this arrangement. In many cases, of course, surrogacy may bring satisfaction, not only to the infertile couple, but to the surrogate mother herself. The fact, however, that many women may not perceive surrogacy negatively but rather see it as an opportunity does not diminish its potential for devastation to other women.
>
> In sum, the harmful consequences of this surrogacy arrangement appear to us all too palpable. In New Jersey the surrogate mother's agreement to sell her child is void. Its irrevocability infects the entire contract, as does the money that purports to buy it.

Id. at 1250. The court affirmed the trial court decision that the best interests of the child justified awarding custody to the Sterns but reversed that part of trial court's decision that would have terminated Mrs. Whitehead's parental rights based on the contract.

Although it appears that the contract in *R.R. v. M.H.* was designed to avoid some of the problems in the *Baby M* case, the court still finds the agreement to be unenforceable. Do you think you could draft an agreement that would be enforceable in Massachusetts in light of the court's opinion in *R.R. v. M.H.*?

3. *Gestational surrogacy and public policy.* As the *R.R. v. M.H.* opinion indicates, the California Supreme Court rendered a decision after the *Baby M* case that essentially held a surrogate parenting agreement to be enforceable in a case involving "gestational surrogacy." Johnson v. Calvert, 851 P.2d 776, *cert. denied*, 510 U.S. 874, and *cert. dismissed sub nom.* Baby Boy J. v. Johnson, 510 U.S. 938 (1993). Anna Johnson, the surrogate, did not supply the egg for the baby. Rather, the Calverts provided both the sperm and the egg that were used to form an embryo, which was implanted by in vitro fertilization. The California Supreme Court held that state law would recognize only one natural mother and framed the key issue as whether

Crispina Calvert, as the egg donor, or Anna Johnson, as the gestational surrogate, was "the mother" of the resulting child. Id. at 781. The case thus presented the challenge of applying traditional policy concepts to advances in reproductive technology.

The *Johnson* court stated that it would use the surrogacy contract to decide who had the better claim as mother of the child. In contrast to the *Baby M* court, the California court rejected a number of public policy arguments against the enforceability of the contract. First, the court reasoned that gestational surrogacy does not involve surrender of parental rights for money because the surrogate is being paid for gestating services and not for surrender of parental rights. Second, the court held that the contract did not involve involuntary servitude that would be inconsistent with the Thirteenth Amendment to the United States Constitution because the contract recognized that the surrogate could terminate the pregnancy by abortion. The court also rejected the arguments that surrogacy contracts would lead to exploitation of women of lesser economic status and to treatment of children as commodities, stating that the limited data available on surrogate contracts reflected an absence of adverse effect on such parties. And finally, the court declared that the argument that a woman cannot knowingly and intelligently enter into a contract to gestate and surrender a baby as carrying "overtones of the reasoning that for centuries prevented women from attaining equal economic rights and professional status under the law." Id. at 783-785. Are you more persuaded by the *Johnson* or *Baby M* court on the import of the policy concerns?

Notably, the only woman on the California Supreme Court at that time, Justice Joyce Kennard, filed the lone dissent in the *Johnson* case. Justice Kennard agreed with the majority that both the genetic and the gestational mothers had valid claims to be the legal mother of the child but rejected that idea that the surrogacy contract should be used to break the tie. Justice Kennard reasoned instead that the best interest of the child should be used to determine parental rights. 851 P.2d at 799. Justice Kennard emphasized that children are not "the personal property of anyone, and their delivery cannot be ordered as a contract remedy on the same terms as a court would, for example, order a breaching party to deliver a truckload of nuts and bolts." Id. at 796-797. Justice Kennard agreed with the majority, however, that the legislature should act to provide guidance in this area. In the absence of such statutory resolution, are you persuaded that the majority in *Johnson* reached the correct decision in the case? Do you think that gender differences between judges are likely to make a difference in how such a case is viewed?

4. *Scholarly commentary.* The surrogacy cases have generated a wealth of commentary. E.g., Carmel Shalev, Birth Power (1989), reviewed by Marci L. Smith, Book Note, 1991 B.Y.U. L. Rev. 709; Martha A. Field, Surrogate Motherhood (1988), reviewed by Lori A. Demond, Book Note, 1991 B.Y.U. L. Rev. 685; Barbara L. Atwell, Surrogacy and Adoption: A Case of Incompatibility, 20 Colum. Hum. Rts. L. Rev. 1 (1988); Christine L. Kerian, Surrogacy: A Last Resort Alternative for Infertile Women or a Commodification of Women's Bodies and Children?, 12 Wis. Women's L.J. 113 (1997); Richard A. Posner, The Ethics and Economics of Enforcing Contracts of

Surrogate Motherhood, 5 J. Contemp. Health L. & Poly. 21 (1989). Many scholars argue for outright prohibition of such contracts. E.g., Judith Areen, *Baby M* Reconsidered, 76 Geo. L.J. 1741 (1988). Others argue for enforcement, but for a variety of reasons. Judge Richard Posner, using principles of economic analysis, contends that surrogacy contracts should be enforced for the same reasons that other private agreements are upheld: They increase the welfare of the contracting parties. Carmel Shalev argues for enforcement of such contracts on feminist grounds, so that women can gain control of their bodies and eliminate the use of a dual standard in matters of sex. By contrast, Martha Field adopts a middle ground. She argues that surrogacy contracts should be legally valid, but unenforceable. Under Field's approach, surrogacy contracts would not be illegal, but at the same time they could not be enforced against the surrogate mother, who would retain the right to refuse to honor the contract until the surrogate couple actually received the baby.

5. *Remedial options.* Courts will not necessarily deem void and completely unenforceable a contract that is inconsistent with a statute or other basis of public policy. Rather, the courts may enforce the contract or, more likely yet, may grant restitutionary relief to one of the parties if a benefit has been conferred. The Restatement (Second) adopts an approach that requires the weighing of a number of factors before denying enforcement of a contract or refusing restitutionary relief on public policy grounds, including assessing the nature of the public policy involved, the degree of resulting forfeiture, and whether denial of relief would further the policy. Restatement (Second) of Contracts §§178, 197. See also Trees v. Kersey, 56 P.3d 765 (Idaho 2002) (contracts made in violation of public works licensing act were void, but court would not allow party who committed fraud to keep benefit of performance without liability); CitaraManis v. Hallowell, 613 A.2d 964 (Md. 1992) (lease for rental property made without proper license would not necessarily be unenforceable; courts must consider strength of public policy, degree of violation, and whether refund of rent would be disproportionate penalty).

6. *"In pari delicto."* If both parties willfully engage in wrongful conduct, and therefore are "in pari delicto" (equally culpable), the courts usually take the position that the parties should be left where the court finds them and will give no remedy to either party, even if one has received a benefit from the other. See Joseph M. Perillo, Calamari & Perillo on Contracts §22.1, at 844 (5th ed. 2003). This rule is applied particularly where the contract involves serious illegal conduct. See, e.g., Al-Ibrahim v. Edde, 897 F. Supp. 620 (D.D.C. 1995) (employee who claimed gambling winnings of employer in plan to avoid federal income tax could not enforce employer's promise of reimbursement of taxes paid; judicial process cannot be used to further illegal acts); Evans v. Luster, 928 P.2d 455 (Wash. Ct. App. 1996) (where contractor and property owner purposely schemed to avoid compliance with permit law, "court will leave the parties as it finds them" and grant no relief to unpaid contractor). But see Maudlin v. Pacific Decision Sciences Corp., 40 Cal. Rptr. 3d 724 (Ct. App. 2006) (former employee who resold stock to company was not in pari delicto where he was aware that employer structured deferred payments to evade taxes but employee derived no

benefit from scheme and would have suffered forfeiture of almost $1.7 million if court left the parties where found).

PROBLEM 7-3

Arturo Guillen is president and the majority stockholder in Hydrazone Systems, Inc., a small company that manufactures and installs patented equipment designed to simulate ocean waves. Hydrazone is incorporated in the state of New London and is a duly licensed contractor in that state. Mirage Waterpark Company owns and operates a water-oriented amusement park in the neighboring state of Ada. On January 15, 2006, Guillen contracted on behalf of Hydrazone with Mirage to design and manufacture for the park a 29,000-square-foot "surfing pool" using Hydrazone wave equipment. Mirage was represented by its president, Anna Patton. The contract provided for a price of "$750,000 for equipment" and "a maximum of $250,000 in fees for services as necessary to assist in installation." The contract provided that Hydrazone would charge an agreed hourly rate for the services of its employees in assisting with installation. The contract stated that delivery was to be completed in time to allow for installation by May 15, 2006. Patton said that Mirage would primarily use its staff in installation and use a local contractor, if necessary. Mirage was entitled to hold back "10% of total charges as retainage," pending satisfactory completion and operation of the pool.

After signing the contract with Mirage, Guillen became concerned about Ada's contractor licensing statute, which he understood would apply to the new installation. Guillen wrote to Patton on February 1, 2006, stating that Hydrazone wished only to sell and deliver its equipment and to avoid involvement in installation or construction of the pool because of the licensing law. In a letter dated February 9, 2006, Patton responded that "Hydrazone's expertise is essential to proper installation of the equipment" and that Mirage would "hold Hydrazone to its commitment to assist in construction." Patton also promised that she would arrange for a friend who was an Ada licensed contractor "to sign any necessary paperwork and accept any formal liability for the work." After this exchange of correspondence, Hydrazone started delivery of the equipment and began assisting Mirage staff in initial layout on March 1, 2006.

By March 15, Guillen became concerned again that no state licensed contractor was involved in the installation. Upon inquiry by Guillen, Patton stated that her friend was tied up but would start assisting later. Guillen then stated that Hydrazone would cease any work until a licensed contractor was brought on board. Patton responded by stating that Mirage would refuse further payment, even for the $250,000 of equipment that had been delivered, and would hold Hydrazone liable for any lost profits if the wave pool was not operational by the beginning of the 2006 summer season. Because his company was fully extended financially due to three concurrent projects, Guillen needed prompt payment from Mirage to meet his regular operating expenses. Thus, although he continued to complain regularly, Guillen directed Hydrazone employees to continue with the installation. By

May 15, the pool was completely installed, primarily by Hydrazone employees. Guillen had charged the full $1,000,000 for equipment and services, and had been paid $800,000. Patton never arranged for an Ada contractor to work with Hydrazone.

The wave pool performed as specified in the contract during the 2006 summer season. After requesting payment of the $200,000 balance, Guillen received on August 1, 2006, a check for $100,000, which he had his financial manager deposit. Patton, however, refused to release the final $100,000 in retainage that had not been paid to Hydrazone. When Guillen complained to Patton, she told him that his last progress payment of $100,000 had been accompanied by a letter that stated it was final payment in full discharge of the contract. Guillen checked his files and discovered in fact that a form letter with a great deal of fine print had been enclosed with the check and that it had included such language. Neither Guillen nor his financial officer had read the form letter before negotiating the check. Hydrazone then filed suit against Mirage to collect the final $100,000.

Assume that you are a law clerk for the magistrate who will be supervising a settlement conference to be held with the parties. The magistrate would like your assessment of the legal issues that are likely to arise if the case goes to trial and the arguments that may be presented to each side to encourage settlement. The state licensing law is given below. What is your assessment?

Business & Professions Code §7031:

(1) No individual person, partnership or corporate entity engaged in the business or acting in the capacity of a contractor, may bring or maintain any action in an Ada court to recover compensation for the performance of any act or contract for which a contractor's license is required without alleging and proving the maintenance of status as a duly licensed contractor at all times during the performance of act or contract.

(a) A license is required for any erection, construction, or renovation of a fixed structure upon real property.

(b) A license may be obtained by satisfactory completion of the contractor's competency examination and payment of a fee of $500 for individuals and $1000 for partnerships or corporate persons.

(2) The penalty for noncompliance with this provision shall be a fine equal to double the fees that should have been properly paid.

PROBLEM 7-4

You are an attorney with the local legal services program, where you handle a general caseload comprising consumer, welfare, and domestic matters. A 17-year-old girl, Samantha Brown, has come into your office and tells you the following story.

About 18 months ago, Samantha became pregnant. When her mother learned about this, she was furious. Her boyfriend offered to get her an abortion, but Samantha refused, saying that it was wrong. Her pregnancy was extremely difficult, and she was hospitalized for two weeks before giving birth to a daughter, named DeAnna. Because of Samantha's difficult pregnancy, her doctor said that she would need to take it easy for several weeks and that she must have someone to take care of the baby. Unfortunately, Samantha did not have anyone who could help her. (Samantha's mother, who works full time, was unable to do so.)

The next few weeks were almost a total disaster for Samantha. The baby seemed to cry nonstop. Samantha couldn't sleep at night and was constantly exhausted during the day. Samantha lost weight. The baby wouldn't eat properly and hardly gained any weight at all. About a month after the baby was born, a Mrs. Wallace, who said she was from the welfare department, came with Samantha's mother to visit her. Her mother said that Mrs. Wallace had come to take care of the baby because Samantha couldn't do so and the baby was getting sick. Samantha agreed she needed help. Mrs. Wallace told Samantha that Samantha needed to sign a paper to allow Mrs. Wallace to take care of the baby, which Samantha did. Mrs. Wallace left, taking DeAnna with her.

A few weeks of rest did wonders for Samantha. When she felt better, she told her mother that she was going to see DeAnna. On the paper that Mrs. Wallace left with her was the name of an agency where she was able to reach Mrs. Wallace on the telephone. When Samantha said that she would like to visit DeAnna, Mrs. Wallace said that was not possible because once a baby was placed for adoption, the natural mother was not allowed to visit the baby. Samantha cried out that she had not given her baby for adoption. Mrs. Wallace explained that the paper she signed gave up her parental rights and authorized the agency to place the baby for adoption. Confused, Samantha turned to her mother, who said that she had contacted the agency because Samantha was too young to have a child, that she couldn't take care of the baby, and that being a single mother would ruin her life. Samantha said she wanted her baby back, that she could take care of her. Her mother asked her to wait, and think about it for a while.

That was about six months ago. Samantha says she didn't do anything about the baby during that time. For a while she didn't know what to do. Then she returned to high school and found a part-time job that took up a lot of her time. Now she really wants the baby back, she says. She wants to know whether you can help her regain custody of DeAnna.

At this point, of course, you as an attorney could not yet give an opinion; fact investigation and legal research would be necessary before doing so. Suppose you begin by contacting Mrs. Wallace; she gives you a copy of the paper that Samantha signed, which is entitled "Consent to Adoption." The document states that by signing the paper the mother is authorizing the agency to place the child for adoption and that the mother is releasing all parental rights, including any right to visit the child or know the name of the parents. Mrs. Wallace tells you that she explained the adoption to Samantha, who fully understood what she was doing. Mrs. Wallace says that it is not unusual for the mother in such cases to change her mind later. She also informs you that the adoptive parents have begun judicial proceedings, as required by local law, to adopt DeAnna legally.

You then research the state statute governing adoption by consent. Its provisions include the following:

An adoption of a child may be decreed when there have been filed written consents to adoption executed by:

(a) . . .

(b) the mother, regardless of age, if the child is illegitimate, and by the child's natural father if he has consistently on a continuing basis exercised rights and performed duties as a parent. . . .

State law also provides that after entry of a final decree of adoption, any consent is irrevocable. Prior to entry of a final decree, however, a consent may be declared to be ineffective for any reason that would be sufficient to avoid an ordinary contract.

Based on this investigation and research, what advice would you give your client about her right to regain custody of DeAnna? Would further investigation or research be necessary? If so, what would you do?

8 | Justification for Nonperformance: Mistake, Changed Circumstances, and Contractual Modifications

Many of the various defenses surveyed in Chapter 7 have a common basis in the asserted misconduct of one party — misconduct resulting in the bargain being either surprisingly different from what the other party believed it to be or oppressively unfair to that party (perhaps both). Although suggestions of such misconduct may also be found in some of the cases in this chapter, the kinds of excuses from performance here at issue are those arising not from overreaching or deception by either party, but from changes in circumstance that have either occurred or come to light since the original agreement was made.

It is clear from our study thus far that executory contracts are frequently entered into for the purpose of protecting against various risks. Indeed, an insurance contract has (at least for the insured party) no other purpose. Even contracts that have as their main purpose the definition of some mutually beneficial exchange of performances (the sale of goods for money, for instance) may have as a subsidiary function the protection of one or both parties against the risk that certain unfavorable events may occur before the time when performance is to take place (a rise in the market price of the goods, for instance, which in the absence of an existing fixed-price contract would require the buyer to pay more than the presently available price, or a fall in the market, which could similarly force the seller to sell his goods at less profit, or even at a loss). In light of this risk-shifting function that contracts perform, it would not be surprising to find contract law generally resistant to the suggestion that a contractual obligation might be avoided just because unforeseen or unprovided-for circumstances made it less favorable to one of the parties than had been originally contemplated. And indeed it is resistant to such excuses, as we shall see. Nevertheless, there are a variety of established legal categories that hold out the possibility of such an excuse from performance, in appropriate cases.

These categories grow from different strands of case law and have different labels, such as "mistake," "impossibility," "impracticability," or "frustration." Modern contract theory, however, is inclined to stress their similarities rather than their differences, since in most cases the underlying question is the same: If for one of the parties a circumstance not expressly provided for in the contract has adversely affected either performance itself or the value thereof, should that party be permitted as a result to escape the obligation of performance the contract would otherwise impose?

A. MISTAKE

Like most words, *mistake* can be used to describe a variety of things. It may refer simply to a decision that with hindsight turns out to have been clearly wrong. (It was a mistake, for instance, for Napoleon to invade Russia; it was a mistake to have that fourth piece of pizza at bedtime.) Or it may describe a decision that, although not clearly disastrous, has nevertheless turned out to be at least arguably not the best choice that could have been made. Even if not always "20/20," as popular wisdom would have it, hindsight is at least apt to be clearer than foresight, and many a contracting party has later regretted her choice to enter into a particular deal, wishing that she had insisted on better terms, expressly protected herself against some contingency, or even forgone the deal entirely.

We have seen already that contract law sometimes has to deal with the parties' mistaken belief that they were using language with the same intention when in fact they attached different meanings to the terms they employed (recall the *Frigaliment* case in Chapter 5). Occasionally such a misunderstanding will cause the court to hold that no binding contract exists, although as we have seen the more usual judicial response is to choose one of the intended meanings and apply it in enforcing the contract. Should the law permit one party to escape a contractual obligation merely because she later regrets the deal she has made — views it, in effect, as a mistake? Ordinarily, the answer would be "No," for the reason suggested in the introduction to this chapter: Parties make contracts with the aim of binding each other *despite* the myriad changes of circumstance that may occur before the time for performance arrives. Sometimes, however, the court finds that a more particular type of mistake has been made, which lifts the case above the ordinary run. The materials that follow explore various situations in which this extraordinary type of relief has been sought and, sometimes, awarded.

| **Lenawee County Board of Health v. Messerly**
Michigan Supreme Court
417 Mich. 17, 331 N.W.2d 203 (1982)

RYAN, Justice.

In March of 1977, Carl and Nancy Pickles, appellees, purchased from appellants, William and Martha Messerly, a 600-square-foot tract of land upon which is located a three-unit apartment building. Shortly after the transaction was closed, the Lenawee County Board of Health condemned the property and obtained a permanent injunction which prohibits human habitation on the premises until the defective sewage system is brought into conformance with the Lenawee County sanitation code.

We are required to determine whether appellees should prevail in their attempt to avoid this land contract on the basis of mutual mistake and failure of consideration. We conclude that the parties did entertain a mutual misapprehension of fact, but that the circumstances of this case do not warrant rescission.

I

The facts of the case are not seriously in dispute. In 1971, the Messerlys acquired approximately one acre plus 600 square feet of land. A three-unit apartment building was situated upon the 600-square-foot portion. The trial court found that, prior to this transfer, the Messerlys' predecessor in title, Mr. Bloom, had installed a septic tank on the property without a permit and in violation of the applicable health code. The Messerlys used the building as an income investment property until 1973 when they sold it, upon land contract, to James Barnes who likewise used it primarily as an income-producing investment.[1]

Mr. and Mrs. Barnes, with the permission of the Messerlys, sold approximately one acre of the property in 1976, and the remaining 600 square feet and building were offered for sale soon thereafter when Mr. and Mrs. Barnes defaulted on their land contract. Mr. and Mrs. Pickles evidenced an interest in the property, but were dissatisfied with the terms of the Barnes-Messerly land contract. Consequently, to accommodate the Pickleses' preference to enter into a land contract directly with the Messerlys, Mr. and Mrs. Barnes executed a quit-claim deed which conveyed their interest in the property back to the Messerlys. After inspecting the property, Mr. and Mrs. Pickles executed a new land contract with the Messerlys on March 21, 1977. It provided for a purchase price of $25,500. A clause was added to the end of the land contract form which provides:

> 17. Purchaser has examined this property and agrees to accept same in its present condition. There are no other or additional written or oral understandings.

Five or six days later, when the Pickleses went to introduce themselves to the tenants, they discovered raw sewage seeping out of the ground. Tests conducted by a sanitation expert indicated the inadequacy of the sewage system. The Lenawee County Board of Health subsequently condemned the property and initiated this lawsuit in the Lenawee Circuit Court against the Messerlys as land contract vendors, and the Pickleses, as vendees, to obtain a permanent injunction proscribing human habitation of the premises until the property was brought into conformance with the Lenawee County sanitation

---

1. James Barnes was married shortly after he purchased the property. Mr. and Mrs. Barnes lived in one of the apartments on the property for three months and, after they moved, Mrs. Barnes continued to aid in the management of the property.

code. The injunction was granted, and the Lenawee County Board of Health was permitted to withdraw from the lawsuit by stipulation of the parties.

When no payments were made on the land contract, the Messerlys filed a cross-complaint against the Pickleses seeking foreclosure, sale of the property, and a deficiency judgment. Mr. and Mrs. Pickles then counterclaimed for rescission against the Messerlys, and filed a third-party complaint against the Barneses, which incorporated, by reference, the allegations of the counterclaim against the Messerlys. In count one, Mr. and Mrs. Pickles alleged failure of consideration. Count two charged Mr. and Mrs. Barnes with willful concealment and misrepresentation as a result of their failure to disclose the condition of the sanitation system. Additionally, Mr. and Mrs. Pickles sought to hold the Messerlys liable in equity for the Barneses' alleged misrepresentation. The Pickleses prayed that the land contract be rescinded.

After a bench trial, the court concluded that the Pickleses had no cause of action against either the Messerlys or the Barneses as there was no fraud or misrepresentation. This ruling was predicated on the trial judge's conclusion that none of the parties knew of Mr. Bloom's earlier transgression or of the resultant problem with the septic system until it was discovered by the Pickleses, and that the sanitation problem was not caused by any of the parties. The trial court held that the property was purchased "as is," after inspection and, accordingly, its "negative . . . value cannot be blamed upon an innocent seller." Foreclosure was ordered against the Pickleses, together with a judgment against them in the amount of $25,943.09.

Mr. and Mrs. Pickles appealed from the adverse judgment. The Court of Appeals unanimously affirmed the trial court's ruling with respect to Mr. and Mrs. Barnes but, in a two-to-one decision, reversed the finding of no cause of action on the Pickleses' claims against the Messerlys. Lenawee County Board of Health v. Messerly, 98 Mich. App. 478, 295 N.W.2d 903 (1980). It concluded that the mutual mistake between the Messerlys and the Pickleses went to a basic, as opposed to a collateral, element of the contract,[6] and that the parties intended to transfer income-producing rental property but, in actuality, the vendees paid $25,500 for an asset without value.[7]

We granted the Messerlys' application for leave to appeal. 411 Mich. 900 (1981).

II

We must decide initially whether there was a mistaken belief entertained by one or both parties to the contract in dispute and, if so, the resultant legal significance.

6. Mr. and Mrs. Pickles did not appeal the trial court's finding that there was no fraud or misrepresentation by the Messerlys or Mr. and Mrs. Barnes. Likewise, the propriety of that ruling is not before this Court today.

7. The trial court found that the only way that the property could be put to residential use would be to pump and haul the sewage, a method which is economically unfeasible, as the cost of such a disposal system amounts to double the income generated by the property. There was speculation by the trial court that the adjoining land might be utilized to make the property suitable for residential use, but, in the absence of testimony directed at that point, the court refused to draw any conclusions. The trial court and the Court of Appeals both found that the property was valueless, or had a negative value.

A contractual mistake "is a belief that is not in accord with the facts." 1 Restatement Contracts, 2d, §151, p.383. The erroneous belief of one or both of the parties must relate to a fact in existence at the time the contract is executed. Richardson Lumber Co. v. Hoey, 219 Mich. 643, 189 N.W. 923 (1922); Sherwood v. Walker, 66 Mich. 568, 580, 33 N.W. 919 (1887) (Sherwood, J., dissenting). That is to say, the belief which is found to be in error may not be, in substance, a prediction as to a future occurrence or non-occurrence. . . .

The Court of Appeals concluded, after a de novo review of the record, that the parties were mistaken as to the income-producing capacity of the property in question. 98 Mich. App. 487-488, 295 N.W.2d 903. We agree. The vendors and the vendees each believed that the property transferred could be utilized as income-generating rental property. All of the parties subsequently learned that, in fact, the property was unsuitable for any residential use.

Appellants assert that there was no mistake in the contractual sense because the defect in the sewage system did not arise until after the contract was executed. The appellees respond that the Messerlys are confusing the date of the inception of the defect with the date upon which the defect was discovered.

This is essentially a factual dispute which the trial court failed to resolve directly. Nevertheless, we are empowered to draw factual inferences from the facts found by the trial court. GCR 1963, 865.1(6).

An examination of the record reveals that the septic system was defective prior to the date on which the land contract was executed. The Messerlys' grantor installed a nonconforming septic system without a permit prior to the transfer of the property to the Messerlys in 1971. Moreover, virtually undisputed testimony indicates that, assuming ideal soil conditions, 2,500 square feet of property is necessary to support a sewage system adequate to serve a three-family dwelling. Likewise, 750 square feet is mandated for a one-family home. Thus, the division of the parcel and sale of one acre of the property by Mr. and Mrs. Barnes in 1976 made it impossible to remedy the already illegal septic system within the confines of the 600-square-foot parcel.[10]

Appellants do not dispute these underlying facts which give rise to an inference contrary to their contentions.

Having determined that when these parties entered into the land contract they were laboring under a mutual mistake of fact, we now direct our attention to a determination of the legal significance of that finding.

A contract may be rescinded because of a mutual misapprehension of the parties, but this remedy is granted only in the sound discretion of the court. Harris v. Axline, 323 Mich. 585, 36 N.W.2d 154 (1949). Appellants argue that the parties' mistake relates only to the quality or value of the real estate transferred, and that such mistakes are collateral to the agreement and do not

10. It is crucial to distinguish between the date on which a belief relating to a particular fact or set of facts becomes erroneous due to a change in the fact, and the date on which the mistaken nature of the belief is discovered. By definition, a mistake cannot be discovered until after the contract is executed. If the parties were aware, prior to the execution of a contract, that they were in error concerning a particular fact, there would be no misapprehension in signing the contract. Thus stated, it becomes obvious that the date on which a mistaken fact manifests itself is irrelevant to the determination whether or not there was a mistake.

justify rescission, citing A & M Land Development Co. v. Miller, 354 Mich. 681, 94 N.W.2d 197 (1959).

In that case, the plaintiff was the purchaser of 91 lots of real property. It sought partial rescission of the land contract when it was frustrated in its attempts to develop 42 of the lots because it could not obtain permits from the county health department to install septic tanks on these lots. This Court refused to allow rescission because the mistake, whether mutual or unilateral, related only to the value of the property.

> There was here no mistake as to the form or substance of the contract between the parties, or the description of the property constituting the subject matter. The situation involved is not at all analogous to that presented in Scott v. Grow, 301 Mich. 226; 3 N.W.2d 254; 141 A.L.R. 819 (1942). There the plaintiff sought relief by way of reformation of a deed on the ground that the instrument of conveyance had not been drawn in accordance with the intention and agreement of the parties. It was held that the bill of complaint stated a case for the granting of equitable relief by way of reformation. In the case at bar plaintiff received the property for which it contracted. The fact that it may be of less value than the purchaser expected at the time of the transaction is not a sufficient basis for the granting of equitable relief, neither fraud nor reliance on misrepresentation of material facts having been established.

354 Mich. 693-694, 94 N.W.2d 197.

Appellees contend, on the other hand, that in this case the parties were mistaken as to the very nature of the character of the consideration and claim that the pervasive and essential quality of this mistake renders rescission appropriate. They cite in support of that view Sherwood v. Walker, 66 Mich. 568, 33 N.W. 919 (1887), the famous "barren cow" case. In that case, the parties agreed to the sale and purchase of a cow which was thought to be barren, but which was, in reality, with calf. When the seller discovered the fertile condition of his cow, he refused to deliver her. In permitting rescission, the Court stated:

> It seems to me, however, in the case made by this record, that the mistake or misapprehension of the parties went to the whole substance of the agreement. If the cow was a breeder, she was worth at least $750; if barren, she was worth not over $80. The parties would not have made the contract of sale except upon the understanding and belief that she was incapable of breeding, and of no use as a cow. It is true she is now the identical animal that they thought her to be when the contract was made; there is no mistake as to the identity of the creature. Yet the mistake was not of the mere quality of the animal, but went to the very nature of the thing. A barren cow is substantially a different creature than a breeding one. There is as much difference between them for all purposes of use as there is between an ox and a cow that is capable of breeding and giving milk. If the mutual mistake had simply related to the fact whether she was with calf or not for one season, then it might have been a good sale; but the mistake affected the character of the animal for all time, and for her present and ultimate use. She was not in fact the animal, or the kind of animal, the defendants intended to sell or the plaintiff to buy. She was not a barren cow, and, if this fact had been known, there would have been no contract. The mistake affected the substance of the whole consideration, and it must be considered that there was no contract to sell or sale of the cow as she actually was. The thing sold and bought had

in fact no existence. She was sold as a beef-creature would be sold; she is in fact a breeding cow, and a valuable one.

The court should have instructed the jury that if they found that the cow was sold, or contracted to be sold, upon the understanding of both parties that she was barren, and useless for the purpose of breeding, and that in fact she was not barren, but capable of breeding, then the defendants had a right to rescind, and to refuse to deliver, and the verdict should be in their favor.

66 Mich. 577-578, 33 N.W. 919.

As the parties suggest, the foregoing precedent arguably distinguishes mistakes affecting the essence of the consideration from those which go to its quality or value, affording relief on a per se basis for the former but not the latter. See, e.g., Lenawee County Board of Health v. Messerly, 98 Mich. App. 478, 492, 295 N.W.2d 903 (1980) (Mackenzie, J., concurring in part).

However, the distinctions which may be drawn from *Sherwood* and *A & M Land Development Co.* do not provide a satisfactory analysis of the nature of a mistake sufficient to invalidate a contract. Often, a mistake relates to an underlying factual assumption which, when discovered, directly affects value, but simultaneously and materially affects the essence of the contractual consideration. It is disingenuous to label such a mistake collateral. McKay v. Coleman, 85 Mich. 60, 48 N.W. 203 (1891). Corbin, Contracts (one vol. ed.), §605, p.551.

Appellant and appellee both mistakenly believed that the property which was the subject of their land contract would generate income as rental property. The fact that it could not be used for human habitation deprived the property of its income-earning potential and rendered it less valuable. However, this mistake, while directly and dramatically affecting the property's value, cannot accurately be characterized as collateral because it also affects the very essence of the consideration. "The thing sold and bought [income generating rental property] had in fact no existence." Sherwood v. Walker, 66 Mich. 578, 33 N.W. 919.

We find that the inexact and confusing distinction between contractual mistakes running to value and those touching the substance of the consideration serves only as an impediment to a clear and helpful analysis for the equitable resolution of cases in which mistake is alleged and proven. Accordingly, the holdings of *A & M Land Development Co.* and *Sherwood* with respect to the material or collateral nature of a mistake are limited to the facts of those cases.

Instead, we think the better-reasoned approach is a case-by-case analysis whereby rescission is indicated when the mistaken belief relates to a basic assumption of the parties upon which the contract is made, and which materially affects the agreed performances of the parties. . . . 1 Restatement Contracts, 2d, §152, pp.385-386.[11] Rescission is not available, however, to relieve a party who has assumed the risk of loss in connection with the

11. The parties have invited our attention to the first edition of the Restatement of Contracts in their briefs, and the Court of Appeals cites to that edition in its opinion. However, the second edition was published subsequent to the issuance of the lower court opinion and the filing of the briefs with this Court. Thus, we take it upon ourselves to refer to the latest edition to aid us in our resolution of this case.

Section 152 delineates the legal significance of a mistake.

mistake. . . . Corbin, Contracts (one vol. ed.), §605, p.552; 1 Restatement Contracts, 2d, §§152, 154, pp.385-386, 402-406.[12]

All of the parties to this contract erroneously assumed that the property transferred by the vendors to the vendees was suitable for human habitation and could be utilized to generate rental income. The fundamental nature of these assumptions is indicated by the fact that their invalidity changed the character of the property transferred, thereby frustrating, indeed precluding, Mr. and Mrs. Pickles' intended use of the real estate. Although the Pickleses are disadvantaged by enforcement of the contract, performance is advantageous to the Messerlys, as the property at issue is less valuable absent its income-earning potential. Nothing short of rescission can remedy the mistake. Thus, the parties' mistake as to a basic assumption materially affects the agreed performances of the parties.

Despite the significance of the mistake made by the parties, we reverse the Court of Appeals because we conclude that equity does not justify the remedy sought by Mr. and Mrs. Pickles.

Rescission is an equitable remedy which is granted only in the sound discretion of the court. . . . A court need not grant rescission in every case in which the mutual mistake relates to a basic assumption and materially affects the agreed performance of the parties.

In cases of mistake by two equally innocent parties, we are required, in the exercise of our equitable powers, to determine which blameless party should assume the loss resulting from the misapprehension they shared.[13] Normally that can only be done by drawing upon our "own notions of what is reasonable and just under all the surrounding circumstances."

Equity suggests that, in this case, the risk should be allocated to the purchasers. We are guided to that conclusion, in part, by the standards announced in §154 of the Restatement of Contracts 2d, for determining when a

---

§152. When Mistake of Both Parties Makes a Contract Voidable

(1) Where a mistake of both parties at the time a contract was made as to a basic assumption on which the contract was made has a material effect on the agreed exchange of performances, the contract is voidable by the adversely affected party unless he bears the risk of the mistake under the rule stated in §154.

(2) In determining whether the mistake has a material effect on the agreed exchange of performances, account is taken of any relief by way of reformation, restitution, or otherwise.

12. ### §154. When a Party Bears the Risk of a Mistake

A party bears the risk of a mistake when
(a) the risk is allocated to him by agreement of the parties, or
(b) he is aware, at the time the contract is made, that he has only limited knowledge with respect to the facts to which the mistake relates but treats his limited knowledge as sufficient, or
(c) the risk is allocated to him by the court on the ground that it is reasonable in the circumstances to do so.

13. This risk-of-loss analysis is absent in both *A & M Land Development Co.* and *Sherwood,* and this omission helps to explain, in part, the disparate treatment in the two cases. Had such an inquiry been undertaken in *Sherwood,* we believe that the result might have been different. Moreover, a determination as to which party assumed the risk in *A & M Land Development Co.* would have alleviated the need to characterize the mistake as collateral so as to justify the result denying rescission. Despite the absence of any inquiry as to the assumption of risk in those two leading cases, we find that there exists sufficient precedent to warrant such an analysis in future cases of mistake.

party bears the risk of mistake. See footnote 12. Section 154(a) suggests that the court should look first to whether the parties have agreed to the allocation of the risk between themselves. While there is no express assumption in the contract by either party of the risk of the property becoming uninhabitable, there was indeed some agreed allocation of the risk to the vendees by the incorporation of an "as is" clause into the contract which, we repeat, provided:

> Purchaser has examined this property and agrees to accept same in its present condition. There are no other or additional written or oral understandings.

That is a persuasive indication that the parties considered that, as between them, such risk as related to the "present condition" of the property should lie with the purchaser. If the "as is" clause is to have any meaning at all, it must be interpreted to refer to those defects which were unknown at the time that the contract was executed. Thus, the parties themselves assigned the risk of loss to Mr. and Mrs. Pickles.

We conclude that Mr. and Mrs. Pickles are not entitled to the equitable remedy of rescission and, accordingly, reverse the decision the Court of Appeals.

WILLIAMS, C.J., and COLEMAN, FITZGERALD, KAVANAGH and LEVIN, JJ., concur.

RILEY, J., not participating.

Notes and Questions

1. *Factual Context.* Additional facts in the *Lenawee* case can be found in the intermediate appellate court opinion. Testimony at trial established that when the Messerlys initially purchased the property in June 1971, Bloom, the previous owner, made an affirmative statement that there had never been a problem with the sanitation system. Bloom failed to disclose, however, that he had replaced the prior septic tank with a relatively small 500-gallon septic tank and had failed to obtain a required permit from the county agency. Lenawee County Board of Health v. Messerly, 295 N.W.2d 903, 904 (Mich. Ct. App. 1980). County health officials testified that the five-bedroom property did not have the minimum of 2000 square feet for a drain field that would be needed for a normal septic system and that two septic tanks of at least 1000 gallons would be needed for a costly "pump and haul" system. 295 N.W.2d at 907. The Messerlys never lived at the property, rarely visited there, had the septic tank cleaned once without incident, and never received any complaints or noticed any problems. Prior to executing the land contract, Mr. Pickles did ask the Barneses about the septic tank. Mr. and Mrs. Barnes responded that they had lived in an apartment for three months in early 1974, had visited the property only occasionally after that, had the septic tank cleaned once without notice of irregularity other than some odor in one bathroom, and received no complaints from tenants. 295 N.W.2d at 905, n. 3. Do these additional facts alter your impression of the case?

2. *Lack of consistency in mutual mistake cases.* In Gartner v. Eikill, 319 N.W.2d 397 (Minn. 1982), a purchaser of land sought rescission on the ground of

mutual mistake, claiming that unknown to him the land had in the past been subjected to a special zoning restriction making it unuseable for the purpose for which he had purchased it. The contract of purchase stated that the seller would convey marketable title subject to, inter alia, "Building and zoning laws, ordinances, State and Federal regulations. . . . " Neither party at the time of the sale was aware of the restriction. Relying on prior Minnesota cases as well as *Sherwood v. Walker* (discussed in the principal case), the court in *Gartner* allowed rescission on the basis of "*mutual mistake of fact.*" *Gartner* and *Lenawee* obviously reach opposing outcomes; are they necessarily inconsistent decisions? Can they be harmonized so that both cases may be regarded as rightly decided? Or was one of them wrongly decided? Is it possible that *both* were wrongly decided? Additional examples of cases with similar facts reaching apparently contrary results in this area can be found: Compare Nichols v. City of Evansdale, 687 N.W.2d 562 (Iowa 2004) (rescission would be available to both parties where neither knew that sewer lines ran beneath transferred property and the error had a material effect on the agreed exchange), with Maloney v. Sargisson, 465 N.E.2d 296 (Mass. App. Ct. 1984) (rescission denied where purchasers discovered that concrete drain line ran under street fronting their land, precluding building because it made installation of septic tank impossible). See also Harris v. Rudin, Richman & Appel, 116 Cal. Rptr. 2d 552 (Ct. App. 2002) (claimant asserted sufficient basis for rescission due to mutual mistake in allegation that parties executed settlement agreement without knowledge that applicable law had changed 13 days prior).

3. *Limiting earlier court decisions.* In analyzing the character of the "mistake" made by the buyers in *Lenawee*, the Michigan Supreme Court discusses and quotes at length from two earlier Michigan decisions, A & M Land Development Co. v. Miller and the "famous 'barren cow' case," Sherwood v. Walker. The *Lenawee* court does not expressly overrule either *Sherwood* or *A & M Land Development Co.*, but it limits the holding of each to its facts, effectively destroying their value as precedent, at least in Michigan. Why did the court so hold? Is the mode of analysis applied by the court in *Lenawee* preferable to that employed in those cases?

4. *Effect of "as is" clause.* Like the Michigan Supreme Court in *Lenawee*, a number of other courts have denied relief on mutual mistake and other grounds when the contract contained an "as is" or similar clause. See Man Roland, Inc. v. Quantum Color Corp., 57 F. Supp.2d 576 (N.D. Ill. 1999) (holding "as is" clause would shift all risks to buyer and preclude mutual or unilateral mistake in sale of equipment); Miller v. Varilek, 342 N.W.2d 94 (Mich. Ct. App. 1983) (purchasers who bought property with inoperable sewage system denied rescission on basis of clause stating that buyer had "personally examined" and accepted the property "in its present condi- tion"). There are other decisions, however, which deny such conclusive effect to "as is" provisions. See Shore Builders, Inc. v. Dogwood, Inc., 616 F. Supp. 1004 (D. Del. 1985) (since mutual mistake arises in situations beyond contemplation of contracting parties, all-purpose boilerplate "as is" clauses should be regarded as ineffective because parties lack adequate notice of what is being bargained for); Lesher v. Strid, 996 P.2d 988 (Or. Ct. App. 2000) (claim of mutual mistake not barred by "as is" clause where seller's

representation of water rights was incorporated into contract for sale of land).

5. *Conscious ignorance.* Another form of assumption of risk is based on a party's conscious ignorance of all relevant facts before entering an agreement, as suggested by the Restatement (Second) of Contracts §154(b) quoted in *Lenawee.* An example is Estate of Nelson v. Rice, 12 P.3d 238 (Ariz. Ct. App. 2000), in which the representatives of an estate sold two paintings for $60 without having them appraised by an appropriate expert and the paintings later proved to be worth more than $1 million. Relying on §154(b), the court rejected the estate's claim of mutual mistake because the representatives were aware of the possibility that the estate might include fine art but failed to employ a qualified expert before making the sale. See also CPL, L.L.C. v. Conley, 40 P.3d 679 (Wash. Ct. App. 2002) (relying on §154(b) in rejecting claim of mutual mistake by buyer of skilled nursing facility that had notice of deficiencies in financial information about transaction but still proceeded to make related payment agreement).

6. *Mistake in written expression.* When the mutual mistake consists of the failure of the written contract to state accurately the actual agreement of the parties, reformation of the contract to express the parties' mutual intent is the normal remedy. E.g., United Bank v. Ashland Development Corp., 792 P.2d 775 (Ariz. Ct. App. 1990) (property line descriptions in deeds reformed for mutual mistake); Omaha Door Co. v. Mexican Food Manufacturers of Omaha, Inc., 439 N.W.2d 776 (Neb. 1989) (repayment schedule in lease reformed because evidence was clear and convincing that landlord's accountant made "scrivener's error"). See also Berezin v. Regency Savings Bank, 234 F.3d 68 (1st Cir. 2000) (parol evidence rule would not bar evidence that promissory note failed to state correct interest rate and resulted in overpayment of nearly $1 million, but evidence of mistake must be clear and convincing).

7. *Equitable relief.* The relief available for mutual mistake other than a mistake in the writing is ordinarily rescission, along with any restitution that may appear appropriate. E.g., Renner v. Kehl, 722 P.2d 262 (Ariz. 1986) (mutual mistake justified rescission; rescinding buyer entitled to return of down payment and credit for increased value of land due to improvements made, but seller entitled to payment for rental value of land during period of buyer's ownership). As relief for mutual mistake is an equitable remedy, traditionally an area of greater judicial discretion, courts occasionally exercise creative ingenuity in fashioning a remedy to fit the nature of the mistake. For example, in Donohue v. Picinich, 852 F. Supp. 144 (D. Conn. 1994), both parties to a land purchase contract were mistaken about something—the buyers thought they were getting a tract of land including a pond, although the pond was really on an adjoining lot not intended by the seller to be included in their purchase; on the other hand, the seller's attorney had mistakenly drafted the contract to include all of that additional lot, and both parties had signed it. The court reformed the contract so as to give the purchasers the pond on the adjoining tract, but leaving the rest of that tract as the property of the seller. But see Rancourt v. Verba, 678 A.2d 886 (Vt. 1996) (where lot turned out not to be buildable for residential purposes, error for lower court to remedy mutual mistake with abatement of purchase price; purchasers should have been granted the rescission they sought).

8. *Personal injury settlement cases.* Claims of mutual mistake are also frequently made by litigants seeking to overturn releases or settlement agreements. A common fact pattern involves settlement of a personal injury claim that the plaintiff later regrets because the injuries turn out to be worse than they were thought to be at the time of the settlement. Such cases involve tension between the social policies of finality of litigation and fair compensation for injury. Not surprisingly, courts differ in the degree to which they will allow such releases to be set aside. Compare Kendrick v. Barker, 15 P.3d 734 (Wyo. 2001) (rescission based on mutual mistake not available to injured party who settled claim with knowledge that extent of closed head injury was uncertain and with assistance of counsel), with Gibli v. Kadosh, 717 N.Y.S.2d 553 (App. Div. 2000) (to "avoid grave injustice," relief for mutual mistake would be available if plaintiff could demonstrate that injury was of different nature than both parties believed it to be at the time of release).

Wil-Fred's, Inc. v. Metropolitan Sanitary District
Illinois Appellate Court
57 Ill. App. 3d 16, 372 N.E.2d 946 (1978)

PERLIN, Justice.

In response to an advertisement published by the Metropolitan Sanitary District of Greater Chicago (hereinafter Sanitary District) inviting bids for rehabilitation work at one of its water reclamation plants, Wil-Fred's Inc. submitted a sealed bid and, as a security deposit to insure its performance, a $100,000 certified check. After the bids were opened, Wil-Fred's, the low bidder, attempted to withdraw. The Sanitary District rejected the request and stated that the contract would be awarded to Wil-Fred's in due course. Prior to this award, Wil-Fred's filed a complaint for preliminary injunction and rescission. After hearing testimony and the arguments of counsel, the trial court granted rescission and ordered the Sanitary District to return the $100,000 bid deposit to Wil-Fred's. The Sanitary District seeks to reverse this judgment order.

The Sanitary District's advertisement was published on November 26, 1975, and it announced that bids on contract 75-113-2D for the rehabilitation of sand drying beds at the District's West-Southwest plant in Stickney, Illinois, would be accepted up to January 6, 1976. This announcement specified that the work to be performed required the contractor to remove 67,500 linear feet of clay pipe and 53,200 cubic yards of gravel from the beds and to replace these items with plastic pipe and fresh filter material. Although plastic pipes were called for, the specifications declared that "all pipes . . . must be able . . . to withstand standard construction equipment."

The advertisement further stated that "[t]he cost estimate of the work under Contract 75-113-2D, as determined by the Engineering Department of the . . . Sanitary District . . . is $1,257,000.00."

A proposal form furnished to Wil-Fred's provided:

The undersigned hereby certifies that he has examined the contract documents . . . and has examined the site of the work. . . .

The undersigned has also examined the Advertisement, the "bidding requirements," has made the examinations and investigation therein required. . . .

The undersigned hereby accepts the invitation of the Sanitary District to submit a proposal on said work *with the understanding that this proposal will not be cancelled or withdrawn.*

It is understood that in the event the undersigned is awarded a contract for the work herein mentioned, and shall fail or refuse to execute the same and furnish the specified bond within thirteen (13) days after receiving notice of the award of said contract, then the sum of One Hundred Thousand Dollars ($100,000.00), deposited herewith, shall be retained by the Sanitary District as liquidated damages and not as a penalty, it being understood that said sum is the fair measure of the amount of damages that said Sanitary District will sustain in such event.

[Emphasis added.]

On December 22, 1975, the Sanitary District issued an addendum that changed the type of sand filter material which was to be supplied by the contractor. During the bidding period the District's engineering department discovered that the material originally specified in the advertisement was available only out of state and consequently was extremely expensive. This addendum changed the filter material to a less expensive type that could be obtained locally.

On January 6, 1976, Wil-Fred's submitted the low bid of $882,600 which was accompanied by the $100,000 bid deposit and the aforementioned proposal form signed on behalf of the company by Wil-Fred's vice president. Eight other companies submitted bids on January 6. The next lowest bid was $1,118,375, and it was made by Greco Contractors, Inc.

On January 8, 1976, Wil-Fred's sent the Sanitary District a telegram which stated that it was withdrawing its bid and requested return of its bid deposit. This telegram was confirmed by a subsequent letter mailed the same day.

On January 12, 1976, Wil-Fred's, at the request of the Sanitary District, sent a letter setting forth the circumstances that caused the company to withdraw its bid. The letter stated that upon learning the amount by which it was the low bidder, Wil-Fred's asked its excavating subcontractor, Ciaglo Excavating Company, to review its figures; that excavation was the only subcontracted trade in Wil-Fred's bid; that the following day Ciaglo informed Wil-Fred's that there had been a substantial error in its bid, and therefore it would have to withdraw its quotation since performing the work at the stated price would force the subcontractor into bankruptcy; that Wil-Fred's then checked with other excavation contractors and confirmed that Ciaglo's bid was in error; that Wil-Fred's had used Ciaglo as an excavating subcontractor on many other projects in the past, and Ciaglo had always honored its previous quotations; that Ciaglo had always performed its work in a skillful fashion; that because of these facts Wil-Fred's acted reasonably in utilizing Ciaglo's quoted price in formulating its own bid; and that with the withdrawal of Ciaglo's quotation Wil-Fred's could not perform the work for $882,600.

On February 2, 1976, Wil-Fred's received a letter from Thomas W. Moore, the Sanitary District's purchasing agent. Moore's letter stated that in his opinion the reasons cited in Wil-Fred's letter of January 12 did not justify withdrawal of the bid. For this reason Moore said that he would recommend to the Sanitary District's general superintendent that the contract be awarded to Wil-Fred's at the original bid price.

At a February 20 meeting between representatives of the Sanitary District and Wil-Fred's, the company was informed that the District's board of trustees had rejected its withdrawal request, and that it would be awarded the contract. In response to this information, Wil-Fred's filed its complaint for preliminary injunction and rescission on February 26, 1976. The complaint alleged that the company would be irreparably injured if required to perform the contract at such an unconscionably low price or if forced to forfeit the $100,000 bid deposit. The hearing on this complaint commenced on March 10, 1976.

At the hearing William Luxion, president of Wil-Fred's, testified that the company had been in business for 18 years; that Wil-Fred's did 13 to 14 million dollars worth of business in 1975; that 95% of the company's work was done on a competitive bid basis; that Wil-Fred's never had withdrawn a competitive bid in the past; and that he personally examined the company's bid prior to its submission. Luxion further stated that he told Wil-Fred's chief estimator to review the company's quotation immediately after he was notified on January 6 that Wil-Fred's bid was more than $235,000 below the next lowest bid. At this time he also requested that Ciaglo Company review its figures.

The reexamination by the chief estimator revealed that there was no material error in the portion of the bid covering work to be done by Wil-Fred's. However, the president of Ciaglo contacted Luxion on January 8 and stated that his bid was too low on account of an error and that, because of this, he was withdrawing his quotation. Upon receiving this information, Luxion sent the Sanitary District the telegram and letter in which he informed the District of this error, withdrew Wil-Fred's bid and requested a return of the company's bid deposit.

Lastly, Luxion testified that a loss of the $100,000 security deposit would result in the company's loss of bonding capacity in the amount of two to three million dollars; that Wil-Fred's decided not to attempt to force Ciaglo to honor its subcontract because the company felt that Ciaglo was not financially capable of sustaining a $150,000 loss; and that he was aware of the Sanitary District's cost estimate before Wil-Fred's submitted its bid. However, Luxion stated that he took the addendum changing the filter material into account when calculating the price of the bid and concluded that this alteration would result in a cost savings of over $200,000.

Dennis Ciaglo, president of Ciaglo Excavating, Inc., also testified on behalf of Wil-Fred's and stated that prior to January 6, 1976, his company submitted a quote of $205,000 for the removal of the existing material in the sand beds, for digging trenches for the new pipe and for spreading the new filter materials. Ciaglo further stated that a representative of Wil-Fred's called him on January 6 and asked him to review his price quotation. During his examination the witness discovered that he underestimated his projected costs by $150,000. Ciaglo said that this error was caused by his assumption that heavy equipment could be driven into the beds to spread the granular fill. Although he was aware that plastic pipes were to be used in the beds, Ciaglo still presumed that heavy equipment could be employed because the specifications called for the utilization of standard construction equipment. Ciaglo first learned that the plastic pipes would not support heavy equipment when, as part of his review of the price quote, he contacted the pipe manufacturer.

Ciaglo testified additionally that his company probably would have to file for bankruptcy if forced to take a $150,000 loss; that Ciaglo Excavating Co. had never before withdrawn a price quotation given to Wil-Fred's or any other company; and that in his opinion the change in the filter material called for by the second addendum would cause a $300,000 reduction in "the cost of the material for the bids. . . . "

Only one witness testified for the Sanitary District. Leslie Dombai, a registered structural engineer for the District, stated that the Sanitary District's cost estimate was based directly upon the expense of the material specified in the advertisement, and he confirmed that the filter material was changed because the type initially called for was expensive and was not available locally. However, Dombai claimed that this substitution increased the District's original cost estimate by $40,000.

By bidding on the Sanitary District's rehabilitation project, Wil-Fred's made a binding commitment. Its bid was in the nature of an option to the District based upon valuable consideration: the assurance that the award would be made to the lowest bidder. The option was both an offer to do the work and a unilateral agreement to enter into a contract to do so. When the offer was accepted, a bilateral contract arose which was mutually binding on Wil-Fred's and the Sanitary District. . . . When Wil-Fred's attempted to withdraw its bid, it became subject to the condition incorporated in the proposal form furnished by the Sanitary District. Under this condition, the company's bid deposit was forfeited when it refused to execute the contract within the specified time period.

The principal issue, therefore, is whether Wil-Fred's can obtain rescission of its contract with the Sanitary District because of its unilateral mistake. Wil-Fred's argues that the mistake was material to the contract; that this error was directly caused by the Sanitary District's misleading specifications; that the Sanitary District did not alter its position in reliance upon the erroneous bid because the company promptly notified the District of the mistake; and that under these circumstances it would be unconscionable to enforce the contract or to allow the Sanitary District to retain the security deposit.

As a general rule, it is often said that relief will not be granted if but one party to a contract has made a mistake. . . . (Restatement of the Law of Contracts §503 (1932).) However, Professor Williston in his treatise on contracts indicates that unilateral mistake may afford ground for rescission where there is a material mistake and such mistake is so palpable that the party not in error will be put on notice of its existence. 13 Williston on Contracts §1578 (3d ed. Jaeger 1970).

In Illinois the conditions generally required for rescission are: that the mistake relate to a material feature of the contract; that it occurred notwithstanding the exercise of reasonable care; that it is of such grave consequence that enforcement of the contract would be unconscionable; and that the other party can be placed in statu quo. . . . Evidence of these conditions must be clear and positive. . . .

If Ciaglo's misestimation was established by competent evidence, it is apparent that the error was material. This determination is based on the fact that the $150,000 mistake represents approximately 17% of Wil-Fred's bid. . . .

However, the Sanitary District contends that Wil-Fred's failed to support its claim of materiality with clear and positive evidence. The District points out that neither of the plaintiff's two witnesses described the proper method for spreading the new filter material on the plastic pipes, and it argues that because of this omission Wil-Fred's failed to introduce sufficient evidence to substantiate Dennis Ciaglo's conclusion that the correct procedure would have cost $150,000 more than the system he had planned to use.

We do not find this argument persuasive. It is manifest from the trial court's judgment order that the trier of fact decided that Ciaglo's mistake related to a material feature of the rehabilitation contract and that this condition was supported by clear and positive evidence. After carefully examining the record, we are in agreement with this finding.

Dennis Ciaglo testified that he gave Wil-Fred's a price quotation of $205,000 for his work allotment, and he indicated that the amount of this bid was based directly upon his incorrect assumption that heavy trucks could be driven into the sand drying beds and onto the plastic pipes. This testimony is corroborated by the subcontractor's price estimate sheet which was introduced into evidence by the Sanitary District.

It is true, nevertheless, that plaintiff's witnesses failed to describe the correct spreading method, and that Ciaglo made only a conclusionary statement to the effect that employment of the proper procedure would have increased his original quotation by $150,000. However, the District did not cross-examine the subcontractor concerning this matter, and it failed to produce any evidence, testimonial or otherwise, that contravened his statement. Consequently, Ciaglo's conclusion stands uncontradicted.

Furthermore, it is our opinion that the accuracy of the estimated error is supported by the fact that Ciaglo had eight years experience in the excavating business and by the fact that he confirmed this figure by checking with other contractors who had submitted bids on the same portion of the project. Under these particular circumstances we feel that Wil-Fred's produced sufficient evidence to sustain its claim of a $150,000 error.

In addition to satisfying the first condition for rescission, Wil-Fred's has decidedly fulfilled two of the three remaining requirements. The consequences of Ciaglo's error were grave. Since the subcontractor was not capable of sustaining a $150,000 loss, Wil-Fred's stood to lose the same amount if it performed the contract for $882,600. Wil-Fred's will forfeit $100,000 if the contract is enforced. A loss of $100,000 will decrease the plaintiff's bonding capacity by two to three million dollars. It is evident, therefore, that either deprivation will constitute substantial hardship. The Sanitary District was not damaged seriously by the withdrawal of the bid. When the subcontractor's mistake was discovered 48 hours after the bid opening, Wil-Fred's promptly notified the District by telegram and declared its intention to withdraw.

The rehabilitation contract had not been awarded at this time. Accordingly, the District suffered no change in position since it was able, with no great loss other than the windfall resulting from Ciaglo's error, to award the contract to the next lowest bidder, Department of Public Works.

The central question, therefore, is whether the error occurred despite the use of reasonable care. The Sanitary District asserts that the mistake itself evidences Wil-Fred's failure to use ordinary care in the preparation of its bid and argues that rescission is not warranted under such circumstances.

We cannot agree with this contention. Wil-Fred's unquestionably exercised due care when it selected Ciaglo Excavating Company as its subcontractor. Ciaglo Excavating Company had been in business for five years; its president had eight years experience in the excavating field; the company had worked for Wil-Fred's on 12 previous occasions; it had never failed to honor a prior quotation; and it had always performed its assignments in a highly skilled manner. Also, Dennis Ciaglo testified that prior to submitting his bid to Wil-Fred's, he inspected the jobsite and carefully examined the specifications with plaintiff's estimators. Taking into account the experience and preparations of the subcontractor, the prior business dealings between the two companies and the high quality of Ciaglo Excavating Company's past performance, we conclude that Wil-Fred's was justified in relying on the subcontractor's quotation in formulating its own bid.

Similarly, we feel that Wil-Fred's exercised reasonable care in the preparation of its portion of the total bid. The plaintiff made two separate reviews of its price quotation. The first was conducted prior to the bid's submission, and it took into account the addendum that substituted a cheaper filter material for the type originally called for by the specifications.[3] The second examination was made immediately after Wil-Fred's president learned that his company's bid was the lowest quotation. It revealed that plaintiff had not erred in estimating expenses for its part of the rehabilitation project.

The question of due care is a factual question to be determined by the trial court, and such determination will not be disturbed unless it is against the manifest weight of the evidence. . . . For the aforementioned reasons we feel that the record supports the trial court's finding of due care on the part of Wil-Fred's.

The Sanitary District asserts that even if due care was exercised by Wil-Fred's, Illinois courts have granted relief only in cases where the bid has contained a clerical or mathematical error. Defendant argues that the trial court's grant of rescission should not be upheld because Ciaglo's mistake was not a factual error but an error in business judgment.

---

3. We believe that the change in filter material explains why the Sanitary District's cost estimate was $374,000 higher than Wil-Fred's quotation. Plaintiff's witnesses testified that the substitution of cheaper material would result in a cost savings of $200,000 to $300,000. Additionally, the Sanitary District's engineer stated that the District's estimate was based directly upon the cost of the material specified in the advertisement, and he admitted that the initial type of filter material was very expensive because it was not available locally. In view of this testimony we must conclude that the large discrepancy would not necessarily have alerted Wil-Fred's president to the fact that there was a substantial error in his company's bid.

Regarding the District's argument, it is the opinion of this court that Ciaglo's error amounts to a mixed mistake of judgment and fact. Ciaglo's belief that the plastic pipes would support heavy trucks was judgmental in nature and in this narrow sense his mistake was one of business judgment. However, his belief was predicated on a misunderstanding of the actual facts occasioned, at least in part, by his reliance on the Sanitary District's misleading specifications which stated that all pipes had to be able to withstand standard construction equipment.

Generally, relief is refused for errors in judgment and allowed for clerical or mathematical mistakes. . . . Nonetheless, we believe, in fairness to the individual bidder, that the facts surrounding the error, not the label, i.e., "mistake of fact" or "mistake of judgment," should determine whether relief is granted. White v. Berrenda Mesa Water District of Kern County (1970), 7 Cal. App. 3d 894, 907, 87 Cal. Rptr. 338, 347-348.

The testimonial evidence reveals that Wil-Fred's acted in good faith and that Ciaglo's error occurred notwithstanding the exercise of reasonable care. Furthermore, it was established that Wil-Fred's quotation was $235,775 lower than the next lowest bid. It is apparent that such a sizable discrepancy should have placed the Sanitary District on notice that plaintiff's bid contained a material error. . . . Accordingly equity will not allow the District to take advantage of Wil-Fred's low offer.

We are aware of the importance of maintaining the competitive bidding system which is used in the letting of municipal construction contracts. Consequently we do not mean to imply by affirming the trial court's order that a bidder who has submitted the lowest quotation on a municipal contract may cavalierly disregard the contract's irrevocability clause and seek rescission. Allowing such action would be unfair to the other bidders and would result in the destruction of the system's integrity. However, we are certain that the courts of this state are capable of preventing such a result by refusing to grant rescission where, unlike the present circumstances, the facts do not justify relieving the lowest bidder from his bid. See Calnan Co. v. Talsma Builders, Inc. (1977), 67 Ill. 2d 213, 10 Ill. Dec. 242, 367 N.E.2d 695, in which our supreme court, although not dealing with a municipal construction contract, recently denied rescission of a plumbing subcontract where the subcontractor failed to include the cost of the entire water supply system in its bid, a concededly material feature of the subcontract. The supreme court held that the subcontractor had not exercised reasonable care by failing to utilize its own bid preparation review system and by not discovering its error until four months after acceptance of its bid. The court also found that the general contractor could not be placed in statu quo since work had begun and the general contractor had no options; it either had to account for the error ($31,000) or had to negotiate another subcontract, at a greater cost with lack of continuity in work.

We note but do not consider the Sanitary District's other arguments which we find to be without merit.

For the above stated reasons, the trial court's order granting rescission and the return of Wil-Fred's security deposit is affirmed.

Affirmed.

STAMOS, P.J., and PUSATERI, J., concur.

Notes and Questions

1. *"Palpable" nature or unconscionable effect of mistake.* Early cases granting relief on grounds of unilateral mistake required that the mistake be "palpable"—so obvious that the other party in the circumstances either knew or should have known that a mistake had been made. In such cases, the mistake is truly "unilateral" (i.e., the other party knows or has reason to know the true facts, or at least to know that there is a mistake). E.g., Belk v. Martin, 39 P.3d 592 (Idaho 2001) (lease agreement reformed on grounds of unilateral mistake where lessee knew that written lease amount should have been $14,768 instead of $1476.80). Sometimes it is said that one party may not "snap up" an offer that is "too good to be true." (Recall that if one party is in fact aware of the other's material mistake, this would be a factor militating in favor of a duty of disclosure. Restatement (Second) §161.) Later cases have relaxed any requirement that the mistake be palpable, however. Restatement (Second) §153, which permits avoidance of a contract for "mistake of one party," requires either (a) that the mistake be such that enforcement of the contract would be unconscionable, or (b) that the other party either have reason to know of, or be responsible for causing, the mistake. Although as we have seen, "unconscionability" in the context of Restatement (Second) §208 or UCC §2-302 is a complex and somewhat amorphous concept, "unconscionable" in the context of §153 seems to mean merely severe enough to cause substantial loss. See the *Wil-Fred's* case ("substantial hardship"). See also Marana Unified Sch. Dist. v. Aetna Casualty & Sur. Co., 696 P.2d 711 (Ariz. Ct. App. 1984) (surveying relative amount of mistake in similar cases and concluding that $400,000 mistake in bid of $4.8 million would make enforcement of contract unconscionable).

2. *Mistake of fact vs. mistake of judgment.* As indicated by the discussion in *Wil-Fred's*, it is often said that rescission in such cases will be permitted for "clerical errors" or other "mistakes of fact," but not for "mistakes in judgment." What policy underlies this distinction? Many of the cases have indeed involved clerical, or "mechanical," errors. See, e.g., First Baptist Church of Moultrie v. Barber Contracting Co., 377 S.E.2d 717 (Ga. Ct. App. 1989) (rescission granted when contractor made $118,776 error in adding cost of materials on its work sheets); Kenneth E. Curran, Inc. v. State, 215 A.2d 702 (N.H. 1965) (hand-operated adding machine could not record more than $99,999, causing bidder to lose $100,000 in its calculations when total exceeded that amount). More recent cases have, like *Wil-Fred's*, been less disposed to insist on the rigidity of the fact-judgment distinction and more inclined to concentrate on the strength of the proof that a genuine and identifiable mistake was made (rather than merely a poor prediction as to how profitable the contract would turn out to be); but see Mid-States General & Mechanical Contracting Corp. v. Town of Goodland, 811 N.E. 2d 425,435-436 (Ind. Ct. App. 2004) (contractor who misunderstood unambiguous specifications and made error in bid not entitled to relief; relief is available for clerical error but not mistake of judgment).

3. *Effect of negligence.* Must a unilateral mistake be "non-negligent" in order to form a basis for relief? Many courts have so held, but, again, there is a clear tendency to relax this requirement where the proof of mistake is strong

and the effect of enforcement will be devastating or at least severely injurious to the mistaken party. See, e.g., Roberts & Schaefer Co. v. Hardaway Co., 152 F.3d 1283,1292 (11th Cir. 1998) (observing that relief for unilateral mistake is available provided that error does not result from "inexcusable lack of due care" and that Florida courts interpret standard "generously" to benefit of erring party); White v. Berenda Mesa Water District, 87 Cal. Rptr. 338 (Ct. App. 1970) (only "gross" negligence will defeat avoidance); and the *Kenneth E. Curran* case, cited in Note 2 above; but see Shoreline Communications, Inc. v. Norwich Taxi, 797 A2d 1165 (Conn. App. Ct. 2002) (lessee assumed risk by failing to ascertain whether space would be adequate for its radio transmission equipment before undertaking contractual obligation); Stamato v. Stamato, 818 So.2d 662 (Fla. Dist. Ct. App. 2002) (failure of party to "bother" to learn that trial court had ruled in her favor on motion for punitive damages constituted "inexcusable neglect" and barred rescission of settlement agreement on grounds of unilateral mistake). In §157, the Restatement (Second) expressly negates any requirement that the mistaken party be non-negligent, requiring only that its conduct not fall below the level of good faith and fair dealing.

4. *Effect of reliance by nonmistaken party.* Recall the *Baird* and *Drennan* cases in Chapter 2, involving the enforcement of subcontract bids after attempted revocation. On the basis of the principles illustrated in *Wil-Fred's* and the other cases discussed above, should the subcontractors in those cases have been able to obtain relief from enforcement on the theory of unilateral mistake? See the discussion of the *Calnan* case at the end of the *Wil-Fred's* opinion; to the same effect is Rotenberry v. Hooker, 864 So.2d 266 (Miss. 2003) (relief for unilateral mistake available where parties can be returned to status quo). If it had chosen to do so, could plaintiff Wil-Fred's have held subcontractor Ciaglo to its subcontract bid? If Ciaglo had been capable of responding to a judgment for damages in a breach of contract action, should Wil-Fred's have been denied rescission against the defendant sanitary district, on the ground that enforcement against Wil-Fred's would not in the circumstances have been unconscionable?

5. *Unilateral mistake as to content of writing.* In Chapter 2, we first encountered the "objective theory" of contracts, and its corollary, the "duty to read," which generally binds those who manifest agreement to what they know is intended to be a contract, even if they are ignorant of its contents (recall the Ray v. Eurice Bros. case). But the duty to read is not a principle that always carries the day, as we have since learned; it may be overcome by a variety of other protective doctrines, such as lack of capacity, fraud (recall the *Park 100* case in Chapter 7), or unconscionability. Where the parties are both equally mistaken about the accuracy of the agreement (it contains a typographical error, or a provision has been mistakenly omitted), the remedy of reformation may be available, as discussed in the notes following the *Lenawee County* case, above. But what if only one party is mistaken, because the agreement says just what the other party meant it to say? Can unilateral mistake provide an avenue of escape for the party who failed to read (or to understand) what he or she signed?

In Nauga, Inc. v. Westel Milwaukee Co., 576 N.W.2d 573 (Wis. Ct. App. 1998), defendant Westel, a cellular telephone company, and plaintiff Nauga, one of its selling agents, were involved in two separate lawsuits over alleged breaches by Westel of its agency agreement with Nauga. The existence of these disputes had not, however, resulted in a severance of the agency relationship between Nauga and Westel. While both of those suits were still in litigation, Westel submitted to Nauga and its other Wisconsin agents a proposed new agency agreement, to replace existing contracts. One clause of the proposed agreement was a release of any claims that the agent might have against Westel under their prior agreements or relationship. Believing that its agreement to this clause would result in Nauga's surrender of its pending claims against Westel, Nauga's attorney added to the proposed agency agreement a clause providing for the payment by Westel to Nauga of $250,000 for the settlement of all existing claims. The revised agreement was ultimately signed by Westel, assertedly without either its lawyers or its officers having noticed the existence and effect of the payment clause. (Nauga apparently conceded the truth of Westel's assertion that Westel never intended to assent to the payment term, and was surprised to learn later of its existence.) Westel refused to make the $250,000 payment, and Nauga moved to enforce the settlement agreement. The trial court held that although Nauga was not guilty of fraud, the two parties' minds had not met, and the contract was not enforceable. A divided appellate court reversed, and gave judgment for plaintiff Nauga. In the absence of ambiguity, fraud, or mutual mistake, enforcement might "seem harsh," the court conceded, but nevertheless was "based on sound principles." Id. at 578. A strong dissent argued that the trial court should have been upheld in its conclusion that no enforceable agreement existed, because of Nauga's violations of good faith, fair dealing, and the duty to cooperate.

Nauga is of course complicated by the fact that the actors primarily responsible for the events leading to the dispute were lawyers. Like many law students, you may sometimes wear a sweatshirt quoting Shakespeare's famous line from *Henry VI, Part II:* "The first thing we do, let's kill all the lawyers." You may be aware that in that speech, Shakespeare was not in fact damning lawyers; the line is spoken by one of a gang of villains, and was intended to express the idea that for evil to triumph, it would first be necessary to deprive society of the protection of the law. But most of your fellow citizens, sadly, probably take those words at face value—and perhaps agree with them.

6. *Effect of unilateral mistake in an advertisement.* As noted above, the *Baird* and *Drennan* cases from Chapter 2 exemplify the category of cases in which a unilateral mistake is contained in an offer submitted by a subcontractor or supplier, and in those cases the mistaken party is not likely to be excused. Another recurrent type of case involves a published newspaper ad that contains a mistake. In Donovan v. RRL Corp., 27 P.3d 702 (Cal. 2001), a car dealer offered a used Jaguar for sale in a newspaper ad for about $12,000 less than the intended price of $38,000 due to errors made by the newspaper's staff in composing the ad. The plaintiff soon appeared at the dealership and, after test driving the car and comparing it to similar cars offered at higher prices by another dealer, he attempted to buy the car at the published price. Although the court acknowledged that newspaper ads usually constitute invitations to negotiate rather than offers, the court decided that the ad in this

case would constitute an offer, at least when viewed in light of a California consumer protection statute which requires that a dealer have available for sale any car which is advertised at a specific price and on specific terms. (Recall the *Izadi* case in Chapter 2 which also addressed the possibility that an ad may constitute an offer.) The plaintiff, having no notice of the mistake, could thus accept the offer by tendering the full advertised price before any published time limit expired. The court then ruled, however, that the resulting contract was subject to rescission on grounds of unilateral mistake. The erroneous price related to a basic assumption upon which the contract was made and had a material adverse effect on the mistaken party since the published price was about 32% less than intended. The court further held that the dealer's failure to discover the mistake in the ad did not amount to a "neglect of legal duty" that would bar rescission when the other party suffers no loss. Id. at 717-719. The court identified the dealer's error as failing to proofread the ad and relying on the newspaper staff to perform that function. How does the *Donovan* case compare with the decision in *Wil-Fred's* or the outcome in *Drennan,* an earlier California case? With *Izadi?*

B. CHANGED CIRCUMSTANCES: IMPOSSIBILITY, IMPRACTICABILITY, AND FRUSTRATION

As we have seen, the defense of mistake is commonly characterized as resting on a mistake by one or both parties as to a fact existing at the time their contract was made. The three doctrines considered in this section — "impossibility," "impracticability," and "frustration of purpose" — are usually thought of as involving changes in circumstance that occur between the making of the contract and the time set for performance (although there are cases in which the circumstance in question already existed at the time of contracting, not being discovered until later). Of the three, the earliest to evolve was the notion of "impossibility of performance."

In order to consider why and when impossibility should constitute a defense to a duty of performance, it may be appropriate first to consider why it should *not.* To a nonlawyer, it might appear that the duty to perform a contractual obligation would naturally be excused whenever it should appear that the performance itself was literally impossible. To understand why that has not been the case, it is necessary to recall that contractual liability is historically a form of "strict" liability: Nonperformance is actionable simply because the defendant has failed to perform what he or she promised, not because that nonperformance is also "culpable" in any sense. So any failure to perform a contractual obligation — whether willful, negligent, or innocent — should in theory give the aggrieved party a cause of action. If that obligation was in fact impossible to perform, then the remedy for breach obviously could not be specific performance; however, the court still could and presumably would award damages to compensate the plaintiff for the lost value of the defendant's expected performance.

The English courts first recognized this principle of strict contractual liability in Paradine v. Jane, 82 Eng. Rep. 897 (K.B. 1647). The case arose during the English Civil War. Jane had leased land from Paradine for a term of years but was dispossessed by a certain Prince Rupert and his army. Jane did not regain possession of the land for almost three years, during which time he paid no rent. When Paradine sued for the unpaid rent, Jane's defense was that he should be excused from his obligation to pay rent during the period of dispossession. The court held, however, that the plea was insufficient:

> [W]hen the party by his own contract creates a duty or charge upon himself, he is bound to make it good, if he may, notwithstanding any accident or inevitable necessity, because he might have provided against it by his contract.

Id. at 897-898.

The first notable line of exceptions to this rule of strict liability is generally traced to a much later English case, Taylor v. Caldwell, 122 Eng. Rep. 309 (K.B. 1863). (There are indications that earlier decisions gave relief from liability for nonperformance where this was occasioned by an Act of God. See Alfred W.B. Simpson, A History of the Common Law of Contract 525-526 (1987). However, Taylor v. Caldwell is generally regarded as the "fountainhead of the modern law of impossibility." E. Allan Farnsworth, Contracts §9.5, at 621 (4th ed. 2004). In *Taylor*, the defendant Caldwell had agreed to rent a music hall to plaintiff Taylor for several days, so that Taylor might present musical performances there. The hall burned down shortly before the first performance was to take place, and Taylor sued for breach of contract. The court absolved Caldwell of liability, holding that because the hall itself was "essential" to the performance of the contract, and the parties had contracted "on the basis of [its] continued existence," Caldwell's duty of performance should be excused by its accidental destruction.

The principle of Taylor v. Caldwell has been applied to contracts for personal service or for the sale of specific goods: When a person or thing "necessary for performance" of the agreement dies or is incapacitated, is destroyed or damaged, the duty of performance is accordingly excused. See Restatement (Second) §§262, 263; UCC §2-613 ("casualty" to goods "identified when the contract is made" which contract "requires for its performance"). The principle is ordinarily easy to apply to destruction of unique goods (such as a racehorse); its application may be more dubious in cases involving specific goods of a fungible type, because the party seeking excuse will have to convince the court that the contract required for its performance the particular goods that were destroyed. See, e.g., Bende & Sons, Inc. v. Crown Recreation, Inc., 548 F. Supp. 1018 (E.D.N.Y. 1982), *aff'd*, 722 F.2d 727 (2d Cir. 1983) (seller not excused from duty to deliver combat boots by destruction of boots in train wreck; no showing that contract required those particular boots for its performance). Another situation commonly characterized as a form of "impossibility" (although not involving impossibility in any literal sense) is the prohibition of performance by governmental action. See Restatement (Second) §264; UCC §2-615(a) and Comment 10.

As suggested above, the doctrine of excuse for impossibility required for its application a showing of *literal* impossibility — the thing promised simply could not be performed at all. Such a requirement is often referred to as "objective" impossibility — "no one could do it" — as opposed to "subjective" impossibility — "*I* cannot do it." See first Restatement §455. This rule therefore would not serve to excuse a party merely because performance had come to be more difficult or expensive or because the contract itself had lost its value to that party. Another English case, decided 40 years after Taylor v. Caldwell, presented the latter situation. In Krell v. Henry, [1903] 2 K.B. 740 (C.A.), the defendant had agreed to pay the plaintiff for the use of a room overlooking the route that the coronation procession of King Edward VII would travel. The sudden illness of the king forced the cancellation of his coronation, however, making the plaintiff's room useless to the defendant for that purpose on that day. The court held that the defendant was excused from his duty of payment.

Although the court in *Krell* cited and relied on Taylor v. Caldwell and other "impossibility" cases, the result in *Krell* is generally not viewed as involving any true impossibility ("objective" or otherwise), because the promises of each party could literally have been performed. *Krell* is explained rather as a case of "frustration of purpose"; the exchange called for by the contract had lost all value to the defendant, because of a supervening change in extrinsic circumstances. (Note here the overlap of doctrines; if, unknown to Krell and Henry, the king's illness had already occurred at the time the contract was made, the case could also have been analyzed as one of "mutual mistake.") For a comprehensive discussion and criticism of the conventional treatment of the English law of impossibility, see John D. Wladis, Common Law and Uncommon Events: The Development of the Doctrine of Impossibility of Performance in English Contract Law, 75 Geo. L.J. 1575 (1987).

The doctrine of frustration was endorsed by the first Restatement in §288 ("frustration of object or effect"). The case law actually applying the doctrine remained sparse, however. See Nicholas R. Weiskopf, Frustration of Contractual Purpose — Doctrine or Myth? 70 St. John's L. Rev. 239, 265 (1996) (noting "lack of widespread decisional support"). And indeed, it does appear that the doctrine has been often advanced but seldom applied. See, e.g., Lloyd v. Murphy, 153 P.2d 47 (Cal. 1944) (en banc) (onset of World War II and consequent legal restrictions on new car sales would not excuse defendant lessee's performance of its obligations under lease of premises for conduct of auto sales agency).

The third of this trilogy of excuses from performance is — like a number of other innovations in contract law — generally attributed to a decision of the California Supreme Court. In Mineral Park Land Co. v. Howard, 156 P. 458 (Cal. 1916), the defendant contractor had agreed to purchase and extract from plaintiff's land, at fixed prices (varying with the amounts taken), all the gravel required for the construction of a concrete bridge. The defendant procured some of the gravel used in the bridge from another source and was thereupon sued for its failure to take all of its gravel requirements from plaintiff's land. The defendant showed that it had removed from plaintiff's land all the gravel that was above water-level, and that removal of that which lay below water-level would have entailed not only a different means of extraction, but 10 to 12 times as great a cost. The court held that the extreme increase in the cost of extraction justified the defendant's nonperformance. Even though performance clearly was not literally impossible (indeed, it was not even "subjectively" impossible), it was sufficiently different from what the parties had both contemplated at the time of contracting as to be "impracticable."

As did the first Restatement, the Restatement (Second) incorporates the doctrines of impossibility (§§262, 263, 264), impracticability (§§261, 266), and frustration (§§265, 266). As we have already noted, the Uniform Commercial Code also has a rule covering traditional impossibility (§2-613); it also provides in §§2-615 and 2-616 for complete or partial excuse from the duty of performance in cases of impracticability. The ambit of UCC §2-615 is apparently broad enough to encompass instances of both traditional impossibility and impracticability, as well as frustration of purpose.

The parties to a modern contractual dispute — and the court that must resolve that dispute — therefore have available to them several strands of doctrine that may apply to reduce or entirely excuse the liability that would ordinarily flow from nonperformance. They also can make use of myriad cases and commentaries in which the justification for, and application of, those various doctrines is considered. The following cases are typical recent examples in which these doctrines have been invoked by defendants in an effort to avoid liability for nonperformance.

Karl Wendt Farm Equipment Co. v. International Harvester Co.

United States Court of Appeals
931 F.2d 1112 (6th Cir. 1991)

Before JONES, RYAN and BOGGS, Circuit Judges.

NATHANIEL R. JONES, Circuit Judge.

Plaintiff Karl Wendt Farm Equipment Company ("Wendt") appeals and defendants International Harvester Company and International Harvester Credit Corp. (collectively "IH") cross-appeal from a deficiency judgement and preceding trial verdicts in this contract action relating to a dealer sales and service agreement. For the reasons set forth below, we reverse and remand in part and affirm in part.

I.

This diversity action arises out of IH's decision to go out of the farm equipment business after a dramatic downturn in the market for farm equipment. In the fall of 1974, Wendt and IH entered into a "Dealer Sales and Service Agreement" ("agreement") which established Wendt as a dealer of IH goods in the area of Marlette, Michigan. The agreement set forth the required method of sale, provisions for the purchase and servicing of goods, as well as certain dealer operating requirements. The agreement also provided specific provisions for the termination of the contract upon the occurrence of certain specified conditions.

In light of a dramatic recession in the farm equipment market, and substantial losses on the part of IH, IH negotiated an agreement with J.I. Case Co. and Tenneco Inc. ("Case/Tenneco") to sell its farm equipment division to Case/Tenneco. The sale took the form of a sale of assets. The base purchase price was $246,700,000.00 in cash and $161,300,000.00 to be paid in participating preferred stock in Tenneco. While IH asserts that it lost $479,000,000.00 on the deal, it also noted that this was a "paper loss" which will result in a tax credit offsetting the loss. J. App. at 405.

In its purchase of IH's farm equipment division, Case/Tenneco did not acquire IH's existing franchise network. Rather, it received "access" to IH dealers, many of whom eventually received a Case franchise. However, there were some 400 "conflicted areas" in which both a Case and an IH dealership were located. In these areas Case offered only one franchise contract. In nearly two-thirds of the conflicted areas, the IH dealer received the franchise. However, Marlette, Michigan was such a "conflicted area" and Wendt was not offered a Case franchise.

Wendt filed this action alleging breach of IH's Dealer Agreement and several other causes of action, but all Wendt's allegations save the breach of contract action were disposed of before trial. IH filed a counter-claim against Wendt for debts arising out of farm equipment and parts advanced to Wendt on credit.

At trial, the court allowed IH's defense of impracticability of performance to go to the jury on the contract action. The jury returned a verdict of no cause of action on the contract and the district court denied Wendt's motion for J.N.O.V./new trial, which was based on the invalidity of the impracticability defense. These actions by the court form a substantial basis of Wendt's appeal. In addition, however, the court ordered a directed verdict for Wendt as to IH's defenses of frustration of purpose, an implied covenant limiting the duration of the contract and a defense relating to whether Section 2 of the agreement permitted IH to cease production of all its product lines. The court's directed verdict on the viability of these defenses forms the basis of IH's cross-appeal. . . .

II.

We review the trial court's interpretation of a contract de novo. . . .

Wendt asserts a number of errors surrounding the district court's allowing the defense of impracticability of performance to go to the jury. Wendt first contends that the defense of impracticability due to extreme changes in market conditions is not a cognizable defense under Michigan law. In the alternative, Wendt argues that there was insufficient evidence to withstand Wendt's motion for a directed verdict on impracticability. The jury's verdict of no cause of action against IH based on the impracticability defense also forms the basis of Wendt's motions for J.N.O.V. and new trial.

To determine whether the doctrine of impracticability is applicable under Michigan law based on the circumstances presented in this case, the court must first look to any controlling decisions of the Michigan Supreme Court. . . .

The district court . . . asserted that the Michigan Supreme Court's recognition of the doctrine of impossibility was not altered by its adoption of the U.C.C. in 1964 and further that the doctrine of impossibility was broadened by the Michigan Court of Appeals in Bissell v. L.W. Edison Co., 9 Mich. App. 276, 156 N.W.2d 623 (1967) to excuse future performance when circumstances make performance impracticable. . . .

In *Bissell*, the Michigan Court of Appeals, relying on the Restatement of Contracts section 457, concluded that the doctrine of impossibility is a valid defense not only when performance is impossible, but also when supervening circumstances make performance impracticable. Section 457 of the Restatement of Contracts, now section 261 of the Restatement (Second) of Contracts (1981) provides:

Discharge by Supervening Impracticability

> Where, after a contract is made, a party's performance is made impracticable without his fault by the occurrence of an event the non-occurrence of which was a basic assumption on which the contract was made, his duty to render that performance is discharged, unless the language or the circumstances indicate the contrary.

Although *Bissell* did not involve non-performance due to economic causes, the court relied extensively on section 457 which defines impossibility to include, "not only strict impossibility but impracticability because of extreme and unreasonable difficulty, expense, injury and loss involved." *Bissell*, 9 Mich. App. at 285, 156 N.W.2d at 626. In the instant case the district court relied heavily on the language of section 457 quoted in *Bissell* to conclude that the extreme downturn in the market for farm products was "unreasonable and extreme" enough to present a jury question as to the defense under Michigan law. See J. App. at 47.

Recognizing that *Bissell* suggests that an impracticability defense may be cognizable under Michigan law in some circumstances, we must turn to the question of whether under Michigan law, the defense of impracticability was appropriately presented to the jury under the circumstances involving a dramatic downturn in the market for farm equipment which led to the contract action before us in this case. The commentary to section 261 of the Restatement (Second) provides extensive guidance for determining when economic circumstances are sufficient to render performance impracticable. Comment *d* to section 261 makes clear that mere lack of profit under the contract is insufficient: "'[I]mpracticability' means more than 'impracticality.' A mere change in the degree of difficulty or expense due to such causes as increased wages, prices of raw materials or costs of construction, unless well beyond the normal range, does not amount to impracticability since it is this sort of risk that a fixed price contract is intended to cover." Comment *d* also provides:

> A severe shortage of raw materials or of supplies due to war, embargo, local crop failure, unforeseen shutdown of major sources of supply, or the like, which either causes a marked increase in cost or prevents performance altogether may bring the case within the rule stated in this Section.

More guidance is provided in Comment *b* to section 261. Comment *b* states: "In order for a supervening event to discharge a duty under this Section, the non-occurrence of that event must have been a 'basic assumption' on which both parties made the contract." Comment *b* goes on to provide that the application of the "basic assumption" criteria

> is also simple enough in the cases of market shifts or the financial inability of one of the parties. The continuation of existing market conditions and of the financial situation of one of the parties are ordinarily *not* such assumptions, so that mere market shifts or financial inability do not usually effect discharge under the rule stated in this Section.

(Emphasis added). Comment *b* also provides two helpful examples. In Illustration 3 of Comment *b*, *A* contracts to employ *B* for two years at a set salary. After one year a government regulation makes *A*'s business unprofitable and he fires *B*. *A*'s duty to employ *B* is not discharged due to impracticability and *A* is liable for breach. In Illustration 4, *A* contracts to sell *B* a machine to be delivered by a certain date. Due to a suit by a creditor, all of *A*'s assets are placed in receivership. *A* is not excused for nonperformance under the doctrine of impracticability.

In our view, section 261 requires a finding that impracticability is an inappropriate defense in this case. The fact that IH experienced a dramatic downturn in the farm equipment market and decided to go out of the business does not excuse its unilateral termination of its dealership agreements due to impracticability. IH argues that while mere unprofitability should not excuse performance, the substantial losses and dramatic market shift in the farm equipment market between 1980 and 1985 warrant the special application of the defense in this case. IH cites losses of over $2,000,000.00 per day and a drop in the company's standing on the Fortune 500 list from 27 to 104. IH Brief at 7 (citing trial record). IH also put on evidence that if it had not sold its farm equipment division, it might have had to declare bankruptcy. While the facts suggest that IH suffered severely from the downturn in the farm equipment market, neither market shifts nor the financial inability of one of the parties changes the basic assumptions of the contract such that it may be excused under the doctrine of impracticability. Restatement (Second) of Contracts, section 261, Comment *b*. To hold otherwise would not fulfill the likely understanding of the parties as to the apportionment of risk under the contract. The agreement provides in some detail the procedure and conditions for termination. IH may not have been entirely responsible for the economic downturn in the company, but it was responsible for its chosen remedy: to sell its farm equipment assets. An alternative would have been to terminate its Dealer Agreements by mutual assent under the termination provisions of the contract and share the proceeds of the sale of assets to Case/Tenneco with its dealers. Thus, we find that IH had alternatives which could have precluded unilateral termination of the contract. Further, application of the impracticability defense in this case would allow IH to avoid its liability under franchise agreements, allow Case/Tenneco to pick up only those dealerships its sees fit and leave the remaining dealers bankrupt. In such circumstance, application of the doctrine of impracticability would not only be a misapplication of law, but a windfall for IH at the expense of the dealers.

We find this understanding of the doctrine of impracticability to be more consistent with Michigan law than the district court's interpretation. In applying the doctrine of impossibility, the Michigan Supreme Court has repeatedly held that economic loss or hardship was not enough to excuse performance. See *Sheldon,* 319 Mich. at 408, 29 N.W.2d at 835 (a government regulation which placed a ceiling on the price of scooter bikes making their manufacture unprofitable did not excuse performance on a contract for sale of scooter bikes); *Chase,* 241 Mich. at 484, 217 N.W. at 567 (increased labor, materials and construction costs due to the unexpected economic hardship brought on by World War I did not excuse performance even when performance cost some 40% more than the contract price); and *Milligan,* 296 Mich. at 71, 295 N.W. at 563 (market conditions which made the manufacture of bricks unprofitable did not excuse performance). As recently as 1986, this principle was recognized by the Michigan Court of Appeals in In the Matter of Yeager Bridge Culvert Co., 150 Mich. App. 386, 398, 389 N.W.2d 99, 104 (1986) (mere changes in market conditions which render performance unprofitable do not justify releasing a party from its obligation to perform). The fact that IH's losses in this case involved millions of dollars does not change the scope of the doctrine as the proportional effect of those changes is equivalent to the hardship imposed on the small businesses in the impossibility cases just described.

In the end, IH simply asserts that it would have been unprofitable to terminate its agreements with its dealers by invoking the six-month notice and other termination procedures embodied in the Dealer Agreement, or by sharing the proceeds of its sale of its farm equipment assets with dealers. This assertion does not excuse IH's performance under the agreement.

As *Bissell* did not address the question of economic circumstances which excuse performance under the doctrine of impracticability and neither the case law of the Supreme Court of Michigan nor the Restatement (Second) of Contracts suggests that the economic circumstances in this case would be sufficient to excuse performance, we hold that while the Supreme Court of Michigan might recognize the defense of impracticability, it would not do so in the circumstances of this case as a matter of law. Accordingly, we find that the district court erred in permitting the defense of impracticability to go to the jury and that Wendt was entitled to a directed verdict on this issue as a matter of law.

III.

In its cross-appeal, IH asserts that the court improperly granted a directed verdict for Wendt on its other affirmative defenses. Specifically, IH objects to the court's grant of a directed verdict on IH's defense of frustration of purpose, its defense based upon Section 2 of the Dealer Agreement and its defense based upon an implied covenant that the contract was not perpetual. We will address IH's defenses seriatim.

A. FRUSTRATION OF PURPOSE.

It is undisputed that Michigan law recognizes the defense of frustration of purpose. See Molnar v. Molnar, 110 Mich. App. 622, 625-26, 313 N.W.2d

171, 173 (1981) (allowing the defense of frustration of purpose in a suit to discontinue child support payments when the beneficiary child died). However, the district court in the instant case determined that the defense was unavailable. In making this determination, the court relied on section 265 of the Restatement (Second) of Contracts which provides:

> Where, after a contract is made, a party's principal purpose is substantially frustrated without his fault by the occurrence of an event the non-occurrence of which was a basic assumption on which the contract was made, his remaining duties to render performance are discharged, unless the language or the circumstances indicate the contrary.

In interpreting this provision, the district court relied on the Supreme Court of South Dakota's analysis of this same defense when raised by IH in a suit by a dealer for breach of the same dealer agreement in Groseth Intl. v. Tenneco, 410 N.W.2d 159 (S.D. 1987).

In *Groseth,* the court found that under the Restatement (Second), the defense of frustration requires the establishment of three factors. The first is that the purpose frustrated by the supervening event must have been the "principal purpose" of the party making the contract. Quoting section 265, Comment *a,* the court noted, "'It is not enough that [the contracting party] had in mind a specific object without which he would not have made the contract. The object must be so completely the basis of the contract that, as both parties understand, without it the transaction would make little sense.'" Id. at 165. The court interpreted this passage to require an inquiry into the principal purpose of the contract and a finding that the frustrating event destroys the primary basis of the contract. Id.

According to the *Groseth* court, the second factor required under the Restatement is that the frustration be "substantial." Once again quoting Comment *a* to section 265, the court stated: "'It is not enough that the transaction has become less profitable for the affected party or even that he will sustain a loss. The frustration must be so severe that it is not fairly to be regarded as within the risks that he assumed under the contract.'" Id. The court added, "[t]he fact that performance has become economically burdensome or unattractive is not sufficient to excuse performance." Id. (citations omitted).

Finally, according to *Groseth,* the third factor required to make out a defense of frustration under the Restatement is that the frustrating event must have been a "basic assumption" of the contract. See Restatement (Second) of Contracts, section 265 Comment *a.* In analyzing this element, Comment *a* states that the analysis is the same as under the defense of impracticability. Id. (referencing section 261, Comment *b*). . . .

Applying these three factors in the instant case, the district court found that the primary purpose of the Dealer Agreement was stated in section 1 of the agreement. Section 1 provides,

> The general purposes of the agreement are to establish the dealer of goods covered by this agreement, and to govern the relations between the dealer and the company in promoting the sale of those goods and their purchase and sale by the dealer, and in providing warranty and other service for their users.

J. App. 506 (quoting agreement). The court interpreted this language to mean that the primary purpose of the agreement was to establish the dealership and the terms of interaction and was not "mutual profitability" as asserted by IH. Therefore, the court reasoned that a dramatic down-turn in the farm equipment market resulting in reduced profitability did not frustrate the primary purpose of the agreement. Id. at 505-07. The court went on to suggest that continuity of market conditions or the financial situation of the parties were not basic assumptions or implied conditions to the enforcement of a contract. Id. at 507. Thus, following *Groseth,* it held that the doctrine of frustration was not applicable to this case. Id.

IH does not offer any arguments which challenge the correctness of the *Groseth* decision or the district court's analysis. Rather, IH challenges the court's finding that the primary purpose of the contract was not "mutual profitability." In our view, the district court had substantial grounds for so finding and we affirm the district court's grant of a directed verdict for Wendt on the frustration defense. If IH's argument were to be accepted, the "primary purpose" analysis under the Restatement would essentially be meaningless as "mutual profitability" would be implied as the primary purpose of every contract. Rather, like the doctrine of impracticability, the doctrine of frustration is an equitable doctrine which is meant to fairly apportion risks between the parties in light of unforeseen circumstances. It is essentially an implied term which is meant to apportion risk as the parties would have had the necessity occurred to them. See *Groseth,* 410 N.W.2d at 166; Patch v. Solar Corp., 149 F.2d 558, 560 (7th Cir. 1945), *cert. denied,* 326 U.S. 741, 66 S. Ct. 53, 90 L. Ed. 442 (1945). In this case, the frustrating event was IH's decision to sell its farm equipment assets and go out of that line of business. While IH might have determined that such a move was economically required, it may not then assert that its obligation under existing agreements are discharged in light of its decision.[2] For these reasons, we affirm.

B. SECTION 2 OF THE DEALER AGREEMENT.

Section 2 of the Dealer Agreement provides, in relevant part:

> The agreement shall cover all those items of agricultural tractors, machines, equipment and attachments, which appear in the agricultural equipment price list issued by the company, and service parts for such goods. The company reserves the right to make additions to and eliminations from such list, including but not limited to reductions resulting from the discontinued production of a line or lines of such tractors, machines, equipment and attachments, without incurring any responsibility to the dealer.

---

2. In addition to an examination of whether the "primary purpose" of the contract was frustrated, Section 265 of the Restatement also requires that the frustrating event occur without the "fault" of the party seeking discharge. It does not seem to us a stretch to conclude that since the frustrating event was IH's decision to sell its farm equipment assets without following the termination provisions of the contract, the frustration of the contract was IH's fault. IH would of course assert that it had no choice but to sell the assets, but we have covered this ground before. Thus, IH's fault in the frustration of its dealer agreements provides an additional reason for the inapplicability of the doctrine.

J. App. at 545. IH asserts that this provision authorizes IH to completely withdraw from the market. The theory is that if IH may withdraw some of its product lines it may also withdraw all of them.

Authority is split as to whether IH's asserted interpretation is correct. In J.I. Case Co. v. Berkshire Implement Co., No. S86-555, slip op. at 7-10 (N.D. Ind. March 3, 1987) (following St. Joseph Equipment v. Massey-Ferguson, Inc., 546 F. Supp. 1245 (W.D. Wis. 1982)), the court interpreted a provision very similar to section 2 of the Dealer Agreement as enabling the manufacturer to eliminate all its product lines and go out of business. In *Groseth*, 410 N.W.2d 159 (S.D. 1987), however, the court read section 2 of the same Dealer Agreement to allow IH to eliminate or change certain products or product lines, but not to eliminate its farm products altogether.

In the instant case, the district court followed the *Groseth* view of section 2 of the Dealer Agreement and we find that interpretation to be the correct one. Section 2, by its terms, seems to be intended to allow IH to make shifts in its product lines and to discontinue product lines without changing the binding force of the agreement. We find it quite a stretch to believe that the parties intended this provision to function as an alternative means for termination of the contract. This interpretation is reenforced by the fact that the agreement provides specific conditions and provisions for termination. See J. App. 555-61 (Section of the contract entitled "Termination of the Agreement"). As we find the court's interpretation of section 2 of the agreement correct as a matter of law, we affirm.

C. AN IMPLIED TERM THAT THE AGREEMENT WAS OF
   LIMITED DURATION.

Finally, IH asserts that the district court erred in refusing to find that an implied term of every dealership agreement is the ability of the manufacturer to go out of business. For this position, IH relies on dicta from the Supreme Court of Michigan in Lichnovsky v. Ziebart Intl. Corp., 414 Mich. 228, 324 N.W.2d 732 (1982). The court in *Lichnovsky*, held that while it might be appropriate to imply a term for termination of an agreement when no termination provisions existed in the contract, it would not imply such a term in a contract which provided for termination of the agreement for cause. Id. at 414 Mich. at 242-43, 324 N.W.2d at 739-40. In response to the argument that the Court's holding would create a perpetual franchise agreement, the Court stated:

> There are relatively few enterprises that last even fifty or a hundred years, let alone forever. Just as an agreement for life employment (terminable for cause) is subject to the vicissitudes of human mortality, so too a franchise agreement is subject to the vicissitudes of the market[.] . . .
>   At some point, that which Ziebart and Lichnovsky agreed upon may no longer be viable. The life of the subject matter of their agreement will be at an end.

414 Mich. at 243-44, 324 N.W.2d at 740. Using this language, IH urges this court to imply a term which would allow termination of a franchise agreement when the manufacturer goes out of business. IH cites as precedent for this

proposition Delta Truck & Tractor v. J.I. Case, Co., No. 85-2606, 1990 WL 294415, slip op. at 2-3 (W.D. La. 1990), which, relying on *Lichnovsky,* holds that in the absence of a specified duration of performance in the contract a reasonable time will be implied. The court held that a reasonable time in the circumstance of the IH franchise agreement was the period in which IH manufactured farm equipment. Hence, the court implied a term that when IH ceased to manufacture such equipment, the agreement was terminated. We find the court's invocation of *Lichnovsky* in *Delta Truck* misplaced as the Dealer Agreement, like the contract in *Lichnovsky* has provisions for its termination for cause. Following *Lichnovsky* would require that no term be implied when the contract itself provides the circumstances for its own termination in its termination provisions.

As noted above, courts will use their equitable power to imply terms into contracts in circumstances which would apportion the risk of loss as the parties would have had they thought to include such a provision. See, e.g, *Groseth,* 410 N.W.2d at 166; *Patch,* 149 F.2d at 560. In this case, the evidence supports the conclusion that while either party might have anticipated market shifts neither party anticipated that IH would go out of the farm equipment business completely. Implying a term which enables IH to terminate its franchise agreement unilaterally without following the termination conditions of the agreement and without incurring a breach places all the risk on the dealer. Rather, if economic circumstances require that IH leave the market for farm products, it should properly seek to terminate its agreement under the terms of the agreement. This is precisely the same conclusion the *Lichnovsky* court arrived at in determining that a franchise agreement was not terminable at will, but rather terminable only for cause by its terms. See *Lichnovsky,* 414 Mich. at 242-43, 324 N.W.2d at 739-40. As there is no evidence which suggests that IH sought to terminate its agreement with Wendt by mutual agreement under the terms of the agreement, the district court properly granted a directed verdict for Wendt on this defense. . . .

V.

As the district court erred in allowing the defense of impracticability of performance to go to the jury in this case under Michigan law, we reverse and remand for a new trial only on the question of damages for IH's breach of its Dealer Agreement with Wendt. With respect to all other assignments of error by the parties, we affirm.

RYAN, Circuit Judge (dissenting).

The court has held that the district court erred in submitting the defendants' defense of impracticability of performance to the jury. I disagree.

The court concedes, correctly I think, that the Michigan Supreme Court "might" recognize the impracticability doctrine, but the court says, "it would not do so in the circumstances of this case as a matter of law." . . .

It appears that the majority opinion rejects the impracticability defense "in the circumstances of this case" because, in the court's view, the economic reverses confronted by International Harvester were not so "extreme and unreasonable," severe, or catastrophic as to excuse performance of the franchise agreement with the plaintiffs. Although claiming to recognize that whether impracticability of performance has been proved is a question of fact for the jury, Michigan Bean Co. v. Senn, 93 Mich. App. 440, 287 N.W.2d 257 (1979), the court appears to disagree with the jury that International Harvester was confronted with economic circumstances sufficiently disastrous to justify discharge for impracticability. There were "alternatives," the court says, "which might have precluded unilateral termination of the contract." One such alternative open to International Harvester, the court suggests, might have been "to terminate [the] Dealer Agreements by mutual assent under the termination provisions of the contract and share the proceeds of the sale of assets to Case/Tenneco with its dealers."

Whether the "alternative" the court suggests ever occurred to International Harvester's management, or, if considered, was a feasible business solution, is entirely irrelevant on this appeal because it is the jury, not this court, that is empowered to determine whether International Harvester proved impracticability of performance as that defense was defined by the trial court.

The district court correctly recognized that the standard for determining whether there was a jury submissible issue of impracticability is set forth in Restatement (Second) of Contracts §261 (1981). . . .

When all facts and reasonable inferences therefrom are taken in a light most favorable to International Harvester, they reveal a sudden, unforeseen, nationwide collapse of the farm implement industry so severe and so widespread that International Harvester, after losing over $2 billion in four years, was faced, in its business judgment, with no alternative but bankruptcy or selling off its farm implement division. *Those* are the facts as we must view them for purposes of this appeal. The question for us, then, is whether "reasonable people could differ" that those facts amounted to "an event, the non-occurrence of which was a basic assumption on which the contract was made." Restatement (Second) of Contracts, supra. Manifestly, they could. The majority opinion is an indication of that.

Since there is nothing in the jurisprudence of the impracticability defense to suggest that a market collapse of the kind shown by International Harvester is not, as a matter of law, within the doctrine, we are not free to disturb the jury's verdict.

Notes and Questions

1. *Comparison of impracticability and frustration doctrines.* While the doctrines of impracticability of performance and frustration of purpose are separate grounds for relief from a contract, the elements of the doctrines are essentially identical. In fact, Professor Farnsworth refers to the Restatement synthesis of the two doctrines as "strikingly similar." E. Allan Farnsworth, Contracts §9.7, at 635 (4th ed. 2004). Both require the disadvantaged party to show: (1) substantial reduction of the value of the contract ("performance is made impracticable"; "a party's principal purpose is substantially frustrated"); (2) because of the occurrence of an event, the nonoccurrence of which was a basic assumption of the contract; (3) without the party's fault; and (4) the party seeking relief does not bear the risk of that occurrence of the event either under the language of the contract or the surrounding circumstances. Compare Restatement (Second)

§§261 (impracticability) and 265 (frustration of purpose). UCC §2-615 is similar (not surprisingly, as it predated the Restatement (Second), and was the model for those Restatement sections).

2. *Increased cost as a basis for relief.* Like the court in *Karl Wendt Farm Equipment*, most courts have refused to grant relief under either the impracticability or the frustration of purpose doctrines to a party who seeks to avoid a contract that has become more expensive or less profitable due to change in market conditions. See, e.g., Seaboard Lumber Co. v. United States, 308 F.3d 1283 (Fed. Cir. 2002) (buyers who contracted to purchase timber at fixed prices could not claim impracticability when slump in market prices made contracts unprofitable); Ecology Services, Inc. v. GranTurk Equipment, Inc., 443 F. Supp. 2d 756 (D. Md. 2006) (allegations that shortage of steel led to increase in price of steel was not sufficient to establish impracticability that would excuse late delivery of garbage trucks).

As noted in the text before the *Karl Wendt Farm Equipment* case, however, the seminal impracticability case, Mineral Park Land Co. v. Howard, did grant relief due to a tremendous increase in cost of performance (10 to 12 times greater than anticipated) resulting from unexpected developments other than a change in market conditions. Other courts also occasionally find impracticability resulting from an unexpected event that causes an overwhelming increase in the cost of performance. See, e.g., Cape-France Enterprises v. Estate of Peed, 29 P.3d 1011 (Mont. 2001) (impracticability excuse granted after notice from government that underground water pollution plume had spread near seller's land and that the drilling of a test well required by land sale contract could exacerbate groundwater contamination and expose seller to liability for "unquantifiable" amount of clean-up costs); Iannuccillo v. Material Sand&Stone Corp., 713 A.2d 1234 (R.I. 1998) (excuse granted for impracticability after discovery of unanticipated rock in area designated for excavation would have effectively increased cost of performance from $5000 to about $65,000).

3. *Natural disaster or war as a basis for relief.* Natural disaster or war have been the basis for claimed relief from a contract under the doctrines of impracticability and frustration, but here also the courts have been generally unwilling to grant relief. E.g., American Trading & Production Corp. v. Shell International Marine, Ltd., 453 F.2d 939 (2d Cir. 1972) (shipowners denied relief for increased expense under doctrine of impracticability when Suez Canal was closed due to war; while parties contemplated use of Suez Canal, that route was not basic assumption of contract and shippers were required to use alternative means when contemplated route became impracticable); Moody v. Lea, 83 S.W.3d 745 (Tenn. Ct. App. 2001) (farmer denied relief from contract to rent equipment that was made unusable by flooding of Mississippi River; flooding in the area was foreseeable). But see Opera Company of Boston, Inc. v. Wolf Trap Foundation for the Performing Arts, 817 F.2d 1094 (4th Cir. 1987) (impracticability established when electrical storm caused power outage and safety concerns that led to cancellation of outdoor performance; dissenting judge would have denied relief because Wolf Trap failed to provide for auxiliary power equipment and neglected to include contractual provision providing for relief due to power outage).

4. *Impracticability based on terrorism.* A recent variation of an impracticability claim based on war or hostilities can be found in a case related to the September 11, 2001, terrorist attack on the World Trade Center in New York City. In Bush v. ProTravel International, Inc., 746 N.Y.S. 2d 790 (Civ. Ct. 2002), the plaintiff sought refund of a $1,500 deposit on a planned honeymoon safari trip scheduled for November 2001 even though the contract provided for refund of the deposit only if cancellation notice was received by September 14, 2001, and the plaintiff's cancellation was not received until September 27, at the earliest. The plaintiff sought to excuse the late cancellation notice on grounds of impracticability due to travel and communication difficulties in New York City in the aftermath of September 11. In denying the defendants' motion for summary judgment, the court noted that in addition to New York City being under a government-imposed state of emergency in the days immediately following September 11, the plaintiff alleged that damage to telephone systems made it almost physically impossible to place a telephone call from Staten Island, where the plaintiff had retreated, to the travel agent's office in Manhattan. The court thus decided that the plaintiff should have the opportunity to prove temporary impossibility that would have suspended the cancellation date. Id. at 797. (See Restatement (Second) §269 on temporary impracticability and frustration.)

In *Bush,* the defendant travel companies asserted that the plaintiff was simply "skiddish [sic] to travel after September 11," and that such concerns were an insufficient basis to excuse performance under the contract. Id. at 794. Should fears for personal safety after a terrorist attack constitute a valid basis for a claim of impracticability? See Restatement (Second) Contracts §261, cmt. *d* (performance may be impracticable because it will involve a risk of injury to person or property); but see 7200 Scottsdale Road General Partners v. Kuhn Farm Machinery, 909 P.2d 408 (Ariz. Ct. App. 1995) (conference organizer's good faith apprehension of terrorism danger to attendees traveling by domestic airlines because of 1991 United States involvement in hostilities in Iraq was not substantial enough to rise to the level of impracticability or frustration and excuse late cancellation of hotel; perception of danger must be "objectively reasonable").

5. *Death or incapacity of particular person necessary for performance.* Where the difficulty in performance stems not merely from unprofitability of the enterprise, however, but from the physical impossibility or difficulty of performance, there is somewhat more likelihood of excuse. If a particular person or thing is necessary for performance, the death or incapacity of the person, or the destruction of the thing, will excuse performance. Restatement (Second) §262 (death or incapacity of person); Restatement (Second) §263 (destruction of thing); UCC §2-613 (casualty to identified goods). See, e.g., CNA International Reinsurance Co. v. Phoenix, 678 So. 2d 378 (Fla. Dist. Ct. App. 1996) (whether or not drug usage contributed to death of actor River Phoenix, rule that death constitutes excusing impossibility of personal service contract would be applied); Hilton Oil Transport v. Oil Transport Co., 659 So. 2d 1141 (Fla. Dist. Ct. App. 1995) (tug charter contract would not be discharged by seizure of both tug and charterer's barge in a

commercial dispute, but would be discharged by subsequent destruction of barge during storm).

6. *Role of foreseeability.* What part should the element of "foreseeability" play in the court's application of the doctrines of frustration or impracticability, as reflected in either the common law or the Uniform Commercial Code? Some courts have tended to require a showing that the event complained of was at least unforeseen — perhaps even unforeseeable — at the time the parties made their contract. Reflecting the traditional preference for self-protection over paternalism (it should be recalled that the parties seeking excuse in these cases tend to be significant commercial enterprises, not consumers or "Mom and Pop" stores), some courts have felt that any party who can foresee an adverse event has the burden of contracting for protection against it. See, e.g., Waldinger Corp. v. CRS Group Engineers, Inc., 775 F.2d 781 (7th Cir. 1985) (in absence of provision otherwise, party assumed to bear burden of any risk foreseeable at time of contracting). Most courts, however, have held that relief under the doctrines of impracticability or frustration of purpose should not be denied simply because the event may have been foreseeable. As one court explained:

> Foreseeability or even recognition of a risk does not necessarily prove its allocation. Parties to a contract are not always able to provide for all the possibilities of which they are aware, sometimes because they cannot agree, often simply because they are too busy. Moreover, that some abnormal risk was contemplated is probative but does not necessarily establish an allocation of the risk of the contingency which actually occurs.

Transatlantic Financing Corp. v. United States, 363 F.2d 312, 318 (D.C. Cir. 1966). Accord Specialty Tires of America v. CIT Group/Equipment Financing, Inc., 82 F. Supp. 2d 434 (W.D. Pa. 2000) (quoting the *Transatlantic Financing Corp.* case); see also Comment *c* to Restatement (Second) §261 (other factors may explain failure to expressly contract against foreseeable risk). The UCC does not in §2-615 expressly impose any "unforeseeability" requirement, although Comment 1 to §2-615 does refer to "unforeseen supervening events."

The commentators agree that foreseeability of an event should not prevent relief. Professor Farnsworth, for example, has argued that "the principle of foreseeability has no merit as a general rule and should be discarded." E. Allan Farnsworth, Disputes over Omission in Contracts, 68 Colum. L. Rev. 860, 887 (1968). See also Sheldon W. Halpern, Application of the Doctrine of Commercial Impracticability: Searching for "The Wisdom of Solomon," 135 U. Pa. L. Rev. 1123, 1140-1154 (1987); Stephen G. York, Re: The Impracticability Doctrine of the U.C.C., 29 Duq. L. Rev. 221, 229-235 (1991).

7. *Economic analysis of impracticability.* In an important article applying principles of economic analysis to the doctrines of impracticability and frustration of purpose, Professors Posner and Rosenfeld argued that the doctrines should be applied to assign the risk of the event to the "superior risk bearer." When the contract specifically allocates the risk to a party, that party is the superior risk bearer. In the absence of a contractual

provision, the risk should be assigned to the party who is in the best position to prevent the event from occurring, or if prevention is not possible, to minimize its consequences at the lowest cost, typically by purchasing insurance. Richard A. Posner & Andrew M. Rosenfeld, Impossibility and Related Doctrines in Contract Law: An Economic Analysis, 6 J. Legal Stud. 83 (1977). Judge Posner applied this approach in Northern Indiana Public Service Co. v. Carbon County Coal Co., 799 F.2d 265 (7th Cir. 1986), to deny relief to a power company that sought to avoid a fixed-price contract for the purchase of coal due to escalating market prices. He held that a fixed-price contract is "an explicit assignment of the risk of market price increases to the seller and the risk of market price decreases to the buyer." Id. at 278. Judge Posner contrasted the case before him with ones involving the destruction of crops:

> Suppose a grower agrees before the growing season to sell his crop to a grain elevator, and the crop is destroyed by blight and the grain elevator sues. Discharge is ordinarily allowed in such cases. The grower has every incentive to avoid the blight; so if it occurs, it probably could not have been prevented; and the grain elevator, which buys from a variety of growers not all of whom will be hit by blight in the same growing season, is in the better position to buffer the risk of blight than the grower is.

Id. Do you agree with this approach? Why? How would it apply to *Karl Wendt Farm Equipment*? For criticism of Judge Posner's opinion in the *Northern Indiana Public Service* case, see Susan E. Wuorinen, Case Comment, Northern Indiana Public Service Co. v. Carbon County Coal Company: Risk Assumption in Claims of Impossibility, Impracticability, and Frustration of Purpose, 50 Ohio St. L.J. 163 (1989) (arguing for judicial consideration of totality of circumstances). The economic approach to impracticability is also criticized in Robert L. Birmingham, Why Is There *Taylor v. Caldwell*? Three Propositions About Impracticability, 23 U.S.F. L. Rev. 379 (1989).

It might be noted, incidentally, that despite the above-stated assumption by Judge Posner that excuse is (and should be, according to his analysis) "ordinarily allowed" in cases of crop destruction, some courts have been surprisingly stingy with excuse in such cases. E.g., Clark v. Wallace County Cooperative Equity Exchange, 986 P.2d 391 (Kan. Ct. App. 1999) (farmer not excused from contract to sell quantity of corn based on freeze which severely damaged his crop; corn to be delivered under contract was not specified to come from his land). The UCC in Comment 9 to §2-615 suggests that crop failure may be regarded as excusing either under that section or under §2-613 ("Casualty to Identified Goods") where a farmer has contracted to sell "crops to be grown on designated land."

8. *Decision by judge or jury.* The Restatement takes the position that a defense such as mistake, impracticability, or frustration of purpose should be decided by the court as a question of law, rather than being submitted to a jury for a finding of fact, as suggested by dissenting Judge Ryan in *Karl Wendt Farm Equipment*. The Restatement explains that treating the doctrines as a question of law will contribute to "stability and predictability of contractual relations." Restatement (Second) of Contracts, §212, Comment *d*. Do you

think having the courts assess claims of impracticability contributes, rightly or wrongly, to the frequent lack of success for the claimants on the grounds noted above?

Mel Frank Tool & Supply, Inc. v. Di-Chem Co.
Supreme Court of Iowa
580 N.W.2d 802 (1998)

Considered by McGIVERIN, C.J., and HARRIS, LAVORATO, SNELL, and ANDREASEN, JJ.

LAVORATO, Justice.

City authorities informed a lessee, a chemical distributor, that it could no longer use its leased premises to store its hazardous chemicals because of a recently enacted ordinance. The lessee vacated the premises, and the lessor sued for breach of the lease and for damages to the premises. The district court awarded the lessor judgment for unpaid rent and for damages to the premises. The lessee appeals, contending that the district court should have found that the city's actions constituted extraordinary circumstances rendering the performance of the lease impossible. The lessee also contends that language in the lease releases it from liability. In addition, the lessee challenges a district court finding that a real estate agent represented the lessee and prepared the lease on its behalf. We affirm.

I. FACTS.

Di-Chem Company is a chemical distributor. In May 1994, Di-Chem began negotiating with Mel Frank Tool & Supply, Inc. to lease a storage and distribution facility in Council Bluffs, Iowa. Mel Frank's real estate agent handled the negotiations so there were no actual face-to-face negotiations between the parties. However, a day before the lease was executed, Mel Frank's owner, Dennis Frank, talked with Di-Chem representatives who were touring the premises. Frank asked them what Di-Chem was going to be selling and was told chemicals. The agent brought the lease to Frank for his signature.

The lease appears to be an Iowa State Bar Association form. See Iowa State Bar Association Official Form No. 164. The lease was to start June 1, 1994 and end May 31, 1997. The lease limited Di-Chem's use of the premises to "storage and distribution."

Some of the chemicals Di-Chem distributes are considered "hazardous material." There was no testimony that Dennis Frank was aware of this at the time the lease was executed. A Di-Chem representative, who was present during the earlier-mentioned conversation with Dennis Frank, testified that hazardous materials did not come up in the conversation.

The lease contained several provisions that bear on the issues in this appeal. One requires Di-Chem to "make no unlawful use of the premises and . . . to comply with all . . . City Ordinances." There is also a destruction-of-premises provision that allows either party to terminate the lease under certain circumstances.

On July 21, 1995, the city's fire chief and several other city authorities inspected the premises. Following the inspection, the city's fire marshal wrote Di-Chem, stating:

> At the time of the inspection the building was occupied as Hazardous Materials Storage. I have given you a copy of 1994 Uniform Fire Code, which the City has adopted, covering Hazardous Material Storage. As you can see the building does not comply with the Code requirements which creates Health and Life Safety Hazards. The Hazardous Materials must be removed within seven (7) days to eliminate the hazard.

The letter also informed Di-Chem of the following code deficiencies: complete fire sprinkler system, mechanical exhaust system, spill control, and drainage control. Both Frank and Di-Chem representatives testified they understood the letter to mean that if these deficiencies were eliminated, Di-Chem could continue to store hazardous material. There was testimony that the changes in the code occurred after Di-Chem took occupancy of the premises.

On August 2 Di-Chem informed Mel Frank by letter of the city's action and enclosed a copy of the city's July 25 letter to Di-Chem. In its August 2 letter Di-Chem informed Mel Frank of its intention to re-locate "as soon as possible to avoid civil and criminal proceedings at the hands of the city." Di-Chem also stated

> we believe the city has overreacted and probably has no authority to order us to remove our materials from the property. . . . Nevertheless, we are not willing to contest the city's position, and we feel compelled to remove our operation beyond the city limits.

Di-Chem also stated it intended to pay the rental for the month of August and vacate the premises by September 1.

Thereafter Dennis Frank and Di-Chem representatives met with city officials about what it would take to correct the various code deficiencies to allow Di-Chem to continue storing hazardous materials. Di-Chem representatives and Dennis Frank briefly considered bringing the building up to code. There was talk about the possibility of Di-Chem splitting the costs with Mel Frank, but Dennis Frank felt the cost was prohibitive.

On October 23 Di-Chem notified Mel Frank by letter of its intention to vacate the premises by the end of October. The letter in part stated: "The city's position that we cannot legally store all of our inventory at this site prior to extensive alteration of the building makes the structure useless to us as a chemical warehouse." True to its word, Di-Chem vacated the premises.

II. PROCEEDINGS.

Later, Mel Frank sued for breach of the lease and for damages to the property. Di-Chem asserted several affirmative defenses: mutual mistake, illegal contract, failure to mitigate damages, fraud in the inducement, and impossibility.

The parties tried the case to the court. In its ruling the court stated the issue this way:

> The principal issue to be determined is whether the defendant may voluntarily terminate the lease agreement based upon defendant's position that the warehouse could not be used for storing hazardous materials [resulting from] the inspection of various departments of the City of Council Bluffs. The conclusion of this issue must be based upon the intention of the litigating parties as well as the terms and conditions of the written lease agreement.

The court found for Mel Frank. The court found that Mel Frank had "no reason to believe or [know] that chemicals classified as hazardous would be stored in the warehouse." The court relied on the testimony of Norm Wirtala, an officer of Di-Chem:

> Mr. Wirtala testified he would be in a "superior position of knowledge" concerning the items to be stored in the building and that he had a general understanding of fire code requirements for the storage of hazardous materials due to his experience in the business although [neither] he nor his agents claimed to have examined the Council Bluffs' fire codes as they may have related to hazardous materials and building specifications for storage of hazardous materials.

With this the court concluded that there was

> clear and conclusive [evidence] that the plaintiff made no representations to the defendant that the warehouse was suitable for any specific purpose, nor were any discussions or representations made concerning the character of the products to be stored by the defendant. Consequently, this Court concludes the lease was breached by the defendants for vacating the premises and failing to pay the balance of the lease term as required by its terms and conditions and the defendants owe the sum of $55,913.77 for rent [and $2,357.00 for damage to the property].

III. SCOPE OF REVIEW.

The action here was one at law. Our review is therefore for correction of errors. Iowa R. App. P. 4. The district court's findings of fact have the force of a special jury verdict and are binding if supported by substantial evidence. See Iowa R. App. P. 14(f)(1). Evidence is substantial if a reasonable mind could find it adequate to reach the same finding. Pierce v. Farm Bureau Mut. Ins. Co., 548 N.W.2d 551, 553 (Iowa 1996). We are not, however, bound by the district court's application of legal principles or the court's conclusions of law. Hagan v. Val-Hi, Inc., 484 N.W.2d 173, 175 (Iowa 1992).

IV. IMPOSSIBILITY OF PERFORMANCE.

A. THE LAW.

The introduction to the Restatement (Second) of Contracts covers impossibility of performance but with a different title: impracticability of performance and frustration of purpose. See Restatement (Second) of Contracts ch. 11, at 309 (1981) [hereinafter Restatement]. According to the Restatement,

[c]ontract liability is strict liability. . . . The obligor is therefore liable in damages for breach of contract even if he is without fault and even if circumstances have made the contract more burdensome or less desirable than he had anticipated. . . . The obligor who does not wish to undertake so extensive an obligation may contract for a lesser one by using one of a variety of common clauses: . . . he may reserve a right to cancel the contract. . . . The extent of his obligation then depends on the application of the rules of interpretation. . . .

Id.

Even though the obligor has not restricted his or her obligation by agreement, a court may still grant relief: "An extraordinary circumstance may make performance so vitally different from what was reasonably to be expected as to alter the essential nature of that performance." Id. In these circumstances, "the court must determine whether justice requires a departure from the general rule that the obligor bear the risk that the contract may become more burdensome or less desirable." Id. at 310. Whether extraordinary circumstances exist justifying discharge is a question of law for the court. Id.

The Restatement recognizes three distinct grounds for the discharge of the obligor's contractual duty:

First, the obligor may claim that some circumstance has made his own performance impracticable. . . . Second, the obligor may claim that some circumstance has so destroyed the value to him of the other party's performance as to frustrate his own purpose in making the contract. . . . Third, the obligor may claim that he will not receive the agreed exchange for the obligee's duty to render that agreed exchange, on the ground of either impracticability or frustration.

Id.

The rationale behind the doctrines of impracticability and frustration is whether the nonoccurrence of the circumstance was a basic assumption on which the contract was made. Restatement (Second) of Contracts ch. 11, at 310-311 (1981). The parties need not have been conscious of alternatives for them to have had a "basic assumption." Restatement (Second) of Contracts ch. 11, at 311 (1981). The Restatement gives an example: Where an artist contracts to paint a painting and dies, the artist's death is an "event the nonoccurrence of which was a basic assumption on which the contract was made, even though the parties never consciously addressed themselves to that possibility." Id.

Under the Restatement's rationale,

the obligor is relieved of his duty because the contract, having been made on a different "basic assumption," is regarded as not covering the case that has arisen. It is an omitted case, falling within a "gap" in the contract. Ordinarily, the just way to deal with the omitted case is to hold that the obligor's duty is discharged, in the case of changed circumstances, or has never arisen, in the case of existing circumstances, and to shift the risk to the obligee.

Id.

B. DISCHARGE BY SUPERVENING FRUSTRATION.

For reasons that follow, we think the facts of this case fall within the parameters of section 265 of the Restatement. Section 265 provides:

> Where, after a contract is made, a party's principal purpose is substantially frustrated without his fault by the occurrence of an event the nonoccurrence of which was a basic assumption on which the contract was made, his remaining duties to render performance are discharged, *unless the language or the circumstances indicate the contrary.*

(Emphasis added.) . . .

The rule deals with the problem that arises when a change in circumstances makes one party's performance virtually worthless to the other, frustrating the purpose in making the contract. Id. §265 cmt. a, at 335. The obligor's contractual obligation is discharged only if three conditions are met:

> First, the purpose that is frustrated must have been a principal purpose of that party in making the contract. It is not enough that he had in mind some specific object without which he would not have made the contract. The object must be so completely the basis of the contract that, as both parties understand, without it the transaction would make little sense. *Second, the frustration must be substantial. It is not enough that the transaction has become less profitable for the affected party or even that he will sustain a loss. The frustration must be so severe that it is not fairly to be regarded as within the risks that he assumed under the contract.* Third, the non-occurrence of the frustrating event must have been a basic assumption on which the contract was made. . . . The foreseeability of the event is . . . a factor in that determination, but the mere fact that the event was foreseeable does not compel the conclusion that its non-occurrence was not such a basic assumption.

Id. (emphasis added).

Under this Restatement section, the following pertinent illustration appears:

> A leases a gasoline station to B. A change in traffic regulations so reduces B's business that he is unable to operate the station except at a substantial loss. B refuses to make further payments of rent. If B can still operate the station, even though at such a loss, his principal purpose of operating a gasoline station is not substantially frustrated. B's duty to pay rent is not discharged, and B is liable to A for breach of contract. The result would be the same if substantial loss were caused instead by a government regulation rationing gasoline or a termination of the franchise under which B obtained gasoline.

Id. §265 cmt. a, illus. 6, at 336.

Iowa case law is in accord with Restatement section 265. See Conklin v. Silver, 187 Iowa 819, 822-23, 174 N.W. 573, 574 (1919). The facts in *Conklin* parallel those in illustration 6 set out above.

In *Conklin,* the lease provided that the lessees were "to only use the premises for iron, metal, and rag business." Id. at 820, 174 N.W. at 573. The lease also prohibited the lessees from "engaging in or permitting any unlawful business on the premises, nor to permit the premises to be occupied for any business deemed extra hazardous on account of fire." Id.

About a month into the lease, the Iowa legislature passed a statute declaring as a nuisance the storage of rags "within the fire limits of any city, unless it be in a building of fireproof construction." Id. at 821, 174 N.W. at 573. The statute applied to the lessees because the premises were within the fire limits of the city and were not of fireproof construction. Id. For this reason, the lessees claimed the statute made its business unlawful, exposed them to criminal prosecution, and deprived them of any substantial or beneficial use of the property thereby releasing them from further obligation to pay rent. Id.

This court rejected the lessees' contention and affirmed a directed verdict in favor of the plaintiff-lessor for the unpaid rent. There was evidence that the lessee also dealt in junk metal. For this reason the court concluded:

> Altogether, we are satisfied that, while the operation of the statute mentioned served to narrow or restrict, to some extent, the scope of the business of the lessees, we think the evidence is insufficient to sustain a finding that it deprives them of the beneficial use of the leased property; and, as the defense is an affirmative one, the burden of establishing which is upon the party pleading it, the trial court did not err in refusing to submit it to the verdict of the jury.

Id. at 822, 174 N.W. at 574. The court continued:

> The right to buy, sell, store, and ship junk metals of all kinds, not only in the building but upon the entire lot, is not, in any sense, a mere incident of the rag business, and that a loss of the privilege of using the building for the handling of rags does not deprive the lessees of the beneficial enjoyment of the property for the other specified uses. It may possibly render the use less valuable or less profitable, but there is no rule or principle of law which makes that fact a matter of defense or of counterclaim in an action upon the lease.

187 Iowa at 822-23, 174 N.W. at 574.

The Restatement and *Conklin* represent the prevailing view:

> The parties to a lease may lawfully agree or stipulate that if by reason of a subsequent prohibitory or restrictive statute, ordinance, or administrative ruling, the tenant is prevented from legally using the premises for the purpose for which it was contemplated, the tenant may surrender or terminate the lease for which it was contemplated and be relieved from further liability for rent. In the absence of such a provision for termination, however, there is some uncertainty as to the effect of subsequent legal prohibition or restriction on the use of the premises. *It may generally be said that in the absence of any such stipulation, a valid police regulation which forbids the use of rented property for certain purposes, but leaves the tenant free to devote the property to other legal uses not forbidden or restricted by the terms of the lease, does not invalidate the lease or affect the rights and liabilities of the parties to the lease. And, even though the lease by its terms restricts the tenant's use of the premises to certain specified purposes, but not to a single purpose, the prevailing view is that the subsequent enactment of the legislation prohibiting the use of the premises for one, or less than all, of the several purposes specified does not invalidate the lease or justify the tenant in abandoning the property, even though the legislation may render its use less valuable. If there is a serviceable use for which the property is still available consistent with the limitations of the demise, the tenant is not in a position to assert that it is totally deprived of the benefit of the tenancy.*

49 Am. Jur. 2d Landlord & Tenant §531, at 442-43 (1995) (emphasis added).

Based on the foregoing authorities, we reach the following conclusions. A subsequent governmental regulation like a statute or ordinance may prohibit a tenant from legally using the premises for its originally intended purpose. In these circumstances, the tenant's purpose is substantially frustrated thereby relieving the tenant from any further obligation to pay rent. The tenant is not relieved from the obligation to pay rent if there is a serviceable use still available consistent with the use provision in the lease. The fact that the use is less valuable or less profitable or even unprofitable does not mean the tenant's use has been substantially frustrated.

C. THE MERITS.

It is clear from the pleadings and testimony that Di-Chem was asserting a defense of frustration of purpose. Di-Chem had the burden of persuasion to prove that defense. See *Conklin*, 187 Iowa at 822, 174 N.W. at 574. The district court's decision in favor of Mel Frank is a determination that Di-Chem did not carry its burden on this defense.

Di-Chem produced no evidence that *all* of its inventory of chemicals consisted of hazardous material. In fact, its own correspondence to Mel Frank indicates otherwise. For example, Di-Chem's October 23 letter to Mel Frank stated: "The city's position that we cannot legally store *all* of our inventory at this site prior to extensive alteration of the building makes the structure useless to us as a chemical warehouse." (Emphasis added.) A reasonable inference from this statement is that not all of Di-Chem's inventory consisted of hazardous material.

Testimony from one of Di-Chem's representatives corroborates this inference:

> Q. Were you involved at all in the discussions with the City of Council Bluffs relative to the various code deficiencies that existed at the building? A. My involvement was that the city had pointed out that there was some deficiencies with the building and asked us to remove *what* chemicals they found objective [sic; objectionable?].

(Emphasis added.) Another Di-Chem representative testified that Di-Chem's product line included industrial chemicals and *food additives*. Presumably, food additives are not hazardous materials.

Given the posture of this appeal, Di-Chem has to establish as a matter of law that its principal purpose for leasing the facility — storing and distributing chemicals — was substantially frustrated by the city's actions. Di-Chem presented no evidence as to the nature of its inventory and what percentage of the inventory consisted of hazardous chemicals. The company also failed to show what its lost profits, if any, would be without the hazardous chemicals. Thus, there is no evidence from which the district court could have found the city's actions substantially frustrated Di-Chem's principal purpose of storing and distributing chemicals. Put another way, there is insufficient evidence that the city's action deprived Di-Chem of the beneficial enjoyment of the property for other uses, i.e., storing and distributing nonhazardous chemicals.

Simply put, Di-Chem failed to establish its affirmative defense of what it has termed impossibility. We must therefore affirm the district court's decision as to this issue.

V. LEASE LANGUAGE.

Di-Chem also relies on language in the lease which it claims releases it from further obligation to pay rent. The language is found in clause 13 of the lease, which is entitled "Fire and Casualty, Partial Destruction of Premises," and provides:

(a) In the event of a partial destruction or damage of the leased premises, which is a business interference, that is, which prevents the conducting of a normal business operation and which damage is reasonably repairable within sixty (60) days after its occurrence, this lease shall not terminate but the rent for the leased premises shall abate during the time of such business interference. In the event of partial destruction, Landlord shall repair such damages within 60 days of its occurrence unless prevented from so doing by acts of God, the elements . . . or other causes beyond Landlord's reasonable control.

(b) **Zoning.** Should the zoning ordinance of the city . . . make it impossible for Landlord, using diligent and timely effort to obtain necessary permits and to repair and/or rebuild so that Tenant is not able to conduct its business on these premises, then such partial destruction shall be treated as a total destruction as in the next paragraph provided.

(c) **Total Destruction of Business Use.** In the event of a destruction or damage of the leased premises . . . so that Tenant is not able to conduct its business on the premises or the then current legal use for which the premises are being used and which damages cannot be repaired within sixty (60) days this lease may be terminated at the option of either the Landlord or Tenant. Such termination in such event shall be effected by written notice of one party to the other, within twenty (20) days after such destruction. Tenant shall surrender possession within ten (10) days after such notice issues, and each party shall be released from all future obligations hereunder. . . .

Di-Chem contends that because it was not able to store and distribute the hazardous chemicals, it was "not able to conduct its business on the premises," as specified in clause 13(b). Di-Chem concludes, therefore, that a "total destruction of business use" occurred in accordance with clause 13(c) and for that reason each party was released from all future obligations under the lease.

There is not even a hint of recognition of clause 13 in the district court's ruling. The reason is obvious: clause 13 simply does not apply to the facts of this case. Clause 13 must be read in its entirety and construed in context.

As the title in clause 13 suggests, the clause's language covers the situation where there has been a temporary interruption of the tenant's business because of a partial destruction of the premises. In these circumstances, the lease gives the landlord a period of time to repair or rebuild. During this period the tenant's rent abates but the lease continues in force.

Clause 13 also covers the situation where the landlord cannot rebuild or repair the premises because of some zoning prohibition. A common example involves a nonconforming use. Typically, zoning ordinances prohibit an owner from rebuilding if, for example, fifty percent of the building has been destroyed. In these circumstances, the tenant cannot legally continue in business on the premises and for this reason the lease considers the tenant's business use has been totally destroyed. In this situation, both the landlord and the tenant have the option to terminate the lease with no further obligation on either's part.

One cannot reasonably interpret clause 13 to cover the situation where a subsequent governmental regulation prohibits the use of the premises for one of several purposes specified in the lease. The district court was correct in ignoring clause 13.

VI. DISTRICT COURT FINDING THAT REAL ESTATE AGENT REPRESENTED DI-CHEM.

We agree with Di-Chem that the district court erroneously found that the real estate agent represented Di-Chem and prepared the lease on its behalf. There is no evidence to support such a finding; in fact, the evidence is the other way. Nevertheless, we find the error harmless, because Di-Chem has not established any ambiguity in the terms of the lease that affect the outcome of this case. Thus, there was simply nothing to construe against Mel Frank. See Iowa Fuel & Minerals, Inc. v. Board of Regents, 471 N.W.2d 859, 862-63 (Iowa 1991) (holding that ambiguities in a contract are construed against the drafter).

VII. DISPOSITION.

In sum, we conclude Di-Chem has failed to establish—as a matter of law—that it is entitled to relief via its impossibility defense or the terms of the lease. The district court's erroneous finding that the real estate agent represented Di-Chem was harmless. We affirm.

AFFIRMED.

Notes and Questions

1. *Governmental regulation as basis for excuse.* Although the lessee in *Mel Frank* did not succeed, the courts have been much more willing to grant relief when the event on which the claim of impracticability or frustration rests is some form of supervening governmental action rather than cases in which the event is war, natural disaster, or market change. Indeed, the UCC in §2-615 makes specific mention of "compliance in good faith with any applicable foreign or domestic governmental regulation or order" as a basis for relief. See also Restatement (Second) of Contracts §264 (recognizing compliance with foreign or domestic governmental order as a basis for excuse under the doctrine of impracticability). Examples include Harriscom Svenska, AB v. Harris Corp., 3 F.3d 576 (2d Cir. 1993) (seller of radio equipment excused on grounds of impracticability after government regulations on transfer of military equipment to Iran led to compromise with U.S. government that required discontinuation of sales to plaintiff distributor; not necessary that the law indisputably required or prohibited conduct, as long as party seeking relief acted in good faith compliance with government's clear determination to prohibit the sales); M.J. Paquet, Inc. v. N.J. DOT, 794 A.2d 141 (N.J. 2002) (contract excused for impracticability

because revised OSHA regulations governing refurbishment of bridges painted with lead-based paint would have resulted in substantial, unanticipated increase in cost of performance).

Despite a receptiveness to claims of excuse where performance is prevented by supervening governmental action, courts will still impose stringent limits on such relief in that category of frustration cases as well as any other, as demonstrated by the *Mel Frank* decision. Those limits include the requirement that frustration be quite substantial. The *Mel Frank* court stated that the performance must be rendered "virtually worthless" and other courts have similarly stated that the principal purpose of the contract must be substantially undermined. See, e.g., Wheelabrator Environmental Systems v. Galante, 136 F. Supp. 2d 21 (D. Conn. 2001) (contract for "waste-to-energy resource recovery" was made less profitable by court decision invalidating mandatory municipal waste disposal ordinances but not excused because principal purpose was not "utterly defeated"). Additionally, courts may also deny relief on the basis of frustration if the supervening event was foreseeable and the complaining party did not guard against the occurrence or otherwise assumed the risk. See City of Starkville v. 4-County Electric Power Ass'n., 819 So. 2d 1216 (Miss. 2002) (frustration excuse not available because possible change in eminent domain laws that rendered contract less profitable was foreseeable at the time contract was made).

2. *Relief under the UCC.* As noted in the introduction to this section of Chapter 8, UCC §2-615 is broad enough to encompass impracticability as well as frustration. The Code section expressly addresses excuse of performance by a seller on the ground of impracticability but does not mention relief to a buyer. Nonetheless, the courts have been willing to grant relief to buyers as well as sellers. See Comment 9 to §2-615, suggesting the section could properly be applied to buyers in appropriate circumstances. See Power Engineering & Manufacturing, Ltd. v. Krug Int'l, 501 N.W.2d 490 (Iowa 1993) (although Code section expressly mentions only sellers, impracticability defense is equally available to buyers; however, inability of buyer to make planned shipments to Iraq did not establish impracticability).

3. *Force majeure clauses.* The lessee in *Mel Frank* also sought to escape the contract based on a portion of the contract which addressed the possibilities of partial or total destruction of the leased facility or a change in zoning law. As one might expect, such "force majeure" clauses are extremely common, particularly where the contract at issue has been drafted by the "performing" (as opposed to the "paying") party. They typically provide for excuse where performance is prevented or delayed by circumstances "beyond the control" of the party seeking excuse. Besides governmental regulation, force majeure clauses are likely to enumerate other particular types of excusing events, such as natural events (windstorm, fire, flood, etc.—often called "acts of God"), prevention by outside forces (war, riot, civil commotion, etc.), and strikes and labor disputes. (In an earlier era of stormier labor relations, such clauses were often dubbed "strike clauses," labor disputes being particularly likely to disrupt contract performance.) To a large extent, force majeure clauses merely track ground now covered by UCC §2-615 and corresponding provisions of the Restatement. (See, e.g., Comment 5 to UCC §2-207.) They may attempt to go further, however, to provide an excuse where the law would

not do so. Cases and commentators have concluded that this is permissible under the Code. R&B Falcon Drilling Co. v. American Exploration Co., 154 F. Supp. 2d 969 (S.D. Tex. 2000); William D. Hawkland, The Energy Crisis and Section 2-615 of the Uniform Commercial Code, 79 Com. L.J. 75 (1974). The law generally does not favor such "exculpatory" clauses, however, particularly as these are apt to become sweeping generalizations expressed in boilerplate provisions. Not only are such clauses likely to be subjected to application of the maxim *contra proferentem*, they also may be tested against the concepts of good faith and unconscionability in the provisions of UCC §§1-102(3), 1-203, and 2-302. See Eastern Air Lines, Inc. v. McDonnell Douglas Corp., 532 F.2d 957, 991 n. 96 (5th Cir. 1976). Do you agree with the court's interpretation of the force majeure clause in the *Mel Frank* opinion?

4. *Nature of relief.* In our earlier study of the rule permitting avoidance for mistake, we noted that the normal remedy is rescission of the contract, along with restitution of any benefits conferred. Impossibility, impracticability, and frustration of purpose have similarly been viewed as grounds on which a still-executory duty of performance might be excused, but not as a basis for reformation or other remedies (such as compensation for reliance). Rather than deciding the issue simply as one of excuse versus no excuse, should a court have the power to go further and actually readjust the parties' contract so that the performance obligation of each will continue, but on a revised basis, taking into account the changes in circumstance that adversely affected performance under the initial agreement? In Aluminum Co. of America v. Essex Group, Inc., 499 F. Supp. 53 (W.D. Pa. 1980), the court did just that, granting "reformation" of a long-term contract for the supply of aluminum processing services to take into account cost increases not adequately reflected in the price-increase formula the parties had initially negotiated. Other courts, however, uniformly rejected the *Alcoa* approach. Paula Walter, Commercial Impracticability in Contracts, 61 St. John's L. Rev. 225, 249-259 (1987). Indeed, the *Alcoa* decision itself is no longer binding precedent since the district court opinion was vacated as part of a settlement of that case. John D. Wladis, Impracticability as Risk Allocation: The Effect of Changed Circumstances Upon Contract Obligations for the Sale of Goods, 22 Ga. L. Rev. 503, 586 n.333 (1988).

PROBLEM 8-1

You are an attorney in Garrett's Landing, a small city in one of the southern states. You have just been consulted by Arthur Barlow, proprietor of a florist shop in your city, who tells you the following story:

"Several years ago I went to work for Sam and Martha Stewart as a clerk in their florist shop, over by Good Samaritan Hospital, on Mackenzie Street. I'd only been out of high school a few years, had a few jobs, none of which seemed likely to go anywhere much; this seemed like a chance to learn a business from the inside, and from people who were getting on in years and might be willing to take me in as a partner eventually. Well, the business did well enough, and they paid me a decent salary, so I stayed on, and just when I was getting up enough nerve to ask whether they might be willing to take me in as a partner,

Martha died very unexpectedly. Naturally, this threw Sam pretty badly, and for a while there I pretty much ran the business single-handed.

"When Sam got on his feet again I was about to make him an offer when he surprised me by making *me* one. He said he'd decided to retire, said he thought he might sell his house, go and live with his daughter over in Marshallsburg, and did I want to buy the business? I said I sure did, if the price was right. We talked it over, and he said there were eight years to go on his lease, and he was sure Mrs. Duval, the owner of the building, would agree to his assigning the lease to me, and that he'd sell me the business for $100,000 — that is, $80,000 for the fixtures, office equipment, and inventory and $20,000 for good will. That struck me as a real good price, knowing what I did about the earnings of the shop. I said the figure was all right with me, provided I could pay him $20,000 now and $20,000 a year over the next four years; that way I could pay him out of the earnings of the business. He said that was acceptable to him, and he showed me the bill of sale that Jonah Cartwright's lawyer had drawn up nearly 30 years ago when old Cartwright sold the business to Sam. (It was called Good Samaritan Florist Shop then, just like it is now.) I read it through and said it sounded okay to me and told Sam to draw up one just like it, and that would be our contract. I raised the $20,000 by borrowing from my uncle, and I took over the shop.

"Well, all that happened last March, and since then I've been running the shop myself, with one helper. So far it's gone pretty good. This week, though, I got a real shock. The Board of Trustees of Good Samaritan Hospital announced — maybe you saw the story in the paper? — that the hospital was merging with Mercy Hospital, over on the other side of town, that a new wing would be built on Mercy, and the old Good Samaritan Building would be torn down. I don't have to tell you, I guess, what a bad piece of news that is for me. My shop is in an old part of town, and the best part of my business is from people who come to visit sick folks at the hospital; both the new shopping centers in town have florists, and I can't compete with them for the suburban trade. Without the hospital, I'm dead. It's been there for 80 years; I never dreamed it wouldn't be there forever. What really gravels me, though, is old Sam Stewart. I can see now why he made me such a good price for the business. I'm sure he knew the hospital was planning to close. A decision like that, it isn't made overnight, they must have been considering it as long ago as last March. And Sam's cousin, Maureen Leonard, she's a doctor at Good Samaritan, and she's on the governing board there. Sam saw the handwriting on the wall and unloaded on me, I know he did. And what I want to know is, what can I do about it?"

Before attempting to answer his question, you ask Barlow to show you the "Bill of Sale," signed by Stewart and Barlow as Seller and Buyer. It recites that Stewart is selling to Barlow "all the assets, stock in trade, fixtures, and good will of the business presently operated by Seller as 'Good Samaritan Flower Shop,' on Mackenzie Street, in Garrett's Landing." It also contains the following language: "Seller represents and warrants that he is the owner of, and has full power to convey, the property which is the subject of this Bill of Sale. Seller makes no other representations or warranties whatever with respect to this property, and Buyer's acceptance of this Bill of Sale so acknowledges." The document also contains a promise by Barlow to pay

Stewart $20,000 on delivery and $20,000 a year for the next four years; the promise is not qualified or conditioned by any reference to the earnings of the business.

What causes of action could Mr. Barlow assert to rescind the agreement with Mr. Stewart? How would you evaluate the likelihood of success of these causes of action?

PROBLEM 8-2

Suppose Mr. Barlow authorizes you to file a lawsuit against Sam Stewart seeking rescission of the contract of sale. Draft a complaint in this action. In doing so, assume that the Federal Rules of Civil Procedure govern.

C. MODIFICATION

We have earlier studied the doctrine of consideration (as a basis for enforcement of a promise), the implied obligation of good faith (both under the UCC and as an element of general contract law), and the concept of duress (as a defense to liability for nonperformance of what would otherwise be an enforceable promise). We have also surveyed a variety of doctrines designed to give relief from the effect of changed circumstances, where those have deprived one of the contracting parties of what may appear to be the benefit fairly to be expected from the originally agreed-to exchange. And we have addressed the statute of frauds, a set of rules requiring writing for enforceability. In this section we will consider a situation in which a number of these doctrines and rules may be brought to bear in deciding the relative rights and duties of the parties: the modification of a preexisting executory contract.

As an introduction, consider the following:

PROBLEM 8-3

You are vice-president and general counsel for Associated Department Stores, Inc., which owns and operates "Schweitzer's," a large department store in your city. Schweitzer's has recently been in the throes of some remodeling, reorganizing, and overall image-upgrading, dropping some lines of goods, adding others, and generally attempting to create a more high-fashion atmosphere in the store. Today you receive a call from Edna Carmody, another Associated executive, who has general responsibility for planning and coordinating the organization and remodeling of the various women's apparel departments. She tells you the following story:

"You probably know that the new women's designer salon on three is scheduled to open at the end of this month; we've had promotions in the papers and on local TV for days about the celebrity fashion show and the charity cocktail party we're throwing for the benefit of the county historical society. Well, virtually everything is done except the laying of the new flooring, which we purposely had left until after the new ceiling tiles and lighting tracks had been installed, and the wallpaper hung, so it wouldn't get the wear of several sets of workmen over it right away. Waller Brothers agreed to do the floor for us — to provide the labor and flooring material and to have the whole job done by next Thursday at the latest. They are the local distributors for EverWare floor tile, which is probably the best product for our needs, and they contracted to install EverWare in the 'Starship' pattern, which we picked to complement the wallpaper and lighting fixtures we had selected.

"Just now I had a call from Jack Waller, who told me that the EverWare Company has notified them that every shipment of EverWare tile from now on — including the lot for our store, which is on its way to the Wallers' now — will be billed to them at a 30 percent increase over the previous prices, due to a settlement EverWare had to make with its employees to prevent a strike, they said. Jack told me that the increase was more than he and Ralph could absorb, and that they had talked it over and agreed that they would have to charge us at least 20 percent more per foot for the Starship tile we ordered. I told him I certainly sympathized with their problem, but I didn't feel they had any right to ask us to agree to a price increase at this point, since for five weeks we had had a firm written contract with them for an agreed price. Jack didn't exactly quarrel with that, but he said he was surely sorry we didn't see things their way, and then he went on to say that these rising costs really had them in a bind, and they thought they'd probably have to lay off some of their help, and it might be pretty difficult to get their work done on schedule under those conditions. Then he said why didn't I think it over for a while, and talk it over with some of the other people here at Schweitzer's; he said he felt sure then I'd see things his way, and that he'd expect me to call him back in a few hours.

"Even if he's telling me the truth about their being hit with a surprise price increase, it seems to me they're way out of line in expecting us to absorb it. Do we have to? And if we say no, what happens if they pull a slowdown on us? Lots of faces are going to be red around here, mine in particular, if all that promotion effort for the new women's shop goes out the window because the redecorating isn't done. I haven't tried yet, of course, but I'm sure we can't get someone else to do the floor on such short notice. Even if we could, no one else stocks the pattern we need to do the job right; the Wallers are exclusive distributors for EverWare in this town. Do they have us over a barrel?"

Obviously, before attempting to advise Ms. Carmody how she might proceed in this situation, you will want to consider the effect of the original agreement with Waller Brothers. You know that there is indeed a "firm written contract . . . for an agreed price" between Associated Department Stores, Inc., and Waller Brothers, because at your direction all agreements with contractors for the renovation were made on purchasing order forms used by Associated. You know that this form contains a standard "force majeure" clause, and also that it contains the following language: "This is the entire agreement of the parties, superseding all prior agreements. No additions or modifications to, or any waivers of provisions contained in, this agreement shall be binding unless in writing and signed by both parties."

Before deciding on the course of action Associated should pursue, you will need to consider the following questions (and perhaps others as well): (1) Can Waller Brothers rely on changes in circumstance occurring since the agreement was made to justify nonperformance on its part? (2) If Associated should (for whatever combination of legal and/or practical reasons) agree to pay Waller Brothers a higher price for the tile work, could it later refuse to pay the amount of the increase, on the ground that its agreement to that increase either was void for lack of consideration, or was entered into as a product of bad faith or duress on Waller Brothers' part? (3) Even if an agreement to pay the increased price would otherwise be enforceable, if you can avoid putting it in writing, can Associated later refuse to pay on the basis of the contractual language quoted above?

On the basis of what we have seen so far, and the materials that follow, how would you answer those questions? Based on your answers, how would you advise Ms. Carmody?

Alaska Packers' Association v. Domenico
United States Court of Appeals
117 F. 99 (9th Cir. 1902)

Ross, Circuit Judge. The libel in this case was based upon a contract alleged to have been entered into between the libelants and the appellant corporation on the 22d day of May, 1900, at Pyramid Harbor, Alaska, by which it is claimed the appellant promised to pay each of the libelants, among other things, the sum of $100 for services rendered and to be rendered. In its answer the respondent denied the execution, on its part, of the contract sued upon, averred that it was without consideration, and for a third defense alleged that the work performed by the libelants for it was performed under other and different contracts than that sued on, and that, prior to the filing of the libel, each of the libelants was paid by the respondent the full amount due him thereunder, in consideration of which each of them executed a full release of all his claims and demands against the respondent.

The evidence shows without conflict that on March 26, 1900, at the city and county of San Francisco, the libelants entered into a written contract with the appellant, whereby they agreed to go from San Francisco to Pyramid Harbor, Alaska, and return, on board such vessel as might be designated by the appellant, and to work for the appellant during the fishing season of 1900, at Pyramid Harbor, as sailors and fishermen, agreeing to do "regular ship's duty, both up and down, discharging and loading; and to do any other work whatsoever when requested to do so by the captain or agent of the Alaska Packers' Association." By the terms of this agreement, the appellant was to pay each of the libelants $50 for the season, and two cents for each red salmon in the catching of which he took part.

On the 15th day of April, 1900, 21 of the libelants signed shipping articles by which they shipped as seamen on the Two Brothers, a vessel chartered by the appellant for the voyage between San Francisco and Pyramid Harbor, and also bound themselves to perform the same work for the appellant provided for by the previous contract of March 26th; the appellant agreeing to pay them therefor the sum of $60 for the season, and two cents each for each red salmon in the catching of which they should respectively take part. Under these contracts, the libelants sailed on board the Two Brothers for Pyramid Harbor, where the appellant had about $150,000 invested in a salmon cannery. The libelants arrived there early in April of the year mentioned, and began to unload the vessel and fit up the cannery. A few days thereafter, to wit, May 19th, they stopped work in a body, and demanded of the company's superintendent there in charge $100 for services in operating the vessel to and from Pyramid Harbor, instead of the sums stipulated for in and by the contracts; stating that unless they were paid this additional wage they would stop work entirely, and return to San Francisco. The evidence showed, and the court below found, that it was impossible for the appellant to get other men to take the places of the libelants, the place being remote, the season short and just opening; so that, after endeavoring for several days without success to induce the libelants to proceed with their work in accordance with their contracts, the company's superintendent, on the 22d day of May, so far yielded to their demands as to instruct his clerk to copy the contracts executed in San Francisco, including the words "Alaska Packers' Association" at the end, substituting, for the $50 and $60 payments, respectively, of those contracts, the sum of $100, which document, so prepared, was signed by the libelants before a shipping commissioner whom they had requested to be brought from Northeast Point; the superintendent, however, testifying that he at the time told the libelants that he was without authority to enter into any such contract, or to in any way alter the contracts made between them and the company in San Francisco. Upon the return of the libelants to San Francisco at the close of the fishing season, they demanded pay in accordance with the terms of the alleged contract of May 22d, when the company denied its validity, and refused to pay other than as provided for by the contracts of March 26th and April 5th, respectively. Some of the libelants, at least, consulted counsel, and, after receiving his advice, those of them who had signed the shipping articles before the shipping commissioner at San Francisco went before that officer, and received the amount due them thereunder, executing in consideration thereof a release in full, and the others being paid at the office of the company, also receipting in full for their demands.

On the trial in the court below, the libelants undertook to show that the fishing nets provided by the respondent were defective, and that it was on that account that they demanded increased wages. On that point, the evidence was substantially conflicting, and the finding of the court was against the libelants, the court saying:

> The contention of libelants that the nets provided them were rotten and unserviceable is not sustained by the evidence. The defendant's interest required that libelants should be provided with every facility necessary to their success as

fishermen, for on such success depended the profits defendant would be able to realize that season from its packing plant, and the large capital invested therein. In view of this self-evident fact, it is highly improbable that the defendant gave libelants rotten and unserviceable nets with which to fish. It follows from this finding that libelants were not justified in refusing performance of their original contract. [112 Fed. 554.]

The evidence being sharply conflicting in respect to these facts, the conclusions of the court, who heard and saw the witnesses, will not be disturbed. . . .

The real questions in the case as brought here are questions of law, and, in the view that we take of the case, it will be necessary to consider but one of those. Assuming that the appellant's superintendent at Pyramid Harbor was authorized to make the alleged contract of May 22d, and that he executed it on behalf of the appellant, was it supported by a sufficient consideration? From the foregoing statement of the case, it will have been seen that the libelants agreed in writing, for certain stated compensation, to render their services to the appellant in remote waters where the season for conducting fishing operations is extremely short, and in which enterprise the appellant had a large amount of money invested; and, after having entered upon the discharge of their contract, and at a time when it was impossible for the appellant to secure other men in their places, the libelants, without any valid cause, absolutely refused to continue the services they were under contract to perform unless the appellant would consent to pay them more money. Consent to such a demand, under such circumstances, if given, was, in our opinion, without consideration, for the reason that it was based solely upon the libelants' agreement to render the exact services, and none other, that they were already under contract to render. The case shows that they willfully and arbitrarily broke that obligation. As a matter of course, they were liable to the appellant in damages, and it is quite probable, as suggested by the court below in its opinion, that they may have been unable to respond in damages. But we are unable to agree with the conclusions there drawn, from these facts, in these words:

> Under such circumstances, it would be strange, indeed, if the law would not permit the defendant to waive the damages caused by the libelants' breach, and enter into the contract sued upon,—a contract mutually beneficial to all the parties thereto, in that it gave to the libelants reasonable compensation for their labor, and enabled the defendant to employ to advantage the large capital it had invested in its canning and fishing plant.

Certainly, it cannot be justly held, upon the record in this case, that there was any voluntary waiver on the part of the appellant of the breach of the original contract. The company itself knew nothing of such breach until the expedition returned to San Francisco, and the testimony is uncontradicted that its superintendent at Pyramid Harbor, who, it is claimed, made on its behalf the contract sued on, distinctly informed the libelants that he had no power to alter the original or to make a new contract; and it would, of course, follow that, if he had no power to change the original, he would have no authority to waive any rights thereunder. The circumstances of the present case bring it, we think, directly within the sound and just observations of the supreme court of Minnesota in the case of King v. Railway Co., 61 Minn. 482, 63 N.W. 1105:

> No astute reasoning can change the plain fact that the party who refuses to perform, and thereby coerces a promise from the other party to the contract to pay him an increased compensation for doing that which he is legally bound to do, takes an unjustifiable advantage of the necessities of the other party. Surely it would be a travesty on justice to hold that the party so making the promise for extra pay was estopped from asserting that the promise was without consideration. A party cannot lay the foundation of an estoppel by his own wrong, where the promise is simply a repetition of a subsisting legal promise. There can be no consideration for the promise of the other party, and there is no warrant for inferring that the parties have voluntarily rescinded or modified their contract. The promise cannot be legally enforced, although the other party has completed his contract in reliance upon it.

In Lingenfelder v. Brewing Co., 103 Mo. 578, 15 S.W. 844, the court, in holding void a contract by which the owner of a building agreed to pay its architect an additional sum because of his refusal to otherwise proceed with the contract, said:

> It is urged upon us by respondents that this was a new contract. New in what? Jungenfeld was bound by his contract to design and supervise this building. Under the new promise, he was not to do anything more or anything different. What benefit was to accrue to Wainwright? He was to receive the same service from Jungenfeld under the new, that Jungenfeld was bound to tender under the original contract. What loss, trouble, or inconvenience could result to Jungenfeld that he had not already assumed? No amount of metaphysical reasoning can change the plain fact that Jungenfeld took advantage of Wainwright's necessities, and extorted the promise of five per cent, on the refrigerator plant as the condition of his complying with his contract already entered into. Nor had he even the flimsy pretext that Wainwright had violated any of the conditions of the contract on his part. Jungenfeld himself put it upon the simple proposition that "if he, as an architect, put up the brewery, and another company put up the refrigerating machinery, it would be a detriment to the Empire Refrigerating Company," of which Jungenfeld was president. To permit plaintiff to recover under such circumstances would be to offer a premium upon bad faith, and invite men to violate their most sacred contracts that they may profit by their own wrong. That a promise to pay a man for doing that which he is already under contract to do is without consideration is conceded by respondents. The rule has been so long imbedded in the common law and decisions of the highest courts of the various states that nothing but the most cogent reasons ought to shake it. [Citing a long list of authorities.] But it is "carrying coals to Newcastle" to add authorities on a proposition so universally accepted, and so inherently just and right in itself.
> . . . What we hold is that, when a party merely does what he has already obligated himself to do, he cannot demand an additional compensation therefor; and although, by taking advantage of the necessities of his adversary, he obtains a promise for more, the law will regard it as nudum pactum, and will not lend its process to aid in the wrong.

. . . It results from the views above expressed that the judgment must be reversed, and the cause remanded, with directions to the court below to enter judgment for the respondent, with costs. It is so ordered.

Notes and Questions

1. *Identifying the parties*. The terminology of *Alaska Packers'* is apt to be a bit confusing, since the same party — the Packers' Association — is at different places referred to as the "appellant" and the "respondent." The explanation lies in the nature of the case as an admiralty claim, or "libel"; the plaintiffs are referred to as "libelants," and the defendant, responding to the libel, is the "respondent." The defendant/respondent is also the "appellant," because the petitioners prevailed below.

2. *Pre-existing duty rule*. The *Alaska Packers'* decision reflects the fundamental tenet that merely promising to perform an existing obligation will not serve as valid consideration for additional return compensation from the other party. This rule continues to be applied, at least as a starting point, even though courts accept even a small or modest addition to or alteration of performance as enough to satisfy the rule. Compare Aerel, S.R.L. v. PCC Airfoils, L.L.C., 448 F.3d 899 (6th Cir. 2006) (alleged promise to pay additional commissions for services already required by contract would constitute unenforceable, one-sided modification), with Oscar v. Simeonidis, 800 A.2d 271 (N.J. Super. Ct. App. Div. 2002) (even insignificant or slight new consideration in modification of lease agreement, such as paying rent one day in advance, would be valid to support modification). If the plaintiffs in *Alaska Packers'* had by good fortune had a lawyer among their number, could they with his counsel have formulated a wage-increase agreement with their employer that would have satisfied the consideration test applied by the court in the above opinion? How? If so, who would have won the case? Could the defendant's other arguments have been foreseen and forestalled by informed lawyering?

3. *Policing coercive behavior*. In discussing the pre-existing duty rule as a barrier to enforcement of a contract modification, Professor Farnsworth refers to *Alaska Packers'* (along with the *Lingenfelder* case, quoted and discussed in *Alaska Packers'*) as a case where "particularly outrageous threats" were made to coerce a one-sided modifying agreement. E. Allan Farnsworth, Contracts §4.22, at 273 n.15 (4th 2004). In Selmer Co. v. Blakeslee-Midwest Co., 704 F.2d 924, 927 (7th Cir. 1983), Judge Posner offers his own approbation of *Alaska Packers'*:

> It undermines the institution of contract to allow a contract party to use the threat of breach to get the contract modified in his favor not because anything has happened to require modification in the mutual interest of the parties but simply because the other party, unless he knuckles under to the threat, will incur costs for which he will have no adequate legal remedy. If contractual protections are illusory, people will be reluctant to make contracts. Allowing contract modifications to be voided in circumstances such as those in *Alaska Packers' Assn.* assures prospective contract parties that signing a contract is not stepping into a trap, and by thus encouraging people to make contracts promotes the efficient allocation of resources.

The Farnsworth and Posner view of this case is more likely to seem appropriate the more strongly one is persuaded that the plaintiffs there were actually lying about their working conditions. Although the evidence on that point was "sharply conflicting," the trial court found on this issue for the defendants, apparently in large measure because plaintiffs' testimony that the defendant had not provided them with serviceable nets was "highly improbable," the defendant's interest requiring that the plaintiffs be supplied with "every facility necessary to their success as fishermen." Do you agree? To the extent that the pre-existing duty rule serves essentially as a guard against coercive behavior, would it better to police that conduct directly and otherwise to enforce all consensual modifications? For a study suggesting such an approach would be desirable, see Kevin M. Teeven, Consensual Path to Abolition of Preexisting Duty Rule, 34 Val. U. L. Rev. 43 (1999) (advocating enforcement of modifications without requirement of new consideration but subject to policing mechanisms of economic duress, unconscionability, and good faith).

4. *Historical context.* The *Alaska Packers'* courts, as well as the commentators discussed above, discounted the possibility that a rational, profit-seeking enterprise would choose not to replace badly depreciated nets, but a recent examination of the case suggests reasons why that might well have happened. In her article, A Fish Story: Alaska Packers' Association v. Domenico, 2000 Utah L. Rev. 185, Professor Debora L. Threedy reviewed not only the opinions in the *Alaska Packers'* trial and appellate decisions, but also explored the salmon fishing and canning industry at the time of the dispute. Among Professor Threedy's key revelations are the facts that the Pyramid Harbor location was only one of eighteen canneries operated by the Association, the canneries purchased fish caught by local native tribes in addition to the catch of the crew, the Association's crew received lower pay than those at nearby competitors, and that the nets at Pyramid Harbor were in fact partially reused while the other Association canneries purchased new nets each year. Most of her findings supporting the claims of the fishing crew about the substandard nets are capsulated in a critique of the crew's lawyer. Professor Threedy writes:

> Hindsight, of course, has perfect vision, but if Banning [the crew's lawyer] had focused on the cannery's capacity and had been able to establish that the 1900 catch met or exceeded the cannery's capacity, then he would have established a motive for the cannery to limit the fishermen's catch. Similarly, if he had been able to bring out the disparities between Pyramid Harbor and other canneries in cost per case and expenditures for fishing gear, along with the extent to which Pyramid Harbor relied on the local tribes, he could have suggested a motive to cut corners on the nets. Either strategy would have bolstered the credibility of the fishermen who testified that the nets were substandard. Moreover, if Banning had been able to bring out the extent to which local tribal fishermen contributed to the cannery's operation, he would have been able to argue that the cannery could have operated even if the fishermen had refused to work during the season.

Id. at 214. Without reaching a firm conclusion on the issue, Professor Threedy questions whether the Association in fact might have decided to supply defective or inefficient nets even if that meant its workers had to expend much greater effort in the performance of their duties. It is also notable that in 1902, when *Alaska Packers'* was decided, the temper of the times (and of the courts) was generally friendly to capital and management, and hostile to labor and collective bargaining. Does the additional information offered by Professor Threedy suggest only that the facts may have been wrongly determined or do they raise concerns about the legal principles applied by the courts?

5. *Modification of employment contracts. Alaska Packers'* can be examined from more than one perspective. If *Alaska Packers'* is regarded as a "labor" case, that does not mean contract principles could not play their part in resolving the dispute. The prospect of an employee union engaging in a strike to obtain a promise of higher pay played out more recently in Contempo Design v. Chicago & Northeast Illinois Dist. Council of Carpenters, 226 F.3d 535 (7th Cir. 2000). Notwithstanding an applicable "no strike" provision within the current contract, the unionized employees struck at a time when the employer was pursuing a multi-year, multi-million-dollar contract with a major new client, Bank of America, and was facing pressure from an overdue loan. The employer agreed to a pay raise and other benefits but reserved its right to sue the union. Relying heavily on *Alaska Packers'* to develop federal common law, the court's majority held that the modified agreement was unenforceable for lack of consideration and noted that the pre-existing duty rule served to "prevent coercive modifications." Id. at 549-50. The four dissenting judges conceded that the union had the employer "over a barrel" but would have enforced the modified contract because of the view that the union had a good faith, though erroneous, belief that it was not bound by the no strike clause. Id. at 555-57. Should the modified agreement in *Alaska Packers'* have been enforceable if the fishing crew held an honest but erroneous belief that the nets were substandard?

Another, more frequent scenario requiring the courts to review the enforceability of a contract modification occurs within the context of non-unionized at-will employment, as typified by the *Donahue v. Federal Express Corp.* case and the following notes in Chapter 6. Frequently these cases will involve an employer's promises of job security or fair treatment contained in a personnel manual that are deemed to become binding through the unilateral-contract formation process. E.g., Doyle v. Holy Cross Hospital, 708 N.E.2d 1140 (Ill. 1999). If the employer later promulgates a new version of its manual, abrogating those earlier promises, should that revision be viewed as a "one-sided" modification of an existing contract, requiring fresh consideration to be effective? And if so, what could constitute the requisite consideration? Several courts have held that such an attempt by an employer to modify its personnel handbook was ineffective because unsupported by any consideration. E.g., Demasse v. ITT Corp., 984 P.2d 1138 (Ariz. 1999); Brodie v. General Chemical Corp., 934 P.2d 1263 (Wyo. 1997); contra Asmus v. Pacific Bell, 999 P.2d 71 (Cal. 2000) (employer may unilaterally terminate announced policy, if employer makes the change after a reasonable time, on reasonable notice, and without interfering with employees' vested benefits; given those limitations, no additional consideration is required); Bankey v. Storer Broadcasting, 443 N.W.2d 112 (Mich. 1989) (employer may unilaterally replace previous for-cause termination policy with employment at-will; issue is not one of contract formation but of employment policy).

6. *Other exceptions to the pre-existing duty rule.* As discussed in Note 2, courts generally require that a modification be supported by new consideration on both sides, even if very minimal or slight. Court decisions reveal, however, a number of exceptions to the requirement of new consideration. The first exception is that of "unforeseen circumstances." This concept is included in Restatement (Second) §89(a) which states that a promise of modification is

binding if "fair and equitable in view of circumstances not anticipated by the parties when the contract was made." The concept may be applicable even if the unforeseen circumstances would not fully qualify for excuse based on the impracticability doctrine as discussed in Section B of this chapter. See §89, Illustration 1 (when solid rock unexpectedly encountered making removal nine times more expensive, owner's promise to pay increased amount for excavation is binding); see also Roussalis v. Wyoming Medical Center, Inc., 4 P.3d 209 (Wyo. 2001) (modification that increased the size of promised medical building would be enforceable without additional consideration in light of need to resolve unforeseen safety concerns not addressed by original architect plans).

Second, Restatement (Second) §89(c) recognizes "reliance" on a promised modification as another basis for enforcing a modifying agreement despite the absence of fresh consideration. This is one of several Restatement (Second) provisions in which the principle of §90 is given a more focused application in the context of a particular problem. See generally Charles L. Knapp, Reliance in the Revised *Restatement:* The Proliferation of Promissory Estoppel, 81 Colum. L. Rev. 52 (1981). What kind of reliance will serve this purpose? Should it be sufficient to make a modification binding that the party seeking enforcement of the modification has "relied" by performing its duties as promised under the original agreement? Neither the comments nor illustrations to §89 are particularly helpful on this issue. The cited article suggests that in light of the apparent intention of §89 to liberalize the consideration requirement for such modifying agreements, the answer may be that simply to perform as originally promised might constitute such reliance as would satisfy §89(c). It seems possible that the drafters of Restatement (Second) §89 would have really preferred to take the approach of UCC §2-209(1) in largely dismissing the pre-existing duty rule, as discussed in the case and notes which follow, but felt unable to make such a complete break with the common law tradition on this point.

Third, many courts also recognize the concept of "mutual release" as another exception to the pre-existing duty rule. In Schwartzreich v. Bauman-Basch, Inc., 131 N.E. 887 (N.Y. 1921), an employee, originally hired as a coat designer for a fixed period at a stated salary, was promised an increase in pay when he reported to his employer that another firm had offered him a higher salary to come with it. The parties tore up their old contract and replaced it with a new one, providing for the promised increase. The employee was later discharged and sued to recover damages based on the increased salary rate. The New York Court of Appeals held that the new contract could be upheld as being the product of a mutual rescission, followed by a new and valid contract. But as the Restatement (Second) points out, in Comment *b* to §89, such a rationale is "fictitious" when the "rescission" and new contract are simultaneous (as they were in *Schwartzreich*). Despite the legal sleight-of-hand involved in its decision, *Schwartzreich* might nevertheless be justified as a case in which the element of coercion was absent and circumstances had changed unexpectedly (the employee later discovered his services were worth more on the market than he had originally anticipated), and the employee had justifiably relied on the promise of a raise (at least by remaining instead of choosing to breach, and possibly also by increased devotion to his efforts on his employer's behalf).

Kelsey-Hayes Co. v. Galtaco Redlaw Castings Corp.
United States District Court
749 F. Supp. 794 (E.D. Mich 1990)

OPINION AND ORDER

COHN, District Judge.

I.

This is a breach of contract case. Plaintiff, Kelsey-Hayes Company (Kelsey-Hayes), alleges defendant, Galtaco Redlaw Castings Corporation (Galtaco), breached a three-year agreement (the 1987 contract) for the purchase of castings. In addition to the damages allegedly suffered as a result of the breach of the 1987 contract, Kelsey-Hayes seeks a declaratory judgment that it does not have to pay Galtaco price increases to which it agreed in 1989. Kelsey-Hayes asserts the 1989 contract modifications (1989 agreements) containing the price increases (1) were agreed to by Kelsey-Hayes under duress, (2) were unconscionable, (3) were demanded by Galtaco in bad faith and (4) constitute unjust enrichment to Galtaco. Galtaco says in response that Kelsey-Hayes waived its breach of contract claims and, in addition, argues that the defenses Kelsey-Hayes raises regarding the validity of the 1989 agreements have no merit. Galtaco also counterclaims for the monies owed under the 1989 agreements. Also before the Court is Kelsey-Hayes' motion for leave to file a second amended complaint. Fed. R. Civ. P. 15(a).

Galtaco has moved for summary judgment, Fed. R. Civ. P. 56, on Kelsey-Hayes' claims and its counterclaim. For the reasons which follow, Galtaco's motion will be denied. In addition, the Court will grant Kelsey-Hayes' motion for leave to file a second amended complaint.

II.

The following facts as gleaned from the affidavits, deposition testimony and documents in the record are not in dispute.

Kelsey-Hayes makes brake assemblies that it sells to auto manufacturers, including Chrysler and Ford. For several years prior to 1987, Galtaco supplied castings to Kelsey-Hayes which incorporated them into the brake assemblies. In 1987, Galtaco and Kelsey-Hayes signed a three-year "requirements" contract. Under the contract, Galtaco was to be the sole source to Kelsey-Hayes of certain types of castings through April 1990. In return, Galtaco was to charge fixed prices for 1987, and scheduled price reductions for 1988 and 1989, respectively. . . .

A.

By the spring of 1989, Galtaco had been experiencing continued monetary losses for several years. Kelsey-Hayes was aware of Galtaco's financial condition. For the seven months ending in April 1989, Galtaco's foundry operations had losses totalling $2,410,000. As a result, on May 10, 1989, Galtaco's Board of Directors made final a decision to discontinue its foundry operations and cease production of castings. Galtaco recognized that an immediate shut down of its foundry operations would seriously inconvenience its customers, because they would need additional castings before they could cover from other sources. Therefore, Galtaco offered all of its customers, including Kelsey-Hayes, an agreement to keep its foundries operating for "several months" in exchange for price increase of 30 percent effective with shipments of May 15, 1989.

If Galtaco were to have immediately terminated its foundry operations, Kelsey-Hayes concluded that it would not have been able to obtain a sufficient supply of castings from alternative sources for 18-24 weeks. As a result, Kelsey-Hayes determined that declining to accept Galtaco's offer would have the effect of shutting down the assembly plants of two of its major clients, Chrysler and Ford. Kelsey-Hayes was Ford's sole source of certain brake assemblies, and Ford had no significant bank of those parts. Any interruption of the supply of brake assemblies longer than five to ten days would likely have resulted in the halting of Ford production of a vehicle line. On May 12, 1989, Kelsey-Hayes accepted Galtaco's offer to continue supplying castings for a time, at a 30 percent price increase for all castings delivered to all plants. Before entering into the 1989 agreements, Kelsey-Hayes did not reserve any rights under the 1987 contract when it accepted Galtaco's offer.

On June 9, 1989, Galtaco informed Kelsey-Hayes it required an additional 30 percent price increase in order to keep its foundry operations going. By this time, Galtaco's other customers had found alternative sources of castings. The additional price increase was asked for to offset the rising fixed costs Galtaco would continue to incur if it were to remain in operation for Kelsey-Hayes' sole benefit. Since Kelsey-Hayes had not yet found another source for castings, it accepted Galtaco's offer to continue providing castings for an additional 30 percent price increase. Again, Kelsey-Hayes did not reserve any rights under the 1987 contract when it entered into the June 1989 agreement.

B.

Between May 15 and August 30, 1989, Galtaco made 282 shipments to Kelsey-Hayes. Galtaco's foundries closed down after the final shipment to Kelsey-Hayes.

Kelsey-Hayes accepted all of the shipments, and it timely paid for the first 197 deliveries according to the terms of the 1989 agreements. However, Kelsey-Hayes failed to pay Galtaco for 84 of the remaining 85 casting shipments. The price for the 84 shipments for which Kelsey-Hayes has not paid approximates the $2 million price increase to which Kelsey-Hayes agreed under the 1989 agreements.

At no time did Kelsey-Hayes explicitly state that it would sue Galtaco; however, Kelsey-Hayes did strenuously protest Galtaco's actions as a breach of the 1987 contract.

III.

As stated, supra, Kelsey-Hayes' claim is based on several alternative theories of liability. However, in order to dispose of the pending motion, the

Court must only decide whether Kelsey-Hayes has presented enough evidence to allow a reasonable finder of the facts to conclude the 1989 agreements were executed under duress.[4]

A.

Galtaco says Kelsey-Hayes cannot sue for breach of the 1987 contract, because it entered into the superseding 1989 agreements. It is true that under Michigan law, entering a superseding, inconsistent agreement covering the same subject matter rescinds an earlier contract and operates as a waiver of any claim for breach of the earlier contract not expressly reserved. Joseph v. Rottschafer, 248 Mich. 606, 610-611, 227 N.W. 784 (1929); Culver v. Castro, 126 Mich. App. 824, 827-828, 338 N.W.2d 232 (1983). However, a subsequent contract or modification is invalid and therefore does not supersede an earlier contract when the subsequent contract was entered into under duress. Lafayette Dramatic Production v. Ferentz, 305 Mich. 193, 217-219, 9 N.W.2d 57 (1943). There is sufficient evidence to allow a reasonable finder of the facts to determine that Kelsey-Hayes was under duress when it executed the 1989 agreements. Thus, Galtaco's motion for summary judgment will be denied.

B.

Courts in Michigan have recognized the doctrine of economic duress or "business compulsion" for more than a century. Hackley v. Headley, 45 Mich. 569, 8 N.W. 511 (1881). Galtaco relies on early statutory and judicial general expressions of the doctrine stating that in order to make a claim of duress, a person must be subjected to the threat of an unlawful act in the nature of a tort or a crime. See Burke v. Gould, 105 Cal. 277, 281-283, 38 P. 733 (1894). However, the doctrine of duress has been greatly expanded since its common-law origin.[5] Now, a contract is voidable if a party's manifestation of assent is induced by an improper threat by another party that leaves the victim no reasonable alternative. Rich & Whillock v. Ashton Development, 157 Cal. App. 3d 1154, 204 Cal. Rptr. 86, 89 (1984); Systems Technology Associates, Inc. v. United States, 699 F.2d 1383, 1387 (Fed. Cir. 1983); Restatement (Second) of Contracts, §175(1) (1982). In other words, economic duress can exist in the absence of an illegal threat; the threat must merely be wrongful. Even acts lawful and non-tortious may be wrongful depending on the circumstances. S. Williston & W. Jaeger, Williston on Contracts §1606 (3rd ed. 1972); Fowler v. Mumford, 48 Del. 282, 102 A.2d 535 (Del. Super. 1954).

4. As to the claim of unconscionability, as distinguished from duress, it appears to lack merit. See Northwest Acceptance Corp. v. Almont Gravel, Inc., 162 Mich. App. 294, 412 N.W.2d 719 (1987). The claim of bad faith likewise appears to lack merit, see Genesee Merchants Bank & Trust Co. v. Tucker Motor Sales, 143 Mich. App. 339, 372 N.W.2d 546 (1985), as does the claim of unjust enrichment, see Hollowell v. Career Decisions, Inc., 100 Mich. App. 561, 570, 298 N.W.2d 915 (1980).

5. A survey of Michigan cases involving duress reveals that there has never been a decision that explicitly adopts the modern formulation of duress. . . .

Nevertheless, the Court is satisfied that if the Michigan Supreme Court looked at the issue today, it would rule that economic duress need not stem from an "illegal" threat. . . . See Dunbar v. United States Insurance Co. of America, 557 F. Supp. 228 (E.D. Mich. 1983) (in diversity cases, federal court must make educated guess what state Supreme Court would decide if question was presented to it, and decisions of state trial and appellate courts, while they may be considered, cannot serve as precedent).

C.

1

Kelsey-Hayes has alleged wrongful acts of Galtaco in its complaint and has offered proof of them in affidavits. Specifically, Kelsey-Hayes says Galtaco threatened to breach its contract and go out of business, stopping production and delivery of castings, unless Kelsey-Hayes agreed to significant price hikes. Austin Instrument, Inc. v. Loral Corp., 29 N.Y.2d 124, 324 N.Y.S.2d 22, 272 N.E.2d 533 (1971) (threat by one party to breach contract by not delivering required items is wrongful).

2

Kelsey-Hayes has also presented a triable issue of fact that it had no reasonable alternative other than acquiescing to Galtaco's demand for a contract modification. Affidavits and deposition testimony in the record show Kelsey-Hayes contacted six other casting manufacturers, but none were able to immediately provide an alternate source of castings to meet Kelsey-Hayes' delivery requirements.[6] As a result, Kelsey-Hayes might reasonably have believed a brief interruption in casting shipments would force at least one of its major customers, Ford, to halt production of a vehicle line. Such an occurrence, Kelsey-Hayes could reasonably fear, would injure its business reputation and subject it to large monetary damages.[7] The facts in this case parallel *Austin Instrument,* supra, in which a government contractor faced a genuine possibility of substantial liquidated damages as a result of a subcontractor's threat to stop deliveries unless prices were increased. In *Austin Instrument,* 324 N.Y.S.2d at 26-27, 272 N.E.2d at 537-538, the court held that a company in this position was deprived of its free will and had no alternative other than acquiescing to the demands of the party threatening to breach its contract. Similarly, faced with the imminent shutdown of its major customer's plants, Kelsey-Hayes may have had no alternative other than agreeing to Galtaco's "requests" for price increases.[8] See also Pittsburgh Steel

6. By the time Galtaco demanded the second 30 percent price increase, most of its other customers other than Kelsey-Hayes were able to acquire alternate supplies of castings. Galtaco says this suggests Kelsey-Hayes also could have obtained another source of supply, and thus it was not under economic duress when it assented to the latter 1989 agreement. But this merely presents an issue to be resolved by the trier of fact. Moreover, when seeking alternate supplies of castings, Kelsey-Hayes may have faced more difficulty than Galtaco's other customers. Kelsey-Hayes had to source 30 different safety related castings representing perhaps 45%-50% of the total output of the Galtaco foundries.

7. Given the changing nature of the automobile industry, Galtaco's actions are more likely to constitute duress. It is well known that in an effort to promote efficiency, car manufacturers are reducing the size of their reserve banks of parts. As a result, component parts are often incorporated into a finished product within a few hours of their delivery. A supplier's failure to make scheduled shipments may have immediate and dramatic consequences. Aware of this, companies in the position of Kelsey-Hayes will face more pressure to agree to the extortionate demands of suppliers who breach their contractual obligations. Thus, a breach of contract in the automotive industry may be more coercive than in other industries.

8. The facts here also mirror an example of economic duress cited in Restatement (Second) of Contracts, §175 comment b, illustration 5 (1982):

A, who has contracted to sell goods to B, makes an improper threat to refuse to deliver the goods to B unless B modifies the contract to increase the price. B attempts to buy substitute goods elsewhere but is unable to do so. Being in urgent need of the goods, he makes the modification. See Uniform Commercial Code §2-209(1). B has no reasonable alternative, A's threat amounts to duress, and the modification is voidable by B.

Co. v. Hollingshead & Blei, 202 Ill. App. 177 (1916); Ross System v. Linden Dari-Delite, 35 N.J. 329, 173 A.2d 258 (1961); Rose v. Vulcan Materials Co., 282 N.C. 643, 194 S.E.2d 521 (1973); King Construction Co. v. W.M. Smith Electric Co., 350 S.W.2d 940 (Tex. Civ. App. 1961).

It is hardly necessary to add that Kelsey-Hayes' normal legal remedy of accepting Galtaco's breach of the contract and then suing for damages would have been inadequate under the circumstances. Kelsey-Hayes might reasonably have feared that if it shunned the 1989 agreements and instead sued for breach of the 1987 contract then Galtaco would have stopped supplying it with castings.[9] As stated, supra, evidence in the record strongly suggests Kelsey-Hayes would not have been able to locate an alternate supply of castings. As a result, Kelsey-Hayes' business reputation may have suffered and its major customers may have been forced to shut down its automobile production lines.

3

In order to state a claim of economic duress a buyer coerced into executing a modification to an existing agreement must "at least display some protest against the higher price in order to put the seller on notice that the modification is not freely entered into." United States v. Progressive Enterprises, 418 F. Supp. 662, 665 (E.D. Va. 1976) (in contract modification situations, the parties must be able to rely on objective, unequivocal manifestations of assent). Galtaco says Kelsey-Hayes executed the 1989 agreements with the secret intention to never pay the higher prices. However, it is undisputed Kelsey-Hayes vigorously objected to Galtaco's breach of the 1987 contract and its demand for price increases. While Kelsey-Hayes did not expressly reserve the right to sue under the 1987 contract, a reasonable trier of the facts could determine its protests effectively put Galtaco on notice that the 1989 agreements were agreed to under duress.

D.

Galtaco argues, in effect, that the common law doctrine of economic duress no longer applies to cases like the one at bar. Instead, Galtaco says, the doctrine has been subsumed by the Uniform Commercial Code's "good faith" test, M.C.L. §440.2209, for determining the enforceability of agreements modifying contracts for the sale of goods. This contention is frivolous. Galtaco relies on a single case, Roth Steel Products v. Sharon Steel Corp., 705 F.2d 134 (6th Cir. 1983), to support its contention that a well-established tenet of law has been abandoned. Moreover, the Court of

9. Galtaco's chief operating officer, T. Cook, testified as follows:

We had conveyed to all of our customers that we needed a written acceptance of the 30 percent price increase or we would not make shipments on May 15th, which was a Monday. The Monday shipments were prepared on Friday night and were shipped out Sunday night. Our shipping supervisors had instructions that those shipments were not to be made unless they had been given approval by me or through someone designated by me that we had, in fact, received those written approvals. Late on Friday we still had not received those from anyone in Kelsey-Hayes. And Ron Olwean called me to find out what he had and how to do it.

Appeals for the Sixth Circuit in *Roth Steel* never even held that a person can no longer rely on the doctrine of economic duress to invalidate a contract modification. Finally, M.C.L. §440.1103 states that, absent explicit language to the contrary, the Uniform Commercial Code merely supplements the common law of duress and coercion. M.C.L. §440.2209 contains no such language. . . .

V.

Galtaco's motion for summary judgment is denied. Kelsey-Hayes' motion to amend is granted.

So ordered.

Notes and Questions

1. *Modification without consideration under Article 2.* The judge writing the opinion in *Kelsey-Hayes* never raises the pre-existing duty rule as a possible reason for denying effect to the modification. The judge's discussion at the beginning of section III. A. may be read to suggest that this case is an example of mutual rescission followed by a new agreement, as discussed in Note 6 after the *Alaska Packers'* case. In any event, the court's citation to Michigan's version of the Uniform Commercial Code indicates that this case falls under UCC §2-209(1), which states that a modification "needs no consideration to be binding." The drafters of the UCC appear to be expressing the view that parties regularly modify agreements without having new consideration on both sides, and that such "one-sided" modifications should be routinely enforced except in the presence of special circumstances. Do people in business indeed routinely agree to such one-sided modifications, and if so, why? Consider Comment 1 to §2-209: "This section seeks to . . . make effective all necessary and desirable modifications of sales contracts without regard to the technicalities which at present hamper such adjustments." A comprehensive survey of the Code's approach to contract modification can be found in two studies by Professor Robert Hillman: Policing Contract Modifications under the UCC: Good Faith and the Doctrine of Economic Duress, 64 Iowa L. Rev. 849 (1979); A Study of Uniform Commercial Code Methodology: Contract Modification under Article Two, 59 N.C. L. Rev. 335 (1981). Professor Irma S. Russell has included a more recent critique of §2-209 in her article, Reinventing the Deal: A Sequential Approach to Analyzing Claims for Enforcement of Modified Sales Contracts, 53 Fla. L. Rev. 49 (2001).

2. *Good faith as a limitation on modification under Article 2.* Assuming that the drafters of the UCC were right to take the position that one-sided contract modifications are by and large an everyday affair, not to be burdened with technicalities of contract law, there remains the question of how the law can "police" against the possibility that one party will exploit developing circumstances to coerce the other party's agreement to a modification. While §2-209(1) itself does not directly address that issue, Comment 2 provides that the obligation of good faith serves as a bar to

"extortion" of a modifying agreement "without legitimate commercial reason." In an oft-cited case discussed briefly at the end of the *Kelsey-Hayes* opinion, the Court of Appeals in Roth Steel Products v. Sharon Steel Corp., 705 F.2d 134 (6th Cir. 1983), upheld a district court's determination that a price-increase modification was unenforceable because it had been procured by bad faith. The *Roth* court applied a two-part test. First, it declared that a party may in good faith seek a modification when "unforeseen economic exigencies existed which would prompt an ordinary merchant to seek a modification in order to avoid a loss on the contract." Second, it held that even where circumstances do justify asking for a modification, it is nevertheless bad faith conduct to attempt to *coerce* one, by threatening a breach. On this point, the court conceded that the inference of bad faith arising when a breach is threatened may be rebutted by a showing that the party threatening not to perform did honestly believe it had a legal defense to the duty of performance. In *Roth*, however, the court held that the inference of bad faith had not been rebutted, principally because it appeared that the legal justification for nonperformance was not offered at the time the modification was sought but only as an afterthought in the context of litigation. This, the court held, was not the "honesty in fact" that the UCC good faith obligation requires. 705 F.2d 145-148. Under the test applied in *Roth*, should the modification agreement asserted by Galtaco be regarded as the product of bad faith?

3. *Economic duress as a limitation on modification under Article 2.* We have already seen, in connection with the *Totem Marine* case in Chapter 7, that economic duress may generally be grounds under the common law for avoiding an agreement. The *Kelsey-Hayes* court holds that UCC §2-209(1) does not preclude application of the duress doctrine to sales of goods cases, and observes that modern formulations of the duress doctrine no longer require the presence of an "illegal" threat. As also reflected in the *Totem Marine* case, most courts now accept that a "wrongful" threat may leave a party without reasonable alternatives and thereby invoke duress as grounds to excuse enforcement of a contract. Thus, the *Kelsey-Hayes* court anticipated that the Michigan Supreme Court would adopt the modern view of duress if confronted with the question and move away from its early statements which required an illegal threat. The Michigan Supreme Court, however, appears not to have confronted that issue since the time of *Kelsey-Hayes* and the intermediate state appellate opinions still require an illegal threat. See, e.g., Farm Credit Services of Michigan's Heartland, P.C.A. v. Weldon, 591 N.W.2d 438, 447 (Mich. Ct. App. 1998) (state duress law requires "unlawful" or "illegal" coercion); but see Stefanac v. Cranbrook Educational Community, 458 N.W.2d 56, 74 n.40 (Mich. 1990) (Levin, J. dissenting) (observing that Michigan law on duress may have lagged behind expansion of the doctrine in the majority of states and also noting that the state's precedent has been interpreted to require an "unlawful or wrongful" act). If the judge in *Kelsey-Hayes* had deemed state law to require an "illegal" threat to establish duress, would that change lead to a different outcome in the case? If so, would you agree with that resolution of the case?

In footnote 4 the *Kelsey-Hayes* opinion summarily held that a claim of bad faith was not supported, while at the same time accepting the argument that the modification may have been the result of economic duress, citing Austin Instrument, Inc. v. Loral Corp., perhaps the leading modern case for this type of duress. While it seems likely that where contract modification is at issue, the law of "duress" and the law of "good faith" will often tend to merge, the two theories may involve somewhat different considerations. See Meredith R. Miller, Revisiting Austin v. Loral: A Study in Economic Duress, Contract Modification and Framing, 2 Hastings Bus. L. J. 357, 411 (2006) (noting that good faith analysis would focus more on a party's reasons for seeking and the fairness of a proposed modification whereas duress analysis looks at alleged threat and lack of choices). Other cases have considered the issues of duress and good faith in the context of an Article 2 case, though claimants seem to succeed only rarely. See, e.g., Sonfast Corp. v. York International Corp., 875 F. Supp. 1099 (M.D. Pa. 1995) (finding neither economic duress nor breach of duty of good faith in making modification; buyer could have insisted on seller honoring existing contract, and had adequate legal remedy if it did not); Gross Valentino Printing Co. v. Clarke, 458 N.E.2d 1027 (Ill. App. Ct. 1983) (claimant failed to establish economic duress; no evidence that alleged threat was sufficient to overcome the will of claimant and failed to show legal redress was inadequate).

4. *Protest of a bad faith modification.* If ties of good faith bind each party to the other under the UCC (and under general contract law as well; see Restatement (Second) §205), they bind not only the party seeking to enforce a modification but also the one who would resist it. In *Kelsey-Hayes,* the buyer at first performed under the modification, but later repudiated it; the seller pointed to this as evidence that the buyer had acted with a "secret intention to never pay the higher prices," suggesting that this might amount to bad faith on the buyer's part. Some courts in similar cases have held that the party agreeing to an assertedly coerced modification has a good faith duty to make plain that it is acting under protest, so that the other party will not be deceived as to its intention eventually to resist enforcement or seek redress. E.g., United States ex rel. Crane Co. v. Progressive Enterprises, Inc., 418 F. Supp. 662 (E.D. Va. 1976) (buyer's secret intention never to pay higher price not in keeping with good faith's requirement of "honesty in fact"); but cf. T & S Brass & Bronze Works, Inc. v. Pic-Air, Inc., 790 F.2d 1098 (4th Cir. 1986) (buyer's failure to make formal protest did not bar later objection to modification; *Crane* distinguished as applying only where other party had acted in good faith in seeking modification). Did the court in *Kelsey-Hayes* appropriately resolve this issue in the buyer's favor?

5. *Revisiting Problem 8-3.* Recall the questions posed in Problem 8-3, above. If Associated Departments Stores were now to agree to pay Waller Brothers an increased amount for the installation of tile in its department store, would that agreement be supported by consideration? Does it need to be? Could enforcement of such an agreement be avoided on grounds of bad faith or duress (or any other ground we have studied, such as fraud, mistake, or undue influence)? To answer these questions, do you

need more facts? What facts would you need, and how might they be discovered?

ORDER

KENT, District Judge.

This is a breach of contract dispute in which Plaintiff Brookside Farms ("Brookside") alleges that Defendant Mama Rizzo's Inc. ("MRI") breached its contract with Brookside to purchase 91,000 pounds of fresh basil leaves. Before the Court now are Plaintiff's Motion for Partial Summary Judgment and Defendant's Motion for Summary Judgment. For the reasons discussed below, the Court finds that Defendant's Motion is denied and Plaintiff's Motion is granted in part and denied in part.

BACKGROUND

On October 13, 1993, Brookside Farms and MRI entered into a requirements contract for the sale of fresh basil leaves from Brookside to MRI. Under the contract, MRI agreed to buy a minimum of 91,000 pounds of fresh basil leaves for a one-year term. Delivery was to be made daily, five days per week, in lots ranging from a minimum of 350 pounds to a maximum of 800 pounds. MRI agreed to pay for the basil it accepted within fifteen days of delivery date.

The price for the basil leaves under the contract was seasonally based, with one price applicable during the domestic growing season, and a higher price applicable during the non-growing season, when Brookside would look to Mexican growers to supply the basil it would need to fulfill its obligations under the contract. The original price for basil delivered during the domestic growing season — between June 1 and September 30 — was $3.80 per pound; the original price for basil delivered during the non-growing season — October 1 to May 31 — was $5.00 per pound. ·

It is undisputed that Mike Franklin, the vice-president of MRI, requested Wayde Burt, Brookside's general partner, to remove additional parts of the stems of the basil leaves, a task not specifically required under the original contract. Brookside agreed to do this work in exchange for a $0.50 per pound increase for the remainder of the contract term. The undisputed testimony shows that, because the original contract contained a clause forbidding oral modification, Franklin promised to make a notation of future price changes on MRI's copy of the original contract. The new price terms were also reflected on MRI's internally-generated purchase orders, Brookside's invoices, and MRI's payment checks. Between October 27, 1993, and November 16, 1993, MRI issued twelve separate purchase orders for shipments of basil at $5.50 per pound, and Brookside filled each order and invoiced MRI at the new price.

Between November 17, 1993, and January 9, 1994, MRI discontinued its order of basil leaves, and Brookside reduced its purchase of basil from its Mexican suppliers as a result. Consequently, Brookside was forced to pay higher prices for its supply of Mexican basil leaves when MRI resumed its orders under the contract. Two price modifications in the contract then followed in close sequence. Initially, Franklin and Burt agreed that MRI would pay $6.23 [sic] per pound for imported basil. Between January 10 and January 21, 1994, MRI issued fifteen separate purchase orders for shipments of basil at $6.25 per pound, and Brookside filled each order and invoiced MRI at that price. MRI paid all these invoices at the higher price. In mid-January, MRI agreed to pay $6.75 per pound for the basil Brookside imported from Mexico and issued sixty-seven separate purchase orders for shipments at that price. Each of these shipments was filled and paid without protest.

Between March 14, 1994, and May 17, 1994, MRI issued twenty-one purchase orders for basil at $6.75 per pound and issued a check to Brookside for $10,260 in payment for eight of those invoices. Unfortunately for both parties, this check was dishonored by MRI's bank for insufficient funds. Brookside has brought this suit on the claims that Defendant has breached the executory portion of the contract by refusing to accept the minimum amount of basil it agreed to and that Defendant is also liable to Plaintiff for the 3,041 pounds of basil it accepted but did not pay for. MRI contends that no payment is due because Brookside itself breached the contract by raising prices in violation of the contract's express language that no modification would be binding unless it was reduced to written form. . . .

ANALYSIS

THE PRICE MODIFICATION ISSUE

The parties in this case vigorously dispute the question of whether they entered into a valid modification of the price of fresh basil leaves. Plaintiff has submitted undisputed affidavit testimony that several oral agreements to modify the original contract price for basil occurred. Within one week of the contract's formation, MRI discovered that the stems on the basil leaves would need to be removed before they could be properly used—a task not required by the original contract. As stated above, MRI's vice-president contacted Plaintiff's general partner, and both parties agreed that Plaintiff would remove the basil stems before shipping the leaves and increase the purchase price by $0.50 per pound.

Both parties were aware that the contract contained a clause forbidding oral modifications of the contract's terms. Section 19 of the contract states:

> This Agreement may be modified only by a writing signed by the party against whom or against whose successors and assigns enforcement of the modification is sought.

Consequently, MRI's vice-president agreed to make a notation of the price change on MRI's copy of the original contract. (See Burt Affidavit, Instrument #7, at 2). Several subsequent price hikes were also agreed to by the parties, and MRI accepted and paid for 21,389 pounds of basil at purchase prices ranging from the original price to $6.75 per pound and accepted, but refused to pay for, an additional 3,041 pounds.[1] Plaintiff currently seeks payment on this 3,041 pounds of basil at the purchase price of $6.75 per pound. MRI contends that no payment is due because Plaintiff itself breached the contract by raising prices in violation of the contract's express language that no modification would be binding unless it was reduced to written form. The Court disagrees.

Neither party in this case has properly pointed out that the contract in dispute falls within the Statute of Frauds under §2.201 of the Texas Business and Commerce Code. That statute provides that "a contract for the sale of goods for the price of $500 or more is not enforceable by way of action or defense unless there is some writing sufficient to indicate that a contract for sale has been made between the parties and signed by the party against whom enforcement is sought." Clearly, the original contract between MRI and Brookside meets these requirements.

It is a general rule of Texas law that oral agreements that materially modify a written agreement within the Statute of Frauds are not enforceable. Tex. Bus. & Comm. Code Ann. §26.01; King v. Texacally Joint Venture, 690 S.W.2d 618, 619 (Tx. App. — Austin, 1985, writ ref'd n.r.e.); Dracopoulas v. Rachal, 411 S.W.2d 719 (Tex. 1967). However, not all modifications are prohibited. If the oral changes do not materially alter the underlying obligations, for example, they are not barred. Horner v. Bourland, 724 F.2d 1142, 1148 (5th Cir. 1984); Group Hospital Services, Inc. v. One and Two Brookriver Center, 704 S.W.2d 886, 890 (Tx. App. — Dallas, 1986, n.w.h.). Second, the Texas Supreme Court has adopted the doctrine of promissory estoppel in some cases to forbid reliance on the Statute of Frauds as a defense to the validity of oral agreements. In specific, the Court has held that where one party reasonably relies on the oral promise of another to reduce an oral agreement to writing, the failure to create such a writing will not prevent the relying party from taking the modification out of the Statute of Frauds.[2] "Moore" Burger, Inc. v. Phillips Petroleum Co., 492 S.W.2d 934, 937 (Tex. 1972); see also, Foster v. Mutual Savings Assoc., 602 S.W.2d 98, 101 (Tx. App. — Ft. Worth, 1980, n.w.h.).

Finally, both parties in this case have also failed to note that Texas has adopted an exception to the Statute of Frauds contained in the Uniform Commercial Code. Sections 2.201(c) & (c)(3) of the Tex. Bus. & Comm. Code state in part that:

---

1. MRI originally tendered payment on this series of shipments, but its bank dishonored the check for insufficient funds.

2. The Court specifically invoked both §§90 and 178, comment F of the Restatement, Contracts. Section 178, comment F reads:

Though there has been no satisfaction of the Statute, an estoppel may preclude objection on that ground in the same way that objection to the nonexistence of other facts essential for the establishment of a right or a defence may be precluded. A misrepresentation that there has been such satisfaction if substantial action is taken in reliance on the representation, precludes proof by the party who made the representation that it was false.

(c) A contract which does not satisfy the requirements of Subsection (a) [the general Statute of Frauds provision] but which is valid in other respects is enforceable
. . .

(3) with respect to goods for which payment has been made and accepted or which have been received and accepted.

Thus, an oral modification that would itself form a binding contract in the absence of Statute of Frauds considerations can be binding on the parties to a sale of goods over $500 insofar as specific goods have been received and accepted. See Tex. Bus. & Comm. Code §2.209.

The Court finds that a valid oral modification of the contract between MRI and Brookside occurred on both estoppel and statutory grounds. As stated above, it is undisputed that the parties agreed to alter the purchase price of the basil leaves. On each occasion, MRI issued separate purchase orders and Brookside filled each order and invoiced MRI on the price. In each case, MRI paid the invoiced price without protest. At the time the first price modification occurred, MRI's vice-president and Brookside's general partner discussed whether or not they needed to redraw the contract to account for the price changes in light of the fact that the contract did not allow for oral modifications. It is undisputed that MRI's vice-president assured Plaintiff that he would make a notation of price changes on MRI's copy of the contract and that this notation would be sufficient. (See Burt Affidavit, at 2).

The Court finds that such behavior clearly brings these parties within the estoppel theory adopted by the Texas Supreme Court in *"Moore" Burger,* 492 S.W.2d at 937. The promised notation would have constituted a valid written modification of the contract's terms. A valid writing under the Statute of Frauds requires only "some writing" signed by the party against whom it is to be enforced, namely, MRI. Tex. Bus. & Comm. Code §2.201(a). In addition, given that the intent of the oral agreement to modify the written form of the contract was clearly designed to bring it within the controlling language of the contract, Plaintiff could have reasonably relied on Defendant's implied promise to initial or sign the price change to indicate its intent to adopt the change; without such an implied promise, MRI's agreement to alter the written price terms would have been a mere fraud on the Plaintiff. Comment 6 to §2.201(a) makes clear that such a writing need not be delivered to any other party; MRI could have made the notation on its signed copy of the contract and retained possession of it. It is also clear that MRI's promise to do so induced Brookside Farms to continue shipping basil leaves at the agreed price changes.[3]

Based on these actions, the Court finds that MRI cannot now invoke the no-oral-modification clause of the contract to bar Plaintiff's claim that a valid modification occurred in this case. To do so would be to reach the

3. Mr. Burt's affidavit states that MRI promised to make the price change notations in regards to the first $0.50 per pound price increase. The Court notes that Burt does not specifically state that the parties agreed to alter the contract with each subsequent price change. Nevertheless, given the sophistication of the parties involved in this case and their extended course of conduct with one another, it is entirely reasonable to expect that, once having promised to make such changes, and having acted on these changes by shipment and subsequent payment, Plaintiff could have relied on MRI's initial promise to make a written notation to allow their commercial dealings to go forward.

inequitable result that thousands of dollars could change hands over an extended period of commercial dealings between the parties, during which the Defendant knowingly and wilfully refrained from acting on the promise that induced the Plaintiff to continue shipments and then object to the course of dealing only when it has issued a bad check. The Court notes that the Uniform Commercial Code, which governs the transaction in question, has codified the contractual duty of good faith and fair dealing in commercial settings like the one presently before the Court. Tex. Bus. & Comm. Code §1.203 provides that "[e]very contract or duty within this title imposes an obligation of good faith in its performance or enforcement." Where the party is a merchant, its standard of good faith performance requires honesty in fact and the observance of reasonable commercial standards of fair dealing in the trade. Adolph Coors Co. v. Rodriguez, 780 S.W.2d 477, 481 (Tx. App. — Corpus Christi, 1989, writ denied).[4] For the Court to allow Defendant to invoke the no-oral-modification clause after MRI itself induced and participated in the extended course of action it now complains of would be to convert the sale of basil leaves into a "basil sale carcinoma" that would devour all reasonable commercial standards of behavior between merchants.

The Court also finds that a valid modification of the contract's price terms occurred on statutory grounds. As stated above, oral modifications to contracts within the Statute of Frauds are generally forbidden. In addition, the Texas Business and Commerce Code specifically provides that signed contracts that exclude modifications that are not in the form of signed writings are valid in this state. Tex. Bus. & Comm. Code §2.209(b). Nevertheless, comment 4 to §2.209 clearly states that such provisions do not limit the "actual later conduct" of parties that have entered into non-written modifications, despite a contract's provision that all modifications must be in writing. In this case, it is undisputed that the "actual later conduct" of these parties involved the order, shipment, and acceptance of 24,430 pounds of basil leaves, 3,041 pounds of which were paid for by a bad check on MRI's part.

Nevertheless, MRI argues that under the contract's "no waiver" clause, it did not waive its right to insist on the contract's initial terms and that, therefore, it now continues to have the right to demand that all modifications to this contract have been in writing to be valid. The Court disagrees.

Section 21 of the contract in question states:

> The failure of either party to this Agreement to demand full performance of any of its provisions by the other party shall not constitute a waiver of performance unless the party failing to demand performance states in a writing signed by party that the party is waiving that performance. The waiver of any breach of any of the provisions of this Agreement by the parties shall not constitute a continuing waiver or a waiver of any subsequent breach by either party of the same or any other provision of this Agreement.

(Defendant's Motion for Summary Judgment, Instrument # 12, Exhibit A, at 4). The Court agrees with MRI that this "no-waiver" clause protects

---

4. The Court realizes, of course, that the duty of good faith and fair dealing under §1.203 does not state an independent cause of action. Rather, it is designed to make an agreement's promises effective and defines other duties which grow out of specific contractual obligations. See id. at 482.

Defendant from a waiver of the "no-oral-modification" clause of the contract. Indeed, comment 4 of §2.209, quoted above, explicitly relies on the theory that "later conduct" of the parties to a contract "waives" contractual obligations. By agreeing that a failure to demand full performance does not give rise to a waiver, the parties in this case have effectively agreed to their own private Statute of Frauds for modifying the contract. As comment 3 of Tex. Bus. & Comm. Code §2.209 states, agreements to modify a contract's terms only in written form "permits the parties in effect to make their own Statute of Frauds as regards any future modification of the contract. . . ." Like the general Statute of Frauds, §2.209(b) is designed "to protect against false allegations of oral modifications." Id.

However, this does *not* protect MRI under these facts. Indeed, in one sense it destroys MRI's entire case, for if the failure to object to full performance reserves the right to demand such performance, then Brookside's failure to object to MRI's initial request for de-stemmed leaves reserves Plaintiff's right to demand full performance of the original contract's terms, which apparently allowed basil to be shipped with stems still attached. More importantly, however, the private Statute of Frauds provision of the contract must be analyzed under the rules otherwise applicable to general Statute of Frauds issues, and under this analysis, the Court finds that the parties have entered into an effective agreement for those items Brookside shipped and MRI received and accepted.

Sections 2.201(c) and (c)(3) of the Texas Business and Commerce Code provide:

(c) A contract which does not satisfy the requirements of Subsection (a) [governing the Statute of Frauds] but which is valid in other respects is enforceable

. . .

(3) with respect to goods for which payment has been made and accepted or which have been received and accepted

This provision also governs the private Statute of Frauds contained in the contract before the Court. Assuming arguendo that the agreement between MRI and Brookside to modify the contract's terms did not meet the writing requirements of §2.201(a), §2.201(c) operates to bring the oral agreement within the Statute with respect to those goods MRI actually received and accepted, that is, the 24,430 pounds of basil Brookside shipped, including the 3,041 pounds of unpaid-for basil leaves. See Bagby Land and Cattle Co. v. California Livestock Commission Co., 439 F.2d 315, 317 (5th Cir. 1971) ("receipt and acceptance either of goods or of the price constitutes an unambiguous overt admission by both parties that a contract actually exists."). Under the specific language of §2.201(c), the new contractual price terms were not made enforceable as to future shipments of basil by Brookside, but they are enforceable as to the 3,041 pounds shipped under the agreed price of $6.75 per pound.[5]

---

5. Because of the general paucity of relevant Texas authority presented in the instant Motions, the Court does not rule on the question of whether sufficient written materials are present in this case to bring the oral agreements out of the Statute of Frauds. The Court notes, however, that purchase

For all these reasons, the Court finds that Plaintiff's Motion for Partial Summary Judgment is granted on the claim that MRI is liable to Brookside for $20,526.75 in payment for the 3,041 pounds of basil accepted but not paid for.

Plaintiff also claims that MRI's refusal to accept and pay for the minimum amount of basil it agreed to buy in its requirements contract with Plaintiff constitutes a breach of contract, with the resulting damages to be determined at trial at a later date. In response, MRI claims that it was relieved of any obligation to purchase basil by Brookside's demand for higher prices than provided for in the contract. Having already decided that Plaintiff's price increases were legally justified, the Court now finds that for the same reasons articulated above, Brookside did not breach its contractual obligations and that MRI is liable for a material breach of its obligation to purchase a total of 91,000 pounds of basil from Plaintiff. Consequently, Plaintiff's Motion for Partial Summary Judgment is granted on this point. . . .

CONCLUSION

For all of the reasons stated above, the Court finds that Plaintiff's Motion for Partial Summary Judgment is denied as to any claim for attorney's fees and is granted as to the claims that MRI breached the executory portion of the parties' contract, is liable in the amount of $20,526.75 for the payment of 3,041 pounds of basil accepted but not paid for, and that MRI is liable under the Perishable Agricultural and Commodities Act. For the same reasons, Defendant's Motion for Summary Judgment is denied on all counts, including its counterclaim that MRI is entitled to recover overpayments from Plaintiff for the amounts it paid for basil. Defendant's counterclaim for overpayment is also hereby dismissed with prejudice. All relief not specifically granted herein is also denied. All parties are to bear their own taxable costs incurred in this case to date. It is further ordered that the parties file no further pleadings in the matters determined in this Order, including motions to reconsider and the like. Instead, they are instructed to seek any further relief to which they feel themselves entitled in the United States Court of Appeals for the Fifth Circuit, as may be appropriate in due course.

It is so ordered.

Notes and Questions

1. *Modifications and the statute of frauds.* The first two cases in this section examined primarily the question whether contract modifications must be supported by new consideration and when they will be vulnerable to the defenses of duress or bad faith. In *Brookside Farms,* however, the important question is whether a contract modification must be in writing to be enforceable. Section 2-209(3) of the Code provides that the "requirements of the statute of frauds section of this Article must be satisfied if the contract as

---

orders and invoices were generated for every shipment of basil made and that other courts have found such materials sufficient to satisfy the Statute of Frauds. See Brochsteins, Inc. v. Whittaker Corp., 791 F. Supp. 660, 661 (S.D. Tex. 1992).

modified is within its provisions." The meaning of this provision has produced substantial debate. Many courts have held not only that a writing is required when the modification brings an oral contract within the statute but also that all modifications must be in writing whenever the contract was within the scope of §2-201 originally and remains within the statute after the change. See Beth A. Eisler, Modification of Sales Contracts Under the Uniform Commercial Code: Section 2-209 Reconsidered, 57 Tenn. L. Rev. 401, 430 n.195 (1990). The commentators, however, have disagreed with this view. They point out that UCC §2-201(1) requires a memorandum to specify only the quantity; other terms, such as the price, may be expressed orally. Under this analysis, an oral modification of a written agreement would be enforceable unless the modification would either change the quantity term or increase the price above the $500 UCC threshold. Id. at 430. See also Mark E. Roszkowski, Contract Modification and the Statute of Frauds: Making Sense of Section 2-209 of the Uniform Commercial Code, 36 Ala. L. Rev. 51, 70-71 (1984). The court in *Brookside Farms* finds a middle ground approach to the question of when modifications must be in writing under §2-209(3). What justifies the court's conclusion? Which approach to defining when modifications are required to be in writing is most persuasive?

2. *No-oral-modification clause.* In *Brookside Farms,* the defendant buyer also relied on a provision of the agreement that any modification must be in writing and signed to be effective—a "no-oral-modification," or "NOM" clause. At common law, such clauses were usually held to be ineffective because parties retained the freedom to later modify their agreement by whatever mode they might choose, written or oral. E.g., Williams v. Jader Fuel Co., 944 F.2d 1388 (7th Cir. 1991) (parties may orally modify contract even when provision requires writing); Prime Financial Group, Inc. v. Masters, 676 A.2d 528 (N.H. 1996) (same, but clear proof of waiver of NOM clause may be required). In §2-209(2), however, the Code authorizes parties to employ a NOM clause to create a "private statute of frauds" governing modifications by providing that a "signed agreement which excludes modification or rescission except by a signed writing cannot be otherwise modified or rescinded. . . ." (Comment 3 indicates that both 2-209(2) and (3) are "intended to protect against false allegations of oral modifications.") Thus, §2-209(2) departs from the common law by generally making NOM clauses enforceable.

3. *Reliance and oral modifications.* Both §§2-209(2) and (3) must be read in conjunction with §2-209(4), which provides that "[a]lthough an attempt at modification or rescission does not satisfy the requirements of subsection (2) or (3) it can operate as a waiver." In a leading case in this area, Wisconsin Knife Works v. National Metal Crafters, 781 F.2d 1280 (7th Cir. 1986), the parties entered into a written contract containing a "no oral modification" clause. The seller failed to deliver the goods by the dates required in the contract, and the buyer sued for breach. The seller claimed that the parties had orally agreed to modify the delivery schedule. Writing for the majority and remanding for a new trial, Judge Posner ruled that the seller could establish "waiver" of the clause requiring modifications to be in writing if it could show that it detrimentally relied on the buyer's indications that late delivery would be accepted. Dissenting Judge Easterbrook argued that the term "waiver" should be interpreted traditionally, as a voluntary

relinquishment of a known right, not dependent on a showing of reliance. Nevertheless, Judge Easterbrook would arrive at an outcome similar to the majority because he reasoned that a waiver could be retracted under §2-209(5) except if material reliance on the oral modification had occurred and would make a retraction unjust. Ultimately, the cases do generally support the proposition that the NOM clause may be waived, by oral agreement to that effect, or by some combination of words and conduct that in the circumstances evidences the parties' willingness to dispense with its protection, and that reliance will prevent retraction of the waiver. See, e.g., Mitsubishi Corp. v. Goldmark Plastic Compounds, Inc., 446 F. Supp. 2d 378 (W.D. Pa. 2006); ePresence, Inc. v. Evolve Software, Inc., 190 F. Supp. 2d 159 (D. Mass. 2002).

In addition to the NOM clause, the contract between Brookside and MRI also contained a "no-waiver" clause, intended to insulate the parties (or at least the drafter) from a claim that any provision in the contract, including the NOM clause, had been orally waived. The *Brookside* court rather ingeniously finds the no-waiver clause to be overcome in the same manner that the statute of frauds may be overcome, by actual performance. It may be useful at this point to see the NOM clause (perhaps in conjunction with its sidekick, the no-waiver clause) as playing in this area the same sort of role that a strong merger clause may play with respect to the parol evidence rule. Under the parol evidence rule, a merger clause may protect the drafting party against earlier or contemporaneous agreements (genuine or merely asserted). The NOM clause is intended to exclude allegations of oral terms made after the creation of the parties' written agreement. Hearkening back to formalistic notions of contract law, the combined effect of the merger clause and the NOM clause is to ensure that in the future any dispute between the parties will be resolved on the basis of the writing, and *only* the writing. Arrayed on the other side — in favor of the court's enforcing or at least considering the parties' informal, oral agreements, as evidenced by both words and conduct— are a variety of doctrines characteristic of "modern" contract law: rules proscribing fraud and nondisclosure, the implied obligations of good faith and fair dealing, the concept of estoppel, and perhaps even unconscionability. For a discussion of the reliance issues raised — on both sides — by the parol evidence rule and the NOM clause, see Charles L. Knapp, Rescuing Reliance: The Perils of Promissory Estoppel, 49 Hastings L.J. 1191, 1303–1330 (1998).

4. *Modification through settlement.* A problem with both practical and legal aspects that often arises in the context of settlement negotiations is the "full payment" check question. Suppose that a debtor resists payment of an asserted obligation, claiming that he does not owe as much as the creditor claims. What if at some point the debtor offers the creditor a check for some amount less than she claims, and says, in effect, "Here's a check for what I'm willing to pay, marked 'payment in full.' You can have this now, without a lawsuit, but only if you accept it as a full settlement of your claim." If the creditor accepts and cashes the check, can she later assert a right to payment of the balance of her claim? Pre-Code law was clear on the point: so long as the amount actually owed is either "unliquidated" (generally, not reduced to a dollar amount) or the subject of a good faith dispute, acceptance of a check tendered in full payment will in legal effect amount to an "accord and satisfaction" that discharges any remaining obligation. Agreements to settle a

liquidated, undisputed claim for less than the full amount have traditionally not been binding on the creditor, under the rule of the old English case of Foakes v. Beer, L.R. 9 A.C. 605 (H.L. 1884), an extension of the "pre-existing duty" rule, which is itself a corollary of the general doctrine of consideration. The rule of Foakes v. Beer has been the subject of much critical comment, and modern developments have tended to reduce its importance. E.g., UCC §1-107 (claim arising out of breach can be discharged in whole or part by written waiver or renunciation, without consideration). See generally E. Allan Farnsworth, Contracts §§4.21-4.25 (4th ed. 2004), for a full discussion of the consideration issues that can arise in connection with settlement and discharge agreements.

Suppose the creditor does not simply cash the debtor's "full payment" check, but instead attempts to do so while at the same time reserving its rights to seek the balance due from the debtor. The creditor might send the debtor a letter to that effect, or might endorse the check "under protest" or "with full reservation of rights." What effect will such steps have? Under the traditional common law rule such an attempted reservation would have no effect; the cashing of the check would still amount to acceptance by the creditor of the debtor's offer of an accord and satisfaction. (See Restatement (Second) §281 on accord and satisfaction as performance of agreement to accept substituted performance in lieu of original duty.) Originally, it appeared that the Code might have changed this result in what is now UCC §1-207(1), which provides for performance of contract under reservation of rights. The subsequent addition of §1-207(2) clarified that cashing a full payment check, even with reservation of rights, still constitutes an accord and satisfaction, barring the creditor from collecting the unpaid balance, unless the creditor can establish a ground for avoiding the accord and satisfaction, such as duress. Revised UCC §1-308 has the same effect.

5. *Revisting Problem 8-3.* Recall again the facts of Problem 8-3. Based on all the above, how would you counsel Ms. Carmody to proceed in responding to the Waller Brothers' request for an increase in the price of their tile work? Indicate what courses of action you would consider, which you would recommend, and why.

9 | **Rights and Duties of Third Parties**

In our study thus far of the various issues raised by the creation and enforcement of promissory obligations, we have been concerned almost entirely with the rights and obligations of the original parties—the ones who entered into the contract in question (or, in cases involving the protection of unbargained-for reliance, the promisor and promisee). In this chapter, we address the possibility that other persons may have rights or duties, or both, enforceable by or against them as a result of the making of contracts to which they were not themselves parties. Such persons are frequently referred to as "third parties," to distinguish them from the two persons who, by convention, are visualized as the original makers of a contract. (Of course, a contract may have any number of original parties, but two is the minimum for the making of either a contract or a promise.) In this chapter, we consider first the possibility that third-party rights may arise simply from the making of the original contract; then we discuss the extent to which the rights or duties of the original parties may be later "assigned" or "delegated" by them to other persons.

A. RIGHTS OF THIRD PARTIES AS CONTRACT BENEFICIARIES

In any system that allows persons to compete more or less freely for goods and services and to enter into binding contracts by which such commodities can be bought and sold, it is obvious that the making of a contract is often likely to have effects on persons who are not parties to it. If the supply of commodity X is limited, then a binding commitment by A to sell 10,000 units of X to B will have the result that C—who is also seeking to acquire X on the market—will have the supply of X available to her diminished by 10,000 units. If A agrees to construct a building on land owned by B, this building may have the practical effect of lessening the enjoyment or utility to C of an adjoining lot of land owned by her. In a loose sense, the "rights" of C in such cases may be adversely affected by the making of these contracts, if the word *rights* is used to mean simply the freedom to do as one pleases to the extent not forbidden by law.

Such a characterization is not really accurate, however. When two persons contract, they do not ordinarily have the power under law to affect adversely any *right* of a person who is not a party to their contract, in the sense in which that word is usually employed by lawyers. In the above examples, if C actually had a legal right to those 10,000 units of X, or to the enjoyment of her property undiminished by the proximity of B's building, then any invasion of those rights by A or B would be an actionable wrong — possibly a breach of contract, possibly a tort. Under our system of legal rules, the power to invade or destroy the rights of nonconsenting persons can only be conferred by "public" law. (Such a power may arise by statute — the so-called fair trade laws, for example — or by common law, as for instance the privilege of "necessity" as justification for trespass or other injury to property. W. Page Keeton et al., Prosser and Keeton on the Law of Torts §24 (5th ed. 1984)). "Private" law — i.e., the kind of legally enforceable obligations that result from the making of a private agreement — generally cannot destroy or impair the rights of anyone who is not a party to that agreement; nor can it impose duties on such a person.

It does not follow from this proposition, however, that the parties to a contract should not be able, if they so desire, to *create* by contract a right in some third person. Suppose for instance that one party, A, has loaned money to another, B, on the strength of B's promise later to repay that sum to A. Later, B loans the same amount of money to C. In that case, it may make sense for B to request that C promise in return to make repayment not to B himself, but to B's creditor A. In that event, C's performance of his promise would result in not only the satisfaction of C's obligation to B, but also of B's debt to A. If C does make such a promise to B but later fails to perform it, does A have a cause of action against C, for breach of that promise made to B? Or does A only have his cause of action against B, on the original debt?

These were essentially the facts of the leading case of Lawrence v. Fox, decided by the New York Court of Appeals in 1859. In that case, plaintiff Lawrence (A) had loaned money to one Holly (B); Holly later made a similar loan to Fox (C), who promised Holly that he (Fox) would make repayment to Lawrence. Fox did not keep that promise, however, and Lawrence sued Fox for the amount of the promised payment. Although Lawrence was not a party to the transaction between Holly and Fox — Lawrence was not in "privity" with Fox — the court nevertheless held that the cause of action would lie. The court sought to justify the result by likening the case to ones in which the defendant had been a "trustee" of property under a trust created by another, with instructions to sell the trust property and convey the proceeds to the plaintiff. In such a case, the plaintiff as "beneficiary" of the trust would have the right to enforce the trust obligation against the promisor/trustee, should the latter fail to perform his promise to pay over those proceeds. In Lawrence v. Fox, however, there was no property held in trust (no "res"), merely an in personam obligation imposed on the defendant by contract with the promisee. Nevertheless, a majority of the court held that the plaintiff could enforce the obligation created by that promise, as a kind of beneficiary of the right created by it. (Two judges concurred in the decision based on agency theory and two other judges dissented based on the lack of privity.) *Lawrence v. Fox,* 20 N.Y. 268 (1859). The majority opinion's analysis in *Lawrence* has been generally accepted, and the plaintiff in such cases is typically referred to as a "third party beneficiary" of the defendant's promise. The degree to which *Lawrence* actually broke new ground, however, has been disputed. An interesting account of *Lawrence* as an innovative decision, and its subsequent influence on third party doctrine, can be found in Anthony J. Waters, The Property in the Promise: A Study of the Third Party Beneficiary Rule, 98 Harv. L. Rev. 1109 (1985). Another account suggests that *Lawrence* came to have great popularity not because it was a novel decision, but because of the relative clarity of its opinions and its appearance at a time when courts were becoming more hostile to third party standing. See Melvin Aron Eisenberg, Third-Party Beneficiaries, 92 Colum. L. Rev. 1358 (1992).

In *Lawrence,* the promise sued on had its genesis in the promisee's desire to provide for the satisfaction of an obligation owed by him to a third party, the plaintiff Lawrence. Since the plaintiff in that case was a creditor of the promisee, the *Lawrence*-type plaintiff came to be called a "creditor beneficiary." (In §133(1)(b), the first Restatement defined the "creditor beneficiary" case as one where performance by the promisor would satisfy an "actual or supposed or asserted duty of the promisee to the beneficiary.") Although other jurisdictions followed the example of *Lawrence* in permitting direct suit by the creditor beneficiary, later cases in New York and elsewhere raised the question whether a third party who was not in any legal sense a "creditor" of the promisee might also have a direct cause of action on the promisor's obligation.

In New York, it appeared during the latter part of the nineteenth century that recovery by third parties would be limited to the creditor-beneficiary case exemplified by Lawrence v. Fox. However, later decisions extended recovery to cases where the promisee had apparently sought to confer the benefit of the promisor's performance on a child, a parent, or some other member of the promisee's family. The 1918 New York case of Seaver v. Ransom has come to be the leading example of this latter type of case. In *Seaver* the promisee was Mrs. Beman, an elderly woman in ill health. Mrs. Beman was about to sign a will that had been prepared pursuant to her instructions by her husband, Judge Beman, when she realized that it made insufficient provision for a beloved niece. Mrs. Beman proposed that another will be prepared to remedy this omission, but it appeared that she might not live long enough to execute it. Judge Beman urged his wife to sign the will already prepared (which left him a life estate in certain real property), promising her solemnly that he would see that the niece was amply provided for in his own will. When Judge Beman himself later died, it was discovered that his will made no provision for the niece, and she therefore sued the Judge's estate to enforce the promise he had made to his dying wife. The court pointed out that in similar cases a "constructive trust" had been imposed on the promisor's estate after his death; this was not feasible in *Seaver,* however, because his estate had not been enriched by the wife's actions. (Recall that Beman received only a life estate under his wife's will.) Nevertheless, the court allowed recovery by the niece, holding that the principle of Lawrence v. Fox should be extended to the facts of *Seaver*. In reaching this decision, the court observed that some earlier cases allowed third party standing to children and wives on the basis of the "close relationship" they had with the promisee. Seaver v. Ransom, 120 N.E. 639 (N.Y. 1918). Many courts have since permitted third party enforcement of promises where it appears that the promisee's intention was to make a gift to the plaintiff third party. Such plaintiffs are often referred to as "donee beneficiaries." (See the first Restatement §133(1)(a).) For a history of the development of third party beneficiary law, see Gary L. Monserud, Blending the Law of Sales with the Common Law of Third Party Beneficiaries, 39 Duquesne L. Rev. 111 (2000).

The principle that a third party may have standing to recover on a contract is now universally accepted by American courts. See John E. Murray, Jr., Contracts §129(C), at 875 (4th ed. 2001). The Restatement (Second) continues its approval of this principle (§§302, 304), but the drafters attempted to deemphasize somewhat the distinction between "creditor" and "donee" beneficiaries, stating that the fundamental distinction is between "intended" beneficiaries (who enjoy a right of direct action) and "incidental" ones (who do not). Their aim apparently was to direct courts away from the somewhat mechanical application of those earlier categories, in the direction of more flexibility (particularly in the case of noncreditor beneficiaries, where "donative" intent in the altruistic sense may be lacking). See generally Harry G. Prince, Perfecting the Third Party Beneficiary Standing Rule under Section 302 of the Restatement (Second) of Contracts, 25 B.C.L. Rev. 919, 974-980 (1984); David M. Summers, Third Party Beneficiaries and the Restatement (Second) of Contracts, 67 Cornell L. Rev. 880 (1982). This shift in emphasis is somewhat undercut by the appearance in §302(1)(a) and (b) of slightly altered versions of the old creditor and donee beneficiaries. See Comments *b* and *c*, and the Reporter's Note to §302 (stating somewhat ingenuously that the terms *creditor* and *donee beneficiary* are "not used"). From his survey of the cases decided since the appearance of §302, Professor Prince concluded in 1984 that its provisions had made relatively little impact on the courts' traditional approach to determining the ability of a third party to enforce a contract. 25 B.C.L. Rev. at 990-997. In a subsequent study, Professor Eisenberg agreed that §302 preserves, in essence, the categorical aspects of the first Restatement; he also concluded that §302 adds an "intent to benefit" test that the courts had frequently used with little consistency because of inherent vagueness about how intent should be defined and proved. Melvin Aron Eisenberg, Third-Party Beneficiaries, 92 Colum. L. Rev. 1358, 1378-1384 (1992).

The cases that follow primarily address the threshold issue of third party beneficiary standing. The courts may view the question of standing differently if the promisee is a governmental entity, because of concerns about a promisor assuming open-ended liability to the public. Apart from the determination of standing for third parties, other issues that may arise include the ability of the promisor and the promisee to vary the contract, the defenses that may be raised by the promisor in responding to an action by a third party beneficiary, and the remedies that are appropriate in third party beneficiary cases.

Vogan v. Hayes Appraisal Associates, Inc.
Supreme Court of Iowa
588 N.W.2d 420 (1999)

CARTER, Justice

Hayes Appraisal Associates, Inc. (Hayes Appraisal), the defendant in the district court, had been hired by MidAmerica Savings Bank (MidAmerica) to monitor the progress of new home construction for plaintiffs, Susan J. Vogan and Rollin G. Vogan. The Vogans had obtained a construction loan from MidAmerica. The contractor defaulted after all of the original construction loan proceeds and a subsequent portion of a second mortgage loan had been paid out by the bank.

The Vogans recovered judgment against Hayes Appraisal on a third-party beneficiary theory based on its alleged failure to properly monitor the progress of construction, thus allowing funds to be improperly released by the lender to the defaulting contractor. The court of appeals reversed the judgment on the basis that erroneous progress reports by Hayes Appraisal were not the cause of any loss to the Vogans. After reviewing the record and considering the arguments of the parties, we vacate the decision of the court of appeals and affirm the judgment of the district court.

In June 1989 the Vogans moved to Des Moines. They wanted to build a home in West Des Moines. They met with builder Gary Markley of Char Enterprises, Inc. Markley agreed to build the home for $169,633.59. The Vogans contacted MidAmerica for a mortgage. MidAmerica orally contracted with Hayes Appraisal to do the initial appraisal and make periodic appraisals of the progress of the construction. The home, according to the plans, and lot were appraised at $250,000.

Thereafter, the Vogans obtained a $170,000 mortgage from MidAmerica. MidAmerica was to disburse progress payments to Markley based on progress reports received from Hayes Appraisal. On November 6, 1989, the Vogans purchased the lot for $66,000 with their own funds. Construction began on November 22, 1989. On December 28, 1989, Hayes Appraisal issued a progress report to MidAmerica that twenty-five percent of the home had been completed.

There were cost overruns on the job, and in February 1990 MidAmerica determined that there was less than $2000 remaining of the $170,000 loan proceeds. Markley determined that at this point it would take another $70,000 to complete the home. The Vogans then took out a second mortgage on the home for $42,050 and turned that money plus some of their own funds over to the bank to continue making progress payments to Markley based on Hayes Appraisal's progress reports. Prior to completion of the home, the Vogans decided to sell it rather than to occupy it.

On March 20, 1990, Hayes Appraisal certified that the home was sixty percent complete. Only eight days later, Hayes Appraisal issued another progress report indicating that ninety percent of the work had been completed on the home. During the trial, witnesses testified for the Vogans that this was an inaccurate report overstating the extent of the contractor's progress on the job. As late as October 1990, substantial additional work was required on the house. At this point, Markley defaulted on the job after having been paid all of the initial $170,000 and much of the additional monies raised by the Vogans. Another contractor estimated the completion of the home would cost an additional $60,000.

The Vogans stopped making mortgage payments, and MidAmerica brought an action to foreclose the mortgage. The Vogans counterclaimed, alleging that the bank had improperly authorized payment of funds to Markley. Allegedly, MidAmerica did not follow its loan procedure for disbursement of funds. At least thirty percent of the loan amount was to be retained until completion. An undisclosed settlement was reached in the litigation between Vogans and MidAmerica.

The Vogans then filed a petition against Hayes Appraisal, contending it negligently certified the extent of the construction that had been completed. Hayes Appraisal filed a motion for summary judgment, arguing, in part, that even if the March 28, 1990 appraisal was negligently issued, it could not have proximately caused harm to the Vogans because MidAmerica had already released most of the loan funds prior to receiving the March 1990 progress reports. The court denied the motion. On reconsideration, the court again denied the motion and stated that the Vogans' claims were based upon other oral and written appraisals that led to the disbursement of the additional money that had been raised to cover cost overruns.

The case proceeded to jury trial on a contract theory. The court denied Hayes Appraisal's motions for directed verdict in which it argued the Vogans were not third-party beneficiaries of its contract with MidAmerica and the March 1990 progress reports did not proximately cause the damages alleged. The jury returned a verdict for the Vogans. Hayes Appraisal's motion for judgment notwithstanding the verdict was denied.

Hayes Appraisal appealed. It contended the evidence was insufficient to prove the Vogans were third-party beneficiaries or that its conduct proximately caused any damage to the Vogans. It believed the trial court erred in failing to grant its motions for summary judgment, directed verdict, and judgment notwithstanding the verdict on these issues.

The court of appeals reversed. It concluded the March 1990 progress reports did not result in any damage to the Vogans because the bank had already released more funds than recommended in those reports. The court concluded the use of the appraisal was to manage the disbursement of only the $170,000 loan, not any monies above that amount. Based upon this disposition, the court of appeals did not address the third-party beneficiary issue. We granted further review.

I. WHETHER THE VOGANS WERE THIRD-PARTY BENEFICIARIES OF THE CONTRACT BETWEEN MIDAMERICA AND HAYES APPRAISAL

A. STANDARD OF REVIEW

In assessing a motion for judgment notwithstanding the verdict, this court's only inquiry is whether there is sufficient evidence to justify submitting the case to the jury. Tredrea v. Anesthesia & Analgesia, P.C., 584 N.W.2d 276,

280 (Iowa 1998). If there is substantial evidence to support a plaintiff's claims, a motion for judgment notwithstanding the verdict should be denied. Id. Evidence is substantial when a reasonable mind would find the evidence presented adequate to reach the same findings. Id. In order to avoid a defendant's motion for judgment notwithstanding the verdict, a plaintiff must present more than a "mere scintilla of evidence." Id. . . . This court views the evidence in the light most favorable to the party against whom the motion was made and takes into consideration every legitimate inference that may fairly and reasonably be made. . . .

B. ARGUMENTS

The Vogans argue that they presented ample evidence to generate a jury question concerning whether they were third-party beneficiaries of the contract between MidAmerica and Hayes Appraisal. The Vogans assert that the court should look to the intent of the parties and the surrounding circumstances and argue that the bank's intent was to protect the Vogans' money as construction progressed. The Vogans claim that Hayes Appraisal knew they were owners of the property and that they would benefit from the progress reports.

Hayes Appraisal, however, claims that the verbal contract between MidAmerica and Hayes had no provision or intent to make the Vogans third-party beneficiaries. Hayes Appraisal claims that the Vogans presented no evidence of intent on behalf of the bank to benefit the Vogans and so failed to meet their burden of proof. Hayes Appraisal argues that this failure of proof entitles them to a directed verdict or judgment notwithstanding the verdict on this issue.

C. ANALYSIS

This court has adopted the following principles from the Restatement (Second) of Contracts that are applicable to third-party beneficiary cases:

> (1) Unless otherwise agreed between promisor and promisee, a beneficiary of a promise is an intended beneficiary if recognition of a right to performance in the beneficiary is appropriate to effectuate the intention of the parties and either
>
> (a) the performance of the promise will satisfy an obligation of the promisee to pay money to the beneficiary; or
>
> (b) *the circumstances indicate that the promisee intends to give the beneficiary the benefit of the promised performance.*
>
> (2) An incidental beneficiary is a beneficiary who is not an intended beneficiary.

See *Tredrea*, 584 N.W.2d at 281 (quoting Restatement (Second) of Contracts §§302 (1979)) (emphasis added); Midwest Dredging Co. v. McAninch Corp., 424 N.W.2d 216, 224 (Iowa 1988) (same). This court has determined that the primary question in a third-party beneficiary case is whether the contract manifests an intent to benefit a third party. *Tredrea*, 584 N.W.2d at 281; *Midwest Dredging Co.*, 424 N.W.2d at 224. However, this intent need not be to benefit a third party directly. *Tredrea*, 584 N.W.2d at 281.

In *Tredrea* we explained

[w]hen a contract is made, the two or more contracting parties have separate purposes; each is stimulated by various motives, some of which he may not be acutely conscious. . . . A third party who is not a promisee and who gave no consideration has an enforceable right by reason of a contract made by two others . . . if the promised performance will be of pecuniary benefit to [the third party] and the contract is so expressed as to give the promisor reason to know that such benefit is contemplated by the promisee as one of the motivating causes of his making the contract.

Id. at 281-82 (quoting 4 Arthur Linton Corbin, A Comprehensive Treatise on the Working Rules of Contract Law §§776, at 15-16, 18 (1951)). In the present case, MidAmerica is the promisee, who stands to benefit from Hayes Appraisal's performance, and Hayes Appraisal is the promisor, who agreed to provide periodic inspections to the bank.

The promised performance of Hayes Appraisal to MidAmerica will be of pecuniary benefit to the Vogans, and the contract is so expressed as to give Hayes reason to know that such benefit is contemplated by MidAmerica as one of the motivating causes of making the contract. The inspection reports and invoices that Hayes Appraisal provided MidAmerica contained not only the location of the project, but also the Vogans' name as the home purchasers. This information gave Hayes Appraisal reason to know that the purpose of MidAmerica obtaining the periodic progress reports from Hayes was to provide the Vogans with some protection for the money they had invested in the project. If we apply the *Tredrea* standard to these circumstances, the Vogans qualify as third-party beneficiaries of the agreement between MidAmerica and Hayes Appraisal.

II. WHETHER THE FAULTY INSPECTION REPORTS WERE A CAUSE OF INJURY TO THE VOGANS

The court of appeals determined that Hayes Appraisal did not cause any damage to the Vogans by reason of their faulty progress reports. That court found that the periodic completion reports submitted by Hayes Appraisal were only for purposes of disbursement of the initial $170,000 construction loan and did not pertain to the additional funds that the Vogans deposited with the bank for periodic disbursement to the contractor. The court of appeals concluded that the bank had already distributed the original $170,000 to the contractor prior to receiving the March 1990 periodic progress reports from Hayes Appraisal that were deemed to be erroneous.

Susan Vogan prepared a spreadsheet, admitted into evidence, that showed both debits and credits on the Vogans' construction account, including the monies added to the original $170,000. The Vogans testified that based on this analysis the bank disbursed a portion of the additional funds raised by the Vogans to cover cost overruns based on the March 1990 progress reports showing that the project was ninety percent completed.

Questions of proximate cause are ordinarily questions of fact that, only in exceptional cases, may be taken from the jury and decided as a matter of law. . . . We believe the facts that we have just detailed would permit the jury to find that the purpose of Hayes Appraisal's reports on the progress of the work was to assist the bank in disbursing all funds on deposit that were intended for application to the Vogans' home construction. Consequently, although the initial $170,000 construction loan might have been disbursed prior to the faulty completion estimate, the erroneous reporting of the project's completion in March 1990 caused the bank to disburse other funds of the Vogans that would have been retained had the report been accurate.

Consequently, we disagree with the conclusion of the court of appeals that the jury could not have found that Hayes Appraisal's faulty progress report caused any injury to the Vogans.

III. WHETHER THE VOGANS' RECOVERY VIOLATES THE RULE OF
    HADLEY V. BAXENDALE

Hayes Appraisal suggests that, even if its conduct could be found to be a proximate cause of injury to the Vogans, it should not be held liable for dissipation of any funds after the $170,000 construction loan had been exhausted. It bases this argument on the rule in Hadley v. Baxendale, 9 Exch. 341 (1854). In that case, the British Court of Exchequer stated:

> Where two parties have made a contract which one of them has broken, the damages which the other party ought to receive in respect of such breach of contract should be such as may fairly and reasonably be considered either arising naturally, *i.e.*, according to the usual course of things, from such breach of contract itself, or such as may reasonably be supposed to have been in the contemplation of both parties, at the time they made the contract, as the probable result of the breach of it. Now, if the special circumstances under which the contract was actually made were communicated by the plaintiffs to the defendants, and thus known to both parties, the damages resulting from the breach of such a contract, which they would reasonably contemplate, would be the amount of injury which would ordinarily follow from a breach of contract under these special circumstances so known and communicated.

Hadley, 9 Exch. at 344. We have approved this principle as a rule of Iowa law. . . .

In applying this rule to the circumstances of the present case, we are convinced that, to the extent the Vogans' recovery included sums advanced to Markley by the bank based on an inaccurate progress report from Hayes Appraisal, that element of recovery was not beyond Hayes' contemplation at the time its contract with the bank was made. If the bank had scrupulously honored its construction loan procedures and there had been no adjustments based on cost overruns, a substantial portion of the $170,000 construction loan would have been retained at the time that Hayes Appraisal inaccurately reported that the project was ninety percent completed. The portion of Vogans' recovery based on improper payments to the contractor by the bank thus did not violate the rule of Hadley v. Baxendale. Of course, much of the Vogans' recovery was for items of consequential damage. Hayes Appraisal has not lodged any challenge to the claims of consequential damage other than its general claim that the Vogans were not a third-party beneficiary of the bank's contract. We have previously rejected that contention.

We have considered all issues presented and conclude that the decision of the court of appeals should be vacated. We affirm the judgment of the district court.

Decision of Court of Appeals Vacated; District Court Judgment Affirmed.

Notes and Questions

1. *Whose intent determines standing?* Probably the most perplexing question involved in third party beneficiary cases is determination of the intent necessary for a third party to be an intended beneficiary with rights under the contract. Restatement (Second) §302 is unclear. The section begins by indicating that the intention of both parties is necessary: "a beneficiary of a promise is an intended beneficiary if recognition of a right to performance in the beneficiary is appropriate to effectuate the *intention of the parties*" (emphasis added). But the section then focuses on the intention of the promisee: "(a) the performance of the promise will satisfy *an obligation of the promisee* to pay money to the beneficiary; or (b) the circumstances indicate that the *promisee intends* to give the beneficiary the benefit of the promised performance" (emphasis added).

Three lines of authority have developed. Some courts have held that both the promisor and promisee must intend to give the third party rights under the contract. See Grigerik v. Sharpe, 721 A.2d 526 (Conn. 1998) (under dual intent standard, buyer of real property not third party beneficiary of contract between seller and engineer to perform soil tests and design sewage system). Other courts have concluded that the intention of the promisee controls. See E. Allan Farnsworth, Contracts §10.3, at 658 (4th ed 2004). Finally, a number of decisions hold that the promisor must know or at least have reason to know of the promisee's intent to benefit the third party, even if the promisor has no particular desire to confer a benefit on or create an obligation to the third person. See KMART Corp. v. Balfour Beatty, Inc., 994 F. Supp. 634, 637 (D.V.I. 1998) ("the increasingly more modern view hold[s] that it is enough that the promisor . . . understood that the promisee had an intent to benefit the third party"); Joseph M. Perillo, Calamari & Perillo on Contracts, §17.3, at 668 (5th ed. 2003) (modern cases require intent of promisee and promisor's knowledge of that intent). What test does the court use in *Vogan*? What arguments support each of the three positions?

Related to the question of whose intent controls is the issue of the nature of the benefit sufficient for a third party to be a beneficiary of a contract. The court in *Vogan* refers to the need for a "pecuniary benefit," but it might be argued that such a requirement is too restrictive. For example, the Restatement provides: "if the beneficiary would be reasonable in relying on the promise as manifesting an intention to confer a right on him, he is an intended beneficiary." Restatement (Second) §302, cmt. *d.*

2. *Evidence of intent.* What evidence should be used to determine the intention of the parties? On occasion the contract will specifically confirm or negate standing for a third party beneficiary. E.g., Mission Oaks Ranch, Ltd. v. County of Santa Barbara, 77 Cal. Rptr. 2d 1 (Ct. App. 1998) (contract expressly provided that consultant would be accountable solely to county and not to any third person); In re Estate of Cohen, 629 N.E.2d 1356, 1357 (N.Y. 1994) (contract for mutual wills provided that "every named legatee . . . is hereby made a third party beneficiary of this Agreement"). Recent cases indicate that in the absence of a clear contractual provision, a totality of the circumstances approach will often be used. Courts generally will consider the language and provisions of the agreement, the background of the contract,

and considerations of fairness and practicality. See Sazerac Co. v. Falk, 861 F. Supp. 253 (S.D.N.Y. 1994); Sisters of St. Joseph v. Russell, 867 P.2d 1377 (Or. 1994). Some courts, however, apply a presumption against third party standing that will be overcome only by clear evidence to the contrary found in the contract. E.g., Swavely v. Freeway Ford Truck Sales, Inc., 700 N.E.2d 181 (Ill. App. Ct. 1998) (strongly presumed that people contract only for themselves, but wife expressly named in employment contract to receive commissions upon death of husband held donee beneficiary); Marine Creek Partners, Ltd. v. Caldwell, 926 S.W.2d 793 (Tex. Ct. App. 1996) (presumption against standing not overcome by tenant injured on swing set who sought third party standing on contract between landlord and seller).

Professor Eisenberg has criticized the intent to benefit test for its vagueness. He proposes that courts adopt the following principle to determine whether a third party has a right to enforce a contract:

A third-party beneficiary should have power to enforce a contract if, but only if:
(I) allowing the beneficiary to enforce the contract is a necessary or important means of effectuating the contracting parties' performance objectives, as manifested in the contract read in the light of surrounding circumstances; or
(II) allowing the beneficiary to enforce the contract is supported by reasons of policy or morality independent of contract law and would not conflict with the contracting parties' performance objectives.

Melvin Aron Eisenberg, Third-Party Beneficiaries, 92 Colum. L. Rev. 1358, 1384 (1992). See also Orna S. Paglin, Criteria for Recognition of Third Party Beneficiaries' Rights, 24 New Eng. L. Rev. 63 (1989). How would *Vogan* be decided under Professor Eisenberg's principle?

3. *Incidental beneficiaries.* In what may appear to be rather circular reasoning, the Restatement (Second) of Contracts §§302(2) and 315 provide, in essence, that an "incidental beneficiary" is a party who benefits from a contract between others but who is not an intended beneficiary. Illustration 16 to §302 provides an example of a party who is expected to benefit from a contract but clearly not intended by the contracting parties to have standing to enforce it:

B contracts with A to erect an expensive building on A's land. C's adjoining land would be enhanced in value by the performance of the contract. C is an incidental beneficiary.

Cf. Devine v. Roche Biomedical Laboratories, 659 A.2d 868 (Me. 1995) (employee who received false positive drug test was not intended beneficiary of contract between employer and testing lab even though employee would clearly be affected by lab's breach; there was no evidence of intent to give employee standing to enforce contract); First Tennessee Bank National Ass'n. v. Thoroughbred Motor Cars, Inc., 932 S.W.2d 928 (Tenn. Ct. App. 1996) (creditor was not intended beneficiary of contract between debtor and party who agreed to purchase portion of debtor's business, even though creditor would have received the payment). See also Joseph M. Perillo, Calamari & Perillo on Contracts, §17-3, at 669 (5th ed. 2003) (observing that courts often determine third party standing primarily on the basis of social and economic policy).

4. *Liability of attorneys for negligent will drafting.* Apart from "true creditor" and "true donee" cases, one can identify categories of recurrent third party standing cases, including: will drafting contracts; construction contracts involving owners, contractors, and sureties; government contracts; and contracts affecting employees. See Harry G. Prince, Perfecting the Third Party Beneficiary Standing Rule under Section 302 of the Restatement (Second) of Contracts, 25 B.C.L. Rev. 919, 946-973 (1984).

One frequently litigated issue is whether an intended legatee has standing as a third party beneficiary to sue an attorney for breach of the will-drafting contract with the testatrix. A majority of jurisdictions allow a party who was intended to receive a bequest under a will to sue the drafting attorney for errors that defeat the intended bequest. See Ronald E. Mallen, Duty to Nonclients: Exploring the Boundaries, 37 S. Tex. L. Rev. 1147, 1149-1150 (1996). Courts allowing such actions have often emphasized that granting standing to the disappointed legatee aligns contract rights with economic interest. While the personal representative of the decedent's estate, as successor to the decedent's contract rights, could maintain a contract action against the lawyer, the representative's function is to collect and distribute assets. The representative ordinarily does not have an economic interest in bringing suit against a lawyer who may have negligently drafted a will. The disappointed legatee, although not a party to the contract with the lawyer, does have the economic interest to bring suit. See Mieras v. DeBona, 550 N.W.2d 202 (Mich. 1996).

The courts that allow an action to proceed against an attorney by intended legatees, or analogous third parties, have recognized actions based on contract, tort, or both. See Noble v. Bruce, 709 A.2d 1264, 1272 (Md. 1998) (citing varying approaches of the courts). Whether the action is based in tort or in contract can be significant for issues such as the statute of limitations, application of comparative fault rules, and the measure of damages. The standard for determining liability, however, will probably be the same regardless of how the action is categorized. In tort, attorneys have the duty to exercise the degree of skill and care customarily exercised by members of the profession. In contract, courts have generally held that lawyers impliedly promise to exercise the same degree of reasonable care in carrying out their drafting agreement. See Mieras v. DeBona, 550 N.W.2d 202 (Mich. 1996); Leyba v. Whitley, 907 P.2d 172 (N.M. 1995). As a consequence of this standard, not every mistake of an attorney will result in liability to the third party. See, e.g., Lucas v. Hamm, 364 P.2d 685 (Cal. 1961) (intended legatees had standing in tort and contract, but alleged error concerning obscure "rule against perpetuities" was mistake that might be made by lawyer using requisite level of skill, prudence, and diligence).

Not all jurisdictions have recognized standing for intended beneficiaries to sue for breach of a contract to draft a will. See, e.g., Noble v. Bruce, 709 A.2d 1264 (Md. 1998); Barcelo v. Elliott, 923 S.W.2d 575 (Tex. 1996); Copenhaver v. Rogers, 384 S.E.2d 593 (Va. 1989). The courts that decline to do so often cite concerns that liability to third parties would expose attorneys to potentially unlimited liability and that the potential liability might interfere with attorneys' duty of undivided loyalty to their clients. It should be noted that attorneys who engage in fraud can be held liable to third parties even without privity. See generally John P. Freeman & Nathan M. Crystal, Scienter in Professional Liability Cases, 42 S.C. L. Rev. 783 (1991).

5. *Defenses available to promisor.* Even if the court rules in favor of the plaintiff on the issue of third party standing, this is not the end of the case. Recall that in the example of Lucas v. Hamm, cited in Note 4, above, the court found the third parties had standing, but held that the promisor had not breached the contract. The defendant/promisor may also be able to raise a number of defenses against the intended beneficiary. All the rules of contract formation still apply, as do the rules relating to fraud, duress, mistake, and the like. See Restatement (Second) §309; Moorings Development Co. v. Porpoise Bay Co., 487 So. 2d 60 (Fla. Dist. Ct. App. 1986) (alleged third party beneficiary was subject to defense that contract was unenforceable on grounds of public policy). The third party beneficiary's right may also be limited by provisions or conditions in the contract, such as the obligation to submit disputes to arbitration. See, e.g., Borsack v. Chalk & Vermillion Fine Arts, Ltd., 974 F. Supp. 293 (S.D.N.Y. 1997) (intended beneficiary of licensing contract must arbitrate dispute); Johnson v. Pennsylvania Natl. Insurance Cos., 594 A.2d 296 (Pa. 1991) (intended beneficiary under uninsured motorist policy subject to arbitration clause). However, if the promisor undertakes an unqualified obligation to render a performance to the third party beneficiary, then the promisor will not be able to use a defense against the beneficiary that might have been asserted by the promisee. See XL Disposal Corp. v. John Sexton Contractors Co., 659 N.E.2d 1312 (Ill. 1995) (promisor bound by unqualified promise to pay finders' fee, regardless whether promisee was actually obligated to pay third party).

6. *Vesting of rights of third party beneficiaries.* An important question concerning third parties is at what time the rights of an intended beneficiary "vest" and are therefore no longer subject to change by agreement of the promisor and promisee. The first Restatement of Contracts §142 provided that the rights of a donee beneficiary vested immediately upon the making of the contract, but §143 stated that the rights of a creditor beneficiary did not vest until there was reliance. Given that Restatement (Second) §302 discards the distinction between creditor and debtor beneficiaries, §311 makes a complementary change by treating vesting for all intended beneficiaries essentially the way that creditor beneficiaries were treated under the first Restatement. Unless the contract prohibits modification by the promisor and promisee, §311 permits variation of the rights of the intended beneficiaries until the third party does one of three things: manifests assent at the invitation of the promisor or promisee, materially changes position in justifiable reliance on the promise, or brings suit on the promise. See Olson v. Etheridge, 686 N.E.2d 563 (Ill. 1997) (adopting §311). Contra Biggins v. Shore, 565 A.2d 737 (Pa. 1989) (immediate vesting of donee's rights found in First Restatement is more consistent with concept of gift than position of Second Restatement).

7. *Causation and foreseeability.* Having concluded that the Vogans were third party beneficiaries of the contract between Hayes and MidAmerica, the court must still consider whether Hayes's breach of contract caused them damages and whether their damages were reasonably foreseeable at the time

of contract formation under the doctrine of Hadley v. Baxendale. Chapter 11 examines these and other issues involved in determining damages.

Zigas v. Superior Court
California Court of Appeal
120 Cal. App. 3d 827, 174 Cal. Rptr. 806 (1981), cert. denied,
455 U.S. 943 (1982)

FEINBERG, Associate Justice.

This case is before us on a petition for writ of mandate. Because the issues involved appeared to be of considerable public importance and of first impression, we issued an alternative writ. We now hold that the relief sought should be granted.

Petitioners are tenants of an apartment building at 2000 Broadway in San Francisco, which was financed with a federally insured mortgage in excess of $5 million, pursuant to the National Housing Act (12 U.S.C. §§1701 et seq.) (the Act) and the regulations promulgated thereunder (24 C.F.R. §§207 et seq.). They seek in a class action, inter alia, damages for the landlords' (real parties in interest) violation of a provision of the financing agreement which requires that the landlords charge no more than the Department of Housing and Urban Development (HUD) approved schedule of rents. The trial court has sustained demurrers without leave to amend to 5 causes of action of 15 alleged, apparently on the ground that there is no right in the tenants to enforce the provisions of an agreement between their landlords and the federal government.

Petitioners allege that their landlords were required under their contract with HUD to file a maximum rental schedule with HUD and to refrain from charging more than those rents without the prior approval of the Secretary of HUD. Petitioners further allege that real parties are, and have been, charging rent in excess of the maximums set out in the rental schedule; the complaint avers that real parties have collected excessive rents and fees in an amount exceeding $2 million.

In addition to sustaining demurrers as to the third party causes of action, the trial court granted real parties' motion to strike all references to the Act, the regulations promulgated thereunder, and the terms of the agreement between HUD and real parties. It is these orders sustaining the demurrers and granting the motion to strike that petitioners seek to have set aside.

The issues presented include: (1) whether federal or state law applies; (2) whether petitioners have standing to sue, and (3) whether the action has become moot as a result of real parties' repayment of the HUD insured loan.

FEDERAL OR STATE LAW

Real parties appear to argue at one point that whether petitioners have standing to sue is to be determined by federal law because a federal contract arising under a federal statute is involved. In so arguing, real parties misconceive the nature of the complaint in the case at bar. The complaint does *not* allege a federal cause of action, i.e., arising out of the National Housing Act. What it alleges, in substance, is that pursuant to the Act, an agreement was entered into between HUD and real parties whereby real parties promised not to charge as rent more than that approved by HUD. Real parties did so charge and petitioners, *under California law*, seek redress as the parties aggrieved. . . .

We turn now to the question of whether petitioners have a cause of action under California law.

STANDING TO SUE — THIRD PARTY BENEFICIARY

California law clearly allows third party suits for breaches of contract where no government agency is a party to the contract. (Civ. Code, §1559.) Whether such suits are allowed when the government contracts with a private party depends upon analysis of the decisions in Shell v. Schmidt (1954) 126 Cal. App. 2d 279, 272 P.2d 82, and Martinez v. Socoma Companies, Inc., supra, 11 Cal. 3d 394, 113 Cal. Rptr. 585, 521 P.2d 841.

In *Shell,* plaintiffs sued as third party beneficiaries to defendant's contract with the Federal Housing Authority (FHA). The contract entailed an agreement by the defendant to build homes for sale to veterans according to plans and specifications submitted by the defendant to FHA in return for which FHA gave priorities to the defendant to secure the materials necessary for the building.

In deciding that plaintiffs had standing to enforce the terms of the contract between the defendant and the FHA, the *Shell* court relied on common law principles as embodied in Civil Code section 1559, which states: "A contract, made expressly for the benefit of a third person, may be enforced by him at any time before the parties thereto rescind it." Applying this provision to the facts before it, the *Shell* court observed:

> Once it is established that the relationship between the contractor and the government is contractual, it follows that veterans purchasing homes, that is, the class intended to be protected by that contract, are third party beneficiaries of that contract. As already pointed out, the statute and the regulations passed thereunder resulting in the contract were passed to aid and assist veterans and for their benefit. Purchasing veterans constitute the class intended to be benefitted, and the contract must therefore be for their benefit.

Id., 126 Cal. App. 2d at p.290, 272 P.2d 82.

It is evident that petitioners are entitled to maintain a third party cause of action under the *Shell* rationale. Real parties do not dispute the contractual nature of their relationship with HUD. And it is clear that a requirement of HUD approval of rent increases could *only* benefit the tenants.

Furthermore, even the most cursory review of the statutes and regulations which resulted in the contract in the present case leads to the conclusion that the tenants constitute the class which Congress intended to benefit. As stated in 12 United States Code section 1701t: "The Congress affirms the national goal, as set forth in section 1441 of Title 42, of 'a decent home under a suitable living environment for every American family.'" Section 1713(b) of Title 12, United States Code, also provides, in part:

> *The insurance of mortgages under this section is intended to facilitate particularly the production of rental accommodations, at reasonable rents, . . . The Secretary is, therefore,*

authorized . . . to take action, by regulation or otherwise, which will direct the benefits of mortgage insurance hereunder primarily to those projects which make adequate provision for families with children, and *in which every effort has been made to achieve moderate rental charges.*

Emphasis added, see also 24 C.F.R. §207.19(e).

This national goal, along with the purposes enunciated throughout the Act and the regulations promulgated thereunder, can leave no doubt that petitioners are members of the class which this legislation was intended to benefit. Under *Shell*, this conclusion, coupled with the uncontested contractual relationship between real parties and HUD, is sufficient to support the tenants' standing to sue as third party beneficiaries to a government contract.

In the subsequent case of Martinez v. Socoma Companies, Inc., supra, 11 Cal. 3d 394, 113 Cal. Rptr. 585, 521 P.2d 841, the court approved of the result in *Shell* but, at the same time, applied a different standard.[2] Plaintiffs in *Martinez* sought to enforce the terms of a contract between Socoma Companies, Inc. and the Secretary of Labor. Under this agreement, defendants received government funds in exchange for a promise to hire and train "hard core unemployed" residents of a "Special Impact Area" in East Los Angeles. Defendants failed to perform, and plaintiffs, who were residents of East Los Angeles and members of the class which the government intended to benefit, sought to recover under the contract.

In holding that the plaintiffs had no standing to sue as third party beneficiaries, the *Martinez* court adopted a more restrictive standard than that embodied in Civil Code section 1559, choosing instead to be guided by the principles set forth in section 145 of the Restatement of Contracts:

> A promisor bound to the United States or to a State or municipality by contract to do an act or render a service to some or all of the members of the public, is subject to no duty under the contract to such members to give compensation for the injurious consequences of performing or attempting to perform it, or of failing to do so, unless, . . . *an intention is manifested in the contract,* as interpreted in the light of the circumstances surrounding its formation, *that the promisor shall compensate members of the public for such injurious consequences* . . . .

Martinez v. Socoma Companies, Inc., supra, at pp.401-402, 113 Cal. Rptr. 585, 521 P.2d 841; City & County of San Francisco v. Western Air Lines, Inc. (1962) 204 Cal. App. 2d 105, 121, 22 Cal. Rptr. 216; Rest., Contracts, supra, §145.[3]

---

2. The *Martinez* court approved of the result in *Shell*, based upon a finding that the legislation under which the homes in *Shell* were built included a provision empowering the government to obtain payment by the contractor to the veteran purchasers for deficiencies resulting from failure to comply with specifications. (*Martinez*, supra, at p.403, 113 Cal. Rptr. 585, 521 P.2d 841.) Thus, the intent to compensate which Restatement, Contracts, section 145 requires was present. However, the *Shell* court made no mention of section 145.

3. It has been suggested that section 145 was meant only to preclude lawsuits for *consequential* damages arising out of government contracts, because the resulting potential liability may be disproportionately burdensome in relation to the value of the promised performance. (See Rest., Contracts, supra, §145, Illus. 1 and 2; 44 A.L.I. Proceedings 331 (1967).) Thus, the underlying rationale of section 145 is inapplicable where, as here, the money sought is not a *consequence* of the breach, it is the breach. In such a situation, standard third-party beneficiary doctrines should apply. (See Note, 88 Harv. L. Rev. 646, 650-651.)

Thus, under *Martinez,* standing to sue as a third party beneficiary to a government contract depends on the intent of the parties as manifested by the contract and the circumstances surrounding its formation. "Insofar as intent to benefit a third person is important in determining his right to bring an action under a contract, it is sufficient that the promisor must have understood that the promisee had such intent. [Citations.] No specific manifestation by the promisor of an intent to benefit the third person is required." (Lucas v. Hamm (1961) 56 Cal. 2d 583, 591, 15 Cal. Rptr. 821, 364 P.2d 685.) We therefore must determine, from the terms of the contract between HUD and real parties and the attendant circumstances, whether there was manifested an intention that petitioners be compensated in the event of real parties' nonperformance. Mindful of the rule that "[w]hen a complaint is based on a written contract which it sets out in full, a general demurrer to the complaint admits not only the contents of the instrument but also any pleaded meaning to which the instrument is reasonably susceptible. [Citation.]" (Martinez v. Socoma Companies, Inc., supra, 11 Cal. 3d at p.400, 113 Cal. Rptr. 585, 521 P.2d 841) and focusing upon the precepts of *Martinez* as to standing, we are of the view that the case falls within *Shell;* that is to say, appellants were direct beneficiaries of the contract and have standing, and not, as in *Martinez,* incidental beneficiaries without standing.

We explicate:

1. In *Martinez,* the contract between the government and Socoma provided that if Socoma breached the agreement, Socoma would refund to the government that which the government had paid Socoma pursuant to the contract between them. Thus, it is clear in *Martinez* that it was the government that was out of pocket as a consequence of the breach and should be reimbursed therefor, not the people to be trained and given jobs. In the case at bench, as in *Shell,* the government suffered no loss as a consequence of the breach, it was the renter here and the veteran purchaser in *Shell* that suffered the direct pecuniary loss.

2. Unlike *Martinez,* too, in the case at bench, no governmental administrative procedure was provided for the resolution of disputes arising under the agreement. Thus, to permit this litigation would in no way affect the "efficiency and uniformity of interpretation fostered by these administrative procedures." (Martinez v. Socoma Companies, Inc., supra, 11 Cal. 3d at p.402, 113 Cal. Rptr. 585, 521 P.2d 841.) On the contrary, as we earlier noted, lawsuits such as this promote the federal interest by inducing compliance with HUD agreements.

3. In *Martinez,* the court held that "To allow plaintiffs' claim would nullify the limited liability for which defendants bargained and which the Government may well have held out as an inducement in negotiating the contracts." (At p.403, 113 Cal. Rptr. 585, 521 P.2d 841, fn. omitted.) Here, there is no "limited liability." As we shall point out, real parties are liable under the agreement, *without limitation,* for breach of the agreement.

4. Further, in *Martinez,* the contracts "were designed not to benefit individuals as such but to utilize the training and employment of disadvantaged persons as a means of improving the East Los Angeles neighborhood." (At p.406, 113 Cal. Rptr. 585, 521 P.2d 841.) Moreover, the training and employment programs were but one aspect of a "broad, long-range objective" (id.)

contemplated by the agreement and designed to benefit not only those to be trained and employed but also "other local enterprises and the government itself through reduction of law enforcement and welfare costs." (Id.)

Here, on the other hand, as in *Shell,* the purpose of the Legislature and of the contract between real parties and HUD is narrow and specific: to provide moderate rental housing for families with children; in *Shell,* to provide moderate priced homes for veterans.

5. Finally, we believe the agreement itself manifests an intent to make tenants direct beneficiaries, *not* incidental beneficiaries, of real parties' promise to charge no more than the HUD approved rent schedule.

Section 4(a) and 4(c) of the agreement, providing that there can be no increase in rental fees, over the approved rent schedule, without the prior approval in writing of HUD, were obviously designed to protect the tenant against arbitrary increases in rents, precisely that which is alleged to have occurred here. Certainly, it was not intended to benefit the Government as a guarantor of the mortgage.

Furthermore, the provision in section 11(d) of the agreement, authorizing the Secretary of HUD to "[a]pply to any court . . . for specific performance, . . . for an injunction against any violation . . . or *for such other relief as may be appropriate*" (emphasis added) would entitle the secretary to seek restitution on behalf of the tenants overcharged, for such relief would surely be "appropriate." (See Porter v. Warner Co. (1946) 328 U.S. 395, 66 S. Ct. 1086, 90 L. Ed. 1332.) Thus, there was an intent upon the part of the government in executing the agreement with real parties, to secure the return of any rents exacted in excess of the rent schedule.

We are supported in our view by section 17 of the Agreement which specifically provides that real parties are personally liable, "(a) for funds . . . of the project coming into their hands which, by the provisions [of the Agreement] *they are not entitled to retain;* and (b) for their own acts and deeds or acts and deeds of other [sic] which they have authorized in violation of the provisions [of the Agreement]." (Emphasis added.)

By the allegations of the complaint, real parties have "retained" in excess of two million ($2,000,000) dollars in violation of the Agreement. Therefore, they are liable for that sum. To whom should they be liable? To ask the question is to answer it. It is not the government from whom the money was exacted; it was taken from the tenants. Therefore, it should be returned to the tenants.

In the face of this evidence of intent to direct the benefits of mortgage insurance to the tenants of the facilities involved, real parties argue that petitioners have no standing to sue because enforcement of the agreement is vested solely in the Secretary. They point to 12 United States Code section 1731a, which empowers the Secretary to refuse the benefits of participation to any mortgagor who violates the terms of the agreement. However, section 1731a's authorization does not constitute the exclusive remedy for enforcement of the agreement by the Secretary or by third parties. As stated by the court in Shell v. Schmidt, supra, 126 Cal. App. 2d at p.287, 272 P.2d 82:

> This fundamental purpose would, in many cases, be defeated if the statute were
> interpreted so as to deprive the veterans of their normal remedies to the benefit of

defaulting contractors — the very class it was the purpose of the statute to protect the veterans against. It must be held, therefore, that the enumeration of remedies in the statute merely created new enumerated remedies and was not intended to and did not deprive the veterans of any action for fraud or breach of contract that they might have under general contract principles.

Similarly, it would be anomalous if a congressional program, and the regulatory agreement formed thereunder, all of which was designed to assist in providing housing for low and moderate income families, were construed so as to provide cheap financing for the housing industry while at the same time denying tenants any means of protecting the benefits which they were intended to receive.

Real parties direct this court's attention to Falzarano v. United States (1st Cir. 1979) 607 F.2d 506, in which the court denied relief to tenants of a similar project. However, *Falzarano* and other similar cases cited by real parties, involved situations where tenants were contesting HUD-approved rent increases. (See Fenner v. Bruce Manor, Inc. (D. Md. 1976) 409 F. Supp. 1332; Harlib v. Lynn (7th Cir. 1975) 511 F.2d 51; Feldman v. HUD (E.D. Pa. 1977) 430 F. Supp. 1324.) These cases are therefore inapposite; a requirement of tenant *approval* to a rent increase or a tenant suit to challenge a HUD-approved increase could easily frustrate the Secretary's policy of maintaining a reasonable return of mortgagor's investments and promoting the financial stability of the housing projects. In contrast, as we have noted, maintenance of petitioners' action in this case will only serve to effectuate the policies of the Act.

Thus, for reasons we have set forth, appellants are entitled to maintain a third party beneficiary action against real parties.

STANDING TO SUE — RESTITUTION

We can do no better than to quote the Supreme Court of New Jersey in a case substantially on all fours with the case at bench.

> Accepting as we must for present purposes, the plaintiffs' version of the transaction there was an illegal and unjust exaction of rent in excess of the maximum expressly prescribed by the Administrator's [presently the Secretary of HUD] regulations and in violation of the terms embodied therein. . . . This exaction resulted in the unjust enrichment of the defendants at the plaintiffs' expense and, special defenses aside, entitles the plaintiffs to restitution under settled equitable principles cognizable in the lower court.

Brinkmann v. Urban Realty Co., Inc. (1952) 10 N.J. 113, 119, 89 A.2d 394.

CONCLUSION

Surely it would be unconscionable if a builder could secure the benefits of a government guaranteed loan upon his promise to charge no more than a schedule of rents he had agreed to and then find there is no remedy by which the builder can be forced to disgorge rents he had collected in excess of his agreement simply because the Government had failed to act.

Insofar as appellants sought specific performance of the contract between real parties and HUD or an injunction against breach of that contract by real parties, it appears that such relief has become moot because the contract has expired. Thus, we have not addressed the question as to whether appellants have standing to seek such remedies.

Let a writ of mandate issue directing the trial court to set aside its orders sustaining the general demurrers and granting the motion to strike. The matter is remanded for such further proceedings as may be appropriate and not inconsistent with the views expressed herein.

WHITE, P.J., and SCOTT, J., concur.

Notes and Questions

1. *Special requirements for third party beneficiaries of government contracts.* Restatement (Second) §313 sets forth special rules making it more difficult for plaintiffs to establish they are third party beneficiaries of government contracts. As the court points out in footnote 3 to *Zigas*, §313(2) (formerly §145 of the first Restatement) appears to be concerned primarily with liability to third parties for consequential damage: A promisor contracting with a governmental entity may not reasonably expect to assume liability to members of the public who may be affected by a breach. The classic case dealing with this situation is H. R. Moch Co. v. Rensselaer Water Co., 159 N.E. 896 (N.Y. 1928), which appears as the following illustration in the Restatement:

> B, a water company, contracts with A, a municipality, to maintain a certain pressure of water at the hydrants on the streets of the municipality. A owes no duty to the public to maintain that pressure. The house of C, an inhabitant of the municipality, is destroyed by fire, owing to B's failure to maintain the agreed pressure. B is under no contractual duty to C.

Restatement (Second) §313, illus. 2. While some cases have reached contrary conclusions, most jurisdictions follow *Moch.* Compare Vaughan v. Eastern Edison Co., 719 N.E.2d 520 (Mass. Ct. App. 1999) (utility did not owe duty to individual injured because of inoperative street light), with Harris v. Board of Water & Sewer Commissioners, 320 So.2d 624 (Ala. 1975) (recovery as beneficiary of contract and in tort for negligence). In explaining in Comment *a* to §313 its continued adherence to the result in *Moch*, the Restatement (Second) identifies as relevant factors "arrangements for governmental control over the litigation and settlement of claims, the likelihood of impairment of service or of excessive financial burden, and the availability of alternatives such as insurance." Assuming that the rule of §313(2) should continue to be applied to defeat third party recovery in cases like *Moch*, should that rule have been applied in *Zigas* to deny the plaintiffs their cause of action? Are there significant differences between the classes of potential third party beneficiaries in the two cases? Cf. Schuerman v. United States, 30 Fed. Cl. 420 (1994) (noting that policy rationale supporting §313(2) is applicable to contracts that benefit community as whole but not government contracts that benefit specific individuals).

2. *Split of authority in housing cases.* Some federal courts have rejected the reasoning of *Zigas* and have held that tenants are only incidental beneficiaries

of regulatory agreements between HUD and property owners. The *Zigas* court attempted to distinguish the contrary authority on the grounds that the cases involved government approved rent increases. Some of the contrary authority, however, rather clearly involved facts similar to *Zigas*. For example in Perry v. Housing Authority of Charleston, 664 F.2d 1210 (4th Cir. 1981), the plaintiffs were residents of a low-income housing project who alleged that the municipal housing authority had breached contracts with the federal government by allowing the housing to fall into a general state of disrepair. More specifically, the tenants alleged hazards from lead-based paint, deterioration of roofing and flooring, inadequate lighting and security patrols, and an infestation of rats and other vermin. The court very summarily concluded that the tenants were at best incidental beneficiaries of the contract between the housing authority and the federal agency. In addressing the question of standing based on federal law in other portions of the opinion, the court emphasized that the primary objective of the subsidized housing scheme was to benefit the states and that there was no indication that Congress had a legislative intent to give tenants a cause of action against their municipal landlords. See also Reiner v. West Village Associates, 600 F. Supp. 233 (S.D.N.Y. 1985), *aff'd*, 768 F.2d 31 (2d Cir. 1985); Price v. Pierce, 823 F.2d 1114 (7th Cir. 1987), *cert. denied*, 485 U.S. 960 (1988). In contrast, other federal courts have reached decisions similar to that in *Zigas* and held that tenants are intended beneficiaries of contracts between HUD and landlords providing rent subsidies pursuant to Section 8 of the United States Housing Act or other federal housing subsidy programs. E.g., Ashton v. Pierce, 716 F.2d 56 (D.C. Cir. 1983); Holbrook v. Pitt, 643 F.2d 1261 (7th Cir. 1981). With which line of cases do you agree? Why?

3. *The Ayala case.* An interesting case study of not only third party beneficiary issues in the public housing context, but also the potential for interaction between the courts, the legislature, and subsequent contracting parties, is found in Ayala v. Boston Housing Authority, 536 N.E.2d 1082 (Mass. 1989), and its aftermath. The plaintiffs in *Ayala* were a mother and her two minor children who sued the Boston Housing Authority (BHA) after the children suffered lead poisoning from exposure in a BHA certified apartment rented under Section 8 of the United States Housing Act of 1937, 42 U.S.C. §§1437 et seq. The court determined that BHA specifically promised in its agreement with HUD "to inspect the apartments which were the subject of the contract and to require the owners to keep the apartments in decent, safe, and sanitary condition." Id. at 1089. Nevertheless, BHA never inspected the apartment and never sought to remedy the lead hazard. The court held that the plaintiffs had standing to sue as third party beneficiaries of the BHA-HUD contract. The court reasoned:

> Recognizing a right to enforce these promises against the BHA "is appropriate to effectuate the intention of the parties." . . . When faced with liability for breach of its contractual duty to inspect for, and oversee the remedying of, lead paint hazards, the BHA will have a strong incentive to achieve the goals of the Federal statutes and regulations. We conclude also that HUD, the promisee, intended the plaintiffs to benefit. . . . To rule that these plaintiffs were not intended beneficiaries would mock the very goals which Congress and HUD set out to achieve through the Section 8

program, at least as to the lead paint provision: to afford children of families of meager means a decent, safe, and sanitary place to live.

Id. at 1089. The *Ayala* decision led to two reactions. First, as reflected in a subsequent case, the Massachusetts state legislature enacted legislation that restricted the outcome in *Ayala*, insulating the housing authorities from liability except where an "explicit and specific assurance[] of safety [is] made to the direct victim or a member of his family." Barnes v. Metropolitan Housing Authority, 679 N.E.2d 545, 548-549 (Mass. 1997). The same case also revealed that the defendant housing authority had altered its standard contract to state expressly that no third party standing rights would be created in the tenants or any other nonparty to the contract. Id. Do these developments after *Ayala* cast doubt on the propriety of courts granting standing in the subsidized housing cases?

4. *Scholarly analysis.* In his article, The Property in the Promise: A Study of the Third Party Beneficiary Rule, 98 Harv. L. Rev. 1109, 1176-1192 (1985), Professor Anthony Jon Waters analyzed *Zigas* and other cases as involving a new kind of "property," the right to various "statutory entitlements" created by federal laws affecting housing, education, welfare, and other public programs. Waters concluded that the third party beneficiary rule is "poised on the fringes of public law . . . perfectly suited to reversing the trend whereby intended beneficiaries of public programs have increasingly been denied access to the courts. . . ." 98 Harv. L. Rev. at 1210. For a more pessimistic analysis after Congress enacted welfare reform legislation in 1996, see Michele Estrin Gilman, Legal Accountability in an Era of Privatized Welfare, 89 Calif. L. Rev. 569 (2001) (exploring the federal and state bases for enforcing accountability after welfare reform, including third party beneficiary doctrine, and concluding that rights of welfare recipients are greatly reduced).

B. ASSIGNMENT AND DELEGATION OF CONTRACTUAL RIGHTS AND DUTIES

As has been the case with other aspects of contract law discussed in these pages, we must begin by treating in a few sentences what took the English courts of law and equity hundreds of years and gallons of ink to accomplish. Just as a long period of growth proved necessary before the courts were willing to enforce the executory bilateral agreement, so there was an initial resistance on their part to the notion that rights of parties to any contract might be transferred, or "assigned," to persons not originally privy to the agreement. In the postfeudal age, when wealth and power were still largely bound up in land, it was undoubtedly natural to think of any contract as creating an essentially personal relationship between individuals, not as giving rise to rights that could be handed from person to person like cabbages. With the growth of mercantile capitalism, it became increasingly apparent that wealth could come from the production and distribution of goods, and also from the financing of such activity; the corporation, whose shareholders enjoy limited liability for corporate obligations, came to be the typical vehicle for such commercial enterprise. In such an environment, it became easier to think of a contract right — particularly the right to a payment of money — as constituting a kind of property, which could itself be the subject of sale or exchange.

Consider, for example, the merchant. One who sells goods is likely to find that more goods are sold, and sold more quickly, if credit is extended to buyers, allowing them to take delivery now and pay later. Of course, selling on credit requires the merchant to run the risk of getting no payment at all (although that risk may seem minimal in the case of customers whose solvency and integrity are beyond question); it also involves a delay in receipt of payment in any case. Since procuring more stock in trade may require cash, however, the merchant who sells on credit may be in a bind — may have, as we say, a "cash-flow" problem. One solution is to find someone who is willing to buy the credit accounts, for cash; this purchase will ordinarily be at something less than the face value of those accounts, to reflect the burden of collection and the risk of default. Or, the merchant may find a bank or other financer willing to lend money (to be repaid with interest) against the security of the accounts receivable (using them as "collateral"). Assignability of contract rights can thus serve as a lubricant to the production-distribution process. Indeed, in a modern credit economy, the availability of credit to commercial and consumer buyers and borrowers is more than just a lubricant; it has become an essential part of the economic machinery. However, for such transactions as these to be part of the accepted mode of doing business, they will generally require the backstop of potential legal enforceability by the "assignee" — the one to whom the merchant's accounts have been sold or pledged.

Given the commercial justification for assignability (at least of money obligations), it is not surprising that the English courts eventually came around to the notion that contract rights were indeed assignable. Equally unsurprising should be the fact that this process was long and tortuous, involving the interplay of law and equity courts and the use of legal fictions. Originally unwilling to recognize assignment as such, the courts of law were eventually persuaded to consider the person whom we would now call an "assignee" as having at least a "power of attorney" — a kind of agency — to collect on behalf of the original obligee (the "assignor"). When thus characterized as a power of attorney, the right of the would-be assignee was subject to certain infirmities: It could be revoked at will by the assignor and was automatically terminated on the latter's death or bankruptcy. During the seventeenth century, the courts of equity began to enforce assignments despite the intervening occurrence of such events. The law courts eventually followed suit. Today in every American jurisdiction it is generally true — either by statute or court decision, or both — that the assignee of a contract right may bring suit to enforce the assigned right, without regard to distinctions between law and equity. Statutes or rules of court usually permit — indeed, usually *require* — that such a suit be brought in the name of the "real party in interest," the assignee. A fuller account of the events so rapidly sketched above can be found in William S. Holdsworth, The History of the Treatment of *Choses* in

Action by the Common Law, 33 Harv. L. Rev. 997 (1920). A compilation of statutory references is contained in the Introductory Note to Restatement (Second) Chapter 15, Assignment and Delegation.

Before proceeding to survey some of the ramifications of contract transferability, we should first note the terminology employed in this area, as developed in the writings of Professor Corbin and others. See Arthur L. Corbin, Assignment of Contract Rights, 74 U. Pa. L. Rev. 207 (1926). As we know, bilateral contracts create both "rights" and "duties" (both parties having one or more of each). A contract *right* (i.e., the ability to require the other party either to perform or to pay damages) can today be "assigned." Restatement (Second) §317(2). Such an assignment at once creates in the assignee a new right, while at the same time extinguishing the corresponding right previously held by the assignor. Restatement (Second) §317(1). The assignment of a right is thus in practical effect a transfer in the true sense: It results in the moving of something from one person to another, just as does the passing of a football or a baton.

The transferring of a contractual *duty,* however, is quite another matter. In many cases, a person who is subject to a duty of performance may properly "delegate" that duty, that is, may satisfy it by employing others to perform it for her. Restatement (Second) §318(1). (This is particularly true of a corporation, whose every performance must obviously be through agents of some kind.) Such delegation of performance is not always permissible, however; whether it is will depend in a given case on the degree to which individual performance was called for by the contract that created the duty in question. Restatement (Second) §318(2). In any event, the mere procuring of a substitute to render performance — even in a case where such delegation of performance is proper — does not by itself extinguish the duty of performance created by the contract. The person originally bound to perform will remain subject to that duty (unless released by the obligee) until performance is actually rendered. Restatement (Second) §318(3). Do you see why this should be so? The essential difference between assignment and delegation lies here, in its effect on the original party. If assigning a right is like passing a football, then delegating a duty resembles more the communication of a catchy tune or a bad cold: Passing it on is not the same as getting rid of it.

In any case where assignment or delegation has been attempted by one or both of the original contracting parties, sorting out the rights and duties of all concerned can be a complicated process. First, you must ascertain the nature of what has been done (or attempted): Was it an assignment of rights? A delegation of duties? Or both? Next, you must test its validity against the terms of the contract itself and also against any other applicable rules of law. As we shall see, an assignment or delegation may be improper even if not expressly forbidden by the terms of the original contract. Conversely, it may in some cases achieve its intended result — may be "effective," to use the terminology suggested by Restatement (Second) §317, Comment *a* — even though the terms of the contract *do* expressly forbid it. If the assignment or delegation is indeed effective, this will create a new set of rights and duties among three persons: the assigning/delegating party; the other original party to the contract; and the new, third party. The cases below illustrate some of the complexities of sorting out these rights and duties, under the rules of the common law and the UCC.

Herzog v. Irace
Maine Supreme Court
594 A.2d 1106 (Me. 1991)

BRODY, Justice.

Anthony Irace and Donald Lowry appeal from an order entered by the Superior Court (Cumberland County, Cole, J.) affirming a District Court (Portland, Goranites, J.) judgment in favor of Dr. John P. Herzog in an action for breach of an assignment to Dr. Herzog of personal injury settlement proceeds[1] collected by Irace and Lowry, both attorneys, on behalf of their client, Gary G. Jones. On appeal, Irace and Lowry contend that the District Court erred in finding that the assignment was valid and enforceable against them. They also argue that enforcement of the assignment interferes with their ethical obligations toward their client. Finding no error, we affirm.

The facts of this case are not disputed. Gary Jones was injured in a motorcycle accident and retained Irace and Lowry to represent him in a personal injury action. Soon thereafter, Jones dislocated his shoulder, twice, in incidents unrelated to the motorcycle accident. Dr. Herzog examined Jones's shoulder and concluded that he needed surgery. At the time, however, Jones was unable to pay for the surgery and in consideration for the performance of the surgery by the doctor, he signed a letter dated June 14, 1988, written on Dr. Herzog's letterhead stating:

> I, Gary Jones, request that payment be made directly from settlement of a claim currently pending for an unrelated incident, to John Herzog, D.O., for treatment of a shoulder injury which occurred at a different time.

Dr. Herzog notified Irace and Lowry that Jones had signed an "assignment of benefits" from the motorcycle personal injury action to cover the cost of surgery on his shoulder and was informed by an employee of Irace and Lowry that the assignment was sufficient to allow the firm to pay Dr. Herzog's bills at the conclusion of the case. Dr. Herzog performed the surgery and continued to treat Jones for approximately one year.

In May, 1989, Jones received a $20,000 settlement in the motorcycle personal injury action. He instructed Irace and Lowry not to disburse any funds to Dr. Herzog indicating that he would make the payments himself. Irace and Lowry informed Dr. Herzog that Jones had revoked his permission to have the bill paid by them directly and indicated that they would follow Jones's directions. Irace and Lowry issued a check to Jones for $10,027 and disbursed the remaining funds to Jones's other creditors. Jones did send a check to Dr. Herzog but the check was returned by the bank for insufficient funds and Dr. Herzog was never paid.

---

1. This case involves the assignment of proceeds from a personal injury action, not an assignment of the cause of action itself.

Dr. Herzog filed a complaint in District Court against Irace and Lowry seeking to enforce the June 14, 1988 "assignment of benefits." The matter was tried before the court on the basis of a joint stipulation of facts. The court entered a judgment in favor of Dr. Herzog finding that the June 14, 1988 letter constituted a valid assignment of the settlement proceeds enforceable against Irace and Lowry. Following an unsuccessful appeal to the Superior Court, Irace and Lowry appealed to this court. Because the Superior Court acted as an intermediate appellate court, we review the District Court's decision directly. See Brown v. Corriveau, 576 A.2d 200, 201 (Me. 1990). . . .

VALIDITY OF ASSIGNMENT

An assignment is an act or manifestation by the owner of a right (the assignor) indicating his intent to transfer that right to another person (the assignee). See Shiro v. Drew, 174 F. Supp. 495, 497 (D. Me. 1959). For an assignment to be valid and enforceable against the assignor's creditor [sic—debtor?] (the obligor), the assignor must make clear his intent to relinquish the right to the assignee and must not retain any control over the right assigned or any power of revocation. Id. The assignment takes effect through the actions of the assignor and assignee and the obligor need not accept the assignment to render it valid. Palmer v. Palmer, 112 Me. 149, 153, 91 A. 281, 282 (1914). Once the obligor has notice of the assignment, the fund is "from that time forward impressed with a trust; it is . . . impounded in the [obligor's] hands, and must be held by him not for the original creditor, the assignor, but for the substituted creditor, the assignee." Id. at 152, 91 A. 281. After receiving notice of the assignment, the obligor cannot lawfully pay the amount assigned either to the assignor or to his other creditors and if the obligor does make such a payment, he does so at his peril because the assignee may enforce his rights against the obligor directly. Id. at 153, 91 A. 281.

Ordinary rights, including future rights, are freely assignable unless the assignment would materially change the duty of the obligor, materially increase the burden or risk imposed upon the obligor by his contract, impair the obligor's chance of obtaining return performance, or materially reduce the value of the return performance to the obligor, and unless the law restricts the assignability of the specific right involved. See Restatement (Second) Contracts §317(2)(a) (1982). In Maine, the transfer of a future right to *proceeds* from pending litigation has been recognized as a valid and enforceable equitable assignment. McLellan v. Walker, 26 Me. 114, 117-18 (1896). An equitable assignment need not transfer the entire future right but rather may be a partial assignment of that right. Palmer, 112 Me. at 152, 91 A. 281. We reaffirm these well established principles.

Relying primarily upon the Federal District Court's decision in *Shiro*, 174 F. Supp. 495, a bankruptcy case involving the trustee's power to avoid a preferential transfer by assignment, Irace and Lowry contend that Jones's June 14, 1988 letter is invalid and unenforceable as an assignment because it fails to manifest Jones's intent to permanently relinquish all control over the assigned funds and does nothing more than request payment from a specific fund. We disagree. The June 14, 1988 letter gives no indication that Jones attempted to retain any control over the funds he assigned to Dr. Herzog. Taken in context, the use of the word "request" did not give the court reason to question Jones's intent to complete the assignment and, although no specific amount was stated, the parties do not dispute that the services provided by Dr. Herzog and the amounts that he charged for those services were reasonable and necessary to the treatment of the shoulder injury referred to in the June 14 letter. Irace and Lowry had adequate funds to satisfy all of Jones's creditors, including Dr. Herzog, with funds left over for disbursement to Jones himself. Thus, this case simply does not present a situation analogous to *Shiro* because Dr. Herzog was given preference over Jones's other creditors by operation of the assignment. Given that Irace and Lowry do not dispute that they had ample notice of the assignment, the court's finding on the validity of the assignment is fully supported by the evidence and will not be disturbed on appeal.

ETHICAL OBLIGATIONS

Next, Irace and Lowry contend that the assignment, if enforceable against them, would interfere with their ethical obligation to honor their client's instruction in disbursing funds. Again, we disagree.

Under the Maine Bar Rules, an attorney generally may not place a lien on a client's file for a third party. M. Bar R. 3.7(c). The Bar Rules further require that an attorney "promptly pay or deliver to the client, as requested by the client, the funds, securities, or other properties in the possession of the lawyer which the client is entitled to receive." M. Bar R. 3.6(f)(2)(iv). [Substantially similar to Model Rule of Professional Conduct 1.15(b). — EDS.] The rules say nothing, however, about a client's power to assign his right to proceeds from a pending lawsuit to third parties. Because the client has the power to assign his right to funds held by his attorney, McLellan v. Walker, 26 Me. at 117-18, it follows that a valid assignment must be honored by the attorney in disbursing the funds on the client's behalf. The assignment does not create a conflict under Rule 3.6(f)(2)(iv) because the client is not entitled to receive funds once he has assigned them to a third party. Nor does the assignment violate Rule 3.7(c), because the client, not the attorney, is responsible for placing the incumbrance upon the funds. Irace and Lowry were under no ethical obligation, and the record gives no indication that they were under a contractual obligation, to honor their client's instruction to disregard a valid assignment. The District Court correctly concluded that the assignment is valid and enforceable against Irace and Lowry.

The entry is:

Judgment affirmed.

All concurring.

Notes and Questions

1. *Limitations on assignments in general; statutory restrictions.* As discussed previously, the law now generally recognizes the validity of assignments of contract rights, but various limitations remain. The Restatement (Second) §317(2) identifies three bases for restricting assignment of rights: conflict with statute or public policy, material adverse effect on the other party, and valid preclusion by contract term.

Assignment of some contract rights may be expressly prohibited either by state or federal statute. Almost every state has some form of statutory restriction on assignment of wages. Federal statutes restrict the assignment of any public contract or order and of any claim against the government. 41 U.S.C. §15; 31 U.S.C. §3727. See generally Statutory Note, Restatement (Second) of Contracts, ch. 15.

2. *Public policy limitations.* The *Herzog* opinion implicitly addresses a potential public policy limit in footnote 1 by underscoring that the assignment involves proceeds from a personal injury action and "not the cause of action itself." The distinction is important because courts often have held that parties may not assign a prejudgment tort claim but may assign the proceeds of such a claim. The basis for the distinction is that "assignment of a claim gives the assignee control of the claim and promotes champerty" (stirring up lawsuits by financing litigation). See Charlotte-Mecklenburg Hosp. Authority v. First of Georgia Ins. Co., 455 S.E.2d 655, 657 (N.C. 1995); but see Midtown Chiropractic v. Illinois Farmers Ins. Co., 847 N.E.2d 942 (Ind. 2006) (assignment of proceeds of injury claim not enforceable because essentially the same in substance as an assignment of the claim itself, which is prohibited by statute; this is a "distinction without a difference"; authorities on both sides discussed). Compare Mallios v. Baker, 11 S.W.3d 157 (Tex. 2000) (most jurisdictions have held that assignment of legal malpractice claims violates public policy).

3. *Material adverse effect on obligor.* In addition to the statutory and public policy restrictions on assignment of rights, an assignment of a contract right may be invalid if the assignment would have a material adverse effect on the other party to the original contract (the obligor). Restatement (Second) §317(2)(a) provides that a contract can be assigned unless "the substitution of a right of the assignee for the right of the assignor would materially change the duty of the obligor, or materially increase the burden or risk imposed on him by his contract, or materially impair his chance of obtaining return performance, or materially reduce its value to him." UCC §2-210(2) contains similar limitations. In light of the public policy in favor of assignability, however, courts will generally be reluctant to find that the assignment would have a material adverse effect on the obligor. E.g., Clark v. B.P. Oil Co., 137 F.3d 386 (6th Cir. 1998) (assignment of gasoline supply contract from producer to regional distributor resulted only in immaterial price increases and credit term changes for retailer); Somont Oil Co., Inc. v. Nutter, 743 P.2d 1016 (Mont. 1987) (assignment of right to exploit mineral interest did not materially impair nonassigning party's chance of obtaining expected performance).

The assignment of rights under a personal services contract may raise questions of material adverse effect on the obligor because of the potential change in the performance to be rendered. See E. Allan Farnsworth, Contracts §11.4, at 693 (4th ed. 2004). See also Munchak Corp. v. Cunningham, 457 F.2d 721 (4th Cir. 1972) (purchasers of basketball franchise could enforce player's contract because he was not obligated to perform differently for the plaintiffs than for the previous owner of the same club). See generally Larry A. DiMatteo, Depersonalization of Personal Service Contracts: The Search for a Modern Approach to Assignability, 27 Akron L. Rev. 407 (1994) (suggesting that general rule prohibiting assignment of personal services contracts should be replaced with presumption of assignability).

Personal services or employment contracts often involve express covenants not to compete after termination (as discussed in the *Valley Medical Specialists* case in Chapter 7). The courts are divided on whether an employer may assign its rights under such a covenant to a successor that buys the business and for which the employee often continues to work for some period of time. Compare J. H. Renarde, Inc. v. Sims, 711 A.2d 410 (N.J. Super. Ch. Div. 1998) (covenant not to compete was assignable and enforceable against employee who remained with new employer for five years), with All-Pak, Inc. v. Johnston, 694 A.2d 347 (Pa. Super. Ct. 1997) (covenant not to compete not assignable to purchaser of business even though employee continued more than five years; restrictive covenants are not favored and new owner could have obtained employee's consent to assignment of covenant).

Some early cases held that the typical requirements contract was not assignable because of the seller's substantial interest in the particular circumstances and creditworthiness of the buyer. E.g., Crane Ice Cream Co. v. Terminal Freezing & Heating Co., 128 A. 280 (Md. 1925). Without attempting to state a blanket rule applicable to all such cases, Comment 4 to UCC §2-210 suggests strongly that the application of §§2-306 and 2-609 should ordinarily overcome this objection, unless "material personal discretion" is involved. Questions related to the adverse impact of an assignment on the other original party are discussed further in the next case, Sally Beauty Co. v. Nexxus Products Co., and the accompanying notes.

4. *Partial assignments.* The *Herzog* facts also suggest the potential for adverse impact on the obligor that may result from a partial transfer of rights. At common law, the obligor's assent to a "partial assignment" was required to make it effective because of concerns about the inconvenience to the obligor of splitting its performance and the exposure of the obligor to multiple lawsuits. Partial assignments, however, were enforceable in equity. See E. Allan Farnsworth, Contracts §11.3, at 689-690 (4th ed. 2004). In light of modern procedural rules allowing joinder of parties in a single action, the rationale for restricting enforcement of partial assignments has largely disappeared. Therefore, the *Herzog* opinion accurately reflects the willingness of many courts to enforce partial assignments in the same manner as a full transfer. The Restatement (Second) §326 also takes this approach, subject to some procedural limitations. Nevertheless, some courts still deny enforcement to partial assignments of rights made without the obligor's consent. See, e.g., Service Adjustment Co., Inc. v. Underwriters at Lloyd's London, 562 N.E.2d 1046, 1049 (Ill. App. Ct. 1990) (although rule against partial assignments has been questioned, it has never been "squarely rejected" in Illinois). The possibility also remains that the splitting of rights into many, partial assignments could impose a material adverse burden on the obligor and therefore be ruled ineffective.

5. *Contractual prohibitions on assignment.* Reflecting a huge departure from the common law position of general nonassignability of contract rights, both the UCC and the Restatement allow assignment of some contractual rights even in the face of contract language expressly providing otherwise. UCC §§2-210(2) and 9-406(d), (f) provide that in some cases the right to payment of

money can always be assigned even though the contract may attempt to prohibit such transfer. While Restatement (Second) §317(2) suggests that contract terms may preclude assignment, §322 modifies that limitation. Under §322 a "no assignment" clause will be first construed only to prohibit delegation of duties, and, alternatively, will be read to constitute a promise not to assign rights that might lead to damages for breach but will not render the assignment ineffective. The Restatement (Second) §322 preference for interpreting a nonassignment clause would be applied "unless a different intention is manifested," suggesting that some language might be strong enough to actually prohibit assignment of rights. In Owen v. CNA Insurance/Continental Cas. Co., 771 A.2d 1208 (N.J. 2001), the New Jersey Supreme Court held that a clause limiting assignment of the proceeds of a structured settlement would be construed as a covenant not to assign, for which the assignor would be liable in damages, but not a prohibition on the assignment. To be effective to prevent assignment, the court indicated that the clause must use magic words:

> To meet that standard, the non-assignment provision generally must state that non-conforming assignments (i) shall be "void" or "invalid," or (ii) that the assignee shall acquire no rights or the non-assigning party shall not recognize any such assignment. Id. at 1214.

See also E. Allan Farnsworth, Contracts §11.4, at 694-695 (4th ed. 2004) (anti-assignment clauses are generally enforced but narrowly construed where possible).

6. *Defenses against assignee.* The *Herzog* decision reflects the basic principle that once the obligor receives notice of an effective assignment of rights, performance must be rendered to the assignee and payment to the assignor will not defeat the assignee's rights. See also UCC §9-406(a). Suppose that Mr. Jones had informed his attorneys that he considered Dr. Herzog's services unsatisfactory. Would that make a difference in the attorneys' obligation to honor the assignment? See Restatement (Second) §336(4). What should the attorneys have done in such a situation?

Sally Beauty Co. v. Nexxus Products Co.
United States Court of Appeal
801 F.2d 1001 (7th Cir. 1986)

CUDAHY, Circuit Judge.

Nexxus Products Company ("Nexxus") entered into a contract with Best Barber & Beauty Supply Company, Inc. ("Best"), under which Best would be the exclusive distributor of Nexxus hair care products to barbers and hair stylists throughout most of Texas. When Best was acquired by and merged into Sally Beauty Company, Inc. ("Sally Beauty"), Nexxus cancelled the agreement. Sally Beauty is a wholly-owned subsidiary of Alberto-Culver Company ("Alberto-Culver"), a major manufacturer of hair care products and a competitor of Nexxus'. Sally Beauty claims that Nexxus breached the contract by cancelling; Nexxus asserts by way of defense that the contract was not assignable or, in the alternative, not assignable to Sally Beauty. The district court granted Nexxus' motion for summary judgment, ruling that the contract was one for personal services and therefore not assignable. We affirm on a different theory—that this contract could not be assigned to the wholly-owned subsidiary of a direct competitor under section 2-210 of the Uniform Commercial Code.

I

Only the basic facts are undisputed and they are as follows. Prior to its merger with Sally Beauty, Best was a Texas corporation in the business of distributing beauty and hair care products to retail stores, barber shops and beauty salons throughout Texas. Between March and July 1979, Mark Reichek, Best's president, negotiated with Stephen Redding, Nexxus' vice-president, over a possible distribution agreement between Best and Nexxus. Nexxus, founded in 1979, is a California corporation that formulates and markets hair care products. Nexxus does not market its products to retail stores, preferring to sell them to independent distributors for resale to barbers and beauticians. On August 2, 1979, Nexxus executed a distributorship agreement with Best, in the form of a July 24, 1979 letter from Reichek, for Best, to Redding, for Nexxus:

Dear Steve:

It was a pleasure meeting with you and discussing the distribution of Nexus [sic] Products. The line is very exciting and we feel we can do a substantial job with it—especially as the exclusive distributor in Texas (except El Paso).

If I understand the pricing structure correctly, we would pay $1.50 for an item that retails for $5.00 (less 50%, less 40% off retail), and Nexus will pay the freight charges regardless of order size. This approach to pricing will enable us to price the items in the line in such a way that they will be attractive and profitable to the salons.

Your offer of assistance in promoting the line seems to be designed to simplify the introduction of Nexus Products into the Texas market. It indicates a sincere desire on your part to assist your distributors. By your agreeing to underwrite the cost of training and maintaining a qualified technician in our territory, we should be able to introduce the line from a position of strength. I am sure you will let us know at least 90 days in advance should you want to change this arrangement.

By offering to provide us with the support necessary to conduct an annual seminar (i.e., mailers, guest artisit [sic]) at your expense, we should be able to reenforce our position with Nexus users and introduce the product line to new customers in a professional manner.

To satisfy your requirement of assured payment for merchandise received, each of our purchase orders will be accompanied by a Letter of Credit that will become negotiable when we receive the merchandise. I am sure you will agree that this arrangement is fairest for everybody concerned.

While we feel confident that we can do an outstanding job with the Nexus line and that the volume we generate will adequately compensate you for your continued support, it is usually best to have an understanding should we no longer be distributing Nexus Products—either by our desire or your request. Based on our discussions, cancellation or termination of Best Barber & Beauty Supply Co., Inc. as a distributor can only take place on the anniversary date of our original appointment as a distributor — and then only with 120 days prior notice. If Nexus terminates us, Nexus will buy back all of our inventory at cost and will pay the freight charges on the returned merchandise.

Steve, we feel that the Nexus line is exciting and very promotable. With the program outlined in this letter, we feel it can be mutually profitable and look forward to a long and successful business relationship. If you agree that this letter contains the details of our understanding regarding the distribution of Nexus Products, please sign the acknowledgment below and return one copy of this letter to me.

> Very truly yours,
> /s/*Mark E. Reichek*
> President

Acknowledged /s/ *Stephen Redding*
Date 8/2/79

Appellant's Appendix at 2-3.

In July 1981 Sally Beauty acquired Best in a stock purchase transaction and Best was merged into Sally Beauty, which succeeded to Best's rights and interests in all of Best's contracts. Sally Beauty, a Delaware corporation with its principal place of business in Texas, is a wholly-owned subsidiary of Alberto-Culver. Sally Beauty, like Best, is a distributor of hair care and beauty products to retail stores and hair styling salons. Alberto-Culver is a major manufacturer of hair care products and, thus, is a direct competitor of Nexxus in the hair care market.[1]

Shortly after the merger, Redding met with Michael Renzulli, president of Sally Beauty, to discuss the Nexxus distribution agreement. After the meeting, Redding wrote Renzulli a letter stating that Nexxus would not allow Sally Beauty, a wholly-owned subsidiary of a direct competitor, to distribute Nexxus products:

> As we discussed in New Orleans, we have great reservations about allowing our NEXXUS Products to be distributed by a company which is, in essence, a direct competitor. We appreciate your argument of autonomy for your business, but the fact remains that you are totally owned by Alberto-Culver. Since we see no way of justifying this conflict, we cannot allow our products to be distributed by Sally Beauty Company.

Appellant's Appendix at 475.

· · ·

II

Sally Beauty's breach of contract claim alleges that by acquiring Best, Sally Beauty succeeded to all of Best's rights and obligations under the distribution agreement. It further alleges that Nexxus breached the agreement by failing to give Sally Beauty 120 days notice prior to terminating the agreement and

---

1. The appellant does not appear to dispute the proposition that Alberto-Culver is Nexxus' direct competitor, see Reply Brief at 8-10; rather it disagrees only with Nexxus' contention that performance by Sally Beauty would necessarily be unacceptable. See infra.

by terminating it on other than an anniversary date of its formation. Complaint, Count III, Appellant's Appendix at 54-55. Nexxus, in its motion for summary judgment, argued that the distribution agreement it entered into with Best was a contract for personal services, based upon a relationship of personal trust and confidence between Reichek and the Redding family. As such, the contract could not be assigned to Sally without Nexxus' consent.

In opposing this motion Sally Beauty argued that the contract was freely assignable because (1) it was between two corporations, not two individuals and (2) the character of the performance would not be altered by the substitution of Sally Beauty for Best. It also argued that "the Distribution Agreement is nothing more than a simple, non-exclusive contract for the distribution of goods, the successful performance of which is in no way dependent upon any particular personality, individual skill or confidential relationship." Appellant's Appendix at 119.

In ruling on this motion, the district court framed the issue before it as "whether the contract at issue here between Best and Nexxus was of a personal nature such that it was not assignable without Nexxus' consent." It ruled:

> The court is convinced, based upon the nature of the contract and the circumstances surrounding its formation, that the contract at issue here was of such a nature that it was not assignable without Nexxus's consent. First, the very nature of the contract itself suggests its personal character. A distribution agreement is a contract whereby a manufacturer gives another party the right to distribute its products. It is clearly a contract for the performance of a service. In the court's view, the mere selection by a manufacturer of a party to distribute its goods presupposes a reliance and confidence by the manufacturer on the integrity and abilities of the other party. . . .
> In addition, in this case the circumstances surrounding the contract's formation support the conclusion that the agreement was not simply an ordinary commercial contract but was one which was based upon a relationship of personal trust and confidence between the parties. Specifically, Stephen Redding, Nexxus's vice-president, travelled to Texas and met with Best's president personally for several days before making the decision to award the Texas distributorship to Best. Best itself had been in the hair care business for 40 years and its president Mark Reichek had extensive experience in the industry. It is reasonable to conclude that Stephen Redding and Nexxus would want its distributor to be experienced and knowledgeable in the hair care field and that the selection of Best was based upon personal factors such as these.

Memorandum Opinion and Order at 56 (citation omitted). The district court also rejected the contention that the character of performance would not be altered by a substitution of Sally Beauty for Best: "Unlike Best, Sally Beauty is a subsidiary of one of Nexxus' direct competitors. This is a significant distinction and in the court's view, it raises serious questions regarding Sally Beauty's ability to perform the distribution agreement in the same manner as Best." Id. at 7.

We cannot affirm this summary judgment on the grounds relied on by the district court. . . . Although it might be "reasonable to conclude" that Best and Nexxus had based their agreement on "a relationship of personal trust and confidence," and that Reichek's participation was considered essential to Best's performance, this is a finding of fact. . . . Since the parties submitted conflicting affidavits on this question,[3] the district court erred in relying on Nexxus' view as representing undisputed fact in ruling on this summary judgment motion. . . .

We may affirm this summary judgment, however, on a different ground if it finds support in the record. United States v. Winthrop Towers, 628 F.2d 1028, 1037 (7th Cir. 1980). Sally Beauty contends that the distribution agreement is freely assignable because it is governed by the provisions of the Uniform Commercial Code (the "UCC" or the "Code"), as adopted in Texas. Appellants' Brief at 46-47. We agree with Sally that the provisions of the UCC govern this contract and for that reason hold that the assignment of the contract by Best to Sally Beauty was barred by the UCC rules on delegation of performance, UCC §2-210(1), Tex. Bus. & Com. Code Ann. §2-210(a) (Vernon 1968).

III

[The court concluded that although the contract involved some services, it was predominantly a contract for the sale of goods and therefore came within the scope of Article 2 of the UCC. — EDS.]

IV

The fact that this contract is considered a contract for the sale of goods and not for the provision of a service does not, as Sally Beauty suggests, mean that it is freely assignable in all circumstances. The delegation of performance under a sales contract (whether in conjunction with an assignment of rights, as here, or not) is governed by UCC section 2-210(1), Tex. Bus. & Com. Code §2-210(a) (Vernon 1968). The UCC recognizes that in many cases an obligor will find it convenient or even necessary to relieve himself of the duty of performance under a contract, see Official Comment 1, UCC §2-210 ("[T]his section recognizes both delegation of performance and assignability as normal and permissible incidents of a contract for the sale of goods."). The Code therefore sanctions delegation except where the delegated performance would be unsatisfactory to the obligee: "A party may perform his duty through a delegate unless otherwise agreed to or unless the other party has a substantial interest in having his original promisor perform or control the acts required by the contract." UCC §2-210(1), Tex. Bus. & Com. Code Ann.

---

3. Reichek stated the following in an affidavit submitted in support of Sally Beauty's Memorandum in Opposition to Nexxus' Motion for Summary Judgment:

> At no time prior to the execution of the Distribution Agreement did Steve Redding tell me that he was relying upon my personal peculiar tastes and ability in making his decision to award a Nexxus distributorship to Best. Moreover, I never understood that Steve Redding was relying upon my skill and ability in particular in choosing Best as a distributor.
>
> I never considered the Distribution Agreement to be a personal service contract between me and Nexxus or Stephen Redding. I always considered the Distribution Agreement to be between Best and Nexxus as expressly provided in the Distribution Agreement which was written by my brother and me. At all times I conducted business with Nexxus on behalf of Best and not on my own behalf. In that connection, when I sent correspondence to Nexxus, I invariably signed it as president of Best.
>
> Neither Stephen Redding nor any other Nexxus employee ever told me that Nexxus was relying on my personal financial integrity in executing the Distribution Agreement or in shipping Nexxus products to Best. . . .

Affidavit of Mark Reichek, pars. 19-21, Appellant's Appendix at 189-190.

§2-210(a) (Vernon 1968). Consideration is given to balancing the policies of free alienability of commercial contracts and protecting the obligee from having to accept a bargain he did not contract for.

We are concerned here with the delegation of Best's duty of performance under the distribution agreement, as Nexxus terminated the agreement because it did not wish to accept Sally Beauty's substituted performance.[6] Only one Texas case has construed section 2-210 in the context of a party's delegation of performance under an executory contract. In McKinnie v. Milford, 597 S.W.2d 953 (Tex. Civ. App. 1980, *writ ref'd, n.r.e.*), the court held that nothing in the Texas Business and Commercial Code prevented the seller of a horse from delegating to the buyer a pre-existing contractual duty to make the horse available to a third party for breeding. "[I]t is clear that Milford [the third party] had no particular interest in not allowing Stewart [the seller] to delegate the duties required by the contract. Milford was only interested in getting his two breedings per year, and such performance could only be obtained from McKinnie [the buyer] after he bought the horse from Stewart." Id. at 957. In *McKinnie,* the Texas court recognized and applied the UCC rule that bars delegation of duties if there is some reason why the non-assigning party would find performance by a delegate a substantially different thing than what he had bargained for.

In the exclusive distribution agreement before us, Nexxus had contracted for Best's "best efforts" in promoting the sale of Nexxus products in Texas. UCC §2-306(2), Tex. Bus. & Com. Code Ann. §2-306(b) (Vernon 1968), states that "[a] lawful agreement by either buyer or seller for exclusive dealing in the kind of goods concerned imposes unless otherwise agreed an obligation by the seller to use best efforts to supply the goods and by the buyer to use best efforts to promote their sale." This implied promise on Best's part was the consideration for Nexxus' promise to refrain from supplying any other distributors within Best's exclusive area. See Official Comment 5, UCC §2-306. It was this contractual undertaking which Nexxus refused to see performed by Sally.

In ruling on Nexxus' motion for summary judgment, the district court noted: "Unlike Best, Sally Beauty is a subsidiary of one of Nexxus' direct competitors. This is a significant distinction and in the court's view, it raises serious questions regarding Sally Beauty's ability to perform the distribution agreement in the same manner as Best." Memorandum Opinion and Order at 7. In Berliner Foods Corp. v. Pillsbury Co., 633 F. Supp. 557 (D. Md. 1986), the court stated the same reservation more strongly on similar facts. Berliner was an exclusive distributor of Haagen-Dazs ice cream when it was sold to Breyer's, manufacturer of a competing ice cream line. Pillsbury Co., manufacturer of Haagen-Dazs, terminated the distributorship and Berliner sued. The court noted, while weighing the factors for and against a

---

6. If this contract is assignable, Sally Beauty would also, of course, succeed to Best's rights under the distribution agreement. But the fact situation before us must be distinguished from the assignment of contract rights that are no longer executory (e.g., the right to damages for breach or the right to payment of an account), which is considered in UCC section 2-210(2), Tex. Bus. & Com. Code Ann. §2-210(b) (Vernon 1968), and in several of the authorities relied on by appellants. The policies underlying these two situations are different and, generally, the UCC favors assignment more strongly in the latter. See UCC §2-210(2) (non-executory rights assignable even if agreement states otherwise).

preliminary injunction, that "it defies common sense to require a manufacturer to leave the distribution of its products to a distributor under the control of a competitor or potential competitor." Id. at 559-60. We agree with these assessments and hold that Sally Beauty's position as a wholly-owned subsidiary of Alberto-Culver is sufficient to bar the delegation of Best's duties under the agreement.

We do not believe that our holding will work the mischief with our national economy that the appellants predict. We hold merely that the duty of performance under an exclusive distributorship may not be delegated to a competitor in the market place — or the wholly-owned subsidiary of a competitor — without the obligee's consent. We believe that such a rule is consonant with the policies behind section 2-210, which is concerned with preserving the bargain the obligee has struck. Nexxus should not be required to accept the "best efforts" of Sally Beauty when those efforts are subject to the control of Alberto-Culver. It is entirely reasonable that Nexxus should conclude that this performance would be a different thing than what it had bargained for. At oral argument, Sally Beauty argued that the case should go to trial to allow it to demonstrate that it could and would perform the contract as impartially as Best. It stressed that Sally Beauty is a "multi-line" distributor, which means that it distributes many brands and is not just a conduit for Alberto-Culver products. But we do not think that this creates a material question of fact in this case. When performance of personal services is delegated, the trier merely determines that it is a personal services contract. If so, the duty is per se nondelegable. There is no inquiry into whether the delegate is as skilled or worthy of trust and confidence as the original obligor: the delegate was not bargained for and the obligee need not consent to the substitution. And so here: it is undisputed that Sally Beauty is wholly owned by Alberto-Culver, which means that Sally Beauty's "impartial" sales policy is at least acquiesced in by Alberto-Culver — but could change whenever Alberto-Culver's needs changed. Sally Beauty may be totally sincere in its belief that it can operate "impartially" as a distributor, but who can guarantee the outcome when there is a clear choice between the demands of the parent-manufacturer, Alberto-Culver, and the competing needs of Nexxus? The risk of an unfavorable outcome is not one which the law can force Nexxus to take. Nexxus has a substantial interest in not seeing this contract performed by Sally Beauty, which is sufficient to bar the delegation under section 2-210, Tex. Bus. Com. Code Ann. §2-210 (Vernon 1968). Because Nexxus should not be forced to accept performance of the distributorship agreement by Sally, we hold that the contract was not assignable without Nexxus' consent.[10]

The judgment of the district court is affirmed.

POSNER, Circuit Judge, dissenting.

My brethren have decided, with no better foundation than judicial intuition about what businessmen consider reasonable, that the Uniform Commercial Code gives a supplier an absolute right to cancel an exclusive-dealing contract

_____

10. This disposition makes it unnecessary to address Nexxus' argument that Sally Beauty breached the distribution agreement by not giving Nexxus 120 days' notice of the Best-Sally Beauty merger.

if the dealer is acquired, directly or indirectly, by a competitor of the supplier. I interpret the Code differently.

Nexxus makes products for the hair and sells them through distributors to hair salons and barbershops. It gave a contract to Best, cancellable on any anniversary of the contract with 120 days' notice, to be its exclusive distributor in Texas. Two years later Best was acquired by and merged into Sally Beauty, a distributor of beauty supplies and wholly owned subsidiary of Alberto-Culver. Alberto-Culver makes "hair care" products, too, though they mostly are cheaper than Nexxus's, and are sold to the public primarily through grocery stores and drugstores. My brethren conclude that because there is at least a loose competitive relationship between Nexxus and Alberto-Culver, Sally Beauty cannot — as a matter of law, cannot, for there has been no trial on the issue — provide its "best efforts" in the distribution of Nexxus products. Since a commitment to provide best efforts is read into every exclusive-dealing contract by section 2-306(2) of the Uniform Commercial Code, the contract has been broken and Nexxus can repudiate it. Alternatively, Nexxus had "a substantial interest in having his original promisor perform or control the acts required by the contract," and therefore the delegation of the promisor's (Best's) duties to Sally Beauty was improper under section 2-210(1).

. . .

The fact that Best's president has quit cannot be decisive on the issue whether the merger resulted in a delegation of performance. The contract between Nexxus and Best was not a personal-services contract conditioned on a particular individual's remaining with Best. Compare Jennings v. Foremost Dairies, Inc., supra, 235 N.Y.S.2d at 574. If Best had not been acquired, but its president had left anyway, as of course he might have done, Nexxus could not have repudiated the contract.

No case adopts the per se rule that my brethren announce. The cases ask whether, as a matter of fact, a change in business form is likely to impair performance of the contract. . . .

My brethren find this a simple case — as simple (it seems) as if a lawyer had undertaken to represent the party opposing his client. But notions of conflict of interest are not the same in law and in business, and judges can go astray by assuming that the legal-services industry is the pattern for the entire economy. The lawyerization of America has not reached that point. Sally Beauty, though a wholly owned subsidiary of Alberto-Culver, distributes "hair care" supplies made by many different companies, which so far as appears compete with Alberto-Culver as vigorously as Nexxus does. Steel companies both make fabricated steel and sell raw steel to competing fabricators. General Motors sells cars manufactured by a competitor, Isuzu. What in law would be considered a fatal conflict of interest is in business a commonplace and legitimate practice. The lawyer is a fiduciary of his client; Best was not a fiduciary of Nexxus.

Selling your competitor's products, or supplying inputs to your competitor, sometimes creates problems under antitrust or regulatory law — but only when the supplier or distributor has monopoly or market power and uses it to restrict a competitor's access to an essential input or to the market for the competitor's output. . . . There is no suggestion that

Alberto-Culver has a monopoly of "hair care" products or Sally Beauty a monopoly of distributing such products, or that Alberto-Culver would ever have ordered Sally Beauty to stop carrying Nexxus products. Far from complaining about being squeezed out of the market by the acquisition, Nexxus is complaining in effect about Sally Beauty's refusal to boycott it!

How likely is it that the acquisition of Best could hurt Nexxus? Not very. Suppose Alberto-Culver had ordered Sally Beauty to go slow in pushing Nexxus products, in the hope that sales of Alberto-Culver "hair care" products would rise. Even if they did, since the market is competitive Alberto-Culver would not reap monopoly profits. Moreover, what guarantee has Alberto-Culver that consumers would be diverted from Nexxus to it, rather than to products closer in price and quality to Nexxus products? In any event, any trivial gain in profits to Alberto-Culver would be offset by the loss of goodwill to Sally Beauty; and a cost to Sally Beauty is a cost to Alberto-Culver, its parent. Remember that Sally Beauty carries beauty supplies made by other competitors of Alberto-Culver; Best alone carries "hair care" products manufactured by Revlon, Clairol, Bristol-Myers, and L'Oreal, as well as Alberto-Culver. Will these powerful competitors continue to distribute their products through Sally Beauty if Sally Beauty displays favoritism for Alberto-Culver products? Would not such a display be a commercial disaster for Sally Beauty, and hence for its parent, Alberto-Culver? Is it really credible that Alberto-Culver would sacrifice Sally Beauty in a vain effort to monopolize the "hair care" market, in violation of section 2 of the Sherman Act? Is not the ratio of the profits that Alberto-Culver obtains from Sally Beauty to the profits it obtains from the manufacture of "hair care" products at least a relevant consideration?

Another relevant consideration is that the contract between Nexxus and Best was for a short term. Could Alberto-Culver destroy Nexxus by failing to push its products with maximum vigor in Texas for a year? In the unlikely event that it could and did, it would be liable in damages to Nexxus for breach of the implied best-efforts term of the distribution contract. Finally, it is obvious that Sally Beauty does not have a bottleneck position in the distribution of "hair care" products, such that by refusing to promote Nexxus products vigorously it could stifle the distribution of those products in Texas; for Nexxus has found alternative distribution that it prefers — otherwise it wouldn't have repudiated the contract with Best when Best was acquired by Sally Beauty.

Not all businessmen are consistent and successful profit maximizers, so the probability that Alberto-Culver would instruct Sally Beauty to cease to push Nexxus products vigorously in Texas cannot be reckoned at zero. On this record, however, it is slight. And there is no principle of law that if something happens that trivially reduces the probability that a dealer will use his best efforts, the supplier can cancel the contract. Suppose there had been no merger, but the only child of Best's president had gone to work for Alberto-Culver as a chemist. Could Nexxus have canceled the contract, fearing that Best (perhaps unconsciously) would favor Alberto-Culver products over Nexxus products? That would be an absurd ground for cancellation, and so is Nexxus's actual ground. At most, so far as the record shows, Nexxus may have had grounds for "insecurity" regarding the performance by Sally Beauty of its obligation to use its best efforts to promote Nexxus products, but if so its remedy was not to cancel the contract but to demand assurances of due performance. See UCC §2-609; Official Comment 5 to §2-306. No such demand was made. An anticipatory repudiation by conduct requires conduct that makes the repudiating party unable to perform. Farnsworth, Contracts 636 (1982). The merger did not do this. At least there is no evidence it did. The judgment should be reversed and the case remanded for a trial on whether the merger so altered the conditions of performance that Nexxus is entitled to declare the contract broken.

Notes and Questions

1. *Effect of general language.* The court noted that the attempted assignment in *Sally Beauty* included a transfer of both rights and duties of the assignor. The language used in assignments does not always make explicit whether the intent is to both assign rights and delegate duties. Restatement (Second) §328 states that general language of assignment will include both assignment of rights and delegation of duties unless the circumstances indicate otherwise. The UCC takes the same approach in §2-210(5). See also Hyosung America, Inc. v. Sumagh Textile Co., Ltd., 137 F.3d 75 (2d Cir. 1998) (general language in transfer of contracts for sale of goods included both assignment of rights and delegation of duties; transaction was not merely assignment of rights for financing purposes); Rosenberg v. Son, Inc., 491 N.W.2d 71 (N.D. 1992) (general language in sale of business included both assignment of rights and delegation of duties).

2. *Delegation of personal service obligations.* Where a contract imposes on an individual the duty of personal service, that duty is almost always regarded as inherently undelegable, unless the other party assents. See, e.g., Restatement (Second) §318, Illustrations 5 (school teacher) and 6 (radio singer); compare Illustration 3 (*A* will build a building "in accordance with specifications"; delegable by *A*) with Illustration 7 (*A* will "personally cut the grass on *B's* meadow"; not delegable by *A*). The principle applies to contracts involving artists and professionals. See Rosetti v. City of New Britain, 303 A.2d 714 (Conn. 1972) (citing as nondelegable duties personal services of artists, physicians, lawyers, and possibly architects, depending upon intent of parties). It has also been extended to business contracts when the promisee has a substantial interest in performance by a particular individual. See Hy King Associates, Inc. v. Versatech Manufacturing Industries, Inc., 826 F. Supp. 231 (E.D. Mich. 1993) (holding that exclusive distributorship agreement for automotive parts was not assignable because it was based on manufacturer's confidence in personal skill and abilities of individual with whom contract was formed); UCC §2-210(1); Restatement (Second) §318(2). The court in *Sally Beauty* appears to accept this principle, but it disagrees with the trial court's decision on motion for summary judgment that the distribution contract between Sally Beauty and Nexxus was a personal service contract as a matter of law. Do you agree with the appellate court on this point, or was the trial judge correct in finding as a matter of law that the contract was a personal service contract?

3. *Economic analysis.* In his stinging dissent Judge Posner characterizes the majority opinion as having "no better foundation than judicial intuition about what businessmen consider reasonable." Do you agree? Can you articulate a justification for the decision based on principles of economic analysis?

4. *Effect of clause requiring consent to delegation.* The contract in *Sally Beauty* did not expressly prohibit delegation of duties, but suppose that it had, would such a clause be effective? The notes after *Herzog* underscored the difficulty of prohibiting assignment of rights, but Restatement (Second) §322(1) and UCC §2-210(4) reflect the general view that courts are likely to enforce a clause prohibiting delegation of a duty. Real property leases and franchise agreements present settings in which the ability to assign rights and delegate duties is particularly important. The courts are divided on whether to allow a landlord or franchisor to refuse arbitrarily to approve assignment when the contract expressly requires their consent. A number of courts have imposed a standard of reasonableness in the decision to approve an assignment of a lease or franchise, unless the contract expressly states that the nonassigning party may exercise unfettered discretion. See Larese v. Creamland Dairies, Inc., 767 F.2d 716 (10th Cir. 1985) (transfer of franchise); Julian v. Christopher, 575 A.2d 735 (Md. 1990) (real property lease). Other courts take just the opposite position that a contract requiring consent to assignment grants "an unrestricted right to withhold approval" if the lessor or franchisor acts honestly and the clause does not expressly provide that consent cannot be unreasonably withheld. Taylor Equipment, Inc. v. John Deere Co., 98 F.3d 1028, 1034 (8th Cir. 1996) (implied obligation of good faith did not apply to manufacturer's refusal to consent to assignment of equipment dealership); First Federal Savings Bank v. Key Markets, Inc., 559 N.E.2d 600 (Ind. 1990) (landlord had unlimited right to withhold approval). Can you think of policy reasons that support or oppose the view that a clause requiring consent to an assignment should be construed to allow withholding of consent for any reason whatsoever?

5. *Effect of delegation or assignment on rights and duties of the parties.* In those situations that involve a permissible delegation of a duty, the obligee generally has rights against the original obligor and the delegate. The original obligor remains liable to the obligee until the performance is rendered by the delegate, unless the obligee agrees to release the original obligor (referred to as "novation"), but evidence of the novation must be clear. See Rosenberg v. Son, Inc., 491 N.W.2d 71 (N.D. 1992) (an obligor cannot escape its liability by merely delegating duties); Restatement (Second) §§280, 318, Comment *d*. The obligee also can bring suit against the delegate as a third party beneficiary of the agreement by which the delegate promises to assume the original obligor's duty. See Gateway Co. v. DiNoia, 654 A.2d 342 (Conn. 1995).

If the transaction involves an assignment of rights rather than a delegation of duties, generally the assignee "stands in the shoes" of the assignor. See, e.g., Board of Managers of the Medinah v. Bank of Ravenswood, 692 N.E.2d 402 (Ill. App. Ct. 1998). Thus, the assignee will be subject to any claims or defenses of the obligor that arise out of the contract assigned. See Smith v. Cumberland Group, Ltd., 687 A.2d 1167 (Pa. Super. Ct. 1997); UCC §9-404(a)(1); Restatement (Second) §336(1). When the assignor and the obligor have done business together over a period of time, it is possible that the obligor may also have claims against the assignor arising from contracts other than the one assigned. The rights of the assignee under the contract assigned will be subject as well to claims and defenses of the obligor arising from these other contracts, but only as to claims or defenses that "accrue" before the obligor receives notification of the assignment. E.g., Seattle-First National Bank v. Oregon Pacific Industries, Inc., 500 P.2d 1033 (Or. 1972) (assignee bank not subject to claim arising from unassigned plywood contract that accrued after notice of assignment; "accrue" defined to mean when breach of contract occurs); UCC §9-404(a)(2); Restatement (Second) §336(2). The assignee may, however, be protected from claims or defenses if the obligor has signed an enforceable "waiver of claims and defenses," UCC §9-403, or if the assignee is a holder in due course of a negotiable instrument. UCC §3-302. Courses in Commercial Paper and Secured Transactions examine these issues.

PROBLEM 9-1

Recall the facts of Problem 6-2, page 493, in which you were asked by your client, Francis Fallon, to review the terms of his proposed contract with Captain Donut, Inc. Assume that you are visited again by Fallon, who has decided to retire after five years of the ten-year franchise period because his pension rights and savings will adequately support him and his household for the foreseeable future. Fallon poses to you a number of questions about his rights under the franchise agreement.

First, Fallon wants to know if he can simply retire from the doughnut business and terminate the franchise without liability to Captain Donut?

Second, since the franchise represents a considerable initial investment on Fallon's part, he is also interested in the possibility of selling the property and his business (including his rights under the franchise agreement) to Carlos Cruz, his assistant store manager for the last three years. Is Fallon likely to be able to make the sale to Cruz?

Third and last, Fallon is interested in the possibility of turning over the business to his daughter Teresa, who is now a 21-year-old college senior. Is Fallon likely to be able to transfer the business to Teresa?

Fallon also mentions that six months ago Captain Donut was acquired by Gigantic Corporation through a stock purchase arrangement. To date, Gigantic has not made any changes in the standard operating procedures for franchisees except that franchise fees are now mailed directly to Gigantic's corporate offices. Does the change in ownership of Captain Donut have any relevance to Fallon's rights and duties?

You should consider the provisions of the franchise agreement as set out in Problem 6-2 in answering Fallon's questions.

While in earlier chapters we have focused on defenses to the contract as a whole, we turn now to a consideration of the performance obligations that a contract imposes. The Restatement (Second) in §235(2) defines "breach" as "any non-performance" of a contractual duty at a time "when performance of [that] duty . . . is due." Comment b to that section states that performance is not due if for any reason nonperformance is "justified." In one way or another, the sections of this chapter address those central questions: When is one party's performance due, so that failure to perform will be a breach? When is nonperformance justified?

The first section of this chapter addresses the question whether, by the express terms of the parties' agreement, performance by one party is a presently due obligation. This might involve simply the question of whether the time stated for performance has arrived—the day, perhaps even the hour. Often, however, the express terms of the agreement will state that performance is not due unless and until some specified event has taken place. If the agreement does so provide, then the performance is said to be "conditioned," and the happening of that event is an "express condition" to the duty of performance. The use of express conditions as a drafting device is designed to protect one party (or possibly both parties) against various types of risk, involving the possibility that performance will be less advantageous than hoped for, or will be more difficult or even impossible in ways that might not otherwise offer an excuse from liability for nonperformance. For example, the typical contract for the purchase of residential real estate contains a clause making the buyer's purchase obligation conditional on the buyer's obtaining financing from a lending institution. If the buyer is unable to obtain financing despite a good faith effort, the buyer will not be obligated to purchase the property.

We will see, however, that sometimes a party does have a present duty of performance even though an express condition to that party's duty has not occurred. The nonoccurrence of a condition can be "excused" for a variety of reasons. For instance, if the buyer in our example made no effort whatever to obtain financing, a court might well hold that the buyer was bound to purchase the property, the financing condition being excused because of his bad faith. (Of course, the seller might — particularly if the buyer's financial condition was uncertain — elect to find another buyer, rather than seeking specific performance, but that would not preclude her pursuing the first buyer for any damages flowing from the breach.) As this example shows, it is analytically important to distinguish between excused and unexcused failure of a condition: When an express condition has simply failed to occur, the conditional duty never arises and the promisor is therefore justified in not performing. When nonoccurrence of the condition is *excused*, however, the conditional duty becomes an *un*conditional one, and the promisor's failure to perform amounts to a breach.

The second situation we will address in this chapter involves the relationship between the parties' performance obligations. As we have seen, although some contracts are "unilateral" in form, the vast majority are probably "bilateral," mutual exchanges of promises of future performance. (Or, in the cumbersome phrase employed by the Restatement (Second) in §231, "performances to be exchanged under an exchange of promises.") In such a case, when the time for performance arrives, one party may fail to render all or some of its promised performance. What effect does that have on the performance obligation of the other? In a construction contract, for instance, the contractor agrees to construct a building according to certain specifications, while in return the owner agrees to pay the contractor, typically in installments of stated amounts payable at the completion of specified portions of the work. Suppose the owner fails to make one of those progress payments when it comes due. What effect does this have on the contractor? Does he simply have to continue construction and hope the owner will eventually make that payment as promised? Can he keep working, but at the same time bring suit for the promised payment? Can he (with or without bringing suit for that payment) call the construction work to a halt until the delinquent payment is made? Can the contractor even go so far as to declare the contract at an end, sue the owner for damages, and go on to another job? Similar questions may arise from the other side as well. Suppose the contractor has ostensibly finished the construction as promised and has gone on to another project, but the owner finds the work done to be incomplete or inadequate. Is the owner nevertheless bound to pay the balance of the contract price? Can she offset that claim with a damage claim of her own? Can she simply withhold all payments not yet made until full performance is rendered?

Of course, the answers to questions like these are often found in the terms of the contract itself. If not, they will have to come from the rules of contract law, as applied to the court's understanding of what is often a complicated and highly contested series of events. Those rules speak sometimes of "partial," "total," or "material" breach, sometimes of "constructive" or "concurrent conditions," and sometimes of "substantial performance." Despite these variations in terminology, however, the law tends to focus on the same underlying issues: What is the magnitude of the breach? What is its effect on the other party? What is the likelihood that the breach will be cured? In light of such factors as these, the law determines what responses by the non-breaching party are or are not permissible.

The final section of this chapter will address a related but distinct situation: Where the time for performance has not yet arrived, but the likelihood of nonperformance appears substantial. Sometimes one party to a contract will declare in advance, in no uncertain terms, his unwillingness or inability to perform his duties under that contract. Does the other party have to wait until the time for performance actually arrives before taking any legal action? Or can she treat this "repudiation" as the equivalent of a present breach of contract and act accordingly? The situation may not be this clear-cut, of course. Even where a duty of performance has not been repudiated, it will sometimes appear to the other party that performance is for some reason unlikely to occur when due. How can that party guard against this prospect of nonperformance, without herself being in breach for nonperformance or repudiation? Here again, the express terms of the contract might answer the question. If they do not, however, the law has rules by which the parties can be guided in taking measures for self-protection. One of the most useful services a lawyer can render for her client is to help him navigate safely between the Scylla and Charybdis of under- and over-reaction to a breach of contract, present or prospective.

A. EXPRESS CONDITIONS

In this section of Chapter 10, we address the seemingly more clearcut case where the parties have expressly agreed that the duty of one party (or, perhaps, both of them) should depend on the happening of one or more specified events. The conditioning event might be all or part of one party's performance, but it could just as well be some event completely outside the control of either party. Often it will be an event over which one party has some control, albeit limited.

When an express condition is spelled out in a contract, it will often be a condition to the duty of only one of the parties, because that term has been included in the agreement to protect that party from having to perform in a situation where performance is for some reason less advantageous for her. Thus, for example, a real estate buyer's performance obligation may be conditioned on its ability to obtain a favorable zoning variance, without which the property will be less useful to it. The buyer of a business may condition its duty to complete the purchase on the accuracy of the seller's financial statements at the time of closing. Sometimes one party's duty is conditioned on the other party's giving certain types of notice or providing certain types of information in a particular form, or by a stated time. (This is particularly common in insurance contracts, but it is found in countless other situations as well.) Whatever the motive behind its insistence on a conditioning term, the party whose performance is so conditioned will be referred to in this context as the "obligor," the one whose performance obligation is at issue. The other party will thus be the "obligee"—the one to whom the performance obligation is owed, and the one who is presumably attempting to enforce it.

Oppenheimer & Co. v. Oppenheim, Appel, Dixon & Co.
New York Court of Appeals
86 N.Y.2d 685, 660 N.E.2d 415, 636 N.Y.S.2d 734 (1995)

OPINION OF THE COURT

CIPARICK, Justice.

The parties entered into a letter agreement setting forth certain conditions precedent to the formation and existence of a sublease between them. The agreement provided that there would be no sublease between the parties "unless and until" plaintiff delivered to defendant the prime landlord's written consent to certain "tenant work" on or before a specified deadline. If this condition did not occur, the sublease was to be deemed "null and void." Plaintiff provided only oral notice on the specified date. The issue presented is whether the doctrine of substantial performance applies to the facts of this case. We conclude it does not for the reasons that follow.

I.

In 1986, plaintiff Oppenheimer & Co. moved to the World Financial Center in Manhattan, a building constructed by Olympia & York Company (O & Y). At the time of its move, plaintiff had three years remaining on its existing lease for the 33rd floor of the building known as One New York Plaza. As an incentive to induce plaintiff's move, O & Y agreed to make the rental payments due under plaintiff's rental agreement in the event plaintiff was unable to sublease its prior space in One New York Plaza.

In December 1986, the parties to this action entered into a conditional letter agreement to sublease the 33rd floor. Defendant already leased space on the 29th floor of One New York Plaza and was seeking to expand its operations. The proposed sublease between the parties was attached to the letter agreement. The letter agreement provided that the proposed sublease would be executed only upon the satisfaction of certain conditions. Pursuant to paragraph 1(a) of the agreement, plaintiff was required to obtain "the Prime Landlord's written notice of confirmation, substantially to the effect that [defendant] is a subtenant of the Premises reasonably acceptable to Prime Landlord." If such written notice of confirmation were not obtained "on or before December 30, 1986, then this letter agreement and the Sublease . . . shall be deemed null and void and of no further force and effect and neither party shall have any rights against nor obligations to the other."

Assuming satisfaction of the condition set forth in paragraph 1(a), defendant was required to submit to plaintiff, on or before January 2, 1987, its plans for "tenant work" involving construction of a telephone communication linkage system between the 29th and 33rd floors. Paragraph 4(c) of the letter agreement then obligated plaintiff to obtain the prime landlord's "written consent" to the proposed "tenant work" and deliver such consent to defendant on or before January 30, 1987. Furthermore, if defendant had not received the prime landlord's written consent by the agreed date, both the agreement and the sublease were to be deemed "null and void and of no further force and effect," and neither party was to have "any rights against nor obligations to the other." Paragraph 4(d) additionally provided that, notwithstanding satisfaction of the condition set forth in paragraph 1(a), the parties "agree not to execute and exchange the Sublease unless and until . . . the conditions set forth in paragraph (c) above are timely satisfied."

The parties extended the letter agreement's deadlines in writing and plaintiff timely satisfied the first condition set forth in paragraph 1(a) pursuant to the modified deadline. However, plaintiff never delivered the prime landlord's written consent to the proposed tenant work on or before the modified final deadline of February 25, 1987. Rather, plaintiff's attorney telephoned defendant's attorney on February 25 and informed defendant that the prime landlord's consent had been secured. On February 26, defendant, through its attorney, informed plaintiff's attorney that the letter agreement and sublease were invalid for failure to timely deliver the prime landlord's written consent and that it would not agree to an extension of the deadline. The document embodying the prime landlord's written consent was eventually received by plaintiff on March 20, 1987, 23 days after expiration of paragraph 4(c)'s modified final deadline.

Plaintiff commenced this action for breach of contract, asserting that defendant waived and/or was estopped by virtue of its conduct[1] from insisting on physical delivery of the prime landlord's written consent by the February 25 deadline. Plaintiff further alleged in its complaint that it had substantially performed the conditions set forth in the letter agreement.

At the outset of trial, the court issued an order in limine barring any reference to substantial performance of the terms of the letter agreement. Nonetheless, during the course of trial, the court permitted the jury to consider the theory of substantial performance, and additionally charged the jury concerning substantial performance. Special interrogatories were submitted. The jury found that defendant had properly complied with the terms of the letter agreement, and answered in the negative the questions whether defendant failed to perform its obligations under the letter agreement concerning submission of plans for tenant work, whether defendant by its conduct waived the February 25 deadline for delivery by plaintiff of the landlord's written consent to tenant work, and whether defendant by its conduct was equitably estopped from requiring plaintiff's strict adherence to the February 25 deadline. Nonetheless, the jury answered in the affirmative the question, "Did plaintiff substantially perform the conditions set forth in the Letter Agreement?," and awarded plaintiff damages of $1.2 million.

Defendant moved for judgment notwithstanding the verdict. Supreme Court granted the motion, ruling as a matter of law that "the doctrine of substantial performance has no application to this dispute, where the Letter Agreement is free of all ambiguity in setting the deadline that plaintiff concededly did not honor." The Appellate Division reversed the judgment on the law and facts, and reinstated the jury verdict. The Court concluded that

1. Plaintiff argued that it could have met the deadline, but failed to do so only because defendant, acting in bad faith, induced plaintiff into delaying delivery of the landlord's consent. Plaintiff asserted that the parties had previously extended the agreement's deadlines as a matter of course.

the question of substantial compliance was properly submitted to the jury and that the verdict should be reinstated because plaintiff's failure to deliver the prime landlord's written consent was inconsequential.

This Court granted defendant's motion for leave to appeal and we now reverse.

II.

Defendant argues that no sublease or contractual relationship ever arose here because plaintiff failed to satisfy the condition set forth in paragraph 4(c) of the letter agreement. Defendant contends that the doctrine of substantial performance is not applicable to excuse plaintiff's failure to deliver the prime landlord's written consent to defendant on or before the date specified in the letter agreement and that the Appellate Division erred in holding to the contrary. Before addressing defendant's arguments and the decision of the court below, an understanding of certain relevant principles is helpful.

A condition precedent is "an act or event, other than a lapse of time, which, unless the condition is excused, must occur before a duty to perform a promise in the agreement arises" (Calamari and Perillo, Contracts §11-2, at 438 [3d ed.]; see, Restatement [Second] of Contracts §224; see also, Merritt Hill Vineyards v. Windy Hgts. Vineyard, 61 N.Y.2d 106, 112-113, 472 N.Y.S.2d 592, 460 N.E.2d 1077). Most conditions precedent describe acts or events which must occur before a party is obliged to perform a promise made pursuant to an existing contract, a situation to be distinguished conceptually from a condition precedent to the formation or existence of the contract itself (see, M. K. Metals v. Container Recovery Corp., 645 F.2d 583). In the latter situation, no contract arises "unless and until the condition occurs" (Calamari and Perillo, Contracts §11-5, at 440 [3d ed.]).

Conditions can be express or implied. Express conditions are those agreed to and imposed by the parties themselves. Implied or constructive conditions are those "imposed by law to do justice" (Calamari and Perillo, Contracts §11-8, at 444 [3d ed.]). Express conditions must be literally performed, whereas constructive conditions, which ordinarily arise from language of promise, are subject to the precept that substantial compliance is sufficient. The importance of the distinction has been explained by Professor Williston:

> Since an express condition . . . depends for its validity on the manifested intention of the parties, it has the same sanctity as the promise itself. Though the court may regret the harshness of such a condition, as it may regret the harshness of a promise, it must, nevertheless, generally enforce the will of the parties unless to do so will violate public policy. Where, however, the law itself has imposed the condition, in absence of or irrespective of the manifested intention of the parties, it can deal with its creation as it pleases, shaping the boundaries of the constructive condition in such a way as to do justice and avoid hardship. (5 Williston, Contracts §669, at 154 [3d ed.].)

In determining whether a particular agreement makes an event a condition courts will interpret doubtful language as embodying a promise or constructive condition rather than an express condition. This interpretive preference is especially strong when a finding of express condition would increase the risk of forfeiture by the obligee (see, Restatement [Second] of Contracts §227 [1]).

Interpretation as a means of reducing the risk of forfeiture cannot be employed if "the occurrence of the event as a condition is expressed in unmistakable language" (Restatement [Second] of Contracts §229, comment a, at 185; see, §227, comment b [where language is clear, "(t)he policy favoring freedom of contract requires that, within broad limits, the agreement of the parties should be honored even though forfeiture results"]). Nonetheless, the nonoccurrence of the condition may yet be excused by waiver, breach or forfeiture. The Restatement posits that "[t]o the extent that the non-occurrence of a condition would cause disproportionate forfeiture, a court may excuse the non-occurrence of that condition unless its occurrence was a material part of the agreed exchange" (Restatement [Second] of Contracts §229).

Turning to the case at bar, it is undisputed that the critical language of paragraph 4(c) of the letter agreement unambiguously establishes an express condition precedent rather than a promise, as the parties employed the unmistakable language of condition ("if," "unless and until"). There is no doubt of the parties' intent and no occasion for interpreting the terms of the letter agreement other than as written.

Furthermore, plaintiff has never argued, and does not now contend, that the nonoccurrence of the condition set forth in paragraph 4(c) should be excused on the ground of forfeiture.[2] Rather, plaintiff's primary argument from the inception of this litigation has been that defendant waived or was equitably estopped from invoking paragraph 4(c). Plaintiff argued secondarily that it substantially complied with the express condition of delivery of written notice on or before February 25th in that it gave defendant oral notice of consent on the 25th.

Contrary to the decision of the Court below, we perceive no justifiable basis for applying the doctrine of substantial performance to the facts of this case. The flexible concept of substantial compliance "stands in sharp contrast to the requirement of strict compliance that protects a party that has taken the precaution of making its duty expressly conditional" (2 Farnsworth, Contracts §8.12, at 415 [2d ed. 1990]). If the parties "have made an event a condition of their agreement, there is no mitigating standard of materiality or substantiality applicable to the non-occurrence of that event" (Restatement [Second] of Contracts §237, comment d, at 220). Substantial performance in this context is not sufficient, "and if relief is to be had under the contract, it must be through excuse of the non-occurrence of the condition to avoid forfeiture" (id.; see, Brown-Marx Assocs. v. Emigrant Sav. Bank, 703 F.2d 1361, 1367-1368 [11th Cir.]; see also, Childres, Conditions in the Law of Contracts, 45 N.Y.U. L. Rev. 33, 35).

Here, it is undisputed that plaintiff has not suffered a forfeiture or conferred a benefit upon defendant. Plaintiff alludes to a $1 million licensing fee it allegedly paid to the prime landlord for the purpose of securing the latter's consent to the subleasing of the premises. At no point, however, does plaintiff claim that this sum was forfeited or that it was expended for the purpose of accomplishing the sublease with defendant. It is further

---

2. The Restatement defines the term "forfeiture" as "the denial of compensation that results when the obligee loses [its] right to the agreed exchange after [it] has relied substantially, as by preparation or performance on the expectation of that exchange" (§229, comment *b*).

undisputed that O & Y, as an inducement to effect plaintiff's move to the World Financial Center, promised to indemnify plaintiff for damages resulting from failure to sublease the 33rd floor of One New York Plaza. Consequently, because the critical concern of forfeiture or unjust enrichment is simply not present in this case, we are not presented with an occasion to consider whether the doctrine of substantial performance is applicable, that is, whether the courts should intervene to excuse the nonoccurrence of a condition precedent to the formation of a contract.

The essence of the Appellate Division's holding is that the substantial performance doctrine is universally applicable to all categories of breach of contract, including the nonoccurrence of an express condition precedent. However, as discussed, substantial performance is ordinarily not applicable to excuse the nonoccurrence of an express condition precedent.

Our precedents are consistent with this general principle. In Maxton Bldrs. v. Lo Galbo, 68 N.Y.2d 373, 509 N.Y.S.2d 507, 502 N.E.2d 184, the defendants contracted on August 3 to buy a house, but included in the contract the condition that if real estate taxes were found to be above $3,500 they would have the right to cancel the contract upon written notice to the seller within three days. On August 4 the defendants learned that real estate taxes would indeed exceed $3,500. The buyers' attorney called the seller's attorney and notified him that the defendants were exercising their option to cancel. A certified letter was sent notifying the seller's attorney of that decision on August 5 but was not received by the seller's attorney until August 9. We held the cancellation ineffective and rejected defendants' argument that reasonable notice was all that was required, stating: "It is settled . . . that when a contract requires that written notice be given within a specified time, the notice is ineffective unless the writing is actually received within the time prescribed" (id., at 378, 509 N.Y.S.2d 507, 502 N.E.2d 184). We so held despite the fact that timely oral notice was given and the contract did not provide that time was of the essence.

In Jungmann & Co. v. Atterbury Bros., 249 N.Y. 119, 163 N.E. 123, the parties entered into a written contract for the sale of 30 tons of casein. The contract contained the following clause: "Shipment: May-June from Europe. Advice of shipment to be made by cable immediately goods are dispatched" (id.). Plaintiff shipped the first 15 tons but gave no notice to the defendant, who rejected the shipment. Plaintiff thereafter shipped the remaining 15 tons to defendant, but again failed to provide notice by cable and instead sent two letters. Defendant rejected the remaining 15 tons. This Court was not persuaded by the argument that the defendant had received notice of shipment by other means and thus suffered no harm. "Even if that be true," we stated, "the fact remains that the plaintiff was obligated under its contract to see that defendant obtained advice of shipment by cable" (id., at 121, 163 N.E. 123). Plaintiff's failure to "perform[ ] all conditions precedent required of it," and "to give notice according to the terms of the contract" barred it from recovery (id., at 122, 163 N.E. 123).

Plaintiff's reliance on the well-known case of Jacob & Youngs v. Kent, 230 N.Y. 239, 129 N.E. 889, is misplaced. . . . The avoidance-of-forfeiture rationale which engendered the rule of *Jacob & Youngs* is simply not present here, and the case therefore "should not be extended by analogy where the reason for the rule fails" (Van Iderstine Co. v. Barnet Leather Co., 242 N.Y. 425, 434, 152 N.E. 250).

The lease renewal and insurance cases relied upon by plaintiff are clearly distinguishable and explicable on the basis of the risk of forfeiture existing therein. For example, in Sy Jack Realty Co. v. Pergament Syosset Corp., 27 N.Y.2d 449, 452, 318 N.Y.S.2d 720, 267 N.E.2d 462, this Court gave effect to a late notice of lease renewal. Importantly, while we reaffirmed the general rule "that notice, when required to be 'given' by a certain date, is insufficient and ineffectual if not received within the time specified," we held that the prior courts properly invoked the rule that equity "relieves against . . . forfeitures of valuable lease terms when default in notice has not prejudiced the landlord" (id., quoting Jones v. Gianferante, 305 N.Y. 135, 138, 111 N.E.2d 419; see also J.N.A. Realty Corp. v. Cross Bay Chelsea, 42 N.Y.2d 392, 397, 397 N.Y.S.2d 958, 366 N.E.2d 1313 ["when a tenant in possession under an existing lease has neglected to . . . renew, he might suffer a forfeiture if he has made valuable improvements on the property"]). We stated: "Since a long-standing location for a retail business is an important part of the good will of that enterprise, the tenant stands to lose a substantial and valuable asset" (id., 27 N.Y.2d, at 453, 318 N.Y.S.2d 720, 267 N.E.2d 462).

III.

In sum, the letter agreement provides in the clearest language that the parties did not intend to form a contract "unless and until" defendant received written notice of the prime landlord's consent on or before February 25, 1987. Defendant would lease the 33rd floor from plaintiff only on the condition that the landlord consent in writing to a telephone communication linkage system between the 29th and 33rd floors and to defendant's plans for construction effectuating that linkage. This matter was sufficiently important to defendant that it would not enter into the sublease "unless and until" the condition was satisfied. Inasmuch as we are not dealing here with a situation where plaintiff stands to suffer some forfeiture or undue hardship, we perceive no justification for engaging in a "materiality-of-the-nonoccurrence" analysis. To do so would simply frustrate the clearly expressed intention of the parties. Freedom of contract prevails in an arm's length transaction between sophisticated parties such as these, and in the absence of countervailing public policy concerns there is no reason to relieve them of the consequences of their bargain. If they are dissatisfied with the consequences of their agreement, "the time to say so [was] at the bargaining table" (*Maxton*, supra, at 382, 509 N.Y.S.2d 507, 502 N.E.2d 184).

Finally, the issue of substantial performance was not for the jury to resolve in this case. A determination whether there has been substantial performance is to be answered, "if the inferences are certain, by the judges of the law" (Jacob & Youngs v. Kent, 230 N.Y. 239, 243, 129 N.E. 889 supra).

Accordingly, the order of the Appellate Division should be reversed, with costs, and the complaint dismissed.

KAYE, C.J., and SIMONS, TITONE, BELLACOSA, SMITH and LEVINE, JJ., concur.

Order reversed, etc.

Notes and Questions

1. *Language sufficient to create an express condition.* In any case where the defendant obligor asserts the nonoccurrence of an express condition to his duty as a defense to liability for his nonperformance, a threshold issue will be whether the duty in question is indeed so conditioned. In *Oppenheimer,* the court spends little time on that issue. The critical language, it finds, is "unambiguous," because the parties have used the "unmistakable language of condition" — words and phrases like "if" and "unless and until." Although the court does not belabor the point, the language in the written contract is actually a good deal stronger than that; rather that just saying "if A does this, then B will do that," it goes on to indicate that failure of the conditioning event (timely delivery of certain notices) will cause the agreement to be "of no further force and effect." In such event, the agreement continues, "neither party shall have any rights against nor obligations to the other."

2. *Distinction between express conditions and promises.* Not all agreements are as clear as the one in *Oppenheimer.* One issue of interpretation that frequently arises involves the distinction between a condition and a promise. As analyzed by the court, plaintiff's failure to make timely delivery of either of the specified notices would have the effect of a failure of condition, releasing defendant from any duty to proceed with the transaction. Would the delivery term also be interpreted as a promise by the plaintiff to make timely delivery of the notices, the breach of which would give rise to a cause of action against the plaintiff for breach of contract? The court says that pursuant to the agreement the plaintiff "was required to" or "obligated to" deliver the notices as stated. If plaintiff had second thoughts about going ahead, could it simply withhold delivery of one or the other of the notices?

However one interprets the contract in *Oppenheimer,* there is no principled reason why a contractual term cannot be interpreted as *both* a promise and an express condition. See, e.g., Internatio-Rotterdam, Inc. v. River Brand Rice Mills, Inc., 259 F.2d 137 (2d Cir. 1958) (buyer's promise to give shipping instructions to seller at least two weeks prior to shipment was a "promissory condition"); 3A Corbin on Contracts §633. If an event is a "promissory condition," failure of the event to occur justifies the obligor in treating her obligations as discharged, and also subjects the obligee to liability for damages.

3. *Interpreting the contract language.* The preceding discussion indicates that a contract term might be interpreted by a court as either an express condition or as a promise, or possibly as both. On the other hand, a term that defines a performance obligation by reference to the happening of some event may be *neither* a promise nor a condition. Thus, in cases where the language of the contract in some fashion links a subcontractor's right to payment for work performed to the general contractor's receipt of payment from the owner (sometimes referred to as a "pay-when-paid" clause), the majority of courts have preferred to interpret such language as merely calling for payment within a reasonable time, and not as also conditioning the subcontractor's right to payment on such prior receipt of payment by the general. To rule otherwise, the courts have pointed out, would require the sub to assume the risk of the owner's credit, with the accompanying possibility of

forfeiture. To achieve that result, strong language to that effect will be needed (and even then may be not effective). For example, in Galloway Corp. v. S.B. Ballard Const. Co., 464 S.E.2d 349 (Va. 1995), the court stated: "[W]e hold that in the absence of a clear and unambiguous statement of the parties' intent as to the meaning of the time of payment provision in a construction subcontract, an absolute 'pay when paid' defense is available to a general contractor only if it can establish by parol evidence that the parties mutually intended the contract to create such a defense." Id. at 356. See also Federal Ins. Co. v. I. Kruger, Inc., 829 So.2d 732 (Ala. 2002) (clause did not create condition precedent but was merely timing mechanism, allowing contractor reasonable time to pay but not relieving it from liability to sub because of nonpayment by owner); but see MidAmerica Constr. Management, Inc. v. MasTec North America, Inc., 436 F.3d 1257 (10th Cir. 2006) (under either Texas or New Mexico case law, clause would be given effect as "pay-*if*-paid" rather than merely "pay-when-paid"; subcontractor not entitled to recover from general when general goes unpaid because of owner's bankruptcy). Some states regulate such clauses by statutes, which generally protect the subcontractor in varying degrees. See generally Margie Alsbrook, Contracting Away an Honest Day's Pay: An Examination of Conditional Payment Clauses in Construction Contracts, 58 Ark. L. Rev. 353 (2005).

4. *Distinction between express and constructive conditions*. In the course of its opinion, the *Oppenheimer* court refers to the early New York case of Jacob & Youngs v. Kent, 129 N.E. 889 (N.Y. 1921) (opinion by Cardozo, J.). The *Jacob & Youngs* case is reprinted later in this chapter as a principal case, and we will discuss it in detail then. At this point, it is enough to know that in that case, the New York court was applying what is usually known as the doctrine of "constructive conditions," which addresses the question of whether performance by one party is in effect an implied condition to the other party's duty of performance. The rule of "substantial performance," which was applied in that case, has generally no application to cases like *Oppenheimer*, where the court is considering the effect of what is clearly an "express condition" spelled out in the parties' contract.

5. *Which party's duty is conditional?* In some cases, the court must decide whether a given event stated as a condition should be regarded as conditioning *both* parties' duties of performance under the contract, in which case either one can insist on its nonoccurrence as a ground for nonperformance, or whether it properly conditions the duty of only one party, in which case it is waivable by that party acting alone. See, e.g., De Freitas v. Cote, 174 N.E.2d 371 (Mass. 1961) (where contract stated "this sale is subject to [federal] loan," buyer who obtained financing from other sources could enforce contract against seller; condition was clearly for benefit of buyer only and thus waivable by him); McDermott v. Burpo, 663 S.W.2d 256 (Mo. Ct. App. 1983) (vendors held in breach where they failed to show up for closing even though purchasers had notified them of willingness to pay price in cash, rather than obtaining mortgage financing). In *Oppenheimer,* if the prospective sublessor (plaintiff in the actual case) had been unable to obtain one or both of the required consents, could the sublessee have waived the condition, and enforced the sublease agreement anyway?

6. *Effect of nonoccurrence of condition.* Once the court has determined that the contract term in question really does expressly condition the defendant's duty of performance on the occurrence of some event, what will be the effect of its nonoccurrence? Until the conditioning event does occur, the duty does not arise; at the point when it cannot (or for some reason clearly will not) occur, the defendant is discharged. Restatement (Second) §225. Although the "strict enforcement" approach to express conditions may be characteristic of classical contract law, it is alive and well today, as the *Oppenheimer* opinion demonstrates. The court in *Oppenheimer* relies principally on two earlier New York decisions. One of those, Maxton Builders v. Lo Galbo, is a relatively recent decision (1986). (You might be interested to know that the attorney in *Maxton* who failed to give the requisite written notice of cancellation on behalf of his client was later held to have thereby committed actionable malpractice as a matter of law, despite assertions that he relied on the other attorney's assurances that oral notice was sufficient. LoGalbo v. Plishkin, Rubano & Baum, 558 N.Y.S.2d 185 (App. Div. 1990).) The Restatement (Second) continues the general rule of strict enforcement of express conditions, and Comment *d* to §237, quoted by the court in *Oppenheimer,* rejects the application of a "substantial performance" qualification to that rule. (As the court indicates, there are a variety of bases on which an express condition might be deemed "excused." Some of those are discussed in the Notes below, and in J.N.A. Realty Corp. v. Cross Bay Chelsea Inc., the case which follows.)

7. *Scholarly commentary.* The court in *Oppenheimer* also cites an article by Professor Robert Childres, Conditions in the Law of Contracts, 45 N.Y.U. L. Rev. 33 (1970). After examining scores of decisions citing the conditions provisions of the first Restatement, Childres concluded that almost all modern courts (as of 1970, that is) in practice would insist on strict performance of conditions only when the conditioning events are material to the agreement of the parties and the risks created thereby. Conditions that are merely "technical" — that is, not related in substance to the real reason for the defendant's nonperformance but asserted solely for the purpose of defeating the plaintiff's claim — he found to be generally excused under various theories such as adverse interpretation, waiver, prevention, or avoidance of forfeiture. While applauding modern courts for this approach to technical conditions, Professor Childres criticized the judicial technique of using such theories of excuse because "the failure to articulate the real ground of decision misleads the profession and thereby promotes uncertainty and litigation." He recommended that courts abandon these theories in favor of a broader rule: Only material conditions should be strictly enforced.

At least some courts appear to share Professor Childres's belief that the issue of materiality should be relevant to the question of how strictly a condition should be enforced. See, e.g, Sahadi v. Continental Illinois National Bank & Trust Co., 706 F.2d 193, 198 n.2 (7th Cir. 1983) (slight delay in making interest payments would not trigger failure of condition, accelerating payment of entire debt obligation; earlier precedents to the contrary were "decided in the salad days of American legal formalism which were marked by an unprecedented adherence to the letter of contractual text — a jurisprudential posture that has since been eclipsed by the kind of materiality approach embodied in [later Illinois cases]"); Jenkins v. U.S.A. Foods, Inc, 912

F. Supp. 969 (E.D. Mich. 1996) (no acceleration permitted; payments slightly late, but substantial performance present). Adopting *arguendo* Professor Childres's approach, does it appear to you that the condition involved in the *Oppenheimer* case was material?

8. *Waiver and estoppel of condition.* In *Oppenheimer*, the court appears to accept as fact that the plaintiff did inform defendant's attorney that the landlord's consent had been obtained. (The court says only that plaintiff's attorney "informed defendant . . . that the consent had been secured," which might suggest merely a voicemail message. The lower court, however, states that defendant's attorney "was notified on that day and, as with prior deadlines, told the landlord's attorney that he would get back to him." See 613 N.Y.S.2d, at 623.) Should the Court of Appeals have given that fact more weight in deciding whether to reverse the lower court? An obligor whose duty is expressly dependent on a condition may be under a duty to perform despite the nonoccurrence of that condition, if a court finds that he has, by word or conduct, "waived" the right to insist on fulfillment of the condition before performing the duty. Restatement (Second) §84(1) expresses the concept of waiver (the term itself is not used in the section, but see Comment *b*). As usually defined, waiver is "an intentional relinquishment of a known right." As expressed in §84(1), a waiver is effective without either consideration or reliance, but only if the condition waived was not either a material part of the performance that the obligor was to receive in exchange or a material part of the risk assumed. Compare Radiation Systems, Inc. v. Amplicon, Inc., 882 F. Supp. 1101 (D.D.C. 1995) (requirement that certain certificates be delivered by one party was purely technical, and could be overcome by showing of waiver or course of conduct amounting to contract modification), with Rose v. Mitsubishi International Corp., 423 F. Supp. 1162 (E.D. Pa. 1976) (condition of clear and marketable title not waivable, because material part of agreed exchange).

If the condition in *Oppenheimer* was merely minor — "procedural or technical" — it could be waived by the defendant-obligor's expression of intention to do so. If it were not minor, but material, it could still be overcome by an estoppel, based on the obligor's expression of intention not to insist on it, followed by the plaintiff-obligee's prejudicial reliance on that manifestation of intention. Justice Ciparick's opinion simply fails to address the issue of waiver or estoppel at all, discussing only the issue of "substantial performance," possibly because this was the basis of the lower appellate court's reversal. Does it appear to you that arguments of waiver or estoppel had potential merit as a basis for overcoming defendant's failure-of-condition argument?

9. *Prevention of condition.* Similar to the concept of waiver is the doctrine of "prevention," which states that a condition is excused if the promisor wrongfully hinders or prevents the condition from occurring. E.g., Shear v. National Rifle Assn. of America, 606 F.2d 1251 (D.C. Cir. 1979) (real estate broker stated cause of action for payment of commission, even though under terms of brokerage contract payment of commission was contingent on closing of sale, where broker alleged that management committee prevented defendant's board of directors from having opportunity to approve contract of sale). See Restatement (Second) §245. Where the conditioning event is to

some extent within the obligor's control, the obligor is likely to have at least the obligation to attempt to cause the condition to occur. E.g., Stendig, Inc. v. Thom Rock Realty Co., 558 N.Y.S.2d 917 (App. Div. 1990) (where both parties' obligations under lease of showroom space in design center were conditioned on landlord's having rented minimum amount of square feet of space, landlord subject to implied duty to use "good faith best efforts" to obtain tenants, citing Wood v. Lucy, Lady Duff-Gordon). Even if the event is not within the obligor's control, she may be under an obligation (express or implied) to cooperate with the obligee in causing the condition to happen, or at the minimum not to impede those efforts. E.g., Fateh v. Rich, 481 A.2d 464 (D.C. 1984) (defendant buyers of restaurant business wrongfully prevented condition that liquor authority give its consent to transfer of liquor license by engaging person with criminal record as manager of restaurant business, in violation of liquor authority policy). The question is often a difficult one, however, and courts have frequently held that the possibility of prevention of the condition by the obligor was a risk assumed by the obligee, and thus not "wrongful."

In *Oppenheimer*, if the plaintiff had obtained the landlord's consent, but withheld delivery of written notice to defendant because it wanted to withdraw from this deal and sublease to someone else, would the plaintiff have been in breach of its contract with the defendant? If it had been *unable* to obtain one or the other of those consents, would it have been in breach? If it didn't even *try* to obtain those consents, would it have been in breach?

10. *Avoidance of forfeiture.* In addition to the various possibilities discussed above, a court might justify enforcing a contractual duty, despite the apparent failure of a conditioning event, in order to avoid a forfeiture. This possibility is considered but ultimately rejected in the *Oppenheimer* case; in the course of that discussion, the court cites but distinguishes J. N. A. Realty Corp. v. Cross Bay Chelsea Inc., the next case in these materials. We will address the forfeiture aspect of *Oppenheimer* in our notes following the *JNA* case.

J. N. A. Realty Corp. v. Cross Bay Chelsea, Inc.
New York Court of Appeals
42 N.Y.2d 392, 366 N.E.2d 1313, 397 N.Y.S.2d 958 (N.Y. 1977)

WACHTLER, Judge.

J. N. A. Realty Corp., the owner of a building in Howard Beach, commenced this proceeding to recover possession of the premises claiming that the lease has expired. The lease grants the tenant, Cross Bay Chelsea, Inc., an option to renew and although the notice was sent, through negligence or inadvertence, it was not sent within the time prescribed in the lease. The landlord seeks to enforce the letter of the agreement. The tenant asks for equity to relieve it from a forfeiture.

The Civil Court, after a trial, held that the tenant was entitled to equitable relief. The Appellate Term affirmed, without opinion, but the Appellate Division, after granting leave, reversed and granted the petition. The tenant has appealed to this court.

Two primary questions are raised on the appeal. First, will the tenant suffer a forfeiture if the landlord is permitted to enforce the letter of the agreement. Secondly, if there will be a forfeiture, may a court of equity grant the tenant relief when the forfeiture would result from the tenant's own neglect or inadvertence.

At the trial it was shown that J. N. A. Realty Corp. (hereafter JNA) originally leased the premises to Victor Palermo and Sylvester Vascellero for a 10-year term commencing on January 1, 1964. Paragraph 58 of the lease, which was attached as part of 12-page rider, granted the tenants an option to renew for a 10-year term provided "that Tenant shall notify the landlord in writing by registered or certified mail six (6) months prior to the last day of the term of the lease that tenant desires such renewal." The tenants opened a restaurant on the premises. In February, 1964 they formed the Foro Romano Corp. (Foro) and assigned the lease to the corporation.

By December of 1967 the restaurant was operating at a loss and Foro decided to close it down and offer it for sale or lease. In March, 1968 Foro entered into a contract with Cross Bay Chelsea, Inc. (hereafter Chelsea), to sell the restaurant and assign the lease. As a condition of the sale Foro was required to obtain a modification of the option to renew so that Chelsea would have the right to renew the lease for an additional term of 24 years.

The closing took place in June of 1968. First JNA modified the option and consented to the assignment. The modification, which consists of a separate document to be attached to the lease, states: "the Tenant shall have a right to renew this lease for a further period of Twenty-Four (24) years, instead of Ten (10) years, from the expiration of the original term of said lease. . . . All other provisions of Paragraph #58 in said lease, . . . shall remain in full force and effect, except as hereinabove modified." Foro then assigned the lease and sold its interest in the restaurant to Chelsea for $155,000. The bill of sale states that "the value of the fixtures and chattels included in this sale is the sum of $40,000 and that the remainder of the purchase price is the value of the leasehold and possession of the restaurant premises." At that point five and one-half years remained on the original term of the lease.

In the summer of 1968 Chelsea reopened the restaurant. JNA's president, Nicholas Arena, admitted on the stand that throughout the tenancy it regularly informed Chelsea in writing of its obligations under the lease, such as the need to pay taxes and insurance by certain dates. For instance on June 13, 1973 JNA sent a letter to Chelsea informing them that certain taxes were due to be paid. When that letter was sent the option to renew was due to expire in approximately two weeks but JNA made no mention of this. A similar letter was sent to Chelsea in September, 1973.

Arena also admitted that throughout the term of the tenancy he was "most assuredly" aware of the time limitation on the option. In fact there is some indication in the record that JNA had previously used this device in an attempt to evict another tenant. Nevertheless it was not until November 12, 1973 that JNA took any action to inform the tenant that the option had lapsed. Then it sent a letter noting that the date had passed and, the letter states, "not having heard from you as prescribed by paragraph #58 in our lease we must assume you will vacate the premises" at the expiration of the original term, January 1,

1974. By letter dated November 16, 1973 Chelsea, through its attorney, sent written notice of intention to renew the option which, of course, JNA refused to honor.

At the trial Chelsea's principals claimed that they were not aware of the time limitation because they had never received a copy of paragraph 58 of the rider. They had received a copy of the modification but they had assumed that it gave them an absolute right to retain the tenancy for 24 years after the expiration of the original term. However, at the trial and later at the Appellate Division, it was found that Chelsea had knowledge of, or at least was "chargeable with notice" of, the time limitation in the rider and thus was negligent in failing to renew within the time prescribed.

Chelsea's principals also testified that they had spent an additional $15,000 on improvements, at least part of which had been expended after the option had expired. Toward the end of the trial JNA's attorney asked the court whether it would "take evidence from" Arena that he had negotiated with another tenant after the option to renew had lapsed. However, the court held that this testimony would be immaterial.

It is a settled principle of law that a notice exercising an option is ineffective if it is not given within the time specified (see, e.g., Restatement, Contracts 2d [Tent. Draft No. 1, 1964], §64, subd. [b]; 1A Corbin, Contracts [1963], §264; 1 Williston, Contracts [3d ed. 1957], §87; Sy Jack Realty Co. v. Pergament Syosset Corp., 27 N.Y.2d 449, 318 N.Y.S.2d 720, 267 N.E.2d 462). "At law, of course, time is always of the essence of the contract" (De Funiak, Modern Equity, §80, p.223). Thus the tenant had no legal right to exercise the option when it did, but to say that is simply to pose the issue; it does not resolve it. Of course the tenant would not be asking for equitable relief if it could establish its rights at law.

The major obstacle to obtaining equitable relief in these cases is that default on an option usually does not result in a forfeiture. The reason is that the option itself does not create any interest in the property, and no rights accrue until the condition precedent has been met by giving notice within the time specified. Thus equity will not intervene because the loss of the option does not ordinarily result in the forfeiture of any vested rights. . . . It has been suggested that even when the option has been paid for, nothing is forfeited when it expires, because the amount paid "is the exact agreed equivalent" of the power to exercise the right for the time allotted (see 1 Corbin, Contracts, §35, p.147).

But when a tenant in possession under an existing lease has neglected to exercise an option to renew, he might suffer a forfeiture if he has made valuable improvements on the property. This of course generally distinguishes the lease option, to renew or purchase, from the stock option or the option to buy goods. This was a distinction which some of the older cases failed to recognize. . . . More recently it has been noted that "although the tenant has no legal interest in the renewal period until the required notice is given, yet an equitable interest is recognized and protected against forfeiture in some cases where the tenant has in good faith made improvements of a substantial character, intending to renew the lease, if the landlord is not harmed by the delay in the giving of the notice and the lessee would sustain substantial loss in case the lease were not renewed" (2 Pomeroy, Equity Jurisprudence [5th ed.], §453b, p.296).

The leading case on this point is Fountain Co. v. Stein, 97 Conn.619, 118 A. 47, 27 A.L.R. 976 and the rule has been accepted by noted commentators (see, e.g., 1 Corbin, op. cit., §35, p.146; 1 Williston, Contracts [3d ed.], §76, p.249, n.4; 2 Pomeroy, op. cit., §453b, p.296). It has also been accepted and applied by this court. In Jones v. Gianferante, 305 N.Y. 135, 138, 111 N.E.2d 419, 420, citing the *Fountain* case we held that the tenant was entitled to "the benefit of the rule or practice in equity which relieves against such forfeitures contract of valuable lease terms when default in notice has not prejudiced the landlord, and has resulted from an honest mistake, or similar excusable fault." The rule was extended in Sy Jack Realty Co. v. Pergament Syosset Corp., 27 N.Y.2d 449, 453, 318 N.Y.S.2d 720, 722, 267 N.E.2d 462, 464, supra to preserve the tenant's interest in a "long-standing location for a retail business" because this is "an important part of the good will of that enterprise, [and thus] the tenant stands to lose a substantial and valuable asset."

In neither of those cases were we asked to consider whether the tenant would be entitled to equitable relief from the consequences of his own neglect or "mere forgetfulness" as the court had held in the *Fountain* case, supra. In *Gianferante* the default was due to an ambiguous lease, and in *Sy Jack* the notice was mailed but never delivered. . . . But the principle involved is well established in this State. A tenant or mortgagor should not be denied equitable relief from the consequences of his own neglect or inadvertence if a forfeiture would result (Giles v. Austin, 62 N.Y. 486; Noyes v. Anderson, 124 N.Y. 175, 26 N.E. 316. . . .) The rule applies even though the tenant or mortgagor, by his inadvertence, has neglected to perform an affirmative duty and thus breached a covenant in the agreement (Giles v. Austin, supra; Noyes v. Anderson, supra).

On occasion the court has cautioned that equitable relief would be denied where there has been a willful or gross neglect (Noyes v. Anderson, supra, 124 N.Y. p. 179, 26 N.E. p. 317), but it has been reluctant to employ the sanction when a forfeiture would result. In Giles v. Austin, supra, p. 491, for instance, the landlord sought to recover possession of the premises after the tenant had neglected to pay the taxes as required by a covenant in the lease. We held that although the tenant had not paid the taxes since the inception of the lease in 1859, and had only paid them after suit was commenced in 1868, the tenant's default was not "so willful, or his neglect so inexcusable, that a court of equity should have denied him any relief."

There are several cases in which this court has denied a tenant or mortgagor equitable relief because of his own neglect to perform within the time fixed in the lease or mortgage, but only when it has found that there was "no penalty, no forfeiture" (Graf v. Hope Bldg. Corp., 254 N.Y. 1, 4, 171 N.E. 884, 885 . . .). Cardozo took a different view. He felt that even though there may be no penalty or forfeiture "in a strict or proper sense" equity should "relieve against it if default has been due to mere venial inattention and if relief can be granted without damage to the lender." Even in those cases he would apply the general equitable principle that "the gravity of the fault must be compared with the gravity of the hardship" (Graf v. Hope Bldg. Corp., supra, 254 N.Y. pp.9-10, 13, 171 N.E. p.888 [Cardozo, Ch. J., dissenting]; see, also, 2 Pomeroy, Equity Jurisprudence [5th ed.], §439, p. 220).

Here, as noted, the tenant has made a considerable investment in improvements on the premises—$40,000 at the time of purchase, and an additional $15,000 during the tenancy. In addition, if the location is lost, the restaurant would undoubtedly lose a considerable amount of its customer good will. The tenant was at fault, but not in a culpable sense. It was, as Cardozo says, "mere venial inattention." There would be a forfeiture and the gravity of the loss is certainly out of all proportion to the gravity of the fault. Thus, under the circumstances of this case, the tenant would be entitled to equitable relief if there is no prejudice to the landlord.

However, it is not clear from the record whether JNA would be prejudiced if the tenant is relieved of its default. Because of the trial court's ruling, JNA was unable to submit proof that it might be prejudiced if the terms of the agreement were not enforced literally. Its proof of other negotiations was considered immaterial. It may be that after the tenant's default the landlord, relying on the agreement, in good faith, made other commitments for the premises. But if JNA did not rely on the letter of the agreement then, it should not be permitted to rely on it now to exact a substantial forfeiture for the tenant's unwitting default. This, however, must be resolved at a new trial.

Finally we would note, as the dissenters do, that it is possible to imagine a situation in which a tenant holding an option to renew might intentionally delay beyond the time prescribed in order to exploit a fluctuating market. However, as the dissenters also note, there is no evidence to suggest that that is what occurred here. On the contrary there has been an affirmed finding of fact that the tenant's late notice was due to negligence. Of course a tenant who has intentionally delayed should not be relieved of a forfeiture simply because this tenant, who was merely inadvertent, may be granted equitable relief. But, on the other hand, we do not believe that this tenant, or any tenant, guilty only of negligence should be denied equitable relief because some other tenant, in some other case, may be found to have acted in bad faith. By its nature equitable relief must always depend on the facts of the particular case and not on hypotheticals.

Accordingly, the order of the Appellate Division should be reversed and a new trial granted.

BREITEL, Chief Judge (dissenting). . . .

In this State, as in others, relief has been afforded tenants threatened with loss of an expected renewal period (see, generally, Effect of Lessee's Failure or Delay in Giving Notice Within Specified Time, of Intention to Renew Lease, Ann., 44 A.L.R.2d 1359, esp. 1362-1369). But in New York, as elsewhere, the circumstances conditioning such relief have been carefully limited. It is only where the tenant can show, not mere negligence, but an excuse such as fraud, mistake, or accident, that is, one or more of the categories common and integral to invocation of equity, that courts have, despite the literal agreement and intention of the parties, stepped in to prevent a loss (see, e.g., Jones v. Gianferante, 305 N.Y. 135, 138-139, 111 N.E.2d 419, 420, supra; 1 McAdam, Landlord and Tenant [5th ed.], §156, pp. 721-722).

Even in the case of excusable default by the tenant the court looks to the investment the tenant has made to bolster his right to equitable relief. But the fact of tenant investment alone is not enough to justify intervention. . . . In no case of accepted or acceptable authority . . . were improvements alone enough to help the negligent tenant. . . .

. . . For reasons that are not persuasive [the majority] would distinguish, however, between mere neglect or forgetfulness and gross or willful negligence, whatever that might be. . . . This is not a distinction generally accepted and is hardly a pragmatic one to apply in an area where the opportunities for distortion and manipulation are so great. The instability and uncertainty would be dangerous and would allow for ad hoc dispensations in particular cases without reliable rule so essential to commercial enterprise.

To begin with, under the guise of sheer inadvertence, a tenant could gamble with a fluctuating market, at the expense of his landlord, by delaying his decision beyond the time fixed in the agreement. The market having resolved in favor of exercising the option, the landlord, even though the day appointed in the agreement has passed, could be held to the return set out in the option, although if the market had resolved otherwise, the tenant could not be held to the renewal period.

None of this is to say that the tenant in this case was guilty of any manipulation. Hardly so. But what the court is concerned with is a rule for this case which perforce must cover other cases of like kind, where there will be no assurance that the "forgetfulness" is no more than that. The worst of the matter is that the kind of paltry record made in this case is hardly one on which a new rule with potential for mischief should be based. When the option, especially one requiring notice well in advance of the expiration of the lease, permits of economic manipulation, in commercial fairness the parties, especially if represented by counsel, should be held to their bargain, if plainly expressed.

Considering investments in the premises or the renewal term a "forfeiture" as alone warranting equitable relief would undermine if not dissolve the general rule upon which there is agreement. For, it is difficult to imagine a dilatory commercial tenant, particularly one in litigation over a renewal, who would not or could not point, scrupulously or unscrupulously, to some threatened investment in the premises, be it a physical improvement or the fact of good will. As a practical matter, it is not unreasonable to expect the commercial tenant, as compared with his residential counterpart, to protect his business interests with meticulousness, a meticulousness to which he would hold his landlord. All he, or his lawyer, need do is red-flag the date on which he has to act.

Having established no excuse, other than its own carelessness, Chelsea's claim is unfounded. Even if Chelsea honestly thought it enjoyed a 30-year lease, it does not change the result. Nor is it helpful to argue that Chelsea, always represented by a lawyer, was unable to procure a copy of the entire lease agreement. Indeed, it borders on the utterly incredible that experienced, sophisticated businessmen and their lawyers would not have assembled and scrutinized every relevant document affecting a longterm lease covering, with a renewal, a 30-year period.

That adherence to well-settled principles, like a Statute of Limitations or a Statute of Frauds, works a hardship on some does not, alone, permit a court to depart from sound doctrine and principles. Even if precedent did not control the same doctrines and principles discussed should be applied.

Accordingly, I dissent and vote that the order of the Appellate Division should be affirmed, and the landlord awarded possession of the premises.

GABRIELLI, FUCHSBERG and COOKE, JJ., concur with WACHTLER, J.

BREITEL, C.J., dissents and votes to affirm in a separate opinion in which JASEN and JONES, JJ., concur.

Order reversed, with costs, and a new trial granted.

Notes and Questions

1. *Meaning of forfeiture.* In §229, the Restatement (Second) states as a general proposition that a court may excuse the nonoccurrence of a condition where forfeiture would otherwise result, unless the conditioning event was a material part of the parties' exchange. In Comment *b* to §229, quoted in footnote 2 to the *Oppenheimer* opinion, the Restatement (Second) defines "forfeiture" as "the denial of compensation that results when the obligee loses [its] right to the agreed exchange after [it] has relied substantially, as by preparation or performance on the expectation of that exchange." Can the court's decision in the *JNA* case be explained as an application of that principle? Although the Restatement's definition focuses on the impact on the obligee that would follow from nonenforcement of the promise ("denial of compensation" after substantial reliance), the *Oppenheimer* court in rejecting the plaintiff's forfeiture argument seems to have equated "forfeiture" with "unjust enrichment," pointing out that the defendant in that case was apparently not enriched, unjustly or otherwise, by any actions the plaintiff may have taken in reliance on the prospective sublease. (In the *JNA* case, was JNA enriched by Chelsea's reliance on the prospective renewal of its lease?) But the Restatement definition of forfeiture is broad enough to encompass reliance losses in general, not only those that may have enriched the obligor. Had the plaintiffs in *Oppenheimer* suffered such losses?

2. *Excuse of condition to avoid forfeiture.* Despite the close division of the court, *JNA* appears to have become a leading case for the principle of equitable relief against forfeiture, for tenants seeking to renew and in some other types of cases as well. A number of later New York decisions have followed *JNA* in lease renewal cases, despite late notice of intent to renew or other obstacles to extension; others have distinguished it on various grounds. Compare Souslian Wholesale Beer & Soda, Inc. v. 380-4 Union Avenue Realty Corp., 560 N.Y.S.2d 491 (App. Div. 1990), *appeal denied*, 580 N.E.2d 1057 (N.Y. 1991) (six-month delay in exercise of renewal option, but tenant not otherwise in material breach of lease obligations and delay inadvertent and excusable; tenant had made substantial investment in business which it purchased from landlord), with 95 East Main Street Service Station, Inc. v. H & D All Type Auto Repair, Inc., 556 N.Y.S.2d 385 (App. Div. 1990) (lease required nine months' notice of renewal but tenant gave notice only one day before expiration of term; no showing of investment that would be forfeited or long-standing interest in location, and indication that tenant deliberately

delayed renewing while looking for another location). Courts in other states are divided on the issue whether a tenant's negligent failure to give timely notice to renew should be excusable on some basis. E.g., Finkle v. Gulf & Western Manufacturing Co., 744 F.2d 1015 (3d Cir. 1984) (under Pennsylvania law, mere negligence not sufficient excuse for failing to meet renewal date for lease option).

3. *Conditions of timely notice in options to purchase real estate.* In cases involving options to purchase real estate (as opposed to options to renew leases) courts almost uniformly have denied equitable relief to an option holder who fails to comply with the time period set forth in the option. E.g., Livesey v. Copps Corp., 280 N.W.2d 339 (Wis. Ct. App. 1979) (exercise of option expiring November 15 ineffective when notice of exercise received November 16; deposited acceptance rule does not apply to options). Are there factors that justify treating options to purchase real estate differently from options for lease renewal? A different problem is presented when the option to purchase is contained in a lease, and the prospective purchaser has already been in possession as a lessee. Here some courts have followed *JNA* by giving the prospective purchaser an enforceable right despite some defect in her exercise of the option. E.g., Pitkin Seafood, Inc. v. Pitrock Realty Corp., 536 N.Y.S.2d 527 (A.D. 1989) (lessee's exercise of option to purchase would be upheld despite fact letter was mistakenly sent in individual name of original tenant instead of name of closely held corporation to which she had assigned leasehold; valuable improvements had been made to premises and landlord not misled or prejudiced by honest error).

4. *JNA from the perspective of legal theory.* As the lengthy and vigorously presented views of the majority and dissenting members of the New York Court of Appeals demonstrate, there are persuasive reasons for granting the relief requested by the tenant in the *JNA* case but also persuasive reasons for withholding it. In an article inspired by the presentations of the participants at a 1988 conference at New York University Law School on the general topic "Contract Law: From Theory to Practice," Professor Knapp reviewed the facts and procedural history of the *JNA* case (including facts not contained in the above opinions), in order to consider whether the insights of modern legal theory could inform the decisionmaking process for a judge faced with a case like *JNA*. Charles L. Knapp, Judgment Call: Theoretical Approaches to Contract Decision-Making, 1988 Ann. Surv. Am. L. 307. (The papers and proceedings of the N.Y.U. conference can be found in the 1988 Ann. Surv. Am. L. 1-351. In addition to articles by Professors Crystal and Knapp, the proceedings include principal papers by Professors James J. White (Legal Realism), Jeffrey L. Harrison (Economic Analysis), Peter Linzer (Relational Theory), and Girardeau A. Spann (Critical Legal Studies).) Professor Knapp concluded that each of these theoretical perspectives can contribute to the court's understanding of the values and interests at stake in the decision, but that none appears to provide a sure answer for the judge in search of a just and principled outcome. No rule, no policy, no principle of justice inevitably controls the judge's action in such a case, he observed; in the end, it comes down to a moral decision by the individual judge. If you had sat on the court that decided *JNA*, what would your choice have been?

5. *Counseling clients facing JNA-type issues.* In evaluating the result and reasoning of the *JNA* decision, a factor one might consider is its effect on the ability of attorneys effectively to counsel their clients in transactions of this type. Suppose you had represented the landlord, JNA, at the time when Chelsea's exercise of its renewal option was about to be due (i.e., *before* the New York Court of Appeals had handed down the above opinion). If your client, aware of the fact that Chelsea was in the process of making some improvements to the property but desiring for some reason to terminate that tenancy, had asked you whether it should remind Chelsea of the necessity for timely written exercise of the option, what would you have said? Would it have mattered why your client wanted to terminate that lease? If the time for exercise of the renewal option came and went, with no word from Chelsea, would you have advised JNA that it was then free to rerent the premises to someone else, effective at the expiration of Chelsea's present term? (In preparing his article on the *JNA* case, Professor Knapp surveyed some practicing attorneys on these questions; the results are summarized in 1988 Ann. Surv. Am. L. 321-323.) Suppose you were representing a New York commercial landlord (residential tenancies may have different rules) in a similar situation today. In light of the *JNA* decision, how would you now advise your client, as the time for exercise of the option was approaching? What would you advise if that time had passed and no notice of renewal had been received from Chelsea?

6. *Settlement of JNA.* In addition to surveys of practicing lawyers, Professor Knapp also interviewed the attorneys who represented Chelsea and JNA in the litigation. According to the lawyer for JNA, a substantial increase in property values motivated JNA to claim that Chelsea had lost its right to renew. The increase in property values (as well as the trouble and expense associated with moving) could also explain Chelsea's determination to try to enforce the renewal provision. The parties eventually settled the case by negotiating a long-term lease at an increased rental. See Knapp, 1988 Ann. Surv. Am. L. at 327 n.86.

PROBLEM 10-1

In our discussion of express conditions, we suggested a number of respects in which the proper treatment of conditions might be problematic: The extent to which one party might have the ability by "waiving" the condition to hold the other to her performance obligation; the possibility that one party or the other (or both) might have a duty to cause the conditioning event to happen, or at least to cooperate in bringing it about; the point at which nonoccurrence of the conditioning event might release a party from his duty to perform; etc. The questions below pursue some of these issues, by posing a set of variations based on a simple underlying fact pattern.

BASIC FACTS: Robert Sellar is the owner of a house and lot in the residential area of Smalltown. On March 15, Sellar and Bonnie Byer entered into a written agreement by the terms of which Sellar agreed to sell the house and lot ("the Property") to Byer for a total purchase price of $65,000, and

Byer agreed to buy the property for that price. By the terms of the Sellar-Byer agreement, the closing (transfer of title in exchange for payment of the purchase price) was to take place on or about June 15. In addition, the agreement also contained the following language:

> It is agreed that this transaction is conditioned on the ability of Byer to obtain by June 1, from the Smalltown Zoning Board, a variance permitting Byer to operate on the premises a drug rehabilitation outpatient clinic, of the type currently operated by Byer in Middleburg [a nearby city].

(a) In March, Byer applies to the zoning board of Smalltown for a variance as described above. The board formally denies that request on May 25. On May 26, Byer notifies Sellar of this fact by letter, and states in her letter, "As you can see, this means that my projected purchase of your property will not take place." On June 20, Sellar sells his property to Frank Fallbach for $60,000. Is Byer liable to Sellar in damages for breach of contract?

(b) In March, Byer makes a preliminary application to the zoning board for a variance as described above. In early April, the board furnishes Byer with a set of application forms and a list of documents to be furnished in order for her application to be processed. Byer never completes and files those forms and other papers. On June 5, Byer advises Sellar by letter that no variance was granted, and states, "As you can see, this means that my projected purchase of your property will not take place." On June 20, Sellar sells his property to Fallbach for $60,000. Is Byer liable to Sellar in damages for breach of contract?

(c) In March, Byer makes a preliminary application to the zoning board for a variance as described above. In early April, the board furnishes Byer with a set of application forms and a list of supporting papers to be furnished in order for her application to be processed. Byer completes the forms and files them with the board, and supplies the board with such of the requested additional documents as she can. However, one of the papers requested by the board is a written statement from each adjoining landowner, either giving consent to the variance or specifying the reasons for objection. One of the pieces of adjoining land is also owned by Sellar. At Byer's request, Sellar files with the zoning board a written statement. In his statement, however, Sellar states that he does not consent to the requested variance, but strongly opposes it, because of the negative impact such a clinic would in his opinion have on the neighborhood. The Board denies Byer's request on May 25. On June 10, Sellar sells the property to Fallbach for $75,000. Is Sellar liable to Byer in damages for breach of contract?

(d) In March, Byer applies for the zoning variance described above, but her application is denied in early May. In the meantime, Byer has entered into negotiations with Fallbach concerning the Property. On May 25, Byer and Fallbach enter into an agreement whereby Byer agrees to sell the Property to Fallbach for $75,000, closing to take place on June 30. That agreement contains a clause conditioning Byer's obligation to sell on the consummation and closing of her purchase from Sellar on or before June 25. On May 26, Byer writes Sellar requesting that closing of Byer's purchase of the Property take place on June 15, at a specified time and place. On June 10, Sellar notifies Byer by letter that due to Byer's failure to obtain a zoning variance, the Sellar-Byer contract is terminated. On June 15, Sellar sells the property to Fallbach for $70,000. Is anybody liable to anyone else for anything?

B. MATERIAL BREACH

In earlier chapters of these materials, we have addressed a variety of reasons why the parties may have failed to create an enforceable agreement, or why an apparently complete and binding agreement might be subject to some defense having to do with either the circumstances of its making or some change in circumstances since that time. At this point, however, we are assuming an agreement that meets all the conventional tests for enforceability, binding both parties to an exchange of performances. At some point in the life of such a contract, one party may completely fail to render a performance then due and owing under the contract. Or, she may render that performance, but in an incomplete, defective or untimely manner. The following case is a classic examination of the issue thus raised: When does one party's failure to perform justify the other party in refusing to render a performance of his own?

Jacob & Youngs, Inc. v. Kent
New York Court of Appeals
230 N.Y. 239, 129 N.E. 889 (1921)

CARDOZO, J. The plaintiff built a country residence for the defendant at a cost of upwards of $77,000, and now sues to recover a balance of $3,483.46, remaining unpaid. The work of construction ceased in June, 1914, and the defendant then began to occupy the dwelling. There was no complaint of defective performance until March, 1915. One of the specifications for the plumbing work provides that —

"All wrought-iron pipe must be well galvanized, lap welded pipe of the grade known as 'standard pipe' of Reading manufacture."

The defendant learned in March, 1915, that some of the pipe, instead of being made in Reading, was the product of other factories. The plaintiff was accordingly directed by the architect to do the work anew. The plumbing was then encased within the walls except in a few places where it had to be exposed. Obedience to the order meant more than the substitution of other pipe. It meant the demolition at great expense of substantial parts of the completed structure. The plaintiff left the work untouched, and asked for a certificate that the final payment was due. Refusal of the certificate was followed by this suit.

The evidence sustains a finding that the omission of the prescribed brand of pipe was neither fraudulent nor willful. It was the result of the oversight and inattention of the plaintiff's subcontractor. Reading pipe is distinguished from Cohoes pipe and other brands only by the name of the manufacturer stamped upon it at intervals of between six and seven feet. Even the defendant's architect, though he inspected the pipe upon arrival, failed to notice the discrepancy. The plaintiff tried to show that the brands installed, though made by other manufacturers, were the same in quality, in appearance, in market value, and in cost as the brand stated in the contract — that they were, indeed, the same thing, though manufactured in another place. The evidence was excluded, and a verdict directed for the defendant. The Appellate Division reversed, and granted a new trial.

We think the evidence, if admitted, would have supplied some basis for the inference that the defect was insignificant in its relation to the project. The courts never say that one who makes a contract fills the measure of his duty by less than full performance. They do say, however, that an omission, both trivial and innocent, will sometimes be atoned for by allowance of the resulting damage, and will not always be the breach of a condition to be followed by a forfeiture. Spence v. Ham, 163 N.Y. 220, 57 N.E. 412, 51 L.R.A. 238. . . . The distinction is akin to that between dependent and independent promises, or between promises and conditions. Anson on Contracts (Corbin's ed.) §367; 2 Williston on Contracts, §842. Some promises are so plainly independent that they can never by fair construction be conditions of one another. . . . Others are so plainly dependent that they must always be conditions. Others, though dependent and thus conditions when there is departure in point of substance, will be viewed as independent and collateral when the departure is insignificant. 2 Williston on Contracts, §§841, 842; Eastern Forge Co. v. Corbin, 182 Mass. 590, 592, 66 N.E. 419. . . . Considerations partly of justice and partly of presumable intention are to tell us whether this or that promise shall be placed in one class or in another. The simple and the uniform will call for different remedies from the multifarious and the intricate. The margin of departure within the range of normal expectation upon a sale of common chattels will vary from the margin to be expected upon a contract for the construction of a mansion or a "skyscraper." There will be harshness sometimes and oppression in the implication of a condition when the thing upon which labor has been expended is incapable of surrender because united to the land, and equity and reason in the implication of a like condition when the subject-matter, if defective, is in shape to be returned. From the conclusion that promises may not be treated as dependent to the extent of their uttermost minutiae without a sacrifice of justice, the progress is a short one to the conclusion that they may not be so treated without a perversion of intention. Intention not otherwise revealed may be presumed to hold in contemplation the reasonable and probable. If something else is in view, it must not be left to implication. There will be no assumption of a purpose to visit venial faults with oppressive retribution.

Those who think more of symmetry and logic in the development of legal rules than of practical adaptation to the attainment of a just result will be troubled by a classification where the lines of division are so wavering and blurred. Something, doubtless, may be said on the score of consistency and certainty in favor of a stricter standard. The courts have balanced such considerations against those of equity and fairness, and found the latter to be the weightier. The decisions in this state commit us to the liberal view, which is making its way, nowadays, in jurisdictions slow to welcome it. Dakin & Co. v. Lee, 1916, 1 K.B. 566, 579. Where the line is to be drawn between the important and the trivial cannot be settled by a formula. "In the nature of the case precise boundaries are impossible." 2 Williston on Contracts, §841. The same omission may take on one aspect or another according to its setting. Substitution of equivalents may not have the same significance in fields of art on the one side and in those of mere utility on the other. Nowhere will change be tolerated, however, if it is so dominant or pervasive as in any real or substantial measure to frustrate the purpose of the contract. Crouch v. Gutmann, 134 N.Y. 45, 51, 31 N.E. 271, 30 Am. St. Rep. 608. There is no general license to install whatever, in the builder's judgment, may be regarded as "just as good." Easthampton L. & C. Co., Ltd., v. Worthington, 186 N.Y. 407, 412, 79 N.E. 323. The question is one of degree, to be answered, if there is doubt, by the triers of the facts (Crouch v. Gutmann; Woodward v. Fuller, supra), and, if the inferences are certain, by the judges of the law (Easthampton L. & C. Co., Ltd., v. Worthington, supra). We must weigh the purpose to be served, the desire to be gratified, the excuse for deviation from the letter, the cruelty of enforced adherence. Then only can we tell whether literal fulfillment is to be implied by law as a condition. This is not to say that the parties are not free by apt and certain words to effectuate a purpose that performance of every term shall be a condition of recovery. That question is not here. This is merely to say that the law will be slow to impute the purpose, in the silence of the parties, where the significance of the default is grievously out of proportion to the oppression of the forfeiture. The willful transgressor must accept the penalty of his transgression. Schultze v. Goodstein, 180 N.Y. 248, 251, 73 N.E. 21; Desmond-Dunne Co. v. Friedman-Doscher Co., 162 N.Y. 486, 490, 56 N.E. 995. For him there is no occasion to mitigate the rigor of implied conditions. The transgressor whose default is unintentional and trivial may hope for mercy if he will offer atonement for his wrong. Spence v. Ham, supra.

In the circumstances of this case, we think the measure of the allowance is not the cost of replacement, which would be great, but the difference in value, which would be either nominal or nothing. Some of the exposed sections might perhaps have been replaced at moderate expense. The defendant did not limit his demand to them, but treated the plumbing as a unit to be corrected from cellar to roof. In point of fact, the plaintiff never reached the stage at which evidence of the extent of the allowance became necessary. The trial court had excluded evidence that the defect was unsubstantial, and in view of that ruling there was no occasion for the plaintiff to go farther with an offer of proof. We think, however, that the offer, if it had been made, would not of necessity have been defective because directed to difference in value. It is true that in most cases the cost of replacement is the measure. Spence v. Ham, supra. The owner is entitled to the money which will permit him to complete, unless the cost of completion is grossly and unfairly out of proportion to the good to be attained. When that is true, the measure is the difference in value. Specifications call, let us say, for a foundation built of granite quarried in Vermont. On the completion of the building, the owner learns that through the blunder of a subcontractor part of the foundation has been built of granite of the same quality quarried in New Hampshire. The measure of allowance is not the cost of reconstruction. "There may be omissions of that which could not afterwards be supplied exactly as called for by the contract without taking down the building to its foundations, and at the same time the omission may not affect the value of the building for use or otherwise, except so slightly as to be hardly appreciable." Handy v. Bliss, 204 Mass. 513, 519, 90 N.E. 864, 134 Am. St. Rep. 673. . . . The rule that gives a remedy in cases of substantial performance with compensation for defects of trivial or inappreciable importance has been developed by the courts as an instrument of justice. The measure of the allowance must be shaped to the same end.

The order should be affirmed, and judgment absolute directed in favor of the plaintiff upon the stipulation, with costs in all courts.

McLAUGHLIN, J. I dissent. The plaintiff did not perform its contract. Its failure to do so was either intentional or due to gross neglect which, under the uncontradicted facts, amounted to the same thing, nor did it make any proof of the cost of compliance, where compliance was possible.

Under its contract it obligated itself to use in the plumbing only pipe (between 2,000 and 2,500 feet) made by the Reading Manufacturing Company. The first pipe delivered was about 1,000 feet and the plaintiff's superintendent then called the attention of the foreman of the subcontractor, who was doing the plumbing, to the fact that the specifications annexed to the contract required all pipe used in the plumbing to be of the Reading Manufacturing Company. They then examined it for the purpose of ascertaining whether this delivery was of that manufacture and found it was. Thereafter, as pipe was required in the progress of the work, the foreman of the subcontractor would leave word at its shop that he wanted a specified number of feet of pipe, without in any way indicating of what manufacture. Pipe would thereafter be delivered and installed in the building, without any examination whatever. Indeed, no examination, so far as appears, was made by the plaintiff, the subcontractor, defendant's architect, or any one else, of any of the pipe except the first delivery, until after the building had been completed. Plaintiff's architect then refused to give the certificate of completion, upon which the final payment depended, because all of the pipe used in the plumbing was not of the kind called for by the contract. After such refusal, the subcontractor removed the covering or insulation from about 900 feet of pipe which was exposed in the basement, cellar, and attic, and all but 70 feet was found to have been manufactured, not by the Reading Company, but by other manufacturers, some by the Cohoes Rolling Mill Company, some by the National Steel Works, some by the South Chester Tubing Company, and some which bore no manufacturer's mark at all. The balance of the pipe had been so installed in the building that an inspection of it could not be had without demolishing, in part at least, the building itself.

I am of the opinion the trial court was right in directing a verdict for the defendant. The plaintiff agreed that all the pipe used should be of the Reading Manufacturing Company. Only about two-fifths of it, so far as appears, was of that kind. If more were used, then the burden of proving that fact was upon the plaintiff, which it could easily have done, since it knew where the pipe was obtained. The question of substantial performance of a contract of the character of the one under consideration depends in no small degree upon the good faith of the contractor. If the plaintiff had intended to, and had, complied with the terms of the contract except as to minor omissions, due to inadvertence, then he might be allowed to recover the contract price, less the amount necessary to fully compensate the defendant for damages caused by such omissions. Woodward v. Fuller, 80 N.Y. 312; Nolan v. Whitney, 88 N.Y. 648. But that is not this case. It installed between 2,000 and 2,500 feet of pipe, of which only 1,000 feet at most complied with the contract. No explanation was given why pipe called for by the contract was not used, nor was any effort made to show what it would cost to remove the pipe of other manufacturers and install that of the Reading Manufacturing Company. The defendant had a right to contract for what he wanted. He had a right before making payment to get what the contract called for. It is no answer to this suggestion to say that the pipe put in was just as good as that made by the Reading Manufacturing Company, or that the difference in value between such pipe and the pipe made by the Reading Manufacturing Company would be either "nominal or nothing." Defendant contracted for pipe made by the Reading Manufacturing Company. What his reason was for requiring this kind of pipe is of no importance. He wanted that and was entitled to it. It may have been a mere whim on his part, but even so, he had a right to this kind of pipe, regardless of whether some other kind, according to the opinion of the contractor or experts, would have been "just as good, better, or done just as well." He agreed to pay only upon condition that the pipe installed were made by that company and he ought not to be compelled to pay unless that condition be performed. . . . Smith v. Brady, 17 N.Y. 173, and authorities cited on page 185, 72 Am. Dec. 442. The rule, therefore, of substantial performance, with damages for unsubstantial omissions, has no application. . . .

What was said by this court in Smith v. Brady, supra, is quite applicable here:

> I suppose it will be conceded that every one has a right to build his house, his cottage or his store after such a model and in such style as shall best accord with his notions of utility or be most agreeable to his fancy. The specifications of the contract become the law between the parties until voluntarily changed. If the owner prefers a plain and simple Doric column, and has so provided in the agreement, the contractor has no right to put in its place the more costly and elegant Corinthian. If the owner, having regard to strength and durability, has contracted for walls of specified materials to be laid in a particular manner, or for a given number of joists and beams, the builder has no right to substitute his own judgment or that of others. Having departed from the agreement, if performance has not been waived by the other party, the law will not allow him to allege that he has made as good a building as the one he engaged to erect. He can demand payment only upon and according to the terms of his contract, and if the conditions on which payment is due have not been performed, then the right to demand it does not exist. To hold a different doctrine would be simply to make another contract, and would be giving to parties an encouragement to violate their engagements, which the just policy of the law does not permit. [17 N.Y. 186, 72 Am. Dec. 442].

I am of the opinion the trial court did not err in ruling on the admission of evidence or in directing a verdict for the defendant.

For the foregoing reasons I think the judgment of the Appellate Division should be reversed and the judgment of the Trial Term affirmed.

Hiscock, C.J., and Hogan and Crane, JJ., concur with Cardozo, J. Pound and Andrews, JJ., concur with McLaughlin, J.

Order affirmed, etc.

Notes and Questions

1. *Commercial context.* Does the opinion of the court adequately explain the reasons for the dispute? Richard Danzig's research into the background of the case is revealing. Danzig tried to find out why the contract specified Reading pipe. At that time, two types of pipe, steel and wrought iron, were commonly used in construction. Although wrought iron was approximately 30 percent more expensive, its manufacturers claimed that use of the pipe would achieve substantial savings because of durability and low maintenance. Several companies manufactured wrought iron pipe, but evidence indicates that all of their pipe was of the same quality. However, manufacturers of wrought iron pipe cautioned buyers to specify a particular manufacturer in order to avoid receiving "wrought pipe," a cheaper product produced by steel companies using scrap steel. Considering this background, the contractor's deviation from the specifications seems immaterial since genuine wrought iron pipe (although not of Reading manufacture) was in fact used. Why then did Kent continue to insist on Reading pipe if genuine wrought iron pipe had in fact been used? Kent moved into the house in June 1914, after substantial construction delays. According to Danzig's research, Kent was probably disenchanted with the contractor because of the delay, as well as some other mistakes in the work, and may have been searching for some reason to withhold the balance due on the contract. Richard Danzig & Geoffrey R. Watson, The Capability Problem in Contract Law 109-116 (2d ed. 2004).

2. *The doctrine of constructive conditions.* In deciding the *Jacob & Youngs* case, Judge Cardozo uses the notion of "dependent promises," promises that are treated like "conditions." We have already considered cases where one party's duty of performance has been expressly conditioned on the occurrence of some specified event, in which case that duty of performance will not arise (absent some excuse of the condition) unless and until the conditioning event occurs. In cases like *Jacob & Youngs,* the courts use similar terminology to answer a somewhat different question: When will one party's duty of performance be dependent on (thus in effect "conditioned" on) some performance by the other party? The doctrine of "constructive conditions" was developed over the years by English and American courts in order to achieve just results in cases where it seemed to the court that one party's failure to perform (or even to "tender" performance) should constitute a sufficient justification for the other party's withholding of its performance in return. (The history of the doctrine is discussed further in the Comment that follows these Notes).

3. *Possible application of rules governing express conditions.* In the course of his opinion, Cardozo indicates that the case involves an implied, or "constructive" condition, rather than an express one: "This is not to say that the parties are

not free by apt and certain words to effectuate a purpose that performance of every term shall be a condition of recovery. That question is not here." However, the case could easily have been treated as involving an express rather than a constructive condition. Article IX of the contract provided that the contractor was to be paid by the owner "only upon certificates of the Architect." Richard Danzig & Geoffrey R. Watson, The Capability Problem in Contract Law 98 (2d ed. 2004). The contractor brought suit when the architect failed to issue a final certificate because the contractor refused to replace the non-Reading pipe. Under New York law the result in the case would probably have been the same whether the case was treated as involving an express condition of the architect's certificate or a constructive condition of performance by the contractor. An earlier New York case had held that an architect could not properly refuse to issue a certificate if the contractor had substantially performed. Nolan v. Whitney, 88 N.Y. 648 (1882). In other jurisdictions, however, the result might well be different. According to the majority view, if the contractor's right to receive payment is expressly conditioned on the issuance of the architect's certificate, the condition will be strictly enforced and the contractor denied recovery unless the contractor shows fraud or bad faith by the architect. 3A Corbin on Contracts §§650, 651. See, e.g., American Continental Life Insurance Co. v. Ranier Construction Co., Inc., 607 P.2d 372 (Ariz. 1980) (en banc).

4. *Principle of substantial performance.* Even though *Jacob & Youngs* could have been treated as a case involving express conditions, instead it is recognized as the leading case adopting the principle of "substantial performance." Substantial performance can best be understood as one aspect of the doctrine of constructive conditions. The principle provides that each party's duty of performance is implicitly conditioned on there being no uncured material failure of performance by the other party. Restatement (Second) §237. Minor or immaterial deviations from the contractual provisions do not amount to failure of a condition to the other party's duty to perform. As Justice Cardozo recognizes, even a minor deviation will give the other party a right to recover damages for that nonperformance, but those damages may be negligible. (Was the house worth less on the market because non-Reading pipe was used, when all manufacturers of wrought iron pipe made a product of the same quality?) Does the dissenting judge disagree with Justice Cardozo on the recognition of the doctrine of substantial performance or merely on its application?

5. *Standard for substantial performance.* When is performance "substantial?" In Thomas Haverty Co. v. Jones, 197 P. 105 (Cal. 1921) the California Supreme Court defined substantial performance as follows:

> [T]here is substantial performance where the variance from the specifications of the contract does not impair the building or structure as a whole, and where after it is erected the building is actually used for the intended purpose, or where the defects can be remedied without great expenditure and without material damage to other parts of the structure, but . . . the defects must not run through the whole work, so that the object of the owner to have the work done in a particular way is not accomplished . . . nor be so substantial [that] . . . the allowance out of the contract price will not give the owner essentially what he contracted for.

Id. at 108. In Kreyer v. Driscoll, 159 N.W.2d 680 (Wis. 1968), the Wisconsin Supreme Court held that a contractor had not substantially performed when it had failed to do work costing approximately $4650 under a contract for the construction of a house for approximately $50,000. The court held that "dispensation in favor of the contractor on the theory of substantial performance should be granted in cases of incompleteness only when such details are inconsiderable and not the fault of the contractor." Id. at 682. (The court, however, did allow the contractor to recover in restitution for the reasonable value of the work done, an approach examined in Chapter 12 below.) The magnitude of the defects in performance will of course be important, but other factors may be just as crucial to the question of whether substantial performance has been rendered. E.g., Schneider v. Dumbarton Developers, Inc., 767 F.2d 1007 (D.C. Cir. 1985) (vendor failed to tender substantial performance of realty contract where deadline for performance not met; timely performance ordinarily not of essence in realty contract but both language and circumstances indicated no leeway contemplated for late performance); City School District v. McLane Construction Co., 445 N.Y.S.2d 258 (App. Div. 1981), *appeal denied*, 436 N.E.2d 1345 (N.Y. 1982) (appearance of wooden beams central to aesthetics of swimming pool building's design; defects in cleaning and staining beams neither trivial nor inadvertent).

6. *Measure of damages.* The notion of "substantial performance" as the fulfillment of a "constructive condition" to the other party's duty of performance may be important where the person rendering defective performance is attempting to enforce the other party's return performance, as was the case in *Jacob & Youngs.* But as that case illustrates, this is not the only issue that may turn on the degree and quality of performance rendered. Whether performance is deemed "substantial" or not, it may still be defective in important ways, requiring the court to consider what damage measure will appropriately remedy those defects. Sometimes courts will measure damages in cases of defective performance by the cost of completion or repair. E.g., Lyon v. Belosky Construction Inc., 669 N.Y.S.2d 400 (App. Div. 1998) (where roof of home was misaligned because of negligence of builder, affecting aesthetic appearance of home both inside and out, cost of repairing defects in performance was appropriate measure of damages); Rivers v. Deane, 619 N.Y.S.2d 419 (App. Div. 1994) (where inadequate structural support rendered addition to home unsafe for occupancy, cost of repair was appropriate measure of damages). In *Jacob & Youngs,* what measure of damages did Cardozo employ? We will return to this issue in Chapter 11, in our discussion of expectation damages.

7. *Effect of willful breach.* In his *Jacob & Youngs* opinion, Cardozo states that the "willful transgressor" will not be entitled to recover under the substantial performance doctrine. Professor Corbin criticized this limitation, arguing that willfulness was a vague concept and that even a willful breach should not necessarily prevent recovery. 3A Corbin on Contracts §707. The revised Restatement adopts Professor Corbin's view: A willful breach does not automatically bar recovery, but the motive of the breaching party is a factor to be considered in determining whether performance was substantial. Restatement (Second) §241(e) and Comment *f.* In Roudis v. Hubbard, 574 N.Y.S.2d 95 (App. Div. 1991), plaintiffs sought damages for defendant builder's failure to install styrofoam insulation and footing drains in plaintiffs' new home.

The parties' contract provided that if the final product substantially complied with the plans and specifications, the owners' sole remedy should be market-value damages; defendant argued that because the defects in his performance did not diminish the value of the house, plaintiffs had suffered no compensable damages. The trial court's judgment for plaintiffs was affirmed. Relying on *Jacob & Youngs*, the court held that since defendant apparently had intentionally omitted the drains and insulation called for because he thought them "unnecessary," the proper remedy was the cost of completion. Even if the contractor has substantially performed, it declared, a "diminution in value" measure should be applied only where the contractor's breach was unintentional and constituted substantial performance in good faith.

8. *Other grounds for recovery: restitution and divisibility.* If the contractor has not substantially performed, other bases for recovery may nonetheless exist. Many courts will allow a breaching contractor to recover in restitution (quantum meruit) for the reasonable value of its services. See the Kreyer v. Driscoll discussed in Note 5 above. If the contract is "divisible," a court may allow recovery for the portions that have been completed. See Carrig v. Gilbert-Varker Corp., 50 N.E.2d 59 (Mass. 1943) (contract for construction of 35 houses in groups of 10; contractor who completed 20 houses allowed to recover because contract was divisible). The Restatement (Second) §240 defines the doctrine of divisibility. It provides that two requirements must be met in order for a contract to be divisible. First, it must be possible to apportion the performances of the parties into corresponding pairs of part performances. Second, it must be proper to treat these pairs of part performances as "agreed equivalents." Comment *e* to §240 explains that the second requirement is designed to protect the expectations of the contracting parties:

> This is because fairness requires that a party, having received only a fraction of the performance that he expected under a contract, not be asked to pay an identical fraction of the price that he originally promised on the expectation of full performance, unless it appears that the performance that he actually received is worth to him roughly that same fraction of what full performance would have been worth to him.

Comment: The Doctrine of Constructive Conditions

We have seen in *Jacob & Youngs* that the courts may use the terminology of "conditions" in deciding the consequences of one party's nonperformance or defective performance on the other party's contractual obligations. The use of the "condition" concept here is quite different from the idea of "express" conditions that we studied in the first section of this chapter. While express conditions result from the agreement of the parties, "constructive conditions" are judicially created devices, used to determine the consequences of breach when the parties have failed to spell that out in their agreement. (It is, of course, possible to argue that the rules of constructive conditions actually reflect the agreements that the parties probably would have reached had they actually bargained about the matter.)

The modern rules of constructive conditions examined in these materials have a long lineage. The English courts of the early seventeenth century originally rejected the idea that one party's duty to perform was conditioned on performance by the other, holding that mutual promises in bilateral contracts were "independent." Under this view, even if one party failed to perform his promise, the other was not justified in refusing to perform. An early case exemplifying this approach was Nichols v. Raynbred, 80 Eng. Rep. 238 (K.B. 1615), where the Court of King's Bench held that in an action by a seller against a buyer for the purchase price of a cow, the seller was not required to plead that the cow had been delivered. The buyer could, of course, bring an independent action against the seller for breach of his promise to deliver the cow, but the buyer could not raise that fact as a defense in the seller's action to recover the price. The promises of the buyer and seller were said to be "independent."

There is some evidence that the rule of independent promises was not firmly established in the English common law. William H. McGovern, Jr., Dependent Promises in the History of Leases and Other Contracts, 52 Tul. L. Rev. 659 (1978) (contending that the English courts in fact held that promises in many types of contracts were dependent). Nevertheless, the conventional view is that the rule of independent promises remained the law until Lord Mansfield decided the case of Kingston v. Preston, reported as part of the argument in Jones v. Barkley, at 99 Eng. Rep. 437 (K.B. 1773). In *Kingston* the defendant, a silk merchant, agreed to sell his business to the plaintiff, his apprentice, who promised in return to pay the purchase price in monthly installments and to provide "good and sufficient security" to be approved by the defendant. The buyer brought suit, alleging that the seller had failed to honor his promise to complete the sale of the business. The seller pleaded in response that the buyer had failed to provide the promised security for his payment of the purchase price. The buyer demurred to this defense, arguing that the covenants were independent. Lord Mansfield's analysis of the case is reported as follows:

> There are three kinds of covenants: 1. Such as are called mutual and independent, where either party may recover damages from the other, for the injury he may have received by a breach of the covenants in his favour, and where it is no excuse for the defendant, to allege a breach of the covenants on the part of the plaintiff. 2. There are covenants which are conditions and dependent, in which the performance of one depends on the prior performance of another, and, therefore, till this prior condition is performed, the other party is not liable to an action on his covenant. 3. There is also a third sort of covenants, which are mutual conditions to be performed at the same time; and, in these, if one party was ready, and offered, to perform his part, and the other neglected, or refused, to perform his, he who was ready, and offered, has fulfilled his engagement, and may maintain an action for the default of the other; though it is not certain that either is obliged to do the first act. — His Lordship then proceeded to say, that the dependence, or independence, of covenants, was to be collected from the evident sense and meaning of the parties. . . . That, in the case before the Court, it would be the greatest injustice if the plaintiff should prevail: the essence of the agreement was, that the defendant should not trust to the personal security of the plaintiff, but, before he delivered up his stock and business, should have good security for the payment of the money. The giving of such security, therefore, must necessarily be a condition precedent. — Judgment was accordingly given for the defendant, because the part to be performed by the plaintiff was clearly a condition precedent.

A subsequent English case, Morton v. Lamb, 101 Eng. Rep. 890 (K.B. 1797), added an important refinement to Mansfield's doctrine of conditions. In *Morton* the plaintiff brought an action for failure to deliver corn. The defendant argued in arrest of judgment that the plaintiff had not declared that he was ready to pay for the corn. The court held that when two performances can be rendered at the same time, it should be presumed (in the absence of express agreement otherwise) that the parties intended them to be performed simultaneously, so that neither party would be required in effect to extend credit to the other. In such a case the party who sues for non-performance must declare that he either performed, or at least was ready to perform, his own obligation. In other words, if acts can be performed at the same time, the readiness of each party to perform is a "concurrent condition" to the other party's duty of performance. The court noted that in some kinds of contracts—construction and service contracts, for example—performances could not be rendered simultaneously. In such cases the performance requiring the longer period of time (rendering of services) is a "condition precedent" to the performance requiring the shorter period of time (payment of money).

Except for changes in terminology, the Restatement (Second) continues the rules of "constructive conditions" developed by Lord Mansfield and subsequent English cases. The revised Restatement abandons the use of the terms *independent covenant, concurrent condition, condition precedent,* and *condition subsequent.* Following an analysis developed by Professor Corbin, the Restatement divides conditions into three categories: express conditions, implied-in-fact conditions (inferred from the conduct of the parties), and constructive conditions (created by a court for reasons of justice). Restatement (Second) §226, Comments *a, b.* (Although the Restatement draws a distinction between implied-in-fact and constructive conditions, the distinction is difficult to maintain and may often be unnecessary. Professor Farnsworth, the chief reporter for the revised Restatement, has written that the distinction is "of little practical importance." E. Allan Farnsworth, Contracts §8.2, at 505 n.11 (4th ed. 2004). See also 3A Corbin on Contracts §632.)

Restatement (Second) §234 sets forth the conventional rules on order of performance, as developed in Morton v. Lamb. Performances that can be rendered at the same time are due simultaneously. Restatement (Second) §234(1). See also Restatement (Second) §238. Under §234(2), if performances cannot be rendered at the same time, the performance requiring the longer period of time must be rendered before the performance requiring the shorter period of time will be due. Contracts for the conveyance of land or for the sale of goods are viewed by the law as being capable of simultaneous performance; absent agreement otherwise, they will be construed as calling for simultaneous rendition of performances. Under the rule of §234(1), it will thus be necessary for either party to such a contract—buyer or seller—to show that she has at least tendered performance on her part, in order to maintain an action for breach against the other party. To the same effect are UCC §§2-507 (tender of delivery a condition to buyer's duty to accept and pay for goods) and 2-511 (tender of payment a condition to seller's duty to deliver). Like the Restatement rules, the UCC provisions are rules of construction only and are not applicable if the parties' agreement provides otherwise. (Note that Comment 1 to §2-511 observes that the requirement of payment against delivery has "no application" to most commercial contracts for the sale of goods, which commonly extend credit to the buyer.) On the other hand, construction contracts and employment contracts are ordinarily construed as requiring performance of the work to be completed before payment is due, under the rule of §234(2). Again, it must be remembered that this is merely a rule of construction, applicable unless the language of the contract itself or the circumstances indicate otherwise; ordinarily such contracts do call for payment at stated intervals as the services are performed, or the work progresses.

As thus elaborated, the doctrine of constructive conditions provides an analytic framework for the courts in various cases where one party claims he did not yet have a duty to perform because of the other party's failure to render her performance. Use of the "condition" device in this fashion has had other consequences, however, and in some cases it has appeared to work against the interests of justice. A well-known early example is Stark v. Parker, 19 Mass. 267 (1824). Plaintiff Stark had contracted to work for a year as a laborer on defendant Parker's farm, in exchange for the sum of $120. (A seemingly trivial sum, but this was 1824, remember; also, plaintiff probably received room and board.) For some reason not disclosed in the report of the case, the plaintiff had left the defendant's service shortly before the year was up. Plaintiff was held not entitled to recover any part of his wages for the year and was also denied any recovery in quantum meruit for the value of the services performed. Full rendition of the entire performance contracted for, the court held, was a condition precedent to the right to recover *any* of the promised compensation, either "on the contract" or on a quantum meruit (restitutionary) basis. Stark v. Parker was generally followed, although some courts did hold otherwise on similar facts, permitting the employee at least to bring an action in quantum meruit for the reasonable value of the work performed, less damages for any loss that the employer could show was suffered as a result of the employee's breach. E.g., Britton v. Turner, 6 N.H. 481 (1834). As exemplified in Britton v. Turner, the doctrine of restitution thus offers one way to ameliorate the possible harshness of the "constructive condition" approach. (We will return to this point in Chapter 12.) The other method devised by the courts to temper the effect of the doctrine of constructive conditions is of course the concept of "substantial performance" (which we saw in action in *Jacob & Youngs*), permitting recovery "on the contract" by a party whose breach is not material.

Sackett v. Spindler
California Court of Appeal
248 Cal. App. 2d 220, 56 Cal. Rptr. 435 (1967)

MOLINARI, Presiding Justice.

Plaintiff and cross-defendant, Sheldon Sackett, appeals from the judgment of the trial court determining that he take nothing on his complaint for money had and received and further awarding defendant and cross-complainant, Paul

Spindler, $34,575.74 plus interest on his cross-complaint against Sackett for breach of contract. Sackett's contentions on appeal are as follows: (1) the evidence reveals no "actionable breach" on his part; (2) damages were incorrectly computed; (3) certain evidence was improperly excluded; (4) the trial court's findings as to mitigation of damages by Spindler are not supported by the evidence; and (5) the trial court erred in awarding interest to Spindler.

THE RECORD

As of July 8, 1961, Spindler was the owner of a majority of the shares of S & S Newspapers, a corporation which, since April 1, 1959, had owned and operated a newspaper in Santa Clara known as the Santa Clara Journal. In addition, Spindler, as president of S & S Newspapers, served as publisher, editor, and general manager of the Journal. On July 8, 1961, Spindler entered into a written agreement with Sackett whereby the latter agreed to purchase 6,316 shares of stock in S & S Newspapers, this number representing the total number of shares outstanding. The contract provided for a total purchase price of $85,000 payable as follows: $6,000 on or before July 10, $20,000 on or before July 14, and $59,000 on or before August 15. In addition the agreement obligated Sackett to pay interest at the rate of 6 percent on any unpaid balance. And finally, the contract provided for delivery of the full amount of stock to Sackett free of encumbrances when he made his final payment under the contract.

Sackett paid the initial $6,000 installment on time and made an additional $19,800 payment on July 21. On August 10 Sackett gave Spindler a check for the $59,200 balance due under the contract; however, due to the fact that the account on which this check was drawn contained insufficient funds to cover the check, the check was never paid. Meanwhile, however, Spindler had acquired the stock owned by the minority shareholders of S & S Newspapers, had endorsed the stock certificates, and had given all but 454 shares to Sackett's attorneys to hold in escrow until Sackett had paid Spindler the $59,200 balance due under the contract. However, on September 1, after the $59,200 check had not cleared, Spindler reclaimed the stock certificates held by Sackett's attorney.

Thereafter, on September 12 Spindler received a telegram from Sackett to the effect that the latter "had secured payments our transaction and was ready, willing and eager to transfer them" and that Sackett's new attorney would contact Spindler's attorney. In response to this telegram Spindler, by return telegram, gave Sackett the name of Spindler's attorney. Subsequently, Sackett's attorney contacted Spindler's attorney and arranged a meeting to discuss Sackett's performance of the contract. At this meeting, which was held on September 19 at the office of Sackett's attorney, in response to Sackett's representation that he would be able to pay Spindler the balance due under the contract by September 22, Spindler served Sackett with a notice to the effect that unless the latter paid the $59,200 balance due under the contract plus interest by that date, Spindler would not consider completing the sale and would assess damages for Sackett's breach of the agreement. Also discussed at this meeting was the newspaper's urgent need for working capital. Pursuant to this discussion Sackett on the same date paid Spindler $3,944.26 as an advance for working capital. However, Sackett failed to make any further payments or to communicate with Spindler by September 22, and on that date the latter, by letter addressed to Sackett, again extended the time for Sackett's performance until September 29. Again Sackett failed to tender the amount owing under the contract or to contact Spindler by that date, the next communication between the parties occurring on October 4 in the form of a telegram by which Sackett advised Spindler that Sackett's assets were now free as a result of the fact that his wife's petition to impress a receivership on his assets had been dismissed by the trial court in which divorce proceedings between Sackett and his wife were pending; that he was "ready, eager and willing to proceed to . . . consummate all details of our previously settled sale and purchase"; and that the decision of the trial court dismissing his wife's petition for receivership "will clear way shortly for full financing any unpaid balance." Accordingly, Sackett, in this telegram, urged Spindler to have his attorney contact Sackett's attorney "regarding any unfinished details." In response to this telegram Spindler's attorney, on October 5, wrote a letter to Sackett's attorney stating that as a result of Sackett's delay in performing the contract and his unwillingness to consummate the agreement, "there will be no sale and purchase of the stock. . . ." Following this letter Sackett's attorney, on October 6, telephoned Spindler's attorney and offered to pay the balance due under the contract over a period of time through a "liquidating trust." This proposal was rejected by Spindler's attorney, who, however, informed Sackett's attorney at that time that Spindler was still willing to consummate the sale of the stock provided Sackett would pay the balance in cash or its equivalent. No tender or offer of cash or its equivalent was made and Sackett thereafter failed to communicate with Spindler until shortly before the commencement of this action.

Beginning during the period scheduled for Sackett's performance of the contract Spindler found it increasingly difficult to operate the paper at a profit, particularly due to the lack of adequate working capital. In an attempt to remedy this situation Spindler obtained a loan of approximately $4,000 by mortgaging various items of personal property owned by him. In addition, in November, Spindler sold half of his stock in S & S Newspapers for $10,000. Thereafter, in December, in an effort to minimize the cost of operating the newspaper, Spindler converted the paper from a daily to a weekly. Finally, in July 1962 Spindler repurchased for $10,000 the stock which he had sold the previous November and sold the full 6,316 shares for $22,000, which sale netted Spindler $20,680 after payment of brokerage commission.

BREACH OF CONTRACT

. . . To begin with, the undisputed evidence shows that of the $85,000 due from Sackett to Spindler under the purchase agreement the total amount which the former paid to the latter up to the time of trial was $29,744.26. Moreover, the purchase agreement reveals that Sackett's promise to pay Spindler $85,000 was an unconditional one once the respective dates on which the payments were due had arrived. Accordingly, since the trial court found that it was not impossible for Sackett to perform the subject contract either by virtue of his illness and hospitalization or his pending divorce litigation, it is clear that his failure to tender the balance due under the contract constituted a breach of the agreement, a breach being defined as an unjustified or unexcused failure to perform all or any part of what is promised in a contract. (Rest., Contracts, §§312, 314, pp.462, 465.) The question remains, therefore, as to whether Sackett's duty to consummate the contract or to respond to Spindler in damages for the former's failure to perform the subject contract was in any way discharged by Spindler's conduct. . . .

. . . [W]ith regard to Sackett's claim that Spindler "repudiated" the contract on October 5, it is clear that the letter which Spindler's attorney wrote to Sackett's attorney on that date informing the latter that as a result of the "many delays" on the part of Sackett "there will be no sale and purchase of the [newspaper] stock" constituted notification to Sackett that Spindler considered his own duty of performance under the contract discharged as a result of Sackett's breach of the contract and that Spindler was thereby terminating the contract and substituting his legal remedies for his contractual rights. Such action was justifiable on Spindler's part if, but only if, Sackett's breach could properly be classified as a total, rather than a partial, breach of the contract. (Rest., Contracts, §313, p.464; 4 Corbin on Contracts, §946, p.809.) If, on the other hand, Sackett's breach at that time was not total so that Spindler was not entitled to consider himself discharged under the contract, then Spindler's action would constitute an unlawful repudiation of the contract, which would in turn be a total breach of the contract sufficient to discharge Sackett from any further duty to perform the contract. (6 Corbin on Contracts, §1253, pp.7, 13-16.)

Whether a breach of contract is total or partial depends upon its materiality. (Rest., Contracts, §317, p.471.) In determining the materiality of a failure to fully perform a promise the following factors are to be considered:

> (1) The extent to which the injured party will obtain the substantial benefit which he could have reasonably anticipated; (2) the extent to which the injured party may be adequately compensated in damages for lack of complete performance; (3) the extent to which the party failing to perform has already partly performed or made preparations for performance; (4) the greater or less hardship on the party failing to perform in terminating the contract; (5) the wilful, negligent, or innocent behavior of the party failing to perform; and (6) the greater or less uncertainty that the party failing to perform will perform the remainder of the contract. (Rest., Contracts, §275, pp.402-403.)

In the instant case, although Sackett had paid part of the purchase price for the newspaper stock and although his delay in paying the balance due under the contract could probably be compensated for in damages, we are of the opinion that Spindler was justified in terminating the contract on October 5 on the basis that despite Sackett's "offers" to perform and his assurances to Spindler that he would perform, it was extremely uncertain as to whether in fact Sackett intended to complete the contract. In addition, in light of Spindler's numerous requests of Sackett for the balance due under the contract, the latter's failure to perform could certainly not be characterized as innocent; rather it could be but ascribed to gross negligence or wilful conduct on his part. . . .

. . . [I]n the instant case although Sackett at no time repudiated the contract and although he frequently expressed willingness to perform, the evidence was such as to warrant the inference that he did not intend to perform the subject contract. Certainly, the state of the record was such as to justify the conclusion either that it was unlikely that Sackett would tender the balance due or that he would do so at his own convenience. Spindler was not required to endure the uncertainty or to await Sackett's convenience and was therefore justified in treating the latter's nonperformance as a total breach of the contract. Accordingly, we conclude that the letter which Spindler's attorney wrote to Sackett's attorney on October 5 did not constitute an unlawful repudiation of the contract on Spindler's part, was therefore not a breach of the contract by him, and thus did not discharge Sackett's duty to perform the contract or, alternatively, to respond to Spindler in damages.

In any event, even if Spindler was not justified in treating Sackett's breach as total as of October 5, the latter's contention that his duty to perform was discharged by Spindler's repudiation of the contract as of that date is untenable. Since Spindler was not obligated to perform his promise at that time due to Sackett's failure to tender the balance due under the contract, Spindler's repudiation was, at best, anticipatory in nature. Its effect was nullified by Sackett's disregard of it and his treating the contract as still in force as evidenced by his attempt, through his attorney, to arrange an alternative method of financing the balance due under the agreement. (See Cook v. Nordstrand, 83 Cal. App.2d 188, 195, 188 P.2d 282; Rest., Contracts, §319, p.481.) Moreover, Spindler's repudiation was itself retracted by his attorney who, on Spindler's behalf, told Sackett's attorney in the same conversation at which the latter suggested an alternative method of financing that Spindler was still willing to consummate the sale provided Sackett would pay the balance due in cash or its equivalent. Such a retraction constitutes a nullification of the original effectiveness of the repudiation. (Rest., Contracts, §319, p.481.) . . .

The judgment is modified by deleting therefrom the award of interest from September 29, 1961 to the date of the entry of judgment. As so modified, the judgment is affirmed. Respondent Spindler to recover costs.

Sims and Bray, JJ., concur.

Hearing denied; Sullivan, J., not participating.

Notes and Questions

1. *Total and partial breach.* The court holds that Sackett committed a breach when he failed to tender the balance due under the contract. The court indicates, however, that once this breach had occurred, Spindler's rights depended on whether the breach was "total" or "partial." The term *total breach* does not mean that a party has breached all of her obligations under the contract. A breach is total if the breach is sufficiently serious to justify discharging the nonbreaching party from her obligations to perform the contract. Restatement (Second) §242 identifies various factors to guide courts in making this determination. The distinction between total and partial breach is significant in two ways: It determines the effect of the breach on the performance obligations of the nonbreaching party; it also affects the measurement of that party's damages. First, a total breach relieves or "discharges" the nonbreaching party from his duties under the contract; after

a total breach the nonbreaching party is justified in refusing to perform his obligations and may even enter into alternative contracts. (Spindler, for example, was justified in selling his stock to another purchaser.) See Restatement (Second) §243(1). A partial breach does not discharge the nonbreaching party, who must continue to perform his obligations under the contract. Second, after a total breach, the injured party is entitled to recover not only actual damages accrued as a result of the breach but also any future damages that will reasonably flow from the breach; a partial breach produces a right to damages only for the actual harm that has resulted to date, not for future harm. Restatement (Second) §243(4).

2. *Material and total breach.* Although the terms "material" and "total" breach are often used interchangeably, the Restatement (Second) distinguishes between them in terms of the effect on the other party: When an uncured "material" breach by one party occurs, Restatement (Second) §237 treats this as in effect the nonoccurrence of a (constructive) condition to the other party's duty to render any performance not yet due, and performance by that party may therefore be suspended until the breach is cured. The materiality of a breach is to be decided in light of the factors listed in Restatement (Second) §241. When a material breach becomes "total," under the rule of Restatement (Second) §242 it has the effect of discharging the other party's remaining duties of performance and permitting that party to proceed immediately to pursue a claim for damages from total breach (§236(1)).

You may also find it helpful to consider the relationship between the concept of total breach and the substantial performance doctrine announced by *Jacob & Youngs*. If performance is substantial but defective, nonperformance would be only a partial breach. The breaching party must answer in damages for the partial breach, but the nonbreaching party is not discharged. Thus, Kent could not refuse to pay Jacob & Youngs the balance of the purchase price. Kent had the theoretical right to recover damages for Jacob & Youngs's partial breach, its failure to use Reading pipe. The measure of damages for partial breach used by the court, however, did not result in Kent receiving any actual damages.

The first question to be addressed in such cases, therefore, is: Is the other party's breach material? In *Sackett* the court refers to §275 of the first Restatement for a list of factors to be used in deciding whether a breach is material. Section 241 of the revised Restatement adopts a similar list. How would the factors in §241 apply to the facts of *Sackett*? Does the Restatement (Second) test offer sufficient guidance to the court in determining whether a breach was material? A careful application of the §241 test can be found in Milner Hotels, Inc. v. Norfolk & Western Ry., 822 F. Supp. 341 (S.D. W. Va. 1993), aff'd, 19 F.3d 1429 (4th Cir. 1994), in which the court held plaintiff hotel had materially breached its long-term contract to provide rooms to defendant's employees by declining to make needed repairs to the hotel, justifying defendant's refusal to continue the relationship.

3. *Other tests for materiality.* Some federal courts have employed a somewhat different, four-factor test for determining the materiality of a breach: (1) whether the breach operated to defeat the bargained-for objective of the parties; (2) whether the breach caused disproportionate prejudice to the

nonbreaching party; (3) whether custom and usage consider such a breach to be material; and (4) whether the allowance of reciprocal nonperformance will result in the accrual of an unreasonable and unfair advantage. Compare Eastern Illinois Trust & Savings Bank v. Sanders, 826 F.2d 615 (7th Cir. 1987) (trial court could find bank's breach of guaranty agreement not material; Small Business Administration therefore not released from its guaranty obligation), with First Interstate Bank v. Small Business Administration, 868 F.2d 340 (9th Cir. 1989) (SBA justified in refusing to honor its guarantee of loan by bank's improper use of excessive amount of loan funds to repay borrower's preexisting debt to bank; bank's breach held to be material both under Restatement (Second) §241 and Seventh Circuit's four-factor test of materiality).

Commentators have advocated simpler approaches. E.g., Amy B. Cohen, Reviving *Jacob & Youngs, Inc. v. Kent:* Material Breach Doctrine Reconsidered, 42 Vill. L. Rev. 65 (1997) (courts should focus on three factors: the harm caused by one party's breach, the harm that the breaching party would suffer were the other party to be excused from performing, and the good faith of both parties).

4. *When does a material breach become total?* Having determined that the breaching party's failure to perform was indeed material, justifying the other party's suspension of performance, the next step for a court in applying the Restatement (Second) analysis is to determine whether the material breach had become total, entitling the other party to be released from its obligations under the contract. Section 242 indicates that the totality of a breach will depend on the "materiality" factors listed in §241, plus two other considerations: the extent to which further delay appears likely to prevent or hinder the making of substitute arrangements by the nonbreaching party, and the degree of importance that the terms of the agreement attach to performance without delay. Comment *b* to §242 suggests an additional relevant consideration: In applying the discharge rule of that section, "the reasonableness of the injured party's conduct in communicating his grievances and in seeking satisfaction is a factor to be considered." See, e.g., McClain v. Kimbrough Construction Co., 806 S.W.2d 194 (Tenn. Ct. App. 1990) (despite asserted defects in subcontractor's performance, general contractor materially breached by declaring contract terminated without giving subcontractor reasonable notice of its claim of defective performance and opportunity to cure). Under the rule of Restatement (Second) §242, at what point (if any) did Sackett's breach become total, justifying Spindler in treating his further duties under their contract as discharged and entitling Spindler to seek damages for total breach?

5. *Risks facing the nonbreaching party.* As the *Sackett* opinion demonstrates, there are substantial risks involved for the party who elects to treat the other party's nonperformance as a material or total breach, justifying suspension of performance or even termination on her part. In the *Sackett* case, it came out (except for the costs of litigation) satisfactorily for Spindler; not all litigating parties are as fortunate. E.g., Health Related Services, Inc. v. Golden Plains Convalescent Center, Inc., 806 S.W.2d 102 (Mo. Ct. App. 1991) (although management company may have performed defectively in various ways, convalescent center failed to demonstrate material breach by management

company, justifying its discharge; center liable for damages for total breach). (The *Golden Plains* case is one of those discussed at length by Professor Amy Cohen in her article cited in Note 2, above.) Suppose Spindler had been found to have "jumped the gun" in treating Sackett's breach as total: What effect would that have had on Spindler's rights and obligations?

6. *Effect of "time of essence" clause.* If you had represented Spindler at the time he entered into the contract with Sackett, could you have helped him avoid the necessity for litigation with Sackett by providing that timely performance by Sackett was to be "of the essence" under their contract? Comment *d* to Restatement (Second) §242 suggests that such "stock phrases" as "time is of the essence" in the contract will not necessarily mean that any delay in performance must be deemed material; such phrases are to be considered "along with other circumstances" in deciding this question. See, e.g., Foundation Development Corp. v. Loehmann's, Inc., 788 P.2d 1189 (Ariz. 1990) (en banc) ("time is of the essence" clause in lease did not entitle landlord to terminate lease; two-day delay in paying common area charge both inadvertent and trivial). On the other hand, Comment *d* to Restatement (Second) §242 also indicates that the parties may make performance by a stated date a "condition to their agreement," in which case delay beyond that date (unless the condition is excused) will result in discharge. See Elda Arnhold and Byzantio, L.L.C. v. Ocean Atlantic Woodland Corp., 284 F.3d 693 (7th Cir. 2002) ("drop dead" clause in settlement agreement enforced even though purchaser missed deadline for closing by only one day and would suffer $1.7 million loss if contract not enforced; court uses two-part test focusing on intention of parties and equitable factors in deciding whether to enforce time-of-essence clause). Thus, as Spindler's attorney you might have employed the language of express conditions, providing in the Spindler-Sackett contract that Sackett's failure to tender payment in full by a stated date would amount to failure of an express condition to Spindler's duty of performance under their contract, releasing him from any further potential duty to Sackett (except perhaps to refund all or some portion of the price already paid). Would such a provision have provided Spindler with full protection against the adverse consequences of delayed performance by Sackett? Can you think of other provisions that might have helped Spindler avoid his dispute with Sackett? Do you think Sackett would have agreed to their inclusion in the agreement?

C. ANTICIPATORY REPUDIATION

By virtue of the rules of constructive conditions, if one party commits a total breach when his performance is due, the other party is justified in treating her performance obligations as discharged. Suppose, however, that something happens *before* the date specified for performance — something that causes the second party to have serious doubts about either the willingness or the ability of the first party to perform. For example, the first party could clearly indicate that he will not perform; this advance refusal to perform, or "anticipatory repudiation," could be expressed orally, in writing, or by conduct showing an unwillingness to perform. Or, even if the first party does not actually repudiate his obligations, circumstances might give the second party reasonable grounds for "insecurity" about the ability of the first party to perform on time (financial difficulty or shortage of materials, for example). In such cases must the party who learns of an anticipatory repudiation, or who has reasonable grounds for insecurity of performance, wait until the time specified for performance to exercise her legal rights, or does the law give her the right to act immediately? The materials that follow address this question.

Truman L. Flatt & Sons Co. v. Schupf
Appellate Court of Illinois
271 Ill. App.3d 983, 649 N.E.2d 990; cert. denied,
163 Ill. 2d 590, 657 N.E.2d 640 (1995)

Presiding Justice KNECHT delivered the opinion of the court:

Plaintiff Truman L. Flatt & Sons Co., Inc., filed a complaint seeking specific performance of a real estate contract made with defendants Sara Lee Schupf, Ray H. Neiswander, Jr., and American National Bank and Trust Company of Chicago (American), as trustee under trust No. 23257. Defendants filed a motion for summary judgment, which the trial court granted. Plaintiff now appeals from the trial court's grant of the motion for summary judgment. We reverse and remand.

In March 1993, plaintiff and defendants entered a contract in which defendants agreed to sell plaintiff a parcel of land located in Springfield, Illinois. The contract stated the purchase price was to be $160,000. The contract also contained the following provisions:

1. This transaction shall be closed on or before June 30, 1993, or upon approval of the relief requested from the Zoning Code of the City of Springfield, Illinois, whichever first occurs ("Closing Date"). The closing is subject to contingency set forth in paragraph 14.
. . .

14. This Contract to Purchase Real Estate is contingent upon the Buyer obtaining, within one hundred twenty (120) days after the date hereof, amendment of, or other sufficient relief of, the Zoning Code of the City of Springfield to permit the construction and operation of an asphalt plant. In the event the City Council of the City of Springfield denies the request for such use of the property, then this contract shall be voidable at Buyer's option and if Buyer elects to void this contract Buyer shall receive a refund of the earnest money paid.

On May 21, plaintiff's attorney sent a letter to defendants' attorney informing him of substantial public opposition plaintiff encountered at a public meeting concerning its request for rezoning. The letter concluded:

The day after the meeting all of the same representatives of the buyer assembled and discussed our chances for successfully pursuing the re-zoning request. Everyone who was there was in agreement that our chances were zero to none for success. As a result, we decided to withdraw the request for rezoning, rather than face almost certain defeat.

The bottom line is that we are still interested in the property, but the property is not worth as much to us a 35-acre parcel zoned I-1, as it would be if it were zoned I-2. At this juncture, I think it is virtually impossible for anyone to get that property re-zoned I-2, especially to accommodate the operation of an asphalt plant. In an effort to keep this thing moving, my clients have authorized me to offer your clients the sum of $142,500.00 for the property, which they believe fairly represents its value with its present zoning classification. Please check with your clients and advise whether or not that revision in the contract is acceptable. If it is, I believe we can accelerate the closing and bring this matter to a speedy conclusion. Your prompt attention will be appreciated. Thanks.

Defendants' attorney responded in a letter dated June 9, the body of which stated, in its entirety:

In reply to your May 21 letter, be advised that the owners of the property in question are not interested in selling the property for $142,500 and, accordingly, the offer is not accepted.

I regret that the zoning reclassification was not approved.

Plaintiff's attorney replied back in a letter dated June 14, the body of which stated, in its entirety:

My clients received your letter of June 9, 1993[,] with some regret, however upon some consideration they have elected to proceed with the purchase of the property as provided in the contract. At your convenience please give me a call so that we can set up a closing date.

After this correspondence, plaintiff's attorney sent two more brief letters to defendants' attorney, dated June 23 and July 6, each requesting information concerning the status of defendants' preparation for fulfillment of the contract. Defendants' attorney replied in a letter dated July 8. The letter declared it was the defendants' position plaintiff's failure to waive the rezoning requirement and elect to proceed under the contract at the time the rezoning was denied, coupled with the new offer to buy the property at less than the contract price, effectively voided the contract. Plaintiff apparently sent one more letter in an attempt to convince defendants to honor the contract, but defendants declined. Defendants then arranged to have plaintiff's earnest money returned.

Plaintiff filed a complaint for specific performance and other relief against defendants and American, asking the court to direct defendants to comply with the terms of the contract. Defendants responded by filing a "motion to strike, motion to dismiss or, in the alternative, motion for summary judgment." The motion for summary judgment sought summary judgment on the basis plaintiff repudiated the contract.

Prior to the hearing on the motions, plaintiff filed interrogatories requesting, among other things, information concerning the current status of the property. Defendants' answers to the interrogatories stated defendants had no knowledge of any third party's involvement in a potential sale of the property, defendants had not made any offer to sell the property to anyone, no one had made an offer to purchase the property or discussed the possibility of purchasing the property, and defendants had not sold the property to, received any offer from, or discussed a sale of the property with, any other trust member.

After a hearing on the motions, the trial court granted the defendants' motion for summary judgment without explaining the basis for its ruling. Plaintiff filed a post-trial motion to vacate the judgment. The trial court denied the post-trial motion, declaring defendants' motion for summary judgment was granted because plaintiff had repudiated the contract. Plaintiff now appeals the trial court's grant of summary judgment, arguing the trial court erred because (1) it did not repudiate the contract, and (2) even if it did repudiate the contract, it timely retracted that repudiation.

Plaintiff contends the trial court erred in granting summary judgment. Summary judgment is proper when the resolution of a case hinges on a question of law and the moving party's right to judgment is clear and free from doubt. . . . Here, there are no facts in dispute. Thus, the question is whether the trial court erred in declaring defendant was entitled to judgment as a matter of law based on those facts.

Plaintiff first argues summary judgment was improper because the trial court erred in finding plaintiff had repudiated the contract.

> The doctrine of anticipatory repudiation requires a clear manifestation of an intent not to perform the contract on the date of performance. . . . That intention must be a definite and unequivocal manifestation that he will not render the promised performance when the time fixed for it in the contract arrives. [Citation.] Doubtful and indefinite statements that performance may or may not take place are not enough to constitute anticipatory repudiation. (In re Marriage of Olsen (1988), 124 Ill. 2d 19, 24, 123 Ill. Dec. 980, 982, 528 N.E.2d 684, 686.)

These requirements exist because "[a]nticipatory breach is not a remedy to be taken lightly." (*Olsen,* 124 Ill. 2d at 25, 123 Ill. Dec. at 983, 528 N.E.2d at 687.) The Restatement (Second) of Contracts adopts the view of the Uniform Commercial Code (UCC) and states "language that under a fair reading 'amounts to a statement of intention not to perform except on conditions which go beyond the contract' constitutes a repudiation. Comment 2 to Uniform Commercial Code §2-610." (Restatement (Second) of Contracts §250, Comment *b*, at 273 (1981).) Whether an anticipatory repudiation occurred is a question of fact and the judgment of the trial court thereon will not be disturbed unless it is against the manifest weight of evidence. . . .

As can be seen, whether a repudiation occurred is determined on a case-by-case basis, depending on the particular language used. Both plaintiff and defendants, although they cite Illinois cases discussing repudiation, admit the cited Illinois cases are all factually distinguishable from the case at hand because none of those cases involved a request to change a term in the contract. According to the commentators, a suggestion for modification of the contract does not amount to a repudiation. (J. Calamari & J. Perillo, Contracts §12-4, at 524-25 n.74 (3d ed. 1987) (hereinafter Calamari), citing Unique Systems Inc. v. Zotos International, Inc. (8th Cir. 1980), 622 F.2d 373.) Plaintiff also cites cases in other jurisdictions holding a request for a change in the price term of a contract does not constitute a repudiation. (Wooten v. DeMean (Mo. Ct. App. 1990), 788 S.W.2d 522; Stolper Steel Products Corp. v. Behrens Manufacturing Co. (1960),

10 Wis. 2d 478, 103 N.W.2d 683.) Defendants attempt to distinguish these cases by arguing here, under the totality of the language in the letter and the circumstances surrounding the letter, the request by plaintiff for a decrease in price clearly implied a threat of nonperformance if the price term was not modified. We disagree.

The language in the May 21 letter did not constitute a clearly implied threat of nonperformance. First, although the language in the May 21 letter perhaps could be read as implying plaintiff would refuse to perform under the contract unless the price was modified, given the totality of the language in the letter, such an inference is weak. More important, even if such an inference were possible, Illinois law requires a repudiation be manifested clearly and unequivocally. Plaintiff's May 21 letter at most created an *ambiguous implication* whether performance would occur. Indeed, during oral argument defense counsel conceded the May 21 letter was "ambiguous" on whether a repudiation had occurred. This is insufficient to constitute a repudiation under well-settled Illinois law. Therefore, the trial court erred in declaring the May 21 letter anticipatorily repudiated the real estate contract as a matter of law.

Moreover, even if plaintiff had repudiated the contract, the trial court erred in granting summary judgment on this basis because plaintiff timely retracted its repudiation. Only one published decision has discussed and applied Illinois law regarding retraction of an anticipatory repudiation, Refrigeradora Del Noroeste, S.A. v. Appelbaum (1956), 138 F. Supp. 354 (holding the repudiating party has the power of retraction unless the injured party has brought suit or otherwise materially changed position), aff'd in part & rev'd in part on other grounds (1957), 248 F.2d 858. The Restatement (Second) of Contracts states:

> The effect of a statement as constituting a repudiation under §250 or the basis for a repudiation under §251 is nullified by a retraction of the statement if notification of the retraction comes to the attention of the injured party before he materially changes his position in reliance on the repudiation or *indicates* to the other party that he considers the repudiation to be final. (Emphasis added.) (Restatement (Second) of Contracts §256(1), at 293 (1981).)

The UCC adopts the same position:

> Retraction of Anticipatory Repudiation.
> (1) Until the repudiating party's next performance is due he can retract his repudiation unless the aggrieved party has since the repudiation cancelled or materially changed his position or otherwise *indicated* that he considers the repudiation final. (Emphasis added.) (810 ILCS 5/2-611(1) (West 1992).)

Professors Calamari and Perillo declare section 2-611 of the UCC:

> . . . is in general accord with the common law rule that an anticipatory repudiation may be retracted until the other party has commenced an action thereon or has otherwise changed his position. The Code is explicit that no other act of reliance is necessary where the aggrieved party *indicates* "that he considers the repudiation final." (Emphasis added.) (Calamari §12.7, at 528.) The majority of the common law cases appear to be in accord with this position. (Calamari §12.7, at 528 n.93.)

Other commentators are universally in accord. Professor Farnsworth states: "The repudiating party can prevent the injured party from treating the contract as terminated by retracting before the injured party has *acted* in response to it." (Emphasis added.) (2 E. Farnsworth, Contracts §8.22, at 482 (1990).) Professor Corbin declares one who has anticipatorily repudiated his contract has the power of retraction until the aggrieved party has materially changed his position in reliance on the repudiation. (4 A. Corbin, Corbin on Contracts §980, at 930-31 (1951) (hereinafter Corbin).) Corbin goes on to say the assent of the aggrieved party is necessary for retraction only when the repudiation is no longer merely anticipatory, but has become an actual breach at the time performance is due. (4 Corbin §980, at 935.) Williston states an anticipatory repudiation can be retracted by the repudiating party "unless the other party has, before the withdrawal, *manifested* an election to rescind the contract, or changed his position in reliance on the repudiation." (Emphasis added.) 11 W. Jaeger, Williston on Contracts §1335, at 180 (3d ed. 1968) (hereinafter Williston).

Defendants completely avoid discussion of the common-law right to retract a repudiation other than to say Illinois is silent on the issue. Defendants then cite . . . [three Illinois decisions] as well as Williston §1337, at 185-86. These authorities stand for the proposition that after an anticipatory repudiation, the aggrieved party is entitled to choose to treat the contract as rescinded or terminated, to treat the anticipatory repudiation as a breach by bringing suit or otherwise changing its position, or to await the time for performance. The UCC adopts substantially the same position. (810 ILCS 5/2-610 (West 1992).) Defendants here assert they chose to treat the contract as rescinded, as they had a right to do under well-settled principles of law.

Plaintiff admits the law stated by defendants is well settled, and admits if the May 21 letter was an anticipatory breach, then defendants had the right to treat the contract as being terminated or rescinded. However, plaintiff points out defendants' assertions ignore the great weight of authority, discussed earlier, which provides a right of the repudiating party to retract the repudiation *before* the aggrieved party has chosen one of its options allowed under the common law. . . . Plaintiff argues defendants' letter of June 9 failed to treat the contract as rescinded, and absent *notice* or *other manifestation* defendants were pursuing one of their options, plaintiff was free to retract its repudiation. Plaintiff is correct.

Defendants' precise theory that plaintiff should not be allowed to retract any repudiation in this instance is ambiguous and may be given two interpretations. The first is Illinois should not follow the common-law rule allowing retraction of an anticipatory repudiation before the aggrieved party elects a response to the repudiation. This theory warrants little discussion, because the rule is well settled. Further, defendants have offered no public policy reason to disallow retraction of repudiation other than the public interest in upholding the "sanctity of the contract."

The second possible interpretation of defendants' precise theory is an aggrieved party may treat the contract as terminated or rescinded *without* notice or other indication being given to the repudiating party, and once such a decision is made by the aggrieved party, the repudiating party no longer has the right of retraction. It is true no notice is required to be given to the repudiating party if the aggrieved party materially changes its position as a result of the repudiation. (See, e.g., Calamari §12-7, at 528 n.92, citing Bu-Vi-Bar Petroleum Corp. v. Krow (10th Cir. 1930), 40 F.2d 488, 493.) Here, however, the defendants admitted in their answers to plaintiff's interrogatories they had not entered another agreement to sell the property, nor even discussed or considered the matter with another party. Defendants had not changed their position at all, nor do defendants make any attempt to so argue. As can be seen from the language of the Restatement, the UCC, and the commentators, shown earlier, they are in accord that where the aggrieved party has not otherwise undergone a material change in position, the aggrieved party must *indicate to the other party* it is electing to treat the contract as rescinded. This can be accomplished either by bringing suit, by notifying the repudiating party, or by in some other way manifesting an election to treat the contract as rescinded. Prior to such indication, the repudiating party is free to retract its repudiation. The Restatement (Second) of Contracts provides the following illustrations:

> 2. On February 1, A contracts to supply B with natural gas for one year beginning on May 1, payment to be made each month. On March 1, A repudiates. On April 1, before B has taken any action in response to the repudiation, A notifies B that he retracts his repudiation. B's duties under the contract are not discharged, and B has no claim against A.
>
> . . .
>
> 4. The facts being otherwise as stated in Illustration 2, on March 15, B *notifies* A that he cancels the contract. B's duties under the contract are discharged and B has a claim against A for damages for total breach. . . ." (Emphasis added.) Restatement (Second) of Contracts §256, Comments *a, c* (1981).

This rule makes sense as well. If an aggrieved party could treat the contract as rescinded or terminated without notice or other indication to the repudiating party, the rule allowing retraction of an anticipatory repudiation would be eviscerated. No repudiating party ever would be able to retract a repudiation, because after receiving a retraction, the aggrieved party could, if it wished, simply declare it had already decided to treat the repudiation as a rescission or termination of the contract. Defendants' theory would effectively rewrite the common-law rule regarding retraction of anticipatory repudiation so that the repudiating party may retract an anticipatory repudiation only upon assent from the aggrieved party. This is not the common-law rule, and we decline to adopt defendants' proposed revision of it.

Applying the actual common-law rule to the facts here, plaintiff sent defendants a letter dated June 14, which clearly and unambiguously indicated plaintiff intended to perform under the contract. However, defendants did not notify plaintiff, either expressly or impliedly, of an intent to treat the contract as rescinded until July 8. Nor is there anything in the record demonstrating any indication to plaintiff, prior to July 8, of an intent by defendants to treat the contract as rescinded or terminated. Thus, assuming plaintiff's May 21 request for a lower purchase price constituted an anticipatory repudiation of the contract, plaintiff successfully retracted that repudiation in the letter dated June 14 because defendants had not yet materially changed their position or indicated to plaintiff an intent to treat the contract as rescinded. Therefore, because plaintiff had timely retracted any alleged repudiation of the contract, the trial court erred in granting summary judgment for defendants on the basis plaintiff repudiated the contract. Defendants were not entitled to judgment as a matter of law.

The trial court's grant of summary judgment for defendants is reversed, and the cause is remanded.

Reversed and remanded.

COOK and MCCULLOUGH, JJ., concur.

Notes and Questions

1. *History of anticipatory repudiation.* The doctrine of anticipatory repudiation is usually traced to the English case of Hochster v. De La Tour, 118 Eng. Rep. 922 (Q.B. 1853). In *Hochster,* defendant had contracted to employ plaintiff as a courier for three months beginning June 1. On May 11 defendant informed plaintiff that he had changed his mind and that plaintiff's services were not required. Plaintiff brought suit on May 22. Between May 22 and June 1 plaintiff obtained other employment. The court held that in light of defendant's unequivocal repudiation of the contract, the plaintiff had the right to bring suit even before the date set for performance. The court reasoned that unless the plaintiff could bring suit at once, he would be required to hold himself ready to perform; to the court, it was more rational for the law to allow the injured party to enter into substitute contracts after the other party clearly expressed the intention not to perform.

The doctrine is generally accepted by American courts; it is included in both Restatement (Second) §253(1) and UCC §2-610. See Keith A. Rowley, A Brief History of Anticipatory Repudiation in American Contract Law, 69 U. Cin. L. Rev. 565 (2001).

2. *Expressions sufficient to be an anticipatory repudiation.* In discussing whether the plaintiff's communication to the defendants amounted to a repudiation of his contract to purchase their land, the court quotes authority to the effect that a manifestation of intent not to perform must be "definite and unequivocal" in order to constitute an anticipatory breach; mere "doubtful and indefinite statements that performance may or may not take place" will not be so regarded. The Restatement takes the same approach. Restatement (Second) §250, Comment *b*. Why does the law apply so stringent a test? The cases generally reflect this approach. See, e.g., Swanson v. Image Bank, Inc. 43 P.3d 174 (Ariz. Ct. App. 2002) (statements by employee's counsel to employer regarding termination, demanding more compensation under employment contract, did not constitute anticipatory repudiation entitling employer to withhold severance pay). On the other hand, an anticipatory repudiation can occur even if the party does not say in so many words that she will not perform the contract. The Restatement (Second) in Comment *b* to §250 goes on to echo the Uniform Commercial Code (Comment 2 to UCC §2-610) in declaring that "language that under a fair reading 'amounts to a statement of intention not to perform except on

conditions which go beyond the contract' constitutes a repudiation." In Millis Construction Co. v. Fairfield Sapphire Valley, Inc., 358 S.E.2d 566 (N.C. Ct. App. 1987), plaintiff contractor sued for wrongful termination of its building contract with defendant real estate developer. The trial court's judgment on a jury verdict for plaintiff was reversed on appeal because of the trial court's refusal to charge the jury that it could find plaintiff was the first party in material breach of contract. Before defendant terminated plaintiff's work on the job, plaintiff had told defendant he was "belly up" and "busted," and would be financially unable to complete the job unless he was given advance payments to which he was not yet entitled; this could have been viewed as a refusal to perform except on a condition outside the terms of the contract and therefore as an anticipatory breach.

3. *Conduct amounting to an anticipatory repudiation.* Although a repudiation must be sufficiently definite and unequivocal to justify treating it as a breach, it may consist of conduct rather than words. Suppose the defendants in the *Truman Flatt* case had regarded the plaintiff's letter of May 21 as a repudiation, and contracted to sell their property to someone else. What would have been the respective rights of the parties? As Restatement (Second) §250(b) indicates, conduct that "renders the obligor unable or apparently unable to perform" may amount to a repudiation. For mere conduct to constitute an anticipatory repudiation, however, it must indicate that performance is a practical impossibility. Compare 4 Corbin on Contracts §984 (conveyance of tract of land constitutes an anticipatory repudiation of contract for sale of land), with §974 (expressions of difficulty or unwillingness to perform do not amount to anticipatory repudiation). Financial difficulty, even to the level of insolvency, does not constitute an anticipatory repudiation. 4 Corbin on Contracts §985; Restatement (Second) §252, Comment *a.* However, insolvency does constitute a ground for demand of adequate assurance of performance. (Hornell Brewing Co. v. Spry, the next principal case, examines the doctrine of adequate assurances of performance.) If a party files a petition in bankruptcy, federal law determines the effect of the bankruptcy on the rights of the other party to the contract. See Restatement (Second) §250, Comment *c.*

4. *Retraction of anticipatory repudiation.* As the *Truman Flatt* case amply demonstrates, a party who commits an anticipatory repudiation may change her mind and retract the repudiation so long as the other party has not relied to his detriment on the repudiation or notified the repudiating party that he is treating the repudiation as final. Restatement (Second) §256(1), UCC §2-611. Suppose you had represented the defendants at the time plaintiff's letter of May 21 was received, and that the defendants by that time had received inquiries from another buyer who was apparently prepared to pay somewhat more for the property than the $142,500 that plaintiff had agreed to pay. You would of course be aware that if the plaintiff had effectively repudiated its obligation by the letter of May 21, the defendants could make that repudiation final and nonretractible, either by notifying the plaintiff of their intent to do so, or simply by selling their property to someone else. On the other hand, you would also be aware that if the plaintiff had *not* effectively repudiated by the letter of May 21, such an action by the defendants would constitute a repudiation by them, entitling plaintiff to treat them as having materially breached, and to claim damages flowing from their breach. How would you proceed?

5. *Effect of express condition in parties' agreement.* The court's opinion in *Truman Flatt* suggests that both parties, and the court as well, treated the plaintiff's letter of May 12 as one that might have been an anticipatory repudiation, except for its lack of definiteness. But even if the letter of May 12 had been an unequivocal "repudiation," asserting clearly plaintiff's intention not to proceed with the purchase of defendant's property, would that repudiation necessarily have been a wrongful breach of the contract? Or should the plaintiff have been able to argue successfully that in the circumstances of the case, Paragraph 14 of their contract released it from further obligation?

Hornell Brewing Co. v. Spry
Supreme Court of New York County
174 Misc. 2d 451, 664 N.Y.S.2d 698 (1997)

LOUISE GRUNER GANS, Justice.

Plaintiff Hornell Brewing Co., Inc. ("Hornell"), a supplier and marketer of alcoholic and non-alcoholic beverages, including the popular iced tea drink "Arizona," commenced this action for a declaratory judgment that any rights of defendants Stephen A. Spry and Arizona Tea Products Ltd. to distribute Hornell's beverages in Canada have been duly terminated, that defendants have no further rights with respect to these products, including no right to market and distribute them, and that any such rights previously transferred to defendants have reverted to Hornell.

In late 1992, Spry approached Don Vultaggio, Hornell's Chairman of the Board, about becoming a distributor of Hornell's Arizona beverages. Vultaggio had heard about Spry as an extremely wealthy and successful beer distributor who had recently sold his business. In January 1993, Spry presented Vultaggio with an ambitious plan for distributing Arizona beverages in Canada. Based on the plan and on Spry's reputation, but without further investigation, Hornell in early 1993 granted Spry the exclusive right to purchase Arizona products for distribution in Canada, and Spry formed a Canadian corporation, Arizona Iced Tea Ltd., for that express purpose.

Initially, the arrangement was purely oral. In response to Spry's request for a letter he needed to secure financing, Hornell provided a letter in July 1993 confirming their exclusive distributorship arrangement, but without spelling out the details of the arrangement. Although Hornell usually had detailed written distributorship agreements and the parties discussed and exchanged drafts of such an agreement, none was ever executed. In the meantime, Spry, with Hornell's approval, proceeded to set himself up as Hornell's distributor in Canada. During 1993 and until May 1994, the Hornell line of beverages, including the Arizona beverages, was sold to defendants on 10-day credit terms. In May 1994, after an increasingly problematic course of business dealings, Hornell de facto terminated its relationship with defendants and permanently ceased selling its products to them.

The problem dominating the parties' relationship between July 1993 and early May 1994 was defendants' failure to remit timely payment for shipments of beverages received from plaintiff. Between November and December 1993,

834 | Chapter 10. Consequences of Nonperformance

and February 1994, defendants' unpaid invoices grew from $20,000 to over $100,000, and their $31,000 check to Hornell was returned for insufficient funds. Moreover, defendants' 1993 sales in Canada were far below Spry's initial projections.

In March and April 1994, a series of meetings, telephone calls, and letter communications took place between plaintiff and defendants regarding Spry's constant arrearages and the need for him to obtain a line and/or letter of credit that would place their business relationship on a more secure footing. These contacts included a March 27, 1994 letter to Spry from Vanguard Financial Group, Inc. confirming "the approval of a $1,500,000 revolving credit facility" to Arizona Tea Products Ltd., which never materialized into an actual line of credit; Spry sent Hornell a copy of this letter in late March or early April 1994.

All these exchanges demonstrate that during this period plaintiff had two distinct goals: to collect the monies owed by Spry, and to stabilize their future business relationship based on proven, reliable credit assurances. These exchanges also establish that during March and April, 1994, Spry repeatedly broke his promises to pay by a specified deadline, causing Hornell to question whether Vanguard's $1.5 million revolving line of credit was genuine.

On April 15, 1994, during a meeting with Vultaggio, Spry arranged for Vultaggio to speak on the telephone with Richard Worthy of Metro Factors, Inc. The testimony as to the content of that brief telephone conversation is conflicting. Although Worthy testified that he identified himself and the name of his company, Metro Factors, Inc., Vultaggio testified that he believed Worthy was from an "unusual lending institution" or bank which was going to provide Spry with a line of credit, and that nothing was expressly said to make him aware that Worthy represented a factoring company. Worthy also testified that Vultaggio told him that once Spry cleared up the arrears, Hornell would provide Spry with a "$300,000 line of credit, so long as payments were made on a net 14 day basis." According to Vultaggio, he told Worthy that once he was paid in full, he was willing to resume shipments to Spry "so long as Steve fulfills his requirements with us."

Hornell's April 18, 1994 letter to Spry confirmed certain details of the April 15 conversations, including that payment of the arrears would be made by April 19, 1994. However, Hornell received no payment on that date. Instead, on April 25, Hornell received from Spry a proposed letter for Hornell to address to a company named "Metro" at a post office box in Dallas, Texas. Worthy originally sent Spry a draft of this letter with "Metro Factors, Inc." named as the addressee, but in the copy Vultaggio received the words "Factors, Inc." were apparently obliterated. Hornell copied the draft letter on its own letterhead and sent it to Metro over Vultaggio's signature. In relevant part, the letter stated as follows:

Gentlemen:

Please be advised that Arizona Tea Products, Ltd. (ATP), of which Steve Spry is president, is presently indebted to us in the total amount of $79,316.24 as of the beginning of business Monday, April 25, 1994. We sell to them on "Net 14 days" terms. Such total amount is due according to the following schedule: . . .

Upon receipt of $79,316.24. (which shall be applied to the oldest balances first) by 5:30 P.M. (EST) Tuesday, May 2, 1994 by wire transfer(s) to the account described below, we shall recommence selling product to ATP on the following terms:

1) All invoices from us are due and payable by the 14th day following the release of the related product.

2) We shall allow the outstanding balance owed to us by ATP to go up to $300,000 so long as ATP remains "current" in its payment obligations to us. Wiring instructions are as follows: . . .

Hornell received no payment on May 2, 1994. It did receive a wire transfer from Metro of the full amount on May 9, 1994. Upon immediate confirmation of that payment, Spry ordered 30 trailer loads of "product" from Hornell, at a total purchase price of $390,000 to $450,000. In the interim between April 25, 1994 and May 9, 1994, Hornell learned from several sources, including its regional sales manager Baumkel, that Spry's warehouse was empty, that he had no managerial, sales or office staff, that he had no trucks, and that in effect his operation was a sham.

On May 10, 1994, Hornell wrote to Spry, acknowledging receipt of payment and confirming that they would extend up to $300,000 of credit to him, net 14 days cash "based on your prior representation that you have secured a $1,500,000. US line of credit." The letter also stated,

Your current balance with us reflects a 0 balance due. As you know, however, we experienced considerable difficulty and time wasted over a five week time period as we tried to collect some $130,000 which was 90-120 days past due.

Accordingly, before we release any more product, we are asking you to provide us with a letter confirming the existence of your line of credit as well as a personal guarantee that is backed up with a personal financial statement that can be verified. Another option would be for you to provide us with an irrevocable letter of credit in the amount of $300,000.

Spry did not respond to this letter. Spry never even sent Hornell a copy of his agreement with Metro Factors, Inc., which Spry had signed on March 24, 1994 and which was fully executed on March 30, 1994. On May 26, 1994, Vultaggio met with Spry to discuss termination of their business relationship. Vultaggio presented Spry with a letter of agreement as to the termination, which Spry took with him but did not sign. After some months of futile negotiations by counsel this action by Hornell ensued.

At the outset, the court determines that an enforceable contract existed between plaintiff and defendants based on the uncontroverted facts of their conduct. Under Article 2 of the Uniform Commercial Code, parties can form a contract through their conduct rather than merely through the exchange of communications constituting an offer and acceptance. . . . Section 2-204(1) states: "A contract for sale of goods may be made in any manner sufficient to show agreement, including conduct by both parties which recognizes the existence of such a contract." Sections 2-206(1) and 2-207(3) expressly allow for the formation of a contract partly or wholly on the basis of such conduct. 1 White & Summers, Uniform Commercial Code, ibid.

Here, the conduct of plaintiff and defendants which recognized the existence of a contract is sufficient to establish a contract for sale under Uniform Commercial Code sections 2-204(1) and 2-207(3). Both parties' undisputed actions over a period of many months clearly manifested mutual recognition that a binding obligation was undertaken. Following plaintiff's agreement to grant defendant an exclusive distributorship for Canada, defendant Spry took certain steps to enable him to commence his distribution operation in Canada. These steps included hiring counsel in Canada to form Arizona Tea Products, Ltd., the vehicle through which defendant acted in Canada, obtaining regulatory approval for the labelling of Arizona Iced Tea in conformity with Canadian law, and obtaining importation approvals necessary to import Arizona Iced Tea into Canada. Defendants subsequently placed orders for the purchase of plaintiff's products, plaintiff shipped its products to defendants during 1993 and early 1994, and defendants remitted payments, albeit not timely nor in full. Under the Uniform Commercial Code, these uncontroverted business dealings constitute "conduct . . . sufficient to establish a contract for sale," even in the absence of a specific writing by the parties. UCC §2-207(3). . . .

Notwithstanding the parties' conflicting contentions concerning the duration and termination of defendants' distributorship, plaintiff has demonstrated a basis for lawfully terminating its contract with defendants in accordance with section 2-609 of the Uniform Commercial Code. Section 2-609(1) authorizes one party upon "reasonable grounds for insecurity" to "demand adequate assurance of due performance and until he receives such assurance . . . if commercially reasonable suspend any performance for which he has not already received the agreed return." The Official Comment to section 2-609 explains that this

> section rests on the recognition of the fact that the essential purpose of a contract between commercial men is actual performance and they do not bargain merely for a promise, or for a promise plus the right to win a lawsuit and that a continuing sense of reliance and security that the promised performance will be forthcoming when due, is an important feature of the bargain. If either the willingness or the ability of a party to perform declines materially between the time of contracting and the time for performance, the other party is threatened with the loss of a substantial part of what he has bargained for. A seller needs protection not merely against having to deliver on credit to a shaky buyer, but also against having to procure and manufacture the goods, perhaps turning down other customers. Once he has been given reason to believe that the buyer's performance has become uncertain, it is an undue hardship to force him to continue his own performance.

McKinney's Consolidated Laws of NY, Book 62 1/2, UCC §2-609 Official Comment 1, at 488.

Whether a seller, as the plaintiff in this case, has reasonable grounds for insecurity is an issue of fact that depends upon various factors, including the buyer's exact words or actions, the course of dealing or performance between the parties, and the nature of the sales contract and the industry. White & Summers, Uniform Commercial Code, supra §6-2 at 286; see also, Phibro Energy, Inc. v. Empresa De Polimeros De Sines Sarl, 720 F. Supp. 312, 322 (S.D.N.Y. 1989); S & S Inc. v. Meyer, 478 N.W.2d 857, 863 (Iowa App. 1991);

AMF, Inc. v. McDonald's Corp., 536 F.2d 1167, 1170 (7th Cir. 1976). Subdivision (2) defines both "reasonableness" and "adequacy" by commercial rather than legal standards, and the Official Comment notes the application of the good faith standard. White & Summers, id., at 287; McKinney's Consolidated Laws of NY, Book 62 1/2, UCC §2-609 Official Comment at 488, 489; Turntables, Inc. v. Gestetner, 52 A.D.2d 776, 382 N.Y.S.2d 798 (1st Dep't 1976).

Once the seller correctly determines that it has reasonable grounds for insecurity, it must properly request assurances from the buyer. Although the Code requires that the request be made in writing, UCC §2-609(1), courts have not strictly adhered to this formality as long as an unequivocal demand is made. White & Summers, Uniform Commercial Code, supra §6-2 at 288; see, e.g., ARB, Inc. v. E-Systems, Inc., 663 F.2d 189 (D.C. Cir. 1980); Toppert v. Bunge Corp., 60 Ill. App. 3d 607, 18 Ill. Dec. 171, 377 N.E.2d 324 (1978); AMF, Inc. v. McDonald's Corp., supra. After demanding assurance, the seller must determine the proper "adequate assurance." What constitutes "adequate" assurance of due performance is subject to the same test of commercial reasonableness and factual conditions. McKinney's Consolidated Laws of NY, Book 62 1/2, UCC §2-609 Official Comment at 489.

Applying these principles to the case at bar, the overwhelming weight of the evidence establishes that at the latest by the beginning of 1994, plaintiff had reasonable grounds to be insecure about defendants' ability to perform in the future. Defendants were substantially in arrears almost from the outset of their relationship with plaintiff, had no financing in place, bounced checks, and had failed to sell even a small fraction of the product defendant Spry originally projected.

Reasonable grounds for insecurity can arise from the sole fact that a buyer has fallen behind in his account with the seller, even where the items involved have to do with separate and legally distinct contracts, because this "impairs the seller's expectation of due performance." McKinney's Consolidated Laws of NY, Book 62 1/2, UCC §2-609 Official Comment 2, at 488; see also Waldorf Steel Fabricators, Inc. v. Consolidated Systems, Inc., 1996 WL 480902 (S.D.N.Y.) (n.o.r.); Turntables, Inc. v. Gestetner, supra; American Bronze Corp. v. Streamway Products, 8 Ohio App. 3d 223, 456 N.E.2d 1295 (1982).

Here, defendants do not dispute their poor payment history, plaintiff's right to demand adequate assurances from them and that plaintiff made such demands. Rather, defendants claim that they satisfied those demands by the April 15, 1994 telephone conversation between Vultaggio and Richard Worthy of Metro Factors, Inc., followed by Vultaggio's April 18, 1994 letter to Metro, and Metro's payment of $79,316.24 to Hornell, and that thereafter plaintiff had no right to demand further assurance.

The court disagrees with both plaintiff and defendants in their insistence that only one demand for adequate assurance was made in this case to which there was and could be only a single response. Even accepting defendants' argument that payment by Metro was the sole condition Vultaggio required when he spoke and wrote to Metro, and that such condition was met by Metro's actual payment, the court is persuaded that on May 9, 1994, Hornell had further reasonable grounds for insecurity and a new basis for seeking further adequate assurances.

Defendants cite White & Summers, Uniform Commercial Code, §6-2 at 289, for the proposition that "[i]f a party demands and receives specific assurances, then absent a further change of circumstances, the assurances demanded and received are adequate, and the party who has demanded the assurances is bound to proceed." Repeated demands for adequate assurances are within the contemplation of section 2-609. See McKinney's Consolidated Laws of NY, Book 62 1/2, UCC §2-609 Official Comment at 490.

Here, there was a further change of circumstances. Vultaggio's reported conversation with Worthy on April 15 and his April 25 letter to Metro both anticipate that once payment of defendants' arrears was made, Hornell would release *up to* $300,000 worth of product on the further condition that defendants met the 14 day payment terms. The arrangement, by its terms, clearly contemplated an opportunity for Hornell to test out defendants' ability to make payment within 14-day periods.

By placing a single order worth $390,000 to $450,000 immediately after receipt of Metro's payment, Spry not only demanded a shipment of product which exceeded the proposed limit, but placed Hornell in a position where it would have *no* opportunity to learn whether Spry would meet the 14-day payment terms, before Spry again became indebted to Hornell for a very large sum of money.

At this point, neither Spry nor Worthy had fully informed Hornell what assurance of payment Metro would be able to provide. Leaving aside the question whether the factoring arrangement with Metro constituted adequate assurance, Hornell never received any documentation to substantiate Spry's purported agreement with Metro. Although Spry's agreement with Metro was fully executed by the end of March, Spry never gave Hornell a copy of it, not even in response to Hornell's May 10, 1994 demand. The March 27, 1994 letter from Vanguard coincided with the date Spry signed the Metro agreement, but contained only a vague reference to a $1.5 million "revolving credit facility," without mentioning Metro Factors, Inc. Moreover, based on the Vanguard letter, Hornell had expected that payment would be forthcoming, but Spry once again offered only excuses and empty promises.

These circumstances, coupled with information received in early May (on which it reasonably relied) that Spry had misled Hornell about the scope of his operation, created new and more acute grounds for Hornell's insecurity and entitled Hornell to seek further adequate assurance from defendants in the form of a documented line of credit or other guarantee. Cf. Creusot-Loire Int'l Inc. v. Coppus Engineering Corp., 585 F. Supp. 45, 50 (S.D.N.Y. 1983). Defendants' failure to respond constituted a repudiation of the distributorship agreement, which entitled plaintiff to suspend performance and terminate the agreement. UCC §2-609(4); Turntables, Inc. v. Gestetner, supra; Creusot-Loire Int'l v. Coppus Engineering Corp., supra; AMF, Inc. v. McDonald's Corp., supra; ARB, Inc. v. E-Systems, Inc., supra; Toppert v. Bunge Corp., supra; Waldorf Steel Fabricators, Inc. v. Consolidated Systems, Inc., supra.

Even if Hornell had seen Spry's agreement with Metro, in the circumstances of this case, the agreement did not provide the adequate assurance to which plaintiff was entitled in relation to defendants' $390,000-$450,000 order. Spry admitted that much of the order was to be retained as inventory for the summer, for which there would be no receivables to factor within 14 days.

Although the question of whether every aspect of Hornell's May 10 demand for credit documentation was reasonable is a close one, given the entire history of the relationship between the parties, the court determines that the demand was commercially reasonable. This case is unlike Pittsburgh-Des Moines Steel Co. v. Brookhaven Manor Water Co., 532 F.2d 572 (7th Cir. 1976), cited by defendants, in that plaintiff's demand for credit assurances does not modify or contradict the terms of an elaborated written contract.

The court notes in conclusion that its evaluation of the evidence in this case was significantly influenced by Mr. Spry's regrettable lack of credibility. See Spanier v. New York City Transit Authority, 222 A.D.2d 219, 634 N.Y. S.2d 122 (1st Dep't 1995). The court agrees with plaintiff, that to an extent far greater than was known to Hornell in May 1994, Mr. Spry was not truthful, failed to pay countless other creditors almost as a matter of course, and otherwise engaged in improper and deceptive business practices.

For the foregoing reasons, it is hereby

Ordered and adjudged that plaintiff Hornell Brewing Co., Inc. have a declaratory judgment that defendants Stephen A. Spry and Arizona Tea Products, Ltd. were duly terminated and have no continuing rights with respect to plaintiff Hornell Brewing Co.'s beverage products in Canada or elsewhere.

Notes and Questions

1. *Right to demand adequate assurances of performance.* As the cases in this chapter show, under common law doctrine it was often difficult to determine when a party had committed a total breach of a contract. Was a non-performance material or insubstantial? What type of conduct was sufficient to amount to an anticipatory repudiation? Such uncertainty meant that a party to a contract ran the risk that she would be held to have breached the contract by acting in response to what she perceived to be a material breach or anticipatory repudiation. Aware of this dilemma, the drafters of the Uniform Commercial Code created a new right, codified in §2-609, by which a party who has "reasonable grounds for insecurity" can demand "adequate assurance of due performance" from the other party. The failure to give such assurances constitutes an anticipatory repudiation of the contract. UCC §2-609(4). Although §2-609 only applies to contracts for the sale of goods, the Restatement has adopted a similar concept. Restatement (Second) §251. A comprehensive account of the history and application of these two provisions is given by Professor R. J. Robertson, Jr., in The Right to Demand Adequate Assurance of Due Performance: Uniform Commercial Code Section 2-609 and Restatement (Second) of Contracts Section 251, 38 Drake L. Rev. 305 (1988-1989).

2. *Reasonable grounds for insecurity.* The case law and comments to the UCC and the Restatement provide some guidance as to the factors that will give the other party reasonable grounds for insecurity. Significant financial difficulties will ordinarily amount to reasonable grounds for insecurity. Erwin Weller Co. v. Talon Inc., 295 N.W.2d 172 (S.D. 1980) (buyer's growing debt to seller coupled with failure to respond to seller's requests to discuss debt). Failure to

perform important obligations under the contract may be a reasonable basis for insecurity. AMF, Inc. v. McDonald's Corp., 536 F.2d 1167 (7th Cir. 1976) (seller's failure to deal with product defects, coupled with evidence that further deliveries would be substantially late). On occasion courts have found that circumstances having nothing to do with the other party's conduct can give rise to reasonable grounds for insecurity. See Top of Iowa Co-op. v. Sime Farms, Inc., 608 N.W.2d 454 (Iowa 2000) (jury question whether buyer had reasonable grounds for insecurity when, due to market conditions, producer would face significant loss if it chose to deliver grain under contracts and attorney general had publicly questioned legality of contracts). On the other hand, unreliable rumors or insignificant risks do not constitute reasonable grounds for insecurity. Compare BAII Banking Corp. v. UPG, Inc., 985 F.2d 685 (2d Cir. 1993) (oil company did not have reasonable grounds for insecurity based on rumors about processor's bankruptcy when boats containing oil had arrived or were about to arrive in port), with Clem Perrin Marine Towing, Inc. v. Panama Canal Co., 730 F.2d 186 (5th Cir. 1984) (phone call from individual who had played major role in brokering deal for sale of vessel stating his company·rather than seller was making mortgage payments gave buyer reasonable ground for insecurity).

The demand for adequate assurance must be based on circumstances that arise after the contract was formed, not on the situation that was known when the contract was formed. In the *Pittsburgh-Des Moines Steel* case, cited and distinguished by the court in *Hornell*, the party demanding adequate assurances had earlier agreed to extend credit to the buyer, and failed to show a sufficient change in circumstances since the making of the contract to justify a demand for additional security or payment in advance of delivery.

3. *Assurances that may be demanded.* Assuming that a party has reasonable grounds for insecurity, what assurances may she demand? UCC §2-609, Comment 4 indicates that an "adequate assurance" may range from a mere verbal guarantee to the posting of a bond, depending on the circumstances. Restatement (Second) §251, Comment *d* adopts a similar "facts and circumstances" approach. See, e.g., Creusot-Loire International, Inc. v. Coppus Engineering Corp., 585 F. Supp. 45 (S.D.N.Y. 1983) (letter of credit adequate assurance when customary in international transactions); Hope's Architectural Products, Inc. v. Lundy's Construction, Inc., 781 F. Supp. 711 (D. Kan. 1991), *aff'd,* 1 F.3d 1249 (10th Cir. 1993) (seller not justified in withholding delivery of windows merely because buyer threatened to withhold part of purchase price to compensate for late delivery; buyer's action probably justified under UCC §2-717, and in any event seller's demand for payment before delivery went beyond what was needed for adequate assurance of buyer's performance). In addition, both the UCC and the Restatement indicate that a demand for assurances must be made in good faith. UCC §2-609, Comment 4; Restatement (Second) §251, Comment *d.*

4. *Necessity for a written demand.* Must a demand for adequate assurances be made in writing? UCC §2-609(1) states that a party who has reasonable grounds for insecurity may "in writing" demand adequate assurances. (Revised §2-609 amends this to "in a record".) Courts are divided on whether

a written demand is mandatory or optional. See Atwood-Kellogg, Inc. v. Nickeson Farms, 602 N.W.2d 749, 753 (S.D. 1999) (reviewing authorities and concluding that "more convincing authority exists that a written demand for adequate assurances is not necessary . . . as long as the demand provides a 'clear understanding' of the insecure party's intent to suspend performance until receipt of adequate assurances"). The Restatement adopts a flexible approach: "The demand need not be in writing. Although a written demand is usually preferable to an oral one, if time is of particular importance the additional time required for a written demand might necessitate an oral one." Restatement (Second) §251, Comment *d*. However, where justice appears to favor the party seeking assurances, a court may be lenient in interpreting communications to satisfy the §2-609 requirement. E.g., Smyers v. Quartz Products Works Corp., 880 F. Supp. 1425 (D. Kan. 1995); cf. James J. White, Eight Cases and Section 251, 67 Cornell L. Rev. 841 (1982) (courts may use "right to adequate assurances" as tool for achieving substantial justice where issue is which party was first in material breach).

5. *Whether demand is permissive or compulsory.* Professor Robert Hillman has argued that in some circumstances the demand should be required:

> Where the aggrieved party could otherwise cancel or seek damages under the Code, the policies of the Code will be greatly served by holding that Section 2-609 requires the aggrieved party to demand adequate assurance first. A party who is in a position to explain the difficulties which have caused the insecurity and to give adequate assurance should have the opportunity to do so. The alternative — permitting the injured party to cancel arbitrarily — is inconsistent with the Code's policy of fostering the completion of commercial agreements and with the mitigation principles urged as proper in this article.

Robert A. Hillman, Keeping the Deal Together After Material Breach — Common Law Mitigation Rules, the UCC, and the Restatement (Second) of Contracts, 47 U. Colo. L. Rev. 553, 591-592 (1976). See also Arthur I. Rosett, Contract Performance: Promises, Conditions and the Obligation to Communicate, 22 UCLA L. Rev. 1083 (1975) (arguing for duty to communicate whenever problems develop in contractual relationship). Compare Northwest Lumber Sales, Inc. v. Continental Forest Products, Inc., 495 P.2d 744 (Or. 1972) (dictum that demand for adequate assurances required), with Copylease Corp. of America v. Memorex Corp., 403 F. Supp. 625 (S.D.N.Y. 1975) (demand optional). Which view is more consistent with the language of UCC §2-609 and Restatement (Second) §251? As a matter of policy, should demand be mandatory?

6. *Time allowed for reasonable assurances.* Under the Code, after a justified demand for adequate assurances, the demanding party must wait a reasonable time not to exceed 30 days. (Note that this is the maximum period; circumstances may well make it reasonable to demand a faster response.) If adequate assurances are not given within that time, the demanding party may treat the failure to respond as an anticipatory repudiation. UCC §2-609(4). The Restatement requires a party to respond to a demand for assurances within a "reasonable time" but does not set a maximum time period.

PROBLEM 10-2

David Mason is a well-known producer of entertainment programs for stage and screen. NBS is a major television network. In early 2006 Mason acquired the motion picture and television rights to the novel, *Blood, Gore and More*. NBS negotiated with Mason for the right to do a miniseries based on the novel and on August 1, 2006, the parties entered into a written agreement. Mason agreed to grant NBS the right to do a miniseries based on the novel and to supervise production of the series. NBS agreed to pay Mason $1.5 million, $500,000 at the time the agreement was signed and the balance in installments as various stages of production were completed. The agreement provided that NBS would employ a writer and engage in preproduction preparation for the series. Paragraph 14 of the agreement provided as follows:

> 14. NBS shall notify Mason by August 1, 2007, whether it plans to proceed with production of the series. In the event NBS so notifies Mason, it shall submit the screenplay and preproduction report to him for his approval. In the event NBS decides not to proceed with the series (or fails to notify Mason of its intent to proceed), this agreement shall terminate and the parties shall have no further obligations hereunder. In no event, however, shall Mason be required to refund the Advance Payment.

If NBS decided to proceed with the series, the agreement provided that the parties would meet within 30 days to develop a budget and production schedule.

In May 2007 NBS notified Mason that the preparation of the screenplay and other preproduction work had been delayed; NBS sent Mason an agreement modifying the original contract by extending the notification date from August 1, 2007, to February 1, 2008. Mason returned the modification agreement unsigned to NBS.

On August 1 NBS notified Mason that it had elected to proceed with the series, but NBS failed to submit either the screenplay or the preproduction report because both were incomplete. NBS then asked Mason to meet with its representatives to discuss budget and planning. On August 24 Mason met with representatives of NBS to discuss these issues. At the meeting Mason asked when the screenplay and preproduction report could be expected. NBS informed Mason that they expected these documents to be completed within three months. Mason informed NBS that the delay caused him problems because he had "other commitments." One week after the August 24th meeting, Mason's lawyers wrote to NBS to inform it that because of NBS's failure to submit the screenplay or preproduction report on time, Mason had no further obligations under the contract. The letter stated that because the contract was terminated, all rights to the book had reverted to Mason.

NBS has retained your firm in connection with this matter and informs you that it could employ someone other than Mason to supervise the production. It is primarily interested in determining whether it has any legal basis for claiming the television rights to the book or recovering the $500,000 paid to Mason.

PROBLEM 10-3

The class has been divided into two-lawyer teams representing Mason and NBS. Secret written instructions have also been given to each of the teams. The teams should meet and attempt to negotiate a settlement of the dispute consistent with their instructions. If a settlement is reached, the teams should prepare and sign a written settlement agreement.

Until now, our study has focused for the most part on the process by which contractual agreements are reached, the methods courts use to interpret (and, where appropriate, supplement) those agreements, and the possible justifications for their nonperformance. In this chapter and the next, we address generally the question of what remedies should be available to a party who has been injured by the other party's unjustified failure to perform her contractual obligation. For this purpose, we will assume a binding contract has been made and that one party has committed an actionable "breach"—unjustified nonperformance—of some duty imposed by that contract. This assumption of breach does not mean that the court necessarily will or should be indifferent to the cause of the nonperformance, as we shall see; it does mean, however, that the party aggrieved by that nonperformance will ordinarily be entitled to some remedy, even if only "nominal damages." Restatement (Second) §346(2) ("a small sum fixed without regard to the amount of loss"). See Khiterer v. Bell, 800 N.Y.S. 2d 348 (N.Y. Civ. Ct. 2005) (patient who proved breach of contract for dental services, but did not prove harm, may recover only nominal damages). Except where the plaintiff is seeking some sort of vindication (e.g., the plaintiff in a libel action who has been publicly and wrongly accused of some criminal or unsavory activity), lawsuits are not brought with the aim of recovering merely nominal damages, nor is it likely that any plaintiff would regard such an outcome as anything more than a Pyrrhic victory. Much more interesting and significant, therefore, is the follow-up question: What kinds of remedies are available to give the plaintiff not merely symbolic justice but actual redress for the injury caused by the defendant's breach?

In Chapter 12, we will consider the possibility that a court may be willing to order "specific performance" of the defendant's promise. In the majority of cases arising out of breach of contract, however, specific relief is not at issue because the plaintiff merely seeks (and in any event, would probably only be awarded) money damages. A question of prime importance, then, is the way in which such damages are to be computed.

In 1936 Professor Lon Fuller and his associate William Perdue advanced the thesis that there are three basic interests that the law may seek to protect in fashioning remedies for breach of contract. Their analysis has become the standard exposition of what might be considered the "modern" approach to contract remedies.

It is convenient to distinguish three principal purposes which may be pursued in awarding contract damages. These purposes, and the situations in which they become appropriate, may be stated briefly as follows:

First, the plaintiff has in reliance on the promise of the defendant conferred some value on the defendant. The defendant fails to perform his promise. The court may force the defendant to disgorge the value he received from the plaintiff. The object here may be termed the prevention of gain by the defaulting promisor at the expense of the promisee; more briefly, the prevention of unjust enrichment. The interest protected may be called the *restitution interest.* For our present purposes it is quite immaterial how the suit in such a case be classified, whether as contractual or quasi-contractual, whether as a suit to enforce the contract or as a suit based upon a rescission of the contract. These questions relate to the superstructure of the law, not to the basic policies with which we are concerned.

Secondly, the plaintiff has in reliance on the promise of the defendant changed his position. For example, the buyer under a contract for the sale of land has incurred expense in the investigation of the seller's title, or has neglected the opportunity to enter other contracts. We may award damages to the plaintiff for the purpose of undoing the harm which his reliance on the defendant's promise has caused him. Our object is to put him in as good a position as he was in before the promise was made. The interest protected in this case may be called the *reliance interest.*

Thirdly, without insisting on reliance by the promisee or enrichment of the promisor, we may seek to give the promisee the value of the expectancy which the promise created. We may in a suit for specific performance actually compel the defendant to render the promised performance to the plaintiff, or, in a suit for damages, we may make the defendant pay the money value of this performance. Here our object is to put the plaintiff in as good a position as he would have occupied had the defendant performed his promise. The interest protected in this case we may call the *expectation interest.* . . .

It is obvious that the three "interests" we have distinguished do not present equal claims to judicial intervention. It may be assumed that ordinary standards of justice would regard the need for judicial intervention as decreasing in the order in which we have listed the three interests. The "restitution interest," involving a combination of unjust impoverishment with unjust gain, presents the strongest case for relief. . . .

On the other hand, the promisee who has actually relied on the promise, even though he may not thereby have enriched the promisor, certainly presents a more pressing case for relief than the promisee who merely demands satisfaction for his disappointment in not getting what was promised him. . . . It is as a matter of fact no easy thing to explain why the normal rule of contract recovery should be that which measures damages by the value of the promised performance. Since this "normal rule" throws its shadow across our whole subject it will be necessary to examine the possible reasons for its existence.

Lon L. Fuller & William R. Perdue, Jr., The Reliance Interest in Contract Damages I, 46 Yale L.J. 52, 53-57 (1936).

Some scholars have criticized the usefulness of Fuller and Perdue's three interests. See David W. Barnes, The Net Expectation Interest in Contract

Damages, 48 Emory L.J. 1137 (1999); Richard Craswell, Against Fuller and Perdue, 67 U. Chi. L. Rev. 99 (2000); Christopher W. Frost, Reconsidering the Reliance Interest, 44 St. Louis U.L.J. 1361 (2000). However, in Restatement (Second) §344, the drafters have adopted the Fuller and Perdue analysis and terminology. As Chapter 12 will demonstrate, both the reliance and restitution interests can be, and often are, a basis for assessing damages against a breaching defendant. It has long been the policy, however, for the court in a breach-of-contract suit to attempt, if possible, to compute and award damages so as to give plaintiff her expectation of gain under the contract: the "benefit of the bargain" that plaintiff would have realized had the agreement been fully performed. See Restatement (Second) §347. This strong preference for expectation damages means that an award may be revised on appeal if it appears that the court below has awarded the plaintiff less than the value of her lost expectation. See, e.g., Sampley Enterprises, Inc. v. Laurilla, 404 So. 2d 841 (Fla. Dist. Ct. App. 1981) (error to restrict plaintiff contractor to recovery of out-of-pocket expenses when amount of expected profit on contract with defendant had been proven with sufficient certainty). On the other hand, it may also be reversible error to render judgment for *more* than the injury to plaintiff's expectation. See, e.g., Wright v. Stevens, 445 So. 2d 791 (Miss. 1984) (error to award damages of $13,000 based on jury's verdict for defects in swimming pool construction when evidence only supported recovery of something less than $10,000).

In this chapter we survey the particular rules by which expectation damages are commonly computed in various types of cases and note some important limitations on such awards. Our discussion below demonstrates that the law is not always as rigid in this regard as the "general rule" might suggest; nevertheless, the rule of expectation damages survives as the stated norm for contract actions. As we proceed, keep in mind two questions raised by this historical preference for protection of the "expectation interest": Why should the law regard the value of the plaintiff's lost expectation as the minimum amount that plaintiff should receive as damages for defendant's breach? Conversely, why should the law regard the value of that lost expectation as the *maximum* permissible award? In the last section of this chapter, we return to these two questions.

A. COMPUTING THE VALUE OF PLAINTIFF'S EXPECTATION

As suggested above, the "expectation" that the court seeks to protect in its award of contract damages is the gain the plaintiff would have realized if the contract between plaintiff and defendant had been fully performed, as promised by both parties. Where the plaintiff has fully performed her obligation under the contract and the only unperformed obligation of the defendant is to pay a stated amount of money in return, the injury to the plaintiff's expectation ordinarily is simply the defendant's failure to pay the promised sum; that amount (perhaps with interest) is therefore a sufficient award of damages to compensate the injury to the plaintiff's expectation. (The judgment in such a case is also a kind of "specific performance," since it orders the defendant to do precisely what he promised.) Where the performance defendant has failed to render is something other than the payment of money (the conveyance of property, perhaps, or the performance of service), it may be more difficult to place a dollar value on the plaintiff's expectation of gain. The case will be further complicated if the plaintiff's own performance was incomplete when the defendant's breach occurred and remains incomplete when the plaintiff's claim for damages is adjudicated. Because the aim of the law is to put the plaintiff in as good a position as she would have occupied had the contract been fully performed *on both sides,* the "expectation" to be protected is the plaintiff's "net" expectation — the value of the performance defendant had promised to render, less the cost of the performance plaintiff had promised in return as the "price" of defendant's performance.

In §347 the Restatement (Second) states a formula by which damages based on the injury to the plaintiff's expectation interest may be computed. In his treatise, Professor Farnsworth (who served as Reporter for the revised Restatement) elaborates on the various components of the Restatement formula.

> **General Measure of Damages.** How is the injured party's expectation to be measured in terms of money? What sum will put the injured party in as good a position as if the contract had been performed? The answer depends on whether the injured party has terminated the contract, refused to render any further return performance, and is claiming damages for total breach or has not terminated, stands ready to perform to render any remaining return performance, and is claiming damages for partial breach.
>
> . . .
>
> A claim of damages for total breach may have four elements because the breach may affect an injured party in four ways. . . .
>
> First, the breach may cause the injured party a loss by depriving that party, at least to some extent, of the performance expected under the contract. The difference between the value to the injured party of the performance that should have been received and the value to that party of what, if anything, actually was received will be referred to as the *loss in value.* If, for example, a buyer of goods has a claim for damages for partial breach because the goods were nonconforming, the *loss in value* equals the difference between the value to the buyer of the goods that were to have been delivered and the value of the goods that were actually delivered. (In addition the Vienna Convention gives a buyer in this situation a right to price reduction, a remedy unknown to the common law, as an alternative to damages for partial breach.[4]) If the buyer has a claim for damages for total breach because no goods were tendered or goods tendered were not accepted, the *loss in value* is simply the value to the injured party of the goods that were to have been tendered. . . . In many situations the *loss in value* depends on the circumstances of the injured party or those

---

4. CISG 50. . . .

of that party's enterprise. If the injured party's expected advantage consists of the realization of profit, it may not be difficult to express that party's *loss in value* in terms of money. In other situations, such as those involving personal satisfaction, the task may be virtually impossible. . . .

Second, the breach may cause the injured party loss other than *loss in value*, and the party is also entitled to recovery for this, subject again to limitations such as that of unforeseeability. Such loss will be referred to as *other loss* and is sometimes said to give rise to "incidental" and "consequential" damages. Incidental damages include additional costs incurred after the breach in a reasonable attempt to avoid loss, even if the attempt is unsuccessful. If, for example, the injured party who has not received the promised performance pays a fee to a broker in a reasonable but unsuccessful attempt to obtain a substitute, that expense is recoverable. Consequential damages include such items as injury to person or property caused by the breach. If, for example, services furnished to the injured party are defective and cause damage to that party's property, that loss is recoverable. The terms used to characterize the loss should not, however, be critical, for the general principle is that all loss, however characterized, is recoverable.

What has been said in the two preceding paragraphs applies regardless of whether or not the injured party chooses to treat the breach as total. It applies to both claims for partial breach and claims for total breach. If the injured party does terminate the contract, however, the breach may have a third or fourth effect, because that party is relieved of the duty of rendering whatever remains of its own performance. What is said in the two following paragraphs applies only to claims for total breach.

Third, then, if the injured party terminates and claims damages for total breach, the breach may have a beneficial effect on that party by saving it the further expenditure that would otherwise have been incurred. This saving will be referred to as *cost avoided*. If, for example, the injured party is a builder that stops work after terminating a construction contract because of the owner's breach, the additional expenditure the builder saves is *cost avoided*.

Fourth, if the injured party terminates and claims damages for total breach, the breach may have a further beneficial effect on that party by allowing it to avoid some loss by salvaging and reallocating some or all of the resources that otherwise it would have had to devote to performance of the contract. The saving that results will be referred to as *loss avoided*. If, for example, the injured party is a builder that, after stopping work after terminating a construction contract, uses some of the leftover materials on another contract, the resulting saving to the builder is *loss avoided*. Or if the injured party is an employee who, after being wrongfully discharged by an employer, takes other employment, the net amount that has been earned or will be earned from that employment is *loss avoided*. If the injured party has actually saved money, the saving is treated as *loss avoided* even though another person might not have been able to effect that saving. If, for example, the injured party happens to make especially favorable arrangements to dispose of leftover materials, and thereby avoids more loss than another person might have succeeded in doing, the *loss avoided* will be based on the actual favorable arrangements. . . .

The general measure of damages for total breach can therefore be expressed in terms of these four effects, two of which (*loss in value* and *other loss*) are adverse to the injured party and therefore increase damages, and two of which (*cost avoided* and *loss avoided*) are beneficial to the injured party and therefore decrease that party's damages. Formula (A) therefore reads:

(A) *general measure* = *loss in value* + *other loss* − *cost avoided* − *loss avoided*

In the case of claim for damages for partial breach, only the first two terms apply.

E. Allan Farnsworth, Contracts §12.9, at 764-768 (4th ed. 2004).

Using Professor Farnsworth's formula, how would you compute the plaintiff's expectation damages in the following hypothetical cases:

Case 1. Owner hires builder to construct a building for a total price of $200,000. The estimated total cost of construction is $180,000. The owner breaches by unjustifiably terminating the contract when the work is partly done. At the time of termination the owner has paid the builder $70,000 for work done, and the builder has spent a total of $95,000 for labor and materials (some of which are incorporated in the partially completed building). After the owner's breach the builder is able to resell $10,000 of materials purchased for the project.

Case 2. Employer hires employee under a two-year employment contract for a salary of $50,000 per year, payable in installments at the end of each month. Six months after the employee starts work, the employer wrongfully discharges her. The employee looks for work for three months, but is unable to find a job. Finally, she hires an employment agency, paying it a fee of $1000. Three months later she obtains a job (similar to the one from which she was fired) paying $45,000 per year.

In this chapter we try generally to use the terminology employed in Restatement (Second) §347 to describe the process by which the plaintiff's damages are computed. It should be noted, however, that the computation of expectation damages may be articulated in different ways, although the end results should be identical. For example, in contracts for the sale of real estate, courts often state that expectation damages are measured by the *difference between the contract price and the market price at the time of breach*. In construction contracts, the measure of expectation damages for a breach by the owner is frequently stated to be the builder's *expected net profit on the entire contract plus the builder's unreimbursed expenses at the time of breach*. In the material that follows we will consider these and other alternative statements of the expectation damage measure.

Case 3. Compute the builder's expectation damages in Case 1, using the formula of expected net profit on the entire contract plus unreimbursed expenses at the time of breach.

The formula of Restatement (Second) §347, while not without its problems in application, works relatively easily in cases where the party in breach is the "paying" party: the one whose promised performance was to consist of one or more payments of money. Thus, where the plaintiff is a wrongfully discharged employee, the first factor, "loss in value," will simply be the excess of salary originally promised over the salary actually paid. Where the defendant is the defaulting buyer of property, the "loss in value" will be the difference between the amount the purchaser promised to pay and the amount (if any) the vendor has actually received. It should not be assumed, of course, that this calculation fixes the amount of the plaintiff's damage, as the rest of the Restatement's formula indicates. In any of these cases, there may in addition be items of "consequential" loss (sometimes referred to as "special" damages); on the other hand, from the aggregate of "total loss" there are likely to be deductions based on the amounts that plaintiff saved (or reasonably should have saved) either as costs avoided or by operation of the principle of "mitigation of damages" (discussed later in this chapter).

Where the defendant's promised performance is to be something other than payment of money, however, the threshold question of loss in value is not so easily answered. Suppose, in Case 1 above, that the breaching party is not the owner, but the builder. If the builder repudiates before construction even begins, then the owner has received no performance at all; how should we compute his loss in value? Is it simply an amount equal to the full contract price? Or should we somehow attempt to put a "value" on the building that was to be constructed? If performance has begun, and the builder unjustifiably stops work halfway through, the situation is even more complicated: How can we put a price tag on the half-completed building that the owner has received? The same question may arise where an employee has rendered part of the service called for by a contract and then wrongfully stops performance. If the loss in value is the difference in value between what was promised and what was performed, how can those two be computed? The cases that follow illustrate some of the approaches that may be used in such cases.

Roesch v. Bray
Ohio Court of Appeals
46 Ohio App. 3d 49, 545 N.E.2d 1301 (1988)

Per Curiam Opinion.
This cause is before the court on an appeal from a judgment rendered by the Erie County Court of Common Pleas.
Appellants filed a timely notice of appeal asserting the following as their sole assignment of error:

The court erred in restricting the plaintiffs' award to consequential damages. The court failed to include the expectancy damage amount, suffered by the plaintiffs, in the judgment.

Appellees filed a cross-appeal asserting the following as their sole assignment of error:

The court erred in awarding the plaintiffs damages for the costs of holding the property for resale and interest upon the cash which would have been generated from the breached contract.

On August 18, 1982, appellants, John C. and L. Janie Roesch, entered into a written contract for the sale of appellants' home located at 516 Lincoln Avenue, Huron, Ohio, with appellees, Harry H. and Carol L. Bray. Approximately five days after the contract was entered into, appellees informed appellants that they would not be able to perform on the contract.
Prior to the breach of the contract, appellants had entered into a contract to purchase another home in Huron. Appellee Harry H. Bray, father of appellant L. Janie Roesch, had encouraged appellants to purchase other real estate in order that he and his wife could move into the property located on Lincoln Avenue.

The contract entered into between appellants and appellees provided for a purchase price of $65,000, $45,000 to be paid at the time of closing and $20,000 to be paid upon the sale of appellees' home with no interest to be charged on said amount.

Due to the breach of the contract to purchase by appellees, appellant John Roesch borrowed $65,000 from a third party at sixteen percent interest in order to meet his obligations under the contract for the purchase of his new home. Appellants ultimately resold the property located on Lincoln Avenue in August 1983 for $63,500.

On November 26, 1985, the trial court granted appellants' motion for partial summary judgment on the issue of breach of contract. The issue of damages was tried before a referee. The referee recommended an award of money damages in the amount of $9,163.06. Said amount included payments for utilities, insurance, real estate taxes, yard maintenance, advertising, and interest on the $45,000 that was payable to appellants from appellees at the proposed closing date, at the rate of sixteen percent interest. The trial judge adopted the referee's report, allowing for interest on the amount awarded at the rate of ten percent from the date of the breach.

Appellants now contend that the trial court erred in failing to award damages for the difference between the contract price agreed to by appellees and the resale price of the home in August 1983. Appellants state that they realized "net proceeds" in the amount of $52,149.20 from the sale of the property. However, appellees contend that the actual purchase price of the home in August 1983 was $63,500; and, therefore, the maximum amount that appellants are entitled to recover in addition to what has been awarded is $1,500 plus interest.

Generally, under Ohio law, when a purchaser defaults upon a contract for the sale of real estate, the seller may recover the difference between the contract price and the market value of the property at the time of the breach. See 54 Ohio Jurisprudence 2d (1962) 731, Vendor and Purchaser, Section 181; 77 American Jurisprudence 2d (1975) 616, Vendor and Purchaser, Section 491; McCarty v. Lingham (1924), 111 Ohio St. 551, 146 N.E. 64, paragraph three of the syllabus.

In the case *sub judice*, the trial court held that there was no evidence introduced to establish the market value of the Lincoln Avenue property at the time of the breach. The trial court further concluded that the ultimate sale price of the home received one year after the breach of the contract and upon different terms should not be admitted as evidence of the market value at the time of breach.

It has been held that when the sale of real estate after a breach of contract is made " . . . within a reasonable time and at the highest price obtainable after the breach, [it] is evidence of the market value on the date of the breach. Kemp [v. Gannett (1977)], 50 Ill. App. 3d 429, 431." Gryb v. Benson (1980), 84 Ill. App. 3d 710, 712, 406 N.E. 2d 124, 126.

At the time of appellees' breach in the instant case, the housing market was moving rather slowly since interest rates were very high. Therefore, it would not be unreasonable to assume that the resale price tendered in August 1983 was the best indicator of the market value of the home in 1982. Furthermore, we cannot conclude that the resale of the home one year after appellees' breach was unreasonable due to the market condition. It is also apparent that the resale price obtained by appellants, $63,500, was, in fact, very close to the purchase price offered by appellees. That is, the eventual sale price in 1983 is a measure of the value of the property in August 1982, and this value is most favorable to appellees. Based on the evidence before us, we conclude that the resale price is as " . . . favorable a bid as the value of the property will admit of. . . . " Lucke v. Eisenstadt (1914), 17 Ohio N.P. (N.S.) 209, 211, 26 Ohio Dec. 529, 531, reversed on other grounds sub nom. Eisenstadt v. Lucke (1915), 35 Ohio C.D. 244, 25 Ohio C.C.(N.S.) 225 (sale at public auction rather than sale on the open market).

Based on the foregoing, we conclude that appellants are entitled to the benefit of their bargain: the contract price less the actual resale price. We further conclude that the resale price is $63,500, rather than $52,149.20. The latter figure represents the "net proceeds" of the sale. The actual purchase price of the home, however, is $63,500. It would be contrary to established law to award appellants the difference between the 1982 contract price, not adjusted for expenses, and the 1983 contract price adjusted for expenses.

Accordingly, we find appellants' sole assignment of error well-taken.

Appellees argue in their cross-appeal that the trial court erred in awarding appellants damages for the costs of holding the property until resale and for interest on the $45,000.

The Ohio courts have not considered in great detail what additional losses may be compensated for in the way of damages pursuant to a breach of a real estate contract. Generally, damages on a breach-of-contract action are limited to losses that are reasonably to be expected as a probable result of the breach. See Roegge v. Wertheimer (Super. Ct. 1923), 1 Ohio Law Abs. 834; and Dudock v. Alexander (App. 1928), 6 Ohio Law Abs. 136.

In the case *sub judice*, the damages awarded by the trial court include maintenance and utility expenses for several months, plus certain costs for resale. However, to allow recovery for expenses of this kind could lead to harsh consequences. Such expenses " . . . could mount indefinitely to unlimited amounts if [the sellers] . . . failed to use, rent or resell their property. . . . " Kauder v. Thompson (May 9, 1986), Montgomery App. No. 9265, unreported, at 11. Therefore, we conclude that these expenses are incidental to ownership. Although appellees might have been able to foresee that certain expenses would be incurred in maintaining the property until future resale, the duration and extent of those expenses could only be speculated upon. Were we to hold otherwise, a breaching party could be subjected to liability for similar expenses for months or even years on end.

Accordingly, appellees' sole cross-assignment of error is found to be well-taken.

On consideration whereof, the court finds substantial justice has not been done the parties complaining, and the judgment of the Erie County Court of Common Pleas is reversed. Pursuant to App. R. 12(B), we hereby enter judgment in favor of appellants in the amount of $ 1,500 plus ten percent interest from the date of the breach. This cause is remanded to said court for execution of judgment. It is ordered that appellants and appellees pay the court costs of this appeal equally.

Judgment accordingly.

Resnick, P.J., and Handwork and Glasser, J.J., concur.

Notes and Questions

1. *Measure of damages for breach of real estate contracts.* Assuming that the disappointed seller or purchaser of land has established the fact of breach and the court is willing to award damages based on the injury to plaintiff's expectation interest, how should such damages be computed? As stated in the *Roesch* opinion, damages for the loss of bargain in such cases are ordinarily calculated as the difference between the contract price and the market value of the property at the time of breach. Thus, where the seller claims damages for the purchaser's wrongful repudiation, she must show that at the time of the breach the property was in fact worth less (on the market) than the contract price. See, e.g., Lawson v. Menefee, 132 S.W.3d 890 (Ky. Ct. App. 2004) (contract price was $265,000 and market value was $274,000, based on resale price as best evidence, thus seller suffered no damages). Conversely, when it is the seller who has breached, the disappointed purchaser must show that at the time of breach the property had a market value of *more* than the contract price. See, e.g., Horning v. Shilberg, 29 Cal. Rptr. 3d 717 (Ct. App. 2005) (nonbreaching buyer entitled to damages based on "contract price-market value" differential but failed to present evidence of value on date set for performance).

In many cases, such as *Roesch*, the contract price and market value at the time of the breach will be reasonably close or perhaps the same. Why would this equivalence often be the case? In many cases the plaintiff will also seek to recover "consequential" or "incidental" damages, as did the sellers in *Roesch*. As that court indicated, such damages are subject to certain requirements and limitations, including:

(a) the requirement that damages be reasonably foreseeable (i.e., breaching party had reason to foresee the harm as a probable result at the time of the contract);

(b) the prohibition on speculative damages (i.e., damages must be proven with reasonable certainty); and

(c) the duty to mitigate damages (i.e., damages may not be recovered to the extent that they could have been avoided or minimized by reasonable efforts).

These concepts are examined in more detail in subsequent sections of this chapter. Based on the general descriptions of these limitations above, is it clear that the *Roesch* court was correct in reversing the trial court's award of damages for maintaining and reselling the property? Cf. Turner v. Benson, 672 S.W.2d 752 (Tenn. 1984) (granting recovery to seller for foreseeable expenses incurred in borrowing funds and maintaining two homes until resale about sixteen months after buyer's breach).

As we mentioned in the introduction, courts often use alternative measures of expectation damages rather than the general formula set forth in Restatement §347. Can the damage award in *Roesch* be explained in terms of the general Restatement formula?

2. *Proof of market value.* The contract price minus market value formula requires proof of market value. Real estate appraisers or other people who are

qualified by education, training, or experience can provide testimony about market value. Courts also usually allow the owner of property to testify about its market value even though the owner may not be qualified as an expert on real estate values. See Seale v. Pearson, 736 So. 2d 108 (Ala. Civ. App. 1999); Valigore v. Cuyahoga County Board of Revision, 825 N.E.2d 604 (Ohio 2005) (recognizing "owner-opinion" rule). Can you think of any disadvantage to using an owner's testimony rather than that of a real estate expert? As in *Roesch*, many courts have also allowed the resale price of the property as evidence of its market value at the time of the breach, provided the resale takes place within a reasonable period of time in an arm's length transaction. See, e.g., Kemp v. Gannett, 365 N.E.2d 1112 (Ill. 1977); but see Piroschak v. Whelan, 106 P.3d 887 (Wyo. 2005) (trial court should have considered all relevant evidence of market value such as appraisals and sales prices of comparable property; resale price is not conclusive).

3. *English and American rules when seller breaches.* As indicated above, the "benefit of the bargain" rule of damages could be applied equally to cases of breach by the purchaser (as in *Roesch*) and to cases where the seller is the breaching party. Where the seller is in breach, however, many courts have traditionally restricted the plaintiff purchaser to restitution of any payments made on the purchase price, unless the defendant seller has breached in "bad faith." This rule, known as the "English rule," appears to have grown up at a time when searching land titles was an extremely difficult process, and a seller frequently contracted to sell in ignorance of some later-discovered "cloud" on title, which prevented him from conveying the good (or "marketable") title called for by the contract. See Avellone v. Mehta, 544 So. 2d 1122 (Fla. Dist. Ct. App. 1989) (well-settled state law that damages for nonbreaching buyer are any payments of purchase price with interest and cost of investigating title if seller acts in good faith); Beard v. S/E Joint Venture, 581 A.2d 1275 (Md. 1990) (recognizing "English rule" but finding it inapplicable because seller's breach had nothing to do with title defect; purchasers allowed to recover benefit of bargain damages).

The competing "American rule" would generally award expectation damages for any unexcused failure to convey, regardless of the good faith or bad faith of the seller. The English rule has been generally criticized by American commentators, and the American rule appears to be gaining adherents. See, e.g., Burgess v. Arita, 704 P.2d 930 (Haw. Ct. App. 1985); McGehee v. Elliot, 849 N.E.2d 1180 (Ind. Ct. App. 2006); Donovan v. Bachstadt, 453 A.2d 160 (N.J. 1982). The latter rule is of course in line with the traditional general rule of contract law that unless the cause of nonperformance falls within one of the recognized categories of legal excuse, an expectation-based remedy will normally be available. On the other hand, the English rule does have the potentially attractive feature of adjusting the remedy for breach in light of the willfulness of the breaching party, an approach that some modern commentators have advocated. See Patricia H. Marschall, Willfulness: A Crucial Factor in Choosing Remedies for Breach of Contract, 24 Ariz. L. Rev. 733 (1982). In §2-510 of the Uniform Land Transactions Act, the Commissioners on Uniform State Laws have offered a rule that would generally award loss-of-bargain damages to a disappointed purchaser, but would limit the remedy to restitution of payments (plus incidental damages) in cases where the seller's failure to convey stemmed from a title defect of which he had no knowledge at the time of contracting. 13 U.L.A. 558 (1986).

4. *UCC damage rules.* Damages for breach of a contract to buy or sell goods under the UCC may also be measured by the difference between the market price and the contract price of the goods. UCC §2-708(1) measures the seller's damages for nonacceptance or repudiation by buyer as "the difference between the market price at the time and place for tender and the unpaid contract price together with any incidental damages provided in this Article (§2-710), but less expenses saved in consequence of the buyer's breach." Similarly, UCC §2-713 provides that the measure of the buyer's damages for nondelivery or repudiation by the seller is "the difference between the market price at the time when the buyer learned of the breach and the contract price together with any incidental and consequential damages provided in this Article (§2-715), but less expenses saved in consequence of the seller's breach." The UCC provides some flexibility on proof of market price. See §2-723.

The drafters of the Code thought, however, that application of the market measure of damages often did not accurately determine the loss suffered because the reaction of the nonbreaching party will often involve making a substitute contract that may be at a price other than the market price. In the case of breach by the buyer, UCC §2-706 provides for "seller's resale." That section allows the seller who complies with its provisions to recover from a breaching buyer damages measured by the difference between the contract price and the seller's resale price. Similarly, in the case of breach by the seller, UCC §2-712(1) allows the buyer to "cover" her loss by purchasing substitute goods and to measure her damages by the difference between the cost of those goods and the contract price. Section E of this chapter further explores these rules along with other remedies available to buyers and sellers under the UCC. The revised version of UCC Article 2 continues to apply these basic concepts, with only minor changes.

5. *Prejudgment and postjudgment interest.* The trial court in *Roesch* awarded the plaintiffs interest on the amount of cash due from the defendants, beginning on the closing date. There are a variety of types of "interest" claims that might be reflected in a judgment for contract damages. When the plaintiff is successful in recovering any judgment in a court action (whether for breach of contract or on other grounds), *postjudgment interest* will under local law usually accrue with respect to the amount of that judgment at least from its date of entry, perhaps from the date of the verdict. See, e.g., 28 U.S.C. §1961; N.Y. Civ. Prac. Law §§5003, 5004 (McKinney 2006).

Should the plaintiff also be entitled to *prejudgment interest* with respect to the period between the accruing of the cause of action and the date of judgment? Agreements that call for the payment of a sum of money on or before a fixed date or on the happening of a specified event (for example, a promissory note) commonly provide that this sum will bear interest at some stated rate if timely payment is not made. Such a provision will be given effect in the judgment unless it violates some "usury" statute. See, e.g., Peterson v. Gustafson, 584 N.W.2d 660 (Minn. Ct. App. 1998) (attorney retainer agreement providing for 1.5 percent interest per month on unpaid fees not usurious). Even in the absence of contract language so providing, the successful plaintiff may sometimes recover prejudgment interest. However, interest of this latter type is usually awarded only in cases where at the time of the breach the plaintiff's claim was for a "liquidated" sum. In Blair Const., Inc. v. McBeth, 44 P.3d 1244 (Kan. 2002), the court stated: "A claim becomes liquidated when both the amount due and the date on which such amount is due are fixed and certain or when the same become definitely ascertainable by mathematical calculation." Id. at 1251. The court also ruled that the award of prejudgment interest was discretionary and that the existence of a good faith controversy about the amount of damages would not necessarily preclude prejudgment interest.

Handicapped Children's Education Board v. Lukaszewski
Supreme Court of Wisconsin
112 Wis. 2d 197, 332 N.W.2d 774 (1983)

CALLOW, Justice.

This review arises out of an unpublished decision of the court of appeals which affirmed in part and reversed in part a judgment of the Ozaukee county circuit court, Judge Warren A. Grady.

In January of 1978 the Handicapped Children's Education Board (the Board) hired Elaine Lukaszewski to serve as a speech and language therapist for the spring term. Lukaszewski was assigned to the Lightfoot School in Sheboygan Falls which was approximately 45 miles from her home in Mequon. Rather than move, she commuted to work each day. During the 1978 spring term, the Board offered Lukaszewski a contract to continue in her present position at Lightfoot School for the 1978-79 school year. The contract called for an annual salary of $10,760. Lukaszewski accepted.

In August of 1978, prior to the beginning of the school year, Lukaszewski was offered a position by the Wee Care Day Care Center which was located not far from her home in Mequon. The job paid an annual salary of $13,000. After deciding to accept this offer, Lukaszewski notified Thomas Morrelle, the Board's director of special education, that she intended to resign from her position at the Lightfoot School. Morrelle told her to submit a letter of resignation for consideration by the Board. She did so, and the matter was discussed at a meeting of the Board on August 21, 1978. The Board refused to release Lukaszewski from her contract. On August 24, 1978, the Board's attorney sent a letter to Lukaszewski directing her to return to work. The attorney sent a second letter to the Wee Care Day Care Center stating that the Board would take legal action if the Center interfered with Lukaszewski's performance of her contractual obligations at the Lightfoot School. A copy of this letter was sent to the Department of Public Instruction.

Lukaszewski left the Wee Care Day Care Center and returned to Lightfoot School for the 1978 fall term. She resented the actions of the Board, however, and retained misgivings about her job. On September 8, 1978, she discussed her feelings with Morrelle. After this meeting Lukaszewski felt quite upset about the situation. She called her doctor to make an appointment for that afternoon and subsequently left the school.

Dr. Ashok Chatterjee examined Lukaszewski and found her blood pressure to be high. Lukaszewski asked Dr. Chatterjee to write a letter explaining his medical findings and the advice he had given her. In a letter dated September 11, 1978, Dr. Chatterjee indicated that Lukaszewski had a hypertension problem dating back to 1976. He reported that on the day he examined Lukaszewski she appeared agitated, nervous, and had blood pressure readings up to 180/100. It was his opinion that, although she took hypotensive drugs, her medical condition would not improve unless the situation which caused the problem was removed. He further opined that it would be dangerous for her to drive long distances in her agitated state.

Lukaszewski did not return to work after leaving on September 8, 1978. She submitted a letter of resignation dated September 13, 1978, in which she wrote:

> I enclose a copy of the doctor's statement concerning my health. On the basis of it, I must resign. I am unwilling to jeopardize my health and I am also unwilling to become involved in an accident. For these reasons, I tender my resignation.

A short time later Lukaszewski reapplied for and obtained employment at the Wee Care Day Care Center.

After Lukaszewski left, the Board immediately began looking for a replacement. Only one qualified person applied for the position. Although this applicant had less of an educational background than Lukaszewski, she had more teaching experience. Under the salary schedule agreed upon by the Board and the teachers' union, this applicant would have to be paid $1,026.64 more per year than Lukaszewski. Having no alternative, the Board hired the applicant at the higher salary.

In December of 1978 the Board initiated an action against Lukaszewski for breach of contract. The Board alleged that, as a result of the breach, it suffered damage in the amount of the additional compensation it was required to pay Lukaszewski's replacement for the 1978-79 school year ($1,026.64). A trial was held before the court. The trial court ruled that Lukaszewski had breached her contract and awarded the Board $1,249.14 in damages ($1,026.64 for breach of contract and $222.50 for costs).

Lukaszewski appealed. The court of appeals affirmed the circuit court's determination that Lukaszewski breached her contract. However, the appellate court reversed the circuit court's damage award, reasoning that, although the Board had to pay more for Lukaszewski's replacement, by its own standards it obtained a proportionately more valuable teacher. Therefore, the court of appeals held that the Board suffered no damage from the breach. We granted the Board's petition for review.

There are two issues presented on this review: (1) whether Lukaszewski breached her employment contract with the Board; and (2) if she did breach her contract, whether the Board suffered recoverable damages therefrom.

I

It is undisputed that Lukaszewski resigned before her contract with the Board expired. The only question is whether her resignation was somehow justified. Lukaszewski argues that, because she resigned for health reasons, the trial court erred in finding a breach of contract. According to Lukaszewski, the uncontroverted evidence at trial established that her employment with the Board endangered her health. Therefore, her failure to fulfill her obligation under the employment contract was excused. . . .

. . . In order to excuse Lukaszewski's nonperformance, the trial court would had to have made a factual finding that she resigned for health reasons. The oral decision and supplemental written decision of the trial court indicate that it found otherwise. . . .

. . . We conclude that the trial court's findings of fact are not against the great weight and clear preponderance of the evidence and, therefore, must be upheld. Accordingly, we affirm that portion of the court of appeals' decision which affirmed the circuit court's determination that Lukaszewski breached her employment contract.

II

This court has long held that an employer may recover damages from an employee who has failed to perform an employment contract. Walsh v. Fisher, 102 Wis. 172, 179, 78 N.W. 437 (1899). Damages in breach of contract cases are ordinarily measured by the expectations of the parties. The nonbreaching party is entitled to full compensation for the loss of his or her bargain — that is, losses necessarily flowing from the breach which are proven to a reasonable certainty and were within contemplation of the parties when the contract was made. Lommen v. Danaher, 165 Wis. 15, 19, 161 N.W. 14 (1917); Pleasure Time, Inc. v. Kuss, 78 Wis. 2d 373, 385, 254 N.W.2d 463 (1977). Thus damages for breach of an employment contract include the cost of obtaining other services equivalent to that promised but not performed, plus any foreseeable consequential damages. Roth v. Speck, 126 A.2d 153, 155 (D.C. 1956); Annot., 61 A.L.R.2d 1008 (1958).

In the instant case it is undisputed that, as a result of the breach, the Board hired a replacement at a salary exceeding what it had agreed to pay Lukaszewski. There is no question that this additional cost ($1,026.64) necessarily flowed from the breach and was within the contemplation of the parties when the contract was made. Lukaszewski argues and the court of appeals held, however, that the Board was not damaged by this expense. The amount a teacher is paid is determined by a salary schedule agreed upon by the teachers' union and the Board. The more education and experience a teacher has the greater her salary will be. Presumably, then, the amount of compensation a teacher receives reflects her value to the Board. Lukaszewski argues that the Board suffered no net loss because, while it had to pay more for the replacement, it received the services of a proportionately more valuable teacher. Accordingly, she maintains that the Board is not entitled to damages because an award would place it in a better position than if the contract had been performed.

We disagree. Lukaszewski and the court of appeals improperly focus on the objective value of the services the Board received rather than that for which it had bargained. Damages for breach of contract are measured by the expectations of the parties. The Board expected to receive the services of a speech therapist with Lukaszewski's education and experience at the salary agreed upon. It neither expected nor wanted a more experienced therapist who had to be paid an additional $1,026.64 per year. Lukaszewski's breach forced the Board to hire the replacement and, in turn, to pay a higher salary. Therefore, the Board lost the benefit of its bargain. Any additional value the Board may have received from the replacement's greater experience was imposed upon it and thus cannot be characterized as a benefit. We conclude that the Board suffered damages for the loss of its bargain in the amount of additional compensation it was required to pay Lukaszewski's replacement.

This is not to say that an employer who is injured by an employee's breach of contract is free to hire the most qualified and expensive replacement and then recover the difference between the salary paid and the contract salary. An injured party must take all reasonable steps to mitigate damages. Kuhlman, Inc. v. G. Heileman Brewing Co., 83 Wis. 2d 749, 752, 266 N.W.2d 382 (1978). Therefore, the employer must attempt to obtain equivalent services at the lowest possible cost. In the instant case the Board acted reasonably in hiring Lukaszewski's replacement even though she commanded a higher salary. Upon Lukaszewski's breach, the Board immediately took steps to locate a replacement. Only one qualified person applied for the position. Having no alternative, the Board hired this applicant. Thus the Board properly mitigated its damages by hiring the least expensive, qualified replacement available.

We hold that the Board is entitled to have the benefit of its bargain restored. Therefore, we reverse that portion of the court of appeals' decision which reversed the trial court's damage award.

The decision of the court of appeals is affirmed in part and reversed in part.

DAY, Justice (dissenting).

I dissent. The majority opinion correctly states, "The only question is whether her resignation is somehow justified." I would hold that it was.

Elaine Lukaszewski left her employment with the school board. She suffered from high blood pressure and had been treated for several years by her physician for the condition. She claimed her hypertension increased due to stress caused when the Board refused to cancel her teaching contract. Stress can cause a precipitous rise in blood pressure. High blood pressure can bring on damage to other organs of the body. . . .

It seems clear from the trial judge's comments that if he had found her physical condition had been caused by the Board's "harassment," he would have let her out of the contract. This is the only logical conclusion from the statement by the trial judge that, "The Court finds that the defendant's medical excuse was a result of the stress condition she had created by an attempted repudiation of her contract, and was not the product of any unsubstantiated, so-called, harrassment [sic] by the plaintiff's board."

In either instance, whether "caused" by the Board or "self induced" because of her gnawing feeling of being unfairly treated, the objective symptoms would be the same.

Either, in my opinion, should justify termination of the contract where the physical symptoms are medically certifiable as they admittedly are here. . . .

What the trial court said was that the desire to take the better job brought on the physical symptoms when release from her contract by the Board was refused.

If the trial court had found that she quit merely for the better job and *not* because of her health problems brought on by the high blood pressure, this would be an entirely different case. However, that is *not* what the trial court found in my opinion. The trial court found her medical problems were self induced and concluded they were therefore unworthy of consideration.

I would reverse the court of appeals decision that held she breached her contract.

Because I would hold that on this record there was no breach, I would not reach the damage question.

Notes and Questions

1. *Measurement of damages in* **Lukaszewski.** As we shall see, the courts will almost never order "specific performance" by an employee of the services promised in a contract of employment. The measure of damages applied in *Lukaszewski* is therefore probably the only potentially useful remedy in most cases where an employee "walks off" the job without legal justification. Is it appropriate? Would some other measure of damages (or no damages at all) be a better solution?

You will recall that many employment contracts are "at will." As we have seen, there are a number of potential limitations on the employer's right to terminate such at will relationships, however, there appears to be no movement toward similar restrictions on termination by the employee. The rule applied in *Lukaszewski* will thus have application only in cases where the employee has by contract bound herself to the employer for some stated period of time. In what fields of employment are such fixed-term contracts likely to be common?

2. *Illness as a defense to breach of an employment contract.* In Chapter 8 we examined the doctrine of impracticability and related concepts. In a personal service contract, the death or incapacity of a person necessary for performance may excuse nonperformance. See Restatement (Second) §262. Moreover, performance may be impracticable because it will involve undue risk of injury to a person. Restatement (Second) §261. cmt. *d*. Do you agree with the dissent that even if Ms. Lukaszewski's high blood pressure was "self induced" by "her gnawing feeling of being unfairly treated," she should have been excused from performance? If so, should that feeling have to meet an objective "reasonable-ness" test? Or should it be enough that she did indeed suffer from such a condition because of her honest belief that she had been dealt with unjustly?

American Standard, Inc. v. Schectman
New York Supreme Court
80 A.D.2d 318, 439 N.Y.S.2d 529 (App. Div.), appeal denied,
427 N.E.2d 512 (1981)

HANCOCK, Justice.
Plaintiffs have recovered a judgment on a jury verdict of $90,000 against defendant for his failure to complete grading and to take down certain

foundations and other subsurface structures to one foot below the grade line as promised. Whether the court should have charged the jury, as defendant Schectman requested, that the difference in value of plaintiffs' property with and without the promised performance was the measure of the damage is the main point in his appeal. We hold that the request was properly denied and that the cost of completion — not the difference in value — was the proper measure. Finding no other basis for reversal, we affirm.

Until 1972, plaintiffs operated a pig iron manufacturing plant on land abutting the Niagara River in Tonawanda. On the 26-acre parcel were, in addition to various industrial and office buildings, a 60-ton blast furnace, large lifts, hoists and other equipment for transporting and storing ore, railroad tracks, cranes, diesel locomotives and sundry implements and devices used in the business. Since the 1870's plaintiffs' property, under several different owners, had been the site of various industrial operations. Having decided to close the plant, plaintiffs on August 3, 1973 made a contract in which they agreed to convey the buildings and other structures and most of the equipment to defendant, a demolition and excavating contractor, in return for defendant's payment of $275,000 and his promise to remove the equipment, demolish the structures and grade the property as specified.

We agree with Trial Term's interpretation of the contract as requiring defendant to remove all foundations, piers, headwalls, and other structures, including those under the surface and not visible and whether or not shown on the map attached to the contract, to a depth of approximately one foot below the specified grade lines.[2] The proof from plaintiffs' witnesses and the exhibits, showing a substantial deviation from the required grade lines and the existence above grade of walls, foundations and other structures, support the finding, implicit in the jury's verdict, that defendant failed to perform as agreed. Indeed, the testimony of defendant's witnesses and the position he has taken during his performance of the contract and throughout this litigation (which the trial court properly rejected), viz., that the contract did not require him to remove all subsurface foundations, allow no other conclusion.

We turn to defendant's argument that the court erred in rejecting his proof that plaintiffs suffered no loss by reason of the breach because it makes no difference in the value of the property whether the old foundations are at grade or one foot below grade and in denying his offer to show that plaintiffs succeeded in selling the property for $183,000 — only $3,000 less than its full fair market value. By refusing this testimony and charging the jury that the

---

2. Paragraph 7 of the Agreement states in pertinent part:

   7. After the Closing Date, Purchaser shall demolish all of the Improvements on the North Tonawanda Property included in the sale to Purchaser, cap the water intake at the pumphouse end, and grade and level the property, all in accordance with the provisions of Exhibit "C" and "C1" attached hereto.

   Exhibit "C" (Notes on demolition and grading) contains specifications for the grade levels for four separate areas shown on Map "C1" and the following instruction:

   Except as otherwise excepted all structures and equipment including foundations, piers, headwalls, etc. shall be removed to a depth approximately one foot below grade lines as set forth above. Area common to more than one area will be faired to provide reasonable transitions, it being intended to provide a reasonably attractive vacant plot for resale.

cost of completion (estimated at $110,500 by plaintiffs' expert), not diminution in value of the property, was the measure of damage the court, defendant contends, has unjustly permitted plaintiffs to reap a windfall at his expense. Citing the definitive opinion of Chief Judge Cardozo in Jacob & Youngs, Inc. v. Kent, 230 N.Y. 239, 129 N.E. 889, he maintains that the facts present a case "of substantial performance" of the contract with omissions of "trivial or inappreciable importance" (p. 245, 129 N.E. 889), and that because the cost of completion was "grossly and unfairly out of proportion to the good to be attained," (p. 244, 129 N.E. 889), the proper measure of damage is diminution in value.

The general rule of damages for breach of a construction contract is that the injured party may recover those damages which are the direct, natural and immediate consequence of the breach and which can reasonably be said to have been in the contemplation of the parties when the contract was made (see 13 N.Y. Jur., Damages, §§46, 56; Chamberlain v. Parker, 45 N.Y. 569; Hadley v. Baxendale, 9 Exch. 341, 156 Eng. Reprint 145; Restatement, Contracts, §346). In the usual case where the contractor's performance has been defective or incomplete, the reasonable cost of replacement or completion is the measure (see, Bellizzi v. Huntley Estates, 3 N.Y.2d 112, 164 N.Y.S.2d 395, 143 N.E.2d 802; . . . Restatement, Contracts, §346). When, however, there has been a substantial performance of the contract made in good faith but defects exist, the correction of which would result in economic waste, courts have measured the damages as the difference between the value of the property as constructed and the value if performance had been properly completed. . . . *Jacob & Youngs* is illustrative. There, plaintiff, a contractor, had constructed a house for the defendant which was satisfactory in all respects save one: the wrought iron pipe installed for the plumbing was not of Reading manufacture, as specified in the contract, but of other brands of the same quality. Noting that the breach was unintentional and the consequences of the omission trivial, and that the cost of replacing the pipe would be "grievously out of proportion" (Jacob & Youngs, Inc. v. Kent, supra, 230 N.Y. p. 244, 129 N.E. 889) to the significance of the default, the court held the breach to be immaterial and the proper measure of damage to the owner to be not the cost of replacing the pipe but the nominal difference in value of the house with and without the Reading pipe.

Not in all cases of claimed "economic waste" where the cost of completing performance of the contract would be large and out of proportion to the resultant benefit to the property have the courts adopted diminution in value as the measure of damage. Under the Restatement rule, the completion of the contract must involve "unreasonable economic waste" and the illustrative example given is that of a house built with pipe different in name from but equal in quality to the brand stipulated in the contract as in Jacob & Youngs, Inc. v. Kent (supra) (Restatement, Contracts, §346, subd. [1], par. [a], cl. [ii], p. 573; Illustration 2, p. 576). In Groves v. John Wunder Co., 205 Minn. 163, 286 N.W. 235, plaintiff had leased property and conveyed a gravel plant to defendant in exchange for a sum of money and for defendant's commitment to return the property to plaintiff at the end of the term at a specified grade — a promise defendant failed to perform. Although the cost of the fill to complete the grading was $60,000 and the total value of the property, graded as specified in the contract, only $12,160 the court rejected the "diminution in value" rule, stating:

> The owner's right to improve his property is not trammeled by its small value. It is his right to erect thereon structures which will reduce its value. If that be the result, it can be of no aid to any contractor who declines performance. As said long ago in Chamberlain v. Parker, 45 N.Y. 569, 572: "A man may do what he will with his own, . . . and if he chooses to erect a monument to his caprice or folly on his premises, and employs and pays another to do it, it does not lie with a defendant who has been so employed and paid for building it, to say that his own performance would not be beneficial to the plaintiff."

(Groves v. John Wunder Co., supra, 205 Minn., p.168, 286 N.W. 235).

The "economic waste" of the type which calls for application of the "diminution in value" rule generally entails defects in construction which are irremediable or which may not be repaired without a substantial tearing down of the structure as in *Jacob & Youngs*. . . .

Where, however, the breach is of a covenant which is only incidental to the main purpose of the contract and completion would be disproportionately costly, courts have applied the diminution in value measure even where no destruction of the work is entailed (see, e.g., Peevyhouse v. Garland Coal & Min. Co., 382 P.2d 109 [Okla.], *cert. denied*, 375 U.S. 906, 84 S. Ct. 196, 11 L. Ed. 2d 145, holding [contrary to Groves v. John Wunder Co., supra] that diminution in value is the proper measure where defendant, the lessee of plaintiff's lands under a coal mining lease, failed to perform costly remedial and restorative work on the land at the termination of the lease. The court distinguished the "building and construction" cases and noted that the breach was of a covenant incidental to the main purpose of the contract which was the recovery of coal from the premises to the benefit of both parties; and see Avery v. Fredericksen & Westbrook, 67 Cal. App. 2d 334, 154 P.2d 41).

It is also a general rule in building and construction cases, at least under *Jacob & Youngs* in New York . . . , that a contractor who would ask the court to apply the diminution of value measure "as an instrument of justice" must not have breached the contract intentionally and must show substantial performance made in good faith (Jacob & Youngs, Inc. v. Kent, supra, 230 N.Y. pp. 244, 245, 129 N.E. 889).

In the case before us, plaintiffs chose to accept as part of the consideration for the promised conveyance of their valuable plant and machines to defendant his agreement to grade the property as specified and to remove the foundations, piers and other structures to a depth of one foot below grade to prepare the property for sale. It cannot be said that the grading and the removal of the structures were incidental to plaintiffs' purpose of "achieving a reasonably attractive vacant plot for resale" (compare Peevyhouse v. Garland Coal & Min. Co., supra). Nor can defendant maintain that the damages which would naturally flow from his failure to do the grading and removal work and which could reasonably be said to have been in the contemplation of the parties when the contract was made would not be the reasonable cost of completion (see 13 N.Y. Jur., Damages, §§46, 56; Hadley v. Baxendale, supra). That the fulfillment of defendant's promise would (contrary to plaintiffs' apparent expectations) add little or nothing to the sale value of the property does not excuse the default. As in the hypothetical case posed in Chamberlain v. Parker, 45 N.Y. 569, supra (cited in Groves v. John Wunder Co., supra), of the man who "chooses to erect a monument to his caprice or folly on his premises, and employs and pays another to do it," it does not lie with defendant here who has received consideration for his promise to do the work "to say that his own performance would not be beneficial to the plaintiff[s]" (Chamberlain v. Parker, supra, p. 572).

Defendant's completed performance would not have involved undoing what in good faith was done improperly but only doing what was promised and left undone (compare Jacob & Youngs, Inc. v. Kent, supra; Restatement, Contracts, §346, Illustration 2, p. 576). That the burdens of performance were heavier than anticipated and the cost of completion disproportionate to the end to be obtained does not, without more, alter the rule that the measure of plaintiffs' damage is the cost of completion. Disparity in relative economic benefits is not the equivalent of "economic waste" which will invoke the rule in Jacob & Youngs, Inc. v. Kent (supra) (see Groves v. John Wunder Co., supra). Moreover, faced with the jury's finding that the reasonable cost of removing the large concrete and stone walls and other structures extending above grade was $90,000, defendant can hardly assert that he has rendered substantial performance of the contract or that what he left unfinished was "of trivial or inappreciable importance" (Jacob & Youngs, Inc. v. Kent, supra, 230 N.Y. p. 245, 129 N.E. 889). Finally, defendant, instead of attempting in good faith to complete the removal of the underground structures, contended that he was not obliged by the contract to do so and, thus, cannot claim to be a "transgressor whose default is unintentional and trivial [and who] may hope for mercy if he will offer atonement for his wrong" (Jacob & Youngs, Inc. v. Kent, supra, p. 244, 129 N.E. 889). We conclude, then, that the proof pertaining to the value of plaintiffs' property was properly rejected and the jury correctly charged on damages.

The judgment and order should be affirmed.

Judgment and order unanimously affirmed with costs.

SIMONS, J.P., and DOERR, DENMAN and SCHNEPP, JJ., concur.

Notes and Questions

1. *Rationale for cost-to-complete measure of damages.* As we have seen, the basic principle for determining damages for breach of contract allows the injured party to recover an amount sufficient to give that party the benefit of the bargain. As a general matter, the cost-to-complete measure of damages seems more consistent with this principle than the diminution-in-value measure because the injured party can expend the damages to receive the bargained-for performance. Another reason for choosing the cost-to-complete measure is that the actual injury to the plaintiff may not be adequately reflected by the market-value comparison. Thus, where the plaintiff contemplates a personal use for the property (e.g., personal residence, family farm), it may be that the property has "idiosyncratic" value to the plaintiff that

is not reflected in the market value of the property, in which case damages based on diminished value will clearly undercompensate the plaintiff, perhaps by a substantial but unquantifiable amount. On the other hand, where the plaintiff is a business enterprise, idiosyncratic value is much less likely, and the diminished market value of the property may appear more likely to be an accurate measure of the plaintiff's true injury. If this factor should be viewed as controlling, was *American Standard* correctly decided? Professor Timothy Muris argues that in choosing between remedies in such cases the courts should take into account the presence of "nonpecuniary" (or "subjective") value to the plaintiff; his survey of the decided cases suggests that indeed courts frequently do so, without necessarily adverting to that factor in their opinions. Timothy J. Muris, Cost of Completion or Diminution in Market Value: The Relevance of Subjective Value, 12 J. Legal Stud. 379 (1983). Are there any other factors that would favor cost-to-complete over diminution in market value?

2. *Justification for diminution in market value damages.* Using the *Groves* case (also discussed in *American Standard*) as his example, Judge Posner has suggested that in such cases damages should be based on the diminished value of the land, on grounds of efficiency. Richard A. Posner, Economic Analysis of Law 121 (6th ed. 2003). Posner argues that the award of cost-to-restore damages overcompensates the owner; if the owner had truly wanted restoration of the property, he could have brought an action for specific performance. Posner notes that in *Groves* the plaintiff, who received a cost-to-restore award, did not in fact use the money to restore the land to its original condition. This argument is a corollary of the general notion of encouraging the "efficient breach," a topic to which we return later in this chapter.

If the injured party does not use the award to restore the property, does it follow that the injured party has been overcompensated, as Posner suggests? In Emery v. Caledonia Sand & Gravel Co., 374 A.2d 929 (N.H. 1977), the defendant road construction company had breached a contract to restore the excavated area on defendant's farm. The trial court awarded the plaintiffs damages in the amount necessary to complete the restoration as promised. The Supreme Court of New Hampshire affirmed. While recognizing that there were some cases in which an award of cost-to-complete damages could result in overcompensation or economic waste, the court rejected the argument that the mere fact that the plaintiffs might pocket the money was sufficient to show unjust enrichment: "A valuable income-producing asset has been rendered unproductive; the damages awarded constitute a reasonable means of bringing that asset back to life. If the plaintiffs choose to 'pocket' their recovery, they will have foregone the restoration of their land; they will not have been unjustly enriched." Id. at 933. See also Corbello v. Iowa Production, 850 So. 2d 686 (La. 2003) (upholding jury award of $33 million for breach of contract to restore land worth $108,000 even though owners of land had no obligation to use award for cleanup).

In *American Standard* the court indicates that in some cases "economic waste" would justify an award of diminution in market value rather than cost to complete. When would the economic waste doctrine apply?

By the time of the decision in *American Standard,* the plaintiffs had sold the land at only $3,000 less than its market value. Did the court give too little weight to this fact? Why? Should the cost-to-restore remedy be limited to cases in which it appears that the plaintiff can and will use the damages recovered for this purpose?

3. *The Peevyhouse case.* Peevyhouse v. Garland Coal & Mining Co., the Oklahoma case cited and discussed in *American Standard,* is the leading case applying the diminished-value measure of damages for the defendant's failure to restore the plaintiffs' land as promised after completion of its strip-mining operations.

In a comprehensive case study, Professor Judith Maute provides important insights about the background and litigation of *Peevyhouse.* Judith L. Maute, *Peevyhouse v. Garland Coal & Mining Co.* Revisited: The Ballad of Willie and Lucille, 89 Nw. U. L. Rev. 1341 (1995). Professor Maute's monograph explores the negotiations leading up to the lease, the context of strip mining in Oklahoma, the lawyering strategies and failures at various levels of the case, allegations of bribery that have surrounded the case for many years, and the continuing impact of the decision. For scholars who have long complained that appellate opinions are an inadequate source for teaching law, Professor Maute's article provides a rich resource.

Maute's research supplies factual background that bears on the choice between diminution in market value or cost to restore as the measure of damages for breach of contract:

> The Peevyhouses were opposed to permitting any mining on their land. An earlier mining operation stopped at their property line, leaving behind the disturbed land, including a dangerous pit, highwall, and unsightly burden. . . . Because they wanted the land restored to usable condition after the mining, they agreed to forego payment of $3000 . . . in exchange for Garland's promise to do remedial work. Willie explained his view that it was not right to take money for land and allow work to be done on it that would make the land worthless in the future.

Id. at 1358-1363. The Peevyhouses obtained a judgment of $300, far less than the $3,000 amount that they had waived. After payment of litigation costs, they received nothing. As of 1995, the Peevyhouses still lived on the property, which had not been restored. Id. at 1348, 1405. For Maute's discussion of the remedial issues in *Peevyhouse,* see 89 Nw. U. L. Rev. at 1426-1446.

In Rock Island Improvement Co. v. Helmerich & Payne, Inc., 698 F.2d 1075 (10th Cir.), *cert. denied,* 461 U.S. 944 (1983), a case governed by Oklahoma law, the facts were nearly identical to those in *Peevyhouse,* except that the plaintiff was apparently a land-developing company, rather than an individual farmer. The cost to restore the property to its original condition was approximately $375,000, while the diminution in value was estimated to be $7,000. Id. at 1077. The Tenth Circuit affirmed a judgment based on a jury verdict for the cost to restore. The court predicted that the Oklahoma Supreme Court would no longer follow *Peevyhouse* because the public policy of the state as reflected in its statutory law had changed to provide greater protection to the environment. The Tenth Circuit was wrong in its prediction. In Schneberger v. Apache Corp., 890 P.2d 847 (Okla. 1994), the Oklahoma Supreme Court reaffirmed its holding in *Peevyhouse* and rejected claims that statutory changes had undermined the rule of the case. The facts in

Schneberger were quite extreme, however. The plaintiffs sought to recover $1.3 million, the cost to remedy water pollution caused by the defendant's oil drilling activities, while the diminution in value of the land was approximately $5,175. The court in *Schneberger* also indicated that the decision might have been different if the parties had specified the measure of damages in their contract. Id. at 854.

4. *The Restatement approach.* The Restatement (Second) provides in §348(2) that if the loss in value to the injured party is not proved with sufficient certainty, damages may be measured by either (a) the diminution in market value or (b) by the reasonable cost of completing performance or of remedying the defects if that cost "is not clearly disproportionate to the probable loss in value to him." How does the Restatement rule compare to the holding in *American Standard?*

5. *Case law and scholarly analysis.* In ordinary cases of defective or unfinished construction work, the courts appear to be generally inclined to award cost-to-complete damages, e.g., Flom v. Stahly, 569 N.W.2d 135 (Iowa 1997). Cases are collected in John P. Ludington, Annotation, Modern Status of Rule as to Whether Cost of Correction or Difference in Value of Structures Is Proper Measure of Damages for Breach of Construction Contract, 41 A.L.R.4th 131 (1985). See also Carol Chomsky, Of Soil Pits and Swimming Pools: Reconsidering the Measure of Damages for Construction Contracts, 75 Minn. L. Rev. 1445 (1991) (arguing that courts should generally award cost-to-complete damages because that measure ordinarily provides full compensation for loss, but recognizing that in some cases cost-to-complete measure may overcompensate).

Other commentators have suggested that the courts have been too rigid in restricting the choice to either cost to complete or diminution in market value. See E. Allan Farnsworth, Legal Remedies for Breach of Contract, 70 Colum. L. Rev. 1145, 1175 (1970) (trier of fact should have discretion to fix any "not unreasonable" compromise award between two extremes). See also Robert L. Birmingham, Damage Measures and Economic Rationality: The Geometry of Contract Law, 1969 Duke L.J. 49, 69-70 and Peter Linzer, On the Amorality of Contract Remedies — Efficiency, Equity, and the Second *Restatement,* 81 Colum. L. Rev. 111, 134-138 (1981) (both articles suggest that courts should award specific performance rather than damages; in cases where owner wants restoration, specific performance will provide full compensation; in other cases, parties will negotiate a buy-out of owner's right to specific performance).

B. RESTRICTIONS ON THE RECOVERY OF EXPECTATION DAMAGES: FORESEEABILITY, CERTAINTY, AND CAUSATION

In its formula for calculating expectation damages, Restatement (Second) §347 distinguishes between two positive components of plaintiff's recovery: "loss in value" (computed with respect to the value of the performance actually received from the defendant) and "other loss." There are many types of "loss" that are in a sense extrinsic to the valuation of the defendant's performance, but that nevertheless are significant. Losses of this sort are commonly referred to as "consequential," and recovery for such losses is subject to certain controls not applied to ordinary damages. These restrictions are traditionally said to originate with the following English decision, one of the few cases that probably all students of contract law have learned to remember by name, even if (as may be likely) they eventually forget what it stands for.

Hadley v. Baxendale
Court of Exchequer
156 Eng. Rep. 145 (1854)

At the trial before Crompton, J., at the last Gloucester Assizes, it appeared that the plaintiffs carried on an extensive business as millers at Gloucester; and that, on the 11th of May, their mill was stopped by a breakage of the crank shaft by which the mill was worked. The steam-engine was manufactured by Messrs. Joyce & Co., the engineers, at Greenwich, and it became necessary to send the shaft as a pattern for a new one to Greenwich. The fracture was discovered on the 12th, and on the 13th the plaintiffs sent one of their servants to the office of the defendants, who are the well known carriers trading under the name of Pickford & Co., for the purpose of having the shaft carried to Greenwich. The plaintiffs' servant told the clerk that the mill was stopped, and that the shaft must be sent immediately; and in answer to the inquiry when the shaft would be taken, the answer was, that if it was sent up by twelve o'clock any day, it would be delivered at Greenwich on the following day. On the following day the shaft was taken by the defendants, before noon, for the purpose of being conveyed to Greenwich, and the sum of 2*l*. 4s. [2 pounds, 4 shillings — EDS.] was paid for its carriage for the whole distance; at the same time the defendants' clerk was told that a special entry, if required, should be made to hasten its delivery. The delivery of the shaft at Greenwich was delayed by some neglect; and the consequence was, that the plaintiffs did not receive the new shaft for several days after they would otherwise have done, and the working of their mill was thereby delayed, and they thereby lost the profits they would otherwise have received.

On the part of the defendants, it was objected that these damages were too remote, and that the defendants were not liable with respect to them. The learned Judge left the case generally to the jury, who found a verdict with 25*l*. damages beyond the amount paid into Court.

Whateley, in last Michaelmas Term, obtained a rule nisi for a new trial, on the ground of misdirection.

ALDERSON, B. We think that there ought to be a new trial in this case; but, in so doing, we deem it to be expedient and necessary to state explicitly the rule which the Judge, at the next trial, ought, in our opinion, to direct the jury to be governed by when they estimate the damages.

It is, indeed, of the last importance that we should do this; for, if the jury are left without any definite rule to guide them, it will, in such cases as these, manifestly lead to the greatest injustice. The Courts have done this on several occasions; and, in Blake v. Midland Railway Company (18 Q.B. 93), the Court granted a new trial on this very ground, that the rule had not been definitely laid down to the jury by the learned Judge at Nisi Prius.

"There are certain established rules," this Court says, in Alder v. Keighley (15 M. & W. 117), "according to which the jury ought to find." And the Court, in that case, adds: "and here there is a clear rule, that the amount which would have been received if the contract had been kept, is the measure of damages if the contract is broken."

Now we think the proper rule in such a case as the present is this: — Where two parties have made a contract which one of them has broken, the damages which the other party ought to receive in respect of such breach of contract should be such as may fairly and reasonably be considered either arising naturally, i.e., according to the usual course of things, from such breach of contract itself, or such as may reasonably be supposed to have been in the contemplation of both parties, at the time they made the contract, as the probable result of the breach of it. Now, if the special circumstances under which the contract was actually made were communicated by the plaintiffs to the defendants, and thus known to both parties, the damages resulting from the breach of such a contract, which they would reasonably contemplate, would be the amount of injury which would ordinarily follow from a breach of contract under these special circumstances so known and communicated. But, on the other hand, if these special circumstances were wholly unknown to the party breaking the contract, he, at the most, could only be supposed to have had in his contemplation the amount of injury which would arise generally, and in the great multitude of cases not affected by any special circumstances, from such a breach of contract. For, had the special circumstances been known, the parties might have specially provided for the breach of contract by special terms as to the damages in that case; and of this advantage it would be very unjust to deprive them. Now the above principles are those by which we think the jury ought to be guided in estimating the damages arising out of any breach of contract. It is said, that other cases such as breaches of contract in the non-payment of money, or in the not making a good title to land, are to be treated as exceptions from this, and as governed by a conventional rule. But as, in such cases, both parties must be supposed to be cognisant of that well-known rule, these cases may, we think, be more properly classed under the rule above enunciated as to cases under known special circumstances, because there both parties may reasonably be presumed to contemplate the estimation of the amount of damages according to the conventional rule. Now, in the present case, if we are to apply the principles above laid down, we find that the only circumstances here communicated by the plaintiffs to the defendants at the time the contract was made, were, that the article to be carried was the broken shaft of a mill, and that the plaintiffs were the millers of that mill. But how do these circumstances shew reasonably that the profits of the mill must be stopped by an unreasonable delay in the delivery of the broken shaft by the carrier to the third person? Suppose the plaintiffs had another shaft in their possession put up or putting up at the time, and that they only wished to send back the broken shaft to the engineer who made it; it is clear that this would be quite consistent with the above circumstances, and yet the unreasonable delay in the delivery would have no effect upon the intermediate profits of the mill. Or, again, suppose that, at the time of the delivery to the carrier, the machinery of the mill had been in other respects defective, then, also, the same results would follow. Here it is true that the shaft was actually sent back to serve as a model for a new one, and that the want of a new one was the only cause of the stoppage of the mill, and that the loss of profits really arose from not sending down the new shaft in proper time, and that this arose from the delay in delivering the broken one to serve as a model. But it is obvious that, in the great multitude of cases of millers sending off broken shafts to third persons by a carrier under ordinary circumstances, such consequences would not, in all probability, have occurred; and these special circumstances were here never communicated by the plaintiffs to the defendants. It follows, therefore, that the loss of profits here cannot reasonably be considered such a consequence of the breach of contract as could have been fairly and reasonably contemplated by both the parties when they made this contract. For such loss would neither have flowed naturally from the breach of this contract in the great multitude of such cases occurring under ordinary circumstances, nor were the special circumstances, which, perhaps, would have made it a reasonable and natural consequence of such breach of contract, communicated to or known by the defendants. The Judge ought, therefore, to have told the jury, that, upon the facts then before them, they ought not to take the loss of profits into consideration at all in estimating the damages. There must therefore be a new trial in this case.

Rule absolute.

Notes and Questions

1. *What did the clerk know?* The Hadley v. Baxendale opinion has had universal acceptance in Anglo-American law as stating an appropriate rule of limitation on damages that would otherwise be recoverable under an unrestricted "expectation" rule. Does the decision itself appear to be sustainable on the facts of the *Hadley* case? In Victoria Laundry (Windsor) Ltd. v. Newman Industries, Ltd., [1949] 2 K.B. 528, 537 (C.A.), a later English court expressed the opinion that the headnote to *Hadley* is "definitely misleading in so far as it says that the defendants' clerk, who attended at the office, was told that the mill was stopped and that the shaft must be delivered immediately." If the court in *Hadley* had actually regarded that as established, it was asserted, then it is "reasonably plain" from Baron Alderson's opinion in *Hadley* that it would have decided that case "the other way round." On the other hand, it has been suggested that the opinion in *Hadley* can be viewed as consistent with the facts as stated in the headnote if one assumes that the clerk was not told either that the stoppage of the mill was solely due to the shaft's being broken or that no other shaft was available in the meantime. Charles T. McCormick, The Contemplation Rule as a Limitation upon Damages for Breach of Contract, 19 Minn. L. Rev. 497, 500-501 (1935). Richard Danzig concludes that there is evidence both ways on the question of whether the

Hadleys indeed "served notice on the . . . clerk of their extreme dependence on the shaft," but suggests that in any event the "rudimentary law of agency" as it then existed might have required notice to be served on Baxendale himself, or at least on some agent more exalted than a mere receiving clerk. Richard Danzig, Hadley v. Baxendale, A Study in the Industrialization of the Law, 4 J. Legal Stud. 249, 262-263 (1975). Danzig's article (substantially incorporated also in his book with Geoffrey R. Watson, The Capability Problem in Contract Law (2d ed. 2004)) explores the context in which the *Hadley* case was decided. Besides the now conventional notion that the *Hadley* decision was more or less consciously an attempt to protect infant industries in the early stages of the industrial revolution, Danzig sees a number of other factors reflected in that decision: tensions between Parliament and the courts, between different courts, and between judge and jury; differences over the proper extent of liability of common carriers, and about the way in which their activities should be regulated; and the still rudimentary state in 1854 of both commercial and agency law. Id. at 64-79

2. *General and consequential damages.* In *Hadley* the court refers to two types of damages: those that arise naturally from the breach of contract and those that result from special circumstances communicated at the time the contract was formed. These two types of damages have various labels. Damages that arise naturally are often referred to as "general" or "direct" damages. Damages flowing from special circumstances are usually called "consequential" damages although the term "special" damages is sometimes used. (You should also be aware that in tort law a different terminology is employed. Special damages in tort refer to out-of-pocket medical expenses, while general damages refer to pain and suffering.)

The plaintiff need not make any special showing to recover general damages. For example, in a contract for the sale of land, the difference between the contract price and the market value constitutes general damages.

The most important type of consequential damages in commercial cases is lost profits arising from collateral contracts. (Note that lost profit on the contract that is breached, as opposed to other contracts, is treated as general rather than consequential damages). Consequential damages also include injury to person or property caused by goods that fail to comply with contractual warranties. On the distinction between general and consequential damages, see American List Corp. v. U.S. News & World Report, Inc., 549 N.E.2d 1161 (N.Y. 1989) (lost profits on contract that was breached rather than on collateral contract are general damages not subject to rule of Hadley v. Baxendale).

3. *Foreseeability.* The modern formulation of the rule of Hadley v. Baxendale is now stated in terms of the foreseeability of the loss. See Restatement (Second) of Contracts §351 and UCC §2-715(2). Several aspects of the foreseeability standard should be noted. As the court in *Hadley* states, the recoverability of consequential damages depends on whether such damages were in the contemplation of the parties "at the time they made the contract." It might plausibly be contended that liability for the foreseeable consequences of breach of contract ought to be based on the breacher's knowledge as of the time the *breach* occurs, just as the law of torts generally makes the tortfeasor's knowledge at the time of the tortious conduct the test

for liability based on foreseeability of harm. However, application of the *Hadley* test is uniformly understood to depend on the defendant's knowledge at the time the contract is made. Why should this be so?

Second, it is only necessary that the type of loss be foreseeable, not the manner in which the loss occurs. Third, while courts sometimes refer to risks that are within the contemplation of both parties, the focus of foreseeability is on the breaching party. Fourth, the standard for foreseeability is at least in part objective. The breaching party is liable for losses about which it had reason to know. Finally, the loss must be foreseeable as a "probable" result of the breach. Liability is not limited to losses that are necessary or inevitable, but it does not extend to remote losses. See E. Allan Farnsworth, Contracts §12.14, at 795-796 (4th ed. 2004); Restatement (Second) Contracts §351, Comment *a*.

4. *The **Hadley** rule under the CISG.* With regard to international transactions, Article 74 of the CISG provides as follows:

> Damages for breach of contract by one party consist of a sum equal to the loss, including loss of profit, suffered by the other party as a consequence of the breach. Such damages may not exceed the loss which the party in breach foresaw or ought to have foreseen at the time of the conclusion of the contract, in the light of the facts and matters of which he then knew or ought to have known, as a possible consequence of the breach of contract.

See Delchi Carrier SpA v. Rotorex Corp., 71 F. 3d 1024 (2d Cir. 1995) (applying CISG Article 74 and finding that seller from U.S. was liable to buyer in Italy after defective compressors delivered under contract led to cancellation of the agreement and buyer lost sales to third parties). How does this principle compare to the *Hadley* rule?

5. *The tacit agreement test.* At the beginning of the twentieth century, Justice Holmes advocated a "tacit agreement" test for recovery of consequential damages. This test would have limited the availability of consequential damages even more than the rule of Hadley v. Baxendale. Under the tacit agreement test the injured party would have been required to show not only that the special circumstances were brought to the attention of the other party, but also that the other party "assumed consciously" the liability in question. Globe Refining Co. v. Landa Cotton Oil Co., 190 U.S. 540, 544 (1903). Modern contract law has largely rejected the tacit agreement test. See Rexnord Corp. v. DeWolff Boberg & Assoc., Inc., 286 F.3d 1001 (7th Cir. 2002); Restatement (Second) of Contracts §351, Comment *a;* UCC §2-715, Comment 2.

Professor Richard Epstein, however, has criticized the modern rejection of the "tacit agreement" test and the general application of the rule of Hadley v. Baxendale. He argues that determination of the amount of contract damages should be viewed as a question of contract interpretation. When the contract specifies the measure of damages, the contractual provision should be enforced, absent fraud, duress, or some other invalidating conduct. When the contract is silent on the measure of damages, the court should adopt the "default rule" of damages that the parties would most likely have agreed on had they considered the issue of damages. Relying on commercial practice, reflected in various types of contracts, which limits expectation damages below the amount that would be fixed by the *Hadley* rule (for example, consumer goods are typically sold with a "repair or replace" warranty), Epstein argues that the appropriate default rule will often be less than the amount determined under a *Hadley* approach. Richard A. Epstein, Beyond Foreseeability: Consequential Damages in the Law of Contract, 18 J. Legal Stud. 105 (1989).

By contrast, Professor Melvin Eisenberg reaches conclusions that are diametrically opposed to Epstein's. Melvin A. Eisenberg, The Principle of *Hadley v. Baxendale*, 80 Cal. L. Rev. 563 (1992). Eisenberg argues that the utility of the *Hadley* rule depends on communication of information by buyers and use by sellers of such information in setting prices to reflect risk. Id. at 587-588. This process is unlikely to occur, however, particularly with regard to standardized products, because of the costs of communicating and utilizing information. Id. at 592. Thus, Eisenberg concludes, the costs of the *Hadley* rule are likely to exceed its benefits. Id. at 597-598. He advocates a rule that would allow recovery of all losses that are proximately caused by a breach (in essence, the tort standard), subject to contractual allocation of risk and principles of fair disclosure of contractual limitations on liability. Id. at 598.

Florafax International, Inc. v. GTE Market Resources, Inc.
Supreme Court of Oklahoma
933 P.2d 282 (1997)

LAVENDER, Justice.

We consider the appropriateness of a jury award of lost profits over a two year time period in favor of . . . Florafax International, Inc. against . . . GTE Market Resources, Inc., for breaching a contract requiring GTE to provide telecommunication and/or telemarketing services for Florafax. The profits were those Florafax claimed it stood to make from a collateral contract it had with a third party, but allegedly lost when the collateral contract was canceled purportedly because GTE breached its contract with Florafax. . . .

I. STANDARD OF REVIEW. . . .

II. FACTS.

Florafax is generally a flowers-by-wire company acting as a clearinghouse to allow the placement and receipt of orders between florists throughout the United States and internationally. . . .

In addition to the above activities, Florafax solicits agreements with third party clients such as supermarket chains, American Express and other entities that advertise the sale of floral products by various methods (e.g., television, radio, newspapers, billing circulars, mass mailings to consumers) which allow a consumer to order floral arrangements via the use of a 1-800 telephone call, with Florafax agreeing to handle the actual inbound and outbound communication aspects of the transactions. . . .

One client that signed up for an arrangement like that described immediately above was Bellerose Floral, Inc., d/b/a Flora Plenty, a leading marketer of floral products advertising sales through use of the telephone number 1-800-FLOWERS. Florafax and Bellerose entered a contract in early October 1989 whereby Florafax and/or its designee would accept direct consumer orders (i.e. inbound calls and orders) placed via the 1-800-FLOWERS number and, of course, it also agreed to handle the outbound placement of orders either by telephone or computer transmission. The Florafax/Bellerose contract provided Florafax would be paid certain fee (s) per order. As we read the contract its initial term was for one year, to be automatically renewed from month to month thereafter, but that either party, with or without cause, could terminate the agreement upon sixty (60) days written notice.

GTE, on the other hand, was a company providing telecommunication and/or telemarketing services for other businesses. It provided for other businesses a call answering center where telemarketing sales representatives (TSRs) physically answered telephones when orders from promotional activities came in from consumers and took care of transmitting the orders by telephone or computer for fulfillment. For certain management and business-related reasons Florafax subcontracted out much of the telecommunication and telemarketing services of its business.

In mid-October 1989, about two weeks after Florafax signed its agreement with Bellerose, the Florafax/GTE contract was entered. In essence, it provided GTE would via a call answering center (apparently located in the Dallas, Texas area) handle much, if not all, of the activities connected with taking incoming orders and placing outgoing calls or computer transmissions directed to it by Florafax associated with the purchase and fulfillment of floral orders throughout the United States and internationally. The agreement required Florafax to pay GTE certain fees for this service depending on the type of order.

The Florafax/GTE contract generally ran for a term of three years from the effective date the parties anticipated Florafax would begin directing calls to GTE for floral orders — a date anticipated to be in early December 1989. It also contained certain provisions that in essence might result in termination after a two year period based upon application of a price/fee renegotiation clause. In answer to one of the questions submitted via a special verdict form, the jury determined the Florafax/ GTE contract could be terminated after two years based on this clause.

The contract further contained a clause concerning lost profits providing in pertinent part:

20. Termination

    a. Termination for cause Any non-defaulting party shall have the right to terminate this agreement at any date not less than forty-five (45) days after an event of default occurs and so long as it continues. In the event GTE [ ] ceases to perform its duties hereunder after a notice of termination is given or otherwise, Florafax may suffer tremendous damage to its business. GTE [ ] agrees to pay Florafax consequential damages and lost profits on the business lost.

The contract also specifically noted GTE would be providing services not only for Florafax, but for others.

In addition to the above express contractual provisions, evidence was presented that officials with GTE knew prior to signing the contract that GTE would be providing its services not only directly for Florafax, but that Florafax had been soliciting business from entities such as Bellerose, business that was anticipated to be at least partially directed through GTE's call answering center. In fact, competent evidence exists in this record showing GTE specifically knew when it signed the contract with Florafax that Bellerose was considering turning over a portion of its inbound and outbound business to Florafax, and that Bellerose received somewhere between 100,000-200,000 orders annually. Evidence was also presented that showed GTE, prior to contract execution, considered it a positive aspect of entering the agreement that Florafax was constantly marketing and promoting its business by the addition of outside clients and that this addition of clients would lead to revenue increases. Evidence also existed that Bellerose was Florafax's largest customer and that it had been an ongoing business for at least sixteen (16) years prior to the date of trial.

Evidence was also submitted showing that before GTE entered the contract, its director of finance and administration did a financial analysis of the Florafax/GTE contract and determined GTE would make little or no money from it. His immediate supervisor (the general manager of GTE) was informed of the analysis. GTE, however, made the decision to enter the contract, apparently because it needed new customers and/or in the hope this financial analysis was wrong.

Although from December 1989 through Valentine's Day in February 1990 certain problems surfaced in regard to the adequacy of GTE's performance, at some point after Valentine's Day the problems appeared to worsen. At some time after Valentine's Day and leading up to Mother's Day in May 1990, the latter holiday being described as the largest floral holiday of the year, the adequacy of GTE's performance became subject to serious question. What appears from the evidence to be the most glaring breach on GTE's part was a failure during the week leading up to Mother's Day to provide sufficient TSRs to answer calls anticipated to be directed to it by Florafax, including calls from Bellerose. Without adequate TSRs to take the calls, floral product orders would obviously be lost and Florafax income lost in the process.

Coupled with this evidence of a failure to adequately staff for anticipated calls, there was also evidence that during the term of the contract GTE's project manager for the Florafax account admitted to Florafax's off-site manager stationed at the GTE facility to look out for Florafax's interests there, that GTE no longer wanted the Florafax account — in essence, because GTE was not making money under the contract's pricing scheme. . . .

In addition, evidence was presented that GTE's failure to perform caused Bellerose to terminate its agreement with Florafax and Bellerose ceased its relationship with Florafax apparently some time in July 1990, directing no more calls from its 1-800-FLOWERS number through GTE after that time. The President of Bellerose essentially testified that he anticipated his agreement with Florafax to be a long-term relationship if things worked out and, although his testimony was not absolute in such regard, that he pulled out of his relationship with Florafax because of the poor performance of GTE. . . .

As a result of GTE's breach, in addition to losing Bellerose as a client, Florafax incurred costs primarily associated with taking steps necessary to set up its own call answering center in Tulsa to perform the duties GTE was supposed to handle so that it would not lose other clients or business relationships as it had lost Bellerose. Florafax finally left the GTE facility at the end of September 1990.

In addition to seeking damages attributable to costs associated with performing the services GTE was supposed to perform, Florafax sought lost profits it claimed would have been realized from the Florafax/Bellerose contract. In support of and in opposition to the lost profit claim the parties presented conflicting economic projections through expert witnesses (Florafax through an economist, GTE through a Certified Public Accountant) as to how much profit, if any, Florafax would have made from the Bellerose contract over varying lengths of time. . . .

One major difference between the experts' projections was that the Florafax expert increased the Bellerose sales volume from 1990 to 1991 one hundred percent (100%), while the GTE expert kept the call and order volumes flat in his projections. The one hundred percent (100%) increase was based on evidence the Bellerose sales volume increased about this percentage over the 1990 year levels. GTE's expert, in contrast, used a flat growth rate because a general floral industry survey indicated declining volumes in the floral industry from the late 1980s through 1991.

The Florafax expert estimated the Bellerose loss at $1,921,028.00 for a period extended out to three years, i.e. for the period of time that remained in the term of the Florafax/GTE contract at the time Bellerose canceled. The GTE expert estimated the Bellerose loss over the same time frame to be $505,731.00 if the fees to be paid to GTE by Florafax remained constant for this period of time. The GTE expert also gave an alternative figure that coincided with the remaining part of a two year period beginning in December 1989 based on the view the Florafax/GTE contract would be subject to termination at such time in view of the price renegotiation provisions of that contract. The loss of profits for this period was estimated to be $294,044.00. These figures of the two experts took into consideration that the fees Florafax had to pay to GTE for its services would have to be deducted from the income or revenue Florafax would have received from Bellerose orders.[5]

The jury determined GTE breached its contract with Florafax and, in addition to other damages, awarded Florafax $750,000.00 in lost profits that would have been earned under the Florafax/Bellerose contract over a two year period of time. Other damages awarded to Florafax included a little over $820,000.00, the majority of which reflected costs and expenses associated

5. Although there was some dispute as to whether Florafax's expert properly deducted all of the expenses that should have been deducted to reach a net lost profit figure, it is clear from the evidence that the amounts reflected in the text from both experts did take into consideration the necessity of deducting the fees that Florafax would have had to pay to GTE for its services. Of course, only net profits — as opposed to gross profits — are recoverable and depending on the particular transactions involved, what does or does not have to be deducted to reach a net lost profit figure may vary. See H. Hunter, Modern Law of Contracts, Breach & Remedies, ¶7.03[4][c] at 7-20/7-23 (1986). GTE, on appeal, does not attack the lost profit award on the basis that it is not a net figure. . . .

with setting up and/or expanding a call center in Tulsa, Oklahoma to perform those functions GTE was supposed to perform under the Florafax/GTE contract. On appeal, GTE, although not admitting liability — i.e. that it breached its contract with Florafax — does not contest the jury determination that it did breach the contract. We now turn to the lost profit damage issues to be reviewed.

III. Lost Profits from a Collateral Contract May Be Recovered as a Proper Element of Damage for Breach of Contract.

GTE raises two basic arguments on the propriety of the recovery of lost profits. These are: 1) lost profit damages cannot include profits from third-party collateral contracts or, if they are recoverable, Florafax failed to prove entitlement to them because it failed to show the prospect of profits from the Florafax/Bellerose contract or, conversely, the loss of such profits upon GTE's breach, were in the contemplation of GTE and Florafax at the time they entered the Florafax/GTE contract; and, 2) if lost profits from the Florafax/Bellerose contract are recoverable they must be limited to a sixty (60) day period, because profits beyond this time must be deemed too remote, speculative or uncertain, and Florafax could not be said to be reasonably assured of any profits from its relationship with Bellerose for any longer period, given the Florafax/Bellerose contract clause allowing either Florafax or Bellerose the right to terminate that contract upon sixty (60) days notice. In our view, each argument is without merit.

III(A). Collateral Contracts and Lost Profits.

GTE asserts Oklahoma jurisprudence has not squarely addressed the question of whether a party suing for breach of contract may recover lost profits arising from a collateral contract. Although this Court may not have used the exact phrase "lost profits from third-party collateral contracts" a review of Oklahoma law makes clear if such damages are properly proved they are recoverable. Thus, GTE's apparent view that lost profits from a collateral contract are never recoverable for breach of contract because as a matter of law they are inherently too remote, speculative and/or unforeseeable, is mistaken.

The time-honored general rules on recovery of damages for breach of contract are found in Hadley v. Baxendale, 9 Ex. 341, 156 Eng. Rep. 145 (1854). . . . The lost profits involved here fall under the second branch of the Hadley v. Baxendale formulation.

Generally speaking, this Court has long espoused the view that loss of future or anticipated profit — i.e. loss of expected monetary gain — is recoverable in a breach of contract action: 1) if the loss is within the contemplation of the parties at the time the contract was made, 2) if the loss flows directly or proximately from the breach — i.e. if the loss can be said to have been caused by the breach — and 3) if the loss is capable of reasonably accurate measurement or estimate. Groendyke Transport, Inc. v. Merchant, 380 P.2d 682 Second Syllabus (Okla. 1962). An award in the form of a loss of profits, in fact, is generally considered a common measure of damages for breach of contract, it frequently represents fulfillment of the non-breaching party's expectation interest, and it often closely approximates the goal of placing the innocent party in the same position as if the contract had been fully performed. H. Hunter, Modern Law of Contracts, Breach & Remedies, ¶7.02[2] at 7-5/7-6 (1986).

Our cases also recognize that where there is sufficient evidence presented on the issue of the recovery of special damages — including lost profits — what was or was not in the contemplation of the parties at the time of contracting is a question of fact to be determined by the trier of fact. Home-Stake Production Company v. Minnis, 443 P.2d 91, 103 (Okla. 1968). . . .

Here, there is clearly sufficient competent evidence to show GTE had within its contemplation at the time of contracting the potential for profits from a Florafax association with Bellerose. As we noted in section II. FACTS above, GTE knew it would be providing services not only directly for Florafax, but for others on behalf of Florafax. It knew Florafax was soliciting other entities to use the services of a call answering center like GTE's and, in fact, GTE looked upon Florafax's solicitation of these other entities as a positive aspect of a contractual relationship with Florafax because of the potential for increased revenue.

Trial evidence also showed the Florafax/Bellerose contract was entered two weeks prior to the Florafax/GTE agreement and that GTE officials knew either before or contemporaneously with signing the latter contract that Bellerose was considering turning over a portion of its inbound and outbound business via its 1-800-FLOWERS network to Florafax — business GTE also knew consisted of 100,000-200,000 orders annually. Further, as already noted, a clause in the Florafax/GTE contract itself expressly reflects the parties' contemplation of the recovery of lost profits by Florafax should GTE cease to perform its duties and obligations during the term of the contract — and, as also noted, evidence exists in this record that GTE intentionally failed to perform during part of the term of the contract, a failure on its part we conclude would support a determination the lost profit clause of the Florafax/GTE contract was implicated. . . .

III(B). THE SIXTY (60) DAY TERMINATION CLAUSE IN
THE FLORAFAX/BELLEROSE CONTRACT DOES NOT
PRECLUDE THE RECOVERY OF LOST PROFITS
BEYOND THE SIXTY (60) DAY PERIOD.

GTE, in addition to arguing no lost profits are proper, alternatively asserts that if their recovery is appropriate, they must be limited to a period of sixty (60) days because of the termination notice clause of the Florafax/Bellerose contract which allowed either party to that agreement to terminate that contract, with or without cause, upon sixty (60) days written notice. For this position prime reliance is placed on Osborn v. Commanche Cattle Industries, Inc., 545 P.2d 827 (Okla. Ct. Civ. App. 1975), an opinion of the Oklahoma Court of Civil Appeals. Although we believe the rule of law laid down in *Osborn* is sound, the rule is not controlling here.

Osborn involved a situation where plaintiff had contracted with a feedlot to perform certain [services]. The contract was for a term of three years, but contained a clause allowing either party to terminate the agreement by giving the other thirty (30) days advance notice. . . . The trial court allowed the lost profit issue to go to the jury with instructions allowing their recovery for the entire three year period, over defendant's objection only nominal damages were appropriate because either party to the contract had the right to terminate it upon thirty (30) days notice.

The *Osborn* court found error in submitting the lost profit issue to the jury for a longer period than the thirty (30) day notice time frame based on the following rule of law: no party to a contract may recover more in damages for a breach of the contract than might have been gained by full performance. *Osborn*, supra, 545 P.2d at 831. . . . In other words, in *Osborn* it was absolutely certain plaintiff could not establish lost profits for any greater period of time because the defendant had an absolute right to terminate the contract upon giving the agreed notice and exercise of this right would have provided full performance on the defendant's part.

The situation here is quite different. . . . GTE had no right to terminate either the Florafax/GTE or Florafax/Bellerose contracts upon any short specified notice provision. That right belonged only to Florafax and Bellerose, and only in relation to the latter contract. Thus, full performance could not have been supplied by the simple expediency of GTE giving sixty (60) days notice to Florafax that it was terminating their agreement. Instead, the Florafax/GTE contract, according to the unchallenged finding of the jury, had a minimum term of two years based on the effect of the price renegotiation provisions of the contract, i.e. Florafax was guaranteed performance by GTE for a full two years.

. . . In fact, competent evidence exists supporting the view it is probable some additional profits would have been made from the Bellerose relationship for a longer period of time. Further, application of the *Osborn* rule here would improperly allow GTE to benefit from a cancellation right it had no ability to exercise. Accordingly, the rule of *Osborn* does not preclude Florafax's recovery of lost profit damages associated with the loss of the Bellerose relationship in excess of a sixty (60) day period.

III(C). COMPETENT EVIDENCE EXISTS TO SUPPORT THE AWARD OF LOST PROFIT DAMAGES TO A REASONABLE CERTAINTY.

Even though the rule of *Osborn* is inapplicable, GTE's arguments as to the termination notice clause of the collateral contract do, however, implicate the legal principle that before lost profit damages are recoverable it must be adequately shown such profits were reasonably certain to have been made by the non-breaching party absent breach. We believe the answer to the reasonable certainty question is not one subject to decision as a matter of law under this record, but was one of fact to be decided by the trier of fact — here the jury.

In order for damages to be recoverable for breach of contract they must be clearly ascertainable, in both their nature and origin, and it must be made to appear they are the natural and proximate consequence of the breach and not speculative and contingent. Chorn v. Williams, 186 Okla. 646, 99 P.2d 1036, 1037 (1940). It is not necessary, however, for the recovery of lost profits shown to have been caused by a breach of contract, that the profits be established with absolute certainty and barring any possibility of failure, but it is only required that it be established with reasonable certainty that profits would have been made had the contract not been breached. Megert v. Bauman, 206 Okla. 651, 246 P.2d 355, 358 (1952). In essence, what a plaintiff must show for the recovery of lost profits is sufficient certainty that reasonable minds might believe from a preponderance of the evidence that such damages were actually suffered. . . .

Once it is made to clearly appear that loss of business profits has been suffered by virtue of the breach, it is proper to let the jury decide what the loss is from the best evidence the nature of the case admits. . . . When a breach of a contractual obligation with resulting damages has been established, although the amount of damages may not be based on mere speculation, conjecture and surmise alone, the mere uncertainty as to the exact amount of damages will not preclude the right of recovery. . . . It is sufficient if the evidence shows the extent of damage by just and reasonable inference. . . . We believe sufficient evidence was presented so that Florafax carried its burden to prove the fact, cause and amount of its lost profit damages with the requisite degree of reasonable certainty.

The fact of lost profit damage beyond merely a sixty (60) day period is shown by the testimony of Bellerose's President. Although not absolute, his testimony was, in essence, he considered the relationship with Florafax a long-term one had things worked out and that the most important issues to him in making the decision to terminate were issues concerning performance. This testimony showed the relationship in all probability would have continued long after it was terminated had GTE adequately performed. Although it is true — given the existence of the sixty (60) day notice provision — Bellerose might have terminated the Florafax/Bellerose contract at some point in time even had GTE performed, the state of this record does not require a conclusion Bellerose would have exercised its right of termination for some other reason.

We are also of the view the fact of damage is partially shown by the projections for profits of both the damage experts presented by the parties. Although they differed in their ultimate conclusions as to the extent or amount of lost profits, both presented estimates that Florafax could have made profits from the Florafax/ Bellerose relationship had it survived.

Causation is also shown by sufficient competent evidence, evidence that partially overlaps with that of the fact of damage in this case. There is enough evidence to support a reasonable determination that Bellerose's decision to cancel or terminate its relationship with Florafax was the direct result of GTE's failure to render adequate performance and, that GTE's breach of the Florafax/GTE contract caused the cancellation. Therefore, there is sufficient evidence in this record upon which reasonable minds might rely that profits from the Florafax/Bellerose relationship would have actually been made by Florafax beyond a sixty (60) day period and that GTE's breach of its contract with Florafax caused the loss of Bellerose as a client.

As to the exact extent or amount of damages, the record contains sufficient evidence to take the matter out of the realm of mere speculation, conjecture or surmise. A track record existed which showed the calls coming to GTE from Bellerose during the five to seven months Bellerose business was actually being routed to GTE. There was also evidence that although the business relationship between Florafax and Bellerose was relatively new,

Bellerose had been in business for a number of years, and it had experienced 100,000-200,000 orders annually. Such evidence clearly was appropriate to consider on the issue of the extent of lost profits. Although this case is not exactly like our cases dealing with the destruction of an established business by a breach of contract, it is sufficiently close to be analogized to the established business situation, where we have allowed the recovery of lost profits. . . .

Evidence also existed which showed that Bellerose, after terminating its relationship with Florafax, experienced a substantial increase in its sales volume in 1991. In other words, there was not only evidence tending to show a certain volume of orders prior to the breach, but evidence tending to show that level of sales would have in all probability increased substantially during part of the term of the Florafax/GTE contract had Bellerose continued its relationship with Florafax. This post-breach evidence is proper to be considered at arriving at a reasonable estimate of the loss caused by a breach of contract . . . because all facts which would reasonably tend to make certain the amount of injury inflicted are admissible. . . . Although the jury apparently did not totally credit the testimony or documentation presented by either Florafax's or GTE's experts as to their projections of profits lost, the $750,000.00 awarded for the two year period was within the range of the estimates of the two experts. Accordingly, not only was the fact and causation of lost profit damages adequately shown to a reasonable certainty, but the amount of lost profit damages awarded was sufficiently shown through competent evidence contained in this record to take the matter out of the realm of mere speculation, conjecture and surmise.

IV. CONCLUSION.

The award of the jury of lost profit damages associated with the Florafax/Bellerose contract was an appropriate remedy for GTE's breach of its contract with Florafax. It was consistent with our substantive law as to the recovery of lost profits for a breach of contract and was supported by competent evidence. . . . Trial court judgment is affirmed as to the award of lost profits.

KAUGER, C.J., SUMMERS, V.C.J., and WILSON and WATT, JJ., concur.

HODGES, SIMMS and HARGRAVE, JJ., dissent.

Notes and Questions

1. *Applying **Hadley v. Baxendale.*** In applying the rule of Hadley v. Baxendale, the court in *Florafax International* points out that the Florafax/Bellerose contract was signed two weeks before the Florafax/GTE agreement. Would the result in the case have been different if the Florafax/Bellerose contract had been signed after the Florafax/GTE agreement?

Lost profits from the Bellerose contract were subject to the second prong of the *Hadley* test because they arose from a *collateral contract* rather than from breach of the Florafax/GTE agreement itself. Since Florafax was a recipient rather than a provider of telecommunications services, it did not expect to receive a profit on its contract with GTE. In cases where the plaintiff seeks lost profits it would have made *on the contract sued on*, these damages will be subject to the first rather than the second prong of the *Hadley* test, and will be recoverable (as "general" or "direct" damages) without the need to show foreseeability. It may also be easier to prove such damages with reasonable certainty. See Lewis Jorge Construction Management, Inc. v. Pomona Unified School Dist., 102 P. 3d 257 (Cal. 2004) (contractor could recover lost profits on contract breached by school district but not for alleged lost profits on future, collateral contracts that were never made due to loss in bonding capacity; other types of transactions might justify lost profits on collateral contracts).

2. *Contractual limitations on consequential damages.* How can a contracting party avoid potentially large liability for consequential damages flowing from the breach of a contract? In *Florafax International* the Florafax/GTE contract specifically provided that GTE would be liable for consequential damages in the event the contract was terminated for cause. Was this provision essential to Florafax International's recovery of lost profits? Contractual assumptions of liability for consequential damages are, however, somewhat unusual. Much more common are contractual disclaimers or limitations of liability for consequential damages. Transactions governed by the UCC have specific rules governing contractual disclaimers of warranties or limitations of remedies for breach of warranty. See UCC §§2-316 (exclusion or modification of warranty), 2-719 (modification or limitation of remedy). Courses on UCC Article 2 examine these concepts in more detail. Statutes at both the federal and state level may regulate disclaimers and limitations of remedies in consumer transactions. For transactions in which the UCC and other statutory law are not applicable, general contractual principles apply. Can you think of any reason why GTE would have agreed to assume liability of a potentially unknown amount for consequential damages? As a lawyer for GTE could you have suggested a modification of this clause that would provide it protection against catastrophic damages?

3. *Limitation of consequential damages to prevent injustice.* In subsection (3) of §351, the drafters of Restatement (Second) have proposed a limitation on consequential damages (and perhaps on other forms of damage as well) in addition to the *Hadley* rule, in cases where "justice so requires in order to avoid disproportionate compensation." Comment *f* expands somewhat on this open-ended criterion, by indicating that the limitation is intended to apply in cases where there is extreme disproportion between the price charged by the defendant under the contract in question and the liability sought to be imposed on it. The comment also suggests that informality of agreement and a noncommercial setting ought to be factors tending toward application of the suggested limitation. Professor Farnsworth, Reporter for this portion of Restatement (Second), concedes that §351(3)'s "frank recognition of the judicial reluctance" to award damages that are disproportionate to the consideration paid is "untraditional." He explains the proposed rule as being designed to permit the courts to do overtly what they have in many cases accomplished covertly through particularly rigorous application of the foreseeability and certainty tests. E. Allan Farnsworth, Contracts §12.17, at 808-810 (4th ed. 2004). Because Section 351(3) is unconventional, only a few courts have relied on it to limit recovery of consequential damages. See Maine Rubber International v. Environmental Management Group, Inc., 324 F. Supp. 2d 32 (D. Me. 2004); Alaska Tae Woong Venture, Inc. v. Westward Seafoods, Inc., 963 P.2d 1055 (Alaska 1998). For scholarly commentary,

see Larry T. Garvin, Disproportionality and the Law of Consequential Damages: Default Theory and Cognitive Reality, 59 Ohio St. L.J. 339 (1998); William B. Harvey, Discretionary Justice Under the Restatement (Second) of Contracts, 67 Cornell L. Rev. 666 (1982); M. N. Kniffin, A Newly Identified Contract Unconscionability: Unconscionability of Remedy, 63 Notre Dame L. Rev. 247 (1988).

4. *Speculative damages.* As the court points out, an injured party cannot recover damages that are "speculative." Plaintiffs must prove their damages with "reasonable certainty." See Restatement (Second) of Contracts §352. In applying this limitation, courts often draw a distinction between uncertainty about the *fact* of damage and uncertainty regarding the *amount* of damage. When the plaintiff establishes the fact of damage, the jury is given wide leeway in awarding compensation. See V.A.L. Floors, Inc. v. Westminster Communities, Inc., 810 A. 2d 625, 630 (N.J. Super. Ct. 2002) (where it is certain that damage has occurred, only fair and reasonable estimate of amount is required). Consider Contemporary Mission, Inc. v. Famous Music Corp., 557 F.2d 918 (2d Cir. 1977), in which the plaintiff claimed that the defendant had breached a contract to produce and promote recordings of songs composed by members of the plaintiff (a nonprofit corporation formed by a small group of Roman Catholic priests). The Court of Appeals held that the plaintiff could recover lost profits resulting from the defendant's failure to promote plaintiff's record, "Fear No Evil," noting that "[e]ven after the promotional efforts ended, [and] the record was withdrawn from the marketplace, it was carried, as a result of its own momentum, to an additional 10,000 sales and to a rise from approximately number 80 on the 'Hot Soul Singles' chart of Billboard magazine to number 61." These facts established that it was "certain" that the plaintiff had suffered some damage, even though the amount was unclear. On the other hand, the court ruled that claimed damages for lost tours were too speculative to be recovered:

> The same is not true, however, of the existence of damage in the form of lost opportunities for concert tours, theatrical tours or similar benefits. While it is certain that some sales were lost as a result of the failure to promote, we cannot believe that . . . the New York courts would accept what Famous' counsel aptly described at trial as Contemporary's "domino theory" of prospective damages. The theory is that if "Fear No Evil" had become a "hit," its success would have stimulated additional sales of the full two-record VIRGIN album and would have generated sufficient popular acceptance to enable Contemporary to obtain bookings for a nationwide concert tour. We hold that these additional benefits are too dependent upon taste or fancy to be considered anything other than speculative and uncertain, and, therefore, proof of damage in the form of such lost benefits was properly excluded by Judge Owen.

Id. at 926-927. Was the distinction between fact and amount of damage significant in *Florafax International*?

5. *Proof of lost profits.* As *Florafax International* shows, proof of lost profits typically requires expert testimony, and experts can vary widely in their assumptions and in their resulting projections of future lost profits. In computing expected lost profits, the plaintiff is only entitled to recover net as

opposed to gross profits. See footnote 5 of the opinion. Why should this be the case? The court in *Florafax International* affirmed the jury's award of $820,000 in expenses for setting up a call center to perform functions that GTE had contracted to perform. Was the award of these expenses inconsistent with the principle that the injured party is only entitled to recover net profits?

Breach of a commercial contract can lead to lost profit as in *Florafax International*. Sometimes the injured party will claim that the breach of contract resulted in a decline of the value of that party's business. In such cases care must be taken to avoid double recovery. The plaintiff is generally not entitled to recover both the decline in market value of its business and the present value of the future net income from the business because these two methods are normally alternative ways of measuring the same injury. "According to economic theory, . . . market price should be approximately equal to the present value of all the income that can be derived far into the future from the business." Johnson v. Oroweat Foods Co., 785 F.2d 503, 507 (4th Cir. 1986). In practice, however, these two measures may differ quite substantially. For example, in Protectors Insurance Service, Inc. v. U.S. Fidelity & Guar. Co., 132 F.3d 612 (10th Cir. 1998), the plaintiff's expert testified that the decline in market value of the plaintiff's insurance agency resulting from the defendant's breach of contract was $35,000. Other evidence projected plaintiff's lost profits at $809,650. The Tenth Circuit reversed the jury's special verdict allowing both measures of damages and instead awarded the plaintiff $35,000. The court indicated that decline in market value was the preferred measure, and that lost profits should be awarded only "where no other reliable method of valuing the business is available." Id. at 618.

6. *The new business rule.* Plaintiffs have traditionally encountered great difficulty in recovering lost profits in a new business venture, or at least a new one for the plaintiff, with no history of prior profitability. Over the years courts have been unreceptive to such claims, often denying recovery as a matter of law for lost profits suffered by new businesses, an approach that came to be referred to as the "new business rule." Many recent decisions, however, have rejected a strict application of this rule and have allowed new businesses to recover lost profits provided that they are proved with reasonable certainty. See Humetrix, Inc., v. Gemplus S.C.A., 268 F.3d 910 (10th Cir. 2001) (under California law, new business may recover lost profits if both occurrence and extent can be proven with reasonable certainty); International Telepassport Corp. v. USFI, Inc., 89 F.3d 82 (2d Cir. 1996) (under New York law, new business rule is not per se rule forbidding award of lost profits to new businesses but, rather, evidentiary rule that creates higher level of proof needed to achieve reasonable certainty as to amount of damages). Cf. RSB Laboratory Services, Inc. v. BSI, Corp., 847 A.2d 599 (N.J. Super. Ct. 2004) (New Jersey continues to be among minority of states that adhere to the new business rule).

7. *Consequential damages in other cases.* Consequential damage claims can arise in a wide variety of cases. In a lending contract, the borrower may claim that the lender's breach of the contract caused it to lose not only a favorable interest rate on the loan (general damages) but also profits from transactions that were prevented because the funds from the loan were unavailable. Such

claims may run afoul of the requirements of mitigation (the borrower should have and could have borrowed money elsewhere, even if it had to pay a higher rate of interest, to mitigate the injury from the lender's breach) or foreseeability (the lender did not have reason to foresee that the borrower would be unable to obtain needed funds from any other source). The Restatement in comment *e* to §351 indicates that consequential damages may be recovered in some cases for breach of a contract to lend money and courts have allowed such awards if the requirements of mitigation, foreseeability, and certainty have been met.

For breach of an employment contract an employee may recover as general damages the wages that she would have received under the contract less the amount of wages that she could have earned from comparable employment found through reasonable efforts. In some cases employees have claimed as consequential damages harm to their reputation flowing from the employer's breach. Such claims have usually been made by employees in professions where reputation is particularly important, such as acting or the media. English courts have allowed such claims, but American courts have been much less willing to do so unless the employee can show the loss of a particular opportunity, not simply harm to the employee's general reputation. Compare Herbert Clayton & Jack Waller, Ltd. v. Oliver, [1930] A.C. 209 (employee entitled not only to lost salary but also to compensation for the loss of valuable publicity), with Ericson v. Playgirl, Inc., 140 Cal. Rptr. 921, 926 (Ct. App. 1977) (defendant not liable to plaintiff for failure to feature his nude photo on cover of its Best of Playgirl magazine, as promised; value to plaintiff of lost publicity too "speculative and conjectural"—"as unpredictable as the lottery and the roulette wheel"), and Redgrave v. Boston Symphony Orchestra, Inc., 855 F.2d 888 (1st Cir. 1988), *cert. denied,* 488 U.S. 1043 (1989) (actress could recover consequential damages for loss of "identifiable professional opportunities," as contrasted with harm to her general reputation, when symphony canceled her appearance allegedly because of political statements; recovery of damages not subject to higher standard applicable to First Amendment claims because BSO's cancellation was not "symbolic speech").

C. RESTRICTIONS ON THE RECOVERY OF EXPECTATION DAMAGES: MITIGATION OF DAMAGES

In the preceding section we considered various rules that courts may employ to calculate the amount of the plaintiff's "loss in value" or "other loss," as Restatement (Second) §347 uses those terms. There are, however, a number of off-setting factors that may have the effect of reducing the plaintiff's recovery or even eliminating it altogether. At this point, we turn our attention to those minus factors, items that are to be subtracted from "total loss" in calculating the damages the plaintiff ought to receive. Restatement (Second) §347 refers to these generally as "cost avoided" and "loss avoided"; they are often referred to in the cases and commentary as instances of "mitigation of damages."

The field of tort law is studded with principles that—whether expressed in terms of "contributory negligence," "comparative negligence," "assumption of the risk," or some other label—reflect a common theme: Even if the defendant's actions have caused harm to the plaintiff, the defendant need not compensate the plaintiff to the extent that the plaintiff's own actions were a contributing cause of her injury. Given the apparent strength of this principle in Anglo-American jurisprudence, it should not be surprising to find the same notion expressed in the rules of contract law. Here, however, the principle is commonly stated as one of "mitigation" (sometimes "minimization") of damages: The plaintiff may not recover for those injurious consequences of the defendant's breach that the plaintiff herself could by reasonable action have avoided. This principle is also referred to—for obvious reasons—as the doctrine of "avoidable consequences."

We have seen in the example considered earlier that when the owner without justification repudiates a partially completed construction contract, the breach will represent a "loss in value" to the builder (the unpaid portion of the total price), but it will also present an opportunity for savings. Thus, the builder will be freed from the necessity of expending whatever additional sums it would have cost to complete its own performance ("cost avoided"); it may also have the ability to recoup some of the expenditures already made, by reselling materials purchased, or by applying them to some other job ("loss avoided"). These savings are to be deducted from the aggregate loss suffered in order to compute the plaintiff's net recovery.

These principles of loss avoidance will be honored throughout the area of contract remedies, but their application will vary according to the type of case under consideration. Thus, personal service contracts present different opportunities for loss avoidance than do other types of contracts; land transactions have their own traditional governing rules; difficult problems of cost allocation may be presented where an enterprise is involved in performing several different contracts at once. The cases and materials below explore some of these problems.

Rockingham County v. Luten Bridge Co.
United States Court of Appeals
35 F.2d 301 (4th Cir. 1929)

PARKER, Circuit Judge. This was an action at law instituted in the court below by the Luten Bridge Company, as plaintiff, to recover of Rockingham county, North Carolina, an amount alleged to be due under a contract for the construction of a bridge. The county admits the execution and breach of the contract, but contends that notice of cancellation was given the bridge company, before the erection of the bridge was commenced, and that it is liable only for the damages which the company would have sustained, if it had abandoned construction at that time.

[Plaintiff Luten Bridge Co. had entered into a contract to build a bridge for Rockingham County. This contract had been originally authorized by a 3 to 2 vote of the Rockingham County Commission. For some reason, feelings apparently ran high on this topic within the Commission—so high, in fact, that one of the three-member majority that voted for the Luten contract resigned his seat shortly thereafter. Although he later changed his mind and attempted to retract that resignation, neither he nor the other two proponents of the Luten contract attended any further meetings. As a result, the two-person minority, augmented by a new third member, undertook to function as the County Commission. Instructing Luten to stop work on the bridge contract, they took the position that the contract was not binding on the county and that in any case it would not be honored. Luten, gambling perhaps on the possibility that the earlier majority would act to regain control of the Commission, continued with the construction of the bridge. In Luten's eventual suit to recover damages for the county's asserted breach of contract, it was held on appeal that the repudiation of Luten's contract amounted to a total breach of contract on the part of the county. The court then had to consider what damages the plaintiff should recover for this breach.—Eds.]

Coming, then, to the third question—i.e., as to the measure of plaintiff's recovery—we do not think that, after the county had given notice, while the contract was still executory, that it did not desire the bridge built and would not pay for it, plaintiff could proceed to build it and recover the contract price. It is true that the county had no right to rescind the contract, and the notice given plaintiff amounted to a breach on its part; but, after plaintiff had received notice of the breach, it was its duty to do nothing to increase the damages flowing therefrom. If *A* enters into a binding contract to build a house for *B*, *B*, of course, has no right to rescind the contract without *A's* consent. But if, before the house is built, he decides he does not want it, and notifies *A* to that effect, *A* has no right to proceed with the building and thus pile up damages. His remedy is to treat the contract as broken when he receives the notice, and sue for the recovery of such damages as he may have sustained from the breach, including any profit which he would have realized upon performance, as well as any other losses which may have resulted to him. In the case at bar, the county decided not to build the road of which the bridge was to be a part, and did not build it. The bridge, built in the midst of the forest, is of no value to the county because of this change of circumstances. When, therefore, the county gave notice to the plaintiff that it would not proceed with the project, plaintiff should have desisted from further work. It had no right thus to pile up damages by proceeding with the erection of a useless bridge.

The contrary view was expressed by Lord Cockburn in Frost v. Knight, L.R. 7 Ex. 111, but, as pointed out by Prof. Williston (Williston on Contracts, vol. 3, p.2347), it is not in harmony with the decisions in this country. The American rule and the reasons supporting it are well stated by Prof. Williston as follows:

There is a line of cases running back to 1845 which holds that, after an absolute repudiation or refusal to perform by one party to a contract, the other party cannot continue to perform and recover damages based on full performance. This rule is only a particular application of the general rule of damages that a plaintiff cannot hold a defendant liable for damages which need not have been incurred; or, as it is often stated, the plaintiff must, so far as he can without loss to himself, mitigate the damages caused by the defendant's wrongful act. The application of this rule to the matter in question is obvious. If a man engages to have work done, and afterwards repudiates his contract before the work has been begun or when it has been only partially done, it is inflicting damage on the defendant without benefit to the plaintiff to allow the latter to insist on proceeding with the contract. The work may be useless to the defendant, and yet he would be forced to pay the full contract price. On the other hand, the plaintiff is interested only in the profit he will make out of the contract. If he receives this it is equally advantageous for him to use his time otherwise.

The leading case on the subject in this country is the New York case of Clark v. Marsiglia, 1 Denio (N.Y.) 317, 43 Am. Dec. 670. In that case defendant had employed plaintiff to paint certain pictures for him, but countermanded the order before the work was finished. Plaintiff, however, went on and completed the work and sued for the contract price. In reversing a judgment for plaintiff, the court said:

> The plaintiff was allowed to recover as though there had been no countermand of the order; and in this the court erred. The defendant, by requiring the plaintiff to stop work upon the paintings, violated his contract, and thereby incurred a liability to pay such damages as the plaintiff should sustain. Such damages would include a recompense for the labor done and materials used, and such further sum in damages as might, upon legal principles, be assessed for the breach of the contract; but the plaintiff had no right, by obstinately persisting in the work, to make the penalty upon the defendant greater than it would otherwise have been.

And the rule as established by the great weight of authority in America is summed up in the following statement in 6 R.C.L. 1029, which is quoted with approval by the Supreme Court of North Carolina in the recent case of Novelty Advertising Co. v. Farmers' Mut. Tobacco Warehouse Co., 186 N.C. 197, 119 S.E. 196, 198:

> While a contract is executory a party has the power to stop performance on the other side by an explicit direction to that effect, subjecting himself to such damages as will compensate the other party for being stopped in the performance on his part at that stage in the execution of the contract. The party thus forbidden cannot afterwards go on, and thereby increase the damages, and then recover such damages from the other party. The legal right of either party to violate, abandon, or renounce his contract, on the usual terms of compensation to the other for the damages which the law recognizes and allows, subject to the jurisdiction of equity to decree specific performance in proper cases, is universally recognized and acted upon.

. . . We have carefully considered the cases . . . upon which plaintiff relies; but we do not think that they are at all in point. . . . In the opinions in all of these some language was used which lends support to plaintiff's position, but in none of them was the point involved which is involved here, viz. whether, in application of the rule which requires that the party to a contract who is not in default do nothing to aggravate the damages arising from breach, he should not desist from performance of an executory contract for the erection of a structure when notified of the other party's repudiation, instead of piling up damages by proceeding with the work. As stated above, we think that reason and authority require that this question be answered in the affirmative.

It follows that there was error in directing a verdict for plaintiff for the full amount of its claim. The measure of plaintiff's damage, upon its appearing that notice was duly given not to build the bridge, is an amount sufficient to compensate plaintiff for labor and materials expended and expense incurred in the part performance of the contract, prior to its repudiation, plus the profit which would have been realized if it had been carried out in accordance with its terms. See Novelty Advertising Co. v. Farmers' Mut. Tobacco Warehouse Co., supra.

Our conclusion, on the whole case, is that there was error in failing to strike out the answer of Pruitt, Pratt, and McCollum, and in admitting same as evidence against the county, in excluding the testimony offered by the county to which we have referred, and in directing a verdict for plaintiff. The judgment below will accordingly be reversed, and the case remanded for a new trial.

Reversed.

Notes and Questions

1. *Counseling Luten.* As noted in the summary of facts above, plaintiff Luten appears to have gambled that its friends would be able to reestablish their control over the Rockingham County Commission. While that never happened, the action of the remaining county commissioners in repudiating the county's contract with the plaintiff was held eventually to have been a breach of that contract (albeit a valid exercise of governmental authority). If the court had held instead that this attempted repudiation of the Luten contract was not in legal contemplation an act of the county commission, what would have been the outcome of this suit? If you represented a modern-day Luten Bridge Co., facing such turmoil in the county commission, what course of action would you advise?

2. *The mitigation principle.* The principle applied by the court in *Rockingham County* is often referred to as the "duty to mitigate damages." As numerous commentators have pointed out, however, it is not strictly speaking a "duty" at all, in the legal sense, any more than the plaintiff in a tort action has a "duty" not to add to his own injury by being contributorily negligent. It is rather a limitation on the plaintiff's right to recover damages. If the plaintiff in a contract action reasonably could have mitigated his damages, but fails to do so, then — as in the *Rockingham County* case — he will be unable to shift that portion of his loss to the defendant and will be forced to absorb it himself. See Corbin on Contracts §1039; Restatement (Second) §350, Comment b.

Havill v. Woodstock Soapstone Company, Inc.
Supreme Court of Vermont
177 Vt. 297, 865 A.2d 335 (2004)

JOHNSON, Justice.

Defendant Woodstock Soapstone Company appeals the trial court's conclusions that plaintiff Lois Havill had an implied employment contract with defendant and that defendant breached that contract when it discharged plaintiff without adhering to the procedures for just cause firings detailed in defendant's personnel policies. Defendant also appeals various aspects of the trial court's damage award of front and back pay as excessive or unwarranted. Plaintiff cross-appeals the trial court's damage award because it makes no provision for bonuses and wages plaintiff might have earned but for her improper discharge and because plaintiff claims the court made other errors calculating her award. We affirm the trial court's conclusions regarding the existence of the implied contract and defendant's liability for violating that contract, but remand for a recalculation of damages.

I. CONTRACTUAL LIABILITY

Defendant manufactures wood-burning and gas-burning stoves. Plaintiff began working for defendant in 1982. She worked part-time at first and then full-time, until she was terminated in April 1987 when the company was experiencing financial difficulties. Plaintiff resumed employment with defendant in 1990 working initially as an independent contractor from her home and later that year as a part-time employee in defendant's office. Defendant made plaintiff a full-time employee in August 1994.

In 1994, defendant also issued and distributed personnel policies, which were the functional equivalent of a personnel manual. The policies detailed a process whereby an employee was entitled to two written warnings in a twelve-month period prior to termination for "willful or repeated violations, or exaggerated behavior not in the best interest of the company or its employees." Most significantly, the policies established a "just cause" requirement for the termination of defendant's employees with problems such as unauthorized absences, violation of safety procedures, theft, careless or faulty work, and incompatibility with other employees. According to the policies, employees' "responsibilities will often change, and responsibilities will often be broad and/or overlapping with responsibilities of other employees."

The trial court found that when plaintiff resumed employment with defendant in 1990 her duties included data entry, database maintenance, and mailings to prospective customers. The trial court's findings detail the expansion of plaintiff's responsibilities into the area of customer service and sales, primarily on the telephone and occasionally in the showroom. The trial court estimated, based on testimony of both plaintiff and defendant, that sales and customer service activities were twenty-five percent of plaintiff's work by 1997. Plaintiff received "very positive" performance reviews in 1995 and 1996 as well as a $1000 bonus in August 1997. . . .

Meanwhile, defendant's business was declining seriously for various market-related reasons. Many of defendant's competitors went out of business. This led defendant's president, Tom Morrissey, to reorganize the company by adding a line of gas-burning stoves and outsourcing in-house functions, including many of the letter shop and order fulfillment functions that comprised much of plaintiff's workload. As part of this reorganization, defendant hired Laura Scott to streamline the operation. There is no dispute that this reorganization was warranted by outside economic factors, that it actually occurred, and that it had a positive effect on the business.

All parties agree that tension developed between plaintiff and Scott soon after Scott's arrival. Plaintiff felt humiliated by the way Scott dealt with her. Scott and Morrissey began to perceive that plaintiff was resisting the reorganization. The conflict between Scott and plaintiff manifested itself in instances of plaintiff's "rude" and "insubordinate" conduct towards Scott. In response, Morrissey sent plaintiff a letter dated September 30, 1997, in which he stated, "As a courtesy to you, and in light of the length of time you have worked here, you are not being issued a written warning now," although a newer employee would have received one. The letter goes on to reprimand plaintiff for her unacceptable behavior toward Scott the prior week, to indicate that she was being temporarily relieved of her customer service duties, and criticized her for not voluntarily participating in a team building lunch for all employees.

The letter was written forty-one days before plaintiff was terminated. Nonetheless, Morrissey's letter states that "to accommodate any additional growth we need customer service people who are flexible, professional, and cooperative team players. I need to know if you will make a commitment to accommodate our needs. This decision is really yours to make." The letter also states that if plaintiff "cannot make this commitment now, and regularly in the future, then we will do everything we reasonably can to help [plaintiff] secure another job," but that Morrissey "would like to have [plaintiff] continue to work here" because Morrissey valued her hard work and dedication and considered her a friend.

On October 1, 1997, plaintiff entered into a written agreement with Morrissey and Scott in which they all pledged to cooperate as team members in the best interests of the company. Despite these efforts, defendant terminated plaintiff on November 10, 1997. According to plaintiff's testimony as recounted in the court's findings, when plaintiff asked Morrissey the reason for her termination, he replied "I don't know why. You just are." Plaintiff did not receive any written warnings prior to termination. Subsequently, plaintiff obtained her personnel file, which contained a memo dated November 10, 1997, indicating that her position had been eliminated due to lack of work. The memo also indicated that defendant would not object to plaintiff's application for unemployment benefits and that the company would provide a written recommendation letter for plaintiff.

Defendant did in fact provide a recommendation letter for plaintiff authored by Morrissey. The trial court noted that the letter speaks of plaintiff in "fairly glowing terms." The letter lauds plaintiff as someone who would be a "big asset in a busy office which requires organization, dedication, and sound office skills." Two weeks after providing plaintiff with the letter, defendant placed an ad in the Valley News seeking an "office whiz" who would be "a well organized person with fast and accurate typing and keyboard ability, basic computer literacy, and sound office skills." The advertisement indicated that the position was full-time with benefits, generous pay and incentives, and the company was growing. The evidence shows that Heather Dahlin responded to this advertisement and was hired. She worked for the company handling telephone inquiries, taking and processing orders, bookkeeping, and other miscellaneous tasks until she quit in November 1998.

By January 1998, defendant had hired three new customer service representatives. The trial court found that the new employees performed some of the functions that plaintiff had previously performed, though they were expected to be more aggressive in turning routine inquiries into sales. The new customer service representatives received training and certification in defendant's products. Defendant did not offer plaintiff the opportunity to undergo such training.

[The Vermont Supreme Court upheld the trial court's finding that the defendant employer intended to be bound by its announced personnel policies that employees would be terminated only for "just cause" and in accordance with the "progressive discipline" procedures, including two written warnings. Moreover, the Supreme Court upheld the lower court's finding that any assertion that the plaintiff was terminated because her job had been eliminated was mere "pretext." Thus, the Supreme Court held that the defendant breached the employment contract by terminating the plaintiff without warning and was therefore liable for damages. — EDS.]

II. DAMAGES

After concluding that defendant was liable for damages in contract, the trial court awarded plaintiff a total of $74,644 in principal damages plus $15,040 in prejudgment interest. Both parties have appealed various aspects of the damages award. Before addressing those arguments, we review the trial court's findings as they relate generally to the issue of damages.

Plaintiff worked for defendant for approximately ten years over the period from 1982 to 1997. For some of that time she worked as either an independent contractor or part-time employee, and for the final three years she worked full-time. At the time of her termination, she earned $10.75 per hour while working forty hours per week at defendant's office. Plaintiff earned a total of $23,360, including an August bonus, working for defendant in 1997. The trial court estimated that she would have earned a total of $24,060, including an anticipated $700 December bonus, had she finished out the year in defendant's employ. The week before defendant terminated her, plaintiff told Morrissey that she was in good health, enjoyed her work, and planned to work for the company another ten years.

Plaintiff was able to find work at Morgan's Plumbing only three days after her termination. She worked thirty hours per week for a rate of $9.00 per hour. This work, which was always understood as temporary, ended in June 2000. Plaintiff was fifty-eight years old when defendant terminated her, and sixty-one when her employment ended at Morgan's. At this point, she decided to become self-employed because she was unable to find other work.

Plaintiff's self-employment consisted of performing typing for two businesses. She began working in 1990 with OT, now called Therapeutic Dimensions, and had continued to work for them while she worked for defendant as a supplement to her income. It does not appear from the record that she worked increased hours for Therapeutic after she became fully self-employed. Her second client, Wilson Associates, now known as Quest, hired her within days of her termination from Morgan's. Between these two clients, she works, on average, forty hours per week without benefits.

A. DAMAGES PERIOD

The trial court calculated plaintiff's damages for the period beginning in calendar year 1998[1], and ending in 2004 — a total period of seven years. This includes five years of back pay, i.e., lost wages up to the time of judgment, and two years of front pay — damages for lost future wages accruing after the date of judgment. See Haynes v. Golub Corp., 166 Vt. 228, 238, 692 A.2d 377, 383 (1997) (defining front and back pay). "When front pay is allowed, the damages must be limited to a reasonable period of time, and the amount must not be speculative." Id. . . .

Defendant first challenges the damages award because, in its view, the damages period was twice as long as plaintiff's tenure as a full-time employee, and thus is unreasonable. We have previously recognized that the length of employment prior to termination is a factor bearing on the determination that a front pay damage award is reasonable and not too speculative. . . . In the present case, we are satisfied that the overall relationship between employer and employee was sufficiently long-term to support the damages period. Defendant would have us focus narrowly on the approximately three and one-half years prior to plaintiff's termination, the period for which plaintiff was a full-time employee. In its first finding, however, the trial court detailed an employment relationship that began almost fifteen years before the date of termination, and comprised a total of ten and one-half years of service by plaintiff to defendant as an independent contractor, part-time employee, and finally as a full-time employee.

Defendant also argues that this award is excessive because the period upon which it is based is unreasonable in light of its argument that plaintiff's job was eliminated by January 1999 at the latest. This argument is based largely on the same assertions and evidence defendant cited to contest the trial court's conclusion on liability. We have already affirmed the trial court's disposition and will not revisit the underlying issues as they pertain to damages.

Nonetheless, we remand to the trial court to consider another factor that could, in the trial court's discretion, support a damages award — with special attention to front pay — that spans a shorter period than that which it chose. Specifically, the trial court may assess whether defendant's evidence in any other way supported its claim that plaintiff would not have remained in defendant's employ until or beyond the normal retirement age of sixty-five. See Barbour v. Merrill, 310 U.S. App. D.C. 419, 48 F.3d 1270, 1280 (D.C. Cir. 1995) (court may consider, among other discretionary factors, defendant's evidence that indicates plaintiff would not have remained in the job until retirement) . . . . In the instant case, plaintiff has prevailed by showing that she was discharged for some reason other than economic circumstances, specifically, incompatibility with a supervisor. . . . Accordingly, the trial court should be allowed to balance this evidence against plaintiff's statements of her subjective intent to remain employed with defendant beyond her normal retirement age.

Plaintiff has also challenged the period over which damages were awarded as too short in light of the evidence. The trial court found that

---

1. The trail court's decision not to calculate damages from the date of termination was made in light of the generous serverance package that defendant granted plaintiff. Neither party challenges this aspect of the award.

plaintiff intends to work until age seventy, and that she told Morrissey that she had planned to work for defendant until she was sixty-eight. After noting these findings, the trial court stated that "in her post-trial memorandum, plaintiff suggests an award 'based on the normal retirement age of sixty-five.'" (citation omitted). The trial court analyzed defendant's argument and then concluded that "plaintiff is reasonable in requesting compensation until she reached the age of 65."

Plaintiff contends that the trial court misunderstood her request. Our review of the post-trial memorandum supports plaintiff's position. . . . [The memo] is not susceptible to the trial court's reading of it.

Notwithstanding the trial court's misapprehension of plaintiff's request, plaintiff is not automatically entitled to the additional damages she requests. In *Haynes*, we implied, in dicta, that a front pay award extending beyond the normal retirement age might be reasonable in that case if it was supported by evidence that plaintiff planned to work beyond the retirement age. 166 Vt. at 238, 692 A.2d at 383. While such evidence is cited in the court's findings here, our law does not compel the trial court to award damages that are co-extensive with the period that a plaintiff intends to work. The trial court's only responsibility is to make an award that is limited to a reasonable time and that is not too speculative when viewing all the evidence in the light most favorable to the plaintiff. Id.

Trial courts should be given considerable discretion in calculating awards for lost future income, because such awards are "inherently speculative and are intrinsically insusceptible of being calculated with mathematical certainty." Williams v. Rubicon, Inc., 808 So. 2d 852, 862 (La. Ct. App. 2002) (internal citation omitted). This deference, however, is limited by the principle that the trial court's findings must sufficiently demonstrate how it exercised its discretion in light of the evidence. The findings here indicate that plaintiff planned to work for defendant beyond the age at which the trial court capped her damages, but also that plaintiff had performance-related issues that may have eventually led to her discharge at some earlier point. Accordingly, the issue of how many years worth of damages plaintiff should be awarded is remanded to the trial court.

B. MITIGATION

Defendant next contends that the court erred in holding that plaintiff had fully mitigated her damages. An employee claiming wrongful discharge has a general duty to mitigate damages. In re Lilly, 173 Vt. 591, 593, 795 A.2d 1163, 1168 (2002) (mem.). Mitigation, in the context of an employment dispute, requires that the employee make a "good faith effort to find suitable alternative employment." *Schnabel*, 168 Vt. at 361, 721 A.2d at 119. When an employer is claiming that the employee did not properly attempt to mitigate damages, the burden of proof is on the employer to show such failure. . . . This requires that the employer show both that suitable work existed and that the employee did not make reasonable efforts to obtain it. Id. Suitable employment is that which is "substantially equivalent to the position lost and suitable to a person's background and experience." Id. at 593, 795 A.2d at 1169.

In the trial court's view, plaintiff had sufficiently mitigated her damages through her work first with Morgan's Plumbing, and later by getting typing work from Quest. The trial court concluded that plaintiff was "very conscientious about mitigating her damages by obtaining other work in a timely manner" even though she no longer worked full time for any one employer after defendant terminated her. The trial court's conclusion is supported by its finding that plaintiff immediately entered the job market and found comparable, albeit lower paying, work three days after defendant terminated her. Moreover, as the trial court found, plaintiff was nearly sixty-one years old when her Morgan's job ended. Being so close to retirement, it is highly unlikely that another employer would have taken a chance on hiring and training her for work comparable to what she was doing for defendant. In this light, her decision to become self-employed was reasonable. Again, plaintiff was able to secure a client for her home typing business within a matter of days after her employment at Morgan's ended. It appears that plaintiff acted with the utmost good faith in trying to keep herself employed after defendant terminated her, and that was all that was required of her. . . .

Assuming, arguendo, that we agreed with defendant's contention that plaintiff could have been more diligent in finding work, defendant has failed to carry its burden of demonstrating that plaintiff's diligence would have been rewarded with a substantially equivalent position available to a person of plaintiff's age and with her experience. Defendant has not called our attention to, nor does the record reflect, any evidence that defendant introduced at trial regarding the job market in plaintiff's area at the time she allegedly failed to mitigate. See id. at 593-94, 795 A.2d 1168-69. Accordingly, the trial court's conclusion on mitigation must be affirmed.

Defendant further contends that the trial court erred by not deducting money that plaintiff earned working at home for OT/Therapeutic Dimensions from her final damage award. "'The measure of damages for wrongful termination of an employment contract is the amount that the plaintiff would have earned absent the breach, less what [plaintiff] actually earned or could have earned by the exercise of reasonable diligence during the contract period after [plaintiff's] termination.'" Benoir v. Ethan Allen, Inc., 147 Vt. 268, 272, 514 A.2d 716, 719 (1986) (citation omitted). As noted, plaintiff had been working for Therapeutic since 1990 and continued to do so up until the time of trial. Her income from Therapeutic did not rise dramatically after her termination. When plaintiff worked for both defendant and Therapeutic, she worked between fifty-five and sixty hours per week with only forty hours of that work attributable to defendant. The trial court found that after she became self-employed she worked only forty hours a week — the same amount she worked for defendant. She testified that, at this point, she has all the work she can handle. Thus, when plaintiff worked for defendant, and then for Morgan's, the income from Therapeutic was mainly supplemental income. After leaving Morgan's, Therapeutic became one of two primary sources of income. This change in character must be reflected in the calculation of damages. From defendant's perspective, defendant should not be responsible for compensating plaintiff for what appears to be a voluntary choice to work less total hours now than she did when she worked for defendant. Although the amount of income from Therapeutic did not change, its role in plaintiff's overall income picture did. By excluding the Therapeutic income from the damages picture, the trial court unfairly placed the burden on defendant to make up for the shortfall in plaintiff's income that resulted more from her voluntary choice to work fewer hours than defendant's decision to fire plaintiff. Accordingly, the trial court shall treat income from Therapeutic in the same manner it treats income from Quest for the period after her termination from Morgan's.

C. VACATION TIME

Defendant also challenges the trial court's decision to augment plaintiff's base pay damages by including additional funds to compensate plaintiff for paid vacation time. Plaintiff would have been contractually entitled to two weeks of paid vacation for the years 1998 through 2000, and to three weeks of paid vacation time for the years 2001 through 2004. Thus in calculating the net damages for those years, the trial court multiplied the number of vacation hours plaintiff could have taken by her hourly wage and added that number to each year's total damages. This resulted in her damages being increased by $860 for each of the first three damage years and $1,290 for each of the last four damage years. As the trial court noted, plaintiff did not receive the benefit of paid vacation time in her current employment.

Defendant argues that plaintiff is essentially receiving a double benefit for this vacation because the trial court's base pay calculation compensates plaintiff for fifty-two weeks worth of salary. In defendant's view, those fifty-two weeks already incorporate paid vacation, six paid holidays and five paid sick days. Accordingly, plaintiff is made whole by the fact that if she had worked for defendant she would have been paid for fifty-two weeks even though she would not have been required to work those fifty-two weeks.

We cannot say that the trial court erred in giving plaintiff some additional monetary benefit for vacation time that her subsequent jobs did not afford her. Nonetheless, the trial court's decision to provide plaintiff full credit for all the vacation she would have been entitled to without any findings on plaintiff's past behavior as it relates to vacation time was error. The conclusion on this issue is not reasonably supported by the findings and thus this portion of the damages award is remanded for further findings and such recalculation of damages that may be warranted by the findings.

D. BONUSES AND RAISES

In calculating base pay damages, the trial court included $700 to account for one anticipated bonus, but did not include any amount for anticipated raises. Defendant contends that the court erred by including the anticipated bonus because defendant was not contractually bound to pay plaintiff bonuses. Plaintiff also claims error in the trial court's failure to account for anticipated future raises. The trial court's findings show that plaintiff received a raise of $.25 per hour in 1995 and another raise of $.50 per hour in 1996. The findings also indicate that plaintiff received bi-annual bonuses since becoming a full-time employee in 1994. The only exception being that she did not receive her December bonus of $700 in 1997 because she was terminated in November. The trial court also found that "defendant has apparently continued its practice of awarding pay raises and bonuses since plaintiff was terminated." These findings are supported by Morrissey's own testimony. With regard to bonuses, Morrissey testified that defendant "likes to give away money, and we do it if we can, and yes, we have succeeded almost every August and December." On the topic of annual raises, Morrissey testified that some employees got annual raises and some people did not. He testified that both bonuses and raises were "heavily merit related," although he did concede that during the five year period from plaintiff's termination in 1997 to the trial in 2002, customer service representatives did receive annual pay raises. By Morrissey's own testimony, the business has doubled in size since 1997.

Based on those findings, we cannot conclude that the trial court's decision to include a reasonably anticipated bonus was too speculative. The decision was based on undisputed evidence about plaintiff's prior employment history and the company practices and finances in the period after termination. See *Benoir*, 147 Vt. at 273, 514 A.2d at 719 ("evidence of plaintiff's past employment history, coupled with proof of the company's operating history during the post-discharge period" provides fact-finder with a conservative estimate of employee's damages). Though plaintiff was not contractually entitled to bonuses it appears certain that she would have continued to receive bonuses as she had regularly in the past, and thus the trial court was within its discretion to provide plaintiff the bonuses.

The issue of annual raises presents a more difficult question. Unlike bonuses, which plaintiff received every year since becoming a full-time employee, plaintiff did not receive raises every year. Specifically, plaintiff did not receive a raise in either her first, or her last year of full-time employment with defendant. We can see why the trial court felt that automatically granting plaintiff an annual raise was more speculative than granting annual bonuses. The issue of timing is especially difficult. The evidence shows that bonuses were granted every August and December. By contrast, plaintiff has not called our attention to any evidence that would assist the trial court in determining at what point in the year raises should be granted. This information is key because, unlike bonuses that can be expressed in consistent lump sums, raises affect the rate of pay that is in turn multiplied by the number of hours worked. Thus, a raise granted in January is far more valuable than a raise granted in November because it applies to a greater number of hours worked. Timing is not the only problem. While Morrissey's testimony does indicate that both bonuses and raises were "heavily merit based," the evidence shows that plaintiff did receive bonuses in 1994 and 1997, but did not receive raises in those years. Thus, the evidence suggests that the employer's standard for granting bonuses was more liberal than its standard for granting raises. Plaintiff's track record indicates that while she always met the standard for bonuses, for whatever reason, she did not always receive a raise. The trial court's conclusion that granting plaintiff annual raises would have been too speculative is reasonably supported by the findings and the evidence.

E. OTHER CLAIMS

Plaintiff appeals the trial court's use of anticipated gross income figures to calculate her income from Quest for the purposes of deducting this amount from her base damages as mitigation. . . . As plaintiff's counsel concedes, the trial court's damage calculations with respect to her income from this source was based on plaintiff's own exhibit. . . . The trial court did not abuse its discretion by relying on plaintiff's own calculation.

Defendant claims error in the trial court's decision not to include income plaintiff receives as compensation for working for her husband's business approximately five hours per week at a rate of $10.00 per hour. Plaintiff testified that this amounted to a gross income of about $2,600 per year since 2001. Plaintiff testified that she reports this income on her taxes. Despite this testimony, the trial court failed to discuss this amount in its opinion. Therefore, on remand, the trial court shall consider the appropriate treatment of this income, and if necessary, adjust the damage award in light of its eventual conclusion with respect to this income.

The trial court's judgment with respect to defendant's liability is affirmed. The trial court's damages award is affirmed in part and reversed in part, and the matter is remanded for further findings and a reconsideration and recalculation of damages consistent with the views expressed herein.

Notes and Questions

1. *Measuring damages for breach by an employer.* At this point in our study, we have seen a number of employment cases that have involved a breach by one party or the other. How does the nature of the employment agreement in *Havill* compare with the agreements in Donahue v. Federal Express Corp. in Chapter 6 and Handicapped Children's Education Board v. Lukaszewski in the first section of this chapter? Are you convinced that the employer in *Havill* breached the contract by terminating Lois Havill?

Once the employee's breach was established in the *Lukaszewski* case, the measurement of damages for the employer seemed fairly straightforward: the additional salary paid to a comparable substitute employee plus the incidental costs incurred in making the hire. In contrast, the measurement of damages for Lois Havill as a nonbreaching employee seems fairly complex. The *Havill* court has to deal with a number of factors including the proper rate for back pay, the duration for the award of front pay, accounting for vacation benefits, the possibility of mitigating contracts, etc. Are you persuaded that the court addressed all these factors correctly or were some elements improperly assessed?

2. *Employer's burden of proof regarding mitigation.* The employer in *Havill* argued, though perhaps not vigorously, that Lois Havill had failed to make effective mitigation. Most courts agree with the *Havill* court that the burden of proving whether the employee made reasonable efforts to mitigate her damages rests with the employer. See, e.g., Collado v. City of Albuquerque, 45 P.3d 73 (N.M. Ct. App. 2002) (mitigation is an "affirmative defense"; burden of proof is on employer). In many cases, the question of mitigation is strenuously contested and the evidence is disputed. For that reason, it is often determinative that a breaching employer will bear the burden of proof on this issue. See, e.g., Boehm v. American Broadcasting Co., 929 F.2d 482 (9th Cir. 1991) (whether employee made reasonable efforts to mitigate damages was question of fact and burden of proof that efforts were unreasonable rested at all times with employer; fact that employee moved from Los Angeles to Pebble Beach did not establish that he removed himself form the job market as radio executive). Indeed, some courts have imposed on the employer the burden of

showing that not only had the employee failed to act reasonably in seeking other jobs but also that such efforts were likely to have been successful. See Stewart v. Board of Education of Ritenour Consolidated School District, 630 S.W.2d 130 (Mo. Ct. App. 1982) (even though teacher made no effort to seek another job, school district did not carry its burden of proof because it failed to show that it was "reasonably likely" that the teacher would have obtained comparable job). Do you agree that the burden of proof regarding mitigation should be allocated to the employer? Why?

3. *Breaching party's offer to mitigate.* In Fair v. Red Lion Inn, 943 P.2d 431 (Colo.1997) (en banc), Red Lion discharged Fair shortly after she returned to work from a medical leave that she had been granted to recover from injuries suffered in an automobile accident. After some negotiations, Red Lion offered to give Fair her old job back, but it refused to accept certain conditions that Fair had proposed because she was now pregnant and because she feared for her job security. Fair brought suit; the jury found Red Lion liable for $140,000 plus interest. The Colorado Supreme Court reversed. The court stated that it did not "question the reasonableness of Fair's apprehensions," but any employee (or for that matter any contracting party) would have apprehensions about the other party' performance after a breach. The court concluded:

> Nonetheless, sound principles of contract law in the commercial and employment setting . . . ordain the principles we acknowledge today: The injured party claiming breach of an employment agreement has a duty to mitigate or minimize damages. In the employment agreement context, such duty includes the acceptance of an unconditional offer of reinstatement where no special circumstances exist to justify rejection.

Id. at 442. See also West v. Bechtel Corp., 117 Cal. Rptr. 2d 647 (Ct. App. 2002) (employee was terminated in breach of contract but failed to mitigate by refusing multiple offers from same employer of comparable jobs). What "special circumstances" would justify rejection of an employer's unconditional offer of reemployment? See Restatement (Second) of Contracts §350(1); Boehm v. American Broadcasting Co., 929 F.2d 482 (9th Cir. 1991) (affirming jury's finding that offer of another position from breaching employer was not comparable position when the compensation and duties were different, employee would have reported to his replacement, and position was created just before offer to employee and was never filled).

4. *The **Parker** case.* In discussing the issue of mitigation, the court in *Havill* also espouses the commonly held view that the employee need only mitigate with alternative work that is "substantially equivalent to the position lost." This limitation on the duty to mitigate was the central issue in the widely discussed decision of the California Supreme Court in Parker v. Twentieth Century-Fox Film Corp., 474 P.2d 689 (Cal. 1970) (en banc). In *Parker,* plaintiff (known professionally as Shirley MacLaine) sued to recover damages for the defendant's breach of a contract to employ her as the star of a major musical motion picture entitled "Bloomer Girl"; the defendant argued that the plaintiff had rejected a postbreach offer from the defendant to star in a nonmusical motion picture for identical compensation and for that reason should not recover any damages. A majority of the California Supreme Court

upheld the trial court's ruling that the second offer was not a truly comparable one, principally because the two pictures were of different types and because the second opportunity did not provide the plaintiff with the same approvals of director, and the like, that she would have had under the first one. In a vigorous dissent, Justice Sullivan had the following to say about the extent of the plaintiff's "duty" to mitigate the loss of her contracted-for employment:

> [The employee need not accept] employment which is of a *different kind*. . . . It has never been the law that the mere existence of *differences between two jobs in the same field* is sufficient, as a matter of law, to excuse an employee wrongfully discharged from one from accepting the other in order to mitigate damages. Such an approach would effectively eliminate any obligation of an employee to attempt to minimize damage arising from a wrongful discharge. The only alternative job offer an employee would be required to accept would be an offer of his former job by his former employer.
>
> Although the majority appear to hold that there was a difference "in kind" between the employment offered plaintiff in "Bloomer Girl" and that offered in "Big Country". . . , an examination of the opinion makes crystal clear that the majority merely point out differences between the two *films* (an obvious circumstance) and then apodically [sic — apodictically?] assert that these constitute a difference in the *kind* of *employment*. The entire rationale of the majority boils down to this: that the *"mere circumstances"* that "Bloomer Girl" was to be a musical review while "Big Country" was a straight drama "demonstrates the difference in kind" since a female lead in a western is not "the equivalent of or substantially similar to" a lead in a musical. This is merely attempting to prove the proposition by repeating it. . . .

Id. at 696. Justice Sullivan also observed that many of the early cases held that an employee is not required to accept employment in an "inferior rank or position nor work which is more menial or arduous." He suggested that the rule may therefore "have had its origin in the bourgeois fear of resubmergence in lower economic classes." Id. at 695 n.2. Is the dissenting justice in *Parker* right in suggesting that this rule is an outmoded relic of concern for "bourgeois" interests? Or are there persuasive reasons for maintaining such an approach today?

The facts of *Parker* are more complex than the opinions in that case suggest. The original "Bloomer Girl" was a 1944 Broadway musical comedy set at the time of the Civil War and suggested by the career of Amelia Jenks ("Dolly") Bloomer, a nineteenth-century crusader for women's rights. Although essentially light entertainment, it did have strong themes of both feminism and racial justice. Plaintiff Parker (MacLaine) has publicly professed strong commitment to both causes. Would these facts have been relevant to the question of whether for her the second film was indeed a "comparable employment"? (It might also be noted that the full title of the substitute, "western-type" film offered to MacLaine was "Big Country, *Big Man*" (emphasis supplied).) For further discussion of the issues in *Parker,* see Mary Joe Frug, Re-Reading Contracts: A Feminist Analysis of a Contracts Casebook, 34 Am. U.L. Rev. 1065, 1114-1125 (1985).

Professor Victor Goldberg has argued that the *Parker* court was wrong even to apply the doctrine of mitigation of damages because her contract had a "pay-or-play" clause. Such clauses, which are common in many fields, give one party (Fox in this case) what amounts to an option to either perform under the contract or to pay the amount set forth in the clause. (Recall Sondra Locke's agreement with Warner Brothers discussed in the *Locke* case in Chapter 6.) As Professor Goldberg sees the case, Fox had the right to have MacLaine perform in "Bloomer Girl" or to pay her the contractually agreed upon amount; application of the doctrine of mitigation would have been inappropriate because it would have deprived Parker of a contractual entitlement. Victor P. Goldberg, Bloomer Girl Revisited or How to Frame an Unmade Picture, 1998 Wis. L. Rev. 1051.

5. *Recovery of incidental damages.* In seeking substitute employment, a wrongfully discharged employee may have to spend money in various ways, such as travel costs seeking other employment and fees to employment agencies. These will be "incidental expenses," for which recovery may be sought from the employer. See W.D.I.A. Corp. v. Mc Graw-Hill, Inc., 34 F. Supp. 2d 612 (S.D. Ohio 1998) (nonbreaching party may recover expenses for reasonable efforts to mitigate, even if unsuccessful); Restatement (Second) §347, Comment *c*. Should the ability of the employee to recover for such expenditures depend on his success at finding other employment?

6. *Effect of other income.* Even though the wrongfully discharged plaintiff has no "duty" to mitigate by taking employment that is not comparable to that promised by the defendant, if she does indeed take another different job, the amounts earned therefrom are likely to be set off against her damages recoverable for breach of contract. See, e.g., Marshall School District v. Hill, 939 S.W.2d 319 (Ark. Ct. App. 1997) (wrongfully discharged teacher's recovery reduced by income earned from other jobs, including work in shirt factory). Why should this be the case? Does this rule undercut the policy, discussed above, of not requiring an employee to seek dissimilar employment when wrongfully discharged? There are, however, some situations in which a new contract entered into after breach will not be considered to be a mitigating one. The next principal case, Jetz Service Co. v. Salina Properties, explores this issue.

Should an employee's recovery be reduced by compensation received from a state unemployment insurance fund or other similar source? In tort cases, most courts recognize a "collateral source" rule. Under this rule an injured party's recovery against the tortfeasor is not reduced by payments received from sources that are wholly unrelated to the tortfeasor, such as payments under disability income policies. In Corl v. Huron Castings, Inc., 544 N.W.2d 278 (Mich. 1996), the Michigan Supreme Court refused to extend the collateral source rule to contract cases and held that the amount of an employee's unemployment compensation should reduce the amount of damages recovered from the employer. Does it make a difference that unemployment compensation typically comes from a fund to which employers make contributions, and the amount of the employer's contribution is affected by the amount of payments charged to the employer's account? In Masterson v. Boliden-Allis, Inc., 865 P.2d 1031 (Kan. Ct. App. 1993), the Kansas Court of Appeals agreed that the amounts of unemployment insurance would reduce the employee's damage award, but the court also held that amounts received by the employee in social security and pension payments would not be a reduction. The court focused on the fact that unemployment insurance was funded solely by employer contributions while social security and pension payments were based on joint employer/employee contributions. See also Stacy v. Batavia Local School District, 829 N.E. 2d 298 (Ohio 2005) (collateral-source rule not applicable to contract action; retirement benefits would be deducted from back-pay award).

7. *Mitigation in the UCC.* Although the Uniform Commercial Code has no provision imposing a general responsibility of mitigation on the parties to a sales contract, Comment 1 to UCC §1-106 indicates this notion was intended to be subsumed in the more general principle that remedies are to be limited to compensation. See Revised UCC §1-305. The Comment also suggests that minimization of damages may be implicit in the more general obligation of good faith imposed by §1-203. See Revised UCC §1-304. The remedies provisions of Article 2 contain a number of specific references to actions by the buyer or the seller intended to have the effect of minimizing the loss or damage incurred by reason of the other party's breach. E.g., §§2-704(2) (seller's privilege to complete manufacture where commercially reasonable despite buyer's repudiation, "for the purposes of avoiding loss and of effective realization"), 2-706(1) (seller's privilege of resale in commercially reasonable manner), 2-709(1)(b) and (2) (attempts at resale as prerequisite to seller's action for price), 2-712 (buyer's attempt to "cover" by substitute purchase), 2-715(2)(a) (buyer not entitled to consequential damages unless loss "could not reasonably be prevented by cover or otherwise"), and 2-716(3) (buyer's right to specific performance conditioned on inability to effect cover). These and other remedies under Article 2 are discussed in more detail in Section E of this Chapter.

8. *Mitigation in real estate leases.* As we saw in the first section of this chapter, damages for nonperformance of a contract to buy or sell real estate are ordinarily based on a comparison of contract price with market value, a rule which in most cases roughly approximates the loss suffered by a promptly reselling vendor or a promptly covering purchaser. Real estate leases, however, have historically been a different matter. Reflecting the principle that a lease of land was considered as a conveyance of an interest in real property (rather than merely a contract to permit its occupancy by someone not the owner), defaulting tenants were traditionally held to their obligation to pay the rent in full, with no obligation on the landlord's part to minimize loss by attempting to re-rent to another. See Restatement (Second) of Property §12.1(3) (1977). More recently, most American jurisdictions have by decision or statute adopted the position that real estate leases should be treated more like other contracts, with the landlord in the event of the tenant's abandonment having a "duty to mitigate" similar to that imposed on other contracting parties. See Frenchtown Square Partnership v. Lemstone, 791 N.E. 2d 417 (Ohio 2003). Not all courts agree, however. In 1995 a unanimous New York Court of Appeals adhered to the traditional rule that a landlord does not have a duty to mitigate damages. Holy Properties Ltd. v. Kenneth Cole Productions, Inc., 661 N.E.2d 694 (N.Y. 1995); but see 29 Holding Corp. v. Diaz, 775 N.Y.S. 2d 807 (N.Y. Sup. Ct. 2004) (holding that duty to mitigate would apply to "residential" lease and that contrary precedent should be limited to "commercial" leases). See generally Christopher Vaeth, Annotation, Landlord's Duty, on Tenant's Failure to Occupy, or Abandonment of,

Premises, to Mitigate Damages by Accepting or Procuring Another Tenant, 75 A.L.R.5th 1 (2000).

Jetz Service Co. v. Salina Properties
Kansas Court of Appeals
19 Kan. App. 2d 144, 865 P.2d 1051 (1993)

LARSON, Judge:
Salina Properties appeals the damages awarded to Jetz Service Co., Inc., resulting from breach of the parties' lease of space in which coin-operated laundry equipment was installed in an apartment complex.

Jetz Service supplies and maintains coin-operated laundry equipment in approximately 2,000 locations in an eight-state area. It constantly seeks locations for installation of laundry equipment which is furnished from several warehouses in which an inventory of approximately 1,500 used washers and dryers is always available.

In May of 1987, Salina Properties' predecessor in title leased 175 square feet of an apartment complex to Jetz Service for use as a coin-operated laundry facility. Five washing machines and five dryers were installed in November of 1987.

The lease was for a six-year term. Jetz Service paid an initial $3,000 decorating allowance and was entitled to the first $300 per month or 50%, whichever was greater, of the gross receipts from the machines during the term of the lease. The lease stated the parties assumed the duties of a landlord and tenant under the laws of Kansas.

In July of 1992, with 16 months remaining on the term of the lease, Salina Properties disconnected all of Jetz Service's equipment and replaced it with its own laundry equipment.

Jetz Service retrieved its property at a cost of $187.50 and stored the washers and dryers in one of its warehouses. Four sets of the laundry equipment were re-leased in the Kansas City area in January 1993, although other suitable laundry equipment was available to complete this transaction.

Jetz Service sued Salina Properties to recover its lost profits for the remaining 16 months of the lease. It requested damages equal to one-half of the anticipated gross income for the remainder of the lease. Salina Properties raised numerous defenses but essentially relied on its argument that Jetz Services had failed to mitigate its damages and should only recover the cost of moving its equipment.

The trial court determined Jetz Service was a "lost volume" lessee and had sustained loss of profits and damages in the amount Jetz Service requested. Salina Properties received credit for one month of unpaid rent but Jetz Service was granted judgment for damages of $6,383.08 and $2,165 in attorney fees.

Salina Properties appeals the award of damages. It does not contest the trial court's finding that it was subject to the lease and that its actions in removing Jetz Service's property constituted a breach of the lease agreement.

The two principal contentions Salina Properties raises by this appeal are that Jetz Service (1) failed, as a matter of law, to mitigate its damages and (2) failed to prove the requisite elements to recover lost profits. The underlying issue of most importance, however, is the trial court's finding that Jetz Service should be treated as a "lost volume" lessee and is entitled to recover its expected gross receipts for the remaining term of the lease notwithstanding the fact it utilized part of the laundry equipment before the term of the Salina lease expired.

In deciding this case, we must remain mindful of several basic concepts in the assessment of damages.

> The purpose of awarding damages is to make a party whole by restoring that party to the position he or she was in prior to the [breach]. Cerretti v. Flint Hills Rural Electric Co-op Ass'n, 251 Kan. 347, Syl. P 6, 837 P.2d 330 (1992). [T]he injured party should be placed, so far as can be done by a money award, in the same position that he or she would have occupied if the contract had been performed. M & W Development, Inc. v. El Paso Water Co., 6 Kan. App. 2d 735, Syl. P 4, 634 P.2d 166 (1981).

. . .

Kansas courts have long held that lost profits may be recoverable as damages.

> This court follows the general rule that loss of profits resulting from a breach of contract may be recovered as damages when such profits are proved with reasonable certainty, and when they may reasonably be considered to have been within the contemplation of the parties. [Citations omitted.] Recovery for loss of profits caused by a breach of contract depends upon the facts and circumstances of each particular case. Vickers v. Wichita State University, 213 Kan. 614, 618, 518 P.2d 512 (1974).

. . .

Our courts further recognize the general rule of law "that one injured by reason of a breach of contract by another is under a duty to exercise reasonable care to avoid loss or to mitigate and minimize the resulting damage. The injured party is bound to protect himself if he can do so with reasonable exertion or at trifling expense, and can recover from the delinquent party only such damages as he could not, with reasonable effort, have avoided." In re Estate of Stannard, 179 Kan. 394, Syl. P 1, 295 P.2d 610 (1956).

. . .

If we assume a factual finding that Jetz Service made reasonable efforts to reuse the laundry equipment but was unable to do so until January of 1993, the trial court's award of damages for the first six months subsequent to the breach is easily affirmed. We would be required, however, to reduce the award for the damages awarded for the breach of the final 10 months of the lease because 80% (8 of the 10 machines) of the laundry equipment was placed into usage in the Kansas City area lease. We are not willing to reach this result because we agree with the trial court's determination that Jetz Service is a "lost volume" lessee, a concept which has not previously been considered by our Kansas courts.

The term "lost volume" seller is credited to Professor Robert J. Harris of the University of Michigan Law School. See Harris, A Radical Restatement of the Law of Seller's Damages: Sales Act and Commercial Code Results Compared, 18 Stan. L. Rev. 66 (1965); . . . Snyder v. Herbert Greenbaum & Assoc., 38 Md. App. 144, 154 n.3, 380 A.2d 618 (1977).

The "lost volume seller" measure of damages "refers to the lost volume of business the non-breaching seller incurs on buyer's breach. When the seller resells the entity he expected to sell to the original buyer, he usually deprives himself of something of value — the sale to a new buyer of another similar entity." 38 Md. App. at 154 n.3, 380 A.2d 618.

The meaning of the term is shown by the following example:

> To illustrate, assume a contract for the sale of a washing machine with a list price of $500. Assume further that the seller has or can obtain more machines than he can sell. The buyer breaches, and the seller resells that washing machine at the same list price the buyer had been willing to pay. However, the resale buyer is one of seller's regular customers who had intended to purchase a washing machine from him anyway. If the seller's total cost per machine was $300, he stood to gain an aggregate profit of $400, that is, $200 profit from each of two sales. Clearly the 2-708 contract-market differential formula is inadequate in this situation since it gives no damages to the seller who has lost a $200 profit because of the breach. In such a case the damage award should be the lost profit, that is, $200, for this will place the seller "in as good a position as performance would have done." 1 White & Summers, Uniform Commercial Code §7-9, p.358 (3d ed. 1988).

Salina Properties argues forcefully that the lost volume theory of damage recovery may only be invoked where K.S.A. 84-2-708(2) of the Uniform Commercial Code applies, which it does not in this case because we are dealing with a provider of "services" and not a seller of "goods." K.S.A. 84-2-102. We agree that Jetz Service does not sell goods, but the underlying concept is analogous; adequate authority exists to apply the lost volume rule to volume providers of services.

. . .

The Restatement (Second) of Contracts §350 Comment d (1979) has this to say:

> Lost volume. The mere fact that an injured party can make arrangements for the disposition of the goods or services that he was to supply under the contract does not necessarily mean that by doing so he will avoid loss. If he would have entered into both transactions but for the breach, he has "lost volume" as a result of the breach. See Comment f to §347. In that case the second transaction is not a "substitute" for the first one.

Section 347 Comment f of the Restatement (Second) of Contracts (1979) provides:

> Lost volume. Whether a subsequent transaction is a substitute for the broken contract sometimes raises difficult questions of fact. If the injured party could and would have entered into the subsequent contract, even if the contract had not been broken, and could have had the benefit of both, he can be said to have "lost volume"

and the subsequent transaction is not a substitute for the broken contract. The injured party's damages are then based on the net profit that he has lost as a result of the broken contract. Since entrepreneurs try to operate at optimum capacity, however, it is possible that an additional transaction would not have been profitable and that the injured party would not have chosen to expand his business by undertaking it had there been no breach. It is sometimes assumed that he would have done so, but the question is one of fact to be resolved according to the circumstances of each case. See Illustration 16. . . .

Illustration:

16. A contracts to pave B's parking lot for $10,000. B repudiates the contract and A subsequently makes a contract to pave a similar parking lot for $10,000. A's business could have been expanded to do both jobs. Unless it is proved that he would not have undertaken both, A's damages are based on the net profit he would have made on the contract with B, without regards to the subsequent transaction.

We were not furnished nor did our research reveal any Kansas cases directly on point. We therefore turn to several cases from other jurisdictions, the first being startlingly similar factually.

Although not so named, the status of lost volume lessor was found to apply to a plaintiff who was engaged in the business of leasing coin-operated equipment in Seaboard Music Co. v. Germano, 24 Cal. App. 3d 618, 101 Cal. Rptr. 255 (1972). Seaboard's lease of a coin-operated juke box and pool table was breached by a tavern operator. The tavern owner claimed that Seaboard was required to mitigate damages by re-leasing the equipment. The California court determined the duty to minimize damages did not apply to contracts "'which do not preclude plaintiff from undertaking and being engaged in the performance contemporaneously of other contracts.'" 24 Cal. App. 3d at 623, 101 Cal. Rptr. 255.

The court found the evidence showed that Seaboard "was engaged in the business of leasing coin-operated equipment; it had a warehouse full of equipment similar to that leased to Ohmer from which it serviced its customers and from which it could service any additional leases negotiated, irrespective of whether Ohmer fulfilled or breached his obligation." 24 Cal. App. 3d at 623, 101 Cal. Rptr. 255.

The court concluded the duty to mitigate damages could not be imposed to deprive Seaboard of the benefit of subsequent contracts which would had been available to it irrespective of the original breach, and the defendants' liability would not be reduced by requiring Seaboard to forego profits that it would otherwise have made in the normal course of business.

In Wired Music, Inc. v. Clark, 26 Ill. App. 2d 413, 168 N.E.2d 736 (1960), the Appellate Court of Illinois determined that when a distributor of music by telephone wires had an unlimited supply of music and was limited in its distribution only by the number of contracts it could secure, the distributor could recover lost profits for the remaining months under a contract from a customer who discontinued service before expiration of the contract period. The fact that the distributor entered into another contract for service at the same location with a new tenant for a higher fee did not relieve the original customer of liability for damages.

. . .

Here, there was substantial competent evidence to support the trial court's determination that Jetz Service was a "lost volume" lessee. The evidence showed that Jetz Service is in the business of supplying coin-operated laundry equipment; it has several warehouses in which it has available for lease about 1,500 used washers and dryers; it continually looks for new locations in which to install laundry equipment; it would have been able to fulfill the Kansas City lease without using the machines from Salina Properties; and it is uncontroverted Jetz Service would have been able to enter into both transactions irrespective of the breach by Salina Properties.

Under appropriate facts such as exist here, lost volume status should be conferred upon one engaged in a service-oriented business. As a lost volume lessee, Jetz Service was not required to mitigate damages by using the equipment in another lease and Salina Properties is not relieved of the liability to pay damages even though Jetz Service did utilize four of the five sets of laundry equipment six months after Salina Properties' breach.

In Haag v. Dry Basement, Inc., 11 Kan. App. 2d 649, 654, 732 P.2d 392, rev. denied 241 Kan. 838 (1987), we stated:

> The determination of the amount of damages is a factual issue, and the trial court's calculation will be upheld if supported by substantial competent evidence. In order for the evidence to be sufficient to warrant a recovery of damages, there must be some reasonable basis for computation which will enable the factfinder to arrive at an approximate estimate thereof.

The calculation of lost future profits was based upon historical past profits generated during the seven month period preceding Salina Properties' breach. We find the amount claimed was proven with reasonable certainty.

Although the parties did not discuss lost profits when the lease was executed, lost profits are presumed to have been contemplated by the parties. The written agreement shows that the lease payments to Salina Properties were based upon the profits expected to be generated under the lease agreement. In this situation, lost profits would have naturally flowed from a breach of the lease agreement. See Farnsworth, Young & Jones, Cases and Materials on Contracts p.527 (2d ed. 1972).

Salina Properties claims the trial court erred by failing to reduce the damage award by the direct costs of maintenance and insurance Jetz Service saved by its breach. The record shows these were fixed costs not affected by Salina Properties' breach. Fixed expenses or overhead are the continuous expenses of the business, irrespective of the outlay on a particular contract, and includes such expenses as executive and clerical salaries, property taxes, general administrative expenses, etc. Farnsworth, Young & Jones, pp.474-75. Fixed expenses or overhead are not deducted when computing lost profits. Farnsworth, Young & Jones, p.475.

We hold the trial court properly applied the status of lost volume lessee to Jetz Service under the facts of this case. There was substantial competent evidence to justify the trial court's findings and judgment.

Affirmed.

Notes and Questions

1. *Mitigating versus additional contracts.* In order for the breaching party to obtain a deduction from its damage liability for income received by the plaintiff from another contract, the breaching party must show that the other contract was a *mitigating contract,* that is, a contract that the plaintiff was able to perform only because the defendant's breach freed the plaintiff from the obligation to perform the original contract. If the court finds that the new contract is an *additional contract* rather than a mitigating one, however (as was the case in *Jetz Service*), the plaintiff is entitled to the profit from both contracts, and the defendant will not have the benefit of any deduction from its damage liability. As the court in *Jetz Service* indicates, whether the contract is mitigating or additional is a question of fact. In Rodriguez v. Learjet, Inc., 946 P.2d 1010 (Kan. Ct. App. 1997), the Kansas Court of Appeals amplified its holding in *Jetz Service.* To establish its status as a lost volume seller, the plaintiff must prove "(1) that it possessed the capacity to make an additional sale, (2) that it would have been profitable for it to make an additional sale, and (3) that it probably would have made an additional sale absent the buyer's breach." Id. at 1015. *Rodriguez* involved a breach of contract to purchase a commercial jet airplane. On the facts of the case Learjet was able to establish that it was a lost volume seller because: (1) it was operating at 60% of capacity, (2) accounting evidence showed that additional sales could be made profitably, and (3) the company sold the jet that was the subject of the contract to another purchaser at a profit.

2. *Lost volume sellers under the UCC.* The Learjet contract in *Rodriguez* was governed by Article 2 of the Uniform Commercial Code since the plane was an item of "goods" as defined in UCC §2-105(1). The courts have been almost unanimous in holding that lost volume sellers of goods, such as Learjet, are entitled to recover their profit under UCC §2-708(2). See James J. White & Robert S. Summers, Uniform Commercial Code §7-9 (5th ed. 2000) (listing cases that have applied §2-708(2) to lost volume sellers). For a recent exchange on whether §2-708(2) is properly interpreted to allow recovery of profit by lost volume sellers and, if so, on the fairness of this rule, see John M. Breen, The Lost Volume Seller and Lost Profits under U.C.C. §2-708(2): A Conceptual and Linguistic Critique, 50 U. Miami L. Rev. 779 (1996); Daniel W. Matthews, Comment, Should the Doctrine of Lost Volume Seller Be Retained? A Response to Professor Breen, 51 U. Miami L. Rev. 1195 (1997). The various remedies available to sellers and buyers under the UCC are discussed later in this chapter.

3. *Application of the mitigation principle to service contracts.* The application of the mitigation principle to service contracts turns on several factors. If the contract is for personal services or employment (as in the *Havill* case), a new contract entered into after the breach will generally be considered to be a mitigating one since an individual has a limited capacity to perform personal services. In some cases, however, it may be possible for the employee or other provider of services to perform both contracts; in that case the second contract will not be considered a mitigating one. For example, in Gianetti v. Norwalk Hosp., 833 A.2d 891 (Conn. 2003), the plaintiff was a staff plastic surgeon at the defendant hospital, but was also on staff at four other hospitals.

The defendant hospital was held to have breached its contract with the plaintiff by failing to renew his appointment. The Connecticut Supreme Court then rejected the defendant's argument that the physician could not possibly be a "lost volume seller" as a matter of law. The court held that the plaintiff, as a general proposition, could have continued to perform his contract with the defendant hospital in addition to his contracts with the other hospitals. 833 A.2d at 902. See also Restatement (Second) §347, Comment *e*, Illustration 13. Ultimately, the *Gianetti* case was remanded for a further factual determination whether the plaintiff could have continued to sell his services to the defendant in light of the fact that he apparently increased his number of hours at the other hospitals. 833 A.2d at 907-908.

When the contract does not require personal services (as was the case in *Jetz Service*), the courts may find it even easier to conclude that a second contract entered into after breach of the first contract is not a mitigating one because the provider of services has the capacity to perform both contracts. The Restatement supports this view. Illustration 10 to §350 provides: "*A* contracts to pay *B* $20,000 for paving *A*'s parking lot, which would give *B* a net profit of $3,000. *A* breaks the contract by repudiating it before *B* begins work. If *B* would have made the contract with *A* in addition to other contracts, *B*'s efforts to obtain other contracts do not affect his damages. *B*'s damages for *A*'s breach of contract include his $3,000 loss of profit." The courts have reached similar decisions. See, e.g., Koplin v. Faulkner, 293 S.W.2d 467 (Ky. 1956) (plaintiff entitled to lost profits on contract to drill an oil well when landowner breached; plaintiff could have realized profits from other contracts and performed the beached contract); Harvey v. Timber Resources, Inc., 37 S.W.3d 814 (Mo. Ct. App. 2001) (plaintiff contractor entitled to lost profits on timber cutting contract; could have performed both the breached contract and a subsequent contract in the requisite time frame).

4. *Calculation of lost profit.* If the new contract is viewed as an additional rather than a mitigating contract, the plaintiff is entitled to her "lost profit" from the original contract without deduction of the amount received from the new contract. The determination of lost profit, however, can be tricky. According to standard accounting principles, "profit" means gross income minus cost of the transaction. What is included in the term "cost"? Certain types of costs vary with the particular transaction ("variable costs," in accounting terminology), while other costs, such as mortgage expenses, officers' salaries, and general administrative expenses are "fixed costs." The court in *Jetz Service* awarded the plaintiff its "gross profit," defined as gross income less variable costs but without any deduction for a portion of fixed costs that could be allocated to the transaction. Other courts agree with this approach. See P.C. Data Centers of Pa., Inc. v. Federal Express Corp. 113 F. Supp. 2d 709 (M.D. Pa. 2000) (fixed expenses are not avoidable and are therefore not deducted in determining damages); Magnet Resources, Inc. v. Summit MRI, Inc. 723 A.2d 976 (N.J. Super. App. Div. 1998) (administrative expenses and plant overhead allocable to contract not deducted in determining damages unless they were saved as result of breach). See also James J. White & Robert S. Summers, Uniform Commercial Code §7-13, at 289-290 (5th ed. 2000). Should fixed costs be deducted in determining the profit awarded to a lost volume seller? Why?

D. NONRECOVERABLE DAMAGES: ITEMS COMMONLY EXCLUDED FROM PLAINTIFF'S DAMAGES FOR BREACH OF CONTRACT

It was earlier suggested that the conventional rule governing contract damages implies both a floor and a ceiling: A plaintiff should ordinarily recover *at least* her expectation damages; on the other hand, a plaintiff should not recover anything *more* than that. As we have seen, a plaintiff's claim for expectation damages will be weighed in light of the doctrine of avoidable consequences; it will also be limited by the requirement that damages be foreseeable (at least where they are "special" or "consequential") and proven with reasonable certainty. As a result, in many cases the damages actually recoverable will in fact fall short of the true "expectation" of gain that the contract created.

In this section, we consider three types of damage recovery usually denied to a plaintiff in ordinary actions at common law for breach of contract (although they may be recoverable in other kinds of actions or specifically provided for by statute): damages to compensate the plaintiff for amounts expended on attorney fees; damages for mental distress (and related types of intangible, "noneconomic" injury); and "punitive" (or "exemplary") damages. In some instances, denial of such recovery will further depress the plaintiff's award of damages below the level that true expectation would require. (E.g., inability of the plaintiff to recover the full cost of litigation occasioned by the breach means that even if an otherwise fully compensatory damage award is granted, the plaintiff necessarily will be left worse off than she would have been if the contract had been performed.) In other cases, to award such damages might well bring the plaintiff's recovery *above* the net-expectation level. (This is particularly likely to be true of a sizeable award of punitive damages.) Recent developments suggest that these conventional rules of nonliability are not beyond question. Some evidence of this gradual shift in attitudes may be seen in the materials that follow.

Zapata Hermanos Sucesores, S.A. v. Hearthside Baking Company, Inc.

United States Court of Appeals
313 F.3d 385 (7th Cir. 2002), cert. denied,
540 U.S. 1068 (2003)

POSNER, Judge.

Zapata, a Mexican corporation that supplied Lenell, a U.S. wholesale baker of cookies, with cookie tins, sued Lenell for breach of contract and won. The district judge ordered Lenell to pay Zapata $550,000 in attorneys' fees. From that order, which the judge based both on a provision of the Convention on Contracts for the International Sale of Goods, Jan. 1, 1988, 15 U.S.C.App., and on the inherent authority of the courts to punish the conduct of litigation in bad faith, Lenell appeals.

The Convention, of which both the U.S. and Mexico are signatories, provides, as its name indicates, remedies for breach of international contracts for the sale of goods. Zapata brought suit under the Convention for money due under 110 invoices, amounting to some $900,000 (we round liberally), and also sought prejudgment interest plus attorneys' fees, which it contended are "losses" within the meaning of the Convention and are therefore an automatic entitlement of a plaintiff who prevails in a suit under the Convention. At the close of the evidence in a one-week trial, the judge granted judgment as a matter of law for Zapata on 93 of the 110 invoices, totaling $850,000. Zapata's claim for money due under the remaining invoices was submitted to the jury, which found in favor of Lenell. Lenell had filed several counterclaims; the judge dismissed some of them and the jury ruled for Zapata on the others. The jury also awarded Zapata $350,000 in prejudgment interest with respect to the 93 invoices as to which Zapata had prevailed, and the judge then tacked on the attorneys' fees—the entire attorneys' fees that Zapata had incurred during the litigation.

Article 74 of the Convention provides that "damages for breach of contract by one party consist of a sum equal to the loss, including loss of profit, suffered by the other party as a consequence of the breach," provided the consequence was foreseeable at the time the contract was made. Article 7(2) provides that "questions concerning matters governed by this Convention which are not expressly settled in it are to be settled in conformity with the general principles on which it is based or, in the absence of such principles, in conformity with the law applicable by virtue of the rules of private international law [i.e., conflicts of law rules]." There is no suggestion in the background of the Convention or the cases under it that "loss" was intended to include attorneys' fees, but no suggestion to the contrary either. Nevertheless it seems apparent that "loss" does not include attorneys' fees incurred in the litigation of a suit for breach of contract, though certain prelitigation legal expenditures, for example expenditures designed to mitigate the plaintiff's damages, would probably be covered as "incidental" damages. Sorenson v. Fio Rito, 90 Ill.App.3d 368, 45 Ill.Dec. 714, 413 N.E.2d 47, 50-52 (1980); cf. Tull v. Gundersons, Inc., 709 P.2d 940, 946 (Colo. 1985); Restatement (Second) of Contracts §347, comment *c* (1981).

The Convention is about contracts, not about procedure. The principles for determining when a losing party must reimburse the winner for the latter's expense of litigation are usually not a part of a substantive body of law, such as contract law, but a part of procedural law. For example, the "American rule," that the winner must bear his own litigation expenses, and the "English rule" (followed in most other countries as well), that he is entitled to reimbursement, are rules of general applicability. They are not field-specific. There are, it is true, numerous exceptions to the principle that provisions regarding attorneys' fees are part of general procedure law. For example, federal antidiscrimination, antitrust, copyright, pension, and securities laws all contain field-specific provisions modifying the American rule (as do many other field-specific statutes). An international convention on contract law *could* do the same. But not only is the question of attorneys' fees not "expressly settled" in the Convention, it is not even mentioned. And there are no "principles" that can be drawn out of the provisions of the Convention for determining whether "loss" includes attorneys' fees; so by the terms of the Convention itself the matter must be left to domestic law (i.e., the law picked out by "the rules of private international law," which means the rules governing choice of law in international legal disputes).

U.S. contract law is different from, say, French contract law, and the general U.S. rule on attorneys' fee shifting (the "American rule") is different from the French rule (loser pays). But no one would say that French contract law differs from U.S. *because* the winner of a contract suit in France is entitled to be reimbursed by the loser, and in the U.S. not. That's an important difference but not a contract-law difference. It is a difference resulting from differing procedural rules of general applicability.

The interpretation of "loss" for which Zapata contends would produce anomalies; this is another reason to reject the interpretation. On Zapata's view the prevailing plaintiff in a suit under the Convention would (though presumably subject to the general contract duty to mitigate damages, to which we referred earlier) get his attorneys' fees reimbursed more or less automatically (the reason for the "more or less" qualification will become evident in a moment). But what if the defendant won? Could he invoke the domestic law, if as is likely other than in the United States that law entitled either side that wins to reimbursement of his fees by the loser? Well, if so, could a winning plaintiff waive his right to attorneys' fees under the Convention in favor of domestic law, which might be more or less generous than Article 74, since Article 74 requires that any loss must, to be recoverable, be foreseeable, which beyond some level attorneys' fees, though reasonable ex post, might not be? And how likely is it that the United States would have signed the Convention had it thought that in doing so it was abandoning the hallowed American rule? To the vast majority of the signatories of the Convention, being nations in which loser pays is the rule anyway, the question whether "loss" includes attorneys' fees would have held little interest; there is no reason to suppose they thought about the question at all.

For these reasons, we conclude that "loss" in Article 74 does not include attorneys' fees, and we move on to the question of a district court's inherent authority to punish a litigant or the litigant's lawyers for litigating in bad faith. The district judge made clear that he was basing his award of attorneys' fees to Zapata in part on his indignation at Lenell's having failed to pay money conceded to be owed to Zapata. Although the precise amount was in dispute, Lenell concedes that it owed Zapata at least half of the $1.2 million that Zapata obtained in damages (not counting the attorneys' fees) and prejudgment interest. Lenell had no excuse for not paying that amount, and this upset the judge.

Firms should pay their debts when they have no legal defense to them. *Pacta sunt servanda*, as the saying goes ("contracts are to be obeyed"). In the civil law (that is, the legal regime of Continental Europe), this principle is taken very seriously, as illustrated by the fact that the civil law grants specific performance in breach of contract cases as a matter of course. But under the common law (including the common law of Illinois, which is the law that choice of law principles make applicable to any issues in this case not covered in express terms by the Convention), a breach of contract is not considered wrongful activity in the sense that a tort or a crime is wrongful. When we delve for reasons, we encounter Holmes's argument that practically speaking the duty created by a contract is just to perform or pay damages, for only if damages are inadequate relief in the particular circumstances of the case will specific performance be ordered. In other words, and subject to the qualification just mentioned, the entire practical effect of signing a contract is that by doing so one obtains an option to break it. The damages one must pay for breaking the contract are simply the price if the option is exercised. See Oliver Wendell Holmes, Jr., The Common Law 300-02 (1881); Holmes, "The Path of the Law," 10 Harv. L.Rev. 457, 462 (1897).

Why such lenity? Perhaps because breach of contract is a form of strict liability. Many breaches are involuntary and so inapt occasions for punishment. Even deliberate breaches are not necessarily culpable, as they may enable an improvement in efficiency — suppose Lenell had a contract to take a certain quantity of tins from Zapata and found that it could buy them for half the price from someone else. Some breaches of contract, it is true, are not only deliberate but culpable, and maybe this was one — Lenell offers no excuse for failing to pay for tins that it had taken delivery of and presumably resold with its cookies in them. Refusing to pay the contract price after the other party has performed is not the kind of option that the performing party would willingly have granted when the contract was negotiated. The option of which Holmes spoke was the option not to perform because performance was impossible or because some more valuable use of the resources required for performance arose after the contract was signed. Zapata argues, moreover, perhaps correctly (we need not decide), that Lenell refused to pay in an effort to extract a favorable modification of the terms of the parties' dealings, which would be a form of duress if Zapata somehow lacked an effective legal remedy. Professional Service Network, Inc. v. American Alliance Holding Co., 238 F.3d 897, 900-01 (7th Cir. 2001); Alaska Packers' Ass'n v. Domenico, 117 F. 99, 100-04 (9th Cir. 1902). But Zapata did not charge duress, and probably couldn't, since it had a good remedy — this suit.

It is true that nowadays common law courts will sometimes award punitive damages for breach of contract in bad faith. But outside the field of insurance, where refusals in bad faith to indemnify or defend have long been punishable by awards of punitive damages to the insured, the plaintiff must show that the breach of contract involved tortious misconduct, such as duress or fraud or abuse of fiduciary duty. See, e.g., Miller Brewing Co. v. Best Beers of Bloomington, Inc., 608 N.E.2d 975, 982-83 (Ind. 1993); Story v. City of Bozeman, 242 Mont. 436, 791 P.2d 767, 776 (1990); E. Allan Farnsworth, Contracts §12.8, pp. 788-89 (3d ed. 1999). This is the rule in Illinois, Morrow v. L.A. Goldschmidt Associates, Inc., 112 Ill.2d 87, 96 Ill.Dec. 939, 492 N.E.2d 181, 183-86 (1986), and Zapata has not tried to come within it. For that matter, it did not ask for punitive damages, and the judge had no authority to award attorneys' fees in lieu of such damages. He could not have awarded punitive damages if Zapata had asked for them but had been unable to prove tortious misconduct by Lenell, and even more clearly he could not award them when they had not been requested.

The decision whether punitive damages shall be a sanction for a breach of contract is an issue of substantive law, and under the *Erie* doctrine a federal court is not authorized to apply a different substantive law of contracts in a diversity case from the law that a state court would apply were the case being litigated in a state court instead. And obviously that rule must not be circumvented by renaming punitive damages "attorneys' fees." United States ex rel. Treat Bros. Co. v. Fidelity & Deposit Co. of Maryland, 986 F.2d 1110, 1119-20 (7th Cir. 1993); see also Chambers v. NASCO, Inc., 501 U.S. 32, 52-55 (1991). . . . It is true that this is not a diversity case, but the *Erie* doctrine applies to any case in which state law supplies the rule of decision, see, e.g., O'Melveny & Myers v. FDIC, 512 U.S. 79, 83-85, 87-88 (1994), here by incorporation in the Convention.

The inherent authority of federal courts to punish misconduct before them is not a grant of authority to do good, rectify shortcomings of the common law (as by using an award of attorneys' fees to make up for an absence that the judge may deem regrettable of punitive damages for certain breaches of contract), or undermine the American rule on the award of attorneys' fees to the prevailing party in the absence of statute. Morganroth & Morganroth v. DeLorean, 213 F.3d 1301, 1318 (10th Cir. 2000); Association of Flight Attendants, AFL-CIO v. Horizon Air Industries, Inc., supra, 976 F.2d at 548-50 (9th Cir. 1992); Shimman v. International Union of Operating Engineers, Local 18, 744 F.2d 1226, 1232-33 and n. 9 (6th Cir. 1984) (en banc). These cases and others we could cite make clear that it is a residual authority, to be exercised sparingly, to punish misconduct (1) occurring in the litigation itself, not in the events giving rise to the litigation (for then the punishment would be a product of substantive law—designed, for example, to deter breaches of contract), and (2) not adequately dealt with by other rules, most pertinently here Rules 11 and 37 of the Federal Rules of Civil Procedure, which Lenell has not been accused of violating.

Insofar as he focused on Lenell's behavior in the litigation itself, which, to repeat, is the only lawful domain of the relevant concept of "inherent authority"—the authority could not constitutionally be extended to give parties remedies not available to them under the law of the state that furnishes the substantive rules of decision in the case—the judge punished Lenell for having failed to acknowledge liability and spare Zapata and the judge and the jury and the witnesses and so on the burden of a trial. But as it happens, the fault here was in no small measure the judge's. Well before the trial, and long, long before Zapata's lawyers had run the tab up to $550,000, they had moved for partial summary judgment, claiming that Lenell in answer to Zapata's requests for admission had acknowledged liability for $858,000 of the $890,000 sought in the complaint. The judge had denied the motion on the ground that partial summary judgment cannot be granted unless the grant would give rise to an appealable judgment. This was error. [The court then discusses how Rule 56 allows for partial summary judgment whether the judgment is appealable or not.—EDS.]

Since the challenged award of $550,000 in attorneys' fees cannot stand, we need not pick through the record to see whether some of the counterclaims or other moves by Lenell during the trial were sanctionable apart from Rule 11 and Rule 37. But it may be useful in guiding further proceedings on remand to point out that to the extent that those rules place limits on the award of sanctions under them (for example by the provision of safe harbors in Rule 11), those limitations are equally limitations on inherent authority, which may not be used to amend the rules. Kovilic Construction Co. v. Missbrenner, 106 F.3d 768, 772-73 (7th Cir. 1997). For federal rules of procedure have the force of statutes. See id.; 28 U.S.C. §2072(b).

One issue remains for discussion. Although we have treated the appeal so far as if the only issues concerned attorneys' fees, Lenell also argues that the jury verdict should be set aside because the judge by his comments in open court signaled to the jury his scorn for Lenell's case. There were only a couple of such comments (many more, however, at sidebars outside the jury's hearing), and we do not think they could have changed the outcome. But we also think that judges should be very cautious about making comments in the hearing of a jury about the quality of a party's case or lawyers. For if he signals to the jury his opinion as to how the case should be decided, he undermines the jury's authority. . . .

From what we have just reported about the judge's statements during the trial and from the tone of a number of other statements that he made in the course of this litigation, we think it best that the further proceedings that we are ordering be conducted before a different judge, in accordance with 7th Cir. R. 36.

AFFIRMED IN PART, REVERSED IN PART, AND REMANDED.

Notes and Questions

1. *CISG as grounds for recovery of attorney fees.* As stated by the *Zapata* court, the "English (or British)" rule concerning attorney fees is that the loser in litigation pays those fees for the prevailing party. This "fee-shifting" approach is also found in most civil law countries. In contrast, the "American rule" dictates that parties pay their own attorney fees. There are exceptions to the American rule, however, that justify the awarding of attorney fees to the prevailing party, including the possibilities that the parties may have a valid contract term allowing for attorney fees, there may be an applicable statute granting such fees, or there may an established court rule that allows for recovery. The primary issue facing the court in *Zapata* was whether the Convention for the International Sale of Goods (CISG), as a treaty that is tantamount to federal legislation, should be interpreted to provide for recovery of attorney fees.

The CISG applied in *Zapata*, of course, because the plaintiff had its place of business in Mexico, the defendant had its place of business in the United States, and both countries are signatories to the CISG. (Most of the United States' major trading partners, with the exception of the United Kingdom and Japan, are parties to the CISG. See the Rules Supplement, Editors' Note on Contracts for the International Sale of Goods.) The trial court in *Zapata* held that attorney's fees are recoverable under CISG Article 74 if they are foreseeable, and the defendant in *Zapata* stipulated that attorney fees were a foreseeable result of its failure to pay for the tins that it ordered. Perhaps more importantly, the trial court based its decision on the considerations that the "American rule" on attorney fees is a minority rule in the world community and, as reflected in its Preamble and Article 7, the CISG has a goal of promoting uniformity and certainty in the law. See Zapata

Hermanos Sucesores, S.A. v. Hearthside Baking Company, Inc., 2001 WL 1000927 (N.D. Ill. 2001). Thus, one could argue that the trial court's decision to allow attorney fees was consistent with central tenets of the CISG. On the other hand, Judge Posner's opinion fits nicely into a syllogism: The CISG deals with the substantive law of contracts not procedure. Attorney fees are a matter of procedure not substance. Therefore, the CISG does not authorize the recovery of attorney fees. Are you persuaded by the Seventh Circuit's reasoning? Does the court offer enough actual drafting history of the treaty to support its conclusion? For favorable commentary on this aspect of the Seventh Circuit opinion, see Harry Flechtner & Joseph Lookofsky, Viva Zapata! American Procedure and CISG Substance in a U.S. Circuit Court of Appeal, 7 Vindobona J. Int'l Com. L. & Arb. 93 (2003). See also Harry M. Flechtner, Recovering Attorneys' Fees as Damages under the U.N. Sales Convention (CISG): The Role of Case Law in the New International Commercial Practice, with Comments on Zapata Hermanos v. Hearthside Baking, 22 Nw. J. Int'l L. & Bus. 121 (2002) (praising the effort of the *Zapata* trial court to take international practice into account but concluding that the trial court misinterpreted Article 74 as supporting an award of attorney fees).

2. *Statutory exceptions for attorney fees, including the UCC.* As noted above, attorney fees may be awarded when a statute specifically provides for such recovery. Numerous federal statutes, covering the entire range of economic activity — consumer protection, civil rights, environmental protection, employment law, and securities regulation, to name just a few — authorize courts to grant attorney fees. Statutes are collected in 3 Mary Francis Derfner & Arthur D. Wolf, Court Awarded Attorney Fees (Shirey rev. 2001). Similarly, at the state level, a variety of statutes provide for recovery of attorney fees. E.g., Cal. Civ. Code §86 (West 1982) (Fair Dealership Law); N.Y. Gen. Bus. Law §691 (McKinney 1996) (Franchise Law); S.C. Code Ann. §39-5-140 (Law. Coop. 1976) (Unfair Trade Practices Act).

While the transaction in *Zapata* came under the CISG, a sale of goods between two American companies would be governed by the UCC. It has been occasionally contended that the UCC provides for or at least permits the award of attorney fees to a victorious plaintiff, either as incidental or consequential damages. UCC §§2-710, 2-715. Such claims have usually been unsuccessful. The courts have indicated that a clearer legislative statement is needed to overcome the presumption in favor of the American rule. See, e.g., Indiana Glass Co. v. Indiana Michigan Power Co., 692 N.E.2d 886 (Ind. Ct. App. 1998); James J. White & Robert S. Summers, Uniform Commercial Code §7-16, at 300 n.7 (5th ed. 2000); contra Cady v. Dick Loehr's, Inc., 299 N.W.2d 69 (Mich. Ct. App. 1980).

3. *Court rules as basis for attorney fees.* In addition to the statutory provisions discussed in the previous note, court rules may also allow the recovery of attorney fees. The Federal Rules of Civil Procedure, which constitute the model for most state procedural systems, contain a number of provisions allowing courts to award attorney fees against an attorney or party who engages in improper litigation conduct. Probably the best known of these is Rule 11 of the Federal Rules of Civil Procedure. Rule 11 provides, essentially, that by presenting a pleading, written motion, or paper to a court, an attorney or unrepresented party is certifying "to the best of the person's knowledge,

information, and belief" that the litigation is not being presented for any improper purpose, that the claims and legal contentions are not frivolous and supported by the available evidence, and that any denials of factual contentions are warranted. Similar to Rule 11, a federal statute, 28 U.S.C. §1927, provides for sanctions against an attorney who "multiplies the proceedings in any case unreasonably and vexatiously." As an alternative basis for awarding attorney fees, the trial court in *Zapata* relied on 28 U.S.C. §1927 and Chambers v. NASCO, Inc., 501 U.S. 32 (1991), a Supreme Court decision that established that federal courts have inherent power to impose sanctions for bad faith conduct in specific situations. See also EIU Group, Inc., v. Citibank Delaware, Inc., 429 F. Supp. 2d 367 (D. Mass. 2006) (providing extensive history of American rule on attorney fees and bad faith exception under federal law). States courts have reached a similar conclusion. See, e.g., Maris v. McGrath, 850 A.2d 133 (Conn. 2004) (state courts have inherent authority to impose attorney fees as sanction for dilatory, bad faith, and harassing litigation even in absence of violation of a specific rule or order).

Apart from the question of CISG interpretation, the Seventh Circuit held that the trial court also erred in awarding attorney fees to sanction bad faith or vexatious conduct by the defendant. The Seventh Circuit concluded that a federal court's inherent authority to award fees is limited to conduct occurring during the course of the litigation and not covered by other rules of procedure or statutes. In its opinion, the Seventh Circuit cited *Chambers*, but not as being relevant to this particular issue. In the *Chambers* case, petitioner Chambers agreed to sell his television station and broadcast license to NASCO, but then changed his mind. NASCO sued for specific performance of the contract. Both before and after the lawsuit was filed Chambers engaged in a series of actions — in court, outside of court, and in collateral proceedings — designed to prevent the sale from going forward. The district court in *Chambers* imposed sanctions in the amount of $1 million, NASCO's litigation costs in the matter, based on its inherent authority, because it concluded that much of Chambers's conduct was not covered by either rule or statute. The U.S. Supreme Court affirmed the award of sanctions in a 5-4 decision, holding that federal courts have inherent authority to award sanctions for litigation abuse, including fraud, even when the conduct occurs outside the courtroom and is not sanctionable under rules of procedure or statutory law. Is the Seventh Circuit's decision in *Zapata* consistent with *Chambers*?

4. *Contract terms as basis for attorney fees.* Since a principal policy of contract law is to enforce the reasonable expectations created by the contract, it would appear that where the contract at issue expressly provides for an award of attorney fees to the prevailing party in a dispute, the court should enforce that promise. See, e.g., Sholkoff v. Boca Raton Community Hospital, Inc., 693 So. 2d 1114 (Fla. Dist. Ct. App. 1997) (agreement to pay attorney fees must unambiguously state intention and clearly identify matter to which clause applies); Parks v. MBNA America Bank, 204 S.W.3d 305 (Mo. Ct. App. 2006) (where contract provides for attorney fees for prevailing party, it is error not to enforce). But see Vermeer of Southern Ohio, Inc., v. Argo Construction Co., Inc., 760 N.E.2d 1, 5-6 (Ohio Ct. App. 2001) (general rule under Ohio law is that a contract provision permitting recovery of attorney fees is unenforceable as against public policy, but courts have carved out an

exception when the agreement to pay fees comes from a "free and understanding negotiation" between "parties of equal bargaining power and similar sophistication"). See generally 1 Mary Francis Derfner & Arthur D. Wolf, Court Awarded Attorney Fees §6.02 (Shirey rev. 2001). In a notable combination of the statutory and contract exceptions, California has enacted legislation which provides that if a contract grants attorney fees to one party, the agreement will be applied to also allow attorney fees for the other party if it should prevail in litigation. See Cal. Civ. Code §1717(a).

5. *Attorney fees available in other situations.* While contract provision, statutory mandate, and court rule constitute the three major exceptions to the American rule, some courts have recognized other exceptions. When the defendant's breach of contract causes the plaintiff to engage in "collateral litigation," the plaintiff may recover as consequential damage for breach of the principal contract the attorney fees incurred in the collateral litigation. The American rule only bars recovery of the litigation expenses in the case against the defendant. See, e.g., Carlund Corp. v. Crown Center Redevelopment Corp., 910 S.W.2d 273 (Mo. Ct. App. 1995) (subcontractor may recover from contractor legal fees incurred by subcontractor in collateral litigation with subsubcontractor caused by contractor's breach of contract); see also Double Oak Construction, L.L.C. v. Cornerstone Development International, L.L.C., 97 P.3d 140 (Colo. Ct. App. 2003) (court distinguishes between legal fees that are "damages" resulting from the breach and legal fees that are the "cost" of the litigation). Can you offer any justification for this distinction?

In some states courts have allowed an insured who incurs attorney fees in forcing an insurance company to honor its contractual obligations to recover these expenses. These courts usually rely on the special relationship that exists between insurer and insured. Compare Preferred Mutual Insurance Co. v. Gamache, 686 N.E.2d 989 (Mass. 1997) (attorney fees incurred by insured in obtaining declaratory judgment that insured had coverage under homeowners policy were recoverable), with Bernhard v. Farmers Insurance Exchange, 915 P.2d 1285 (Colo. 1996) (en banc) (attorney fees incurred in securing judgment against insurer for bad faith breach of insurance contract not recoverable in absence of contractual provision).

6. *Justifications and criticisms of the American rule.* The American rule denying recovery of attorney fees has usually been defended on the basis of access to the court system and the burden on judicial administration:

> [S]ince litigation is at best uncertain one should not be penalized for merely defending or prosecuting a lawsuit, and . . . the poor might be unjustly discouraged from instituting actions to vindicate their rights if the penalty for losing included the fees of their opponents' counsel. . . . Also, the time, expense, and difficulties of proof inherent in litigating the question of what constitutes reasonable attorney's fees would pose substantial burdens for judicial administration.

Fleischmann Distilling Corp. v. Maier Brewing Co., 386 U.S. 714, 718 (1967). The American rule has been subject to extensive criticism, however. Among other arguments, opponents claim that the rule fails to provide full compensation for the prevailing party and prevents the assertion of meritorious small claims. See W. Kent Davis, The International View of

Attorney Fees in Civil Suits: Why Is the United States the "Odd Man Out" in How It Pays Its Lawyers?, 16 Ariz. J. Intl. & Comp. L. 361 (1999). Moreover, critics point out that the failure to require the loser to pay attorney fees for the other side may actually encourage frivolous litigation by parties who realize they have little chance of winning. See Jonathan Fischbach & Michael Fischbach, Rethinking Optimality in Tort Litigation: The Promise of Reverse Cost-Shifting, 19 BYU J. Pub. L. 317 (2005).

As discussed above, the American rule is subject to numerous exceptions, but it nonetheless remains applicable in the garden variety breach of contract or tort case. Whatever the merits of the rule, it is clear that in practice it deprives the successful plaintiff in an ordinary breach of contract action of full expectation damages, as the cost of litigation will not be reimbursed. Of course, the winning plaintiff in a tort case also may have to pay a substantial fraction of her damage recovery to her attorney (who was probably employed on a contingent fee basis), but it seems likely that the jury when it fixes damages in a tort case often takes that factor into account and increases the plaintiff's recovery for such intangibles as "pain and suffering." The damage rules of contract law, however, are not so susceptible to manipulation in this respect; a damage award couched in pure expectation terms is unlikely to make provision (directly or indirectly) for attorney fees unless one of the exceptions to the American rule applies.

7. *Ethical obligations of lawyers regarding litigation.* Lawyers who engage in improper litigation tactics may be subject to professional discipline as well as sanctions under the rules of civil procedure. Rule 3.1 of the American Bar Association's Model Rules of Professional Ethics states that a "lawyer shall not bring or defend a proceeding, or assert or controvert an issue therein, unless there is a basis in law and fact for doing so that is not frivolous, which includes a good faith argument for an extension, modification or reversal of existing law." Rule 3.2 requires lawyers to "make reasonable efforts to expedite litigation consistent with the interests of the client." Rule 3.4(d) states that a lawyer shall not "in pretrial procedure, make a frivolous discovery request or fail to make reasonably diligent effort to comply with a legally proper discovery request by an opposing party." Rule 4.4(a) provides that in "representing a client, a lawyer shall not use means that have no substantial purpose other than to embarrass, delay, or burden a third person, or use methods of obtaining evidence that violate the legal rights of such a person." See generally Nathan M. Crystal, Limitations on Zealous Representation in an Adversarial System, 32 Wake Forest L. Rev. 671 (1997).

Erlich v. Menezes
Supreme Court Of California
21 Cal.4th 543, 981 P.2d 978, 87 Cal.Rptr.2d 886 (1999)

BROWN, J.

We granted review in this case to determine whether emotional distress damages are recoverable for the negligent breach of a contract to construct a house. A jury awarded the homeowners the full cost necessary to repair their home as well as damages for emotional distress caused by the contractor's negligent performance. Since the contractor's negligence directly caused only economic injury and property damage, and breached no duty independent of the contract, we conclude the homeowners may not recover damages for emotional distress based upon breach of a contract to build a house.

I. FACTUAL AND PROCEDURAL BACKGROUND

Both parties agree with the facts as ascertained by the Court of Appeal. Barry and Sandra Erlich contracted with John Menezes, a licensed general contractor, to build a "dreamhouse" on their ocean-view lot. The Erlichs moved into their house in December 1990. In February 1991, the rains came. "[T]he house leaked from every conceivable location. Walls were saturated in [an upstairs bedroom], two bedrooms downstairs, and the pool room. Nearly every window in the house leaked. The living room filled with three inches of standing water. In several locations water 'poured in [ ] streams' from the ceilings and walls. The ceiling in the garage became so saturated . . . the plaster liquefied and fell in chunks to the floor."

Menezes's attempts to stop the leaks proved ineffectual. Caulking placed around the windows melted, "'ran down [the] windows and stained them and ran across the driveway and ran down the house [until it] . . . looked like someone threw balloons with paint in them at the house.'" Despite several repair efforts, which included using sledgehammers and jackhammers to cut holes in the exterior walls and ceilings, application of new waterproofing materials on portions of the roof and exterior walls, and more caulk, the house continued to leak—from the windows, from the roofs, and water seeped between the floors. Fluorescent light fixtures in the garage filled with water and had to be removed.

"The Erlichs eventually had their home inspected by another general contractor and a structural engineer. In addition to confirming defects in the roof, exterior stucco, windows and waterproofing, the inspection revealed serious errors in the construction of the home's structural components. None of the 20 shear, or load-bearing walls specified in the plans were properly installed. The three turrets on the roof were inadequately connected to the roof beams and, as a result, had begun to collapse. Other connections in the roof framing were also improperly constructed. Three decks were in danger of 'catastrophic collapse' because they had been finished with mortar and ceramic tile, rather than with the light-weight roofing material originally specified. Finally, the foundation of the main beam for the two-story living room was poured by digging a shallow hole, dumping in 'two sacks of dry concrete mix, putting some water in the hole and mixing it up with a shovel.'" This foundation, required to carry a load of 12,000 pounds, could only support about 2,000. The beam is settling and the surrounding concrete is cracking.

According to the Erlichs' expert, problems were major and pervasive, concerning everything "related to a window or waterproofing, everywhere that there was something related to framing," stucco, or the walking deck.

Both of the Erlichs testified that they suffered emotional distress as a result of the defective condition of the house and Menezes's invasive and unsuccessful repair attempts. Barry Erlich testified he felt "absolutely sick" and had to be "carted away in an ambulance" when he learned the full extent of the structural problems. He has a permanent heart condition, known as superventricular tachyarrhythmia, attributable, in part, to excessive stress. Although the condition can be controlled with medication, it has forced him to resign his positions as athletic director, department head and track coach.

Sandra Erlich feared the house would collapse in an earthquake and feared for her daughter's safety. Stickers were placed on her bedroom windows, and alarms and emergency lights installed so rescue crews would find her room first in an emergency.

Plaintiffs sought recovery on several theories, including breach of contract, fraud, negligent misrepresentation, and negligent construction. Both the breach of contract claim and the negligence claim alleged numerous construction defects.

Menezes prevailed on the fraud and negligent misrepresentation claims. The jury found he breached his contract with the Erlichs by negligently constructing their home and awarded $406,700 as the cost of repairs. Each spouse was awarded $50,000 for emotional distress, and Barry Erlich received an additional $50,000 for physical pain and suffering and $15,000 for lost earnings.

By a two-to-one majority, the Court of Appeal affirmed the judgment, including the emotional distress award. The majority noted the breach of a contractual duty may support an action in tort. The jury found Menezes was negligent. Since his negligence exposed the Erlichs to "intolerable living conditions and a constant, justifiable fear about the safety of their home," the majority decided the Erlichs were properly compensated for their emotional distress.

The dissent pointed out that no reported California case has upheld an award of emotional distress damages based upon simple breach of a contract to build a house. Since Menezes's negligence directly caused only economic injury and property damage, the Erlichs were not entitled to recover damages for their emotional distress.

We granted review to resolve the question.

II. DISCUSSION

A. In an action for breach of contract, the measure of damages is "the amount which will compensate the party aggrieved for all the detriment proximately caused thereby, or which, in the ordinary course of things, would be likely to result therefrom" (Civ. Code, §3300), provided the damages are "clearly ascertainable in both their nature and origin" (Civ. Code, §3301). In an action not arising from contract, the measure of damages is "the amount which will compensate for all the detriment proximately caused thereby, whether it could have been anticipated or not" (Civ. Code, §3333).

"Contract damages are generally limited to those within the contemplation of the parties when the contract was entered into or at least reasonably foreseeable by them at that time; consequential damages beyond the expectation of the parties are not recoverable. [Citations.] This limitation on available damages serves to encourage contractual relations and commercial activity by enabling parties to estimate in advance the financial risks of their enterprise." (Applied Equipment Corp. v. Litton Saudi Arabia Ltd. (1994)

7 Cal.4th 503, 515, 28 Cal.Rptr.2d 475, 869 P.2d 454 *(Applied Equipment)*.) "In contrast, tort damages are awarded to [fully] compensate the victim for [all] injury suffered. [Citation.]" (Id. at p. 516, 28 Cal.Rptr.2d 475, 869 P.2d 454.)

"'[T]he distinction between tort and contract is well grounded in common law, and divergent objectives underlie the remedies created in the two areas. Whereas contract actions are created to enforce the intentions of the parties to the agreement, tort law is primarily designed to vindicate "social policy." [Citation.]'" (Hunter v. Up-Right, Inc. (1993) 6 Cal.4th 1174, 1180, 26 Cal. Rptr.2d 8, 864 P.2d 88, quoting Foley v. Interactive Data Corp. (1988) 47 Cal.3d 654, 683, 254 Cal.Rptr. 211, 765 P.2d 373 *(Foley)*.) While the purposes behind contract and tort law are distinct, the boundary line between them is not (Freeman & Mills, Inc. v. Belcher Oil Co. (1995) 11 Cal.4th 85, 106, 44 Cal.Rptr.2d 420, 900 P.2d 669 (conc. and dis. opn. of Mosk, J.) *(Freeman & Mills)*) and the distinction between the remedies for each is not "'found ready made.'" (Ibid., quoting Holmes, The Common Law (1881) p.13.) These uncertain boundaries and the apparent breadth of the recovery available for tort actions create pressure to obliterate the distinction between contracts and torts—an expansion of tort law at the expense of contract principles which Grant Gilmore aptly dubbed "con*torts*." In this case we consider whether a negligent breach of a contract will support an award of damages for emotional distress—either as tort damages for negligence or as consequential or special contract damages.

B. In concluding emotional distress damages were properly awarded, the Court of Appeal correctly observed that "the same wrongful act may constitute both a breach of contract and an invasion of an interest protected by the law of torts." . . . Here, the court permitted plaintiffs to recover both full repair costs as normal contract damages and emotional distress damages as a tort remedy.

The Court of Appeal also noted that "[a] contractual obligation may create a legal duty and the breach of that duty may support an action in tort." This is true; however, conduct amounting to a breach of contract becomes tortious only when it also violates a duty independent of the contract arising from principles of tort law. (*Applied Equipment,* supra, 7 Cal.4th at p. 515, 28 Cal.Rptr.2d 475, 869 P.2d 454.) "'"An omission to perform a contract obligation is never a tort, unless that omission is also an omission of a legal duty."'" (Ibid., quoting Jones v. Kelly (1929) 208 Cal. 251, 255, 280 P. 942.)

Tort damages have been permitted in contract cases where a breach of duty directly causes physical injury . . . ; for breach of the covenant of good faith and fair dealing in insurance contracts . . . ; for wrongful discharge in violation of fundamental public policy . . . ; or where the contract was fraudulently induced. . . . In each of these cases, the duty that gives rise to tort liability is either completely independent of the contract or arises from conduct which is both intentional and intended to harm. . . .

Plaintiff's theory of tort recovery is that mental distress is a foreseeable consequence of negligent breaches of standard commercial contracts. However, foreseeability alone is not sufficient to create an independent tort duty. "'Whether a defendant owes a duty of care is a question of law. Its existence depends upon the foreseeability of the risk and a weighing of policy considerations for and against imposition of liability.' [Citation.]" (Burgess v. Superior Court (1992) 2 Cal.4th 1064, 1072, 9 Cal.Rptr.2d 615, 831 P.2d

1197.) Because the consequences of a negligent act must be limited to avoid an intolerable burden on society . . . , the determination of duty "recognizes that policy considerations may dictate a cause of action should not be sanctioned no matter how foreseeable the risk." . . . "[T]here are clear judicial days on which a court can foresee forever and thus determine liability but none on which that foresight alone provides a socially and judicially acceptable limit on recovery of damages for [an] injury." (Thing v. La Chusa (1989) 48 Cal.3d 644, 668, 257 Cal.Rptr. 865, 771 P.2d 814.) In short, foreseeability is not synonymous with duty; nor is it a substitute.

The question thus remains: is the mere negligent breach of a contract sufficient? The answer is no. It may admittedly be difficult to categorize the cases, but to state the rule succinctly: "[C]ourts will generally enforce the breach of a contractual promise through contract law, except when the actions that constitute the breach violate a social policy that merits the imposition of tort remedies." (*Freeman & Mills,* supra, 11 Cal.4th at p. 107, 44 Cal.Rptr.2d 420, 900 P.2d 669 (conc. and dis. opn. of Mosk, J.).) The familiar paradigm of tortious breach of contract in this state is the insurance contract. There we relied on the covenant of good faith and fair dealing, implied in every contract, to justify tort liability. . . . In holding that a tort action is available for breach of the covenant in an insurance contract, we have "emphasized the 'special relationship' between insurer and insured, characterized by elements of public interest, adhesion, and fiduciary responsibility." (*Freeman & Mills,* supra, 11 Cal.4th at p. 91, 44 Cal.Rptr.2d 420, 900 P.2d 669. . . .)

The special relationship test, which has been criticized as illusory and not sufficiently precise . . . has little relevance to the question before us. Menezes is in the business of building single-family homes. He is one among thousands of contractors who provide the same service, and the Erlichs could take their choice among any contractors willing to accept work in the area where their home would be constructed. Although they undoubtedly relied on his claimed expertise, they were in a position to view, inspect, and criticize his work, or to hire someone who could. Most significantly, there is no indication Menezes sought to frustrate the Erlichs' enjoyment of contracted-for benefits. He did build a house. His ineptitude led to numerous problems which he attempted to correct. And he remains ultimately responsible for reimbursing the cost of doing the job properly.

Moreover, since, as *Foley* noted, the insurance cases represented "a major departure from traditional principles of contract law," any claim for automatic extension of that exceptional approach whenever "certain hallmarks and similarities can be adduced in another contract setting" should be carefully considered. (*Foley,* supra, 47 Cal.3d at p. 690, 254 Cal.Rptr. 211, 765 P.2d 373.)

Our previous decisions detail the reasons for denying tort recovery in contract breach cases: the different objectives underlying tort and contract breach; the importance of predictability in assuring commercial stability in contractual dealings; the potential for converting every contract breach into a tort, with accompanying punitive damage recovery, and the preference for legislative action in affording appropriate remedies. . . . The same concerns support a cautious approach here. Restrictions on contract remedies serve to protect the "'freedom to bargain over special risks and [to] promote contract formation by limiting liability to the value of the promise.'" . . .

Generally, outside the insurance context, "a tortious breach of contract . . . may be found when (1) the breach is accompanied by a traditional common law tort, such as fraud or conversion; (2) the means used to breach the contract are tortious, involving deceit or undue coercion or; (3) one party intentionally breaches the contract intending or knowing that such a breach will cause severe, unmitigable harm in the form of mental anguish, personal hardship, or substantial consequential damages." (*Freeman & Mills,* supra, 11 Cal.4th at p. 105, 44 Cal.Rptr.2d 420, 900 P.2d 669 (conc. and dis. opn. of Mosk, J.).) Focusing on intentional conduct gives substance to the proposition that a breach of contract is tortious only when some independent duty arising from tort law is violated. . . . If every negligent breach of a contract gives rise to tort damages the limitation would be meaningless, as would the statutory distinction between tort and contract remedies.

In this case, the jury concluded Menezes did not act intentionally; nor was he guilty of fraud or misrepresentation. This is a claim for negligent breach of a contract, which is not sufficient to support tortious damages for violation of an independent tort duty.

It may ultimately be more useful, in attempting to develop a common law of tortious breach, to affirmatively identify specific practices utilized by contracting parties that merit the imposition of tort remedies (*Freeman & Mills,* supra, 11 Cal.4th at p. 107, 44 Cal.Rptr.2d 420, 900 P.2d 669 (conc. and dis. opn. of Mosk, J.)) instead of comparing each new claim to a template for exceptions. In the interim, however, it is sufficient to note that more than mere negligence has been involved in each case where tort damages have been permitted. The benefits of broad compensation must be balanced against the burdens on commercial stability. "[C]ourts should be careful to apply tort remedies only when the conduct in question is so clear in its deviation from socially useful business practices that the effect of enforcing such tort duties will be . . . to aid rather than discourage commerce." (*Freeman & Mills,* supra, 11 Cal.4th at p. 109, 44 Cal.Rptr.2d 420, 900 P.2d 669 (conc. and dis. opn. of Mosk, J.).)

C. Even assuming Menezes's negligence constituted a sufficient independent duty to the Erlichs, such a finding would not entitle them to emotional distress damages on these facts. "The fact that emotional distress damages may be awarded in some circumstances (see Rest.2d Torts, §905, pp. 456-457) does not mean they are available in every case in which there is an independent cause of action founded upon negligence." (Merenda v. Superior Court (1992) 3 Cal.App.4th 1, 7, 4 Cal.Rptr.2d 87 (*Merenda*).) "No California case has allowed recovery for emotional distress arising solely out of property damage" (Cooper v. Superior Court (1984) 153 Cal.App.3d 1008, 1012, 200 Cal.Rptr. 746); moreover, a preexisting contractual relationship, without more, will not support a recovery for mental suffering where the defendant's tortious conduct has resulted only in economic injury to the plaintiff. . . .

[The court then discussed with approval two decisions of the California Court of Appeals denying recovery for emotional distress damages to clients who had been injured by their attorneys' negligence. One case involved litigation; the other dealt with tax planning. The court of appeals concluded in both cases that damages for emotional distress could not be recovered because the harm flowed from inherently economic activity. — EDS.]

In Lubner v. City of Los Angeles (1996) 45 Cal.App.4th 525, 53 Cal. Rptr.2d 24, two artists lost a substantial portion of their life's work when a city trash truck, which had been parked on a hilltop, rolled down and crashed into their home, damaging the house, two cars, and much of their artwork. The Lubners filed a negligence action and sought damages for their emotional distress. Recognizing that the artwork may have been extremely important to the Lubners, the court nevertheless found they were not entitled to recover for emotional distress caused by injury to property. (Id. at p. 532, 53 Cal. Rptr.2d 24.) The court based its ruling primarily on the absence of a preexisting relationship between the parties, but separately considered whether the defendant breached a duty of care to the plaintiffs. Noting that the moral blame on the defendant was only that which attends ordinary negligence and nothing in the record indicated bad faith or reckless indifference to the Lubners' emotional tranquillity, the court concluded liability for negligent infliction of emotional distress was unwarranted. (Id. at p. 534, 53 Cal.Rptr.2d 24.)

Public policy supports a similar limit where the negligence concerns the construction of a home. In Blagrove v. J.B. Mechanical, Inc. (Wyo.1997) 934 P.2d 1273 (*Blagrove*), the homeowners sued a plumbing contractor to recover damages for mental anguish caused when flooding from a faulty plumbing connection damaged their home and destroyed personal possessions. The Wyoming Supreme Court held that, absent physical injury, emotional distress damages can be recovered only in limited circumstances involving intentional torts, constitutional violations, and the breach of the covenant of good faith and fair dealing in insurance contracts, and concluded a contrary rule would be poor public policy.

. . .

Here, the breach — the negligent construction of the Erlichs' house — did not cause physical injury. No one was hit by a falling beam. Although the Erlichs state they feared the house was structurally unsafe and might collapse in an earthquake, they lived in it for five years. The only physical injury alleged is Barry Erlich's heart disease, which flowed from the emotional distress and not directly from the negligent construction.

The Erlichs may have hoped to build their dream home and live happily ever after, but there is a reason that tag line belongs only in fairy tales. Building a house may turn out to be a stress-free project; it is much more likely to be the stuff of urban legends — the cause of bankruptcy, marital dissolution, hypertension and fleeting fantasies ranging from homicide to suicide. As Justice Yegan noted below, "No reasonable homeowner can embark on a building project with certainty that the project will be completed to perfection. Indeed, errors are so likely to occur that few if any homeowners would be justified in resting their peace of mind on [its] timely or correct completion. . . ." The connection between the service sought and the aggravation and distress resulting from incompetence may be somewhat less tenuous than in a malpractice case, but the emotional suffering still derives from an inherently economic concern.

D. Having concluded tort damages are not available, we finally consider whether damages for emotional distress should be included as consequential or special damages in a contract claim. "Contract damages are generally limited to those within the contemplation of the parties when the contract was entered into or at least reasonably foreseeable by them at the time; consequential damages beyond the expectations of the parties are not recoverable. [Citations.] This limitation on available damages serves to encourage contractual relations and commercial activity by enabling parties to estimate in advance the financial risks of their enterprise." (*Applied Equipment,* supra, 7 Cal.4th at p. 515, 28 Cal.Rptr.2d 475, 869 P.2d 454.)

"'[W]hen two parties make a contract, they agree upon the rules and regulations which will govern their relationship; the risks inherent in the agreement and the likelihood of its breach. The parties to the contract in essence create a mini-universe for themselves, in which each voluntarily chooses his contracting partner, each trusts the other's willingness to keep his word and honor his commitments, and in which they define their respective obligations, rewards and risks. Under such a scenario, it is appropriate to enforce only such obligations as each party voluntarily assumed, and to give him only such benefits as he expected to receive; this is the function of contract law.'" (*Applied Equipment,* supra, 7 Cal.4th at p. 517, 28 Cal.Rptr.2d 475, 869 P.2d 454.)

Accordingly, damages for mental suffering and emotional distress are generally not recoverable in an action for breach of an ordinary commercial contract in California. (Kwan v. Mercedes-Benz of North America, Inc. (1994) 23 Cal.App.4th 174, 188, 28 Cal.Rptr.2d 371) (*Kwan*). . . . "Recovery for emotional disturbance will be excluded unless the breach also caused bodily harm or the contract or the breach is of such a kind that serious emotional disturbance was a particularly likely result." (Rest.2d Contracts, §353.) The Restatement specifically notes the breach of a contract to build a home is not "particularly likely" to result in "serious emotional disturbance." (Ibid.)

Cases permitting recovery for emotional distress typically involve mental anguish stemming from more personal undertakings the traumatic results of which were unavoidable. (See, e.g., Burgess v. Superior Court, supra, 2 Cal.4th 1064, 9 Cal.Rptr.2d 615, 831 P.2d 1197 [infant injured during childbirth]; Molien v. Kaiser Foundation Hospitals (1980) 27 Cal.3d 916, 167 Cal.Rptr. 831, 616 P.2d 813 [misdiagnosed venereal disease and subsequent failure of marriage]; Kately v. Wilkinson (1983) 148 Cal.App.3d 576, 195 Cal.Rptr. 902 [fatal waterskiing accident]; Chelini v. Nieri (1948) 32 Cal.2d 480, 196 P.2d 915 [failure to adequately preserve a corpse].) Thus, when the express object of the contract is the mental and emotional well-being of one of the contracting parties, the breach of the contract may give rise to damages for mental suffering or emotional distress. (See Wynn v. Monterey Club (1980) 111 Cal.App.3d 789, 799-801, 168 Cal.Rptr. 878 [agreement of two gambling clubs to exclude husband's gambling-addicted wife from clubs and not to cash her checks]; Ross v. Forest Lawn Memorial Park (1984) 153 Cal.App.3d 988, 992-996, 203 Cal.Rptr. 468 [cemetery's agreement to keep burial service private and to protect grave from vandalism]; Windeler v. Scheers Jewelers (1970) 8 Cal.App.3d 844, 851-852, 88 Cal.Rptr. 39 [bailment for heirloom jewelry where jewelry's great sentimental value was made known to bailee].)

Cases from other jurisdictions have formulated a similar rule, barring recovery of emotional distress damages for breach of contract except in cases involving contracts in which emotional concerns are the essence of the contract. (See, e.g., Hancock v. Northcutt (Alaska 1991) 808 P.2d 251, 258 ["contracts pertaining to one's dwelling are not among those contracts which, if breached, are particularly likely to result in serious emotional disturbance"; typical damages for breach of house construction contracts can appropriately be calculated in terms of monetary loss]. . . .

Plaintiffs argue strenuously that a broader notion of damages is appropriate when the contract is for the construction of a home. Amici curiae urge us to permit emotional distress damages in cases of negligent construction of a personal residence when the negligent construction causes gross interference with the normal use and habitability of the residence.

Such a rule would make the financial risks of construction agreements difficult to predict. Contract damages must be clearly ascertainable in both nature and origin. (Civ. Code, §3301.) A contracting party cannot be required to assume limitless responsibility for all consequences of a breach and must be advised of any special harm that might result in order to determine whether or not to accept the risk of contracting. . . .

Moreover, adding an emotional distress component to recovery for construction defects could increase the already prohibitively high cost of housing in California, affect the availability of insurance for builders, and greatly diminish the supply of affordable housing. The potential for such broad-ranging economic consequences — costs likely to be paid by the public generally — means the task of fashioning appropriate limits on the availability of emotional distress claims should be left to the Legislature. (See Tex. Prop. Code Ann. §27.001 et seq. (1999); Hawaii Rev. Stat. §663-8.9 (1998).)

Permitting damages for emotional distress on the theory that certain contracts carry a lot of emotional freight provides no useful guidance. Courts have carved out a narrow range of exceptions to the general rule of exclusion where emotional tranquillity is the contract's essence. Refusal to broaden the bases for recovery reflects a fundamental policy choice. A rule which focuses not on the risks contracting parties voluntarily assume but on one party's reaction to inadequate performance, cannot provide any principled limit on liability.

The discussion in *Kwan*, a case dealing with the breach of a sales contract for the purchase of a car, is instructive. "[A] contract for [the] sale of an automobile is not essentially tied to the buyer's mental or emotional well-being. Personal as the choice of a car may be, the central reason for buying one is usually transportation. . . . In spite of America's much-discussed 'love affair with the automobile,' disruption of an owner's relationship with his or her car is not, in the normal case, comparable to the loss or mistreatment of a family member's remains [citation], an invasion of one's privacy [citation], or the loss of one's spouse to a gambling addiction [citation]. In the latter situations, the contract exists primarily to further or protect emotional interests; the direct and foreseeable injuries resulting from a breach are also primarily emotional. In contrast, the undeniable aggravation, irritation and anxiety that may result from [the] breach of an automobile warranty are secondary effects deriving from the decreased usefulness of the car and the frequently frustrating process of having an automobile repaired. While [the] purchase of an automobile may sometimes lead to severe emotional distress, such a result is not ordinarily foreseeable from the nature of the contract." (*Kwan,* supra, 23 Cal.App.4th at p. 190, 28 Cal.Rptr.2d 371.)

Most other jurisdictions have reached the same conclusion. (See . . . City of Tyler v. Likes (Tex. 1997) 962 S.W.2d 489, 497 [mental anguish based solely on property damage is not compensable as a matter of law].)

We agree. The available damages for defective construction are limited to the cost of repairing the home, including lost use or relocation expenses, or the diminution in value. . . . The Erlichs received more than $400,000 in traditional contract damages to correct the defects in their home. While their distress was undoubtedly real and serious, we conclude the balance of policy considerations—the potential for significant increases in liability in amounts disproportionate to culpability, the court's inability to formulate appropriate limits on the availability of claims, and the magnitude of the impact on stability and predictability in commercial affairs—counsel against expanding contract damages to include mental distress claims in negligent construction cases.

DISPOSITION

The judgment of the Court of Appeal is reversed and the matter is remanded for further proceedings consistent with this opinion. . . .

Notes and Questions

1. *Amicus Curiae. Erlich* was a significant case not only for the parties but also for builders, insurance companies, and consumer advocates. The case attracted *amicus curiae* briefs from, among others: the American Insurance Association, the National Association of Independent Insurers, the Association for California Tort Reform, the Building Industry Legal Defense Foundation, the California Building Industry Association, and Consumer Attorneys of California. Do you think the case would have been decided differently if there had been no amicus briefs for the court to consider?

2. *Scope of court's holding on tort liability.* In part II(B) of the opinion, the court holds that negligent breach of a contract is not sufficient to justify recovery of damages for emotional distress. Do you agree that negligent performance of a residential construction contract should never be sufficient to justify an award of damages for emotional distress? Consider Restatement (Second) of Torts §§436 and 436A, which deal with negligent infliction of emotional distress. Under these sections an actor who is negligent is liable for damages for emotional distress if the distress is accompanied by bodily harm or other compensable damage but is not liable if the negligence produces only emotional distress.

Suppose a builder's breach goes beyond ordinary negligence to gross negligence or recklessness. Would a higher level of negligence support a recovery of damages for emotional distress? Consider Restatement (Second) of Torts §46, which provides as follows:

One who by extreme and outrageous conduct intentionally or recklessly causes severe emotional distress to another is subject to liability for such emotional distress, and if bodily harm to the other results from it, for such bodily harm.

Cf. Robinson Helicopter Co., Inc. v. Dana Corp., 102 P.2d 268 (Cal. 2004) (tort damages would be available when seller breached contract by intentionally providing false certificates of conformance for helicopter parts; fraud is a tort independent of contract breach). Would you characterize Menezes's breach of contract as merely negligent or does it rise to a higher level?

3. *Mitigation of damages.* In part II(C) of the opinion, the court makes the following point: "Although the Erlichs state they feared the house was structurally unsafe and might collapse in an earthquake, they lived in it for five years." The court seems to be suggesting that the Erlichs could have avoided emotional distress by moving out of the house. Should the Erlichs have moved out? Consider the following background information:

> Why didn't they move out, rather than remaining in perpetual fear for their safety, and if the house was in imminent danger of collapse? The simple reality was that the Erlichs could not afford to mitigate their damages, even though they might properly have recovered the expenses incurred for doing so. (Respondent's Brief at 14; (R.T. 478-479). It was a practical impossibility for them to achieve real mitigation, because they were effectively trapped in their nightmare home.
>
> The Erlichs had taken out a loan from the San Luis Obispo School District Credit Union for $300,000 to pay for the $258,000 house construction and for the separate contract to build a swimming pool. The land itself was still encumbered by a $300,000 loan.

Ronnie Wagner, Sand Castles: A Case Study of *Erlich v. Menezes* 22 (unpublished student paper on file with Professor Knapp).

4. *Contract cases in which damages for emotional distress may be recovered.* In part II(D), the court cites Restatement (Second) §353 as identifying two types of cases in which damages for emotional distress may be recovered in an action for breach of contract. In the first type of case, the breach of contract also causes bodily harm. E.g., Sullivan v. O'Connor, 296 N.E.2d 183 (Mass. 1973) (breach of contract action against surgeon who had promised to enhance appearance of plaintiff's nose; damages for emotional distress recoverable when operation disfigured nose). In the second category of cases, emotional distress is a "particularly likely" consequence of the breach. Comment *a* to §353 sets forth certain types of contracts in which the courts have found emotional distress to be particularly likely: contracts of carriers and innkeepers with passengers and guests, contracts dealing with the carriage or disposition of dead bodies, and contracts for the delivery of messages concerning death. The court's opinion gives several other examples.

Outside of these established exceptions, numerous contract cases have denied such recovery even though the breach appears to have caused the plaintiff substantial emotional distress. See, e.g., Dunkin v. Boskey, 98 Cal. Rptr. 2d 44 (Ct. App. 2000) (contract between domestic partner and mother granting domestic partner paternity rights was enforceable, but as a matter of public policy domestic partner not entitled to recover damages for emotional distress resulting from loss of relationship with child under either contract or tort theory); St. Charles v. Kender, 646 N.E.2d 411 (Mass. App. Ct. 1995) (damages for emotional distress may not be recovered from physician who breached contract with patient by not returning telephone calls for two days while patient was having miscarriage).

5. *Restatement test.* As noted above, Restatement (Second) §353 suggests that unless bodily harm was also caused by the defendant's breach, recovery for emotional disturbance should be granted only where either the contract or the breach in question was "of such a kind that serious emotional disturbance was a particularly likely result." In Illustration 1 to §353, the drafters suggest that recovery for "nervousness and emotional distress" resulting from "delays and departures from specifications" in the building of a house should be denied, even where the defendant had notice that the plaintiff buyer was "in delicate health."

In Brooks v. Hickman, 570 F. Supp. 619, 620 (W.D. Pa. 1983), plaintiff sought damages for emotional distress resulting from the defendant's breach of its contract to provide investment management services, causing loss of the plaintiff's savings. In denying recovery, the District Court observed:

> Plaintiffs argue that emotional distress was a particularly likely result of a breach in this case because plaintiffs sought to build a nest egg for retirement, and defendants were aware of this goal. The instant case is simply not of the same class as the cases cited above. The plaintiffs have not suffered disfigurement, anxiety over death or the birth of an unwanted, crippled child. They have only lost money, and not so much of it as to force personal bankruptcy or impoverishment. See, Restatement (Second) of Contracts, §353, comment. Although loss of money is often disturbing, it does not ordinarily give rise to a claim of emotional distress. We find no Pennsylvania decision permitting recovery of such damages on breach of a contract which caused only a monetary loss, and we hesitate to so extend the rule. Furthermore, even if recovery for emotional distress on such a breach is permitted as intimated in the Comment to §353, the plaintiffs have not alleged such an extreme loss from the breach, and while loss of a nest egg may cause anxiety, it does not appear particularly likely to cause *serious* emotional distress.

What test does the *Erlich* court use to determine when contract damages for emotional distress may be awarded? How does this test compare to the one in the Restatement?

6. *Scholarly commentary.* Commentators have generally favored liberalization of the rules dealing with recovery of damages for emotional distress in actions for breach of contract. See, e.g., Ronnie Cohen & Shannon O'Byrne, Cry Me a River: Recovery of Mental Distress Damages in a Breach of Contract Action — A North American Perspective, 42 Am. Bus. L. J. 97 (2005) (reviewing U.S. and Canadian reluctance to award mental distress damages for breach of contract and asserting the approach fails to recognize that many contracts contain promise of nonpecuniary benefit); Charlotte K. Goldberg, Emotional Distress Damages and Breach of Contract: A New Approach, 20 U. C. Davis L. Rev. 57 (1986) (recovery should be allowed when contract involves emotional subjects, but not when it is purely profit-making).

Scholars who employ principles of economic analysis have also argued that the rule denying recovery of damages for emotional distress is unsound because it allows a breaching party to avoid the full costs of his breach and thus produces "inefficient breach." (The concept of "efficient breach" is examined in section F of this chapter.) E.g., John A. Sebert, Jr., Punitive and Non-pecuniary Damages in Actions Based upon Contract: Toward Achieving the Objective of Full Compensation, 33 UCLA L. Rev. 1565 (1986). See also Samuel A. Rea, Jr., Nonpecuniary Loss and Breach of Contract, 11 J. Legal Stud. 35 (1982).

Comment: Recovery of Punitive Damages for Bad Faith Breach of Contract

In *Erlich* the California Supreme Court concluded that damages for emotional distress should not be awarded to compensate for a negligent breach of contract under either a tort or a contract theory of recovery. The relationship between tort and contract law also arises with regard to the possible recovery of punitive damages.

In a tort action, an injured party may recover punitive damages in addition to actual damages when the wrongdoer's conduct is "outrageous, because of the defendant's evil motive or his reckless indifference to the rights of others." Restatement (Second) of Torts §908(2). Punitive damages are generally not available, however, for an ordinary breach of contract. Restatement (Second) of Contracts §355 states: "Punitive damages are not recoverable for a breach of contract unless the conduct constituting the breach is also a tort for which punitive damages are recoverable."

Why should punitive, or exemplary, damages be available in tort actions, but not for breach of contract? The standard answer is twofold: First, the damage remedies available in contract are only such as will compensate the plaintiff for harm actually caused and should not put the injured party in a better position than she would have occupied if the contract had been performed. Second, contract law is a system founded not on "fault" but on "strict liability" for the consequences of breach; since culpability plays no part in determining liability it should also play no part in fashioning the remedy. See E. Allan Farnsworth, Contracts §12.8, at 760-761 (4th ed. 2004). To these observations, many modern commentators would add a third: Contract remedies (like the law of contract in general) should promote "efficiency," and therefore should deter only "inefficient" breaches of contract; punitive damage awards (or, for that matter, any award of more than pure "expectation" damages) could deter even "efficient" breaches, which ought rather to be encouraged. See id. §12.3, at 736. We return to this notion of "efficient breach" in the final section of this chapter.

One of the major exceptions to the principle that punitive damages are not recoverable for breach of contract involves insurance contracts. Courts around the country have held insurance companies liable in tort to their insureds for bad faith refusal to honor claims brought by third parties. Automobile accidents are common examples of occurrences that generate third party claims. Companies have been held liable not only for amount of dishonored claims but also for punitive damages. Many courts have extended liability to cases where insurers failed to act in good faith in refusing to pay claims brought by the insured (known as "first party claims") rather than ones filed by third parties. A claim by an insured for fire damage under a homeowners policy is an example of a first party claim. See Douglas R. Richmond, An Overview of Insurance Bad Faith Law and Litigation, 25 Seton Hall L. Rev. 74, 80 n.33 (third party claims) and 104 n.170 (first party claims) (1994). See also Roger C. Henderson, The Tort of Bad Faith in First-Party Insurance Transactions After Two Decades, 37 Ariz. L. Rev. 1153, 1153-1154 (1995).

In justifying the imposition of tort liability on insurance companies, the courts have focused on several factors:

> The special nature of an insurance contract has been recognized by courts and legislatures for many years. A whole body of case and statutory law has been developed to regulate the relationship between insurer and insured. An insurance policy is not obtained for commercial advantage; it is obtained as protection against calamity. . . . In securing the reasonable expectations of the insured under the insurance policy there is usually an unequal bargaining position between the insured and the insurance company. . . . When the loss insured against occurs the insured expects to have the protection provided by his insurance. Often the insured is in an especially vulnerable economic position when such a casualty loss occurs. The whole purpose of insurance is defeated if an insurance company can refuse or fail, without justification, to pay a valid claim.

Noble v. National American Life Insurance Co., 624 P.2d 866, 867-868 (Ariz. 1981) (en banc). See also Giampapa v. American Family Mutual Insurance Co., 64 P.3d 230 (Colo. 2003) (in addition to coverage for loss, insured is paying for peace of mind and security); McEvoy v. Group Health Co-op. of Eau Claire, 570 N.W.2d 397 (Wis. 1997) (rationale of doctrine is to encourage fair treatment and penalize corrupt practices by insurers; court extends doctrine to HMOs as well as insurance companies).

Should liability for bad faith breach of contract be extended beyond insurance contracts to other agreements? In Seaman's Direct Buying Service, Inc. v. Standard Oil Co., 686 P.2d 1158 (Cal. 1984), the California Supreme Court agreed that in some situations bad faith breach of contract should be treated as a tort for which punitive damages could be recovered. While *Seaman's* was widely discussed by scholars and generated litigation in other states, few courts followed its holding. In fact, the California Supreme Court soon retreated from the decision. Four years later the Court limited the holding in *Seaman's,* declaring that it did not apply to employment contracts. See Foley v. Interactive Data Corp., 765 P.2d 373 (Cal. 1988) (en banc). Finally, in Freeman & Mills, Inc. v. Belcher Oil Co., 900 P.2d 669 (1995), the Court overruled *Seaman's* and held that recovery of punitive damages for bad faith breach of contract was limited to insurance contracts.

In his concurring and dissenting opinion in *Freeman & Mills,* Justice Mosk agreed that the holding in *Seaman's* was too broad, but he argued that recovery of punitive damages for breach of some contracts was appropriate:

> The majority would displace *Seaman's* with "a general rule precluding tort recovery for noninsurance contract breach, at least in the absence of violation of 'an independent duty arising from principles of tort law' [citation] other than the bad

faith denial of the existence of, or liability under, the breached contract." . . . I agree that the bad faith denial of the existence of a contract or contractual liability, *alone*, cannot give rise to tort liability. I agree as well with the tautological proposition that a breach of contract is made tortious only when some "independent duty arising from tort law" is violated.

In my view, however, this "independent duty arising from tort law" can originate from torts other than those traditionally recognized at common law. There are some types of intentionally tortious behavior unique to the contractual setting that do not fit into conventional tort categories. Allowing for the possibility of tort causes of action outside conventional categories is consistent with the malleable and continuously evolving nature of the tort law. . . .

. . . [A] tortious breach of contract outside the insurance context may be found when (1) the breach is accompanied by a traditional common law tort, such as fraud or conversion; (2) the means used to breach the contract are tortious, involving deceit or undue coercion or; (3) one party intentionally breaches the contract intending or knowing that such a breach will cause severe, unmitigatable harm in the form of mental anguish, personal hardship, or substantial consequential damages. . . .

. . . [P]ublic policy does not always favor a limitation on damages for *intentional* breaches of contract. The notion that society gains from an efficient breach must be qualified by the recognition that many intentional breaches are not efficient. . . .

In addition to fully compensating contract plaintiffs and discouraging inefficient breaches, the imposition of tort remedies for certain intentional breaches of contract serves to punish and deter business practices that constitute distinct social wrongs independent of the breach. . . .

. . . [T]he rationale for limiting actions for intentional breaches of contract to contract remedies — that such limitation promotes commercial stability and predictability and hence advances commerce — is not invariably a compelling one. Breaches accompanied by deception or infliction of intentional harm may be so disruptive of commerce and so reprehensible in themselves that the value of deterring such actions through the tort system outweighs the marginal loss in the predictability of damages that may result. . . .

In sum, . . . an intentional breach of contract may be found to be tortious when the breaching party exhibits an extreme disregard for the contractual rights of the other party, either knowingly harming the vital interests of a promisee so as to create substantial mental distress or personal hardship, or else employing coercion or dishonesty to cause the promisee to forego its contractual rights. These cases illustrate the recognition by a number of jurisdictions that an intentional breach of contract outside the insurance context, and not accompanied by any conventional tortious behavior such as promissory fraud, may nonetheless be deemed tortious when accompanied by these kinds of aggravating circumstances. . . . 900 P.2d at 681-687.

In *Freeman & Mills* the court referred to scholarly criticism of its decision in *Seaman's*. It is inaccurate, however, to conclude that scholars have rejected the fundamental point on which *Seaman's* rests — that tort liability is appropriate to deter some egregious breaches of contract. A number of commentators have argued that, as a matter of policy, liability for punitive damages should be imposed to deter some flagrant breaches of contract, and that such liability is fully consistent with the principle of economic efficiency. See e.g., Thomas A. Diamond, The Tort of Bad Faith Breach of Contract: When, if at All, Should It Be Extended Beyond Insurance Transactions?, 64 Marq. L. Rev. 425 (1981) (if tort is limited to those breaches that are economically inefficient, its recognition will promote contract theory);

A. Mitchell Polinsky & Steven Shavell, Punitive Damages: An Economic Analysis, 111 Harv. L. Rev. 869, 936-939 (1998) (punitive damages are appropriate in contract cases in which likelihood of escaping liability is substantial, either because breach is hidden or costs of enforcement too great).

In The Case for Punitive Damages in Contracts, 48 Duke L.J. 629 (1999), Professor William Dodge argues that economic efficiency supports a rule that allows punitive damages for any willful breach of contract. Professor Dodge divides willful breaches into two categories: opportunistic and efficient. An opportunistic breach involves an attempt by the breaching party to gain at the expense of the nonbreaching party, for example, by coercing a settlement because the breaching party knows that the other party cannot afford to litigate. An efficient breach occurs when the breaching party seeks to engage in another transaction that is more profitable than the existing contract. Professor Dodge agrees with a number of other commentators who have concluded that punitive damages should be awarded to deter opportunistic breaches because such breaches by definition do not increase social wealth. He goes further, however, and argues that punitive damages should be available even in cases of efficient breach because the imposition of punitive damages gives the breaching party an incentive to negotiate with the nonbreaching party to obtain a release from the contract. From an efficiency perspective, negotiation of a release is likely to involve fewer transaction costs than assessment of the nonbreaching party's damages through litigation. Negotiation of a release also forces the breaching party to share some of the efficiency gains from the new transaction with the nonbreaching party, rather than capturing all of those gains for itself.

While recovery of punitive damages for bad faith breach of a non-insurance contract is unlikely in almost all jurisdictions, it should be remembered that punitive damages can be recovered if the defendant's conduct goes beyond bad faith to amount to an independent tort for which punitive damages are recoverable. Cases that involve fraud or breach of fiduciary duty are likely candidates for such treatment. See, e.g., Formosa Plastics Corp. U.S.A. v. Presidio Engineers & Contractors, Inc., 960 S.W.2d 41 (Tex. 1998) (claim that one party fraudulently induced other party to enter into contract states cause of action in tort justifying award of punitive damages). See generally Timothy J. Sullivan, Punitive Damages in the Law of Contract: The Reality and the Illusion of Legal Change, 61 Minn. L. Rev. 207 (1977) (surveying cases in which defendant's conduct amounted to independent tort as well as breach of contract). For a review of the development of the law around the country regarding the award of punitive damages for breach of contract, see the article by Professor Dodge, discussed above.

PROBLEM 11-1

In 1975, Gordon and Amy Tan opened a drug store in the city of Newton. During the next 30 years, the Tans devoted themselves to developing their business and to raising their four children. In 2005, when their youngest child graduated from college, the Tans decided that it was time to sell their business, which had grown to 12 stores, and to retire. Through their lawyer,

Stewart Taylor, the Tans employed Miranda Evans, a business broker, to assist them in the sale of the business. The Tans and Evans entered into a brokerage contract in which the Tans agreed to pay Evans 5 percent of the sales price of their business as a commission. Under the terms of the contract, 25 percent of the commission was due when the contract was signed, with the balance payable at the closing of the sale.

In June 2006, Evans succeeded in finding a purchaser, Simpson's, Inc., a large regional chain of drug stores. On June 19, 2006, the parties signed a contract of sale in which Simpson's agreed to purchase the Tans' 12 stores for a price of $4.5 million. The contract provided for a closing on October 15, 2006. Simpson's paid an earnest money deposit to Taylor of $250,000. With the approval of the Tans and Simpson's, Taylor paid from this deposit $56,250 to Evans as payment of the commission due Evans, leaving a balance held by Taylor of $193,750.

On September 15, 2006, the Tans received a letter from Simpson's stating that as a result of its due diligence investigation of the Tans' business, it would no longer be in a position to go forward with the purchase of the Tans' stores. The Tans immediately consulted with Taylor and Evans about how to proceed. Evans suggested that she would investigate informally what had happened to cause Simpson's to change its plans. Taylor advised the Tans that they should write to Simpson's to put it on formal notice that the Tans would insist on their contract rights. They decided, however, to delay this letter for a few days pending the results of Evans's contacts.

A few days later Evans met with Taylor and the Tans. Evans informed them that she had learned that a dramatic restructuring of the retail drug industry was under way, with many existing companies and new entrants beginning to offer drugs over the Internet. Apparently, Simpson's had decided to follow this route and would be closing, rather than opening or acquiring, new retail outlets.

Taylor immediately wrote to Simpson's stating that Simpson's was bound contractually to purchase the Tans' stores, that the Tans insisted on strict compliance with the contract, and that the Tans were ready, willing, and able to proceed with the sale. He demanded that Simpson's proceed with the closing as scheduled. They received no response to this letter.

On October 15, the Tans and Taylor appeared at the closing, but no one appeared on behalf of Simpson's. Taylor immediately wrote to Simpson's informing it that Simpson's had committed a total breach of the contract by failing to appear at the scheduled closing. Taylor informed Simpson's that the Tans would use their best efforts to attempt to resell the business, but that their sales efforts were with full reservation of all rights to seek to enforce the contract against Simpson's by action for specific performance or damages.

After consultation with Taylor and Evans, the Tans decided to place their stores on the market again and to proceed with a lawsuit against Simpson's seeking to enforce the contract. The Tans signed a new commission contract with Evans, which contained terms identical to the first contract. Taylor filed suit on behalf of the Tans against Simpson's for breach of contract.

In January 2007, Evans informed the Tans that she had received an offer to purchase their stores from Rite-Buy, a large national chain of retail drug stores for a price of $2.5 million. Evans told the Tans that she thought that Rite-Buy was "bottom fishing" because it knew about the failed deal with Simpson's.

The Tans were in a state of shock and bewilderment from this news. They both believed that the price was grossly inadequate. But, after talking with Taylor and being advised of the "uncertainties of litigation," they finally concluded that they couldn't take a chance on being able to find a better offer. They decided to sell to Rite-Buy and to try to hold Simpson's responsible for damages.

The Tans' sale to Rite-Buy was originally scheduled to close on March 3, 2007, but it was twice delayed, finally closing on May 15, 2007. Meanwhile, the lawsuit against Simpson's proceeded through discovery toward trial. The stress of these matters had an effect on the Tans, both of whom worried constantly about Rite-Buy changing its mind and about the lawsuit. Gordon was especially affected by these events. He treated Simpson's refusal to go forward with the contract as a personal insult. In late May, shortly after he gave a deposition in the case, Gordon suffered a heart attack, which was fortunately a relatively mild one.

As part of discovery, Simpson's has served interrogatories on the Tans. One of the interrogatories asks them to state the amount and basis of the damages that they claim in the case. In answer to this interrogatory, Taylor has listed the following elements of damage:

1. The purchase price of the contract totaling $4.5 million.
2. Interest on this amount from October 15, 2006, at the market rate of interest available on U.S. Treasury bonds on that date (approximately 5 percent).
3. Loss of the investment appreciation on the purchase price of $4.5 million if this amount had been invested in the Chambers U.S. Treasury Bond Mutual Fund on October 15, 2006, as the Tans planned to do. Taylor's answer showed that had the Tans invested $4.5 million in that fund on October 15, 2006, the amount would have appreciated by $526,000 as of the time the answer to the interrogatory was given.
4. Commissions paid to Evans totaling $181,250.
5. Attorney fees incurred in litigation with Simpson's.
6. Damages for emotional distress suffered by the Tans as a result of Simpson's willful breach of contract in an amount determined by the jury.
7. Punitive damages for fraudulent, willful, and malicious breach of contract in an amount to be determined by the jury.

Assuming the Tans can establish a breach of contract by Simpson's, how should their damages be computed?

E. BUYERS' AND SELLERS' REMEDIES UNDER THE UNIFORM COMMERCIAL CODE

In the previous sections we have studied the general principles governing remedies for breach of contract with only brief references to the Uniform Commercial Code. In this section we study buyers' and sellers' remedies for breach of contracts governed by UCC Article 2. While Article 2 does contain a number of innovations, the Code also continues many of the basic principles concerning remedies that we have already studied.

As a preliminary matter, you may remember that an amended version of Article 2 was promulgated in 2003 by the American Law Institute and the National Conference of Commissioners on Uniform State Laws. This amended version had not been adopted by any state as of January 2007 and it is unclear when, if ever, a sizable number of states will enact the changes into law. Consequently, the discussion that follows is based on the unamended version of Article 2 of the UCC. The Rules Supplement contains the amended version of Article 2, which makes only modest changes in the sections discussed below.

1. Buyers' Remedies

A seller may commit a breach of contract in two general ways. First, a seller may deliver goods that fail to "conform" to the contract in some way (breach of an express or implied warranty relating to the "quality" of the goods, most likely). Second, the seller may fail to make a proper "tender" of the goods, such as failing to deliver on time, delivering too few or too many, or failing to deliver at all. When the buyer does not have the goods because the seller fails to deliver or the buyer rightfully rejects (§§2-601, 2-602) or revokes acceptance (§2-608), the buyer may recover any part of the price that has been paid under §2-711 and also obtain cover damages under UCC §2-712 or market damages under UCC §2-713. Alternatively, the buyer may pursue specific performance to compel delivery of the goods under §2-716. When the buyer has accepted and retained goods despite a nonconformity, the buyer's damages are determined under §2-714. In addition to the foregoing remedies, the buyer may be able to recover consequential and incidental damages under §2-715.

a. Cover, UCC §2-712

The traditional rule for measuring damages for a seller's breach is the contract price–market price difference, similar to that applied to the land sale contract in the *Roesch* case earlier in this chapter. The drafters of Article 2 thought that the market measure of damages was often arbitrary in its application, sometimes overcompensating the buyer who purchased substitute goods at a price lower than the relevant market price, and sometimes undercompensating the buyer when the buyer bought substitute goods at a price greater than the relevant market price. Accordingly, the drafters created a new "cover" measure of damages in UCC §2-712. Roy R. Anderson, The Cover Remedy, 6 J.L. & Commerce 155 (1986). If the buyer complies with the requirements of §2-712, she may recover the difference between the cover price and the contract price, plus incidental and consequential damages. UCC §2-715.

To recover damages under §2-712, the covering purchase must be made "in good faith and without unreasonable delay." As Comment 2 indicates, the buyer need not purchase identical goods, only commercially reasonable substitutes. If the buyer purchases superior or significantly different goods, the purchase will not qualify as cover. Some courts have been willing to expand the scope of the cover section to include situations in which the buyer internally manufactures substitute goods rather than purchase the goods on the market. See Cives Corp. v. Callier Steel Pipe & Tube, Inc., 482 A.2d 852 (Me. 1984) (after seller failed to deliver steel tubing under contract and buyer was unable to locate another supplier, buyer allowed to recover the difference between the cost of manufacturing the tubing in-house and the contract price); but see Chronister Oil Co. v. UNOCAL Refining & Marketing, 34 F.3d 462 (7th Cir. 1994) (criticizing courts that allow the buyer to "self-cover" because buyer cannot make a "purchase" from itself).

UCC 2-712(3) provides that cover is elective and failure to cover does not bar the buyer from any other remedy. However, this section must be read in light of the principle of mitigation of damages, expressed in UCC §2-715(2)(a), which allows a buyer to recover consequential damages that meet the foreseeability test of *Hadley v. Baxendale*, provided the damages "could not reasonably be prevented by cover or otherwise." Thus, the buyer's failure to cover will preclude recovery of consequential damages only if she fails to act reasonably.

b. Market Damages, UCC §2-713

If the buyer has elected not to purchase substitute goods as cover under UCC §2-712, the buyer may instead recover damages under UCC §2-713. That section provides a basic measure of damages based on the "difference between the market price at the time when the buyer learned of the breach and the contract price." Under §2-713(2) the relevant market is the place for tender and the place of tender depends on where the seller completes its delivery obligations with respect to the goods. In "shipment" contracts the seller tenders by placing the goods in the hands of a carrier, while in "destination" contracts tender takes place when the goods are delivered to a designated point, often the buyer's place of business or locale. UCC §2-503. The typical commercial contract will contain a delivery term that will define the seller's delivery obligations and thereby identify the relevant market price for measuring damages.

Suppose the buyer has covered, but the market price at the time and place of delivery is more than the cover price. May the buyer elect to forgo damages under the cover section and recover the greater amount of damages under the market damage section? The Code seems unclear on this point.

Comment 3 to §2-712 states, "The buyer is always free to choose between cover and damages for nondelivery under the next section." However, Comment 5 to §2-713 provides that the market value rule applies "only when and to the extent that the buyer has not covered." Moreover, UCC §1-106 (Revised UCC §1-305) provides that the purpose of remedies under the Code is to place "The aggrieved party . . . in as good a position as if the other party had fully performed." Most commentators agree that in this situation the buyer should be limited to damages measured under the cover section. See, e.g., John A. Sebert, Jr., Remedies Under Article Two of the Uniform Commercial Code: An Agenda for Review, 130 U. Pa. L. Rev. 360, 380-383 (1981).

Suppose the seller has committed an anticipatory repudiation and the buyer fails or elects not to cover. As of what point in time should the market measure of damages be determined? This question has proved difficult for the courts because of uncertainty about the meaning of the phrase *learned of the breach* in §2-713. Three interpretations have been offered, each of which has its scholarly advocates and its support in case law:

1. the date when the buyer learns of the repudiation;
2. the date when the buyer learns of the repudiation plus a commercially reasonable time thereafter;
3. the date when actual performance by the seller is due under the contract.

The plain meaning of the section supports the first interpretation. The buyer's right to await performance by a repudiating party for a commercially reasonable time under UCC §2-610(a) supports the second approach. White and Summers argue for the third alternative based on legislative history and comparison with other Code provisions. See White & Summers, Uniform Commercial Code (5th ed. 2000) §6-7, at 241.

c. Damages for Accepted Goods, UCC §2-714

Even though nonconforming goods have been accepted, the buyer may still be entitled to recover damages under §2-714(1). Under that section, the buyer may recover those damages that result "in the ordinary course of events from the seller's breach." More specifically, if the damages are caused by a breach of warranty, UCC §2-714(2) provides that the measure of damages is "the difference at the time and place of acceptance between the value of the goods accepted and the value they would have had if they had been as warranted, unless special circumstances show proximate damages of a different amount." For example, if an automobile is delivered with a different and lower priced set of tires than specified in the contract, the buyer would be able to recover the difference in the value (probably based on market prices) between the two sets of tires. Section 2-714(3) goes on to authorize incidental and consequential damages. It is important to note that if the buyer retains the goods despite nonconformity in the goods or the seller's tender, the buyer must give notice to the seller within reasonable period of time, under §2-607 (3)(a), in order to preserve the right to collect a remedy.

d. Specific Performance, UCC §2-716

You may recall from an earlier overview of remedies in Chapter 2 and other discussion in this book that the principal alternative remedies for a nonbreaching party are money damages or equitable relief. The most common form of equitable remedy is specific performance, a judicial decree compelling the breaching party to render the performance required by the contract. In Chapter 12 we will see that the common law imposes various restrictions on the award of specific performance, particularly the requirement that the remedy of money damages be inadequate. In §2-716 the drafters of the Code made an effort to liberalize the award of specific performance. Under that section, specific performance "may" be decreed in the buyer's favor where the goods are "unique," or in "other proper circumstances." If goods are readily available on the market, a court applying the Code is likely to deny specific performance. Klein v. Pepsico, Inc., 845 F.2d 76 (4th Cir. 1988) (error to award specific performance of contract to sell airplane when comparable planes available on the market). Where substitute goods or a substitute contract is not available, the courts may be more willing to grant the remedy. See, e.g., Laclede Gas Co. v. Amoco Oil Co., 522 F.2d 33 (8th Cir. 1975) (specific performance granted of long-term requirements contract to supply propane; while propane was currently available to plaintiff under short-term contracts with other suppliers, it had "no assurance" that this situation would continue).

e. Incidental and Consequential Damages, UCC §2-715

After breach by the seller, the buyer is entitled to recover both incidental and consequential damages under UCC §2-715 in addition to other more immediate damages. Incidental damages consist of out-of-pocket expenses incurred by the buyer to deal with the consequences of the seller's breach. UCC §2-715(1). Consequential damages include:

(a) any loss resulting from general or particular requirements and needs of which the seller at the time of contracting had reason to know and which could not reasonably be prevented by cover or otherwise; and

(b) injury to person or property proximately resulting from any breach of warranty.

UCC §2-715(2).

The section makes a distinction between economic or commercial loss, such as lost profits (subsection (a)), and damage to person or property (subsection (b)). The former is subject to the foreseeability test of Hadley v. Baxendale, which we studied in Section B of this chapter ("which the seller at the time of contracting had reason to know") and to the mitigation principle ("would not reasonably be prevented by cover or otherwise"). The Code rejects the "tacit agreement" formulation of the foreseeability test as discussed in the notes after the *Hadley v. Baxendale* case. UCC §2-715, Comment 2. Under subsection (b), damages for injury to person or property are not subject to the foreseeability test. Comment 4 to §2-715 states that damages must be proved by the buyer with reasonable certainty but not mathematical precision.

PROBLEM 11-2

Bing Industries is engaged in the manufacturing and fabrication of parts and components for the automotive industry. Last August it ordered 98,195 pounds of high-carbon cold-rolled steel from Southern Steel, Inc., for use in the fabrication of springs used in the assembly of automobile clutches. The purchase order set forth the specifications of the steel, which were critical because of the requirements for manufacture of the springs. Southern delivered the steel in coils to Bing on January 26 and 28. In accordance with its usual practice, Bing checked the steel for dimensional accuracy and chemical content and began partial fabrication of the steel into "blanks." It then stored the blanks, awaiting orders from its customers. Recently Bing removed the pieces from storage and resumed the fabrication process. During this processing, Bing noticed that the springs exhibited cracks and other failures. Bing immediately gave notice of the problem to Southern, which did extensive testing of the steel. A dispute has developed: Southern claims that Bing improperly processed the steel, while Bing contends that the steel was defective. Because of the problem with the steel, Bing is late on delivery of springs under a contract and runs the risk of having the contract canceled. Bing has sought your advice about how to proceed legally. What advice would you give?

2. Sellers' Remedies

In the section on buyers' remedies, we saw that the Code has modified the common law rules in several ways; in particular, a buyer has the option of recovering damages under the Code's rule on cover rather than under the traditional rule of market damages. For sellers, the Code adopts a similar provision, the right of "resale." UCC §2-706. In addition, the Code includes a new rule allowing a seller, under certain circumstances, to recover damages based on his lost profit. UCC §2-708(2). Analysis of sellers' remedies begins with §2-703, which outlines the seller's rights in the event the buyer breaches the contract. The measurement of the seller's damages depends partly on whether the buyer has accepted the goods based on the definition of acceptance in §2-606. If not, the seller may recover either resale damages, UCC §2-706, market damages, UCC §2-708(1), or lost profit, UCC §2-708(2). If the goods have been accepted, or are not reasonably subject to resale, the seller may recover the contract price under UCC §2-709.

a. Resale Damages, UCC §2-706

Section 2-706 allows a seller to resell goods after a breach by the buyer and "recover the difference between the resale price and the contract price." This remedy is the equivalent of the buyer's right to cover. The seller must follow three basic steps to recover damages under §2-706. First, the seller must identify the goods being resold as the same ones under the contract that was breached. Second, the seller must give the buyer proper notice of resale.

For private sales, "the seller must give the buyer reasonable notification of his intention to resell." UCC §2-706(3). For public sales, the seller must give the buyer reasonable notice of the time and place of the resale except in the case of goods which are perishable or otherwise may quickly decline in value. UCC §2-706(4)(b).

Third, the seller's resale must be made in good faith and in a commercially reasonable manner. UCC §2-706(1). If the seller engages in a "sham" resale to a friendly purchaser or an affiliated entity, the court should not allow the seller to recover damages under the section. E.g., Coast Trading Co. v. Cudahy Co., 592 F.2d 1074 (9th Cir. 1979) (seller entered into a "paper contract apparently intended to serve only as basis for calculating resale damages"). The fact that in hindsight a better price could have been obtained, however, does not make a sale unreasonable. Finnish Fur Sales Co. v. Juliette Shulof Furs, Inc., 770 F. Supp. 139 (S.D.N.Y. 1991) (seller sold at regularly scheduled auctions at prevailing prices; unreasonable for seller to suspend its operations to await higher world prices).

b.   Market Damages, UCC §2-708(1)

As is the case with buyers, the Code contains a traditional contract price minus market value damage formula for sellers in UCC §2-708(1). The major problem in interpreting this section is the interrelationship between it and §2-706, the resale section. Suppose a seller has in fact resold goods identified to the contract. May the seller recover damages under §2-708(1) if that section would produce a greater recovery than the formula of §2-706? This situation can arise when the market price at the time and place for tender is less than the resale price. On the one hand, Comment 2 to §2-706 suggests that a seller who fails to follow the requirements for resale under that section is left to the remedy under §2-708(1). On the other hand, Professors White and Summers argue that a seller who has resold should not be entitled to recover greater damages under §2-708(1) than under §2-706. In their view, such a result would contravene the principle of awarding only compensatory damages as expressed in §1-106 (revised UCC §1-305). White & Summers, §7-7, at 271. See Tesoro Petroleum Corp. v. Holborn Oil Co., 547 N.Y.S.2d 1012 (Sup. Ct. 1989) (following the White and Summers approach).

c.   Lost Profits, UCC §2-708(2)

As an alternative to the market price measure of damages, UCC §2-708(2) authorizes courts to award lost profits to sellers if the market measure of damages set forth in §2-708(1) is "inadequate to put the seller in as good a position as performance would have done." Case law and commentary have identified three situations in which §2-708(2) should apply. The first of these is usually referred to as the case of the "lost volume seller." Recall the *Jetz Service* case earlier in this chapter. If the buyer breaches and the seller makes a resale of the same item, the seller may collect lost profits if it can prove that it had the capacity to make both sales and that both sales would have been profitable. For example, a dealer who sells rather fungible new cars may argue that it has practically unlimited supply. The burden of proving its status as a lost volume seller is on the seller.

Note that Section 2-708(2) requires "due credit for payments or proceeds of resale." This phrase has proved troublesome in the "lost volume seller" cases. If the total proceeds of the seller's resale are deducted, the profit recovery under §2-708(2) would be negated because the resale price also includes seller's profit. Courts have avoided this problem by interpreting the "due credit" language to apply only when the seller sells uncompleted or otherwise unmarketable goods for scrap. See R. E. Davis Chemical Corp. v. Diasonics, Inc., 826 F.2d 678, 684 (7th Cir. 1987).

The second situation in which §2-708(2) has been applied involves a seller who is in the process of assembling a product for sale when the buyer breaches. While the seller could complete manufacture of the product and attempt to resell it on the open market, it might not be commercially reasonable to do this (for example, if the goods were specialty items without an established market). See UCC §2-704(2). Awarding lost profits based on the contract price minus the cost of production would be perhaps the only way to compensate the seller.

Finally, §2-708(2) has been applied in the case of the "jobber," a middle person who purchases goods for resale. If the buyer from a jobber breaches before the jobber has acquired the goods, courts may award lost profits as the best measure of the seller's harm. See Blair International, Ltd. v. LaBarge, Inc., 675 F.2d 954 (8th Cir. 1982) (jobber of oil casings allowed to recover lost profits); TCP Industries, Inc. v. Uniroyal, Inc., 661 F.2d 542 (6th Cir. 1981) (intermediary for chemicals allowed to recover lost profits).

Section 2-708(2) states that it applies if the market value measure of damages is "inadequate" to put the seller in as good a position as full performance by the buyer. May a seller elect to recover market value damages under §2-708(1), if the measure of recovery under that section *exceeds* his lost profit in the transaction? We have previously encountered similar questions concerning whether a covering buyer or a reselling seller elect market damages if that measure would produce a greater recovery? In each situation, the same arguments have reappeared. The language and legislative history of the Code favor allowing the election by the nonbreaching party, while the principle of compensation supports the opposite view. The courts are divided. See Nobs Chemical, U.S.A., Inc. v. Koppers Co., 616 F.2d 212 (5th Cir. 1980) (acknowledging ambiguity in §2-708 and limiting seller to lost profit even though market damages would have been greater).

d. Seller's Action for the Price, UCC §2-709

The seller may recover the price of the goods from the buyer as damages under §2-709 in three situations. First, if the buyer has accepted the goods, then the seller may recover the price under §2-709(1)(a). Second, under the same section, the seller may recover the price if the goods are damaged after the risk of loss has passed to the buyer. In both of these situations, the buyer has effectively received the goods and thus should pay the contract price.

Third, the seller may recover the price under §2-709(1)(b), and essentially force the goods onto the buyer, if the seller is unable to resell the goods with reasonable effort. Although neither §2-709(1)(b) nor its comments use the phrase *specific performance*, it appears that the section is the analogue of §2-716, which makes specific performance available to the buyer. See Schumann v. Levi, 728 F.2d 1141 (8th Cir. 1984) ("the equitable remedy of specific performance and the Uniform Commercial Code's action for the price are virtually identical").

e. Seller's Incidental and Consequential Damages, UCC §2-710

All of the above remedial sections also allow the seller to recover incidental damages under §2-710. Incidental damages include a variety of out-of-pocket expenses incurred by the seller to deal with the buyer's breach, such as cost of storage or transportation of the goods. Section 2-710 does not contain any reference to consequential damages, perhaps because the drafters of the Code were persuaded that sellers rarely suffer consequential damages that would not be compensated by the damage measures discussed above. White and Summers argue that, despite the language of §2-710, courts should rely on common law principles via §1-103 (Revised UCC §1-103(b)) and allow sellers to recover consequential damages in appropriate cases. White & Summers, §7-16, at 300-303. Note that Revised UCC §2-710 expressly allows for the seller to receive consequential damages.

PROBLEM 11-3

On July 1, Henry T. Johnson Food Distributors, Inc., entered into a written contract with McBride Farms to purchase 5,000 bushels of "large" peaches at $4 per bushel, delivery to be made on or before August 15. At 9 A.M. on August 15 McBride's trucks pulled up at the Johnson facility. Charlotte McBride gave an invoice to the Johnson agent at the unloading docks. She pointed out that the invoice showed 4800 bushels of "large" peaches and 200 bushels of "small" peaches. (In the trade, small peaches are not as marketable as large ones, selling to buyers like Johnson Food for approximately $2 per bushel.) She also noted that the invoice price ($19,600) had been adjusted by $400 to reflect the small peaches. The agent said he would have to "check with the boss." He returned a few minutes later to say that the peaches were unacceptable and could not be unloaded. McBride asked to talk with the boss, who told her that he was "sick and tired" of "farmers making deliveries any way they wanted." He said that McBride should have obtained approval first, not just "showed up" with the small peaches. She offered to leave only the large peaches, but he refused and ordered her to leave. McBride returned with the peaches to her farm, and left them at the McBride Cannery, a subsidiary operation that cans unmarketable peaches. On its books, the Cannery recorded a credit of $5,000 for McBride

Farms, treating the peaches as costing $1 per bushel. Subsequently, the Cannery completed canning the peaches; its manufacturing costs for doing so were $3,000. McBride has now brought suit against Johnson Food Distributors for breach of contract. Analyze McBride's rights to recover damages. If additional facts are needed, explain what they are and why they are legally significant.

F. JUSTIFICATIONS FOR THE EXPECTATION DAMAGE RULE

At the beginning of our survey of the rules governing contract damages, we posed—but did not then attempt to answer—two questions about the expectation-damage principle: Why should the law of contract proclaim as its stated norm for damage recovery the plaintiff's full expectation of gain under the breached contract, even in cases where the plaintiff has not yet performed, expended any resources on preparations for performance, or substantially relied in any other way on the contract at issue? Conversely, why should the law ordinarily award *no more than* expectation damages for breach of contract, denying to most contract plaintiffs the sorts of exemplary or punitive damages often available in tort actions? In this section, we will consider some answers that have been given to these questions.

1. Protecting the Expectation Interest Under a Wholly Executory Contract

In many cases where enforcement of a contractual obligation is sought, it is clear that the party seeking enforcement has relied in a variety of ways, substantial and insubstantial, on her expectation that the defendant's promised performance would be rendered. In many such cases, the defendant promisor has also received some benefit from the plaintiff's actions, so that the defendant would be unjustly enriched if his promise were to go completely unenforced. In such cases, the plaintiff's reliance or restitution interest may therefore appear to require compensation in damages. But not every breach of contract will necessarily involve such injury. Since the law recognizes an exchange of purely executory promises as sufficient in itself to create a contract, there is no theoretical barrier to enforcement where the defendant promisor has breached his promise at a time when the plaintiff promisee had neither performed nor relied (in any but a purely psychological way) on the defendant's promise of performance. In such a case, the only remedial interest that has been injured is the plaintiff's expectation interest. Aside from the internal logic of the rule-structure itself, what justifies the law's willingness to award an expectation-based remedy to a plaintiff who has not been demonstrably injured in any quantifiable or even tangible way by the defendant's breach?

In their landmark 1936 article, Professor Lon Fuller and his associate William Perdue attempted to answer that question in the following passage:

Why Should the Law Ever Protect the Expectation Interest?

Perhaps the most obvious answer to this question is one which we may label "psychological." . . . Whether or not he has actually changed his position because of the promise, the promisee has formed an attitude of expectancy such that a breach of the promise causes him to feel that he has been "deprived" of something which was "his." Since this sentiment is a relatively uniform one, the law has no occasion to go back of it. It accepts it as a datum and builds its rule about it.

The difficulty with this explanation is that the law does in fact go back of the sense of injury which the breach of a promise engenders. No legal system attempts to invest with juristic sanction all promises. Some rule or combination of rules effects a sifting out for enforcement of those promises deemed important enough to society to justify the law's concern with them. . . . Therefore, though it may be assumed that the impulse to assuage disappointment is one shared by those who make and influence the law, this impulse can hardly be regarded as the key which solves the whole problem of the protection accorded by the law to the expectation interest.

A second possible explanation for the rule protecting the expectancy may be found in the much-discussed "will theory" of contract law. This theory views the contracting parties as exercising, so to speak, a legislative power, so that the legal enforcement of a contract becomes merely an implementing by the state of a kind of private law already established by the parties. . . .

. . . This attitude finds a natural application to promises to pay a definite sum of money. But certainly as to most types of contracts it is vain to expect from the will theory a ready-made solution for the problem of damages.

A third and more promising solution of our difficulty lies in an economic or institutional approach. . . . In a society in which credit has become a significant and pervasive institution, it is inevitable that the expectancy created by an enforceable promise should be regarded as a kind of property, and breach of the promise as an injury to that property . . . .

It is a cure for these losses in the sense that it offers the measure of recovery most likely to reimburse the plaintiff for the (often very numerous and very difficult to prove) individual acts and forbearances which make up his total reliance on the contract. If we take into account "gains prevented" by reliance, that is, losses involved in foregoing the opportunity to enter other contracts, the notion that the rule protecting the expectancy is adopted as the most effective means of compensating for detrimental reliance seems not at all far-fetched. Physicians with an extensive practice often charge their patients the full office call fee for broken appointments. Such a charge looks on the face of things like a claim to the promised fee; it seems to be based on the "expectation interest." Yet the physician making the charge will quite justifiably regard it as compensation for the loss of the opportunity to gain a similar fee from a different patient. This foregoing of other opportunities is involved to some extent in entering most contracts, and the impossibility of subjecting this type of reliance to any kind of measurement may justify a categorical rule granting the value of the expectancy as the most effective way of compensating for such losses. . . .

In seeking justification for the rule granting the value of the expectancy there is no need, however, to restrict ourselves by the assumption, hitherto made, that the rule can only be intended to cure or prevent the losses caused by reliance. A justification can be developed from a less negative point of view. It may be said that there is not only a policy in favor of preventing and undoing the harms resulting from reliance, but also a policy in favor of promoting and facilitating reliance on business agreements.

Lon L. Fuller & William R. Perdue, Jr., The Reliance Interest in Contract Damages (Pt. I), 46 Yale L.J. 52, 57-62 (1936).

In 1999 Professor David Barnes presented a comprehensive review and critique of the reliance-based justification for expectation damages offered by Fuller and Perdue. Barnes argues that "the ultimate effect of their work was to confuse and complicate the law of contract damages." David W. Barnes, The Net Expectation Interest in Contract Damages, 48 Emory L.J. 1137, 1138 (1999). He contends that damages should be measured by the net expectation interest of the injured party, even in cases of fully executory contracts. Protection of this interest "reflects contracting parties' interest in improving their well-being." Id. at 1139.

Conversely, English historian P. S. Atiyah has asserted that the law's readiness to protect a promisee's expectation under a completely executory bilateral contract (i.e., one that has been neither performed nor relied on) is a relatively recent development. Atiyah has also argued that cases where enforcement of a completely executory contract is sought are much rarer in real life than in contract theory:

> [A]lthough this form of liability must be treated as promise-based, we are entitled to ask how extensive it is in relation to the rest of the law, and whether it deserves to occupy the central role in Contract and even in promissory theory that it occupies today. It is, I think, worth observing that wholly executory contracts are generally nothing like as binding in practice as legal theory might suggest. Consumers and even business men often expect to be able to cancel executory agreements with the minimum of penalty, paying perhaps only for actual expenses laid out in reliance on the promise. And such reliance expenditures would, by definition, not exist if the arrangement were still wholly executory. And even in strict law, it must be stressed that the expectations protected by executory contracts are limited. They are not generally expectations of performance but expectations of profit. Where there is no difference in the market price of the goods or services which are the subject of the contract, and the market price of comparable goods or services, the contract may in law be broken with impunity. In practice this must comprise a high proportion of cases in which executory arrangements are broken. Then again, the binding force of wholly executory contracts is normally of an ephemeral nature. Executory contracts do not normally remain executory for very long. Even if made well before the time for performance, the whole purpose of making them is frequently to enable the parties to make preliminary arrangements in confident reliance on reciprocal performance. Thus action in reliance is likely to follow hard on the heels of the making of most executory contracts, and it is only in the rare cases where cancellation is sought very soon after making the contract, or where, despite the lapse of some longer period of time no action in reliance has been commenced, that the source of the obligation has to be rested in the promise alone. Whatever the paradigm of actual Contract may be, there can be no doubt that the paradigm of *a breach of contract* is not the breach of a wholly executory contract. And this surely reflects the intentions of most parties who enter into executory contracts. The primary purpose of making such a contract is usually to agree upon the terms which are to regulate a contemplated exchange, when and if it is carried through; it is surely a subordinate and less obvious purpose that the contract binds both parties to see that the exchange is indeed carried through.

P. S. Atiyah, Contracts, Promises and the Law of Obligations, 94 L.Q. Rev. 193, 211-212 (1978). Based on these conclusions, Atiyah predicts that modern emphasis on protection of the reliance and restitution interests may produce a corresponding decline in the law's willingness to protect the plaintiff's expectation under a completely executory contract.

In a 1982 article, The Bargain Principle and Its Limits, 95 Harv. L. Rev. 741, Professor Melvin Eisenberg critically examines in a variety of situations the principle that bargained-for promises should be enforced to the full extent of the expectation created thereby. He considers first the half-completed contract, where one party has rendered full performance and seeks the return performance (or its value) from the other. In this case, he argues, both fairness and efficiency are served by full enforcement of the defendant's promise rather than a mere restitutionary award to the plaintiff of the "fair value" of her performance. Where the defendant has received the full benefit of the plaintiff's promised performance, fairness clearly requires *some* measure of compensation to the plaintiff; moreover, full enforcement increases efficiency by relieving the court of the burden of valuing the plaintiff's performance.

Next, Eisenberg notes that in some cases, the contract at issue appears to have been to some degree the product of factors that he collectively describes as "unconscionability": fraud, duress, undue influence, knowingly taking advantage of the other's ignorance, etcetera. In such cases, neither fairness nor efficiency appear to be served by full enforcement of even the half-completed bargain. Either partial enforcement (on a restitutionary basis) or no enforcement at all may be the appropriate response.

Eisenberg then addresses the case where the plaintiff has not performed at all, even partially. Assuming that the contract in question is not in any degree tainted by some form of unconscionability, should the plaintiff's expectation interest be protected by enforcing the contract? Eisenberg asserts that at least three policies can be identified that may justify full-bargain enforcement: (1) assured protection of the full cost of reliance (which Eisenberg calls the "surrogate-cost theory"); (2) facilitation of planning (by deterring breach in most cases); (3) protection of a risk-allocation that the contract was created to effectuate (e.g., a contract for future delivery at a fixed price, made in order to allocate the risk of price changes between the time of contract and the time set for performance). He then applies this analysis to a number of contracts between business concerns and concludes that in most cases full-bargain enforcement can be justified on the basis of one or more of these policies. The following is one of Eisenberg's examples:

> Take first a contract for the sale of relatively homogeneous goods in which the seller is a dealer, the buyer is a business concern, and the seller breaches, as in the following hypothetical:
>
>> *Paper Buyer I.* Seller is in the business of selling office supplies to large users. Buyer is a financial corporation. On May 1, Seller and Buyer enter into a contract for the sale of one hundred ten-ream cases of a standard grade of typing paper at a price of $4,000, delivery on July 1, payment on August 1. On July 1, Seller repudiates.
>
> The argument for applying the bargain principle in cases like *Paper Buyer I* is very strong. The buyer's expectation damages in such a case are normally measured by the difference between the replacement price and the contract price — a type of

measure that will hereinafter be called a replacement-price formula. But a recovery that measured the buyer's damages by cost (the reliance measure) would usually be just as great. This is because the market for relatively homogeneous goods normally has continuity and depth — that is, purchases and sales can normally be made at any time, in significant quantities, at a price very close to the price at which the last such transaction was closed. . . . Given the nature of the market, however, the forgone price will normally equal the contract price. Accordingly, application of the bargain principle can be justified in such cases under the surrogate-cost theory, on the ground that the buyer's expectation damages will normally equal his cost or reliance damages and are much easier to determine.

The planning and risk theories point the same way. Business firms make forward purchase contracts at fixed prices to ensure supply and to shift the risk of price changes from the buyer to the seller. A replacement-price formula helps ensure supply by making breach unprofitable, and effectuates the intended shift of risk.

Melvin A. Eisenberg, The Bargain Principle and Its Limits, 95 Harv. L. Rev. 741, 788-789 (1982).

Suppose, however, that the contract at issue is not between two commercial concerns, but between a merchant and a consumer. Here Eisenberg's analysis produces somewhat different results.

> Assume now a contract for the sale of relatively homogeneous services by a merchant to a consumer, as in the following hypothetical:
>
> > *Dance Lessons. E,* an electrical engineer, wants to learn to dance. *S* operates a dancing school. On May 1, *E* signs a contract with *S* to take Dancing 1, a group class, which begins on July 1. Dancing 1 meets two hours a week, runs twenty-six weeks, and costs $500. *E* understands all the provisions of the contract and considered the matter in a deliberative frame of mind, but knows nothing about damage rules. On June 15, *E* changes his mind and repudiates.
> >
> > *S* incurs little or no incremental out-of-pocket costs for group classes, since its instructors work on full-year contracts and it owns its own studios. *S's* classes usually don't fill to capacity. The capacity of Dancing 1 is twenty students. On June 15, sixteen students had enrolled. No additional students enrolled thereafter.
>
> When the buyer breaches a contract for the sale of services, the seller's expectation damages are normally measured under a net-proceeds formula, that is, contract price minus the seller's out-of-pocket cost of performance. On facts like those in *Dance Lessons,* however, performance by the seller does not entail any incremental out-of-pocket cost. Accordingly, the seller's expectation damages under a net-proceeds formula equal the entire contract price, despite the fact that the buyer has received no benefit.
>
> Such a recovery is not easy to justify under the surrogate-cost theory when the seller has incurred no cost in reliance on the buyer's promise. In considering whether it is justified by the risk theory, two related questions must be asked. The first question is, why would *E* make a contract on May 1, rather than wait until July 1? Consumers normally do not make contracts like that in *Dance Lessons* for the purpose of allocating the risk of price changes or speculating in the market for dancing lessons. Rather, the typical purposes of such advance contracting are to ensure supply (that is, to ensure a place in the class) and, perhaps, to make a self-commitment. The second question is, would the parties have agreed to a provision permitting the seller to measure damages under a net-proceeds formula if they had consciously

adverted to the issue? Given the buyer's assumed motivation for contracting, the answer pretty clearly seems to be no. . . .

The final question is whether a net-proceeds formula is required to enable a seller like S to plan effectively. This is an empirical issue on which firm evidence is lacking. However, random evidence suggests that firms selling services to consumers can plan effectively without being entitled to damages measured by a net-proceeds formula. For example, the problem raised by *Dance Lessons* is characteristic of any contract for tuition, and such contracts often involve relatively large amounts. Nevertheless, many and perhaps most schools provide for refunding tuition on a declining basis if the student drops out. Indeed, under FTC regulations, if a student in a proprietary vocational school cancels his enrollment contract, the "school shall not receive, demand, or retain more than a pro rata portion of the total contract price" plus a relatively small registration fee. . . .

Most important, even assuming that planning does require a consumer in E's position to suffer some loss, requiring such a consumer to pay damages equal to the entire contract price seems excessive to the task, particularly if it is assumed that the consumer would not have agreed to such damages at the time the contract was made. Rather, the seller's damages should be measured by what might be called a cancellation charge. Such a recovery should be based on the amount necessary to reimburse the seller for incidental costs, to provide enough deterrent to facilitate planning, and to pay for the benefit of having had a place reserved. The measurement required need not be as difficult as it may seem, since the law could leave it to the seller to fix such an amount in the contract by way of liquidated damages, or might treat a deposit by the buyer as a tacit cancellation charge even if the contract does not so provide.

Id. at 794-797. See also Robert Cooter & Melvin A. Eisenberg, Damages for Breach of Contract, 73 Cal. L. Rev. 1432 (1985).

If Professor Atiyah's observations above are as correct as intuitively they seem to be, the number of cases in which a court is asked to enforce a completely executory agreement (both unperformed and unrelied on) will be relatively few. In the absence of injury to either the reliance or the restitution interest of the plaintiff, the arguments for full-bargain enforcement seem much less compelling. When such a case does arise, therefore, it should not be surprising to find the court seeking some basis for denying enforcement—particularly where, as in the last of Eisenberg's examples above, the defendant is a consumer who may not have prepared for or even foreseen the possibility of substantial liability.

2. Encouraging Breach of Contract: The Theory of "Efficient Breach"

The rules governing remedies for breach of contract have often been referred to (sometimes with favor, sometimes not) as "amoral." Perhaps the most frequently quoted passage in support of this view is from an address delivered in 1897 by Oliver Wendell Holmes, then Justice of the Massachusetts Supreme Judicial Court, at the dedication of a new hall at the Boston University School of Law. Speaking first of the necessity for law students to avoid the fallacy of assuming "law" and "morality" to be synonymous, Holmes went on to give some examples of the divergence between them.

Nowhere is the confusion between legal and moral ideas more manifest than in the law of contract. . . . The duty to keep a contract at common law means a prediction that you must pay damages if you do not keep it — and nothing else. If you commit a tort, you are liable to pay a compensatory sum. If you commit a [breach of] contract, you are liable to pay a compensatory sum unless the promised event comes to pass, and that is all the difference. But such a mode of looking at the matter stinks in the nostrils of those who think it advantageous to get as much ethics into the law as they can.

Oliver Wendell Holmes, The Path of the Law, in Collected Legal Papers 174-175 (1920). Holmes voiced similar views elsewhere: "It is true," he observed in his lecture on the Elements of Contract,

that in some instances equity does what is called compelling specific performance. But . . . [t]his remedy is an exceptional one. The only universal consequence of a legally binding promise is, that the law makes the promisor pay damages if the promised event does not come to pass. In every case it leaves him free from interference until the time for fulfillment has gone by, and therefore free to break his contract if he chooses.

Oliver Wendell Holmes, The Common Law 236 (Mark DeWolfe Howe ed. 1963).

To Holmes, it may be that these statements represented an effort to direct our thinking about law away from the twin perils of "moralizing" and "metaphysics," and toward the possibility that law is primarily the product of social forces whose nature as "good" or "evil" may be debatable, but whose existence and effect cannot be denied. This thought is most pithily expressed in what are perhaps Holmes's best-known words: "The life of the law has not been logic; it has been experience." Id. at 1. Others, however, have seen in Holmes's observations about contract law a challenge to both morals and logic. If indeed the law of contract does take an "amoral" view of contract-breaking behavior, why has this been so? And, indeed, *should* it be so?

In recent years, the view that Holmes's observation is correct both historically and philosophically has been most energetically advanced by writers of the law and economics school, led by Richard Posner. Holmes's statement that the breaching party is merely required to choose between performance and compensation contains, Posner asserts, "an important economic insight." Richard A. Posner, Economic Analysis of Law 131 (5th ed. 1998). "In many cases," Posner continues,

it is uneconomical to induce completion of performance of a contract after it has been broken. I agree to purchase 100,000 widgets custom-ground for use as components in a machine that I manufacture. After I have taken delivery of 10,000, the market for my machine collapses. I promptly notify my supplier that I am terminating the contract, and admit that my termination is a breach. When notified of the termination he has not yet begun the custom grinding of the other 90,000 widgets, but he informs me that he intends to complete his performance under the contract and bill me accordingly. The custom-ground widgets have no use other than in my machine, and a negligible scrap value. To give the supplier a remedy that induced him to complete the contract after the breach would waste resources. The law is alert to this danger and, under the doctrine of mitigation of damages, would not give the supplier damages for any costs he incurred in continuing production after notice of termination. . . .

Now suppose that the widget contract is broken by the seller rather than the buyer. I really need those 100,000 custom-ground widgets for my machine but the supplier, after producing 50,000, is forced to suspend production because of a mechanical failure. Other suppliers are in a position to supply the remaining widgets that I need but I insist that the original supplier complete his performance of the contract. If the law compels completion (by ordering specific performance, a form of injunction), the supplier will have to make arrangements with other producers to complete his contract with me. Probably it will be more costly for him to procure an alternative supplier than for me to do so directly (after all, I know my own needs best); otherwise he would have done it voluntarily, to minimize his liability for the breach. To compel completion of the contract (or costly negotiations to discharge the promisor) would again result in a waste of resources, and again the law does not compel completion but confines the victim to simple damages.

But what *are* simple contract damages? Usually the objective of giving the promisor an incentive to fulfill his promise unless the result would be an inefficient use of resources (the production of the unwanted widgets in the first example, the roundabout procurement of a substitute supplier in the second) can be achieved by giving the promisee his expected profit on the transaction. If the supplier in the first example receives his expected profit from making 10,000 [sic 100,000?] widgets, he will have no incentive to make the unwanted 90,000. We do not want him to make them; no one wants them. In the second example, if I receive my expected profit from dealing with the original supplier, I become indifferent to whether he completes his performance.

Id. at 131-133.

It should be remembered at this point that in many cases where performance is in some sense "impossible" or even "impracticable," the law will in fact excuse the nonperforming party from the duty of performance, in which case no damages at all would be awarded. (Recall our discussion in Chapter 8.) But Posner's analysis is not limited to cases where the breach is "involuntary." The same result should follow, he continues, even in some cases where the breaching party could perform, but chooses not to do so.

[I]n some cases a party is tempted to break his contract simply because his profit from breach would exceed his profit from completion of the contract. If it would also exceed the expected profit to the other party from completion of the contract, and if damages are limited to the loss of that profit, there will be an incentive to commit a breach. But there should be. Suppose I sign a contract to deliver 100,000 custom-ground widgets at 10 apiece to A for use in his boiler factory. After I have delivered 10,000, B comes to me, explains that he desperately needs 25,000 custom-ground widgets at once since otherwise he will be forced to close his pianola factory at great cost, and offers me 15 apiece for them. I sell him the widgets and as a result do not complete timely delivery to A, causing him to lose $1,000 in profits. Having obtained an additional profit of $1,250 on the sale to B, I am better off even after reimbursing A for his loss, and B is also better off. The breach is Pareto superior. True, had I refused to sell to B he could have gone to A and negotiated an assignment to him of part of A's contract with me. But this would have introduced an additional step, with additional transaction costs. . . .

Id. at 133.

Although Posner himself did not dub this analysis the theory of "efficient breach," others have employed that term. See, e.g., Richard Craswell, Contract Remedies, Renegotiation, and the Theory of Efficient Breach, 61 S. Cal. L. Rev. 629 (1988); Charles J. Goetz & Robert E. Scott, Liquidated Damages, Penalties and the Just Compensation Principle: Some Notes on an Enforcement Model and a Theory of Efficient Breach, 77 Colum. L. Rev. 554 (1977); Lewis A. Kornhauser, An Introduction to the Economic Analysis of Contract Remedies, 57 U. Colo. L. Rev. 683 (1986). Many commentators have echoed Posner's view that when nonperformance (in order to permit entry into a substitute, more profitable transaction) would be "efficient," the law should not only permit breach but indeed regard it as appropriate behavior to be encouraged rather than condemned. Thus, in their article cited above, Professors Goetz and Scott observe that contract damages are apparently not designed to "prevent breach" but merely to compensate for any injury that results. So long as compensation to the nonbreaching party adequately "mirrors the value of performance," they conclude, the conventional damage rule will produce "a result superior to performance, since one party receives the same benefits as performance while the other is able to do even better." Goetz & Scott, above, at 558.

Professor Robert Birmingham has applied a similar analysis to the contract for performance of personal service, concluding that in certain circumstances breach by either the employee or the employer could be regarded as appropriate. Breach by the employee, he argues,

> should be encouraged where gain to the employee will exceed loss to the employer. Such a situation will normally arise where the particular skills of the employee can be more fully utilized in his second position. Here transfer will produce social gain through more efficient allocation of labor.

Robert L. Birmingham, Breach of Contract, Damage Measures, and Economic Efficiency, 24 Rutgers L. Rev. 273, 288-289 (1970). On the other hand, Birmingham asserts, breach by the employer may also be economically efficient. Noting the central role of the mitigation principle in this situation, he goes on to consider the circumstances in which discharge of the employee, even in breach of an existing employment contract, might be viewed as socially desirable.

> Limitation of recovery through adherence to the general damage measure implies award of the difference between the contract wage and what the worker is able to earn through available comparable employment. Application of this rule, adopted by the court, promotes mobility of labor essential to competitive efficiency. If the value of a worker hired at a salary of $10,000 falls to $8,000, an employer will gain through repudiation of their agreement when the resulting cost to him is less than $2,000. If transaction costs are disregarded, breach will thus be profitable to the employer if and only if the worker can obtain another job paying more than $8,000. A new employer will not normally pay the worker more than what he anticipates his services will contribute to the undertaking. The rule therefore encourages breach where the product of the worker would be greater in an alternative position and discourages breach where the product would be less. . . .

Id. at 291.

Criticism of the doctrine of efficient breach as thus propounded has taken a number of forms. Professor Joseph Perillo argues that advocates of the concept of efficient breach have misread Holmes. Holmes supported an objective analysis of legal concepts but he did not, as the efficient breach theorists claim, contend that parties had the right to breach a contract. Perillo's article also includes a useful summary of the various arguments made against the theory of efficient breach. See Joseph M. Perillo, Misreading Oliver Wendell Holmes on Efficient Breach and Tortious Interference, 68 Fordham L. Rev. 1085 (2000).

Even commentators who accept the methodology of economic analysis have pointed out that many of the examples used to support the Posnerian argument are based on assumptions that run counter to the realities of contracting behavior. Of primary importance in this respect is the often-assumed absence of "transaction costs." As many commentators have pointed out, the transaction costs of postbreach behavior for the nonbreaching party are likely to include such items as attorney fees, whether for litigation or for negotiation of a settlement; to assume the absence of such costs is to create a "model" that is very different from the real world of contracting parties. See, e.g., Daniel A. Farber, Reassessing the Economic Efficiency of Compensatory Damages for Breach of Contract, 66 Va. L. Rev. 1443, 1448 (1980).

Critics also point to the traditional limitations on expectation damages (including not only the denial of reimbursement for litigation costs, but also the requirements of foreseeability and certainty) as virtually guaranteeing that the nonbreaching party will be undercompensated if breach does occur. In the case of a discharged employee, for example, noncompensable damages might include injury to the employee's reputation or harm to her psychic well being or that of members of her family. In addition, the theory of efficient breach has been faulted for failing to take into account idiosyncratic injuries, that is, types of harm suffered by the nonbreaching party that are not reflected in the market values of the goods or services involved (and may indeed not be quantifiable at all). See generally Daniel A. Farber, Reassessing the Economic Efficiency of Compensatory Damages for Breach of Contract, 66 Va. L. Rev. 1443 (1980); Richard Schiro, Prospecting for Lost Profits in the Uniform Commercial Code: The Buyer's Dilemmas, 52 S. Cal. L. Rev. 1727 (1979); Alan Schwartz, The Case for Specific Performance, 89 Yale L.J. 271 (1979).

In order to counter these weaknesses in the basic efficient breach doctrine, various modifications in traditional remedial principles have been proposed. Professor Daniel Farber would in some cases award "super-compensatory" damages, calculated to compensate the plaintiff for some of the major transaction costs incurred as a result of breach (such as attorney fees) but not ordinarily recoverable under present rules. 66 Va. L. Rev. at 1443-1445. Professor Richard Schiro suggests a substantial loosening of the present rules limiting the recovery of "nonforeseeable" or "speculative" damages, to increase the likelihood that the actual injury resulting from breach will be fully compensated. 52 S. Cal. L. Rev. at 1757, 1769. Professor Alan Schwartz argues for an expanded availability of specific performance. 89 Yale L.J. at 305-306. See also Joshua Cender, Knocking Opportunism: A Reexamination of Efficient Breach of Contract, 1995 Ann. Surv. Am. L. 689 (to deter opportunistic breach, existing rules on compensatory damages should be altered to reflect all losses resulting from breach of contract).

Other writers have made direct assaults on the notion that the law does and should encourage the efficient breach of contract. Professor Ian Macneil argues that the doctrine is "fundamentally fallacious" in a number of respects. Even in its "simple" form (with transaction costs completely omitted), the doctrine assumes that the maximally "efficient" outcome will be produced only by breach. In fact, Macneil argues, that same outcome can and will be reached even under a rule of "specific performance" (i.e., a breaching party will be ordered to specifically perform his contractual duty), because in that case the parties will bargain among themselves to reach the "efficient" result: The party who has available a more profitable second contract will then buy his way out of the first one (rather than simply breaching it). Thus, the goods will still end up being allocated to their most highly valued use, but some of the resulting gain will have gone to the other party to the original contract. Ian R. Macneil, Efficient Breach of Contract: Circles in the Sky, 68 Va. L. Rev. 947, 951-952 (1982). (The commentators cited above also note that the remedial rules they propose could have the effect of forcing the "efficient" breacher to share with the innocent nonbreacher the gain that the former's breach will enable him to realize. Schiro, 52 S. Cal. L. Rev. at 1743-1744; Schwartz, 89 Yale L.J. at 285-286.)

Moreover, when the efficient-breach analysis is expanded to allow for some transaction costs, Macneil asserts that it cannot possibly be accurate unless it considers *all* potentially significant transaction costs under each proposed damage rule, including the costs of precontract planning, prebreach planning, postbreach negotiation and litigation, "relational costs" (including reputational injury), and so forth. Unless all such factors are included in the model, he argues, the analysis is useless. Ian R. Macneil, Efficient Breach of Contract: Circles in the Sky, 68 Va. L. Rev. 947, 961 (1982).

As his parting shot, Macneil has the following to say about "neoclassical" economic theory:

> The final question is the nature of the bias of the simple-efficient-breach theory. That bias is in favor of individual, uncooperative behavior as opposed to behavior requiring the cooperation of the parties. The whole thrust of the Posner analysis is breach first, talk afterwards. Indeed, this may be an overstatement of the level of cooperation, since Posner pays singularly little attention to talking afterwards. Although he stresses the transaction costs of negotiations needed to reach efficient results under the specific performance rule, he pays no attention to the transaction costs of talking after a breach. And this is so despite the fact that "talking after a breach" may be one of the more expensive forms of conversation to be found, involving, as it so often does, engaging high-priced lawyers, and gambits like starting litigation, engaging in discovery, and even trying and appealing cases.
>
> The bias against cooperation demonstrated by the simple-efficient-breach theory should surprise no one familiar with the neoclassical model. Such a bias is not limited to this particular fallacy, but is one towards which the neoclassical model inevitably and always tends. That model postulates individuals acting as if the relations in which those individuals exist have no effect on their behavior. Cooperative behavior postulates relations. A model assuming away relations slips with the greatest of ease at any stage into favoring uncooperative and — ironically enough — highly inefficient human behavior.

Id. at 968-969. See also Ian R. Macneil, Economic Analysis of Contractual Relations: Its Shortfalls and the Need for a "Rich Classificatory Apparatus," 75 Nw. U.L. Rev. 1018 (1981).

In a vein similar to Macneil's, Professor Daniel Friedmann argues that the theory of efficient breach is based on fallacious arguments. The concept fails to recognize that contractual rights, like property rights, are entitlements of which a person should not be deprived without his consent. Moreover, Friedmann argues that the efficient breach theory fails even on efficiency grounds because it increases transaction costs. To illustrate this point he considers a contract between A and B in which C values the property subject to the contract more highly than B:

> If A performs his contract with B, there will be only one additional transaction, that between B and C. If, however, A is "allowed" to break his contract with B, there will be two transactions: one between A and C over the sale of the property promised to B, and the other a dispute between A and B regarding the measure of damages. The implied assumption in Posner's analysis is that the payment of damages by A to B entails no transaction costs. This, however, is totally unrealistic. The payment of damages is hardly ever a standard transaction of the type the parties are routinely engaged in. It is likely to follow protracted negotiations, or even litigation, over difficult questions of fact and law. Finally, the breach may lead to an expensive tort action for inducement of breach of contract by the promisee (B) against the third party (C). This claim may breed another transaction between C and A regarding A's liability for losses suffered by C.

Daniel Friedmann, The Efficient Breach Fallacy, 18 J. Legal Stud. 1, 6-7 (1989).

Other scholars have been even more critical of the theory of efficient breach. Professor Patricia Marschall argues that promotion of economic efficiency is neither a "realistic" nor a "proper" goal for contract law. She urges courts to distinguish between willful and nonwillful breaches, awarding either specific performance or the highest measure of compensatory damages for the former. In addition, punitive damages should be available when the breach is not only willful, but also made in unreasonable disregard of the other party. Patricia H. Marschall, Willfulness: A Crucial Factor in Choosing Remedies for Breach of Contract, 24 Ariz. L. Rev. 733, 761 (1982). Professor Peter Linzer stresses that while economic efficiency is an important value in the law, fairness and justice are more important. He calls on courts to award specific performance for breach of promise rather than a "diluted substitute" of money damages. Peter Linzer, On the Amorality of Contract Remedies — Efficiency, Equity and the Second *Restatement,* 81 Colum. L. Rev. 111, 139 (1981). Professor George Cohen claims that the theory of efficient breach fails: Courts do not always award expectation damages and the theory does not explain when courts choose expectation damages over other remedies. Cohen argues instead for a fault-based theory of contract damages. He contends this theory is consistent with the actual decisions of courts and is sound economically because it creates the proper incentives for contracting parties regarding performance and breach. George M. Cohen, The Fault Lines in Contract Damages, 80 Va. L. Rev. 1225 (1994).

While the theory of efficient breach has been debated and used by academics for several decades, it remains true that few courts have explicitly relied on the doctrine in deciding cases. See Craig S. Warkol, Note, Resolving the Paradox Between Legal Theory and Legal Fact: The Judicial Rejection of the Theory of Efficient Breach, 20 Cardozo L. Rev. 321 (1998). Mr. Warkol offers four reasons for this lack of judicial acceptance:

> First, the theory improperly assumes that people are rational and efficient economic actors. Second, the theory is shortsighted because it fails to consider the value of morality. Third, the theory fails to recognize that contracts are risk allocation devices. Finally, and most critically, the theory fails to account for the existence of noneconomic damages that may be difficult to quantify and compensate.

Id. at 343.

In a recent review of the results produced by scholars applying principles of economic analysis to contract law generally, one of the leading scholars in the field, Professor Eric Posner, points to some successes but ultimately reaches a surprisingly negative conclusion: "[T]he economic approach does not explain the current system of contract law, nor does it provide a solid basis for criticizing and reforming contract law." Eric A. Posner, Economic Analysis of Contract Law after Three Decades: Success or Failure?, 112 Yale L.J. 829, 830 (2003). Despite Posner's criticisms, economic analysis of contract law will undoubtedly remain vibrant.

Roth v. Speck
District of Columbia Municipal Court of Appeals
126 A.2d 153 (1956)

QUINN, Associate Judge.

This suit was brought by plaintiff (employer) against defendant (employee) for breach of a written contract of employment. Trial by the court resulted in a finding and judgment for plaintiff for one dollar. Plaintiff appeals.

Plaintiff testified that he was the owner of a beauty salon in Silver Spring, Maryland; that his business was seasonal; and that on April 15, 1955, by a written contract he agreed to employ defendant as a hairdresser for one year. Defendant's salary was to be $75 a week or a commission of fifty percent on the gross receipts from his work, whichever sum was greater. Defendant remained in his employ for approximately six and one-half months and then left. Plaintiff testified that from the beginning defendant earned his salary, needed no special training, and soon built up and maintained a following because of his exceptional skill and talent.

Plaintiff also testified that his net profit was seven percent of the gross receipts per hairdresser. To substantiate this he introduced defendant's statement of earnings, which reflected gross receipts and salary paid to him. Plaintiff testified that in an effort to mitigate his damages he employed another person "to whom he paid $350, which was a complete loss and he had to let this employee go." He then hired still another operator who even at the date of trial was not earning his salary, and was thus employed at a loss to plaintiff. A witness for plaintiff testified that he had been the owner of a beauty salon for many years; that defendant had been in his employ since November 1, 1955, at a weekly salary of $100; and that defendant was a very good operator.

Defendant testified that he left because conditions in plaintiff's shop were unbearable; that he complained to plaintiff on numerous occasions; that he had asked for more money but that salary was not the main reason for his leaving; and that he was presently earning $100 per week.

The sole question presented is what damages plaintiff was entitled to under these circumstances. Plaintiff argues that the trial court did not consider the value of defendant's services or the profits lost by plaintiff and therefore erroneously limited the award to nominal damages. It is established law that where a plaintiff proves a breach of a contractual duty he is entitled to damages; however, when he offers no proof of actual damages or the proof is vague and speculative, he is entitled to no more than nominal damages. While the facts warrant application of this principle to plaintiff's claim concerning lost profits, we think there was proof of actual damage and that the evidence with regard to the value of defendant's services provided an accurate measure of such damage.

The measure of damages for breach of an employment contract by an employee is the cost of obtaining other service equivalent to that promised and not performed. Compensation for additional consequential injury may be recovered if at the time the contract was made the employee had reason to foresee that such injury would result from his breach. However, we need not concern ourselves with the foreseeability of lost profits resulting from defendant's breach since plaintiff's proof on this point was at most conjectural and speculative. He introduced defendant's statement of earnings, which reflected gross receipts and salary paid to defendant, and testified that his net profit was seven percent of such gross receipts per hairdresser. However, he also testified that his business was seasonal. The matter was further complicated by the testimony of both plaintiff and defendant to the effect that an employee assigned the customers and that some customers requested a particular operator. It can be seen then that defendant's gross receipts, and hence plaintiff's seven percent profit, depended on a number of contingencies — the seasonal fluctuations of business, defendant's skill and industry, and the judgment of the employee who assigned the operators. There was no criterion by which the trial court could have estimated plaintiff's profits with the degree of certainty necessary to allow their recovery; therefore they were not within the range of recoverable damages.

There remains the question as to the value of defendant's services. Defendant was evidently a hairdresser of exceptional talent. This is demonstrated not only by the fact that he experienced no difficulty in securing and retaining another position at a higher salary, but also by plaintiff's own testimony that he was unable to hire a satisfactory substitute. Defendant did not claim that he was required to render services other than those in his original contract with plaintiff in order to obtain a higher salary from his new employer, nor did plaintiff prove by expert testimony how much such services would bring in the market. But plaintiff did prove the amount defendant actually received. Under such circumstances, there was some evidence of the value of defendant's services and therefore of the cost of replacement. As was said in Triangle Waist Co. v. Todd, 223 N.Y. 27, 119 N.E. 85, 86:

> If one agrees to sell something to another, and then, the next day, sells it to someone else at an advance, the new transaction is not to be ignored in estimating the buyer's loss. . . . The rule is not different when one sells one's labor. The price received upon a genuine sale either of property or of service is some evidence of value. . . .

Twenty-four weeks yet remained when defendant abandoned his contract and obtained employment elsewhere at a higher salary. Until this new compensation is disproved as the value of his services, it may be presumed to be the fair value. That it was the fair value of defendant's services was partially supported by plaintiff's unsuccessful efforts to obtain a comparable replacement. Seemingly, plaintiff would have had to pay $100 a week in order to obtain an equally talented hairdresser, if one could have been found. If this be so, plaintiff, having contracted for defendant's services at a guaranteed wage of $75 per week, would be entitled to the difference between the two salaries for the remainder of the contract period. The fact that defendant was entitled to a fifty-percent commission on his gross receipts — if such receipts were more than his salary — should not be a deterrent to the application of this measure of damages. It was defendant's duty to prove facts in mitigation of the damage he caused by his breach. If he believed his damages would be lessened by proving that if he had stayed for the remainder of his contract the fifty-percent commission on his gross receipts would have been higher than his guaranteed salary, it was his burden to offer such proof. Though such facts may be difficult to prove, one who breaches his contract "'cannot wholly escape on account of the difficulty which his own wrong has produced of devising a perfect measure of,' or method of proving, damages."

The judgment will be reversed with instructions to grant a new trial, limited to the issue of damages.

Reversed with instructions.

Notes and Questions

1. *Roth* **and** *Lukaszewski* **compared.** Recall the measure of damages employed in Handicapped Children's Education Board v. Lukaszewski, section A of this chapter. Does the court in *Roth* recognize that rule? Should that measure have been used to compute the plaintiff's damages in *Roth*? Conversely, could the measure employed in *Roth* have been used in *Lukaszewski*? Should it have been?

2. *Use of market value measure of damages.* In computing damages for a seller's wrongful refusal to convey land, the court may employ as a measure of "market value" the higher price that the seller received in selling to another

(a sale that would not have been possible, of course, if the seller had not breached his earlier contract with the plaintiff). See Ament v. One Las Olas, Ltd., 898 So. 2d 147 (Fla. 2005) (long-standing precedent establishes that breaching seller should be liable to buyer for any profit made on subsequent sale). This result shifts to the innocent original purchaser the gain that the seller was able to realize as a result of the seller's breach. In *Roth,* the court carries that approach over to a case involving breach of an employment contract. Is this appropriate? Or are there factors, not present in the sale-of-land cases, that militate against using this approach to computation of damages in cases like *Roth?*

3. *The disgorgement principle.* Should the measure of damages used in *Roth* and in the sale-of-land cases be more generally employed, so as to give the plaintiff in most breach-of-contract cases the option of having her damages computed with reference to the gain the defendant was enabled to realize by virtue of his breach? Some commentators have observed that this factor, while not overtly provided for in orthodox contract-remedy doctrine, may be covertly at work in some types of cases. Besides sale-of-land contracts, Professor John Dawson cites as an example contracts for construction in which the owner's damages for defective performance are measured by the cost of completion rather than by the diminution in value occasioned by the breach. John P. Dawson, Restitution or Damages?, 20 Ohio St. L.J. 175, 185-189 (1959). (Recall *American Standard,* section A of this chapter.) More recently, other commentators have argued that the principle of "disgorgement" traditionally employed in cases of tortious conversion and breach of fiduciary duty should be further extended into the area of breach of contract. See Daniel Friedmann, Restitution of Benefits Obtained Through the Appropriation of Property or the Commission of a Wrong, 80 Colum. L. Rev. 504 (1980). (This form of remedy is commonly referred to as a species of "restitution," although it is clear that this is to some extent a misnomer, since the gain realized by the defendant was not received from the plaintiff.) Professor Friedmann argues that such restitution of gain may be proper in two types of cases: those involving appropriation of some "property" or "quasi-property" interest rightly belonging to the plaintiff and those in which "deterrence" is a major factor.

> In some instances a wrongdoer's profits may have been derived not from the plaintiff's property (even in the broadest sense) but from the property, labor, or skill, of the wrongdoer himself, even though it was the perpetrating of a wrong that enabled him to use his property, labor, or skill to obtain those profits. Because the gains were not derived from the plaintiff's property, the plaintiff cannot be regarded as "entitled" to them, and restitution cannot be founded upon the property theory elaborated in the previous section. Nevertheless, where the property approach falls short, considerations of deterrence and punishment, coupled with the basic idea that a man ought not to profit from his own wrong, have led to the development of rules governing forfeiture of ill-gotten gains.
>
> Application of the deterrent approach to justify restitution depends upon a number of considerations, including the reprehensibility of the defendant's conduct and the importance of the duty he breached. Other considerations that should be taken into account are the extent of the defendant's contribution and the justification for granting the plaintiff a windfall in the amount involved.

Friedmann, above, at 551. Among various hypothetical cases, Friedmann considers the following:

Illustration 2. A contracts to purchase from *B* 50,000 units of a certain article manufactured by *B*, at $10 per unit, for a total of $500,000. *B*'s cost of production is $9 per unit; his expected profit is therefore $50,000. *C* induces *A* to break his contract with *B* and buy the same article at the same price from him. *C*'s cost of production is $8 per unit. *B* is able to mitigate the loss and sell the goods at $9.60 per unit, for a total of $480,000. The reduction in profit to *B* is thus $20,000, while *C* has gained $100,000.

As we have seen, where one appropriates performance under a contract to which another is entitled, a claim for restitution may be made under the property approach. In this case, however, there are two different contracts. *C*'s profits from his contract result from his own resources and ability and are not derived from the appropriation of *B*'s contract rights. At most it can be said that only by the destruction of *B*'s contract was *C* able to form his own. Under these circumstances the property approach would not warrant *B*'s recovery of profits *C* made over and above *B*'s potential gain.

Nonetheless, should considerations of deterrence permit recovery of the additional $80,000 earned by *C*? That is, should *B* be permitted to "waive" the tort and seek restitution of all profits derived by *C* from his action? On balance, a negative answer seems proper. Allowing *B* to recover, beyond damages, the profit that *C* was able to reap would give *B* the benefit of *C*'s greater efficiency in production. In view of the broader economic and social implications of this approach, concern for the deterrence of interference with contractual relations would not justify a restitutionary award in this type of case.

It is conceivable that in exceptional circumstances deterrent considerations may justify restitution not only against the third party who induced the breach but also against the other party to the contract. Traditionally, contractual rights were accorded modest protection. But modern courts show greater sensitivity to contractual discipline, as evidenced by the liberalization of the remedy of specific performance and the development of the breach of contract tort, for which punitive damages may sometimes be awarded. Recognition of a right of restitution would be consistent with the same trend and make possible forfeiture of benefits unjustly obtained through breach of contract, even when the breach did not involve appropriation of the other party's right to performance.

Id. at 553-554. For a further discussion of disgorgement by Professor Friedmann, see Restitution for Wrongs: The Measure of Recovery, 79 Tex. L. Rev. 1879 (2001). Professor Friedmann's article is part of a symposium on issues in restitution and unjust enrichment. Is disgorgement of profit in such a case inconsistent with the theory of efficient breach? If so, which should prevail?

4. *Farnsworth's analysis of the disgorgement principle.* Professor Farnsworth has carried forward the discussion of whether and when the defendant should be required to make "restitution" to the plaintiff of gains made possible by breach. E. Allan Farnsworth, Your Loss or My Gain? The Dilemma of the Disgorgement Principle in Breach of Contract, 94 Yale L.J. 1339 (1985). Taking issue with a number of Friedmann's conclusions, Farnsworth advocates an even more cautious approach, stressing the fact that in many cases it is at least an oversimplification, if not an outright inaccuracy, to say that the defendant's gain is the "result" of his breach of contract. Id. at 1343-1350.

Farnsworth also notes that where there is a functioning market for the goods or services involved, application of market-value remedies will frequently result in effect in disgorgement of substantially all of the breacher's gain. Id. at 1370-1378. He does conclude, however, that a limited extension of the disgorgement principle is appropriate in cases of what he calls "abuse of contract." Farnsworth gives the following example:

> Suppose that I contract to build a house for you according to your plans for $150,000. I then find that by substituting cheaper materials I can do the job for $25,000 less than if I follow the plans. I make the switch, but you do not discover this until the house is built and you have paid me the $150,000. The price at which you can sell your house on the market is diminished by $10,000, and it would now cost $60,000 to replace the materials to conform to the plans, largely because of the cost of undoing and redoing the work.
>
> It is unlikely that a court would award you damages in the amount of $60,000, your cost of obtaining full performance ("cost to complete"), since the cost to complete will consist in large part of the expense of undoing my defective performance. A court will probably . . . award you damages based on the diminution in the price at which you can sell your house on the market, that is, $10,000. But can you require me to disgorge the $25,000 that I have saved by switching material in breach of our contract?

Id. at 1382. Going on to distinguish the stated case from one in which it is practicable for the innocent party to mitigate by obtaining a substitute on the market, Farnsworth concludes that perhaps in the example given, the remedy of disgorgement is appropriate because there is a "strong moral argument" in its favor, and because the breach has created a "significant risk of undercompensation." Id. at 1384-1386. For a case relying on Professor Farnsworth's analysis, see Earthinfo, Inc. v. Hydrosphere Resource Consultants, Inc., 900 P.2d 113 (Colo. 1995) (en banc) (in software development contract, defendant's conscious and intentional breach by refusing to make royalty payments justified plaintiff's rescission of contract and also disgorgement of profits received by defendant under derivative software contracts; case remanded for apportionment of profits between parties). See also University of Colorado Foundation, Inc. v. American Cyanamid Co., 342 F.3d 1298 (Fed. Cir. 2003) (following the *Earthinfo* precedent and upholding damage award based on disgorgement of profits resulting from misconduct related to patent as proper measure of restitution under Colorado law).

The disgorgement concept has also been advocated by a number of scholars in recent writings. Professor Melvin Eisenberg has asserted that not only can disgorgement be found in actual contract case law but also that it is appropriate in certain circumstances, including when necessary to provide incentive for performance and to avoid unjust enrichment by a breaching party. Melvin A. Eisenberg, The Disgorgement Interest in Contract Law, 105 Mich. L. Rev. 559 (2006). Similarly, Professor John D. McCamus has predicted and supported application of the disgorgement principle in breach of contract cases involving "wrongful" conduct such as commission of a tort or crime or breach of confidence or fiduciary duty. John D. McCamus, Disgorgement for Breach of Contract: A Comparative Perspective, 36 Loyola L.A. L. Rev. 943 (2003). See also Andrew Kull, Disgorgement for Breach, the "Restitution Interest," and the Restatement of Contracts, 79 Tex. L. Rev. 2021, 2052-53 (2001) (making distinction between remedies that restore value to nonbreaching party and those that address breaching party's gain; advocating use of disgorgement when the breach is both profitable to the breaching party and opportunistic). In light of the materials we have studied in this chapter, does it appear that a deliberate breach of contract will in many other types of cases also create for the other party a "significant risk of undercompensation?" In the next chapter, we consider some of the more orthodox applications of the restitutionary principle in the area of contract damages, along with other alternatives to the award of expectation damages.

PROBLEM 11-4

You are an attorney representing a variety of clients involved in different phases of the motion picture and television industries. Not long ago you assisted one of your clients, Robin Green, with the negotiation of a contract for her services next season as a performer in a weekly dramatic television series, "Operating Room," in which she was to play the continuing featured role of a doctor, for a salary of $30,000 per week, for a minimum of 13 and maximum of 39 weeks of installments. Before that contract was negotiated and signed, Green had performed a featured role in a theatrical motion picture, *Frat Men in Space*. When *Frat Men* was subsequently released, it became the surprise hit of the summer season, grossing many millions of dollars for its producers and winning acclaim and attention for all its featured performers, particularly Green. Green has now received informal and indirect word from the producer of an established television comedy series, "Flying High," that she is being considered to replace one of the three principal players in that series, in the role of an airline pilot. She has been led to believe (and your experience confirms this) that such a role would be compensated at $75,000 or more per weekly episode. However, Green's fulfillment of her existing contract for "Operating Room" would be inconsistent with a role in "Flying High," both legally and practically, since either role would require a full-time commitment to filming during the coming television season. Green now asks you whether she can and should pursue the possibility of a role in "Flying High." Specifically, she asks you what would be the legal consequences if she breached her contract for "Operating Room," and — in light of your conclusions on that point — whether you would advise her to do so, if necessary, in order to obtain the better and more remunerative contract.

In light of the preceding material on damage remedies, what would you tell her?

12

Alternatives to Expectation Damages: Reliance and Restitutionary Damages, Specific Performance, and Agreed Remedies

In Chapter 11 we examined the principles governing the award of expectation damages in actions for breach of contract. In this chapter we analyze several alternatives to expectation damages: reliance and restitutionary damages, specific performance, and agreed remedies. In addition, we consider the measure of recovery when the basis of liability is either the doctrine of promissory estoppel or restitution, rather than conventional breach of contract.

A. RELIANCE DAMAGES

We have seen that modern contract law recognizes three interests as the basis for awarding damages: expectation, reliance, and restitution. (Recall the excerpt from the Fuller and Perdue article quoted in the introduction to Chapter 11.) When and how should damages based on the reliance rather than the expectation interest be determined? The following materials explore these questions.

Wartzman v. Hightower Productions, Ltd.
Court of Special Appeals of Maryland
53 Md. App. 656, 456 A.2d 82 (1983)

JAMES S. GETTY, Judge (Specially Assigned).

Woody Hightower did not succeed in breaking the Guinness World Record for flagpole sitting; his failure to accomplish this seemingly nebulous feat, however, did generate protracted litigation. We are concerned here with whether Judge Robert L. Karwacki, presiding in the Superior Court of Baltimore City, correctly permitted a jury to consider the issue of "reliance damages" sustained by the appellees. Additionally, we are requested by the appellees, as cross-appellants, to determine if the trial court's refusal to permit the jury to consider prejudgment interest is error.

Hightower Productions Ltd. (appellees and cross-appellants) came into being in 1974 as a promotional venture conceived by Ira Adler, Frank Billitz and J. Daniel Quinn. The principals intended to employ a singer-entertainer who would live in a specially constructed mobile flagpole perch from April 1, 1975, until New Years Eve at which time he would descend in Times Square in New York before a nationwide television audience having established a new world record for flagpole sitting.

The young man selected to perform this feat was to be known as "Woody Hightower." The venture was to be publicized by radio and television exposure, by adopting a theme song and by having the uncrowned champion make appearances from his perch throughout the country at concerts, state fairs and shopping centers.

In November, 1974, the three principals approached Michael Kaminkow of the law firm of Wartzman, Rombro, Rudd and Omansky, P.A., for the specific purpose of incorporating their venture. Mr. Kaminkow, a trial attorney, referred them to his partner, Paul Wartzman.

The three principals met with Mr. Wartzman at his home and reviewed the promotional scheme with him. They indicated that they needed to sell stock to the public in order to raise the $250,000 necessary to finance the project. Shortly thereafter, the law firm prepared and filed the articles of incorporation and Hightower Productions Ltd. came into existence on November 6, 1974. The Articles of Incorporation authorized the issuance of one million shares of stock of the par value of 10 cents per share, or a total of $100,000.00.

Following incorporation, the three principals began developing the project. With an initial investment of $20,000, they opened a corporate account at Maryland National Bank and an office in the Pikesville Plaza Building. Then began the search for "Woody Hightower." After numerous interviews, twenty-three year old John Jordan emerged as "Woody Hightower."

After selecting the flagpole tenant, the corporation then sought and obtained a company to construct the premises to house him. This consisted of a seven foot wide perch that was to include a bed, toilet, water, refrigerator and heat. The accommodations were atop an hydraulic lift system mounted upon a flat bed tractor trailer.

Hightower employed two public relations specialists to coordinate press and public relations efforts and to obtain major corporate backers. "Woody" received a proclamation from the Mayor and City Council of Baltimore and after a press breakfast at the Hilton Hotel on "All Fools Day" ascended his home in the sky.

Within ten days, Hightower obtained a live appearance for "Woody" on the Mike Douglas Show, and a commitment for an appearance on the Wonderama television program. The principals anticipated a "snowballing" effect from commercial enterprises as the project progressed with no substantial monetary commitments for approximately six months.

Hightower raised $43,000.00 by selling stock in the corporation. Within two weeks of "Woody's" ascension, another stockholders' meeting was scheduled, because the corporation was low on funds. At that time, Mr. Wartzman informed the principals that no further stock could be sold, because the corporation was "structured wrong," and it would be necessary to obtain the services of a securities attorney to correct the problem. Mr. Wartzman had acquired this information in a casual conversation with a friend who recommended that the corporation should consult with a securities specialist.

The problem was that the law firm had failed to prepare an offering memorandum and failed to assure that the corporation had made the required disclosures to prospective investors in accordance with the provisions of the Maryland Securities Act Article 32A. (The Act was repealed and re-enacted in 1975 as CA Sec. 11-101 to 11-805). Mr. Wartzman advised Hightower that the cost of the specialist would be between $10,000.00 and $15,000.00. Hightower asked the firm to pay for the required services and the request was rejected.

Hightower then employed substitute counsel and scheduled a shareholders' meeting on April 28, 1975. At that meeting, the stockholders were advised that Hightower was not in compliance with the securities laws; that $43,000.00, the amount investors had paid for issued stock, had to be covered by the promoters and placed in escrow; that the fee of a securities specialist would be $10,000.00 to $15,000.00 and that the additional work would require between six and eight weeks. In the interim, additional stock could not be sold, nor could "Woody" be exhibited across state lines. Faced with these problems, the shareholders decided to discontinue the entire project.

On October 8, 1975, Hightower filed suit alleging breach of contract and negligence for the law firm's failure to have created a corporation authorized to raise the capital necessary to fund the venture. At the trial, Hightower introduced into evidence its obligations and expenditures incurred in reliance on the defendant law firm's creation of a corporation authorized to raise the $250,000.00, necessary to fund the project. The development costs incurred included corporate obligations amounting to $155,339 including: initial investments by Adler and Billitz, $20,000; shareholders, excluding the three promoters, $43,010; outstanding liabilities exclusive of salaries, $58,929; liability to talent consultants, $25,000; and accrued salaries to employees, $8,400.

Individual liabilities to the three promoters, Adler, Billitz and Quinn, totaled $88,608, including loans to the corporation $44,692; repayment of corporate debt to Maryland National Bank, $8,016; and loss of salaries $36,000. The trial court disposed of the individual suit filed by the promoters, Adler, Billitz and Quinn and the cross complaint filed by the appellants. The only claim submitted for the jury's consideration was the claim of the corporation, Hightower, against the defendant law firm.

The jury returned a verdict in favor of Hightower in the amount of $170,508.43. Wartzman, Rombro, Rudd and Omansky, P.A., appealed to this Court. Hightower filed a cross appeal alleging that the jury should have been permitted to consider prejudgment interest.

The appellants raise four issues for our consideration:

1. The trial court erred in permitting Hightower to recover "reliance damages" or "development costs."

2. If "reliance damages" were recoverable, the trial court failed to properly instruct the jury on the law concerning their recovery.

3. The trial court erred in refusing to instruct the jury on the duty to mitigate damages.

4. The trial court erroneously permitted a member of the plaintiff's law firm to testify as a witness in the case.

RELIANCE DAMAGES

The appellants first contend that the jury verdict included all of Hightower's expenditures and obligations incurred during its existence resulting in the law firm being absolute surety for all costs incurred in a highly speculative venture. While they do not suggest the analogy, the appellants would no doubt equate the verdict as tantamount to holding the blacksmith liable for the value of the kingdom where the smith left out a nail in shoeing the king's horse, because of which the shoe was lost, the horse was lost, the king was lost and the kingdom was lost. Appellants contend that there is a lack of nexus or causation between the alleged failure of Mr. Wartzman to discharge his duties as an attorney and the loss claimed by Hightower. Stated differently, an unjust result will obtain where a person performing a collateral service for a new venture will, upon failure to fully perform the service, be liable as full guarantor for all costs incurred by the enterprise.

Ordinarily, profits lost due to a breach of contract are recoverable. Where anticipated profits are too speculative to be determined, monies spent in part performance, in preparation for or in reliance on the contract are recoverable. 5 Corbin, Contracts, Sec. 1031, Restatement of Contracts, Sec. 333, cited with approval in Dialist Co. v. Pulford, 42 Md. App. 173, 399 A.2d 1374 (1979).

In *Dialist,* supra, a distributor, Pulford, brought suit for breach of an exclusive contract that he had with Dialist. Pulford paid $2500.00 for the distributorship, terminated his employment with another company and expended funds in order to begin developing the area where the product was to be sold. When Pulford learned that another distributor was also given part of his territory he terminated his services.

This Court upheld the award of development costs to Pulford which included out of pocket expenses, telephone installation, office furniture, two months of forfeited salary and the value of medical insurance lost. The Court determined that the expenditures were not in preparation for or part performance of a contract, but in reliance upon it. "Such expenditures are not brought about by reason of the breach. They are induced by reliance on the contract itself and rendered worthless by its breach." Id. at 181, 399 A.2d 1374.

Recovery based upon reliance interest is not without limitation. If it can be shown that full performance would have resulted in a net loss, the plaintiff cannot escape the consequences of a bad bargain by falling back on his reliance interest. Where the breach has prevented an anticipated gain and made proof of loss difficult to ascertain, the injured party has a right to damages based upon his reliance interest, including expenditures made in preparation for performance, or in performance, less any loss that the party in breach can prove with reasonable certainty the injured party would have suffered had the contract been performed. Restatement, Second, Contracts, Sec. 349, Holt v. United Security Life Ins. & Trust Co., 76 N.J. 585, 72 A. 301 (1909); In Re Yeager Company, 227 Fed. Supp. 92 (N.D. Ohio, E.D. 1963).

The appellants' contention that permitting the jury to consider that reliance damages in this case rendered the appellants insurers of the venture is without merit. Section 349 of the Restatement, cited above, expressly authorizes the breaching party to prove any loss that the injured party would have suffered had the contract been performed. Such proof would avoid making the breaching party a guarantor of the success of the venture.

As Judge Learned Hand stated in Albert & Son v. Armstrong Rubber Company, 178 F.2d 182 (2d Cir. 1949),

> It is often very hard to learn what the value of the performance would have been; and it is a common expedient, and a just one, in such situations to put the peril of the answer upon that party who by his wrong has made the issue relevant to the rights of the other. On principle therefore the proper solution would seem to be that the promisee may recover his outlay in preparation for the performance, subject to the privilege of the promisor to reduce it by as much as he can show that the promisee would have lost if the contract had been performed.

In the present case the appellants knew, or should have known, that the success of the venture rested upon the ability of Hightower to sell stock and secure advertising as public interest in the adventure accelerated. Appellants' contention that their failure to properly incorporate Hightower was collateral and lacked the necessary nexus to permit consideration of reliance damages is not persuasive. The very life blood of the project depended on the corporation's ability to sell stock to fund the promotion. This is the reason for the employment of the appellants. In reliance thereon, Hightower sold stock and incurred substantial obligations. When it could no longer sell its stock, the entire project failed. No greater nexus need be established. Aside from questioning the expertise of the promoters based upon their previous employment, the appellants were unable to establish that the stunt was doomed to fail. The inability to establish that financial chaos was inevitable does not make the appellants insurers and does not preclude Hightower from recovering reliance damages. The issue was properly submitted to the jury.

Appellants contend that the appellees should be limited to the recovery of damages under traditional contract and negligence concepts, citing Meyerberg, Sawyer and Rue v. Agee, 51 Md. App. 711, 446 A.2d 69 (1982).

Meyerberg, supra, involved a breach of contract action for certification of a title that was not marketable. The trial judge permitted the jury, in assessing damages, to consider:

1. Economic loss occasioned by increased costs of construction and financing.
2. Attorneys' fees expended to establish access to the property.
3. Capital gains taxes paid for failure to purchase another property within the time limitations prescribed by law.
4. The amount of earned hazard insurance premium the appellees were required to purchase.

In affirming the decision of the trial court, this Court acknowledged that a contracting party is expected to take account of only those risks that are foreseeable at the time he makes the contract and is not liable in the event of breach for loss that he did not at the time of contracting have reason to foresee as a probable result of such a breach. This limitation is set forth in Restatement, Contracts, (2d), Sec. 351.

In *Meyerberg*, we noted that exceptional perception is not relevant to the test of foreseeability when applied to an attorney who is relied upon by a layman to protect his investment from pitfalls which are not readily apparent to those in foreign fields of endeavor.

Relying on Cochrane v. Little, 71 Md. 323, 18 A. 698 (1889), we further stated:

> A client who has employed an attorney has a right to his diligence, his knowledge and his skill; and whether he had not so much of these qualities as he was bound to have, or having them, neglected to employ them, the law properly makes him liable for the loss that has accrued to his employer.

We find little solace for the appellants' cause in the cases cited above. . . .

INSTRUCTIONS ON RELIANCE DAMAGES

Appellants' primary exception to the court's damage instruction relates to the failure to include suggested instruction 23b which states:

> You are instructed that you may not award any damages for unpaid expense of Hightower unless you find that these expenses were incurred by Hightower in justifiable reliance on the defendant's causing Hightower to comply with the securities laws. If you find that the expenses were not incurred in reliance on the defendant's performance, or if such reliance was not justified, then you may not award unpaid expenses as damages.

The Court instructed the jury that in order to find liability that the plaintiff must prove three things:

> First, the employment of the defendants in behalf of the Plaintiff and the extent of the duties for which the Defendants were employed; secondly, that the Defendants neglected the duties undertaken in the employment and, thirdly, that such negligence resulted in and was the proximate cause of loss by the Plaintiff, that is that the Plaintiff was deprived of any right or parted with anything of value in reliance upon the negligence of the Defendants.

The instruction given fairly apprised the jury of the Plaintiffs' burden and adequately covered the reliance damage concept. Additionally, the court instructed the jury that they could not consider unpaid salaries due its officers or employees or amounts invested by stockholders as recoverable damages.

Appellants further object to the court's refusal to grant its suggested instructions 23C and D designed to forbid recovery if the jury found that Hightower would not have been able to secure funds to remain in business regardless of the defendants' breach. The instruction was properly refused. The very nature of reliance damages is that future gain cannot be measured with any reasonable degree of reliability. Had Hightower been able to show lost profits the theory of their right to recover may not have been development costs in reliance on the contract but loss based upon expectation interest instead. Appellants had the opportunity to minimize the recovery by showing that the venture could not succeed. This was difficult, but their failure to do so does not entitle them to an instruction that requires the jury to speculate on the ultimate success of the venture. We find no error in the instructions given by Judge Karwacki.

DUTY TO MITIGATE DAMAGES

Appellants further except to the trial court's refusal to grant any instruction on the issue of Hightower's obligation to mitigate its damages. The instruction offered by appellants is a correct statement of the law. Correctness alone, however, is insufficient to require the court to grant the prayer; there must be evidence to support the proposition to which it relates. Dorough v. Lockman, 224 Md. 168, 167 A.2d 129 (1961).

The evidence in this case establishes that Hightower did not have the $43,000.00 to place in escrow covering stock sold, did not have the $10,000.00 or $15,000.00 to employ a securities specialist and could not continue stock sales or exhibitions to obtain the necessary funds. Mr. Wartzman's offer to set up an appointment for Hightower with an expert in security transactions at Hightower's expense can hardly be construed as a mitigating device that Hightower was obligated to accept. The party who is in default may not mitigate his damages by showing that the other party could have reduced those damages by expending large amounts of money or incurring substantial obligations. *Meyerberg*, supra. Since such risks arose because of the breach, they are to be borne by the defaulting party. 22 Am. Jur. 2d, Damages, Sec. 37, Griffin v. Bredouw (Okla.), 420 P.2d 546 (1966).

The doctrine of avoidable consequences, moreover, does not apply where both parties have an equal opportunity to mitigate damages. Appellants had the same opportunity to employ and pay a securities specialist as they contend Hightower should have done. They refused. Having rejected Hightower's request to assume the costs of an additional attorney, they are estopped from asserting a failure by Hightower to reduce its loss. See D. Dobbs, Remedies, Sec. 37, (1973), 11 Williston, Contracts Sec. 1353, (1979).

There is no evidence in this case that the additional funds necessary to continue the operation pending a restructuring of the corporation were within the financial capabilities of Hightower. The Court properly declined to instruct the jury on the issue of mitigation. . . .

PREJUDGMENT INTEREST

Hightower, in its cross-appeal, alleges that the issue of pre-judgment interest should have been presented to the jury for its consideration. Applicable Maryland law provides that where a claim is for unliquidated damages, interest may run from the date of the judgment, but not before. *Affiliated Distillers*, 213 Md. 509, 132 A.2d 582 (1957), Taylor v. Wahby, 271 Md. 101, 314 A.2d 100 (1974).

The reliance damages sought in this case are not subject to pre-judgment valuation. "Reasonable and justified" damages incurred by reason of

Mr. Wartzman's representation of Hightower were not reasonably ascertainable until the jury rendered its verdict. Refusal to permit the jury to consider prejudgment interest, therefore, was not an abuse of discretion.

In conclusion, the final comment of Judge Lowe in *Meyerberg,* supra, is equally apposite here.

> The unfortunate oversight on which this case was based was a costly one, but it was made by one who was hired precisely for the purpose of averting the consequent losses. It is he, and his firm, who must bear them.

Judgment affirmed.
Costs assessed to appellants.

Notes and Questions

1. *Reliance damages as a substitute remedy.* Even if expectation damages would in theory be recoverable, they may not be proveable with reasonable certainty. In such a case, the plaintiff's fall-back position will usually be to seek recovery of reliance damages. See, e.g., United States v. Behan, 110 U.S. 338 (1884) (contractor allowed to recover expenditures in part-performance where lost profits too speculative because cost of completion not provable with reasonable certainty); Hollywood Fantasy Corp. v. Gabor, 151 F.3d 203 (5th Cir. 1998) (promoter of "fantasy vacations" for movie fans allowed to recover out-of-pocket expenses from breaching celebrity despite inability to prove lost profits for new venture). The revised Restatement also adopts this rule in §349. In *Wartzman,* what could the plaintiff's expectation damages have consisted of? What were the obstacles to establishing a claim for such damages?

2. *Contract price as limit on reliance damages.* The report of the *Wartzman* case does not indicate the amount the defendants charged for their legal services, but in light of the indication that a "securities specialist" would have cost no more than $15,000, it seems obvious that the defendants' bill for legal fees was far less than the $170,000 awarded to the plaintiffs. Should this factor bear on the availability of reliance damages? Under the original Restatement, reliance damages as an alternative to expectation damages were stated to be "not recoverable in excess of the full contract price promised by the defendant." Restatement §333(a). Fuller and Perdue criticized this limitation. They argued that a distinction should be drawn between the costs of performance of the contract (which they labeled "essential reliance") and the costs incurred in collateral transactions related to the contract ("incidental reliance"). The contract price should limit the recovery only of essential reliance damages. To the extent that essential reliance exceeds the contract price, the contract would be a losing one. An award of essential reliance damages in excess of the contract price would put the injured party in a better position than if the contract had been fully performed. The contract price should not, however, limit the recovery of incidental reliance damages. Lon L. Fuller & William R. Perdue, Jr., The Reliance Interest in Contract Damages, 46 Yale L.J. 52, 77-78 (Pt. I) (1936).

For example, in Maine Rubber International v. Environmental Management Group, Inc., 324 F. Supp. 2d 32 (D. Me. 2004), the plaintiff paid the defendant $1900 to perform an environmental assessment of a prospective business site. After the defendant falsely reported that the property was free of problems, the federal and state governments found environmental hazards and the plaintiff lost more than $211,000 in wasted expenditures when a move to the site was aborted. The court held that these amounts could be recovered as reasonably foreseeable reliance damages even though their total greatly exceeded the contract price.

Several commentators have criticized the terminology used by Fuller and Perdue, while accepting their reasoning. E.g., Robert E. Hudec, Restating the "Reliance Interest," 67 Cornell L. Rev. 704, 724-726 (1982) (ambiguity latent in this terminology; more useful distinction would probably be "direct" and "consequential"); Stewart Macaulay, *The Reliance Interest* and the World Outside the Law Schools' Doors, 1991 Wis. L. Rev. 247, 268 (concept of "incidental reliance" makes important contribution in widening our view of compensable reliance to include investment in other transactions necessary to "unlock the contract's value"; however, decided cases do not make much of the distinction, and courts often do not provide enough information about damages claimed and awarded to enable reader to classify them under the Fuller/Perdue terminology).

3. *Limitations on recovery of reliance damages.* The revised Restatement indicates that the doctrines that normally apply to limit recovery of expectation damages — foreseeability, causation, certainty, and mitigation — should also apply to recovery of reliance damages. E.g., Restatement (Second) §352, Comment *a* (requirement of certainty). See also L. Albert & Son v. Armstrong Rubber Co., 178 F.2d 182 (2d Cir. 1949) (in contract for sale of rubber reconditioning machines, buyer denied damages for investment in rubber reclaiming department and for cost of scrap rubber because of showing that delay in delivery by seller was only one of several possible causes of loss); Interfilm, Inc. v. Advanced Exhibition Corp., 672 N.Y.S.2d 309 (App. Div. 1998) (reliance damages for breach of contract to finance film properly precluded for failure to prove reliance harm with certainty); Cities Services Co. v. Gulf Oil Corp., 980 P.2d 116 (Ok. 1999) (reliance damages have goal of undoing harm that was foreseeable and can be measured with reasonable certainty).

As we have seen, one of the principal damage-limiting factors is the possibility that the plaintiff could have mitigated the injury resulting from the defendant's breach. In *Wartzman*, the court held that the plaintiffs had no obligation to mitigate their damages by paying the amount necessary to hire an attorney specialized in securities law, because the defendants had the same opportunity as the plaintiffs to take that action. This "equal opportunity" exception to the requirement of mitigation has been applied by other courts, although some have expressed doubt about its utility. Compare Chicago Title Insurance Co. v. Huntington National Bank, 719 N.E.2d 955 (Ohio 1999) (failure to mitigate will not limit damages when defendant title company had equal opportunity to that of plaintiff bank to bid on foreclosed home to prevent sale below market value after title company breached contract), with Cates v. Morgan Portable Building Corp., 780 F.2d 683 (7th Cir. 1985) (plaintiff's obligation to mitigate not offset by fact that defendant had "equal opportunity" to complete performance of installing buildings for plaintiff's motel facility; defendant could mitigate only by performing as promised while plaintiff had variety of other options, and application of "questionable" equal opportunity rule would remove incentive for plaintiff to act reasonably in mitigation). Did the *Wartzman* court properly reject the defendant's mitigation argument?

4. *Losing contracts.* In the course of its opinion in *Wartzman*, the court notes another potential limitation on the recovery of reliance expenses, quoting from Restatement (Second) §349: recovery should be offset by "any loss that the party in breach can prove with reasonable certainty the injured party would have suffered had the contract been performed." The defendant, however, would have the burden of showing that the contract would have been a losing one for the plaintiff. See, e.g., Doering Equipment Co. v. John Deere Co., 815 N.E.2d 234 (Mass. Ct. App. 2004) (equipment distributor could not collect reliance damages where evidence established that contract was a losing contract, apart from alleged breach by manufacturer).

5. *Precontract reliance.* Courts may not allow a party to recover for reliance costs incurred before the contract was made. See Chicago Coliseum Club v. Dempsey, 265 Ill. App. 542 (1932) (fight promoter not allowed to recover expenses incurred before defendant signed contract to perform); Drysdale v. Woerth, 153 F. Supp. 2d 678 (E.D. Pa. 2001) (tenant may not recover reliance damages for improvements made to property while tenant occupied property under one-year lease prior to negotiation of 20-year lease renewal, but tenant may recover in restitution for increase in market value of defendant's property as result of improvements); E. Allan Farnsworth, Contracts §12.16, at 805. But see Security Stove & Manufacturing Co. v. American Railway Express Co., 51 S.W.2d 572 (Mo. Ct. App. 1932) (shipper allowed to recover precontract expenses from carrier who failed to deliver goods to exhibition, thus causing expenses to be wasted); John E. Murray, Jr., Murray on Contracts §121(D) at 795 (4th ed. 2001) (suggesting the recovery of precontract damages depends on test of certainty).

6. *Forgone opportunities as reliance damages.* Ordinarily, reliance damages are thought of as out-of-pocket expenditures made by the plaintiff. Sometimes, however, protection of the injury to the plaintiff's reliance extends further, taking into account the gains the plaintiff would have made had she not relied on the promises of the defendant. See Dialist Co. v. Pulford, 399 A.2d 1374, 1382 (Md. Ct. Spec. App. 1979) (after breach of exclusive territory provision, plaintiff permitted to recover not only initial franchise fee but also amount of lost salary after quitting his original job until reemployed; court asserted that "giving up one's livelihood in reliance on, in preparation for and in performance of, a contractual obligation can be as real a detriment as out-of-pocket expenditures"). See also Designer Direct, Inc. v. Deforest Redevelopment Authority, 368 F.3d 751 (7th Cir. 2004) (plaintiff allowed to recover reliance damages, including "overhead" expenses, that could have been recovered under alternative contracts that were available).

Walser v. Toyota Motor Sales, U.S.A., Inc.
United States Court of Appeals
43 F.3d 396 (8th Cir. 1994)

HANSEN, Circuit Judge.

The plaintiffs, Paul Martin Walser and Philip Martin McLaughlin, appeal from a jury verdict in this diversity case awarding them $232,131 in damages on their promissory estoppel claim against Toyota Motor Sales. The plaintiffs argue that the district court erred by instructing the jury that the plaintiffs' damages on their promissory estoppel claim were limited to out-of-pocket expenses. The plaintiffs also argue that the district court erred in declining to award specific performance as an alternative remedy on their promissory estoppel claim, in denying their motion for judgment as a matter of law on their contract claim, in instructing the jury on their contract claim, in requiring them to accept payment from Toyota for $.89 less than the amount of damages and interest awarded, in granting summary judgment on their claim under the Minnesota Motor Vehicle Sale and Distribution Regulations, and in precluding them from taxing costs prior to a final determination of this case on appeal. We affirm.

I.

In 1987, Toyota Motor Sales, U.S.A., conducted market surveys throughout the United States to identify the best markets for the new line of "Lexus" automobiles that Toyota planned to introduce in 1989. The market studies identified the Minneapolis/St. Paul, Minnesota, metropolitan area as a two-dealership market and recommended establishing dealerships in two suburban areas—Wayzata and the Bloomington/Richfield area.

In April 1988, Toyota issued letters of intent for the prospective dealerships in the two locations. The recipient of the letter for the Bloomington/Richfield dealership was unwilling or unable to comply with the conditions of the letter of intent and returned it to Toyota in early 1989. Soon after, Toyota began to search anew for a dealer for the Bloomington/Richfield location. Lexus Central Region Area Manager, James Melton, asked Stephen Haag, the Central Region Market Manager, to contact Walser, who was then co-owner with McLaughlin of a BMW dealership and a Lincoln-Mercury dealership both located in Bloomington. Both Walser and McLaughlin met with Haag and indicated that they would be interested in obtaining the Lexus dealership.

Toyota had instituted a three-step process to establish dealerships. First, the prospective dealer would fill out a formal application and propose a dealership plan to Toyota. If acceptable, then Toyota would issue a letter of intent signed by the head of the Lexus division and to be signed by the prospective dealer, which would contain final conditions that had to be satisfied before the agreement was finalized. If all conditions were satisfied, then a formal dealership agreement would be approved by Toyota and signed by the parties to establish the dealership.

[After Walser and McLaughlin formally applied for the Lexus dealership, Haag told Walser in October 1989 that the letter of intent would soon be approved. Subsequently, in December 1989, Haag told Walser that "you're our dealer" and that the letter of intent had been formally approved by Lexus management. A few days later Haag called Walser to tell him that a mistake had been made, that the letter had not been finally approved, and that additional financial information would be necessary. In the meantime Walser's father, R.J. Walser, had agreed to purchase property for the proposed Lexus dealership. In February 1990, Haag informed Walser that Lexus would not be issuing the letter of intent to him and McLaughlin. — Eds.]

On March 7, 1990, Walser and McLaughlin filed a seven-count complaint in Minnesota state court against Toyota. Walser and McLaughlin sought relief under the following theories: breach of the Minnesota motor vehicle franchise statute (count I); breach of contract (count II); promissory estoppel (count III); joint venture (count IV); fraud (count V); intentional interference with contractual relations (count VI); and interference with a prospective business advantage (count VII). Toyota removed this action to the United States District Court for the District of Minnesota.

The district court granted Toyota's motion for partial summary judgment and dismissed the claims for breach of the Minnesota motor vehicle franchise statute and for recovery on a joint venture theory. Prior to trial, the parties filed a joint stipulation to dismiss without prejudice the claims for intentional interference with contractual relations and interference with a prospective business advantage. The case went to trial in February 1992 on the breach of contract, promissory estoppel, and fraud claims. Walser and McLaughlin sought approximately $7,600,000 in damages, which included expected lost profits. The jury returned a verdict in favor of Toyota on the contract and fraud claims but in favor of Walser and McLaughlin on the promissory estoppel claim. The jury awarded Walser and McLaughlin $232,131 in accordance with the district court's instruction to limit damages on the promissory estoppel claim to Walser and McLaughlin's out-of-pocket expenses.

. . .

II.

. . .

A.

Walser and McLaughlin's principal argument in this appeal is that the district court erred in instructing the jury that damages on their promissory estoppel claim were limited to the out-of-pocket expenditures they made in reliance on Toyota's promise. The jury awarded $232,131 in out-of-pocket expenses. Walser and McLaughlin argue that under Minnesota law, the court should have allowed the jury to consider awarding lost profits of up to $7,600,000 allegedly flowing from Toyota's failure to keep its promise.

Minnesota has adopted the statement of the doctrine of promissory estoppel found at Restatement (Second) of Contracts §90 (1981). Christensen v. Minneapolis Mun. Employees Retirement Bd., 331 N.W.2d 740, 749 (Minn. 1983). Section 90 provides, in relevant part:

> A promise which the promisor should reasonably expect to induce action or forbearance on the part of the promisee or a third person and which does induce

such action or forbearance is binding if injustice can be avoided only by enforcement of the promise. The remedy granted for breach may be limited as justice requires.

Restatement (Second) of Contracts §90(1) (1981); see also Cohen v. Cowles Media Co., 479 N.W.2d 387, 391-92 (Minn. 1992) (relying on and quoting from portions of section 90); *Christensen,* 331 N.W.2d at 749 (quoting section 90). Of particular significance to this case is the meaning of the last phrase of the quoted section: "The remedy granted for breach may be limited as justice requires." The commentary to section 90 elaborates on the nature of the remedy available for breach based on promissory estoppel:

> A promise binding under this section is a contract, and full-scale enforcement by normal remedies is often appropriate. But the same factors which bear on whether any relief should be granted also bear on the character and extent of the remedy. *In particular, relief may sometimes be limited to restitution or to damages or specific relief measured by the extent of the promisee's reliance rather than by the terms of the promise.*

Restatement (Second) of Contracts §90 cmt. *d* (emphasis added). Minnesota courts have incorporated the underlined language stating: "When a promise is enforced pursuant to section 90 '[t]he remedy granted for breach may be limited as justice requires.' Relief *may be limited* to damages measured by the promisee's reliance." Grouse v. Group Health Plan, 306 N.W.2d 114, 116 (Minn. 1981) (alterations in original) (emphasis added). The Minnesota Court of Appeals, relying on *Grouse,* further stated that "relief *may be limited* to the party's out-of-pocket expenses made in reliance on the promise." Dallum v. Farmers Union Cent. Exch., Inc., 462 N.W.2d 608, 613 (Minn. Ct. App. 1990) (emphasis added).

The critical question in this case is whether the language of section 90 as interpreted by the Minnesota courts authorized the district court to limit damages to Walser and McLaughlin's out-of-pocket expenses. We conclude that it did. This language is permissive — courts *may* limit relief as justice requires. The Minnesota Court of Appeals specifically stated that "relief *may* be limited to the party's out-of-pocket expenses made in reliance on the promise." *Dallum,* 462 N.W.2d at 613 (emphasis added). This permissive language and the Minnesota courts' interpretation of it indicate to us that Minnesota courts, like the other courts addressing this issue, treat the damages decision under section 90 as being within the district court's discretion. See, e.g., Chedd-Angier Prod. Co., Inc. v. Omni Publications Int'l, Ltd., 756 F.2d 930, 937 (1st Cir. 1985) (in determining damages under section 90 "whether to charge full contract damages, or something less, is a matter of discretion delegated to district courts"); Green v. Interstate United Management Serv. Corp., 748 F.2d 827, 831 (3d Cir. 1984) (concluding that district court did not abuse its "equitable discretion" under section 90 "in refusing to allow full-scale enforcement of the promise"); Signal Hill Aviation Co. v. Stroppe, 96 Cal. App. 3d 627, 158 Cal. Rptr. 178, 186 (1979) ("California Supreme Court appeared to emphasize . . . the exercise of judicial discretion in promissory estoppel cases to fashion relief to do justice") (citing C & K Eng'g Contractors v. Amber Steel Co., 23 Cal. 3d 1, 151 Cal. Rptr. 323, 587 P.2d 1136 (1978)); Gerson Elec. Constr. Co. v. Honeywell, Inc.,

117 Ill. App. 3d 309, 72 Ill. Dec. 851, 453 N.E.2d 726, 728 (1983) (decision under section 90 whether the damage award prevents injustice is a policy decision and "necessarily embraces an element of discretion").

We are left then to determine only whether the district court abused its discretion in limiting the damages to out-of-pocket expenses. We will not disturb a district court's discretionary decision if that decision remains within "the range of choice" available to the district court, accounts for all relevant factors, does not rely on any irrelevant factors, and does not constitute a "clear error of judgment." Kern v. TXO Prod. Corp., 738 F.2d 968, 970 (8th Cir. 1984). We cannot find that the district court abused its discretion in limiting the award of damages on the promissory estoppel claim to out-of-pocket expenses.

. . . .

Our review of the record . . . also reveals that the district court did not make a "clear error of judgment" in finding that justice required limiting Walser and McLaughlin to out-of-pocket expenses. Toyota presented evidence that the dealership was far from a certainty and that Walser and McLaughlin would have great difficulty in meeting the capitalization requirements. The negotiations were still in a preliminary stage and broke down at that point. The promise on which they relied did not guarantee that they would get the dealership, as there were other conditions in the letter of intent that still would have had to be satisfied. Walser and McLaughlin could have relied on the promise for only a short period of time, as they were informed by Haag only a couple of days later that he had misinformed them about the status of the letter of intent. Moreover, Walser and McLaughlin have not demonstrated any opportunity they lost by virtue of relying on the promise by Toyota. Accordingly, the district court did not make a clear error of judgment in limiting Walser and McLaughlin's damages on their promissory estoppel claim to out-of-pocket expenses.

. . .

B.

Walser and McLaughlin next argue that the district court erred in limiting out-of-pocket expenses to "the difference between the actual value of the property and the price paid for it." (Jury Instr. No. 34.) They argue that they should have been allowed to "recoup" at least the full amount of the "unamortized capital investments" they made in attempting to obtain the dealership. They claim the full value of their investment totals more than $1,000,000 including the $676,864 they paid for the land and the various expenses in maintaining it.

. . .

. . . [W]e find no error in the district court's instruction to the extent that it defined their out-of-pocket expenses to be only the difference between the actual value and the amount paid for the property. Such an instruction reflects the amount of damage Walser and McLaughlin suffered from relying on Toyota's promise. For example, while the purchase price of the land totaled $676,864 Walser acknowledged in his trial testimony that the land still had significant value, worth at least $550,000. (Tr. Vol. VI at 23-24.) Their *damage* from relying on Toyota's promise is essentially the difference between the two amounts. Accordingly, the district court committed no error in instructing the jury on how to determine the damage award.

. . . .

III.

For the foregoing reasons, the judgment of the district court is affirmed.

Notes and Questions

1. *Measuring damages in promissory estoppel actions.* In the first case in this section, we saw that an injured party may recover reliance damages for breach of contract even if she is unable to prove expectation damages with reasonable certainty. Suppose, however, that liability is based on the doctrine of promissory estoppel and the plaintiff has suffered expectation damages (lost profits, for example), which the plaintiff is able to prove with reasonable certainty. Should the plaintiff be entitled to recover these expectation damages, or should the plaintiff's recovery always be limited to the amount of her actual reliance? Or is the best approach the one adopted by the *Walser* court, allowing the trial court discretion to award a full range of remedies for promissory estoppel, including expectation or reliance based recovery, as justice seems to require?

In assessing the merits of these various remedial approaches, it may help to recall that the doctrine of promissory estoppel was viewed originally as a substitute for consideration rather than an independent theory of recovery. The logical consequence of this view was that the injured party would be entitled to recover full expectation damages. This approach to the scope of recovery under the theory of promissory estoppel was advocated by Professor Williston in 1926 when the American Law Institute debated adoption of Restatement §90. Williston was asked to give his opinion of the measure of damages if an uncle promised his nephew $1,000 to buy a car and the nephew detrimentally relied by purchasing a car for $500. He responded that the uncle would be liable for $1,000: "Either the promise is binding or it is not. If the promise is binding it has to be enforced as it is made." 4 A.L.I. Proc. 103-104 (Appendix) (1926), reprinted in Peter Linzer, A Contracts Anthology 339-349 (2d ed. 1995).

2. *View that damages should be limited to protection of reliance interest.* As the use of promissory estoppel became more widespread, some commentators questioned whether recovery of expectation damages was just. Writing in 1950, Professor Benjamin Boyer stated: "There is no real need for the courts to restrict themselves to giving only complete enforcement. It is to be hoped that the trend will be towards a protection of the reliance interest of the promisee without the injustice to the promisor that is often patent when complete enforcement is granted." Benjamin F. Boyer, Promissory Estoppel: Requirements and Limitations of the Doctrine, 98 U. Pa. L. Rev. 459, 497 (1950). A number of significant, relatively early promissory estoppel cases did limit recovery to reliance damages. See Goodman v. Dicker, 169 F.2d 684 (D.C. Cir. 1948) (reliance on promise that radio franchise would be awarded; recovery limited to expenses incurred preparing to do business); Wheeler v. White, 398 S.W.2d 93 (Tex. 1965) (reliance on promise to procure or make a

loan to develop property; recovery limited to losses incurred in reliance on promise); Hoffman v. Red Owl, 133 N.W.2d 267 (Wis. 1965) (promissory estoppel adopted and applied to precontract reliance but recovery limited to reliance damages). The court in *Wheeler* explicitly stated that expectation damages would not be recoverable even if they could be proven with reasonable certainty and based its holding, in part, on the reasoning that the promisee "in such cases is partially responsible for his failure to bind the promisor to a legally sufficient contract." 398 S.W.2d at 97.

The jury in *Walser* found Toyota liable solely on promissory estoppel grounds and, in accordance with the trial judge's instructions, awarded damages based solely on the plaintiffs' "out-of-pocket" expenses. Notwithstanding the appellate court's more flexible reasoning, the trial judge's instructions may well have been based on the perception that recovery for promissory estoppel should always be limited to the amount of actual reliance. Some contemporary courts appear to take that restrictive approach. See, e.g., Hi-Pac, Ltd. v. Avoset Corp., 26 F. Supp. 2d 1230, 1237 n.5 (D. Haw. 1997) (recovery of damages for promissory estoppel should be limited to promisee's reliance damages); Sammons Communications of Indiana, Inc. v. Larco Cable Construction, 691 N.E.2d 496 (Ind. Ct. App. 1998) (remedy under promissory estoppel limited to reliance damages as a matter of law).

3. *View that courts should have discretion in determining measure of damages.* As reflected by citations in its opinion, a number of other courts agree with the appellate court in *Walser* that a trial court has discretion to award expectation, reliance, or some other form of remedy when the basis of recovery is promissory estoppel. In addition to the cases cited in *Walser,* the court emphasized that the position of the Restatement (Second) appears to endorse a flexible approach in Comment *d* to §90. This reading of §90 is tempered somewhat by Illustration 10, based on Hoffman v. Red Owl, cited above in Note 2. The illustration reads:

> *A*, who owns and operates a bakery, desires to go into the grocery business. He approaches *B*, a franchisor of supermarkets. *B* states to *A* that for $18,000 *B* will establish *A* in a store. *B* also advises *A* to move to another town and buy a small grocery to gain experience. *A* does so. Later *B* advises *A* to sell the grocery, which *A* does, taking a capital loss and foregoing expected profits from the summer tourist trade. *B* also advises *A* to sell his bakery to raise capital for the supermarket franchise saying "Everything is ready to go. Get your money together and we are set." *A* sells the bakery taking a capital loss on this sale as well. Still later, *B* tells *A* that considerably more than an $18,000 investment will be needed, and the negotiations between the parties collapse. At the point of collapse many details of the proposed agreement between the parties are unresolved. The assurances from *B* to *A* are promises on which *B* reasonably should have expected *A* to rely, and *A* is entitled to his actual losses on the sales of the bakery and for his moving and temporary living expenses. Since the proposed agreement was never made, however, *A* is not entitled to lost profits from the sale of the grocery or to his expectation interest in the proposed franchise from *B*.

The exclusion of expectation damages and lost profits in the illustration may suggest that such damages should usually be denied in promissory estoppel cases. See Sykes v. Payton, 441 F.Supp.2d 1220 (M.D. Ala. 2006) (full range of contract remedies are available for promissory estoppel, but reliance damages are the preferred remedy); Toscano v. Greene Music, 21 Cal.Rptr.3d 732 (Ct. App. 2004) (the damages available for promissory estoppel are the same as for an enforceable contract, including lost profits from job given up in reliance on the unfulfilled promise). See generally Charles L. Knapp, Reliance in the Revised *Restatement:* The Proliferation of Promissory Estoppel, 81 Colum. L. Rev. 52, 57-58 (1981) (noting lack of clarity in comments and illustrations to §90 regarding when expectancy damages should be available).

4. *View that expectation damages should ordinarily be awarded.* Despite some contrary authority, a review of decisions reveals that courts have often awarded lost profits or other forms of expectation damages in promissory estoppel cases rather than limiting damages to plaintiff's reliance interest. E.g., ZBS Industries, Inc. v. Anthony Cocca Videoland, Inc., 637 N.E.2d 956 (Ohio Ct. App. 1994) (buyer allowed to recover lost profits for breach of seller's promise to extend credit in promissory estoppel action where promise extended into the future and damages were proved with reasonable certainty); Skebba v. Kasch, 724 N.W.2d 408 (Wis. Ct. App. 2006) (granting full performance of promise to pay employee $250,000 bonus; reversing trial court that would have limited employee to reliance damages and construing *Hoffman v. Red Owl* to require full performance as remedy for promissory estoppel). If the court in *Walser* had been willing to give expectancy relief, could the plaintiffs' expectation interest have been measured with reasonable certainty?

5. *Scholarly commentary.* As discussion of the proper remedy for promissory estoppel has continued, some writers have argued that expectation damages may often be the appropriate remedy in promissory estoppel cases. While rejecting the formalistic justification given by Professor Williston, these writers claim that an award of expectation damages may be the best way of compensating the injured party for reliance damages that may be difficult to prove. In commercial cases, such reliance could take the form of forgone contractual opportunities, including numerous and difficult to prove acts or forbearances that may be deemed to make up the "total reliance" of the plaintiff. Comment, Once More into the Breach: Promissory Estoppel and Traditional Damages Doctrine, 37 U. Chi. L. Rev. 559, 566-567 (1970). Professor Melvin Eisenberg has argued that even in cases involving purely gratuitous promises, as compared with promises made during precontract negotiations as in *Walser,* reliance may involve subtle changes or forms of nonfinancial costs that may be very difficult to measure. Melvin A. Eisenberg, Donative Promises, 47 U. Chi. L. Rev. 1, 29 (1979).

In a 1987 study of this area, Professor Mary Becker found that expectation-based remedies are commonly and routinely awarded in promissory estoppel cases and concluded that where recovery is limited to reliance damages, this is usually not because promissory estoppel is the basis of recovery, but because an expectation-based recovery would fail to satisfy one of the other requirements, such as certainty or foreseeability. Mary E. Becker, Promissory Estoppel Damages, 16 Hofstra L. Rev. 131 (1987). By contrast, Professor Robert A. Hillman's study of cases from 1994 to 1996 strongly undercuts the argument that courts routinely grant expectancy relief. Hillman observed that the cases did not clearly show a judicial preference for reliance or expectancy damages in promissory estoppel actions, but he did conclude that the cases establish "that courts take seriously the admonition of the second Restatement to award damages as justice requires." Robert A. Hillman, Questioning the "New Consensus" on Promissory Estoppel: An Empirical and Theoretical Study, 98 Colum. L. Rev. 580, 610 (1998). In an even more exhaustive review of cases, Professor Eric Holmes reached a similar conclusion that courts consider the remedy for promissory estoppel as discretionary and award a "full range of remedies" that includes expectation and reliance damages. Eric Mills Holmes, Restatement of Promissory Estoppel, 32 Willamette L. Rev. 263, 295-296 (1996).

6. *Specific performance in promissory estoppel actions.* As we shall see later in this chapter, cases involving land are usually good candidates for specific performance or other types of equitable relief. Such literal enforcement of the defendant's obligation is in one sense the most purely expectation-based remedy. The Restatement (Second) apparently contemplates the award of specific performance in promissory estoppel cases involving land (see §90, Illustration 11). See also Jackson v. Morse, 871 A.2d 47 (N.H. 2005) (full range of remedies are available for promissory estoppel, including specific performance in appropriate circumstances); Satcher v. Satcher, 570 S.E.2d 535 (S.C. Ct. App. 2002) (specific performance available for promise of land when established by clear and convincing evidence). Section C of this chapter will offer more detailed discussion of specific performance.

7. *Measure of recovery in construction bidding cases.* We saw in Chapter 3 that courts have generally followed the lead of the California Supreme Court in Drennan v. Star Paving Co., awarding damages on a promissory estoppel theory to the general contractor injured by the withdrawal of a subcontractor's bid, despite the failure of the parties to conclude a formal contract binding the general contractor as well. As the *Drennan* case itself illustrates, the damage award in such cases will typically be computed by subtracting the defendant's bid price from the price the plaintiff had to pay another subcontractor for the goods or services in question. Such a recovery might be regarded as reliance based, but it seems apparent that the courts in such cases are really awarding a conventional expectation-based remedy, whatever the terminology they employ. See Mary E. Becker, Promissory Estoppel Damages, 16 Hofstra L. Rev. 131, 143-144 (1987) (noting difficulty of measuring general's actual reliance based on the amount general would have bid but for subcontractor's withdrawn bid, and thus concluding that expectation damages are the only effective way to protect general's reliance interest). See also W. David Slawson, The Role of Reliance in Contract Damages, 76 Cornell L. Rev. 131, 222 (1990) (noting virtual impossibility of proving true reliance damages in these cases and observing that if plaintiff Drennan had been required to prove precisely the degree of injury to his reliance interest "his lawyer would have advised him to forget it").

It has been commonly assumed that the expectation interest is greater than the reliance interest, and that where full compensation is given for injury to the plaintiff's expectation, any injury to the reliance interest will automatically be thereby redressed. As the preceding discussion may suggest, however, in many cases a "full" reliance remedy will be virtually identical to a remedy based on lost expectation. See e.g., Tipton County Farm Bureau

Cooperative Assn., Inc. v. Hoover, 475 N.E.2d 38 (Ind. Ct. App. 1985) (promise to guarantee debts of son to plaintiff induced extension of credit after earlier denial, and enforcement on promissory estoppel basis necessary to overcome statute of frauds; amount of debt that will go unpaid unless guarantee is enforced equals both measure of detrimental reliance and expectation interests).

B. RESTITUTIONARY DAMAGES

As we saw in the first section of this chapter, if a party cannot prove expectation damages with reasonable certainty, she may still recover damages measured by her reliance interest. Restatement (Second) §349. Modern contract law also allows a nonbreaching party to elect recovery of restitutionary rather than expectation damages for breach of contract. Restatement (Second) §373. Even a breaching party may in some cases be entitled to restitution by virtue of the benefit conferred on the other party by part performance. Restatement (Second) §374. Moreover, if the performance obligations imposed by the contract have been "discharged" for some reason, such as incapacity or impracticability, either or both of the parties may be entitled to restitutionary relief. Restatement (Second) §§375 (restitution when contract is unenforceable because of the statute of frauds); 376 (restitution when contract is voidable because of lack of capacity, mistake, misrepresentation, duress, undue influence, or breach of fiduciary duty); 377 (restitution when contract is discharged due to impracticability, frustration of purpose, or failure of condition).

The materials in this section explore the restitutionary principle at work in a variety of contractual situations. The principal cases address some of the possibilities enumerated above: restitution as a remedy for breach; the possibility of restitution in favor of a party who is herself in breach; and the role of restitution where the contract has been rendered unenforceable.

United States ex rel. Coastal Steel Erectors, Inc. v. Algernon Blair, Inc.
United States Court of Appeals
479 F.2d 638 (4th Cir. 1973)

CRAVEN, Circuit Judge:
May a subcontractor, who justifiably ceases work under a contract because of the prime contractor's breach, recover in quantum meruit the value of labor and equipment already furnished pursuant to the contract irrespective of whether he would have been entitled to recover in a suit on the contract? We think so, and, for reasons to be stated, the decision of the district court will be reversed.

The subcontractor, Coastal Steel Erectors, Inc., brought this action under the provisions of the Miller Act, 40 U.S.C.A. §270a et seq., in the name of the United States against Algernon Blair, Inc., and its surety, United States Fidelity and Guaranty Company. Blair had entered a contract with the United States for the construction of a naval hospital in Charleston County, South Carolina. Blair had then contracted with Coastal to perform certain steel erection and supply certain equipment in conjunction with Blair's contract with the United States. Coastal commenced performance of its obligations, supplying its own cranes for handling and placing steel. Blair refused to pay for crane rental, maintaining that it was not obligated to do so under the subcontract. Because of Blair's failure to make payments for crane rental, and after completion of approximately 28 percent of the subcontract, Coastal terminated its performance. Blair then proceeded to complete the job with a new subcontractor. Coastal brought this action to recover for labor and equipment furnished.

The district court found that the subcontract required Blair to pay for crane use and that Blair's refusal to do so was such a material breach as to justify Coastal's terminating performance. This finding is not questioned on appeal. The court then found that under the contract the amount due Coastal, less what had already been paid, totaled approximately $37,000. Additionally, the court found Coastal would have lost more than $37,000 if it had completed performance. Holding that any amount due Coastal must be reduced by any loss it would have incurred by complete performance of the contract, the court denied recovery to Coastal. While the district court correctly stated the "'normal' rule of contract damages," we think Coastal is entitled to recover in quantum meruit.[2]

In United States for Use of Susi Contracting Co. v. Zara Contracting Co., 146 F.2d 606 (2d Cir. 1944), a Miller Act action, the court was faced with a situation similar to that involved here — the prime contractor had unjustifiably breached a subcontract after partial performance by the subcontractor. The court stated:

> For it is an accepted principle of contract law, often applied in the case of construction contracts, that the promisee upon breach has the option to forego any suit on the contract and claim only the reasonable value of his performance.

146 F.2d at 610. The Tenth Circuit has also stated that the right to seek recovery under quantum meruit in a Miller Act case is clear. Quantum meruit recovery is not limited to an action against the prime contractor but may also be brought against the Miller Act surety, as in this case. Further, that the

---

2. Where there is a distinction between federal and state substantive law, federal law controls in actions under the Miller Act. United States for Use and Benefit of Astro Cleaning & Packaging Co. v. Jamison Co., 425 F.2d 1281, 1282 n.1 (6th Cir. 1970). But in this case the result would be the same, we think, under either state or federal law. Compare United States for Use of Susi Contracting Co. v. Zara Contracting Co., 146 F.2d 606 (2d Cir. 1944), with Gantt v. Morgan, 199 S.C. 138, 18 S.E.2d 672 (1942).

complaint is not clear in regard to the theory of a plaintiff's recovery does not preclude recovery under quantum meruit. Narragansett Improvement Co. v. United States, 290 F.2d 577 (1st Cir. 1961). A plaintiff may join a claim for quantum meruit with a claim for damages from breach of contract.

In the present case, Coastal has, at its own expense, provided Blair with labor and the use of equipment. Blair, who breached the subcontract, has retained these benefits without having fully paid for them. On these facts, Coastal is entitled to restitution in quantum meruit.

> The "restitution interest," involving a combination of unjust impoverishment with unjust gain, presents the strongest case for relief. If, following Aristotle, we regard the purpose of justice as the maintenance of an equilibrium of goods among members of society, the restitution interest presents twice as strong a claim to judicial intervention as the reliance interest, since if A not only causes B to lose one unit but appropriates that unit to himself, the resulting discrepancy between A and B is not one unit but two.

Fuller and Perdue, The Reliance Interest in Contract Damages, 46 Yale L.J. 52, 56 (1936).

The impact of quantum meruit is to allow a promisee to recover the value of services he gave to the defendant irrespective of whether he would have lost money on the contract and been unable to recover in a suit on the contract. Scaduto v. Orlando, 381 F.2d 587, 595 (2d Cir. 1967). The measure of recovery for quantum meruit is the reasonable value of the performance, Restatement of Contracts §347 (1932); and recovery is undiminished by any loss which would have been incurred by complete performance. 12 Williston on Contracts §1485, at 312 (3d ed. 1970). While the contract price may be evidence of reasonable value of the services, it does not measure the value of the performance or limit recovery.[7] Rather, the standard for measuring the reasonable value of the services rendered is the amount for which such services could have been purchased from one in the plaintiff's position at the time and place the services were rendered.

Since the district court has not yet accurately determined the reasonable value of the labor and equipment use furnished by Coastal to Blair, the case must be remanded for those findings. When the amount has been determined, judgment will be entered in favor of Coastal, less payments already made under the contract. Accordingly, for the reasons stated above, the decision of the district court is

Reversed and remanded with instructions.

---

7. . . .

> It should be noted, however, that in suits for restitution there are many cases permitting the plaintiff to recover the value of benefits conferred on the defendant, even though this value exceeds that of the return performance promised by the defendant. In these cases it is no doubt felt that the defendant's breach should work a forfeiture of his right to retain the benefits of an advantageous bargain.

Fuller and Perdue, supra, at 77.

Notes and Questions

1. *Actions under the Miller Act.* Plaintiff's claim was based on the Miller Act, which provides that in any contract for construction, alteration, or repair of any public building or public work of the United States in an amount in excess of $100,000 the contractor is required to furnish both "performance" and "payment" bonds issued by satisfactory sureties (normally insurance companies). 40 U.S.C. §270a. A performance bond protects the government against the contractor's improper performance; if the contractor breaches, the government may demand that the surety complete or pay for performance of the contract. A payment bond protects subcontractors who supply labor or materials to the project against nonpayment by the contractor. If a subcontractor is not paid, he may bring suit against the contractor and surety under the payment bond. The suit is styled on behalf of the United States for the use of the subcontractor. As the court points out in footnote 2, while federal rather than state law governs claims brought under the Miller Act, both federal and state law recognize the right of the injured party to elect to recover restitutionary rather than expectation damages. See also United States ex rel. Wallace v. Flintco Inc., 143 F.3d 955 (5th Cir. 1998) (after general contractor breached by actively interfering with performance, subcontractor allowed to treat contract as rescinded and recover under quantum meruit for full value of work done).

2. *Market value restitution.* Although the defendant owed $37,000 on the contract, the district court held that the plaintiff was not entitled to recover damages because the plaintiff would have lost more than that amount if the plaintiff had completed performance. The court of appeals reversed, holding that when a plaintiff elects restitution as a remedy for breach of contract by the defendant, the "measure of recovery . . . is the reasonable value of the performance . . . and recovery is undiminished by any loss which would have been incurred by complete performance." Several arguments have been made to support the rule of "market value restitution" followed by the court. If the plaintiff elects to rescind the contract and recover in restitution, the contract no longer legally "exists"; any loss that would have resulted from performance of the contract, therefore, should not act as a limitation on the amount of recovery. George E. Palmer, The Contract Price as a Limit on Restitution for the Defendant's Breach, 20 Ohio St. L.J. 264, 273 (1959). In addition, it seems unfair to allow the defendant, who is after all the breaching party, to retain the benefit of the bargain. 1 George E. Palmer, Law of Restitution §4.4 at 393 (1978).

Critics of the rule of market value restitution argue that labels should not control results. Even though the action is classified as restitutionary, it amounts to a claim for damages for breach of contract. Accordingly, they argue that the normal rules of contract damages should apply, including the rule that a court should not place the injured party in a better position than that party would have been in had performance been completed. Moreover, the critics contend that the rule of market value restitution ignores the risk allocation function of modern commercial contracts. Robert Childres & Jack Garamella, The Law of Restitution and the Reliance Interest in Contract, 64 Nw. U. L. Rev. 433, 440-441 (1969). See also Andrew Kull, Restitution as a

Remedy for Breach of Contract, 67 S. Cal. L. Rev. 1465 (1994) (criticizing remedy on both historical and efficiency grounds). For a more philosophical criticism of the rule of market value restitution, see Henry Mather, Restitution as a Remedy for Breach of Contract: The Case of the Partially Performing Seller, 92 Yale L.J. 14 (1982) (rule of market value restitution inconsistent with liberal principles of justice).

3. *Cases adopting rule of market value restitution.* Despite such criticisms, a majority of courts apparently still follows the rule of market value restitution applied in *Algernon Blair.* See also Bausch & Lomb Inc. v. Bressler, 977 F.2d 720 (2d Cir. 1992) (restitution looks to value of benefit conferred and is not governed by terms of agreement; therefore, restitution is available even if nonbreaching party would have lost money on contract); IT Corp. v. Motco Site Trust Fund, 903 F. Supp. 1106 (S.D. Tex. 1994) (after breach of environmental remediation contract for $32 million, nonbreaching contractor allowed to recover more than $43 million in restitution; no Texas authority to limit recovery to contract price); Mather, Note 2 above, at 17 n.9. See also Restatement (Second) §373, Comment *d* (adopting majority rule permitting restitution in excess of contract price).

4. *Effect of contract price in measuring restitution.* In Constantino v. American S/T Achilles, 580 F.2d 121 (4th Cir. 1978), the plaintiff contracted to clean 33 grain storage tanks for a price of $30,000. When the plaintiff had completed work on 24 tanks, the defendant terminated the contract without justification. The plaintiff then brought suit on a quantum meruit theory, seeking the reasonable value of its services, which was claimed to be $69,000. The trial court awarded the plaintiff 24/33 of the contract price. The Fourth Circuit affirmed: "Since the contract price unquestionably is probative in ascertaining damages in quantum meruit, . . . we cannot say the district court abused its discretion in relying upon admittedly admissible evidence as the measure of Constantino's recovery." Id. at 123. Dissenting Judge Winter argued that the trial judge abused his discretion because he was clearly basing his award of damages on the contract price. Does the approach of allowing the contract price as probative evidence of market value substantially erode the significance of the rule of market value restitution?

5. *Full performance exception to market value restitution.* The right of a nonbreaching party to elect restitution in situations like that presented in *Algernon Blair* is subject to an important exception. If the nonbreaching party has fully performed his obligations under the contract and the breaching party's only remaining duty of performance is the payment of a liquidated or specified sum of money, the nonbreaching party may not elect a restitutionary recovery but is limited to expectation damages. Restatement (Second) §373(2). A leading case applying this "full performance" exception is Oliver v. Campbell, 273 P.2d 15 (Cal. 1954). In *Oliver* an attorney agreed for a fee of $750 to defend a husband in an action for separate maintenance brought by his wife. After the husband discharged the lawyer at the end of the trial, the lawyer sued to recover $10,000 in restitution as the reasonable value of his services. Although the California Supreme Court recognized the general rule of market value restitution as an alternative remedy for breach of contract, the court held that the full performance exception applied and limited recovery to the contract price. Id. at 20. But see Chodos v. West Publishing Co., Inc., 292 F.3d

992 (9th Cir. 2002) (after defendant breached contract by declining to publish finished manuscript, plaintiff author could elect to recover in quantum meruit because publisher's obligation to pay percentage of gross revenue was not a "liquidated" debt). The Restatement asserts that the exception is justified because it protects the nonbreaching party's expectation interest while eliminating the judicial burden of determining the market value of the performance. Restatement (Second) §373, Comment *b*. Is this persuasive?

Lancellotti v. Thomas
Superior Court of Pennsylvania
341 Pa. Super. 1, 491 A.2d 117 (1985)

SPAETH, President Judge.

This appeal raises the question of whether a defaulting purchaser of a business who has also entered into a related lease for the property can recover any part of his payments made prior to default. The common law rule precluded a breaching buyer from recovering these payments. Today, we reject this rule, which created a forfeiture of the breaching buyer's payments and unjustly enriched the nonbreaching seller, and adopt §374 of the Restatement (Second) Contracts (1979), which permits limited restitution. This case is remanded for further proceedings so that the trial court may apply the Restatement rule.

1

On July 25, 1973, the parties entered into an agreement in which appellant agreed to purchase appellees' luncheonette business and to rent from appellees the premises on which the business was located. Appellant agreed to buy the name of the business, the goodwill, and equipment; the inventory and real estate were not included in the agreement for the sale of the business. Appellees agreed to sell the business for the following consideration: $25,000 payable on signing of the agreement; appellant's promise that only he would own and operate the business; and appellant's promise to build an addition to the existing building, which would measure 16 feet by 16 feet, cost at least $15,000, and be 75 percent complete by May 1, 1973.[1]

It was also agreed that appellees would lease appellant the property on which the business was operated for a period of five years, with appellant having the option of an additional five-year term. The rent was $8,000 per year for a term from September 1, 1973, to August 31, 1978. A separate lease providing for this rental was executed by the parties on the same date that the agreement was executed. This lease specified that the agreement to build the existing building was a condition of the lease. In exchange for appellant's promise to build the addition, there was to be no rental charge for the property until August 31, 1973. Further, if the addition was not constructed as agreed, the lease would terminate automatically. An addendum, executed by the parties on August 14, 1973, modified this agreement, providing that "if the addition to the building as

---

1. The parties agree that this date was incorrect, and that the date the parties intended was May 1, 1974.

described in the Agreement is not constructed in accordance with the Agreement, the Buyer shall owe the Sellers $6,665 as rental for the property . . . " for the period from July 25, 1973, to the end of that summer season. The addendum also provided that all the equipment would revert to appellees upon the appellant's default in regard to the addition.

Appellant paid appellees the $25,000 as agreed, and began to operate the business. However, at the end of the 1973 season, problems arose regarding the construction of the addition. Appellant claims that the building permit necessary to construct the addition was denied. Appellees claim that they obtained the building permit and presented it to appellant, who refused to begin construction. Additionally appellees claim that appellant agreed to reimburse them if they built the addition. At a cost of approximately $11,000, appellees did build a 20 feet by 40 feet addition. In the spring of 1974 appellees discovered that appellant was no longer interested in operating the business. There is no evidence in the record that appellant paid any rent from September 1, 1973, as the first rental payment was not due until May 15, 1974. Appellees resumed possession of the business and, upon opening the business for the 1974 summer season, found some of their equipment missing.

Appellant's complaint in assumpsit demanded that appellees return the $25,000 plus interest. Appellees denied that appellant was entitled to recovery of this sum and counterclaimed for damages totalling $52,000; $6,665 as rental for the property for the 1973 summer season and the remainder as compensation for "grievous damage to [appellees'] business, its good-will and its physical operation . . ." and appellee Lillian Thomas suffering "nervous illness, pain and suffering inclusive of serious bodily injury and necessitating bed rest and physicians' supervision for one year after [appellant's] default." Defendants' Counterclaim and New Matter, paras. 9-11. In his answer, Appellant only conceded liability for the $6,665 rent under the terms of the addendum. Plaintiff's Answer to Counterclaim and New Matter, para. 9. The trial court, sitting without a jury, found against appellant on the original claim, allowing appellees to retain the $25,000 paid by appellant, and for appellees on the counterclaim, allowing them to recover the $6,665 rent.

2

At one time the common law rule prohibiting a defaulting party on a contract from recovering was the majority rule. J. Calamari and J. Perillo, The Law of Contracts §11-26, at 427 (2d ed. 1977). However, a line of cases, apparently beginning with Britton v. Turner, 6 N.H. 481 (1834), departed from the common law rule. The merit of the common law rule was its recognition that the party who breaches should not be allowed "to have advantage from his own wrong." Corbin, The Right of a Defaulting Vendee to the Restitution of Instalments Paid, 40 Yale L.J. 1013, 1014 (1931). As Professor Perillo states, allowing recovery "invites contract-breaking and rewards morally unworthy conduct." Restitution in the Second Restatement of Contracts, 81 Colum. L. Rev. 37, 50 (1981). Its weakness, however, was its failure to recognize that the nonbreaching party should not obtain a windfall from the breach. The party who breaches after almost completely performing should not be more severely penalized than the party who breaches by not acting at all or after only beginning to act. Under the common law rule the injured party retains more benefit the more completely the breaching party has performed prior to the default. Thus it has been said that "to allow the injured party to retain the benefit of the part performance . . . , without making restitution of any part of such value, is the enforcement of a penalty or forfeiture against the contract-breaker." Corbin, supra, at 1013.

Critics of the common law rule have been arguing for its demise for over fifty years. See Corbin, supra. See also Calamari and Perillo, supra, at §11-26; 5A Corbin on Contracts §§1122-1135 (1964); 12 S. Williston, A Treatise on the Law of Contracts §§1473-1478 (3d ed. 1970). In response to this criticism an alternative rule has been adopted in the Restatement of Contracts.

The first Restatement of Contracts (1932) adopted the following rule:

§357. Restitution in Favor of a Plaintiff Who is Himself in Default

(1) Where the defendant fails or refuses to perform his contract and is justified therein by the plaintiff's own breach of duty or non-performance of a condition, but the plaintiff has rendered a part performance under the contract that is a net benefit to the defendant, the plaintiff can get judgment, except as stated in Subsection (2), for the amount of such benefit in excess of the harm that he has caused to the defendant by his own breach, in no case exceeding a ratable proportion of the agreed compensation, if

(a) the plaintiff's breach or non-performance is not wilful and deliberate; or

(b) the defendant, with knowledge that the plaintiff's breach of duty or nonperformance of condition has occurred or will thereafter occur, assents to the rendition of the part performance, or accepts the benefit of it, or retains property received although its return in specie is still not unreasonably difficult or injurious.

(2) The plaintiff has no right to compensation for his part performance if it is merely a payment of earnest money, or if the contract provides that it may be retained and it is not so greatly in excess of the defendant's harm that the provision is rejected as imposing a penalty.

(3) The measure of the defendant's benefit from the plaintiff's part performance is the amount by which he has been enriched as a result of such performance unless the facts are those stated in Subsection (1b), in which case it is the price fixed by the contract for such part performance, or, if no price is so fixed, a ratable proportion of the total contract price.

In 1979, this rule was liberalized. [The court quotes Restatement (Second) of Contracts §374 (1979) — EDS.] . . . Thus the first Restatement's exclusion of the willful defaulting purchaser from recovery was deleted, apparently in part due to the influence of the Uniform Commercial Code's permitting recovery by a buyer who willfully defaults.[2] Id., Reporter's Note at 218. Professor Perillo suggests that the injured party has adequate protection without the common law rule.[3] Choosing "the just path," he therefore rejects the common law rule,

---

2. [The court quotes UCC §2-718 — EDS.]

3. He identifies four types of protection:

First, the defaulting party's right to recovery is subject to the aggrieved party's right to offset his damages. Second, the measure of benefit is limited to the actual enrichment and cannot exceed a ratable portion of the contract price. Third, restitution is denied to the extent that the criteria for a valid liquidated damages clause are present. Fourth, restitution is denied if the aggrieved party seeks and is entitled to specific performance.

Perillo, supra, at 50 (footnotes omitted).

explaining this choice by saying that times have changed. "What appears to be just to one generation may be viewed differently by another." Perillo, supra, at 50. See also 12 S. Williston, supra, §1473, at 222 ("The mores of the time and place will often determine which policy will be followed.").

Many jurisdictions have rejected the common law rule and permit recovery by the defaulting party. See, e.g., Amtorg Trading Corp. v. Miehle Printing Press and Manufacturing Co., 206 F.2d 103 (2d Cir. 1953) (noting with approval §357 of Restatement (First) of Contracts); . . . Kulseth v. Rotenberger, 320 N.W.2d 920 (North Dakota 1982) (following rule in Restatement (Second) of Contracts §374); . . . Hartford Elevator, Inc. v. Lauer, 94 Wis. 2d 571, 289 N.W.2d 280 (1980) (approving of §357 of Restatement (First) of Contracts).

This development has been called the modern trend. See Quillen v. Kelley, 216 Md. 396, 140 A.2d 517 (1958). See also 12 S. Williston, supra, §1473, at 222 (cases permitting recovery are now the weight of the authority); 5A Corbin on Contracts, supra, §1122, at 3 (common law rule is broad statement not supported by the actual decisions). But see 1 G. Palmer, The Law of Restitution 568 (1978) (no valid generalization may be made regarding when a defaulting vendee can recover). It may be that the growing number of jurisdictions permitting recovery have been influenced by the widespread adoption of the Uniform Commercial Code §2-718. See, e.g., Maxey v. Glindmeyer, 379 So. 2d 297 (Miss. 1980) (allowing recovery of excess of seller's actual damages in land sale contract by following the logic of the state statute equivalent to §2-718 of the Uniform Commercial Code). Indeed, the common law rule is no longer intact even with respect to land sales contracts. See, e.g., Honey v. Henry's Franchise Leasing Corp., 64 Cal. 2d 801, 415 P.2d 833, 52 Cal. Rptr. 18 (1966); . . . and see 1 G. Palmer, supra, at 596 n.15 (citing cases).

In Pennsylvania, the common law rule has been applied to contracts for the sale of real property. Kaufman Hotel & Restaurant Co. v. Thomas, 411 Pa. 87, 190 A.2d 434 (1963); Luria v. Robbins, 223 Pa. Super. 456, 302 A.2d 361 (1973). In such cases, however, the seller has several remedies against a breaching buyer, including, in appropriate cases, an action for specific performance or for the purchase price. See Trachtenburg v. Sibarco Stations, Inc., 477 Pa. 517, 384 A.2d 1209 (1978). See also 5A Corbin on Contracts, supra, §1145. As long as the seller remains ready, able, and willing to perform a contract for the sale of real property, the breaching buyer has no right to restitution of payments made prior to default. See 5A Corbin on Contracts, supra, at §1130.

The common law rule has also been applied in Pennsylvania to contracts for the sale of goods. Atlantic City Tire and Rubber Corp. v. Southwark Foundry & Machine Co., 289 Pa. 569, 137 A. 807 (1927). However, Pennsylvania has since adopted the Uniform Commercial Code, which, as to contracts for the sale of goods, has modified the common law rule by 13 Pa. C.S. §2718(b), which permits a breaching party to recover restitution. See note 2, supra.

The viability of the common law rule permitting forfeiture has also been undermined in other areas of Pennsylvania law. In Estate of Cahen, 483 Pa. 157, 168 n.10, 394 A.2d 958, 964 n.10 (1978), the Supreme Court held that assuming that a breaching fiduciary could recover in unjust enrichment, the basis would be Restatement of Contracts §357 (1932), which allows recovery by a breaching party to the extent that the benefits exceed the losses sustained by the other party.[4]

3

In regard to the present case, §374 of the Restatement (Second) of Contracts represents a more enlightened approach than the common law rule. "Rules of contract law are not rules of punishment; the contract breaker is not an outlaw." Perillo, supra, at 50. The party who committed a breach should be entitled to recover "any benefit . . . in excess of the loss that he has caused by his own breach." Restatement (Second) of Contracts §374(1).

This conclusion leads to the further conclusion that we should remand this case to the trial court. The trial court rested its decision on the common law rule. Slip op. of trial court at 7-8. Thus it never considered whether appellant is entitled to restitution, Restatement (Second) of Contracts §374(1), nor, if appellant is not entitled to restitution, whether retention of the $25,000 was "reasonable in the light of the anticipated or actual loss caused by the breach and the difficulties of proof of loss," id., §374(2).[5]

Remanded for further proceedings consistent with this opinion. Jurisdiction relinquished.

TAMILIA, Judge, dissenting:

I strongly dissent. In the first instance, the majority does not and cannot cite *any* Pennsylvania authority adopting the rule cited in §374 of the Second Restatement of Contracts. Although the ostensible basis for remand is the trial court's reliance on outmoded law, the majority relies on law so new as to be virtually unknown in this jurisdiction. The law in Pennsylvania has been and continues to be that where a binding contract exists, and there is no allegation that the contract itself is void or voidable, a breaching party is not entitled to recovery. Luria v. Robinson, 223 Pa. Super. 456, 302 A.2d 361 (1978). While our Supreme Court may yet abrogate the forfeiture principle in this Commonwealth, it has not yet seen fit to do so, and we may not usurp its prerogatives, particularly when the result would be unjust.

Secondly, the Uniform Commercial Code §2718, cited by the majority in (partial) support, is applicable only to the sale of goods, and, while it and some of the equally inapplicable cases referred to by the majority may be part of a trend, the mainstream of contract law in Pennsylvania has not yet been

---

4. The assertion in the dissenting opinion that "the majority does not and cannot cite *any* Pennsylvania authority" allowing a breaching party recovery, dissent op. at 122, fails to acknowledge the Supreme Court's decision in *Cahen.* While not citing *Cahen,* the dissenting opinion does cite Luria v. Robbins, 223 Pa. Super. 456, 302 A.2d 361 (1973), but as we have already discussed, we find *Luria* distinguishable.

5. We do not share the view expressed in the dissenting opinion that "the most important determinant of the proper result in this case is the trial judge's assessment of the witness[es]' credibility." Dissent op., at 122. To the contrary, as we have discussed, the trial court did not base its decision on an assessment of credibility but on the common law rule. Thus the court did not even consider the possibility of recovery by the breaching plaintiff. We are remanding so that the trial court may consider whether appellant is entitled to restitution. If the trial court again finds that it was the intention of the parties that the $25,000 be retained in the event of a breach, see slip op. of trial court at 7, then the court must determine whether this sum is reasonable. If the sum is unreasonable, appellant is entitled to restitution. See Restatement (Second) of Contracts §374 Comment *c.*

diverted by it. Indeed the identification of the jurisdictions cited as the vanguard of change is for the most part questionable, as of those states relied upon to confer legitimacy on the majority's somewhat arbitrary conclusion, only one may be termed authoritative.

Lastly, and given the current state of the law, the most important determinant of the proper result in this case is the trial judge's assessment of the witness' credibility, here resolved in appellee's favor. The majority, far from according these findings their due, ignores them, contrary to law and our mandate. Knepp v. Nationwide Insurance Co., 324 Pa. Super. 479, 471 A.2d 1257 (1984).

The trial court correctly points out that the understanding of the parties is clearly evidenced by the agreements they signed. In breaching those agreements, appellant has engaged in what might charitably be termed sharp practice. The facts reasonably support the inference that appellant learned the hoagie business, benefited from the acquired trade and good will at appellees' place of business, then conducted the hoagie business at its previously owned pizza shop in the following season. Restitution in this instance constitutes a wholly unmerited reward for bad faith. We do not feel that such a result is consistent with the intent of law or the expectations of equity.

Notes and Questions

1. *Origin of breaching party's right to restitution.* In 1931 Professor Arthur Corbin collected and analyzed the cases dealing with the right of a defaulting purchaser in a land contract to recover in restitution. He concluded that the right had been recognized in "too many thousands of cases to deny such a right to a vendee merely because he is in default." Arthur L. Corbin, The Right of a Defaulting Vendee to the Restitution of Installments Paid, 40 Yale L.J. 1013, 1015 (1931). Corbin's work led to the inclusion of §357 in the original Restatement, which recognized a general right to restitution in favor of a party in default. Section 374 of the Restatement (Second) is the current version of this doctrine.

2. *Case law.* The court in *Lancellotti* cites several modern cases allowing a breaching party to recover in restitution, and decisions adopting the rule of Restatement (Second) §374 have continued to appear. E.g., Alstom Power, Inc. v. RMF Industrial Contracting, Inc., 418 F.Supp.2d 766 (W.D. Pa. 2006) (even if subcontractor breached contract for installation of boilers, it could recover in restitution for benefit conferred in excess of harm to other party); United Coastal Industries, Inc. v. Clearheart Construction Co. Inc., 802 A.2d 901 (Conn. App. Ct. 2002); Ducolon Mechanical Inc. v. Shinstine/Forness, Inc., 893 P.2d 1127 (Wash. Ct. App. 1995). Not all jurisdictions agree, however. Two notable exceptions are Massachusetts and New York. Albre Marble & Tile Co. v. Goverman, 233 N.E.2d 533 (Mass. 1968) (subcontractor not allowed to recover in quantum meruit for tile work that did not comply with contract specifications; quantum meruit recovery available only if party "can prove both substantial performance of the contract and an endeavor on his part in good faith to perform fully"); Intermetal Fabricators, Inc. v. Losco Group, Inc., 2000 WL 1154249 (S.D.N.Y. 2000) (under New York law, builder

who defaults on construction contract may not recover either under contract or on quantum meruit basis unless builder has substantially performed the contract). In support of the modern rule, the *Lancellotti* court also cites UCC §2-718, which provides for a right of restitution on behalf of a defaulting purchaser of goods. Do you think the modern rule is superior to the common law rule? Why? Based on the Pennsylvania cases cited in the opinion, did the court in *Lancellotti* exceed its authority as an intermediate appellate court by adopting the modern rule?

3. *Effect of willful breach.* As the court points out, the original Restatement provided that a defaulting party could not recover in restitution if the breach was willful and deliberate. Professor Corbin took issue with this portion of the section; this requirement, he asserted, showed a "childlike faith in the existence of a plain and obvious line between the good and the bad, between unfortunate virtue and unforgiveable sin." 5A Corbin on Contracts §1123, at 7. Other commentators have agreed with Corbin. Robert J. Nordstrom & Irwin F. Woodland, Recovery by Building Contractor in Default, 20 Ohio St. L.J. 193, 211-224 (1959). The language of §374 of the Restatement (Second) does not mention willfulness. Comment *b* to that section indicates, however, that an intentional variation from the terms of the contract (as distinguished from an intentional nonperformance) will preclude restitution: "A party who intentionally furnishes services or builds a building that is materially different from what he promised is properly regarded as having acted officiously and not in part performance of his promise and will be denied recovery on that ground even if his performance was of some benefit to the other party." Does the dissenting opinion in *Lancellotti* suggest another possible doctrine that might limit the right of a breaching party to recover in restitution?

4. *Measure of restitution.* We have seen in the *Jacob & Youngs* case that a court may permit a party who has substantially performed a contract to recover "on the contract" even though his performance in some respect involves an immaterial breach. What should the measure of the restitutionary interest be when recovery is given to a party who has committed a material breach? Since the breaching party is seeking relief, not surprisingly, recovery is limited. The Restatement (Second) §374, Comment *b*, provides that recovery should be limited to the lesser of either (a) the value of the benefits conferred or (b) the defendant's increase in wealth. In addition, to prevent the breaching party from recovering more than her expectation interest, the Restatement also provides that "in no case will the party in breach be allowed to recover more than a ratable portion of the total contract price where such a portion can be determined." Restatement (Second) §374, Comment *b* and Illustration 3. Finally, to ensure protection of the nonbreaching party's expectation interest, any damages suffered by that party must be deducted from the amount of the restitutionary award. Restatement (Second) §374(1).

In some cases, a breaching party's recovery in restitution will not differ markedly from the recovery that would have followed if the plaintiff had the benefit of the doctrine of substantial performance. E.g., Kreyer v. Driscoll, 159 N.W.2d 680 (Wis. 1968) (trial court found contractor had substantially performed and awarded contract price of house, less deductions for work not performed; appellate court holds that magnitude of work not done precluded finding of substantial performance but affirms award below on quantum meruit theory). In many cases, however, the plaintiff even if eligible for §374 recovery will receive little on its quantum meruit claim. E.g., Denver Ventures, Inc. v. Arlington Lane Corp., 754 P.2d 785 (Colo. Ct. App. 1988) (subcontractor entitled to no quantum meruit recovery because in light of large cost of completion, damages from breach exceeded benefit conferred).

Ventura v. Titan Sports, Inc.
United States Court of Appeals
65 F.3d 725 (8th Cir. 1995), cert. denied, 516 U.S. 1174 (1996)

MAGILL, Circuit Judge.

This appeal arises out of a match between wrestler/commentator Jesse "The Body" Ventura and Titan Sports, Inc., which operates "The World Wrestling Federation" (WWF). Titan appeals the district court's judgment in favor of Ventura, arguing that (1) Ventura was not entitled to recovery under quantum meruit because an express contract covers the subject matter for which Ventura sought recovery; and (2) the district court erroneously admitted and relied upon the testimony of Ventura's damages expert. Ventura cross-appeals the district court's denial of prefiling interest. We affirm in all respects.[1]

I. BACKGROUND

During July 1984, Titan entered into a licensing agreement with LJN Toys authorizing LJN Toys to manufacture dolls using the images of WWF wrestlers. Titan also entered a "master licensing" agreement with DIC Enterprises that resulted in WWF T-shirts, trading cards, calendars, a computer game and numerous other items. In December 1984, Titan entered into a licensing agreement with A & H Video Sales (d/b/a Coliseum Video) for the production of videotapes of WWF matches. Agreements with A & H and Columbia House resulted in the production of approximately ninety videotapes of WWF performances involving Ventura.

Ventura began wrestling for Titan in Spring 1984 under an oral contract with Vincent K. McMahon, Titan's President and sole shareholder. In late 1984, Ventura suffered medical problems and ceased to work as a wrestler, although Titan continued to pay him during his convalescence. After Ventura recovered, he returned to work for Titan as a "color" or "heel"[2] commentator under an oral agreement with Titan. He was paid a flat rate of $1000 per week and there was no discussion of videotape royalties or licenses. Shortly after returning to work for Titan, Ventura executed a "Wrestling Booking

---

1. We refer to the contracts negotiated by Ventura's agent, Barry Bloom, during the 1987-90 period as "post-Bloom" contracts. The earlier oral agreements between Ventura and [Vincent K.] McMahon we refer to as the "pre-Bloom" contracts.

2. A color commentator provides the story of the wrestling match, which is in essence a stage show. A heel commentator is a color commentator who plays the role of "the bad guy."

Agreement" (WBA) with an effective date of January 1, 1985. Ventura subsequently resumed wrestling for Titan, for which he was paid according to the terms of the WBA. In March 1986, Ventura terminated his relationship with Titan in order to pursue an acting career.

Ventura's foray into movies was moderately successful, but in fall 1986 he returned to Titan as a commentator, again under an oral agreement that made no mention of videotape royalties or licenses. In fall 1987, Ventura hired Barry Bloom as his talent agent. Bloom negotiated on Ventura's behalf with Dick Ebersol, Titan's partner in producing the "Saturday Night's Main Event" show. However, the negotiations quickly broke down, and as a result, the first show of the 1987-88 season aired without Ventura. A few weeks later, Titan's Vice-President of Business Affairs, Dick Glover, contacted Bloom concerning Ventura and represented to Bloom that Titan's policy was to pay royalties only to "feature" performers. Because Ventura was interested in working for Titan, Bloom thought it wise not to attempt to "break the policy." Ventura returned to work for Titan under a new contract that waived royalties and continued to work as a commentator for Titan until August 1990. Since that time he has worked as a commentator for WCW, Titan's main competitor.

In December 1991, Ventura filed an action in Minnesota state court seeking royalties for the use of his likeness on videotapes produced by Titan. The original complaint contained causes of action for fraud,[3] misappropriation of publicity rights and quantum meruit. Titan removed the case to federal court, and the case was tried before a jury. Although only the quantum meruit claim was submitted to the jury, the jury was given a special verdict form concerning misrepresentation. Using this form, the jury found that Titan had defrauded Ventura and that $801,333.06 would compensate Ventura for Titan's videotape exploitation of his commentary. The jury also determined that Titan exploited Ventura's name, voice or likeness as a commentator in other merchandise and concluded that $8,625.60 would compensate Ventura for this exploitation.

After the jury rendered its verdict, the district court concluded that Ventura was not entitled to a jury trial on his quantum meruit claim. Accordingly, the court vacated the jury verdict and entered findings of fact and conclusions of law that were consistent with the verdict. The court denied Ventura's request for prefiling interest but granted prejudgment interest from the time the suit was filed. Titan appealed, and Ventura cross-appealed the denial of prefiling interest.

II. DISCUSSION

Titan raises three claimed errors on appeal. First, Titan argues that Ventura was not entitled to quantum meruit recovery of royalties for the videotape[4] exploitation of his performance as color commentator during the 1985-87 (pre-Bloom) period because Ventura provided his commentating

---

3. The fraud pleaded in Ventura's Complaint and Second Amended Complaint is that Titan fraudulently misrepresented to Ventura that Ventura was employed for no purpose other than a live performance. Second Amended Complaint ¶42.

4. For the sake of simplicity, we discuss the issues only in terms of the videotapes. However, the principles applied to videotape licenses and royalties apply equally to other merchandise.

services under an express contract. Second, Titan claims that the district court erroneously applied the law of quantum meruit when it rescinded an express contract and awarded Ventura royalties for the videotape exploitation of his performance as color commentator during the 1987-90 (post-Bloom) period. Third, Titan alleges that the district court abused its discretion in qualifying and relying upon Ventura's expert witness in awarding damages. Ventura's cross-appeal presents a single issue: whether the district court clearly erred when it denied Ventura's request for prefiling interest. We address each of these issues in turn.

A. IS QUANTUM MERUIT AVAILABLE DURING THE PRE-BLOOM PERIOD?

Minnesota law determines the rights of the parties in this diversity action, and we review the district court's interpretation of Minnesota law de novo. Salve Regina College v. Russell, 499 U.S. 225, 231, 111 S. Ct. 1217, 1221, 113 L. Ed. 2d 190 (1991). The basic contours of the law of quantum meruit, or unjust enrichment, are well settled under Minnesota law:

> An action for unjust enrichment may be based on failure of consideration, fraud, mistake, and situations where it would be morally wrong for one party to enrich himself at the expense of another. However, a claim of unjust enrichment does not lie simply because one party benefits from the efforts or obligations of others, but instead lies where one party was unjustly enriched in the sense that the term 'unjustly' could mean illegally or unlawfully.

Hesselgrave v. Harrison, 435 N.W.2d 861, 863-64 (Minn. App. 1989) (internal quotations and citation omitted). Although the applicable law is well settled, the facts of this case are rather unique and therefore require us to address some preliminary issues.

The first unique aspect of this appeal involves defining the benefit received (allegedly unjustly) by Titan. Titan makes much of the fact that Ventura provided no services for Titan other than pursuant to the Ventura-Titan contracts. While it is true that the Ventura-Titan contracts governed all the services provided by Ventura (i.e., his acts of appearing at the wrestling match and commentating), the agreements do not necessarily address all the benefits created by Ventura's services. Ventura's services created several varieties of intellectual property rights. In defining the "benefit" conferred upon Titan, the proper focus is not merely Ventura's labor as he performed, but must also include the intellectual property rights created by Ventura's performance. Thus, we find that the intellectual property rights to Ventura's commentary are benefits upon which an action for unjust enrichment may be based.

We next must determine whether Titan, in taking this benefit, was *unjustly* enriched. Ventura's quantum meruit claim may succeed only if Titan's rights to use Ventura's performance are limited so that Titan is not entitled to use the performance without Ventura's consent. We believe that Titan's rights are limited by Ventura's right to publicity. In determining the law of the State of Minnesota concerning publicity rights, we are bound by the decisions of the Minnesota Supreme Court. If the Minnesota Supreme Court has not addressed the issue, we must determine what that court would probably hold were it to decide the issue. The parties have identified, and we have discovered, no case in which the Minnesota Supreme Court has either accepted or rejected the tort of misappropriation of publicity rights. We must therefore attempt to predict the decision of the Minnesota Supreme Court. In making our prediction, we may consider relevant state precedent, analogous decisions, considered dicta, scholarly works and any other reliable data. B.B. v. Continental Ins. Co., 8 F.3d 1288, 1291 (8th Cir. 1993).

We believe that the Minnesota Supreme Court would recognize the tort of violation of publicity rights. . . . The right to publicity protects the ability of public personae to control the types of publicity that they receive. The right to publicity protects pecuniary, not emotional, interests. [Uhlaender v. Henricksen, 316 F. Supp. 1277, 1280-81 (D. Minn. 1970)]. . . . Thus, we believe that the Minnesota courts would recognize the right to publicity, and Titan's violation of this right makes Titan's use of Ventura's commentary without his consent unjust.[6]

However, quantum meruit is not available simply because Titan may have been unjustly enriched. Minnesota law is clear that "[w]here an express contract exists, there can be no implied [in law] contract with respect to the same subject matter." Reese Design v. I-94 Highway 61 Eastview Center Partnership, 428 N.W.2d 441, 446 (Minn. App. 1988); accord Sharp v. Laubersheimer, 347 N.W.2d 268, 271 (Minn. 1984). On the other hand, if an existing contract does not address the benefit for which recovery is sought, quantum meruit is available regarding those items about which the contract is silent. Holman v. CPT Corp., 457 N.W.2d 740, 745 (Minn. App. 1990); Frankson v. Design Space Int'l, 394 N.W.2d 140, 145 (Minn. 1986); Sagl v. Hirt, 236 Minn. 281, 52 N.W.2d 721, 725 (1952).[7]

Between 1985 and 1987, Ventura performed services for Titan under two different agreements. Ventura's services as a wrestler are governed by the WBA; his services as a commentator are governed by his oral agreements with McMahon. Thus, two contracts existed between Ventura and Titan between 1985 and March 1986, when the WBA was terminated. Whether quantum meruit recovery was proper depends upon whether or not the two agreements between Ventura and Titan were of limited scope, addressing only televised live performances, or also included subsequent videotape releases of the performances. The district court found that the WBA precluded royalties for the videotape exploitation of Ventura's performance *as a wrestler*. The district court also found that Ventura and Titan had no agreement concerning the payment of royalties for videotape exploitation of Ventura's performance *as a*

---

6. We are troubled by the fact that section 301(a) of the copyright code (Title 17) preempts Ventura's claims that are "equivalent to any of the exclusive rights within the general scope of copyright as specified by section 106," such as the production of videotapes of Ventura's televised commentary. Baltimore Orioles, Inc. v. Major League Baseball Players Ass'n, 805 F.2d 663, 675 (7th Cir. 1986) (baseball players' challenge to television broadcast of live games without their consent as a violation of their publicity rights preempted), cert. denied, 480 U.S. 941, 107 S. Ct. 1593, 94 L. Ed. 2d 782 (1987). However, Titan has not timely raised the issue of preemption on appeal, and has therefore waived it. . . .

7. A corollary of this rule is that quantum meruit is available if the benefit is conferred unknowingly, but not if the benefit is conferred merely as part of a bad bargain. Galante v. Oz, Inc., 379 N.W.2d 723, 726 (Minn. App. 1986). For the reasons discussed below, we conclude that Ventura conferred the videotape rights upon Titan unknowingly.

commentator. This finding concerns the intent of the parties, Cepeda v. Swift & Co., 415 F.2d 1205, 1207-08 (8th Cir. 1969), and as such, is a factual finding which we review only for clear error. 1 Steven A. Childress & Martha S. Davis, Federal Standards of Review §2.23 (2d ed. 1991) ("The clearly erroneous rule generally applies to a finding regarding the intent of the contracting parties, at least where the contract is ambiguous.").

We have reviewed the record, and are left with no definite and firm conviction that a mistake has been made. From 1985 to 1987, there was no discussion of Titan's right to use Ventura's color commentary. At least initially,[8] Ventura was not aware of the impending videotape sales, as merchandising was not part of the industry practice. These facts support the conclusion that Ventura's contract for commentating services did not contemplate a license for videotape distribution. Accordingly, we hold that the district court's finding that the pre-Bloom Ventura-Titan contracts did not address videotape licenses or royalties is not clearly erroneous. See Anderson v. Bessemer City, 470 U.S. 564, 105 S. Ct. 1504, 84 L. Ed. 2d 518 (1985). We believe that the judgment of the district court was correct insofar as it awarded damages for the exploitation of Ventura's pre-Bloom commentating performances.

B. IS QUANTUM MERUIT AVAILABLE FOR THE POST-BLOOM PERIOD?

The post-Bloom contracts pose different issues. It is clear that Ventura performed commentating services between 1987 and 1990 pursuant to a series of contracts with Titan. It is also clear that the post-Bloom Ventura-Titan contracts included an arrangement concerning videotape royalties. Bloom specifically inquired about royalties and was told of the Titan policy. In reliance upon this purported policy, Ventura waived his rights to royalties. Titan contends that Ventura is not entitled to recovery in quantum meruit for the post-Bloom period because of the existence of express contracts waiving royalties. See *Sharp*, 347 N.W.2d at 271 ("'It is fundamental that proof of an express contract precludes recovery in quantum meruit.'" (quoting Breza v. Thaldorf, 276 Minn. 180, 149 N.W.2d 276 (Minn. 1967))). Thus, the question reduces to whether Ventura may avoid the express contract waiving royalties and recover these royalties under quantum meruit. We believe that the district court correctly concluded that Ventura was entitled to avoid the fraudulently induced contracts and to recover the reasonable value of the royalties.

. . .

It is well established under Minnesota law that unjust enrichment and quantum meruit may arise from fraud or several other predicates. See, e.g., *Holman,* 457 N.W.2d at 745; *Hesselgrave,* 435 N.W.2d at 863; Timmer v. Gray, 395 N.W.2d 477, 478 (Minn. App. 1986); Anderson v. DeLisle, 352 N.W.2d 794, 796 (Minn. App. 1984). Nothing in these Minnesota cases requires that all elements of a cause of action for fraud must be proved in order to use fraud as a stepping stone for quantum meruit. However, we begin with the elements of a cause of action for fraud under Minnesota law as a useful guide. See Davis v. Re-Trac Mfg. Corp., 149 N.W.2d 37, 38-39 (Minn. 1967) (listing elements of cause of action for fraud). Titan argues that the evidence was insufficient to

---

8. Ventura stated that he was aware that tapes were being distributed in 1985. App. at 99-100.

support the necessary findings of materiality, inducement, justifiable reliance, causation and damages. We disagree. . . .

The evidence demonstrates that in 1987, Ventura hired Bloom to negotiate with Titan on his behalf. During negotiations, Glover told Bloom that Titan's policy was to pay royalties only to talent featured in their own videotapes, such as the "Best of" videotapes. Believing it difficult to break Titan's policy, Bloom negotiated an agreement under which Ventura agreed to perform for Titan as a commentator. The agreement did not entitle Ventura to royalties for videotapes of his performances, unless he was the featured performer. Ventura's compensation did not include any payment based on videotape sales.

Between 1987 and 1990, Glover and Bloom met annually, in person or by telephone, to negotiate Ventura's performance fees for each broadcast season, and occasionally for special performances. During each negotiation, Bloom asked Glover whether Titan had changed its policy regarding the payment of videotape royalties, and each time Glover reiterated that no talent received videotape royalties unless they were the featured performer on a videotape. Glover also told Ventura of this policy. Bloom and Ventura relied on Glover's statements concerning Titan's royalty policy, and understood that by entering into fee agreements they waived any right Ventura had to royalties. Despite these representations, Titan simultaneously made numerous royalty payments which were inconsistent with the purported policy of not paying royalties except to featured performers.[10]

In light of this evidence concerning Titan's representations and its history of royalty payments, the district court concluded that from 1987 through 1990, Titan's representations to Ventura that its policy was to pay videotape royalties only to featured performers were false. The district court also found that had Ventura known that Titan did not abide by its stated policy, he would not have accepted a deal which did not compensate him for the reproduction and sale of his performances on videotape. The court further found that Ventura justifiably relied on Titan's fraudulent misrepresentations of its royalty policy, and as a result Ventura suffered damages. Thus, the district court rescinded the 1987-1990 agreements, and permitted Ventura to recover in quantum meruit. In light of the abundance of supporting evidence, we find no basis for concluding the district court's findings were clearly erroneous or lacked sufficient evidentiary support.

C. DID THE DISTRICT COURT ABUSE ITS DISCRETION WHEN IT RELIED UPON THE TESTIMONY OF VENTURA'S DAMAGES EXPERT?

[The court first concluded that the testimony of Ventura's expert, Weston Anson, pertained to a material issue, the reasonable value of the services rendered by the plaintiff or the benefit to the defendant. — EDS.]

_____

10. In 1985, 1986 and 1987, Titan paid videotape royalties to Hulk Hogan and Marvel Comics for "Wrestlemania I," "II" and "III," despite the fact that there was no featured performer in these productions. During 1988, Titan paid videotape royalties to all 54 wrestlers appearing in the "Survivor Series," to all 57 wrestlers appearing in "Wrestlemania IV" and to all 38 wrestlers appearing in "Summer Slam '88." Again, these payments were inconsistent with Titan's stated policy because none of these videotapes had one featured performer. Beginning in December 1988, Titan paid royalties to all wrestlers appearing in videotapes of pay-per-view events.

We now turn to the related question whether Anson's testimony was reliable. Titan argues that Anson's testimony is unreliable because it is impermissibly speculative. In order to assess whether Anson's testimony is reliable, we must focus on the methodology and principles underlying the testimony, not the conclusions they generate. *Sorensen,* 31 F.3d at 648. Anson arrived at his estimate of damages by applying a royalty percentage to Titan's revenues from wholesale distribution of the tapes. The sales figures for the ninety videotapes upon which Ventura appeared were not available, but net profits (a more conservative measure) were established to the penny ($25,733,527.94). The main dispute concerns the royalty rate applied to this figure to generate the royalty that is the measure of damages. Titan's expert figured damages in a similar fashion, applying varying royalty percentages and formulas to base amounts keyed to sales. Anson testified that a five percent royalty was the minimum that he would be satisfied with as an agent and was the single most likely rate, but that rates could range from 3.5% to 7.5%. When applied to the profits figure, these rates yield: $865,723.00 (3.5%), $1,236,747.00 (5%), and $1,855,121.00 (7.5%).

We believe that Anson's methodology in arriving at the royalty percentages was reliable. Anson based his opinion as to the reasonable royalty upon a survey of thousands of licensing agreements. It is common practice to prove the value of an article (e.g., a videotape license) by introducing evidence of transactions involving other "substantially similar" articles (i.e., other licenses). 2 John H. Wigmore, Wigmore on Evidence §463, at 616-30 (James H. Chadbourn rev. 1979). Anson surveyed licensing agreements involving numerous sports and entertainment figures, App. at 487a (NFL), 489a (major league baseball), as well as various other types of characters. Although no individual arrangement examined by Anson was "on all fours" with the predicted Ventura-Titan license, in the aggregate, the licenses provided sufficient information to allow Anson to predict a royalty range for a wrestling license. We believe that this methodology is sufficiently reliable to support the admission of Anson's testimony.

. . .

III. CONCLUSION

The district court did not clearly err when it determined that Ventura's pre-Bloom contracts did not address videotape licensing and royalties. Accordingly, it did not err in permitting quantum meruit recovery of videotape royalties for the pre-Bloom period. Nor did the district court err when it awarded quantum meruit recovery for the post-Bloom period. We also find that the district court did not abuse its discretion in qualifying Anson, nor did it abuse its discretion in determining that Anson's testimony was relevant and that the methods used by Anson were reliable. We further find that the district court did not clearly err in denying Ventura's request for prefiling interest where Ventura's potential damages varied by over 200% and where the amount was contingent upon the factfinder's determination of unresolved issues.

MORRIS SHEPPARD ARNOLD, Circuit Judge, dissenting.

I dissent from so much of the court's opinion as allows Mr. Ventura a recovery for royalties before Mr. Bloom negotiated a contract for him. To state a cause of action for unjust enrichment in Minnesota, a plaintiff must show either on legal or equitable grounds, or based on principles of natural justice, that a defendant's retention of a benefit would be unjust. Mehl v. Norton, 201 Minn. 203, 205-07, 275 N.W. 843, 844-45 (1937). In the court's view, Mr. Ventura was deprived of a legal right to additional compensation because Titan infringed his right of publicity. I believe that the court has mistakenly allowed this recovery, however, because I do not think that a right of publicity exists under Minnesota law.

The court finds a right of publicity under Minnesota law in the absence of any evidence that Minnesota's courts would welcome this cause of action — and, indeed, a Minnesota Supreme Court case indicates to me that they would not. Minnesota has not adopted the tort of appropriation of name or likeness or any of the other torts collectively known as invasion of privacy, Hendry v. Conner, 303 Minn. 317, 319, 226 N.W.2d 921, 922-23 (Minn. 1975), and a right to one's likeness is virtually indistinguishable from a right of publicity. . . . [I]t is highly significant that, in the year 1995, when everyone not only wants his or her fifteen minutes of fame but the concomitant television rights as well, no Minnesota state court has yet discovered a right of publicity in Minnesota law. The court has thus cited no "reliable data," B.B. v. Continental Ins. Co., 8 F.3d 1288, 1291 (8th Cir. 1993), to indicate that Minnesota would recognize such a right. Titan was therefore not enriched in violation of a legal right recognized in Minnesota.

Nor has Mr. Ventura shown that it would be inequitable or violate natural justice for Titan to reproduce and sell the videotapes that it produced and on which Mr. Ventura was already paid to appear as an announcer without paying him additional consideration. The doctrine of unjust enrichment, it is true, may provide recovery for performing extra services not specified in an original contract, Sagl v. Hirt, 236 Minn. 281, 287, 52 N.W.2d 721, 725 (1952), but Mr. Ventura does not argue that he performed any duties in addition to his commentary. One may also recover to prevent unjust enrichment if a benefit is conferred "unknowingly" or "unwillingly," Galante v. Oz, Inc., 379 N.W.2d 723, 726 (Minn. App. 1986), but Mr. Ventura's own testimony shows that he did not confer the alleged benefit unknowingly or unwillingly. More important, it is hardly unjust, from an economic viewpoint, that Titan should receive the full benefit from selling copies of the videotapes that it created. Titan, as entrepreneur, staged the wrestling matches, hired the various wrestlers, hired the announcers, and, above all, took the risks that the venture would fail to turn a profit. Now that Titan has been successful, Mr. Ventura wants additional compensation for having performed no additional work. If there is any unjust enrichment in this case, it is in allowing Mr. Ventura a recovery under these circumstances.

Plaintiff cites Frankson v. Design Space Int'l, 394 N.W.2d 140, 145 (Minn. 1986), and Holman v. CPT Corp., 457 N.W.2d 740, 745 (Minn. App. 1990), for the proposition that when there is a lack of full agreement concerning compensation an employee may still recover in quantum meruit. That is no doubt so. But those cases are inapposite because each involved performances that had concededly not been compensated. The issue in each was whether sales employees would be allowed to recover commissions. In *Frankson,* the court held that the parties never reached an agreement about commissions and that therefore the plaintiff should be allowed a quantum meruit recovery. In *Holman,* plaintiff was terminated before she realized a commission on a sale that was virtually complete but still pending when she was fired, and the contract was silent with respect to whether a commission was due under the circumstances. Mr. Ventura, by contrast, performed and was compensated for his performances. He made an agreement to be paid a weekly sum rather than royalties for announcing wrestling events, and while he now regrets this less favorable arrangement, his regrets are not actionable under Minnesota law because one cannot recover for an unfavorable bargain. See *Galante,* 379 N.W.2d at 726.

Nelson v. Radio Corp. of Am., 148 F. Supp. 1 (S.D. Fla. 1957) is an instructive case. Nelson, a vocalist, was hired to perform with the Glenn Miller Orchestra. Miller paid him weekly according to union scale. Nelson sang six selections for a recording session and two more for a broadcast that also was recorded. Miller assigned all his rights in the records to the defendant, and in due course, defendant made copies of the recordings for sale. Nelson sued for an accounting for the sale of the recordings on which he sang, a 5 percent royalty on the records, as well as injunctive relief and damages. The evidence established that Nelson had no agreement with Miller entitling him to receive any royalties on the sale of phonograph records. The court ruled that "any right in and to phonograph records or other recordings in connection with the production of which plaintiff worked were the property of the plaintiff's employer Miller. . . ." 148 F. Supp. at 3. The court therefore rejected Nelson's claim for royalties.

The reasoning of *Nelson* is highly persuasive and our case is strikingly similar to it. Mr. Ventura agreed to receive weekly pay to perform wrestling commentary. He does not dispute, as far as I can discern, that the videotapes belong to Titan. Mr. Ventura, like Nelson, is suing for a royalty on the sales of the recordings on which he performed. And like Nelson, Mr. Ventura deserves no recovery because he and Titan both performed under their contract and the recordings of Mr. Ventura's performances now belong to Titan and it may profit from them as it sees fit.

Finally, even if Minnesota recognized a cause of action for the breach of a right of publicity, and even if this case could be properly characterized, as the court seems to believe, as a dispute over the scope of a license of intellectual property rights (that is, publicity rights), I still doubt that Mr. Ventura should recover. Mr. Ventura himself testified that he was employed to "broadcast wrestling." The agreement was therefore clearly susceptible to the construction that it authorized the sale of videotapes to end users. According to a leading copyright treatise, the preferred rule for copyright contracts when the intent of the parties is unclear is that the licensee may properly pursue any uses that may reasonably be said to fall within the medium as described in the license. 3 Melville B. Nimmer & David Nimmer, Nimmer on Copyright §10.10[B] at 10-93 (1993). It follows "that a grant of the right to exhibit a motion picture by 'television' in its unambiguous core meaning refers to over-the-air television broadcasts, but in its ambiguous penumbra includes any device by which the motion picture may be seen on television screens, including cable television and videocassette uses." Id. at 10-94. The ambiguity ought to favor the licensee because "it is surely more arbitrary and unjust to put the onus on the licensee by holding that he should have obtained a further clarification of a meaning that was already present than it is to hold that the licensor should have negated a meaning that the licensee might then or thereafter rely upon." Id. I believe that this principle is recommended by reason and is applicable here because a right of publicity does not differ in any material way from a copyright. See Baltimore Orioles, Inc. v. Major League Baseball Players Ass'n, 805 F.2d 663, 679 (7th Cir. 1986), cert. denied, 480 U.S. 941, 107 S. Ct. 1593, 94 L. Ed. 2d 782 (1987). Mr. Ventura testified that he was hired to perform commentary for television broadcasts. "Television broadcasts" under these circumstances must reasonably include dissemination of the videotapes containing the commentary that Mr. Ventura performed as part of his employment. Indeed, this seems to me utterly implicit in the original contractual arrangement.

For the foregoing reasons, I believe that Mr. Ventura's claim for additional compensation for his announcing duties in the period before Mr. Bloom negotiated a contract for him fails as a matter of law. I would therefore reverse that part of the judgment allowing Mr. Ventura's recovery for his role as a commentator before he entered into the written contract.

Notes and Questions

1. *Governor Ventura.* Plaintiff Jesse Ventura eventually left professional wrestling and entered the political arena where he served as mayor of Brooklyn Park, Minnesota, before being elected governor of Minnesota in 1998. After serving one term, he decided not to seek reelection.

2. *Types of restitutionary claims in **Ventura**.* The majority and the dissent make a distinction between plaintiff Ventura's claims for restitution arising during the time that he had oral contracts and his claims from the period when he had written contracts negotiated by Bloom. How do these two claims for restitution compare with the theories advanced in the first two cases in this section? The dissent disagrees with the majority only about the "pre-Bloom" claims for restitution. Part of the disagreement focuses on whether there is a right of publicity in Minnesota in the absence of a clear ruling by the state courts. Beyond that dispute about state law, however, the dissent also disagrees with the majority's holding on whether Titan was unjustly enriched. Are you more persuaded by the majority or the dissent? More specifically, are you persuaded that Ventura conferred an uncompensated benefit "unknowingly" in the pre-Bloom performances?

The "post-Bloom" claim exemplifies a case in which restitution is sought after a contract has been rendered unenforceable due to fraud. As noted in the introduction to this section, the same reasoning applies if a contract is unenforceable for other reasons, such as mistake, incapacity, impossibility, duress, etc. What measure of restitution would be appropriate in such cases? See the following note.

3. *Measuring the restitutionary interest: enrichment or benefit.* In the late nineteenth century, when commentators first began developing the theory of restitution, it was often said that the basis of restitution was "unjust

enrichment." In the first major treatise on restitution, published in 1893, Professor William Keener stated, "By far the most important and most numerous illustrations of the scope of quasi contract are found in those cases where the plaintiff's right to recover rests upon the doctrine that a man shall not be allowed to enrich himself unjustly at the expense of another." William A. Keener, A Treatise on The Law of Quasi-Contracts 19 (1893). See also Arthur L. Corbin, Quasi Contractual Obligations, 21 Yale L.J. 533, 550 (1912). Other commentators argued, however, that courts often awarded recovery in restitutionary actions even if the defendant was not in fact enriched. In his 1913 treatise on quasi contracts, Professor Woodward suggested that the measure of recovery should be based on the "receipt of benefit" rather than enrichment. Frederic C. Woodward, The Law of Quasi Contracts (1913). While the use of the word *benefit* seems to imply enrichment, the term was intended to refer to the value of what was received rather than the increase in the defendant's wealth. The Restatement of Restitution, which was published in 1937, adopted this concept of benefit as the measure of recovery. Comment *e* to §1 provided that "a person who has been unjustly deprived of his property or its value or the value of his labor may be entitled to maintain an action for restitution against another although the other has not in fact been enriched thereby."

The Restatement (Second) of Contracts §371 recognizes both means of measuring restitution (reasonable value of the performer's services and value of increase to the recipient's property) and indicates that relief may be measured as justice requires. Cf. Maglica v. Maglica, 78 Cal. Rptr. 2d 101 (Ct. App. 1998) (after jury awarded $84 million, appellate court reversed, holding that quantum meruit could be measured only by "reasonable value of the services rendered" and not by the "impact" on the business). Would these measures necessarily be different? Which measure would be more appropriate in *Ventura*?

4. *Recovery of reliance damages in restitution.* A number of commentators have argued that courts should have the power under the theory of restitution to compensate for reliance damages or order some other equitable adjustment of the rights of the parties when a contract has been discharged because of impracticability or other similar cause. See John P. Dawson, Restitution Without Enrichment, 61 B.U. L. Rev. 563 (1981); Jeffrey L. Harrison, A Case for Loss Sharing, 56 S. Cal. L. Rev. 573 (1983). The Restatement (Second) appears to authorize courts to engage in such loss sharing, albeit in a somewhat roundabout fashion. Section 371 provides that in an action for restitution a court may "as justice requires" measure recovery either by the value of the performance rendered (the benefit theory) or the increase in value of the defendant's property or interests (the enrichment theory). Comment *b* to §371 provides that the measure of recovery excludes expenditures "to the extent that they conferred no benefit." This comment notwithstanding, other sections of the Restatement allow a court to award reliance damages when a contract is discharged for reasons such as impracticability. See Restatement (Second) §§158 (mistake), 272 (impracticability). See generally Joseph M. Perillo, Restitution in the Second Restatement of Contracts, 81 Colum. L. Rev. 37 (1981); William F. Young, Half Measures, 81 Colum. L. Rev. 19 (1981).

There appears to be little case law applying the proposed "restitutionary reliance" remedy provided for in §§158 and 272 of the revised Restatement. Given that recovery of expanded restitution under those sections would not be available in every case, what factors might be relevant to an award of such damages? See Heyl & Patterson International, Inc. v. F. D. Rich Housing, Inc., 663 F.2d 419 (3d Cir. 1981) (after holding that construction contract between plaintiff general contractor and defendant real estate developer was excused by mutual mistake, court awarded plaintiff substantial sum to compensate for expenses undertaken in reliance on contract because developer was more responsible for error as to legality of the contract); Earhart v. William Low Co., 600 P.2d 1344 (Cal. 1979) (when services are rendered on request, party rendering the services may obtain restitution for expenses incurred in justifiable reliance); Hart v. Arnold, 884 A. 2d 316 (Pa. Super. Ct. 2005) (even though acts in reliance did not benefit buyer, seller of parcel of land was entitled to restitution plus reliance damages after governmental regulations made performance by buyer of promise to build lake impracticable but buyer failed to timely inform seller of the changed circumstances).

5. *Proving restitutionary damages with reasonable certainty.* The defendant in *Ventura* challenged the sufficiency of the evidence offered to measure the restitutionary interest of the plaintiff. Is it surprising to find here the same problem of "certainty" that we have seen in connection with claims for expectation and reliance damages? Are you persuaded that the majority reached the correct conclusion on this issue? An example of the potential difficulty in measuring restitution damages with certainty is found in ATACS Corp. v. Trans World Communications, Inc., 155 F.3d 659 (3d Cir. 1998), *remanded at* 2002 U.S. Dist. LEXIS 15070 (E.D. Pa. 2002). After the plaintiff subcontractor entered into a preliminary "teaming agreement" with the defendant to produce the successful bid for a Greek government contract worth more than $23 million, the defendant breached by unexpectedly awarding a contract to one of the plaintiff's competitors for the work the plaintiff expected to perform. After finding that the plaintiff's expectancy relief would be too speculative, the trial court also ruled that it could not quantify the value of the plaintiff's services rendered in enhancing the defendant's winning bid and thus awarded nominal damages of $1. The plaintiff did not seek and the trial court did not address a reliance-based measure of damages. Id. at 670. The Third Circuit Court of Appeals reversed on the issue of restitutionary damages, ruling that the trial court should have invited the parties to offer expert evidence about the reasonable value of technical and consulting services in the market of government contracting and should have considered dollar savings realized by the defendant in later subcontracts made possible by the plaintiff's earlier services. In remanding and essentially urging the trial court to make a greater effort to give relief to the nonbreaching party, the court of appeals stated that "equitable considerations must predominate over a parochial approach" to the remedies issue. Id. at 671. On initial remand, the trial court rejected the plaintiff's request for more than $4 million in restitution damages as a disguised claim for lost profits and awarded the plaintiff only $18,900 based on the defendant's calculation of the plaintiff's costs in preparing technical submissions. After the appellate court rejected that award and remanded

again, the trial court awarded the plaintiff restitutionary damages of $230,000 as a reasonable commission for facilitating the contract and another $20,000 as the reasonable value to the defendant of technical submissions provided by the plaintiff.

PROBLEM 12-1

Big Burger, Inc., is a corporation that franchises hamburger restaurants throughout the country. In June 2004 Emily Michaels approached Big Burger about obtaining a franchise. After reviewing literature from the company, Michaels visited several Big Burger franchises in other cities and hired a lawyer to represent her in negotiations; she spent a total of $15,000 in traveling expenses and legal fees.

In August the parties signed an agreement in which Big Burger granted Michaels a franchise to sell hamburgers under its corporate name and agreed to construct and lease a restaurant to her. Michaels agreed to pay Big Burger a franchise fee of $100,000 and to lease the restaurant for a ten-year term at a fixed rental plus a percentage of sales. After resigning her job as a manager of a local restaurant, where she had been earning $40,000 per year, to devote full time to her franchise, Michaels purchased equipment for the restaurant from suppliers approved by Big Burger at a cost of $50,000. In January 2005 the restaurant was ready for operation.

Within six months after the restaurant opened, disputes developed between Michaels and Big Burger. Michaels objected to the quality of some of the products she received from the company and to the company's failure to honor a commitment to run a major advertising campaign. She also complained that her income did not meet company projections. During negotiations Big Burger had shown Michaels financial reports from comparable restaurants indicating an average net profit of $75,000 per year in addition to an average owner's salary of $50,000 per year. After paying Michaels a salary of $20,000 per year, the restaurant was just breaking even.

By late 2006 Michaels had become so dissatisfied with her situation that she decided to give up the restaurant. When negotiations with the company were unsuccessful, she decided to bring suit.

(a) Assume Michaels can establish that Big Burger committed a material breach of the franchise agreement. How might her damages be computed?

(b) Suppose Michaels's complaint includes a count seeking rescission and restitution. At a pretrial conference the judge stated that he would require the plaintiff to "elect" between the claim for damages for breach of contract and the claim for rescission because the causes of action were inconsistent. In some jurisdictions a plaintiff must elect between inconsistent remedies in order to avoid double recovery and jury confusion. Which theory — restitution or damages — should Michaels's lawyer elect to pursue?

(c) At a pretrial conference the judge asks the lawyers for Michaels and Big Burger to prepare proposed jury instructions on the issue of damages for breach of contract. Write proposed jury instructions for either Michaels or Big Burger. In doing so, you may obtain guidance from model civil jury instructions for state or federal courts in your jurisdiction.

C. SPECIFIC PERFORMANCE

As we saw in Chapter 11, some types of injury are not compensable in money damages at all, while the doctrines of foreseeability, certainty, causation, and mitigation may prevent recovery of damages even for compensable types of harm. It seems natural to wonder whether the plaintiff should not be able to avoid all these problems by simply asking the court to order the defendant to perform as promised. In the Anglo-American legal tradition, however, "specific performance" is not a remedy to which the plaintiff is automatically entitled, even when an unexcused breach has been clearly established. The following discussion by Professor Farnsworth explains the nature and genesis of the various limitations on the availability of specific relief.

> The early common law courts did know specific relief, for many of the first suits after the Norman Conquest were proprietary in nature, designed to regain something of which the plaintiff had been deprived. Even the action of debt was of this character, since it was based on the notion of an unjust detention of something belonging to the plaintiff. But it became the practice in these actions to allow money damages for the detention in addition to specific relief, and with the development of new forms of action, such as assumpsit, that were in no way proprietary, substitutional relief became the usual form.
>
> The typical judgment at common law declared that the plaintiff recover from the defendant a sum of money, which in effect imposed on him a new obligation as redress for the breach of the old. The new obligation required no cooperation on his part for its enforcement since, if the sum was not paid, a writ of execution would issue empowering the sheriff to seize and sell so much of the defendant's property as was required to pay the plaintiff. . . . The judgment itself was seen as a mere declaration of rights as between the parties, and the process for its execution was directed not at the defendant but at the sheriff, ordering him to put the plaintiff in possession of real or personal property or to seize the defendant's property and sell such of it as was necessary to satisfy a money judgment.
>
> The enforcement of promises in equity developed along very different lines. . . .
>
> Under the influence of the canon law (for the early chancellors were usually clerics), decrees in equity came to take the form of a personal command to the defendant to do or not to do something. His cooperation was assumed, and if he disobeyed he could be punished not only for criminal contempt, at the instance of the court, but also for civil contempt, at the instance of the plaintiff. This put into the plaintiff's hands the extreme sanction of imprisonment, which might be supplemented by fines payable to the plaintiff and sequestration of the defendant's goods. So it was said that equity acted in personam, against the person of the defendant, while the law acted in rem, against his property. But it did not follow that the chancellor stood ready to order every defaulting promisor to perform his promise. Equitable relief was confined to special cases in light of both practical and historical limitations.
>
> The practical limitations grew out of the problems inherent in coercion. Our courts, like those of civil law countries, will not undertake to coerce a performance that is personal in nature—to compel an artist to paint a picture or a singer to sing a song. . . . Our courts have also been reluctant to order specific performance where difficulties of supervision or enforcement are foreseen, e.g., to order a building

contractor specifically to perform his contract to repair a house. It has been suggested that in their origins these ideas carried a load of snobbery, expressed in distaste for menial tasks — "how can a Master judge of repairs in husbandry?" Today they are more often justified as a means of avoiding conflict and unfairness where no clear standards can be framed in advance. The practical exigencies of drafting decrees to guide future conduct under threat of contempt have also moved courts to require that contract terms be expressed with somewhat greater certainty if specific performance is to be granted than if damages are to be awarded. But these practical limitations are on the whole far less significant than the historical ones.

The most important of the historical limitations derives from the circumstance that, since the chancellor had first granted equitable relief in order to supply the deficiencies of the common law, equitable remedies were readily characterized as "extraordinary." When, during the long jurisdictional struggle between the two systems of courts, some means of accommodation were needed, an "adequacy" test was developed to prevent encroachment by the chancellor on the powers of the common law judges. Equity would stay its hand if the remedy at law was "adequate." To this test was added the gloss that the money damages awarded by the common law courts were ordinarily "adequate" — a gloss encouraged by the philosophy of free enterprise, since in a market economy money ought to enable an aggrieved promisee to arrange a substitute transaction. . . .

So it came to be that, in sharp contrast to the civil law approach, money damages were regarded as the norm and specific relief as the deviation, even where the law could easily have provided specific relief without any cooperation from the defaulting promisor.

Land, which the common law viewed with particular esteem, was singled out for special treatment. Each parcel, however ordinary, was considered to be "unique," and from this it followed that if a vendor defaulted on his promise to convey land, not even money would enable an injured purchaser to find a substitute. The remedy at law being in this sense "inadequate," a decree of specific performance would ordinarily issue. Although the case for allowing the vendor to have specific performance when the purchaser defaulted was less compelling, equity also granted him relief. But no such reason applied to the contract for the sale of goods, for in a market economy it was supposed that, with rare exceptions for such "unique" items as heirlooms and objects of art, substantially similar goods were available elsewhere. . . .

A second historical limitation, or group of limitations, is premised on the notion that equitable relief is "discretionary." Since the chancellor was to act according to "conscience" (a circumstance that prompted the famous charge that his conscience might vary with the length of his foot), he might withhold relief where considerations of "fairness" or "morality" dictated. Some of the most renowned of these equitable restrictions are embodied in equity's colorful maxims: "he who seeks equity must do equity"; "he who comes into equity must come with clean hands"; and "equity aids the vigilant." . . .

The historical development of the parallel systems of law and equity may afford an adequate explanation of the reluctance of our courts to grant specific relief; it is scant justification for it. A more rational basis might be the severity of the sanctions available under the contempt power for their enforcement. In any event, the current trend is clearly in favor of the extension of specific relief. The fusion of law and equity into a single court system at least facilitates a major change in this direction, and commentators have urged such a change. . . .

Still, for the present, the promisee must ordinarily be content with money damages.

E. Allan Farnsworth, Legal Remedies for Breach of Contract, 70 Colum. L. Rev. 1145, 1149-1156 (1970).

In 1990, Professor Douglas Laycock published a major study of equitable remedies entitled The Death of the Irreparable Injury Rule. As his title suggests, Professor Laycock contends that regardless of what courts say by way of justifying their decisions, they do not in fact limit access to equitable relief by requiring the plaintiff to demonstrate that otherwise an "irreparable injury" will result (or that there is "no adequate remedy at law," a principle that he equates with the requirement of "irreparable injury"). Instead, Laycock concludes that although this requirement is often invoked, it is virtually never decisive in fact: Courts grant or withhold equitable relief on the basis of a number of other, more particular policies, such as hardship to the defendant or others, hostility to the merits of the plaintiff's case, or values such as freedom of speech or freedom from compulsory service. The work of additional scholars is discussed in the Notes that follow the cases below.

City Stores Co. v. Ammerman
United States District Court
266 F. Supp. 766 (D.D.C. 1967), aff'd,
394 F.2d 950 (D.C. Cir. 1968)

GASCH, District Judge.

The plaintiff, City Stores Company, seeks specific performance of a contract wherein defendants allegedly promised to offer plaintiff a lease as a major tenant in defendants' shopping center in Tyson's Corner, Fairfax County, Virginia. By the terms of the contract, the defendants were to give plaintiff an opportunity to accept a lease on terms at least equal to those offered to other major department stores in the center. The court granted a preliminary injunction to prevent the defendants from leasing the last available department store site to another department store. Now the court is called upon to decide whether there is a valid contract and, if so, whether it is sufficiently definite so that specific performance of it should be decreed.

Defendants desired to construct a large shopping center on a tract of land near Tyson's Corner, in Fairfax County, Virginia. In order to build the center, they had to persuade the Board of County Supervisors of Fairfax County to rezone the property for that use. By the time plaintiff came into the picture, defendants' prospects for securing the necessary zoning were not good: the Fairfax County Planning Commission and the Planning Commission Staff had voted against defendants' requested zoning. Defendants had to persuade the Board that these advisory groups were wrong in their recommendations. Moreover, defendants had an extremely strong competitor, the Rouse-Reynolds group, for another shopping center in the same general area. There was a zoning application for the Rouse-Reynolds center pending before the Board of Supervisors at the same time. Hearing on defendants' application was set for May 31, 1962.

During a period of time prior to May 31, Lansburgh's Department Store, which is owned by City Stores Company, the plaintiff herein, had been negotiating the terms of a lease of a store site in the Wheaton Plaza shopping center with defendants Lerner and Gudelsky. In the course of meetings with Mr. Lerner, or Messrs. Lerner and Gudelsky together, Lansburgh's president, Mr. Jagels, learned of the Tyson's Corner proposal. Mr. Lerner asked for a letter from Lansburgh's expressing a desire to participate in defendants' Tyson's Corner project, which could be used in the hearing before the Fairfax County Board of County Supervisors. Mr. Lerner had sought similar letters from other department stores in Washington, but found them unwilling to express a preference for defendants' Tyson's Corner site over the nearby proposed site of the Rouse-Reynolds group. Under normal circumstances, Lansburgh's also would have been unwilling to express a preference for one site over the other. It was eager to obtain suburban department store sites for expansion purposes. But, for a reason which is a matter of dispute between plaintiff and defendants, Mr. Jagels wrote a letter to Mr. Lerner and Mr. Gudelsky (Plaintiff's Exhibit E) in which he stated that it was Lansburgh's conclusion that the Tyson's Corner site was preferable to any other in the area and expressing Lansburgh's great interest in becoming a major tenant at a Lerner-Gudelsky shopping center if they were successful in their zoning application.

Defendants contend that plaintiff wrote this letter in order to secure defendants' help in obtaining necessary permission from other department store tenants in the Wheaton Plaza shopping center for plaintiff to become another major tenant there. However, I find that this contention is not supported by the evidence. The evidence shows that during the period in question, plaintiff and Lerner-Gudelsky had not themselves reached agreement on rental and other terms for plaintiff to become a tenant in the Wheaton Plaza center, and that they were engaged in negotiations. It was not until November of 1962, by defendant Lerner's own correspondence records, which are part of the evidence herein, that either plaintiff or defendants became aware that there would be an objection raised to plaintiff's tenancy by Montgomery Ward, one of the major tenants at Wheaton Plaza with right of approval of other lessees.

Plaintiff contends, on the other hand, that the Jagels letter to Lerner and Gudelsky was written at Lerner's request in exchange for a promise that plaintiff would be given an opportunity to become a major tenant at Tyson's Corner on terms at least equal to those of other major tenants at the center.

I find that on or about May 29, 1962, the Lerner-Gudelsky interests promised to give Lansburgh's an opportunity to become a major tenant at the Tyson's Corner center on terms at least equal to those granted other major department store tenants in exchange for assistance from Lansburgh's in securing the necessary zoning for the tract. I further find that on or about May 29, 1962, the defendants Lerner and Gudelsky signed and gave to Lansburgh's president Jagels the following letter concerning the defendants' promise, and that this letter, together with plaintiff's full performance of the requested services, is a sufficient writing to satisfy the Statute of Frauds, §12-302 D.C. Code. The letter is Plaintiff's Exhibit B, and states:

Dear Mr. Jagels:

We very much appreciate the efforts which you have expended in endeavoring to assist Mr. Gudelsky and me in our application for zoning at Tyson's Corner for a Regional Shopping Center.

You have our assurance that in the event we are successful with our application, that we will give you the opportunity to become one of our contemplated center's major tenants with rental and terms at least equal to that of any other major department store in the center.

Sincerely yours,
/s/*Isadore M. Gudelsky*
/s/*Theodore N. Lerner*

I also find that the services plaintiff performed for defendants, particularly the letter from Mr. Jagels which defendants used to support their case in the zoning hearing on May 31, constituted adequate consideration for a valid unilateral contract which was binding on defendants thereafter.

I

The plaintiff contends that this unilateral contract is an option for an opportunity to accept or reject a lease for a store at Tyson's Corner on terms at least equal to those granted to other major tenants. Defendants deny that the agreement is an option contract and contend that, even if it were, it would not be sufficiently definite to be specifically enforced by this court.

In determining the nature and consequences of this contract, it should be observed first that a typical option contract is a continuing offer for a fixed period of time (or a reasonable time if no time is specified) which is binding on the offeror because given for a valuable consideration. As noted by Williston, the word "option" is a business and not a strictly legal term. 5 Williston on Contracts §1441 (Rev. ed. 1937). An option contract is a unilateral contract as is the contract at issue. Generally, however, an option contract describes specifically the subject offered and all its material terms. The offeree knows at the time he receives the option exactly what has been offered and what he may accept or reject. It is obvious that the contract between Lerner-Gudelsky and Lansburgh's is not of this description, and further analysis is needed to decide whether or not it may be classified as an option, despite its superficial dissimilarity to the usual form.

In this case, it is clear that an option in typical form could not have been offered by Lerner-Gudelsky, because they had nothing but a contingency to offer at the time the contract was made. Any specific terms they might have included in their letter to Jagels would have been meaningless in view of the fact that they had neither received the necessary permission to construct their center, nor had they entered into leases with other major tenants which were to be the measure of the lease offered to Lansburgh's. Yet it does not follow from this that what they did promise to offer Lansburgh's was without substance. What we have here is a contract with certain conditions precedent to its operation.

The first condition precedent to the Lerner-Gudelsky obligation to Lansburgh's was the securing of necessary zoning for its Tyson's Corner tract, without which it could not construct a shopping center at all. The second condition precedent was its entering into leases with other major tenants for stores in the center, so the terms of those leases could provide the essential terms of a lease to be offered to plaintiff. Defendants did secure the zoning, and they did, in the latter half of 1965, enter into leases with Woodward & Lothrop and Hecht department stores. At the time it secured those leases, defendants were under an immediate contractual obligation to tender plaintiff a lease which in all its material terms would be at least as favorable to plaintiff as the two other leases were to their respective stores. That this would have been possible is entirely clear from the record: both the Hecht and Woodward & Lothrop leases, Plaintiff's Exhibit F, contain clauses to the effect that their terms will be at least equal to those offered to other lessees in the center. Thus, even though none of the stores in the center will be identical in design, it is apparent from defendants' own leases that complete equality of material terms governing occupancy, including amount of space and cost per square foot, and substantially equal terms on less material aspects of the lease, is within the customary contemplation of parties entering into shopping center agreements of the type at issue in this case. When it is recognized that a lessor's success in a shopping center is directly tied to the success of all of his lessees, it must be conceded that as a practical business matter it is to the lessor's advantage that one tenant be given no distinct competitive advantage over another traceable to the terms of the leases entered into.

I therefore hold as a matter of law that the Lerner-Gudelsky letter was a binding unilateral contract, which gave plaintiff an option to accept a lease at Tyson's Corner, and that the existence of express and implied conditions precedent did not render it invalid or too indefinite to be a contract. . . .

II

Whether the option contract secured by plaintiff in this case is sufficiently definite to be the subject of a decree for specific performance is quite another question, which does not concern the validity or existence of the contract but only the nature of the remedy available to plaintiff.

It is not contested by the plaintiff that if it were to accept a lease tendered by defendants in accordance with the contract, there would be numerous complex details left to be worked out. The crucial elements of rate of rental and the amount of space can readily be determined from the Hecht and Woodward & Lothrop leases. But some details of design, construction and price of the building to be occupied by plaintiff at Tyson's Corner would have to be agreed to by the parties, subject to further negotiation and tempered only by the promise of equal terms with other tenants. The question is whether a court of equity will grant specific performance of a contract which has left such substantial terms open for future negotiation.

The defendants have cited a number of cases in support of their argument that a court of equity will not grant specific performance of a contract in which some terms are left for further negotiations by the parties, or which would require a great deal of supervision by the court. I have examined those cases cited which were decided in this jurisdiction, because unless the precedents here establish a clear policy one way or the other, this court may exercise its discretion in fashioning an equitable decree. Moreover, this is an area of law in which not all jurisdictions are in agreement, and whichever way this court were to decide the case, there would be cases holding to the contrary in other parts of the country. . . .

Thus, defendants have cited no cases in this jurisdiction that would support the contention that an option contract involving further negotiations on details and construction of a building may not be specifically enforced.

On the other hand, the 1926 case of Morris v. Ballard, 56 App. D.C. 383, 16 F.2d 175, 49 A.L.R. 1461, held that an option to purchase property which contained a provision as to price "on terms to be agreed upon" was specifically enforceable by a court of equity. The court in that case held that "it became the duty of defendant, upon proper demand, either to accept the agreed purchase price in cash or to specify such terms as were acceptable to him. He had no right to refuse arbitrarily and unconditionally to accept payment solely for the purpose of defeating the option. Such a refusal would operate as a fraud upon the plaintiff." The court further held that the clause "on terms to be agreed upon" "*was in good conscience a stipulation that he would in fact agree with plaintiff upon reasonable terms of payment, and would not arbitrarily refuse to proceed with the sale. . . .*" [Emphasis added.] 56 App. D.C. 383, 384, 16 F.2d 175, 176. The court also quoted Pomeroy, Specific Performance §145 to the following effect: "when a contract has been partly performed by the plaintiff, and the defendant has received and enjoys the benefits thereof, and the plaintiff would be virtually remediless unless the contract were enforced, the court, from the plainest considerations of equity and common justice, does not regard with favor any objections raised by the defendant merely on the ground of the incompleteness or uncertainty of the agreement." 56 App. D.C. 383, 384, 16 F.2d 175, 176. I therefore hold as a matter of law that the mere fact that a contract, definite in material respects, contains some terms which are subject to further negotiation between plaintiff and defendant will not bar a decree for specific performance, if in the court's discretion specific performance should be granted. Walsh v. Rundlette, supra, adds further support to this position. See also 5 Williston on Contracts §1424 (Rev. ed. 1937).

The question whether a contract which also calls for construction of a building can or should be specifically enforced apparently never has been decided before in this jurisdiction. The parties have cited no cases on this point.

At the outset, it should be noted that where specific performance of such contracts has been granted the essential criterion has not been the nature or subject of the contract, but rather the inadequacy or impracticability of legal remedies. See 5 Williston on Contracts §1423 (Rev. ed. 1937); 4 Pomeroy's Equity Jurisprudence §§1401-1403 (5th ed. 1941). Contracts involving interests in land or unique chattels generally are specifically enforced because of the clear inadequacy of damages at law for breach of contract. As Pomeroy says:

The foundation and measure of the jurisdiction is the desire to do justice, which the legal remedy would fail to give. . . .

. . . The jurisdiction depending upon this broad principle is exercised in two classes of cases: 1. Where the subject-matter of the contract is of such a special nature, or of such a peculiar value, that the damages, when ascertained according to legal rules, would not be a just and reasonable substitute for or representative of that subject-matter in the hands of the party who is entitled to its benefit; or in other words, where the damages are *inadequate;* 2. Where, from some special and practical features or incidents of the contract inhering either in its subject matter, in its terms, or in the relations of the parties, it is impossible to arrive at a legal measure of damages at all, or at least with any sufficient degree of certainty, so that *no* real compensation can be obtained by means of an action at law; or in other words, where damages are *impracticable.*

It is apparent from the nature of the contract involved in this case that even were it possible to arrive at a precise measure of damages for breach of a contract to lease a store in a shopping center for a long period of years—which it is not—money damages would in no way compensate the plaintiff for loss of the right to participate in the shopping center enterprise and for the almost incalculable future advantages that might accrue to it as a result of extending its operations into the suburbs. Therefore, I hold that the appropriate remedy in this case is specific performance.

Some jurisdictions in the United States have opposed granting specific performance of contracts for construction of buildings and other contracts requiring extensive supervision of the court, but the better view, and the one which increasingly is being followed in this country, is that such contracts should be specifically enforced unless the difficulties of supervision outweigh the importance of specific performance to the plaintiff. 5 Williston on Contracts §1423 (Rev. ed. 1937). This is particularly true where the construction is to be done on land controlled by the defendant, because in that circumstance the plaintiff cannot employ another contractor to do the construction for him at defendant's expense. In the case at bar, the fact that more than mere construction of a building is involved reinforces the need for specific enforcement of the defendants' duty to perform their entire contractual obligation to the plaintiff.

Cases from an early date have granted specific performance of construction contracts. In Jones v. Parker, 163 Mass. 564, 40 N.E. 1044 (1895), Justice Holmes commented:

> There is no universal rule that courts of equity never will enforce a contract which requires some building to be done. They have enforced such contracts from the earliest days to the present time. [163 Mass. 564, 40 N.E. 1044, 1045.]

Joy v. City of St. Louis, 138 U.S. 1, 11 S. Ct. 243, 34 L. Ed. 843 (1890), is the leading Supreme Court case on specific performance of contracts where the relations between the parties were of a complex nature and might require continuous supervision by the court granting the decree. The Court said on this point:

> In the present case, it is urged that the court will be called upon to determine from time to time what are reasonable regulations to be made by the Wabash Company for the running of trains upon its tracks by the Colorado Company. But this is no more

than a court of equity is called upon to do whenever it takes charge of the running of a railroad by means of a receiver. Irrespectively of this, the decree is complete in itself, and disposes of the controversy; and it is not unusual for a court of equity to take supplemental proceedings to carry out its decree, and make it effective under altered circumstances. 138 U.S. 1, 47, 11 S. Ct. 243, 257.

. . . See also Union Pacific Railway Co. v. Chicago, Rock Island & Pacific Railway Co., 163 U.S. 564, 16 S. Ct. 1173, 41 L. Ed. 265 (1896), where the Supreme Court commented in a case involving a similarly complex situation: "It must not be forgotten that, in the increasing complexities of modern business relations, equitable remedies have necessarily and steadily been expanded, and no inflexible rule has been permitted to circumscribe them. . . ."

The defendants contend that the granting of specific performance in this case will confront the court with insuperable difficulties of supervision, but after reviewing the evidence, I am satisfied that the standards to be observed in construction of the plaintiff's store are set out in the Hecht and Woodward & Lothrop leases with sufficient particularity (Plaintiff's Ex. F) as to make design and approval of plaintiff's store a fairly simple matter, if the parties deal with each other in good faith and expeditiously, as I shall hereafter order.

For example, Article VIII, Sec. 8.1, Paragraph (G) of the Hecht lease (the Woodward & Lothrop lease contains a similar provision) says:

> The quality of (i) the construction, (ii) the construction components, (iii) the decorative elements (including landscaping irrigation systems for the landscaping) and (iv) the furnishings; and the general architectural character and general design, the materials selection, the decor and the treatment values, approach and standards of the Enclosed Mall shall be comparable, at minimum, to the qualities, values, approaches and standards as of the date hereof of the enclosed mall at Topanga Plaza Shopping Center, Los Angeles, California. . . .

The existing leases contain further detailed specifications which will be identical to those in the lease granted to plaintiff. The site for plaintiff's store has already been settled by the design of the center. Although the exact design of plaintiff's store will not be identical to the design of any other store, it must be remembered that all of the stores are to be part of the same center and subject to its overall design requirements. If the parties are not in good faith able to reach an agreement on certain details, the court will appoint a special master to help settle their differences, unless they prefer voluntarily to submit their disagreements to arbitration.

III

The defendants contend that specific performance of this contract will result in hardship to them, and invoke the maxim that equity will not grant specific performance if the hardship to the defendants is greater than the potential benefit to the plaintiff. Defendants point to the fact that they agreed with Woodward & Lothrop and Hecht in their leases to limit the number of major department stores in the center to three. That means that if a lease is granted to Lansburgh's, defendants will be unable to negotiate a lease with

Sears, which has expressed a willingness to be the center's third department store tenant. The Sears lease would be more valuable to them, defendants claim, because the lease would be for a larger amount of space, and also because Sears would be expected to do a larger business than Lansburgh's, and defendants would receive a percentage share of its profits over a certain minimum amount as part of the agreed rental.

The defendants have not contended that performance of their obligation to Lansburgh's would be impossible or would ruin them financially. In effect, their contention is only that they can make more money by dealing with Sears than with Lansburgh's. This is not a reason for denying specific performance. Willard v. Tayloe, 75 U.S. 557, 8 Wall. 557, 19 L. Ed. 501 (1869). 5 Williston on Contracts §1425 (Rev. ed. 1937).

Moreover, the defendants need not have executed leases with both Hecht and Woodward & Lothrop to the exclusion of Sears as a possible additional tenant; nor need they have agreed with Hecht and Woodward & Lothrop that there would be no more than three stores in the center. Plaintiff was not responsible for these actions of defendants and should not be made to suffer irreparable loss due to the limitations which defendants have written into their contracts with Hecht and Woodward & Lothrop and which they now assert as a basis for their refusal to honor their obligation to plaintiff.

The defendants do contend that plaintiff was indirectly responsible, however, in failing to "press its claim" in May of 1964 when defendants advised it by letter that they considered themselves under no contractual obligation to plaintiff. First of all, I find from the record that at all material times the plaintiff through its officers did inform the defendants that it intended to hold them to their contract. Secondly, the defendants in effect imply that the plaintiff, by not "pressing its claim," gave up its rights under the contract, or waived them. But it is elementary contract law that a release of a contractual right (as distinguished from waiver of a condition) is not valid unless made for a valuable consideration. Finally, in May of 1964 defendants' obligation to tender a lease to plaintiff had not yet ripened because one of the conditions precedent to that obligation — execution of leases with other major tenants — had not yet been satisfied. Plaintiff could not have brought an action for anticipatory breach because of the impossibility of assessing damages; it certainly could not have brought an action for specific performance because as yet there was no specifically enforceable contract right. Plaintiff did contact defendants again when it learned that the Hecht and Woodward & Lothrop leases had been executed; and it brought this suit in a timely manner to prevent the defendants from entering into a lease with Sears which would have precluded them from performing their contract with plaintiff. I therefore hold that plaintiff neither gave up its contractual rights nor unnecessarily delayed its assertion of them in this court. . . .

During the course of this proceeding, the plaintiff has examined the leases executed between defendants and Hecht and Woodward & Lothrop and has indicated its willingness to accept a lease with terms equal to the Hecht lease. I therefore find that the plaintiff has exercised its option, and is entitled to specific performance of a lease on terms equal to those contained in the Hecht lease.

Notes and Questions

1. *Effect of indefiniteness on specific performance.* The court in *City Stores* begins its analysis by determining that an enforceable contract did exist, utilizing concepts familiar to us from our earlier discussions of agreement formation and consideration. The court then proceeds to decide whether the obligations imposed by the contract were sufficiently certain and definite to be susceptible to specific performance. Specific relief will not be denied merely because the parties have left some matters out of their agreement, or left some issues to be agreed on in the future, particularly when the parties have agreed on all material terms and other equitable factors are present. See Restatement (Second) §362 and Comment *b*. On the other hand, failure to agree on material terms may result in the denial of specific relief, though lines are difficult to draw. Compare Oglebay Norton Co. v. Armco, Inc., 556 N.E.2d 515 (Ohio 1990) (long-term contract for shipping of iron ore on Great Lakes specifically enforceable despite failure of agreed-on pricing mechanism; injury to plaintiff impossible to remedy by damages), with Honolulu Waterfront Ltd. Partnership v. Aloha Tower Development Corp., 692 F. Supp. 1230 (D. Haw. 1988), *aff'd*, 891 F.2d 295 (9th Cir. 1989) (four-page letter agreement did constitute binding agreement for real estate development but left too many material matters for future agreement to be specifically enforceable; virtually every provision contemplated further negotiation). Does the court in *City Stores* adequately weigh the indefiniteness factor in granting the relief requested?

2. *Inadequacy of damages at law.* As the discussion by Professor Farnsworth indicated, contracts involving land are prime candidates for specific enforcement because land has been regarded in the Anglo-American legal tradition as unique, presumptively justifying equitable relief under the traditional rule that equity will act only where the remedy at law is "inadequate." Modern American courts will routinely grant specific performance to purchasers of real estate. See, e.g., Sullivan v. Porter, 861 A.2d 625 (Me. 2004) (court may assume inadequacy of money damages in contract for purchase of real estate and order specific performance without actual showing of singular character of the realty); but see Meikle v. Watson, 69 P.3d 100 (Idaho 2003) (denying specific performance to buyer who merely planned to resell land). Restatement (Second) §360, comment *e* indicates that specific performance has traditionally been available to both buyers and sellers. Cases awarding specific performance to sellers, however, are not very common. Compare Humphries v. Ables, 789 N.E.2d 1025 (Ind. Ct. App. 2003) (granting specific performance to sellers of property with a liquor store, based on mutuality of remedy principle and contract term that contemplated specific performance for the sellers, but also noting that only small number of cases grant the remedy to sellers), with Wolf v. Anderson, 334 N.W.2d 212 (N.D. 1983) (specific performance available to sellers only when equitable considerations warrant award).

Besides the possibility that a land-related contract will be specifically enforced because of the "uniqueness" of its subject matter, the Restatement (Second) in §360 identifies other circumstances which support a claim that damages are inadequate. These include the difficulty of proving damages with certainty, the difficulty of procuring a suitably equivalent substitute performance, and the likelihood that a damage award would not be collectible. See, e.g., Sokoloff v. Harriman Estates Development Corp., 754 N.E.2d 184 (N.Y. 2001) (plaintiffs properly stated cause of action for specific perfomance to obtain allegedly unique architect plans that were based on plaintiffs' concept). To what extent are these factors concerning adequacy of money damages at work in the *City Stores* decision?

3. *Specific performance of development contract.* If *City Stores* represented an earlier trend of retail stores and other businesses moving from the city to suburban areas, an example of a more recent return of business to urban areas is reflected in Franklin Point, Inc. v. Harris Trust & Savings Bank, 660 N.E.2d 204 (Ill. App. Ct. 1995). *Franklin Point* involved a plan to develop a parcel of land near downtown Chicago, pursuant to which the defendant, Harris Bank, agreed to purchase a portion of the property and construct a high-rise office building. Not surprisingly, many details of the construction plans were not established by the contract, but the agreement did establish an architectural review board to approve construction decisions not within the discretion of Harris Bank. Harris Bank purchased the property but failed to construct the building and the remainder of the project was not developed. The appellate court decided that the trial court erred in its ruling that "specific performance of a construction contract is barred as a matter of law." Id. at 206. Citing *City Stores* and similar precedent, the court held that specific performance might be available if the presence of the review board would prevent the court from becoming embroiled in ongoing supervision of construction disputes. Id. at 208. Cf. Mayor's Jewelers, Inc. v. State of California Employees' Retirement System, 685 So.2d 904 (Fla. Ct. App. 1996) (denying request for specific performance of lease by tenant because court would be required to supervise future performance). If it is assumed that Harris Bank was expected to be the "anchor" business of the Franklin Point development, how does the case for specific performance compare to that in *City Stores*?

Ordinary building contracts are unlikely to be specifically enforced, both because of the difficulties of supervision and because construction services can readily be purchased on the market with a money award in damages. As cases such as *City Stores* and *Franklin Point* suggest, however, the courts are probably more willing than they were at an earlier day to decree specific performance in cases where some degree of service or labor will have to be performed by the defendant. See E. Allan Farnsworth, Contracts §12.7, at 754 (4th ed. 2004). Drawing a comparison to complex civil rights cases, Professor Farnsworth suggests that courts have discovered that the burden of supervision is not as great as might be feared. How does the test used by the *City Stores* court compare to that prescribed in Restatement (Second) §366 to determine when to grant specific performance even though court supervision will be required?

4. *Other factors affecting award of specific performance.* Besides the question of adequacy of the remedy "at law" and the problem of difficulty of supervision, courts of equity traditionally consider various other factors in deciding whether specific relief should be available. Some of these are listed in Restatement (Second) §364. These include the possibility that the contract was

the product of mistake or unfair practices, or that the exchange it calls for is grossly inadequate or the terms of the contract are otherwise unfair. These factors are reflected in the doctrine that equity will not aid one who comes to the court with "unclean hands." See, e.g., Ingram v. Kasey's Associates, 531 S.E.2d 287 (S.C. 2000) (tenant denied specific performance of option contract because he had unclean hands; tenant misled landlord into believing that he would not exercise option and he had ulterior motive for doing so).

Another factor to be considered is the question whether specific relief would cause unreasonable hardship or loss to the party in breach. See, e.g., Webster Trust v. Roly, 802 A.2d 795 (Conn. 2002) (denying specific performance of "right of first refusal" contract allegedly triggered by intra-family transfer for $100,000 while land had $340,000 fair market value; sale to plaintiffs at lower price would have been "inequitable" and plaintiffs could still exercise option if land was sold in "market place" before the right's expiration); Kilarjian v. Vastola, 877 A.2d 372 (N.J. Super. Ch. Div. 2004) (declining to award specific performance for buyers where seller's health had declined significantly due to spinal muscular atrophy after contract was made, even though buyers were faultless and there is virtual presumption that nonbreaching buyers should receive specific performance). Should the potential hardship to the defendants have militated against the grant of specific relief to the plaintiff in *City Stores*?

5. *Effect on third parties.* Besides the possibility that specific relief may disproportionately affect the defendant, the court in some cases must consider the possible impact of its decree on third parties. Restatement (Second) §364(1)(b). Compare Craven v. TRG-Boyton Beach, Ltd., 925 So.2d 476 (Fla. Ct. App. 2006) (denying award of specific performance to tenant in building project where enforcing commitment for location of plaintiff's store would have required destruction of five new townhouses valued at $5 million, dispossessing the residents, and would have required judicial supervision), with Ruddock v. First National Bank of Lake Forest, 559 N.E.2d 483 (Ill. App. Ct. 1990) (specific performance of contract to purchase rare clock improperly denied where subsequent purchaser from defendant took with notice of plaintiff's claim). The court in *City Stores* had previously granted a temporary injunction to prevent the defendants from leasing to someone else the last available site suitable for the plaintiff's department store in the Tyson's Corner shopping center, pending disposition of the plaintiff's claim. If in the absence of such an order the defendants had actually entered into a binding lease agreement with another tenant, should that fact have precluded specific relief for plaintiff City Stores?

6. *Scholarly analysis.* A number of writers have addressed the question whether there should be greater availability of specific performance as a remedy for breach. Writing in 1978, Professor Anthony Kronman presented an economic analysis of the rules of specific performance and concluded that the present approach is "efficient," partly because specific performance is awarded only when the subject of the contract is unique and judicial computation of damages would be extremely difficult and expensive. Anthony T. Kronman, Specific Performance, 45 U. Chi. L. Rev. 351, 360-361 (1978). Professor Edward Yorio reached a similar conclusion that increased use of

specific performance would ignore the interests of promisors in fair treatment and the interests of courts in not having their decrees flouted or in becoming the instruments of oppressive conduct. Edward Yorio, In Defense of Money Damages for Breach of Contract, 82 Colum. L. Rev. 1365 (1982). Professor Yorio's views were further elaborated in Edward Yorio, Contract Enforcement: Specific Performance and Injunctions 517-557 (1989), in which he argued on both economic and noneconomic grounds that the existing limitations on specific relief afford a better balance of the interests of the promisee, the promisor, and the court system than would a regime in which specific relief was freely available for the asking.

In contrast, Professor Alan Schwartz has asserted that the test of "uniqueness" is too narrow and argued that specific performance should be the normal remedy for breach of contract because money damages are often undercompensatory. Alan Schwartz, The Case for Specific Performance, 89 Yale L.J. 271, 276-277 (1979). Schwartz also argued that increased availability of specific performance would actually produce efficiency gains by eliminating litigation of complex damage issues. Id. at 291. See also Peter Linzer, On the Amorality of Contract Remedies — Efficiency, Equity, and the Second *Restatement*, 81 Colum. L. Rev. 111 (1981) (arguing that increased availability of specific performance is supported both by reasons of economic efficiency and by fairness of holding promisors to their obligations). In his article broadly advocating more frequent award of punitive damages for breach of contract, discussed in the Comment in Section D of Chapter 11, Professor William Dodge also argued in favor of specific performance. Dodge contended that specific performance will often be the most desirable remedy when it is practical because it gives the promisee exactly what he bargained for; when specific performance is not practical, however, the threat of an award of punitive damages is necessary to promote post-breach negotiations. William S. Dodge, The Case for Punitive Damages, 48 Duke L.J. 629, 685 (1999).

7. *Specific performance under the UCC.* In §2-716 the UCC declares that specific performance "may" be decreed for a buyer where the goods are "unique," or "in other proper circumstances." Comment 1 to §2-716 states that the section is intended generally to continue "prior policy," but with a "more liberal attitude than some courts have shown" toward the granting of specific performance of contracts for the sale of goods. The comparable provision for sellers, §2-709(1)(b), allows goods to be forced on the buyer and the price obtained when the goods are not reasonably subject to resale to others. Under the Code's approach, courts will still face the question whether the goods contracted for are sufficiently "unique" to justify specific enforcement. Compare International Casings Group, Inc. v. Premium Standard Farms, Inc., 358 F. Supp. 2d 863 (W.D. Mo. 2005) (specific performance of contract for hog casings appropriate for buyer where comparable goods were not available in market place and harm to buyer could be irreparable), with I. Lan Systems, Inc. v. Netscout Service Level Corp., 183 F. Supp. 2d 328 (D. Mass. 2002) (if UCC is treated as applicable by analogy to software licensing agreements, software at issue was not sufficiently unique to warrant specific performance).

Reier Broadcasting Company, Inc. v. Kramer
Supreme Court of Montana
316 Mont. 301, 72 P.3d 944 (2003)

Justice W. William Leaphart delivered the Opinion of the Court.

Reier Broadcasting Company, Inc., appeals from the order of the Eighteenth Judicial District Court, Gallatin County, denying Reier's motion for relief from judgment. We affirm.

The following issue is raised on appeal:

Whether the District Court correctly concluded that Reier Broadcasting was not entitled to injunctive relief to prevent a breach of its employment agreement with Michael Kramer.

FACTUAL AND PROCEDURAL BACKGROUND

Appellant, Reier Broadcasting Company, Inc., owns several radio stations in Gallatin County and, until 2002, had exclusive rights to broadcast Montana State University athletic events. Respondent, Michael Kramer, is the head football coach at MSU. In January 2001, Reier Broadcasting and Kramer entered into an employment contract at the behest of MSU, whereby Reier agreed to pay Kramer $10,020 per year in exchange for exclusive broadcast rights with Kramer. Pursuant to the contract, Reier agreed to employ Kramer as an announcer and talent on the weekly, one-hour "Cat Chat" program, which airs during the MSU football season. [The Montana State football team is known as the "Bobcats."—EDS.] In addition, Kramer agreed to record commercials for several of Reier's advertisers. The agreement remains in force and effect until November 2004. Section Two of the contract contains an exclusivity clause that provides the following:

> That Coach shall diligently and faithfully serve Station in such capacity, shall devote his entire skill and energies to such service, and shall not perform on or permit his name to be used in connection with any other radio or television station or program, or to accept any other engagement which will conflict with his performance or effectiveness for Station, without prior approval and consent in writing by the Station.

Reier Broadcasting had earlier purchased exclusive broadcast rights to all MSU athletic events. These rights expired in the summer of 2002, at which time MSU began seeking competitive bids from other broadcasting companies. After reviewing MSU's Request for Proposal, under which these bids were to be obtained, Reier notified the university that there was a potential conflict between the Request for Proposal and Reier's contract with Kramer. According to Reier, the Request for Proposal required the successful offeror to broadcast interviews and conduct a commentary program with Kramer in violation of Section Two of the Reier-Kramer employment agreement, under which Kramer was contractually prohibited from announcing, or otherwise providing talent for Reier's competitors.

MSU declined to amend the Request for Proposal to address this conflict. MSU then disqualified Reier Broadcasting as a potential bidder, and awarded broadcast rights to the university's athletic events to Clear Channel

Communications. MSU also notified Kramer that he was expected to provide interviews to Clear Channel despite the exclusivity clause contained in his contract with Reier.

Reier Broadcasting subsequently filed a Complaint and Application for Temporary Restraining Order with the Eighteenth Judicial District Court in an effort to protect its rights under the employment agreement, and to prevent Kramer from providing services to Clear Channel. The District Court granted the request for a TRO, pending an evidentiary hearing on the matter. In August 2002, the court held an evidentiary hearing on the question of whether or not to convert the TRO into a preliminary injunction. The TRO was later amended to allow Kramer to "engage in audio, video or printed media obligations in connection with his coaching job. . . ."

After hearing testimony and reviewing the parties' pleadings, the court concluded that §27-19-103(5), MCA [Montana Code Annotated], prohibited the issuance of an injunction under the circumstances. The court also dissolved the TRO. Reier Broadcasting moved to alter or amend the court's judgment. The court denied the motion, and Reier appealed.

STANDARD OF REVIEW

Generally, when reviewing a trial court's grant or denial of an injunction, our standard of review is for abuse of discretion. Spoklie v. Montana Dep't of Fish, Wildlife & Parks, [311 Mont. 427, 56 P.3d 349]. However, when a trial court "'bases its decision to grant such relief upon its interpretation of a statute, no discretion is involved and we review the [ ] court's conclusion of law to determine whether it is correct.'" [Spoklie, 56 P.3d 352-353]. . . .

DISCUSSION

This appeal concerns the scope and effect of §27-19-103(5), MCA, which provides the following: "An injunction cannot be granted: . . . (5) to prevent the breach of a contract the performance of which would not be specifically enforced. . . ." The paramount issue raised by the appellant, Reier Broadcasting, is whether, within the context of a personal services contract such as the employment agreement between Reier and Kramer, the language of §27-19-103(5), MCA, may be interpreted as prohibiting the use of injunctive relief to prevent one of the contracting parties (in this case, Kramer) from performing services elsewhere during the life of the contract.

Characterizing the Reier-Kramer employment agreement as a personal services contract and not subject to specific enforcement, the District Court concluded that the prohibition contained in §27-19-103(5), MCA, precluded the issuance of the injunction sought by Reier. The court relied, in part, on §27-1-412(1), MCA, which states that, "[t]he following obligations cannot be specifically enforced: (1) an obligation to render personal service. . . ." Combining this restriction with the language of §27-19-103(5), MCA, the court concluded that it "may not enjoin one from doing something in violation of a contract if the [c]ourt cannot enforce the contract by specific performance. . . . The [a]greement between Kramer and [Reier] is a personal services contract and cannot be enforced by specific performance." The court explained that it could not prevent Kramer from violating the terms of that contract without improperly enforcing the affirmative obligations of the Reier-Kramer agreement through indirect means.

Reier Broadcasting argues that neither §27-1-412(1), MCA, nor §27-19-103(5), MCA, applies in the present case. Reier contends that by seeking an injunction, the company did not intend to require Kramer to render personal services, but rather to prevent Kramer from providing the same services to Clear Channel. Accordingly, Reier asserts that §27-1-412(1), MCA, and its prohibition against the specific enforcement of personal services contracts, has no bearing on the present case, and thus §27-19-103(5), MCA, is equally irrelevant.

Reier characterizes its request for an injunction as an attempt to enforce a negative covenant which, according to Reier, is appropriate given that Kramer's services are special or unique. According to Reier, contracts based on special or unique personal services, or in which a person holds a unique position, may be indirectly enforced by restraining the person from providing services to another. In support of this, Reier cites Volume 71, Section 165 of the American Jurisprudence, Second Edition, which states the following:

> Contracts calling for personal services or acts of a special, unique, or extraordinary character, or by persons in eminence in their profession or calling who possess special and extraordinary qualifications, may be indirectly enforced by restraining the person employed from rendering services to another. . . .

71 Am.Jur.2d Specific Performance §165, 213 (1973).

Reier also cites a 1972 decision, Nassau Sports v. Peters (E.D.N.Y.1972), 352 F.Supp. 870, 875 (citations omitted), in which the federal district court for the eastern district of New York noted that "it has long been settled that injunctive relief may be granted to restrain an employee's violation of negative covenants in a personal services contract. . . ." On this basis, Reier concludes that although Kramer should not be forced to fulfill his contractual obligations to the company, he nonetheless may be prevented from providing his unique services to Reier's competitors until the employment agreement expires in 2004.

We discussed the proper application of §27-19-103(5), MCA, in Westland Enterprises, Inc. v. Boyne, USA, Inc. (1989), 237 Mont. 186, 772 P.2d 309. Although we held that an injunction against the defendant was improperly issued for reasons not associated with §27-19-103(5), MCA, we set forth the rationale for the statute, and articulated the circumstances under which it would apply. We stated the following:

> Injunctions are rarely used to enforce contract rights or prevent breaches, and applicable court decisions concerning the propriety of this tactic are scarce. However, the legislature has set forth statutory guidelines for the use of injunctions. An applicable guideline is found at §27-19-103(5), MCA. Under this section, an injunction cannot be obtained "to prevent the breach of a contract the performance of which would not be specifically enforced." A list of "obligations which cannot be specifically enforced" is found at §27-1-412, MCA.

Westland Enterprises, 237 Mont. at 191, 772 P.2d at 312.

Reier appears to accept this general premise from *Westland* that §27-1-412(1), MCA, identifies those contracts that cannot be specifically enforced, and that §27-19-103(5), MCA, prohibits the use of injunctive relief to enforce the affirmative covenants contained in such agreements. That said, the point of contention, here, is whether these statutory prohibitions also apply to the enforcement of negative covenants, such as the exclusivity clause contained in the Reier-Kramer employment agreement. Given the absence of any relevant Montana case law, we turn to the California and Arizona courts, which have interpreted statutes similar to §27-19-103(5), MCA, to prevent the enforcement of negative covenants in personal services contracts.

In Anderson v. Neal Institutes Co. (1918), 37 Cal.App. 174, 173 P. 779, the California Court of Appeals construed an early version of §3423 of the California Civil Code, which provided that "[a]n injunction may not be granted . . . to prevent the breach of a contract the performance of which would not be specifically enforced. . . ." In *Anderson,* the court of appeals identified two conflicting lines of authority under which §3423 could have been construed at the time. The first suggested that although a court cannot specifically enforce an affirmative agreement by compelling one party to perform, the court can enjoin a party from breaching a negative covenant and performing elsewhere. *Anderson,* 37 Cal.App. at 177, 173 P. at 780. The second line of authority suggested that since a court cannot enforce the positive part of a personal services contract, it cannot restrain by injunction the negative part. 37 Cal.App. at 178, 173 P. at 780. The court of appeals adopted the later rationale, concluding that in light of the unambiguous language of §3423, a court cannot "interfere by injunction to prevent the violation of an agreement of which, from the nature of the [contract], there could be no decree of specific enforcement." 37 Cal.App. at 178-79, 173 P. at 781.[1]

The Arizona Supreme Court followed *Anderson* in Titus v. Superior Court, Maricopa County (1962), 91 Ariz. 18, 368 P.2d 874. The court reasoned that §12-1802(5) of the Arizona Revised Statutes, like §3423 in California, was intended "to deprive the court of jurisdiction to enjoin breaches of covenants not to compete during the original term of the contract (where enforcement would indirectly enforce the promise to render services)." *Titus,* 91 Ariz. at 23, 368 P.2d at 878. The court noted that the purpose of this rule is to prevent parties from "seeking injunctive relief to force the course of affirmative action." *Titus,* 91 Ariz. at 21, 368 P.2d at 876.

---

1. Immediately following *Anderson,* the California Legislature modified §3423 to allow for the use of injunctive relief to enforce a negative covenant where the promised service is of a unique character the loss of which cannot be adequately compensated in damages. In its current form, the statute states, "[a]n injunction may not be granted . . . to prevent the breach of a contract the performance of which would not be specifically enforced . . . other than a contract in writing for the rendition of personal services . . . where the promised service is of a special, unique, [or] unusual . . . character, which gives it peculiar value. . . ." Construing this new version of the statute in Motown Record Corp. v. Brockert (1984), 160 Cal.App.3d 123, 138, 207 Cal.Rptr. 574, 584, the California Court of Appeals stated that for reasons of public policy, a negative covenant (an exclusivity clause in that case), can be enforced by injunction when the contract is with a performer of requisite distinction as measured by the compensation the employer is willing to pay. Although *Motown* establishes the appropriate application of §3423 in its current form, that case is of no consequence here given that §27-19-103(5), MCA, is identical to the earlier version of §3423.

We determine that §27-19-103(5), MCA, like its California and Arizona counterparts, prohibits the use of injunctive relief to prevent a party to a personal services contract from performing services elsewhere during the life of the contract. The exclusivity clause in the Reier-Kramer employment agreement, if enforced vis a vis an injunction, would prevent Kramer from performing for Clear Channel or any of Reier's other competitors until the summer of 2004 when the Reier-Kramer agreement expires. Thus, if Kramer were to perform at all, he would have to perform for Reier. In that sense, an injunction would amount to the indirect enforcement of the affirmative part of the contract. It was this sort of indirect enforcement that the California court sought to avoid in *Anderson,* stating that "to enjoin one from doing something in violation of his contract is an indirect mode of enforcing the . . . contract." *Anderson,* 37 Cal.App. at 178, 173 P. at 780.

Following the lead of California and Arizona, we conclude that the issuance of an injunction, preventing Kramer from working for Clear Channel during the period remaining on his contract with Reier, would result in the indirect specific enforcement of the Reier-Kramer employment agreement. Contrary to the dissent's characterization, we do not hold that the underlying contract was invalid. The issue presented is not whether the contract is valid, but rather, whether the contract can be specifically enforced by means of an injunction. We conclude that pursuant to the explicit language of §27-19-103(5), MCA, Montana courts may not enjoin the violation of a contract, the specific enforcement of which is barred by Montana law. The issue of whether Reier has other legal remedies for the alleged breach of contract is not before the Court.

CONCLUSION

In summary, we hold that §27-19-103(5), MCA, prohibits the use of injunctive relief to enforce negative covenants contained in personal services contracts. Accordingly, the District Court correctly concluded that Reier Broadcasting was not entitled to enjoin Kramer from performing services elsewhere during the life of the contract.

We concur: Karla M. Gray, C.J., James C. Nelson and Jim Regnier, J.J.

Justice Patricia O. Cotter dissents.

I dissent. As requested by RBC, I would reverse the District Court's order dissolving the TRO and remand this case for a determination of whether or not a preliminary injunction should issue to prevent Kramer from providing his services to others in violation of the agreement between Kramer and RBC.

I would conclude that the enforcement of the negative covenant in the contract between RBC and Kramer would not run afoul of §27-19-103(5), MCA. The court properly recognizes that the exclusivity clause in the agreement, if enforced by way of an injunction, would prevent Kramer from performing for Clear Channel or any of Reier's other competitors until the summer of 2004 when the Reier-Kramer agreement expires. I disagree, however, with the ensuing conclusion the Court reaches, which is that an injunction would amount to the indirect enforcement of the affirmative part of the contract because, if Kramer were to perform at all, he would have to perform for Reier. I respectfully submit that this is a stretch. RBC is not seeking to compel Kramer to perform under the contract. It is simply seeking to prevent him from violating the non-competition provisions of the contract-provisions which were specifically bargained for by Kramer, at the encouragement and behest of MSU.

In addition, I find the position taken by MSU in this litigation offensive. As the majority notes, RBC and Kramer entered into an employment contract "at the behest of MSU." RBC alleges, and MSU does not deny, that representatives of MSU approached RBC for purposes of securing additional compensation for Kramer, after Kramer had been hired by MSU. An agreement was reached whereby Kramer would receive $10,200 from RBC, and in exchange would broadcast with RBC and no one else. MSU actively sought this benefit for Kramer and approved of the terms of the contract. A little more than a year later, MSU decided to award the exclusive rights to broadcast its athletic events to RBC's competitor, Clear Channel Communications. It was only at this point — when the deal between RBC and Kramer ceased serving MSU's interests — that MSU began to cry foul, claiming that the contract, which it solicited in the first place, should be declared unenforceable. Laid bare, theirs is an argument born of convenience, not virtue.

RBC has fully and in good faith performed its obligations under its contract with Kramer, and for the first year, MSU and Kramer both accepted the benefits of the contract as well. Now, they want this Court to assist them in their breach. Many years ago this Court recognized that "[a] party who has secured to himself the benefits of a contract, and has accepted and used these benefits, has estopped himself in the courts from denying the validity or binding force of the instrument, or from setting up or asserting the contrary." Brundy v. Canby (1915), 50 Mont. 454, 148 P. 315 (citations omitted). Numerous other courts have embraced this same legal premise: Once a contract is performed and a party has received the benefits of it, that party is estopped from claiming invalidity in order to avoid the contract's burdens. See Seay v. Dodge (N.D.Ill.1998), 1998 U.S. Dist. LEXIS 12005, 1998 WL 460273; Silling v. Erwin (S.D.W.Va.1995), 885 F.Supp. 881; Smith v. Hornbuckle (1977), 140 Ga.App. 871, 232 S.E.2d 149.

Although the resolution I favor [allowing enforcement of the covenant not to compete for the duration of the contract] could stand alone, I would also conclude that MSU and Kramer were estopped from challenging the contract's enforceability. For these reasons, I dissent.

Justice Jim Rice concurs in the foregoing dissent.

Notes and Questions

1. *Equitable remedies and personal service contracts.* The parties in the *Reier Broadcasting* case did not dispute that the respondent Kramer contracted to provide services for the radio station or that he intended to breach that agreement. Rather, the dispute focused on whether an equitable remedy for breach would be available to Reier Broadcasting. You will recall from the *City Stores* case that one form of equitable relief is specific performance, in which a court compels a party to render a promised performance, based primarily on a showing that money damages would be an inadequate remedy. Without any

need to address the adequacy of money damages, the *Reier Broadcasting* court briefly notes that Montana statutes prohibit specific enforcement of a personal services contract. The Restatement (Second) §367(1) is equally succinct: "A promise to render personal services will not be specifically enforced." Why should there be such an absolute ban on enforcement of a personal services contract through specific performance? Comment *a* to §367 states the prohibition is based on reasons of both policy and practicality: the undesirability of forcing parties to continue in a relationship that has soured, potential concerns about involuntary servitude, and the difficulty of a court enforcing a decree for specific performance. Considering the nature of the contract in *Reier Broadcasting*, is it possible that Kramer could have been compelled to render the promised performance?

While specific performance of a personal service contract will not be available, some courts have been willing to grant "negative enforcement" by way of injunction that prohibits a breaching party from performing for anyone other than the nonbreaching party. Such an injunction might be based on implied promise that a party, such as the respondent in *Reier Broadcasting*, would not perform for another employer during the contract period. Alternatively, an injunction might be based on an express covenant not to work for others during the term of employment. See American Broadcasting Co. v. Wolf, 420 N.E.2d 363 (N.Y. 1981) (historically injunctions were initially available only if based on an express covenant not to compete with employer during the contract, but later became available if based on clear implication not to work elsewhere). The dissent in *Reier Broadcasting* founded its proposed resolution primarily on the presence of an express covenant not to compete. Is the dissent persuasive in its argument that Reier Broadcasting should have been allowed to seek an injunction?

2. *Historical perspective: Lumley v. Wagner.* The granting of relief by way of injunction may be traced back to the early English chancery case of Lumley v. Wagner, 42 Eng. Rep. 687 (1852). In that case, defendant Johanna Wagner had contracted to appear in several operas in London at the opera house of the plaintiff, Benjamin Lumley, during three months of the 1852 season; as part of that agreement she promised not to appear for any other opera company in London during that time. Wagner thereafter agreed, in violation of her contract with Lumley, to appear in the Royal Italian Opera at London's Covent Garden (for a salary higher than the sum that plaintiff had agreed to pay her). Lumley sought an injunction restraining Wagner from singing for his competitor, and the court granted him the requested relief. In the course of his decision, the Lord Chancellor conceded that under established principles his court would not have granted specific performance by ordering Wagner to sing for the plaintiff as promised. Nevertheless, the defendant had also expressly promised to refrain from singing for any competitor of the plaintiff during the period in question, which in the Lord Chancellor's opinion made the requested relief appropriate.

> It was objected that the operation of the injunction in the present case was mischievous, excluding the defendant J. Wagner from performing at any other theatre while this Court had no power to compel her to perform at Her Majesty's Theatre. It is true, that I have not the means of compelling her to sing, but she has no

cause of complaint, if I compel her to abstain from the commission of an act which she has bound herself not to do, and thus possibly cause her to fulfil her engagement. The jurisdiction which I now exercise is wholly within the power of the Court, and being of opinion that it is a proper case for interfering, I shall leave nothing unsatisfied by the judgment I pronounce. The effect too of the injunction, in restraining J. Wagner from singing elsewhere may, in the event of an action being brought against her by the plaintiff, prevent any such amount of vindictive damages being given against her as a jury might probably be inclined to give if she had carried her talents and exercised them at the rival theatre; the injunction may also, as I have said, tend to the fulfilment of her engagement; though, in continuing the injunction, I disclaim doing indirectly what I cannot do directly.

Id. at 693. This portion of the Lumley v. Wagner opinion acknowledges that an injunction might force a party to perform a contract that could not be specifically enforced, but seems to permit that outcome. In contrast, the state law cited in *Reier Broadcasting* seems clearly to prohibit an injunction as an indirect way of compelling specific performance. See also Restatement (Second) §367(2) (injunction will not be issued if probable result would be to compel an "undesirable" continuance of personal relations or "to leave the employee without other reasonable means of making a living"). What do you think would have been the practical effect if an injunction had been issued against the respondent in *Reier Broadcasting*?

Whatever the artistic merits of Wagner's vocal performances, her dispute with Lumley has guaranteed her at least a kind of immortality in legal circles. Besides the decision quoted above, making injunctive relief available in such cases, Wagner's attempt to forsake Lumley for his competitor also generated a lawsuit by Lumley against that competing impresario, which culminated in the decision in Lumley v. Gye, 118 Eng. Rep. 749 (1853), establishing the modern tort of intentional interference with contract—and thus paving the way for Pennzoil v. Texaco, discussed in Chapter 2. See also Lea S. VanderVelde, The Gendered Origins of the Lumley Doctrine: Binding Men's Consciences And Women's Fidelity, 101 Yale L.J. 775 (1992) (discussing historical context of Lumley v. Wagner and observing that disproportionate number of early cases allowing injunctive relief in personal services contracts involved women defendants).

3. *Requirement that services be unique.* The majority opinion in *Reier Broadcasting* interpreted the applicable Montana statutes in a manner that would always bar injunctive relief in a personal services contract. While the court cited California statutes and case law as supporting its holding, the majority opinion also acknowledged in footnote 1 that the law in California was subsequently changed to allow for a possible injunction when an employee's "service is of a special, unique, [or] unusual . . . character, which gives it peculiar value." Indeed, in jurisdictions where injunctive relief is a possibility, courts will likely deny a request if the personal services are not unique. Injunctive relief may be available against employees whose services are not easily replaceable, such as athletes, artists, or media personalities, particularly when the employee plans to work for a competing enterprise. *Lumley* was such a case. See, e.g., Marchio v. Letterlough, 237 F. Supp. 2d 580 (E.D. Pa. 2002) (preliminary injunction issued against boxer to prevent breach

of contract with promoter; boxer was unique talent and there existed risk of irreparable injury to plaintiff); Arias v. Solis, 754 F. Supp. 290 (E.D.N.Y. 1991) (preliminary injunction issued against boxer competing in imminently scheduled bout in violation of contract with plaintiff boxing manager).

Writing in 1967, Professor James Brennan concluded that the case law had reached a point where professional athletes of "better than average," "average," or even "marginal" ability would be held sufficiently "unique" to warrant their being judicially restrained from playing for any other team; he contended, however, that such judicial willingness to grant "indirect specific performance" is not justified:

> While the language of the cases speaks of exceptional knowledge, skill or ability, the cases in fact ignore the limitations inherent in this language. The reason appears to be an undemonstrated and unlitigated assumption on the part of the courts that professional athletics would collapse as an industry economically or competitively if injunctions against breach were not issued. Personally, I see little justification and no proof for this assumption.

James T. Brennan, Injunction Against Professional Athletes' Breaching Their Contracts, 34 Brooklyn L. Rev. 61, 70 (1967). See also Sharon F. Carton, Damning with Fulsome Praise: Assessing the Uniqueness of an Artist or Performer as a Condition to Enjoin Performance of Personal Service Contracts in Entertainment Law, 5 Vill. Sports & Ent. L.J. 197 (1998).

4. *Equitable relief against other types of parties.* It is possible that services of employees other than entertainers or athletes may also be deemed unique, depending on the circumstances, and therefore warrant the grant of injunctive relief. See Ticor Title Ins. Co. v. Cohen, 173 F.3d 63 (2d Cir. 1999) (services of former senior vice president of title insurance company were unique based on special relationships with clients). More generally, you may recall from the discussion of express covenants not to compete in conjunction with the Valley Medical Specialists v. Farber case in Chapter 7 that post-employment covenants not to compete may be enforceable in situations where the employer has a valid, protectible interest and the restrictions are reasonable. See, e.g., The 7's Enterprises, Inc. v. Rosario, 143 P.3d 23 (Haw. 2006) (injunction granted to enforce three year express non-compete agreement against ex-employee where employer gave unique training that constituted a protectible interest and ex-employee was not precluded from pursuing other work); Washel v. Bryant, 770 N.E.2d 902 (Ind. Ct. App. 2002) (enforcing covenant against hair stylist that prohibited her from opening a competing shop within ten miles for two years after leaving employment). Cf. Falk v. Axiam Inc., 944 F. Supp. 542 (S.D. Tex. 1996) (court granted buyer specific performance against seller that had contracted to send engineer to China to install piston gauge and train personnel for unique and highly specialized equipment; performance to be rendered was "corporate obligation" rather than "personal" and there was no adequate remedy at law).

5. *Specific performance or reinstatement on behalf of employees.* Can a court ever order, against a breaching employer, specific performance on behalf of a wrongfully discharged employee? Although some of the policy problems relating to specific enforcement *against* the employee would not apply in this

reverse situation (most notably the prohibition against "involuntary servitude"), the courts have nevertheless traditionally been unwilling to grant such relief. See, e.g., Nicholas v. Pennsylvania State University, 227 F.3d 133 (3d Cir. 2000) (tenured professor could not obtain reinstatement under breach of contract claim because court of equity will not grant specific performance of personal service contracts); Quadron Software International Corp. v. Plotseneder, 568 S.E.2d 178 (Ga. Ct. App. 2002) (employee not entitled to specific performance of software development contract absent showing of irreparable harm or inadequacy of damage remedy). When the employee's claim is based on violation of a statutory provision prohibiting discrimination in employment, such as Title VII of the Civil Rights Act of 1964, 42 U.S.C. §2000e et seq., however, reinstatement is authorized and usually ordered. See generally Pollard v. E.I. du Pont de Nemours & Co., 532 U.S. 843 (2001) (discussing award of reinstatement and alternative remedies).

6. *Problem 11-4 reconsidered.* Recall Problem 11-4. In light of the materials in this section, should injunctive relief be available to the producers of "Operating Room" if Green accepts a contract with "Flying High"?

D. AGREED REMEDIES

Once a nonperformance (or defective performance) of an existing contract has occurred, it is within the power of the parties to agree to compromise or "settle" their dispute. By doing so the parties will in effect be agreeing on the remedy for breach. Absent some element of fraud, mistake, or duress, that agreement will almost surely be the final settlement of the dispute, with no occasion for judicial readjustment. Alternatively, it would be possible in such a case for the parties to stipulate between them the amount of damages that the one party had suffered from the other's nonperformance, litigating only the issue of whether that nonperformance was indeed an unexcused breach of their contract. Again, if such an agreement is free from fraud, mistake, or other bargaining defects, it is unlikely to be judicially condemned: Such agreements save all those concerned — the parties and the court — the time and money that would otherwise have to be expended on a full trial of all the issues material to their dispute.

Suppose, however, that the parties as part of their original agreement (as opposed to a settlement agreement entered into after breach) specify the remedy to be awarded in the event of its breach. One might assume that such an agreement should simply be viewed as another bargained-out compromise of liability, to be accorded the respect that any freely bargained contract enjoys in our system. Indeed, in light of our studies so far, it could be plausibly contended that such an originally agreed-on remedy term represents the "expectation interest" in its purest, most easily ascertainable form and thus should enjoy the highest degree of enforceability. The agreed-remedy provision (often referred to as a "liquidated damages" clause, where a fixed or determinable sum of money has been specified in advance as the remedy for a particular type of breach) has not been so warmly received by the courts, however. Despite the obvious advantages that such terms can have for the parties and the court system, they are subject to judicial scrutiny and will not be enforced unless they meet certain traditional tests. As reflected in the following case, courts make a distinction between a term aimed at compensation, and therefore enforceable, and a clause intended to penalize, and therefore unenforceable.

‖ **Westhaven Associates, Ltd. v. C.C. of Madison, Inc.**
Wisconsin Court of Appeals
257 Wis. 2d 789, 652 N.W.2d 819 (2002)

Before DYKMAN, DEININGER and LUNDSTEN, J.J.
LUNDSTEN, J.

C.C. of Madison, Inc. (Cost Cutters) rented space in a mall owned by Westhaven Associates, Ltd. (Westhaven). Cost Cutters breached its lease by vacating, and Westhaven sought to enforce various lease provisions. The parties dispute whether stipulated damages provisions in the lease are reasonable, and thus enforceable liquidated damages provisions, or unreasonable, and thus unenforceable penalty provisions. Following the terminology used in the seminal case on this topic, Wassenaar v. Panos, 111 Wis. 2d 518, 521, 331 N.W.2d 357 (1983), we use the term "stipulated damages" to mean the damages specified in the lease and "liquidated damages" to mean reasonable and enforceable stipulated damages. The parties also dispute whether the lease permits Westhaven to recover attorneys' fees it incurred in its attempt to enforce various lease provisions against Cost Cutters.

The circuit court concluded that the stipulated damages provisions were unreasonable and therefore unenforceable penalty provisions. The circuit court also awarded attorneys' fees to Westhaven relating solely to Westhaven's attempt to enforce lease provisions against Cost Cutters. We reverse both decisions and remand.

BACKGROUND

The parties stipulated to the facts necessary for the resolution of this case. Westhaven owns the Westhaven Village Shopping Center (Shopping Center). On July 28, 1997, Cost Cutters entered into a lease with Westhaven. Cost Cutters leased about 17% of the available rentable space in the Shopping Center. The lease term was ten years.

On October 9, 1999, Cost Cutters closed its store without Westhaven's approval. At this time, the lease rate was $49.58 per day. Before the parties entered into the lease on July 28, 1997, the Shopping Center's occupancy rate was 71%. The Shopping Center's occupancy rate fluctuated after the parties signed the lease, dropping to 53% in October 1999 prior to Cost Cutters' departure. By March 2000, the occupancy rate increased to 72%. From February 1, 2000, forward, Cost Cutters did not pay rent. In accordance with the lease, Westhaven attempted to find a new tenant for the Cost Cutters space. The space remained vacant until it was leased to a third party beginning December 1, 2000.[2] Westhaven then sued Cost Cutters seeking attorneys' fees, rent, and contract damages relating to the approximately thirteen-month period the space remained unoccupied.

Westhaven sought relief under paragraph 14.00 of the lease entitled "Default by Tenant." Paragraph 14.00 sets forth Westhaven's remedies in the event Cost Cutters "defaults in the payment of Minimum Rent or other charges or in the performance of any other of Tenant's obligations hereunder, and fails to remedy such default within ten (10) days after written notice from Landlord...." Paragraph 14.00 presents Westhaven with two options if Cost Cutters fails to remedy its default: first, Westhaven can terminate the lease, reenter the premises, and recover from Cost Cutters "any sums due Landlord for rent or otherwise to the date of such entry," and liquidated damages; second, Westhaven can choose to not terminate the lease and attempt to relet in its own name for the remainder of the term and then recover from Cost Cutters "any deficiency... between the amount for which the premises were relet, less expense of reletting, including all necessary repairs and alterations and reasonable attorney's fees and the rent provided hereunder."

Westhaven exercised the second option under paragraph 14.00. There was no dispute that under this paragraph Westhaven was entitled to the lease rate of $49.58 for each day between October 9, 1999, when Cost Cutters vacated, and December 1, 2000, when the space was sublet. However, the parties dispute whether Westhaven was entitled to certain attorneys' fees pursuant to paragraph 14.00. Westhaven sought $15,670 in attorneys' fees consisting solely of fees relating to its litigation with Cost Cutters.

In addition, Westhaven's exercise of the second option under paragraph 14.00 permits Westhaven to seek stipulated damages under paragraphs 3.02 and 8.00(n) of the lease. Paragraph 3.02 requires Cost Cutters to pay Westhaven $20 per day if Cost Cutters fails to keep its premises open for business during "normal business hours." Westhaven argued that it was entitled to $20 per day for each violation of paragraph 3.02 from October 14, 1999, to November 30, 2000. Paragraph 8.00(n) of the lease requires Cost Cutters to pay a sum equal to Cost Cutters' normal daily rent for each day Cost Cutters fails to keep its premises open for business during specified "minimum hours."[3] Westhaven argued that it was entitled to an amount equal to the daily rent for each violation of paragraph 8.00(n) from October 14, 1999, to November 30, 2000.

Both parties sought summary judgment. Cost Cutters argued that the attorneys' fees sought by Westhaven are not covered under paragraph 14.00 because those fees were not incurred for the purpose of finding a new tenant for the space vacated by Cost Cutters. Cost Cutters also argued that

---

2. By agreement of the parties, Cost Cutters sublet its space on December 1, 2000. Whether the space was sublet or relet is not pertinent to our inquiry.

3. Westhaven contends "normal business hours" and "minimum hours" are two different concepts under the contract. In Westhaven's view, normal business hours are the typical business hours of a business such as Cost Cutters, while "minimum hours" are the specified hours the Shopping Center is open for business. Westhaven argues that the two provisions target two different activities and are thus not penalty clauses. Cost Cutters disagrees with this analysis. For reasons we discuss below, we need not address this issue.

paragraphs 3.02 and 8.00(n) (collectively the "failure to do business" provisions) are unenforceable penalty provisions.

The circuit court determined that Westhaven was entitled to recover attorneys' fees as a result of Cost Cutters' breach of the lease. But the circuit court ruled that the "failure to do business" provisions contained in paragraphs 3.02 and 8.00(n) were unreasonable and, therefore, unenforceable.

Cost Cutters appeals the circuit court's award of attorneys' fees and Westhaven cross-appeals the circuit court's determination that the "failure to do business" provisions were unenforceable.

DISCUSSION

Cost Cutters appeals and Westhaven cross-appeals the circuit court's grant of summary judgment. We review summary judgment decisions *de novo*, applying the same methodology as the circuit court. . . .

A. COST CUTTERS' APPEAL OF THE AWARD OF ATTORNEYS' FEES

The parties agree that under the lease, attorneys' fees are recoverable only as an expense of reletting. However, they disagree as to whether the attorneys' fees claimed in this action constitute an expense of reletting. . . .

We are required to determine whether the attorneys' fees incurred by Westhaven as a result of this action are properly characterized as an expense of reletting. Wisconsin follows the American Rule, under which "parties to litigation are generally responsible for their own attorney's fees unless recovery is expressly allowed by either contract or statute, or when recovery results from third-party litigation." DeChant v. Monarch Life Ins. Co., 200 Wis. 2d 559, 571, 547 N.W.2d 592 (1996). We "will not construe an obligation to pay attorneys' fees contrary to the American Rule unless the contract provision clearly and unambiguously so provides." Hunzinger Constr. Co. v. Granite Res. Corp., 196 Wis. 2d 327, 340, 538 N.W.2d 804 (Ct. App. 1995).

. . . [T]he lease language limits recovery of attorneys' fees to those related to efforts to "relet." We conclude that litigation expenses in a suit against Cost Cutters are not expenses related to an attempt to relet to a third party. The record reveals that Westhaven's attorneys' fees were incurred as a result of litigation against Cost Cutters. Therefore, Westhaven is unable to collect any of the attorneys' fees, and we reverse the circuit court's decision.

B. WESTHAVEN'S CROSS-APPEAL ON THE ENFORCEABILITY OF THE "FAILURE TO DO BUSINESS" PROVISIONS

Westhaven argues that the uncontested facts show that the "failure to do business" provisions are not unenforceable penalty provisions. The review of a stipulated damages provision is a mixed question of law and fact. *Wassenaar*, 111 Wis. 2d at 525. Normally, "because the trial court's legal conclusion, that is, whether the clause is reasonable, is so intertwined with the factual findings supporting that conclusion, the appellate court should give weight to the trial court's decision, although the trial court's decision is not controlling." Id. However, where the parties have stipulated to the facts, and thus the circuit court makes no factual findings, only legal issues remain and, therefore, our review is *de novo*. . . .

A stipulated damages provision will be enforced if it is reasonable under the totality of the circumstances. *Wassenaar,* 111 Wis. 2d at 526. The court looks at several factors to determine reasonableness: "(1) Did the parties intend to provide for damages or for a penalty? (2) Is the injury caused by the breach one that is difficult or incapable of accurate estimation at the time of contract? and (3) Are the stipulated damages a reasonable forecast of the harm caused by the breach?" Id. at 529-30 (footnotes omitted). Essentially, we must look at both the "harm anticipated at the time of contract formation and the actual harm at the time of breach." Id. at 532. The factors are not meant to be mechanically applied, and courts may give some factors greater weight than others. Id. at 533.

Courts generally assume that "bargains are enforceable and that the party asking the court to intervene to invalidate a bargain should demonstrate the justice of his or her position." Id. at 526. At least in situations like the one before us, where neither party complains of inequity in bargaining power, see id. at 536, the party seeking to avoid a stipulated damages provision bears both the "burden of proving facts which would justify the trial court's concluding that the clause should not be enforced" and the burden of persuading the court that the provision should not be enforced. Id. at 526, 539-40. . . . Thus, here, where the facts are uncontested, Cost Cutters bears the burden of persuading this court that the stipulated damages provisions are unreasonable.

1. Whether the Parties Intended the Provision to be a Liquidated Damages Provision or a Penalty

The first factor we examine when determining the reasonableness of a stipulated damages provision is whether the parties intended the provision to provide liquidated damages or to provide a penalty. As explained in Koenings v. Joseph Schlitz Brewing Co., 126 Wis. 2d 349, 377 N.W.2d 593 (1985), this factor is "rarely helpful" because the parties' intent has "little relevance to what is reasonable in law." Id. at 362. Nevertheless, we examine this topic because "the parties' intent may have some evidentiary value." Id.

Cost Cutters argues that the "failure to do business" provisions impose two different fees on the same conduct, evincing a punitive intent. In addition, Cost Cutters contends that the provisions are penalties because the provisions were part of a form lease and not geared to the particular circumstances of Cost Cutters. However, Cost Cutters fails to explain why the presence of two form provisions prohibiting the same conduct turns the provisions into an impermissible penalty. Even assuming the provisions prohibit the same conduct, it does not follow that the provisions thus become penalties. Neither case law nor logic requires a stipulated damages provision to appear but once in a contract in order to be enforceable. Moreover, the stipulated damages provisions, taken together, set the damages at an amount tied to Cost Cutters' base rent, which is presumably based on the amount and location of the space leased by Cost Cutters. Therefore, the provisions, taken together, are at least somewhat tailored to the space leased by Cost Cutters.

Cost Cutters also argues that because neither provision requires mitigation by the landlord, the provisions are penalties, citing Frank Nero

Auto Lease, Inc. v. Townsend, 64 Ohio App. 2d 65, 18 Ohio Op. 3d 44, 411 N.E.2d 507 (Ohio Ct. App. 1979). *Townsend* involved a motor vehicle lease agreement that allowed the lessor to repossess an automobile and accelerate future rents upon the lessee's default. 411 N.E.2d at 511. In addition, the lease permitted the lessor to regain possession of the vehicle and relet or resell the vehicle while collecting the full rent from the lessee for the life of the contract without any obligation to mitigate. Id. However, the fact that the "failure to do business" provisions do not contain mitigation clauses is not controlling in this case because a mitigation clause is contained elsewhere in the lease, unlike the lease in *Townsend*. Westhaven was required to attempt mitigation under the second option in paragraph 14.00.[4] Thus, *Townsend* is easily distinguished.

We do not regard the parties' arguments relating to the first factor as particularly helpful, and we move on to the other two factors.

2. Whether the Damages Were Ascertainable at the Time of Contracting, and Whether the Stipulated Damages Reasonably Forecasted the Actual Damages

The second factor used to determine the reasonableness of a stipulated damages provision examines whether the damages can be estimated *at the time of contracting*. The third factor examines whether the stipulated damages provisions are a reasonable forecast of the *harm caused by the breach*. See *Wassenaar*, 111 Wis. 2d at 530-31. The *Wassenaar* court stated that these two "factors are intertwined, and both use a combined prospective-retrospective approach." Id. at 531.

Although the second and third factors both use a prospective-retrospective approach, the fact remains that they require two distinct inquiries: the reasonableness of the stipulated damages provision at the time of contracting and the reasonableness of the provision when compared with actual damages after a breach. See Pollack v. Calimag, 157 Wis. 2d 222, 240-41, 458 N.W.2d 591 (Ct. App. 1990); see also *Koenings*, 126 Wis. 2d at 371 ("The touchstone of the reasonableness under the totality of the circumstances test must still be the relationship of anticipated and actual harm to the stipulated amount of damages, as expressed in the *Wassenaar* factors."). We first address whether the "failure to do business" provisions were reasonable at the time of contracting.

a. Time of Contracting

Cost Cutters first argues that the stipulated damages provisions were unreasonable at the time of contracting because the parties should have been able to predict there would be no harm beyond lost rent if Cost Cutters breached. Cost Cutters reasons that because Westhaven collects a fixed rent from Cost Cutters, rather than a variable rent based on Cost Cutters' sales,

---

4. If Westhaven had chosen the first option under paragraph 14.00, there would have been no mitigation requirement, but at the same time had Westhaven chosen that first option, it could not have collected damages under paragraph 3.02 or paragraph 8.00(n).

Westhaven is entitled to the same rental income whether or not Cost Cutters vacates. We disagree with Cost Cutters' reasoning.

Westhaven's managing general partner testified by affidavit about the harm caused by vacating businesses:

> When a business fails to keep its business open, other tenants are harmed because each tenant brings potential customer foot traffic into the mall who then may shop the other businesses. Failing to remain open has a slow but certain negative effect on the value of the property because as tenants lose business and customers patronize competitor malls the rent the landlord may charge to future tenants decreases and renewal rate of existing tenants decreases. . . . Over time, the very economic viability of the shopping center is threatened because the costs of operating the mall outweigh the rents received.

In addition, at his deposition Cost Cutters' president acknowledged the harm caused by vacancies in malls: "Why don't I build freestanding buildings? I like the traffic. They, Hollywood Video, . . . they have a lot of people every single day. That hurt my business when they went out."

As tenants vacate, a shopping center receives less customer traffic, potentially causing other tenants to vacate or go out of business. These consequential damages are often difficult to prove, but that does not prevent sophisticated parties from including consequential damages when estimating the damages at the time of contracting. See *Wassenaar*, 111 Wis. 2d at 535-36 (stating that parties may reasonably include in their estimates damages that reflect actual harm, rather than just the harm that may be proved in court).

Next, Cost Cutters argues that the provisions are unreasonable because Cost Cutters has no opportunity to cure a minor or justifiable breach. Cost Cutters alleges that such default clauses are unenforceable when any violation could trigger them, citing Mayfield v. Hicks, 575 S.W.2d 571 (Tex. Civ. App. 1978). Cost Cutters' reliance on *Mayfield* is misplaced. In *Mayfield*, an equipment lease permitted the lessor to declare a breach of the lease "upon the occurrence of even a minor default." Id. at 575. That court found that "the coupling of repossession with acceleration of rent, irrespective of the type of breach, is the defect in this provision." Id. In contrast, under the lease here, Westhaven must give Cost Cutters written notice as well as ten days to remedy the violation before declaring a breach of the lease. Thus, a minor violation of the "failure to do business" provisions will not automatically breach the lease. Although a minor violation may lead to money damages, a minor violation cannot lead to the "repossession with acceleration of rent" to which the *Mayfield* court objected.

Furthermore, Cost Cutters argues that the provisions are unreasonable because the "failure to do business" fees accrue regardless of the tenant mix, and would be assessed even if Cost Cutters were the only store left in the mall. This hypothetical scenario is too speculative to render the provisions unreasonable at the time of contracting. Furthermore, if this scenario had come to pass, it would have been more properly analyzed by comparing the stipulated damages provisions to the actual harm caused.

Cost Cutters has failed to persuade us that the "failure to do business" fees were an unreasonable estimation of Westhaven's damages. Cost Cutters did not, for example, present expert testimony that the stipulated damages provisions were unusually harsh as compared with stipulated damages provisions found in other multi-tenant retail commercial leases. To the contrary, in this case Cost Cutters' president, in his deposition testimony, admitted that similar "failure to do business" provisions are common in leases with other shopping malls.

b. After Breach

Next, we turn to the question whether the stipulated damages are reasonable in light of the actual damages caused by the breach. See *Wassenaar*, 111 Wis. 2d at 530. As stated above, it is incumbent on Cost Cutters to persuade us that the damages it must pay under the contract do not reasonably relate to the actual harm suffered by Westhaven. Cost Cutters fails to meet this burden.

Cost Cutters argues that Westhaven suffered no harm and thus the provisions unreasonably penalize Cost Cutters. Cost Cutters contends that the lack of evidence of the Shopping Center's property value before or after Cost Cutters closed means that Westhaven did not establish any harm. However, Cost Cutters fails to appreciate that it had the burden of producing evidence of unreasonableness. Westhaven was not required to present evidence on value. See id. at 526 ("Placing the burden of proof on the challenger is consistent with giving the non-breaching party the advantage inherent in stipulated damages clauses of eliminating the need to prove damages. . . . ").

Cost Cutters also argues that because the occupancy rate at the Shopping Center was low before Cost Cutters departed and actually rose after Cost Cutters left, it is obvious that Westhaven suffered no harm as a result of Cost Cutters' departure. The occupancy rate just prior to Cost Cutters' departure was 53%. About five months later, occupancy had risen to 72%. However, we are not persuaded by the occupancy rate information. Simply because the occupancy rate rose after Cost Cutters' breach does not mean that the breach caused Westhaven no harm. Based on the record before us, the most reasonable inference is that occupancy would have been even higher had Cost Cutters remained in the Shopping Center. When a mall has a low occupancy rate, it does not follow that the mall suffers no harm when a significant tenant vacates. The record contains a letter from another tenant commenting on the harm caused by Cost Cutters' vacating:

> I have just recently learned that Cost Cutters, a solid anchor in this mall, will be moving down the street.
>
> . . . I do not believe that myself or PD Meats will be able to survive without both a full, thriving mall with tenants that compliment each other and also an anchor . . .
>
> I am afraid soon I'll be the only one here and [the Shopping Center] will become not a shopping destination, but a place to avoid because businesses fail and close.

In a subsequent letter, the same tenant stated: "My market study was based on the fact that there was a video store and a hair care business as [an] anchor and a draw to this Center. These businesses have closed and moved, which has a significant impact on my bottom line."

We conclude that Cost Cutters has failed to meet its burden of persuasion. Cost Cutters has not shown that the stipulated damages provisions in the lease were unreasonable under the totality of the circumstances.

CONCLUSION

We conclude that the plain language of the lease does not permit Westhaven to recover its attorneys' fees incurred in this suit because they are not expenses of reletting. Additionally, we conclude that Cost Cutters has failed to show that the stipulated damages provisions in the lease were unreasonable. Westhaven is entitled to stipulated damages under both paragraphs 3.02 and 8.00(n). Therefore, we reverse both decisions of the circuit court and remand for further proceedings consistent with this opinion.

Notes and Questions

1. *Test for enforcement of liquidated damage clauses.* As reflected in the *Westhaven* opinion, courts traditionally have used a three-pronged test to determine the validity of clauses providing for agreed remedies: (1) the damages to be anticipated from the breach must be uncertain in amount or difficult to prove; (2) the parties must have intended the clause to liquidate damages rather than operate as a penalty; and (3) the amount set in the agreement must be a reasonable forecast of just compensation for the harm flowing from the breach. E. Allan Farnsworth, Contracts §12.18, at 813-814 (4th ed. 2004). Consistent with the analysis in *Westhaven*, Professor Farnsworth has observed that the "intent" prong of the test has atrophied in light of the courts' disinclination to allow the parties' own characterization of their agreement to be controlling. Farnsworth, above, at 817. Similarly, Restatement (Second) §356 states a two-part test: A provision for liquidated damages will be enforceable if the amount fixed is reasonable in light of the "anticipated or actual loss" and the "difficulties of proof of loss." Comment *b* to §356 provides, "[t]he greater the difficulty either of proving that loss has occurred or of establishing its amount with the requisite certainty . . . , the easier it is to show that the amount fixed is reasonable." Thus, the difficulty in quantifying harm resulting from a breach is pivotal in many cases. See, e.g., Travelodge Hotels, Inc. v. Kim Shin Hospitality, Inc., 27 F. Supp. 2d 1377 (M.D. Fla. 1998) (liquidated damages clause in hotel licensing agreement enforceable in light of great difficulty estimating future profitability of hotel at time contract was made); City of Davenport v. Shewry Corp., 674 N.W.2d 79 (Iowa 2004) (enforcing liquidated damages in economic development contract; it would be difficult, if not impossible, to measure harm resulting to plaintiff city from defendant company's failure to create jobs that would contribute to city's economy and tax base).

In determining the validity of a liquidated damage clause, many courts have also adopted the position expressed in *Westhaven* that a liquidated damage clause is presumed to be valid and the burden of proof is on the party seeking to invalidate the provision. Where adopted, this presumption is seen as a corollary of the "freedom of contract" principle. See, e.g., Willard Packaging Company, Inc. v. Javier, 899 A.2d 940 (Md. Ct. Spec. App. 2006) (most jurisdictions place burden on party challenging clause, but allocation of burden may depend on whether parties had equal bargaining power); TAL Financial Corp. v. CSC Consulting, Inc., 844 N.E.2d 1085 (Mass. 2006) (majority of states place burden of proof on party seeking to avoid clause; doubts resolved in favor of enforcement). On the other hand, if a clause appears to have no relationship to anticipated harm, a court may readily deny enforcement. See Energy Plus Consulting, LLC v. Illinois Fuel Company, LLC, 371 F.3d 907 (7th Cir. 2004) (holding unenforceable a lump sum stipulated remedy of $720,000 to be awarded without regard to timing or severity of breach).

2. *Evaluating provision in light of anticipated or actual harm.* The traditional position has been that a liquidated damage clause should be judged only as of the time that the contract was made, and some courts still take the approach. Under this view, proof of a low amount of actual damage would have only limited relevance. See, e.g., Kelly v. Marx, 705 N.E.2d 1411 (Mass. 1999) (noting sharp division among jurisdictions on the issue but holding that stipulated remedy should be evaluated only in light of circumstances at time of contract formation; the expectations of parties and efficiency considerations support "single look" approach). The court in *Westhaven,* however, reflects the modern trend toward assessing reasonableness either at the time of formation or after the breach. See also Wasserman's Inc. v. Township of Middletown, 645 A.2d 100 (N.J. 1994) (adopting modern approach, noting "that hindsight is frequently better than foresight" and that a court cannot avoid being influenced by its knowledge of subsequent events).

As noted above, the Restatement (Second) §356 states that a liquidated damage clause must be reasonable in light of the "anticipated or actual loss." Also contributing to the current trend, UCC §2-718 provides that damages may be liquidated "only at an amount which is reasonable in the light of the anticipated or actual harm." The impact of this two-fold perspective, however, is less than clear. In Wassenaar v. Panos, 331 N.W.2d 357 (Wis. 1983), a decision heavily relied on in *Westhaven,* the court stated that a clause producing liquidated damages "grossly disproportionate to the actual harm" may thus be determined to be unreasonable. This approach suggests that a liquidated damages clause should be *denied* enforcement if it is unreasonable in light of the actual harm even if it appeared reasonable at contract formation. The Ninth Circuit court applied a different approach in California & Hawaiian Sugar Co. v. Sun Ship, Inc., 794 F.2d 1433 (9th Cir. 1986), *cert. denied,* 484 U.S. 871 (1987). In that case, the court interpreted the disjunctive language in the Restatement (Second) and the UCC to mean that a liquidated damage clause should be *upheld* if the clause was reasonable either in light of anticipated harm or in light of the actual harm. Thus, the Ninth Circuit court enforced a clause resulting in recovery of more than $4 million because it was a reasonable forecast of what might have happened, even though the actual harm was apparently less than $400,000. The Ninth Circuit court also emphasized that the parties to the contract were sophisticated and that the precise extent of actual harm was difficult to measure. Id. at 1439. See also XCO International, Inc. v. Pacific Scientific Co., 369 F.3d 998 (7th Cir. 2004) (rule against penalty clauses is "anachronism," especially in contracts between commercial enterprises; clause will be enforceable if reasonable in light of actual harm even if not reasonable forecast at time contract was made). Do you agree with the approach of the Ninth Circuit in *California & Hawaiian Sugar Co.?*

3. *Necessity of actual loss.* The defendant in *Westhaven* argued, unsuccessfully, that the plaintiff landlord suffered no actual harm from the breach. If it did appear that there had been no injury at all, should a liquidated damage clause then be enforced? Under the traditional approach of determining enforceability solely at the time the contract was made, as noted above, even a total absence of loss or injury might well be irrelevant. See, e.g., Frick Co. v. Rubel Corp., 62 F.2d 765 (2d Cir. 1933) (actual harm not relevant); Wallace Real Estate Investment, Inc. v. Groves, 881 P.2d 1010 (Wash. 1994) (proof of actual damage not prerequisite to upholding liquidated damages clause, but unconscionably disproportionate actual damage may be used in evaluating reasonableness of pre-estimate). A number of courts have held, however, that the complete absence of actual loss or injury will make a clause invalid as a penalty. See, e.g., Colonial at Lynnfield, Inc. v. Sloan, 870 F.2d 761 (1st Cir. 1989); Jones v. Hryn Development, Inc., 778 N.E.2d 245 (Ill. App. Ct. 2002). See also Restatement (Second) §356, Comment *b* (where "it is clear that no loss at all has occurred," a provision fixing substantial damages should be unenforceable because of the absence of "difficulty of proof").

4. *Liquidated damages in construction contracts.* Clauses providing for liquidated damages in the event of delay in completion are common in construction and similar contracts; such clauses typically measure the amount recoverable by some daily or weekly rate, with perhaps an outside time limit, and are usually held to be enforceable in light of the various kinds of injury — both tangible and intangible — that can result from such delays. See, e.g., Miami Valley Contractors, Inc. v. Town of Sunman, Indiana, 960 F. Supp. 1366 (S.D. Ind. 1997) (liquidated damage provisions of $1,000 and $500 per day for failure to timely complete work under contract for construction of wastewater treatment facility were enforceable; damages to town would be difficult to measure); see also American Multi-Cinema, Inc. v. Southroads, L.L.C., 119 F.Supp.2d 1190 (D. Kan. 2000) (enforcing portion of liquidated damage clause that allowed four days of free rent for each day that shopping center was late in turning over site for construction of movie "mega-plex" by tenant; provision was reasonable estimate of likely harm).

Occasionally a clause will be held to provide a measure of damages so far in excess of any injury conceivably resulting from such delay that it amounts to a penalty and will not be enforced. See, e.g., Rohlin Construction Co. v. City of Hinton, 476 N.W.2d 78 (Iowa 1991) (provision in highway contract for $400 daily liquidated damages for delay held to be unenforceable penalty; while slight damage might have occurred, amount in contract bore no reasonable relation to anticipated or actual loss).

5. *Liquidated damages in employment contracts.* In the preceding section of this chapter we saw that courts will not grant specific performance of personal service contracts and are even reluctant to provide injunctive relief. Because of this judicial tendency, employment contracts may contain liquidated damage clauses that apply in the event of breach by the employee. See, e.g., Vanderbilt v. DiNardo, 174 F. 3d 751 (6th Cir. 1999) (liquidated damage clause requiring college football head coach to pay sum equal to net annual salary for breach was enforceable; amount was reasonable in light of tangible and intangible harm

resulting from discontinuity in football program if coach did not complete five-year term). Of course, such clauses must still survive judicial determination of whether they operate as a penalty. Compare Ashcraft & Gerel v. Coady, 244 F.3d 948 (D.C. Cir. 2001) (liquidated damage clause in contract between attorney and law firm imposing $400,000 payment for attorney's breach held to be reasonable in light of estimated loss from breach), with Equity Enterprises, Inc. v. Milosch, 633 N.W.2d 662 (Wis. Ct. App.), *rev. denied,* 635 N.W.2d 784 (Wis. 2001) (forfeiture of sales commissions by former insurance agent for breach of covenant not to compete was not a reasonable liquidated damage provision). Notably, provision for liquidated damages in an employment contract or covenant not to compete will not preclude a court from granting injunctive relief if the facts warrant.

Employment contracts may also include a liquidated damage clause that provides a remedy for the employee in the event of breach by the employer. In *Wassenaar*, cited in Note 2 above and in the *Westhaven* case, the plaintiff entered into a written, three-year employment contract, agreeing to serve as the general manager of the defendant's hotel. If the defendant terminated the contract prior to its expiration, defendant agreed to be "responsible for fulfilling the entire financial obligation as set forth within this agreement for the full period of three (3) years." The employer discharged the plaintiff 21 months before the expiration of the contract. The plaintiff was unemployed for approximately two and one-half months, but then obtained a job, which he held until the time of trial. The Wisconsin Supreme Court held that the employee was entitled to his full compensation for the remainder of the three-year term as liquidated damages with no deduction for the pay he received from the other job. The court reasoned that the standard measure of damages for the employer's breach of an employment contract (the contract amount + expenses of seeking other employment − earnings received from other employment) does not compensate for certain consequential damages, such as harm to reputation and emotional stress; accordingly, the clause could be upheld as a reasonable forecast of uncertain damages.

6. *Liquidated damages by other names.* Sometimes a lease agreement or other contract will also provide for "late charges" or other fees if a payment is not made when due. In light of the law's tendency to assume that money is always available in the marketplace (at market rates of interest) and the conventional requirement that liquidated remedies be in lieu of damages that are difficult of computation, it is not surprising that such clauses are likely to be held invalid as penalties. E.g., Sun Ridge Investors, Ltd. v. Parker, 956 P.2d 876 (Okla. 1998) (daily charge of $5 for late payment of rent, on top of $20 late fee, was penalty unrelated to actual harm). Such late fees may also violate consumer protection laws. See Woodhaven Apartments v. Washington, 942 P.2d 918 (Utah 1997) (liquidated damages clause in apartment lease held unenforceable because not based on reasonable forecast of harm; lease also found subject to consumer protection statute).

In a similar vein, real estate contracts typically require purchasers to make "earnest money" deposits and often provide for retention of the deposit by the seller if the purchaser breaches. Courts are divided on how to treat such provisions. Many courts will not allow a breaching purchaser to recover any portion of an earnest money deposit. See Star Financial Corp. v. Howard

Nance Co., 508 S.E.2d 534 (N.C. Ct. App. 1998), *aff'd*, 516 S.E.2d 381 (1999) (North Carolina adheres to common law rule, followed by majority of jurisdictions, that breaching purchaser cannot recover any portion of consideration paid). Other courts treat such provisions as liquidated damage clauses subject to judicial scrutiny under the tests discussed above. See, e.g., Palmieri v. Partridge, 853 A.2d 1076 (Pa. Super. Ct. 2004) (clause requiring forfeiture of $225,000 deposit on purchase price of $2,250,000 was a reasonable liquidated damage provision and not a penalty; forfeitures of up to 10 percent have often been found to be reasonable).

7. *Liquidated damage clauses and other remedial options* Should the presence of a liquidated damage clause bar the granting of specific performance of a real estate contract? The courts have been divided on this question. Compare Allen v. Smith, 114 Cal. Rptr. 2d 898 (Ct. App. 2002) (liquidated damage clause will not bar action for specific performance in real estate contract), with O'Shield v. Lakeside Bank, 781 N.E.2d 1114 (Ill. App. Ct. 2002) (liquidated damage clause does preclude action for specific performance in real estate contract, based on clear intent of parties). Moreover, some jurisdictions hold that a valid liquidated damage clause will also bar access to remedies at law. See Blue Mountain Mushroom Co., Inc. v. Monterey Mushroom, Inc., 246 F. Supp. 2d 394 (E.D. Pa. 2002) (under Pennsylvania contract law a party that retains legally enforceable liquidated damages will be barred from seeking actual damages).

The court in *Westhaven* found that the contract terms imposed on the plaintiff landlord a duty to mitigate. In other cases, however, it has been less clear how the mitigation principle should interact with a liquidated damage clause. In Lake River Corp. v. Carborundum Co., 769 F.2d 1284 (7th Cir. 1985), a case involving a contract for distribution services between two commercial entities, the court held that any savings from mitigation should not be deducted from recovery under a liquidated damages clause. Writing for the court, Judge Posner explained that mitigation is inconsistent with the underlying premise that such clauses allow parties to fix the amount of damages with certainty. But see Browning Ferris Industries of Nebraska, Inc. v. Eating Establishment — 90th & Fort, Inc., 575 N.W.2d 885 (Neb. Ct. App. 1998) (failure of nonbreaching party to produce evidence relating to mitigation precluded determination of actual harm and whether liquidated damages clause was reasonable estimate; clause held unenforceable).

8. *Under-liquidated damages.* Most often, liquidated damage clauses are scrutinized in light of the possibility that they might greatly overcompensate the plaintiff for defendant's breach. Can an agreed remedy also be invalid because it will *under*compensate the plaintiff? Restatement (Second) §356 states that a term that provides for "unreasonably large liquidated damages" will be treated as a "penalty," but does not refer expressly to a clause that fixes damages at an amount that is unreasonably small; Comment *a* to §356 suggests that a term fixing an "unreasonably small amount" of damages might be unenforceable as "unconscionable." UCC §2-718(1) and its Comment 1 are to the same effect as the Restatement on this point. UCC §2-719, which deals with limitation of remedy, suggests that a limitation-of-damages clause could be invalid on grounds of "unconscionability," but does not expressly subject such a clause to the sort of test applied by §2-718(1) to "liquidated damage" clauses.

This disparity in treatment between "over-liquidated" and "under-liquidated" damages appears not to be an oversight but rather to reflect different policies applicable to the two situations. The rule traditionally applied to "liquidated damages" denies enforcement to those clauses that have an "in terrorem" effect — clauses that in effect compel a party to perform instead of breaching. However, where contracting parties have agreed on a damage-limitation clause, this ordinarily represents their agreement that liability in the event of breach should be fixed at something less than the real cost of the resulting injury. For this reason, one court has asserted that damage-limitation clauses cannot and should not be tested by a "reasonableness" standard, because to do so would "swallow up" the general rule that such clauses are potentially valid devices for reallocating the risks attendant on contractual nonperformance. Tharalson v. Pfizer Genetics, Inc., 728 F.2d 1108, 1112 (8th Cir. 1984). See also Rainbow Country Rentals & Retails, Inc. v. Ameritech Publishing, Inc., 706 N.W.2d 95 (Wis. 2005) (agreeing with majority of jurisdictions that clause limiting liability for error in telephone directory is enforceable stipulated remedy in light of difficulty in assessing actual harm).

9. *Scholarly commentary.* A considerable body of scholarly writing has questioned the wisdom of the "penalty" limitation on the enforceability of liquidated damage clauses. In an early, influential article Professors Charles Goetz and Robert Scott pointed out that conventional damage rules often do not fully compensate the injured party because these rules ignore idiosyncratic value (subjective value attached to the contract but not reflected in market value) and fail to include certain damages, such as emotional harm or attorney fees. Because of this systematic undercompensation, Goetz and Scott argued that the penalty limitation on liquidated damage clauses should be abolished; such clauses should be enforced unless they are the product of some defect in the bargaining process. Charles J. Goetz & Robert E. Scott, Liquidated Damages, Penalties and the Just Compensation Principle: Some Notes on an Enforcement Model and a Theory of Efficient Breach, 77 Colum. L. Rev. 554 (1977). See also Larry A. DiMatteo, A Theory of Efficient Penalty: Eliminating the Law of Liquidated Damages, 38 Am. Bus. L.J. 633 (2001) (advocating a strong presumption of enforceability for liquidated damage clauses, subject to the unconscionability doctrine as primary ground for avoidance). Other scholars, however, have concluded that the penalty limitation should be continued, although perhaps redefined. See Kenneth W. Clarkson, Roger LeRoy Miller, & Timothy J. Muris, Liquidated Damages v. Penalties: Sense or Nonsense?, 1978 Wis. L. Rev. 351 (under economic analysis penalty limitation should be applied to situations where there may be opportunity and incentive to induce breach; in other cases clause should be upheld without regard to whether it is penalty).

PROBLEM 12-2

In June 2005 Waste Disposal, Inc., entered into a contract with Yamini Chemical Company, a chemical manufacturer, for the transportation and disposal of waste chemicals from Yamini's manufacturing operations. The contract was for a five-year term. Paragraph 7 of the agreement provided as follows:

> 7. *Price.* The price for the first year of this agreement has been set under paragraph 6 above. For subsequent years, the price shall be set by mutual agreement of the parties not more than thirty (30) days before the anniversary of the execution of this contract. Adjustment in price from the previous year's price shall be based on the amount of any cost increases incurred by Waste Disposal during the previous year. The parties agree to negotiate in good faith to agree on price.

In February 2007 Waste Disposal notified Yamini that it was terminating the contract effective June 30 of that year because changes in federal and state regulations governing waste disposal had made the business so difficult and expensive that Waste Disposal found it commercially impracticable to continue performance. After receiving this notification, Yamini contacted other waste disposal companies to determine if it could obtain alternative services. While two other companies are willing to enter into contracts with Yamini, both insist on a right of termination on 30 days' notice and demand that Yamini agree to indemnify them against any liability arising from the contract. (Yamini's contract with Waste Disposal does not have an indemnification provision.)

Yamini has asked your advice concerning its legal rights against Waste Disposal. In particular, Yamini wants to know whether it could require Waste Disposal to specifically perform the contract. What advice would you give?

PROBLEM 12-3

Albertson & Yee is a professional partnership of two doctors, Sally Albertson and Joanne Yee, engaged in the practice of medicine and specializing in dermatology. Albertson and Yee have decided to take in a third doctor, Ron Newsome, as an associate in the practice, with plans that he will eventually become a partner. The doctors have negotiated the terms of an employment contract, including salary and benefits. They have agreed that at the end of three years a decision will be made whether Newsome will be admitted as a partner. While Albertson and Yee expect that they will decide to admit Newsome into the partnership, they are concerned about the possible impact on their practice if they decide not to admit him, or if he leaves on his own, taking with him a number of their patients. Albertson and Yee want you to draft a provision for Newsome's employment contract to protect the partnership in the event Newsome leaves. Draft such a provision. In doing so you may obtain some guidance from form books such as Am. Jur. 2d, Legal Forms.

Table of Cases

Table of Uniform Commercial Code Provisions (UCC)

Note: ALI and the NCCUSL have adopted a revised version of Article 2, but as of late 2006, the revision has not been adopted by any state. The materials cite both the prior version of Article 2, which remains governing law with some variations in all states, and Revised Article 2 when the revised version makes significant changes.

Table of Provisions from Restatement (Second) of Contracts

Table of Provisions from Restatement (First) of Contracts

Table of Provisions
from Other
Restatements

Table of Other Acts, Codes, and Rules

Table of Secondary Authorities

Index